MEXICO AND THE UNITED STATES

A STUDY OF SUBJECTS AFFECTING THEIR POLITICAL,
COMMERCIAL, AND SOCIAL RELATIONS, MADE
WITH A VIEW TO THEIR PROMOTION

BY

MATIAS ROMERO

———

VOLUME I.

———

G. P. PUTNAM'S SONS
NEW YORK AND LONDON
The Knickerbocker Press
1898

The Knickerbocker Press, New York

PREFACE.

At two different periods I have been in Washington as the official representative of Mexico in the United States. My first sojourn began on December 24, 1859, when I came as First Secretary of the Mexican Legation, continuing as such until August 14, 1860, the day on which Minister Mata left Washington on leave, and I became Chargé d' Affaires and continued in that capacity until October 29, 1863. On that day I presented to President Lincoln my credentials as Envoy Extraordinary and Minister Plenipotentiary of Mexico, in which capacity I remained in Washington until July 16, 1868, when I took my departure for Mexico. I was therefore in Washington during nearly two years of Mr. Buchanan's administration, the whole of Mr. Lincoln's first and second administrations, and of his successor, Mr. Johnson. I, therefore, was fortunate enough to be in this capital during the most serious crises that this government ever passed through, that is, during the preparation for the secession of the Southern States, during the secession, the Civil War that it brought about, and the Reconstruction Period, as well as during the whole period of the French Intervention in Mexico, which was an incident closely connected with the Civil War in the United States. It was my fortune to meet the most prominent men of this country, both in political and social life, and to hold very friendly personal relations with many of them, such as Secretary Seward and General Grant.[1]

[1] The extent of the personal friendship with which Mr. Seward favored me, appears from the following official communication dated at Washington, October 7, 1867, in which he tendered me a public vessel of the United States to convey me and my friends from Charleston, South Carolina, to the port of Veracruz in Mexico, on my return home. Governor Morton, of Indiana, and General Banks had intended to go to Mexico with me, but could not leave when I started, and I only left with my family.

DEPARTMENT OF STATE,
WASHINGTON, *Oct. 7, 1867.*

To Señor Don Matias Romero
  etc., etc., etc.

SIR: You are aware of the intention of the Government to provide you with a passage to Mexico in a public vessel of the United States. I now have the honor to acquaint you that in a letter of this date, the Secretary of the Treasury informs me

Preface.

The second period of my service in Washington extends from March 7, 1882, to the present time, and it has continued without interruption excepting from May, 1892, to February, 1893, when I discharged, while absent on leave, the duties of Secretary of the Treasury of Mexico, filling that office for the third time.

During the years which elapsed between these periods I served at two different times as Secretary of the Treasury in Mexico, and for a few months as Postmaster-General of that country, although that office is not in Mexico, as in the United States, a cabinet position; and during the intervals I travelled in different parts of Mexico and spent about three years in agricultural pursuits in the District of Soconusco, State of Chiapas, bordering upon Guatemala, an incident which gave me the opportunity of becoming familiar with the political and social conditions of Guatemala, a country which I twice visited, and which furnished me practical knowledge of the boundary question between Mexico and that republic, which several times threatened to disturb the peace between the two countries.

During my second official residence in the City of Washington, I have contributed to the Press of this country several papers relating to Mexican affairs, prepared with a view to correct misapprehensions concerning the laws of Mexico, and its social, political, industrial, and commercial conditions, the feelings and disposition of its people towards the United States, and several other subjects affecting the relations between the two Republics, and to furnish information on matters concerning Mexico, which ought to be better understood in the United States. It has been my special desire to do whatever might lie in my power to lessen the risk of misunderstandings and to further the knowledge of each country by the other, and thus to develop friendly political, commercial, and social relations between the two nations, and establish the basis of lasting peace between them. The contiguity of the two Republics, the peculiarities of each, and the special advantages which, in certain respects, each possesses over the other, are such as to promote and preserve, in the near future, the strongest ties of interest, respect, and friendship. It was with the view of furthering such a result that these articles were originally written, and it is the same purpose that has induced me to reissue them in book form.

that the Revenue Cutter *Wilderness* will be ordered to Charleston, South Carolina, for the purpose of receiving you and your friends and of making the voyage referred to.

If, therefore, you should reach Charleston by the 14th of this month, it is probable that you may then embark in the *Wilderness* there.

I will avail myself of the occasion to renew the assurance of my high consideration.

WILLIAM H. SEWARD.

I had enough letters from General Grant to fill a volume, and may use some of them hereafter.

Preface.

These contributions have now become quite numerous, and because of the frequent demands received for copies, I have considered it advisable to revise and publish them in book form, in such manner as to make the collection a convenient source of knowledge and reference for citizens of the United States who desire to have a more intimate knowledge of Mexican affairs. At first I thought that I would group my papers in the chronological order of their publication in this country; but after further consideration I decided to follow the order in which they now appear.

I have carefully revised the articles embraced in this volume with the view of making them parts of a comprehensive work. When I began to prepare these papers I thought it would be proper to begin the same with a short description of Mexico, and I used for the purpose a paper I published in the *Bulletin of the American Geographical Society* of New York on December 31, 1896, adding to it considerably, so as to embrace the more recent geographical and statistical information on Mexico that could be obtained, and in that way the first paper of this set came out in a more voluminous way than I had intended. The several articles I had published bearing on historical affairs concerning Mexico were grouped together under the head of *Historical Notes on Mexico,* and followed the one containing geographical and statistical data, and those of a miscellaneous character are grouped together rather on my theory of their importance than on the date of their publication.

As each article was written with a certain purpose, a repetition of some facts and views on a given subject has at times been unavoidable, because the statement of such facts, or the expression of such views, was in each case indispensable to a thorough knowledge of the subject-matter of the article. I have tried to avoid these repetitions as much as possible, but I have found that I could not altogether succeed in doing so.

I feel constrained to say that my stay in Washington has been so long, and my acquaintance with the leading public men of this country so intimate, that I can state with truth that I know a great deal of the unwritten history of this country, which if carefully collected would afford material for very interesting personal memoirs. Although these articles are far from having that character, they contain facts which throw light upon some incidents of the inside political history of the times, and which have not heretofore been within the reach of the general public. I trust therefore that for this reason these papers will be found of interest to those who may wish to know something of the workings of the great Government of the United States as viewed by friendly foreign eyes.

This book makes no pretensions to literary merit. I have been in this country long enough to learn something of the English language, but of course I cannot aspire to as perfect a knowledge and command of it as if it were my mother tongue. These articles were written by me originally in English, as they were intended to be read by the people of this country, and although I have submitted them to friends of mine for correction of the style, the corrections that have been made have been of small importance, and the style, therefore, remains my own. I know very well that it is far from being perfect, or even as terse or correct as I could reasonably desire, but I have done my best to make it as good as I knew how.

I know that it is something new and a rather delicate undertaking for a diplomatic representative of a foreign country to write articles for the Press of the country to which he is accredited, and I am well aware that to an European diplomat this would be considered a serious breach of etiquette; but the conditions in this country are so different from those prevailing elsewhere, and the relations between Mexico and the United States are so exceptional, that I have felt myself justified in following this course, and so far I have had no occasion to regret it. I have found, besides, that some of my colleagues, not only representing American, but even European countries, have acted in a similar manner; the former Brazilian Minister in Washington, Señor Mendonça, who is a very accomplished diplomat, the former Argentine Minister, Señor Zeballos, the former Belgian Minister, Monsieur Le Ghait, an able man of very wide diplomatic experience, representing a very conservative European State, and also two Japanese Ministers, Messrs. Tateno and Kurino, have published articles on important subjects relating to their respective countries.[1] I am also able to cite as a precedent the example of the diplomatic representatives of the United

---

[1] The articles referred to are two from Señor Don Salvador de Mendonça, published in the *North American Review*, one in January, 1894, entitled "Republicanism in Brazil," and the other in the February number of the same year, entitled "Latest Aspects of the Brazilian Rebellion"; one from Señor Don Estanislao S. Zeballos, published in the August, 1894, number of the same paper, entitled "Civil Wars in South America"; two from Mon. Alfred Le Ghait, one published in the March, 1892, number of the *North American Review*, entitled "The Anti-Slavery Conference," and another published in November, 1893, entitled "The Revision of the Belgian Constitution"; one from Mr. G. Tateno, published in the January, 1893, number of the same paper, entitled "Japan at the World's Fair"; and two from Mr. S. Kurino, one published in November, 1894, entitled "The War in the Orient," and the other published in May, 1895, entitled "The Future of Japan."

Señor Zeballos published besides, in 1894, while he was Argentine Minister in Washington, a book of 656 pages entitled *La Concurrencia Universal y la Agricultura de Ambas Américas*, which he prepared in the shape of a report to the State Department of his country on the agricultural conditions of the United States. I understand this book was published simultaneously in English and Spanish, but it was written in Spanish, and I have only seen the Spanish edition of the same.

States in England. This country bears towards England, in some respects, relations similar to those borne by Mexico towards the United States; and it may therefore not be considered extraordinary that the Mexican representative in Washington should feel justified in following their example. If a representative of an European Government should make public addresses in London on subjects of common interest to his own and the British Government, or on other subjects of a political character, public opinion in Europe would find ample ground for criticism, and he would possibly even be reprimanded by his Government; but the peculiar position of the United States representative at the Court of St. James has been held to justify the course taken by Ambassadors Bayard and Hay and their predecessors during their mission in Great Britain.

I have also thought that the presentation of trustworthy information for the purpose of avoiding misunderstandings between two sister Republics, and of furthering satisfactory and friendly relations, was not only a privilege permissible, but a duty of the representative of Mexico in the United States. Besides, in this case I have only collected in book form, papers which I have already published in this country, some of them as early as 1883, and I cannot see any impropriety in reprinting them. The American public has very kindly received my papers, and with perhaps a single exception, in which I touched on a question which was at the time paramount in a hot political discussion in the United States, which preceded a Presidential election, they all have been commented upon in a great deal more kindly and complimentary manner than I had any reason to expect.

My experience in dealing with two peoples of different races, speaking different languages and with different social conditions, has shown me that there are prejudices on both sides, growing out of want of sufficient knowledge of each other, which could be dispelled, and by so doing, a better understanding be secured. This fact was very plainly shown to me during the Pan-American Conference, which met in Washington from October, 1889, to April, 1890, where serious prejudices prevailing among some of the delegates regarding the various countries were dispelled by the close contact with their respective representatives at the Conference. I have often witnessed in Washington very serious misunderstandings to the prejudice of the Latin-American nations, and especially in regard to Mexico, resulting from want of proper information on the questions involved, and I thought that I would render a service both to Mexico and the Latin-American countries at large, as well as to the United States, if I did what I could to dispel those errors, and so obtain a more satisfactory understanding between the two races inhabiting the American continent.

On account of my long residence in the United States, the greater part of my life having been spent here, many people in Mexico, and especially those who are unfriendly to this country, have thought that pleasant and agreeable associations may have imperceptibly influenced and controlled my judgment and methods of thought. While this belief may be perfectly correct, in so far as a full knowledge and appreciation of the American people and their institutions and tendencies is concerned, it is not true that I am the less jealous of the rights and interests of my own country. The peculiar position which I thus occupy enables me to judge correctly of the conditions of the two countries, and of the manner in which such obstacles as are in the way of a better understanding of each other may best be removed.

I do not need, of course, to say that I publish this book in my personal character as a Mexican citizen, and not in my official capacity as a diplomatic representative of the Mexican Government in Washington. Everything that it contains is therefore said on my own personal responsibility, and in no case should the Mexican Government be held responsible for any views or statements of mine.

Although the first term of my residence in Washington was the more important of the two—both because of the Civil War in this country and of the French Intervention in Mexico which took place during that time—it would swell this book to unreasonable proportions were I to collect here all my writings, speeches, interviews, and other papers written during that trying period; and therefore I shall include in this work only such matter as has been published during the second period, excepting a few short papers that I think I ought to present now.

My correspondence with the United States Government during my first sojourn in Washington, which I consider of great importance, was sent by Presidents Lincoln and Johnson to Congress, and published in several volumes, containing a record of important events then occurring in Mexico. I append a list of the different Messages sent by the President of the United States to Congress during the French Intervention in Mexico, bearing on Mexican affairs. Most of that correspondence, together with my official letters to the Mexican Government, and the instructions from that Government to the Mexican Legation at Washington, from 1859 to 1867, I published in Spanish in Mexico, in ten large volumes, some of them of over 1,000 pages, containing data in my opinion indispensable to write an accurate history of the events which took place in Mexico during that eventful period.[1] As those papers are already printed I do not think it advisable to include them here, notwithstanding that they belong to a most interesting historical period.

[1] The extent of the labor I accomplished during that period, appears from the following extract of a statement of work done by the Mexican Legation at Washington, from August 16, 1860, when I became Chargé d'Affaires, to December 31, 1866, which I published on that date :

Preface.

As an instance illustrating the importance of those documents, I append to this Preface an autograph letter from Mr. Lincoln, dated at Springfield, Ill., on January 21, 1861, addressed to me after a short visit that I made to him at his home, a few weeks before his inauguration as President of the United States. This letter, which has not before seen public light, shows his feelings towards Mexico, and is quite typical of that great man.

It is hardly necessary to say that in the publication of these papers, I have had no thought of pecuniary profit. I have often been asked by the editors of the periodicals in which they were originally printed to consent to receive an honorarium, which I have always declined. My object in writing them was, as already stated, to diffuse important information, and not to make money, and I considered that the periodicals which published my papers did me a favor, as they contributed to the accomplishment of that object. I have now decided to print the book containing them through a leading New York and London editorial house, because that is the only effective way of putting it within the reach of the general public for continued reading and reference. If I had printed this volume for private circulation it would have reached comparatively few readers, and my object would not have been accomplished.

I shall be well satisfied if I succeed in my purpose of placing within reach of the people of the United States a knowledge of Mexican affairs which is the result of many years of experience and of an intimate acquaintance with the condition of things in my own country, and will feel still more pleased if I succeed in accomplishing my object of contributing to establish a lasting friendship between the two Sister Republics.

WASHINGTON, July, 1898.

AGGREGATE STATEMENT OF WORK.

	LETTERS AND EN-CLOSURES TO	PAGES.	LETTERS AND EN-CLOSURES FROM	PAGES.
Department of State of Mexico..................	6,643	23,791	1,905	4,834
Department of State of the United States............	1,720	8,948	483	721
Mexican Consulates, Legations, etc................	1,301	1,729	1,379	1,951
Private Letters.............	7,430	14,920	7,405	16,678
Total................	17,094	49,388	11,172	24,184

TOTALS.

	LETTERS AND ENCLOSURES.	
	Number.	Pages.
From the Legation..............................	17,094	49,388
To the Legation................................	11,172	24,184
Total...	28,266	73,572

Springfield, Ill. Jan. 21. 1861

Mr. Matias Romero.

My dear Sir:

Allow me to thank you for your polite call, as Charge d'Affaires of Mexico— While, as yet I can do no official act on behalf of the United States, as one of its citizens, I tender the expression of my sincere wishes for the happiness, prosperity, and liberty of yourself, your government, and its people—

Your Obt. Sevt

A. Lincoln

Facsimile of autograph letter of Abraham Lincoln, written a few weeks before his inauguration as President of the United States, to express his sympathy for Mexico. This letter was written on note paper 7⅞ by 5⅛ inches.

PARTIAL LIST OF SPECIAL MESSAGES ON MEXICO SENT BY THE PRESIDENTS OF THE UNITED STATES TO CONGRESS DURING THE PERIOD OF THE FRENCH INTERVENTION.[1]

1862.

President's Message to the House of Representatives of April 14, 1862, enclosing papers on the present condition of Mexico. (House of Representatives, Ex. Doc. No. 100, 37th Congress, 2d Session.) 434 pages.

1863.

President's Message to the House of Representatives of January 5, 1863, in relation to the alleged interference of the United States Minister to Mexico in favor of the French. (House of Representatives, Ex. Doc. No. 23, 37th Congress, 3d Session.) 27 pages.

President's Message to the Senate of January 20, 1863, enclosing correspondence between the United States Government and Mexican Minister in relation to the exportation of articles contraband of war for the use of the French army in Mexico. (Senate, Ex. Doc. No. 24, 37th Congress, 3d Session.) 17 pages.

President's Message to the House of Representatives of February 4, 1863, enclosing report of Secretary of State and accompanying papers on present condition of Mexico. (House of Representatives, Ex. Doc. No. 54, 37th Congress, 3d Session.) 802 pages.

1864.

President's Message to the Senate of June 16, 1864, enclosing papers relative to the condition of affairs in Mexico. (Senate, Ex. Doc. No. 11, 38th Congress, 1st Session.) 496 pages.

[1] This list was made from a set of the President's Special Messages on Mexico, from 1862 to 1867, which I kept at the time for my personal use and have bound in seven volumes. Fearing that some messages might have escaped me, notwithstanding that I was very careful to collect them all, I requested Mr. Cliffton Warden, Assistant Librarian of the United States Senate Library, a very competent person, to make a complete list, and to revise mine. He furnished me with a list which is fuller than mine, and which appears at the end of the volume. He adds to my list messages sent confidentially by the President to the Senate, to which I had no access, and gives of others more details than I do.

President's Message to the House of Representatives of April 23, 1866, on the evacuation of Mexico by the French. (House of Representatives, Ex. Doc. No. 93, 39th Congress, 1st Session.) 47 pages.

President's Message to the House of Representatives of May 10, 1866, on discriminations against American commerce by the so-called Maximilian government. (House of Representatives, Ex. Doc. No. 110, 39th Congress, 1st Session.) 2 pages.

President's Message to the Senate of June 15, 1866, regarding the departure of troops from Austria for Mexico. (Senate, Ex. Doc. No. 54, 39th Congress, 1st Session.) 21 pages.

President's Message to the House of Representatives of June 18, 1866, regarding the despatch of military forces from Austria for service in Mexico. (House of Representatives, Ex. Doc. No. 130, 39th Congress, 1st Session.) 1 page.

President's Message to the House of Representatives of June 22, 1866, regarding employment of European troops in Mexico. (House of Representatives, Ex. Doc. No. 137, 39th Congress, 1st Session.) 2 pages.

President's Message to the House of Representatives of December 8, 1866, on the occupation of Mexican territory by United States troops. (House of Representatives, Ex. Doc. No. 8, 39th Congress, 2d Session.) 4 pages.

President's Message to the House of Representatives of December 20, 1866, on the attempt of Santa Anna and Ortega to organize armed expeditions in the United States to overthrow the national government of Mexico. (House of Representatives, Ex. Doc. No. 17, 39th Congress, 2d Session.) 179 pages.

1867.

President's Message to the House of Representatives of January 14, 1867, on the occupation of Mexico by United States troops. (House of Representatives, Ex. Doc. No. 37, 39th Congress, 2d Session.) 6 pages.

President's Message to the House of Representatives of January 29, 1867, on the condition of affairs in Mexico, and the evacuation of the French troops. (House of Representatives, Ex. Doc. No. 76, 39th Congress, 2d Session.) 735 pages.

President's Message to the Senate of February 11, 1867, on grants to American citizens for railroad and telegraph lines through Mexico. (Senate, Ex. Doc. No. 25, 39th Congress, 2d Session.) 30 pages.

President's Message to the House of Representatives of March 20, 1867, on the withdrawal of the French troops from Mexico. (House of Representatives, Ex. Doc. No. 11, 40th Congress, 1st Session.) 2 pages.

President's Message to the Senate of April 12, 1867, on the prisoners of war taken by the belligerents in the Mexican Republic. (Senate, Ex. Doc. No. 5, Special Session, U. S. Senate.) 4 pages.

President's Message to the House of Representatives of July 10, 1867, on the United States, European, and West Virginia Land and Mining Company and the Republic of Mexico. (House of Representatives, Ex. Doc. No. 23, 40th Congress, 1st Session.) 250 pages.

President's Message to the House of Representatives of July 11, 1867, enclosing correspondence between the Department of State and United States Ministers to Mexico. (House of Representatives, Ex. Doc. No. 30, 40th Congress, 1st Session.) 76 pages.

President's Message to the Senate of July 12, 1867, enclosing correspondence between the Department of State and Hon. Lewis D. Campbell, United States Minister to Mexico. (Senate, Ex. Doc. No. 15, 40th Congress, 1st Session.) 1 page.

President's Message to the Senate of July 18, 1867, enclosing correspondence relating to recent events in Mexico. (Senate, Ex. Doc. No. 20, 40th Congress, 1st Session.) 298 pages.

President's Message to the House of Representatives of July 18, 1867, on the capture and execution of Maximilian and the reported arrest and execution of Santa Anna in Mexico. (House of Representatives, Ex. Doc. No. 31, 40th Congress, 1st Session.) 1 page.

CONTENTS.

Contents.

Contents.

Contents.

XX

Contents.

Contents

Contents.

Contents.

Contents.

Contents.

Contents.

ILLUSTRATIONS.

GEOGRAPHICAL AND STATISTICAL NOTES
ON MEXICO

GEOGRAPHICAL AND STATISTICAL NOTES ON MEXICO.[1]

(Corrected to June 30, 1897.)

FOR a long time past I have felt the need of a short treatise containing geographical and statistical information about Mexico, to answer the many queries received on that subject by the Mexican Legation in Washington. A statistical abstract about Mexico, such as most nations publish every year, is greatly needed, especially now when the attention of business men and young men is awakening to the possibilities of Mexico. It was partly with the purpose of supplying that need that I prepared this article, which will, I hope, at least serve

---

[1] This article first appeared in the *Bulletin of the American Geographical Society of New York* of December 31, 1896. A club of the City of Washington requested me, in January, 1888, to deliver a lecture on Mexico, and, as I had not time to prepare one, I consented to give an informal talk on the subject, which I did on January 16th of that year. Most of my talk was taken down by a stenographer, and was the basis of the article which appeared in the *Bulletin of the American Geographical Society of New York*. That Society did me the honor of electing me one of its honorary members, at the request of Honorable Frederick A. Conkling, on January 25, 1870, and I have ever since felt that I owed it a debt which I could only pay by sending it a contribution about Mexico. The pressure of my official duties in Washington on the one hand, and my inability to treat properly the many subjects connected with a description of Mexico, added to the difficulty of compressing them into a few pages; on the other, delayed that work much longer than I desired or expected. I have added considerably to this article in the present edition, especially in that part which embraces statistical information about Mexico, and I am sure that in so far as concerns the fulness of that information and the most recent data, my article stands above any previous publication on the subject.

to call attention to that country, and awaken a desire for reading other and better monographs and books on Mexico written by more competent men. I have borrowed from the descriptions of others, especially in what appears under the heading of Geology, Orography, and Fauna.

PART I.

GEOGRAPHY

I. GEOGRAPHY.

Location.—Mexico is situated between 14° 30′ 42″ and 32° 42′ north latitude, and between 86° 46′ 8″ and 117° 7′ 31″ 89 longitude west of the meridian of Greenwich, embracing therefore 18° 11′ 18″ of latitude and 30° 21′ 23″ 89 of longitude. It has an area of 767,326 square miles. It is bounded on the north by the United States of America, on the southeast by Guatemala and Belize, on the south and west by the Pacific Ocean, and on the north and east by the Gulf of Mexico and the Carribean Sea.

Boundary with the United States.—The boundary with the United States is fixed by the treaties of February 2, 1848, and December 30, 1853, and begins at the mouth of the Rio Grande River on the Gulf of Mexico, follows the river for 1136 miles, to the point where it strikes parallel 31° 47′ north latitude, beyond El Paso, Texas, and from there runs along said parallel for a distance of one hundred miles, and thence south to parallel 31° 20′ north latitude ; from there west along this parallel as far as the 111th meridian of longitude west of Greenwich ; thence in a straight line to a point on the Colorado River, twenty English miles below the junction of the Gila ; thence up the middle of the said River Colorado to the intersection with the old line between Upper and Lower California, and thence to a point on the Pacific Ocean, distant one marine league due south of the southern-most point of the Bay of San Diego on the Pacific ; the total distance from El Paso to the Pacific being 674 miles. The whole extent of the boundry line between the two countries is 1833 miles.

The boundary line with the United States runs from southeast to northwest, the mouth of the Rio Grande being in 25° 57′ 14″ 74‴ north latitude ; while the line reaches on the Pacific latitude 32° 32′ 1″ 34‴ ; the point where the boundary line strikes the Colorado River is farther north, reaching 32° 42′ of north latitude. Mexico has, therefore, on the western, or Pacific side, 6° 34′ 46″ 20‴ of latitude more than on the eastern or the Gulf of Mexico side.

Boundary with Guatemala.—The boundary with Guatemala is fixed
by the treaties of September 27, 1882, and April 1, 1895, and runs from
a point on the Pacific coast three leagues distant from the upper mouth
of the River Zuchiate, and thence, following the deepest channel
thereof, to the point at which it intersects the vertical plane which
crosses the highest point of the volcano of Tacaná, and distant twenty-
five miles from the southernmost pillar of the gate of Talquian, leaving that gate in the territory of Guatemala ; the determinate line by
the vertical plane defined above until it touches the River Zuchiate at
the point of its intersection with the vertical plane which passes the
summit of Buenavista and Ixbul ; the determinate line by the vertical
plane which passes the summit of Buenavista, determined by the astro-
nomical observations, and the summit of the Ixbul hill from where it
intersects the former to a point four kilometres beyond said hill ;
thence to the parallel of latitude which crosses the last-named point,
and thence eastward until it reaches the deepest channel of the Chixoy
up to its junction with the Usumacinta River, following that river
until it reaches the parallel situated twenty-five kilometres to the south
of Tenosique in Tabasco, to be measured from the principal square of
that town ; the parallel of latitude referred to above, from its intersection with the deepest channel of the Usumacinta, until it intersects
the meridian which passes at one third of the distance between the
centres of the Plazas of Tenosique and Sacluc, this distance being
calculated from Tenosique ; from this meridian, from its intersection
with the parallel above mentioned to the latitude of 17° 49′ ; and from
the intersection of this parallel with the latter meridian indefinitely
toward the east.

The southern end of the Guatemalan line on the Pacific is in 14° 24′
north latitude, while the northern end, on the Caribbean Sea, is in 17°
49′ north latitude, being a difference of 3° 25′ in favor of the latter.
The calculated length of the southern boundary is 642 miles.

Boundary with Belize.—To the southeast of Yucatan extends the
territory of Belize, occupied by a British settlement under a permit
granted to them by the Spanish Government to cut wood within the
limits mentioned in the treaty concluded between the Kings of Great
Britain and Spain on November 3, 1783, and amended on July 14,
1786.

British Honduras, according to Mr. George Gil, F.R.G.S., in his
book, "British Colonies," published in London in 1896, was declared
a separate colony of Great Britain, under a Lieutenant-Governor subordinate to the Governor of Jamaica, in the year 1862, previous to
which time it had been a dependency of Jamaica. In 1884 a Governor
and Commander-in-Chief was appointed, by Letters Patent, and thus
the colony became independent of Jamaica. On April 30, 1859, Great

Britain signed a treaty with Guatemala, within whose boundaries most of British Honduras was situated, defining the boundary of that colony.

The limits between Mexico and Belize are defined by a treaty signed at the City of Mexico on July 8, 1893, as follows : " Beginning at Boca Bacalar Chica, the strait which separates the State of Yucatan from the Ambergris Cay and its dependent isles, the boundary-line runs in the centre of the channel between the above-mentioned cay and the main-land, southwestward as far as the parallel 18° 9' north, and then north-west midway between two cays, as marked on the annexed map (to the treaty), as far as the parallel of 18° 10' north ; then turning to the west-ward, continues across the adjoining bay, first westward to the meridian of 88° 2' west, then north to the parallel 18° 25' north, again westward to the meridian 88° 18' west, and northward along that meridian to latitude 18° 28½' north, in which is situated the mouth of the River Hondo, which it follows in its deepest channel, passing west of Albion Island, continuing up Blue Creek until the said creek crosses the meridian of Garbutt's Falls at a point due north of the point where the boundary lines of Mexico, Guatemala, and British Honduras intersect ; and from that point it runs due south to latitude 17° 49' north, the boundary-line between the Republics of Mexico and Guatemala, leav-ing to the north, in Mexican territory, the so-called River Snosha, or Xnohha."

Cession of Mexican Territory to the United States.—Mexico has ceded to the United States, by the treaty of Guadalupe-Hidalgo of February 2, 1848, and the Gadsden Treaty of December 30, 1853, 930,590 square miles, comprising over one-half of her former territory. The same cession is considered in the United States under three heads—first under the boundary treaty signed in Washington on April 25, 1838, between the United States of America and the Republic of Texas, under which Texas was annexed to the United States in 1845; second, under the cession of the Guadalupe-Hidalgo Treaty, and the third under the Gadsden Treaty.

As Mexico did not recognize the independence of Texas until the treaty of Guadalupe-Hidalgo was signed, we consider that she only gave her consent to that annexation by said treaty, and therefore that the cession of territory made then to the United States embraced also Texas.

Mr. S. W. Lamoreaux, former Commissioner of the General Land Office, published in 1896 a map of the United States, which contained in detail the different sections of territory annexed to the same in dif-ferent periods from France, Spain, Mexico, and Russia, where the Mexican annexations are clearly defined. From official data of that office, I take the following figures representing the area of each of the Mexican cessions :

First, annexation of Texas, which embraces in whole or in part the following States and Territories :

	Sq. Miles.	
Texas	265,780	
Colorado, in part	18,000	
Kansas, in part..........................	7,766	
New Mexico.............................	65,201	
Oklahoma...............................	5,740	
Total		362,487

Second, cession by the Guadalupe-Hidalgo Treaty, embracing in whole or in part the following States and Territories :

	Sq. Miles.	
Arizona	82,381	
California	157,801	
Colorado, in part.......................	29,500	
Nevada	112,090	
New Mexico..........................	42,000	
Utah.................................	84,476	
Wyoming, in part......................	14,320	
Total		522,568

Third, cession by the Gadsden Treaty, containing additions to the following Territories :

	Sq. Miles.	
Arizona	31,535	
New Mexico..........................	14,000	
Total		45,535

Grand Total in Square Miles........ 930,590

General Characteristics.—Mexico is bounded on the east by the long curve of the Gulf of Mexico and by the Caribbean Sea, and its eastern coast is 1727 miles long ; on the west it is washed by the Pacific Ocean, its coast describing the arc of a still larger circle, for a length of 4574 miles ; but after passing the latitude of the City of Mexico, about the meridian 19° of north latitude, going south, the continent makes a decided turn towards the east, the Gulf of Mexico forming the northern border, and the Pacific Ocean the southern border.

Mexico has the shape of a cornucopia, with its narrowest end tapering toward the southwest, its convex and concave sides facing the Pacific and the Atlantic, respectively, and its widest end toward the north, or the United States. I look forward to the time, which I do not think far distant, considering our continuity of territory to the United States and our immense elements of wealth, when we shall be able to provide the United States with most of the tropical products, such as sugar, coffee, tobacco, india-rubber, etc.,[1] which they now import from several other countries.

The widest portion of Mexico is, therefore, its northern extremity, or its boundary with the United States. The narrowest point is the Isthmus of Tehuantepec, about one hundred miles from one ocean to the other ; and after passing it the country expands again to the southeast towards Yucatan and Chiapas until it reaches the boundary with Guatemala and Belize.

Yucatan resembles but little in its configuration Mexico proper, as it is a level country formed by coral reefs and beds, and whose ruins show it to have been the seat of a high civilization and an advanced people.

Although the greater part of Mexico is on the North American continent proper, as the Isthmus of Panama divides North from South America, a large portion of it lies in Central America. Geographically speaking, Central America is the portion of North America embraced between the Isthmus of Tehuantepec and Panama, and of this vast territory Mexico holds about one-third. In a paper published in the *Bulletin of the American Geographical Society of New York*, of March 31, 1894, I dealt especially with this subject.[2]

The broken surface of Mexico formerly made travelling there very difficult, for which reason the country was but little known, even by Mexicans themselves, as its configuration did not allow of the building of good roads, and to travel any considerable distance it was necessary to go by mule paths, without comfortable inns, and running great risks, owing to the disturbed condition of the country. It required, therefore, time, expense, endurance, and an object in view to travel widely there. I was always desirous of knowing as much as possible of the country, and I have made long trips, many of them on horseback, solely for the purpose of studying certain regions, and I think that before the railway era, I was perhaps one of the Mexicans who knew

---

[1] In his *Notes on Mexico*, Lempriere, a distinguished traveller and historian, says : "The merciful hand of Providence has bestowed on the Mexicans a magnificent land, abounding in resources of all kinds—a land where none ought to be poor, and where misery ought to be unknown—a land whose products and riches of every kind are abundant and as varied as they are rich. It is a country endowed to profusion with every gift that man can desire or envy ; all the metals from gold to lead ; every sort of climate, from perpetual snow to tropical heat, and of inconceivable fertility."

[2] A copy of that paper is appended to this article.

most of the country and who could, therefore, most clearly realize the difficulty of knowing it thoroughly.   From this it can be readily understood how difficult it would be for a foreigner, without any previous knowledge of the country and ignorant of its language, to know it by a few days' sojourn there.   Yet many travellers who have been in Mexico only a few days write about it on their return home, just as if they knew it perfectly, making necessarily many serious and sometimes laughable mistakes.

The natural beauties of Switzerland are well known ; but to me that country is hardly to be compared with Mexico, as everything in Mexico is on a much grander scale.   In the latitude in which Switzerland is situated the snow line is quite low, and, therefore, most of the peaks of the Swiss mountains, while not so high as the Mexican mountains, are covered with perpetual snow, which embellishes the country, and which, melting in summer, supplies the beautiful lakes of that country with fresh water.   Therefore, only in the beauty of many snow peaks, beautiful fresh-water lakes, good roads, and fine hotels has Switzerland the superiority over Mexico.

Historians, travellers, and writers of the present day compare Mexico with Egypt.   There is no doubt that between the legends and romance with which the history of each of these countries abounds there is a striking resemblance.   The pyramids and ancient relics in the form of buildings, images, and undeciphered hieroglyphics on stones, coins, etc., found in both countries, all contribute to the general belief that, centuries ago, the people of Mexico and Egypt were connected by some tie, were in some way of the same race and had the same ideas. To-day in Mexico, the manner of living, of cultivating the soil, and many other peculiarities in the manners and customs of the Mexican people forcibly remind the traveller of Upper and Lower Egypt.[1]

---

[1] In a very bright article about Mexico by Mr. Charles Dudley Warner, published in *Harper's Illustrated Monthly Magazine* for June, 1897, I find the following sentence supporting my assertion :

" In the cities he is reminded of Spain, and often of Italy (since the Catholic Church prevails), but in the country and in small towns the appearance is Oriental, or rather Egyptian.   This resemblance to Egypt is due to the color or colors of the inhabitants, to the universal use of the donkey as a beast of burden, to the brown adobe walls and mud huts covered with cane, to the dust on the foliage, the clouds of dust raised in all the highways, and to a certain similarity of dress, so far as color and rags can give it, and the ability of men and women to squat all day on the ground and be happy."

Mr. Theodore W. Noyes, of Washington, in a descriptive article on Mexico, published in December, 1895, makes the following parallel between Mexico and Egypt :

" . . . The Egyptian shaduf finds its counterpart in the well sweep of Irapuato where strawberries are grown and sold every day in the year, and where irrigation is resorted to, systematized, and on a grand scale.   In the absence of trees and rocks

I, myself, although I have only visited Lower Egypt, and that as a tourist in a very hasty manner and for a very few days, was greatly struck by the great similarity that I found between the two countries and between the habits of the native Egyptian and the Mexican Indians. The Egyptian plows are used by the Mexican Indians, and they are drawn in Mexico as in Egypt by oxen whose yokes are fastened to their horns, while in other countries they are fastened on their necks. Several of the agricultural products of Egypt and Mexico are exactly the same, and the way in which foods are prepared in both countries is, too, very similar; and I also found similar traits and race characteristics between the Egyptian Copts and some tribes of the Mexican Indians.

The great difference between Egypt and Mexico is that Mexico lacks "irrigation," which has made Egypt—that small corner of the earth—the most remarkable and productive country in the world. Owing to the great stretch of latitude from the Rio Grande to the Guatemala boundary, everything that grows in Egypt, and in fact in any other part of the world, can be produced in Mexico by the aid of irrigation.

the Egyptian shaduf is small, is composed of prepared timbers, and the counterpoise to the well bucket is an immense chunk of dried, hardened Nile mud. The Mexican shaduf utilizes a forked tree and swings across it a long tapering tree trunk or branch, and the counterpoise consists of a large sink stone or mass of stones fastened together. Although Mexico stretches farther south than Egypt, the two countries lie, generally speaking, between the same parallels of latitude, but the altitude of Irapuato is 5000 feet above the sea-level of the Nile, so that the same degree of undress is not expected or found in the Mexicans as in the Egyptian shaduf workers. I saw, however, in the neighborhood of Irapuato two Indians at well sweeps working side by side who were dressed only in white cotton loin cloths, who looked like the twin brothers of shaduf workers whom I have seen photographed on the Nile. . . . The water-carrier of Cairo is much like his brother of Guanajuato, where a long earthen jar is used. The groups about the fountains with jars of water bodily borne on the women's heads or on a protecting turban-like ring, or balanced on the men's shoulders, are also Oriental. Corn is ground between two stones in Asiatic fashion.

"Egyptian sand spouts are common. Also Egyptian types of domestic utensils of pottery. The Mexican woman with a baby at her back securely fastened in the reboso, which throws the infant's weight on the mother's shoulders, is to be compared with the Egyptian woman whose reboso covers her face while the child straddles her shoulders, holding to her head and leaving her hands unfettered as in the Mexican fashion. There are no Egyptian camels, but even more numerous donkeys, the patient burros. The Indian villages, either of adobe or bamboo, the thatched roofs and organ cactus fences, and alive with goats, donkeys, or snarling curs, are African in effect. There Aztecs picture writings resemble the Egyptian, the paper being made from the maguey instead of the papyrus. The Aztecs employed captives on great public works as in Egypt. Mexico thus has pyramids with much broader base than those of Egypt, though not nearly so high, and idols quite as ugly. Gold ornaments, beads, and other highly prized antiquities are found in the tombs as in Egypt."

GEOLOGY.

The geology of Mexico has been but imperfectly studied. In the higher ranges the prevailing formations are granite, which seem also to form the foundations of the plateaus, above which rise the traps, basalts, mineral-bearing porphyries, and more recent lavas. Hence, Lyell's theory that Mexico consisted originally of granite ranges with intervening valleys subsequently filled up to the level of the plateaus by subterranean eruptions. Igneous rocks of every geologic epoch certainly form to a large extent the superstructure of the central plateau. But the Mexican table-land seems to consist mainly of metamorphic formations which have been partly upheaved, partly interpenetrated, and overlaid by igneous masses of all epochs, and which are chiefly represented by shales, greywacke, greenstones, silicious schists, and especially unfossiliferous limestones. All these formations are alike remarkable for the abundance and variety of their metalliferous ores, such as silver, silver glance, copper, and gold. Gneiss and micaceous schists prevail in Oaxaca and on all the southern slopes facing both oceans. But the highest ranges are formed mainly of plutonic and volcanic rocks, such as granites, syenites, diorites, mineral-bearing trachytes, basalts, porphyries, obsidian, pearlstone, sulphur, pumice, lavas, tufa, and other recent volcanic discharges. Obsidian (itzli) was the chief material formerly used by the natives in the manufacture of their cutting implements, as shown by the quarries of the Cerro de las Navajas (Knife Cliff), near Real del Monte and Pachuca in the State of Hidalgo. Vast deposits of pumice and the purest sulphur are found at Huichapam and in many of the craters. But immeasurably the most valuable rocks are the argentiferous porphyries and schists of the central plateau and of Sinaloa, unless they are destined to be rivalled by the auriferous deposits of Sonora. Horizontal and stratified rocks, of extremely limited extent in the south, are largely developed in the northern states, and chalk becomes very prevalent towards the Rio Grande and Rio Gila valleys. To this chalk and to the sandstones are probably due the sandy plains which cover vast tracts in North Mexico, stretching thence far into New Mexico and Texas. Here the Bolson de Mapimi, a vast rocky wilderness inhabited until recently by wild tribes, occupies a space of perhaps 50,000 square miles in Coahuila and parts of the surrounding States.

None of the horizontal layers seem to be very rich in ores, which are mainly found in the metamorphic, palæozoic, and hypogene rocks of Durango, Chihuahua, and the south. Apart from Sinaloa and Sonora, which are now known to contain vast stores of the precious metals, nearly all the historical mines lie on the south central plateau at elevations of from 5500 to 9500 feet. A line drawn from the capital to Guanajuato, and thence northwards to the mining town of Guadalupe y Calvo of Chihuahua, and southwards to Oaxaca, thus cutting the main axis of upheaval at an angle of 45°, will intersect probably the richest known argentiferous region in the whole world.

Of other minerals the most important are copper, found in a pure state near the city of Guanajuato, and associated with gold in Chihuahua, Sonora, Guerrero, Jalisco, Michoacan, and elsewhere ; iron in immense masses in Michoacan and Jalisco, and in Durango, where the Cerro del Mercado is a solid mountain of magnetic iron ore ; lead associated with silver, chiefly in Oaxaca ; tin in Michoacan and Jalisco ; sulphur in many craters ; platinum, recently found in Hidalgo ; cinnabar, also recently found in Morelos and Guerrero ; " steppe salt " in the sandy districts of the north ; "bitter salt " at Tepeyac and many other places ; coal at various points ; bismuth in many parts ; marble, alabaster, gypsum, and rock-salt in great abundance throughout the plateaus and the sierras.

MINING.

Mexico is, perhaps, the richest mining country in the world, and the production of silver—notwithstanding the imperfect methods and other drawbacks with which it has contended—represents over one-third of the product of the world, according to official statistics. Almost all the mountains of Mexico are of the metalliferous character, but those which seem richest in mining deposits are the western cordillera, extending from the State of Oaxaca to Sonora, a distance of about 1600 miles from northwest to southeast.

Humboldt gave as his opinion that Mexico would be " the treasure house of the world." Subsequent history has, in a great measure, confirmed the opinion of the great savant of his time. Still a more conservative authority has quite lately asserted that only one-tenth of the mining resources of Mexico is known. This last estimate, I am sure, is inside rather than outside of the facts. Mexico has always been considered the great silver producer, and, considering her area, and taking the century as a measure, she is the greatest silver producer of the world.

Silver.—The central group of mines in the three mining districts of Guanajuato, Zacatecas, and Catorce, in the States of Guanajuato, Zacatecas and San Luis Potosi, which have yielded more than half of all the silver heretofore found in Mexico, lies between 21° and 24° 30' N., within an area of about 13,000 square miles. Here the Veta Madre lode of Guanajuato alone produced $252,000,000 between 1556 and 1803.

In the beginning of this century Humboldt found two Guanajuato mines—the famous " Conde de Valenciana " and the " Marques de Rayas "—producing annually 550,000 marks, 4,400,000 ounces, of silver, one-seventh or one-eighth of the entire American output.   From January 1, 1787, to June 11, 1791, the Valenciana yielded 13,896,416 ounces of silver, its ore averaging a little over 100 ounces to the ton.   Though flooded, this fine old mine is still far from exhausted.

Gold occurs chiefly, not on the plateau in association with silver, but on the slopes facing the Pacific, and apparently in greatest abundance in Sonora, near the auriferous region of Lower California.   The production would have been larger if an improved process of reducing the metals had been used, but during the whole colonial period and up to the present time, we have used the patio system, which consists in grinding the ore, stirring it until it is reduced to a fine dust and mixing it then with salt and copper amalgam ; after the paste dries somewhat, salt is added in proportion to the amount of silver supposed to be in the ore ; the material is then mixed with shovels and trodden by mules, and, after a day or two, another mixture of copper, vitriol, and salt is added ; after that it is mixed and trodden again ; then quicksilver is finally added, and then more mixing and treading.   This process is repeated from five to fifteen times until the silver and quicksilver unite to form an amalgam, which is gathered into bags, and that requires about forty days.   Most of the quicksilver is squeezed out and the rest is evaporated and run off into tubs.   This method saves 50 or 60 per cent. of rich ore and, besides being very long, is rather imperfect, as it leaves a great deal of silver in the ore, and only rich ores could be treated by it ; but it was on the whole the easiest and cheapest.

Some of the old mines were worked until finally they became so deep that, with the methods then used, as buckets were employed instead of pumps, and steam had not been employed as power, it was impossible to drain them.   Naturally in a deep mine the water flows in from springs, and the deeper a mine becomes the more water it has.   These mines were worked until it was seen that it was impossible to drain them, and then they were abandoned, even though they were rich in metals.   During our war of independence almost all the mines were abandoned for the want of guarantee to life and property, and the mining industry, therefore, declined considerably ; but recently the old mines have been worked again and the production of silver has increased very considerably.[1]

[1] Mr. J. A. R. Waters of the firm of Waters Bros., Mining Engineers of the City of Mexico, said of his visit to the Jesus Maria District of the State of Chihuahu, where he went to examine the mine worked by the Pinos Altos Co., as follows :

" The district is very thoroughly mineralized and is pierced by veins more frequently than any district I ever saw.   The general formation is very similar to that of Cripple Creek, with the exception that it is not traversed by the great porphyry dikes that occur there and in other parts of Colorado.   The country formation is largely braccia.   The ore is generally free milling, and is treated with stamps and pan amalgamation, the finer ores being treated with Huntington mills.   There is little waste of values."

Real del Monte Company.—It would be interesting to refer briefly to the ups and downs of one of the mining enterprises of Mexico—the Real del Monte—as a typical case which exemplifies what has happened with many other of our mines, namely, that sometimes they yield large profits, and soon afterwards they cause tremendous losses. The Real del Monte is located about three miles from Pachuca, a large mining centre and the capital of the State of Hidalgo, distant about sixty miles southeast of the City of Mexico.

In 1739, a Biscayan, by the name of Don Pedro Jose Romero de Terreros, came from Santander and settled in Queretaro. He acquired a fortune of $60,000 in a small store in 1749, closed up his affairs, and started to return to his native land. On reaching Pachuca he met an old mining friend, Don Jose Alejandro Bustamante, who called his attention to the Real del Monte. In company with Bustamante he staked out the Biscaina, Santa Brigida, and Guadalupe mines and began to get the water out, but they soon exhausted their united funds. However, they succeeded in raising money in the City of Mexico on hard terms and drained their properties by a tunnel, which started at Moran, on the northern slope of the mountains, and, running 9000 feet through hard porphyry rock, struck the vein at a depth of 600 feet. This was accomplished a few years later in 1759. Bustamante by this time had died, but Terreros continued the work. On striking the vein he drained it, and in 1760 began the erection of the Hacienda de Regla, to work the rich ore he was taking out. He took out $15,000,000 at a small cost, repaid his advances, built and presented to the King of Spain a man-of-war and 4700 bars of silver, for which he was created Conde de Regla. He lived in grand style in the City of Mexico, and built a palatial residence on Cadena Street.

He died in 1781, and was succeeded by his son, the second Conde, who from 1774 to 1783 struggled with the water, which, as depth was attained, was very severe ; according to Ward, twenty-eight horse-whims were employed in the drainage at great expense and unsuccessfully. However, they had gotten down to 324 feet below the Moran adit on the Biscaina vein in the Guadalupe and Santa Teresa shafts. The production was $400,000 per year, drainage costing $250,000 per year, and sinking was abandoned, and the work was confined to drifting above water level.

From 1801 to 1809, $300,000 per year was taken out, but the cost of extraction was severe. Humboldt visited the property, and in 1810 the war of independence broke out, and all operations were suspended. Meanwhile the water rose and the Moran tunnel caved in, and so allowed the water to rise to an enormous height, and the district went to rack and ruin.

In 1822 the Conde's administrator, Don Ignacio Castelazo, made a report, and by his Italian mining friend, Rivafinoli, sent it to the Conde, who was living in England.

That country was only too anxious to reap for themselves some of the spoils that Spain had gleaned from Mexican mines. Here was their opportunity, many became interested, and the celebrated mining expert of that day, Mr. John Taylor, the founder of the present London firm now so heavily interested in South Africa, Taylor Bros., was sent to make an examination, and in 1824 the English Real del Monte Company was formed on the following terms :—The company leased the mines and haciendas for twenty-one years : 1st. The capital invested was to be returned from the products of the mines with interest ; 2d. The Conde was then to have one-half of the remaining proceeds yearly ; 3d. Meanwhile he was to receive $16,000 per year as an advance against his portion or anticipated profits. In case of failure of this third clause the lease would be cancelled and everything revert to the Conde. As the outlay amounted to over $5,000,000 and no profit ensued, it amounted to a rent of $16,000 per year.

In 1824 Captain Vetch, of the Royal Engineers, was sent out as manager. He brought three ships filled with one thousand tons of machinery, pumps, etc., and after untold trials in transportation and erection, finally got them to their destination. All this was done by English engineers, machinists, miners, and workmen, nearly all Cornishmen, under the direction of Colonel Colquhoun, a Peninsular veteran, who finally died of yellow fever with over fifty of his men. After unheard-of troubles they got everything by 1826 safely landed in the Real del Monte. The magnitude of the task may be understood when the almost roadless condition of the country is considered, and the bringing up of the machinery from the coast was a splendid example of British tenacity and pluck.

Captain Vetch had now cleaned out the Moran adit and the Dolores shaft, and the machinery was at once erected. The stock now rose from $500 to $8000 per share. The Conde had, in the meanwhile, borrowed money from the company and made the twenty-one-year lease perpetual, the annual rent of $16,000 remaining in force.

By 1829 Captain Vetch had grappled with the water question, and with an annual cost of $30,000 had accomplished what the first Count had paid $250,000 for, and extracted metal 324 feet below the Moran adit.

Captain Tindall, R.E., succeeded Captain Vetch, and a new shaft (1830) was commenced on the Santa Teresa and called the Terreros shaft. It was 1140 feet to the vein and was started at four points, and was connected in 1834 by drifts run from several levels, and then raised and sunk on. The work came out as true as if it had been done from the surface, thanks to the correctness of the plans of the English mine surveyors.

A 54-inch engine was erected, and with it they sank to 720 feet below the Moran adit. At this point water overpowered them. This was in 1838, and Captain John Rule, who had succeeded Captain Tindall, put in a 75-inch engine at Dolores, and removed the 54-inch one to Acosta. Captain Rule enjoyed a salary of £10,000 per year, and all other payments were in proportion. He struck two bunches of rich ore, one on the Santa Brigida, near Acosta, and the other on La Biscains, near Dolores. From these two and one at Torreros they had produced $10,481,475 at a cost of $15,381,633 or nearly $5,000,000 loss in twenty-three years. By 1846 the stock had fallen to $12.50 from $8000 a share.

In 1848, Mr. J. H. Buchan arrived, representing the English stockholders. He found water in the mines and increasing; a heavy debt of $5,000,000, bearing a tremendous interest; no money on hand and no ore. So in October, 1848, by order of the bondholders he turned over the business to a Mexican company—the present one—composed of Manuel Escandon, Antonio and Nicanor Beistegui, Mr. Mackintosh, and others for the paltry sum of $130,000. The haciendas, stock, and ores on hand were worth millions, but the English company could not dispose of them.

This was the end of the famous English Real del Monte Company. Their Mexican successors reduced expenses, completed the adit from Omotitlan commenced by the first Conde, which, running 13,500 feet, cut the mines 1110 deeper and struck immediately the *bonanza* in the Rosario, which tradition says had previously been discovered and covered up by Captain Rule.

New Mines, Topia.—We have now a great many districts that were not known by the Spaniards and have recently been discovered. Notable among them is the Sierra Mojada district in the State of Coahuila. The State of Durango has, on the west slope of the Sierra Madre mountains, the mining camps of Topia, Sianori, Birimoa, Gusanillas, Canelas, Ventanos, El Pando, Rodeo, and San Fernando; and with the exception of San Fernando they are close together, a square, one of whose sides is forty miles, would almost cover them all. This section has all the elements to form the basis of a great mining and smelting centre, as is evident by the great deposits of galena in the Topia district; in fact, this is the only place on the coast where lead ore is found in abundance; and smelting, if done at all, must rely on Topia for its supply of lead ores. In no other part of Mexico are lead ores so cheap, because of the fact that to realize on them at all they must be transported on mule-back to Culiacan in the State of Sinaloa, a distance of 106 miles, at a rate of $26.40 silver per ton, and from there by rail to Altata, a distance of thirty-nine miles; and from Altata by steamer to San Francisco, or to Guaymas, and thence by rail to the smelters in the United States, very much at the same cost. La Liona mine of this district is a very rich mine, its vein being almost vertical, and is tapped from both sides of the mountain, with tunnels at right angles to the vein. Where the tunnels intersect the vein, the vein is driven on in both directions from the tunnels ; stopes are opened, and chutes for ore are put in every seventy-five feet. The vertical distance between the tunnels is 125 metres. This mine can easily produce one thousand tons per month of clean galena, and would produce that much metal if there was a market for it.

There are other mines as large and perhaps better than La Liona, as, for instance, La Madrugada mine, formerly owned by Santa Fé Railroad employees, but now controlled by Mr. Charles Miller, of Franklin, Pa., connected with the Standard Oil Company. Topia is a great dry-ore camp as well. One thousand tons of dry ores can easily be mined there per month, were there a market for them, such as a commercial smelter located centrally to treat the ores of this and adjoining districts. Such smelter would have the advantage of an inexhaustible supply of good water the year round, fine iron ore, and limestone for fluxes.

At Topia there are four mills for the treatment of zincy ores, and dry ores assaying below one hundred ounces silver per ton. The lixiviation process by hyposulphite of soda is employed in the four mills or haciendas, two of them employ occasionally the patio process as well. Two of the mills and two mines are lighted by electricity ; the dynamo that furnishes light for one of the mills and both of the mines is driven by water power. Below the mills operated by water power, there is sufficient fall and sufficient water to furnish the power to operate compressed-air drills in all the large mines.

The other mining camps of this district, although not so well developed as Topia, are also in process of development and in a very good condition. Velardeña is also in the State of Durango, but on the other or eastern side of the mountains, and is located in a comparatively new district, where the previous owners had failed. Mr. James F. Mathews purchased the Velardeña property, erected a smelter after the International Railroad Company had extended their main line from Torreon to the city of Durango, passing near the mine, and from the beginning has run five of the six furnaces almost continuously. During 1896 the Velardeña smelter smelted on an average 175 tons of ore per day.

Li Hung Chang and the Mexican Silver Mines.—When Li Hung Chang, the Chinese Viceroy, was in Washington, in August, 1896, he inquired of me about the production of the Mexican mines, and I, trying to be conservative, informed him that they produced about $50,000,-000 a year. He then inquired how long they would continue yielding that amount. I answered that it was uncertain, but that, judging from present appearances, it could safely be said that it might be for one hundred years. This seemed incredible to him, and he said that I had been so long absent from Mexico—for he had previously asked me how long I had been in this country—I could not know the real wealth and abundance of our mines, and he was very positive that I had made a mistake. He assured me that the silver mines in China yielded occasionally something, but soon were exhausted, and it was impossible to get any silver out of them, and judging the Mexican silver mines from those he had seen at home, he was, of course, incredulous as to their yield.

Some years ago, and when the Mexican mines only yielded about $20,000,000 a year, I predicted that their annual yield would reach $100,000,000, and that prediction is about being verified, as the present product exceeds $60,000,000.

Gold.—Gold was used freely in Mexico before the Spanish conquest, and history teaches us how Cortez induced Montezuma to deliver to him his gold treasury.

As soon as Mexico was conquered, Bernal Diaz del Castillo, one of the cotemporary historians, tells us that Cortez inquired very carefully about the place where the Indians obtained their gold, whether there were placers, mines, or washings, and his agents were taken to some localities in the State of Oaxaca, where they were told was the gold supply, but, whether the Indians concealed the real location of the gold deposits, or for other reasons, the Spaniards did not obtain much gold. I have known recently of unavailing efforts having been made of persons from the United States who have tried to ascertain the localities where the Indians obtained their gold, that is—the places which were shown to Cortez in Oaxaca as gold deposits.

There is a river in the State of Guerrero which flows over a country with hills abundant in gold formation, which carries nuggets that the natives find without any difficulty, and it is called for that reason the Gold River. That river passes over some mountains where gold is found, and then comes to a place where a natural dam is formed, and the gold carried by the washings in the rainy season sinks when reaching that place, and every indication shows that there must be a very large deposit of gold there. A military engineer suggested, the last time I was Secretary of the Treasury in Mexico, that the bed of the river be changed by the Mexican Government, a work which did not present serious obstacles, and thus allow excavations to be made and the gold deposits found. It was thought advisable to make some preliminary examinations in the way of boring, and for that purpose the necessary orders were issued to send soldiers there, but I understand the project was given up and nothing was accomplished. I have no doubt that at some future time that matter will be taken up, and a great deal of gold will be found there.

Our production of gold has so far been comparatively small, because the mining and reduction of gold are more difficult and expensive than the same operations in silver, and our gold production has really been the amount of gold which has been found in our silver. For many years, when the amount was small, it was not separated, and for that reason old Mexican dollars have in China greater value than newly coined ones; but recent improvements have made it easy and cheap to make the separation of the two metals. Now that gold has risen so much in value, its mining is beginning to be developed in Mexico on a comparatively large scale, and I have no doubt that before long Mexico will be one of the largest gold producers of the world.

Mexico is an undeveloped country, in fact there are parts of Mexico as unknown as was Central Africa a few years back. From the Sonora gold district, south, on the west side of the Sierra Madre, to the State of Oaxaca, there is a gold belt as rich as California, Alaska, and South Africa combined. It is known that in the State of Sinaloa there are gold placers and gold washings, and that they are also found in every State from there south on the line of this belt.[1]

The gold output of Sonora, now beginning to attract attention, is only the first contribution of Mexico to the world's stock of the yellow metal. The west side of the Sierra Madre has a belt rich in gold, and when the world discovers this fact capital will flock to Mexico to dig it out, and Mexico will become one of the first gold producers of the world, as she has been in silver.

Specimens of " float " rich in gold have been brought from the State of Guerrero. These indications of gold have not been followed up, because no one has been progressive enough to advance the means necessary to prospect this belt. To prospect in a country where often water fit to drink must be carried, where food for man and beast must be carried, and where in many places roads must be cut with machete and axe, cannot be done without the spending of money in outfit and expenses.

The principal gold-producing States will be Sonora, Sinaloa, Guerrero, and Oaxaca, but in all of them gold-mining is yet in its beginning.

[1] I take from a report of Mr. Cramer, a mining engineer sent to Mexico by the Geological Society of Washington, D. C., as Commissioner to explore the gold fields of that Republic, the following, which refers to only one of the many new gold fields that are being found there :

" There exists an extensive ' gold placer' situated about thirty miles from Durango in the mountain devoid of vegetation ; the rock that is found in greater quantities is porphyry. I estimate that one ton of ore will yield at least $50 of gold.

" Gold is found all over the mountain, though in such imperceptible filaments that it is hard to recognize it with the naked eye ; however, every piece of stone contains the same proportion of gold."

Coinage of the Precious Metals.—Mexico has produced about one-half of the silver supply of the world. In the statistical portion of this paper I shall give full details of the production of gold and silver in Mexico, coinage, etc., and here I will only append the total coinage of gold, silver, copper, and nickel according to official statistics of the Mexican Government, which is the following :

COINAGE OF MEXICO FROM THE ESTABLISHMENT OF THE MINTS IN 1537 TO THE END OF THE FISCAL YEAR OF 1896.

COLONIAL EPOCH.	GOLD.	SILVER.	COPPER.	NICKEL.	TOTAL.
Unmilled coin from 1537 to 1731...................	$ 8,497,950 00	$ 752,067,456 54	$ 200,000 00	....	$ 760,765,406 54
Pillar coin 1732 to 1771.....	19,889,014 00	441,629,211 45	....	....	461,518,225 45
Bust coin 1772 to 1821.....	40,391,447 00	888,563,989 45	342,893 37	....	929,298,329 82
INDEPENDENCE.	$ 68,778,411 00	$2,082,260,657 44	$ 542,893 37	....	$2,151,581,961 81
Iturbide's Imperial Bust from 1822 to 1823.......	$ 557,392 00	$ 18,575,569 69	....	....	$ 19,132,961 69
Republic from 1824 to June 30, 1896...........	55,748,559 50	1,247,289,651 59	$6,511,350 36	$4,000,000	1,313,549,561 45
	$ 56,305,951 50	$1,265,865,221 28	$6,511,350 36	$4,000,000	$1,332,682,523 14
Total coinage from 1537 to June 30, 1896........	$125,084,362 50	$3,348,125,878 72	$7,054,243 73	$4,000,000	$3,484,264,484 95

SUMMARY.

Colonial Epoch............1537 to 1821...........$2,151,581,961 81

Independence.............1821 to 1896........... 1,332,682,523 14

Total.............$3,484,264,484 95

Iron.—Iron, the most useful of all the metals, is found in such vast abundance in Mexico that, could it be even partially utilized, that Republic would become one of the wealthiest of modern communities. One of the largest mines was discovered by Gines Vazquez del Mercado, in Durango, in 1562, and its appellation of "*Cerro del Mercado*" still preserves his name. The hill, which is 4800 feet long by 1100 feet in width and 640 feet in height, is almost a solid mass of mineral, averaging about seventy per cent. of metal and from which could be extracted more than 300,000,000 tons of solid ore ; this only to the level of the plain, beneath which it probably extends to an unknown depth.

The iron is also magnetic to a high degree and its power is greater when the grain is fine. This may delay fusion, but the result is an excellent wrought iron, with none of the inconveniences caused by earthy substances mixed with the iron. I have no doubt that when the coal mines are developed the iron industry will make great strides and that we will be able to manufacture most of at least the low grades of the iron goods required for our comsumption. In several other places besides our Iron Mountain we have iron with very little phosphorus, which makes first-class steel and is as good as the best produced in Cuba or Spain.

The deposits of iron in Mexico are sufficient to supply the universe for centuries to come. There is but one thing lacking, and that thing is—cheap fuel. Nature never works by halves ; those immense deposits of iron never were put where they are without the means near at hand for their utilization. Coal exists, but it has not been mined yet on a large scale, as it will be hereafter.

But even at the present time the principal supply of pig-iron comes from native ore, the output being consumed by the producers in the manufacture of iron goods. The main iron mines now being worked are located at Durango, Zimapán, Zacualtipán, Tulancingo, and Leon. For the most part these mines are found in the midst of great forests, in consequence of which cheap fuel is found in the form of charcoal, the iron made from which being of very superior quality, free from phosphorous, and, price and other things being equal, is always preferred to the imported pig. It is manufactured in charcoal furnaces exclusively.

There is, however, quite a considerable amount of pig imported, principally from Alabama, and Scotch pig from England. The great drawback to importations heretofore has been the immense quantity of scrap iron, which, during the lapse of centuries, had accumulated, unused, throughout the Republic. This, however, is becoming well-nigh exhausted ; and for that reason the demand for imported pig is increasing, the native output not keeping pace with the need for it. Much scrap iron also has come from railroads, another source of supply which is not increasing with the demand.

Imported pig ranges in price in the City of Mexico from $50 to $60 silver per ton, the native producers aiming to keep their price just about the same.

Iron Foundries.—There are in the City of Mexico, in addition to several small ones, seven large foundries, as follows : the Mexican Central Railroad foundry, the Mexican National Railroad foundry, the Artistic, the Delicias, Charreton Bros., V. Elcoro & Co., and Hipolito David. There are also large foundries at Pachuca, Puebla, Chihuahua, Durango, and Monterey, as well as smaller ones at Irapuato, Guanajuato, Zacatecas, Veracruz, Guadalajara, Mazatlán, Oaxaca, and Morelia.

Copper.—Copper is now quite an important product of Mexico, and is used to a certain extent in the country, but as the supply far exceeds the home demand, it is exported to the United States and Europe. That which finds its way to this country enters chiefly in the form of matte, and is refined into casting or electrolytic copper. What goes to Europe is blister copper, or approximately so, from the Boleo mine in Lower California, where a French company is working a large group of copper mines. The point of most activity is Santa Rosalia, on the

Gulf of California, where the company treats the ore in its own smelting plant adjoining. The matte, or black copper, is sent to Europe in the same vessels that bring out coke. The company gives employment to thousands of hands directly and indirectly, owns its own steamers, and solicits workmen all along the coast. But this enterprise, large as it is, shows the progress that has been made and the difficulties overcome by individuals. The country itself is arid and sterile, and there is little encouragement for others to prospect, or even develop, when found, apparently good prospects, owing to the natural difficulties to be overcome and the vast capital necessary to successfully carry on mining operations ; as success is hardly to be obtained except by treating the ores on the ground, as the Boleo Company has done.

At the same time the enterprising firm of Guggenheim has established its works at Aguas Calientes, adding very considerably to the copper product, and the increase of matte shipments from San Luis Potosi and Monterey makes a large difference from former returns. To judge from the official figures, the amount of copper produced in 1896 was not less than 22,000 metric tons, the greater production being from the Boleo mines.

Quicksilver.—The production of quicksilver can only be approximated from imports, as the native production is far short of the requirements of the country. In 1895 the amount imported was 818,704 kilos, with a value of $541,664, while during the past year the amount imported was 854,526 kilos, with a value of $574,153. The only inference to be drawn from these figures is that the production in Mexico in the past year as compared with 1895 has not increased, and the figures of production given in the *Engineering and Mining Journal* of 1895 may be accepted as correct for 1896.

Coal.—Fuel is perhaps the greatest and most pressing need of Mexico. For centuries the population of the whole country has used wood for fuel, until the most thickly inhabited portions of the country are completely destitute of trees. This condition of things is a very serious objection to the increase of manufacturing, as it is impossible to manufacture cheaply when fuel commands a very high figure. Coal, which has to be transported sometimes for thousands of miles before it reaches the centre of the country, becomes very expensive. At present rates the cost of wood in the City of Mexico is equal to $14 a cord, while coal ranges from $16 to $22 per ton according to grade, and one source of supply is the artificial fuel of compressed coal dust brought from England, and in use not alone on the Veracruz Railway, but in various local industries, while coal also comes from West Virginia, Alabama, etc. The distances of the sources of coal supply and its consequent cost led to the attempt of utilizing the peat deposits which

are of great extent and practically inexhaustible within ten miles of
the City of Mexico.

In the Tlahualilo district of the State of Coahuila, for instance,
owing to the distance from the nearest coal mines, the question of fuel
is very important, as there are at present more than three hundred
horse-power in constant use, and the amount is steadily increasing.
The main supply is from the mesquite brush, which is cleared from the
new lands as the work of ditching and preparation advances. The
hulls of the cotton seed also make a hot but quick fuel for some of
the larger stationary engines. The wheat, straw and cotton bushes are
utilized for brick-burning and for the domestic purposes of the laboring population.

Those acquainted with industrial conditions in Mexico and making
investigations with a view to the establishment of new industries in
that Republic, are consequently impressed with the fact that, in spite
of the cheap labor, favorable climatic conditions, and good home
markets, the lack of cheap fuel is exceedingly detrimental to a large
proportion of the industries of this country ; but fortunately large deposits of coal are now being discovered in the Republic. At Salinas,
in the State of Coahuila, a large bed of coal is being worked by the
International Railroad Company, which furnishes fuel for that road
and even for a portion of the Southern Pacific Railroad and for some
of the manufactories in Monterey. In the district of Tlaxiaco, in the
State of Oaxaca, a very rich coal-field has been discovered, but for the
present it is inaccessible and before a railroad can be built to tap it
it cannot be used, as the expense of transportation would be exceedingly high. Sonora contains a carboniferous area, several miles in extent, with innumerable veins from five to sixteen feet in thickness, of
hard, clean, anthracite coal, carrying as high a percentage in fixed carbon as the best coal mined in Wales. The ledge is thirty miles in
length and averages sixteen feet in width, showing a quantity sufficient
to supply the entire Pacific coast with anthracite coal of the first quality
for years to come. The configuration of that State and the proximity
of the sea make it comparatively easy to work it.

At Jiquilpan, State of Michoacan, almost immediately south from
Negrete station on the Guadalajara branch of the Mexican Central
Railroad, a large coal-field has been discovered. While it is not probable that either anthracite or first-class bituminous coal will be found
in these fields, still the great value of even an ordinary class of coal
will be appreciated by those acquainted with industrial conditions in
Mexico. The coal measures of the Chapala district probably belong
to the tertiary period, and lie in stratified rock overlaid by an outflow
of basalt or lava, at an elevation of 250 or 300 feet above Lake Chapala. The general series of rocks has been examined and pronounced

as coal-bearing by an eminent geologist. The measures are quite extensive, being easily traced from Yurecuaro to near Ameca with occasional interruptions through volcanic intrusion. The developments already made, show that the coal or lignite veins extend over perhaps thirty square miles. How much beyond these limits, it would be impossible to state. It exists in considerable quantities. There are a number of veins overlying each other, and varying from two inches to fifty inches in width ; but, as the explorations have not yet found the veins in place, it is impossible to say exactly what their condition will be. A feature which adds considerably to the value of these deposits is an extensive deposit of bog iron in the immediate vicinity. If further exploration discovers considerable quantities of commercially valuable coal, it is easy to estimate the results to the industries. Other beds of coal have been discovered but of less consequence, and in several of the northern states of Mexico there are known to exist large deposits.

Mexican industries will be completely revolutionized when they can use cheap coal instead of wood for all purposes, thus cheapening the cost of manufacturing by using cheaper fuel, which is so important an item of expense in manufacturing.

Mexican Miners.—While the laborers employed in Mexico will not compare in efficiency with the labor of the miner in the United States, it must be borne in mind that the American miner works eight hours and receives $3 per day, or $6 in Mexican money, and $6 in Mexican money will employ from eight to twelve Mexicans, wages varying from 50c. to 75c. per day. As for the climatic conditions, it is only necessary to say that in all the mining districts of Mexico a miner can work 365 days in the year. There is never any snow or cold weather in winter, and the heat in the summer is not so extreme as in St. Louis, Chicago, or New York, and never enervating. A pair of blankets at night are indispensable every night in the year.

Mining Laws. — The mining laws of Mexico issued during the Spanish rule, which were kept in force until 1884, were both liberal and wise, and were intended to encourage mining. The domain of the mines remained in the Government and it gave temporary titles to anybody who discovered one, and who was willing to work it, but only as long as work was done in the mine. When the discoverer or owner could not for any reason continue to work it, and allowed a certain time to elapse without doing any work, the mine reverted to the Government and anybody else willing to work it could obtain a temporary title over it. This system was changed, by our Mining Code of 1884, to the effect of giving the mines in fee simple to the discoverers of the same, whether they were worked or not by those who denounced them, and the only cause for forfeiting the title is the failure to pay a tax of $10 per pertenencia, a "pertenencia" being our unit of a mining property and consisting of a hectare or a square 100 metres on each side, equivalent to 2.47 acres. The rights of the owner of the land are not interfered with, and in case anybody discovers a mine upon another man's property, the landlord continues to own the surface, and all the discoverer is entitled to is the mineral underground and so much of the surface as is necessary to work it, for buildings and other mining requirements, and for that the owner of the ground is compensated by agreement, or, if no amicable agreement can be reached, by arbitration.

Mining litigation is quite rare in Mexico, and it does not take long to get a final decision, as mining cases are tried before a single judge, and appeals lie to the Supreme Courts of the different states, and to the Federal Supreme Court in Mexico. To the honor of the courts in Mexico be it said, as may also be said of the judiciary in the States and the United States Federal Courts, they are above reproach.

A concise statement of the provisions of the present mining laws of Mexico will not be out of place here.

The law grants to all inhabitants of the country the right to acquire and work mines. He has to denounce a new mine. A denouncement means making a location. When the location of a claim has been determined upon, all possible data are obtained concerning it before the denouncement is made. It may be a rich old mine, and yet if the law has not been complied with it is subject to relocation. The law grants to any inhabitant of the Republic the right to explore for mineral. All districts have their mining agents and all the prospector has to do is to have the regular form of petition used in making out a denounce-ment, as it is called, made out and submitted to the mining agent of the district. If there does not happen to be a mining agent in the district, the petition is presented to the local postmaster. The expense of registering the petition is $1. After registering the petition, the mining agent has thirty days in which to appoint an expert to examine the property, who has eight days in which to reply to the summons, and if he accepts the service, the mining agent issues in duplicate a document stating that the claim has been denounced and directing objecting parties to make known their prior claims within a period of four months from the date of the denouncement, or forfeit any right to the property.

The charge of the expert for making a report upon the claim, to-gether with the plans, is about $15 per claim and travelling expenses. The expert has sixty days in which to send in his plans and report. The notification that the property has been denounced is published in the official journal of the district, the cost of which varies in the different states, from $2 to $4 being the usual fee.

The cost of making up a mining title is from $10 to $12. Titles, when once granted, unless fraud is shown, are irrevocable so long as the taxes are paid, which are ten dollars per year on each "pertenencia," and no work or manual labor is necessary to hold the same. The taxes may be paid quarterly or annually, at the discretion of the holder, to the mining agent of the district in which the property is denounced, or by special arrangement they may be paid at the office of the Federal Treasury in the City of Mexico. After the title is granted, it must be registered in the district where the denouncement is made, and also entered upon the books of the stamp office, for which no fees are charged.

MINTS AND DUTIES ON SILVER.

Under the Spanish laws all silver paid a duty; and as most of it was coined, that duty was levied on coinage, and the exportation of bullion was prohibited; but of course a great deal was smuggled, both during the Spanish rule and still more when Mexico was opened to foreign trade after our Independence. When I occupied for the first time the Treasury Department of Mexico in 1868, it seemed to me an outrage against the mining industry of the country to require the miners—especially those who were far removed from the mints—to take their bullion from the mints, at a heavy expense and risk, coin it there and take it back to the mines, and from there to the ports to be exported to London, where it was often again turned into bullion; and as the contracts made with the lessees of the mints did not allow the free exportation of bullion, I proposed and succeeded in having enacted a law for the purpose of allowing bullion to be exported, provided that it paid the coinage duty at the respective custom-houses for the benefit of the mint's lessees; and this condition of things, extraordinary as it may seem, was a great relief to the silver producers, and continued until the Mexican Government could recover all the mints and be free to legislate on the subject, which it was able to do partially during my last incumbency of the Treasury Department; they all since having been recovered.

We had thirteen mints in the country to coin the silver extracted from our mines, which, in the precarious condition of the Mexican Treasury, were sometimes rented to private parties who advanced a sum that seemed large at that time, although it was a trifle in comparison to their profits, as they collected a duty of nearly $4\frac{1}{2}$ per cent. upon the amount of bullion coined, and they credited to the Government only $1\frac{1}{2}$ per cent. of the same, the laws requiring that only coined silver could be exported. But now that silver can be transported easily from the mine to the mint, since a railway system has been built, the mints have been reduced to four,—one in the City of Mexico, which is the principal one ; one at each of the cities of Guanajuato, Zacatecas, and Culiacan, the last being the capital of Sinaloa.

Besides the mint or coinage duties, silver was taxed in Mexico with an export duty which sometimes was as high as twelve per cent. on the value of the silver, which, together with the mint duty, amounted to seventeen per cent., not taking into account other taxes and local duties. Only the rich character of the Mexican mines could stand that burden.

The duties on silver have been readjusted and reduced considerably, until now they only amount, as established by the law of March 27, 1897, to a coinage duty of two per cent. and a stamp duty of three per cent., which are paid at the Assay Office of the Mint when coined, or at the custom-house when exported in bullion, ores, or other compounds. When exported in ores in their crude condition, the duty has a rebate of ten per cent. A small duty representing the cost of the operation is also charged for assaying, refining, smelting, and separating the metals.

SMELTING PLANTS.

The Tariff Act of October 1, 1890, having levied a duty upon lead ore, which prevented that Mexican product from coming into the United States in the shape it had come before, the American companies, who had been developing the lead ore in Mexico, established smelting plants in the country for the purpose of treating there the lead ore, and sending it as pig-lead to the United States.

The smelting plants that have been established in Mexico, and their capacity and output, taken from official data received from the Mexican Government, up to December 31, 1896, are the following :

Mexican Metallurgical Company.—This company, of which Mr. Robert S. Towne is president, obtained a charter from the Mexican Government on March 20, 1890, to establish five smelting plants in Mexico, two with the minimum capacity of 200 tons a day, two of 150 tons, and one of 100 tons. The first one is located at Morales, five kilometres west of the city of San Luis Potosi. During the fiscal year 1895 to 1896, this plant received 62,370 and 020/1000 metric tons of ore from the States of Chihuahua, Coahuila, Durango, Guanajuato, Jalisco, Mexico, Michoacan, Nuevo Leon, Queretaro, San Luis Potosi, and Zacatecas. This plant yielded during the same year 16,019 and 070/1000 metric tons of base lead bullion, with 3,198,924.14 troy ounces of silver, valued at $4,882,177.50 ; and 8268 and 37/100 troy ounces of gold, valued at $161,338.63.

National Mexican Smelter at Monterey.—This company, whose president is Mr. Daniel Guggenheim, obtained a charter from the Mexican Government on October 9, 1890, to establish three smelting plants in Mexico, two with a minimum capacity of 300 tons per day, and one with 100 tons. The first plant is located in the outskirts of the city of Monterey, has ten furnaces of the water-jacket system, and seven smelting furnaces for lead ore. From July, 1892, to June, 1896, this plant has smelted 521,809 and 769/1000 metric tons of ore, yielding 78,067 and 141/1000 tons of lead, with 515,382 kilograms of silver, with a value of $21,824,597.93, having used foreign coke to the value of $1,474,385.81, and Mexican coke to the value of $73,268.08.

Central Mexican Smelter.—The second smelter of the Guggenheim Company is located at Aguascalientes. It has a department for concentrating copper ores, one for smelting the same ores, consisting of three furnaces, and another with four furnaces for smelting lead ores. This plant smelted from the 26th of December, 1895, 606 and 190/1000 tons of lead, containing 6502 kilograms of silver and 28 and 71/100 kilograms of gold, with a value of $341,091.

Velardeña Mining Company.—This company, whose president is Mr. Edward W. Nash, obtained a charter from the Mexican Government on May 15, 1893, for the construction of two smelting plants in Mexico, with a capacity of 200 tons a day each. From November 30, 1893, to June 30, 1896, this plant smelted 110,000 tons of ore, yielding 9069 and 680/1000 tons of lead containing 1,850,685 troy ounces of silver and 6192 ounces of gold.

The Chihuahua Mining Company.—This company, whose president is Mr. John B. Shaw, obtained a charter from the Mexican Government May 26, 1893, and is located near the city of Chihuahua. Up to July 28, 1896, it had smelted 28,555 tons of lead ore, yielding 3761 tons of lead and 529,450 troy ounces of silver.

The Mazapil Copper Company, Limited.—This company established a plant at Concepcion del Oro, Zacatecas, and has smelted 5000 tons of lead ore containing silver.

Sabinal Mining and Smelting Company, Chihuahua.—This company owns the mines of Santa Juliana and Santa Inez, which yield 30 per cent. of lead, with a mixture of silver, and smelts their ore, notwithstanding that the cost of a ton of coke amounts to $37.50.

La Preciosa.—A smelter under that name has been established at Tepeyahualco, State of Puebla, but I do not have any data about the company owning it, and the date of its contract with the Mexican Government, nor the amount of ore smelted there.

The Boleo Smelter.—I have already spoken of this plant, which smelts copper ores at Santa Rosalia, Lower California.

OROGRAPHY.

Mexico is traversed by two cordilleras or high ranges of mountains running almost parallel to the coast, one along the Gulf of Mexico and the other along the Pacific Ocean. The former runs from ten to one hundred miles from the coast, leaving an imperceptibly inclined plane from the sea to the foot of the mountains ; while the cordillera on the Pacific side runs, on the whole, very near the coast, leaving a very narrow strip of land between the same and the sea, and from this run several branches in different directions. The most continuous range is the Sierra Madre of the Pacific, which may be traced, at a mean elevation of over 10,000 feet, from Oaxaca to Arizona. Parallel to this is the Lower Californian range (Sierra de la Giganta) 3000 feet, which, however, falls abruptly eastwards, like the Atlantic escarpments. The California peninsula seems to have been detached from the mainland when the general upheaval took place which produced the vast chasm now flooded by the Gulf of California. Corresponding with the Sierra Madre on the west are the more interrupted eastern scarps of the central plateau, which sweep around the Gulf of Mexico as the Sierra Madres of Nuevo Leon and Tamaulipas at an elevation of about 6000 feet. These are crossed by the routes from Tula to Tampico, the highest pass being 4820 feet ; from Saltillo to Monterey 3400, and at several other places.

Of the central cross ridges the most important orographically and historically is the Cordillera de Anahuac, which surrounds the Mexican (Tenochtitlan) and Puebla valleys, and which is supposed to culminate with Popocatepetl and Ixtacihuatl. But these giants belong to a different or rather more recent system of igneous upheaval, running from sea to sea between 18° 59′ and 19° 12′ N. in almost a straight line east and west, consequently nearly at right angles to the main axis of the central plateau. The line is clearly marked by several extinct cones and by five active or quiescent volcanoes, of which the highest is Popocatepetl, lying south of the capital, nearly midway between the Pacific and the Atlantic. East of the central point of the system are Citlaltepetl, better known as the peak of Orizaba, on the coast south of Veracruz, to which correspond on the west the recently upheaved Jorullo in Michoacan, Colima (12,800) near the coast in Jalisco, and the volcanic Revillagigedo group in the Pacific. South of this line and nearly parallel, are the sierras of Guerrero, and southeast of the Tehuantepec Isthmus those of Oaxaca and Chiapas towards the Guatemala frontier. In the same direction run the islands of Cuba and Hayti, which probably belong to the same Central American system.

In the course of centuries these high mountains have become disintegrated by the rains and other natural elements, and a great many spaces between them filled up, forming a series of valleys and other spots quite delightful in climate and very rich in agricultural resources. This series of valleys, which we call the central plateau, runs from about one hundred and fifty miles east of the City of Mexico, traversing all of Mexico in a northwesterly direction. So level is the plateau that even when there were no wagon roads in Mexico one could travel in a carriage from the City of Mexico to Santa Fé. Baron Humboldt and other geologists considered the cordilleras of Mexico as a portion of the Andes of South America, which originate in Patagonia, extending over the whole of that continent; but researches were made specially by a corps of engineers, who surveyed Mexico during the French Intervention, arrived at a different conclusion, and consider that the Andes proper end in Panama, and that the Mexican cordilleras are entirely independent from that lofty chain of mountains.

In contrast with the plains and at times barren districts of the central plateau, it is occasionally broken by depressions of the soil, known as barrancas, descending sometimes one thousand feet and measuring several miles across, which are covered with a luxuriant vegetation of trees and shrubs, and watered by small streams running through the middle of the valley. Among the most remarkable ones are the barranca de Beltran descending the western slope from Guadalajara to Colima, and the barranca de Mochitilte from Guadalajara to Tepic.

One of the pre-eminently interesting features of Mexico is the mountain of Jerullo, in this section, which has been born within recent times. The natives described to Alexander von Humboldt the convulsions of the earth during its birth, and the frightful spectacle of the huge mass thrusting its giant shoulders among its neighbors, making room for itself in their ranks.

The best way to illustrate the broken surface of Mexico is to give the altitudes of some of the principal localities, both from the coast to the interior and from the interior back to the coast, taken from the measurements made by the railroad companies and by the engineers of the Mexican Government in the national wagon roads where railroads are not yet running. I append to this paper a list of such altitudes, with their distances, whenever I have been able to find them, which I consider the best illustration that could be presented on this subject.

MOUNTAINS.	STATES.	ELEVATION IN FEET.
Popocatepetl	Mexico	17,540
Orizaba	Veracruz and Puebla	17,362
Toluca	Mexico	15,019
Ixtacihuatl	Mexico and Puebla	16,076
Colima	Jalisco	14,363
Zapotlan	Jalisco	12,743
San Martin or Tuxtla	Veracruz	4,921
Tancitaro	Michoacan	12,467
Jorullo	Michoacan	4,265
Tacana or Soconusco	Chiapas	7,436
Guarda	Federal District	9,731
Ajusco	Federal District	13,628
Cofre de Perote	Veracruz	13,415
Zempoaltepec	Oaxaca	11,141
Pico de Quinceo	Michoacan	10,905
Veta Grande	Zacatecas	9,140

The above are the principal mountain peaks of Mexico, the first ten being volcanoes, with their heights according to the most recent measurements :

HYDROGRAPHY.

The eastern Mexican coast, washed by the Caribbean Sea and the Gulf of Mexico, is low, flat, and sandy, except near the mouth of the Tabasco River, where at some distance from the coast appear the heights of San Gabriel, extending northeast and southwest for several miles ; but the majestic mountains of Veracruz, especially the volcano of Orizaba, visible for many leagues to seaward, form a picturesque background which relieves the monotony of the shore region of that State. On the Pacific side the coast, although generally low, is here and there roughened by spurs extending from the cordillera to the ocean.

The principal gulfs are those of Mexico, California, and Tehuantepec, the first of which ranks among the largest in the world.

We are not blessed with good harbors on the Gulf coast. Veracruz is an open roadstead, and we are now spending large sums of money in trying to make it a good port. Our best harbors are on the Pacific coast, as Acapulco, which is a large one ; Manzanillo, a very fine although a very small one ; and La Paz, on the Gulf of California. By artificial means we expect to improve our harbors considerably.

The development of the harbor of Tampico is remarkable. A short time ago the depth of the bar roadstead was only eight or nine feet. Now steamships drawing twenty-four feet of water enter the port. The deepening of the entrance to the harbor has been accomplished by means of jetties, just as the mouth of the Mississippi was deepened by the Eads jetties. A very large part of the imports of Mexico enter now by the port of Tampico.

The more noteworthy bays are those of Guaymas, Santa Barbara, Topolobampo and Navachiste, in the Gulf of California ; Concepción, La Paz, and Mulejé, on the west coast of the same gulf ; San Quentin, Magdalena, and Amejas, on the Pacific coast of Lower California ; and San Blas and Valle de Banderas, on the coast of Tepic.

We have no lakes as large as those with which the United States is favored, and the Lake of Chapala, a beautiful spot where country houses are now being built, is the largest lacustrine basin in Mexican territory. The Valley of Mexico has six lakes, two of fresh and six of salt water. The other lakes in Mexico are Catemaco, in the State of Veracruz ; Cairel and Carpintero, in the State of Tamaulipas ; Encantada, in Tabasco ; Bacalar, in Yucatan ; Alcuzague, in Colima ; Cuitzeo, Tacascuaro, and Patzcuaro, in Michoacan ; Yuriria, in Guanajuato ; and Meztitlan, in Hidalgo.

Mexico has a great many islands, situated near the coast, although not any of very great area, the greater number being uninhabited, although some of them are very fertile, and could be the seat of a large population. Among the most important are : El Carmen, the largest in the Gulf of Mexico ; San Juan de Ulua and Sacrificios, opposite the port of Veracruz ; Mujeres, in the Caribbean Sea ; Guadalupe, about seventy-five miles from the west coast of Lower California; the Tres Marias group, about thirty miles from the same coast ; the Revillagigedo group, not far from the coast of Colima ; and adjoining the coast of the State of Michoacan, the Alcatraz Island.

As I have already stated, Mexico has a very broken surface, with high mountains, causing streams to run down a very inclined plane, forming torrents with rapid cascades, which contribute to embellish the natural features of the country. These conditions, however, prevent us from having large navigable rivers, and furnishing a cheap way of transportation, which is one of the greatest advantages the United States enjoys, and which so largely contributed in its early days to the development of the country, making transportation to long distances both easy and cheap. While the torrents descending from the mountains afford an immense water-power—which, in the course of time, may be used as a motor for industrial purposes—they meet when they reach a valley and run smoothly there through a ravine until finally they reach the coast, and it is therefore only at a comparatively small distance from the sea that they can be made navigable.

Our principal rivers, measuring their positions from north to south, are the Rio Grande—which from El Paso, Texas, to the sea, is the boundary line between the two countries, and which used to be a large river ; but as it rises in Colorado and passes through New Mexico, and the inhabitants of both have taken for irrigation purposes most of the water that it carries, it becomes entirely dry during the dry season after the freshets, very much to the distress of the inhabitants of its borders from El Paso to Ojinaga, especially on the Mexican side, which has been inhabited for three hundred years, the people using the water for irrigation—on the other side there being hardly any population,— and now they find that their farms are entirely worthless for want of water. After passing Presidio del Norte, now called Ojinaga, the Conchos River and other tributaries of the Rio Grande River supply it with water, although not to the extent it had before the water was taken in Colorado and New Mexico. The Mescala, or Balsas River, rises in the central plateau near the Valley of Mexico, passes by the State of Puebla to the southwest, by Mixteca of Oaxaca, and finally empties into the Pacific at Zacatula. As indicated by its name, it is, to a limited extent, navigable along its lower reaches ; above the bar it is accessible to small craft, which, higher up, are arrested by rapids,

whirlpools, and a high cascade.   The Pánuco River rises north of the
Valley of Mexico.   Under the names of Tula and Montezuma it describes a vast semicircular bend towards the west across the Hidalgo
uplands and collects the waters of the Huasteca of Veracruz and Tamaulipas, beyond which it is joined by the various streams flowing
from Queretaro, and finally empties into the Gulf of Mexico at the
port of Tampico.   The Tampico bar, improved by jetties, is now the
best harbor on our Gulf coast.   The Rio Lerma or Santiago, the
Tololotlan of the Indians, is also a considerable stream.   By the
riverain populations it is, in fact, known as the Rio Grande, while
the inhabitants of Michoacan call it also Cuitzeo, from the large
lake situated in their State.   It rises in the State of Mexico in
the very centre of the Anahuac plateau, and its farthest sources,
issuing from underground galleries, descend from the Nevado de
Toluca down to the twin lake of Lerma, the remains of an inland
sea which formerly filled the Upper Toluca valley north of the Nevado volcano.   At its issue from the lake, or rather marshy lagoon,
the Lerma stands at the great altitude of 8600 feet, and during its
winding northwesterly course across the plateau, the incline is very
slight.   In this upland region it is swollen by several affluents, some of
which, like the main stream itself, flow from lakes dotted over the
table-land.   After completing half of its course at La Barca, the Lerma is still 5600 feet above sea-level.   Here, some 280 miles from its
source, it enters the large Lake Chapala, near its eastern extremity ;
but about twelve miles below the entrance it again emerges through
a fissure on the north side of the lake, and still continues to flow
throughout its lower course in the same northwesterly direction.

The Grijalva and Usumacinta rivers, rising in the State of Chiapas,
after being joined by many others, some of them coming from Guatemala, empty into the Gulf of Mexico by one of its mouths at the city
of Frontera in the State of Tabasco.   The Papaloapam River rises in
the State of Oaxaca, passes through the State of Veracruz, and empties into the Gulf of Mexico at the town of Alvarado, a few miles south
of Veracruz.

The rains increase considerably the amount of water in the rivers,
but as their duration is not very long this soon subsides.   When the
streams rise near the sea, as is the case on the coast of Chiapas on the
Pacific, they become so swollen immediately after the rains that it is
impossible to ford them, and as there are no bridges, it is necessary to
wait until early the next day when the freshet has subsided.

Springs are rare, and some of the rivers run in deep mountain beds,
without receiving smaller tributaries, while the rapid evaporation on a
light soil, covering porous rocks, leaves the surface dry and hot and
unable to support much vegetation beyond the cactus and low grasses.

We are blessed with quite a number of mineral springs, although very few of them are used, most of them being at places not easily accessible ; but in this regard I do not think we have any cause to envy any other country.

CLIMATE.

By looking at the map it will be perceived that Mexico, being intersected by the Tropic of Cancer and stretching across eighteen parallels of latitude, must, from its position alone, necessarily enjoy a great diversity of climate. But from its peculiar configuration this feature is affected far more by the altitude of the land than by its distance from the pole or the equator. This is especially true of the more fertile and populous section lying within the torrid zone, where three distinct climatic regions are distinguished, not according to their horizontal, but according to their vertical position. The warm climate has the heat of the torrid zone and prevails on the sea-coast in the sandy and marshy tracts fringing the Gulf of Mexico and the Pacific Ocean, in other low places below 3000 feet above the level of the sea, and in some of the valleys higher than that, but protected entirely from the winds. But the night breezes refresh the temperature in the evening and make it bearable during the day, the heat never being so oppressive as it is in summer in the more northern latitudes. This region is also much refreshed in summer by the rains, which are abundant and fall regularly during that season. The heat of the sun increases considerably the evaporation from the sea, and when the evaporation reaches the cool atmosphere of the sky, it is naturally condensed into water and falls in this region. The rains begin generally in June, increase considerably in July, and end in November, although this varies in different regions, the rains lasting longer in those near the sea than in the inland districts. They are so abundant that they form the main reliance of the agricultural industry, and there are few regions which use water for irrigation, depending entirely upon the rainfall ; therefore, when in a year by some atmospheric phenomena, the rains are late or very scarce, we had a famine in Mexico, which can now be averted by importing cereals through our railroads, as was the case in 1893. The rains fall regularly and at fixed intervals, that is, about from one to three hours every day, and after the rain is over, the atmosphere is clear and pleasant, and in well drained places the ground becomes dry, so that it causes no inconvenience to the inhabitants.

The rains have such a decided effect on the atmosphere that in most of the country the seasons are divided into the rainy and dry season, and very few realize what spring and fall mean. As our climate is so even, the trees do not lose their leaves at any given time, but one by one as they grow old and die ; and as the leaves die they are replaced gradually and imperceptibly by new ones, so that the phenomenon familiar to northern latitudes, of trees losing all their leaves in the autumn and regaining them in the spring, is quite new to anybody going to a temperature that has both extremes.

The differences of climate depending upon the different degrees of altitude are so great in Mexico that the vegetable products of this vast country include almost all that are to be found between the equator and the polar circle.

The mean temperature in the hot region varies from 77 to 82 degrees, Fahrenheit, seldom falling below 60, but often rising to 100 degrees, and in the sultry districts of Veracruz and Acapulco occasionally to 104 degrees, although the heat is not oppressive as is the summer heat of the eastern portions of the United States. The vegetation is, of course, in consequence entirely tropical. In the southern region the climate on both seaboards may be described as humid, hot, and rather unhealthy, and in places where stagnant water and marshes exist—which are often found on the coast on account of the sea water flowing in and remaining there—intermittent and remittent fevers prevail, and in some localities during the summer yellow fever and black vomit are endemic. These conditions could easily be remedied by proper drainage of the swamps and marshy districts.

The heat of the Gulf of Mexico when the atmosphere begins to cool in the polar regions causes a depression in the barometer, and consequently very strong north winds, which sweep over the coast with terrible force, causing great havoc. They generally begin in September and last until the winter season sets in about December. As the country is narrow, the effect of the north wind is felt all over it and that is the prevailing wind. In the City of Mexico, for instance, notwithstanding its altitude and that it is protected by high mountains from the northern winds, the temperature falls when the northerns prevail on the Gulf coast, and it becomes cloudy and drizzly, and the same effect is felt, more or less, in other portions of the country. As the country narrows towards the southeast, especially at Tehuantepec, the northern wind blows with but small obstacles, and its force and effects are felt all over it. The districts in the mountains bordering the Pacific are affected in the same way as the City of Mexico.

From 3000 to 5000 feet above the level of the sea is located our temperate zone, which succeeds the hot zone in a verticle position, and embraces all the higher terraces, and portions of the central plateaus themselves. The mean temperature is from 62 to 70 degrees, Fahrenheit, varying not more than 4 to 5 degrees during the season, thus making one of the very finest climates on the face of the earth. In this privileged region both extremes of heat and cold are unknown, and it has several cities—Jalapa and Huatusco in the State of Vera-cruz, Chilpancingo in Guerrero, Ameca in Jalisco, and many others too numerous to mention here. As these places are generally located on the slopes of mountains and not far removed from the ocean, the evaporations from the sea form clouds which are detained in their course by the high peaks and are precipitated into rain. In this region the semi-tropical productions are abundant, and with them are often combined the products of tropical and cold regions. I have seen in my own native place, the city of Oaxaca, located in the temperate region, a farm where wheat and sugar-cane were growing on the same piece of ground.

The cold region is located from 7000 feet above the sea-level up-wards, and has a mean temperature of from 59 to 63 degrees, Fahrenheit. Most of the grand central plateau is located in this region, except in such places as are in a great depression of ground and in deep ravines, where a warm temperature and tropical products are found. The rainfall is about five times less than in the temperate zone. This region, of course, produces all the growths of the cold latitudes, as wheat, oats, apples, etc., etc.

The portion of the country that is most thickly inhabited lies in the central plateau, and is quite high above the level of the sea, and so sheltered from the winds and storms by the mountains as to make the climate even, temperate, and delightful. The impression pre-vails in the United States that Mexico, lying to the south and run-ning towards the equator, must be much warmer than this country; but this is not so. Even in warm places, like the lowlands on the coast, we do not have the extreme hot weather that is experienced in summer in the United States. The sea breezes refresh the atmos-phere at night and cool it considerably, making, therefore, a very great contrast with the summer heat in this country. The medium climate of the Valley of Mexico, for instance, which is the one that has been best observed and understood, varies comparatively little between summer and winter, its greatest variations being between day and night on the same day.

The climatic conditions of Mexico are undergoing great changes on account of the destruction of the forests. The country had formerly a great deal of rain and much humidity in the atmosphere, being covered with thick forests; but with the difficulty of transporting the coal already found, the population has had to depend entirely for their supply of fuel upon charcoal, and this has in the course of time denuded the mountains, changing very materially the climatic con-ditions of some regions in the country. But in the lowlands, being thinly inhabited, the case is different, and the country is still so thickly wooded that it is impossible to pass through it, unless an open path is made with a great deal of difficulty, by felling very high trees and low brush and weeds. In this region abound forests of mahogany, cedar, rosewood, etc. I will later state more in detail the conditions of the fuel question in Mexico.

As a whole, the Mexican climate, if not of the most invigorating nature, is certainly one of the most delightful in the world. The zone of temperate lands, oceanic slopes, enjoy an everlasting spring, being exposed neither to severe winter, nor to intolerable summer heats; in every glen flows a rippling stream; every human abode is embowered in leafy vegetation; and here the native plants are intermingled with those of Europe and Africa. Each traveller in his turn describes the valley in which he has tarried longest as the loveliest in the world; nowhere else do the snowy crests or smoking volcanic cones rise in more imposing grandeur above the surrounding sea of verdure, all carpeted with the brightest flowers. In these enchanting regions there is still room for millions and millions of human beings.

The following table prepared by the Meteorological Observatory of the City of Mexico shows the meteorological conditions of the principal Mexican cities during several years, their elevation upon the sea-level being marked in metres and the temperature under the Centigrade scale.

SUMMARY OF THE METEOROLOGICAL OBSERVATIONS TAKEN IN SEVERAL CITIES OF MEXICO DURING SEVERAL YEARS.

LOCALITIES.	N. Lat.	Height above sea-level.	Number of years of observation.	Mean barometrical pressure.	TEMPERATURES IN THE SHADE.			Relative humidity.	CLOUDS.		WIND.		Rainfall. Average for a year.
					Max.	Min.	Mean.		Average.	Prevailing direction.	Prevailing direction.	Mean velocity.	
	° '	m.		mm.	°	°	°						mm.
Monterey, N. L........	25 40	495.6	1	709.1	33.2	11.7	21.0	..	....	....	S.E.	....	3413.5
Saltillo, Coah........	25 25	1633.0	4	632.1	34.0	—2.8	16.8	61	4.4	N.	N.	1.4	527.3
Culiacan, Sin..........	24 48	34.2	1	754.9	35.9	12.5	25.6	62	....	....	....	....	125.2
Mazatlan, Sin.........	24 11	4.0	4	759.3	34.1	10.3	25.2	77	3.4	N.W.	N.W.	1.7	519.2
Zacatecas, Zac........	22 46	2496.0	10	573.4	21.8	6.1	13.2	48	3.2	S.E.	S.E.	2.6	819.1
San Luis Potosi, S. L. P.	22 9	1890.0	9	613.4	33.9	—1.8	17.4	60	4.4	W.	E.	1.3	389.0
Pabellon, Ag.........	22 4	1924.0	10	607.8	24.0	12.2	18.2	57	4.0	S.S.E.	W.S.W.	1.2	537.0
Aguascalientes, Ag.....	21 53	1861.0	1	605.1	29.5	2.8	18.6	..	....	....	N.	....	542.2
Huejutla, Hid.........	21 41	376.0	1	765.1	34.0	10.0	23.0	81	....	....	....	....	2019.3
Leon, Gto.............	21 7	1798.0	14	617.4	35.6	—1.1	18.9	66	4.9	S.W.	N.N.W.	0.6	729.8
Guanajuato, Gto......	21 1	2060.0	5	601.3	30.7	1.3	17.6	58	5.3	....	....	....	964.5
Tuxpam, Ver........	20 59	......	2	763.0	......	......	24.5	82	4.3	N.W.	W.	....	1654.3
Guadalajara, Jal.......	20 41	1567.0	7	636.2	35.5	—4.5	19.7	53	....	....	E.	0.6	861.9
Queretaro, Que.......	20 35	1850.0	3	613.8	33.1	......	18.1	59	4.1	....	....	....	602.2
Pachuca, Hid	20 7	2460.0	1	574.8	27.2	0.6	13.7	59	4.2	S.W.	N.E.	2.4	436.8
San Juan del Rio, Que..	19 49	1976.0	1	......	......	......	18.3	60	3.5	E.	N.E.	....	567.1
Patzcuaro, Mich........	19 31	2138.0	1	......	......	......	16.1	..	4.3	E.	W.	....	1110.4
Mexico, D. F..........	19 26	2282.5	15	586.4	31.6	—1.7	15.4	60	5.0	S.W.	N.W.	0.8	614.8
Tacubaya, D. F........	19 12	2322.6	9	583.6	28.6	0.8	15.5	62	....	....	N.W.	....	668.1
Puebla, Pue..........	19 03	2172.0	14	593.2	31.9	—1.1	15.7	63	4.7	E.N.E.	N.E.	1.9	926.0
Tlacotalpam, Ver.......	18 36	3.5	1	760.4	......	......	25.3	80	4.8	N.	N.E.	....	2264.0
Oaxaca, Oax..........	17 04	1541.0	1	636.6	32.9	6.2	20.6	80	....	....	W.	....	649.3

SUMMARY OF THE METEOROLOGICAL OBSERVATIONS TAKEN IN SEVERAL LOCALITIES OF MEXICO, DURING THE YEAR 1896.

LOCALITIES.	N. Lat.	Altitude above the sea.	BAROMETRICAL PRESSURE REDUCED TO 0°. mean.	max.	min.	TEMPERATURE IN THE SHADE. m'n.	mx.	min.	Humidity.	RAIN. Days of Rain.	Total Rains.	Rainiest Month.	Highest rainfall in 24 hrs.	Mean annual am'nt of rain.	CLOUDS. Dominant direction.	WINDS. Average velocity per second.	Prevailing direction.	Maximum velocity per second.	EVAPORATION. Shade	Open Air
		m.	mm.	mm.	mm.	°	°	°			mm.	mm.	mm.	mm.		m.		m.	mm.	mm.
Aguascalientes	21°49'	1939.0		610.1	601.1	24.8	34.4	-0.8	53	107	82.9	July, 17.6	13 Oct., 81.6	5.1	W.		E. & N. W.	16.7		
Colima (Seminario)	19°11'	487.7	718.3				37.2	9.4	69	71	749.2	Oct., 206.7		5.2	S. W.	2.6	S. W.	6.7	4.2	
Colima	21° 0'	1580.8	634.7	639.7	630.1	25.8	34.1	-1.2	71	112	1597.8	Aug., 379.0	2 April, 125.0	4.8					4.6	7.7
Guadalajara	21° 1'	2060.8	636.1	606.5	596.1	18.4	34.1	2.9	82	107	504.2	June, 100.3	14 Aug., 48.7	4.0	E. & N. E.	0.8	N. E.	10.5	4.0	7.9
Guanajuato	19°31'	1450.0	649.3	618.6	607.9	18.5	33.5	5.6	48	202	1779.4	June, 396.4	5 July, 88.8	6.2	S. E.	1.8	E. N. E.		3.2	
Jalapa	19°21'	1912.5	613.5	618.6	607.9		34.0	-3.6	58	109	395.1	July, 87.8	16 Sept., 25.8	3.9		1.5	N. E.	36.0	2.3	4.3
Lagos	21° 7'	1798.6	617.2	622.8	611.2	17.5	34.7	2.4	47	117	314.0	Oct., 113.4	16 Sept., 33.1	4.9	S. W.	2.1	N. E.	15.6	3.9	8.2
Leon	21° 7'	1508.0				22.0	40.0	1.1				Aug., 100.0			S. W.		S. S. W.			
Magdalena	30°38'		759.8	764.9	749.3	25.4	33.5	11.7	75	70	594.2	July, 180.9	18 Sept., 85.9	3.2	N.	1.7	W.	22.0	2.3	6.9
Mazatlan	23°13'	7.5	750.5	769.9	749.4	25.8	40.5	1.8	72	72	914.7	June, 294.0	21 June, 63.8	4.9	E.	2.0	N. & N. W.	6.2	2.0	7.8
Merida	20°55'	15.3	586.2	591.9	580.5	16.8	31.8	1.5	57	143	452.0	Oct., 105.0	8 Oct., 39.0	5.1	N. E.	1.2	N. E.	15.0	2.3	6.0
Mexico (Central Observat.)	19°26'	2277.5	586.2	591.5	580.5	16.3	31.0	1.0	59	142	424.9	July, 106.0	8 Oct., 31.1	5.0	N. W.		N. W.		4.8	6.0
Mexico (National School of Young Ladies)			714.9	728.7	703.4		43.8	-3.5	60	94	628.0	July, 131.9	4 Oct., 37.4	4.6	W.	1.4	N. E.	11.3	6.9	9.6
Monterey	25°40'	495.6	688.8	613.3	604.1	16.8	31.5	5.5	63	159	619.9	Sept., 112.2	5 June, 47.6	5.5	N. E.	1.5	S. S. W.	18.7	6.1	
Morelia	19°42'	1951.0	636.9	642.2	632.5	21.3	36.0	3.1	60	128	700.2	Sept., 89.7	21 June, 36.6	4.5	N. E. & S. W.	3.3	N. W.	20.0		
Oaxaca	17° 7'	1574.1	573.5	578.9	569.1	14.1	30.7	-0.2	60	57	226.5	June, 146.7	8 Aug., 50.4	3.8		0.5	N. E.	18.0		
Pachuca	20° 7'	2425.0	594.0	598.0	589.0	17.5	31.5	1.8	73	129	687.3	April, 74.5	16 Sept., 24.8	3.7	N. E. & S. W.	1.4	E.	20.0	3.3	9.7
Puebla (Catholic College)	20° 2'	2167.7	616.0	621.4	609.6	13.1	26.5	1.0	58	88	289.7	Aug., 216.0	6 Oct., 47.0	4.1			N. N. E.			
Queretaro	20°36'	1850.0	548.6	552.3	543.0	11.3	34.3	0.1	54	92	435.0	Sept., 41.4	23 June, 40.5		N. E.	1.4	N. & S.	12.2	4.1	
Real del Monte	20° 8'	2772.2	632.3	636.5	624.1	15.2	28.2	-4.2	63	86	713.0	Oct., 86.4	23 June, 33.2	3.7	N. E.	2.3	S. E.	11.7	1.7	3.3
Saltillo	25°25'	1645.5	556.1	560.3	551.9	19.5	32.4	4.0	53	146	618.8	July, 164.0	2 April, 76.8	4.6	N. E.	0.7	W.	10.0	2.4	
San Luis Potosi	22° 9'	1890.3	616.2	621.9	609.3	13.8	28.7	-3.8	58	99	347.5	Sept., 183.4	2 April, 33.2	3.5	N. E.	2.2	W. & W. S. W.	16.7	1.7	3.0
Silao	20°56'	1848.0	556.6	560.5	551.9	25.0	31.0	15.9	76	146	647.8	Sept., 177.5	7 Oct., 34.0	4.6	N. E.		N. E.			
Toluca	19°17'	2625.0	762.5	766.1	760.4	16.1	32.0	-5.2	52	52	1539.1	July, 359.1	7 Oct., 34.0	5.2	E.	2.9	S. W.	17.1	4.0	10.0
Trejo (estate of)	20°56'		572.9	577.4	568.0		35.9	6.0		151	473.4	Nov., 177.5								
Veracruz	19°11'	14.6	636.8	640.4	633.6	20.5	35.9	6.0		151	610.6	July, 260.5	19 Aug., 78.6	5.6	N. E.	2.6	S. E.	18.0	2.1	
Zacatecas	22°46'	2443.0																		
Zapotlan	19°36'	1562.0																		

The table on page 39 shows the results of the meteorological observations taken in the principal cities of Mexico during the year 1896.

Professor Mariano Barcena, director of our National Meteorological Observatory or Weather Bureau, furnished me the following data about the maximum and minimum of temperature and greatest oscillation both in summer and winter of several cities in Mexico, located both at the sea-level like Merida and Mazatlan, at different altitudes like Jalapa, San Luis Potosi, Oaxaca, and at the highest level like the cities of Mexico, Pachuca, and Zacatecas, showing the mildness of the Mexican climate.

CITY OF MEXICO.

Maximum temperature in the shade in summer........ 84.9, May 5th.
Maximum temperature in winter.................... 72.0, December.
Minimum temperature in winter.................... 32.9, January and February.
Greatest oscillation in one day in winter............ 13.7
Greatest oscillation in one day in summer........... 32.9

PUEBLA (STATE OF PUEBLA).

Maximum temperature in the shade in summer .... 83.8, April.
Maximum temperature in winter.................... 74.7, February.
Minimum temperature in winter.................... 32.9, January.
Greatest oscillation in one day in winter............ 36.3
Greatest oscillation in one day in summer........... 34.4

OAXACA (STATE OF OAXACA).

Maximum temperature in the shade in summer........ 93.7, May.
Maximum temperature in winter.................... 83.1, February.
Minimum temperature in winter.................... 39.2, January and December.
Greatest oscillation in one day in winter............ 39.1
Greatest oscillation in one day in summer........... 37.8

JALAPA (STATE OF VERACRUZ).

Maximum temperature in shade in summer........... 89.6, April.
Maximum temperature in winter.................... 87.1, December.
Minimum temperature in winter .... 33.8, February.
Greatest oscillation in one day in winter............ 35.3
Greatest oscillation in one day in summer........... 32.0

QUERETARO (STATE OF QUERETARO).

Maximum temperature in the shade in summer........ 90.1, April and June.
Maximum temperature in winter.................... 80.4, December.
Minimum temperature in winter.................... 32.9, January.
Greatest oscillation in one day in winter............ 39.4
Greatest oscillation in one day in summer........... 34.7

GUANAJUATO (STATE OF GUANAJUATO).

Maximum temperature in the shade in summer........ 91.9, April.
Maximum temperature in winter.................... 82.0, February.
Minimum temperature in winter .... 36.0, January.
Greatest oscillation in one day in winter............ 36.7
Greatest oscillation in one day in summer............ 36.7

LEON (STATE OF GUANAJUATO).

Maximum temperature in the shade in summer. ...... 91.6, May and June.
Maximum temperature in winter.................... 77.0, February.

PACHUCA (STATE OF HIDALGO).

Maximum temperature in the shade in summer........ 80.2, May.
Maximum temperature in winter.................... 77.0, December.
Minimum temperature in winter.................... 32.4, December.
Greatest oscillation in one day in winter 33.3
Greatest oscillation in one day in summer............ 28.6

REAL DEL MONTE (STATE OF HIDALGO).

Maximum temperature in the shade in summer........ 80.2, March.
Maximum temperature in winter.................... 74.1, January.
Minimum temperature in winter.................... 31.6, January.

SALTILLO (STATE OF COAHUILA).

Maximum temperature in the shade in summer........ 89.6, April.
Maximum temperature in winter.................... 75.7, January.
Minimum temperature in winter.................... 12.2, February.
Greatest oscillation in one day in winter............ 32.8
Greatest oscillation in one day in summer........... 25.6

MERIDA (STATE OF YUCATAN).

Maximum temperature in the shade in summer........103.6, April and June.
Maximum temperature in winter.................... 92.8, January.
Minimum temperature in winter.................... 47.8, February.
Greatest oscillation in one day in winter............ 37.1
Greatest oscillation in one day in summer........... 38.7

MAZATLAN (STATE OF SINALOA).

Maximum temperature in the shade in summer........ 91.0, September.
Maximum temperature in winter.................... 84.0, December.
Minimum temperature in winter................... 15.8, February.
Greatest oscillation in one day in winter............ 16.9
Greatest oscillation in one day in summer........... 17.5

MEXICO AS A SANITARIUM.

Although the City of Mexico, on account of its present unsatisfactory sanitary conditions, of which I will treat in speaking of that city and which I am sure will be remedied before long, cannot be considered now as the best place for invalids, there are many other localities in the country presenting great advantages as sanitariums.

The mild nature and evenness of most of our climate is very favorable to certain diseases—especially pulmonary ones—and when that advantage becomes well known the central plateau of Mexico will be the best sanitarium for lung diseases, and especially for tuberculosis. Other lung diseases requiring a warmer climate could find desirable places in certain valleys in the temperate zone like Cuantla, Cuernavaca, Tasco, Iguala, and others. These very conditions, namely, the even and mild climate both in summer and winter, will make it a country visited by thousands of pleasure or health seekers who wish to escape both extremes of the northern climate. Even now we would have a much larger travel from this country if we had convenient accommodations for travellers, but our hotels are not yet as comfortable as those in the United States.

FLORA.

The short and imperfect description of the climate of Mexico, made above, will show that we can raise all the products of the three different zones into which the earth is divided, and the most remarkable thing is that we can raise them almost on the same ground. By going only a few miles, for instance, travelling on horseback four or five hours from a low to a higher locality, we change from the torrid to the temperate zone, and therefore we can have the products of both with comparatively little trouble ; and by going four or five hours higher still, we change from the temperate to the frigid zone, and these are advantages of our geographical position which can be appreciated only by those who have experienced them.[1]

[1] Mr. Charles Dudley Warner, editor of *Harper's Monthly Magazine*, in a brilliant article published in the July, 1897, number of that periodical, gives the following description of the rapid descent from the cold to the temperate and hot regions of Mexico, which may be considered as a specimen of the scenery in many other localities of that country. In many other places, where there are no wagon-roads, but only a footpath, the descent is a great deal more rapid, often 5000 feet in four or five miles, and then the contrast is still greater. At Maltrata for instance, an Indian town about 5000 feet above the level of the sea, the natives offer their tropical fruits to the passengers of the Mexican Railway going from Veracruz to the City of Mexico, and they leave with what they have left after the train starts to climb the mountains to the Central Plateau to an altitude of about 9000 feet, and they reach Esperanza, the first station on the Central Plateau far ahead of the train, which has to describe a long, zigzag course before getting there. I have selected the following extract from Mr. Warner's article because it relates to one of the historical places of Mexico :

" Cuernavaca is distinguished as the actual meeting-place of the pine and the palm. It lies only a little more than fifty miles south of the City of Mexico ; but in order to reach it there is a mountain to be crossed which is at an elevation of over ten thousand feet. A railway climbs up this mountain, over the summit, to a wind-swept plain, in the midst of pine forests, called Tres Marias—marked by the sightly peaks of the Three Marys. By long loops and zigzags it is crawling down the mountain on

The Mexican Southern Railway, from Puebla to Oaxaca, descends in a few hours, by a series of fertile terraces, from an elevation of seven thousand feet to one of about seventeen hundred and fifty feet, when ths wonderful Cañon de los Cues is reached, a region of cocoa-nuts and bananas. But all the valleys and terraces in March are green or yellow with wheat and corn and sugar-cane. It confuses one's ideas to pass a field of wheat, the green blades just springing from the ground, and then a field ripe for harvest, and then a threshing-floor where the grain is being trodden out by mules. This means that you can plant and reap every day in the year, if you can obtain water in the dry season, and do not wait for the regular and copious summer rains.

The magnificent arboreal vegetation embraces one hundred and fourteen different species of building timber and cabinet woods, including oaks, pines, firs, cedars, mahogany, and rosewood ; twelve species of dyewoods ; eight of gum trees : the cacao and india-rubber, copal, liquid-ambar, camphor, turpentine, pine, mezquite yielding a substance

the other side to Cuernavaca. Mexico City has an elevation of seven thousand five hundred feet, Tres Marias of about ten thousand, and Cuernavaca of five thousand. The descent by the wagon-road is in length only twelve miles, but the drop in that distance is five thousand feet, so that the traveller passes very quickly from temperate to tropical conditions. . . .

"From the heights Cuernavaca seems to lie in a plain, but it is really on a promontory between two barrancas, and the whole country beyond is broken, till the terraces fall off into more tropical places, where the view is bordered by purple mountains. Indeed, the little city in the midst of this tumultuous plain is surrounded by lofty mountains. The country around, and especially below to the south, is irrigated, and presents a dozen contrasts of color in the evergreen foliage, the ripening yellow crops of sugar-cane and grain, the clusters of big trees here and there about a village or a hacienda, and the frequent church-towers. All this is loveliness, a mixture of temperate and tropical grace, but there is grandeur besides. Looking to the east, say from the Palace of Cortez, over the fields of purple and green and yellow and brown, where the graceful palms place themselves just as an artist would have them in the foreground of his picture, the view is certainly one of the finest in the world. There is in the left the long mountain range with the peaks of Tres Marias, and along the foot of it haciendas and towers, cones of extinct volcanoes and noble rocky promontories. To form the middle-distance mountains come into the picture, sloping together to lead the eye along from one "value" to another, violet, purple, dark or shining as the sun strikes them, while on the left is a noble range of naked precipices of red rock, always startling in color. It is some two thousand feet up the side of one of these red cliffs that there is the remains of an ancient city of Cliff-dwellers— almost inaccessible now, but once the home of a race that understood architecture and knew how to carve. The lines of this natural picture, the fields, the intervening ledges, the lofty mountains, all converge to the spot the artist would choose for the eye to rest, and there, up in the heavens, are the snow-clad peaks of Popocatepetl and Iztaccihuatl, about seventeen thousand five hundred feet above the sea, volcanic creators of the region, and now undisputed lords of the landscape. In the evening these peaks are rosy in the sun ; in the morning their white immobility is defined against the rosy sunshine."

similar to gum-arabic, dragon trees, and the almacigo or *Callitris quadvalvis*, from which sandarac is extracted. Among the oil-bearing trees and plants, of which there are seventeen varieties, are the olive, cocoa palm, almond, sesame, flax, the tree yielding the balsam of Peru, and others. There are fifty-nine classified species of medicinal plants, and many more are mentioned by botanists as still unclassified by science.

Of the many delicious fruits which grow in the tropical regions, only a few—the pineapple, the banana, and the cocoa-nut—are known in this country, the orange being rather a semi-tropical fruit. The others require, as all fruits do, cultivated taste, and, therefore, if imported here would not find a market. Even those which do come here are of very inferior flavor, owing to the fact that they are cut green so as to prevent their decay during transportation, and they, of course, have a less agreeable taste than in the place where they grow. Of the banana, for instance, we have about twenty varieties, some of which—the richest in my opinion—grow to a size from twelve to fifteen inches in length and from two to three inches in diameter.

We can raise in Mexico all the products of the world because we have all climates, from the perpetual snow to the burning sun of the equator ; but it would take a great deal more space than I can dispose of in this paper, to mention all the agricultural products we can raise, and I will, therefore, confine myself to only such as I think are now of more importance.

Coffee.—Mexico has many localities well suited for the raising of coffee, and the production of that berry can in the future be very largely increased. In the proper locality, namely, zone, ground, and climate, coffee can be raised on a large scale at comparatively small cost, affording always a large profit, whatever may be in the future its price in foreign markets.

I have had personal experience in coffee-raising, having made a coffee plantation in the district of Soconusco, in the State of Chiapas ; and I took especial interest in visiting other plantations, both in Mexico and Guatemala, where coffee had attained a large development. My experience has shown me that the best zone for coffee is located between one and five thousand feet above the level of the sea, as coffee is not a product of the hot but of the temperate zone. On the highlands, as a rule, the quality of the coffee is better and the yield large, while the lowlands give an earlier but smaller yield. There are coffee plantations in Mexico, almost down to the level of the sea, which are yielding coffee, and from that to the elevation of six thousand feet, producing also a very good quality of coffee. For further information on this subject, I refer the reader to a treatise on coffee-raising on the southern coast of the State of Chiapas, which I published in the City of

Mexico in 1874, and which contains detailed information on the several factors affecting that industry.

It is interesting to know the production of coffee in Mexico, taken from some statistics for 1896 :

Cordoba produces..............................10,000,000 lbs.
Huatusco and Coatepec ....10,000,000 "
Oaxaca... 6,000,000 "
Tabasco.. 5,000,000 "
Chiapas .... 3,000,000 "
Other districts................................26,000,000 "

                                    60,000,000 lbs.

Sugar-Cane.—Mexico has many localities where sugar-cane can be raised at a very small cost, and where that industry can be made very lucrative, although we hardly produce enough sugar for our home consumption. From the sea-level to the frost line, which ranges, in different localities, from three to five thousand feet above the sea-level, sugar-cane can be raised in Mexico to great advantage. I have seen the cane in some places, especially in Soconusco, attain a height of twelve feet and a diameter of about five inches ; and in some localities it lasts from ten to eighteen years without need of replanting, and can be cut for grinding twice a year. When it is considered that in some places, like Louisiana, sugar has to be planted, as I believe, every two years, and that it is liable to be destroyed by frosts, the advantages of Mexico for that industry are apparent.

The favorable conditions of Mexico for raising sugar-cane are so great that I have seen the natives in the Indian town of Loxicha, in the State of Oaxaca, plant a small plot of sugar-cane, grind it with primitive wooden mills moved by hand power, using very primitive earthen pans, to evaporate the juice and make brown sugar—losing of course a great part of the saccharine matter in the cane,—transport the sugar, sometimes a distance of thirty miles on mule-back, and sell it at one cent per pound, and still make a profit.

For sugar-cane the lowlands are the best, and the plant is essentially a tropical one. It will grow, however, at very considerable altitudes, but when planted in the mountains it takes a longer time to ripen, and soon ceases to give remunerative crops. There was in southern Veracruz a sugar-cane only six months old which had a circumference of $7\frac{1}{2}$ inches. Where that cane grew the yield of cane per acre was about 80 tons when twelve months old. The elevation was something like 1000 feet. It is true, however, that the bulk of the cane grown in Mexico is to be found above 2000 feet, but I am convinced that a lower altitude would produce even better results.

Tobacco.—Among the tropical products of superior quality that we raise in the hot zone, I should mention tobacco, the Mexican tobacco being, in General Grant's estimation, superior to the Havana article. The natural conditions of soil and temperature are the same in Cuba and Mexico, but we had not the superior experience of the Cubans in curing the leaf until the late insurrection broke out in Cuba, in 1868, when a great many Cubans went to Mexico to plant tobacco. As the land has been planted in Cuba with tobacco for nearly four hundred years, and as tobacco is a very exhausting crop, it has become indispensable to manure the land with guano, while in Mexico we have virgin land, and tobacco being a comparatively new industry, no guano needs to be used. General Grant, whom I consider a competent judge, detected the taste of guano in the Havana cigars, of which ours is free, and he, therefore, preferred to smoke the Mexican cigars.

In Cuba the exhausted soil cannot produce all the leaves that are required for the world's supply of Havana cigars, and the want can only be filled through the use of Mexico leaf tobacco, the weed produced in other countries having similar conditions. The Marquis de Cabañas sent to Sumatra a quantity of seed when it became obvious that the soil of the tobacco region of Cuba was fast being worn out. He sent seed also to Java and to the United States, but it was found that it was impossible to raise tobacco of the quality of that raised in Havana anywhere but in Mexico. That raised in Java from Havana seed was very coarse and rank, replete with nicotine and meconic acid, and devoid of those delicate essential oils that give the Havana and Mexican tobacco their fine aroma.

The tobacco plant is a native of the tropics, and thrives best in the hot lands. It is a hardy plant, however, and will grow well in northern latitudes in the summer time. It often happens that the land in the tropics is actually too rich for the successful cultivation of tobacco.

India-Rubber.—The lowlands of Mexico, especially those adjoining the Pacific Ocean and which have a very warm and moist climate, are very well adapted for the india-rubber tree, which attains a large size and yields a considerable amount of india-rubber. We used to have whole forests of them, which fact shows that they were in their proper conditions of soil and climate, as they could outgrow the rank vegetation of the tropics, and prevent the growth of most of the other large trees in the forests ; but india-rubber gatherers have destroyed most of them, and I imagine that there is a comparatively small number left.

I have always thought that the production of india-rubber would before long cease to be sufficient to supply the demand, and that, therefore, the value of that article would increase with the lapse of time. Now it is to be expected that the enormous expansion during the last few years of the cycle-tire, electrical motor-car, cab, and kindred industries will lead to the bestowal of increased attention on the world's rubber supply, which is so intimately associated with the existence of these industries.

Thinking that a plantation of india-rubber trees would be very remunerative, I devoted considerable attention to that subject, and in 1872 started one of 100,000 trees in a place admirably located for the purpose, bordering on the Pacific Ocean and between two large rivers, in the same district of Soconusco. In an article published in 1872, under the title "India-Rubber Culture in Mexico," I compiled all the information on the subject that I could obtain, supplementing it with the experience that I had acquired. Unfortunately, for reasons of a political nature, I had to abandon that plantation, and when the trees that I had planted grew large enough to yield rubber, they were tapped by the natives and entirely destroyed, but my work gave me an experience which I considered of great value. For further information on this subject I refer the reader to the above mentioned article.

The india-rubber trees that grow in Mexico are not the *Haevea guianensis* that grows in Brazil, but the *Castilloa elastica*, and if we have any of the *Haevea guianensis* I have not seen them.

Enough has been written lately on rubber cultivation to show that the profits, in Mexico at least, would be very great ; indeed, 300 per cent. on the capital invested is a possible return, after five years, from cultivating *Castilloa elastica* in that Republic. This is a return which provides plenty of margin for contingencies. Rubber-growing is no longer in the experimental stage, as witness the plantation of La Esmeralda, in Oaxaca, to which further reference is made below. Cultivated india-rubber plantations are few, for the reason that, in some degree like the coffee plant, the india-rubber tree requires a long period of continuous cultivation before making any return to the cultivator. Mexico affords excellent opportunities for the development of this admittedly profitable industry. On this point the authority of Sir Henry Nevil Dering, the British Minister to Mexico, who, in a recent report to the Foreign Office on the cultivation of india-rubber, says : "The regions most favorable for the growth of this important, yet rarely cultivated, india-rubber tree are the plains of Pochutla, Oaxaca, and also along the banks of the Copalita River where the tree is found in astonishing numbers. Few are the plantations of india-rubber trees existing in the Republic of Mexico. The principal one is La Esmeralda, in Juquila, Oaxaca, which has over 200,000 trees, eight years old." According to the same report the total expense for five years' cultivation of a "rubber plantation of 100,000 trees will not exceed $25,000 in silver and the yield of 100,000 trees at the first year's harvest will bring the planter $120,000, besides the product obtained from the corn, vanilla beans, cacao, and bananas raised from side planting. The net profit on the investment, after deducting the entire cost of the land and all expenses up to the first year of harvesting, will be $95,000, and each of the succeeding harvests, for twenty-five or thirty years, will bring a steady income of over $100,000." This is 400 per cent. per annum net profit on the investment. These calculations are based upon the production of a five-year-old tree, but the report adds that "this product will be gradually increased every year for the next four or five years."

Cotton.—We have many regions in Mexico very favorably located for the cultivation of cotton. I am aware that the cotton-growers of the United States hold that what they call their cotton belt has peculiar conditions for the production of their staple, which, in their opinion, do not exist in any other portion of the globe, and they believe, therefore, that nobody can compete with them in this regard. Without any intention of depreciating the advantages of the cotton belt of this country, I am of the opinion that there are in Mexico lands as well adapted for the production of cotton as the best in this country, and in some regions perhaps better ; yet, notwithstanding these advantages, and although our wages are low, cotton is produced cheaper in the United States, and is sold with profit by the planters for one-half the price that it commands in Mexico. So great is the difference in the price of this staple in the two countries that, notwithstanding an import duty on cotton of eight cents per kilogram, or almost five cents per pound, which is equivalent to fifty cents ad valorem, we import from this country a very large portion of the cotton we manufacture. I do not overlook the fact that cotton is raised here by negro labor, which is considerably cheaper than white labor, but, even assuming that wages in this case be the same in both countries, the difference in cost is so great that some other factor besides labor must enter into the expense of production.

As our cotton manufactories are increasing, more especially because of the protection afforded to home products by the depreciation of silver, we now produce only about one half of the cotton we manufacture, and have to import the other half from the United States ; but I am sure that before long we shall not only produce enough for our own consumption but also for export.

Agave.—The whole central plateau abounds in many species of agave, which are used for several purposes. In the eastern portion of the plateau, that is, from the City of Mexico towards Veracruz, in the region called the Plains of Apam, the agave yields a large quantity of a white juice, similar in appearance to milk, which when fermented is used as a tonic, and is an intoxicating beverage. The amount of alcohol it contains is small—about 7 per cent., I believe—but imbibed in large quantities it is quite intoxicating. The use of this beverage, called pulque, has become very extensive in Mexico, and it must have very superior qualities both as a tonic and nutritive, when many live on nothing but corn and pulque. In the mining districts, where a great deal of nervous force is expended working in a high temperature and under very unhealthy atmospheric conditions, this drink is almost indispensable, and I imagine that when a way is discovered to keep it for some time, and its medicinal qualities become better known, it will be exported in considerable quantities and used by foreign countries. From the agave of other districts a drink is made called mescal, which has some remarkable therapeutic properties, the most celebrated being made in a district of the State of Jalisco called Tequila, from which it takes its name ; and in the very dry and stony regions of Yucatan another species of agave grows, which seems to derive its food wholly from the atmosphere, yielding a very good fibre, much like manilla, which we now export in large quantities, particularly to New York. All the agave yields a first-class fibre as raw material, either for paper or cordage—some of it being rather coarse, like the Yucatan henequen, and some of it almost as fine and glossy as silk, like pita.

Henequen.—By far the most important of our fibre industries is the cultivation and preparation of the fibre known as " Sisal hemp," so called from the name of the port from which it used to be principally exported, and in the United States as "henequen hemp." The plant which produces it is a species of agave which flourishes to best advantage in stony and arid land at the level of the sea. The present prosperity of the state of Yucatan, a large proportion of which is too sterile to yield any other crop, is due almost entirely to the development of this industry. The plant requires very little cultivation, and the separation and cleaning of the fibre is effected very cheaply. The yield of fibre is estimated at the rate of 1000 to 1200 pounds per acre.

Pulque.—The pulque plant is indigenous to Mexico, often growing wild on the uplands, where for months and years at a time no rain falls ; and it is also largely cultivated on the Plains of Apam, a large tract of land lying in the States of Mexico, Puebla, and Hidalgo, about sixty miles east of the City of Mexico. The plants are transplanted when two or three years old with much care, then cultivated in fields especially prepared for the purpose, each acre containing from 360 to 680 plants.

Nature requires the plant to be milked, when the liquor is ready to flow, for the use of man, else the superfluity of juices will cause the growth of a thick stem from the centre of the plant, which shoots up some ten or fifteen feet, putting out branches at the top, with clusters of yellowish flowers. These branches are symmetrical, and the effect is like a lofty, branched candlestick.

When the pulque is first extracted, before the process of fermentation sets in, it is sweet and scentless, and in this state is preferred by

those unaccustomed to the drink.   The fermentation takes place in
tubs constructed for the purpose, and to aid or expedite the process a
little " madre pulque," or pulque mother, is added, which hastens the
chemical change.   At times fermentation is retarded by a cold spell at
the vats.   When the laborer draws the sweet sap with his rude siphon,
made either of a gourd or a calabash and a hollow horn tip, he discharges the contents into a pig- or goat-skin swinging at his back.   The
" agua miel" in this stage is like a green water in appearance and taste.
Soon carbonic acid is formed, and it becomes milky, and resembles in
taste very good cider.   The amount of carbonic acid contained is so
great, and the decomposition so incredibly rapid, that in a few hours
it would become vinegar if not closely watched.   To prevent this the
pulque dulce, or sweet pulque, is poured into a tinacal—an oxhide
strapped to a square wooden frame, and capable of holding a considerable amount of the liquid.   These tinacals are of various sizes, to
meet the emergencies of the situation.

      To the sweet pulque is added an equal proportion of milk, and
then a slight dose of infusion of rennet.   This is not enough to coagu-
late it, but sufficient to induce a slight amount of putrescence, as in
cheese.   The putrid odor and flavor of pulque as sold in the pulque
shops is due to the rennet alone, for the belief that this is caused by
the flavor of the pigskin, in which it is brought to market, is without
foundation.

      From the tinacal it is poured into a hogshead by means of pigskins,
and it is transferred to the barrels of venders from the hogsheads of
the " haciendado " by means of the same skins.

      The plants are wholly independent of rain and storm, and are of a
beautiful deep-green color.   The pulque is carried every day to the
City of Mexico, by special trains, in " barricas," or large tierces, and
by " cueros de pulque," or pigskins filled with the liquid.

      The plant does not arrive at maturity or yield its sap before its
eighth year.   During the growth of the plant a central bulb is formed
for its coming juices.   This is scooped out, leaving a cavity or hole
large enough to hold a few quarts.   This cavity is made in the bottom
and middle of the plant.   The juice exudes into this cavity and is
taken out daily by being sucked into a long-necked gourd on the
siphon principle, by the Indian laborers, and then poured into the tubs
taken to the fields and then removed to the vats.

      The outlay on each plant up to maturity is calculated generally at
about $2, and the return is from $7 to $10, according to the size of the
plant.   Its period of production is about five months, and each plant
supposed to yield from 125 to 160 gallons of liquid during that time.

      The principal regions for the cultivation of the maguey are the arid
limestone chains of hills, and here, in many places, the hole for the

reception of the young plant is made with a sort of crowbar with a sharp point, used principally in the quarrying of tepatate, the chief building material of the Mexican capital. It is usual to aid the young plant by putting some good soil into the hole. These young plants are suckers which the mature maguey throws out on all sides, and which have to be removed before the heart is tapped for the sweet sap, which is the " agua miel," or honey water, of the pulque.

The leaves of the pulque plant are long and pointed, with prickles along the edges. Sometimes these leaves are very large, and the bunches of them springing from the common stalk are enormous. The bruised leaves are made into a kind of paper—a rather tough, stiff, and hard paper—and they are also used in their natural state as a thatch for the roofs of the common huts or houses occupied by the peons. A kind of thread is also made from the fibrous texture of the leaves. A rough needle and pin are made from the thorn, and from the root a cheap and palatable food is made.

Cactus.—Mexico is often called "the land of the cactus," and the multitudinous development of cactus forms in that country cannot be appreciated by any one who has not seen them in their home in the hot land. There is a species known as the giant or candelabra cactus, which has a single stem, from which spring innumerable branches, the whole plant resembling an immense candelabrum. I have seen in Oaxaca, some candelabra cacti about twenty feet in height by thirty in diameter. Some cacti shoot in single, column-like stems, others run like leafless vines, and others resemble needle cushions stuck full of needles.

Cocoa.—Cocoa is produced in several localities. That of Soconusco, in the State of Chiapas, is of so excellent a quality that when Mexico was a colony of Spain it was the only kind used by the Spanish royal family. On account of the expense and difficulty of transportation, and the cultivation of cheaper quality in other localities, the production has dwindled down to an insignificant amount, and now hardly enough is grown to supply the demand in that district ; but it is universally acknowledged that the Soconusco cocoa is the best in the world.

The best elevation for cocoa is from 300 to 1000 feet, and the tree seldom thrives well at an altitude exceeding 3000 feet. Warmth and moisture are necessary for the successful cultivation of this plant.

The State of Tabasco produces a very good quality of cocoa, although it cannot be compared with that of Soconusco. In other places it grows very well also, but for various reasons the production, instead of being developed, has dwindled down until it is not enough for home consumption, and we have to import some, especially from Venezuela and Ecuador. One disadvantage of the cocoa industry is that the tree requires several years to reach maturity and to bear fruit, and few investors can afford to wait the necessary time.

Vanilla.—The vanilla bean grows very luxuriantly on the Gulf coast of Mexico, and it has been for some time a very profitable production, especially in the counties of Papamtla and Misantla, in the State of Veracruz, on account of the excellent quality of the bean and the high price which it brings. It grows in a region which is subject to intermittent and remittent fevers, and sometimes yellow fever, and where labor is very scarce ; for these reasons it has not attained a greater development. I hardly think there is any locality where the vanilla vine grows better than in Mexico.

Vanilla requires a hot, moist climate, and, therefore, the lowlands are best suited for its culture. Very little of the vanilla produced in Mexico is at present grown at an elevation exceeding 1000 feet. At the same time it is claimed that in some places it thrives up to 3000 feet.

The vines will usually produce considerable vanilla in the third year, and they will yield considerably more during the fourth, fifth, sixth, and seventh years, and the production then begins to decrease. But before this time new rootlets have been dropped from the old plants, which form new vines that take the place of the old ones ; thus the plantation is kept in a state of continued production. The central portion of the Isthmus of Tehuantepec is one of the most suitable regions for its cultivation, as much wild vanilla is found growing in the forests there.

The Mexican vanilla dealers have established five grades, namely : First, vanilla "fina," or legal, the beans and pods of six and a half inches long, or upwards, short in the neck, sound and black, and the beans which become split or open, provided they have the foregoing qualities and the split does not extend more than a third of the pod. This class is again divided into "terciada," which is composed of the shortest pods ; "primera chica," "primera grande," "marca menor," and "marca mayor," the largest of all. Second, "vanilla chica," those pods which differ from the "terciada" only in being shorter, two of them counting as one of the first class. Third, vanilla "zacate," the pods of all sizes, which are off color through being gathered before becoming properly ripe, or being over-cured ; "pescozuda," "vana," "cueruda," and "aposcoyonada," names for pods in a more or less damaged condition. Fourth, vanilla "cimarrona," the wild vanilla in good or fair condition, three pods counting as one of the first class. Fifth, the "rezacate," composed of the very short pods ; of those split all the way up to the stalk, of the badly damaged, of the very immature, and of the greatly over-cured ; of this, six pods count as one of the first class.

After the sizing and classification are finished, the pods are tied up in bunches of 100–150, so as to weigh one pound, and wrapped in filtering paper and tin foil.

Silk Culture.—The mulberry-tree and silkworm industries have a very great future in Mexico, and are destined to produce a veritable revolution in the industries of the central plateau of that country. The mulberry tree can be grown in Mexico almost to an unlimited extent, especially in the central plateau, and, as wages are low, the raw silk can be manufactured at a great profit. Several experiments have been made on a small scale, more particularly in the Valley of Mexico, by Mr. Hipolito Chabon, a gentleman of French descent, and he has obtained most satisfactory results. I have no doubt that the time is not far distant when the silk industry will assume great proportions in Mexico, and we will be able to stand among the foremost silk-producing countries of the world.

Cochineal.—The cochineal is a bug which feeds on the cactus ; and which, when fully developed, is brushed off the cactus leaves and roasted to prevent decomposition, being then ready for market. It is raised to great advantage in Mexico, and especially in the valleys of the State of Oaxaca. When it was the only article used to dye red it was very valuable, commanding sometimes between four and five dollars per pound, and it made the wealth of that State. But recent discoveries in chemistry have supplied other substances for dyeing which are very cheap, especially aniline, and the price of cochineal has fallen considerably, so that now it is hardly raised at all. When it had a high price, it was raised in Guatemala, and it was the beginning of the wealth of that State. It is now raised, I understand, in several other countries.

Rice.—Rice grows very well in Mexico, and I have not seen any district where it is necessary to inundate the fields to favor its production, although I understand it is also raised in that way in some localities. It is generally planted just as wheat and barley are in the United States, needing no irrigation and depending entirely on the rainfall. I imagine that raising rice by inundation would be more expensive, and also be dangerous, because it could not fail to affect the salubrity of the country.

Chicle, or Chewing-Gum.—This article, like many others, grows wild in Mexico, where the demand that has arisen for it in the United States has begun to develop its production. For some time past the shipments from Mexico have been on an increasing scale, owing, no doubt, to the comparatively high prices which ruled early in 1896.

Every year a larger extent of forests is worked for chicle, resulting in a steady growth of the production since the gum first became an important commercial article, about ten years ago. Prior to that time 7 or 8 cents a pound was considered a good price, and in 1896 it was sold at 36 cents. The importation into the United States constitutes almost the entire production, and the amounts and values are thus officially reported by the Statistical Bureau of the United States for the fiscal years ending June 30 :

	1894.	1895–96.
Chicle	1,903,655 lbs.	3,618,483 lbs.
Value	$490,438	$1,167,101
Average	25⅘ cents per lbs.	32 cents per lbs.

The following statement has been compiled from official data collected by the Mexican Government, the value of the chewing-gum being in silver :

Year.	Pounds.	Value.
1885–86	929,959	$ 156,402
1886–87	1,254,853	353,641
1887–88	1,542,794	371,673
1888–89	2,037,783	592,810
1889–90	1,827,131	714,242
1890–91	2,457,653	1,284,682
1891–92	2,494,177	703,572
1892–93	1,757,813	705,167
1893–94	2,645,722	803,019
1894–95	1,668,636	679,367
1895–96	3,297,371	1,527,838
Total	21,913,932	$7,892,413

Yuca.—Yuca, or starch-plant, called manioc in South America, is a bush from four to six feet high, having tubers, like horse-radish, six to ten to every plant, and weighing from one to twelve pounds each. It is an important product of Chiapas and may be sown at any time, but it is better to do so from the stems when the rains begin, say in the month of May, by opening ditches five feet apart, and planting the cuttings, eight inches long, in them consecutively, leaving one foot between. Vegetable and sandy soil is best adapted for it, although it can be planted and will thrive in any kind of land. In arid and hard soil it needs plowing. If the land has been thoroughly cleared before planting it requires but little weeding during cultivation. A year after being sown, if the soil is rich, it will begin to yield tubers which must be dug up at the time the tree begins to flower. In replanting after digging the tubers, a slip is left standing and this will bear in twelve months. Besides extracting the starch from the tubers, the leaves are used as fodder for stock.

Sir Henry Dering, the British Minister to Mexico, sent recently to the Foreign Office some practical notes on the cultivation in Mexico of the "Yuca" or cassava plant, pineapple, ginger, "chicle" or chewing-gum, sarsaparilla, jalap, licorice, canaigre, and ramie, and I shall quote here from his notes on some of those products.

The yuca is to the peon, in the tropical section of the Republic, what potatoes are to the poor and working people of Ireland. Yuca is a native of the country, and its rise dates back before the conquest of Hernan Cortez, and it has always formed a portion of the food of the ancient and present Mexicans, especially those living in Veracruz, Oaxaca, Chiapas, Tabasco, and Yucatan. It has been estimated that the returns of yuca cultivation are immense ; the yield of an acre contains more nutritive matter than six times the same area of wheat.

Ginger.—Ginger is found growing wild in various parts of Mexico. The returns from an acre of land vary considerably, but when cultivated under favorable conditions, the crops ought to be 4000 pounds and upward. A ten-acre patch would yield annually from $5000 to $7000.

Canaigre.—Though for years canaigre has been used in Mexico, both for medicinal and tanning purposes, it has but recently attracted the attention of the outside commercial world as a valuable source of tannic acid. The result of investigations has been to create a great demand for canaigre in the tanning business of European countries, and more recently in the leather-making centres of the United States. The only supply now to be obtained of this plant is from the wild growth along the rivers and valleys of Western Texas, New Mexico, and Mexico, and a fear has been felt for some time that with the constantly increasing demand the present sources of supply must become exhausted.

Peppermint.—Water mint (*mentha vulgaris*) thrives very well on the central plateau of Mexico and in some sections of the warm zone, especially along the rivulets and small lakes. There is no reason why the peppermint (*mentha piperita*), as well as spearmint and tansy, should not grow in abundance in Mexico, as they belong to the same family and require the same climatic conditions. As the oil of peppermint is very extensively employed in medicines and the arts, the cultivation of this plant will be profitable to Mexico.

Cabinet and Dye Woods.—In the low, hot countries we have all the cabinet woods growing wild and a great many dye woods, some of which are indigenous to Mexico, like the Campechy wood, not being found in other countries. It would take too long to enumerate the different kinds of cabinet woods we have, and I will only say that it happens with them as with our fruits, that only such of them as have been introduced here, like mahogany, cedar, rosewood, ebony, and a few others, are known in this country and in Europe, while hundreds of other kinds as hard as those and of as fine, if not a finer grain, are found in the wild woods of Mexico.

Grasses.—In the lower regions of Mexico, especially at the sea-level, we have various grasses which can be grown at very little expense and which make very good food for cattle, fattening them very much, and in comparatively short time. While I lived in Soconusco, I used to buy lean cattle, three years old, at $10 per head ; and letting them pasture on the grass, the expense being little more than that of a few men to take care of the cattle, without providing them with any shelter, pens, or anything of that kind, only giving them about once a month some salt, at the end of four or five months they became very fat and could be sold on the spot at $25 a head. The fattening grasses can be very easily cultivated, because they are of such rank growth that they do not allow any other vegetation to spring up on the same spot, and so save the expense of cleaning the ground of weeds ; which, in the hot regions is very great, as vegetation is there very rank.

Alfalfa.—The alfalfa grows very luxuriantly in almost every place in Mexico, and it is so abundant there, that it has very little commercial value. It is nowhere dried and kept for fodder, but of course such use can be made of it. Land good for alfalfa has a very low price, and we are greatly surprised when we hear that in California the alfalfa land is worth $100 an acre.

Cattle Raising.—Mexico has special advantages for the raising of cattle, not only because of its mild climate, which renders unnecessary the many expenses required in the northern section of this continent, but also on account of the grasses that grow in several localities and that constitute very good food for cattle, as I have just stated.

Mexico will be, before long, a very large producer of cattle and other animals, and they will form a large share of her exports. Mexico has sent within two years about 400,000 small undeveloped cattle to the United States at about $15, Mexican silver, per head, and has also sent nearly her entire output of cotton-seed meal to the United States and Europe at about $16, silver, per ton. The meal sent to the United States is fed to cattle. The Mexican cattle sent there take the place of the better stock which is sent to Europe, causing virtually a five-thousand-kilometre railway haul against the short haul in Mexico to reach the coast. In addition we have to pay import duties in the United States. This is a sufficient evidence that a large profit could be made by fattening cattle with the cotton-seed meal in Mexico, and shipping the fattened cattle direct to Europe, even using the best cattle of the country. But rapid improvement should be made in the class of cattle for beef purposes. Cotton-seed meal is the feed to be relied on chiefly. The quantity of it produced already is sufficient to fatten a large number of stock. The cattle should also be fed with a small amount of corn along with the meal during the last month of feeding to harden and whiten the meat, as feeding only with cotton-seed meal makes the meat dark, and militates against its selling value to some extent, and the corn can be easily and profitably supplied. The total cost of fattening a steer should not reach $15 silver. There is an unlimited demand in Europe for choice meats at about 12c., gold, per pound, and no import duties have to be paid. Poor classes of meat are a drug in all markets of the world. With these great advantages placed within easy reach, the producers in Mexico of grain and stock have a guarantee of ready sale at good prices for all they can produce.

Inquiry was made in Liverpool about the possibilities of the Mexican live-animal trade with England, and it was found that the initial difficulty is the small size of the Mexican cattle, as cattle weighing 1200 pounds are considered small by the trade there, and from 900 to 1000 pounds is therefore extremely small. The smallest Texan cattle ever imported in Liverpool averaged 1226 pounds.

The best Mexican steers can be made to weigh 1200 pounds if well fattened. The difference in cost of transportation on account of lighter weight is but small in proportion to the cheapness of Mexican cattle. Cattle breeders in Mexico, on the whole, have not advanced much in developing good breeds of cattle. They do not appreciate their value, nor would they pay one-half their actual cost, though they can be had from the United States at half of what they would cost from Europe. Herefords are the best breed. I am sure that the railroads will do all they can to encourage that industry by charging as low rates as possible, as they would thus develop an industry which in the course of time would become very profitable to them.

A great need of Mexico is a reliable supply of good and healthy water through artificial means, well distributed over the stock ranges to prevent the great loss by death through lack of water, as well as the heavy shrinkage of meat and tallow, by so much unnecessary travelling of stock to water. They cannot grow fairly, much less fatten, and over one-half the annual increase die of exhaustion, while the value of the stock lost in one year would supply permanent water at convenient distances and prevent three-fourths of the loss and shrinkage now sustained. It has been amply proved that stock water can be secured under the most unfavorable conditions.

It would be to the advantage of the breeder to import some English short-horn bulls, with the object of breeding larger cattle, so as to make profitable the export of cattle to England, as animals should weigh from 1200 to 1300 pounds. This has been done in Texas and in the Argentine with beneficial results, and the improvement in the cattle from the latter place has been most marked during the last five years. With the proper attention, the same good results could be achieved in Mexico.

The English steamers that bring a large quantity of merchandise to Mexican ports have trouble in even securing ballast to get out of those ports, and have to traverse the Gulf and United States coasts to secure loads for the return trip.   Their owners are willing and ready to supply facilities for the exportation of live stock and frozen meats if assured of a sufficient traffic to justify them in the expense, for they prefer reloading direct for Europe to going elsewhere for freight.   The time required to return direct from Mexican ports is but little more than from New York and Baltimore, and is sufficiently short to warrant good service in transportation of live stock, and the cost would practically be the same as from United States ports.   The United States is beginning to export beef and stock from Galveston to Europe, which is practically the same distance as from the Gulf ports of Mexico.

Mexico could export annually and easily after the next ten years 400,000 of fattened cattle, which would increase considerably the amount of our exports, and this trade would greatly assist the development of many other industries.

The desired result in question could be hastened by mixing good foreign labor with the native labor.   The latter would be better fed, clothed, and educated, as well as encouraged, taught, and compelled to do better work, and thus the country's physical and mental welfare would be greatly promoted.

Sheep.—The same conditions apply to the sheep and wool industry. It is a great mistake for the Mexican sheep-owners to raise a class of sheep that yield each only from one to two and one-half pounds of very coarse and inferior wool, annually, while they themselves wear goods manufactured from foreign wools, and the domestic-cloth manufacturers are also under the necessity of importing largely of fine wools. Mexico possesses natural resources for producing all the wools of every grade that she needs, with a large quantity over for export, not to speak of choice grain-fed mutton for domestic and foreign consumption.

The custom of killing so much poor stock is a terrible waste of resources, as one well-fattened animal will render twice as much as a thin or poor one.

Products of Cold and Temperate Regions.—I will not speak of the products of the cold and temperate regions of Mexico, such as Indian corn, wheat, oats, barley, and others, because their cultivation is well understood in the United States, and I could say here nothing new to the American reader, but will only state that they all grow very well in the proper regions of Mexico.

FRUITS.

We produce in Mexico a great many tropical fruits that are not sent to the United States because there is no market for them for the reason that they are not known here.   Some of them are delicious, and with the facilities of communication, I have no doubt that they will become known and a taste will be developed for them in this country. I will speak here only of such of our tropical fruits as come to the United States.

The advantage of tropical fruits growing in their proper zone and climate is immense, as the expense of planting and cultivating them outside of their proper limits is very great and there is always danger of their destruction.

Oranges.—Orange trees, like any other fruit trees, depend in Mexico on the rain, and, except in a private garden or private grounds, are not irrigated. While the orange tree is a hardy plant, it thrives best and yields the most luscious fruit in the tropics. Elevation exceeding 2500 feet is not, as a rule, desirable for orange culture.

The advantages of irrigation in orange culture are great in the subtropical regions of Mexico. The fruit of the irrigated orange tree is of a very superior quality, while the tree itself has a longer lease of life and is less subject to attacks from insects and diseases of a fungoid nature. One of the conditions primarily requisite to the growing of a marketable orange is that the trees be watered at judiciously regulated intervals during and for a short time after the blossoming season. Attacks from insect and fungoidal pests, which are most disastrous, and to which the trees are peculiarly subject during the blossoming period, are rendered even more dangerous by the prevalence of a considerable amount of humidity in the atmosphere which is always conducive to the development of parasitic germs or fungoidal spores. An abundance of moisture in the ground but a comparatively small amount in the air is the condition most to be desired during and just after the blossoming season. This is to be had by irrigation, but, generally speaking, not without it. Under irrigation, the soil is also much less subject to deterioration, owing to the superior fertilizing properties of water taken from wells and streams. Rain water, aside from containing a small percentage of ammonia, which it receives from the air, only acts as a medium to transmit the nutriment from the soil to the tree, while water taken from wells or streams holds in solution the renewing materials which are directly communicated to the plant proper.

In the more elevated orange districts of Mexico, the trees should be watered about once every twenty days during the dry season.

In some places our oranges are as sweet as if they had been preserved in sugar, and this, notwithstanding the fact that no attention is paid to their cultivation, that they grow almost wild, and without irrigation.

I think that the distillation of orange blossoms would prove very profitable. The production of flowers per tree is given at from 22 to 55 pounds in the case of sweet oranges, and from 60 to 100 pounds per tree from the bitter variety.

In flavor and productiveness the Mexican orange is unsurpassed. In the majority of the districts but little care or attention is given to the cultivation of the trees. Scientific orange culture in Mexico is practically unknown. The introduction from other countries of different varieties of the plant for experimental purposes is just being commenced.

The price of oranges in Mexico at the present time, in districts reasonably near lines of transportation, is about $11 per thousand, Mexican money, on the tree. It is the practice of the producer to sell the fruit on the trees, the buyer picking, packing, and shipping it at his own expense.

About one hundred trees are usually set out to the acre, the average yield being from 800 to 1000 oranges to the tree. I know of trees in Mexico which have a record of having produced 10,000 oranges. This, however, is very exceptional.

A properly cultivated and prudently managed grove at the end of five years' growth should prove as profitably as a coffee plantation of the same size, at the end of five years.

The production of the orange trees begins in the third or fourth year and increases up to the twelfth, and, in some cases, to the fifteenth or sixteenth year. It is considered best to cut the fruit up to the fifth year, not permitting it to mature.

A book prepared by Frederico Atristain, entitled *Cultivo y explotacion de Naranja*, and published by the Department of Fomento of the Mexican Government, contains a great deal of reliable information on the subject of orange culture in Mexico.

After an orange tree has been yielding sweet oranges for many years, it very likely exhausts the substances of the earth which give the sweet taste to the fruit, and it begins to lose its sweetness, until finally, if the land is not manured, as is almost always the case in Mexico, the oranges become bitter.

A recent cyclone, which lowered considerably the temperature in Florida, destroyed in one day, I understand, about 12,000,000 orange trees, thus causing ruin or serious loss to thousands of men engaged in that large industry, while the orange region in Mexico is entirely free from frosts and consequently from such dangers.

Lemons.—In the hot and temperate regions of Mexico lemons grow very well. There are some districts of the country, like Soconusco, where the natives plant the lemon trees very close together, for the purpose of making a hedge or fence, and, notwithstanding that the trees have not the necessary conditions of sunlight and air for their proper development, they grow very well. I do not know of any place in Mexico where lemons have been cultivated for commercial purposes ; but I am sure they could be made a very lucrative industry.

Limes and Shaddocks.—Lime trees prosper very well in Mexico, bearing large amounts of delicious fruit. I have not seen in the United States any of our limes, at least such as are imported here are not like ours, and I have no doubt that if known our limes would find a good market in this country. The lime should not be planted at an altitude exceeding 1000 feet. We grow also a very large kind of shaddock, which we call "toronja," and which is not imported in this country, but which if known here would find a good demand. It grows very luxuriantly and attains at times a very large size, even eight inches in diameter, having a very thick peel.

Bananas.—The banana thrives anywhere from the sea-level to an elevation of 5000 feet, and is one of the many Mexican fruits which yield to the planter an immense profit. The whole Mexican coast produces the banana spontaneously and in very great abundance. On the lands near the sea, at an elevation of 600 to 700 feet, large planta-tions of bananas can be started at a cost of five cents per plant, in-cluding all expenses. At the end of the first year, the plants begin to bear, and 1000 plants, which have cost $50, will produce $1000 as a minimum. The following year the yield is double that amount, and almost without expense. At the end of one year, the plant produces one bunch which is worth in the United States from 75 cents to $1 gold, the cost to the farmer being not more than 25 cents per bunch in Mexican currency. After the first year, the sprouts from the old plant grow up and give double the first year's yield.

There is perhaps no tropical plant easier of cultivation than the banana. The suckers having been planted out at the commencement of the rainy season, they will grow vigorously, and produce fruit in about a year. The land must be kept free from weeds, and an oc-casional turning up of the soil will prove beneficial. Before the plant throws out its flowering stem, suckers will make their appearance above the ground, and these will require careful attention. While the plant is young, all the suckers except one should be cut away, the best plan being to sever them with a sharp spade. Thus all the vigor of the plant is thrown into the fruiting of the first stem, and the growth of the one to supplant it, and, in this way, fine large bunches can be reckoned on. The second stem usually produces a finer bunch of fruit than the first, but, as the land becomes exhausted, the bunches of course decrease in size, and this shows the necessity for manure in some form or other.

Bananas are used extensively as shade for young coffee and cocoa trees, and in places where an export banana trade has been established, the formation of a cocoa plantation is a very inexpensive matter, as the return in fruit from the bananas will pay for the cultivation of the cocoa until the trees are able to give a small crop.

The important feature, and the one upon which the success and profit of the industry depend largely, is that of cheap and certain transportation facilities. That requisite is easily obtainable ; for instance, there are extensive and cheap lands for sale along the Tampico branch of the Mexican Central Railroad, from which the fruit can be shipped either all by rail, or by rail to Tampico, and thence by boat.

We have many kinds of bananas in Mexico, of different sizes, colors, and flavors, ranging in length from two to eighteen inches, and from one-half of an inch to three inches in diameter. The largest, which in some places are thought unfit for food, are in others, like Soconusco, considered the best ; very likely on account of their different quality. When roasted the latter are very juicy, and taste exactly as if they had been preserved in sugar. Some people on the coast live almost entirely on bananas, this fruit forming their principal food. The banana is likewise a tropical plant, and thrives best on the lowlands.

Pineapple.—The Toltecs and Aztecs knew how to cultivate the pineapple, and when the Spaniards conquered Mexico, they found the fruit in the markets of the towns on their way from Veracruz to the great Tenochtitlan. "From time immemorial," Sir Henry Dering says, "the pineapple has been cultivated in Amatlan, a town five miles south of Cordoba, from where the ancient Mexicans used to get their main supply." Now it is grown in tropical Hidalgo, Puebla, Veracruz, Tabasco, Chiapas, Oaxaca, Morelos, Guerrero, Michoacan, Colima, Jalisco, and Tepic. " Besides the fruit being very delicious and wholesome," Sir Henry Dering says, "a fine wine and vinegar are made of the juice. The leaf furnishes a fibre of extraordinary strength and fineness, making it even more valuable than the fruit. The fibre is made into ropes, cables, binding twine, thread, mats, bagging, hammocks, and paper. A pineapple rope three and a half inches thick can support nearly three tons. A textile fabric as fine and beautiful as silk is made of this fibre too. It is believed that the fine cloth of various colors used by the upper classes among the Aztecs was made of the pineapple fibre. The modern Mexicans do not manufacture it much now, except in the Isthmus, where the Zapotec Indians still make a cloth from it and from wild silk. One cause for its disuse is the slow and wasteful manner in which it is separated." Pineapples will grow at elevations of from 2000 to 3000 feet above the level of the sea, but the best and most delicate fruit is produced on the lowlands.

Cocoa-Nut.—We have in our lowlands near the sea many kinds of palms called corozo, bearing different kinds of fruit, growing in large bunches and the fruit very abundant, being in the shape of a small egg, very rich in oils, and making also a very good food, although it is hardly used now for any purpose. The palm tree bearing the cocoa-nut grows, of course, very luxuriantly, and does not require any care after it is once planted. The cocoa-nut prefers the sea-coast and high temperature. The saline breezes from the sea are very beneficial to it. I have not seen in Mexico the species of palm bearing the date, perhaps because it has not been planted there ; but I am sure that we could raise it, as we have several sections with a climate similar to that of Egypt and Asia Minor, where the date palm grows so well.

Mangos.—The mango is a very fine fruit, but requires a cultivated taste, and is generally disliked the first time it is eaten. It has a very large bone, although that is not the case in fine qualities, called Manilla mango, which has a very thin one and a great deal of pulp. The mango occasionally comes to the United States, but being a very frail fruit, has to be taken from the tree when very green. It does not ripen well, and, if taken when beginning to ripen, it reaches its destination in a decayed condition.

Alligator Pear.—The alligator pear is one of the most delicious fruits that we raise in Mexico, and is properly called vegetable butter, being a good substitute for butter. It is not eaten by itself ; the most usual way to eat it is in salad. We have several kinds and sizes of this fruit. The seed of the alligator pear is oval-shaped and quite large, about 4 inches in length by 1½ in diameter, and of some oily substance, which, I have no doubt, has some good medicinal properties.

Mamey.—The same is the case with the seed of the mamey, a fruit unknown in the United States, having a red pulp, and a very large seed covered with a thin shell. The Indian women extract an oil from that seed and use it for their hair, and I think it must have many more useful medicinal properties.

A great many other of our fruits have seeds containing substances which I have no doubt will be found, when analyzed, to be very valuable to therapeutics.

Zapote.—The zapote is one of our tropical fruits which does not come to this country. I have just heard that the seeds of the zapote have recently been found by a Mexican doctor to be a very good narcotic, which does not produce the ill effects of the drugs now in use.

Papaya.—This fruit, which grows in our hot lands resembles the melon in shape, pulp, and seeds, but its color is of a yellowish-red. It was considered a very common fruit, but recently it was found to be a powerful digestive, and it is already used in Europe as a medicine under the name of Papaine.

Flowers.—Mexico is a favored country for flowers. They grow wild in a great many places, and they can be raised at very little cost, as there is no need of hot-houses or any other expensive appliance to cultivate them. The Indians in the small towns around the City of Mexico make a business of raising flowers, and they sell handsome bouquets, as artistically made as any in this country, for a mere trifle. A bouquet which, for instance, in New York would cost $5 in winter, could be had in the City of Mexico all the year round for 25 cents ; and I look forward to the time when flowers will be exported in large quantities from Mexico to the United States if the protective policy of the country does not interfere.

IRRIGATION.

At the time of the Spanish invasion of Mexico, the Indians in those parts of the country where the population was greatest were dependent upon irrigation for a large part of their cereals, and for cotton, which played so important a part in their economy.   As the same method had been employed from time immemorial in Spain, it followed that on the partition of the soil among the Spanish conquerors, irrigation became an important factor in their agriculture ; but with expansion of population large tracts of land have come to depend entirely upon the rain.

In recent years Mexican agriculture has depended almost altogether on the rainfall, except in a few places well supplied with water, and where irrigation is both cheap and easy ; but the inhabited portions of the country have been depleted of their timber by the natives for the purpose of using the wood for fuel or lumber.   In more recent years, the building of railroads has increased considerably the demand for wood both for sleepers and for fuel for locomotives, and the consequence is that a great change is taking place in the climatic conditions of the country and that fuel is exceedingly high.   In no other country is there so much timber—a good deal of it not yet full grown—consumed annually as in Mexico.   The consumption of timber for railroad purposes alone, not to mention that used in mines, smelters, and as fuel in cities and towns, is incalculable.

Competent authority in Mexico, among whom is the Inspector of Manufactories, created for the purpose of insuring the collection of the internal-revenue tax, considers that only in the Federal District of Mexico the consumption of wood exceeds 4000 English cords daily, used as fuel in the factories, railroads, and other plants of that city.

The consumption of charcoal by private families in the old-style open cooking grates is at least 500,000 pounds in the Federal District of Mexico, which is equivalent to 2,500,000 pounds of wood taken from the scanty forests of the central plateau, and that consumption would be very much reduced if, instead of those old-fashioned grates, iron cooking stoves should be used ; and to encourage their use, when I was last in the Treasury Department of Mexico, I was instrumental in reducing considerably the duties on the same.

Another cause of the destruction of the forest in Mexico consists in the primitive way in which the Indians raise their crops. They own in common a large tract of land, and they begin to till near their towns, commencing by destroying the forests and planting every year in a different locality, because, more especially in the lowlands, the vegetation springs up so rank after the first year's crop that it is very difficult to keep the ground clear of weeds. In this way they clear new land every year, going farther and farther from their town, until sometimes their crops are raised at a distance of as much as thirty or forty miles from their homes. The natural result is the destruction of the forests around the towns and at some considerable distance from the same, and consequently the diminution of the rainfall. I was greatly struck, on my last visit to Mexico, in 1896, by the scantiness of water at an Indian town called San Bernardino, in the sierra district, about five miles north of Teotitlan, the county seat of the district, which I had visited in November, 1855, and found then exceedingly abundant in rainfall and consequently in water, as well as all the mountains north of that place, which extend for about eighty miles to the lowlands on the Gulf of Mexico. On my recent visit, however, I found a great scarcity of water: a small stream of probably not more than one-half an inch in diameter, carried in very primitive wooden troughs, was all the water the town had, and that only during the rainy season, the people being obliged to go a considerable distance for water in the dry season; this being only one illustration of what the destruction of the woods is doing in Mexico.

The city of Oaxaca, at the foot of the Sierra, used to be, in my young days, very well supplied with water, using for that purpose several streams coming from the mountains; but during the last dry season the scarcity of water has been such as to cause a real water famine.

The diminution of the rains, together with other atmospheric phenomena, which takes place from time to time, produces in some years drought that prevents the crops from being raised; as the country produces at present only the corn necessary for its consumption, which cannot be kept from year to year on account of its being eaten by insects. This diminution was very disastrous before the railroad era, causing serious famines. Since the railways were built, we import in such years corn from the United States, spending several millions of dollars in providing ourselves with that staple. All that will be changed, and we shall be able to produce cereals enough not only for home consumption, but even for export, when we begin to use irrigation. The configuration of the country allows dams that will retain sufficient water both for irrigation and manufacturing purposes, to be built at comparatively little expense.

Large tracts of land in Western Asia, Northern Africa, and Southern Europe—countries which, according to historians, were once densely

populated and gardens of the world—are now uninhabited and barren
wildernesses ; and this has been brought about by the wholesale destruction of the forests and the absence of any law to protect them
and provide for their replanting.   In the United States it has been seen
that not only does the decrease of the forest area lessen the rainfall,
but also the fall of snow in the winter months, the consequence being
a marked decrease in the supply of water for irrigation purposes from
the streams and rivers dependent for their supply on the snowy mountain tops.

Along the Mississippi River it is a common observation of the river
pilots and old steamship hands that the summers are becoming more
and more dry and the streams smaller, and that the big river itself has
shown a marked decrease of " navigability " every year during the past
twenty years.   All this is caused by the indiscriminate chopping down
of the forests at the head of the principal tributaries of the big river.
Statistics from Russia, Germany, Spain, Italy, Palestine, Australia, and
India all prove beyond a doubt that the protection of the forests is a
matter of vital importance.

Mexico is not only suffering from an annual decrease in rainfall,
owing to the continual decrease in the timber-bearing area, the rainfall
being more and more unequal every year during the past twenty years
but the winters are becoming more and more severe, and the frosts are
reaching farther and farther south each year.   This is undoubtedly due
to the wholesale destruction of timber now going on throughout that
Republic.

The Government can cope with this matter only by legislation, and
having before it the example of the rest of the world, the Mexican Government should act without delay and in a manner that would benefit, not
only the present, but also future generations ; and I understand it has
been studying the advisability of prohibiting the use of wood for the
locomotives and sleepers.   Experience has shown that in tropical countries iron sleepers last much longer, and are, on the whole, cheaper
than wooden ones, and our supply of coal will soon be ample enough
to furnish all the fuel necessary for the railway and mining industries.

One of the most profitable investments for capital in the near future
will undoubtedly be the construction of reservoirs in the mountains,
dams in the rivers, artesian-well boring, the erection of pumping machinery on a large scale, together with the introduction of modern
devices and appliances that will facilitate the successful cultivation of
the soil and assure crops of all descriptions in all parts of the country
where it has been proved that irrigation must be resorted to.   Not only
are these requirements essential for the conservation of water for irrigation purposes, but many large cities throughout the Republic are without any certain water supply ; and many that have a sufficient supply

show by their death-rates that that supply is bad, and during the greater part of the year is the cause of wide-spread disease.

Again, much is to be gained by the use of these waters for the generating of power for the use of factories, mines, electric lighting, railways, and street cars, even should one hundred miles or more intervene between the generating plant and the machinery it is proposed to apply to it.

It seems marvellous that the Mexico of to-day—presenting, as it does, more natural resources, a greater variety of climate, cheaper labor, and better facilities for the construction of dams, reservoirs, canals, etc., than almost any other country—should be so far behind the times in a matter that has become an absolute necessity before the greater portion of its area can be thoroughly populated. The great increase in value of a piece of land after it is irrigated ought to be inducement enough for capital to be invested in such works. Competent engineers contend that Mexico, owing to its topographical and geological features, will be found to present most favorable conditions for the construction of reservoirs, dams, gravitation canals, the erection of pumping plants driven by wind, steam, gasoline, electricity, or even water power, and also for the cutting off and bringing to the surface of the underflowing waters, which are known to exist in greater abundance there than elsewhere on the face of the globe, as nature has been very prodigal to it in these respects.

Irrigation in arid countries is the corner-stone of civilization, and, to make a country self-sustaining, agriculture should be the first aim of its inhabitants. Agriculture must come first; manufacturing and mining cannot thrive until the food supply is forthcoming.

With the extension of railway lines and the notable impulse given to agricultural enterprise within the last twenty years, Mexican landowners have improved more and more upon the earlier methods, and have, to an increasing extent, applied the principles of engineering science to the methodical cultivation of the large tracts into which their holdings are usually divided.

The Nazas Irrigation.—Some notice of an irrigation enterprise in Mexico will show how much we are now doing in this line.

The great plan of northern Mexico embraces nearly the whole of the States of Chihuahua and Coahuila, being bounded east and west by the sierras of the Pacific and Gulf coasts respectively. It consists of two watersheds,—that of the Rio Grande to the north, and the the so-called desert of the Bolson of Mapimi in the south. It is about four hundred miles wide by six hundred long, and maintains a general level of about four thousand feet above the sea, although much broken by local mountain ranges. The Bolson of Mapimi has much the same formation as the basin of the Great Salt Lake.

It receives the drainage of all the eastern slopes of the Durango sierras and the western slopes of the Coahuila ranges, but possesses no outlet. As a consequence, throughout its whole area, the rivers run into broad, shallow lakes, whence the waters are gradually lost by evaporation during the dry season. Of these rivers, the largest is the Nazas, which has a course of nearly three hundred miles from its source to where it is dispersed over the shallows, called on modern maps Lake Mayran. Sixty or seventy years ago the Nazas discharged its waters into a series of extensive lagoons, occupying what is now the fertile Laguna district of Durango and Coahuila.

At that time a phenomenal and long-continued rainfall so over-charged the, then, bed of the Nazas as to cause it to open a new course, and leave the Cayman lagoons thirty miles on one side. In the course of years these lagoons were converted into a mesquite wilderness, almost dead level, and composed of a deposit of the finest detritus, of unknown depth. The central depression of this lake-bed filled a broad valley running north and south, and surrounded by a parallelogram of mountains. The area thus comprised was about two hundred and ten square miles of pure vegetable loam, locally known as the Lake of Tlahualilo. This cuenca, or bowl, was the spot chosen about six years ago for the establishment of the great irrigation enterprise.

The problems involved called for courage and high administrative qualities, as well as technical engineering knowledge. It had early developed that the lands left dry by the changed course of the river were of extraordinary fertility, and half a century ago these tracts, immediately adjacent to the river, had been taken up and brought under irrigation after the rough methods then practised. The result was that, by 1890, about 250,000 acres of this land were under ditch, and the region was producing the greatest part of the cotton grown in Mexico, as well as heavy crops of corn and wheat. The Tlahualilo basin was known to be the richest portion of this district, but the thirty miles of sun-baked desert separating it from the present course of the river presented an obstacle to utilization which proved too formidable for the cultivators of the Laguna country. In 1889 a project was formulated for carrying a ditch across the intervening desert to the head of the Tlahualilo cuenca, and converting the whole of the latter area into a huge hacienda.

Preliminary survey showed that the lowest level of the basin to be irrigated was about 100 feet below the point on the river Nazas which it was proposed to dam; that the main canal, on account of topographical conditions, would require a development of 39 miles; and that the slope of the lands within the basin was such that about 175 square miles out of the 210 composing the basin could be advantageously irrigated. A company was formed to undertake the work.

A dam of piles and riprap was thrown across the river at a point where it is about 1500 feet wide at flood. From this dam the line of the main canal was traced to the entrance of the Tlahualilo,—a distance of 39 miles. The canal terminated in a distributing tank at the entrance to the irrigable area, whence it bifurcated, one arm being carried along the western side of the basin.

The rainfall in the Bolson of Mapimi is confined to a few days of heavy showers about the beginning of June and the beginning of December. But up in the mountains of Durango, where the Nazas takes its rise, the rainfall at the same season is very heavy and protracted, resulting in high water in the river, which lasts for several weeks at a time. It is during these freshets that the cultivated lands in the Nazas district are irrigated. For the rest of the year they receive no water, except from occasional brief showers. In the Tlahualilo basin, a week or ten days of irrigation is all that is needed in the course of a year, the water soaking easily and quickly through the almost impalpable silt, and the hot sun forming a protecting crust which checks evaporation, and retains the moisture in the subsoil for a surprisingly long time. In fact, owing to their long roots, the cotton plants strictly require irrigation only once every other year, but corn and wheat, of course, must receive it at each planting. The distribution of the waters is regulated by government schedule, each property on the river being allotted its proportion of water, according to priority of settlement. Each canal on the river is permitted to take as many irrigations as it desires during the season of high waters, but in strict rotation. That is, after a property has taken one quota, it cannot repeat the process until all the others have taken theirs, when its second quota is available. Where another property, as often happens, does not care to use all the water to which it is entitled, its further allotments may be used by its neighbor. The waters, on leaving the river, are heavily charged with sediment largely volcanic in its origin, and this is deposited on the lands at each flooding in the shape of extremely fine mud.

Six years of experience with this property demonstrates the fact that irrigation, when applied to fertile land under a carefully planned and thoroughly executed system, where the water supply is owned by the user, puts agriculture among the least dubious of industries. The system adopted by the Tlahualilo Company is especially worthy of attention, because of the notable unity of plan pursued from the inception of the enterprise to its fullest development, and of its resultant economies. It was on this property that a disastrous experiment of colonization from Alabama took place in the year 1896, when hundreds of negroes were taken from Alabama and other points of the southern portion of the United States under the supposition that they could withstand the down-pour of the tropical sun of Mexico, and by their knowledge of the cultivation of cotton succeed in carrying out the purpose of the men who undertook the enterprise. Unused to food conditions in Mexico, especially for want of bacon and corn bread, they were infested with sickness, which caused great mortality among them, and frightened and demoralized they fled from Tlahualilo, this experiment showing very plainly that Mexican planters cannot rely for labor on the colored people of the United States.

The production of cotton and corn in the vicinity of Torreon can be increased eightfold by building reservoirs in the Nazas River and its tributary cañons, to hold the water back for the irrigation of the vast area of fine cotton and corn lands that are yet unproductive, simply through the non-retention of the great amount of water flowing to the sea, unused, annually, and the same result could be obtained by doing the same thing with many other rivers in Mexico. With one-fourth of the water now needed to produce a good crop, the same amount of grain can be produced by good cultivation. The reason is that by the methods now in vogue in most parts of the country, so little soil is loosened by the plow that nearly all the water runs off, where rain is relied on, and only with a great amount of rain can a crop be raised. When irrigation is used, the water required to keep the hard ground moist is entirely in excess of the reservoir, rain, and river supplies. This is the reason of the short grain supply and of the necessity for importing during years of drought large quantities of corn. If the ground were plowed deep and well, it would absorb most of the rainfall and create sufficient surface moisture to meet the moisture from below, which would counteract the dry action of the atmosphere on the soil and roots of the grain, which, by its luxuriant growth, would soon shade the ground, and thus contribute still further to the retention of moisture.

The fact is, taking Mexico as a whole, that there is not a year so dry but that with good cultivation, sufficient grain can be raised to supply domestic demands, while all the excess above that quantity in favorable seasons should be used as feed for stock, which would supply the large quantities of lard, tallow, hard-oil, etc., now being imported, and would leave a large amount for export, together with a consider-able quantity of meat for the same purpose, thus helping to cover the balance of foreign trade and keeping our silver dollars in the hands of the farmers and stockmen, to improve and increase their lands, herds, and flocks.

FAUNA.

The present Mexican fauna belongs, like its flora, to the North American zone, so far as regards the plateau regions, and to the An-tilles in respect to the coast lands round the Gulf, while that of the

Pacific seaboard is intermediate between the Californian and South American. In the general aspect of its terrestrial animals, Mexico is connected more with the United States, whereas in its marine forms the reverse movement has taken place. Thus the prevailing species in the Gulf of Mexico as far as Tamaulipas and Texas, and the Pacific coast northwards to Sonora and Lower California, have migrated from South America. The species in the two oceanic basins differ almost completely ; and, despite the proximity of the Pacific and Atlantic shores, their shells are quite distinct.

The fauna includes three species of large felidæ, the puma or American lion, jaguar, and ocelot ; among the smaller is the wildcat. Wolves are common in the northern States, and also the coyote ; besides which there are bears, wild boars, and bisons. A species of sloth is found in the southern forests, with five varieties of monkeys. Of the other wild animals the principal are hares, rabbits, squirrels, two or three kinds of deer, beavers, moles, martens, and otters.

All the domestic animals introduced by the early Spanish settlers have multiplied prodigiously. The horses, though small, retain the spirit and graceful form of the Andalusian or Arabian stock, from which they mainly sprang.

The waters of the estuaries and coast streams teem with fishes, all the numerous varieties of which differ on the two oceanic slopes, but still present a certain analogy in their general distribution. Turtles are taken in considerable numbers on the coast, and the *carey*, or turtle-shell, of Yucatan and Guerrero is the object of a trade valued at $20,000 yearly.

The ophidians are represented by a few boas in the southern forests, and several species of snakes, some extremely venomous, as the rattle and coral snakes. The largest lizard is the iguana, whose flesh is by some of the natives used as food. Noxious insects infest the hot regions in myriads ; alacranes, or scorpions, in two different varieties, are everywhere feared, and many children were every year killed by their sting in the city of Durango before the proper antidote was found and used. Scolopendras, gigantic spiders, tarantulas, and mosquitoes abound.

Bees are numerous and their wax is an article of export, and the silkworm, though comparatively neglected, yields an annual profit of some importance. The birds of prey are eagles, hawks, and zopilotes, or turkey-buzzards, the scavengers of the coast towns, with three or four species of owls. Domestic fowl are extremely abundant. The parrots, humming-birds, trogons, and so forth, vie in richness of plumage with those of Brazil, and the Mexican songsters, the prince of which is the zenzontle, or mocking-bird, are unequalled by those of any other country.

Of all the Mexican fauna, two only have been domesticated : the huahulotl (*Meleagris Mexicana*), which is a species of duck, and the turkey, introduced into Europe by the Spaniards from the West Indies, hence by the French called "coq d'Inde." The techichi, an edible dumb dog, was soon exterminated when taxed by the Spanish authorities. The other farmyard animals have all been introduced into Mexico by the conquerors.

In the Gulf of California, and especially near La Paz, and the neighboring archipelagoes, extensive beds of pearl oysters are fished. Some other islands in the same gulf are frequented by myriads of various species of aquatic birds, and have already yielded many hundred cargoes of guano.

It is noteworthy that the Pacific islands, lying at some distance from the coast, have all a fauna different from that of the mainland. Thus the little Tres Marias group, about sixty miles off the coast of Jalisco, has a special species of humming-bird. The Revillagigedo Archipelago also forms a separate zoölogical zone, and the island of Guadalupe, over one hundred and fifty miles distant from Lower California, has eleven species of land birds, every one of which differs from the corresponding species on the adjacent continent.

ETHNOLOGY.

Mexico is inhabited by native Indians found there during the Spanish conquest, by descendants of the conquerors of Mexico and other European races, and by a mixture of the two. There are so few inhabitants of African descent that it is hardly worth while speaking of them. The proportion of this population is about as follows : Of European descent, 19 per cent. ; native Indians, 43 per cent. ; mixed races, 38 per cent.

Mexican Indians.—The native Indians found by the Spaniards belong to several nations and tribes, having different features and entirely distinct languages. The principal of these tribes are the following, some of which are now extinct :

Otomi,	Apache,	Tarahumara,
Chichimec,	Irritilas,	Tepehuan,
Huaxtec,	Tamaulioecs,	Sabaibos,
Totonac,	Zacotec,	Acaxee,
Mixtec,	Huastec,	Xixime,
Zapotec,	Zoqué,	Concho,
Mahuas,	Opata,	Manosprietas,
Toltec,	Guaicuri,	Comanche,
Olmecs,	Yaqui,	Cuachichils,
Xicalancs,	Mayo,	Tarascos,
Tula,	Seri,	Mixé.

These tribes have been classified in the following families :

Mexican Family ;

Sonorense Opata-Pima Family ;

Guaicura y Cochimi Laimon Family ;

Seri Family ;

Tarasco Family ;

Zoque-Mixé Family ;

Totonaca Family ;

Mixteco-Zapoteca Family ;

Matlalzinga ó Pirinda Family ;

Maya-Quiche Family ;

Chontal Family :

Huave Family ;

Apache Family ;

Otomi Family.

There is a great deal of similarity between the Mexican Indians and the Malay Asiatic races—especially the Japanese branch—which gives foundation to the idea that the aborigines of Mexico originally came from Asia, or *vice versa*.[1] Their intensely black hair and eyes, their brown or yellow color, their small stature and the slight obliquity

[1] The following extracts from the San Francisco, Cal., *Bulletin* of June 7, 1897, confirm my views on the subject :

" Information is received from Australia concerning the reports of F. W. Christian of the Polynesian Society, who has returned to Sydney after an extended tour of the islands of the South Seas, the Caroline group especially, where he has been on a successful search for ethnological specimens. These reports are of great importance to the scientific world and are said to let much light on a vexed question which has puzzled the most learned savants for years. Mr. Christian has discovered extensive traces of the Chinese and Japanese in the islands of the Pacific, and claims to have discovered evidence pointing to the existence of a civilization of nearly two thousand years ago, which is linked with the ancient civilization in Central America, and will probably explain the origin of the Aztec races.

" Under the auspices of the Polynesian Society, according to advices from Sydney, *via* Honolulu, received per *Coptic* yesterday, Mr. Christian worked. The gentleman spent nearly two years looking for traces of the Chinese in the islands, and was lucky enough to find ancient records, specimens of handiwork and weapons which proved that Asiatic races were extensive traders among the South Sea group thousands of years ago. Evidence of a very decisive nature was secured which shows that a large trade was carried on *via* the islands of the Caroline group, between China and Central America, and that the ancient Chinese were more inclined to emigrate than their latter-day brethren and colonized extensively.

" Extensive inquiries were made as to the traditions of the islanders, and many discoveries were made concerning the early history of the Malays with regard to navigation, all proving that the Torres strait's route to the Pacific was not taken, but that voyages were made to many of the Caroline islands.

" The coincidence is a strange one that a despatch from Hermosillo, Mexico, dated June 6th, reports that a rock recently discovered in the mountains of Magdalena district, State of Sonora, which is covered with Chinese inscriptions, has just been visited by Sen Yup, a well-educated Chinese of Guaymas. He says the inscriptions are Chinese, but are somewhat indistinct. He made a copy of them, and has translated enough of the lines to show that the writing was probably inscribed on the rock at least two thousand years ago."

of their eyes, are features common to the Mexican Indians and the Japanese. When I first came to Washington, at the end of 1859, not having been out of Mexico before, I retained very vivid recollections of the Mexican Indians, with whom I had been somewhat closely associated ; and shortly afterwards the first Japanese Embassy came to this country and was received in a very solemn manner by Mr. Buchanan, then President of the United States. The Embassy consisted of about forty persons altogether, comprising ministers, secretaries, interpreters, servants, etc., and were dressed in their national gala costumes, not having yet adopted the European one. The Diplomatic Corps having been invited to the reception, I attended as a member of the same, and was greatly struck by the remarkable similarity which I found between the Japanese members of the Embassy and the Mexican Indians, whom I had just left. It seemed to me that had I collected at random forty Mexican Indians and dressed them in the same gorgeous costumes that the Japanese wore, nobody could have detected the difference.

Some of the Indian languages seem to me to resemble strongly the Oriental ones, though of course I cannot speak with authority, as I do not know any of those languages and have heard only the Chinese, Japanese, and Korean spoken ; but I am sure that if any educated and intelligent Chinese should go to Mexico and spend some time among the Indians, he would find traces in the language which would contribute greatly to clear up this problem. Mr. Tateno, a former Japanese Minister, who visited Mexico, found, during his short stay in that country, several words that are used in Japan and that have the same meaning in both countries. I am aware that Señor Pimentel, a very learned philologist, who made a special study of the languages of the Mexican Indians, finds no similarity at all between them and the Chinese or other Oriental languages ; and that even the Otomi language, which is monosyllabic, he finds to have no similarity to the Chinese. But, notwithstanding that great authority, I believe that the aborigines of both continents, that is, Asiatic and American, were originally of the same race, and that there must be some relationship between their respective languages.

The Indians of the different tribes do not generally mix with one another, but intermarry among themselves, and this fact contributes largely to their physical decay, and makes very difficult, at least for some time to come, the complete assimilation of all the Mexican population.

The Mexican Indians are on the whole a hard-working, sober, moral, and enduring race, and when educated they produce very distinguished men. Some of our most prominent public men in Mexico, like Juarez as a statesman, and Morelos as a soldier, were pure-blooded

Indians,[1] and fortunately there is no prejudice against their race in Mexico, and so when they are educated they are accepted in marriage among the highest families of pure Spanish blood.[2]

I have been a great deal among them, and my knowledge of their characteristics only increases my sympathy and admiration for them. In the State of Oaxaca, for instance, where I spent the early years of my life, I have seen Indians from the mountain districts, who, when they had to go to the capital, especially to carry money, would form parties of eight or ten to make a ten days' round trip, carrying with them their food, which consists of roasted ground corn, which they take three times a day ; stopping at a brook to mix it with water, and

[1] Sir William Hingston, President of the Surgery Section in the Second Pan-American Medical Congress, held at the City of Mexico in October, 1896, in an interview which was published by *The Gazette* of Montreal, Canada, of December 2, 1896, said, concerning his visit to Mexico, among other things :

" The pure-blooded Indian was seen on all sides. . . .

" The Spaniards would seem to have pursued the same course as was followed by the original French settlers, *they did not shove aside the native Indians as useless lumber, to be gotten out of the way*, as a distinguished Harvard professor puts it, but they treated them as people in possession of the soil, with whom it was not only right but proper to ally in marriage. I have always regarded our North American Indian as the best type of the aborigines in stature. I still believe he is, but not so in intellect. The broad, massive forehead of the native of Mexico, and his soft but prominent and intelligent eye, are evidences of mental power. . . ."

[2] I take from a spicy article published by Mr. Charles Dudley Warner, in *Harper's Magazine* for June, 1896, the following description of the dress of the poorer classes in Mexico :

" Herbert Spencer might extend here his comments on the relation of color to sex. It is the theory that all the males of birds have gay plumage in order to make them attractive to the other sex, while the females go in sober colors. This is also supposed to hold true of barbarous nations. The men who dress at all, or use paint as a substitute, wear bright colors and more ornaments than the women, while the gentle sex is content to be inconspicuous. Needless to say that in what we call civilization, this rule is reversed. The men affect plain raiment, while the women vie with the tropical birds of the male gender. Tried by this test Mexico has not reached the civilization of the United States. The women of the lower orders are uniformly sober in apparel, and commonly wear drawn over the head a reboso in plain colors. The scant dress is usually brown or pale blue. It is the men who are resplendent, even the poorest and the beggars. The tall conical hats give to all of them an " operatic " distinction ; the lower integuments may be white (originally) as also the shirt and the jacket ; or the man may have marvellous trousers, slit down the sides and flapping about so as to show his drawers, or sometimes, in the better class, fastened down with silver buttons ; but every man of them slings over his left shoulder or wraps about him, drawing it about his mouth on the least chill in the air, a brilliantly colored sarape, or blanket, frequently of bright red. Even if he appears in white cotton, he is apt to wear a red scarf round his waist; and if he is of a higher grade, he has the taste of a New York alderman for a cravat. This variety and intensity of color in the dress of the men gives great animation and picturesqueness to any crowd in the streets, and lights up all the dusty highways."

sleeping on the bare ground, preferring always the open air; getting up before daylight and starting on their journey at daybreak immediately after their early meal, speaking no Spanish and travelling about forty miles a day. When they reached the city of Oaxaca, they would remain there one or two days, and go back to their homes without taking part in any dissipation. They prefer to live in the high, cool localities, and they have their patch of ground to raise corn and a few vegetables in the hot lowlands, sometimes thirty miles away from their homes, and carry their crops on their backs for all that distance. They make very good soldiers, and military leaders have used them to great advantage during our revolutions.

Professor Starr's theory that we are all on this Continent assuming the type of the Indian, is, in a measure, true. It is nothing new, for it was already indicated by an English physician travelling in the British colonies before the United States were thought of.

The great task of the Mexican Government is to educate our Indians and make them active citizens, consumers, and producers, elevating their condition. Before we think of spending money to encourage European immigration to Mexico, we ought to promote the education of our Indians, which I consider the principal public need of the country.

Increase of Mexican Population.—In the beginning of the century Baron Humboldt, who visited Mexico and studied very carefully the conditions of the country, thought that the Indian race, which was then very numerous, would continue to increase and would be the preponderant race of Mexico, as far as numbers were concerned, as it showed a large proportion in a census made in 1810 by Don Fernando Navarro y Noriega, and which appears in Baron Humboldt's *Political Essay of New Spain.* According to that census the population of Mexico was then divided as follows :

European and American Spaniards	1,097,928
Indians	3,676,281
Mixed races or castes	1,338,706
Secular ecclesiastics	4,229
Regular ecclesiastics	3,112
Nuns	2,098
Total	6,122,354

Including among the Europeans the ecclesiastics and nuns, the population was, according to that census :—

Europeans	1,107,367	or 18 per cent.	
Indians	3,676,281	" 60 " "	
Mixed races	1,338,706	" 22 " "	
Total	6,122,354	" 100 " "	

In the census of 1875 the following results appear :—

European race and descen-
        dants of the Spaniards......1,899,031 or 20 per cent.
Mixed race..................4,082,918 " 43 " "
Native Indian race...........3,513,208 " 37 " "

        Total.........9,495,157 " 100 " "

The increase of population in the 65 years which elapsed between the two censuses mentioned, deducting from the census of 1810 the inhabitants of Texas, New Mexico, and Upper California, who had passed to the United States, numbering 58,338, was

Population of 1810.........................6,064,016
Census of 1875.............................9,495,157

Increase of the population in the 65 years.....3,431,141

From the preceding data it appears that the European race nearly doubled its population in the space of 65 years, and at the rate of 1.1 per cent. of increase per year ; that the mixed race trebled it at the rate of 3.25 ; and that the native race diminished it at the rate of 0.058 per cent. per annum.

Families in Mexico are generally very large, often having ten or fifteen children. I remember how much surprise it caused in Washington, my stating in the presence of Señor Don Jacobo Blanco, the Mexican Commissioner in the late International Boundary Commission, who was recently here for a year finishing his office work and maps and preparing his report, that he was the twenty-fourth child in his family, his father having been twice married.

Decrease of the Indian Population.—It further appears that the Indian population has been decreasing since the beginning of the present century, notwithstanding the fact that the Indian race on the whole is very prolific.

The causes of the decrease of the Indian population in Mexico are various ; bad nourishment, insufficient shelter from the inclemency of the weather, wretched attendance in sickness, and many others, some of which I shall mention here, having contributed toward the degeneration and decline of the race.

The small-pox, owing to the carelessness or indolence of the parents in regard to vaccination, or their repugnance to it, causes deplorable ravages in this race, more especially among the individuals that live at any considerable distance from the cities.

Indian women, even when far advanced in pregnancy, do not abstain from hard labor, and, without any care for their coming offspring, continue grinding their corn until the moment of parturition. Then, before the proper time for taking the child from the breast, it is fed with food unsuitable for its age and difficult of digestion, which occasions diarrhœa or other maladies that either cause its death or at least contribute to its imperfect development.

Another circumstance which causes the degeneration of the Indians is their premature marriages. In Mexico the marriageable age for women has been fixed by law at eighteen years, and in the tierra caliente, or hot country, at fourteen ; but in some places Indian girls are married at twelve. Every Indian father considers it his duty to marry his children, whether boys or girls, as soon as they are of age, the parents of course making the match to suit themselves.

This used to be the case not only with the Indians, but even with persons of Spanish descent. I once heard General Degollado, a very good and prominent man in Mexico, say, that the day he married he took, immediately after the ceremony was over, his bean-shooter and went to shoot birds, because he had no conception of what he had done, his parents having arranged the match for him ; but he added that he could not possibly have made a better choice of a wife.

The Indians are strong by nature ; and in this is to be found the fact that so many of them reach an advanced age, in spite of their scant and poor food, their unhealthy mode of living, and their damp and unwholesome habitations, consisting of miserable huts where whole families are huddled together.

The Spaniards in Mexico.—The Spaniards are a money-making, wonderfully frugal race, since they have been battling with hard conditions at home for centuries. The Spaniard in Mexico is as Richard Ford who spent thirty years in the peninsula, and who was a close observer, depicts him—a hardy, temperate man, well fitted, under favorable conditions, to become a dominant influence.

In Mexico, the energy of the Spaniard is remarkable. He is forceful of word and phrase, energetic in his movements, immensely vital, tremendously persistent, and wonderfully enduring. After thirty years behind a counter selling groceries, he retires, a man of fortune ; not always large, but sufficient, and is still a man of force and ready for undertakings demanding good brain power and courage. They come over mere lads, from ten to fifteen, toil and moil, feed frugally, and sleep hardly, and they become millionaires, bank directors, great mill owners, farmers on a grand scale, hot-country planters and monopolists, for the Spaniard is born with the " trust " idea ; while his sons are too often dudes and spendthrifts.

The thrifty Spaniard toils and saves, and his ambition is to marry a rich girl, frequently the daughter of a Mexican landowner, and so he lays the foundation for permanent wealth ; for everywhere, the world over, the man who gets the lands and holds on to them is the wealthy man. Speculators and financiers come and go like bubbles on a river, but the landed proprietor keeps a permanent clinch on humanity.

There is one check to the growth of Spanish influence in Mexico, and that is the climate. All Europeans, no matter what their nationality, become physically modified by residence in the new world ; and nowhere is the effect of climate more noticeable than in the tropics. The children of the Spanish residents are less energetic than the parents, and the third generation are altogether Creoles. Just as the Mexican of Spanish descent is, as a rule, less energetic, not so vascular, and less vigorous than the Spaniard, so is the American less full-blooded and leaner than the Englishman. The change that takes place in the human organization, transplanted from the old world to the new, is a profound one.

English and Germans in Mexico.—The present century has seen many changes in the commercial world of Mexico ; the great English houses have almost all disappeared ; especially has this been marked in the dry-goods, or draper's business. The Germans, with superior economy, if with no more of enterprise, drove the English out of that profitable business, and in time themselves succumbed to the still closer methods of the Barcelonettes who gained a foothold in the business which they have successfully maintained. The dry-goods business in the Republic is largely in the hands of men who speak the French language. From the great houses of the capital go forth bright young men, trained to business habits who are established over branch concerns in the interior and coast towns. Their employers become their backers, and a close intimacy is maintained, to the mutual advantage of older and younger merchants.

Very few of the foreigners who settle in Mexico, and especially Spaniards, are educated, as most of them hardly know how to read and write. They very seldom become naturalized Mexicans, and almost always keep their allegiance to the country of their origin. That seemed natural when Mexico was in constant turmoil, and many of the foreigners going there expected to make large fortunes by means of diplomatic claims ; but that reason can hardly hold good now, when the country is at peace, and perfect security is extended to every inhabitant. If the foreigners continue keeping their old nationality when they become permanent settlers of Mexico, some changes may be necessary in the legislation of the country affecting their condition.

Americans in Mexico.—It will be very difficult for the fun-loving, self-indulgent, Anglo-Saxon Englishman of America to compete with these self-denying Spaniards, capable of living with the nose to the grindstone twenty, twenty-five, or thirty years, eating always sparingly, drinking wine, but in moderation, spending no money, dressing poorly, and ever with a fortune accumulating. The American wants to cut a dash and so does the Englishman, else the English would have maintained their commercial supremacy in Mexico. They lost it to the more frugal and economical Germans.

The American is a speculator, a dreamer of golden dreams; he lives for the eyes of other people; he is not capable of the patience that keeps a man tied to a desk or shop for half a lifetime, making a savings bank of himself.

Some Mexicans are afraid that a free influx of citizens from this country may Americanize it. This is true as to the means of transportation, the introduction of electric lights, improved hotel accomodations, and where similar improvements are concerned. But there is no doubt of the persistence of traditions and habits, and the influence of climate. It is difficult to introduce the American push and restlessness in business, and to overcome the habits formed in many centuries of letting the morrow take care of itself. There must be the mid-day siesta, and the number of working days is reduced by several feast days, saints' days, and holidays, besides the Sundays. There is no doubt that the productiveness of nature is an inducement to very leisurely labor, and the lack of any sharp division of seasons is a sort of moral discipline, as well as a stimulus to extra exertion in summer to prepare for winter. What must be the effect upon character when this stimulus is wanting? It is possible, of course, that industry will be stimulated by the inflow of settlers from the north, and that Mexico will take on new enterprise and productive vigor; but I think it is easier for Americans in Mexico to fall into Mexican ways and Mexican moral views than it is to convert the Mexicans to the American view of life. I do not doubt that Mexico has a great industrial, agricultural, and manufacturing future, but I fancy that its power of absorption, like that of Egypt, is greater than its facility of adaptation.

Ruins.—We have in Mexico some of the most ancient and remarkable ruins, and although there are different surmises about the time at which they were built and the people who built them, nothing is known positively about them.

The principal ones are in Uxmal and Chichen Itza in Yucatan, Comalcalco in Tabasco, Teotihuacan and Cholula in Puebla and Tlaxcala, and Mitla in Oaxaca.

Uxmal.—Uxmal is not far from the city of Merida, the capital of the State of Yucatan, supposed to have been built by the Mayas, and different books have been written about them, especially one by Dr. Augustus Le Plongeon, a French savant, who passed many years in Yucatan, studying its magnificent ruins, and published in New York, in 1896, a book entitled *Queen Moó and the Egyptian Sphinx*, in which

he contends that the empire of the Mayas, which had its seat at Yucatan, was the cradle of civilization, and that from there it went to India,
Egypt, and finally to Greece and Western Europe.

Palenque.—Very likely the same Mayas built the large ruins which
still exist in the district of Palenque in the State of Chiapas, and in
some places in Guatemala.

Cholula.—The great pyramid of Cholula, made known to the scientific world by Humboldt, which is eight miles from Puebla, has been
pictured and described. Its base is 1000 feet on each side, and it is
built in two great terraces, the first being 71 feet, and the second 66
feet, in height. The top is 203 by 144 feet. So far as investigations
have revealed, the great pyramid is artificial and is constructed of sun-
dried brick.

Teotihuacan.—Teotihuacan, an ancient city lying twenty-five miles
northeast of the City of Mexico, and occupying an area of about one
and a half or two miles, contains some of the most remarkable series
of ruins. To the north of the ruins is a truncated pyramid, rectangular in form, squared to the points of the compass, and known as the
Pyramid of the Moon. South of it, at a distance of about 1300 yards,
is another pyramid of similar form, known as the Pyramid of the Sun.
Its perpendicular height is 223 feet, and its base measures about 735
feet from east to west. Both pyramids are united by a straight street,
which starts from a circular plaza at the south side of the Pyramid of
the Moon, and loses itself in the barranca south of the Pyramid of the
Sun.

These colossal pyramids are regarded as among the most ancient
monuments of Mexico, far antedating the civilization found by the
Spaniards. They are wonderful illustrations of what perseverance and
time will accomplish. Now even the means which the builders used
for handling the immense blocks of volcanic stone with which they
constructed is unknown. Other ruins, in the character of little
mounds, are found scattered over the extensive plain in which the two
pyramids are situated. The street or avenue which united the latter
is called the "Road of the Dead." Along its entire length, parallel to
it on both sides, there is a terrace constructed of cement, clay, and
broken lava, faced with a coating of mortar or plaster, highly polished,
and painted red and white. Desire Charnay removed the rubbish
from one of the mounds on the side facing this road, and discovered
what he calls a "palace," with two large halls and various small rooms.
In 1886, Señor Don Leopoldo Batres made an excavation in one of
the mounds, and found two polychrome frescos painted on the wall
of the building which was laid bare. The question is naturally asked,
how these monuments came to be covered? Was it by an earthquake,
or by the hands of the builders themselves? Señor Batres inclines to

the latter view, as he found the roofs of the houses perfectly preserved,
while the interior of the rooms was in every case filled with stones
neatly fitted into the spaces, and joined with a clayish cement to form
a compact mass.   His conclusion as to the pyramids is, that they are
two great temples erected to two old Mexican divinities.   Each pyramid consists of five terraces, which diminished in size until the height
of 223 feet was reached.   Each has on one of its sides a stairway six
and one-half feet in width, which makes five zigzag turns, and leads to
the sanctuary or shrine on the summit.   The outer surface of the
pyramids, and perhaps the interior as well, was plastered over with a
mortar of lime, hard and smooth, and decorated with frescoes, representing quasi-historical events and scenes.

The small mounds scattered over the area occupied by the ruins
were, according to Batres, dwellings and small shrines.   Each contained from six to twelve rooms, quadrangular and rectangular in form.
The cornices as well as the walls were beautifully ornamented in colors.
On some as many as twenty tints had been used.   The doors were rectangular, never trapezoidal in form, although the latter style has been
erroneously attributed to ancient American architecture.   They measure eight feet in height by about three feet in width.   The houses had
neither windows nor balconies.   The city was crossed by subterranean
aqueducts constructed of stone, the walls of which were plastered with
firm and smooth mortar.   Near the Pyramid of the Moon, among the
rubbish, there was a monolithic statue of colossal dimensions.   It represents a woman with a characteristic head-dress, and wearing a neck-
lace of four strings of beads.   Travellers in Teotihuacan can find
countless miniature heads modelled in clay anywhere on the freshly-
plowed stretches of level land that lies across the broad, straight
Micoatl, or " Path of the Dead."   They vary in length from one to two
inches, and invariably have nothing more than a neck attached to
them.   They may be distinguished by this peculiarity from those that
are applied as ornaments to terra cotta vases, and from fragments of
" idols."   The features and peculiar head-dresses that adorn these
little heads of Teotihuacan vary greatly, and this diversity has given
rise to, and been quoted in proof of, the migration of tribes, of the mix-
tures of widely differing races, or of their succession to each other in
the occupation of the Valley of Mexico.   Owing to the unfamiliar
aspect of some of these head-dresses, it has been asserted that they
could not be even "Toltec," but must be relics of still more remote
and unknown races of men.   Various uses have been assigned to them,
the commonest supposition being that they were in some way associated
with ceremonies relating to the dead.   There is probably no subject
connected with Mexican archæology, except the calendar, that has given
rise to more discussion.   Dr. E. B. Tylor regarded them as a puzzle,

and Professor F. W. Putnam has spoken of them as the "riddle of the many heads." Desire Charnay saw in some of them Chinese and Japanese masks, and even types of the white race, proving in his opinion how many races must have been mingled or succeeded each other on this old continent.

Mitla.—About twenty miles east of the city of Oaxaca is an Indian town called Mitla, near which still remain the ruins of great edifices and palaces. The temples were built, it is supposed, by the ancient Zapotecas, and are the most interesting relics of the earlier civilizations of Mexico. The first description of these ruins was given by the Spanish priest, Burgoa, who accompanied the conquerors of Montezuma. The interior of the principal hall or room of the main palace is supposed to be the teocali of the high priest. The peculiar architecture and elaborate and grotesque decoration can easily be observed. It is astonishing to see the enormous size of the stones used in the walls of these temples. Professor Bickmore said that he had seen nothing to equal them except at Baalbec, in Syria. At Mitla are found some clay images, mostly miniature, doubtless of gods, but some of them no doubt portraits, and some of these bore a striking resemblance to the little heads found at the pyramids of the Sun and Moon in the Valley of Mexico; that is, some of them had the slant Oriental eyes, and others Ethiopian features, very different from any races we now know in these regions. The ruined temples of Mitla are covered with stucco, which was painted Pompeiian red. There is a pyramid also at Mitla, and there are some elaborately wrought sepulchral chambers.

I borrow from Mr. Vivien Cory the following extracts of his description of the ruins of Mitla.

"There are four of these places; the first is almost entirely destroyed, only some huge monolithic slabs supported horizontally upon tottering piles of broken stones remaining; while everywhere amongst the ruins have sprung up the grass huts of the Mexican Indians, and of the fourth or one farthest from the hamlet nothing but indication of the site is left, upon which the Spaniards have reared a modern church. It is in the two palaces that lie between, each slightly raised above the surrounding country on a separate eminence, that the interest centres.

"One of these is in the form of a double Greek cross, its stem running north and south, and its arms extended east and west. In the centre is the large court, surrounded on all sides by rising ground and ruined mounds of stones: there are traces still remaining of the foundations, that speak of four apartments built upon these mounds to face the court, but of these those on the west and south sides have disappeared; on the east side, only two colossal pillars and a portion of the walls remain, while to the north side the whole apartment forming the head of the cross has been spared and stands almost unharmed in its original beauty and richness. The façade of this apartment extends the whole length of the court, one hundred and forty-one feet, and its height is a little over fifteen feet: the material is freestone, the color a faint, dull, amber tint, soft as the light seen in the sky at evening. In the centre are three square portals and above these forming the head-piece to them all extends one long and narrow panel of carving, a high relief of the natural stone on a crimson ground. The whole façade is composed of a series of these panels, from the straight line of the foundation-stone to the straight line of the summit, nine panels being on each side of the entrance, arranged in three tiers, divided by horizontal bands of the natural stone. In some of the panels, the ground retains still a faint tint of its former rich vermillion, in others, all color has subsided into the soft neutral shade of the freestone. The designs are wonderfully rich and varied, thirteen different patterns being represented on this façade alone ; all these designs are remarkable for the straight lines in which they are executed and the absence of all curves. Throughout all the ruins, upon the walls of which appear twenty-three different models of carving, only two of these represent any curve in their design. In one of these two there is visible the form of the Arabic letter ' L ' placed horizontally, and in the other a double curve ' S,' possibly intended to represent or suggest the snake. With these exceptions the designs are of the Greek key pattern, variations on this, or parallelograms.

" Behind this façade is a narrow court, roofless as all the courts are, and empty, save for six colossal pillars standing at even distances down the centre, and giving to this chamber the name of Hall of the Monoliths. Each pillar is one solid stone, eleven feet high and eleven feet in circumference. A low stone passage leads from this chamber northward to the smallest and richest court of all, entering it at the southeast corner. There is comparatively little trace of the destructiveness of the elements or the iconoclasm of man here. The court and all the four chambers opening from it are perfect and singularly rich in carving. The court is perfectly square and the chambers are entered from it, each through one square doorway, the roof of which is formed by a huge monolith, thirteen feet long and with a richly carved face. Of these four lintels each has a separate design. Each of the four walls has six panels, the uppermost extending the whole length of the wall, two smaller panels being on either side of the entrance, and one long narrow one above it. Between the panels stand out in high relief the horizontal and vertical edges of the freestone, forming a symmetrical frame to each panel.

" Within the four chambers the walls are designed differently, the carving running simply and evenly round the entire room in three straight horizontal bands, each band possessing a separate pattern and being about three feet in width. Beneath these bands of carving was originally, evidently, a dado of vermillion stucco, of such fine and delicate quality that the smooth and polished surface resembles marble. Portions of this delicate stucco still adhere to the crumbling walls in places and are of various colors, scarlet, black and white. In some instances this stucco seems to have been plain, simply bearing a brilliant polish, in others, there remains distinctly traced in white upon a crimson ground, a wierd, fantastic, yet handsome design, the head ; half horse, half dragon, repeated in four inch squares. This latter ornamented stucco, however, does not appear except in the fourth palace, containing the Spanish church, where it is visible on the walls of one of the courts, now used as a stable for the padre's horse. Leaving the richest of the centre palaces, passing through a gap in the ruined wall on the south side, descending the elevation on which it is placed and ascending the opposite eminence, the patio of the second palace is reached. This is almost wholly in ruins ; three of the façades that face the court remain indeed, but the great smooth slabs with which the walls were faced have been torn away at the base, and most of the beautiful panels of carving stripped from the front. Yet it is in this ruined palace that one lingers longest and to which one's feet return, drawn by an irrisistible fascination ; for this palace contains the tomb and the pillar of death.

" This subterranean vault is called by general consent a sepulchre, but there is no line of history, no record, no tradition even, left to explain to us its origin and use. It may have been a torture-chamber, sacrificial hall, or tomb. The excavation is but a little below the surface of the court, now carried down so deeply that the light is wholly excluded. From the entrance there is enough to fill the interior with a sad, gray twilight. The vault is in the form of a simple cross lying north and south ; its walls are massive and heavily decorated with panels of carving let into their sides, while it is roofed by enormous monolithic slabs that reach from wall to wall. In the centre of the cross, just where by descending a few steps one enters the tomb, stands the pillar of death, round which, the Indians say, should a man clasp his arms he must shortly afterwards die. Does not this very tradition, handed down perhaps through the long file of countless years, seem to indicate that this pillar was some ancient stone of sacrifice to which human victims were bound or chained, and from which death alone released them? As one gazes at the massive column, that one man's arms alone could not entirely encircle, the eye notices an indentation round the base where the column sinks into the floor. The stone is corroded and worn away as by the long friction of ropes or chains.

" Most of the panels do not consist of actual carving, though they produce that effect at a few yards' distance ; they are formed in reality by small slabs of the freestone cut perfectly square and inserted edgeways into the wall, the remaining edges standing out at various distances from it and thus forming the different designs. This, although a work of infinite patience, does not necessarily presuppose a high stage of civilization, no instrument sharper than hard stone being required to cut the slabs of soft freestone ; and that only a stone instrument was employed by the workers seems indicated by the fact that, in the large panels where the stone is actually carved, the edges are not sharp, but rounded, as if made with a blunt tool. The effect of the panels of inserted squares of stone, however simply produced, is that of the most finished and clear-cut carving and the designs themselves are rich and elaborate. There is no crudity, no harshness in them, no suggestion of the primitive savage's scratching on his native rock ; but rather that of Greek work on some Athenian temple. The patterns have a complicated elegance and distinction of line that can only be produced by a people of cultivated mind and eye.

" Evidence, too, of what high grade of civilization in some ways at least they must have arrived at, lies in the gigantic stones that they have placed as lintels over their doorways and which in their immense weight and bulk have defied the greed or rage of all the succeeding races to remove or destroy. The mystery here is the Egyptian mystery of the Pyramids ; that these enormous blocks of stone are resting here in positions and elevations where it would require all the modern knowledge of mechanics, engineering skill, and mechanical appliances to place them ; and, as in Egypt, so here the mystery will never be solved, as the builders have passed hence and left no clue. The solid stone rests there upon its supporting pillars before the eye as it has rested for a thousand years, but how the perished hands lifted and placed it there remains its own inviolable secret.

" Leaving the palace court by the south side and following the road to the dry and stony bed of a wide river, if one turns aside here a little to the eastward he finds himself facing a Zapotecan mound, a solid base composed of earth and stones, in which are visible at intervals large slabs of cement, portions of terraces and tiers that originally formed its sides. Ascending this, from the summit one can overlook the whole valley."

LANGUAGES.

About one hundred and fifty different Indian languages are known to have been spoken by the Mexican Indians. The Spanish monks accompanying the conquerors and who went to the country soon afterwards compiled grammars and even dictionaries of some of these languages ; but the Indians falling into a semi-barbarous state after the conquest, having lost their civilization and literature, their languages have either disappeared completely or become very primitive. and it is ascertained that some of them have become entirely extinct.

The Spanish is, of course, the language of the country and most of the Indians speak it, although very imperfectly and incorrectly ; only a small portion of them speaking no language but their own.

The chief languages spoken in Mexico proper, excluding Chiapas and Yucatan, are as follows :

Nahuatl or Mexican (Aztec) with Acaxee, Sabaibo, Xixime, Cochimi, Concho and other members of the same family.

Seri, Upanguaima, and Guaima.

Papago, Opata, Yaqui, Mayo, Tarahumara, Tepehuan, Cora, etc.

Apache or Yavipai, Navajo, Mescalero, Llanero Lipan, etc.

Otomi or Hia-hiu, Pame, Mazahua, etc.

Huaxtec, Totonac.

Tarascan, Matlaltzincan.

Mixtec, Zopotec, Mixé, Zoqué, Chinantec.

Señor Don Manuel Orosco y Berra wrote a treatise on the language of the Indian tribes in Mexico entitled " Geography of Languages," which describes the languages of the races who inhabited Mexico, and Señor Don Francisco Pimentel enlarged upon that work, making philological comparisons, and from the data collected by both authors Señor Don Antonio Garcia Cubas a distinguished Mexican geographer made the following synopsis of the Indian languages spoken in Mexico.

SYNOPSIS OF THE INDIAN LANGUAGES OF MEXICO, FORMED ACCORDING TO THE CLASSIFICATION OF DON FRANCISCO PIMENTEL.

NOTE.—The sign * indicates that the classification is doubtful.

GROUPS.	FAMILIES.	LANGUAGES.	DIALECTS.
		1st Order.—Languages polysyllabic, polysynthetic of sub-flexion.	
MEXICAN-OPATA.	I. MEXICAN.	1. Mexican, Nahuatl or Azteca.................	Conchos, Sinaloense, * Mazapil, Jaliscience, Ahualulco, Pipil, Niquiran.
		*2. Cuitlateco.....................................	
		3. Opata, Teguima or Teguima Sonorense........	
		4. Eudebe, heve or hegue, dohme or dohema-batuco	
		5. Joba, joval ova...............................	
		6. Pima, nevome, ohotama or Otama.............	Tecoripa. Sabaqui. Various.
		7. Pepehuan.....................................	
		8. Papago or Papabicotan.......................	
		9 to 12. El Yuma comprising Cuchan, Cocomaricopa or Opa, Mojave or Mahao, Diegueño, or Cuñeil, Yavipai, Yampai, and yampaio...................................	
		13.* Cajuenche, Cucapa or Jallicuamay..........	
		14. Sobaipure	
		15. Julime.......................................	

GROUPS.	FAMILIES.	LANGUAGES.	DIALECTS.
		1st Order.—Languages polysyllabic, polysynthetic of sub-flexion.	
	II. SONORENSE OR OPATA-PIMA.	16. Tarahumar.....................................	Varogio or Chinipa, Guazapare, Pachera, and others.
		17. Cahita or Sinaloa...........................	Yaqui, Mayo, Tehueco or Zuaque.
		18. Guarave or Vacoregue........................	
		19. Chora, Chota, Cora del Nayarit..............	Muutzicat, Teacucitzin, Ateanaca.
		20. Colotlan....................................	
		21. Tubar......................................	Various.
		22. Huichola...................................	
		23. Zacateco...................................	
		24. Acaxee or Topia, comprising Sabaibo, Tebaca, and Xixime, the last of doubtful classification................................	
	III. COMANCHE SOSHONE.	25. Comanche, Nauni, Paduca, Hietan or Getan. 26. Caigua or Kioway. 27. Shoshone or Chochone. 28. Wihinasht. 29. Utah, Yutah or Yuta. 30. Pah-Utah or Payuta. 31. Chemegue or Cheme-huevi. 32. Cahuillo or Cawio. 33. Kechi. 34. Netela. 35. Kizh or Kij. 36. Fernandeño. 37. Moqui and some others spoken in the United States.....................................	Various.
MEXICAN-ÓPATA.	IV. TEXANA OR COAHUILTECA.	38. Texano or Coahuilteco.......................	Various.
	V. *KERES ZUÑI.	39. Keres or Quera.............................	Kiwomi or Kivome, Cochiteumi or Quime, Acoma and Acuco.
		40. Tesuque or Tegua...........................	Various.
		41. Taos, Piro, Suma, Picori...................	
		42. Jemez, Tano, Peco.........................	
		43. Zuñi or Cibola.............................	
	VI. MUTSUN.	44. Mutsun. 45. Rumsen. 46. Achastli. 47. Soledad. 48. Costeño or Costanos and other languages of California...................................	
	VII. GUAICURA.	49. Guaicura, Vaicura or Monqui. 50. Aripa. 51. Uchita. 52. Cora. 53. Concho or Lauretano.......................	
	VIII. COCHIMI-LAIMON.	54 to 57. Cochimi, divided into four sister languages, viz.: Cadegomo and the languages used in the missions of San Javier, San Joaquin, and Santa Maria................. 58. Laimon or Layamon.........................	
	IX. SERI.	59. Seri or Ceri............................... 60. Guaima or Gayama......................... 61. Upanguaima...............................	
	X. TARASCA.	62. Tarasco .... 63. Chorotega de Nicaragua.....................	
	XI. ZOQUE-MIXE.	64. Mixe...................................... 65. Zoque .... 66. Tapijulapa	Various.

GROUPS.	FAMILIES.	LANGUAGES.	DIALECTS.
	XII. Totonaca.	67. Totonaco (mixed language).................	Four.
		2d Order. Languages polysyllabic polysynthetic of juxtaposition.	
	XIII. Mixteco-Zapo-teca.	68. Mixteco..................................... 69. Zapoteco................................... 70. Chuchon .... 71. Popoloco .... 72. Cuicateco.................................. 73. Chatino .... 74. Papabuco................................... 75. Amusgo .... 76. Mazateco .... *77. Solteco .... *78. Chinanteco	Eleven. Twelve. Two. Two. Two.
	XIV. Pirinda or Ma-tlalzinca.	79. Pirinda or Matlalzinca.;....................	Various.
		3d Order.—Languages Polosyllabic Synthetic.	
	XV. Maya.	80. Yucateco or Maya............................ 81. Punctunc................................... 82. Lacandon or Xochinel .... 83. Peten or Itzae............................ 84. Chañabal, Comiteco, Jocolobal.............. 85. Chol or Mopan .... 86. Chorti or Chorte........................... 87. Cakchi, Caichi, Cachi or Cakgi............. 88. Ixil, Izil................................... 89. Coxoh..................................... 90. Quiché, Utlateco............................ 91. Zutuhil, Zutugil, Atiteca, Zacapula.......... 92. Cachiquel, Cachiquil .. .. 93. Tzotzil, Zotzil, Tzinanteco, Cinanteco....... 94. Tzendal, Zendal............................ 95. Mame, Mem, Zaklohpakap................. 96. Poconchi, Pocoman......................... 97. Atche, Atchi............................... 98. Huaxteco .... *99. Haitiano, Quizqueja or Itis, with their af-finities, Cubano, Borigua and Jamaica......	Various.
	XVI. Chontal.	*100. Chontal doubtful in its morphologic char-acter.....................................	
	XVII. Derivatives of Nicaragua.	*101. Huave, Huazonteca...................... *102. Chiapaneco	
	XVIII. Apache.	103. Apache	North American Apache, Mexi-can Apache, Mimbreño, Pinaleño, Nava-jo, Xicarilla or Faraon, Lipan Mescalero.
		4th Order.—Languages cuasi-mo-nosyllabic.	
	XIX. Otomi.	104. Otomi or Hiahiu........................... 105. Serrano .... 106. Mazahua .... 107. Pame..................................... 108. Jonaz or Meco. (Perhaps the rest of the ancient Chichimeco)...................	Various.

FAMILIES INDEPENDENT AMONG THEMSELVES AND OF THE MEXICAN-OPATA GROUP.

POPULATION.

We have until recently taken a regularly correct census of our population. The first reliable census was made in 1795, under Revillagigedo's viceroyalty, the second in 1810 by Don Fernando Navarro y Noriega, the third one was estimated by Mr. Poinsett, United States Minister in Mexico, in 1824, and the others have been taken by the Mexican Government.

The following is a statement of the general results of our various censuses :

Years.	Inhabitants.
1795	5,200,000
1810	6,122,354
1824	6,500,000
1839	7,044,140
1854	7,853,395
1869	8,743,614
1878	9,384,193
1879	9,908,011
1886	10,791,685
1895	12,570,195

The population of Mexico appears to be, from our last census, taken in 1895, 12,570,195, which would give 16.38 for each square mile ; but from my personal knowledge of the country, I am quite sure that it is not less than 15,000,000. It is very difficult to take a correct census in Mexico, because there is not the proper machinery in operation for that purpose, and especially because a great many districts are inhabited by Indians, who are impressed with the fear that if they inscribe themselves in the census they will be taxed or drafted into the military service, and they try to avoid registration.

A great many of our people live in such remote districts that they are practically cut off from communication with other portions of the country, and in fact are almost isolated ; and this constitutes still another difficulty in the way of taking a correct census. These people generally raise everything they need for their living, as well as for their clothing. They also raise their domestic animals, and wear either cotton or woollen clothes, manufactured by the women. The configuration of the country, which makes transportation very expensive, together with the very sparse population, has caused their isolation, and this explains why some agricultural products which are very cheap in other countries are very dear in certain districts of Mexico, as prices can be easily controlled, there being no possibility of competition. While sugar, for instance, costs 25 cents per pound in some districts, it can be had in others for one cent. This fact shows also that a year of good crops was often a real misfortune to these districts.

The upper lands being the healthiest, most of the population in Mexico is settled in the central plateau ; a relatively small portion lives in the temperate zone, while the torrid zone is very thinly populated. I imagine, at a rough calculation, that about 75 per cent. of the population make their abode in the cold zone, from 15 to 18 per cent. in the temperate zone, and from 7 to 10 per cent. in the torrid zone.

From the synopsis of our censuses, inserted above, it appears that the population in Mexico has duplicated during the last century, and although that increase does not keep pace with the increase in the United States, because this has been really wonderful, it compares favorably with the increase in other countries. Mexico also, as a new country and one full of possibilities, ought to have increased its population more rapidly, but its slow progress can be accounted for in several ways.

Under the head of Ethnology I enumerated the different races inhabiting Mexico and stated the number of inhabitants belonging to each, and I gave at length the reasons for the slow increase of the Indian population, which is the largest in Mexico. I will only add here that while the Indians lead a very abstemious and simple life, marry while very young and generally have a family of several children, they are at the same time subject to epidemics. Notwithstanding that the race on the whole is sturdy and little subject to disease, the mortality is very large among the children for want of proper nutrition and care. The losses caused by our civil wars could not at all explain the slow increase of our population, and the only way in which I can account for it is that they are not so well prepared as the people of the United States and other more advanced countries, to bear the discomforts of life and climate, and that, therefore, they cannot bring up all the children born in the family, among whom there is annually a great mortality.

Classification of Mexican States. Under the Spanish rule Mexico was divided into several provinces, the Spaniards trying to divide the provinces in accordance with the different nationalities of the aborigines found there, and each province possessing a very large extent of territory. After our independence and when we established a Federal government, each province was made a state, and since then some of the largest states have been divided into two or even three smaller ones. In the chapter on Political Organizations I shall give further information on this subject.

The Mexican states are classified in several ways, and generally as Northern, Southern, Central, Pacific, and Gulf States ; but it is difficult to make a proper division of them, because there are several included in two denominations. I will, therefore, divide them into Northern States, calling so those bordering on the United States ; Southern States,

those bordering on Gautemala and Belize ; Gulf, Caribbean Sea, and
Pacific States, those bordering on their respective waters ; and Central
States those which do not belong to any of the above denominations,
although I do not consider this a proper classification, because the
State of Tamaulias included among the Northern States, and the States
of Tabasco, Campeche, and Yucatan among the Southern States, are
all on the Gulf of Mexico, and are, therefore, Gulf States, the latter
being also washed on their southern side by the Caribbean Sea, and
the State of Sonora, classified as a Northern State, borders on the
Pacific ; the State of Chiapas, included among the Southern States, also
borders on the Pacific, and, therefore, is, like Sonora, also a Pacific
State.

Our last official census, taken in 1895, gives the following results
by States, which I compared with the census of 1879.

AREA AND POPULATION OF THE UNITED MEXICAN STATES.

	STATES.	AREA IN SQUARE MILES.	POPULATION in 1879.	POPULATION in 1895.	POPULA-TION PER SQUARE MILE.	CAPITAL.	POPULA-TION.
Northern States bordering on the U.S.	Tamaulipas	32,585	140,137	204,206	6.3	Ciudad Victoria..	14,575
	Nuevo Leon	24,324	203,284	309,607	13.1	Monterey	56,855
	Coahuila	62,376	130,026	235,638	3.7	Saltillo	19,654
	Chihuahua	87,820	225,541	266,831	3.0	Chihuahua	18,521
	Sonora	76,922	115,424	191,281	2.4	Hermosillo	8,376
Southern States bordering on Guatemala.	Yucatan	35,214	302,315	297,507	8.4	Mérida	36,720
	Campeche	18,091	90,413	90,458	5.0	Campeche	16,631
	Tabasco	10,075	104,747	134,794	13.3	S. Juan Bautista..	27,036
	Chiapas	27,230	205,362	313,678	11.5	Tuxtla Gutierrez.	7,882
Atlantic.	Veracruz	29,210	542,918	855,975	29.3	Jalapa	18,173
Pacific.	Oaxaca	35,392	744,000	882,529	24.9	Oaxaca	32,641
	Guerrero	25,003	295,590	417,621	16.7	Chilpancingo	6,204
	Michoacan	22,881	661,534	889,795	38.8	Morelia	32,287
	Colima	2,273	65,827	55,677	24.5	Colima	19,305
	Jalisco	31,855	983,484	1,107,863	34.8	Guadalajara	83,870
	Sinaloa	33,681	186,491	256,414	7.6	Culiacan	14,205
Central.	Aguascalientes	2,951	140,430	103,645	35.1	Aguas Calientes .	31,619
	Durango	38,020	190,846	294,366	7.7	Durango	42,165
	Guanajuato	11,374	834,845	1,047,238	92.1	Guanajuato	39,337
	Hidalgo	8,920.	427,350	548,039	61.6	Pachuca	52,189
	Morelos	2,774	159,160	159,800	57.6	Cuernavaca	8,554
	Mexico	9,250	710,579	838,737	90.7	Toluca	23,648
	Puebla	12,207	784,466	979,723	80.2	Puebla	91,917
	Querétaro	3,558	203,250	227,233	63.9	Querétaro	32,790
	Tlaxcala	1,595	138,988	166,803	104.6	Tlaxcala	2,874
	San Luis Potosí	25,323	516,486	570,814	22.5	San Luis Potosí ..	69,676
	Zacatecas	24,764	422,506	452,720	18.2	Zacatecas	40,026
Territories.	Tepic	11,279	....	144,308	12.8	Tepic	16,266
	Lower California..	58,345	30,208	42,287	0.7	La Paz and	4,737
						Ensenada de Todos Santos ..	1,259
	Federal District ..	463	351,804	484,608	1046.7	City of Mexico...	339,935
	Islands	1,471	....				
	Totals	767,226	9,908,011	12,570,195			

RELIGION.

All Mexicans are born in the Catholic Church, that being the prevailing religion of the country ; but there is no connection between Church and State, and the Constitution guarantees the free exercise of all religions.

While Mexico was a colony of Spain and for many years afterwards, the catholic religion was the only one allowed in the country, and anybody professing any other would expose himself to great hardships if he avowed that he was a dissenter, especially while the Inquisition was in existence.

The clergy became one of the principal pillars of the Spanish domination in Mexico. In the early part of the present century the Church was flourishing, and it was the high-water mark of clerical prosperity. The humble Mexican priests did the hard laborious work, while the Spanish-born ecclesiastics filled the great bishoprics and other great posts and lived at their ease, and the great convents in their most lucrative positions of control were practically in Spanish hands.

Huge convents occupied a considerable part of the site of the City of Mexico, Puebla, Morelia, Guadalajara, Querétaro, and other cities. The incomes of the convents were derived from endowments, amounting to a large sum. To support the high ecclesiastics, great sums were derived from tithes. The archbishop of Mexico had an income of $130,000 a year ; the bishops of Puebla, $110,000 ; of Michoacan, $100,000 ; and of Guadalajara, $90,000. Meantime, the parish priests, who bore the brunt of Christian work among the masses, were living on very moderate sums. The Church erected in Mexico buildings which are remarkable for their dimensions and taste.[1]

---

[1] Mr. Charles Dudley Warner in the Editor's Study of *Harper's Illustrated Monthly Magazine* for July, 1897, speaks in the following way of the church edifices in Mexico :

" Somebody of authority, by the way, ought to explain why Mexico has so many church edifices that go to the heart of the lover of beauty, and why the United States has so few that are interesting. Aside from the great Gothic monuments in Spain, Mexico surpasses Spain in interesting ecclesiastical architecture. It has more variety, more quaint beauty, more originality in towers and façades. The interiors are generally monotonous, and repetitions of each other. The Spaniards, in an age of faith, built churches, convents, monasteries, all over the county, in remote and unimportant Indian villages, and as far north as their patient ministers of religion wandered, even to the bay of San Francisco. In these edifices the Spanish ingenuity and enthusiasm prevailed, but they were largely executed by Indian builders and artists ; and if there is Sarasenic feeling shown, there are also, especially in ornamentation, traces of that aboriginal artistic spirit which, long before the Spanish conquest, executed both in stone and in pottery singularly attractive work. Even within a hundred years of our own time Indian genius has been distinguished. Those who think that this genius is only exhib-

Not all the great dignitaries of the Church exhibited an unchristian selfishness, for many often spent their income in pious and charitable works, and in prosecuting missionary undertakings among the Indians of the remote distances.

The wealth of the Church was loaned out at a moderate rate of interest to landed proprietors, who formed the moral support of the Church among the laity and whose influence was prodigiously strong. The wealth of the Church was mostly in mortgages, while it held a large amount of real estate. In the City of Mexico and other places, the clergy owned a large portion of the real estate and held a great many mortages, and, to its credit be it said, was not at all usurious, exacting only a fair rate of interest and being hardly ever oppressive in dealing with delinquent debtors.

After the Revolution which effected the independence of the country, the ecclesiastical life began to cease having many of the attractions it had before. While many men became friars from genuine inclination and vocation, not a few went into the religious life because it gave them support without hard labor, and because it was one of the best careers opened to young men at the time.

The nunneries sheltered a great many pious women, who effected some good as educators of the young, as almoners for the wealthy, and as nurses of the sick. There were abuses, of course, but on the whole the religious life afforded a refuge for many thousands of good women who felt drawn to works of charity and usefulness. Rich young girls were often over-persuaded to enter the convents, by avaricious and scheming priests, but such abuses are common to all religions. The Liberal party thought that the best way to destroy the Church influence in Mexico was to suppress convents, both of friars and nuns, because they

ited in bizarre forms, and in such small details of design and color as the potter can attain, should see at Querétaro the work of Tresguerras, architect, sculptor, and painter. Any modern architect, who is led away by straining after effect in a grotesque combination of distinct Greek styles with mediæval and early English, having no note of originality anywhere, could study with profit the simple elegance—as simple as the Old Louvre—of the Bishop's Palace in Querétaro, or the wood-carving in the church of the sequestered Convent of Santa Rosa. In my remembrance there is not, on such a great scale, any wood-carving in the world equal to it in freshness and largeness of execution and in beauty of design. It could not have been all done by the hand of Tresguerras, but it was all from his designs and under his superintendence. Of course, as to civic and ecclesiastic architecture, climate and lack of popular taste for the beautiful put limits upon our architectural work, but it is worth the while of the American architect to consider whether he cannot learn more from our sister republic below the Tropic of Cancer than he is likely to get from the well-studied structures of Europe. In many petty and poverty-stricken Indian villages are charming towers and curious façades which would be a most valuable education in the principles of taste to any American community."

were considered a nest of superstition, and they thought that the best
interest of the country required to close them.

During our civil wars the clergy contributed large amounts to the
support of the conservative governments, which it often established.
It is thought that in 1853, General Santa Anna abandoned the Conservative Government, which he then presided over, because the Archbishop of Mexico did not give him all the money he required to carry
on the war waged against him by the Liberal party.

The wealth accumulated by the Church of Mexico was used for the
purpose of supporting the conservative governments, whose policy was
to keep the statu quo, and was therefore opposed to progress of any
kind.   The Church became a very prominent factor in politics, and
could upset and establish governments at its pleasure, fomenting
the many revolutions which were constantly breaking out.   It was
thought necessary, therefore, to destroy the political power of the
Church before we could establish and maintain peace, and that work
was done by what we call our Laws of Reform, issued in 1859, which
established a complete independence between the Church and the
State, and were intended to completely end the domination of the
Catholic Church in civil affairs in Mexico : the Church property was
confiscated, so that even the houses of worship are now the property
of the government ; all convents of friars and nuns were closed, all
religious ceremonies—such as processions and wearing a distinctive
dress,—were ordered to be confined to the interior of the edifices ;
the cemeteries were secularized, and marriage made exclusively a civil
contract.   No religious instruction or ceremony is allowed in the public
schools, and never is a prayer offered as a part of the program of a
national celebration.   In an article, which I published in the *North
American Review*, of January, 1895, entitled " The Philosophy of the
Mexican Revolutions," I dwelt especially on this subject, and to that
article I refer the reader who may desire more detailed information.

The Liberals were not the first to dispose of the Church property
and revenues, as the Spanish Government, under the rule of Godoy, in
1805 and 1806, to secure funds to form a redemption provision for the
royal *vales* or credit notes, pounced on the property of the Church in
Mexico, and that, later on, when the Mexicans rose in their war for
independence, the royal authorities took another part of the Church's
wealth to fight the patriots.

The bigoted Catholic element which used to be decidely opposed to
any liberal government and was always conspiring to overthrow it, has
since the downfall of Maximilian, become satisfied that the condition of things has changed having accordingly changed their course,
and now there are thousands of progressive catholics in Mexico
sincerely devoted to their Church, who see only danger and eventual

disastrous defeat in the adoption of a program of reaction. They go with the times and support the administration of Gen. Diaz because, on the whole, it suits them, and manifests no hostility to their conscientiously held convictions. The pope's influence seems to be directed to assuaging ancient rancors, and to the calming of passionate resentments, which is a great deal better for the Church.

Protestantism in Mexico.—The Liberal party proclaimed as an inherent right of man, freedom of conscience and the free exercise of one's religion ; but the question was really only a theoretical one, since excepting a few foreigners, no one in Mexico had any other religion than the Catholic. The clergy, the Church party, and all strict Mexican catholics were greatly opposed to the introduction of Protestantism, because protestants were looked upon as heretics whose purpose was to divide the Mexican people into different sects, disturbing their religious unity, which they considered a source of national strength, and ultimately aiding in what some Mexicans fear is the aim of this country, that is : the final absorption of Mexico. When the struggles between the Liberal and the Church party terminated in favor of the former in 1867, with the withdrawl of the French army from Mexico and the downfall of Maximilian, the time came to put into practice the principles of the Liberal creed, and protestant organizations in the United States sent missionaries to Mexico for the purpose of establishing and propagating the protestant religion there. The Mexican Government could not refuse to allow the missionaries the free exercise of the Protestant or any other faith, because that right was guaranteed to all men in our constitution, and also because it has been a principle for which the Liberal party had been contending during many years.

But we went, then, further than allowing the Protestants the free exercise and preaching of their religion, and as I am in a measure responsible for that step, I think it proper to give my reasons for the same. My opinion has never been favorable to missionary work, because although I recognize that some religions have higher moral principles than others, I think that on the whole they are all intended to accomplish the same purpose, that all are good, when practised in good faith. It has always seemed to me that Christian missionaries sent to heathen countries would be looked upon in the same manner as would be heathen missionaries sent to Christian countries. But even supposing that it should be proper and desirable for the Christian religion, on account of its high morals and principles, to send missionaries to heathen countries for the purpose of converting them to Christianity, that principle would scaracely hold good in Christian countries of different denominations, and Catholicism is a Christian religion—whatever abuses it may have committed,—and I think the natural tendency of all religions when they are predominant is to absorb and misuse power ; but that Protestants should send missionaries to a Catholic country seems to me inconsistent.   In principle, therefore, Mexico is hardly the proper field for Protestant missionaries, notwithstanding that there is a great deal of room for improvement there, in so far as religious matters are concerned.

After having witnessed the terrible consequences of religious intolerance and political domination of the Catholic Church in Mexico, I was of course greatly impressed with the condition of things existing in the United States, where all religions are tolerated and none attempts to control the political destinies of the country.   I thought that one of the best ways to diminish the evils of the political domination and abuses of the clergy in Mexico was to favor the establishment of other sects, which would come in some measure into competition with the Catholic clergy and thus serve to cause it to refrain from excesses of which it had been guilty before.   When, after having lived for ten years in the United States, from 1859 to 1868, I returned to Mexico and took charge of the Treasury Department there, just at the time when the religious question was being solved, I, therefore, favored the establishment of a Protestant community as planned by Mr. Henry C. Riley, since made a Bishop, a gentleman of English parentage, born in Chili, who had been educated in London and New York and was graduated with high honors at Columbia College, New York, who spoke equally well English and Spanish, and eagerly desired to establish a Mexican National Church in competition with the Roman Catholic, in which undertaking, I understand, he used his own funds. He proposed to buy one of the finest churches, the main church of the Franciscan convent, which had been built by the Spaniards, located in the best section of the City of Mexico, and which could not now be duplicated but for a very large amount of money ; and with the hearty support of President Juarez, who shared my views and who was perhaps a great deal more radical than I was myself on such subjects, I sold the building which had become national property after the confiscation of the Church property, for a mere trifle, if I remember rightly about $4000, most of that amount being paid in Government bonds which were then at a nominal price.

The magnificent building sold to Dr. Riley's community was bought recently by the Catholic Church to restore it as a Catholic temple, for the sum of $100,000, as I understand.   My assistance was rendered to the Protestant cause for the reasons that I have stated, and not because I had adopted the Protestant faith ; therefore the action of the Mexican Government in the matter at the time I speak of, was all the more praiseworthy.   Dr. Butler bought about the same time another part of the same convent of San Francisco, where he established a Methodist Church in a very creditable building.

It is true that a great many Mexicans, namely the Indians, do not know much about religion and keep to their old idolatry, having changed only their idols, that is, replaced their old deities with the images of the Saints of the Catholic Church, but it would be difficult for the Protestant missionaries to reach them. The Spaniards labored zealously to make the natives adopt the Catholic religion, and although they succeeded wonderfully, it was a task too difficult to fully accomplish in the three centuries of the Spanish domination in Mexico.

I do not think that the American Protestant missionaries in Mexico have made much progress, and I doubt very much whether Mexico is a good field for them ; but they are satisfied with their work, and they think that under the circumstances, they have made very good progress.

The number of Catholic churches and chapels in the country was, in 1889, 10,112, while the number of Protestant places of worship was 119. On August 12, 1890, there were in the municipality of Mexico 320,143 Catholics and 2623 Protestants.

The American missionaries, and especially Dr. Riley, whom I consider a very benevolent and unselfish man, have established Protestant schools and asylums for children, spending considerable money in maintaining such institutions. Of course poor parents were glad to send their children to the Protestant schools and asylums when they could not afford to keep them at home or send them to more desirable places, and these Protestant institutions were of a very benevolent character and worthy, therefore, to be encouraged. Parents in such cases declared themselves to be partial to Protestantism, but only for the sake of having their children accepted in the Protestant schools and asylums, and this made the Protestants think they were making a great many converts.

Now and then a Catholic priest would renounce Catholicism and accept Protestantism, and such occurrences were always considered as great triumphs for the Protestant cause, but although in some instances such changes have been made in good faith, in others they were made for selfish purposes, and they never had any great weight with the community.

I have no prejudice against Protestantism ; on the contrary, I admire greatly many of its principles, and in speaking on this subject I consider myself perfectly impartial and unbiassed.

In February, 1888, the Evangelical Assembly, representing the various Protestant denominations and Evangelical Societies conducting missionary operations in the Republic of Mexico, was held in the City of Mexico. They claimed that, notwithstanding the difficulties of language and climate and the other obstacles with which they had to contend, they found that they had over 600 congregations, 192 foreign and 585 native workers, over 7000 in the day schools, and about 10,000

7

in the Sunday-schools, 18,000 communicants and a Protestant community of over 60,000 souls.   Ten small publishing-houses are turning out
millions of pages each year, and their church property is valued at
nearly a million and a quarter dollars in silver.

POLITICAL ORGANIZATION.

Mexico was the largest and richest American colony of Spain, and
for this reason it was called New Spain.   The City of Mexico grew
during the Spanish rule to be larger than Madrid, the capital of the
Spanish Kingdom, the population of the country being estimated in
1810, just before the independence movement began, at 6,122,354 ;
while the public revenue of the whole colony amounted to the very
large sum of $20,000,000 yearly, the only exports of the country
being silver and gold, and commodities of great value in small volume
and weight, such as cochineal, vanilla, indigo, and a few others.

Mexico accomplished her independence in 1821, and since then
has had two Federal Constitutions, both modelled after the Constitution of the United States ; two Central Constitutions, which organized
the country into a centralized republic, and two ephemeral empires,
one under Iturbide, lasting ten months, from 1822 to 1823, and the
other under Maximilian, established by French intervention, lasting
from 1864 to 1867.

Mexico is now organized, under the Constitution of the 5th of
February, 1857, with its several amendments, into a Federal Republic,
composed of twenty-seven states, two territories, and a federal district,
and the political organization is almost identical with that of this
country.   The powers of the Federal Government are divided into
three branches—Legislative, Executive, and Judicial.   The Legislative
is composed of a House of Representatives and a Senate ; the members of the House are elected for two years and the senators for four,
the Senate being renewed by half every two years.   Representatives
are elected by the suffrage of all male adults, at the rate of one member for every 40,000 inhabitants.   The qualifications requisite are to
be at least twenty-five years of age and a resident of the State ; and for
senators thirty years.

The Executive is exercised by a President elected by the electors
popularly chosen, who holds his office for four years, without any
provision forbidding his re-election.   He has a cabinet of seven members, namely : Secretary of Foreign Affairs, of the Interior, of Justice
and Public Instruction, of Fomento, which means promotion of Public Improvements, and includes public lands, patents, and colonization ; of Communications and Public Works, of the Treasury, and
of War and Navy.   No Vice-President is elected, but by an amendment to our Constitution, promulgated April 24, 1896, in the per-

manent or temporary disability of the President, not caused by resignation or by leave, the Secretary of State, and after him the Secretary of the Interior, shall exercise that office until Congress elects a President *pro tempore.* In case of resignation, Congress, accepting it, elects a President *pro tempore,* and in case of leave the President recommends to Congress the person to fill that office.

The Federal Judiciary is composed of a Supreme Court, consisting of eleven Judges, four substitutes, one Attorney-General, and one Fiscal, chosen for six years; three Circuit and thirty-two District Courts.

The States are independent in their domestic affairs, and their governments are similarly divided into three branches : the Governor, the Legislature, and the State Judiciary.

As we adopted the federal system rather to follow the example of the United States than to suit the conditions of Mexico, that system did not work with us so easily or so satisfactorily as it works here ; and the tendency is rather to centralization and to the increasing of the powers given by the Constitution to the Federal Government. In the article above mentioned published in the *North American Review,* for January, 1896, entitled, " The Philosophy of the Mexican Revolutions," [1] I dwelt particularly on the results of our having copied almost literally the political institutions of the United States, and gave a general idea of our political condition.

Political Division.—When the federal system was established in Mexico, in 1824, each of the old provinces under the Spanish rule was organized as a State, and our Constitution of October 4, 1824, enumerated nineteen States. After the war with the United States we lost Texas, New Mexico, and California ; but since then as I stated in the chapter on population some of the larger States have been divided into two, or even three States, as was the case with the old State of Mexico, out of which were formed the three present States of Mexico, Hidalgo, and Morelos. Our present Constitution, of February 5, 1857, enumerates twenty-four States ; but we now have twenty-seven.

The tabular statement published above, under the head of " Population," shows the number of States which form the Mexican Confederation, their area, population, and capital cities.

Army and Navy.—During our civil wars, and for some time later, we had to keep a very large standing army, and our army acquired recently a very high degree of discipline and efficiency. The Liberal party always favored the reduction of the army, while the Church party favored a large army, as our old regular army, on the whole, took sides with the Church. Soon after the restoration of the Republic, in 1867, the Mexican army consisted of : Infantry, 22,964 ; engineers, 766 ; ar-

[1] This article will appear in this volume under the head of " Historical Notes on Mexico."

tillery, 2304 ; cavalry, 8454 ; rural guards of police, 2365 ; gendarmerie, 250 ; total, 37,103 ; and was commanded by 11 Major-Generals, 73 Brigadier-Generals, 1041 Colonels, Lieutenant-Colonels, and Majors, and 2335 Commissioned Officers. The total fighting strength, including reserves, is stated to be 132,000 infantry, 25,000 cavalry, and 8000 artillery. Every Mexican capable of carrying arms is liable for military service from his twentieth to his fiftieth year.

Notwithstanding that General Diaz is himself a soldier, he has followed the policy of the Liberal party of reducing the army as much as possible, and in his report of November 30, 1896, in which he informs his fellow citizens of his results of his sixteen years administration, he gives the following figures, showing the reduction he has been able to accomplish in the army since 1888 :

The army had, in 1888, according to President Diaz's report, the following personnel :

Major-Generals..............................	16
Brigadier-Generals	84
Commissioned Officers........................	1,205
Non-Commissioned Officers....................	2,566
Soldiers	29,367
Total...............................	33,238

In 1896 the personnel had been reduced in the following numbers :

Generals.....................................	24
Commissioned Officers........................	166
Non-Commissioned Officers	299
Soldiers	8,170
Total...............................	8,659

The Mexican navy is now in its inception, as it consists of a fleet of two dispatch vessels, launched 1874, each of 425 tons and 425 horsepower, and severally armed with a four-ton muzzle-loading gun, and four small breech-loaders. A steel training ship, the *Zaragoza*, of 1200 tons, was built at Havre, in 1891 ; four gun-boats are building, and a battle-ship and cruiser are projected ; five first-class torpedo-boats have been ordered in England. The fleet is manned by ninety officers and five hundred men.

EDUCATION.

In 1521, the City of Mexico fell into the hands of the conquering Spaniards, and exactly eight years after that event there was established in the City of Mexico the College of San Juan de Letran, for giving secondary education to intelligent Indians as well as to the sons of the invading race.   Thus, ninety years before the landing of the Pilgrims, the City of Mexico had its " Harvard."

Universities Established by the Spanish Government.—The first vice-roy of New Spain, as Mexico was called then, fourteen years after the conquest, petitioned the King of Spain to permit him to found a university in Mexico, and, anticipating from his knowledge of the good-will of the Spanish-rulers that the desired permission would be given, the viceroy took the responsibility of establishing certain classes in the higher learning, a fact which does not support the commonly held theory that Spain has always been the enemy of education and of popular enlightenment.   Owing to the slow means of communication in those days, and the legal steps necessary to be taken in the mother country, the university was not formally established until 1553, or eighty-three years before Harvard College was opened. The great event of setting on foot the university came under the enlightened rule of the second viceroy, Don Luis de Velasco, who did so many great things for Spain's new dependency.

Later on, in 1573, there were founded in Mexico the colleges of San Gregorio and San Ildefonso, the latter still open, but modernized into the national preparatory school, a really great institution in that city of many schools.   A few years later, long before the 17th century had dawned, came the founding of two more colleges and a divinity school, so that in the first sixty-five years of Spain's control in Mexico no less than seven seats of the higher learning had been established on secure foundations.

No wonder that Mexico's capital became known as the Athens of the new world, producing men of great learning, such as Don Juan Ruiz de Alarcon and such notably erudite women as Juana Inez de la Cruz.   The extensive library of " Americana," belonging to Don Jose de Agreda, of that city, containing over 4000 books, many of them invaluable, attests the literary, antiquarian, scientific and artistic activity of the Spaniards who planted there in a short space of time so much of learning and such vast institutions dedicated to the instruction in all the higher branches of knowledge.

At the outset the University of Mexico gave instruction only in mathematics, Latin and the arts.   Medicine and surgery were not esteemed highly during the middle ages, and it was not until long after the revival of learning in the Renaissance that the physician came to be considered as a true man of science.   So it is not to be marvelled at that the University of Mexico waited until 1578 to establish a chair of medicine—the first in the new world discovered by Columbus.   The first chair of medicine was a morning class, and a single professor carried his students through a four years' course unaided.   In 1599, a second medical professorship was added ; in 1661, anatomy and surgery were added, and, consequently dissection was authorized. At the outset the viceroys appointed the professors, but after a time the candidates for chairs had to win the coveted prizes through competitive examinations.

The early students were not railroaded through. They had to study four years to obtain the diploma of a bachelor of medicine ; then went out into active life, and, on gaining practical knowledge, received, passing a fresh examination, the diploma of licentiate of medicine, and, later, that of doctor of medicine.

School of Medicine.—In 1768 a decree was issued for the establishment in the City of Mexico of a royal college for surgeons, similar to institutions in Cadiz and Barcelona. This college was a very complete one, instruction being given in anatomy and dissection, in physiology, operations, clinical surgery, and medical jurisprudence. There were graduated also from the college all the dentists, bonesetters, phlebotomists, and midwives. A knowledge of Latin was not essential to receive a medical degree until 1803.

In 1821, Mexico having achieved her independence, the same careful watch over education continued, and in 1833 a general revision of educational institutions was ordered under the administration of Don Valentin Gomez Farias a leader of the Liberal party and the university was closed, because it was considered to have conservative tendencies, and a general board of education organized, which, among other things established what was called the School of Medical Science, with ten professors, giving a remarkably complete and modern course. On account of a revolution which occurred in 1834 which overthrew the Gomez Farias Government, the new school of medicine was closed, and the old university reopened ; but, as the officials of the university, on making a careful study of the conditons of the new school of medicine rendered an impartial report, setting forth its manifold advantages it was decided to keep open the institution.

The incessant revolutions and consequent changes of government brought many evil things to pass, and the medical professors at times found themselves without salaries, and nobly devoted themselves to their classes without remuneration. They at one time were deprived of their building and literally thrown into the street. Better times came, however, the successive governments began to give substantial aid to the school, and in 1845 it took the name it still bears, the National School of Medicine. After more vicissitudes, many movings and trials which bore hard on the enthusiastic professors, the National School of Medicine finally was located where it now remains, in a part of the enormous edifice belonging formerly to the Inquisition.

In the chaos of succeeding revolutions the salaries of the professors were often unpaid, but the devoted men of science struggled on, assisted by wealthier students and contributing often out of their own slender means to keep the school alive ; but, in 1857, a better era commenced, and not since then, with rare exceptions, have there been any interruptions in financial aid from the various governments. All the other institutions of learning suffered the same fate and were exposed to similar ups and downs.

School of Engineering.—Our mining college is the best in Spanish America, and it was established when engineering was hardly taught, and endowed by a portion of the taxes levied by the Spanish Government on mines. Its edifice is one of the best built by the Spaniards in their colonies, and still stands as a great monument, embellishing the City of Mexico.

The above given facts will show how early did Mexico open great schools for the higher education, and how solicitous was the Spanish government to maintain them. But, three centuries of devotion to learning, antedating the war for independence, planted there firmly a love of knowledge which is now exhibited in the great government schools, in a city full of students, in innumerable private schools, in the well-filled public primary institutions, in night schools for adults, and in the thirty-five bookstores of that city.

Mexican Technical Schools in the Present Time.—The edifice of the first University in America, founded by the Spanish crown in 1551, is to-day occupied by the National Conservatory of Music. The National Academy of Art, ancient Academy of San Carlos, stands where Fray Pedro de Gante founded, in 1524, the first school of the New World—a school for Indians. The Normal School for males, with its six hundred pupils and its first-class German equipment, occupies the old convent of Santa Teresa, (1678). The Normal School for females has fourteen hundred pupils, an expensive building of 1648. The fine old Jesuit College of San Ildefonso, erected in 1749 at a cost of $400,000 is now filled with a thousand pupils of the National Preparatory School. The National College of Medicine is housed in the old home of the Inquisition (1732), an edifice whose four hanging arches at each corner of the lower corridor are famous. The building was taken for its present purpose in this century, the Holy Office dying in America with the Independence, but the medical college was established by royal decree of 1768. It has now several hundred pupils. San Lorenzo (1598) is now the manual training-school where poor boys are gratuitously taught lithography, engraving, printing, carpentry, and many other trades. The similar institution for girls is of course modern, dating only from 1874. The National Library, with its 200,000 volumes, dwells in the splendid sequestered Church of San Agustin. The National Museum occupies part of the million-dollar building erected in 1731 for the royal mint. And so on through a list that would rival that of any other country. The School of Mines and Engineering, however, stands as one of the first. Its magnificent building of Chiluca, the nearest to granite the valley affords, was built for it by Tolsa in 1793, and cost three millions. The institution named the Colegio de la Paz, better known as the Vizcainas is one of the principal establishments for the education of young women, founded in 1734, at a cost for construction alone of about $2,000,000, subscribed by three Spanish merchants, who also provided funds for its support. These funds, when insufficient to meet expenses, are supplemented by the Federal Government. We have also a very high grade Military School located at the historical grounds of Chapultepec, which educates fine soldiers.

As late as 1824 Humboldt declared, " No city of the New Continent, not excepting those of the United States, presents scientific establishments so great and solid as those of the capital of Mexico." Except as to the buildings, of course, so much could not be said to-day, as wealth and numbers have made other countries take more rapid strides in higher education. Some of the universities of the United States pay even $10,000 a year to professors and they therefore can secure the best talent.

From the time of the Spanish domination in Mexico to but a few years ago, the Mexican Government considered itself bound to give to the people free secondary education, and for this purpose colleges for all literary and scientific professions were established in the City of Mexico, and each State did the same in its respective capital, in so far as its means allowed it, so that anybody who intended to follow a scientific career could do so without any expense to himself.

The result of the free technical schools has been that most of the young men of well-to-do families in Mexico follow a literary career and that does not cost them anything, and we have more lawyers, doctors, engineers than we really need for the country.

Reorganization of the Technical Colleges.—We had before 1868 several higher colleges and in each of them the same careers were taught, as law, medicine, engineering, etc., but in the reorganization of our national colleges which took place in that year, it was thought proper to establish a special college for each career, and a preparatory college for such elementary studies as would be required for all careers, such as elementary mathematics, physics, chemistry, etc., etc., so that we now have in the City of Mexico, supported by the Federal Government a special school for engineering, one for law, one for medicine, another for agriculture, etc., etc., but each State generally supports one technical college where all literary careers are taught.

Primary Education.—Comparatively little attention was paid to the primary education, and the public schools were so deficient that parents of some means did not send their children to them, but to private schools where they were better attended to. The fact that the elevation of the people depends on their primary education has caused common schools to be established in the country, and now the States vie with each other for the purpose of establishing the best system of common schools and increasing their number.

The Mexican Government has been too much disturbed since its independence to earnestly promote the education of the Indians. I consider that one of the first duties of Mexico is to educate the large number of Indians which we have, and when that is accomplished the whole condition of the country will change, as it will be able in a few years to increase by several millions its productive and consuming population.

In 1896 the Federal Congress of Mexico passed a law which was promulgated on June 3d of that year, making primary education obligatory on all the inhabitants of the Federal District and Territories, and placing public education under the control of the Federal Government, having been before under the respective municipalities.

In almost all the States education is free and compulsory, but the law has not been strictly enforced. Primary instruction is mostly at the expense of the municipalities, but the Federal Government makes frequent grants, and many schools are under the care of the beneficent societies.

School Statistics.—Statistical reports on public instruction for 1876 showed an aggregate of 8165 primary schools, with an attendance of 368,754 children of both sexes throughout the Republic. Reports for 1895 show a total number of public schools for both sexes throughout the Republic amounting to 10,915, in which are instructed 722,435 scholars, at an aggregate cost of $5,455,549.60. The proportion of children of both sexes attending the school is, with respect to the general population, nearly five per cent., and that of the children of school age, actually attending school about 27 per cent. with an average yearly outlay per capita of $7.55. The entire number of private schools for both sexes, including those supported by religious and civil associations, is 2585, with a total attendance of 81,221. Adding these to the preceding figures we have an aggregate of 13,500 schools with an attendance of 803,656 scholars. The number of schools in the country for professional technical education is 136, attended by 16,809 pupils of both sexes.

In the Federal District there are 454 public primary schools with an attendance of 44,776 pupils, and 247 private schools with an attendance of 19,334 pupils. In the matter of education Mexico now stands upon a plane as high, if not higher, than any of the Spanish American Republics, out-ranking even Chili and the Argentine Republic, both of which greatly surpassed her in former years.

The statistical part of this paper will contain detailed information about the number of schools established in each State, their cost, etc., during the year 1895, which complements the information embraced in this chapter.

Libraries.—Many great and noteworthy public and private libraries attest the ineradicable love of learning characteristic of the Mexican people. In 1894 there were in the Republic the National Library, with 200,000 volumes, and 102 other public libraries. There were in that year 22 museums for scientific and educational purposes, and 3 meteorological observatories. Our National Library at the City of Mexico collected all the books possessed by the libraries of the different convents when they were suppressed by the National Government, and has therefore a very large number of rare and valuable books.

Newspapers.—The number of newspapers published was 363, of which 94 are published in the capital : 4 in English, 2 in French, and 1 in German, showing that the Press has not attained there the great development that it has in this country.

THE VALLEY OF MEXICO.

The Valley of Mexico is one of the finest spots in the world. Surrounded by high mountains—almost at the foot of the two highest in the country, Popocatepetl and Ixtaccihuatl—with a very rare and clear atmosphere and a beautiful blue sky, especially after a rain ; it is really a centre of magnificent scenery. The rareness of the atmosphere makes distant objects appear to be very near, and when looking from the City of Mexico at the mountains which surround the Valley, one imagines that they are at the end of the City, while some of them are at a distance of forty miles. The view of the Valley from Chapultepec Hill, which is about one hundred and fifty feet high and distant about three miles from the City, towards its western extremity, where our military school now is and where the President has made his summer residence, is one of the most beautiful with which the earth is endowed. I have seen the Bosphorus, Constantinople, the Bay of Naples and other spots in the world which are considered to be most remarkable for their natural beauty, but I think the view of the Valley of Mexico from Chapultepec can be advantageously compared with any of them, if it does not excel them all.

Six lakes are within the limits of the Valley,—Chalco, Zochimilco, Texcoco, Xaltocan, San Cristobal, and Zupango, the two former being of fresh water and the others of salt water—and, as they have no natural outlet the City of Mexico has been deprived for some time of a proper drainage and its health has been affected very materially thereby. But the colossal undertaking of making an artificial outlet is now practically finished. In an article which I published in the *Engineering Magazine* in January, 1895, I dwelt especially on the work done during four centuries to accomplish that great end.[1]

The prevailing wind in the Valley of Mexico is northwest and north-northwest, which blew 250 times during the year 1883 ; while the southern winds, which are very dry, are rare, as they only blew 51 times in that year ; but at the same time they have greater velocity than the others, and the greatest relative velocity of the winds is 3.0. The west and northwest winds are very damp.

At the present stage of industrial development, speaking especially of the Valley of Mexico, the question of a cheaper combustible is the one of supreme importance. In the absence of water-power of importance and permanence of volume, the only solution of the problem so vital to the growth of manufactures there lies in procuring abundant and cheap fuel.

THE CITY OF MEXICO.

The City of Mexico, located in the western end of the valley, on the Anahuac plateau, at an altitude of 7350 feet above the sea level in 19° 26′ north latitude and 99° 07′ 53″ .4 longitude west of Greenwich, covering about twenty square miles, is one of the most ancient cities of this continent, was the capital of the Aztec Empire, of the Spanish Colony of New Spain and now of the Mexican Republic, and of the Federal District of Mexico.

Mexico dates either from the year 1325 or 1327, when the Aztecs, after long wanderings over the plateau were directed by the oracle to settle at this spot. For here had been witnessed the auspicious omen of an eagle perched on a nopal (cactus) and devouring a snake. Hence the original name of the city, Tenochtitlan (cactus on a stone), changed afterwards to Mexico in honor of the war god Mexitli. The eagle holding a snake in her beak and standing on a cactus upon a stone, is the coat-of-arms of the Mexican Republic. With the progress of the Aztec culture the place rapidly improved, and about 1450 the old mud and rush houses were replaced by solid stone structures, erected partly on piles amid the islets of Lake Texcoco, and grouped around the central enclosure of the great teocalli. The city had reached its highest splendor on the arrival of the Spaniards in 1519, when it comprised from 50,000 to 60,000 houses, with perhaps 500,000 inhabitants, and seemed to Cortes, according to Prescott's, " like a thing of fairy creation rather than the work of mortal hands." It was at that time about 12 miles in circumference, everywhere intersected by canals, and connected with the mainland by six long and solidly constructed causeways, as is clearly shown by the plan given in the edition of

---

[1] That article is appended to this paper.

Cortez's letters published at Nuremberg in 1524.[1] After its almost destruction in November, 1521, Cortez employed some 400,000 natives in rebuilding it on the same site; but since then the lake seems to have considerably subsided, for although still 50 square miles in extent, it is very shallow and has retired two and a half miles from the city.

During the Spanish rule the chief event was the revolt in 1692, when the municipal buildings were destroyed. Since then Mexico has been the scene of many revolutions, was captured by the United States Army after the battle of Chapultepec, on September 13, 1847, and by the French Army under Marshall Forey in 1863. But since the overthrow of Maximilian, and the French Intervention in 1867, peace has been established and it has become a great centre of civilizing influences for the surrounding peoples.

The City of Mexico is 263 miles by rail from Veracruz on the Atlantic, 290 from Acapulco on the Pacific, 285 from Oaxaca, 863 from Matamoros on the frontier with the United States, and 1224 miles from El Paso. Mexico is the largest and finest city in Spanish America, and at one time larger than Madrid, the capital of Spain, forming a square of nearly 3 miles both ways, and laid out with perfect regularity, all its six hundred streets and lanes running at right angles north to south and east to west, and covering within the walls an area of about ten square miles, with a population now of 539,935.

The present City of Mexico is almost twice as large as the old one, it having increased towards the northwest, and, strange to say, the new portion is not laid out as regularly as the old one. All the main thoroughfares converge on the central Plaza de Armas, or Main Square, which covers 14 acres, and is tastefully laid out with shady trees, garden plots, marble fountains, and seats. Here also are grouped most of the public buildings, towering above which is the Cathedral, the largest and most sumptuous church in America, which stands on the north side of the plaza on the site of the great pyramidal teocalli or temple of Huitzilopochtli, titular god of the Aztecs. This church, which was founded in 1573 and finished in 1657, at a cost of $2,000,-000, for the walls alone, forms a Greek cross, 426 feet long and 203 feet wide, with two great naves and three aisles, twenty side chapels, and a magnificent high altar supported by marble columns, and surrounded by a tumbago balustrade with sixty-two statues of the same rich gold, silver, and copper alloy serving as candelabra. The elaborately carved choir was also enclosed by tumbago railings made in Macao, weighing twenty-six tons, and valued at about $1,500,000. In the interior, the Doric style prevails, and Renaissance in the exterior, which is adorned by five domes and two open towers 218 feet high. At the foot of the

[1] Reproduced in vol. iv. of H. H. Bancroft's *History of the Pacific States*, San Francisco, 1833, p. 280.

left tower was placed the famous calendar stone, the most interesting relic of Aztec culture, which is now at the National Museum.

The east side of the plaza is occupied by the old vice-regal residence, now the National Palace, with 675 feet frontage, containing most of the Government offices, ministerial, cabinet, treasury, military headquarters, archives, meteorological department with observatory, and the spacious halls of ambassadors, with some remarkable paintings by Miranda and native artists. North of the National Palace, and forming portions of it, are the post-office and the national museum of natural history and antiquities, with a priceless collection of Mexican relics.

Close to the cathedral stands the Monte de Piedad, or national pawnshop, a useful institution, endowed in 1744 by Don Manuel Romero de Terreros with $375,000, and now possessing nearly $10,-000,000 of accumulated funds. Facing the cathedral is the Palacio Municipal, or City Hall, 252 feet by 122, rebuilt in 1792 at a cost of $150,000, and containing the city and district offices, and the merchant's exchange.

Around the Plaza San Domingo were grouped the convent of that name, which contained vast treasures buried within its walls, the old inquisition, now the school of medicine, and for some time the Custom House, which has now been removed to the city boundary. In the same neighborhood are the Church of the Jesuits and the School of Arts, which is, in the language of Brocklehurst, " an immense workshop, including iron and brass foundries, carriage and cart mending, building and masonry, various branches of joinery and upholstery work, and silk and cotton hand-weaving."

Other noteworthy buildings are the national picture gallery of San Carlos, the finest in America, in which the Florentine and Flemish schools are well represented, and which contains the famous *Las Casas*, by Felix Parra ; the national library of St. Augustine, with over 200-000 volumes, numerous MSS., and many rare old Spanish books ; the mint,[1] which since 1690 has issued coinage, chiefly silver, to the amount of nearly $3,000,000,000 ; the Iturbide Hotel, formerly the residence of the Emperor Iturbide ; the Mineria, or schools of mines, with lecture-rooms, laboratories, rich mineralogical and geological specimens, and a fossil horse, three feet high, of the Pleistocene period.

[1] The Spanish Government intended during last century to build a spacious, costly, and magnificent mint in the City of Mexico, and its plans and specifications were approved by the king, but by a mistake of the clerks in Madrid, they were forwarded to Santiago, Chili, instead of being sent to the City of Mexico, and it was in consequence built there. The building was so fine that, not having any mint at Santiago, it was used as the Government House, and it is now the Executive Mansion and Departments, and it is called " La Moneda," an abbreviation of " La Casa de Moneda," which is the Spanish name for mint.

Among the twenty scientific institutes, mention should be made of the Geographical and Statistical Society, whose meteorological department issues charts and maps of unsurpassed excellence.

Owing to the spongy nature of the soil, the Mineria and many other structures have settled out of the perpendicular, thus often presenting irregular lines and a rickety appearance.

Before 1860 half of the city consisted of churches, convents, and other ecclesiastical structures, most of which have been sequestrated and converted into libraries, stores, warehouses, hotels, and even stables, or pulled down for civic improvements. Nevertheless there still remain fourteen parish and thirty other churches, some of large size, with towers and domes. San Francisco Street is the leading thoroughfare, and is rivalled in splendor only by the new Cinco de Mayo Street, running from the National Theatre to the cathedral.

It would take a great deal more space than it is convenient to give in this paper, should I attempt to make a longer description of the City of Mexico which, being one of the oldest on this continent and the largest and principal one during the three centuries of the Spanish rule, it has quite a number of remarkable buildings and monuments and a very important history, a great deal of romance being connected with it.

The City of Mexico is not only the capital of the country, but the real head of the Republic ; and the aim of all other Mexican cities is to follow in its footsteps and imitate as much as possible the City of Mexico, which to them is a beau ideal and a real paradise.

The City of Mexico is now literally encircled with a belt of factories—cotton, paper, linen, etc., packing houses, brick works, cork factories, soap works, etc., and cheaper fuel will add largely to their number. They have been able to show profits under the load of a dear combustible, and they will welcome the introduction of any fuel, which will enable them to work even more successfully.

Climate.—From the official reports of Professor Mariano Barcena, Director of the National Meteorological Observatory of the City of Mexico, of the weather conditions in 1895, it appears that there were 121 cloudy days. But the rains were mostly at night or late in the afternoon, of short duration, and immediately succeeded by sunshine showers. Long periods of rainy weather are unknown there. The total rainfall for the year, less than twenty inches, will convey a fair idea of the dryness of the climate. The mean temperature in the shade for 1895 was 60 degrees, the highest being 65, reached in April, and the lowest 53, in January, a temperature rather which avoids both extremities. The mean temperature for the summer months were : June, 64 degrees ; July, 62 ; August, 62 ; September, 61.

The table on page 112, prepared by the Weather Bureau of the City

of Mexico, contains the average annual climatological data of that city
from the years 1877 to 1895.

More detailed data about the climatological conditions of the City
of Mexico during the year 1896, prepared also by our Weather Bureau,
is appended on page 113.

Mortality in the City of Mexico.—During the year 1896 the total
mortality in the City of Mexico, under a recorded population of 330,698,
was 15,567, not including 1275 still-births, equivalent to 4.70 per cent.
The principal diseases which caused that mortality were those affecting

[1] A BRIEF HISTORICAL SKETCH OF THE METEOROLOGY IN THE MEXICAN REPUBLIC.

Priest José Antonio Alzate stands in the first place among those who have cultivated the meteorological science in our country, being he who first devoted himself to
its study, and made regular observations during more than eight years, as he himself
says in his *Descripcion topográfica de México* (1738 to 1799). Of these observations, he,
unfortunately, only published those belonging to the last nine months of the year 1769,
in his famous *Gaceta de Literatura de México*, 1788 to 1795. He also published many
articles describing some phenomena and instruments, climates of towns, value and
usefulness of observations, as he had done in others of his publications : *Diario Liter-
ario de México*, 1768 ; *Asuntos varios sobre Ciencias y Artes*, 1772 to 1773 ; and *Ob-
servaciones sobre la Física Historia Natural y Artes útiles*, 1787. He was the first in
determining the height of the City of Mexico.

After these labors of Father Alzate, we find in the journal *El Sol* regular series
of observations published, daily, from the 14th of June, 1824, to the 14th of January,
1828. Dr. John Burkart in 1826 ; Sr. Francisco Gerolt from 1833 to 1834, at the
School of Mines ; Sr. José Gómez de la Cortina, Conde de la Cortina, from 1841 to
1845 ; the members of the Geographical Section of the Army Staff from 1842 to 1843 ;
the Astronomer Sr. Francisco Jiménez in 1858 ; the School of Mines in the years
1850, 1856, 1857, and 1858 ; Sr. Ignacio Cornejo, M.E., at the same school from
1865 to 1866 ; and Sr. Juan de Mier y Terán at the " Escuela Preparatoria " from
1868 to 1875, respectively, made some meteorological observations.

A series of observations from 1855 to 1875 were made at the Hacienda de San
Nicolás Buenavista, and another one at the city of Córdoba from 1859 to 1863, by
Dr. José Apolinario Nieto ; Sr. Carlos Sartorius at the Hacienda del Mirador (State
of Veracruz) ; Sr. Miguel Velázquez de León, and his sons, Joaquín and Luis, engineers, from 1869 up to the present, at the Hacienda del Pabellón ; Sr. Gregorio Bar-
reto from 1869 to 1880, at the city of Colima ; General Mariano Reyes, Sr. José
María Romero, engineer, and Sr. Pascual Alcocer, from 1870 to the present date, at
the city of Querétaro ; Sr. Lázaro Pérez from 1874 to 1885, at the city of Guadalajara ;
Sr. Isidoro Epstein at the City of Monterrey, 1855 ; Sr. Vicente Reyes, a civil engineer and architect, at the city of Cuernavaca, 1873, 1874, and 1876 ; Sr. Joaquín de
Mendízabal Tamborrel, an engineer, at the city of Puebla, 1872 to 1873 ; Sr. Augustin
Galindo at the same city, 1875 ; Professor Manuel M. Cházaro at San Juan Michapa
(State of Veracruz), 1872 to 1873 ; Priest Pedro Spina, S. J., at the city of Puebla,
1876, and perhaps many others from whom we have no notice, have devoted themselves to making meteorological observations.

The " Sociedad de Geografía y Estadistica " the most ancient scientific society in
Mexico, distributed, in 1862, some instruments and instructions to observers.

Finally, on the 6th of March, 1877, being President of the Republic, General

CLIMATOLOGICAL DATA OF THE CITY OF MEXICO.
ANNUAL SUMMARIES AND GENERAL SYNOPSIS, 1877–1895.
(ENGLISH MEASURES.)

Lat. N. 19° 26'.   Long. W., Greenwich 6 h. 36 m. 31 s., 56 or 99° 87' 53'' 4.   Height, 7472 (Eng. feet).

METEOROLOGICAL DATUM.	1877.	1878.	1879.	1880.	1881.	1882.	1883.	1884.	1885.	1886.	1887.	1888.	1889.	1890.	1891.	1892.	1893.	1894.	1895.	Average, 1877–1895.
Mean barometrical height reduced to the freezing point	23.10	23.09	23.11	23.10	23.10	23.11	23.09	23.09	23.06	23.07	23.07	23.07	23.08	23.08	23.07	23.07	23.07	23.08	23.09	23.08
Maximum barometrical height	23.31	23.28	23.40	23.32	23.34	23.38	23.32	23.32	23.28	23.29	23.30	23.27	23.27	23.28	23.27	23.28	23.29	23.30	23.23	23.40
Minimum barometrical height	22.89	22.87	22.89	22.89	22.89	22.84	22.88	22.88	22.88	22.89	22.87	22.87	22.87	22.89	22.84	22.84	22.87	22.87	22.86	22.83
Mean temperature in shade	61°9	61°2	59°5	59°5	59°9	59°7	59°4	59°4	59°7	59°7	59°0	59°5	60°1	58°8	59°2	59°9	59°5	59°0	60°3	59°7
Mean temperature in open air	—	—	—	—	—	—	59.5	59.5	60.1	60.1	59.2	59.9	59.4	59.4	59.5	60.0	60.4	60.6	60.8	59.9
Maximum temperature in shade	85.1	88.9	84.2	86.0	85.1	86.9	86.0	86.0	84.4	84.4	83.3	83.3	85.1	84.0	84.0	86.0	84.2	84.0	84.0	88.0
Maximum temperature in open air	106.5	120.5	105.5	112.8	100.6	101.8	100.0	103.1	96.9	93.0	97.7	100.9	99.0	95.0	89.4	93.0	91.0	95.9	98.6	120.5
Minimum temperature in shade	35.2	30.2	30.9	33.1	29.8	32.5	26.0	27.0	32.5	30.0	32.0	36.4	36.5	33.8	31.8	35.5	25.2	25.5	34.3	28.9
Minimum temperature in open air	28.2	19.0	21.9	26.4	27.0	27.5	27.0	—	28.8	30.0	25.0	30.2	31.5	30.0	31.8	28.9	—	—	32.9	19.0
Mean temperature of water in shade	—	—	—	—	—	—	55.8	55.6	56.8	56.0	56.3	56.8	57.2	55.9	56.7	58.5	56.5	56.5	57.6	56.7
Mean humidity of the air, per cent, in shade	59	57	58	59	61	60	62	62	59	62	63	64	60	61	62	58	59	59	57	60
Mean humidity of the air, per cent, in open air	—	—	—	—	—	61	67	62	63	62	65	64	58	62	62	58	59	58	58	57
Mean vapor tension in shade	0.327	0.320	0.306	0.322	0.355	0.319	0.337	0.311	0.329	0.323	0.335	0.347	0.320	0.315	0.320	0.312	0.320	0.315	0.315	0.322
Mean vapor tension in open air	—	—	—	—	—	—	0.320	0.315	0.343	0.319	0.339	0.348	0.302	0.320	0.320	0.312	0.320	0.315	0.315	0.322
Mean evaporation of water in shade	0.083	0.099	0.118	0.103	0.091	0.095	0.087	0.103	0.095	0.095	0.091	0.091	0.111	0.095	0.103	0.107	0.095	0.099	0.099	0.099
Mean evaporation of water in open air	0.268	0.284	0.319	0.323	0.271	0.232	0.209	0.256	0.240	0.244	0.229	0.244	0.280	0.252	0.240	0.276	0.271	0.292	0.217	0.260
Days of rain, total amount	104	120	125	122	162	135	157	123	168	112	161	143	143	155	138	134	136	112	145	145
Rainfall, total amount	15.906	18.787	21.740	23.433	26.024	16.083	23.065	26.602	20.913	31.994	29.130	19.610	25.917	25.917	17.488	22.386	22.012	13.067	22.001	22.915
Greatest precipitation in 24 hours	1.032	2.442	1.288	1.517	1.457	1.575	1.221	1.071	1.686	1.131	2.064	1.138	2.501	1.398	1.595	1.013	1.158	1.639	1.260	2.501
Average cloudiness	4.6	4.4	4.8	4.9	5.3	4.8	5.5	4.7	5.7	4.9	5.3	5.6	5.2	4.9	4.7	4.4	4.6	4.7	5.0	4.9
Prevailing direction of clouds	S. W.	S. W.	W.	W.	S. W.	S. W. & N. E.	N. E.	S. W. & N. E.	W. & S. W.	N. E.	S. W.	S. W.	N. E.	N. E.	S. W.	N. E.	N. E.	N. E.	N. E.	S. W.
Amount of cloudy days	69	108	121	123	116	118	145	107	146	114	142	158	141	112	105	87	109	103	121	118
Amount of clear days	88	142	135	120	99	119	83	113	75	121	110	81	99	108	137	136	135	119	107	114
Prevailing wind	N. W.	N. W.	N. W.	N. W. & N. W.	N. W.	N. W.	N. W.	N. E.	N. W.	N. E.	N. E.	N. W.	N. W.	N. W.	N. W.	N. W.	N. W.	N. W.	N.	N. W.
Mean velocity of wind, per hour (miles)	2.68	2.45	2.23	2.01	2.23	1.56	2.01	2.01	1.79	1.79	0.89	0.89	0.89	1.34	2.23	2.68	2.23	2.68	2.23	2.01
Maximum velocity of wind, per hour (miles)	28.16	40.23	35.76	40.23	32.41	28.61	31.29	27.94	30.96	46.93	40.23	35.76	34.64	33.08	34.64	45.15	35.55	34.41	32.41	46.93
Direction of the wind of maximum velocity	N. W.	N. E.	N. W.	N. W.	N.	N. E. & W.	N. & W.	N.	N. & N. E.	N. E.	S. E.	S. W.	N.	N. & W.	N. W.	N. & N.	N. W.	N. E.	N.	N. W.
Ozone (mean) (0–10)	4.9	3.4	3.8	4.3	4.6	4.7	4.6	4.5	5.0	4.8	4.6	4.2	3.2	1.5	4.5	3.7	3.5	4.2	3.5	4.0
Amount of lightning days	77	118	111	146	160	164	149	161	189	101	138	146	133	150	109	119	142	157	155	138

MARIANO BÁRCENA, *Director.*   JOSÉ ZENDEJAS, *Vice-Director.*

GENERAL SUMMARY OF THE METEOROLOGICAL OBSERVATIONS TAKEN IN THE CENTRAL OBSERVATORY OF THE CITY OF MEXICO DURING THE YEAR 1896.

Lat. N. 19° 26'. Long. W. of Greenwich, 6 h. 36 m. 31 s. 56 or 99° 07' 53" 4. Height of the barometer above sea level, 7472.25 (Eng. feet).

	Jan.	Feb.	March.	April.	May.	June.	July.	August.	Sept.	Oct.	Nov.	Dec.	YEAR. 1896.
Mean barometrical height, reduced to freezing (inches)	23.083	23.039	23.051	23.075	23.071	23.079	23.106	23.122	23.071	23.071	23.091	23.071	23.079
Maximum barometrical height (inches)	23.276	23.181	23.193	23.209	23.177	23.248	23.240	23.240	23.150	23.173	23.240	23.307	23.307
Minimum barometrical height (inches)	22.878	22.854	22.890	22.906	22.941	22.902	22.965	22.992	22.637	22.957	22.957	22.953	22.854
Mean temperature in shade (Fahrenheit)	55.04	55.94	61.52	65.48	67.64	65.48	63.50	62.96	62.42	61.34	58.46	52.70	60.98
Maximum temperature in shade (Fahrenheit)	72.50	75.20	83.48	86.90	89.24	83.48	81.50	78.44	77.36	75.38	71.96	71.60	89.24
Minimum temperature in shade (Fahrenheit)	36.50	37.40	40.10	43.70	50.00	48.60	51.80	50.00	50.00	49.10	47.30	34.70	34.70
Mean temperature in open air (Fahrenheit)	55.94	56.84	62.42	65.84	67.82	66.02	63.86	63.14	62.78	61.88	59.00	52.70	61.52
Maximum temperature in open air (Fahrenheit)	81.14	87.80	94.10	97.16	98.06	95.00	94.10	86.99	89.06	86.00	84.20	78.80	98.06
Minimum temperature in open air (Fahrenheit)	30.20	29.84	31.28	36.63	42.80	36.50	45.68	44.06	42.98	41.72	38.30	23.00	23.00
Maximum daily range in shade	29.70	35.20	37.80	32.04	32.94	34.20	27.00	25.92	33.30	24.84	33.30	30.66	37.80
Maximum daily range in open air	45.90	53.28	54.36	48.60	52.92	48.60	44.28	46.62	42.48	40.86	42.30	46.44	54.36
Mean temperature of soil (33.5 inches deep.)	56.30	55.94	56.66	57.56	61.16	62.78	62.60	62.24	62.24	62.24	61.34	58.64	59.90
Mean temperature of water in shade.	52.16	52.52	57.38	60.80	62.60	60.98	60.26	59.54	59.00	57.92	55.04	52.70	57.56
Mean humidity of the air, per cent, in shade.	54	48	42	46	47	54	65	65	69	71	68	61	57
Mean humidity of the air, per cent, in open air.	54	46	41	46	47	54	65	65	69	70	70	64	58
Mean vapor tension in shade (inches).	0.244	0.221	0.236	0.284	0.311	0.343	0.389	0.382	0.410	0.406	0.354	0.252	0.319
Mean vapor tension in open air (inches).	0.244	0.207	0.229	0.288	0.311	0.347	0.389	0.386	0.410	0.406	0.364	0.271	0.323
Mean evaporation of water in shade (inches).	0.083	0.048	0.107	0.111	0.142	0.130	0.095	0.079	0.079	0.071	0.071	0.055	0.091
Mean evaporation of water in open air (inches).	0.190	0.197	0.264	0.311	0.358	0.331	0.256	0.229	0.232	0.217	0.162	0.118	0.236
Days of rain, total amount.	6	6	7	7	13	13	25	25	17	17	13	4	143
Rainfall, total amount (inches).	0.016	0.039	0.039	0.721	0.473	1.170	3.919	2.555	3.324	4.135	0.795	0.615	17.800
Greatest fall in 24 hours (inches).	0.016	0.035	0.024	0.296	0.197	0.433	0.787	0.394	0.914	1.181	0.300	0.528	1.181
Mean amount of clouds (0-10).	4.1	2.8	2.3	4.1	4.5	5.5	7.1	6.3	7.2	6.4	5.9	5.4	5.1
Prevailing direction of clouds.	S. W.	S. W.	S. W.	S. W.	N. E. & N. W.	N. E.	N. E.	N. E.	N. E.	N. E.	N. E.	S. W.	N. E.
Amount of cloudy days.	6	3	0	2	6	8	16	13	20	15	9	13	111
Amount of clear days.	12	19	21	8	9	3	1	1	0	2	3	5	84
Prevailing wind.	N. W.	N. W.	N.	N.	N.	N.	N.	N. W.	N.	N. W.	N. W.	N. W.	N. & N. W.
Mean velocity of wind per hour (miles).	1.79	2.68	2.68	2.90	3.35	4.69	3.79	3.35	2.68	1.79	1.12	0.67	2.68
Maximum velocity of wind per hour (miles).	30.96	25.25	29.05	25.25	27.94	27.27	33.52	26.37	30.17	20.33	16.76	11.78	33.52
Direction of the wind of maximum velocity.	S.	S. & S. E.	N. E.	N. E.	N. W.	N. W.	N. E.	N. E.	N. E.	N. E.	N. E.	N. W.	N. E.
Ozone [mean] (0-10).	3.4	3.5	3.7	3.7	3.8	3.7	3.5	3.7	3.5	3.3	3.2	2.7	3.5
Amount of lightning days.	0	1	4	13	17	19	26	26	24	21	10	0	161

MARIANO BÁRCENA, *Director.*

JOSÉ ZENDEJAS, *Vice-Director.*

the digestive and respiratory organs, the former amounting to 4472 or 1.35 per cent. of the population and the latter to 3904 or 1.18 per cent. of the population, and both causing 8376 deaths or 53.81 per cent. of the total number of deaths. Deaths by typhus and typhoid fevers and small-pox, which are supposed to make such great ravages in the City of Mexico, were in reality insignificant, the deaths by the former amounting in that year to 480 or 0.14 per cent. of the population, and the deaths by small-pox were, in the Federal District, embracing the City of Mexico and twenty-three suburban towns, 217 or 0.047 per cent. of the population of the District which is 473,820. Small-pox only attacks the very poor people, and, strange to say, also foreigners, even in case they have been vaccinated in their country, and to be free from small-pox they must be vaccinated in Mexico.

The months of the greatest mortality during the same year were from February to May, and of the smallest the month of August, showing that the unhealthy months are the dry months, that is before the rains set in.

The mortality in the City of Mexico is indeed very large, and it is due principally to two causes, first, the want of proper drainage and sewerage for the refuse of the city, a trouble which is now almost com-

Porfirio Díaz, and by the suggestion of General Vicente Riva Palacio, then Secretary of Public Works, the Central Meteorological Observatory was established. From that date up to the present, an uninterrupted hourly observation is regularly taken during the day and the night in the Central Meteorological Observatory. Some magnetical observations have also been made, and the Observatory is now thought of being removed to a more suitable spot.

After the establishment of the Central Meteorological Observatory, some official or private meteorological stations have also been established as follows : Aguascalientes (Instituto del Estado) ; Guadalajara (Escuela de Ingenieros), observer, Augustín V. Pascal ; Guanajuato (Colegio del Estado), observer, Genaro Montes de Oca ; León (Escuela Secundaria), observer, Mariano Leal ; Mazatlán (Observatorio Astronómico y Meteorológico), observer, N. González ; Oaxaca (Colegio del Estado), observer, Dr. A. Domínguez ; Pachuca (Instituto del Estado), observer, Dr. N. Andrade ; Puebla (Colegio Católico and Colegio del Estado), observers, Priest P. Spina and B. G. González respectively ; Querétaro (Colegio Civil), observer, J. B. Alcocer ; San Luis Potosí (Instituto del Estado), observer, Dr. G. Barroeta ; Toluca (Instituto del Estado), observer, S. Enríquez ; Veracruz, observer, G. Baturoni ; Zacatecas (Instituto), J. A. Bonilla. Dr. Manuel Andrade, of Huejutla ; Dr. Matienzo, of Tampico ; Father Pérez, of Morelia ; Father Arreola, of Colima ; Father Castellanos, of Zapotlán ; Sr. Pascual Borbón, of Tacámbaro, are enlightened observers to whom the Central Meteorological Observatory is indebted for their valuable co-operation, and also to the telegraph operators of the " Telegraph system," who send, daily, some weather observations to this office.

The staff of the Central Meteorological Observatory is now as follows: Director, Mariano Bárcena ; Vice-Director, José Zendejas, C.E. ; Second Observer, Francisco Toro ; Assistants, Rafael Aguilar, Francisco Quiroga, Angel Robelo, José Torres, and J. I. Vázquez.

pletely remedied, and the second, the unhygienic way of living of the poor classes, among whom takes place the largest mortality.

The very large number of still-births which occurred in the City of Mexico in 1896, almost exclusively among the poor classes, shows the little care that the poor women take of themselves, and is enough to explain the present large mortality.

RAILWAYS.

For many years the government earnestly endeavored to further the construction of railroads in Mexico, but the broken surface of the country made the building of these roads very expensive. Until 1873 the means of internal locomotion were mainly limited to a few wagon roads, over which travelled twenty-four regular lines of diligences, under one management; and bridle-paths from the central plateau over the sierras and terrace lands down to a few points on both coasts.

In 1854 the first railroad was finished, connecting the City of Mexico with Guadalupe, about three miles in length, and another from Veracruz to Tejeria towards the City of Mexico about twelve miles in length; these being the only railroads that were built, up to 1861. During the French Intervention the French army extended the Tejeria road to Paso del Macho, about thirty-five miles further, to the foot of the mountain, so as to be able to transport their army, with the shortest delay possible, out of the yellow-fever zone, toward the central plateau; and an English Company, which had a grant for a road from the City of Mexico to Veracruz, which was supposed at the time to be the only one that could be built in Mexico, extended the Guadalupe road to Apizaco in the direction of Veracruz and not far from Puebla.

No construction of consequence was done immediately after the French Intervention, because the country was generally in a disturbed condition, although several efforts were made in that direction by President Juarez, under whose administration a new and very liberal grant was given to the Veracruz railway company. The Veracruz road was finished in 1873, during Señor Lerdo de Tejada's Presidency, and when General Diaz became President in 1876 he earnestly promoted railroad building; and we now have two trunk lines connecting the City of Mexico with the United States—the Mexican Central to El Paso, Texas, with a branch from San Luis Potosi to the port of Tampico, and another from Irapuato to Guadalajara, which has recently been extended to Ameca, towards the Pacific; and the Mexican National to Laredo, Texas, with several branches. Another trunk line from Eagle Pass to Torreon and Durango, which it is intended shall finally reach the Pacific, has also been built by Mr. C. P. Huntington and his associates. There is besides a line from Nogales to Guaymas, built and owned by the Atchison, Topeka, and Santa Fé

Company ; and these four lines connect us with the main systems of the United States, our lines being in fact extensions of the United States railway system.

We have now two lines from the City of Mexico to Veracruz, the old Veracruz road passing by Orizaba, and the Interoceanic, which runs from Veracruz by Jalapa and the City of Mexico and is intended to reach the Pacific. All of our roads, excepting the one built by Mr. Huntington, have had large subsidies paid by the Mexican Government, and in one case, that of the Veracruz railroad, the subsidy paid was \$560,000 per year, for twenty-eight years, or about \$57,471 per English mile, although the average subsidy per mile, according to President Diaz's report, dated November 30, 1896, is \$14,380.

The Tehuantepec railway, running from Coatzacoalcos on the Gulf of Mexico to Salina Cruz on the Pacific, about one hundred and thirty miles in length, has been built at great expense and at a great sacrifice by the Mexican Government. I published in the *Engineering Magazine* for March, 1894,[1] an article stating the different efforts made by the Mexican Government to have that road built, and the advantages that we expected from it as a highway of trade between the Atlantic and the Pacific. The Mexican Government has recently made a contract with Messrs. E. Weetman, Pearson & Son, of London, for the building of good harbors at both ends of the road, and when that is accomplished we expect that a great deal of eastern trade will pass through Tehuantepec.

With the exception of the Tehuantepec road, we have not yet any road running from the Atlantic to the Pacific, although several are in process of construction. The descent of the mountains is on the Pacific slope a great deal more difficult than on the Gulf coast, where the large centres of population are located near the Gulf, and this explains why none of the roads have so far been able to reach the Pacific Ocean.

Our railway system extends now, in the direction of Guatemala, as far as the city of Oaxaca, where we are only about five hundred miles away from our frontier with Guatemala. In other directions, our system reaches the principal cities and commercial and mining centres of the country.

The total mileage of railway in 1895 was 6989½ English miles. President Diaz, in his above mentioned report gives, the total mileage of railways in Mexico as 11,469 kilometres or 7126 miles ; and in his message to Congress on April 1, 1897, he stated that the railway mileage had been increased by 238 kilometres 550 metres, finished and received by the Government, and 248 kilometres built, but not yet received officially, making a total mileage of 11,955 kilometres 550 metres, or 7.429 miles.

[1] This paper will appear in this volume.

President Diaz's Railway Policy.—President Diaz deserves a great deal of credit for his efforts to promote in Mexico, material improvements, and especially in railroad building. When he came into power, in 1877, public opinion was very much divided as to the policy of allowing citizens of the United States to develop the resources of the country by building railroads, working mines, etc. Our experience of what took place in consequence of the liberal grants given by Mexico to Texan colonists made many fear that a repetition of that liberal policy might endanger the future of the country by giving a foothold in it to citizens of the United States who might afterward, if circumstances favored them, attempt to repeat the case of Texas. President Lerdo de Tejada seemed to share such fears judging by his policy in this regard. But President Diaz, as a broad-minded and patriotic statesman, believed that the best interest of the country required its material development, and that it would not be advisable to discriminate against citizens of the United States, as that country was more interested than any other, on account of its contiguity to Mexico, in developing the resources of our country by building an extensive system of railways, and would, therefore, be more ready than any other to assist in building them. He trusted, at the same time, that when the resources of the country should be more fully developed, it would become so strong as to be beyond reach of the temptation by foreign states or individuals. The results of the work done in Mexico so far show that General Diaz acted wisely, and proved himself equal to the task before him.

Many in Mexico, and myself among the number, thought that, as the railroads were such lucrative enterprises, especially in a country endowed with so many natural elements of wealth as Mexico, it would not be judicious to give their promoters any pecuniary assistance, in the shape of subsidies or otherwise, the more so as the finances of the country were then in a critical condition, and it would not be wise to increase its burdens by large pecuniary subsidies in aid of private enterprises. My opinion in this case was based mainly on what I had seen in the United States, namely : that long lines of railways are built in this country without any pecuniary assistance from the Government, and that when the Government subsidized any one line it became a source of great dissatisfaction and very unpleasant questions, which are yet unsettled. We feared also that such large subsidies as were asked by the railway promoters would amount in the end to so large a sum as to make it impossible for Mexico to pay it, discrediting the country. But in this case General Diaz's view seems to have been the right one, in so far as that it afforded a great inducement for the immediate building of large trunk lines of railways, which, without subsidy, might have been delayed for several years. He thought it worth while to spend large sums of money for the purpose of having railways built without delay, rather than trust to the fluctuations of confidence and credit in the foreign exchanges, that would enable the prospective companies to obtain the funds necessary to build their roads, trusting, at the same time, that the material development of the country promoted by the railroads would yield revenue enough to pay all the subsidies granted.   Fortunately all railroad subsidies contracted by Mexico have been punctually paid, and their amount forms now a large item of our national debt.   To pay some of them the mistake was made of negotiating a sterling loan on Europe, to pay a silver debt ; but even in that way the transaction is not altogether a bad one.

General Diaz's policy was to give a railway subsidy to anybody asking for it without investigating the responsibility of the concern, with the idea that if the road was built the country would get the benefit of the same, and if it was not built nothing would be lost, as there was in all grants, a clause to the effect that if no building was done within a given time, the grant should by that mere fact be forfeited, the forfeiture to be declared by the Administration.

The system of subsidizing railways has a great many drawbacks, but at the same time commands some decided advantages, like giving the government the strict supervision over the roads who have to submit to it for its approval, tariffs for freights and passengers, the free carrying of the mails, the duty of the company to present to the government a yearly statement of its traffic, receipts, etc., and other similar advantages.   In all grants to subsidized railroads there is a stipulation that at the end of ninety-nine years the road-bed would revert to the Mexican government.

President Diaz's Statistics on Mexican Railways.—Before I close this chapter I think it will not be out of place to quote some remarks of President Diaz concerning our Mexican railroads, which occur in his above-mentioned report.

.   .   .   .

"In 1875 we had 578 kilometres 285 metres of railway, in 1885 we had 5915 kilometres, in 1886, 6018 kilometres, in November, 1888, 7940 kilometres, in June, 1892, 10,233, and including the tramways and other local and private lines, the amount was 11,067 kilometres ; in September, 1894, we had 11,100 kilometres ; in April, 1896, 11,165 kilometres, and now we have 11,469 kilometres. . . .

"We stand first in railroad building of all the Latin-American countries.   During the years 1877 to 1892 Mexico built more railroads than any other Latin-American State, being 11,165 kilometres ; the Argentine Republic takes the second place, with 8108 kilometres, and Brazil the third, with 6193 kilometres, built during the years mentioned.   The average number of kilometres built per annum in Mexico during this period was 689, the maximum having been reached in

1881–82	1938 kilometres
1882–83	1727 "
1887–88	1217 "
1889	1263 "

The number of passengers carried in

1876	4,281,327
1890	19,531,395
1893	22,781,343
1895	24,269,895

The freight handled in

1876	132,915 tons
1890	2,734,430 "
1893	3,798,360 "
1895	4,117,511 "

The gross receipts in

1876	$2,564,870
1890	21,019,960
1893	26,121,624
1895	28,758,450

" The subsidies paid for railroads up to December, 1892, averaged $8935 per kilometre of road built and in operation at that date. This average is much less than that of the subsidies paid by other Latin-American countries, the Republic of Chili having averaged $17,635 per kilometre, and the Argentine Republic $31,396.

" The railroad system of the Republic has given the capital direct and rapid connection with our principal states. Throughout the length of the central plateau to the frontier, Mexico City is connected with the capitals of the states of Querétaro, Guanajuato, Jalisco, Aguascalientes, Zacatecas, Chihuahua, and San Luis Potosi by the Mexican Central Railway, and with Durango by the Mexican International; with the states of Mexico, Guanajuato, Michoacan, San Luis Potosi, Coahuila and Nuevo Leon by the Mexican National; with the cities of Puebla, Orizaba, Cordoba, Veracruz, and Jalapa by the Mexican Railway and by the Interoceanic, and with Tehuacan and Oaxaca by the Mexican Southern from Puebla. Three lines connect the capital with the northern frontier; the Central, which terminates in Ciudad Juarez; the National, which runs to Nuevo Laredo; and the International, which, from its junction with the Central at Torreon, runs to Piedras Negras. And as to our various ports Guaymas is connected with Nogale on the northern frontier; Manzanillo with Colima; Matamoros with Reynosa and San Miguel; Tampico with San Luis Potosi and Monterrey; Veracruz with Jalapa and Mexico; and the first really Interoceanic railway of the Republic across the Isthmus of the Tehuantepec, united the Atlantic and Pacific oceans by connecting the port of Coatzacoalcos, on the gulf, with the port of Salina Cruz on the Pacific coast. Southward from the capital of the Republic the Interoceanic traverses the State of Morelos, and the Mexico, Cuernavaca and Pacific Railway has its line located to the City of Cuernavaca and is pushing on through the state of Guerrero to the port of Acapulco. In the peninsula of Yucatan, the lines connecting Campeche and Merida are nearly finished; while the port of Progreso has rail communication with Merida."

Financial Condition of Mexican Railways.—Our railroads are doing remarkably well, and their traffic, especially domestic, is daily increas-

ing and grows in much larger proportion than the foreign, or international traffic ; and they are paying the interest on their debt, which
is due and paid in gold, notwithstanding that they collect their
freights in silver, which has been for several years at a great discount,
losing at the present rate of exchange about one hundred per cent. in
the operation ; but their business is such that they can afford to suffer
that loss.

In the statistical section of this paper will be found a list of our
railroads, their mileage, earnings, and several other data, showing that
they are in a prosperous condition, all of which will be of interest to
those who desire to have a more intimate acquaintance with the railway
system of Mexico.   I will only insert here the following statement of
the annual building and earnings of the Mexican railways, supplementing it with a comparative statement showing the tonnage
moved by the principal railway lines, for the ten years ending December 31, 1896, which shows a great increase in their business, and consequently in their earnings.

ANNUAL BUILDINGS AND EARNINGS OF MEXICAN RAILWAYS.

YEAR.	MILES OF ROADS BUILT.		ANNUAL EARNINGS.
	Each year.	Total.	
1873...................	— —	359,306	$2,097,104.55
1874...................	5,393	364,699	2,665,496.18
1875...................	47,087	418,001	2,799,696.13
1876...................	2,265	414,052	2,563,241.00
1877...................	3,739	417,791	3,213,434.17
1878...................	40,748	458,539	3,400,799.89
1879...................	91,950	550,488	3,828,718.65
1880...................	120,328	670,817	4,504,135.39
1881...................	429,858	1,100,675	5,679,193.37
1882...................	1,204,118	2,304,792	9,883,719.51
1883...................	1,073,404	3,378,196	12,102,583.34
1884...................	282,523	3,660,719	11,089,136.39
1885...................	73,614	3,734,332	10,656,551.42
1886...................	49,099	3,783,432	11,373,667.63
1887...................	323,084	4,106,516	13,310,218.79
1888...................	756,522	4,863,060	16,121,267.79
1889...................	390,650	5,253,096	18,788,142.29
1890...................	784,744	6,037,752	20,919,287.14
1891...................	495,015	6,532,711	23,762,172.87
1892...................	352,171	6,884,842	25,363,922.29
1893...................	14,829	6,870,015	25,359,244.06
1894...................	118,810	6,888,811	— —

COMPARATIVE STATEMENT, SHOWING APPROXIMATE TONNAGE MOVED
BY THE UNDERMENTIONED RAILWAYS FOR THE TEN YEARS
ENDED DECEMBER 31, 1896.

(Compiled from published reports and information furnished by the respective railway companies.)

YEAR.	CENTRAL RAILWAY.	NATIONAL RAILWAY.	INTEROCEANIC RAILWAY.	MEXICAN RAILWAY.	TOTAL.
	Tons.	Tons.	Tons.	Tons.	Tons.
1887........	346,898	77,935	141,090	273,194	839,117
1888........	477,530	372,800	197,231	318,893	1,366,454
	Inc. 34.4	Inc. 378.3	Inc. 39.7	Inc. 16.7	Inc. 62.7
1889........	540,479	428,314	186,222	354,321	1,509,336
	Inc. 13.1	Inc. 14.8	Dec. 5.5	Inc. 11.1	Inc. 10.4
1890........	609,382	472,045	281,769	384,584	1,747,780
	Inc. 12.7	Inc. 10.2	Inc. 51.3	Inc. 8.2	Inc. 15.7
1891........	867,657	502,856	277,866	409,185	2,057,564
	Inc. 42.3	Inc. 7.3	Dec. 1.3	Inc. .6	Inc. 17.7
1892........	1,091,785	588,505	365,191	367,980	2,413,461
	Inc. 25.8	Inc. 17.	Inc. 31.4	Dec. 10.	Inc. 17.3
1893........	860,187	552,123	380,805	385,923	2,179,038
	Dec. 21.2	Dec. 6.5	Inc. 4.3	Inc. 4.8	Dec. 9.7
1894........	898,484	558,382	444,191	433,637	2,334,694
	Inc. 4.4	Inc. 1.1	Inc. 16.6	Inc. 12.3	Inc. 7.1
1895........	1,047,038	636,193	464,976	453,289	2,601,496
	Inc. 16.5	Inc. 13.9	Inc. 4.4	Inc. 4.5	Inc. 11.4
1896........	1,231,025	782,106	479,744	756,330	3,249,205
	Inc. 17.5	Inc. 22.9	Inc. 3.1	Inc. 66.8	Inc. 24.8
	7,970,465	4,971,259	3,219,085	4,137,336	20,298,145

(S.)   A. BLAKE.

CITY OF MEXICO, May 19, 1897.

TELEGRAPHS.

We have quite a number of miles of telegraph lines in Mexico, and our service is now as good as that of any other country. The first telegraph line built and owned in Mexico by a private company, liberally assisted by the government, extended from Veracruz to the City of Mexico. On November 5, 1851, the first section was inaugurated from the City of Mexico to Nopalucan, and on May 19, 1852, to Veracruz.

In 1853 another company established a line from the City of Mexico towards the north to Leon in the State of Guanajuato, and in 1865 a line was finished to San Luis Potosi.

In 1868 and 1869 a private company, called the " Jalisco Company " established the line between the City of Mexico and Guadalajara, which was soon afterwards extended to Manzanillo and San Blas. After the restoration of the Republic in 1867, the Mexican government began to build lines to the principal centres of population of the country, and in 1890 it bought the Jalisco line, and in 1894 the Veracruz.

From 1869 to 1876 the States of Michoacan, Oaxaca, and Zacatecas established several lines in their respective jurisdictions. When General Diaz became President in 1876, the National Telegraphic Lines only had 7927 kilometres.

In 1885 the Federal Goverment transferred to the States, without any cost, all the telegraphic lines which were considered of local interest, keeping only such as could be called trunk lines.

In 1893 we had 37,880 English miles of telegraph lines, of which 24,840 belonged to the Federal Government, the remainder belonging in about equal parts to the States, private companies and railways.

The following statement, which I take from the *Anuario Estadistico de la Republica Mexicano, 1895*, shows the telegraphic lines belonging to the Federal Government, to the States, to private companies and to railroads :

Federal Lines	43,416	k 780	m
State Lines	5,544	068	"
Private Company Lines	4,730	980	"
Railroad Lines	9,761	611	"
General Total	63,453	k 439	"

On November 30, 1896, the total mileage of our telegraph lines was, according to the President's report of that date, 45,000 kilometres, 27,962 English miles, and that amount was increased, according to the President's message of April 1, 1897, to 45,259 kilometres, 28,123 miles.

In 1891 the operations of the various lines throughout the Republic involved the transmission of 1,050,000 messages, of which about 800,-000 were private, and the remainder official. The receipts from this branch of the public service amounted to $469,305 collected at 767 offices ; the expenditure included for repairs an average of $3 per kilometre, and for salaries a total of $671,431.

The proceeds of the Federal telegraphic lines were, according to President Diaz's report of November 30, 1896, as follows :

Fiscal Year, 1883–1884	$239,051
" " 1890–1891	462,076
" " 1893–1894	524,634
" " 1895–1896	537,308

In the statistical portion of this paper will be found a detail statement of the earnings and expenses of the national telegraphic lines of

Mexico for the 27 fiscal years which elapsed from July 1, 1869, to
June 30, 1896, and such data as it is possible to obtain for the ten
years which elapsed from July 1, 1869, to June 30, 1879.

Cables.—Up to 1887 there was no communication between Mexico
and foreign countries. In 1880 the Mexican Cable Co. built their
cables from Galveston to Tampico, Veracruz and Coatzacoalcos, on
the Gulf of Mexico, and a telegraphic line from Coatzacoalcos to Salina
Cruz, on the Pacific, which was extended to Central and South America. Cables had been laid between Jicalango and El Carmen and between the rivers Grijalva and Coatzacoalcos, and now through those
cables we are in direct communication with the United States and
Europe.

POSTAL SERVICE.

Our postal service has improved considerably of late. It was until
recently quite imperfect on account of the difficult and expensive ways
of communication. It used to be slow and so expensive that it was
almost prohibitory, and up to 1870 the single postage of a letter, weighing one quarter an ounce was 25 cents, and double for any distance exceeding sixty miles. After Mexico entered into the Universal Postal
Union, in 1870, the postage of letters for foreign countries was reduced
to 5 cents, and that reduction made it necessary to reduce the home
postage from 25 to 10 cents. Recently it has been reduced again from
10 to 5 cents.

There were in the whole country, in 1883, one head post-office at
the national capital, 53 first-class post-offices, 265 second class, for
the most part inefficient, and 518 postal agencies, little better than useless. The entire service as it was being rendered at 837 stations. The
evils resulting from the very high postage were further aggravated by
the insecurity of the mails. The revenue of the postal department in
that year amounted to $817,244.

The total number of post-offices and postal agencies in 1893 was
1448, and the mail pouches are now transported on railways over a total
distance of 10,000 kilometres, or more than 6000 miles. Over the remaining distances in the interior the mails are conveyed either by
stages or by foot or mounted carriers.

President Diaz gives in his report of November 30, 1896, the following statistics about our postal services :

	Post Offices.	Postal Agencies.
1877	53	269
1888	356	719
1892	356	1430
1895	469	1471
1896	471	1500

President Diaz states in his same report that the total number of pieces distributed by our mails in the year 1878 was 5,169,892, while in the year 1896 the number increased to 24,000,000.

For the purpose of communicating with foreign countries, especially before railroads were finished, the Mexican government granted large subsidies to steamship companies, running especially between Mexican and United States ports, and their amount increased considerably the expenses of our post-office department.

In the statistical part of this paper I shall insert the statement of the earnings and expenses of the postal service in Mexico, in the twenty-seven years elapsed from July 1, 1869, to June 30, 1896.

PUBLIC LANDS.

The Spanish government considered itself the owner of lands in Mexico, and it granted them to private parties under certain very liberal regulations. The Indians having been the original owners, and needing the lands to raise their food, and textiles for their clothing, could not be entirely deprived of them, and a large portion of the land was left to each municipality to be held generally in common by the inhabitants of the same. Large tracts of land remain, however, which had not been granted either to the Indians nor to the Spanish settlers, and these we called vacant lands—Terrenos Baldios. The Mexican government succeeded Spain in the ownership of public lands, and with a view to make them available for colonization an easy system to dispose of them at a comparatively low price was established.

The greatest difficulty was to find the public lands, as they had never before been surveyed, and a great many were occupied without title by private parties. As such survey would be very expensive, the Mexican government devised a plan of contracting that work with private companies, paying them with one-third of the land measured, and in that way large portions of the public lands have been surveyed.

It appears from President Diaz's report to his fellow-citizens, dated November 30, 1896, that up to 1888 private companies had surveyed 33,811,524, hectares of public lands, for which they received in payment for their work one-third or 11,036,407 hectares. In the four years from 1889 to 1892, 16,820,141 hectares of public lands were surveyed by private companies, of which 11,213,427 hectares belonged to the government, and in that way in less than ten years it was possible to survey 50,631,665 hectares. Out of this amount the government sold to private parties and to colonization companies 1,607,493 hectares, and to private companies who were in possession of public lands held by them without any title, which we call *demacias*, 4,222,991 hectares. At the same time the government has been trying to divide the lands held in common by the Indian towns between the inhabitants of the same, and up to 1888 it had distributed in that manner 67,368 hectares among 2936 titles, and from 1889 to 1892 180,169 hectares among 4560 titles. In accordance with the provisions of our public land laws we sold to private parties, who pre-empted the lands for purchase, which we call *"denuncio,"* 3,635,388 hectares among 1504 titles, and from 1889 to 1892 1,353,137 hectares among 1218 titles. From July 1, 1891, to August 18, 1896, 9,677,689 hectares of land were surveyed, of which 6,504,912 hectares belong to the government, and the balance, 3,172,777 hectares, belong to private companies.

Every year the Department of Fomento publishes under authority of law a price-list of public lands, which have different prices in each state and are sometimes divided into three classes; the first, second, and third having each a different price. The following is the official price of public lands fixed by the Department of Fomento for the fiscal year 1895–1896:

STATES	PRICE PER HECTARE	STATES	PRICE PER HECTARE
Aguascalientes............	$2.25	Oaxaca...............	$1.10
Campeche...............	1.80	Puebla................	3.35
Coahuila	1.00	Queretaro.............	3.35
Colima.................	2.25	San Luis Potosi.........	2.25
Chiapas................	2.00	Sinaloa	1.10
Chihuahua.............	1.00	Sonora................	1.00
Durango	1.00	Tabasco...............	2.50
Guanajuato............	3.35	Tamaulipas............	1.00
Guerrero..............	1.10	Tlaxcala	2.25
Hidalgo...............	2.25	Veracruz..............	2.75
Jalisco................	2.25	Yucatan...............	1.80
Mexico	3.35	Zacatecas.............	2.25
Michoacan	2.25	District federal.........	5.60
Morelos...............	4.50	Territore de Tepic	2.00
New Leon.............	1.00	Territory of Lower Cal...	0.65

In the statistical part of this paper I shall insert some data about the sales of public lands by the Mexican government from 1867 to 1895, and a statement of the titles issued from the years 1877 to 1895.

IMMIGRATION.

It has always been the aim of the Mexican government from the time of the independence of the country, to encourage the immigration of foreigners, because Mexico being so large and the population so scanty, it was considered a necessity to promote the development of the country, to increase the population by inducing the settlement of foreigners, and different laws have been issued for that purpose.

Since the restoration of the Republic new laws have been sanctioned to encourage colonization, which allow colonists and the companies bringing them free importation of their personal goods and such articles as they may need for their subsistence and welfare for a reasonable term of years, exempting them at the same time from all kinds of taxes— federal, state, and municipal,—excepting only the stamp tax, and also exempting them from military and other personal service, and some- times even going so far as to give a bounty for each colonist brought to the country. Under such laws several contracts were made with differ- ent companies, and 32 colonies have been planted in different sections of Mexico, of which 13 have been established by the government and 19 by private parties. In 1892 there were only 1266 families with a total number of 10,985 colonists. On the whole, the efforts made and the expenses incurred by the Mexican government in the establish- ment of those settlements of colonists, have had but unsatisfactory results, but they have paved the way for future experiments on a larger scale, especially if undertaken by private parties, and with only such assistance from the government as can be rendered by liberal legisla- tion.

The principle obstacle which has prevented us from having a large immigration is our low wages. Those who immigrate are generally poor wage earners, who want to better their condition, and they could not go to a country where wages are a great deal lower than in the United States, or even in Europe, as they could never compete with the native labor of our Indians. We have now a surplus of labor and a deficit of capital, and cannot have a large immigration until such conditions are changed.

What Mexico needs is capital to develop her resources and give employment to labor, and then immigration will flow in as naturally as water seeks its level. Mexican credit will be established, so far as im- migration is concerned, when her natural resources are developed, this being the only safe and reliable basis of such credit, and this will never be developed until those who have capital to invest are acquainted with the unparalleled opportunities for safe and profitable investment in Mexico. This will only be accomplished by plain, blunt, matter-of- fact and well-informed press agents, who lay before people who have money to invest the plain facts of the case.

Immigration from the United States.—I have often been asked for my opinion of the chances of Americans going to settle in Mexico, and have always answered that while Mexico is desirous of attracting good settlers, and while that country undoubtedly offers great inducements to foreign settlers, especially to those having some means, there are serious drawbacks which ought to be pointed out to the prospective immigrant from the United States, as a warning against a possible failure and disappointment.

The comforts of life in the rural districts of Mexico, where a settler from this country has the best chances, are scanty compared with similar districts in the United States. The difference of race, language, religion, and education between a young man brought up in this country and the small Mexican farmers, are enough to create difficulties at first sight insuperable to any young man from the United States who settles there. If he establishes himself in a district inhabited only by Indians these difficulties are considerably increased. If the settler prefers the hot lands, which are the most fertile and productive, the severity of the climate is such as to challenge the courage of the bravest. The mosquitoes of several varieties, the flies, and many other insects are very annoying, besides the sickness inherent to such climate.

The question of labor is another great difficulty in the way, because, while it is cheap and abundant in the cold regions, it is generally scarce and unreliable in the hot lands.

The conditions of the two countries are so very different that the change experienced by one brought up in this country who goes into Mexico, is very apt to discourage the strongest and most sanguine, at least in the beginning, as the lapse of time makes anybody adapt himself to existing conditions and to appreciate the advantages of his new home.

The land question is also a serious objection. A large portion of the public lands have already been disposed of, and comparatively little of the public and private lands have been surveyed, and cannot easily be had in small lots. The large land-holders are unwilling to divide their estates, and the Indians holding large tracts of land are very reluctant to part with them at any price.

Coffee raising is undoubtedly one of the most profitable undertakings in Mexico, but at the same time it has serious drawbacks. It takes from three to four years before the trees begin to yield, and the planter must be provided with sufficient means to defray not only his personal expenses, but also those of the plantation, like houses, machinery, cultivation, etc., without receiving any proceeds until the third or fourth year. Besides, if he makes any mistake in the selection of his land, his profits will be considerably reduced. The general impression prevailing in Mexico is that coffee is the product of the hot lands, where the coffee trees need shade ; but a plantation in such lands would cost a great deal more money to make and to keep, and would yield smaller profits than one located in the temperate zone, that is, just below the frost line.[1]

[1] The same views were expressed in Mexico to the State Department by the United States Consuls, and even published in the *Consular Reports* for August, 1894, vol. xlv., No. 167, pp. 628, 629.

"Consular advices received at the Department of State warn Americans about emigrating to Mexico, with a view to permanent settlement, with insufficient means or without informing themselves in a reliable way as to the prospects for earning liveli-

For the American common laborer who looks to his day's pay for his living, Mexico is unquestionably not the proper place to go. He cannot compete with the Mexican laborer, whose usual pay is from 38 to 50 cents a day in silver, and he boards himself. For the man who has no means, unless he is especially qualified in some particular branch, and knows something of the language, and will work harder and longer hours, it is no place. There is room for the steady, sober, industrious mechanic or miner or tradesman who will adapt himself to new conditions and surroundings, leave all social, political, and other ambitions behind him, and who will attend strictly to his own business.

Those who are safest in going to Mexico are those who have a little capital, say from $2000 in gold and upward, which will give them about twice that amount there; who can look around and decide what they propose to do, and where they want to settle. There is an excellent field for the small general farmer of the New England or Middle States type, who will raise a little of everything. Butter, potatoes, hogs, poultry, corn, vegetables, and small grain find a ready sale at good prices. I have seen the common article of corn, which is nearly always a sure crop, sell at from $1 to $1.25 per bushel, Mexican money.

It is always best for the mechanic or miner to first secure a job before going to Mexico, and work for wages several months, and in the meantime study the situation, get acquainted with the language, the customs, and the people before going it alone.

The manner of living there and the customs of the people are totally different from those of the United States. Those going there will have to work harder and longer hours than in the United States, but they can save money. Ten years ago Americans went to Mexico to make money and return to the United States; to-day they go to find homes. I know several Americans who would not live in the United States again.

The climate of Mexico permits a man to work every day in the year. The cost of living and clothing is cheap, and a dollar in Mexican money can be made to go as far there as a dollar in American money in the United States, and a dollar there is easier to get.

In mining, Mexico offers inducements superior to any other coun-

hoods. While there are undoubtedly good opportunities in Mexico for enterprise, frugality, and thrift, it is like other countries, a land of varying conditions, and it often happens that disappointment is the result of emigration undertaken upon insufficient or misleading information, or without resources, which are always necessary for success in a new country. Many Americans have been induced by alluring statements as to the cheapness of coffee raising, etc., to emigrate to Mexico within the past year, and some have lost their all by so doing. For these reasons Consuls desire to caution Americans against the representations of speculators, who are always on the watch for the unwary."

try ; and whether a man has a thousand dollars or a million he can go there and make money if he exercises ordinary precaution and judgment, and if he makes up his mind to stand the discomforts of the country. It is a good country for the prospector, too, because there are no seasons against him, and there are many new fields entirely untouched; but he needs money enough to get there with and enable him to obtain the proper kind of outfit, and time to familiarize himself with the requirements of the law and select some district in which he wants to operate.

For the small capitalist, or for a small syndicate, there is no finer field for the organizing of small legitimate companies for the purposes of opening and working old abandoned mines, which are filled with débris or water, and which it will pay to clean out and work, and of which there are still many to be had. In times gone by they were abandoned because of the refractory condition of the ores, or lack of machinery, or want of transportation, all of which conditions have been removed. There is also a fine opening for capital for the exploration of the new gold-fields in the vicinity of Guadalupe y Calvo, in the range between Sonora and Chihuahua, in the State of Guerrero, and in many other localities.

There are in various parts of Mexico educated, experienced, and thoroughly reliable Americans to be found, who have lived a long while in the country, and know the language, the laws, and the people, and would be willing to give reliable information to young Americans wishing to go there.

PUBLIC DEBT.

The public debt of Mexico is represented by bonds drawing different rates of interest, some payable in gold and others in silver. In 1825, very soon after our independence, we contracted two loans in London, both for 10,000,000 pounds sterling, which we mainly used for buying war-ships and war material. On account of the disturbed condition of the country, the interest on that debt could not be paid punctually, and the bonds naturally fell to a very low nominal price. In 1851, after the war with the United States, we refunded that debt in new bonds, the interest of which was reduced from 5 to 3 per cent., which we expected to pay punctually, but the disturbed condition of the country made it impossible for us to do it. Finally, in 1888, the debt was readjusted and gold bonds bearing 6 per cent. interest issued, and as we have paid since punctually the interest, they have reached par.

We had issued bonds from 1849 to 1856 to pay claims of English, French, and Spanish subjects under certain conventions signed with those countries, and such bonds were exchanged at different rates for the 6 per cent. gold bonds of our foreign debt.

To build the Tehuantepec Railway we negotiated in London, in 1888, another gold loan for 3,000,000 pounds sterling at 5 per cent. interest.

The subsidies granted to railway companies were payable in silver, with a percentage of our import duties, but as they amounted to a considerable sum their payment reduced the revenue considerably, and the Mexican Government contracted in London in 1890 a gold loan at 6 per cent. interest, with which it paid the subsidies due up to that date to most of the railway companies.

We had to issue besides in 1850 what we call domestic or interior bonds, at 3 and 5 per cent. interest in silver, and we had other indebtedness of several kinds, caused by loans and other sources when the revenue of the Government was not enough to pay its expenses. All such debts have been consolidated into new bonds of 3 and 5 per cent. interest, payable in silver. Such railway subsidies as were not paid out of the proceeds of the loan of 1890 have been paid with bonds drawing 5 per cent. interest, paying both capital and interest in silver.

It is very onerous for Mexico when it is on a silver basis to pay in gold the interest of its foreign debt, because we have to buy gold at current prices, and it costs us now more than double its current price. When silver was about 50 cents on the dollar, as compared with gold, 6 per cent. interest of our foreign debt, cost us 12 per cent., and of course the further silver is depreciated the greater will be the cost of paying the interest of our gold debts.

President Diaz gives in his report of November 30, 1896, the following data about the cost to the Mexican Treasury of buying exchange to place in London the funds to pay us the gold interest on our foreign debt :

Fiscal year 1888–1889..................$ 729,178.17
    "   "   1890–1891.................. 2,314,477.77
    "   "   1891–1892.................. 3,225,246.77
    "   "   1892–1893.................. 5,101,223.57

In the second part of this paper I will give a detailed statement showing the different kinds of bonds and obligations which constitute the Mexican debt, and here will only give the figures of the total amount, which are the following :

Sterling Mexican debt................$114,675,895.49
Debt payable in silver................ 88,549,111.80
                                       ———————————
        Total....................$203,225,007.29

It is not possible to fix the exact amount of the debt of Mexico, either in silver or gold, because of the daily changes in the price of silver ; but as silver is the currency of the country, when the Mexican dollar is worth 24 pence in London, the amount of our debt in silver would be equal to our sterling debt, that is : $114,675,895.40 added to our debt will make a grand total in Mexican silver of $317,900,902.78.

BANKING.

Banking in Mexico is in its incipient state. The National Bank of Mexico, established in the City of Mexico in 1882, with its branches in the principal cities of the country, has a monopoly for the issuing of notes in the capital which is only shared by such banks as were in existence before the National Bank of Mexico was chartered, like the Bank of London, Mexico, and South America, established during the French intervention in Mexico and recently remodelled under the name of the Bank of London and Mexico. The Mortgage Bank of Mexico enjoys that privilege also.

On June 3, 1896, a general banking law was issued by the Mexican Congress, which establishes the conditions under which banking institutions can be organized ; but, of course, that does not affect the rights of the National Bank and other banks in the City of Mexico which had been chartered before the date of that law.

Formerly, owing to the expense and dangers of transportation, it was difficult to transport money from one place to another, and therefore exchange between cities in Mexico was very high, sometimes even ten per cent. from one city to another in the country. The rate has been reduced considerably since the railroads were built, but it is still quite high. To draw money from the City of Mexico to the City of Oaxaca, for instance, and vice versa, costs now one per cent. each way ; when money is required to be sent to smaller places the expenses are much higher, as it is necessary to send a man to the nearest town where the money can be placed by the banks, and pay to him a large commission—the expenses sometimes reaching ten per cent. To keep up this rate of exchange the National Bank makes its bills payable at a certain place so that they cannot be paid at any other.

Banking is very profitable in Mexico. The following is a statement of the earnings and dividends of the National Bank of Mexico, which began with a capital of $3,000,000, increased since to $6,000,000, having now a reserve fund of $5,500,000, and is owned almost exclusively by Mexicans, being the fiscal agent of the Government :

	NET PROFITS.	DIVIDENDS.
1891....................................	$1,813,623	23 per cent.
1892....................................	1,839,418	23 " "
1893....................................	2,355,464	29 " "
1894....................................	1,961,801	24 " "
1895....................................	2,200,626	27 " "

The following is a statement, from official sources, of the earnings and dividends of the Bank of London and Mexico. Up to 1891 it had a capital of $1,500,000, which was then increased to $3,000,000 :

	NET PROFITS.	DIVIDENDS EARNED, PER CENT.	DIVIDENDS DECLARED, PER CENT.
1889............	$243,246	16	10
1890............	569,351	36	20
1891............	703,522	46	20
1892........	789,967	26	16
1893....	618,653	20½	16
1894............	603,178	20	14
1895....	557,710	18½	14

Recently the capital stock of this bank was further increased to $10,000,000, without any expense to the stockholders, as the reserve fund, which amounted to about $2,000,000, was used to complete the new capital, and was issued to the regular stockholders as a stock dividend. The balance to complete the $5,000,000 of new stock was offered to the public, the subscriptions amounting to $22,000,000, or $17,000,000 more than was wanted.

From this statement it will be seen that the existing banks are prosperous and in a flourishing condition, but the demand for increased banking facilities is such that new banks are being formed, and the operations of the old banks increased and extended in various directions.

PATENTS AND TRADE-MARKS.

Patents.—On June 7, 1890, the present patent law of Mexico was issued, and its provisions are very similar to the respective laws existing in this country.

Since the date of that law the following patents have been issued by our Department of Fomento :

YEARS.	PATENTS.	INCREASE.	DIMINUTION.
1890........................	63	....	....
1891........................	153	90	....
1892........................	168	15	....
1893........................	122	....	46
1894........................	125	3	....
1895........................	154	29	....
	785		

Trade-Marks.—On November 28, 1889, our present law regulating trade-marks was promulgated, and since then the following trade-marks have been issued by the Department of Fomento :

YEARS.	TRADE-MARKS.	INCREASE.	DIMINUTION.
1890............................	97	....	....
1891............................	112	15	....
1892............................	161	49	....
1893........................ ...	108	....	53
1894............................	79	....	29
1895............................	91	12	....
	648		

SHIPPING.

The mercantile marine of Mexico in 1895 comprised 52 steamers and 222 sailing vessels. The shipping included also many small vessels engaged in the coasting trade.

In 1893–94, in the foreign trade, 1237 vessels of 1,314,625 tons entered, and 1211 vessels of 1,296,834 tons cleared the ports of Mexico. In the coasting trade 7721 of 1,623,371 tons entered and 7708 of 1,592,754 tons cleared. In 1894–95, in the foreign and coasting trade, there entered 9575 vessels of 3,428,973 tons, and cleared 9557 of 3,359,684 tons.

In the statistical portion of this chapter I will give official information about the number of vessels and their tonnage, which have entered and cleared from Mexican ports in recent years, the nations from which they came, and other valuable data.

MONEY, WEIGHTS, AND MEASURES.

The standard of value is silver. There is no paper currency except ordinary bank notes.

The silver peso or dollar of 100 centavos is the unit of coin in Mexico.

The silver peso weighs 27.073 grammes, .902 fine, and thus contains 24.419 grammes of fine silver.

The 10-pesos gold-piece weighs 27.0643 grammes, .875 fine, and thus contains 23.6813 grammes of fine gold.

The weights and measures of the metric system were introduced in 1856 ; but the Indians and other ignorant people use the old Spanish measures. The principal ones are these :

> *Weight.*—1 libra=0.46 kilogramme, 1.014 lbs. avoirdupois.
> 1 arroba=25 libras, 25.357 lbs. avoirdupois.
> *For Gold and Silver.*—1 marco=$\frac{1}{2}$ libra, 4,608 granos.
> 1 ochava=62 tomines.
> 1 tomin=12 granos.
> 20 granos=1 French gramme.
> *Length.*—1 vara—0.837 metre = 2 ft. $8\frac{9}{10}$ English inches.
> 1 legua comun (1 common league) = 5,000 yards.
> 1 legua marina (1 marine league) = 6,666$\frac{2}{3}$ yards.

NON-OFFICIAL PUBLICATIONS.

The following is a partial and rather incomplete list of (principally English) books about Mexico :

ABBOTT, GORHAM D., *Mexico and the United States.* New York, 1869.

BANCROFT, H. H., *A Popular History of the Mexican People.* 8. London. *Resources and Development of Mexico.* San Francisco, 1894.

BROCKLEHURST, T. U., *Mexico To-day.* London, 1883.

BURKE, U. R., *Life of Benito Juarez.* 8. London, 1894.

CASTRO, LORENZO, *The Republic of Mexico in 1882.* New York, 1882.

CHARNAY, D., *Ancient Cities of the New World.* Tr. 8. London.

CHEVALIER, MICHEL, *Le Mexique ancien et moderne.* 18. Paris, 1886.

CONKLING, HOWARD, *Mexico and the Mexicans.* New York, 1883.

CONKLING, A. R. *Appleton's Guide to Mexico.* New York, 1890.

CRAWFORD, CORA HAYWARD, *The Land of the Montezumas.* New York, 1889.

CUBAS, ANTONIO GARCIA, *Mexico, its Trade, Industries, and Resources.* Mexico, 1893.

FLINT, H. M., *Mexico under Maximilian.* 12. Philadelphia, 1867.

GLONER, PROSPER, *Les Finances des Etats Unis Mexicains.* Bruxelles, 1895.

GOOCH, F. C., *Face to Face with the Mexicans.* London, 1890.

GRIFFIN, S. B., *Mexico of To-day.* New York, 1886.

HAMILTON, LEONIDAS, *Border States of Mexico.* Chicago, 1882.

HAMILTON, L. L. C., *Hamilton's Mexican Handbook.* London, 1884.

JANVIER, THOMAS A., *The Mexican Guide.* New York, 1886.

KOZHEVAR, E., *Report on the Republic of Mexico.* London, 1886.

LA BEDOLLIERE, EMILE G. DE, *Histoire de la guerre du Mexique.* 4. Paris, 1866.

LESTER, C. EDWARDS, *The Mexican Republic.* New York, 1878.

NOLL, ARTHUR HOWARD, *A Short History of Mexico.* Chicago, 1890.

OBER, F. A., *Travels in Mexico.* Boston, U. S., 1884.

PRESCOTT, W. H., *History of the Conquest of Mexico.* 8. London.

RATZEL, FRIED., *Aus Mexico, Reiseskizzen aus den Jahren 1874-75.* Breslau, 1878.

RICE, JOHN N., *Mexico, Our Neighbor.* New York. (No date.)

ROUTIER, G., *Le Mexique de nos Jours.* Paris, 1895.

SCHROEDER, SEATON, *The Fall of Maximilian's Empire as seen from a United States Gunboat.* New York, 1887.

SCOBEL, A., "Die Verkehrswege Mexicos und ihre wirtschaftliche Bedeutung." In *Deutsche Geographische Blätter.* Band X, Heft 1. Bremen, 1887.

Through the Land of the Aztecs ; or, Life and Travel in Mexico. By a "Gringo." London, 1892.

WELLS, DAVID A., *A Study of Mexico.* New York, 1887.

PART II.

STATISTICS

II. STATISTICS.

I do not know of any publication in which the latest statistical information about Mexico is compiled in a concise and complete form. One which perhaps is the fullest, published in Berlin by Messrs. Puttkammer & Muhlbrecht, entitled *Les Finances des Etats-Unis Mexicains*, written by Mr. Prosper Gloner, contains a great deal more statistical information than others, and is of later date.

It has required a great deal of work, energy, and time on my part to collect the data contained in this paper, most of which is of an official character, and I am sure it is the most complete ever published, I having tried to make it very concise, so as to take the smallest space possible.

REVENUES AND EXPENSES.

The financial question was for many years the leading and the most difficult one in Mexico, because the urgent needs of the Treasury, especially on account of the disturbed condition of the country, made public expenses considerably exceed the revenue, and this condition did not allow of a thorough overhauling and settlement of the finances, nor did it contribute to establish the credit of the Government ; but peace having prevailed since 1877, a great improvement has taken place in the financial condition of Mexico ; the revenue has increased considerably, and it has finally reached an amount amply sufficient to pay all our expenses.   In fact, at the end of the fiscal year, ended June 30, 1896, we had for the first time in the history of Mexico since its independence, a surplus which amounted to $6,000,000.   The obnoxious tax which we inherited from the Spanish, called *alcabalas*, or interstate duties on domestic and foreign commerce, was a great drawback to internal trade, was finally abolished on July 1, 1896 ; and the country being now in a condition when radical reforms can be introduced without serious disturbances.

Our expenses as an independent nation are necessarily large, and as a comparatively small portion of our population are really producers

137

of wealth, upon them lies the whole burden of such expenses ; that is, we are a nation of from twelve to fifteen millions of inhabitants, with a very large territory and a large coast on both oceans, requiring army, revenue, light-house, and police service, and other expensive institutions proportionate to such extent and population, when the portion which contribute to such expenses is only about one-fourth or one-third of the same.

It is a very difficult task to give a complete and correct statement of the revenues and expenses of the Mexican Government prior to the year 1867. The disturbed condition of the country made it often quite impossible to keep any account at all : such was the case especially from 1858 to 1860, as during that period the City of Mexico and a large part of the country was occupied by the Church party under Miramon, and from 1863 to 1867 by the French Intervention. Besides that cause it was a very difficult matter for us to keep a correct account of public receipts and expenses, in some way for lack of a good system of book-keeping. To make a statement of the revenues and expenses of the Mexican Government since the independence of the country from Spain, I had to rely upon the reports made by Secretaries of the Treasury, which are, however, lacking for many years, and which contain rather an estimate than an account of the revenues and expenses, and I have made in that way the statement which I append under No. 1, which embraces the revenues and expenses from the year 1808, the last of the Spanish rule in Mexico, to the year 1867.

The forming of accounts was under the charge of the Federal Treasury of Mexico, and the Treasury kept its accounts with a very defective system of book-keeping, which prevented them from being correct. To remedy that difficulty, after the restoration of the Republic in 1867, a bureau of accounts was established in the Treasury Department, but its accounts were seldom correct, because it did not have the necessary detailed data to make a complete account, and, as could be expected, the results in the accounts of both bureaus differ widely.

In 1880 the Federal Treasury was reorganized with a large number of clerks with a view to keep a full and correct account of public moneys, and from that year until 1888 their accounts began to be better than before. In 1888 the system was still remodelled and improved, and since then that office has been able to keep correct and complete accounts of our public revenues and expenses.

I also append a statement No. 2 of the revenues and expenses of the Mexican Treasury from July 1, 1867, to June 30, 1888. The first thirteen years in that statement are taken from the data furnished by the Bureau of Accounts of our Treasury Department. The account of the year 1879–1880 was taken from the account of the Federal

Treasury, and the data for the year 1880–1881 from the accounts published by the Liquidating Bureau established by the Mexican Government to close the old accounts and open the new ones under the new system. The accounts of the year 1888–1889, which appear in statement No. 3, are all taken from the Federal Treasury of Mexico, and are complete and correct.

I also append a statement of the appropriations approved by the Federal Congress during the fiscal years from 1868 to 1895. The actual expenses never exceeded the appropriations and the revenue was generally below them.

NO. I.—REVENUE AND EXPENSES OF THE FEDERAL GOVERNMENT OF MEXICO IN 1808 AND FROM 1822 TO JUNE 30, 1867.

	REVENUE.	EXPENSES.
1808, Colonial period...............	$20,075,362 25	....
1822, Independence period..........	9,328,740 00	$13,455,377 00
1823...........................	5,249,858 96	3,030,878 50
1824...........................	15,254,601 03	15,165,876 05
1825 to Sept. 1st	7,903,163 42	13,110,187 24
Sept. 1, 1825, to June 30, 1826....... ..	14,770,733 30	13,112,200 65
1826–27.........................	17,017,016 59	16,364,218 36
1827–28.........................	13,644,974 69	12,982,092 86
1828–29.........................	14,593,307 69	14,016,978 27
1829–30.........................	14,103,773 28	13,728,491 39
1830–31.........................	18,392,134 96	17,601,289 67
1831–32.........................	17,582,929 15	16,937,384 67
1832–33.........................	20,563,360 77	22,392,607 90
1833–34.........................	21,124,216 81	19,934,490 42
1834–35.........................	18,353,283 00	12,724,686 62
1835–36.........................	26,382,303 90	17,766,262 81
1836–37.........................	17,327,706 15	19,181,138 95
1837–38.........................	25,018,121 77	26,588,305 03
1839...........................	29,136,536 64	27,318,729 73
1840...........................	21,227,263 43	21,235,097 67
1841...........................	23,995,766 52	22,997,220 18
1842...........................	30,682,369 40	30,639,711 00
1843...........................	34,138,581 72	34,035,277 13
1844...........................	31,873,019 47	31,260,225 87
1845...........................	24,159,050 04	19,584,812 91
1846...........................	24,026,938 36	27,845,487 28
1847...........................	26,154,222 84	31,251,467 91
1848 to June 30, 1849...............	25,726,737 23	19,742,876 48
1849–50.........................	18,281,835 38	17,291,233 25
1850–51.........................	14,955,535 73	14,477,369 06
1851–52.........................	11,022,291 17	10,475,686 10
1852–53.........................	10,044,298 40	16,287,532 90
1853–54.........................	19,028,975 00	18,726,088 00
1854–55.........................	26,259,970 45	23,396,074 75
1855–56..	15,855,597 47	12,920,257 65
1856–57.........................	16,035,609 81	12,977,265 90
1857–58.....	15,529,887 47	15,927,102 01
1858–59.........................	14,737,763 76	16,005,536 45
1859–60.........................	14,306,675 28	16,589,034 47
1860–61.........................	12,863,500 00	12,750,500 00
1861–62.........................	15,500,000 00	15,300,600 00
1862–63.........................	17,600,000 00	17,595,690 00
1863–64.........................	7,000,000 00	6,990,000 00
1864–65.........................	5,950,000 00	5,945,000 00
1865–66.........................	5,057,500 00	5,053,250 00
1866–67.........................	8,092,000 00	8,085,200 00

NO 2.—REVENUE AND EXPENSES OF THE MEXICAN GOVERNMENT FROM JULY 1, 1867, TO JUNE 30, 1888.

FISCAL YEARS.	RECEIPTS.				EXPENSES.		
	Revenue.	Extraordinary and Incidental.	Loans.	TOTAL.	Expenses authorized by law.	Other expenses.	TOTAL.
1867–1868.				$ 17,736,538 19			$ 14,786,128 51
1868–1869.	$ 2,355,322 95	$ 14,109,931 96		16,465,254 91			16,862,024 12
1869–1870.	2,720,494 53	13,678,241 59		16,398,736 12	$ 13,867,208 59	$ 2,647,820 15	16,515,028 74
1870–1871.	2,674,676 17	16,033,649 71		18,708,325 88	15,080,349 52	2,541,938 90	17,622,288 42
1871–1872.	3,798,734 56	15,285,044 18		19,083,778 74	15,321,071 33	3,657,406 94	18,978,478 27
1872–1873.	4,402,386 91	15,739,239 94		20,141,626 85	15,558,623 89	4,827,965 64	20,386,589 53
1873–1874.	3,327,674 88	17,900,156 10		21,227,830 98	16,369,509 34	4,837,241 82	21,206,751 16
1874–1875.	4,181,077 58	17,597,916 26		21,778,993 84	17,286,167 44	4,081,712 51	21,367,879 95
1875–1876.	3,818,501 22	17,266,228 93		21,084,730 15	18,074,771 02	3,248,089 40	21,322,860 42
1876–1877.	4,741,742 59	18,408,803 80		23,150,546 39	18,183,958 78	5,041,925 63	23,225,584 41
1877–1878.	9,686,555 30	19,772,638 13		29,459,193 43	19,420,113 15	10,125,161 38	29,545,274 53
1878–1879.	11,463,237 47	17,811,124 96		29,274,362 43	17,898,255 20	11,418,550 37	29,316,805 57
1879–1880.	235,097 93	21,936,165 39		22,171,263 32	20,431,896 15		20,431,896 15
1880–1881.	1,789,614 11	24,089,698 07		25,879,312 18	24,092,198 16	160,663 13	24,252,861 29
1881–1882.	30,466,093 74	6,138,642 39	$ 10,283,731 74	46,888,467 87	30,595,891 81	15,600,899 37	46,196,791 18
1882–1883.	32,850,951 25	7,226,397 49	3,438,867 68	43,516,216 42	37,582,604 18	4,459,444 84	42,042,049 02
1883–1884.	37,621,065 29	18,435,299 84	2,697,900 42	58,754,265 55	42,714,229 29	13,696,247 74	56,410,477 03
1884–1885.	30,660,434 24	33,275,909 03	2,636,263 91	66,572,607 18	44,407,386 22	21,535,422 04	65,942,808 26
1885–1886.	28,980,895 76	31,925,011 61	2,332,033 51	63,237,940 88	26,164,198 18	40,526,366 85	66,690,565 03
1886–1887.	32,126,509 07	72,702,037 63	6,949,374 87	111,777,921 57	36,262,962 48	75,085,077 50	111,348,039 98
1887–1888.	40,962,045 23	85,488,474 33	24,039,637 72	150,490,157 28	54,956,554 45	89,552,965 48	144,509,519 93

NO. 3.—REVENUE AND EXPENSES OF THE MEXICAN GOVERNMENT FROM JULY 1, 1888, TO JUNE 30, 1896.

FISCAL YEARS.		REVENUE.				EXPENSES.			
		Cash.	Bonds.	Nominal.	Total.	Cash.	Bonds.	Nominal.	Total.
1888–1889.	Revenue receipts	$34,374,783 32	$20,427,141 26		$54,801,924 58	$49,325,109 50	$20,103,595 45	$4,493,624 48	$73,922,329 43
	Loans	22,478,738 14			22,478,738 14	13,764,470 97		54,272,265 53	68,036,736 50
	Nominal	11,934,096 11		$50,147,312 08	62,081,408 19				
		$68,787,617 57	$20,427,141 26	$50,147,312 08	$139,362,070 91	$63,089,580 47	$20,103,595 45	$58,765,890 01	$141,959,065 93
1889–1890.	Revenue receipts	$38,586,601 69	$22,716,725 61	$605,354 23	$61,908,681 53	$51,641,115 34	$24,167,362 65	$4,350,275 75	$78,158,753 74
	Loans	15,849,706 41			15,849,706 41	4,163,849 84		45,016,373 95	49,180,223 79
	Nominal	19,608,525 81		29,775,715 65	49,384,241 46				
		$74,044,833 91	$22,716,725 61	$30,381,069 88	$127,142,629 40	$55,804,965 18	$22,167,362 65	$49,366,649 70	$127,338,977 53
1890–1891.	Revenue receipts	$37,391,804 99	$932,799 50	$5,818,252 12	$44,142,856 61	$56,928,276 11	$934,799 50	$5,144,053 07	$63,005,128 68
	Loans	26,645,962 80		3,614,283 94	30,260,246 74	10,360,242 26		65,086,034 91	75,446,277 17
	Nominal	3,328,985 36		60,797,551 92	64,126,537 28				
		$67,366,753 15	$932,799 50	$70,230,087 98	$138,529,640 63	$67,288,518 37	$932,799 50	$70,230,087 98	$138,451,405 85
1891–1892.	Revenue receipts	$37,474,879 20	$1,868,171 91	650,692 83	$39,993,743 94	$40,053,990 03	$624,667 92	$2,671,491 67	$43,350,149 62
	Loans	5,485,005 10		19,174,882 70	24,059,887 80	2,876,346 94	1,243,503 99	17,154,083 86	21,273,934 79
		$44,959,884 30	$1,868,171 91	$19,825,575 53	$64,053,631 74	$42,930,336 97	$1,868,171 91	$19,825,575 53	$64,624,084 41
1892–1893.	Revenue receipts	$37,692,293 31	$847,113 46	$115,363 54	$38,654,770 31	$42,813,455 71	$869,887 31	$5,271,629 41	$48,954,972 43
	Loans	4,526,983 82			4,526,983 82	5,161,799 45	773,626 26	12,541,002 83	18,476,419 54
	Nominal	5,484,854 56	796,400 11	17,697,268 70	23,978,523 37				
		$47,704,131 69	$1,643,513 57	$17,812,632 24	$67,160,277 50	$47,975,246 16	$1,643,513 57	$17,812,632 24	$67,431,391 97
1893–1894.	Revenue receipts	$40,211,747 13	$852,565 02	$152,581 36	$41,216,803 51	$41,552,162 16	$361,887 64	$3,799,741 67	$45,713,791 47
	Loans	6,053,794 09	69,800 59	3,390,000 00	9,353,794 09	7,092,362 90	560,477 97	16,074,636 92	23,727,477 79
	Nominal	2,054,225 12		16,421,797 23	18,545,822 94				
		$48,319,766 34	$922,365 61	$19,874,378 59	$69,116,510 54	$48,644,525 06	$922,365 61	$19,874,378 59	$66,441,269 26
1894–1895.	Revenue receipts	$43,945,699 05	$2,530,518 70	$430,995 41	$46,907,123 16	$41,372,264 63	$1,892,958 19	$2,389,803 96	$45,655,026 78
	Loans	4,577,500 00	470,000 00	2,172,500 00	6,750,000 00	9,368,711 42	1,107,560 51	30,104,662 36	40,580,934 29
	Nominal	2,468,360 68		29,891,060 91	32,829,421 59				
		$50,991,559 73	$3,000,518 70	$32,494,466 32	$86,486,544 75	$50,740,976 05	$3,000,518 70	$32,494,466 32	$86,235,961 07
1895–1896.	Revenue receipts	$50,521,470 42	$477,033 98	$241,552 55	$51,240,056 95	$45,070,123 13	$32,727 54		$45,102,850 67
	Loans	708,277 66	5,121,667 46	6,240,637 41	12,070,582 53	5,399,533 73	5,565,973 90	6,482,189 96	17,447,697 59
		$51,229,748 08	$5,598,701 44	$6,482,189 96	$63,310,639 48	$50,469,656 86	$5,598,701 44	$6,482,189 96	$62,550,548 26

FEDERAL APPROPRIATIONS DURING THE FISCAL YEARS FROM 1868 TO 1895.

FISCAL YEARS.	POWERS.			DEPARTMENTS.							TOTALS.
	Legislative.	Executive.	Judicial.	Foreign Affairs.	Interior.	Justice and Education.	Fomento and Colonization.	Communications and Public Works.	Treasury and Public Credit.	War and Navy.	
1868–1869.	$735,360 00	$52,880 00	$488,290 00	$124,540 00	$1,025,080 00	$380,640 75	$2,292,932 00		$5,143,726 24	$8,450,939 86	$18,694,388 85
1869–1870.	754,300 00	46,325 20	265,090 00	148,540 00	1,437,699 84	737,643 18	3,096,180 00		4,870,722 08	6,907,931 92	18,324,432 22
1870–1871.	760,619 99	48,172 40	280,960 00	150,160 00	1,447,512 24	844,587 99	4,341,771 11		4,562,292 80	8,443,306 48	20,879,393 01
1871–1872.	811,920 00	48,172 40	280,960 00	150,166 00	1,626,146 50	879,127 99	4,353,411 55		4,643,922 80	10,144,601 52	22,938,422 76
1872–1873.	811,920 00	48,172 40	280,960 00	150,166 00	1,626,146 50	879,127 99	4,353,411 55		4,643,922 80	10,144,601 52	22,938,442 76
1873–1874.	877,100 00	48,172 40	291,680 00	260,360 00	1,773,886 50	873,127 99	4,557,883 00		5,021,638 75	10,252,522 32	23,956,420 96
1874–1875.	842,610 00	48,172 40	313,490 00	248,560 00	1,954,151 20	890,998 80	5,127,372 00		4,956,317 04	10,632,862 92	24,114,534 36
1875–1876.	1,074,162 00	48,172 40	328,228 00	209,860 00	1,963,475 55	910,533 20	5,623,253 00		4,179,070 79	10,554,747 24	24,891,502 18
1876–1877.	1,044,270 00	48,172 40	328,928 00	195,160 00	2,092,951 12	906,933 20	6,079,584 41		4,253,976 12	10,898,280 68	25,830,255 93
1877–1878.	957,319 12	48,172 40	328,228 00	189,166 00	2,262,105 60	991,513 20	2,777,000 00		4,715,954 61	6,818,645 43	19,088,158 36
1878–1879.	1,051,322 00	48,572 40	332,028 00	193,666 00	2,511,195 40	1,210,035 60	2,722,330 00		4,691,016 56	8,788,742 56	20,748,902 78
1879–1880.	980,242 00	48,832 40	347,878 00	176,666 00	2,488,296 30	1,103,862 20	1,849,722 00		3,895,116 57	8,004,509 18	18,895,198 65
1880–1881.	1,022,842 00	48,832 40	355,878 00	228,466 00	2,574,299 70	1,174,345 20	3,570,077 00		4,366,609 35	9,786,964 95	23,128,218 60
1881–1882.	990,402 00	48,832 40	370,976 00	317,680 00	3,152,697 55	1,352,697 55	6,162,627 00		4,173,585 75	8,648,033 12	25,217,633 82
1882–1883.	1,071,712 00	48,832 40	389,554 00	336,280 00	3,235,118 88	1,215,473 00	7,551,683 00		4,648,377 67	8,514,478 13	27,011,509 08
1883–1884.	1,015,652 00	48,832 40	406,652 00	367,580 00	3,285,577 75	1,243,510 00	11,127,600 00		4,966,261 81	8,252,352 18	30,713,993 14
1884–1885.	1,087,232 00	43,832 40	429,674 00	377,680 00	3,339,213 77	1,234,718 00	6,151,870 00		4,903,438 78	8,252,764 88	25,825,423 83
1885–1886.	1,007,144 15	49,251 50	432,392 90	418,762 60	3,441,616 10	1,254,376 85	8,339,728 25		11,832,644 95	12,138,435 86	38,903,353 16
1886–1887.	1,052,913 45	49,251 50	436,387 80	417,726 00	3,227,529 20	1,431,081 24	2,698,101 39		10,663,485 78	11,559,714 00	31,536,205 27
1887–1888.	1,002,928 75	49,846 45	439,994 00	434,930 66	3,466,882 30	1,398,850 00	4,426,132 17		11,664,391 97	13,386,495 24	30,270,451 48
1888–1889.	1,053,839 40	49,848 19	464,095 45	434,783 20	3,596,320 90	1,421,204 75	5,965,450 54		12,059,535 94	13,482,152 47	36,527,239 84
1889–1890.	1,009,036 50	49,849 45	465,095 55	432,695 70	3,553,128 89	1,350,471 10	6,145,555 69		11,310,380 29	12,449,603 37	36,765,926 54
1890–1891.	1,054,030 50	49,849 45	468,884 25	462,517 25	3,678,679 70	1,303,072 40	7,310,326 50		11,395,207 09	12,656,021 07	38,439,488 21
1891–1892.	1,009,036 50	49,977 20	476,784 50	558,483 54	2,480,806 76	1,630,636 25	672,106 95	$4,399,345 97	14,432,995 81	12,658,101 37	38,377,364 85
1892–1893.	1,050,638 06	49,977 20	1,478,083 90	590,379 84	2,564,151 00	1,657,215 60	951,054 51	4,483,599 25	15,857,292 61	12,684,685 67	41,367,047 64
1893–1894.	1,005,638 00	49,977 20	478,083 00	553,560 80	2,459,301 20	1,614,652 45	822,414 16	3,922,141 60	22,399,405 20	11,329,618 82	44,634,793 33
1894–1895.	1,005,638 00	50,977 30	478,171 50	516,905 50	2,560,741 70	1,547,824 54	655,610 06	4,455,097 15	24,000,570 85	10,378,683 32	45,610,279 92
Totals..	$26,139,868 42	$1,324,956 64	$11,437,427 75	$8,645,445 03	$68,824,781 15	$31,536,283 47	$119,667,202 75	$17,260,153 97	$223,521,911 01	$276,279,966 34	$784,637,936 53

Sources of Revenue.—The Federal revenue of Mexico consists mainly of three sources : import duties, internal revenue, and direct taxes in the Federal District. Under the head of import duties we collect duties on imports, extra import duties which we call additional duties, and duties on exports.

The sources of revenue of the Mexican Federal Treasury during the fiscal year 1895–1896, were :

Imposts on foreign trade................	$23,658,692 61
Internal revenue.....	20,447,096 42
Direct taxes in the Federal District and	
Territories	3,357,611 81
Public services........................	1,811,045 30
Nominal.............................	1,955,301 94
Total........................	$51,229,748 08

Import Duties.—Our tariff is a highly protective one, as we have always maintained a very high rate of import duties, almost prohibitory for a large portion of our population, which under such a system are practically excluded from the use of foreign commodities, to the material detriment of the fiscal revenue, the public wealth at large, and the advancement of the masses of our people. The causes which have induced such a high tariff are twofold : first, that, in a great measure, protective ideas have prevailed ; secondly, and especially, the need of revenue, and the idea that the higher the rate of duties the larger would be the revenue collected. A new source of protection has been created by the depreciation of our currency, which acts as a powerful protection to our home commodities, in favor of our manufacturers to the disadvantage of the great body of consumers.

The protective policy in Mexico has been so deeply rooted that notwithstanding that I lean to freer trade, and that I have been three times at the head of the Treasury Department, and once for five years, I never was able to modify substantially that policy, because the condition of the Treasury was so precarious, that it would have been very rash to attempt any radical change on the face of a great reduction of an insufficient revenue which would have brought about disastrous results. For the same reason I was unable to do away with the obnoxious alcabala tax.

Our present tariff is divided into the following sections : 1st, animal industry ; 2d, agricultural products ; 3d, metals and its manufactures ; 4th, fabrics ; 5th, chemicals, oils, and paints ; 6th, wines, liquors, and fermented drinks ; 7th, paper ; 8th, machinery ; 9th, carriages ; 10th, arms and explosives, and 11th, sundries.

Additional Import Duties.—The additional duties collected by the Custom-houses are 1½ per cent. of the amount of the import duties, which is levied for the respective municipality ; 2 per cent. of the same duties, for harbor improvements ; and 2 per cent. in revenue stamps, making in all 5½ per cent. of the import duties. The custom-houses collect besides the import duties, tonnage and light-house duties, and pilot fees.

Export Duties.—Our export duties are levied upon cabinet and dye-woods, india rubber, cochineal, coffee, henequen, ixtle, indigo, fequila, jalap, tamarind, tobacco, mother-of-pearl, orchilla, vanilla, zacaton, and onyx.

The following statement shows the amount of export duties collected in Mexico from the fiscal year 1881–1882 to 1894–1895, expressing the commodities in which they were collected :

STATEMENT OF THE RECEIPTS FROM EXPORT DUTIES IN MEXICO FROM JULY 1, 1881, TO JUNE 30, 1895.

FISCAL YEAR.	RECEIPTS.	COMMODITIES TAXED.
1881–1882................	$122,462 24	Orchilla, wood.
1882–1883................	144,597 93	" "
1883–1884................	179,439 97	" "
1884–1885................	161,811 47	" "
1885–1886................	107,484 80	" "
1886–1887................	106,859 63	" "
1887–1888................	114,869 04	" "
1888–1889................	81,849 25	" "
1889–1890................	98,386 12	" "
1890–1891................	86,859 86	" "
1891–1892................	96,560 48	" "
1892–1893................	91,475 54	" "
1893–1894................	1,045,105 44	Orchilla, wood, henequen, coffee.
1894–1895................	1,227,719 24	Orchilla, wood, henequen, coffee, skins, zacaton, chewing gum, ixtle, vanilla.

Amount of Import Duties.—It is very difficult to give a correct statement of the receipts of the Mexican custom-houses before the year 1875. I append, however, one made from the reports of the Secretaries of the Treasury of Mexico, especially those of July 25, 1839, and September 16, 1870, and completed from the years 1839–1851, with data obtained from the *Comercio exterior de Mexico,* by D. Miguel Lerdo de Tejada. From the fiscal year 1875–1876, the Statistical Bureau of our Treasury Department began to publish detailed and correct statements of the custom receipts, and I append one embracing the fiscal years from 1875 to 1896 which shows how largely our import duties have increased. In the ten years elapsed from 1878 to 1888 the increase was over 67 per cent. as compared with the corresponding period from 1869–1879, and the increase in the last seven years, 1889–1896, was 16 per cent. as compared with the previous ten years, both periods making an increase of nearly 100 per cent. over the first ten years of said statement :

CUSTOMS RECEIPTS FROM 1823 TO THE FISCAL YEAR ENDING JUNE 20, 1875.

1823. From April 1st to September 30 the receipts were $971,345 77, which for a year of 12 months would be.................................. $1,942,691 54

1825. From the 1st of January to the 1st of August, 1825, the receipts were $4,472,069 37, which for a year of 12 months would be................ 7,666,404 63

1825–1826 From the 1st of September, 1825, to June, 1826, $6,414,383 26, which for a year of 12 months would be........................... 9,621,574 89

1826–1827... 7,828,208 44
1827–1828... 5,692,026 70
1828–1829... 6,497,288 93
1829–1830....,.................................... 4,815,418 25
1830–1831... 8,287,082 92
1831–1832... 7,335,637 76
1832–1833... 7,538,525 47
1833–1834... 8,786,396 94
1834–1835... 8,920,408 28
1835–1836.. 5,835,068 51
1836–1837... 4,377,579 52

From July 1, 1837, to December 31, 1838, $4,258,411 10.
Corresponding to one year of 12 months....... 2,838,940 73

1839.. 5,577,890 67
1840.. 8,309,918 65
1841.. 6,597,912 32
1842.. 6,034,342 29
1843.. 8,507,478 79
1844.. 8,254,141 96
1845.. 5,814,048 69
1846.. 6,747,932 35
1847... 1,394,609 52

From January 1, 1848, to June 30, 1849, 18 months... 6,660,037 96
From July, 1849, to June, 1850.................... 6,338,437 50
1850–1851.. 5,337,068 62
From July 1, 1851, to June 30, 1852.............. 6,108,835 26
1852–1853, according to the calculations of M. Haro y Tamariz average from the preceding five years. 4,906,533 17

1853–1854, according to the report of M. Olazagarre (1855)...............................	8,399,208	93
1854–1855, according to the report of M. Lerdo de Tejada (1857).............................	8,096,208	85
1855–1856, according to the report makes the receipts for the first six months amount to $3,379,761 35, which for the year is........................	6,759,522	70
1856–1857, average for the six years previous........	6,854,061	78
1857–1858 " " " "	6,854,061	78
1858–1859 " " " "	6,854,061	78
1859–1860 " " " "	6,854,061	78
1860–1861 " " " "	6,854,061	78
1861–1862 " " " "	6,854,061	78
1862–1863 " " " "	6,854,061	78
1863–1864 " " " "	6,854,061	78
1864–1865 " " " "	6,854,061	78
1865–1866 " " " "	6,851,061	78
1866–1867 " " " "	6,851,061	78
1867–1868, according to the amount of the receipts....	9,566,360	99
1868–1869 " " "	9,606,491	73
1869–1870...	7,824,525	57
1870–1871...	10,014,277	60
1871–18	8,430,211	00
1872–1873...	11,833,117	52
1873–1874...	13,981,795	42
1874–1875...	11,821,533	49

Total.............................$367,725,836 01
Average in one year......................$7,071,650 69

Internal Revenue.—The Federal Treasury of Mexico depended up to 1867 mainly upon import duties, and as it was not safe to have only that source of revenue, when I occupied for the first time the Treasury Department, I introduced a system of internal revenue through the use of stamps, which met with a great deal of opposition at the time, but which has finally been developed very largely, yielding now almost as much as the import duties. The receipts during the six months from January 1st to June 30th, 1875, amounted to $1,097,-668 28, which in a whole year would make, duplicating it, $2,195,336 56, while in the fiscal year ended June 30, 1896, the receipts amounted to $18,078,952 54, or nearly eight times as much.

We have had since 1861 a comparative large source of revenue called Federal Tax, which up to 1892 was 25 per cent. of all the revenues collected by the States and Municipalities in Mexico. That rate

RECEIPTS OF THE CUSTOM-HOUSES DURING THE TWENTY-SEVEN FISCAL YEARS ENDING JUNE 30, 1896.

FISCAL YEARS.	IMPORT DUTIES. Tariff.	Additional.	Total.	EXPORT DUTIES. Precious metals.	Commodities.	Total.	TOTAL GROSS RECEIPTS.	COST OF COLLECTION. Annual expenditures.	Percentage.	NET RECEIPTS.
1869–1870	$4,036,046 61	$3,203,833 78	$7,239,880 39	$1,270,501 27		$1,270,501 27	$8,510,531 66	$493,346 90	5.796	$8,017,184 76
1870–1871	5,094,768 00	4,316,886 00	9,411,654 59	1,473,299 13		1,473,299 13	10,884,953 72	566,228 51	5.202	10,318,725 21
1871–1872	4,466,410 78	3,681,849 73	8,148,260 51	914,510 72		914,510 72	9,062,771 23	471,690 42	5.205	8,591,080 81
1872–1873	8,048,293 29	132,211 08	8,180,504 37	1,063,700 30		1,063,700 30	9,244,204 67	553,049 99	5.983	8,691,154 68
1873–1874	10,354,158 85	74,347 38	10,428,506 23	881,042 30		881,042 30	11,309,548 53	575,591 80	5.090	10,733,916 73
1874–1875	9,200,033 06	71,236 49	9,271,269 55	854,873 99		854,873 99	10,126,143 54	728,036 74	7.090	9,408,106 80
1875–1876	8,390,636 72	60,306 05	8,450,942 77	726,843 55		726,843 55	9,177,786 32	697,458 27	7.598	8,480,328 05
1876–1877	8,308,293 94	51,555 14	8,359,849 08	957,087 47	$2,736 75	959,824 22	9,319,673 30	632,041 27	6.781	8,687,632 03
1877–1878	12,367,461 71	65,762 21	12,433,223 92	1,009,786 96	6,839 47	1,016,626 43	13,449,850 35	811,493 28	6.042	12,638,357 07
1878–1879	9,518,567 31	60,535 88	9,579,103 19	871,047 37	14,426 70	885,474 07	10,464,577 26	815,888 25	7.796	9,648,689 01
1879–1880	11,718,864 37	69,645 66	11,788,510 03	886,340 75	78,277 92	964,618 67	12,753,128 70	849,564 55	6.662	11,903,564 15
1880–1881	13,768,416 33	81,853 46	13,850,269 79	738,521 03	77,732 00	816,253 03	14,666,522 82	993,055 14	6.775	13,673,467 68
1881–1882	17,001,961 23	656,944 34	17,658,905 57	588,637 95	199,887 52	788,525 47	18,447,431 04	1,141,442 69	6.133	17,305,988 35
1882–1883	18,173,720 89	421,987 31	18,595,708 20	377,873 54	144,597 93	462,471 47	19,058,179 67	1,327,620 19	7.757	17,730,559 48
1883–1884	17,292,567 28	255,225 91	17,547,793 19		129,439 97	129,439 97	17,727,233 16	1,302,472 09	7.685	16,304,761 07
1884–1885	15,429,759 37	165,981 90	15,445,517 27		161,811 47	161,811 47	15,607,382 74	1,501,149 17	9.631	14,106,233 57
1885–1886	14,852,980 15	148,048 87	15,001,029 02		107,484 80	107,484 80	15,108,513 82	1,847,009 10	12.224	13,261,504 72
1886–1887	17,268,650 16	173,108 20	17,441,758 36		106,859 63	106,859 63	17,548,617 99	1,867,313 96	10.811	15,651,304 03
1887–1888	18,958,215 27	216,530 83	19,174,746 10		114,869 04	114,869 04	19,289,615 14	1,928,129 03	9.995	17,361,486 11
1888–1889	18,922,772 12	369,495 71	19,292,267 86		81,849 25	81,849 25	19,374,117 11	1,994,137 23	10.291	17,379,979 88
1889–1890	21,725,839 17	728,315 56	22,454,154 73		98,386 12	98,386 12	22,552,540 85	2,017,168 55	9.070	20,535,372 30
1890–1891	20,178,744 17	685,077 76	20,863,821 93		86,359 86	86,359 86	20,950,181 79	2,077,439 79	9.916	18,873,241 93
1891–1892	20,931,365 52	684,450 14	20,715,815 66		96,560 48	96,560 48	20,812,376 14	2,092,217 10	10.053	18,720,159 04
1892–1893	16,839,276 77	666,644 66	17,505,921 43		91,475 54	91,475 54	17,597,396 97	2,098,397 95	11.397	15,438,999 02
1893–1894	15,333,926 55	546,243 98	15,880,170 57		1,037,110 65	1,037,110 65	16,897,281 22	1,927,912 38	11.409	14,969,368 84
1894–1895	17,738,129 66	716,009 40	18,454,139 06		1,227,360 45	1,227,360 45	19,681,499 51	1,811,243 63	9.208	17,870,255 88
1895–1896	21,492,211 91	853,482 25	22,345,694 16		1,078,861 48	1,078,861 48	23,424,555 64	1,825,178 73	7.795	21,599,376 91
Total in 27 years....	$376,341,901 23	$19,097,570 30	$395,439,471 53	$12,554,066 33	$4,992,927 03	$17,546,993 36	$412,986,614 89	$35,026,276 78	8.048	$379,961,338 11
Average per annum...	$13,938,588 93	$707,317 41	$14,645,906 35	$464,905 42	$184,923 22	$649,888 64	$15,295,857 58	$1,297,269 51	8.482	$14,072,642 15

Abstract of sums and annual averages of the two periods of ten years and the last of seven years.

Totals and averages.	Tariff.	Additional.	Total.	Precious metals.	Commodities.	Total.	Total gross receipts.	Annual expenditures.	Percentage.	Net receipts.
1869-79.—Totals	$79,784,770 27	$11,718,574 33	$91,503,344 60			$10,046,705 98	$101,550,040 58	$6,334,825 43	6.238	$95,215,215 15
„ Average ...	7,978,477 03	1,171,857 43	9,150,334 46			1,004,670 60	10,155,004 06	633,482 54		9,521,521 52
1879-89.—Totals	$163,237,737 17	$2,558,822 22	$165,796,559 39		$1,252,809 53	$3,784,182 80	$169,580,742 19	$14,841,893 15	8.752	$154,738,849 04
„ Average ...	16,323,773 72	255,882 22	16,579,655 94		121,280 95	378,418 28	16,958,074 19	1,434,189 32		15,473,884 90
1889-96.—Totals	$133,319,493 79	$4,820,223 75	$138,139,717 54		$3,717,114 88	$3,717,114 88	$141,856,832 12	$13,849,558 20	9.763	$128,007,273 92
„ Average ...	19,045,641 97	688,603 39	19,734,245 36		531,016 41	531,016 41	20,265,261 73	1,978,508 31		18,286,753 42

was increased in 1893 from 25 to 33⅓ per cent. on account of the deficit caused to the Federal Treasury by the depreciation of silver, and that tax which is paid in Federal stamps, constitutes a very large portion of our internal revenue receipts.

I append a statement of our internal revenue taxes with full details.

INTERNAL REVENUE RECEIPTS FROM JANUARY 1, 1875, TO JUNE 30, 1896.

FISCAL YEARS.	GROSS RECEIPTS.	GROSS RECEIPTS OF THE FEDERAL TAX.	TOTAL RECEIPTS.	COLLECTION EXPENSES.		NET RECEIPTS.
From January 1 to June 30, 1875...	$328,631 26	$769,037 02	$1,097,668 28		Percentage.	
1875–1876.........	$668,930 14	$1,145,624 37	$1,814,554 51	$167,937 42	9.255	$2,247,617 09
1876–1877.........	728,192 71	1,905,806 66	2,633,999 37	120,334 94	4.567	2,513,664 43
1877–1878.........	920,901 29	2,154,249 51	3,075,150 80	302,612 65	9.840	2,772,538 15
1878–1879.........	763,879 23	2,239,267 37	3,003,146 60	300,490 02	10.006	2,702,656 58
1879–1880.........	1,311,463 95	2,336,431 73	3,647,895 68	484,215 36	13.274	3,164,180 32
Average per annum in five years	$878,673 46	$1,956,275 93	$2,834,949 39	$275,118 08	9.705	$2,680,131 31
1880–1881.........	$1,037,730 93	$2,371,369 31	$3,409,100 24	$351,980 01	10.325	$3,057,120 23
1881–1882.........	1,429,655 61	2,775,149 84	4,204,805 45	376,095 30	8.943	3,828,710 15
1882–1883.........	1,591,189 33	3,099,179 93	4,690,369 26	420,132 04	9.000	4,270,237 22
1883–1884.........	1,919,461 99	2,912,967 08	4,832,429 07	441,080 10	9.126	4,391,348 87
1884–1885.........	3,231,872 75	3,127,481 85	6,359,354 60	489,043 89	7.690	5,870,310 71
Average per annum in five years	$1,841,982 12	$2,857,229 60	$4,699,211 72	$415,666 27	8.845	$4,283,545 44
1885–1886.........	$2,761,886 56	$3,115,759 85	$5,877,646 41	$428,390 78	7.288	$5,449,255 63
1886–1887.........	3,930,429 16	3,587,339 96	7,517,769 12	638,011 29	8.486	6,879,757 83
1887–1888.........	4,654,190 93	3,324,937 53	7,979,128 46	728,431 31	9.000	7,250,697 15
1888–1889.........	5,108,911 59	3,679,493 52	8,788,405 11	771,601 95	8.777	8,016,803 16
1889–1890.........	5,575,067 62	3,791,695 27	9,366,762 89	799,721 78	8.538	9,567,041 11
Average per annum in five years	$4,406,097 17	$3,499,845 23	$7,905,942 40	$673,237 42	8.516	$7,432,710 98
1890–1891.........	$5,624,340 94	$3,865,650 49	$9,489,991 43	$853,834 28	8.955	$8,636,157 15
1891–1892.........	5,402,495 76	3,969,987 88	9,372,483 64	868,161 60	9.263	8,504,322 04
1892–1893.........	6,625,265 53	4,431,022 65	11,056,288 18	945,076 71	8.548	10,111,211 47
1893–1894.........	9,164,063 10	5,216,547 31	14,380,610 41	1,120,760 85	7.190	13,259,849 56
1894–1895.........	10,098,795 63	5,471,173 92	15,569,969 55	1,146,419 41	7.363	14,423,550 14
1895–1896.........	12,519,676 93	5,559,255 61	18,078,932 54	1,196,053 14	6.616	16,882,879 40
Average in six years	$8,239,106 31	$4,752,272 98	$12,991,379 29	$1,021,717 67	7.865	$11,969,661 63
Total in 21½ years.	$85,397,032 94	$70,849,428 66	$156,246,461 60	$12,950,384 83	8.288	$143,799,908 39

Direct Taxes.—The third source of revenue of the Mexican Government are direct taxes collected in the Federal District, which includes the City of Mexico. They are levied on real-estate, scientific professions, commercial and industrial establishments, and work-shops. The real-estate for the purpose of this tax is divided into rural and urban, the former paying a tax of 12 per cent. on its rent when occupied, and 3 per cent. when not occupied, and the latter paying 8 per thousand of its registered value.

Taxes on professions vary from 50 cents to $20.00 a month. The tax on commercial and industrial establishments is regulated by law. The commercial establishments, which pay license taxes are commission agencies of all kinds : banking firms ; dry goods, groceries, wines, furniture, and jewelry stores ; insurance companies ; restaurants, hotels, and boarding-houses. Among the industrial establishments are embraced especially railway, telegraph and telephone companies ; cotton, woollen, and silk mills ; factories of all kinds ; iron smelters ; printing, engraving, and photographic establishments ; coffee, corn, and flour mills, etc., etc.

When the alcabalas were abolished a direct tax was established upon some of the articles which paid the largest sums, namely : pulque, wheat flour, and domestic brandy distilled from molasses.

I annex a statement showing the proceeds of Direct Taxes in the Federal District during the last twenty-seven fiscal years.

RECEIPTS FROM DIRECT TAXES IN THE FEDERAL DISTRICT DURING THE TWENTY-SEVEN FISCAL YEARS ENDING JUNE 30, 1896.

FISCAL YEARS.	GROSS RECEIPTS.	COLLECTION EXPENSES.	PER-CENTAGE EXPENSES.	NET RECEIPTS.
1869–1870	$485,451 73	$55,481 65	11.42	$429,970 08
1870–1871	502,146 64	53,924 28	10.74	448,222 36
1871–1872	471,228 78	50,034 37	10.62	421,194 41
1872–1873	477,654 75	51,939 05	9.90	425,715 70
1873–1874	524,494 76	57,205 69	10.90	467,289 07
1874–1875	531,149 09	56,663 64	10.67	474,485 45
1875–1876	1,350,705 56	69,957 24	5.18	1,280,748 32
1876–1877	516,510 80	47,685 23	9.23	468,825 57
1877–1878	538,300 09	37,970 00	7.05	500,330 09
1878–1879	559,217 21	51,160 08	9.15	508,057 13
1879–1880	592,688 44	52,126 21	8.79	540,562 23
1880–1881	634,498 92	52,260 50	8.23	582,238 42
1881–1882	674,973 66	53,161 23	7.87	621,812 43
1882–1883	753,579 80	98,264 24	13.08	655,315 56
1883–1884	830,010 26	100,937 90	12.16	729,072 36
1884–1885	1,092,656 37	89,892 38	8.23	1,002,763 99
1885–1886	1,023,349 52	91,464 07	8.97	931,885 45
1886–1887	1,040,143 16	84,861 27	8.16	955,281 89
1887–1888	1,074,489 54	121,011 50	11.26	953,478 04
1888–1889	1,125,202 97	97,635 14	8.68	1,027,567 83
1889–1890	1,213,458 49	100,134 87	8.25	1,113,323 62
1890–1891	1,306,746 37	103,740 02	7.35	1,203,006 35
1891–1892	1,369,225 30	104,320 34	7.62	1,264,904 96
1892–1893	1,436,875 70	115,817 86	8.06	1,321,057 84
1893–1894	1,445,270 81	110,290 73	7.63	1,334,980 08
1894–1895	1,497,251 90	108,255 57	7.36	1,388,996 33
1895–1896	1,620,480 35	110,347 13	6.81	1,510,133 22
Totals in the 27 years	$24,687,760 97	$2,126,542 19	....	$22,561,218 78
Average per annum	912,028 18	78,760 82	8.65	835,600 69
Totals and Annual averages of the first five years	$2,460,976 66	$268,585 04	....	$2,192,391 62
Annual average	492,195 33	53,717 01	11.14	438,478 32
Total of the second five years	$3,495,882 75	$263,436 19	....	$3,232,446 56
Annual average	699,176 55	52,687 24	7.54	646,489 31
Total of the third five years	$3,485,751 08	$356,750 08	....	$3,129,001 00
Annual average	684,550 38	71,350 02	10.42	625,800 20
Total of the fourth five years	$5,355,841 56	$484,864 36	....	$4,870,977 20
Annual average	1,071,168 31	96,972 87	9.05	974,195 44
Total of the fifth period of five years	$6,771,576 67	$534,303 82	....	$6,237,272 85
Annual average	1,354,315 33	106,860 76	7.89	1,247,454 57
Total of the sixth period of two years	$3,117,732 25	$218,602 70	....	$2,899,129 55
Annual average	1,558,866 13	109,301 35	7.01	1,449,564 78

REVENUES OF THE MEXICAN STATES FROM 1884 TO 1895.

STATES.	1884.	1885.	1886.	1887.	1888.	1889.	1890.	1891.	1892.	1893.	1894.	1895.	TOTAL.
Aguascalientes	$117,672	$103,043	$82,656	$80,400	$81,206	$80,656	$90,095	$144,507	$171,899	$136,615	$101,865	$90,885	$1,290,499
Campeche	136,841	132,938	177,055	190,516	176,553	223,924	239,860	260,419	247,951	252,495	283,777	279,210	2,601,538
Coahuila	222,586	168,211	195,283	185,679	262,725	220,937	431,412	273,318	323,606	333,843	341,093	380,757	3,339,450
Colima	118,237	126,420	126,420	95,870	103,871	116,186	130,237	171,951	178,370	175,383	170,534	163,681	1,657,160
Chiapas	136,015	154,510	125,218	143,322	135,126	163,279	204,332	229,608	274,749	441,520	359,184	421,428	2,808,291
Chihuahua	210,476	317,153	338,187	287,634	335,647	466,415	486,916	697,602	634,422	643,139			4,421,491
Durango	270,398	225,887	238,181	260,254	272,643	288,780	363,660	522,761	539,089	549,007	857,047	820,080	5,297,787
Guanajuato	839,870	967,610	952,017	1,028,064	998,006	1,038,109	1,143,221	1,174,248	1,136,123	1,287,202	1,423,687	1,330,662	13,318,819
Guerrero	221,055	235,578	393,291	286,038	409,785	426,205	443,149	495,556	519,550	530,980	252,072		4,213,259
Hidalgo	423,257	440,445	644,071	668,584	702,288	825,788	1,004,083	1,761,868	1,806,339	2,059,099	1,330,602	2,053,207	13,720,459
Jalisco	1,021,227	1,398,273	1,093,321	1,170,304	1,061,452	1,010,814	1,031,039	1,586,213	1,396,491	1,491,258	1,484,448	1,495,784	15,240,624
México	419,440	440,973	680,124	769,999	739,452	764,863	839,547	1,033,135	1,029,799	1,100,257	963,508	1,182,340	9,963,437
Michoacan	649,167	666,138	683,313	686,995	732,853	706,546	672,545	986,358	1,011,260	1,131,363	822,075	1,231,965	9,980,578
Morelos	328,066	359,053	338,982	338,169	347,233	336,256	359,811	437,187	418,697	436,433	407,824	360,962	4,450,273
New Leon	113,218	113,754	112,964	146,717	134,228	137,361	147,777	162,460	177,087	192,870	206,476	321,589	1,957,001
Oaxaca	680,207	714,471						878,355	1,049,477	1,033,287	982,250	905,504	6,243,551
Puebla	899,854	919,633	889,463	988,163	1,126,934	1,019,703	1,062,274	1,554,890	1,384,428	1,106,544	1,231,527	1,144,999	13,333,412
Querétaro	210,810	216,115	248,271	233,526	245,415	256,692	296,875	374,189	337,363	307,539	422,812	352,344	3,501,951
San Luis Potosí			1,313,582	1,149,522	1,144,234	2,645,298	1,638,341	1,596,576	1,596,791	1,187,854	1,055,791	1,602,899	14,895,008
Sinaloa	355,604	429,792	391,883	497,793	412,857	491,905	499,354	618,284	623,574	704,032	573,994	577,144	6,086,216
Sonora	302,962	296,136	290,959	404,179	342,456	352,568	362,701	561,201	571,263	493,399	374,865	471,753	4,824,652
Tabasco	170,149	185,307	176,831	184,934	253,488	255,832	201,149	298,668	284,208	282,723	336,365	331,537	3,050,141
Tamaulipas			160,938	160,031	114,866	133,029	190,832	192,087	193,458	189,557	215,137		1,535,835
Tlaxcala	131,331	153,362	111,724	116,868	117,912	167,345	166,719	173,966	203,092	182,936	187,379	190,166	1,923,400
Veracruz	722,448	771,516	814,485	730,232	686,818	779,413	866,383	1,039,184	985,395	867,044	572,441		8,833,359
Yucatan	374,466	441,485	452,055	501,450	483,796	510,634	498,162	587,186	621,697	637,749	680,900	696,202	6,485,782
Zacatecas	538,895	756,831	689,962	710,170	744,144	737,427	730,672	1,251,160	1,207,758	1,216,893	1,186,183	726,819	10,487,914
Total	$9,614,261	$10,735,534	$11,718,726	$11,923,413	$12,166,198	$14,186,465	$14,191,158	$19,038,682	$18,892,421	$18,962,076	$16,824,736	$17,131,917	$175,386,487
Federal Treasury	37,442,625	30,359,637	28,797,729	32,126,509	40,962,045	54,801,924	61,908,681	44,142,856	39,993,743	38,654,770	41,216,803	46,907,123	497,314,535
Total	$47,056,886	$41,095,171	$40,516,455	$44,049,922	$53,128,243	$68,988,389	$76,099,839	$63,181,538	$58,886,164	$57,617,746	$58,041,629	$64,039,040	$672,700,022

EXPENSES OF THE MEXICAN STATES FROM 1884 TO 1895.

STATES.	1884.	1885.	1886.	1887.	1888.	1889.	1890.	1891.	1892.	1893.	1894.	1895.	TOTAL.
Aguascalientes	85,564	86,626	81,356	78,400	80,603	89,186	93,475	144,487	166,306	135,384	101,865	90,395	1,233,647
Campeche	134,901	133,426	177,150	189,492	168,558	217,778	244,180	259,866	244,872	244,742	265,180	267,288	2,547,433
Coahuila	234,835	183,489	190,436	176,418	226,093	210,031	232,162	269,094	317,445	320,074	341,093	304,873	3,006,043
Colima	115,030	124,474	124,474	100,348	109,525	144,487	131,770	171,240	162,195	168,548	163,611	152,590	1,638,292
Chiapas	135,370	155,231	125,052	142,815	135,197	181,885	195,972	174,740	268,293	430,949	359,918	423,103	2,728,525
Chihuahua	218,219	282,275	......	......	......	......	......	639,574	614,605	611,159	......	......	2,365,832
Durango	264,619	217,555	235,965	243,311	263,616	282,654	357,368	506,563	516,407	539,315	836,912	799,997	5,064,282
Guanajuato	......	......	......	......	......	1,049,015	1,102,697	1,132,089	1,168,058	1,299,855	2,204,964	1,338,106	9,294,784
Guerrero	216,627	244,522	209,870	220,598	223,819	238,936	235,840	273,100	280,527	340,450	260,693	......	2,742,982
Hidalgo	426,442	455,812	599,701	594,192	642,825	727,283	1,017,407	1,740,351	1,792,792	2,051,629	1,316,470	2,052,213	13,417,207
Jalisco	1,012,909	1,415,211	972,846	1,052,887	1,283,412	994,430	962,737	1,586,213	1,396,491	1,457,104	1,459,535	1,495,928	15,089,703
México	419,440	440,973	625,497	647,467	725,933	716,405	801,950	1,014,974	1,069,427	1,147,155	800,459	1,142,016	9,557,557
Michoacan	632,911	665,949	641,589	708,362	719,088	694,400	703,478	930,135	988,860	1,019,427	883,064	1,249,031	9,788,313
Morelos	327,057	356,038	342,412	326,511	351,425	336,390	355,109	433,756	418,697	436,427	394,229	335,742	4,443,793
New Leon	90,785	103,199	107,245	153,664	131,559	134,578	138,034	146,428	143,861	157,623	151,955	258,649	1,715,580
Oaxaca	748,927	681,918	......	......	......	......	......	749,105	834,411	953,536	973,723	876,536	5,868,156
Puebla	894,686	945,442	889,011	987,925	1,112,660	987,460	1,055,366	1,518,955	1,361,484	1,084,620	1,212,622	1,128,949	13,179,194
Querétaro	212,759	215,702	248,136	228,023	251,004	257,158	294,797	374,185	337,362	307,343	419,501	350,846	3,496,816
San Luis Potosí	......	......	1,309,827	1,156,149	1,156,279	2,580,051	1,699,971	1,524,776	1,561,652	1,162,797	1,046,668	834,262	14,034,432
Sinaloa	353,950	428,201	304,780	401,999	417,246	492,448	495,781	614,419	617,355	692,662	543,784	581,051	6,033,676
Sonora	289,598	326,301	169,781	403,056	235,140	308,416	315,077	535,870	541,439	467,997	354,155	587,153	4,535,913
Tabasco	166,771	188,948	175,993	192,154	229,834	272,042	286,706	303,998	281,405	290,187	335,022	328,366	3,051,386
Tamaulipas	......	......	160,790	158,851	118,357	133,094	191,134	194,977	177,632	180,984	213,019	......	1,526,838
Tlaxcala	135,101	148,311	116,720	118,826	118,723	161,773	172,780	172,509	198,199	189,411	185,960	184,284	1,904,597
Veracruz	708,606	760,873	750,070	739,293	772,118	777,697	742,065	871,260	954,055	799,019	542,615	......	8,417,671
Yucatan	371,562	439,712	449,096	444,200	438,347	487,658	480,315	580,204	620,784	632,999	672,738	679,994	6,297,606
Zacatecas	573,031	761,686	603,294	671,625	784,641	701,522	754,860	1,226,525	1,201,780	1,179,868	1,174,420	750,387	10,383,630
Total	8,759,700	9,759,904	9,701,181	10,136,566	10,697,922	13,149,777	13,061,925	18,089,393	18,236,394	18,301,264	17,214,175	16,211,699	163,329,900
Federal Treasury	42,714,229	44,407,386	26,184,198	36,262,962	54,956,554	73,922,329	78,158,753	63,005,128	43,350,149	48,954,972	45,713,791	45,078,551	602,709,002
Total	51,483,929	54,167,290	35,885,379	46,399,528	65,654,476	87,072,106	91,220,678	81,094,521	61,586,543	67,256,236	62,927,966	61,290,250	766,038,902

REVENUES OF THE MUNICIPALITIES OF MEXICO FROM 1884 TO 1895.

REVENUES.

STATES.	1884.	1885.	1886.	1887.	1888.	1889.	1890.	1891.	1892.	1893.	1894.	1895.	TOTAL.
Aguascalientes..	$60,147	$55,176	$58,989	$59,106	$62,053	$68,260	$71,735	$75,434	$78,138	$64,179	$71,587	$73,140	$797,944
Campeche........	71,336	68,774	80,332	96,295	98,871	83,350	99,145	101,294	96,481	127,908	170,921	142,479	1,237,186
Coahuila........	174,285	206,569	174,837	194,790	239,837	255,036	226,780	393,032	372,664	396,414	446,611	692,720	3,773,575
Colima..........	52,872	54,596	53,237	49,821	47,638	52,861	52,185	67,216	70,460	76,585	62,534	73,447	713,452
Chiapas.........	....	....	....	....	....	....	....	61,096	82,398	103,250	120,103	143,204	510,051
Chihuahua.......	....	....	290,727	287,235	306,604	322,363	384,340	514,369	522,015	540,740	....	....	3,168,393
Durango.........	....	....	....	....	....	....	....	....	....	....	....	....	....
Guanajuato......	591,541	594,347	580,575	556,340	564,435	599,086	630,516	656,913	582,232	558,204	662,419	751,636	7,328,044
Guerrero........	82,943	99,064	105,888	111,781	123,548	117,665	129,431	103,117	115,839	99,792	112,877	142,877	1,201,955
Hidalgo.........	331,716	334,462	307,109	315,772	318,558	310,061	318,057	521,426	532,224	537,685	585,954	586,895	4,999,319
Jalisco.........	498,723	675,100	....	....	....	....	....	....	....	....	....	....	3,586,809
México..........	178,996	210,500	233,671	245,392	246,687	260,793	252,090	254,934	266,080	276,042	299,680	291,911	3,016,776
Michoacan.......	....	....	235,349	226,264	229,174	245,197	256,335	295,700	306,877	348,060	379,043	401,070	2,923,069
Morelos.........	85,012	68,065	98,159	108,042	104,215	111,405	114,459	35,598	34,989	36,488	156,506	184,371	1,138,259
New Leon........	156,773	155,761	160,614	180,819	195,739	240,438	253,524	343,994	336,758	377,011	418,749	433,666	3,247,846
Oaxaca..........	98,804	126,496	103,077	102,108	102,798	104,610	109,473	184,235	216,689	219,065	255,169	248,326	1,870,369
Puebla..........	894,686	945,462	....	....	....	593,061	609,957	656,129	669,291	705,259	754,985	804,682	6,633,512
Querétaro.......	55,529	54,475	....	....	....	....	....	77,041	79,918	65,351	70,387	80,736	472,437
San Luis Potosi.	....	....	319,240	285,009	285,232	283,793	288,699	141,527	145,306	272,070	334,164	394,647	2,749,687
Sinaloa.........	190,144	159,832	397,067	410,575	481,194	495,429	516,366	478,714	470,688	447,745	437,543	473,958	4,509,279
Sonora..........	102,376	87,850	98,351	216,782	212,655	248,216	241,986	220,400	266,858	277,479	254,699	357,089	2,793,957
Tabasco.........	....	....	....	114,291	113,024	124,226	145,322	131,110	144,931	155,985	171,938	167,397	1,556,801
Tamaulipas......	....	....	....	....	....	....	231,949	233,524	266,587	248,395	254,699	....	1,235,064
Tlaxcala........	27,237	39,615	40,013	37,302	47,256	43,058	35,470	47,662	59,084	46,565	51,118	48,298	505,598
Veracruz........	906,016	890,442	1,828,202	2,307,848	2,222,601	2,348,206	2,183,987	2,628,734	2,764,251	2,728,308	3,571,242	293,551	24,439,837
Yucatan.........	140,388	176,854	156,277	209,040	198,411	233,390	159,842	248,678	249,020	261,214	302,015	293,551	2,628,680
Zacatecas.......	438,890	443,054	238,557	396,443	409,053	409,393	427,019	454,396	412,377	431,511	438,904	512,204	5,011,801
Territory of Lower California...	28,249	39,681	32,443	38,870	40,630	49,726	57,220	18,491	20,392	17,772	108,910	19,054	462,488
Territory of Tepic......	127,445	119,717	65,002	82,989	83,795	85,771	85,195	136,501	143,043	158,826	185,491	210,947	1,484,622
Total......	$5,294,108	$5,586,792	$5,857,957	$6,702,049	$6,728,675	$7,691,787	$7,881,082	$9,508,881	$9,760,610	$10,108,656	$10,883,094	$7,903,600	$93,907,291
Federal District.	1,332,403	1,486,645	1,928,324	2,049,063	2,380,238	2,688,081	3,345,267	2,455,435	2,745,401	3,175,992	3,461,919	3,395,638	30,444,406
Total......	$6,626,511	$7,073,437	$7,786,281	$8,751,112	$9,108,913	$10,379,868	$11,226,349	$11,964,316	$12,506,011	$13,284,648	$14,345,013	$11,299,238	$124,351,697

EXPENSES OF THE MUNICIPALITIES OF MEXICO FROM 1884 TO 1895.

STATES.	1884.	1885.	1886.	1887.	1888.	1889.	1890.	1891.	1892.	1893.	1894.	1895.	TOTAL.
Aguascalientes	$60,837	55,922	38,989	59,106	62,053	68,260	71,375	75,677	79,232	64,734	71,769	73,272	$781,226
Campeche	71,162	68,382	77,447	92,147	92,500	81,299	87,160	94,416	89,009	109,245	121,139	110,548	1,094,454
Coahuila	182,873	206,148	182,938	195,358	189,358	258,424	222,151	392,554	372,129	389,368	436,244	678,247	3,705,792
Colima	53,187	54,763	53,712	50,935	48,378	54,217	57,775	66,930	69,744	75,997	62,405	72,803	719,946
Chiapas								60,199	81,712	105,880	115,551	139,728	503,070
Chihuahua			290,727	287,235	306,604	332,363	384,340	502,605	511,012	532,422			3,147,308
Durango													
Guanajuato	594,545	595,280				553,036	639,547	622,072	614,813	571,115	654,363	732,697	5,577,468
Guerrero	82,482	87,432	103,033	108,757	114,481	120,205	125,929	101,936	120,768	99,654	112,314		1,176,991
Hidalgo	327,716	333,898	307,051	310,798	316,290	307,885	318,056	506,200	514,130	517,572	574,836	564,334	4,898,766
Jalisco	498,723	675,100						427,661	476,297	519,867	451,261	503,624	3,553,533
México	178,996	210,500	182,231	188,453	191,771	203,925	205,866	247,166	260,215	275,647	278,323	286,008	2,709,101
Michoacan			224,998	232,164	232,055	243,785	250,208	271,690	287,495	317,662	352,712	360,371	2,782,140
Morelos	84,985	68,586	97,205	107,096	104,361	109,110	116,379	35,374	34,506	35,769	155,822	150,791	1,099,984
New León	160,904	160,949	164,310	175,533	190,876	222,480	232,497	339,169	329,495	352,568	419,594	434,222	3,182,597
Oaxaca	114,073	113,632	96,998	92,852	93,239	94,570	166,527	170,293	202,576	207,028	236,286	234,409	1,762,423
Puebla	585,684	585,809				594,570	594,126	642,015	647,543	682,645	722,863	757,059	5,828,763
Querétaro	55,230	50,807						76,954	70,915	65,348	68,317	79,300	466,671
San Luis Potosí			293,627	226,867	248,330	241,214	303,632	298,779	370,032	299,063	327,764	387,372	2,996,750
Sinaloa	188,730	159,728	387,590	399,388	482,874	491,130	525,973	474,059	470,131	446,146	432,110	475,837	4,585,838
Sonora	82,125	85,537	208,880	217,683	211,318	248,516	240,422	217,209	268,690	277,227	164,777	349,544	2,587,047
Tabasco			96,674	111,758	112,404	123,573	138,024	123,974	135,453	144,473		166,859	1,485,631
Tamaulipas							235,398	223,713	261,597	243,649	255,419		1,219,686
Tlaxcala	27,379	29,071	39,654	37,142	47,756	41,199	34,518	45,609	48,880	46,333	50,320	46,999	494,860
Veracruz	847,470	878,432	1,783,602	2,078,832	2,217,032	2,334,273	2,200,548	2,581,042	2,710,325	2,696,628	3,515,127		23,841,311
Yucatan	136,046	172,005	185,119	233,957	166,712	267,635	230,021	242,913	248,949	257,654	306,279	299,116	2,746,406
Zacatecas	438,368	436,458	247,685	571,760	415,190	439,992	400,048	454,396	412,377	431,511	428,767	495,688	5,171,640
Territory of Lower California	29,237	30,783	31,710	37,494	41,222	45,783	60,088	18,362	20,260	17,638	104,323	18,258	455,158
Territory of Tepic	112,602	110,731	67,364	82,471	94,937	105,001	97,291	129,796	143,193	145,495	168,893	195,869	1,453,643
Total	$4,913,354	$5,169,953	$5,161,014	$5,896,886	$5,981,741	$7,570,001	$7,894,792	$9,443,363	$9,851,328	$9,928,338	$10,587,578	$7,617,955	$90,016,303
Federal District	1,332,451	1,491,055	1,882,825	2,082,296	2,391,464	2,638,093	3,239,286	2,580,074	3,210,371	3,040,865	3,460,845	3,378,695	30,728,320
Total	$6,245,805	$6,661,008	$7,043,839	$7,979,182	$8,373,205	$10,208,094	$11,134,078	$12,023,437	$13,061,699	$12,969,203	$14,048,423	$10,996,650	$120,744,623

STATE AND MUNICIPAL FINANCES.

The best way in which I can give the state and municipal revenues and expenses in Mexico, is by inserting the detail amounts of the last twelve years of the revenues and expenses of each of the Mexican States, and a similar statement of the revenues and expenses of the municipalities of each State. That statement gives also the revenues and expenses of the City of Mexico, which have increased very considerably of late. In the year 1867, after the restoration of the Republic, they only amounted to about $800,000, while in the year 1895, they had increased to $3,395,638. (These statements are on pp. 150–153.)

FOREIGN TRADE.

The foreign trade of Mexico was necessarily very small before the railway era, because transportation was exceedingly high on account of the broken condition of the country, and only articles of great value and comparatively small weight could be profitably exported, while the price of foreign commodities became very high, both on account of transportation charges and high import duties. Therefore, only rich people could afford to consume foreign commodities, and the exports of Mexico were practically reduced to silver and gold, and to a few commodities having small bulk and great value.

The normal cost of transportation on merchandise from the City of Mexico to Veracruz, a distance of one hundred Mexican leagues or 263¾ English miles, used to be, before the railroad connecting both places was built, $68.75 per ton of 2200 pounds, or more than 26 cents per mile and ton ; and in extraordinary circumstances, as during the French Intervention in Mexico from 1861 to 1867, the freight was as high as $330 per ton, or over $1.25 per mile and ton. Therefore, no article could be transported unless it was very much needed and it commanded a very high price. The result was that not only the foreign but also the domestic trade was reduced to its smallest proportions, and that the people raised just enough to provide for the wants of themselves and their immediate neighbors. A fact that may seem incredible is, that for the same reasons, among the farmers, a good crop was considered a great misfortune.

Since the railways have revolutionized transportation, our products, especially agricultural commodities, have begun to be sent to foreign markets, and their exportation is increasing considerably. As yet the precious metals, especially silver, are the main exports from Mexico, representing during the fiscal year ended June 30, 1896, 61 per cent. of our total annual exports ; but other commodities are now exported, and they are in a fair way to exceed, before long, the value of our silver exports. I have no doubt that with the opening of our railroads, if our exports continue to increase in the same proportion as they have recently done, Mexico will be able to supply the United States with most of the tropical products now consumed and not yet produced here, and even with others, that would find a market if they could be cheaply transported.

The same difficulties which prevented us from having correct accounts of our public revenues and expenses, and which I have stated in speaking on that subject, made it very difficult for many years to have correct statistics of our imports and exports.

Imports.—I could not give even a tentative statement, which I could vouchsafe, of our total imports and exports from 1821 to 1867, but the statement of the receipts of our custom-houses from 1823 to 1875, which appears on page 145 gives an approximate idea of our imports, considering that the receipts amount to about from 50 to 60 per cent. of the value of the imports.

I append a detailed statement of the imports and exports in Mexico during the years 1826, 1827, and 1828, and the total imports and exports during the year 1825.

From the fiscal year 1872–1873 our Statistical Bureau began to make its reports, and I have concised them in the three annexed statements comprising most of those years, up to the fiscal year ended June 30, 1896. The commodities are divided in their respective classes in accordance with the different schedules of the tariffs then in force.

MEXICAN IMPORTS AND EXPORTS FROM 1826 TO 1828.

MERCHANDISE.	1826.	1827.	1828.
Imports.			
Linen	$2,384,715	$2,180,191	$1,711,051
Wool	934,295	493,760	245,901
Silk	1,432,578	844,732	398,003
Cotton	5,017,700	6,913,126	3,417,766
Mixed	122,968	107,108	38,654
Wines, liquors, groceries	2,888,066	2,867,320	3,244,498
Haberdashery	728,236	489,402	306,614
Medicines, drugs, and perfumeries	90,779	55,100	20,260
Books, blank and printed, paper	1,430,039	495,743	130,638
China, fine and ordinary, crystal and glass	264,424	311,074	332,819
Furniture, of wood and metal	91,910	103,047	57,187
Machines and instruments for mining, science, and the arts	63,499	22,816	44,123
Furs	912	4,517	318
Gold and silver	444	1,080	....
Total imports	$15,450,565	$14,889,016	$9,947,832
Exports.	Total imports in 1825: $19,093,716.		
Gold and silver	$5,847,795	$9,669,428	$12,387,288
Cochineal	1,356,730	912,049	1,483,746
Indigo, vanilla, jalap, and sarsaparilla	76,440	1,076,528	448,747
Other articles of indigenous products	367,164	513,769	169,005
Total exports	$7,648,129	$12,171,774	$14,488,786
	Total exports in 1825 : $5,085,235.		

IMPORTS IN MEXICO FROM JULY 1, 1872, TO JUNE 30, 1875, AND IN THE YEAR 1884-1885.

	1872-1873.		1873-1874.		1874-1875.		1884-1885.	
	Invoice Value.	Duties.	Invoice Value.	Duties.	Invoice Value.	Duties.	Invoice Value.	Duties.
1. Cottons.......	$7,036,913 45	$4,992,003 53	$8,814,123 34	$6,002,759 46	$7,379,339 12	$5,826,530 86	$6,153,559 86	$5,234,420 08
2. Linens........	1,003,595 70	603,559 96	1,173,572 41	700,445 22	703,052 21	496,896 20	548,191 22	469,798 70
3. Woollens.....	1,031,378 82	676,339 40	1,306,932 77	877,078 29	988,292 75	695,216 55	1,376,365 04	1,066,491 36
4. Silks	401,905 37	260,004 52	337,560 01	217,398 44	274,744 88	189,815 46	337,550 28	281,978 04
5. Mixtures	1,052,553 37	624,126 96	1,174,004 66	715,661 44	796,762 17	539,745 16	1,281,247 44	1,070,162 56
6. Groceries.....	3,613,162 45	2,184,375 85	3,334,152 92	2,058,713 20	2,955,852 55	2,038,344 16	3,761,080 40	2,632,185 86
7. Crystal........	279,216 43	172,154 00	356,770 88	248,030 11	240,825 10	185,952 29	398,154 72	305,172 42
8. Haberdashery.	1,180,194 88	687,282 98	1,376,719 31	828,395 54	1,160,921 85	768,267 32	1,741,956 70	1,278,237 60
9. Chemicals	178,258 75	141,181 29	226,681 92	198,761 67	174,618 02	143,569 70	479,734 38	348,709 22
10. Sundries.......	1,404,297 58	1,125,142 38	1,635,461 81	1,111,199 21	1,322,722 14	898,919 65	1,769,536 32	1,203,434 20
11. Commodities paying 55%..	555,027 91	366,946 65	36,400 00	23,352 84	58,444 09	38,276 14	296,166 38	194,302 24
Free Articles.....	2,429,508 14	....	3,509,918 53	....	2,737,918 73	....	5,643,142 16	....
Total........	$20,166,012 85	$11,833,117 52	$23,282,298 56	$12,981,795 42	$18,793,493 61	$11,821,533 49	$23,786,684 90	$14,084,892 28

IMPORTS IN MEXICO FROM JULY 1, 1885, TO JUNE 30, 1886, AND FROM JULY 1, 1888, TO JUNE 30, 1890.

	1885-1886 (UNDER THE TARIFF OF JANUARY 24, 1885.)		1888-1889 (UNDER THE TARIFF OF MARCH 1, 1887.)		1889-1890.	
	Invoice Value.	Duties.	Invoice Value.	Duties.	Invoice Value.	Duties.
1. Free of duties	$2,682,343 26	......	$13,506,230 23	......	$21,238,598 91	......
2. Cottons	5,520,538 32	$6,953,659 28	7,534,088 70	$7,447,394 70	7,677,131 31	$8,109,445 45
3. Linens	556,115 48	639,234 50	674,029 52	671,590 87	681,879 69	645,276 72
4. Woollens	1,227,327 42	1,737,314 34	1,613,186 22	1,986,020 61	1,995,890 56	2,353,441 00
5. Silks	305,936 48	351,903 84	394,691 60	378,614 57	540,845 12	505,490 35
6. Mixtures	366,755 04	430,279 26	394,889 86	410,419 80	548,298 13	550,578 80
7. Food articles	2,390,360 48	2,037,829 30	4,893,706 49	3,789,270 57	5,954,813 02	4,627,227 87
8. Stones and earths	97,579 84	66,873 18	81,815 68	41,244 81	133,694 20	61,249 16
9. Crystal and porcelain	309,411 14	326,712 90	607,727 18	686,884 84	667,593 16	743,388 64
10. Gold, silver, and platinum	145,551 66	17,690 40	320,843 60	27,967 36	286,680 35	28,792 54
11. Iron and steel	852,065 14	674,270 34	1,510,129 91	1,259,480 12	2,034,625 21	1,507,561 26
12. Leather	363,577 72	238,771 08	593,166 91	324,225 37	705,768 54	428,993 02
13. Tin, lead, and zinc	42,620 20	34,558 16	75,968 92	39,289 76	93,421 20	50,877 98
14. Haberdashery	423,549 42	304,950 50	658,853 68	505,497 81	715,068 53	551,554 20
15. Machines	1,457,236 48	81,014 42	539,582 35	128,205 84	587,478 34	155,459 53
16. Carriages and wagons	75,024 30	41,868 66	213,796 20	116,206 57	272,264 46	150,161 03
17. Arms, ammunition, and gunpowder	285,926 12	141,862 40	280,453 04	172,830 78	348,652 13	200,487 78
18. Wood and its manufactures	202,492 52	171,495 12	473,684 25	368,523 72	620,984 55	480,905 30
19. Paper and its manufactures	951,677 28	626,525 02	1,352,143 12	1,161,250 81	1,359,417 23	1,154,445 55
20. Furs	253,677 12	197,113 18	414,109 54	290,211 92	506,593 83	348,989 86
21. Chemicals	736,830 94	496,131 56	1,697,830 38	997,449 42	1,737,395 37	1,036,988 80
22. Sundries	1,925,372 88	1,534,435 38	2,193,966 94	1,675,382 70	3,311,465 05	2,091,334 04
Total	$21,171,795 24	$17,104,492 82	$40,024,894 32	$22,477,962 95	$52,018,658 89	$25,782,648 88

IMPORTS IN MEXICO FROM THE FISCAL YEAR 1892–1893 TO THE FISCAL YEAR 1895–1896.

	FREE — Invoice Value.				DUTIABLE — Invoice Value.				TOTAL — Invoice Value.			
	1892–1893	1893–1894	1894–1895	1895–1896	1892–1893	1893–1894	1894–1895	1895–1896	1892–1893	1893–1894	1894–1895	1895–1896
1. Animal Industry:												
Live animals	$9,042	$10,797	$3,640	$7,252	$745,321	$260,010	$169,673	$374,655	$754,363	$270,807	$173,313	$381,907
Animal remains	1,523				379,441	302,880	567,391	797,499	380,964	302,880	567,391	797,499
Animal products	12,290	11,922	13,370	26,271	1,243,263	817,868	789,496	1,052,730	1,255,553	829,790	802,866	1,079,001
Animal manufactures	1,865	119	3,366	471	723,029	628,993	674,686	628,993	724,894	629,112	678,052	629,464
Total	$24,720	22,838	$20,376	$33,094	$3,082,054	$2,009,751	$2,201,246	$2,753,877	$3,106,774	$2,032,589	$2,221,622	$2,797,871
2. Agricultural Products:												
Textiles		$13,925	$13,925		2,365,756	2,016,616	2,341,747	1,761,488	$2,365,756	$2,016,616	$2,355,672	$1,761,438
Fruits and grains	$30,847	19,026	16,205	25,716	7,380,439	1,118,146	883,923	1,553,036	7,420,286	1,137,172	900,128	1,578,752
Sundry vegetable substances	199,496	65,710	94,772	98,375	234,350	192,310	211,556	266,237	343,846	258,020	306,338	364,612
Sundry vegetable products	3,583	3,437	9,578	3,137	1,268,458	1,019,067	974,778	1,194,787	1,212,041	1,023,404	984,336	1,197,924
Wood and its products	937,383	675,950	600,512	966,411	341,752	276,838	296,230	391,658	1,279,135	954,788	896,742	1,358,069
Manufactures of sundry vegetable substances	395,958	20	3,225	2,270	225,671	383,698	464,683	380,334	531,629	383,718	467,908	382,604
Furniture					292,011	187,027	216,899	319,662	292,011	187,027	216,899	319,662
Total	$1,387,267	$764,143	$738,217	$1,095,909	$12,057,437	$5,194,602	$5,389,816	$5,867,142	$13,444,704	$5,958,745	$6,128,043	$6,963,051
3. Metals and its Manufactures:												
Gold, silver, and platinum	$200,610	$117,369	$834,472	$59,336	$159,203	$163,655	$201,850	$173,268	$359,813	$281,024	$1,036,322	$232,604
Copper	31,183	24,479	24,670	55,683	497,992	438,503	600,916	676,098	529,175	462,482	625,186	731,781
Tin, lead, and zinc	4,228	3,148	6,115	4,495	69,042	73,377	102,514	128,930	73,270	76,525	108,629	133,425
Iron and steel	1,216,596	441,254	281,165	1,049,435	1,855,228	2,054,929	2,427,516	3,140,837	3,071,824	2,496,183	2,713,681	4,190,272
Other metals	693,525	506,043	541,664	574,153	984	12,131	3,281	4,470	604,509	518,774	544,945	578,623
Stone and earthenware	1,804,277	1,051,373	1,040,790	1,046,402	826,979	614,256	675,187	982,678	2,631,256	1,665,029	1,714,977	2,029,085
Crystal, glass, china, and porcelainware	6,472	6,939	2,851	6,853	545,297	504,073	548,230	867,162	551,769	511,012	551,081	874,015
Total	$3,866,891	$2,151,205	$2,735,727	$2,796,357	$3,954,725	$3,860,924	$4,559,494	$5,973,443	$7,821,616	$6,012,129	$7,295,221	$8,769,800
4. Fabrics:												
Cotton					$4,119,936	$4,198,266	$4,576,433	$5,767,483	$4,119,936	$4,198,266	$4,576,433	$5,767,483
Linen					531,936	489,827	489,690	673,109	531,938	489,827	489,690	673,109
Wool					1,368,129	1,459,060	1,734,418	1,828,491	1,370,262	1,459,060	1,734,418	1,828,491
Silk	$2,133	$4,530	$5,268	$6,053	428,372	393,334	456,681	554,382	434,401	397,864	461,949	560,435
Silk with a mixture of other substances	4,029				405,922	393,123	526,723	596,585	495,922	393,123	526,723	596,585
Total	$6,162	$4,530	$5,268	$6,053	$6,854,297	$6,933,610	$7,783,945	$9,420,050	$6,860,459	$6,938,140	$7,789,213	$9,426,103
5. Chemicals, oils, and paints	$146,659				2,587,505	1,913,161	2,174,460	2,530,249	2,734,164	1,913,161	2,174,460	2,530,249
6. Wines, liquors, fermented and unfermented drinks					1,356,293	1,068,415	1,339,077	1,647,561	1,356,293	1,068,415	1,339,077	1,647,561
7. Paper and its manufactures	156,953	143,557	172,258	217,359	4,097,950	3,401,821	3,562,141	4,994,785	4,254,903	3,545,378	3,734,399	5,212,144
8. Machinery	1,935,081	140,047	157,892	262,224	933,419	174,156	121,623	549,237	2,868,500	314,203	279,515	811,461
9. Carriages	625,324	162,312	141,977	580,050	341,542	443,802	711,714	438,411	966,866	606,114	853,691	1,018,461
10. Arms and Explosives	444,182	1,058			443,505	798,201	909,979	1,114,696	887,687	799,259	909,979	1,114,696
11. Sundries	8,062	979		5,587	1,038,184	1,098,371	1,276,620	1,719,758	1,046,246	1,099,350	1,276,620	1,725,345
Grand Total	$8,601,301	$3,395,690	$3,972,694	$5,004,533	$34,811,830	$26,891,793	$30,027,736	$37,012,209	$43,413,131	$30,287,483	$34,000,440	$42,016,742

I append a statement which shows the imports and exports of Mexico during the two fiscal years 1894–1895 and 1895–1896, both by countries and by custom-houses, and the imports and duties by countries in the fiscal years 1888–1889 and 1889–1890.

Exports.—It would be difficult to make a correct statement of our exports previous to the fiscal year 1867–1868. Their amount was very small for reasons already given, and as they principally consisted in silver, and almost all the silver coined was exported the coinage of which we have exact records, can be taken as the amount of exports, with the addition of from 30 to 40 per cent., representing the silver both in coin and bullion smuggled. I give a correct statement of our exports of agricultural commodities from the fiscal year 1877–1878 to 1895–1896, and also a statement of our exports of other commodities from the fiscal year 1886–1887 to 1895–1896, which shows the rapid pace at which they are increasing.

The exports from Mexico are embraced in the following articles :

MINERALS.

Chapopote.
Coal.
Copper in bars.
Gold and silver coin.
Gold and silver bullion.
Lead in pigs.
Onyx.
Opals.
Ores of silver, copper, and lead.

AGRICULTURAL PRODUCTS.

Beans.
Bitter almonds and various fruits, kernels.
Chick-peas.
Cocoa.
Coffee.
Honey.
India-rubber.
Molasses.
Piloncillo (brown sugar).
Sugar, all grades.

FIBRES.

Henequen.
Ixtle.
Mallows fibre.
Pita.
Ramie.
Sotol.
Wool.

ANIMAL PRODUCTS.

Bones.
Cattle.
Chihuahua terriers.
Donkeys.
Goats.
Hair, horse.
Hair, rabbit.
Heron feathers.
Hides, raw and tanned.
Hoofs.
Horns.
Horses.
Mules.
Ox grease.
Sheep.
Skins of sheep and goat, dressed and undressed.

MANUFACTURES.

Cotton, linen, worsted and silk domestic shawls (rebozos).
Guadalajara earthenware.
Maguey, brandy (Tequila and mescal.
Preserved sweet meats.
Rag puppets and dolls.
Rags (all sorts).
Wax, artificial flowers and figures.
Woollen and worsted Mexican plaids or blankets (Zarapes).

FRUITS.

Bananas.
Cocoanuts.
Lemons.
Limes.
Oranges.
Pine apples.
Walnuts, Nuevo Leon.
Tamarind pulp.

FORESTRY.

Cabinet woods, mahogany, moral, lind-aloe, tepeguaje, cedar, sandal, ebony, and rosewood.
Dye woods, brasil, camphor, moral, and other varieties of logwood.
Orchilla.

SUNDRIES.

Copal, chick, and sundry resinous substances.
Jalap, and other medicinal herbs.
Mother of pearl shells.
Pearls.
Tortoise shell from the Gulf of Cortez.
Vanilla.
Zacaton brush and broom grasses.

IMPORTS IN MEXICO BY COUNTRIES IN THE FISCAL YEARS 1888–1889 AND 1889–1890 AND IMPORTS AND EXPORTS BY COUNTRIES AND CUSTOM HOUSES IN THE FISCAL YEARS 1894–1895 AND 1895–1896.

Imports by Countries

COUNTRIES	1888–1889 VALUE	1888–1889 DUTIES	1889–1890 VALUE	1889–1890 DUTIES	FISCAL YEAR 1894–95 IMPORTS	FISCAL YEAR 1894–95 EXPORTS	FISCAL YEAR 1895–96 IMPORTS	FISCAL YEAR 1895–96 EXPORTS
Arabia	82	24	19	8	1,245		417	
Argelia	13,649	15,907	15,060	14,416	5,358		10,434	
Argentine Republic								
Australia	30	32	600	203	177		189	
Austria	485	216	3,895	77	38,331		4,572	300
Bavaria	96,436	74,814	117,544	87,658	87,615		116,155	20
Belgium	242,083	234,287	553,270	281,198	319,580	380,265	420,015	1,000,393
Bolivia	600	277	400		1,949		2,900	
Brazil	309	230	912	602	342		4,358	
Canada					2,469			
Chili	108	72	220		5,248	30	653	70
China	39,351	26,346	59,001	45,682	44,928		1,734	
Colombia	78,178	32,635	38,666	6,200	71,702	545	51,188	800
Costa Rica	22,425	6,580	24,742	2,928	375		76,804	
Cuba			2,802	588	4,658	71,274	131	85,473
Denmark	1,112	729	1,868		2,062		1,986	
Ecuador	80,451	38,429	118,477	55,156	73,069	6,837	2,870	8,455
Egypt					1,701		63,644	
England	6,337,986	5,083,870	8,535,370	6,259,363	6,668,321	15,261,169	7,005,016	16,467,149
France	4,950,568	3,846,252	6,233,608	4,802,900	5,576,750	15,129,816	6,099,183	2,080,802
Germany	2,844,932	2,310,015	3,678,684	2,588,077	3,361,043	3,113,435	4,363,324	2,968,792
Greece	1,089	462	683	468	1,557		899	
Guatemala	11,548	3,636	218,402	11,448	14,357	887,753	21,874	44,443
Holland	72,009	53,010	160,535	129,319	127,187	65,420	134,284	1,076,442
Honduras			3,251	9		3,502		2,990
India	69,629	123,362	85,490	144,032	151,870	26,814	142,629	
Italy	269,826	121,818	161,505	58,119	121,308	5,850	159,369	123,955
Japan	95	64	1,515	1,139	9,028		12,793	
Morocco					17			
Nicaragua	31,176	33,358	44,462	34,307	40,218	3,615	70,052	4,952
Norway	102	73	366	444	471		668	
Persia	772	347	122	30	674		725	
Peru	9,132	2,656	13,331	4,738	19,400	2,155	32,949	28,247
Portugal	833	386	363	104	7,811		17,789	
Russia	11,385	4,664	3,465	890	19,012		7,861	
Salvador	80	60	150	94	1,110	283,349	1,073	536,525
San Domingo					240			
Senegambia						376,028		
Spain	1,920,042	1,177,177	2,576,289	1,539,561	1,918,661	914,160	2,174,298	813,162
Sweden	1,607	2,295	4,845	6,005	24,992		30,461	122,237
Switzerland	157,444	89,830	238,163	125,579	115,108		158,210	
Turkey	2,327	761	1,205	452	2,136		1,841	
United States	22,669,420	9,169,787	29,080,276	9,554,446	15,130,367	67,322,986	20,145,763	79,651,605
Uruguay	2	10			728	150	45	
Venezuela	73,738	25,435	37,819	14,207	23,950		16,806	
Zanzibar	20	37	80	211	2,626		2,367	
Total	**$40,024,885**	**$22,477,943**	**$52,018,648**	**$25,782,632**	**$34,000,440**	**$90,854,953**	**$42,253,938**	**$105,016,902**

Imports and Exports by Custom Houses

CUSTOM HOUSES	1894–95 IMPORTS	1894–95 EXPORTS	1895–96 IMPORTS	1895–96 EXPORTS
Acapulco	161,684	124,251	178,065	101,672
Altata		32,437	45,897	931,759
Camargo	6,046		6,678	14,380
Campeche	186,397	938,972	258,161	1,097,183
Ciudad Juárez	2,571,977	14,255,800	2,677,525	19,599,797
Ciudad Porfirio Díaz	2,386,451	2,850,062	4,228,658	3,065,014
Coatzacoalcos	40,348	135,670	315,249	328,014
Frontera	321,219	334,136	306,235	428,863
Guaymas	453,199	904,018	557,261	19,994
Guerrero	2,639	21,481	3,645	14,553
Isla del Carmen	67,430	1,273,788	80,277	1,584,421
La Morita	29,641	350,549	50,965	640,444
La Paz	59,433	691,001	119,334	703,944
Laredo	3,449,802	3,016,000	3,868,950	3,311,273
Las Palomas	88,570		21,259	276,594
Manzanillo	189,795	324,146	91,349	246,403
Matamoros		322,111	1,566,087	285,299
Mazatlán	1,458,693	6,285,777		5,451,804
Mier	16,525	73,604	19,403	148,007
Nogales	549,189	2,787,590	656,676	4,937,624
Progreso	1,092,079	7,865,933	1,696,714	8,102,908
Puerto Angel	9,950	388,661	12,794	254,169
Salina Cruz	40,016	56,709	23,627	59,571
San Blas	181,532	669,122	214,894	679,966
Santa Rosalía	331,370	2,235,189	377,235	3,028,030
Soconusco	183,241	825,575	182,690	1,288,956
Tampico	3,642,007	15,546,228	8,685,442	23,920,464
Tijuana	7,438	36,749	14,088	53,443
Todos Santos	132,049	143,241	152,776	164,466
Tonalá	163,651	372,076	182,536	127,566
Túxpam	50,735	382,277	70,332	1,369,380
Veracruz	16,123,505	27,413,009	15,296,544	22,354,298
Zapaluta	3,829	198,241	12,539	366,463
Total	**$34,000,440**	**$90,854,953**	**$42,253,938**	**$105,016,902**

The following is a list of the value of metals and commodities exported from Mexico during the fiscal year 1895–1896, which shows that they are all either mineral or agricultural products, these being only raw materials : The commodities are placed in the order of their relative importance in value.

METALS.

Gold ore	$160,555
Gold coin	169,794
Gold bullion	20,377,663
Silver ore	10,885,479
Silver coin	5,246,418
Silver bullion	26,345,160
Sulphate of silver	1,030,156
Foreign gold and silver and silver in other combinations	623,371
Total	$64,838,596

COMMODITIES.

Coffee	$8,103,302
Henequen	6,763,821
Cabinet and dye woods	4,206,880
Copper	3,909,485
Lead	2,531,624
Live animals	3,546,770
Hides and skins	2,331,999
Chewing gum	1,527,838
Tobacco	1,461,090
Vanilla	1,428,675
Ixtle	690,862
Zacaton—broom root	616,492
Chick-peas	352,737
Coal	270,176
Marble	258,668
Fruits	246,150
Sugar	169,662
Horse hair, beans, and jalap	247,768
All others	1,514,307
Total	40,178,306
	$105,016,902

EXPORTS OF MEXICAN COMMODITIES DURING THE TEN FISCAL YEARS, FROM JULY 1, 1886, TO JUNE 30, 1896.

FISCAL YEARS.	LIVE STOCK.		COCOA.		HIDES AND SKINS.		FRUITS.		WOOL. (raw.)		TOTAL VALUE of exports of domestic produce (not metals).
	Heads.	Value.	Weight, Kilograms.	Value.	Weight, Kilograms.	Value.	Weight, Kilograms.	Value.	Weight, Kilograms.	Value.	
1886–1887............	100,467	$ 470,097	663	$ 425	6,308,820	$2,211,439	1,999,072	$ 74,815	873,951	$169,324	$ 2,926,100
1887–1888............	106,221	506,997	659	397	5,109,243	1,864,471	1,796,278	51,945	56,483	12,518	2,436,338
1888–1889............	84,257	585,894	197	231	4,957,043	2,011,128	1,551,505	53,612	364,013	90,567	2,741,432
1889–1890............	91,913	493,223	7,666	3,633	4,743,326	1,013,129	1,896,515	68,581	124,950	26,826	2,505,392
1890–1891............	30,331	182,620	149	93	4,571,830	1,864,829	2,795,369	103,850	49	30	2,091,422
Totals in five years.......	413,189	$2,238,831	9,334	$4,779	25,690,262	$9,804,996	9,048,739	$352,803	1,419,446	$299,265	$12,700,674
Averages per annum....	82,638	$447,766	1,867	$956	5,138,052	$1,960,999	1,980,743	$70,561	283,889	$59,853	$2,640,135
1891–1892............	7,932	$ 56,589	....	....	5,335,971	$ 1,931,791	2,524,239	$105,395	126	$ 56	$ 2,093,831
1892–1893............	168,164	1,741,161	639	639	5,666,320	2,067,156	2,475,873	104,042	38,648	8,881	3,921,879
1893–1894............	19,054	144,122	1,501	1,983	5,619,227	2,256,460	2,842,523	139,147	68	15	2,541,727
1894–1895............	7,723	137,382	83,877	42,809	4,939,209	2,350,262	2,915,688	125,460	58,759	11,252	2,667,165
1895–1896............	266,838	3,543,549	2,774	2,543	3,929,841	2,422,099	6,488,921	246,150	41,376	5,851	6,220,192
Totals in five years.......	469,711	$5,622,803	88,791	$47,974	25,490,568	$11,027,768	17,247,244	$720,194	138,977	$26,055	$17,444,794
Averages per annum....	93,942	$1,124,560	17,758	$9,595	5,098,113	$2,205,554	3,449,448	$144,039	27,795	$5,211	$3,488,959
Totals in ten years......	882,900	$7,861,634	98,125	$52,753	51,180,830	$20,832,764	27,195,983	$1,072,997	1,558,423	$325,320	$30,145,468
Averages per annum....	88,290	$786,163	9,812	$5,275	5,118,083	$2,083,276	2,719,598	$107,300	155,842	$32,532	$3,014,547

EXPORTS OF MEXICAN COMMODITIES DURING THE TEN FISCAL YEARS, FROM JULY 1, 1886, TO JUNE 30, 1896—(Continued).

FISCAL YEARS.	CABINET WOODS.		DYE WOODS.		COAL.		OTHER ARTICLES (not metals) exported. Value.	TOTAL VALUE of exports of domestic produce (not metals).
	Weight, Kilograms.	Value,	Weight, Kilograms.	Value.	Weight, Kilograms.	Value.		
1886–1887	66,720,699	$ 974,739	48,169,637	$ 869,802	....	....	$10,860,786	$12,705,327
1887–1888	46,902,480	969,322	44,944,581	773,671	402,243	$ 2,177	13,648,223	15,443,393
1888–1889	39,678,782	694,609	36,565,209	684,592	83,552,558	350,171	16,902,344	17,631,716
1889–1890	45,009,669	805,009	44,934,537	921,728	45,149,902	188,507	19,457,462	21,372,706
1890–1891	53,044,251	907,273	39,981,205	811,624	39,482,132	160,702	23,049,002	24,928,601
Totals in five years....	251,436,881	$4,350,952	214,595,169	$4,061,417	168,586,805	$701,557	$83,067,817	$93,081,743
Averages per annum...	50,287,376	$870,190	42,919,034	$812,283	33,717,379	$140,311	$16,793,563	$18,616,349
1891–1892	53,536,153	$ 882,658	39,180,385	$ 767,217	55,069,921	$221,154	$ 22,365,551	$ 24,236,580
1892–1893	46,269,557	746,717	44,133,509	916,512	8,279,968	33,960	26,983,447	28,680,636
1893–1894	44,762,231	673,560	61,233,904	1,399,576	49,729,184	205,605	28,045,199	30,323,940
1894–1895	118,667	631,143	81,694,951	2,056,030	53,192,261	232,919	31,128,063	34,048,155
1895–1896	56,271	971,678	110,239,715	2,912,476	66,174,597	270,176	29,803,784	33,958,114
Totals in five years....	144,742,879	$3,905,756	336,482,464	$8,051,811	233,345,931	$963,814	$138,326,044	$151,247,425
Averages per annum...	28,948,576	$781,151	67,296,493	$1,610,362	46,669,186	$192,763	$27,665,209	$30,249,485
Totals in ten years....	396,179,760	$8,256,708	551,077,633	$12,113,228	401,932,826	$1,665,371	$222,293,861	$244,329,168
Averages per annum...	39,617,976	$825,671	55,107,763	$1,211,323	40,193,283	$166,537	$22,229,386	$24,432,917

STATEMENT OF EXPORTS OF SOME AGRICULTURAL PRODUCTS DURING THE FISCAL YEARS FROM JULY 1, 1877, TO JUNE 30, 1896.

FISCAL YEARS.	ORCHILLA. Weight in Kilograms.	ORCHILLA. Value in Mexican Currency.	HENEQUEN. Weight in Kilograms.	HENEQUEN. Value in Mex. Currency.	IXTLE. Weight in Kilograms.	IXTLE. Value in Mexican Currency.	COFFEE. Weight in Kilograms.	COFFEE. Value in Mex. Currency.	TOBACCO. Weight in Kilograms.	TOBACCO. Value in Mexican Currency.	TOTAL VALUE OF EXPORTS. Successive Annual Increase per ct.	TOTAL VALUE OF EXPORTS. Value.
1877–1878	3,802,343	$ 228,146	11,389,180	$ 1,078,076	2,167,236	$ 257,768	4,867,779	$ 1,242,041	111,211	$ 86,713	....	$ 2,892,744
1878–1879	2,211,203	154,679	13,442,489	1,267,375	1,668,395	191,287	8,654,494	2,230,097	182,995	142,532	+37.723	3,983,970
1879–1880	909,647	54,581	20,574,513	1,945,397	2,454,600	291,978	7,656,267	1,084,473	396,192	310,146	+15.123	4,586,483
1880–1881	255,240	15,315	24,161,197	2,285,389	3,432,676	408,278	8,706,827	2,243,782	477,188	371,674	+16.089	5,324,438
1881–1882	1,582,600	115,618	26,182,071	2,672,107	4,748,979	620,199	10,447,805	2,444,538	351,486	351,253	+15.931	6,173,715
Av'ge in 5 years..	1,752,206	$ 113,268	19,149,890	$ 1,849,651	2,882,359	$ 353,902	8,066,634	$ 2,022,986	304,214	$ 252,464	+21.216	$ 4,592,270
1882–1883	1,189,430	74,629	30,069,409	3,311,063	5,153,025	596,533	8,556,899	1,717,191	265,481	272,160	- 3.274	$ 5,971,576
1883–1884	899,480	75,053	45,538,272	4,165,020	3,523,589	434,431	6,917,720	1,579,021	402,190	307,970	+ 9.879	6,561,495
1884–1885	506,097	73,772	46,173,579	3,988,790	6,190,409	672,583	5,824,276	1,201,673	363,686	412,913	- 3.227	6,349,731
1885–1886	980,999	71,870	40,506,805	2,929,116	6,046,152	523,972	8,385,641	1,699,724	545,916	528,568	- 9.394	5,753,250
1886–1887	1,311,786	116,891	39,536,048	3,991,628	3,881,621	348,842	8,326,215	2,627,477	844,420	850,807	+34.368	7,845,645
Av'ge in 5 years..	979,358	$ 82,443	40,364,841	$ 3,659,123	4,958,959	$ 515,272	7,602,150	$ 1,765,017	480,339	$ 474,484	+ 5.670	$ 6,496,339
1887–1888	1,149,999	106,291	36,754,947	6,229,460	3,570,628	361,687	6,528,086	2,431,025	764,131	830,362	+26.908	9,956,825
1888–1889	149,662	12,536	38,396,970	6,872,593	5,454,944	594,118	9,243,091	3,886,034	969,960	971,886	+23.907	12,337,167
1889–1890	1,312,550	114,797	39,371,774	7,392,245	7,429,770	827,981	10,009,642	4,811,000	1,014,745	948,332	+14.243	14,094,355
1890–1891	17,637	1,351	53,731,679	7,048,557	7,676,926	833,350	14,656,777	6,150,359	1,041,962	1,105,447	+ 7.341	15,129,064
1891–1892	17,982	985	56,337,719	6,358,220	6,610,561	617,300	11,058,279	5,514,355	1,560,610	1,746,928	- 5.891	14,237,788
Av'ge in 5 years..	529,566	$ 47,192	44,918,618	$ 6,780,215	6,148,576	$ 644,887	10,299,175	$ 4,558,554	1,070,282	$ 1,120,591	+13.302	$ 13,151,040
1892–1893	319,751	16,657	60,424,057	8,893,091	6,327,570	588,487	14,514,949	8,727,119	1,391,368	1,459,690	+38.258	19,685,024
1893–1894	540,330	14,019	56,625,651	6,718,667	5,667,424	461,614	18,866,590	11,766,090	1,983,364	1,755,314	+ 5.235	20,715,704
1894–1895	410,454	11,300	67,157,018	7,724,092	4,342,621	349,537	16,512,648	12,670,783	1,310,902	1,460,133	+ 7.242	22,215,845
1895–1896	384,295	10,368	59,342,038	6,768,007	7,154,845	694,922	11,463,558	8,103,302	1,333,109	1,461,090	-23.308	17,037,689
Av'ge in 4 years..	413,207	$ 13,086	60,887,191	$ 7,525,959	5,873,115	$ 523,640	15,339,436	$ 10,316,823	1,504,686	$ 1,534,057	+ 6.882	$ 19,913,565
Total for 19 years	17,958,485	$1,266,358	765,715,506	$91,548,783	93,441,931	$9,664,865	191,197,543	$83,000,084	15,292,916	$15,373,918	....	$200,854,508
Av'ge in 19 years.	945,183	$ 66,677	40,300,816	$ 4,818,357	4,917,996	$ 508,677	10,063,028	$ 4,368,426	804,890	$ 809,153	....	$ 10,571,184

REMARKS.—The records regarding the Exports to which this statement refers, before the year 1877–1878 are not reliable.

The increase of the average yearly amount of exports, on the second period of five years of this statement was 41.462 per cent. as compared with the average of the first period.

    "   "   "   "   "   " third "   five "   "   102.438 "   "   " second "

    "   "   "   "   "   " fourth "   four "   "   51.421 "   "   " third "

The grand total amount of the Exports of the five articles of domestic production specified in this statement was seventy times as much as the amount of the first year 1877–1878.

The average yearly successive increase of the Exports herein specified, was 10.852 per cent.

In record to the decrease of something more than 23 per cent. in the amount of exports registered in the fiscal year 1895–1896, it may be stated that while there was undoubtedly

VALUE OF EXPORTS FROM MEXICO FROM JULY 1, 1882, TO JUNE 30, 1892.

PRECIOUS AND OTHER METALS.

NOMENCLATURE.	1882–1883.	1883–1884.	1884–1885.	1885–1886.	1886–1887.	1887–1888.	1888–1889.	1889–1890.	1890–1891.	1891–1892.
Argentiferous copper		235 00	187 00							317,242 75
Argentiferous lead	$ 13,025 40	5,200 00	8,656 40	25,527 00	3,044 24	51,772 00	19,288 77			1,457,878 32
Base silver		2,450 00	2,016 00	3,450 00	5,400 00	8,102 00	11,957 69	1,810 00	1,382 00	3,900 00
Gold foreign coin	148,055 96	22,047 00	144,457 00	55,674 38	35,820 87	21,578 85	25,426 00	13,204 00	20,594 00	33,684 00
Gold in lingots	548,039 23	696,652 97	490,429 45	290,529 60	284,506 09	347,547 24	349,507 53	457,610 59	612,619 12	751,408 18
Gold Mexican coin	331,708 00	200,816 25	391,097 23	316,938 57	198,758 75	238,104 00	253,255 00	96,592 00	134,219 00	175,524 00
Gold ore		29,832 99	500 00							31,289 00
Silver foreign coin	146,615 59	205,595 75	97,821 50	56,892 37	395,584 37	52,833 83	154,347 02	141,032 70	229,806 85	97,885 00
Silver in lingots	4,773,928 15	5,312,310 49	5,881,178 03	5,014,237 88	5,568,735 85	6,504,451 23	6,629,262 75	7,250,958 68	6,751,419 07	6,559,670 30
Silver Mexican coin	22,969,583 90	25,999,875 68	25,394,262 05	21,969,957 87	21,955,759 85	16,841,117 86	22,686,337 29	23,084,489 40	17,622,171 10	26,478,376 00
Silver mixed with gold			181,118 98	247,263 62	559,503 26	184,807 22	233,247 23	368,871 87	729,134 81	1,294,087 14
Silver ore	592,189 20	896,354 98	1,332,896 91	1,809,836 84	3,737,888 79	5,928,303 97	7,623,589 07	6,394,062 41	8,874,457 24	10,478,293 92
Sulphite of silver	105,512 26	99,862 19	142,430 37	116,092 70	815,506 68	827,769 51	798,556 64	803,058 58	1,280,768 97	1,458,095 37
Total	$29,628,657 69	$33,473,283 30	$33,774,050 92	$29,906,400 83	$33,560,502 56	$31,006,187 71	$38,785,274 99	$38,621,290 23	$36,256,372 16	$49,137,303 98

COMMODITIES.

	1882–1883.	1883–1884.	1884–1885.	1885–1886.	1886–1887.	1887–1888.	1888–1889.	1889–1890.	1890–1891.	1891–1892.
Ale			10,164 00	2,800 00	2,480 00	8,030 10	30,288 56	31,332 50	29,989 03	22,413 45
Bags			5,039 66	22,507 72			13,279 00	23,333 25	3,129 00	2,524 00
Bones			691 96	1,121 00	6,384 00	2,400 00	6,760 00	3,874 25	6,982 00	2,872 00
Brandy	3,430 75	4,650 04	3,603 50	29,888 53	3,510 25	2,441 00	4,117 00	9,316 37	14,323 50	5,097 50
Brown sugar	1,468 95	946 38	5,038 97	4,462 79	6,786 44	39,027 44	8,880 25	12,516 39	29,202 58	41,626 10
Chapapote	32,132 17	11,767 10	10 00			3,771 80	3,567 50	5,628 40	5,735 00	9,083 00
Cheese	653 52	1,570 08	74			1,604 00	13,073 75	12,682 00	790 00	268,939 00
Chewing gum	207 50	18 00	66,809 68	158,757 56	357,413 22	375,956 61	595,636 61	716,746 33	1,286,997 10	703,571 95
Chic peas	82,205 38	134,537 65	4,073 00	11,617 75	38,555 89	33,182 50	27,707 00	98,141 40	98,251 28	283,251 73
Coal	28,855 44	19,715 00	70,436 03	247,348 82	2,434 65	2,177 00	350,170 60	188,507 00	160,702 35	221,154 22
Coffee	3,050 00	766 00	16,960 67	1,699,723 82	2,627,477 11	2,431,024 99	3,886,034 53	4,811,000 48	6,150,358 72	5,514,355 15
Copper	1,717,190 85	1,579,020 83	1,201,673 38	2,330 72	37,560 13	615,666 00	817,089 18	735,183 60	940,920 00	860,378 94
Copper ore	65,996 00	39,297 00					13,775 03	1,857 00	850 00	8,937 55
Corn			25,800 00	7,655 54	18,669 99	25,880 07	818 00	597 00	8,108 80	26,028 31
Cotton	63,684 11	5,488 82	2,253 00					11,781 40	3,331 00	7,633 00
Cotton seed	90 00	2 40					3,175 00		3,138 40	7,449 00
Carried forward	$1,999,564 67	$1,797,773 30	$1,412,553 25	$2,188,288 25	$3,128,620 83	$3,540,461 48	$5,775,271 66	$6,662,497 03	$8,742,308 76	$7,985,334 90

COMMODITIES—(Continued).

NOMENCLATURE.	1882–1883.	1883–1884.	1884–1885.	1885–1886.	1886–1887.	1887–1888.	1888–1889.	1889–1890.	1890–1891.	1891–1892.
Brought forward	$1,999,564 67	$1,797,773 30	$1,412,553 25	$2,188,288 25	$3,128,620 83	$3,540,461 48	$5,775,271 66	$6,662,497 03	$8,742,308 76	$7,985,324 99
Documents	....	....	....	....	....	....	28,211 00	111,535 00	6,464 00	9,654 00
Empty barrels	1430 00	365 25	5,724 00	4,008 00	4,219 00	6,336 00	5,313 00	12,275 00	18,769 50	10,876 00
Equipages	19482 00	12,428 00	14,005 41	19,580 75	23,543 00	12,032 00	24,912 75	15,366 00	39,734 25	19,090 00
Essence of aloes	....	....	....	9,351 75	18,073 00	2,892 66	2,470 00	2,005 00	8,415 00	17,080 00
Feathers	1,372 00	1,900 12	1,055 75	2,255 00	2,960 00	910 00	1,331 00	3,324 00	17,911 00	59,144 22
Fine pearls	18,500 00	40,870 00	38,750 00	7,700 00	19,200 00	58,300 00	35,000 00	88,750 00	17,500 00	19,550 00
Fresh and salted meats	181 00	800 13	4,405 00	10,139 04	18,169 00	3,367 30	2,444 00	1,247 50	66 00	1,180 00
Fruits	78,898 42	78,936 59	74,928 38	73,942 02	74,814 99	51,945 00	53,612 00	68,581 25	103,849 62	105,395 28
Guano	....	1,233 84	6,200 00	6,200 00	....	68,024 14	35,362 30	28,025 00	....	29,000 00
Gypsum	4,010 00	700 00	6,575 00	....	....	....	....	6,842 00	4,629 00	7,992 02
Hats	4,251 12	5,086 02	2,266 25	4,223 25	4,777 65	5,297 47	6,608 82	8,070 75	12,680 77	6,606 50
Henequen	3,311,062 64	4,165,020 35	3,988,799 97	2,929,116 03	3,901,628 19	6,229,459 62	6,872,592 87	7,392,244 69	7,048,556 76	6,358,220 15
Honey	115,817 56	106,262 29	123,547 70	59,455 84	44,649 00	50,455 42	51,789 10	103,266 49	91,874 92	172,722 08
Horse hair	62,007 77	79,704 76	67,661 30	71,133 38	55,401 80	61,038 45	58,884 82	64,207 13	58,477 92	69,410 05
India-rubber	159,382 72	202,496 09	66,367 73	108,488 18	179,529 51	169,385 66	124,547 27	97,245 75	72,558 88	47,584 32
Indigo	630 50	45,855 00	30,156 25	119,086 50	62,862 40	79,226 66	11,987 50	85,305 37	93,143 88	7,979 00
Ixtle	596,533 23	434,430 94	672,583 34	523,972 47	348,841 60	361,682 22	594,118 55	827,980 61	823,349 84	617,300 22
Jalap	34,592 41	56,159 46	36,726 00	24,552 00	13,656 85	10,926 90	11,532 53	10,023 04	67,457 66	42,935 05
Jewels and precious stones	9,730 00	5,499 85	3,955 00	6,129 00	9,779 00	161,093 00	20,913 00	6,850 00	17,574 00	27,514 26
Lard	520	1,705	....	....	....	....	320 00	141 00	31 88	10,575 90
Lead	47,554 83	188,469 73	329,239 96	485,948 14	323,205 27	382,236 33	467,737 52	607,329 70	1,125,468 64	2,363,521 05
Lemons	745 50	877 46	1,596 50	3,283 00	8,307 45	63,079 75	54,029 00	79,988 50	70,675 00	43,280 04
Lima beans	90,641 11	75,518 91	68,486 00	43,501 74	79,969 82	120,839 84	151,145 99	279,839 56	268,506 38	127,552 25
Live animals	634,376 18	620,956 05	496,435 94	624,906 52	471,470 80	508,713 35	587,063 00	500,217 25	184,482 00	59,335 50
Manufactures	7,052 46	16,430 70	13,672 07	11,028 07	12,389 61	18,902 53	14,811 32	15,402 63	13,962 74	12,413 17
Manufactures returned	13,655 00	14,777 98	81,292 00	483,953 75	160,081 60	44,067 50	59,398 23	178,435 40	97,154 69	99,748 00
Marble	8,014 00	4,925 00	14,369 25	8,198 21	15,314 75	35,917 14	51,530 55	162,134 26	87,555 85	169,054 50
Oils	....	125 00	....	....	....	....	1,138 00	50 00	201 00	33,352 00
Orchilla	74,628 68	75,053 20	73,772 50	71,870 30	116,890 86	106,299 52	122,535 60	114,796 68	1,351 00	985 00
Other articles	118,809 84	155,382 49	202,469 79	154,738 50	145,295 13	105,706 95	100,911 13	102,348 85	73,883 44	75,511 82
Paper	8,172 66	5,396 33	3,977 00	10,040 07	9,553 08	11,149 36	12,886 73	19,979 44	22,051 75	20,245 90
Plants	2,200 00	3,273 26	9,103 50	8,636 48	10,235 35	16,692 75	13,635 40	21,969 00	15,151 00	18,336 70
Printed books	1,569 88	3,391 00	3,987 50	3,899 00	5,822 81	7,207 70	11,710 80	15,732 00	3,961 00	5,178 00
Rice	3 50	3 00	3,014 00	....	....	120 00	728 00	2,225 00	10,368 40	8,294 87
Salt	525 00	3,860 00	1,512 00	2,217 00	2,235 00	3,633 25	6,481 00	5,645 00	2,765 25	15,035 68
Carried forward	$7,424,414 68	$8,205,487 10	$7,853,020 34	$8,076,342 72	$9,271,517 35	$12,297,681 35	$15,263,964 44	$17,701,515 88	$19,162,891 82	$18,668,518 43

COMMODITIES—(Continued).

NOMENCLATURE.	1882–1883.	1883–1884.	1884–1885.	1885–1886.	1886–1887.	1887–1888.	1888–1889.	1889–1890.	1890–1891.	1891–1892.
Brought forward	$7,424,414 68	$8,205,487 10	$7,853,020 34	$8,076,342 72	$9,271,517 35	$12,297,681 35	$15,263,964 44	$17,701,515 88	$19,162,891 82	$18,668,518 43
Samples		929 68		3,020 00	1,731 38	2,734 78	98,059 28	26,157 50	9,745 90	17,553 00
Sarsaparilla	50,699 04	37,476 14	53,822 42	119,837 23	69,511 93	168,310 03	27,724 50	15,993 55	31,350 06	44,719 47
Skins	1,653,165 92	1,747,254 96	1,779,957 14	2,133,259 79	2,211,438 34	1,864,469 98	2,011,128 85	1,913,129 05	1,804,888 69	1,931,791 18
Starch		3,020 00	800 00				1,840 00		11,181 00	
Sugar	198,365 16	177,260 11	34,271 26	178,887 00	124,034 24	107,276 98	40,880 36	61,983 80	24,018 40	21,888 59
Tanning wood	6 21				39,683 28	35,078 36	10,532 50	14,484 00	22,163 00	8,892 00
Tin									140 00	11,600 00
Tin ore										14,040 68
Tobacco	272,160 18	307,969 85	412,912 84	528,568 28	850,807 39	830,362 50	971,885 97	948,332 17	1,105,446 73	1,746,927 96
Tortoise shell	48,420 44	50,435 54	67,663 85	20,198 88	6,836 00	199,993 50	32,643 45	30,258 74	24,411 31	26,959 73
Value in paper	27,191 00	19,076 00	159,503 00		16,494 00	1,964 00	31,379 00	43,286 90	2,073,706 50	290,626 00
Vanilla	443,850 75	497,502 75	471,611 52	463,395 25	693,891 05	451,372 53	926,903 25	917,409 66	519,741 04	969,611 58
Vegetables	19,596 60	14,958 55	13,082 79	16,784 68	32,603 24	15,648 05	3,374 95	1,512 25	1,768 61	2,244 53
Wood	1,917,323 67	2,008,913 65	1,754,346 04	1,688,799 14	1,848,792 98	1,754,296 66	1,390,214 71	1,739,138 30	1,725,527 08	1,676,351 40
Wool	306 00	43,148 01	171,859 20	220,071 09	169,324 33	12,518 40	90,566 70	26,826 40	30 00	55 75
Zacaton (broom root)	123,438 01	139,710 46	125,014 00	292,052 51	294,761 98	380,013 55	472,050 07	426,889 26	513,254 04	898,630 67
Total	$12,178,937 66	$13,252,213 12	$12,896,794 08	$13,741,316 57	$15,631,427 49	$17,879,720 67	$21,373,148 03	$23,878,098 46	$27,020,023 18	$26,330,410 97

RESUMÉ OF THE TOTAL EXPORTS.

	1882–1883.	1883–1884.	1884–1885.	1885–1886.	1886–1887.	1887–1888.	1888–1889.	1889–1890.	1890–1891.	1891–1892.
Precious metals	$29,628,657 69	$33,473,283 30	$33,774,050 92	$29,906,400 83	$33,560,502 56	$31,006,187 71	$38,785,274 99	$38,621,290 23	$36,256,372 16	$49,137,303 98
Commodities	12,178,937 66	13,252,213 12	12,896,794 08	13,741,316 57	15,631,427 49	17,879,720 67	21,373,148 03	23,878,098 46	27,020,023 18	26,330,410 97
Total	$41,807,595 35	$46,725,496 42	$46,670,845 00	$43,647,717 39	$49,191,930 05	$48,885,908 38	$60,158,423 02	$62,499,388 69	$63,276,395 34	$75,467,714 95

DESTINATION AND VALUE OF EXPORTS FROM MEXICO IN THE FISCAL YEARS FROM 1882 TO 1892.

PRECIOUS METALS.

DESTINATION.	1882-1883.	1883-1884.	1884-1885.	1885-1886.	1886-1887.	1887-1888.	1888-1889.	1889-1890.	1890-1891.	1891-1892.
Belgium		920 00								18,067 00
Colombia	298,937 55	153,791 00	372,556 98	47,359 00	52,490 00	68,076 21	71,575 00	35,998 85	53,813 40	10,776 00
Costa Rica			3,000 00	1,500 00	225 00	1,000 00		1,000 00		
France	3,561,987 13	2,325,310 78	1,624,728 38	3,447,116 60	4,401,222 74	3,626,489 74	2,729,232 44	2,477,299 29	2,753,395 33	3,830,444 32
Germany	392,955 92	498,591 24	628,028 95	834,628 92	1,289,910 82	1,326,544 72	1,281,805 76	954,722 26	1,764,446 75	2,484,012 02
Great Britain	15,201,600 36	17,265,462 28	13,784,962 91	9,417,463 53	11,122,019 69	7,935,735 71	10,459,405 10	10,865,360 47	8,045,962 89	12,165,795 23
Guatemala	94,975 00	130,915 00	64,400 00	2,000 00	2,300 00	33,881 25	253,996 07	114,385 65	168,691 15	83,573 00
Honduras				2,000 00	7,550 62	2,500 00	6,027 74	8,303 20	4,992 60	
Nicaragua					3,545 00			1,000 00		
Russia							450 00			
Salvador	8,515 40	2,940 00	5,498 00	4,709 33	490 00	490 00	450 00	2,412 30	2,133 00	399 00
Spain	1,035,013 00	273,112 50	889,099 50	654,487 28	104,343 60	97,131 25	335,763 08	63,750 00	52,104 10	90,671 00
United States	9,036,773 33	12,822,240 50	16,494,776 20	15,496,336 17	16,576,120 09	17,915,115 83	23,647,919 80	24,098,147 31	23,400,832 94	30,447,566 41
Total	$29,628,657 69	$33,473,283 30	$33,774,059 92	$29,906,400 83	$33,560,502 56	$31,006,187 71	$38,785,274 99	$38,621,290 23	$36,256,372 16	$49,137,303 98

COMMODITIES.

DESTINATION.	1882-1883.	1883-1884.	1884-1885.	1885-1886.	1886-1887.	1887-1888.	1888-1889.	1889-1890.	1890-1891.	1891-1892.
Argentine Republic										100 00
Austria							520 00			15 00
Belgium	29,040 00	69,329 00	32,370 00	25 00	67,326 42	25,583 16	50,544 00			322,592 97
China	59,229 59	55,394 05	38,087 11	73,188 00	41,757 66	41,883 65	28,422 55	41,603 50	845 00	
Colombia	750 00	750 00		43,603 00	1,242 00	1,882 80	3,000 00		3,602 88	20,272 75
Costa Rica				11,130 00					212 00	1,050 00
Ecuador	200 00									
France	642,918 42	556,688 20	610,728 27	489,160 18	711,298 40	848,233 57	766,805 89	681,960 21	890,156 21	807,941 19
Germany	732,763 29	719,684 89	792,575 65	738,770 28	885,859 29	850,563 37	779,757 33	739,050 89	1,021,428 11	1,860,219 58
Great Britain	2,056,642 25	2,064,689 87	1,582,317 10	2,182,604 21	2,240,166 88	2,605,229 52	2,076,129 89	2,856,762 05	2,836,765 44	3,102,160 45
Guatemala	686 00	1,773 87	400 00	25 00	2,766 90	946 00	2,287 00	3,285 00	25,020 32	60,167 17
Hayti	300 00	30 00	22,189 44			100 00	134,947 35	150,580 08	187,931 65	49,997 63
Holland		14,944 60						2,700 00		4,400 00
Honduras		609 50		10 00	890 00	52 00	50 00	4,555 00	920 00	4,732 89
Italy			70 00		570 00					
Carried forward	$3,521,779 55	$3,483,893 98	$3,078,735 57	$3,538,515 67	$3,951,857 55	$4,374,474 07	$3,842,464 61	$4,480,496 73	$4,966,881 40	$6,233,649 63

COMMODITIES—(Continued).

DESTINATION.	1882-1883.	1883-1884.	1884-1885.	1885-1886.	1886-1887.	1887-1888.	1888-1889.	1889-1890.	1890-1891.	1891-1892.
Brought forward	$3,521,779 55	$3,483,893 98	$3,078,735 57	$3,538,515 67	$3,951,857 55	$4,374,474 07	$3,842,464 61	$4,480,496 73	$4,966,881 40	$6,233,649 63
Nicaragua					670 00	25 00	787 60	266 00	1,296 71	10,914 01
Peru			30 00	600 00						
Russia		10,140 00	300 00		280 00			390 00	4,000 00	26,200 00
Salvador	288 00	12,375 00					685 00		2,502 00	3,120 00
Spain	954,245 74	743,644 09	353,545 67	259,236 50	520,950 24	360,710 77	323,567 88	470,306 37	463,089 64	571,178 86
Switzerland			48 00							
United States	7,702,324 37	9,002,160 05	9,448,284 84	9,933,258 39	11,152,594 70	13,144,510 83	17,205,442 94	18,924,293 36	21,584,253 43	19,485,098 47
Venezuela	300 00		15,850 00	9,706 00	5,075 00		200 00	2,346 00	250 00	250 00
Total	$12,178,937 66	$13,252,213 12	$12,896,794 08	$13,741,316 56	$15,631,427 49	$17,879,720 67	$21,373,148 03	$23,878,098 46	$27,020,023 18	$26,330,410 97

TOTAL EXPORTS.

DESTINATION.	1882-1883.	1883-1884.	1884-1885.	1885-1886.	1886-1887.	1887-1888.	1888-1889.	1889-1890.	1890-1891.	1891-1892.
Argentine Republic							520 00			100 00
Austria	$29,040 00	70,249 00	34,370 00	25 00	67,326 42	25,583 16	50,544 00			15 00
Belgium									845 00	340,659 97
China	358,167 14	209,185 05	410,644 09	90,962 00	94,247 66	109,959 86	99,997 55	77,512 35	57,416 28	31,048 75
Colombia			14,130 00	13,590 00	2,242 00	2,107 80	3,000 00	212 00	212 00	1,050 00
Costa Rica	200 00	750 00								
Ecuador										
France	4,204,905 55	2,881,908 98	2,235,456 65	3,936,276 78	5,112,521 14	4,474,723 31	3,496,038 33	3,159,259 50	3,653,551 33	4,644,385 51
Germany	1,125,719 21	1,218,276 13	1,420,604 60	1,571,399 20	2,175,779 11	2,177,106 09	2,061,563 09	1,693,773 15	2,785,874 86	4,344,231 60
Great Britain	17,258,242 00	19,330,152 15	15,367,280 01	11,600,067 74	13,362,186 57	10,540,965 23	12,535,534 99	13,722,122 52	10,884,728 33	15,207,955 68
Guatemala	93,501 00	132,688 87	64,800 00	2,025 00	5,066 90	34,827 25	255,383 67	117,670 65	193,711 47	143,740 17
Hayti			30 00			100 00				
Holland		14,944 66	24,187 44		870 00		134,947 35	150,586 08	187,931 65	49,997 63
Honduras		609 50	70 00	10 00	570 00	52 00		3,700 00	920 00	4,400 00
Italy	300 00		10 00		8,220 62	2,500 00	50 00	4,555 00	6,289 31	4,732 89
Nicaragua		30 00	600 00	600 00		25 00	6,815 34	8,569 20		10,914 01
Peru										
Russia						490 00	1,135 00	2,802 30	4,000 00	26,200 00
Salvador	8,803 40	15,315 00	5,798 00	4,709 33	280 00				4,655 00	3,519 00
Spain	1,989,258 74	1,016,750 59	1,242,645 17	913,523 78	625,293 84	457,842 02	659,330 96	534,057 27	515,193 74	661,849 86
Switzerland										
United States	16,739,097 70	21,824,400 55	25,853,061 04	25,429,594 56	27,728,714 79	31,059,626 66	40,853,362 74	43,022,440 67	44,983,086 37	49,932,664 88
Venezuela	300 00	15,850 00	15,850 00	9,706 00	5,075 00		200 00	2,346 00	250 00	250 00
Total	$41,807,595 35	$46,725,496 42	$46,670,845 00	$43,647,177 39	$49,191,930 05	$48,885,908 38	$60,158,423 02	$62,499,388 69	$63,276,395 34	$75,467,774 95

TRADE BETWEEN MEXICO AND THE UNITED STATES.

It is quite difficult to make a correct statement of the trade between Mexico and the United States, because the official data of both governments never used to agree, especially on account of the different currencies prevailing in the two countries. As we have the silver standard, all our public accounts are kept in silver, and that makes our exports appear twice as large in value as they really are, when stated in the money of the United States, while we give our imports in the value of the country from whence they come, that is their gold value. That fact, which has often been overlooked, has caused the prevailing idea that there is a very large balance of trade in favor of Mexico, because the exports of United States commodities in Mexico amount to a given figure a year, the imports to this country of Mexican commodities amount to over double that figure ; but it must be borne in mind that the former is in silver while the latter is in gold. For instance, according to the Mexican Bureau of Statistics the imports into Mexico of merchandise from the United States in the fiscal year ended June 30, 1896, amounted to \$20,145,763, while the exports of metals and commodities from Mexico to the United States during the same year amounted to \$79,651,695, the proportion being almost four to one ; but if the imports are doubled as they ought to be, because the Mexican currency is silver, they amount to \$40,291,526, and if the exports of Mexico into the United States, calculated also in silver, are reduced to gold, they will amount to one half or \$39,825,847.50.

In corroboration of this statement I will mention the fact that according to the data of the Statistical Bureau of the United States Treasury Department, the exports to Mexico of commodities and precious metals from the United States during the last fiscal year, ending June 30, 1897, amounted to \$23,535,213 while the imports into the United States of commodities and precious metals amounted to \$30,-714,366. Since March 1893, however, the Statistical Bureau of the United States Treasury Department, has reduced to gold the silver value of the Mexican metals and commodities imported in this country, and its data come now nearer to the mark, as in the year 1896 it gives the total exports of merchandise from this country into Mexico as \$19,450,256, while the total imports of merchandise from Mexico into this country are \$17,456,177.

The figures of our exports appear very large in the Mexican returns, because our merchandise is sold in gold markets, and their gold price is reduced to silver, and increased in the same proportion in which silver depreciates. It is not therefore the amount of merchandise which has increased so much, as that the price has been swollen in reducing it from gold to silver. In that regard the returns from the United States Statistical Bureau are more in conformity with the facts.

Another cause of the discrepancy between the statistics of both countries is that the Statistical Bureau of the United States Treasury Department had not, prior to March 3, 1893, any data of commodities exported to Mexico by way of the frontier, as there was no law which provided for the collection of such data, and a very large portion of the trade between the two countries is carried on by the frontier, especially since the railroads connecting both countries were finished.[1] That deficiency was only in relation to the exports, as the imports were duly declared for the payment of duties, and therefore the statistics of the United States necessarily were deficient and incomplete about the exports to Mexico of United States commodities, and that accounts in a great measure for the discrepancy between the official data published by both governments, and for the great discrepancy between exports and imports which appear in the statistics of the United States for those years.

From the preceding remarks it will be understood why there is such a great discrepancy between the data of the respective Bureaus.

It is very difficult to make a correct statement of the trade between the two countries previous to the organization of the Bureau of Statistics of the United States ; but I found in a book published in Washington in 1860 by Mr. Carlos Butterfield, entitled "The United States and Mexican Mail Steamship Line and Statistics of Mexico," a statement of the imports and exports between Mexico and the United States from 1826 to 1858, taken as he states from official data of the United States Treasury Reports, which I will use.

That statement is complemented by two tables furnished to me by Hon. Worthington C. Ford, Chief of the Bureau of Statistics of the Treasury Department. The first contains a statement of the trade between the United States and Mexico, during the forty-six years from 1851 to 1897, and the second is a full statement of that trade, including gold and silver during the same period. (Pages 174 and 175.)

I have prepared besides from the official publications of the Bureau of Statistics of the United States Treasury Department, a detailed statement of the commodities imported into the United States from Mexico, and exported from the United States to Mexico during the

---

[1] For these reasons the statements of the Statistical Bureau of the United States, previous to the fiscal year ended June 30, 1892, contained the following foot-note :

" In the absence of law providing for the collection of statistics of exports to adjacent foreign territory over railways, the values of exports to Mexico, from 1883 to 1893 inclusive, have been considerably under-stated. Since March, 1893, there has been a law in force for the collection of exports by railways. According to official information from Mexican sources, the value of imports into that country from the United States during the year ending June 30, 1888, was $19,264,673, including precious metals valued at $38,362. Prior to 1866 the figures include gold and silver imported and exported. For 1866 and subsequent years, merchandise only."

years 1858 to 1897, which is complete so far as the records of this government go, and contains very valuable information.

I will give first a partial statement prepared by the Bureau of Statistics of the Mexican Government of the total imports to Mexico and the imports from the United States of America from the fiscal year 1872–1873 to 1895–1896, and then another detailed statement prepared by the same Bureau of the total exports from Mexico and the exports to the United States of America from the fiscal year 1877–1878 to 1895–1896.

From said data it will be seen that the trade of Mexico with the United States is increasing very rapidly, notwithstanding the difficulty thrown in the way by high protective tariffs. Only a few years ago, as will be seen by the appended statement, our largest trade was with Great Britain, the United States occupying the second place, while now the United States occupies the first place, both in amount of our exports and imports.[1]

Value of exports during the fiscal year 1872–1873 with their destination.

Great Britain	$12,479,547.75	Guatemala and Honduras.	80,999.52
United States	11,366,530.76	Italy	17,389.00
France	4,604,417.38	Belgium	4,784.00
Panama (New Grenada)	1,579,015.12	Ecuador	2,931.75
Germany	802,643.83		
Spain and the Island of Cuba	752,891.91	Total	$31,691,151.02

TOTAL IMPORTS TO MEXICO AND IMPORTS FROM THE UNITED STATES FOR THE FISCAL YEARS, 1872–1873 TO 1895–1896.

	IMPORTS FROM THE UNITED STATES.	TOTAL IMPORTS.
	Value.	Value.
1872–1873	$5,231,255	$20,166,013
1873–1874	5,946,614	23,282,299
1874–1875	5,028,636	18,793,494
1884–1885 First 6 months	5,045,531	11,893,342
1885–1886 First 6 months	5,145,736	10,585,898
1888–1889	22,669,421	40,024,894
1889–1890	29,080,276	52,018,659
1892–1893	26,235,963	43,413,131
1893–1894	14,351,785	30,287,489
1894–1895	15,130,367	34,000,440
1895–1896	20,145,763	42,253,938

MEXICO, November, 1896.

[1] This statement is corroborated by the following extract from an official report addressed to Lord Salisbury by Mr. Lionel Carden, British Consul-General at the City of Mexico, on the trade of Mexico during the year 1896:

"The great increase in the imports of American goods this year must be regarded by British merchants and manufacturers as another warning that unless they soon make a serious effort, they will have to give up all hope of profiting by the increase in the Mexican import trade, and may even lose part of the very limited share of it they at present enjoy."

TABLE SHOWING THE TOTAL EXPORTS FROM MEXICO AND THE EXPORTS
TO THE UNITED STATES OF AMERICA FROM THE FISCAL YEAR 1877–
1878 TO THE YEAR 1895–1896.

	EXPORTS TO THE UNITED STATES.			TOTAL EXPORTS FROM MEXICO.		
	Precious Metals.	Commodities.	Total.	Precious Metals.	Commodities.	Total.
1877–1878...	$ 8,664,052	$ 3,676,937	$ 12,340,989	$ 22,663,438	$ 6,622,223	$ 29,285,661
1878–1879...	7,439,815	4,741,724	12,181,539	21,528,938	8,362,540	29,891,478
1879–1880...	6,848,231	6,568,375	13,416,606	22,086,418	10,577,136	32,663,554
1880–1881...	7,601,767	6,556,424	14,158,191	19,354,704	10,573,994	29,928,698
1881–1882...	5,451,731	8,309,131	13,760,862	17,063,767	12,019,526	29,083,293
1882–1883...	9,036,773	7,702,325	16,739,098	29,628,658	12,178,937	41,807,595
1883–1884...	12,822,241	9,002,160	21,824,401	33,473,283	13,252,213	46,725,496
1884–1885...	16,404,776	9,448,285	25,853,061	33,774,051	12,896,794	46,670,845
1885–1886...	15,496,336	9,933,259	25,429,595	29,906,401	13,741,316	43,647,717
1886–1887...	16,576,120	11,152,595	27,728,715	33,560,503	15,631,427	49,191,930
1887–1888...	17,915,116	13,144,511	31,059,627	31,006,188	17,879,720	48,885,908
1888–1889...	23,647,920	17,205,443	40,853,363	38,785,275	21,373,148	60,158,423
1889–1890...	24,098,147	18,924,294	43,022,441	38,621,290	23,878,099	62,499,389
1890–1891...	23,400,833	21,582,253	44,983,086	36,256,372	27,020,023	63,276,395
1891–1892...	30,447,566	19,485,099	49,932,665	49,137,304	26,330,411	75,467,715
1892–1893...	40,113,882	23,723,761	63,837,643	56,504,305	31,004,916	87,509,221
1893–1894...	36,681,273	23,978,970	60,660,243	46,484,360	32,858,927	79,343,287
1894–1895...	38,852,843	28,470,143	67,322,986	52,535,854	38,319,099	90,854,953
1895–1896...	51,071,661	28,580,034	79,651,695	64,838,596	40,178,306	105,016,902
Total....	$392,571,083	$272,185,723	$664,756,806	$677,209,705	$374,698,755	$1,051,908,460

STATEMENT TAKEN FROM THE UNITED STATES TREASURY REPORTS
OF THE COMMERCIAL TRANSACTIONS BETWEEN MEXICO AND THE
UNITED STATES FROM 1826 TO 1850.

YEARS.	EXPORTS FROM MEXICO INTO THE UNITED STATES.	EXPORTS FROM THE UNITED STATES INTO MEXICO.	TOTAL TRADE BETWEEN THE TWO COUNTRIES.
1826....................	$ 3,916,000	$ 6,281,000	$ 10,197,000
1827....................	5,232,000	4,163,000	9,395,000
1828....................	4,814,000	2,886,000	7,700,000
1829....................	5,026,761	2,331,151	7,357,912
1830....................	5,235,241	4,837,458	10,072,699
1831....................	5,167,000	6,178,000	11,345,000
1832....................	4,293,954	3,467,541	7,761,495
1833....................	5,459,818	5,408,091	10,867,909
1834....................	8,666,668	5,265,053	13,931,721
1835....................	9,490,446	9,029,221	18,519,667
1836....................	5,615,819	6,040,635	11,656,454
1837....................	5,654,002	3,880,323	9,534,325
1838....................	3,127,153	2,787,362	5,914,515
1839...................	5,500,707	2,164,097	7,664,804
1840....................	4,175,000	2,515,341	6,690,341
1841....................	3,484,957	2,036,620	5,521,577
1842....................	1,996,694	1,534,493	3,531,187
1843....................	2,782,406	1,471,937	4,254,343
1844....................	2,387,000	1,794,833	4,181,833
1845....................	1,702,936	1,152,331	2,855,267
1846....................	1,836,621	1,531,180	3,367,801
1847....................	746,818	692,428	1,439,246
1848....................	1,581,247	4,058,446	5,639,693
1849....................	2,216,719	2,090,869	4,307,588
1850....................	2,135,336	2,012,827	4,148,163
Total	$102,245,303	$85,610,237	$187,855,540
Average	$4,089,812	$3,424,409	$7,514,222

STATEMENT SHOWING THE COMMERCE IN MERCHANDISE BETWEEN THE UNITED STATES AND MEXICO, BY YEARS AND DECADES, FROM 1851 TO 1897.

YEAR ENDING JUNE 30.	EXPORTS FROM THE UNITED STATES.			IMPORTS INTO THE UNITED STATES.			EXCESS OF EXPORTS (−) OR IMPORTS (+).
	Domestic.	Foreign.	Total.	Free.	Dutiable.	Total.	
1851	$ 1,014,690	$ 567,093	$ 1,581,783	$ 27,666	$ 693,120	$ 720,786	$ −860,997
1852	1,406,372	878,557	2,284,929	20,564	534,700	555,264	−1,729,665
1853	2,529,770	1,029,054	3,558,824	4,148	751,952	756,100	−2,802,724
1854	2,091,870	1,043,616	3,135,486	111,405	826,451	937,856	−2,197,630
1855	2,253,368	668,236	2,921,604	17,508	887,242	904,750	−2,016,854
1856	2,464,692	1,237,097	3,701,789	79,966	773,792	853,758	−2,848,031
1857	3,017,640	597,566	3,615,206	62,307	964,566	1,026,873	−2,588,333
1858	2,782,852	529,973	3,312,825	246,894	861,607	1,108,501	−2,204,324
1959	2,252,162	667,580	2,919,742	234,112	1,009,972	1,244,084	−1,675,658
1860	3,309,379	2,015,334	5,324,713	586,016	1,317,415	1,903,431	−3,421,282
Total 10 years..	$ 23,122,795	$ 9,234,106	$ 32,356,901	$ 1,390,586	$ 8,620,817	$ 10,011,403	$ −22,345,498
1861	$ 1,559,062	$ 651,364	$ 2,210,426	$ 253,703	$ 632,409	$ 886,112	$ −1,324,314
1862	1,840,720	340,454	2,181,174	289,011	441,977	730,988	−1,450,186
1863	7,441,579	1,579,045	9,020,624	446,070	2,597,812	3,043,882	−5,976,742
1864	7,765,133	1,505,464	9,270,597	385,037	5,743,408	6,128,445	−3,142,152
1865	13,819,972	2,530,867	16,350,839	369,915	5,850,959	6,220,874	−10,129,965
1866	3,701,599	871,619	4,573,218	402,568	1,323,524	1,726,092	−2,847,126
1867	4,823,614	572,182	5,395,796	402,779	669,157	1,071,936	−4,323,860
1868	5,048,420	1,392,919	6,441,339	482,228	1,108,439	1,590,667	−4,850,672
1869	3,835,699	1,047,408	4,883,107	511,319	1,824,845	2,336,164	−2,546,943
1870	4,544,745	1,314,955	5,859,700	522,907	2,192,758	2,715,665	−3,144,035
Total 10 years..	$ 54,380,543	$11,806,277	$ 66,186,820	$ 4,065,537	$ 22,385,288	$ 26,450,825	$ −39,735,995
1871	$ 5,044,033	$ 2,568,080	$ 7,612,113	976,117	$ 2,233,571	$ 3,209,688	$ −4,402,425
1872	3,420,658	2,122,931	5,543,589	1,156,257	2,846,663	4,002,920	−1,540,669
1873	3,941,019	2,323,882	6,264,901	3,065,140	1,211,025	4,276,165	−1,988,736
1874	4,016,148	1,930,691	5,946,839	3,026,661	1,319,703	4,346,364	−1,600,475
1875	3,872,004	1,865,278	5,737,282	3,863,302	1,311,292	5,174,594	−562,688
1876	4,700,978	1,499,594	6,200,572	3,920,633	1,229,939	5,150,572	−1,050,000
1877	4,503,802	1,389,692	5,893,494	3,756,191	1,448,073	5,204,264	−689,230
1878	5,811,429	1,649,275	7,460,704	3,723,281	1,528,221	5,251,502	−2,209,202
1879	5,400,380	1,351,864	6,752,244	3,981,402	1,511,819	5,493,221	−1,259,023
1880	6,065,974	1,800,519	7,866,493	4,852,659	2,356,934	7,209,593	−656,900
Total 10 years..	$ 46,776,425	$18,501,806	$ 65,278,231	$ 32,321,643	$ 16,997,240	$ 49,318,883	$ −15,959,348
1881	$ 9,198,077	$ 1,973,161	$ 11,171,238	$ 5,643,176	$ 2,674,626	$ 8,317,802	$ −2,853,436
1882	13,324,505	2,158,077	15,482,582	5,310,796	3,151,103	8,461,899	−7,020,683
1883	14,370,992	2,216,628	16,587,620	4,211,328	3,965,795	8,177,123	−8,410,497
1884	11,089,603	1,614,689	12,704,292	5,334,689	3,681,797	9,016,486	−3,687,806
1885	7,370,599	970,185	8,340,784	5,173,441	4,093,580	9,267,021	+926,237
1886	6,856,077	881,546	7,737,623	6,808,757	3,879,215	10,687,972	+2,950,349
1887	7,267,129	692,428	7,959,557	9,928,122	4,791,718	14,719,840	+6,760,283
1888	9,242,188	655,584	9,897,772	11,042,772	6,287,117	17,329,889	+7,432,117
1889	10,886,288	600,608	11,486,896	13,825,242	7,428,359	21,253,601	+9,766,705
1890	12,666,108	619,179	13,285,287	15,536,100	7,154,815	22,690,915	+9,405,628
Total 10 years..	$102,271,566	$12,382,085	$114,653,651	$ 82,814,423	$ 47,108,125	$129,922,548	$+15,268,897
1891	$ 14,199,080	$ 770,540	$ 14,969,620	$ 23,364,519	$ 3,931,473	$ 27,295,992	$+12,326,372
1892	13,696,531	597,468	14,293,999	23,702,496	4,405,029	28,107,525	+13,813,526
1893	18,891,714	676,920	19,568,634	27,145,469	6,409,630	33,555,099	+13,986,465
1894	12,441,805	400,344	12,842,149	21,560,011	7,166,995	28,727,006	+15,884,857
1895	14,582,484	423,422	15,005,906	12,903,789	2,731,999	15,635,788	+629,882
1896	18,686,797	763,459	19,450,256	13,819,698	3,636,479	17,456,177	−1,994,079
1897	22,726,596	694,468	23,421,064	13,999,017	4,521,555	18,511,572	−4,909,492
Total 7 years..	$115,225,007	$ 4,326,621	$119,551,628	$136,485,999	$ 32,803,160	$169,289,159	$+49,737,531

Treasury Department, Bureau of Statistics,   WORTHINGTON C. FORD,
       September 4, 1897.   *Chief of Bureau.*

STATEMENT SHOWING THE TOTAL COMMERCE BETWEEN THE UNITED STATES AND MEXICO, BY YEARS AND DECADES FROM 1851 TO 1897.

YEAR ENDING JUNE 30.	EXPORTS FROM THE UNITED STATES.			IMPORTS INTO THE UNITED STATES.			EXCESS OF EXPORTS (−) OR IMPORTS (+).
	Merchandise.	Gold and Silver.	Total.	Merchandise.	Gold and Silver.	Total.	
1851	$ 1,581,783	$ 2,652	$ 1,584,435	$ 720,786	$ 1,083,993	$ 1,804,779	$ +220,344
1852	2,284,929	3,255	2,288,184	555,264	1,093,942	1,649,206	−638,978
1853	3,558,824	1,734	3,560,558	756,100	1,411,885	2,167,985	−1,392,573
1854	3,135,486	528	3,136,014	937,856	2,525,334	3,463,190	+327,176
1855	2,921,604	1,200	2,922,804	904,750	1,978,080	2,882,830	−39,974
1856	3,701,789	450	3,702,239	853,758	2,714,923	3,568,681	−133,558
1857	3,615,206	....	3,615,206	1,026,873	4,958,984	5,985,857	+2,370,651
1858	3,312,825	3,000	3,315,825	1,108,501	4,368,964	5,477,465	+2,161,640
1859	2,919,742	72,804	2,992,546	1,244,084	4,095,890	5,339,974	+2,347,428
1860	5,324,713	29,360	5,354,073	1,903,431	5,032,441	6,935,872	+1,581,799
Total 10 years	$32,356,901	$114,983	$32,471,884	$10,011,403	$29,264,436	$39,275,839	$+6,803,955
1861	$ 2,210,426	$ 5,464	$ 2,215,890	$ 886,112	$ 2,803,101	$ 3,689,213	$+1,473,323
1862	2,181,174	....	2,181,174	730,988	1,953,864	2,684,852	+503,678
1863	9,020,624	51,588	9,072,212	3,040,882	1,485,702	4,526,584	−4,545,628
1864	9,270,597	3,410,957	12,681,554	6,128,445	1,755,946	7,884,391	−4,797,163
1865	16,350,839	664,241	17,015,080	6,220,874	1,133,299	7,354,173	−9,660,907
1866	4,573,218	15,000	4,588,218	1,726,092	2,429,511	4,155,603	−432,615
1867	5,395,796	56,452	5,452,248	1,071,936	2,849,038	3,920,974	−1,531,274
1868	6,441,339	12,924	6,454,263	1,590,667	4,525,255	6,115,922	−338,341
1869	4,883,107	2,000	4,885,107	2,336,164	4,895,842	7,232,006	+2,346,899
1870	5,859,700	15,696	5,875,396	2,715,665	10,383,366	13,099,031	+7,223,635
Total 10 years	$66,186,820	$4,234,322	$70,421,142	$26,447,825	$34,214,924	$60,662,749	$−9,758,393
1871	$ 7,612,113	$ 38,500	$ 7,650,613	$ 3,209,688	$14,301,475	$ 17,511,163	$ +9,860,550
1872	5,543,589	35,000	5,578,589	4,002,920	4,504,204	8,507,124	+2,928,535
1873	6,264,901	165,262	6,430,163	4,276,165	12,154,060	16,430,225	+10,000,062
1874	5,946,839	57,531	6,004,370	4,346,364	8,893,541	13,239,905	+7,235,535
1875	5,737,282	33,501	5,770,783	5,174,594	6,460,389	11,634,983	+5,864,200
1876	6,200,572	7,600	6,208,172	5,150,572	7,355,181	12,505,753	+6,297,581
1877	5,893,494	5,239	5,898,733	5,204,264	10,240,319	15,444,583	+9,545,850
1878	7,460,704	32,180	7,492,884	5,251,502	8,394,146	13,645,648	+6,152,764
1879	6,752,244	9,040	6,761,284	5,493,221	8,554,598	14,047,819	+7,286,535
1880	7,866,493	3,371	7,869,864	7,209,593	9,115,824	16,325,417	+8,455,553
Total 10 years	$65,278,231	$387,224	$65,665,455	$49,318,883	$89,973,737	$139,292,620	$+73,627,165
1881	$ 11,171,238	1,500	$ 11,172,738	$ 8,317,802	$ 9,136,324	$ 17,454,126	$ +6,281,388
1882	15,482,582	18,446	15,501,028	8,461,899	6,631,938	15,093,837	−407,191
1883	16,587,620	96,964	16,684,584	8,177,123	9,782,986	17,960,109	+1,275,525
1884	12,704,292	335,635	13,039,927	9,016,486	13,015,901	22,032,387	+8,992,460
1885	8,340,784	79,406	8,420,190	9,267,021	14,919,611	24,186,632	+15,766,442
1886	7,737,623	110,035	7,847,658	10,687,972	16,935,396	27,623,368	+19,775,710
1887	7,959,557	279,812	8,239,369	14,719,840	14,855,765	29,575,605	+21,336,236
1888	9,897,772	319,408	10,217,180	17,329,889	14,032,637	31,362,526	+21,145,346
1889	11,486,896	176,616	11,663,512	21,253,601	17,557,248	38,810,849	+27,147,337
1890	13,285,287	240,912	13,526,199	22,690,915	18,155,809	40,846,724	+27,320,525
Total 10 years	$114,653,651	$1,658,734	$116,312,385	$129,922,548	$135,023,615	$264,946,163	$+148,633,778
1891	$ 14,969,620	$ 227,734	$ 15,197,354	$ 27,295,992	$ 14,297,431	$ 41,593,423	$ +26,396,069
1892	14,293,999	168,584	14,462,583	28,107,525	19,174,034	47,281,559	+32,818,976
1893	19,568,634	473,942	20,042,576	33,555,099	22,951,604	56,506,703	+36,464,127
1894	12,842,149	708,932	13,551,081	28,727,006	12,790,199	41,517,205	+27,966,124
1895	15,005,906	551,064	15,556,970	15,635,788	9,644,160	25,279,948	+9,722,978
1896	19,450,256	926,560	20,376,816	17,456,177	29,166,241	46,622,418	+26,245,602
1897	23,421,064	114,149	23,535,213	18,511,572	12,202,794	30,714,366	+7,179,153
Total 7 years	$119,551,628	$3,170,965	$122,722,593	$169,289,159	$120,226,463	$289,515,622	$+166,793,029

STATEMENT SHOWING THE QUANTITIES AND VALUES OF THE PRINCIPAL AND ALL OTHER ARTICLES OF IMPORTS INTO THE UNITED STATES FROM, AND OF EXPORTS FROM THE UNITED STATES TO, MEXICO, 1858–1883.

IMPORTS OF MERCHANDISE FROM MEXICO.

Year ending June 30—	Breadstuffs and other farinaceous food.*		Coffee.		Copper, pigs, bars, ingots, old, and other unmanufactured.		Chemicals, drugs, dyes and medicines.			Hides and skins other than furs.	Hair unmanufactured.	India rubber and gutta-percha, crude or unmanufactured.		Jute, and other grasses, raw.	
	Indian corn.	All other.	Pounds.	$	Pounds.	$	Cochineal and indigo.	Dye-woods in sticks.	All other.†	$	$	Pounds.	$	Tons.	$
1858..	34,686	$28,198	29,687	$3,259	......	$1,437	†‡ 31,793	$107,649	$1,030	$496,929	$11,261	......	$143	406	$50,173
1859..	45,520	15,794	45,518	6,036	......	3,638	144,437	40,208	1,336	457,297	485	......	......	389	44,861
1860..	28,940	5,124	549,265	64,616	......	10,542	49,651	161,115	110	535,591	2,074	......	107	251	25,114
1861..	19,612	8,445	461,416	59,405	......	1,320	91,645	115,757	411	267,527	2,264	1,586	......	382	35,670
1862..	......	6,399	7,175	1,026	12,958	1,734	49,564	91,976	......	171,905	11,535	......	252	286	23,537
1863..	......	15,048	935,594	122,663	85,796	14,081	91,151	48,094	10,830	383,530	912	......	......	898	44,647
1864..	......	9,818	11,736	2,027	129,810	21,401	123,434	110,299	12,622	563,978	2,140	......	201	843	63,455
1865..	......	6,337	595	109	114,761	16,528	132,959	126,341	7,127	547,109	1,667	......	20	333	36,495
1866..	......	......	524,777	84,428	40,299	5,629	96,362	59,350	40,722	325,186	3,196	......	214	889	104,453
1867..	9,975	5,183	138,005	18,468	20,497	3,001	130,154	108,754	39,024	368,817	2,808	......	228	862	116,455
1868..	34,269	29,599	882,521	112,159	29,536	3,123	144,144	187,337	38,526	411,505	2,613	2,554	600	1,513	237,803
1869..	71,163	53,140	203,048	22,062	57,700	7,326	144,974	207,859	64,510	745,550	2,728	34,842	8,648	2,906	469,235
1870..	79,321	48,551	110,607	13,223	24,197	2,304	‡ 92,836	244,932	28,380	833,743	4,697	98,656	23,594	3,300	631,090
1871..	104,554	68,313	526,495	59,454	161,711	18,608	117,745	36,698	53,306	714,489	6,442	93,046	33,055	3,338	626,044
1872..	74,297	43,114	1,878,301	248,022	2,468	218	104,772	39,660	286,781	1,380,082	15,940	106,417	34,792	4,244	784,809
1873..	53,547	62,720	2,035,540	314,347	39,704	3,120	55,239	27,752	163,745	1,093,387	55,420	184,554	63,269	3,590	534,980
1874..	61,081	37,720	2,930,285	624,611	14,028	2,161	61,964	65,662	70,090	1,561,830	18,625	72,963	23,710	4,867	694,254
1875..	33,628	31,002	2,691,889	485,489	4,611	620	54,510	63,958	158,279	2,077,156	28,784	115,607	35,690	6,185	613,338
1876..	45,990	49,022	3,941,229	713,833	23,050	2,490	39,736	150,413	247,427	1,812,557	79,230	39,835	11,103	6,846	542,756
1877..	25,791	39,411	6,789,663	1,265,970	67,793	7,917	54,726	72,402	219,193	1,529,702	29,317	43,314	13,825	7,428	656,746
1878..	12,321	34,339	6,337,063	1,082,272	68,556	7,082	‡‡ 23,196	112,482	204,135	1,565,546	42,710	40,494	11,364	9,103	889,061
1879..	33,497	56,432	8,307,040	1,371,979	18,443	3,302	62,483	96,877	159,017	1,675,777	34,274	17,500	4,432	10,197	930,396
1880..	65,230	65,192	9,818,525	1,523,658	226	19	68,345	149,651	106,706	1,951,918	36,964	107,026	44,235	14,086	1,324,075
1881..	87,840	43,141	13,911,910	1,730,838	55,740	6,825	20,973	160,070	265,642	2,111,750	39,701	616,742	315,059	17,153	1,634,215
1882..	58,648	41,352	17,020,669	1,817,584	3,562	494	5,813	128,734	198,030	1,525,107	38,810	325,206	164,847	19,233	2,061,939
1883..	22,072	50,192	8,578,532	809,757	124	8	......	211,714	119,681	1,568,645	52,985	241,478	123,484	25,065	2,712,088

* All other breadstuffs comprise barley, barley malt, bread and biscuit, oats, rice, rye, wheat, wheat flour, meal of all kinds, peas and beans ; all other farinaceous food and preparations of breadstuffs.

† All other chemicals, drugs, dyes, and medicines include : Argols ; medicinal barks ; camphor, crude ; gums ; soda, nitrate of ; cutch and catechu ; opium : soda and salts of ; sulphur or brimstone ; chloride of lime or bleaching powder ; all chemicals, not elsewhere specified.　‡ Cochineal only ; no indigo included.

MEXICO, 1858–1883—*Continued.*

IMPORTS OF MERCHANDISE FROM MEXICO—*Continued.*

YEAR ENDING JUNE 30—	LEAD, PIGS, BARS, AND OLD. (POUNDS.)	LEAD, value.	ANIMALS, LIVING.	PRECIOUS STONES.	SALT.	SPICES OF ALL KINDS.	SUGAR AND MOLASSES OF ALL KINDS.	WOOL, RAW AND FLEECE. (POUNDS.)	WOOL, value.	WOOD, UNMANUFACTURED.	OTHER MERCHANDISE.	TOTAL IMPORTS OF MERCHANDISE.
1858	36,517	$ 825	......	......	$ 6,285	$ 1,252	$ 9,569	......	$ 4,137	$ 43,674	$ 275,901	$ 1,108,201
1859	91,440	1,829	......	......	11,331	1,272	8,273	......	9,864	55,949	389,964	1,244,084
1860	320,141	6,203	......	......	22,555	642	55,309	......	15,151	101,392	819,195	1,903,431
1861	57,482	1,150	......	......	12,266	1,835	23,333	......	1,641	102,711	141,120	886,112
1862	......	......	......	......	16,138	1,551	10,886	31,209	3,550	51,415	* 289,510	730,988
1863	295,136	13,988	......	......	40,671	3,959	45,576	1,226,820	155,450	69,014	† 1,984,068	3,043,882
1864	4,609	297	......	......	36,247	22,873	12,019	702,676	96,593	62,342	‡ 4,987,889	6,128,445
1865	648	66	......	......	6,452	10,836	816	......	45,490	83,921	§ 5,188,606	6,220,874
1866	25,152	1,509	......	......	12,326	30,920	79,904	163,297	18,667	82,908	‖ 770,268	1,726,092
1867	......	......	......	......	13,645	19,041	1,693	......	377	106,921	127,392	1,071,936
1868	79,504	2,799	......	......	21,368	40,324	29,735	69,493	4,386	72,973	217,404	1,590,667
1869	523,043	22,211	......	......	13,716	33,841	65,197	716,068	51,838	126,345	225,821	2,336,164
1870	456,516	14,607	......	......	30,235	104,476	28,123	636,459	49,829	107,808	377,916	2,715,665
1871	725,211	23,261	......	......	29,600	124,473	39,877	865,909	68,907	176,724	908,208	3,209,688
1872	461,274	14,653	$188,558	$ 34,449	20,984	10,396	52,007	1,182,481	128,375	279,020	263,991	4,002,920
1873	392,440	19,304	147,512	330	6,963	1,613	11,818	1,182,414	129,475	171,554	550,070	4,276,165
1874	817,579	41,978	134,701	102,048	9,844	2,100	17,682	1,173,099	112,226	324,520	379,557	4,346,364
1875	325,648	16,689	81,439	156,690	8,201	1,882	104,547	1,095,282	119,534	346,923	756,226	5,174,594
1876	837,698	42,253	108,050	63,329	6,803	1,520	164,567	838,798	85,887	247,833	735,763	5,150,572
1877	1,336,641	68,218	129,897	6,355	7,196	5,481	227,543	1,495,983	119,708	133,669	583,176	5,144,264
1878	1,136,453	58,245	132,971	1,540	6,768	1,650	155,700	835,487	72,216	257,853	580,051	5,251,502
1879	407,276	20,839	132,873	3,927	6,138	3,760	76,992	879,784	66,300	224,925	529,001	5,493,221
1880	......	......	175,305	5,416	8,419	9,040	234,055	1,321,674	144,875	408,754	889,136	7,209,593
1881	630,947	27,661	314,272	21,057	7,178	5,219	124,535	1,009,376	99,479	329,295	974,452	8,317,802
1882	1,132,064	44,365	455,917	76,241	802	8,428	104,374	191,666	18,037	499,776	1,212,601	8,461,899
1883	1,191,225	26,919	661,245	55,176	973	10,775	64,527	1,775	257	441,083	1,244,542	8,177,123

* Of this amount $60,497 was the value of unmanufactured cotton.

† Of this amount $1,750,615 was the value of unmanufactured cotton.

‡ Of this amount $4,859,725 was the value of unmanufactured cotton.

§ Of this amount $5,128,875 was the value of unmanufactured cotton.

‖ Of this amount $417,197 was the value of unmanufactured cotton.

MEXICO, 1858–1883—*Continued.*

EXPORTS OF DOMESTIC MERCHANDISE TO MEXICO.

YEAR ENDED JUNE 30—	SHEEP. No.	BREAD AND BREADSTUFFS. Indian corn. Bushels	BREAD AND BREADSTUFFS. Indian corn. $	BREAD AND BREADSTUFFS. Wheat and wheat-flour.	BREAD AND BREADSTUFFS. All others.*	COTTON, RAW OR UNMANUFACTURED. Value	COTTON, RAW OR UNMANUFACTURED. Pounds
1858	.....	49,579	$ 37,676	$ 139,673	$ 3,629	$ 1,074,818	9,084,609
1859	.....	48,932	29,886	184,223	4,137	883,337	5,993,635
1860	.....	80,329	78,063	247,206	8,247	1,076,150	9,043,327
1861	.....	13,877	9,993	109,033	10,920	153,905	1,410,059
1862	.....	18,364	14,017	282,810	31,915	.....	.....
1863	.....	268,653	263,849	777,122	379,727	.....	.....
1864	.....	187,014	255,024	855,772	50,730	.....	.....
1865	280	181,462	347,464	1,089,016	99,238	331,199	417,497
1866	590	158,624	121,553	584,012	66,227	17,611	50,317
1867	740	14,218	16,874	547,965	117,066	934,458	3,310,842
1868	2,253	7,292	9,051	343,205	10,938	1,349,685	8,228,598
1869	(†)	72,216	72,439	278,111	10,923	458,405	2,042,224
1870	2,800	62,859	65,292	209,371	11,911	1,412,863	6,609,707
1871	3,156	173,585	169,350	225,718	14,069	1,586,517	11,309,498
1872	18,189	21,039	27,233	218,279	35,166	128,186	957,209
1873	27,481	104,146	99,166	110,525	22,310	74,352	550,639
1874	36,347	55,881	40,049	96,666	25,449	322,507	2,289,561
1875	27,228	9,862	9,092	102,173	21,532	184,186	1,305,276
1876	25,843	93,487	75,945	108,952	26,580	890,574	6,972,575
1877	59,935	64,776	55,058	88,913	23,756	462,902	3,969,812
1878	57,217	288,109	267,663	171,450	51,885	357,210	3,442,162
1879	110,290	126,613	95,802	129,971	50,001	912,583	9,698,129
1880	111,445	85,702	68,743	69,072	44,126	1,176,067	9,881,543
1881	133,222	352,510	240,182	93,757	60,198	1,494,101	13,386,186
1882	112,553	470,263	332,642	103,528	91,475	1,447,522	12,537,650
1883	95,215	475,453	391,751	178,408	118,744	2,217,259	20,577,771

* Bread and breadstuffs, all other, comprise barley, bread and biscuit, Indian corn-meal, oats, rye, rye-flour, other small grain and pulse, maizena, farina, and all other breadstuffs, or preparations of, used as food.

† Classed under the general heading "Animals, living, all kinds." Animals, living, all kinds," total, $156,773.

EXPORTS OF DOMESTIC MERCHANDISE TO MEXICO—*Continued.*

YEAR ENDED JUNE 30—	COTTON, MANUFACTURES OF.			DRUGS, CHEMICALS, MEDICINES, ACIDS, ASHES, AND DYE-STUFFS.	GLASS AND GLASS-WARE.	IRON AND STEEL, AND MANUFACTURES OF *	LEATHER, AND MANUFACTURES OF.	
	Colored.	Uncolored.	All other.				Boots and Shoes.	All other.
	YARDS.	YARDS.						
1858	......	......	$ 281,504	$ 29,957	$ 8,011	$ 188,214	$ 1,066	$ 4,404
1859	......	......	312,203	34,280	7,637	91,472	9,345	5,873
1860	......	......	641,870	63,727	5,981	329,326	8,929	4,204
1861	......	......	312,695	48,710	5,763	255,327	4,562	6,395
1862	......	......	157,874	75,194	14,486	265,225	9,676	4,607
1863	......	......	1,784,531	118,604	43,224	704,944	289,543	112,334
1864	......	......	717,622	166,741	40,670	1,165,541	373,146	67,404
1865	......	......	2,222,410	326,675	126,447	1,443,571	1,119,848	160,203
1866	......	$ 1,049	58,663	89,660	23,515	420,034	32,131	35,114
1867	141,780	3,718	356,163	68,137	16,813	770,150	21,533	21,639
1868	397,472	45,583	387,610	85,635	27,010	784,897	61,227	23,874
1869	(†)	68,023	341,593	73,572	27,076	811,384	95,590	18,430
1870	1,049,621	601,927	106,373	113,105	21,217	654,298	116,761	11,591
1871	758,338	1,451,727	94,366	96,248	18,905	608,296	91,070	16,970
1872	559,411	1,355,636	38,368	93,734	26,419	803,668	98,565	18,480
1873	500,156	1,258,021	73,244	105,436	26,752	1,043,071	104,377	13,613
1874	277,032	1,086,883	50,337	126,437	20,007	1,073,530	70,417	12,757
1875	569,855	1,019,997	64,189	112,877	37,561	954,961	84,129	26,026
1876	1,210,286	2,143,975	60,595	111,348	20,743	1,062,687	79,153	11,182
1877	6,255,489	5,876,817	64,450	79,799	24,763	786,365	53,383	14,233
1878	10,104,048	5,726,156	87,278	123,069	56,898	1,201,574	60,950	27,719
1879	7,663,001	3,886,748	69,852	127,756	47,831	996,080	58,500	21,124
1880	6,402,170	2,808,228	106,406	145,331	54,781	1,257,731	53,466	25,133
1881	6,874,372	3,657,611	193,630	212,477	87,313	2,582,346	48,207	45,953
1882	6,745,817	3,838,669	296,132	288,824	111,542	4,239,712	85,327	65,557
1883	6,114,541	3,523,873	185,329	265,220	159,099	3,774,287	86,788	65,102

* Including, also, printing presses and type, scales and balances, sewing machines and parts of, steam and other fire engines and apparatus.
† Included in "All other."

EXPORTS OF DOMESTIC MERCHANDISE TO MEXICO.—Continued.

YEAR ENDED JUNE 30—	REFINED ILLUMINATING MINERAL OIL.	ORDNANCE STORES. Cartridges and Fuses.	Gunpowder.	All other.	PROVISIONS.* Bacon and Hams. (POUNDS.)	Bacon and Hams. (Value)	Lard. (POUNDS.)	Lard. (Value)	All other.*	QUICKSILVER.	SUGAR AND MOLASSES.	TOBACCO AND MANUFACTURES OF.	WOOD AND MANUFACTURES OF.	OTHER MERCHANDISE.	TOTAL EXPORTS OF DOMESTIC MERCHANDISE.	TOTAL EXPORTS OF FOREIGN MERCHANDISE.	TOTAL EXPORTS OF MERCHANDISE.
1858	....	....	$7,015	....	49,198	$6,280	526,208	$67,902	$19,382	$77,490	$3,047	$15,387	$62,763	$754,634	$2,782,852	$529,973	$3,312,825
1859	....	....	14,469	....	43,431	5,202	679,033	65,413	19,319	....	7,054	14,163	61,496	502,713	2,252,162	667,580	2,919,742
1860	....	....	66,543	....	60,551	7,709	906,106	103,120	24,305	103,128	21,259	9,527	84,372	425,643	3,309,379	2,015,334	5,324,713
1861	....	....	25,775	....	37,502	4,885	117,487	17,344	16,712	197,765	11,391	9,526	58,465	302,896	1,559,062	651,364	2,210,426
1862	....	....	....	....	69,170	6,453	656,851	56,692	31,093	436,231	51,723	22,700	78,900	342,218	1,840,720	340,454	2,181,174
1863	....	....	4,906	....	487,992	49,440	1,357,512	150,279	110,627	572,436	13,922	202,234	326,014	1,536,634	7,441,579	1,579,045	9,020,624
1864	$15,901	....	6,115	....	321,760	40,781	2,825,411	340,683	191,442	302,222	53,275	270,972	544,885	1,972,979	7,765,133	1,595,404	9,470,597
1865	26,657	....	6,244	....	294,721	59,750	2,334,693	453,797	295,006	207,090	36,364	436,420	872,314	4,525,962	13,819,972	2,530,867	16,350,839
1866	27,687	....	....	....	120,353	28,264	880,408	212,256	134,121	182,120	34,593	26,663	211,876	895,138	3,701,599	871,619	4,573,218
1867	60,887	$34,317	1,759	$34,457	93,418	18,402	931,178	137,262	112,476	379,238	53,699	32,763	137,319	895,571	4,823,614	572,182	5,395,796
1868	92,909	10,790	16,957	26,213	98,490	16,720	630,541	134,619	64,739	335,729	53,847	27,354	179,130	706,039	5,048,420	1,392,919	6,441,339
1869	64,657	....	26,573	....	68,113	12,658	734,683	108,798	40,130	328,117	44,025	91,301	141,477	630,841	3,835,699	1,047,408	4,883,107
1870	157,034	32,839	20,968	6,978	95,852	17,555	764,704	124,107	63,028	225,301	46,254	87,690	151,231	....	4,544,745	1,314,955	5,859,700
1871	90,073	26,756	26,220	2,838	210,770	30,010	1,079,754	121,082	60,149	325,980	13,385	129,567	144,227	793,532	5,044,745	2,568,080	7,612,113
1872	172,280	55,272	24,274	271	296,001	31,686	808,445	83,081	69,843	177,316	33,268	71,239	178,636	744,695	3,426,058	2,122,931	5,543,589
1873	143,149	70,139	40,800	130	277,536	33,918	364,646	36,628	65,749	263,370	138,572	140,750	156,058	842,646	3,941,019	2,323,882	5,204,901
1874	164,160	47,608	46,834	314	269,862	28,052	388,420	52,243	58,118	495,048	127,613	91,218	251,951	674,838	4,016,148	1,930,691	5,946,839
1875	168,368	68,432	23,788	212	110,799	14,909	311,862	41,762	53,456	471,808	59,328	100,499	253,249	765,413	3,872,004	1,865,278	5,737,282
1876	171,348	146,390	28,807	9,746	128,983	19,338	556,718	63,491	61,463	365,097	38,442	109,546	226,816	620,332	4,503,862	1,499,594	5,863,494
1877	221,894	57,578	25,210	302	64,360	9,091	1,255,063	102,052	54,972	352,606	38,485	147,347	161,013	551,574	4,700,978	1,389,692	6,200,572
1878	173,438	118,793	26,672	....	141,505	16,565	1,204,422	125,319	81,543	290,249	75,704	122,844	252,055	729,361	5,811,429	1,649,275	7,460,704
1879	132,438	73,014	34,867	1,141	75,645	9,378	1,508,525	132,597	71,820	344,500	38,800	160,516	240,289	752,535	5,400,380	1,351,864	6,752,244
1880	155,328	80,113	43,742	256	90,496	11,312	1,313,086	163,797	77,512	377,825	41,673	152,791	274,532	871,184	6,065,974	1,800,519	7,866,493
1881	173,155	95,230	49,627	....	169,312	19,765	1,183,647	....	97,534	462,159	63,750	135,174	541,201	1,327,434	9,198,077	1,973,101	11,171,498
1882	226,115	226,125	145,397	....	214,523	31,013	1,392,134	....	136,198	316,714	71,582	142,671	1,426,411	2,506,302	13,324,505	2,158,077	15,482,582
1883	249,404	119,491	393,783	....	243,583	37,955	....	....	142,213	394,572	73,298	141,185	1,385,420	2,821,760	14,370,992	2,216,628	16,587,620

* Provisions, all other, comprise: Beef, salted or cured ; beef, fresh ; butter, cheese, condensed milk ; eggs ; fish, dried, smoked, fresh, pickled, other cured ; meats, preserved mutton, fresh ; oysters ; pickles and sauces ; pork ; onions ; potatoes ; other vegetables ; vegetables, prepared or preserved.

STATEMENT SHOWING THE QUANTITIES AND VALUES OF THE PRINCIPAL AND ALL OTHER ARTICLES OF IMPORTS INTO THE UNITED STATES FROM, AND OF EXPORTS FROM THE UNITED STATES TO, MEXICO, DURING EACH OF THE YEARS SPECIFIED BELOW.

MERCHANDISE.—MEXICO, 1889–1897.

IMPORTS OF MERCHANDISE.

YEAR ENDING JUNE 30—	Breadstuffs and other farinaceous food.		Coffee.		Copper: Pigs, bars, ingots, old, and other unmanufactured.		Chemicals, drugs, dyes, and medicines.			Hides and skins, other than fur skins.	Hair unmanufactured.	India rubber and gutta percha, crude.		Jute and other grasses unmanufactured.		Lead and Manufactures of.	
	Corn.	All other.	POUNDS.		POUNDS.		Cochineal and indigo.	Dyewoods in sticks.	All other.			POUNDS.		TONS.		POUNDS.	
1889..	$1,082	$1,837	18,243,317	$2,895,862	81,471	$4,893	$1,000	$187,862	$1,142,124	$1,526,915	$47,452	233,096	$81,800	41,389	$6,257,610	......	$549,257
1890..	871	3,025	20,666,975	3,542,851	39,607	2,948	12,571	194,532	1,155,350	1,579,250	57,066	177,801	59,826	42,787	5,851,822	......	657,658
1891..	1,463	22,046	28,489,632	5,094,839	283,744	23,560	10,915	162,445	1,888,813	1,646,369	61,098	169,343	56,669	56,360	6,047,593	......	1,847,969
1892..	8,102	3,165	21,921,549	4,037,592	1,106,222	84,175	3,745	119,457	1,396,667	1,704,872	60,557	120,528	41,802	52,021	5,542,985	......	3,596,728
1893..	1,093	2,279	25,417,152	4,297,880	1,521,762	134,997	38,411	145,725	1,340,088	1,653,775	61,711	140,096	41,367	60,550	6,687,947	......	5,646,481
1894..	924	1,828	38,160,641	6,964,034	1,821,163	213,377	681	88,390	1,245,525	1,438,277	57,064	120,415	33,750	52,723	3,949,401	......	6,463,346
1895..	6,920	10,283	35,262,229	5,971,439	2,213,101	155,645	345	102,160	953,185	1,433,945	43,846	160,808	54,868	59,706	3,375,998	......	1,423,150
1896..	1,465	12,201	23,975,477	4,040,443	5,544,429	452,712	318	125,774	2,049,715	1,519,301	43,261	124,343	41,489	65,441	4,239,531	......	1,359,713
1897..	1,046	10,310	28,733,370	4,591,909	7,072,378	580,241	......	124,066	1,537,371	1,778,225	58,228	106,871	32,675	70,692	4,235,624	......	1,435,891

IMPORTS INTO, AND EXPORTS FROM, THE UNITED STATES FROM AND TO MEXICO, ETC.—Continued.
MEXICO, 1889-1897—Continued.

IMPORTS OF MERCHANDISE.

YEAR ENDING JUNE 30—	Animals.	Precious stones.	Salt.	Spices of all kinds.	Sugar and molasses.	Wool, unmanufactured.		Wood, unmanufactured.	Other merchandise.	Total imports of merchandise.
						POUNDS.				
1889	$399,493	$11,956	$2,302	$9,278	$7,022	761,828	$67,711	$301,142	$7,757,003	$21,253,601
1890	417,025	57,614	3,546	16,413	27,129	322,166	30,614	441,620	8,579,184	22,690,915
1891	140,642	3,025	4,659	11,507	35,460	1,709	158	470,564	9,764,647	27,294,441
1892	20,257	911	2,369	12,575	40,790	263	41	699,033	10,731,702	28,107,525
1893	36,391	1,164	11,933	19,891	48,157	92,709	10,727	631,238	12,743,844	33,555,099
1894	24,415	3,672	387	19,595	69,618	5,708	632	360,490	7,791,600	28,727,006
1895	760,000	10,121	440	166	55,156	74,574	3,928	230,499	1,043,700	15,635,794
1896	1,520,044	3,840	2	14,066	63,522	95,834	3,964	595,543	1,378,193	17,456,177
1897	1,954,783	847	1,451	30,135	19,111	140,053	7,668	539,499	1,572,552	18,511,572

EXPORTS OF DOMESTIC MERCHANDISE.

YEAR ENDING JUNE 30—	ANIMALS.		BREADSTUFFS.			All other.	Chemicals, drugs, and medicines.	Cotton, unmanufactured.	
	Sheep.		Corn.		Wheat and wheat flour.				
	NUMBER.		BUSHELS.					POUNDS.	
1889	77,560	$122,193	434,997	$194,778	$185,746	$85,558	$329,487	16,901,267	$1,607,395
1890	26,814	47,047	961,458	481,052	166,769	100,997	362,328	13,047,474	1,217,805
1891	9,147	21,464	675,332	389,619	213,299	125,718	377,586	12,841,122	1,281,972
1892	2,827	5,068	734,548	489,702	184,299	127,443	440,297	22,117,381	1,844,500
1893	1,310	4,682	6,960,356	4,343,777	239,576	144,031	418,452	20,905,980	1,890,461
1894	5,443	9,085	431,516	220,362	197,192	100,508	341,989	17,582,418	1,391,836
1895	909	3,338	179,611	108,272	175,637	80,649	408,795	37,976,422	2,332,299
1896	2,182	9,693	1,676,758	672,093	167,680	85,542	469,193	19,408,420	1,043,183
1897	4,628	11,877	8,825,860	3,233,583	96,794	128,527	481,652	15,103,628	1,236,447

IMPORTS INTO, AND EXPORTS FROM, THE UNITED STATES FROM AND TO MEXICO, ETC.—*Continued.*

MEXICO, 1889–1897.—*Continued.*

EXPORTS OF DOMESTIC MERCHANDISE.

YEAR ENDING JUNE 30—	COTTON, MANUFACTURES OF.			Glass and Glassware.	GUNPOWDER AND OTHER EXPLOSIVES.		Iron and steel, and manufactures of.	LEATHER, AND MANUFACTURES OF.	
	Cloths, colored.	Cloths, uncolored.	All other.		Gunpowder.	All other explosives.		Boots and Shoes.	All other.
	YARDS.	YARDS.							
1889	$461,765	1,845,659	$218,293	$76,833	$10,227	$283,794	$2,290,757	$39,981	$48,648
1890	314,882	2,048,130	179,402	94,697	15,723	348,845	2,700,979	38,959	54,794
1891	317,576	1,706,327	158,053	126,688	18,080	375,320	3,414,397	24,366	48,231
1892	347,687	1,937,489	155,362	123,546	28,589	339,625	3,834,343	21,984	38,702
1893	205,250	1,000,704	140,323	117,979	8,787	410,513	3,862,876	26,731	42,308
1894	197,855	1,368,663	151,575	112,972	6,265	454,775	3,198,597	24,843	58,245
1895	244,114	2,159,210	151,924	121,488	43,028	572,031	3,703,556	26,532	51,648
1896	311,532	2,540,396	322,729	162,628	74,805	587,706	5,239,307	45,115	66,943
1897	231,527	1,706,708	346,719	168,437	75,657	671,036	6,425,645	58,639	63,453

EXPORTS OF DOMESTIC MERCHANDISE.

YEAR ENDING JUNE 30—	Oils: Mineral, refined.	PROVISIONS, COMPRISING MEAT AND DAIRY PRODUCTS.			Quicksilver.	Sugar and molasses.	Tobacco, and manufactures of.	Wood, and manufactures of.	Other merchandise.	Total exports of domestic merchandise.	Total exports of foreign merchandise.
		Bacon and hams.	Lard.	All other.							
		POUNDS.	POUNDS.								
1889	$248,381	$41,289	$128,169	$386,117	$144,734	$66,843	$133,727	$964,310	$2,678,444	$10,886,373	$600,608
1890	234,435	34,021	119,976	433,062	169,341	42,035	130,440	1,393,448	3,919,396	12,666,108	619,179
1891	301,889	38,999	109,816	228,245	68,112	36,493	73,535	1,483,903	5,839,026	15,199,080	770,540
1892	238,952	48,280	142,253	193,414	111,349	34,442	89,394	1,206,672	3,596,236	13,606,531	597,468
1893	198,740	53,008	368,449	234,417	143,381	73,545	126,745	1,200,486	4,671,554	18,891,714	676,920
1894	146,626	34,993	116,198	173,281	361,781	57,452	129,205	998,805	3,846,069	12,441,805	400,344
1895	181,092	33,754	128,779	164,853	381,621	37,402	167,665	1,048,844	4,249,723	14,582,484	423,422
1896	142,819	38,113	209,727	167,490	466,259	38,731	175,541	1,611,477	5,795,658	18,686,797	763,459
1897	174,625	38,125	334,335	160,769	368,463	29,395	122,387	2,163,446	5,972,207	22,726,591	694,468

Increase of trade during the year 1896–97.—The data given in the chapter on Foreign Trade contain detailed statements of the amount of commodities and precious metals exported from Mexico into the United States during the last ten years, and I refer, therefore, to the same, those desiring more detailed information on that subject.

I give, however, a statement of the leading merchandise imported from Mexico into the United States, during the last fiscal year, compared with the fiscal year ended June 30, 1896, embracing only such imports as are not specifically stated in the data taken from the official reports of the United States Statistical Bureau, and which appear on pages 176 and 177. The following data, also taken from the last official report of the same Bureau, shows a comparative increase of trade.

LEADING MERCHANDISE IMPORTS FROM MEXICO.

	FISCAL YEAR 1896–1897.	FISCAL YEAR 1895–1896.
Henequen, tons..................	62,839	51,167
Value......................	$3,809,415	$3,339,180
Ixtle fibre, tons..................	6,313	12,207
Value......................	$335,841	$717,585
Oranges, value...................	$258,340	$212,913
Tobacco, lbs....................	749,560	93,197
Value......................	$297,262	$28,025
Mahogany, feet..................	8,791	10,654
Value......................	$321,800	$414,817
Coal, tons.....................	99,760	72,056
Value......................	$218,456	$146,813

I also append a similar statement of some of the articles exported from the United States into Mexico during the last fiscal year, compared with the previous one, ended June 30, 1896, embracing only such exports as are not specifically stated in the data taken from the official reports of the United States Statistical Bureau, appearing on pages 178 to 183, and which I also take from the last official report of the same Bureau. When it is taken into consideration that the Mexican imports from the United States during the last fiscal year were made on a falling silver market, the annexed statement shows a considerable financial strength.

EXPORTS FROM THE UNITED STATES TO MEXICO.
(Fiscal year 1896–97 and preceding year.)

	1896–97.	1895–96.
Cattle, no.......................	690	1,112
Value......................	$29,186	$39,509
Hogs, no........................	22,164	17,540
Value......................	$263,083	$206,807

	1896–97.	1895–96.
Agricultural implements...........	$130,825	$119,838
Books, maps, etc..................	$161,143	$107,384
Carriages and cars................	$615,468	$687,425
Coal and coke, tons...............	219,111	121,269
Value.....................	$643,715	$377,469
Bicycles	$73,117	$24,278
Fruits and nuts..................	$72,654	$78,497
Hops.	$55,610	$8,289
Hardware.......................	$2,874,283	$2,455,400
Leather........................	$16,456	$24,014
Crude petroleum, gals............	7,090,853	6,779,059
Value...........	$349,021	$392,510
Refined petroleum, gals...........	836,628	631,147
Value.....................	$174,107	$142,761
(Includes lubricating oil.)		
Cotton-seed oil, gals..............	1,616,407	1,588,504
Value..................	$320,496	$337,892
Paraffin, lbs.....................	2,888,475	2,975,476
Value.....................	$144,805	$163,644
Tallow, lbs.....................	997,216	1,783,788
Value.....................	$36,561	$77,050
Hams..........................	$28,976	$29,487
Butter	$40,089	$33,169
Wool, lbs...	1,698,952	2,605,150
Value....................	$140,609	$238,316

Tropical Products Supplied by Mexico to the United States.—It will be interesting to state in what proportion Mexican imports of tropical products figure in the total imports of said commodities into this country.

From 1892 to 1896 the annual average of importation of vanilla beans into the United States was 205,197 pounds, of which Mexico furnished 142,727 pounds, or 69½ per cent. Mexico receives for her vanilla crop, annually, $640,000 gold.

Mexico's average annual exportation of coffee to the United States for the past five years was 28,927,410 pounds, or 4.8 per cent., of the total American purchase of coffee, Brazil furnishing 70 per cent., Central America 7.6 per cent., Venezuela 6.4 per cent., and the British West Indies 1.1 per cent. There is plenty of room for the Mexican coffee-growing industry to expand. Mexico's fine flavored, mild coffees are steadily gaining in favor in the United States.

In henequen, or sisal grass, Mexico takes the leading place in the import trade of the United States, selling, of the total received there, 98.1 per cent. The average annual importation for the past five years was 50,129 tons, of which Mexico furnished 49,195, Cuba 277, British Australia 386, and all other countries 271. Mexico received a yearly average, during the five years, for her henequen, of $4,218,267, gold. All of which went to the State of Yucatan.

In sugar, Mexico holds but an insignificant place in the American importation, which showed an annual average, during the past five years, of 3,827,799,481 pounds, Cuba furnishing 46.5 per cent. and Hawaii 7.9 per cent.

We could expand very largely our sugar production and supply this country with almost all of that product, but as sugar is produced in Louisiana and as Hawaii is likely to belong to the United States the protective policy of this country will not allow us to supply the United States with that commodity on a large scale.

Mexico is sending on an average every year, 1,400,000 pounds of wool to the United States. In 1892 she exported but 190 pounds.

The United States takes, annually, an average of 50,493,000 pounds of goat skins, of which Mexico furnishes 3,007,000, or 5.9 per cent. Of other hides and skins the United States imports 167,993,000 pounds, Mexico's share being 4.3 per cent.

The cattle trade of Mexico with the United States increased considerably under the liberal provisions of the Wilson Bill, which taxed cattle with 20 per cent. ad valorem. The following statement shows how large the increase of that trade was under that bill :

CATTLE EXPORTED TO THE UNITED STATES.

Years.	Number.	Gold Value.
1892	1,438	$ 7,740
1893	2,597	16,376
1894	1,469	11,857
1895	148,431	720,864
1896	216,913	1,481,954

(Fiscal years ended June 30th.)

Mexico has been for at least two years the most important source of supply to the United States for cattle purchased abroad, Canada furnishing, in 1896, cattle to the value of but $18,902, and the United Kingdom $6,684. The cattle trade is one in which American, as well as Mexican capital is embarked, but it will be considerably diminished if not completely destroyed under the highly protective tariff.

COINAGE.

In the chapter on Mining I gave a concise statement of the silver and gold coined in Mexico from the time of its discovery by the Spaniards to the fiscal year ended June 30, 1896, and it appears from the same that the total coinage of silver amounted to $3,398,664,400.

According to the report of the Director of the Mint (page 347) on the " Production of Precious Metals in the United States during the Calendar Year 1895," the last one out as this paper goes to press, the total production of silver of the world from 1493 to 1895 is $10,-345,688,700, the Mexican coinage being over one-third of the whole.

It must be borne in mind that that statement embraces, so far as Mexico is concerned, only the silver coined, and it does not take into consideration the silver used in the arts, which used to be a considerable amount, as almost every well-to-do Mexican had forks, spoons, plates and other table ware and household articles of solid silver. It does not embrace either such silver as was smuggled in bullion, which, considering the large extent of the Mexican sea coast, its scanty population and the general demoralization during our civil wars represents a very large amount. It can, therefore, be safely stated that the production of silver in Mexico, not coined, represents at least from one-fourth to one-third of the amount coined. Therefore, the production of silver by Mexico may be safely estimated at from $5,000,000,000, to $6,000,000,000, which is about one-half of the total product of the world.

The following statement shows the amount of silver coined by the several mints of Mexico from their establishment to June 30, 1895, stating the years in which the coinage was made :

COINAGE BY THE MEXICAN MINTS FROM THEIR ESTABLISHMENT IN 1535 TO JUNE 30, 1895.

PERIOD OF COINAGE.	MINTS.	COINAGE.
1868–1895	Alamos	$ 22,828,869
1863–1866	Catorce	1,321,545
1811–1895	Chihuahua	62,465,756
1846–1895	Culiacan	46,438,169
1811–1895	Durango	67,128,366
1812–1895	Guadalajara	64,127,846
1844–1849	Guadalupe y Calvo	4,375,062
1812–1895	Guanajuato	307,364,150
1852–1895	Hermosilla	19,659,506
1535–1895	Mexico	2,453,110,110
1857–1893	Oaxaca	5,761,045
1827–1893	San Luis Potosi	113,143,358
1810–1812	Sombrerete	1,551,248
1827–1830	Tlalpam	1,162,660
1810–1895	Zacatecas	350,341,499
From 1535 to 1895	Total	$3,520,779,189

I give a statement of the production of gold and silver in Mexico in the fiscal years 1879–1880, 1889–1890 and 1894–1895, which shows a considerable increase in each of those years, and this statement only represents such amounts of the precious metals as were either exported in bullion or taken to the mints, and not the production that is otherwise disposed of.

PRODUCTION OF GOLD AND SILVER IN MEXICO IN THE FISCAL YEARS 1879–1880, 1889–1890 AND 1894–1895.

	1879–1880.			1889–1890.			1894–1895.		
	Kilograms.	Grams.	Value.	Kilograms.	Grams.	Value.	Kilograms.	Grams.	Value.
Gold coined........	772	598	$ 521,826	360	219	$ 243,298	807	260	$ 545,237
Gold exported.....	622	032	420,131	677	524	457,611	6,217	351	4,199,305
Total..........	1,394	630	941,957	1,037	743	700,909	7,024	611	4,744,542
Silver coined,......	587,034	804	24,018,529	594,606	526	24,328,326	675,277	551	27,628,981
Silver exported	74,302	310	3,040,079	362,418	697	14,828,361	747,283	490	30,575,104
Total..........	661,337	114	27,058,608	957,025	223	39,156,687	1,422,561	041	58,204,085
Total of gold and silver..........			$28,000,565			$39,857,596			$62,948,627

The following statement gives the exports of the precious metals from Mexico during the same years embraced in the preceding table.

EXPORT OF PRECIOUS METALS AND MINERALS FROM MEXICO IN THE FISCAL YEARS 1879–1880, 1889–1890 AND 1894–1895.

	VALUE IN MEXICAN DOLLARS.		
	1879–1880.	1889–1890.	1894–1895.
Argentiferous copper.............	....	....	....
Gold ore......................	....	....	59,660
Silver ore....................	....	6,394,662	10,935,353
Foreign gold coined	220,567	13,204	34,887
Mexican gold coined.............	760,683	96,592	164,113
Gold bullion...................	420,132	457,611	4,139,645
Mixed gold....................	....	....	....
Foreign silver coined............	314,537	141,033	485,326
Mexican silver coined............	16,783,317	23,084,489	17,077,119
Base silver....................	....	1,810	50,866
Silver bullion........	3,040,079	7,259,959	18,803,876
Manufactured silver.............	581	....	....
Mixed silver...................	....	368,872	....
Sulphite of silver...............	....	803,058	785,009
Argentiferous lead............ ...	....	....	....
Argentiferous zinc...............	....	....	....
	21,539,896	38,621,290	52,535,854

It may be interesting to state the amount of silver exported and coined in Mexican mints from 1874 to 1896, which is the following :

	EXPORTED.	COINED.
1874–75................................	$ 16,038,215	$ 19,386,958
1875–76................................	....	19,454,054
1876–77................................	....	21,415,128
1877–78................................	20,853,074	22,084,203
1878–79................................	19,339,151	22,162,988
1879–80................................	20,307,563	24,018,529
1880–81................................	17,774,910	24,617,395
1881–82................................	15,700,704	25,146,260
1882–83................................	28,441,212	24,083,922
1883–84................................	32,242,770	25,377,379
1884–85................................	32,770,900	25,840,728
1885–86................................	29,160,835	26,991,805
1886–87................................	32,642,785	26,844,031
1887–88................................	30,286,247	25,862,977
1888–89................................	37,982,948	26,031,223
1889–90................................	37,912,848	24,328,326
1890–91................................	35,259,131	24,237,449
1891–92................................	46,272,391	25,527,018
1892–93................................	44,303,593	27,169,876
1893–94................................	36,012,950	30,185,612
1894–95................................	36,716,870	27,628,981
1895–96................................	46,722,823	22,634,788
	$616,741,920	$541,029,630

The preceding statement gives correct data of the exports of silver from the fiscal year 1874–1875 to the fiscal year 1895–1896, excepting the years 1875–1876 and 1876–1877, which are not included for want of data. The difference between the two amounts for these years is $75,712,290, showing the large proportion of silver which was not coined, and was exported in bullion.

The following statement shows that the export of Mexican silver reached almost its minimum in the year 1887–1888, and its maximum in the year 1892–1893, with the exception of the last one. The minimum coincided with the first sterling loan negotiated by Mexico ; the second sterling loan negotiated in 1890 caused a decrease in the export of Mexican silver coin of 26 per cent., as compared with the previous fiscal year of 1889–1890.

The export of silver bullion has steadily increased since 1872–1873, until it was in 1895–1896 seventeen times as large as in the first named year. During the first fiscal year of those embraced in the above table, the export of silver bullion was 1.4 to 22.6 as compared with silver coin, and in the year 1895–1896 the proportion was 15.3 to 20.5. In the year 1872–1873 the export of silver bullion represented 6 per cent. of the total export of silver, while in the fiscal year 1895–1896 it represented 20 per cent.

The export of silver ore only began in the fiscal year 1886–1887.

EXPORTS OF SILVER FROM JULY 1ST, 1872, TO JUNE 30TH, 1896.

FISCAL YEARS.	COINS.	BULLION.	ORES.	OTHER FORMS.	TOTAL VALUE.
1872–1873	$ 22,626,065	$ 1,459,426	$ 199,596	$ 8,716	$ 24,293,803
1873–1874	17,021,405	1,217,853	240,769	1,359	18,481,386
1874–1875	15,372,254	1,843,523	79,443	3,920	17,299,140
Average in three years	$ 18,339,908	$ 1,506,934	$ 173,269	$ 4,665	$ 20,024,776
1877–1878	$ 18,120,297	$ 2,560,859	$ 19,920	$ 87	$ 20,701,163
1878–1879	16,366,877	2,650,400	....	2,812	19,020,089
1879–1880	16,783,317	3,040,079	....	581	19,823,977
1880–1881	13,183,955	3,976,879	....	376	17,161,210
1881–1882	11,607,888	3,540,994	10,129	5,079	15,163,990
Average in five years	$ 15,212,467	$ 3,153,842	$ 6,010	$ 1,787	$ 18,374,086
1882–1883	$ 22,969,584	$ 4,773,928	$ 30,105	$ 113,537	$ 27,892,154
1883–1884	25,999,876	5,311,310	67,815	111,112	31,490,113
1884–1885	25,394,262	5,899,297	....	153,489	31,446,848
1885–1886	21,969,958	5,261,502	1,809,873	145,070	29,186,403
1886–1887	21,953,759	6,128,239	3,737,883	823,951	32,643,832
Average in five years	$ 23,657,488	$ 5,474,855	$ 1,129,135	$ 269,432	$ 30,531,870
1887–1888	$ 7,794,245	$ 4,771,328	$ 4,547,250	$ 475,942	$ 17,588,765
1888–1889	22,686,337	6,862,510	7,623,589	830,304	38,002,740
1889–1890	23,084,489	7,628,831	6,394,662	804,869	37,912,851
1890–1891	17,622,171	7,480,354	8,874,457	1,282,151	35,259,133
1891–1892	26,478,376	7,853,757	10,478,264	3,237,116	48,047,513
Average in five years	$ 19,533,124	$ 6,919,356	$ 7,583,644	$ 1,326,076	$ 35,362,200
1892–1893	$ 27,170,865	$ 8,126,593	$10,940,750	$ 9,008,215	55,246,423
1893–1894	17,386,338	7,881,897	9,023,596	11,119,345	45,411,176
1894–1895	17,077,119	18,803,876	10,935,353	835,875	47,652,223
1895–1896	20,377,663	26,345,160	10,885,479	1,138,245	58,746,547
Average in four years	$ 20,502,996	$ 15,289,381	$10,446,294	$ 5,525,420	$ 51,764,092
Total in the twenty-two years	$429,047,100	$143,418,595	$85,898,933	$30,102,151	$688,471,479
Average for the twenty-two years	$ 19,502,140	$ 6,519,027	$ 3,904,496	$ 1,368,279	$31,294,158

MEXICAN GOLD EXPORTS.

Our production of gold used to be very small for reasons already given, but the present high price of that metal is increasing considerably our output of the same.

The exports of gold from Mexico in the fiscal year ended June 30, 1896, amounted to $5,800,000, as declared by the Mexican Bureau of Statistics, but even this statement is not correct, as it needs the following additions, shown by experience and reliable authorities: about 15 per cent. for gold exports made without any return, 2 per cent. for undervaluation, 0.5 per cent. used in the arts in Mexico, 1 per cent., possibly more now, with the increasing prosperity of the country, retained in the banks, 2 per cent. in circulation, making a total of 20.5 per cent. to be added to the official return, which brings up the production of gold in Mexico to $6,989,000 for the year 1896 and even this figure is considered very low.

Mexican Gold Exported to the United States.—The United States is our principal market for the gold we produce.

The following statement furnished to me on February 6, 1897, by the Director of the Mint of the Treasury Department of the United States, contains the imports of gold bullion, ore and coin into the United States, as reported by the Collector of Customs, from 1891 to 1895, and from the fiscal years ending June 30, 1892, to June 30, 1896.

"IMPORTS OF GOLD BULLION, ORE AND COIN FROM MEXICO INTO THE UNITED STATES AS REPORTED BY COLLECTORS OF CUSTOMS.

YEARS.	ORE.	BULLION.	COIN.	TOTAL.
1891......................	$ 222,088	$1,192,183	$ 367,015	$ 1,781,286
1892......................	711,672	1,714,440	380,711	2,806,823
1893......................	507,647	1,566,728	265,315	2,339,690
1894......................	673,583	1,064,721	38,376	1,776,680
1895......................	997,221	2,435,296	34,217	3,466,734
Total................	$3,112,211	$7,973,368	$1,085,634	$12,171,213

" For additional information see *Report on Production of Precious Metals*, 1894, page 248, and the same report for 1895, page 289.

" Yours, R. D. Preston,

" Mint Bureau, February 6, 1897."

"IMPORTS OF GOLD ORE, BULLION AND COIN FROM MEXICO INTO THE UNITED STATES AS REPORTED BY COLLECTORS OF CUSTOMS.

FISCAL YEARS ENDING JUNE 30.	ORE.	BULLION.	COIN.	TOTAL.
1892......................	$ 246,849	$1,336,593	$ 542,499	$ 2,125,941
1893......................	886,284	1,923,565	300,012	3,109,861
1894......................	502,023	1,210,757	116,823	1,829,603
1895......................	810,066	1,635,852	36,835	2,482,753
1896......................	1,108,839	2,826,327	72,482	4,007,648
Total................	$3,554,061	$8,933,094	$1,068,651	$13,555,806

" Treasury Department, Mint Bureau, February 6, 1897."

Mr. Preston completed the above information with other data obtained from private parties in the following manner : communicated to me in a letter dated, February 6, 1897, enclosing the two preceding statements.

" I would add, for your information, that from returns received by this Bureau, from private refineries, and the deposits of foreign bullion at the Mints and Assay

Offices of the United States during the calendar years 1894 and 1895 the amount of gold credited to Mexico was reported to be as follows :

1894.

Reported by private refineries as extracted from Mexican ores and
bullion... $2,360,765
Gold bullion deposited at the United States Assay Office at New York...   735,787
Deposited at the Mint at San Francisco................................   290,713

    Total... $3,387,265

1895.

Gold extracted from Mexican ores and bullion by private refineries....... $3,843,783
Gold deposited at the United States Assay Office at New York..........   560,775
Mexican gold bullion deposited at the United States Mint at San Francisco   504,745

    Total.. .... $4,909,303

The preceding official data from the United States Treasury Department was not complete, as will appear from the following table prepared by the Bureau of Statistics of the Mexican Republic :

GOLD EXPORTED FROM MEXICO TO THE UNITED STATES.

CALENDAR YEARS.

	1891.	1892.	1893.	1894.	1895.	1896.
Gold ore................	$ 16,700	$ 100,595	$ 113,548	$ 5,767	$ 87,695	$ 324,305
Coined.................	53,769	45,290	91,936	177,089	109,421	477,505
Bullion [1].............	497,400	279,699	99,415	1,606,152	4,368,898	6,851,564
Mixed [1]...............	....	126,184	257,761	144,515	....	528,460
Cyanide................	....	....	....	....	31,231	31,231
Sulphite...............	....	....	....	....	3,026	3,026
According to information from Mexico.........	$ 567,869	$ 551,768	$ 562,660	$1,933,523	$4,600,271	$8,216,091
According to information from the United States	$1,781,286	2,806,823	2,339,690	1,776,680	3,466,734	12,171,213
Differences.............	+$1,213,417	+$2,255,055	+$1,777,030	− $ 156,843	−$1,133,537	+$3,955,122

FISCAL YEARS.

	1891–1892.	1892–1893.	1893–1894.	1894–1895.	1895–1896.	TOTAL.
Gold ore...............	$ 31,289	$ 145,785	$ 55,799	$ 8,889	$ 160,555	$ 402,317
Coined.................	41,259	74,798	121,915	150,544	147,981	536,497
Bullion [1].............	474,156	115,642	116,994	3,687,872	4,608,959	9,003,623
Mixed [1]...............	....	271,913	256,547	....	....	528,460
Cyanide................	....	....	....	....	80,947	80,947
Sulphite...............	....	....	....	....	31,332	31,332
According to information from Mexico.........	$ 546,704	$ 608,138	$ 551,255	$3,847,305	$5,029,774	$10,583,176
According to information from the United States	2,125,941	3,109,861	1,829,603	2,482,753	4,007,648	13,555,806
Differences.............	+$1,579,237	+$2,501,723	+$1,278,348	− $1,364,552	−$1,022,126	+$2,972,630

[1] From the 1st of July, 1894, the " Bullion " includes the value of the gold contained in the mixed ore.

This instance shows how difficult it is for the commercial statistics of both countries to agree, even when the merchandise is entered with the same value in both as in the present case.

RAILWAYS.

The following table contains a list of all the railways, exclusive of the tramways, built in Mexico up to October 31, 1896, prepared by the Department of Communications of the United Mexican States :

OFFICIAL STATEMENT MADE BY THE DEPARTMENT OF COMMUNICATIONS OF THE MEXICAN GOVERNMENT OF THE RAILROAD MILEAGE IN OPERATION ON OCTOBER 31, 1896.

(1) The initials at the beginning of each line of this table stand for the guage of the railroads ; S. for standard, N. for narrow, and B. for both.

NAME.	DATE OF CONCESSION.	LENGTH.	FROM AND TO.
(1) S. Mexican.	Nov. 27, 1867	292.50	Mexico to Veracruz and Apizaco to Puebla.
S. Mérida to Progreso.	Jan. 17, 1874	22.65	Mérida to Progreso.
N. Hidalgo.	Feb. 2, 1878	92.43	Tepa to Sototlan, Tepa to Pachuca and San Augustin to Tepa.
B. Veracruz to Alvarado.	Mar. 26, 1878	43.75	Veracruz to Medellin and Medellin to Alvarado.
N. Mérida to Peto.	Mar. 27, 1878	68.97	Merida to Ingenio de Sta. Maria.
N. Interoceanic from Acapulco to Veracruz.	Apr. 16, 1878	489.74	Mexico to Veracruz, Mexico to Puente Ixtla by Morelos and branches of Virreyes to Libres and San Nicolas.
N. Puebla to Izucar de Matamoros.	May 6, 1878	52.39	Los Arcos to Cholula, Cholula to Atlixco and Atlixco to Matamoros.
S. Mexican Western.	Aug. 16, 1880	38.48	Culiacan to Altata.
S. Mexican Central.	Sept. 8, 1880	1,877.15	Mexico to Paso del Norte, Silao to Guanajuato, Irapuato to Guadalajara, Aguascalientes to Tampico, San Blas to Huaristemba and Guadalajara to Ameca.
N. Mexican National.	Sept. 13, 1880	1,056.16	Mexico to Laredo, Acambaro to Patzcuaro, Matamoros to S. Miguel, Mexico to Salto, belt tramways from suburbs of Mexico called La Colonia extension to Salto.
N. Mexican National Construction Company.	Sept. 13, 1880	88.30	Manzanillo to Colima and Zacatecas to Ojo Caliente.
S. Sonora.	Sept. 14, 1880	262.40	Guaymas to Nogales.
N. Mérida to Valladolid.	Dec. 15, 1880	67.53	Merida to Valladolid and Progreso to Conkal.
N. Tlalmanalco.	Feb. 3, 1881	16.56	Tlalmanalco to Chalco and Amecameca.
N. Mérida to Campeche.	Feb. 23, 1881	97.80	Mérida to Campeche, Campeche to Calkini and connecting line with the railroad from Mérida to Progreso.

NAME.	DATE OF CONCESSION.	LENGTH.	FROM AND TO.
N. Campeche to Lerma.	Feb. 23, 1881	3.73	Campeche to Lerma.
S. Mexican International.	June 7, 1881	658.28	Porfirio Diaz City to Torreon and Durango, Sabinas to Hondo, Matamoros to Zaragoza, Hornos to San Pedro, branch from Velardeña and Monclova to Cuatro Cienegas.
N. Nautla to San Marcos.	June 25, 1881	47.22	San Marcos toward Nautla and branch to Libres.
N. San Juan Bautista to Paso del Carrizal.	Sept. 17, 1881	3.57	S. Juan Bautista to Tamulte.
S. Chalchicomula.	Sept. 20, 1881	6.43	San Andres Chalchicomula.
S. Orizaba to Ingenio.	Sept. 22, 1881	4.69	Orizaba to Ingenio.
S. Santa Ana to Tlaxcala.	Dec. 11, 1882	5.28	Santa Ana to Tlaxcala.
N. Cardenas to the River Grijalva.	May 12, 1883	4.66	Cardenas to the River Grijalva.
N. Toluca to San Juan de las Huertas.	May 25, 1883	9.77	Toluca to San Juan de las Huertas.
N. Vanegas, Cedral, Matehuala and Rio Verde.	June 11, 1883	40.39	Vanegas to Cedral and branch to Potrero.
S. Tehuacan to Esperanza.	Nov. 28, 1883	31.07	Esperanza to Tehuacan.
S. Mérida to Izamal.	May 15, 1884	40.91	Mérida to Izamal.
S. Chihuahua and Hidalgo to the Sierra Madre.	Nov. 13, 1884	6.83	Chihuahua to the Sierra Madre and Jimenez to Balleza.
N. Southern Mexican.	Apr. 21, 1886	228.00	Puebla to Oaxaca.
S. Tonala to Textla and Frontera.	Dec. 16, 1886	31.07	Tonala to Kilomete.
S. Lower California.	May 25, 1887	16.78	San Quintin to the Colorado River.
S. Monterey to the Gulf.	Nov. 10, 1887	388.12	Monterey to Treviño and Monterey to Tampico.
N. Tecolutla to Espinal.	Dec. 10, 1887	13.04	Tecolutla to Espinal.
S. Córdova to Tuxtepec.	May 19, 1888	31.69	Córdova to Motzorongo.
S. Pachuca to Tampico.	June 5, 1888	6.21	Isolated Branch.
N. Maravatío to Cuernavaca.	Aug. 16, 1888	40.84	Maravatío towards Cuernavaca and branches to Agangueo to Trojes.
N. Mexican Northeastern.	Aug. 28, 1888	31.12	Mexico to Tizayuca.
N. Salamanca to Jaral.	Aug. 30, 1888	21.75	Salamanca to Jaral.
N. Monte Alto.	Aug. 30, 1888	6.21	Tlalnepantla to Pedregal.
N. Veracruz to Boca del Rio.	Aug. 31, 1888	13.67	Veracruz to Boca del Rio.
S. National Tehuantepec.	Government Road.	192.38	Coatzacoalcas to Salina Cruz.
S. Ometusco to Pachuca.	May 25, 1889	28.40	Ometusco to Pachuca.
S. Puebla Industrial.	July 21, 1889	22.21	Puebla to Constancia, Cholula and Huejotzingo.
S. Tula to Pachuca.	Dec. 20, 1889	43.49	Tula to Pachuca.
S. Minero.	Mar. 20, 1890	80.94	Escalon to Sierra Mojada and branches.
S. Mexico to Cuernavaca and the Pacific.	May 30, 1890	58.65	Mexico to Tres Marias and Puente de Ixtla to Mexcala.
N. Mixcalco to Santa Cruz.	June 13, 1890	2.77	Mixcalco to Santa Cruz.

NAME.	DATE OF CONCESSION.	LENGTH.	FROM AND TO.
N. Izucar of Matamoros to Acapulco.	Nov. 21, 1890	24.85	Matamoros towards Acapulco.
N. Toluca to Tenango.	Nov. 24, 1891	4.35	Toluca to Tenango.
N. Hacienda of Xavaleta to the San Rafael Paper Factory.	Mar. 24, 1892	2.49	Hacienda of Xavaleta to San Rafael Paper Mill.
S. Esperanza to Xuchil.	Nov. 29, 1892	15.84	Esperanza to Xuchil Station.
N. Guanajuato to Dolores, Hidalgo and San Luis de la Paz.	May 24, 1893	6.21	Rincon on the National Railroad to San Luis de la Paz.
S. Villa Lerdo to San Pedro de la Colonia.	June 3, 1893	15.84	Villa Lerdo to Sacramento.
N. Celaya to the farms of Roque and Plancarte.	June 2, 1893	9.07	Celaya to the farms of Roque and Plancarte.
N. From La Compañia to the Zoquiapan farm.	June 13, 1893	5.17	La Compañia to the Zoquiapan farm.
S. Cazadero to Solis.	May 24, 1893	18.64	Cazadero to point between the stations of Solis and Tepetongo.
S. Industrial Railroads.	Dec. 18, 1895	1.86	Mexico to Xochimilco.
	Total........	(1) 6,791.30	

(1) This amount does not include the tramways.

RESUME OF RAILWAYS IN MEXICO IN 1895.

	KILOMETERS.	MILES.
Railroads under Federal Grants............	10,723,k 113	6,663,022
Tramways	427, 583	265,687
Surburban Railways connecting towns.......	410, 164	254,863
Railroads belonging to private parties	87, 000	54,059
Portable Railroad, Decauville System.......	242, 252	150,527
Total.................	11,890,k 112	7,388,158

As I have already stated most of the roads built in Mexico have obtained large subsidies from the government, and that fact has contributed very materially to their present prosperous financial condition, as they have used the proceeds of the subsidy, not only to build the roads, but in some cases to pay the interest on their bonds. On the whole Mexican roads are very prosperous, and the following statements taken from the official reports of the principal roads shows their trade and earnings are increasing considerably.

The Mexican roads like the Mexican Government have been very much crippled by their obligation to pay in gold the interest on their bonds and dividends on their shares, and as they collect their freights in silver, they have to buy gold at current prices to pay their gold obligations, and the depreciation of silver causes them a very great loss, but notwithstanding that serious drawback, the increase in their business and earnings has been such as to place them in a position to meet their gold obligations.

I give below a statement of the traffic and receipts of the three principal railways in Mexico, namely : the Mexican Central, Mexican National, and Mexican International, which I have obtained directly from the respective companies. I also give similar statements from the other roads, which I have taken from statements published by the *Anuario Estadistico de la Republica Mexicana* of 1895.

Mexican Central.—The Mexican Central is the largest road so far built in Mexico. The whole of the main line was opened for traffic in 1884, and all figures for traffic previous to July 1, 1884, were thrown into Construction Accounts. The annexed statement of freights and earnings of this road begins therefore in 1885, and shows a decided increase every year. I also append a statement of the traffic and earnings of this road and its branch from Tula to Pachuca, from 1881 to 1895, taken from the *Anuario Estadistico de la Republica Mexicana* of 1895, which has been compiled from data furnished by the company to the Mexican Government. (See first table on page 197.)

EARNINGS OF THE MEXICAN CENTRAL RAILWAY FROM 1885 TO 1896.

MEXICAN CURRENCY.

CALEN-DAR YEAR.	MILEAGE OPERATED.	METRIC TONS FREIGHT.	FREIGHT EARNINGS.	NUMBER OF PASSENGERS.	PASSENGER EARNINGS.	ALL OTHER EARNINGS.	TOTAL GROSS EARNINGS.
1885	1,035.00	226,238	2,087,418 14	312,272	1,100,260 62	171,002 00	3,359,560 76
1886	1,235.90	245,398	2,511,028 78	573,896	1,168,750 24	177,926 83	3,857,705 85
1887	1,235.90	346,898	3,458,006 46	601,393	1,235,284 05	193,288 16	4,886,578 67
1888	1,316.40	507,631	4,244,648 52	581,967	1,321,511 96	208,170 83	5,774,331 31
1889	1,461.85	540,546	4,683,290 74	675,144	1,420,375 76	233,558 88	6,337,225 38
1890	1,527.20	609,382	4,702,142 48	723,928	1,436,317 68	287,233 92	6,425,694 08
1891	1,665.11	867,657	5,625,668 51	742,993	1,470,940 51	277,929 00	7,374,538 02
1892	1,824.83	1,091,785	6,183,149 29	731,425	1,439,571 60	340,532 80	7,963,253 69
1893	1,846.64	860,187	6,130,347 06	792,025	1,443,793 73	407,627 52	7,981,768 31
1894	1,859.83	898,484	6,440,713 23	945,434	1,576,801 33	408,510 72	8,426,025 28
1895	1,859.83	1,047,038	7,145,041 44	1,030,911	1,828,072 61	522,751 63	9,495,865 68
1896	1,869.60	1,231,025	7,646,257 99	1,259,623	1,934,612 78	627,149 62	10,208,020 39
Total	18,938.99	8,472,169	$61,057,704 64	9,171,011	$17,376,300 87	$3,856,561 91	$82,290,567 42

Mexican National.—The Mexican National obtained its first concession from the Mexican Government in 1877, but it was amended from time to time thereafter, until all the amended grants were grouped in the concession approved July 5, 1886, under which the road is now operated. The old companies did not print any reports, and there is no data running back further than the time when the bondholders took possession of the property at the foreclosure sale, which occurred in the City of Mexico on May 23, 1887. I give a statement of the traffic and earnings of the road from 1873 to 1895, taken from the *Anuario Estadistico de la Republica Mexicana* in 1895, which was compiled with data furnished to the Mexican Government by the company.

CENTRAL RAILWAY AND BRANCHES, INCLUDING EARNINGS DURING PERIOD OF CONSTRUCTION.

YEARS.	PASSEN-GERS.	PASSENGER RECEIPTS.	FREIGHT.		MISCELLANEOUS RECEIPTS.	TOTAL RECEIPTS.
			Tons.	Kilos.		
1881.	303,543	$ 62,270 20	7,012	436	$ 33,413 44	$ 95,683 64
1882.	491,985	442,726 54	202,304	993	1,289,387 24	1,732,113 78
1883.	653,669	726,830 09	167,356	565	2,876,906 29	3,603,736 38
1884.	761,687	1,111,906 96	190,423	972	2,662,684 86	3,774,591 82
1885.	694,894	1,111,062 54	331,700	260	2,484,325 68	3,595,388 22
1886.	769,655	1,185,662 53	255,027	111	2,754,613 02	3,940,275 55
1887.	797,693	1,251,743 98	356,448	976	3,721,358 13	4,973,102 11
1888.	756,560	1,337,734 10	519,261	394	4,554,830 53	5,892,564 63
1889.	683,147	1,436,301 06	576,324	408	5,081,628 68	6,517,929 74
1890.	736,730	1,487,086 60	694,966	914	5,212,261 40	6,699,348 00
1891.	753,276	1,512,415 42	1,005,447	237	6,167,092 56	7,679,507 98
1892.	735,363	1,442,310 99	1,100,364	029	6,534,507 42	7,976,818 41
1893.	792,025	1,443,793 73	860,186	545	6,537,974 58	7,981,768 31
1894.	945,434	1,576,801 35	898,484	071	6,849,223 95	8,426,025 28
1895.	1,030,911	1,828,072 61	1,047,037	836	7,767,793 03	9,495,865 68
Total	10,906,572	$17,956,718 70	8,212,346	747	$64,528,000 81	$82,484,719 51

MEXICAN NATIONAL RAILROAD.

YEARS.	PAS-SENGERS.	PASSENGER RECEIPTS.	FREIGHT.		MISCEL-LANEOUS RECEIPTS.	TOTAL RECEIPTS.
			Tons.	Kilos.		
1873.	247,547	$ 17,425 65	....	....	....	$ 17,425 65
1874.	584,075	40,446 01	298	860	$ 298 86	40,744 87
1875.	486,788	43,027 18	221	140	221 14	43,248 32
1876.	486,000	43,437 24	698	245	709 41	44,146 65
1877.	565,572	52,759 84	346	499	275 75	53,035 59
1878.	529,333	71,193 68	3,209	097	3,845 61	75,039 29
1879.	535,806	74,277 07	8,102	920	15,329 07	89,606 14
1880.	466,897	91,505 23	18,191	400	41,983 90	133,489 13
1881.	903,049	124,452 13	26,234	150	47,320 00	171,772 13
1882.	900,855	225,267 21	105,549	146	229,586 51	454,853 72
1883.	1,071,835	341,614 87	140,185	779	366,320 26	707,935 13
1884.	878,878	517,316 80	254,804	000	743,423 74	1,260,740 54
1885.	839,573	492,822 92	177,179	000	803,291 20	1,296,114 12
1886.	891,711	538,359 97	132,661	000	1,018,018 51	1,556,378 48
1887.	884,541	537,520 17	307,435	000	1,120,950 34	1,658,470 51
1888.	907,113	691,915 03	370,300	527	1,880,684 24	2,572,599 27
1889.	929,685	864,309 90	430,166	055	2,640,418 14	3,504,728 04
1890.	937,527	887,437 19	487,598	563	2,684,550 59	3,561,987 78
1891.	998,617	994,951 69	515,164	143	3,057,891 00	4,052,842 69
1892.	1,012,786	973,768 72	605,545	610	3,643,784 47	4,617,553 19
1893.	935,167	972,488 57	571,524	780	3,191,146 37	4,163,634 94
1894.	576,574	865,698 53	527,440	000	3,246,375 07	4,112,073 60
1895.	926,516	1,005,515 55	642,535	071	3,426,841 93	4,432,357 48
Total	17,496,445	$10,467,511 15	5,325,390	985	$28,152,266 11	$38,609,777 26

STATEMENT OF EARNINGS AND EXPENSES OF THE MEXICAN NATIONAL RAILWAY, FROM 1889 TO 1896 INCLUSIVE.

ROAD OPENED FOR THROUGH TRAFFIC IN NOVEMBER, 1888.

MEXICAN CURRENCY.

EARNINGS FROM	1889.	1890.	1891.	1892.	1893.	1894.	1895.	1896.
Freight	$2,612,509 38	$2,654,268 04	$2,956,817 91	$3,474,405 42	$2,956,148 19	$3,087,466 29	$3,129,461 43	$3,871,117 08
Passenger and Mail	869,133 94	902,053 41	1,020,627 10	994,071 43	985,399 34	924,454 28	1,010,047 75	1,010,150 14
Express	127,822 31	129,151 00	156,670 31	179,623 45	199,730 71	227,939 76	262,014 13	278,138 62
Telegraph	17,715 31	20,509 92	23,358 12	24,738 14	22,305 98	25,834 93	34,775 78	58,318 06
Miscellaneous	32,943 30	49,053 99	48,949 30	83,191 50	61,219 89	63,383 39	76,906 82	81,301 87
Total	$3,660,124 24	$3,754,966 36	$4,206,422 74	$4,756,029 94	$4,224,804 11	$4,329,078 65	$4,513,205 91	$5,299,025 77
Operating Expenses	2,993,431 54	2,927,961 89	3,047,401 56	3,055,416 55	2,586,366 45	2,437,116 41	2,441,797 41	2,773,068 06
Net Earnings	666,692 70	827,004 47	1,159,021 18	1,700,613 39	1,638,437 66	1,891,962 24	2,071,408 50	2,525,957 71
Per cent. of Earnings for Operation	81 78	77 97	72 45	64 24	61 22	56 30	54 10	52 33
Expenditure for Extraordinary Repairs and Replacements	....	135,194 15	419,955 87	149,080 83	151,612 22	93,451 32	121,534 70	156,586 37
Gold Purchases taken up in Exchange Account	25,887 88	Gain. 18,358 25	64,745 18	310,777 59	542,802 54	885,149 80	861,681 42	991,760 43

I also append a statement of the freights, passengers, express, telegraphs, and miscellaneous receipts, as well as the expenses and earnings of the road from the year 1889 to 1896, taken from the last official report of the companies. It will be noticed that the traffic and receipts of this road, like the Central, have been steadily increasing from the time at which it began to be operated. (See table on page 198.)

MEXICAN INTERNATIONAL RAILROAD COMPANY.
GROSS EARNINGS IN MEXICAN MONEY.

YEAR.	NO. OF PASS'G'RS.	PASSENGER RECEIPTS.	FREIGHT.		FREIGHT RECEIPTS.	TOTAL RECEIPTS.
			Tons.	Kilos.		
From Dec. 3d, 1883– 1884.....	15,942	$ 32,408 45	15,129	723	$ 37,575 00	$ 69,983 45
1885.....	9,853	25,881 44	50,896	181	118,177 80	144,059 24
1886.....	10,411	29,242 61	55,877	079	144,311 09	173,553 70
1887.....	9,796	32,516 71	86,889	772	189,184 86	221,701 57
1888.....	41,170	125,848 48	116,561	273	459,906 57	585,755 05
1889.....	53,194	140,676 05	180,544	270	691,477 04	832,153 09
1890.....	59,327	149,258 43	222,856	211	894,944 35	1,044,202 78
1891.....	64,641	170,304 00	216,465	739	956,546 91	1,126,850 91
1892.....	60,967	181,378 14	390,802	838	1,836,958 51	2,018,336 65
1893.....	74,577	219,624 38	335,200	769	1,743,140 42	1,962,764 80
1894.....	77,456	208,551 86	376,734	430	1,873,974 91	2,082,526 77
1895.....	102,858	276,514 04	469,641	859	2,197,463 36	2,473,977 40
1896.....	111,480	313,904 13	525,951	874	2,453,223 54	2,767,127 67
Total..	691,672	$1,906,108 72	3,043,552	018	$13,596,884 36	$15,502,993 08

MEXICAN INTERNATIONAL RAILWAY.
(STATEMENT FURNISHED BY THE COMPANY.)

YEAR.	AVERAGE KILOMETRES OPERATED.	GROSS EARNINGS.	AVERAGE EARNINGS PER KILOMETRE.	AVERAGE EARNINGS PER MILE.
1884..................	245.20	$ 103,307 98	$ 421 49	$ 612 37
1885..................	273.58	153,916 18	562 59	905 39
1886..................	273.58	185,150 25	676 76	1,098 11
1887..................	273.58	237,394 13	867 73	1,396 43
1888..................	573.97	656,781 41	1,144 28	1,841 47
1889..................	636.34	911,698 51	1,432 73	2,305 64
1890..................	637.38	1,126,366 41	1,745 64	2,839 77
1891..................	658.30	1,197,856 55	1,819 69	2,924 02
1892..................	746.37	2,095,726 14	2,807 89	4,518 67
1893..................	922.19	2,050,934 01	2,226 15	3,579 04
1894..................	922.19	2,169,121 47	2,352 14	3,785 29
1895..................	947.23	2,664,126 08	2,812 54	4,526 28
1896..................	1,011.02	2,900,925 33	2,869 30	4,617 69
Total.........	8,120.93	$16,453,304 45	$21,738 93	$34,950 17

Mexican International. The Mexican International, which has been built without any subsidy from the Mexican Government, was opened for traffic in 1883, and its traffic and receipts, like the other two roads, have steadily increased. I append two statements of this road; the first, furnished me by the company, embraces its traffic and earnings from 1883 to 1896 ; and the second is another statement furnished me also by the company, showing the average kilometres operated, gross earnings, average earnings per kilometre, and average earnings per mile from the years 1884 to 1896. (See the two tables on page 199.)

Mexican Southern Railway.—I give below a statement of the number of passengers, amount of freight and earnings of the Mexican Southern Railway, furnished to me by the Company, embracing nine months of the year 1893 and the whole of 1894, as before the 1st of April, 1893, the road was run by the Contractors, and the Company has no data in their possession. I also append a statement taken from the *Anuario Estadistico de la Republica Mexicana* of 1895, embracing the traffic and

MEXICAN SOUTHERN RAILWAY.

MONTHS.	PASSEN-GERS.	PASSENGER RECEIPTS.	FREIGHT.		FREIGHT RECEIPTS.	TOTAL RECEIPTS.
			Tons.	Kilos.		
1893.						
January.....	....	....	....	......	....	....
February....	....	....	....	......	....	....
March.......	....	....	....	.....	....	....
April........	12,099	$ 14,647 21	2,554	810	$ 20,243 01	$ 38,172 41
May	9,943	11,683 15	2,262	790	15,421 87	29,506 27
June........	8,154	7,119 78	1,344	950	9,541 00	18,209 89
July........	11,865	8,740 20	1,355	420	5,707 05	16,671 95
August......	10,375	9,577 91	2,568	330	23,762 64	35,959 30
September...	10,405	9,751 47	2,019	000	17,322 40	30,947 32
October	10,897	10,317 54	2,145	150	16,941 41	29,945 71
November...	11,893	12,661 99	3,296	070	16,276 89	31,839 26
December ...	14,452	17,096 43	2,943	420	15,702 01	38,308 76
Total	100,083	$101,595 68	20,489	940	$140,918 28	$269,560 87

Number of Passengers according to official Tables........ 142,919.
"   Tons   "   "   " .... 27,917,510 k.

MONTHS.	PASSEN-GERS.	PASSENGER RECEIPTS.	FREIGHT.		FREIGHT RECEIPTS.	TOTAL RECEIPTS.
			Tons.	Kilos.		
1894.						
January.....	15,255	$ 16,146 67	3,187	880	$ 20,083 75	$ 39,725 34
February....	14,900	14,925 48	3,060	140	22,616 16	40,935 29
March.......	29,545	21,348 92	3,744	290	25,224 36	50,001 11
April........	16,527	17,195 89	4,010	380	25,184 73	45,742 46
May	18,229	14,864 75	4,322	880	21,406 14	39,720 18
June........	20,543	15,173 98	3,942	590	23,279 97	42,037 56
July	19,471	14,023 23	3,828	110	20,637 28	38,168 24
August......	18,218	14,602 85	3,515	420	17,531 15	35,709 56
September...	18,653	15,354 80	3,189	740	16,285 34	35,156 99
October	17,814	14,954 13	2,973	510	19,374 02	38,068 95
November...	16,300	14,257 08	2,453	800	17,145 58	34,691 02
December ...	20,994	18,776 23	2,682	690	17,900 02	40,519 83
Total	226,449	$191,624 01	40,911	430	$246,668 50	$480,476 53

earnings of the Company during the years from 1890 to 1895, taken from data furnished by the Company to the Department of Communications of Mexico.

MEXICAN SOUTHERN.

YEARS.	PASSEN- GERS.	PASSENGER RECEIPTS.	MERCHANDISE.		OTHER RECEIPTS.	TOTAL RECEIPTS.
			Tons.	Kilos.		
1890.........	....	....	.....	.....	....	....
1891.........	76,788	$74,259 78	11,506	820	$ 59,427 26	$ 133,687 04
1892.........	104,296	109,011 90	26,977	490	152,859 11	261,871 01
1893.........	143,037	153,233 01	27,921	510	246,862 75	400,095 76
1894.........	225,447	191,624 01	40,911	430	246,668 50	438,292 51
1895.........	218,213	196,462 34	36,511	210	287,426 59	483,888 93
Total......	767,781	$724,591 04	143,828	460	$993,244 21	$1,717,835 25

Other Railroads. The following statement shows the traffic and earnings of the Mexican, Interoceanic, Sonora, and minor railroads in Mexico, taken from the *Anuario Estadistico de la Republica Mexicana* of 1895, compiled from data furnished by the respective companies to the Department of Communications of the Mexican Government.

MEXICAN RAILROAD.

YEARS.	PASSEN- GERS.	PASSENGER RECEIPTS.	MERCHANDISE.		OTHER RECEIPTS.	TOTAL RECEIPTS.
			Tons.	Kilos.		
1873...	476,287	$ 482,565 39	150,473	812	$ 1,348,344 49	$ 1,830,909 88
1874...	459,601	467,816 73	121,935	229	1,887,028 76	2,354,845 49
1875...	267,776	476,546 91	136,632	65	1,970,008 55	2,446,555 46
1876...	245,675	380,018 73	132,216	831	1,841,717 53	2,221,736 26
1877...	300,591	533,520 58	158,537	56	2,255,466 03	2,788,986 61
1878...	279,893	518,318 74	169,287	672	2,440,513 39	2,958,832 13
1879...	293,179	517,711 92	190,908	638	2,823,013 02	3,340,724 94
1880...	323,088	548,941 72	219,930	162	3,242,343 11	3,791,284 83
1881...	331,749	587,135 85	278,942	924	4,433,648 24	5,020,784 09
1882...	385,621	696,235 87	333,979	556	5,396,090 55	6,092,326 42
1883...	409,098	710,636 88	373,389	634	5,115,639 84	5,826,276 72
1884...	389,421	655,458 83	236,030	480	3,191,916 10	3,847,374 93
1885...	377,512	603,886 11	246,169	949	2,812,764 22	3,416,650 33
1886...	367,260	604,278 41	266,432	333	2,714,082 96	3,318,361 37
1887...	380,153	655,312 23	301,185	300	3,141,903 40	3,797,215 63
1888...	393,679	694,138 08	351,070	36	3,352,439 37	4,046,577 45
1889...	444,149	765,118 71	391,627	274	3,512,566 64	4,277,685 35
1890...	502,139	701,916 00	443,794	979	3,565,083 50	4,266,999 50
1891...	620,988	832,185 94	464,123	453	3,239,764 53	4,071,950 47
1892...	628,591	797,878 35	408,709	417	2,286,389 71	3,084,268 06
1893...	629,892	768,616 68	387,400	277	2,140,061 75	2,908,678 43
1894...	717,076	857,525 26	433,637	485	2,063,486 26	2,921,011 52
1895...	772,139	993,016 63	453,294	579	2,087,844 19	3,080,860 82
Total.	9,995,557	$14,848,780 55	6,649,709	141	$66,862,116 14	$81,710,896 69

INTEROCEANIC RAILWAY.

YEARS.	PASSEN-GERS.	PASSENGER RECEIPTS.	MERCHANDISE.		OTHER RECEIPTS.	TOTAL RECEIPTS.
			Tons	Kilos.		
1880.....	228,053	$65,277 91	11,431	145	$ 36,515 46	$ 101,793 37
1881.....	367,116	105,083 31	49,942	548	159,535 64	264,618 95
1882.....	411,090	111,029 25	53,382	385	258,221 05	369,250 30
1883.....	406,016	223,049 58	56,822	222	356,906 46	579,956 04
1884.....	634,306	247,528 50	131,385	319	407,593 64	655,122 14
1885.....	606,510	240,233 70	167,970	265	436,345 10	676,578 80
1886.....	569,421	224,815 19	148,001	913	482,003 18	706,818 37
1887.....	621,295	239,812 48	174,194	156	570,033 20	809,845 68
1888.....	673,169	254,809 77	200,386	400	658,063 22	912,872 99
1889.....	596,812	271,562 69	190,902	920	710,848 78	982,411 47
1890.....	657,616	383,107 10	288,836	358	1,153,999 13	1,537,106 23
1891.....	795,625	456,635 80	282,311	491	1,176,562 22	1,633,248 02
1892.....	799,487	466,799 31	367,762	660	1,376,488 38	1,843,287 69
1893.....	879,005	486,075 54	383,503	000	1,705,859 74	2,191,935 28
1894.....	881,810	491,914 20	440,648	000	1,912,192 58	2,404,106 78
1895.....	906,550	491,388 67	464,975	000	1,771,268 92	2,262,657 59
Total..	10,033,881	4,759,173 00	3,412,455	782	13,172,436 70	17,931,609 70

SONORA RAILWAY.

1881......	....	$ 11,303 29	....	.....	$ 17,254 95	$ 28,558 24
1882......	....	68,410 83	....	.....	157,694 60	226,105 43
1883......	33,464	99,461 33	24,202	791	119,347 56	218,808 89
1884......	36,428	87,793 47	21,115	382	108,531 43	196,324 90
1885......	47,271	101,918 90	29,927	682	193,189 89	295,108 79
1886......	45,298	98,613 06	33,635	621	191,981 24	290,594 30
1887......	38,189	87,098 20	34,660	670	193,981 40	281,079 60
1888......	38,335	84,143 57	37,621	60	204,146 63	288,290 20
1889... ..	44,691	104,367 85	43,321	710	239,697 67	344,065 52
1890......	48,196	97,662 48	46,147	870	259,360 01	357,022 49
1891......	56,565	112,919 18	53,947	663	332,938 65	445,857 83
1892......	54,621	119,784 37	58,867	359	363,128 91	482,913 28
1893......	52,678	126,657 56	63,687	055	393,319 17	519,976 73
1895......	62,715	141,744 09	69,982	389	469,950 09	611,694 18
Total...	558,451	1,341,878 18	517,117	252	3,244,522 20	4,586,400 38

HIDALGO AND NORTHEASTERN RAILWAY.

1881......	39,759	$ 9,897 17	2,264	000	$ 1,659 36	$ 11,556 53
1882......	30,940	12,270 02	7,624	000	10,442 30	22,712 32
1883......	37,198	25,715 04	17,852	283	33,220 80	58,933 84
1884......	35,209	32,648 22	34,958	222	54,955 16	87,603 38
1885......	51,823	32,295 08	40,960	794	76,710 43	109,005 51
1886.,....	44,666	36,692 27	51,760	395	117,603 55	154,295 82
1887......	53,958	43,582 66	65,524	057	145,702 22	189,284 88
1888......	55,055	45,805 05	77,203	173	161,773 18	207,578 23
1889......	90,241	90,194 56	100,110	733	262,081 27	352,275 83
1890......	113,605	106,397 87	137,467	201	328,124 49	434,522 36
1891......	127,972	120,128 18	176,432	664	404,735 74	524,863 92
1892......	148,540	141,360 09	186,041	471	422,052 91	563,413 00
1893......	168,422	161,908 45	178,174	047	468,566 69	630,475 14
1894......	214,837	178,477 10	200,685	687	643,760 93	822,178 03
1895......	206,194	181,043 96	164,176	000	616,641 61	797,685 57
Total...	1,418,419	$1,218,415 72	1,441,234	727	$3,747,970 64	$4,966,384 36

MÉRIDA AND PROGRESO RAILWAY.

YEARS.	PASSEN-GERS.	PASSENGER RECEIPTS.	MERCHANDISE.		OTHER RECEIPTS.	TOTAL RECEIPTS.
			Tons.	Kilos.		
1881......	56,085	$ 28,639 50	....	......	$ 53,236 00	$ 81,875 50
1882......	84,016	37,642 38	41,934	297	75,242 88	112,885 26
1883......	83,231	36,239 83	59,859	715	108,248 80	144,488 63
1884......	87,159	37,940 54	95,962	902	139,299 59	177,240 13
1885......	64,173	29,078 41	79,611	737	120,389 13	149,467 54
1886......	77,139	33,353 16	58,239	254	78,168 66	111,521 82
1887......	85,044	22,844 42	46,055	714	52,995 68	75,840 10
1888......	109,997	29,812 76	30,872	512	64,291 88	94,104 64
1889......	158,534	56,763 81	44,619	200	97,017 37	153,781 18
1890......	162,701	55,566 97	53,949	818	89,139 81	144,706 78
1891......	129,989	46,155 85	34,486	000	67,460 18	113,616 03
1892......	108,119	36,528 45	28,656	499	83,593 75	120,132 20
1893......	91,291	39,276 08	34,406	476	96,230 47	135,506 55
1894......	79,653	33,387 18	38,659	401	68,513 05	101,900 23
1895......	....	38,228 81	....	......	97,850 38	136,079 19
Total...	1,377,131	$561,458 15	647,313	525	$1,291,677 63	$1,853,135 78

TEHUACAN AND ESPERANZA RAILWAY.

YEARS.	PASSEN-GERS.	PASSENGER RECEIPTS.	MERCHANDISE.		OTHER RECEIPTS.	TOTAL RECEIPTS.
			Tons.	Kilos.		
1884.....	18,343	$ 11,427 64	6,043	813	$ 32,921 87	$ 44,349 51
1885.....	15,049	10,077 20	5,857	257	31,905 66	41,982 86
1886.....	12,942	9,111 04	6,603	705	38,271 80	47,382 84
1887.....	14,848	10,080 15	7,669	730	47,437 77	57,517 92
1888.....	17,116	15,376 57	8,764	045	54,500 93	69,877 50
1889.....	19,385	20,673 00	9,858	360	61,564 09	82,237 09
1890.....	20,462	18,459 96	16,625	870	75,744 37	94,204 33
1891.....	17,426	11,087 06	14,381	340	68,684 08	79,771 14
1892.....	15,102	8,792 35	4,179	510	44,602 09	53,394 44
1893.....	16,096	9,411 51	5,663	530	37,997 45	47,408 96
1894.....	....	....	....	......	....	....
1895.....	19,905	10,941 81	4,062	500	18,724 99	29,666 80
Total...	186,674	$135,438 29	89,709	660	$512,355 10	$647,793 39

MÉRIDA AND PETO RAILWAY.

YEARS.	PASSEN-GERS.	PASSENGER RECEIPTS.	MERCHANDISE.		OTHER RECEIPTS.	TOTAL RECEIPTS.
			Tons.	Kilos.		
1881.....	22,852	$ 3,913 69	....	......	$ 430 60	$ 4,344 29
1882.....	81,102	12,293 58	....	......	2,637 41	14,930 99
1883.....	88,920	14,422 31	5,654	115	4,833 23	19,255 54
1884.....	81,566	17,818 29	11,063	915	11,588 49	29,406 78
1885.....	64,118	16,795 70	16,919	464	20,222 10	37,017 80
1886.....	62,983	16,728 82	17,368	079	21,710 91	38,439 73
1887.....	62,763	15,943 55	15,827	969	26,619 71	42,563 26
1888.....	92,773	22,146 61	20,231	714	37,013 76	59,160 37
1889.....	99,761	25,351 70	25,397	822	52,553 95	77,905 65
1890.....	126,978	24,514 70	30,024	477	69,390 02	93,904 72
1891.....	134,438	55,007 97	27,106	666	85,602 24	140,610 21
1892.....	129,163	59,742 62	28,266	475	118,214 20	177,956 82
1893.....	163,852	71,970 64	36,202	439	128,115 61	200,086 25
1894.....	157,311	70,898 03	32,260	765	121,547 79	192,445 82
1895.....	140,193	67,134 69	37,853	723	118,179 11	185,313 80
Total...	1,508,773	$494,682 90	304,177	623	$818,659 13	$1,313,342 03

SINALOA AND DURANGO (ALTATA TO CULIACAN) RAILWAY.

YEARS.	PASSEN-GERS.	PASSENGER RECEIPTS.	FREIGHT.		MISCELLA-NEOUS RECEIPTS.	TOTAL RECEIPTS.
			Tons.	Kilos.		
1882.....	2,727	$ 3,712 04	1,864	589	$ 5,155 65	$ 8,867 69
1883.....	12,251	7,816 94	3,913	457	18,717 39	26,534 33
1884.....	21,776	8,584 57	5,962	325	25,019 62	33,604 19
1885.....	15,816	8,786 88	4,953	364	19,719 92	28,506 80
1886.....	23,171	10,681 46	4,316	116	20,880 39	31,561 85
1887.....	25,487	10,705 56	5,962	325	16,661 71	27,367 27
1888.....	27,904	11,459 15	6,736	532	23,650 34	35,109 49
1889.....	21,850	9,318 46	6,535	236	25,537 79	34,856 25
1890.....	42,987	14,871 77	4,722	749	18,911 41	33,783 18
1891.....	54,678	19,170 23	7,442	886	25,381 35	44,551 58
1892.....	39,494	14,837 39	10,371	701	28,131 17	42,968 56
1893.....	56,503	14,152 07	12,893	822	35,205 12	49,357 19
1894.....	38,451	14,040 41	12,093	568	38,393 29	52,433 70
1895.....	37,627	15,768 25	8,538	024	29,390 59	45,158 84
Total...	420,722	$163,905 18	96,306	694	$330,755 74	$494,660 92

MÉRIDA AND CAMPECHE RAILWAY.

1883.....	22,944	$ 3,586 10	462	169	$ 1,120 32	$ 4,706 42
1884.....	97,295	13,161 59	3,952	565	5,203 67	18,365 26
1885.....	76,135	12,535 94	7,794	570	9,306 31	21,842 25
1886.....	65,274	10,779 44	6,265	722	9,579 90	20,359 34
1887.....	68,883	11,793 63	8,106	813	13,263 22	25,056 85
1888.....	86,329	22,172 11	11,514	018	21,106 70	43,278 81
1889.....	58,383	17,017 46	12,534	035	28,300 44	45,317 90
1890.....	75,496	28,939 04	6,779	458	19,057 69	47,996 73
1891.....	96,994	35,303 04	17,328	478	36,035 70	71,338 74
1892.....	87,954	33,598 11	17,363	510	39,330 26	72,928 37
1893.....	124,983	56,034 03	21,775	101	53,390 97	109,425 00
1894.....	....	....			....	....
1895.....	139,349	66,174 14	24,699	277	72,923 31	139,097 45
Total...	1,000,019	$311,094 63	138,575	716	$308,618 49	$ 619,713 12

MÉRIDA AND VALLADOLID RAILWAY.

1883.....	18,123	$ 2,570 17	....	.....	$ 609 18	$ 3,179 35
1884.....	75,541	12,595 63	4,248	788	5,287 96	17,883 59
1885.....	100,015	18,548 61	6,040	957	8,487 63	27,036 24
1886.....	132,210	25,798 73	25,181	498	33,276 45	59,075 18
1887.....	176,501	32,298 87	41,496	479	58,096 41	90,395 28
1888.....	183,973	37,957 45	35,975	207	65,864 26	103,821 71
1889.....	280,348	58,691 70	54,206	189	115,032 74	173,724 44
1890.....	295,034	63,485 18	50,781	662	96,611 23	160,096 41
1891.....	264,781	60,366 76	47,064	535	98,212 31	158,579 07
1892.....	254,344	61,573 70	46,124	159	134,209 85	195,783 55
1893.....	244,040	79,223 48	50,633	534	139,384 68	218,608 16
1894.....	....	....			....	....
1895.....	199,670	72,828 22	62,342	134	165,983 26	238,811 48
Total...	2,224,580	$525,938 50	424,095	142	$921,055 96	$1,446,994 46

TLALMANALCO RAILWAY.

YEARS.	PASSEN- GERS.	PASSENGER RECEIPTS.	FREIGHT.		MISCELLA- NEOUS RECEIPTS.	TOTAL RECEIPTS.
			Tons.	Kilos.		
1883.....	39,688	$ 4,022 44	10,813	000	$ 5,564 91	$ 9,587 35
1884.....	40,211	4,596 80	9,641	000	7,276 95	11,873 75
1885.....	41,226	4,577 43	7,466	713	6,830 06	11,407 49
1886.....	41,905	4,621 28	6,845	349	6,360 51	10,981 79
1887.....	47,808	5,098 09	8,083	538	6,788 75	11,886 84
1888.....	46,150	5,076 97	10,722	122	9,164 56	14,241 53
1889.....	49,866	5,536 16	13,710	170	11,566 53	17,102 69
1890.....	55,345	6,654 20	24,988	131	12,019 62	18,673 82
1891.....	61,236	6,765 86	15,469	050	12,684 68	19,450 54
1892.....	62,618	7,225 65	12,303	020	9,853 83	17,079 48
1893.....	60,835	6,492 30	18,572	715	15,430 59	21,922 89
1894.....	....	....	....	.....	....	....
1895.....	71,777	7,358 10	13,824	250	12,284 66	19,642 76
Total...	618,665	$68,025 28	152,439	058	$115,825 65	$183,850 93

SAN JUAN BAUTISTA AND CARRIZAL PASSENGER RAILWAY.

1888.....	99,504	$ 5,123 13	....	.....	....	$ 5,123 13
1889.....	56,880	4,406 10	....	.....	....	4,406 10
1890.....	110,731	6,733 92	1,022	000	$1,022 60	7,756 52
1891.....	105,251	7,923 34	922	000	922 79	8,846 13
1892.....	152,606	9,462 23	1,803	000	1,442 28	10,904 51
1893.....	150,243	9,965 56	2,052	000	1,842 70	11,808 26
1894.....	....	....	....	.....	....	....
1895.....	167,994	12,003 21	3,455	454	3,131 00	15,134 21
Total...	843,209	$55,617 49	9,254	454	$8,361 37	$63,978 86

SAN ANDRÉS AND CHALCHICOMULA RAILWAY.

1882.....	6,851	$ 1,905 53	1,658	614	$ 2,847 76	$ 4,753 29
1883.....	15,053	4,002 51	4,802	280	9,548 51	13,551 02
1884.....	14,218	3,683 23	4,485	960	11,681 15	15,364 38
1885.....	10,928	2,834 42	4,723	310	4,805 87	7,640 29
1886.....	9,994	2,595 58	4,079	294	4,980 84	7,576 42
1887.....	9,794	2,428 25	5,835	696	6,850 94	9,279 19
1888.....	10,173	2,489 80	8,324	735	9,592 88	12,082 68
1889. ...	12,727	3,137 07	5,832	417	7,100 57	10,237 64
1890.....	13,010	3,163 15	4,385	480	6,225 35	9,388 50
1891.....	12,711	3,079 10	6,258	307	8,140 76	11,219 86
1892.....	12,223	6,327 21	7,980	430	9,376 67	15,703 88
1893.....	12,239	3,061 75	10,011	250	11,474 05	14,535 80
1894.....	13,998	3,398 65	7,781	980	9,266 42	12,665 07
1895.....	13,454	3,444 35	....	....	10,383 00	13,827 35
Total..	167,373	$45,550 60	76,159	753	$112,274 77	$157,825 37

ORIZABA AND INGENIO RAILWAY.

YEARS.	PASSEN-GERS.	PASSENGER RECEIPTS.	FREIGHT.		MISCELLA-NEOUS RECEIPTS.	TOTAL RECEIPTS.
			Tons,	Kilos.		
1882.....	38,636	$ 4,473 30	....	....	$	$ 4,473 30
1883.....	91,949	10,645 94	237	168	197 64	10,843 58
1884.....	94,323	10,920 74	360	972	300 82	11,221 56
1885.....	34,921	4,365 12	435	720	363 10	4,728 22
1886.....	86,047	9,962 57	384	813	350 18	10,312 75
1887.....	40,364	4,673 38	121	344	101 12	4,774 50
1888.....	41,945	4,800 00	182	400	152 00	4,952 00
1889.....	46,640	5,400 00	168	000	140 00	5,540 00
1890.....	106,773	12,362 20	504	000	420 00	12,782 20
1891.....	103,011	12,532 10	612	000	510 00	13,042 10
1892.....	99,553	13,303 20	750	000	728 36	14,031 56
1893.....	104,030	13,900 50	....	....	400 00	14,300 50
1894.....	104,019	13,990 77	704	000	528 00	14,518 77
1895.....	132,650	17,438 04	748	000	561 00	17,999 04
Total..	1,124,861	$138,767 86	5,208	417	$4,752 22	$143,520 08

SANTA ANA AND TLAXCALA RAILWAY.

1883.....	58,068	$ 2,860 20	....	....	$ 494 38	$ 3,354 58
1884.....	117,560	8,580 60	....	....	1,494 14	10,074 74
1885.....	174,204	12,714 98	....	....	1,483 00	14,197 98
1886.....	156,676	6,733 14	....	....	1,482 37	8,215 51
1887.....	117,518	8,463 85	....	....	1,373 25	9,837 10
1888.....	120,910	9,179 28	....	....	1,651 02	10,830 30
1889.....	110,574	8,294 98	....	....	1,475 20	9,770 18
1890.....	145,263	8,398 00	....	....	1,469 82	9,867 82
1891....	66,716	9,098 30	....	....	1,769 28	10,867 58
1892.....	55,768	7,011 74	750	000	1,280 03	8,291 77
1893.....	59,127	7,326 40	3,829	003	2,434 13	9,760 53
1894.....	....	....			....	....
1895.....	71,843	8,670 35	2,038	440	2,344 38	11,014 73
Total..	1,254,227	$ 97,331 82	6,617	443	$18,751 00	$116,082 82

CÁRDENAS AND RIO GRIJALVA RAILWAY.

1886.....	....	$ 263 01	....	....	$ 526 00	$ 789 01
1887.....	....	401 43	....	....	722 57	1,124 00
1888.....	....	309 07	....	....	781 13	1,090 20
1889.....	....	216 72	....	....	839 69	1,056 41
1890.....	....	380 00	....	....	839 69	1,219 69
1891.....	....	480 00	....	....	939 69	1,419 69
1892.....	....	....	....	....	....	....
1893.....	....	....	....	....	....	....
1884.....	....	....	....	....	....	....
1895.....	....	....	....	....	....	....
Total..	....	2,050 23	....	....	$4,648 77	$6,699 00

TOLUCA AND SAN JUAN DE LAS HUERTAS RAILWAY

YEARS.	PASSEN-GERS.	PASSENGER RECEIPTS.	FREIGHT.		MISCELLA-NEOUS RECEIPTS.	TOTAL RECEIPTS.
			Tons.	Kilos.		
1885.....	75,052	$ 7,016 39	....	....	$ 1,138 19	$ 8,154 58
1886.....	97,535	9,078 95	6,133	000	5,201 59	14,280 54
1887.....	94,874	8,788 61	9,361	000	6,755 49	15,544 10
1888.....	93,512	8,475 83	7,251	750	4,729 99	13,205 82
1889.....	134,193	12,677 97	13,483	088	8,087 03	20,765 00
1890.....	178,072	16,264 75	18,595	861	12,156 67	28,421 42
1891.....	156,917	15,293 69	13,998	185	11,082 76	26,376 45
1892.....	107,122	13,777 47	13,924	530	11,702 56	25,480 03
1893.....	176,241	16,340 90	14,128	510	11,690 24	28,031 14
1894.....	121,949	15,328 76	13,778	920	11,536 10	26,864 86
1895.....	204,591	18,210 13	13,860	796	10,136 78	28,346 91
Total..	1,440,058	$141,253 45	124,515	640	$94,217 40	$235,470 85

VANEGAS, CEDRAL, MATEHUALA, AND RIO VERDE RAILWAY.

YEARS.	PASSEN-GERS.	PASSENGER RECEIPTS.	FREIGHT.		MISCELLA-NEOUS RECEIPTS.	TOTAL RECEIPTS.
			Tons.	Kilos.		
1889.....	......	$ 449 69	28	540	$ 335 24	$ 784 93
1890.....	10,848	5,763 16	1,840	661	15,492 27	21,255 43
1891.....	36,742	12,783 05	5,939	568	61,513 43	74,296 48
1892.....	44,502	16,083 11	94,112	500	124,565 69	140,648 80
1893.....	46,083	16,030 02	83,115	000	114,505 49	130,535 51
1894.....	35,213	13,798 53	113,384	000	185,649 51	199,448 04
1895....	....	....	....	....	....	....
Total..	173,388	$64,907 56	298,420	269	$502,061 63	$566,969 19

MÉRIDA AND IZAMAL RAILWAY.

YEARS.	PASSEN-GERS.	PASSENGER RECEIPTS.	FREIGHT.		MISCELLA-NEOUS RECEIPTS.	TOTAL RECEIPTS.
			Tons.	Kilos.		
1887.....	42,812	$ 7,280 38	2,729	000	$ 3,954 64	$ 11,235 02
1888.....	78,102	18,981 70	7,871	541	17,656 81	36,638 51
1889.....	106 089	38,330 34	11,633	376	28,069 91	66,400 25
1890.....	106,883	54,462 10	10,146	374	29,995 33	84,457 43
1891.....	80,042	41,891 51	13,775	771	44,798 43	86,689 94
1892.....	94,634	49,729 03	18,094	768	65,565 47	115,294 50
1893.....	96,458	45,684 12	21,476	676	65,714 14	111,398 26
1894.....	....	52,564 78	....	....	61,335 45	113,900 23
1895.....	. .....	49,735 12	....	....	63,295 49	113,030 61
Total..	605,020	$358,659 08	85,727	506	$380,385 67	$739,044 75

SAN MÁRCOS AND NAUTLA RAILWAY.

YEARS.	PASSEN-GERS.	PASSENGER RECEIPTS.	FREIGHT.		MISCELLA-NEOUS RECEIPTS.	TOTAL RECEIPTS.
			Tons.	Kilos.		
1891.....	4,582	$ 3,181 70	5,307	750	$ 5,968 12	$ 9,149 82
1892.....	10,894	5,968 34	12,000	570	17,835 93	23,804 27
1893.....	14,136	7,339 14	19,576	000	27,008 47	34,347 61
1894.....	15,481	7,918 63	....	......	29,519 97	37,438 60
1895.....	17,309	8,195 77	24,452	440	27,603 55	35,799 32
Total...	62,402	$32,603 58	61,336	760	$107,936 04	$140,539 62

MONTEREY AND GULF RAILWAY.

| YEARS. | PASSEN-GERS. | PASSENGER RECEIPTS. | FREIGHT. | | MISCELLA-NEOUS RECEIPTS. | TOTAL RECEIPTS. |
			Tons.	Kilos.		
1889......	16,714	$ 17,144 65	4,197	432	$ 13,440 52	$ 30,585 17
1890......	57,096	70,185 08	168,204	600	791,398 47	861,583 55
1891......	94,052	112,910 64	174,829	706	876,563 75	989,474 39
1892......	99,802	119,390 74	193,437	800	664,072 42	783,463 16
1893......	107,378	141,093 86	238,442	000	820,433 06	961,526 92
1894......	....	....	....	....	....	....
1895......	127,900	150,005 75	329,059	008	1,162,009 39	1,312,015 14
Total..	502,942	$610,730 72	1,108,170	546	$4,327,917 61	$4,938,648 33

CÓRDOVA AND TUXTEPEC RAILWAY.

| YEARS. | PASSEN-GERS. | PASSENGER RECEIPTS. | FREIGHT. | | MISCELLA-NEOUS RECEIPTS. | TOTAL RECEIPTS. |
			Tons.	Kilos.		
1889......	26,537	$ 4,815 27	....	....	$ 1,285 13	$ 6,100 40
1890......	49,142	8,917 06	....	....	2,379 97	11,297 03
1891......	23,542	14,009 84	....	....	5,097 98	19,107 82
1892......	39,885	12,767 51	2,235	571	5,111 19	17,878 70
1893......	46,086	17,433 62	3,730	424	9,828 94	27,262 56
1894......	....	....	....	....	....	....
1895......	....	....	....	....	....	....
Total..	185,192	$57,943 30	5,965	995	$23,703 21	$81,646 51

MARAVATÍO AND CUERNAVACA RAILWAY.

| YEARS. | PASSEN-GERS. | PASSENGER RECEIPTS. | FREIGHT. | | MISCELLA-NEOUS RECEIPTS. | TOTAL RECEIPTS. |
			Tons.	Kilos.		
1890......	3,466	$ 3,389 66	....	....	$ 3,372 10	$ 6,761 76
1891......	6,190	6,283 94	....	....	16,741 42	23,025 36
1892......	9,081	8,047 76	....	....	30,160 42	38,208 18
1893......	12,867	9,418 26	....	....	28,201 99	37,620 25
1894......	15,138	11,235 58	....	....	32,238 33	43,473 91
1895......	13,964	11,364 72	....	....	39,714 80	51,079 52
Total..	60,706	$49,739 92	....	....	$150,429 06	$200,168 98

SALAMANCA AND SANTIAGO VALLEY RAILWAY.

| YEARS. | PASSEN-GERS. | PASSENGER RECEIPTS. | FREIGHT. | | MISCELLA-NEOUS RECEIPTS. | TOTAL RECEIPTS. |
			Tons.	Kilos.		
1889......	4,709	$ 1,486 51	132	270	$ 304 26	$ 1,790 77
1890......	18,836	5,946 04	529	080	1,217 04	7,163 08
1891......	25,432	8,554 11	3,324	430	7,237 67	15,791 78
1892......	21,923	8,020 59	2,815	940	5,325 03	13,345 62
1893......	22,674	7,719 44	3,380	060	8,910 74	16,630 18
1894......	27,496	8,740 90	4,142	690	9,584 17	18,325 07
1895......	30,094	10,376 66	7,799	050	13,969 73	24,346 39
Total..	151,164	$50,844 25	22,123	520	$46,548 64	$97,392 89

Railways.

MONTE ALTO RAILWAY.

YEARS.	PASSEN-GERS.	PASSENGER RECEIPTS.	FREIGHT		MISCELLA-NEOUS RECEIPTS.	TOTAL RECEIPTS.
			Tons.	Kilos.		
1892......	31,080	$ 2,652 89	4,006	000	$1,330 13	$ 3,983 02
1893......	30,888	3,260 28	6,135	000	1,965 72	5,226 00
1894......	31,913	3,318 14	6,221	000	2,002 79	5,320 93
1895......	39,041	4,005 14	5,430	000	1,410 85	5,415 99
Total..	132,922	$13,236 45	21,792	000	$6,709 49	$19,945 94

VALLEY OF MEXICO RAILWAY.

YEARS.	PASSEN-GERS.	PASSENGER RECEIPTS.	FREIGHT		MISCELLA-NEOUS RECEIPTS.	TOTAL RECEIPTS.
			Tons.	Kilos.		
1891......	1,423,652	$ 99,615 09	9,108	000	$ 5,912 38	$105,527 41
1892......	1,639,873	119,379 76	21,154	000	12,310 35	131,690 17
1893......	1,637,135	110,160 60	24,361	000	21,497 48	131,658 08
1894......	....	....	......	....	....	....
1895......	....	....	......	....	....	....
Total..	4,700,660	$329,155 45	54,623	000	$39,720 21	$368,875 66

PUEBLA INDUSTRIAL RAILWAY.

YEARS.	PASSEN-GERS.	PASSENGER RECEIPTS.	FREIGHT		MISCELLA-NEOUS RECEIPTS.	TOTAL RECEIPTS.
			Tons.	Kilos.		
1891......	151,380	$ 23,234 66	....	....	$ 1,398 00	$ 24,632 66
1892......	125,766	20,052 34	....	....	1,239 00	21,291 34
1893......	155,112	24,082 55	....	....	1,380 00	25,462 55
1894......	190,480	31,620 62	....	....	3,149 37	34,769 99
1895......	226,275	36,264 00	14,250	000	11,122 35	47,386 35
Total..	849,013	$135,254 17	14,250	000	$18,288 72	$153,542 89

MEXICAN NORTHERN RAILWAY.

YEARS.	PASSEN-GERS.	PASSENGER RECEIPTS.	FREIGHT		MISCELLA-NEOUS RECEIPTS.	TOTAL RECEIPTS.
			Tons.	Kilos.		
1891......	4,870	$14,802 61	94,726	000	$ 740,122 98	$ 754,925 59
1892......	4,369	14,802 61	177,781	825	1,337,853 47	1,352,656 08
1893......	4,088	13,087 90	176,801	913	1,334,524 47	1,347,612 37
1894......	.....	....	....	...	....	....
1895......	4,274	13,420 18	151,744	929	1,149,069 15	1,162,489 33
Total..	17,601	$56,113 30	601,054	667	$4,561,570 07	$4,617,683 37

MEXICO, CUERNAVACA AND PACIFIC RAILWAY.

YEARS.	PASSEN-GERS.	PASSENGER RECEIPTS.	FREIGHT		MISCELLA-NEOUS RECEIPTS.	TOTAL RECEIPTS.
			Tons.	Kilos.		
1895......	17,209	$19,214 84	84,434	000	$130,662 86	$149,877 70

FEDERAL DISTRICT TRAMWAYS.

YEARS.	PASSENGERS.	PASSENGER RECEIPTS.	FREIGHT.		MISCELLA-NEOUS RECEIPTS.	TOTAL RECEIPTS.
			Tons.	Kilos.		
1873..	3,760,653	$ 232,347 92	......	....	$ 16,421 10	$ 248,769 02
1874..	3,088,808	240,277 12	......	....	29,628 70	269,905 82
1875..	3,597,197	286,248 25	......	....	23,644 10	309,892 35
1876..	3,545,589	278,068 94	......	....	19,289 15	297,358 09
1877..	4,455,595	357,262 43	......	....	14,179 54	371,441 97
1878..	4,605,223	360,175 98	......	....	6,752 49	366,928 47
1879..	5,084,669	390,298 10	......	....	8,089 47	398,387 57
1880..	6,165,461	458,547 60	......	....	19,020 46	477,568 06
1881..	7,675,829	586,167 20	......	....	52,547 54	638,714 74
1882..	9,851,614	703,422 06	......	....	87,584 95	791,007 01
1883..	10,101,302	775,550 34	......	....	90,644 72	866,195 06
1884..	9,926,621	717,264 90	......	....	114,307 69	831,572 59
1885..	9,407,751	690,457 87	......	....	63,423 48	753,881 35
1886..	10,841,928	746,107 46	......	....	134,133 77	880,241 23
1887..	11,121,575	810,974 85	......	....	155,972 22	966,947 07
1888..	12,185,031	881,646 36	......	....	171,418 11	1,053,064 47
1889..	13,533,217	981,922 98	......	....	203,011 13	1,184,934 11
1890..	14,457,203	1,028,871 57	......	....	247,868 09	1,276,739 66
1891..	15,585,919	1,002,224 50	......	....	206,601 54	1,208,826 04
1892..	16,164,644	1,023,617 85	......	....	194,358 01	1,217,975 86
1893..	15,622,879	990,265 03	......	....	217,905 64	1,208,170 67
1894..	15,844,425	1,028,430 01	......	...	230,935 43	1,259,365 44
1895..	18,281,729	1,194,335 17	......	....	229,571 08	1,423,906 25
Total.	224,904,862	$15,764,484 49	......	....	$2,537,308 41	$18,301,792 90

VERACRUZ AND ALVARADO RAILWAY.

1885......	39,078	$ 18,451 01	....	...	$	$ 18,451 01
1886......	37,772	18,673 04	882	500	4,942 00	23,615 04
1887......	29,971	16,677 46	....	...	14,316 16	30,993 62
1888......	58,127	33,174 25	....	...	26,549 26	59,723 51
1889......	63,328	36,779 93	8,500	412	31,779 57	68,559 50
1890......	72,292	42,128 89	11,500	892	34,829 14	76,958 03
1891......	74,317	39,304 87	16,845	178	44,831 36	84,136 23
1892......	73,249	47,831 14	14,498	000	51,025 73	98,856 87
1893......	73,705	47,298 50	22,976	000	49,955 98	97,254 48
1894......	32,964	44,294 74	20,197	000	56,927 90	101,222 64
1895......	87,291	53,050 84	22,764	103	69,450 61	122,501 45
Total..	642,094	$397,664 67	118,164	085	$384,607 71	$782,272 38

Total Traffic and Receipts of Mexican Railways.—Before concluding this chapter, I append a statement of the total traffic and receipts of the Mexican Railways from 1873 to 1895, taken from the *Anuario Estadistico de la Republica Mexicana of 1895,* compiled in the Department of Communication of the Mexican Government from data furnished the same by the respective companies, in compliance with the provisions of their grants.

RAILWAY SUBSIDIES PAID BY THE MEXICAN GOVERNMENT.

I append a statement of the railway subsidies paid by the Mexican Government from the beginning of railway construction to June 30, 1896, which is entirely correct, as it has been obtained from the accounts of the Federal Treasury of Mexico. I insert after that statement a detailed account of each of the railways to whom subsidies have

TRAFFIC AND RECEIPTS OF THE MEXICAN RAILWAYS.

RAILWAYS.	YEARS.	PASSEN-GERS.	PASSENGER RECEIPTS.	FREIGHT. Tons.	FREIGHT. Kilos.	OTHER RECEIPTS.	TOTAL RECEIPTS.
Mexican Railway	1873-1895	9,995,557	$14,848,780 55	6,649,709	141	66,862,116 14	81,710,896 69
District Tramway	1873-1895	225,104,862	15,764,484 49	…	…	2,537,308 41	18,301,792 90
Mexican National	1873-1895	17,496,445	10,457,511 15	4,783,356	914	28,152,266 11	38,609,777 26
Veracruz and Alvarado	1885-1895	64,294	397,664 67	118,164	085	364,607 71	782,272 38
Sonora Railway	1885-1895	568,451	1,341,898 18	517,117	252	3,244,522 20	4,586,400 38
Interoceanic Railway	1880-1895	10,933,881	4,759,173 00	3,412,455	782	13,172,436 70	17,931,609 70
Mexican Central and Branch from Tula to Pachuca	1881-1895	10,916,572	17,956,718 70	8,212,346	747	64,528,000 81	82,484,719 51
Hidalgo and Northeastern	1881-1895	1,418,419	1,218,413 72	1,441,234	727	3,747,970 64	4,966,384 36
Mérida and Progreso	1881-1895	1,377,131	561,468 15	647,333	525	1,291,677 63	1,853,145 78
Tehuacan and Esperanza (Tramway)	1884-1895	186,674	135,438 29	125,709	660	512,355 10	647,793 39
Mérida and Peto	1881-1895	1,508,773	504,682 90	304,177	623	818,659 13	1,323,342 03
Sinaloa and Durango (Altata and Culiacan)	1882-1895	420,722	163,995 18	96,306	694	331,755 74	495,660 92
Mérida and Campeche	1882-1895	1,000,019	311,694 63	138,575	716	308,618 49	619,713 12
Mérida and Valladolid	1883-1895	2,224,580	525,938 50	428,135	142	921,055 96	1,446,904 46
Tlalmanalco	1883-1895	618,665	68,025 28	152,439	058	115,825 65	183,850 93
Mexican International	1891-1895	580,192	1,590,654 34	2,517,600	144	11,143,660 82	12,734,315 16
San Márcos and Náutla	1888-1895	62,392	32,603 58	61,336	760	107,936 04	140,539 62
San Juan Baptista and Paso del Carrizal	1882-1895	843,209	55,617 49	9,154	454	8,361 37	63,978 86
San Andrés and Chalchicomula	1883-1895	167,373	45,550 60	76,159	753	112,274 77	157,825 37
Orizaba and Ingenio	1886-1894	1,124,861	138,767 86	5,208	208	4,752 22	143,520 08
Santa Ana and Tlaxcala	1885-1895	1,254,227	97,927 82	6,617	417	18,755 00	116,682 82
Cárdenas and Rio Grijalva	1889-1894	…	2,050 23	…	443	4,648 77	6,699 00
Toluca and San Juan de las Huertas	1890-1895	1,440,058	141,253 45	124,515	640	94,217 40	235,470 85
Vanegas, Cedral, Matehuala, and Rio Verde	1889-1895	173,388	64,907 56	298,420	269	502,061 63	566,969 19
Mérida and Izamal	1890-1895	605,020	358,659 08	85,727	506	380,385 67	739,044 75
Mexican Southern	1889-1895	767,781	724,591 04	143,828	460	993,244 21	1,717,835 25
Monterey and Gulf	1892-1895	502,942	610,730 72	1,108,170	546	4,327,917 61	4,938,648 33
Córdova and Tuxtepec	1891-1893	185,192	57,943 30	5,965	995	23,793 21	81,646 51
Maravatio and Cuernavaca	1891-1895	60,706	49,739 92	…	…	150,429 06	200,168 98
Salamanca and Valley of Santiago	1891-1895	151,164	50,844 25	12,123	520	46,548 64	97,392 89
Monte Alto		132,022	13,236 45	21,792	000	6,709 49	19,945 94
Valley of Mexico		4,700,660	329,155 45	54,623	000	39,720 21	368,875 66
Puebla Industrial		849,013	135,254 17	14,250	000	18,288 72	153,542 89
Mexican Northern	1891-1895	17,601	56,113 30	601,054	667	4,561,570 17	4,617,683 47
Mexican, Cuernavaca, and Pacific	1895	17,209	19,214 84	84,434	000	130,662 86	149,877 70
Total		296,570,955	$73,589,396 84	32,258,024	640	$209,605,020 29	$283,194,417 13

SUBSIDIES PAID BY THE MEXICAN GOVERNMENT TO RAILWAY COMPANIES UP TO JUNE 30, 1896.

	NAME OF RAILWAY.	DATE OF CONTRACT.	LENGTH OF LINE IN KILOMETRES.	AMOUNT OF SUBSIDY DUE.	PAYMENTS IN Cash.	PAYMENTS IN Certificates.	PAYMENTS IN Bonds.
1	Mexican (Mexico City to Veracruz, via Orizaba and Cordova)	1867, Nov. 27.	614.960	$14,000,000 ..	$13,685,194 59		
2	Progreso & Mérida, Yucatan	1874, Jan. 17.	36.453	218,718 ..	218,718 ..		
3	Hidalgo Ry. (Mexico City to Pachuca)	1878, Feb. 2.	154.011	1,232,088 ..	931,296 37		
4	Veracruz & Alvarado (coast line)	1878, March 26.	55.000	440,000 ..	394,000 ..		
5	Mérida & Peto, Yucatan	1878, March 27.	108.000	648,000 ..	577,445 85		
6	Interoceanic (from Veracruz to Acapulco)	1878, April 6.	743.267	5,570,511 12	2,896,938 ..	$2,673,573 12	
7	Puebla and Matamoros Izucar Railway	1878, May 6.	84.312	674,496 ..	674,496 ..		
8	Tehuantepec Railway	1879, June 2.	309.617	19,181,172 72	5,681,172 72		$13,500,000
9	Sinaloa & Durango R. R. (from Durango City to Mazatlan)	1880, Aug. 16.	61.927	557,343 ..	557,343 ..		
10	Mexican Central (Trunk line and branches, Mexico City to El Paso)	1880, Sept. 8.	2,932.753	26,609,003 50	14,417,936 45	7,108,070 80	
11	Mexican National (Trunk line and branches, Mexico City to New Laredo)	1880, Sept. 13.	1,737.045	12,042,815 ..		11,929,870 ..	
12	Sonora Railway (from Nogales to Guaymas)	1880, Sept. 14.	422.312	2,956,184 ..	2,171,310 60		
13	Mérida & Valladolid R. R. Yucatan	1880, Dec. 15.	108.668	642,068 ..	597,608 ..		
14	Tlalmanalco (Local line in the State of Puebla)	1881, Feb. 3.	26.650	159,900 ..	159,900 ..		
15	Mérida & Campeche Railway (via Calkini, Yucatan)	1881, Feb. 23.	135.152	810,915 ..	766,915 ..		
16	Náutla & San Márcos Railway (States of Puebla and Veracruz)	1881, June 25.	75.000	450,000 ..	70,500 ..		349,000
17	San Juan Bautista & Tamulte-Pass, Railway (State of Tabasco)	1881, Sept. 17.	5.750	20,125 ..	20,125 ..		
18	Chalchicomula Branch Railway (State of Puebla)	1881, Sept. 20.	10.353	22,238 65	22,238 65		
19	Tlaxcala & Santa Ana Railway (State Tlaxcala)	1882, Dec. 11.	8.000	28,000 ..	28,000 ..		
20	Cárdenas & Grijalva River Railway (State Tabasco)	1883, May 12.	7.500	33,750 ..	33,750 ..		
21	Toluca & Las Huertas Railway (State of Mexico)	1883, May 25.	15.721	55,023 50	46,250 ..		
22	Vanegas, Cedral, Matehuala & Rio-Verde (State S. Louis Potosi)	1883, June 11.	65.000	357,500 ..	341,000 ..		
23	Mérida & Soluta (State of Yucatan, via Izamal)	1884, May 15.	65.848	395,088 ..	395,088 ..		
24	Jimenez & Sierra Madre, via Hidalgo District (State Durango)	1884, Nov. 13.	5.000	40,000 ..			
25	Mexican Southern (States of Puebla and Oaxaca)	1886, April 21.	367.000	11,248,805 10	880,805 10		10,368,000
26	Tonala & Frontera (States of Chiapas and Tabasco)	1886, Dec. 16.	50.000	444,444 ..			444,000
27	Monterey & Mexican Gulf (States of N. Leon and Tamaulipas)	1887, Nov. 10.	624.640	5,534,572 24			5,534,572 24
28	Tecolutla (Gulf of Mexico) & Espinal (State of Veracruz)	1887, Dec. 10.	19.000	100,500 ..	40,500 ..		60,000
29	Córdova (State Veracruz) & Tuxtepec Railway	1888, June 19.	51.000	408,000 ..	408,000 ..		
30	Pachuca (State Hidalgo) & Tampico Railway	1888, June 5.	10.000	80,000 ..			80,000
31	Maravatío & Iguala Railway (States Michoacan and Guerrero)	1888, Aug. 16.	50.000	316,666 50	112,000 ..		166,000
32	Mexican Northeastern (State Tamaulipas)	1888, Aug. 28.	50.090	300,540 ..	294,000 ..		
33	Salamanca & Valley of Santiago Railway (State Guanajuato)	1888, Aug. 30.	35.000	280,000 ..	280,000 ..		
34	Veracruz & Boca del Rio Railway	1888, Aug. 31.	11.504	92,032 ..	83,000 ..		
35	Tula, Zacualtipan (State of Hidalgo) & Tampico Railway	1889, Dec. 10.	70.000	560,000 ..			560,000
36	Matamoros Izucar (State of Puebla) & Acapulco (Pacific coast)	1892, March 5.	40.000	988,776 49	111,370 62		
37	Lower California Railway	1894, June 3.	20.000	177,777 77			
38	Monte-Alto branch Railway (State of Mexico)	1894, Sept. 14.	10.000	66,666 66			66,000
			9,196.533	$107,743,660 25	$46,896,901 95	$21,711,513 92	$31,127,572 24

Total, 38 subsidized Railway Concessions.

been paid, stating the number of kilometres built, the amount of subsidy due for the same, and the manner in which the subsidy was paid, that statement being the most complete that has so far been published :

Résumé.—Amount paid in Cash............................. $ 46,896,901 95
         "   " Certificates of Construction (convertible
                    in five per cent. bonds)............ 21,711,513 92
         "   " Bonds............................. 31,127,000 00
         " of Balance due (payable either in cash or Bonds), 8,008,244 38

      Total amount of Subsidies, as per corresponding concessions, $107,743,660 25

The Tehuantepec Railway cost of construction is herein included, in order to give a complete statement of the Government's pecuniary outlay for the construction of railways in the country. As the $13,500,000 amount of the five per cent. Bonds paid on account of the construction of this line to the contractors, McMurdo & Co., represent a gold indebtedness, if reduced at the rate of 24 pence per dollar, the above total cost of railway construction should be increased by an equal amount, say $13,500,000 Mexican currency—or a grand total of $121,243,660.25.

DETAILED STATEMENT OF THE SUBSIDIES PAID BY THE MEXICAN GOVERNMENT TO THE RAILWAY COMPANIES.

1. MEXICAN RAILWAY.—(From Mexico City to Veracruz.)

Subsidy as per original concession, $560,000 per annum, during
    25 years, equal to................................. $14,000,000 00
Paid previous to October 21, 1890........... 10,187,315 79
Balance in favor of the company, on October
    21, 1890, as per special agreement of the
    same date........................... $3,497,878 80
9% deduction, for cash payment, according to
    the second clause of said agreement....... 314,805 41
        Total payment................................. 14,000,000 00

2. HIDALGO RAILWAY.—(From Mexico City to Pachuca, Hid.)

Subsidy, $8000, per kilometre, as per concession............. $1,232,088 00
Paid on account thereof in cash.............. $931,296 37
In 3% and 5% Bonds........................ 300,791 63
        Total payment..................................... 1,232,088 00

3. VERACRUZ & ALVARADO RAILWAY.—(Coast Line between the said ports.)

Subsidy due the Company, $6000 per kilometre, as per con-
    cession.. $440,000 00
Paid on account thereof, in cash............. $394,000 00
In 3% Bonds.............................. 46,000 00 440,000 00

4. MERIDA & PETO RAILWAY.—(Between the two named towns, State of Yucatan.)

Subsidy, due the Company, $6000 per kilometre, as per con-
    cession.. $648,000 00
Paid in cash............................. $577,445 85
In 3% Bonds............................. 70,554 15
        Total payment................................. 648,000 00

5.   INTEROCEANIC RAILWAY.—(Narrow gauge, from Veracruz to Acapulco, Pacific Coast.)

Subsidy due the Company................................ $5,570,511 12

483.$\frac{30}{864}$ Kilometres at $8000............. $3,866,469 12

81.$\frac{000}{}$ "   " 6500............. 526,500 00

140.$\frac{000}{}$ "   " 6000............. 840,000 00

38.$\frac{959}{}$ "   unsubsidized........

Construction bounty earned, as per concession on the Mexico & Cuautla division........ 137,542 00

Construction bounty earned, as per concession on the Jalapa & Veracruz division........ 200,000 00   5,570,511 12

Paid in cash................. $2,896,938 00

In certificates already paid for, out of the 3% of the Customs Receipts... .... 2,673,573 12

Total payment.... .... 5,570,511 12

6.   OCCIDENTAL RAILWAY.—(Between points in the States of Sinaloa and Durango.)

Length of the road, according to the concession 1373 kilometres, subsidy at the rate of $8000, per kilometre, as follows :

From Altata, (Port on the Pacific Coast, Gulf of California), to Culiacan, capital of the State of Sinaloa...... 61.$\frac{927}{}$ kilometres constructed

From Culiacan to Durango and Fresnillo cities 600

A Branch to Guaymas 536

"   "   " Mazatlan 237

_____

1,373

Subsidy due for the first 61.$\frac{927}{}$ kilometres already built............................ $495,416 00

Construction bounty according to concession $1000 per kilometre..................,...... 61,927 00

Total amount due and paid for to the Company.............. $557,343 00

7.   MEXICAN CENTRAL, and sundry branches.—(Trunk-line, from Mexico City to El Paso del Norte, on the Rio Grande River.)

Subsidy due in accordance with the corresponding charter was $26,609,003 50

As follows : for 1970.$\frac{600}{}$ kilometres of the trunk-line, of which 107 kilometres were subsidized at $1500 per kilometre.................... $ 160,500 00

And 1,863.$\frac{600}{}$ kilometres at $9500 per kilometre........ 17,704,200 00 $17,864,700 00

For 258.$\frac{580}{}$ kilometres of the

Gaudalajara branch, which reduced as per special contract of Feb. 25, 1887, to 218.^{580} kilometres at $9500 per kilometre................. .... $2,076,510 00

For 653.^{500} kilometres of the Aguascalientes & Tampico Branch, at $9500 per kilometre.................... 6,208,250 00

For 25 kilometres of the San Blas & Guaristemba at $9500 per kilometre............. 237,500 00   8,522,260 00

For 23.^{373} kilometres of Silao & Guanajuato Branch at $9500 per kilometre............. 222,043 50

     Total payment.................................... $26,609,003 50

This total amount, was settled and paid for in accordance with special agreement entered into by and between the Department of Public Works and the Company, on August 23, 1890, as follows:

Lands, art-works, drafts and plans, etc., due by the Company as per settlement effected December 22, 1881..................... $ 34,204 39

Rebate off the subsidy corresponding to 6600 kilometres of parallel lines, between Zacatecas & Guadalajara, as per agreement therefor 52,800 00

Rebate off the subsidy on 50 kilometres of the line, between Tantoyuquita & Tampico, as per agreement......................... 75,000 00

Cash received by the Government of the State of San Luis Potosi, on account of the old branch line to Tampico................. 48,000 00

Certificates of construction paid at various Custom Houses out of the 8% of the receipts of the same, during the fiscal years 1881–1890 7,108,070 80

Paid with bills of exchange on London out of the proceeds of the loan negotiated in 1890................................... 14,335,732 06

25% discount on $19,820,793 01, amount of the balance acknowledged in favor of the Company, according to the above mentioned agreement, (August 23, 1890)........... 4,955,196 25

     Total payment.................................... $26,609,003 50

8. MEXICAN NATIONAL, and branches. — (Trunk-line from Mexico City to Laredo, Tamaulipas.)

The Company constructed 1737.^{045} kilometres for which the Government owed the following subsidies :—

On 1444.$\frac{045}{}$ kilometres of the trunk line, at the
rate of $7000 per kilometre............ . $10,108,315 00
On 273.$\frac{000}{}$ kilometres of the trunk line, at the
rate of $6500 per kilometre............. 1,774,500 00
On 20 kilometres of the Salto Branch at the rate
of $8000 per kilometre.................. 160,000 00
Total amount of subsidy due............................. $12,042,815 00

The above amount was paid in certificates of construction for..$11,929,870 00
of which the sum of $8,746,722 60 was paid at several Custom-Houses
during the fiscal years 1882–1895, and the balance of $3,183,147 40, was
converted, by special agreement between the Treasury Department and
Messrs. Lionel Carden and H. P. Webb, as representatives of the Company
in 5% Bonds. The balance of $112,945 which in the preceding statement,
appears as pending of payment, was accepted by the Company, as the
value of the Government's shares in the Salto Branch.

9. "SONORA RAILWAY."—(From Guaymas, on the Gulf of California, to Nogales, on the boundary line.)

Subsidy on 422$\frac{812}{}$ kilometres at the rate of $7000 per kilometre, $ 2,956,184 00
Paid to the Company, cash.................. $ 2,071,310 60
Fine against the forfeiture of the concession... 100,000 00
3% Bonds in accordance with the provisions of
the law of September 6th, 1894......... 784,873 40
Total payment................................. $ 2,956,184 00

10. "MERIDA & VALLADOLID RAILWAY," with a branch.—(Between these two towns in the State of Yucatan.)

Subsidy due on 108.$\frac{668}{}$ kilometres at $6000 per kilometre..... $642,008 00
Paid for as follows, cash.................... $ 597,608 00
In 3% Bonds (law of September 6th, 1894).... 44,400 00
Total payment................................. $642,008 00

11. "MERIDA & CAMPECHE RAILWAY," via. Kalkini.—(Between
the capitals of the States of Yucatan and Campeche.)

Subsidy due on 135.$\frac{1525}{}$ kilometres at $6000 per kilometre, $810,915 00
Paid to the Company in cash................ $766,915 00
In 3% Bonds............. .... 44,000 00
Total payment................................. $810,915 00

12. "SAN MARCOS & NAUTLA RAILWAY."—Between San Marcos
station on the Mexican Ry. and Nautla bar on the Gulf
of Mexico.)

Subsidy due on 75 kilometres at $6000 per kilometre.. .... $450,000 00
Paid to the Company as follows: Cash....... $ 70,500 00
In special 5% subsidy Bonds................. 349,000 00
In 3% Bonds according to the provisions of the
law of September 6th, 1894............. 500 00
Rebatement of subsidy on 5 kilometres running
parallel with the "Interoceanic Ry....... 30,000 00
Total payment................................. $450,000 00

13. "TOLUCA & SAN JUAN de las HUERTAS RAILWAY."—(Between the capital of the State of Mexico and the San Juan estate.)

Subsidy due on 15.⁷²¹ kilometres at $3500 per kilometre.......		$55,023 50
Paid to the Company, cash..................	$46,250 00	
In 3% Bonds (law of September 6th, 1894).....	8,773 50	
Total payment..		$55,023 50

14. "VANEGAS, CEDRAL, MATEHUALA & RIO VERDE RAILWAY."— (All townships within the State of San Luis Potosi.)

Subsidy due on 65.⁰⁰⁰ kilometres at $5500 per kilometre.....		$357,500 00
Paid to the Company, cash..................	$341,000 00	
In 5% Bonds (September 6th, 1894)...........	16,500 00	
Total payment.......................................		$357,500 00

15. "JIMENEZ and SIERRA MADRE RAILWAY."—(Through the Hidalgo District, State of Chihuahua.)

Subsidy due on 5.⁰⁰⁰ kilometres at $8000 per kilometre....... $40,000 00
The whole paid to the Company in 3% Bonds (Law of September 6th, 1894.

16. "MEXICAN SOUTHERN RAILWAY."—(367 kilometres from the City of Puebla to Oaxaca.)

Subsidy due under agreement of May 4th, 1892.............		$11,248,805 10
First annuity of interest paid to the Company in conformity with the original concession of April 21st, 1886...................	$880,800 00	
Conversion of the remaining 14 annuities, as per the above named agreement, in special Bonds denominated of the "Oaxaca Trunk Line".............................	8,558,888 55	
Bounty paid to the Company, as per original concession, in Bonds (special)..........	1,809,116 55	
Total payment....................		$11,248,805 10
Of the total amount of special Bonds issued, $10,368,000 00		
Cashed	1,108,000 00	
Outstanding.............................	9,260,000 00	

17. "TONALA" (State of Chiapas, Pacific Coast) and "FRONTERA RAILWAY."—(State of Tabasco, on the Gulf of Mexico.)

Subsidy on 50 kilometres at $8000 per kilometre............ $400,000 00
Paid to the Company with 6% Bonds, valued at
90% of their nominal................... $444,444 00
The balance shown in the preceding statement in favor of the Company for $44,444.00 proceeds from the want of a Bond of less value than $1000 of the corresponding issue.

18. "Monterey" (Capital of the State of Nuevo Leon) and "Mexican Gulf Railway."—(Port of Tampico.)

Subsidy on 624.⁶⁴⁰ kilometres at $8000 per kilometre........ $5,534,572 24[1]

Wholly paid for in 5% Bonds, issued under the law of September 6th, 1894, with the exception of a balance of $572.24, which, on account of the want of bonds of less value than $1000, is still pending of settlement. Of the original issue of special Bonds given to the Company in payment of the subsidy, $235,000 is still pending of conversion.

19. "Tecolutla" (a bar on the Mexican Gulf) and "Espinal Railway."—(Both in the State of Veracruz.)

According to the original concession, the subsidy granted to this Company was on 19 kilometres at the rate of $4500 in cash per kilometre ; but under a new agreement, dated January, 20th, 1892, it was settled as follows :

9 kilometres at the rate of $4500 each in cash,	$40,500 00
10 kilometres in Bonds at $6000 each.........	60,000 00
Total payment................................	$100,500 00

20. "Pachuca" (Capital of the State of Hidalgo) and "Tampico Railway."—(On the Mexican Gulf.)

Subsidy on 10.⁰⁰⁰ kilometres at $8000.................... $80,000 00
Totally paid in Bonds, in accordance with the law of September 6th, 1894.

21. "Maravatio" & "Iguala Railway."—(Towns in the States of Michoacan and Guerrero, respectively.)

Subsidy on 50 kilometres at $3000 in cash and $3000 in special Bonds, under 10% discount off their nominal value, and paid for, cash,	$112,000 00
Bonds..............................	166,000 00
Total payment.................................	$316,666 50[1]

22. "Mexican Northeastern Railway."—(An extension of the "Hidalgo" Ry. to Tizayuca, in the State of that name.)

Subsidy on 50.⁰⁹⁰ kilometres at $6000....................	$300,540 00
Paid for, in cash...........................	$294,000 00
In 3% Bonds.............................	6,540 00
Total payment.................................	$300,540 00

[1] Some of the total payments in this table do not correspond to the amount of subsidy due, because in some of those cases other payments have been made, like bounty, of which no account appears in the respective statement. In some cases a bounty was offered provided the road was finished before the time fixed in the respective grant.

23. "Veracruz & Boca del Rio Railway."

Subsidy acknowledged on 11.<u>504</u> kilometres at $8000 per kilometre $92,032 00
Paid for, cash............................ $83,000 00
In 3% Bonds............................ 9,032 00
  Total payment................................ $92,032 00

24. "Tula, Zacualtipan" (State of Hidalgo), and Tampico Railway.

Subsidy on 70.<u>000</u> kilometres at $8,000 per kilometre......... $560,000 00
The whole amount paid for in 5% Bonds, of which $285,000 were outstanding on the 30th of June, 1896.

25. "Matamoros Izucar" (State of Puebla) and "Acapulco Railway."—(On the Pacific coast.)

Subsidy under contract of March 22d, 1895, on 40 kilometres.. $988,776 49
Paid as follows : cash, for the amount of 2% interest annuities paid to the Company in conformity with the original concession... $111,370 62
In 5% Bonds, according to the above contract................................ 877,405 87
  Total payment................................ $988,776 49

26. "Lower California Railway."—(From the town of San Quintin to a point on the "Mexican Central," Chihuahua.)

Subsidy on 20 kilometres, payable in 6% Bonds at the rate of $8000 per kilometre, the said Bonds, afterwards converted in conformity with the corresponding law of conversion, were taken by the Company under 10% discount off their nominal value.... .... $177,777 77

27. "Monte Alto Railway."—(Starts from the town of Tlalnepantla, on the Salto branch of the "Mexican National," towards Alizapan and Villa del Carbon.)

Subsidy on 10 kilometres at $6000 per kilometre, payable in 6% Bonds taken by the Company at the rate of 90% of their face value................. .... $66,666 66

28. Tehuantepec R. R.—(Between Coatzacoalcos on the Gulf of Mexico, and Salina Cruz, on the Pacific coast.)

COSTS OF CONSTRUCTION TO THE MEXICAN GOVERNMENT.

I. Contractors, Edward Learned & Co.—(Contract of June 2d, 1879.)
35 kilometres, of which only 25 were paid for, at $7500..................... $187,500 00
The Learned contract was rescinded by the Mexican Government on August 16th, 1882 ; but by agreement adjusted with J. Tyng, as representative of the contractors, who received the following payments :

December 21st, 1882, $125,000 00
July 9th, 1883.......   403,618 44
July 19th, 1883......   101,068 48
July 12th, 1888...... 1,075,726 90   1,705,413 82

Total amount paid to Learned & Co................... $1,892,913 82

Of which amount the sum of $230,413.82 represents interest accrued at the rate or 6% per annum ; so that the 35 kilometers built by these contractors actually cost $14,083.25 per kilometre.

2. CONTRACTOR, MR. DELPIN SANCHEZ.—(Agreement of October 5th, 1882.)

This contractor received from the Government the sum of.................. $1,079,135 40

For the purchase of material, which he only accounted for the amount of $908,-910.50 the balance of $170,224 90
Having been donated to the contractor according to special agreement of April 25th, 1888.
The same contractor received in 150 weekly installments of $1900 each during the fiscal years 1885, 1888 .... $285,000 00
Mr. Sanchez delivered as constructed 74 kilometers which were paid to him at the rate of $25,000 each............... $1,850,000 00 $2,305,224 90

3. MAC-MURDO CONTRACT.—(Agreement approved by Decree of October 15th, 1888.)

For the completion of the construction and the furnishing of all the rolling material, etc., and for which the Contractors received in payment in 5% Bonds, special issue, principal and interests payable in sterling currency, £2,700,000,................................. ... $13,500,000 00
This contract was rescinded on the 13th of January, 1892, when the contractors, in settlement of accounts, surrendered to the Government the sum of about $2,000,-000 as surplus proceeding from the sale of the said bonds, and delivered, more or less, 250 kilometres of the lines as built or repaired within the stipulations of the said contract.

4. STANHOPE, HAMPSON & CORTHEL CONTRACT.—(Made under Decree of December 6th, 1893.)

For the construction of 59 kilometres and the completion of all the necessary works for the preservation and working of the whole line, for the fixed sum of,...... $1,483,035 00

Total cost of the line................................ $19,181,173 72

PUBLIC DEBT.

In the first part of this paper I gave a brief statement of the different loans and liabilities which constitute the Mexican debt, and that statement will make it easy to understand the different issues and denominations of our bonds. Here I append a detailed statement of the National Debt of Mexico, up to June 30, 1896, submitted to Congress by the Secretary of the Treasury on the 14th of December, 1896, and a further statement containing the same data in a more concise form.

STATEMENT OF THE NATIONAL DEBT OF MEXICO TO JUNE 30, 1896.

Bonded Debt, Principal and Interest payable in Sterling currency.

Six per cent. interest bearing Bonds for the Loan of 1888, with .. % sinking fund, Capital and Interest........	$51,908,786 50	
Six per cent. interest bearing Bonds for the Loan of 1890, with .. % sinking fund, Capital and Interest.......	30,068,710 25	
Six per cent. interest bearing Bonds for the Loan of 1893, with .. % sinking fund, Capital and Interest.......	15,325,561 50	
Five per cent. interest bearing Bonds for the Construction of the Tehuantepec Railway, 1889, Capital....	13,500,000 00	
Six per cent. (non converted balance) Bonds of the Loan, contracted in London, 1851, Capital....:..........	134,153 12	
Total amount of outstanding Bonds, payable in Sterling currency....................		$110,937,211 37

Bonded Debt, Principal and Interest payable in Mexican Silver currency.

Three per cent. interest bearing Bonds of the Interior Consolidated Debt, Capital and Interest............	$52,464,927 60	
Five per cent. interest bearing Bonds of the Interior Redeemable Debt, first series, Capital and Interest....	19,995,689 48	
Five per cent. interest bearing Bonds of the Interior Redeemable Debt, second series, Capital and Interest.	987,127 15	
Subsidy Bonds, non converted balances, for sundry works and railways, Capital......................	9,792,865 75	
Total	83,240,609 98	
Railway Construction Certificates, pending of conversion, Capital....................................	219 17	
Balance-certificates corresponding to the fiscal years comprehended between 1882 and 1894, Capital pending of conversion................**........	329,221 91	
Total amount of bonded debt, payable in Mexican Silver currency......................		83,570,051 06
Grand Total of Bonded Liabilities..............		$194,507,262 43

Liabilities from various sources, and in forms, other than Bonds, payable in Mexican Silver currency.

To Railway, Harbor Works and Drainage of the Valley of Mexico, Contractors......................	$ 501,741 02	
To Unpaid for Appropriations in the Budgets for the fiscal years between 1891 and 1896....	612,337 82	
To other credits pending of settlement: on account of the same Budgets..................................	600,894 63	
To Balances in Account-current due various Contractors with some of the Executive Departments..........	315,818 95	
To sundry, cash or otherwise executed, Deposits, as guarantee for pending contracts..................	2,681,662 95	
To provisional certificates issued on account of the 1888, 1890 and 1893, Sterling Loans.....................	3,738,684 12	
To cash or other values pending of classification in the corresponding accounts.........................	74,434 57	
To cash Receipts on account of credits, other than fiscal and pending of payment to the corresponding offices.	32,829 68	
To Balance due to Mint-Lessees.....................	48,214 89	
To outstanding Bills Payable.......................	111,186 28	
Total Amount of Liabilities from various sources and in forms other than Bonds....		8,717,804 91
Grand Total of the Mexican National Debt.....		$203,225,067 34

222

Statistical Notes on Mexico.

STATEMENT OF THE FEDERAL PUBLIC DEBT ON JUNE 30, 1896.

	Interest bearing annual.	Sinking fund.	BONDED DEBT.		INDEBTEDNESS SETTLED IN SUNDRY FORMS OTHER THAN BONDS.	
			Principal and interest payable in sterling money.	Payable in Mexican silver currency.	Payable in sterling money.	Payable in Mexican silver currency.
Balance of the loan contracted in London in 1851, not presented to conversion	6 %	..	$ 134,153 12	....	....	....
Loan of 1888 in Berlin and London to refund the loan of 1825	6 "	1⅛	51,908,786 50	....	....	....
Loan of 1889 for the Tehuantepec Railway	5 "	1	13,500,000 00	....	....	....
Loan of 1890 for the payment of railway subsidies	6 "	1¼	30,068,710 25	....	....	....
Loan of 1893 to pay public indebtedness	3 "	..	15,325,561 50	....	....	....
Conversion of 1886 to 1896 of the interior debt			....	$52,464,927 60	....	....
Conversion of 1894 in settlement of railway and public works, claims, first series	5 "	1 "	....	19,995,689 48	....	....
Conversion of 1895 in settlement of railway and public works, claims, second series	5 "	1 "	....	....	....	....
Special subsidy bonds pending conversion under the law of September 6, 1894			....	987,127 15	....	....
Balances of certificates of railway construction			....	9,792,865 75	....	....
Certificates of balances due for public services, pending of conversion			....	....	....	$ 219 17
Balances due to several railways, public works, and drainage of the Valley of Mexico contractors			....	....	....	329,221 91
Unpaid appropriations of 1891 to 1896			....	....	....	501,741 02
Sundry claims on said appropriations pending liquidation			....	....	....	612,337 82
Balance, favor of sundry contracts with the various departments			....	....	....	600,894 63
Sundry deposits to guarantee pending contracts			....	....	....	315,818 95
Provisional certificates—not submitted to conversion—issued on the sterling loans of 1888, 1890, and 1893			....	....	$3,738,684 12	2,681,662 95
Cash receipts on account of municipal dues—pending of payment			....	....	....	32,829 68
Cash receipts pending of classification for the corresponding accounts			....	....	....	74,434 57
Balances due to mint lessees			....	....	....	48,214 89
Outstanding treasury bills			....	....	....	111,186 28
Total	..	..	$110,937,211 37	$83,249,609 98	$3,738,684 12	$5,308,561 87
Grand total	..	..				$203,225,067 34

POST-OFFICE AND TELEGRAPH SERVICE.

I append a statement containing the number of post-offices, and postal agencies in each of the Mexican states in 1895, and the number of postal pieces transported by Mexican mails from the years 1878–1879 to 1894–1895. (See page 225.)

I have prepared a statement of the earnings and expenditures of the post-office and telegraph services in Mexico during the twenty-seven fiscal years elapsed from July 1, 1869, to June 30, 1896. It was not possible to obtain full data of the earnings of the telegraph lines during the first ten years of that period, on account of the defective way in which the books were kept by the Federal Treasury of Mexico. With that exception the data embraced in the following statement is correct, as it has been taken from the official accounts. (See p. 224.)

POST-OFFICES IN MEXICO IN 1895 BY STATES.

STATES.	POST-OFFICE.	POSTAL AGENCIES.		TOTAL.
Aguascalientes	5	5	..	10
Campeche.	8	3	..	11
Chiapas.	7	24	..	31
Chihuahua.	24	58	..	82
Coahuila	25	26	1	52
Colima.	2	9	..	11
Durango	19	42	..	61
Federal District	1	8	10	19
Guanajuato.	27	38	..	65
Guerrero.	13	31	..	44
Hidalgo.	19	43	..	62
Jalisco	35	83	..	118
Lower California.	7	17	..	24
Mexico	14	21	..	35
Michoacan	22	59	..	81
Morelos.	9	9	..	18
New Leon.	18	33	..	51
Oaxaca.	22	39	..	61
Puebla.	27	77	1	105
Querétaro.	7	10	..	17
San Luis Potosí.	18	34	..	52
Sinaloa.	16	28	..	44
Sonora.	14	75	..	89
Tabasco.	5	16	..	21
Tamaulipas.	17	36	..	53
Tepic.	7	13	..	20
Tlaxcala	9	7	..	16
Veracruz.	36	82	..	118
Yucatan.	16	40	..	56
Zacatecas	20	23	1	44
Total	469	989	13	1471

EARNINGS AND EXPENDITURES OF THE POST-OFFICE AND TELEGRAPH SERVICES DURING THE LAST TWENTY-SEVEN FISCAL YEARS, FROM JULY 1, 1869, TO JUNE 30, 1896.

FISCAL YEARS.	POST-OFFICE.		TELEGRAPH.		BOTH SERVICES.—TOTAL.	
	Dr. Expenditure.	Cr. Earnings.	Dr. Expenditure.	Cr. Earnings.[1]	Dr. Expenditure.	Cr. Earnings.[1]
1869–1870...	$ 132,399 06	$ 120,120 24	$ 29,212 73	$ 1,809 53	$ 161,611 79	....
1870–1871...	154,574 90	167,348 85	84,150 00	....	238,724 90	....
1871–1872...	340,324 63	265,440 22	48,379 77	....	388,704 40	....
1872–1873...	457,153 19	474,819 11	72,418 96	....	529,572 15	....
1873–1874...	491,199 48	523,583 09	174,504 32	....	665,703 80	....
Total in five years..	$ 1,575,651 26	$ 1,551,311 51	$ 408,665 78	....	$ 1,984,317 04	....
Average per annum.	$ 315,130 25	$ 310,262 30	$ 81,733 16	....	$ 396,863 41	....
1874–1875...	$ 641,836 35	$ 549,820 14	$ 190,366 06	....	$ 832,202 41	....
1875–1876...	480,299 37	455,473 12	161,795 66	....	642,095 03	....
1876–1877...	530,032 95	441,329 10	134,830 02	....	664,862 97	....
1877–1878...	682,076 21	590,384 36	241,200 00	....	923,276 21	....
1878–1879...	867,789 75	679,392 06	259,095 86	$ 1,789 15	1,126,885 61	....
Total in five years..	$ 3,202,034 63	$ 2,716,398 78	$ 987,287 60	....	$ 4,189,322 23	....
Average per annum.	$ 640,406 93	$ 543,279 76	$ 197,457 52	....	$ 837,864 45	....
1879–1880...	$ 892,856 73	$ 702,080 39	$ 348,290 24	$ 101,064 69	$ 1,241,146 97	$ 803,145 08
1880–1881...	983,606 17	833,830 87	196,542 94	135,144 02	1,180,149 11	968,974 89
1881–1882...	873,200 78	704,766 47	570,155 25	174,301 24	1,443,357 03	879,067 71
1882–1883...	840,354 70	795,122 86	916,657 53	219,384 91	1,757,012 23	1,014,507 77
1883–1884...	878,519 75	698,019 36	677,729 50	239,051 45	1,556,249 25	937,070 81
Total in five years..	$ 4,468,539 13	$ 3,733,819 95	$ 2,709,375 46	$ 868,946 31	$ 7,177,914 59	$ 4,602,766 26
Average per annum.	$ 893,707 83	$ 746,763 99	$ 541,875 09	$ 173,789 26	$ 1,435,582 92	$ 920,553 25
1884–1885...	$ 1,411,183 03	$ 642,660 19	$ 618,829 54	$ 180,820 77	$ 2,030,012 57	$ 823,480 96
1885–1886...	751,227 37	672,329 80	622,858 67	155,442 82	1,374,086 04	827,772 62
1886–1887...	943,332 74	739,732 65	718,821 70	197,478 87	1,662,154 44	937,211 52
1887–1888...	956,701 47	793,873 74	799,074 24	275,856 95	1,755,775 71	1,069,730 69
1888–1889...	1,049,880 10	880,530 93	820,072 05	329,493 13	1,869,952 15	1,210,024 06
Total in five years..	$ 5,112,324 71	$ 3,729,127 31	$ 3,579,656 20	$ 1,139,092 54	$ 8,691,980 91	$ 4,868,219 85
Average per annum.	$ 1,022,464 94	$ 745,825 46	$ 715,931 24	$ 227,818 51	$ 1,738,396 18	$ 973,643 97
1889–1890...	$ 1,126,436 69	$ 994,112 87	$ 872,316 89	$ 388,926 07	$ 1,998,753 58	$ 1,383,038 94
1890–1891...	1,196,329 63	1,084,153 40	972,164 06	462,076 59	2,168,493 69	1,546,229 99
1891–1892...	1,342,437 11	1,127,563 18	1,045,726 44	501,802 33	2,388,163 55	1,629,365 51
1892–1893...	1,278,587 20	1,153,401 20	1,073,105 81	528,881 96	2,351,693 01	1,682,283 16
1893–1894...	1,250,855 82	1,213,309 46	954,864 48	524,634 33	2,205,720 30	1,737,943 79
Total in five years..	$ 6,194,646 45	$ 5,572,540 11	$ 4,918,177 68	$ 2,406,321 28	$11,112,824 13	$ 7,978,861 39
Average per annum.	$ 1,238,929 29	$ 1,114,508 02	$ 983,635 54	$ 481,264 26	$ 2,222,564 83	$ 1,595,772 28
1894–1895...	$ 633,201 36	$ 1,337,691 40	$ 531,949 48	$ 547,308 67	$ 1,165,150 84	$ 1,885,000 07
1895–1896...	1,228,784 30	1,062,415 99	1,025,347 29	622,340 69	2,254,131 59	1,684,756 68
Total in two years..	$ 1,861,985 66	$ 2,400,107 39	$ 1,557,296 77	$ 1,169,649 36	$ 3,419,282 43	$ 3,569,756 75
Average per annum.	$ 930,992 83	$ 1,200,053 70	$ 778,648 38	$ 584,824 68	$ 1,709,641 21	$ 1,784,878 38
Total in the 27 years ...	$22,415,181 84	$19,703,305 05	$14,160,459 49	$ 5,584,009 49	$36,575,641 33	$21,019,604 25
Average per annum.	$ 830,191 92	$ 729,752 04	$ 524,461 46	$ 328,471 14	$ 1,354,653 38	$ 1,236,447 30

[1] The totals and averages per annum in the colums marked "Earnings" and "Total Earnings" only embrace seventeen years, as the returns for the first ten years being very incomplete are not computed.

NUMBER OF PIECES TRANSPORTED BY MEXICAN MAILS FROM 1878–1879 TO 1894–1895.

FISCAL YEARS.	NUMBER OF PIECES.
1878–1879	5,992,611
1879–1880	5,786,790
1880–1881	6,141,790
1881–1882	6,732,504
1882–1883	10,640,516
1883–1884	10,488,518
1884–1885	11,905,209
1885–1886	13,289,591
1886–1887	16,504,034
1887–1888	27,429,018
1888–1889	43,052,800
1889–1890	95,852,939
1890–1891	111,406,893
1891–1892	116,778,853
1892–1893	122,821,359
1893–1894	35,818,148
1894–1895	24,773,636
Total	665,415,209

Printed matter, samples, and parcel post articles in the year 1894–1895, weighed in grammes, 1,107,755,679.

The notable reduction which appears in the last two years is due to the fact that in the preceding years all correspondence was counted, namely : such pieces as were received and sent, and such as came in transit, while in the last two years only are accounted such as were sent.

BANKS.

The following statement contains a list of all the banks existing in Mexico up to December 31, 1895, and their respective condition :

LIST OF MEXICAN BANKS.

STATE.	LOCATION.	NAME OF BANK.	DATE OF CHARTER.
Federal District.	Mexico City....	National Bank of Mexico.....	February, 1882.
" "	" "	International and Hypothecary Bank of Mexico..........	May, 1883.
" "	" "	Bank of London and Mexico..	October, 1886.
Chihuahua.. ...	Chihuahua City..	Mexican Chihuahua Bank....	September, 1888.
"	" " ..	Chihuahua Mining Bank.....	September, 1888.
"	" " ..	Chihuahua Bank............	December, 1889.
"	" " ..	Chihuahua Commercial Bank..	December, 1890.
Yucatan........	Merida.........	Yucateco Bank.............	February, 1890.
"	"	Yucatan Mercantile Bank.....	March, 1890.
Durango	Durango City...	Durango Bank	June 1, 1891.
Zacatecas.......	Zacatecas City..	Zacatecas Bank............	December, 1891.
New Leon......	Monterey	New Leon Bank...........	February 18, 1892.

SITUATION OF THE MEXICAN BANKS ON DECEMBER 31, 1894.

	NATIONAL BANK OF MEXICO.	BANK OF LONDON AND MEXICO.	INTERNATIONAL AND HYPOTHECARY BANK OF MEXICO.	CHIHUAHUA MINING BANK.	MEXICAN CHIHUAHUA BANK.	CHIHUAHUA COMMERCIAL BANK, ON FEBRUARY 15, 1895.
Social capital....	$20,000,000 00	$3,000,000 00	$5,000,000 00	$ 600,000 00	$610,000 00	$600,000 00
Unpaid capital.	12,000,000 00	....	1,500,000 00	....	....	300,000 00
Accumulated capital......	....	....	....	....	50,342 62	....
Reserve funds..	1,796,100 51	1,100,000 00	34,500 00	105,000 00	108,600 00	5,000 00
Emergency funds.........	2,500,000 00	....	....	22,729 55	6,928 00	....
Real estate.....	190,000 00	111,266 94	242,662 76	....	100,855 86	....
Cash	20,630,086 89	7,783,647 78	656,496 33	292,555 01	265,630 62	52,026 61
Cash in hand ...	11,962,994 35	8,892,749 25	1,581,974 19	1,167,942 29	281,713 84	229,199 13
Guarantee advances.......	3,093,555 21	....	....	....	....	....
Advances on mortgages....	....	....	2,788,527 85	....	94,124 01	....
Debtors' current accounts.	12,605,302 02	5,318,895 69	1,854,417 78	264,538 80	786,198 62	222,115 58
Bills in circulation	16,417,061 00	9,195,535 00	....	538,429 25	287,133 28	122,782 00
Mortgage bonds in circulation	....	....	1,947,200 00	....	....	....
Deposits and creditors' current accounts.	21,768,776 96	8,811,024 66	1,642,378 91	458,877 30	465,519 05	75,559 32

	CHIHUAHUA BANK, ON JANUARY 15, 1895.	YUCATECO BANK.	YUCATAN MERCANTILE BANK.	DURANGO BANK.	ZACATECAS BANK.	NEW LEON BANK.
Social capital....	$500,000 00	$1,000,000 00	$ 750,000 00	$500,000 00	$600,000 00	$600,000 00
Unpaid capital.	200,000 00	....	....	....	240,000 00	....
Reserve funds..	5,666 25	22,654 71	17,716 89	3,396 88	6,500 00	8,278 82
Real estate, furniture, etc....	....	....	....	....	....	175,619 63
Cash	40,174 41	475,519 43	508,805 68	178,282 55	250,376 35	240,066 38
Cash in hand...	109,113 11	1,346,715 63	1,001,457 81	603,039 90	565,032 52	600,323 71
Guarantee advances.......	....	....	....	71,894 13	98,196 13	231,094 10
Debtor's current accounts......	285,441 59	172,391 75	426,601 32	322,927 09	339,306 74	118,521 26
Bills in circulation	98,885 00	658,726 00	658,312 00	227,079 00	185,346 00	565,418 00
Deposits and creditors' current accounts.	30,277 86	313,246 10	510,835 92	445,667 79	701,065 74	191,928 26

PUBLIC LANDS.

I append four statements of the titles of public lands issued by the Mexican Government. The first one embraces a résumé of the titles issued without cost, and under the act of December 14, 1874, of the Indian town lands held in common, called in Spanish " Ejidos " to the respective inhabitants of the said towns, from 1877 to 1895 : the second embraces a résumé of the titles issued in 1894 and 1895 for public lands held by private parties as portions of public land bought from the government but which were in excess of the respective titles, which we call in Spanish " Demacias " : the third one embraces a résumé of the titles of public lands issued to private parties in the years 1894 and 1895 : and the fourth contains a résumé of the titles issued by the Mexican Government to surveying companies for one-third of the land respectively surveyed by them in 1894 and 1895, according to law and the respective contracts.

FREE TITLES ISSUED UNDER THE ACT OF DECEMBER 14, 1874, OF THE INDIAN TOWN LANDS TO THE RESPECTIVE INHABITANTS FROM 1877 TO 1895.

YEARS.	TITLES.	AREA.		
		Hectares.	Ares.	Cts.
1877...........................	1	85	06	00
1878...........................	195	3,572	71	41
1879...........................	72	128,144	94	56
1880.......	2	5,000	00	00
1882...........................	195	5,629	29	69
1883...........................	259	14,616	14	13
1884...........................	1,932	61,497	56	94
1885...........................	383	13,068	18	08
1886..........	774	20,662	93	12
1887...........................	254	2,999	85	98
1888...........................	1,524	20,547	73	16
1889...........................	2,237	100,627	65	32
1890...........................	1,130	68,086	31	86
1891...........................	499	6,516	74	22
1892...........................	1,449	15,807	30	95
1893...........................	452	17,709	59	08
1894...........................	791	6,262	71	49
1895...........................	273	6,160	03	65
Total......	12,422	496,994	79	64

TITLES ISSUED FOR UNWARRANTED POSSESSION BY PRIVATE PARTIES OF PUBLIC LANDS IN 1894 AND 1895.

YEARS.	Number of Titles.	AREA.			VALUE.
		Hectares.	Ares.	Cts.	
1894..................	17	34,781	98	04	$21,554 91
1895..................	10	69,557	33	21	20,254 12
	27	104,339	31	25	$41,809 03

TITLES OF PUBLIC LANDS ISSUED TO PRIVATE PARTIES IN 1894 AND 1895.

YEARS.	Number of Titles.	AREA.			VALUE.
		Hectares.	Ares.	Cts.	
1894..................	21	86,385	63	26	$140,067 72
1895..................	19	59,265	24	84	81,883 95
	40	145,650	88	10	$221,951 67

YEARS.	Number of Titles.	AREA.		
		Hectares.	Ares.	Cts.
1894...............................	32	484,257	30	70
1895...............................	29	243,576	11	81
	61	727,833	42	51

EDUCATION.

The following official data received by the Census Bureau of the Mexican Government contains the number of schools in the different States of Mexico, supported by the Federal, State, and municipal administrations, and the number of students attending the same. That statement does not include the States of Mexico and Veracruz, which are among those having the largest number of schools and attendance.

I also append a statement of the number of schools supported by private parties, with the number of pupils attending the same and their cost ; and finally a detailed statement of the public libraries existing in Mexico, and newspapers published in the country, taken from the publication of the Census Bureau in 1895.

NEWSPAPERS PUBLISHED IN MEXICO IN 1895.

Aguascalientes	10	New Leon........................	8
Campeche	4	Oaxaca..........................	5
Chiapas	4	Puebla..........................	17
Chihuahua	19	Queretaro.......................	1
Coahuila........................	6	San Luis Potosí.................	6
Colima..........................	13	Sinaloa..........................	14
Durango........................	7	Sonora	12
Federal District, City of Mexico....	115	Tabasco.........................	14
Guanajuato	14	Tamaulipas	20
Guerrero	6	Territory of Tepic...............	6
Hidalgo	3	Tlaxcala	2
Jalisco	43	Veracruz	24
Lower California (Territory).......	5	Yucatan.........	18
Mexico.........	11	Zacatecas........................	12
Michoacan	30		
Morelos	5	Total.....................	454

These are published in several languages, namely :

English..........................	12	German	1
French	2	Spanish..........................	439
		Total....................	454

Dailies..........................	44	Bi-monthly	3
Semi-weekly.....................	33	Quarterly.......................	5
Tri-weekly.......................	5	Yearly	3
Weekly..........................	185	Unknown........................	10
Semi-monthly....................	79		
Monthly	87	Total....................	454

EDUCATION.

PUBLIC SCHOOLS SUPPORTED BY THE FEDERAL, STATE, AND MUNICIPAL ADMINISTRATIONS OF MEXICO IN 1895.

STATES.	SCHOOLS SUPPORTED BY THE GOVERNMENT.				SCHOOLS SUPPORTED BY THE MUNICIPALITY.				GRADES.			
	Males.	Females.	Both sexes.	Total.	Males.	Females.	Both sexes.	Total.	Primary.	Secondary.	Professional.	Total.
Aguascalientes	1	1		2	20	14		43	43	2		45
Campeche	30	18		48	16	8		27	72	2	1	75
Coahuila	3			3	69	55	5	129	131	1		132
Colima	21	21		42	1			1	43			43
Chiapas	31	27	120	178					177	1	1	178
Chihuahua	71	31	16	118					116	1	1	118
Durango	70	38	8	116					112	2	2	116
Guerrero	266	57		323		47		102	319	2	2	323
Guanajuato	88	77		165	55				263	2	2	267
Hidalgo	122	104	292	518		4		10	515	2	1	518
Jalisco	194	189	92	475	6				479		2	485
Michoacan	194	94		288					285	2	4	288
Morelos	53	54	115	222					221	2	2	222
Nuevo Leon	4	101	1	5	210	90	11	311	311	1	4	316
Oaxaca	512	1		614	18	8		26	638	1		640
Puebla	11	3	4	18	717	286	167	1,170	1,182	1	3	1,188
Querétaro	89	30		119					117	3	1	119
San Luis Potosí	86	81	19	186	36	36	156	156	340	1	1	342
Sinaloa	1	1		1	107	49	180	252	252		1	253
Sonora							6	162	162			162
Tabasco	25	22	32	79	74	41	4	119	77	1	1	79
Tamaulipas	4	66		76					119	6		125
Tlaxcala	132	92	34	232	49	22		71	231		1	232
Yucatan	168		1	261	174	119	132	425	328	1	3	332
Zacatecas	2	2		4	128	116	26	270	425	1	3	429
Federal District	9	6	8	23	58	29	4	91	292		1	293
Territory of Tepic					7	8	13	28	91			91
Lower California Territory, Southern District	2	2	6	10			1	1	28			28
Lower California Territory, Northern District									11			11
Totals	2,189	1,119	748	4,056	1,754	932	708	3,394	7,380	34	36	7,450

EDUCATION.

PUBLIC SCHOOLS SUPPORTED BY THE FEDERAL, STATE, AND MUNICIPAL ADMINISTRATIONS OF MEXICO IN 1895—Continued.

STATES.	ALUMNI INSCRIBED IN THE YEAR			MEDIUM ATTENDANCE DURING THE YEAR			AGES				ADVANCEMENT		
	Males	Females	Total	Males	Females	Total	Under 5 years	From 5 to 10 years	From 10 to 15 years	Over 15 years	Alumni examined	Alumni passing examination	Graduated
Aguascalientes	2,574	1,715	4,289	1,790	1,218	3,008	129	2,479	1,375	306	2,954	2,735	41
Campeche	2,320	1,462	3,782	1,725	1,121	2,846	375	2,540	611	256	3,070	1,074	232
Coahuila	6,472	5,656	12,128	5,199	4,919	10,118	1,046	6,082	4,436	564	7,780	7,206	75
Colima	1,741	1,723	3,464	1,119	1,214	2,333	35	1,817	1,348	264	2,405	1,608	135
Chiapas	1,510	1,284	2,794	…	…	2,540	…	…	…	…	30	30	……
Chihuahua	6,387	4,257	10,644	4,218	2,977	7,195	881	…	…	618	7,816	7,198	14
Durango	5,044	3,664	8,708	3,790	2,968	6,758	387	…	…	977	6,534	5,062	207
Guerrero	9,427	3,743	13,170	3,800	2,490	6,290	221	…	…	216	8,037	6,131	97
Guanajuato	17,837	13,867	31,704	13,397	6,920	20,317	866	…	…	349	12,777	11,824	268
Hidalgo	17,343	8,114	25,457	12,713	6,563	19,276	4,247	…	…	1,298	17,103	14,575	58
Jalisco	19,981	19,779	39,760	14,235	14,445	28,680	380	…	…	146	17,155	16,363	413
Michoacan	14,631	9,765	24,396	10,134	6,754	16,888	273	…	…	3,093	…	14,877	430
Morelos	6,971	5,545	12,516	4,611	4,437	9,048	6,209	…	…	925	…	123	1
Neuvo Leon	13,159	7,309	20,468	9,492	5,251	14,743	1,980	…	…	958	13,899	7,765	815
Oaxaca	54,713	12,181	66,894	19,282	4,625	23,907	4,906	…	…	18,812	19,171	13,751	1,479
Puebla	37,003	17,032	54,035	26,802	12,143	38,945	…	…	…	78	37,499	32,144	584
Querétaro	3,725	1,417	5,142	2,886	1,062	3,948	310	…	…	2,686	3,384	2,925	129
San Luis Potosí	13,936	11,359	25,295	10,882	8,777	19,659	148	…	…	2,140	18,590	14,724	1,933
Sinaloa	7,363	5,077	12,440	5,501	4,160	9,661	103	…	…	353	9,334	8,250	367
Sonora	5,052	4,598	9,650	4,600	4,200	8,800	2,132	…	…	2,632	6,800	3,100	45
Tabasco	3,165	1,630	4,795	4,921	861	5,782	842	…	…	312	67	58	135
Tamaulipas	5,746	3,388	9,134	3,766	2,078	5,844	1,045	…	…	147	5,061	4,942	129
Tlaxcala	7,996	3,720	11,716	7,209	3,002	10,211	798	…	…	862	9,226	8,825	133
Yucatan	9,106	4,998	14,104	9,652	4,491	14,143	90	…	…	2,663	12,846	12,572	1,306
Zacatecas	15,791	12,184	27,975	11,263	8,821	20,084	…	…	…	1,985	16,293	12,604	434
Federal District	17,218	12,610	29,828	12,302	9,559	21,861	…	…	…	82	14,880	13,299	771
Territory of Tepic	3,154	2,323	5,477	2,141	1,540	3,681	…	…	…	…	2,777	1,848	50
Lower California Territory, Southern District	931	927	1,858	575	626	1,201	…	673	1,185	…	1,234	671	……
Lower California Territory, Northern District	200	157	357	172	127	299	…	206	151	…	312	276	……
Totals	310,496	181,484	491,980	208,717	129,349	338,066	27,403	235,887	167,513	42,722	295,705	226,560	10,271

EDUCATION.

SCHOOLS SUPPORTED BY PRIVATE PARTIES.

STATES.	SCHOOLS SUPPORTED BY PRIVATE PARTIES.				SCHOOLS SUPPORTED BY THE CLERGY.				SCHOOLS SUPPORTED BY SOCIETIES.				ALUMNI INSCRIBED DURING THE YEAR.		
	Males.	Females.	Both sexes.	Total.	Males.	Females.	Both sexes.	Total.	Males.	Females.	Both sexes.	Total.	Males.	Females.	Total.
Aguascalientes	6	2		8	1			1					185	80	265
Campeche	4	4		8	1			1					282	83	365
Coahuila	37	25	13	75	4		1	5					1,647	1,473	3,120
Colima			24	24	3	2		5	2	7		9	660	708	1,368
Chiapas													187	133	320
Chihuahua	3	1	2	6	1			1		2		2	2,516	1,526	4,042
Durango	39	13	14	66	3	1		5	5	6		11	1,297	700	1,997
Guerrero	14	9	1	24	4	1		5					3,591	2,351	5,942
Guanajuato	63	47		110	14	14		28					2,471	1,791	4,262
Hidalgo	30	17		47	39	34	9	82	8	3	1	12	12,009	8,914	20,923
Jalisco	89	74	111	274	19	11	4	34					4,516	3,405	7,921
Michoacan	54	58	29	141	2	1		3	1	3		4	894	579	1,473
Morelos	10	5	8	23	2	1		3		2		2	2,010	1,508	3,518
Neuvo Leon	52	31	12	95	12	5		27	1			1	5,972	8,329	14,301
Oaxaca	11	9	20	40	4	6		19					4,515	2,112	6,627
Puebla	27	13	13	53	1	6	21	4	14	10	2	26	1,267	852	2,119
Querétaro	14	10	19	43				2					2,127	1,905	4,032
San Luis Potosí	49	39	336	424					10	9		19			
Sinaloa	10	5		15	1			1					73	29	102
Sonora	1		2	3	6	7		14					740	952	1,692
Tabasco	27	12	3	42					1	1		2	708	486	1,194
Tamaulipas	24	8	14	46	2			2		2		2	427	252	679
Tlaxcala	11	8	3	22	1			1		2		2	1,438	527	1,965
Yucatan	9	9	19	37	7	2		8	9			9	3,802	3,224	7,026
Zacatecas	58	46	35	139	6	5		9	3	2		5	1,690	1,582	3,272
Federal District	14	11	6	31	5			1	2			2	1,504	1,166	2,670
Territory of Tepic	2	3	11	16		1			10	1	6	17	129	16	145
Lower California Territory, Southern District	1	1	2	4											
Totals	659	460	697	1,816	141	92	43	276	78	57	11	146	56,657	44,683	101,340

EDUCATION.

SCHOOLS SUPPORTED BY PRIVATE PARTIES—*Continued.*

STATES.	MEDIUM ATTENDANCE DURING THE YEAR. Males.	Females.	Total.	GRADES. Primary.	Secondary.	Professional.	Total.	AGES. Five years.	From 5 to 10 years.	From 10 to 15 years.	Over 15 years.	ADVANCEMENT. Examined.	Passed.	Graduated.
Aguascalientes	119	14	133	8	1	...	9	14	30	92	129	226	221	7
Campeche	244	78	322	9	...	...	9	14	233	113	161	250	205	3
Coahuila	1,492	1,271	2,763	88	1	...	89	252	1,407	1,300	33	2,556	2,377	101
Colima	570	387	957	32	...	...	32	120	707	508	...	992	962	15
Chiapas	...	...	...	...	...	...	...	...	...	...	...	...	...	...
Chihuahua	132	112	244	4	4	1	9	7	103	133	77	253	233	309
Durango	2,004	1,094	3,008	80	1	1	82	539	2,073	1,205	225	2,699	2,571	44
Guerrero	798	284	1,082	27	1	1	29	407	691	537	362	1,599	1,145	...
Guanajuato	3,109	2,225	5,334	110	...	...	110	...	...	...	...	...	...	...
Hidalgo	1,855	1,433	3,088	74	1	...	75	493	2,112	1,364	293	177	169	3
Jalisco	9,256	7,295	16,551	366	1	1	368	3,224	8,907	6,503	2,289	12,305	9,041	311
Michoacan	3,429	2,721	6,150	170	8	1	179	626	3,274	2,777	1,244	5,141	4,190	268
Morelos	638	507	1,145	26	1	1	28	148	855	404	66	1,296	46	8
Nuevo Leon	...	...	...	93	5	1	99	...	...	...	...	...	...	...
Oaxaca	1,462	939	2,421	93	...	...	93	2,256	4,358	4,581	3,106	1,807	1,107	61
Puebla	3,552	1,530	5,122	85	5	1	91	494	3,127	2,271	735	5,052	4,539	173
Querétaro	1,076	743	1,819	45	1	1	47	307	887	700	225	1,186	1,089	149
San Luis Potosí	2,079	1,896	3,975	445	...	...	445	...	...	...	...	...	...	...
Sinaloa	...	...	...	15	...	...	15	...	...	...	...	...	...	...
Sonora	60	25	85	4	...	...	4	17	48	37	...	...	...	...
Tabasco	652	860	1,512	58	...	...	58	152	859	610	71	651	538	6
Tamaulipas	504	347	851	48	...	...	48	61	684	427	22	523	448	16
Tlaxcala	367	219	586	26	...	...	26	122	384	129	44	1,734	1,907	258
Yucatan	1,215	445	1,661	43	3	1	47	186	543	1,069	167	5,446	4,393	263
Zacatecas	3,013	2,393	5,411	150	1	1	152	377	3,613	2,595	441	1,977	1,812	98
Federal District	1,229	1,246	2,475	42	...	...	42	327	1,880	959	97	1,518	1,119	6
Territory of Tepic	1,111	867	1,978	45	...	...	45	259	1,454	872	85	115	69	...
Lower California Territory, Southern District	103	13	116	5	...	...	5	11	112	22	...	...	...	...
Totals	40,135	28,744	68,879	2,193	34	11	2,238	10,413	38,350	29,208	9,872	47,413	38,181	2,099

PUBLIC LIBRARIES IN MEXICO.

STATES.	NAME OF LIBRARY.	WHERE LOCATED.	NUMBER OF VOLUMES.	ANNUAL NUMBER OF STUDENTS.	HOW SUPPORTED.
Aguascalientes	Scientific Institute	Aguascalientes	3,668	1,037	State funds.
Campeche	Campeche Institute	Campeche	3,408	150	Institute funds.
"	Carmelita Lyceum	Cármen	1,194	......	Carmelita Lyceum funds.
"	Melchor Ocampo	......	......	585	Miguel Hidalgo School funds.
Coahuila	State	Saltillo	2,102	4,400	State funds.
"	Commercial	......	......	......	School funds.
Colima	Public	Colima	355	......	Government funds.
"	Parochial "Christopher Columbus"	"	350	......	Clergy funds.
"	Seminary	......	3,322	......	
Chiapas	Preparatory School	San Cristóbal	3,450	......	Federal Government funds.
"	Public	Tapachula	......	......	"
Chihuahua	Franklin Society	Chihuahua	2,563	775	Franklin Society funds.
"	Literary Institute	"	1,090	......	Institute funds.
"	San Francisco College	......	490	......	College funds.
Durango	Juárez Institute	Durango	5,000	6,000	State funds.
Federal District	National	Mexico	159,000	......	Federal Government funds.
"	Preparatory School	"	10,000	......	"
"	Commercial	"	2,000	......	"
"	Law	"	14,000	......	"
"	Fine Arts	"	2,000	......	"
"	Engineering	"	7,000	......	"
"	Agricultural	"	4,000	......	"
"	Medical	"	3,000	......	"
"	Museum of Natural History	"	2,000	......	"
"	Geographical and Statistical Society	"	4,000	......	"
"	Judicial Archives	"	1,000	......	"
"	General Archives	"	8,000	......	"
"	Normal School for Men	"	400	......	"
"	Normal School for Women	"	400	......	"
"	Conservatory of Music	"	1,021	......	"

PUBLIC LIBRARIES IN MEXICO—*Continued.*

State	Library	City			Funds
Federal District	Arts and Trades for Men	Mexico	2,117	.....	Federal Government funds.
Guanajuato	State College	Guanajuato	12,500	10,900	State funds.
Guerrero	Literary Institute	Chilpancingo	2,346	8,400	"
Hidalgo	Scientific and Literary Institute	Pachuca	2,628	.....	"
Jalisco	State	Guadalajara	.....	16,000	"
Mexico	Municipal	Cuautitlan	300	15	Special donations.
"	"	Coyotepec	38	5	"
"	"	Ixtlahuaca	36	15	"
"	"	San Felipe del Progreso	27	20	"
"	"	Mineral del Oro	13	15	"
"	"	Jilotepec	25	10	"
"	"	Lerma	130	20	"
"	Benito Juárez	Otumba	77	25	"
"	Municipal	Sultepec	16	9	"
"	"	Sacualpan	16	14	"
"	"	Texcaltitlan	15	14	"
"	"	Temascaltepec	64	12	"
"	"	Tejupilco	56	12	"
"	"	San Simon de Guerrero	87	12	"
"	Scientific Institute	Toluca	13,700	12	"
"	Municipal	Bravo Valley	25	10	"
"	"	Asuncion Malacatepec	62	4	"
"	"	Tenango Valley	45	4	"
"	"	Guerrero Valley	10	12	"
Michoacan	Public	Morelia	13,922	8,864	$1 tax on the estate of deceased persons.
"	San Nicolás College	"	.....	.....	College funds.
"	Seminary	"	30,000	3,000	Special donations.
"	Compañia College	Pátzcuaro	1,000	200	"
"	Uruapam	Uruápam	333	43	Municipal funds.
"	Seminary	Zamora	7,000	1,392	Special donations.
Morelos	Public	Cuernavaca	2,348	.....	State funds.
"	Yautepec	Yautepec	30		"
"	Morelos	Cautla	522		"
"	Tetecala	Tetecala	225		"
"	Jojutla	Jojutla	352		"
Nuevo Leon	Public	Monterey	3,458		"
Oaxaca	Public	Oaxaca	15,000		"

PUBLIC LIBRARIES IN MEXICO—*Continued.*

State	Library	Locality			Support
Puebla	Palafoxiana	Puebla		27,000	State funds.
"	Lafragua	"	4,000	21,000	"
"	Serrano	"	15,012	200	Special donations.
"	Benito Juárez	Atlixco	80	400	"
"	Manuel M. Flores	Zacatlan	2,408	350	"
"	"Porfirio Díaz" Municipal	Chalchicomula	100	500	Political Prefect donations.
"	Civil College	Matamoros Izucar	50		Municipal funds.
Querétaro	State	Querétaro		7,743	
San Luis Potosí	State	San Luis Potosí	20,345	13,751	State funds.
Sinaloa	"	Culiacan	495	3,000	"
Sonora	"	Hermosillo	4,870	4,714	"
"	Sonora College			800	"
"	Board of Public Instruction	Guaymas		1,138	Junta
"	Education Society	Sahuaripa		800	State
Tabasco	Juárez Institute	San Juan Bautista		165	"
"	José Eduardo Cárdenas	"		1,800	"
Tamaulipas	State	Ciudad Victoria	3,600	1,650	"
"	Juárez Society	Matamoros		500	"
Tlaxcala	General Archives	Tlaxcala		11,030	Juárez Society funds.
Veracruz	Pueblo	Veracruz	3,000	13,995	State funds.
"	Public	Tlacotálpan	1,100	333	"
"	Preparatory College	Orizaba		9,704	Municipal funds.
"	Preparatory "	Córdova		805	State funds.
"	Normal School	Jalapa		697	"
"	Preparatory College	"		1,377	"
"	Seminary	"		2,796	"
"	Gabino Barreda	Papantla		97	"
"		Tantoyuca		824	"
"		"		400	"
Yucatan	Benito Juárez	Mérida	7,300	2,317	Special funds.
"	Cepeda	Valladolid	720	200	"
"	Iturralde	Mérida		4,000	"
"	Catholic College	Progreso		445	"
"	Eulogio Ancona	Ticul	340	300	"
Zacatecas	Traconis	Zacatecas		22,000	State donations.
"	Public	"	10,000		"
"	Public	Fresnillo	500	2,000	"
Lower California Territory	Municipal	La Paz	50	700	Municipal funds.

SUMMARY OF FACTORIES EXISTING IN MEXICO IN 1893.

STATES	Cotton and woolen mills	Brandy	Mezcal	Beer	Chemical products	Chocolate	Paper	Soap	Tobacco	Matches	Powder	Cake and crackers	Pottery	China	Glass	Starch	Cotton gins	Candles	Artificial stone, bricks, tiles, etc.	Ice	Grape wine	Total
Federal District	13			8	11	8	5	16	22	16		13		2	6	7		118	25	3		273
Aguascalientes	3							2													6	11
Campeche		37																				37
Chiapas	3	13	4																			13
Chihuahua	9		11																			20
Coahuila	3	13						1														10
Colima	7	5	11						4	1			2		1	1						8
Durango	8	24	3	6				1				7					5					48
Guanajuato	1	47	1	8	1	1	2	8	4	4		1						1	1			80
Guerrero	7	77	9	1			1	49	4	2												79
Hidalgo	4	191	50					21				3										263
Jalisco	2	111	56	3		1		24				5										207
Michoacan	15	178		2		2		6		1		3										225
Mexico			4																			72
Morelos	2	44	4					2		1		2										57
Nuevo Leon	19	606	33											1		1				3		625
Oaxaca	4	88	3	3		1	1			1	1	1		1			5					128
Puebla	2	515																				539
Querétaro	2	82						1														87
San Luis Potosí	1	213	36					1												1		256
Sinaloa		147	14					2														166
Sonora	5	71	66																			142
Tabasco	5	21	4																			25
Tamaulipas		13	12																			25
Tlaxcala		17	7																			30
Veracruz	3	137				3	1	4														146
Yucatan	2	42							6	2									1			70
Zacatecas		58	3					8										7		1	2	64
Territory of Tepic	1	31	6																			41
Territory of Lower California		69							1											1	1	73
Total	**123**	**2,899**	**276**	**31**	**12**	**16**	**10**	**146**	**41**	**28**	**1**	**35**	**2**	**3**	**7**	**9**	**10**	**126**	**27**	**9**	**9**	**3,820**

MANUFACTURING ESTABLISHMENTS IN MEXICO IN 1893.

I take from *Les Finances des Etats-Unis Mexicains* of Mr. Prosper Gloner the following table, which purports to give the number of some of the manufacturing establishments in Mexico during the year 1893. Mr. Gloner acknowledges that his table is very deficient, as he says in a note that appears at the foot of it that he failed to receive the data from 117 districts in different states of Mexico, and that besides the manufacturing establishments mentioned in his table there are in the City of Mexico the following : (See page 236.)

Carriages and wagons	11
Wax works	28
Agricultural implements	9
Wall paper	1
Coloring substances	2
Mineral and soda-waters	4
Carriage varnishes	2
Jewelry boxes, etc	9
Mucilage and paste	11
Card-board	6
Scientific instruments	1
Playing cards	1
Pianos, organs, and harmonicas	4
Passementeries	6
Type foundries	1
Gold and silver ribbons	2
Perfumeries	6
Hats	49
Musical instruments	6
Total	159

NAVIGATION.

The total number of vessels, both steamers and sailing vessels, which arrived at and departed from Mexican ports during the year 1895, appears in the following statement.

I also append a statement showing the number of passengers who arrived in and departed from Mexico by sea and rail during the year 1895, mentioning both their nationality and the port of their arrival. The number appears exceedingly small when compared with the very large number coming from Europe to the United States ; but I feel sure that before long we will have a large immigration.

VESSELS ARRIVED AT MEXICAN PORTS IN 1895.

COUNTRIES.	TOTAL NUMBER.			STEAMERS.			SAILING VESSELS.			LOADED.			IN BALLAST.		
	Vessels.	Tons.	Crew.	Vessels.	Tons.	Crew.	Vessels.	Tons.	Crew.	Vessels.	Tons.	Crew.	Vessels.	Tons.	Crew.
Mexican ports	4,042	1,757,700 58	77,290	2,406	1,655,634 69	68,391	1,636	102,065 89	8,899	3,329	1,532,227 11	66,422	713	225,473 47	10,868
United States	466	397,050 07	12,303	317	360,480 20	11,214	149	36,569 87	1,089	408	382,915 97	11,516	58	14,134 10	787
Colombia	14	20,509 34	407	11	19,561 66	440	3	947 68	27	11	19,561 66	440	3	947 68	27
Venezuela	15	5,717 59	140	1	1,387 00	22	14	4,330 59	18	3	1,725 35	35	12	3,992 24	105
Brazil	31	11,121 90	289				31	11,121 90	289				31	11,121 90	289
Guatemala	35	53,720 25	2,284	32	53,064 35	2,249	3	655 90	35	28	46,304 99	1,919	7	7,415 26	365
Norway	16	7,482 81	199	1	1,024 00	24	15	6,458 81	175				16	7,482 81	199
Honduras	1	186 00	9				1	186 00	9	1	186 00	......	1	186 00	9
Costa Rica	10	9,641 95	207	8	9,086 00	191	2	555 95	16	8	9,086 00	191	2	555 95	16
Antilles	2	912 00	22				2	912 00	22				2	912 00	22
Chili	1	446 00	11				1	446 00	11	1	446 00	11			
Hayti	8	12,126 15	326	8	12,126 15	326				8	12,126 15	326			
Holland	5	1,810 56	49				5	1,810 56	49				5	1,810 56	49
Italy	7	8,804 00	184	7	8,804 00	184				7	8,804 00	184			
England	226	217,055 31	4,215	80	137,503 22	2,547	146	79,552 09	1,668	114	181,443 77	3,280	112	35,611 54	935
Germany	36	47,882 01	1,012	23	36,706 22	821	13	11,175 79	191	32	46,460 69	975	4	1,421 32	37
Belgium	6	7,930 00	138	5	7,572 00	127	1	358 00	11	6	7,930 00	138			
France	30	27,973 24	2,191	12	21,944 00	2,023	18	6,029 24	168	15	22,752 90	2,049	15	5,220 34	142
Spain	202	345,314 42	11,426	160	338,264 11	11,084	42	7,050 31	342	155	329,517 91	10,962	47	15,796 51	464
Australia	4	3,475 67	72				4	3,476 67	72	2	2,022 60	41	3	1,454 07	31
Africa	3	807 52	25				3	807 52	25				2	807 52	25
Argentine Republic	2	1,115 23	25				2	1,115 23	25				2	1,115 23	25
Portugal	2	687 32	19				2	687 32	19				2	687 32	19
Unknown	10	7,074 50	167	6	5,223 50	125	4	1,851 00	42	8	6,637 50	151	2	437 00	16
Totals	5,174	2,946,545 42	113,070	3,077	2,668,381 10	99,768	2,097	278,164 32	13,302	4,135	2,609,962 60	98,640	1,039	336,582 82	14,430

VESSELS DEPARTED FROM MEXICAN PORTS IN 1895.

COUNTRIES.	TOTAL NUMBER.			STEAMERS.			SAILING VESSELS.			LOADED.			IN BALLAST.		
	Vessels.	Tons.	Crew.	Vessels.	Tons.	Crew.	Vessels.	Tons.	Crew.	Vessels.	Tons.	Crew.	Vessels.	Tons.	Crew.
Mexican ports	4,109	1,807,250 18	77,942	2,454	1,705,294 55	69,243	1,655	101,955 63	8,699	2,880	1,394,899 85	58,770	1,229	412,350 33	19,172
United States	548	544,768 74	13,685	411	489,504 13	12,460	137	55,264 61	1,225	345	437,468 44	10,592	203	107,300 30	3,093
Colombia	4	4,167 80	196	4	4,167 80	196				1	1,081 75	62	3	3,086 05	134
Guatemala	31	57,619 30	2,085	30	57,332 30	2,075	1	287 00	10	15	26,592 51	1,184	16	31,026 79	901
Honduras	2	548 00	29	2	548 00	29							2	548 00	29
Costa Rica	1	752 60	15				1	752 60	15				1	752 60	15
Nicaragua	1	693 36	14				1	693 36	14				1	693 36	14
Italy	3	962 00	29				3	962 00	29	3	962 00	29			
England	169	85,583 45	2,114	16	29,970 00	556	153	55,613 45	1,558	150	80,515 45	1,950	19	5,068 00	164
Germany	34	39,708 02	985	21	34,783 00	859	13	4,925 02	126	34	39,708 02	985			
Belgium	1	1,565 00	29	1	1,565 00	29				1	1,565 00	29			
France	39	24,757 03	1,585	7	13,279 83	1,265	32	11,477 20	320	38	24,353 03	1,575	1	404 00	10
Spain	193	333,554 71	11,488	160	330,180 15	11,242	33	3,374 56	246	152	314,319 43	10,931	41	19,235 28	557
Russia	21	12,104 48	276				21	12,104 48	276	19	8,984 00	194	2	3,120 48	82
Ecuador	1	241 87	9				1	241 87	9				2	241 87	9
Unknown	2	954 00	13				2	954 00	13				2	954 00	13
Totals	5,159	2,915,230 54	110,494	3,106	2,666,624 76	97,954	2,053	248,605 78	12,540	3,638	2,330,449 48	86,301	1,521	584,781 06	24,193

RÉSUMÉ OF THE YEARS 1885 TO 1895.

ARRIVED.

Year.	Total number of vessels.	In-crease.	De-crease.	Year.	Total number of vessels.	In-crease.	De-crease.
1885	4,456	......	......	1891	5,170	6	......
1886	4,741	285	......	1892	5,675	505	......
1887	5,123	382	......	1893	5,618	......	57
1888	5,448	325	......	1894	5,489	......	129
1889	5,220	......	228	1895	5,174	......	315
1890	5,164	......	56				

DEPARTED.

Year.	Total number of vessels.	In-crease.	De-crease.	Year.	Total number of vessels.	In-crease.	De-crease.
1885	4,396	......	......	1891	5,083	165	......
1886	4,687	291	......	1892	5,640	557	......
1887	5,076	389	......	1893	5,582	......	58
1888	5,293	217	......	1894	5,504	......	78
1889	5,055	......	238	1895	5,159	......	345
1890	4,918	......	137				

FOREIGN PASSENGERS ARRIVED AT MEXICAN PORTS IN 1895.

GULF PORTS.

PORTS.	Total number of passengers.	NATIONALITY.															WHERE THEY COME FROM.											
		Mexicans.	Americans.	Chilians.	English.	French.	Germans.	Chinese.	Italians.	Spanish.	Russians.	Swiss.	Austrians.	Turks.	Colombians.	Other nationalities.	Spain.	United States.	England.	France.	Guatemala.	Germany.	Italy.	Costa Rica.	Colombia.	Belgium.	Salvador.	Other nations.
Alvarado	2		1			1											1	2										
Campeche	1	1																										
Coatzacoalcos																												
Frontera	13	2	3		1	2	2						1					13	1									
Isla del Carmen										6		1					6							1				
Progreso	601	126	55		16	7	5	45	4	295				48			493	104	4	3		1						
Tampico	447	35	74		18	13	11	205	7	40						43	299	97	4	3								
Túxpan	9		8																									
Veracruz	4,072	170	456	5	214	445	164	21	170	2,285		33	10	62	3	34	2,472	732	191	597		52	1		20	7	43	
Total	5,153	334	597	5	250	468	182	271	181	2,628		36	11	110	3	77	3,271	957	200	600		53	1	1	20	7	43	

PACIFIC PORTS.

PORTS.	Total number of passengers.	NATIONALITY.															WHERE THEY COME FROM.											
		Mexicans.	Americans.	Chilians.	English.	French.	Germans.	Chinese.	Italians.	Spanish.	Russians.	Swiss.	Austrians.	Turks.	Colombians.	Other nationalities.	Spain.	United States.	England.	France.	Guatemala.	Germany.	Italy.	Costa Rica.	Colombia.	Belgium.	Salvador.	Other nations.
Acapulco	59	22	10		3		12		3							9		37	1		21							
Guaymas	24		11		4	2		7										20	4									
La Paz	21	5	8		2	3	3											21			9							
Mazatlan	196	107	59	7	1	4	10	7		1			1			2		187			2							
Puerto Angel		2																										
San Blas	15	24	5			2	3											13										
San José del Cabo	87	7	1															4										
Salina Cruz	12		5					55													25							
Santa Rosalía	7	7	8		3													9	2		6	1						
Tonalá	603	179	357		39	9	1	8	10	1								603										58
Todos Santos																												
Total	1,026	353	462	7	52	20	29	77	13	1			1			11		897	7		63	1						58

FOREIGN PASSENGERS DEPARTED FROM MEXICAN PORTS IN 1895.

GULF PORTS.

PORTS.	Total number of passengers.	NATIONALITY.															DESTINATION.											
		Mexicans.	Americans.	Chilians.	English.	French.	Germans.	Chinese.	Italians.	Spanish.	Russians.	Swiss.	Austrians.	Turks.	Colombians.	Other nationalities.	Spain.	United States.	England.	France.	Guatemala.	Germany.	Italy.	Costa Rica.	Colombia.	Belgium.	Salvador.	Other nations.
Alvarado																												
Campeche	2		2															2										
Coatzacoalcos	24	3	5		2	1	2		1							7	11	13										
Frontera																												
Isla del Cármen	453	96	32		9		1	35	18	208	1	1	9				308	115	30									
Progreso	161	19	97		9	7	11	3	6	12		10		29			48	110										
Tampico	139	132	5			4				2							3	136	2									
Túxpan																												
Veracruz	2,261	187	284		45	333	75	5	55	1,192	1	4	1	54	1	24	1,399	407	9	433		13						1
Total	**3,040**	**437**	**425**		**65**	**345**	**89**	**43**	**80**	**1,414**	**2**	**15**	**10**	**83**	**1**	**31**	**1,769**	**783**	**41**	**433**		**13**						**1**

PACIFIC PORTS.

PORTS.	Total number of passengers.	NATIONALITY.															DESTINATION.											
		Mexicans.	Americans.	Chilians.	English.	French.	Germans.	Chinese.	Italians.	Spanish.	Russians.	Swiss.	Austrians.	Turks.	Colombians.	Other nationalities.	Spain.	United States.	England.	France.	Guatemala.	Germany.	Italy.	Costa Rica.	Colombia.	Belgium.	Salvador.	Other nations.
Acapulco	33	4	18		3													27			6							
Guaymas	30	9	14		3		4	4		2								30										
La Paz	33	18	7		3													33			10							
Mazatlan	124	59	34		1	7	11	8	2	2		1						114	9		1							
Puerto Angel	7	1	1				5											7										
San Blas	19	2	13			5			4									18				1						
San José del Cabo	8	7	6															8										
Salina Cruz	44	34	1															8										
Santa Rosalia	61	40	1		20	1												51										
Tonalá	14	14																14			1							
Todos Santos	461	144	266		33	6	1	10	1	2						1	35	457	4									1
Total	**834**	**332**	**361**		**63**	**19**	**23**	**22**	**7**	**6**		**1**				**1**	**35**	**767**	**13**		**17**	**1**						**1**

GENERAL RÉSUMÉ.

	NATIONALITY																DESTINATION											
	Total number of passengers.	Mexicans.	Americans.	Chilians.	English.	French.	Germans.	Chinese.	Italians.	Spanish.	Russians.	Swiss.	Austrians.	Turks.	Colombians.	Other nationalities.	Spain.	United States.	England.	France.	Guatemala.	Germany.	Italy.	Costa Rica.	Colombia.	Belgium.	Salvador.	Other nations.
Arrived	6,179	687	1,059	12	302	488	211	348	194	2,629	...	36	12	110	3	88	3,271	1,854	207	600	63	54	1	1	20	7	43	58
Departed	3,874	769	786	...	128	364	112	65	87	1,420	2	16	10	83	1	31	1,804	1,550	54	433	17	14	...	...	...	...	...	2
Total	10,053	1,456	1,845	12	430	852	323	413	281	4,049	2	52	22	193	4	119	5,075	3,404	261	1,033	80	68	1	1	20	7	43	60
Difference	2,305	82	273	12	174	124	99	283	107	1,209	2	20	2	27	2	57	1,467	304	153	167	46	40	1	1	20	7	43	56

Passengers arrived by the Central Railroad during 1895.......... 9,991
" " National Railroad during 1895.......... 3,387
" " International Railroad during 1895.......... 3,238
    16,616

Passengers departed by the Central Railroad during 1895.......... 9,589
" " National Railroad during 1895.......... 3,126
" " International Railroad during 1895.......... 2,691
    15,406

Total of passengers arrived and departed by rail in 1895.......... 32,022

Difference between passengers arrived and departed by railroads in 1895.......... 1,210

Passengers arrived by the ports.......... 6,179
" " railroads.......... 16,616
    22,795

Passengers departed by the ports.......... 3,874
" " railroads.......... 15,406
    19,280

Total of passengers arrived and departed by ports and rail in 1895.......... 42,075

Difference between passengers arrived and departed by ports and railroads in 1895.......... 3,515

VESSELS ARRIVED AT AND DEPARTED FROM MEXICAN PORTS DURING
THE FISCAL YEARS 1894–95 TO 1895–96.

	ARRIVED.				DEPARTED.			
	Steamers.		Sailing vessels.		Steamers.		Sailing vessels.	
	Ves-sels.	Ton-nage.	Ves-sels.	Ton-nage.	Ves-sels.	Ton-nage.	Ves-sels.	Ton-nage.
Total navigation in the fiscal year 1894–1895............	4,078	3,083,050	5,497	345,923	3,399	3,026,964	5,566	332,720
Total navigation in the fiscal year 1895–1896............	4,471	3,300,444	5,723	395,041	4,378	3,242,711	5,856	390,765
Difference....................	393	217,394	226	49,118	979	215,747	290	58,045

AGRICULTURAL PRODUCTS.

I take from the *Anuario Estadistico de la Republica Mexicana* of 1895
the following table, which gives the total production of some of our
agricultural staples, although I feel perfectly satisfied that they are
very much under-rated in said table, because of the difficulty in obtaining complete data about our agricultural productions, both for want of
a proper machinery to collect it, and because manufacturers conceal
the extent of these products for the purpose of avoiding taxation. I
think if the figures in said table are duplicated they will be nearer
the true production.

RÉSUMÉ OF AGRICULTURAL PRODUCTS IN MEXICO.

ARTICLES.	BUSHELS.	POUNDS AND OTHER MEASURES.	VALUE.
Cereals :			
Rice..........................	....	27,174,320 59	$ 1,400,299 40
Barley......................	4,752,239	....	3,587,682 65
Indian corn................	71,900,598	....	75,695,383 21
Wheat......................	10,034,328	....	13,273,790 50
Leguminous :			
Chickling vetch (Arvejon)...	251,230	....	336,771 40
Beans......................	4,319,834	....	7,269,123 25
Chick-peas................	774,351	....	932,608 60
Lima beans................	561,159	....	624,530 22
Lentils....................	34,123	....	64,441 25
Root plants :			
Sweet potatoes............	2,051,854	....	859,461 50
Huacamote................	235,939	....	108,348 82
Potatoes...................	....	29,472,894 45	879,430 15
Solanaceous :			
Dried pepper..............	....	9,724,443 98	1,731,857 67
Green pepper..............	1,007,049	....	758,199 90
Cane products :			
Sugar cane................	....	5,924,612,232 56	25,692,281 25
Sugar......................	....	316,531,239 02	10,283,994 38
Brown sugar..............	....	152,300,903 95	7,942,787 60
Molasses	....	12,748,079 24	3,304,787 82

ARTICLES.	BUSHELS.	POUNDS AND OTHER MEASURES.	VALUE.
Oleaginous :			
Sesame seed............	214,469	....	$ 144,773 00
Peanuts................	357,569	....	325,413 00
Coquito de Aceite........	69,388	....	130,955 00
Cocoanuts................	....	(310,953,000 cocoanuts)	3,522,789 00
Linseed................	303,425	....	373,115 00
Palma Christi...........	59,460	....	83,434 00
Turnip seed.............	20,708	....	34,806 00
Lime-leaf sago..........	9,968	....	20,168 00
Alcohol and Fermented Drinks:			
Rum....................	....	12,768,716 gals.	5,056,474 82
Pulque whiskey.........	....	270,876 gals.	199,935 00
Mezcal.................	....	6,011,602 gals.	3,078,372 00
Pulque.................	....	54,624,835 gals.	3,562,435 05
Tlachique or unfermented pulque.............	....	24,013,901 gals.	1,294,575 00
Textiles :			
Henequen..............	....	93,427,740 04	4,104,096 00
Ixtle..................	....	9,608,026 79	325,250 95
Cotton................	....	78,511,486 26	10,176,050 50
Grape Products :			
Grape.................	....	3,114,519 05	161,372 25
Wine..................	....	162,816 16 gals.	146,028 70
Brandy................	....	91,656 69 gals.	83,724 80
Dyeing Plants :			
Indigo.................	....	299,761 56	285,530 00
Brazil.................	....	632,135 85	64,795 00
Campeachy.............	....	171,604,086 41	2,110,098 50
Moral.................	....	19,826,253 38	195,300 00
Tanning Plants :			
Cascalote..............	....	4,798,994 96	242,070 25
Tanning bark...........	....	33,036,812 04	457,167 26
Tropical Plants :			
Cocoa.................	....	5,346,718 17	1,123,180 00
Coffee................	....	42,019,015 76	11,565,519 28
Tobacco...............	....	124,852,597 69	6,464,733 50
Pepper................	....	119,273 60	14,055 00
Vanilla................	....	(10,714,000 vanilla beans)	667,145 50
Gums :			
Chewing gum...........	....	3,996,630 32	549,865 50
India rubber...........	....	1,354,851 48	410,290 00
Mesquite gum..........	....	139,896 97	7,292 75
Copal gum.............	....	21,485 47	10,313 55
Medicinal Plants :			
Jalap..................	....	50,099 00	6,945 00
Sarsaparilla............	....	1,514,331 90	100,730 00

CONCLUSION.

It has taken me a great deal of time and required a great deal of effort to obtain and prepare the data contained in this paper. I am sorry I have not been able to make it more complete than it is ; but I hope my article, by giving a general and superficial idea of Mexico, may promote the desire to read other papers and books treating on that subject in a fuller and more complete manner.

ADDENDA.

Since this paper has been printed the Federal Treasury of Mexico finished the accounts of the fiscal year ended June 30, 1897, and I give below the general results, showing the total amount of the Federal revenues and expenses during that year. I also give a statement, taken from the Statistical Bureau of the Treasury Department of Mexico, published since this paper has gone to press, of the imports and exports in the same year, both by countries and custom houses, these two statements completing the data contained in this paper, and finally some data of the trade of both countries during the first nine months of the present calendar year.

FEDERAL REVENUE AND EXPENSES OF MEXICO IN THE FISCAL YEAR 1896–1897.

RECEIPTS.

Duties on imports and exports..................	$23,639,580.91	
Internal revenue.............................	24,323,798.46	
Public services......	2,057,409.92	
Extraordinary and incidental..................	2,084,496.30	
		$52,105,285.59
Extraordinary revenues proceeding from contracts and other sources		2,819.17
		$52,108,104.76

EXPENSES.

1.	Legislative power.......................	$ 989,758.38	
2.	Executive power........................	62,100.26	
3.	Judicial power..........................	428,687.46	
4.	Department of Foreign Affairs............	470,122.37	
5.	Department of Interior...................	3,354,888.95	
6.	Department of Justice and Public Education.	2,184,556.52	
7.	Department of Fomento, Colonization, and Industry............................	611,863.83	
8.	Department of Communications and Public Works............................	5,494,593.34	
9.	Department of the Treasury and Public Credit.............................	24,218,207.75	
10.	Department of War and the Navy.........	10,550,955.18	
	Total..................		$48,365,734.04
	Surplus...........................		$3,742,370.72

245

IMPORTS AND EXPORTS OF MEXICO BY COUNTRIES AND CUSTOM HOUSES IN THE FISCAL YEAR 1896–97.

COUNTRIES.	IMPORTS.	EXPORTS.	CUSTOM HOUSES.	IMPORTS.	EXPORTS.
Algiers......	$ 802	....	Acapulco	$ 206,275	$ 123,481
Arabia......	282	....	Altata	101,159	813,899
Argentine			Camargo.....	6,897	8,735
Republic..	1,897	....	Campeche....	175,027	747,710
Australia....	24,833	....	City of Juarez.	2,910,359	17,929,521
Austria......	128,367	....	City of Porfirio		
Belgium.....	479,850	$ 1,134,325	Diaz.......	4,710,415	2,888,535
Bolivia......	214	....	Coatzacoalcos.	105,148	285,195
Brazil	240	....	Frontera......	246,918	418,352
Canada.....	3,356	17	Guaymas.....	451,959	40,307
Chili........	6,203	20	Guerrero	6,863	15,754
China	51,357	5,396	Isle of Carmen	89,894	1,693,767
Colombia....	64,317	17,675	La Morita....	24,943	498,765
Costa Rica..	....	31,658	La Paz.......	62,937	430,144
Cuba	363	53,503	Laredo	4,693,818	3,701,086
Denmark....	3,614	....	Las Palomas..	18,794	420,011
Ecuador	53,249	....	Manzanillo ...	77,395	221,551
Egypt	10,271	....	Matamoros ...	185,370	312,987
England	6,881,701	14,280,527	Mazatlan	1,572,568	5,808,037
France	4,989,082	1,873,522	Mier........	8,157	78,609
Germany....	4,003,263	4,416,744	Nogales......	944,312	5,776,575
Greece......	1,660	....	Progreso.....	1,463,515	8,443,130
Guatemala ..	46,323	1,197,247	Puerto Angel.	15,150	525,075
Hawaii	....	1,200	Salina Cruz...	11,676	68,114
Holland.....	132,728	57,906	San Blas.....	152,643	638,398
Honduras....	3	....	Sta. Rosalia..	547,726	3,279,390
India	210,845	....	Soconusco....	231,078	1,608,446
Italy........	184,186	10,765	Tampico.....	8,773,275	29,952,441
Japan	23,673	1,660	Tijuana......	14,297	116,238
Nicaragua...	....	2,110	Todos Santos.	140,268	199,367
Norway.....	41,670	....	Tonala	106,494	255,582
Persia.......	784	....	Tuxpam	76,926	1,154,313
Peru........	108	19,690	Veracruz.....	14,036,136	22,484,633
Portugal	22,653	....	Zapaluta.....	35,703	408,346
Russia......	31,387	294,165			
Salvador	452	12,185			
San Domingo	1,071	....			
Senegambia .	902	....			
Spain.......	1,983,794	1,192,328			
Sweden	29,078	180			
Switzerland..	163,293	720			
Turkey	3,267	....			
United States	22,593,860	86,742,951			
Uruguay	33	....			
Venezuela...	27,608	....			
Zanzibar	1,456	....			
Total....	$42,204,095	$111,346,494	Total......	$42,204,095	$111,346,494

A comparison between the foreign trade in the fiscal year 1896–97 with the year before, 1895–96, gives the following results : During the year 1896–97 Mexico's exports increased $6,329,592, but the value of the exports sent to the United States increased $7,091,256. The total of Mexico's imports for the year 1896–97 shows a falling-off of $49,843, but, notwithstanding this fact, Mexico's imports from the United States increased $2,448,097. During the year England's exports to Mexico decreased $1,023,315, and her imports from Mexico show a loss of $2,186,622, a combined loss of over 12 per cent. in her commercial relations with the Republic. Imports to Mexico from France fell off $1,110,101, a loss of one-sixth of all France's exports to Mexico. In 1895–96 the United States imported 75.8 per cent. of the total exports from Mexico ; in 1896–97 American exporters furnished 53½ per cent. of all that Mexico bought abroad, and, more than this, the United States took 47.67 per cent. of all that was exported from Mexico. These figures sustain the prediction made, that any unsettlement or diminution of Mexico's importations either because of fluctuating silver or the increased production of home manufactories would affect American exporters less than those of any other country. The statistics given above show that these causes have affected them less than those of all the other countries combined ; in fact, their loss has been the gain of the United States.

TRADE BETWEEN MEXICO AND THE UNITED STATES DURING THE
FIRST NINE MONTHS OF THE CALENDAR YEAR 1897.

The following data, taken from the publications of the Statistical Bureau of the United States Treasury Department, shows the results of the trade with Mexico in the nine months ended September 30, 1897, as compared with the similar period ended September 30, 1896.

Mexican Exports to the United States.—In the following items the first group of figures represents the amounts and values exported in the first nine months of this year, and the second those of the similar period in 1896 :

Coffee, 30,016,967 pounds, worth $4,574,252 gold, against 19,715,264 pounds, worth $3,333,385. The much lower price of coffee this year accounts for the disproportionate valuation.

The people of the United States, besides being Mexico's chief customers for coffee, are buying more and more of our tobacco, which they now know and appreciate on its merits. The amount exported to the United States was 600,987 pounds, worth in gold $294,536, against 191,303, worth $78,769.

Mexico exported, in the period under consideration, to the United States, hides and skins to the value of $1,534,306 gold, against $1,055,299. The quantities, respectively, were 11,764,000 pounds, and 7,102,465 pounds. No diminution of activity there.

It is worth noting that oranges were shipped out to the value of $22,444 gold against $19,359.

Mexico's great argentiferous lead business did not fall behind, the nine months' exportation being 108,776,560 pounds, worth in gold $1,226,525, against 97,818,833 pounds, worth $949,926. The bulk of the American purchase of lead is from Mexico.

Yucatan is Mexico's henequen-growing region, and the exportation has been heavy, standing at 48,410 tons, worth in gold $2,889,003, against 35,746 tons, worth $2,323,585, a noteworthy increase. The henequen or sisal-grass trade into the United States is overwhelmingly Mexican, " other countries " furnishing but 399 tons in the first nine months of this year !

Mexico both exports and imports coal, and shipped into the United States 85,890 tons, worth in gold $182,416, against 52,674 tons, worth $115,015.

Logwood exports were $44,028, against $15,250.

Mahogany fell off, being $290,044 gold, against $306,715, but this trade is always variable.

Mexican Imports from the United States.—It is worthy of note that, in spite of the extraordinarily heavy gold premium, Mexico should be increasing her buying abroad of electrical apparatus, the purchase from the United States alone, in the first nine months of this year, amounting to $228,000 gold, as against $200,000 in the same period last year. Sewing machines went in to the value of $164,000 gold in the nine-month period, against $154,000 last year. Builders' hardware fell off from $556,600 gold value, in the first nine months of last year, to $424,000 this year, but lumber for builders ran up to $1,079,000 gold, against only $544,000 last year, all coming from the United States. Furniture increased slightly, $141,000 gold, against $126,000.

Carriages, cars, and other vehicles, in the nine-months' period, came from the United States to the value of $664,000 gold, as compared with $463,000 last year. Bicycles amounted to $56,000 gold, as against $37,700.

Other importations were as follows :

	9 mos., 1897.	9 mos., 1896.
Cotton :		
Bales	9,936	23,127
Value	* $411,973	* $1,020,000
Crude petroleum imports :		
Gallons	6,260,164	5,486,667
Value	* $277,300	* $299,422
Refined petroleum :		
Gallons	734,466	588,242
Value	$136,180	$122,447
Cotton seed oil :		
Gallons	1,010,580	912,905
Value	* $199,000	* $195,000

* Gold.

APPENDIX.

In the preceding paper I stated that I would give as an appendix some data concerning several subjects treated in the same, and I now append the documents mentioned ; the first one being a paper published in the *Bulletin of the American Geographical Society of New York* for March 31, 1894, under the title of "Mexico a Central American State," the second, some itineraries of the principal roads in Mexico, which show the broken surface of that country, and the third and last, a paper on the "Drainage of the Valley of Mexico," published by the *Engineering Magazine* of New York, Vol. viii., No. 4, for January, 1895.

MEXICO A CENTRAL AMERICAN STATE.

In the chapter of this paper entitled " Location, Boundaries, and Area," I referred, (page 9) to an article under the above heading, which I published in the *Bulletin of the American Geographical Society of New York* of March 31, 1894, and offered to give it in the appendix.   That paper is the following :

MEXICO A CENTRAL AMERICAN STATE.[1]

There is in this city a social gathering of ladies and gentlemen called " The Travellers' Club," meeting weekly during the winter of each year, for the purpose of studying a foreign country, on the supposition that its members are then travelling in that particular country, and with that view papers are read referring to the same, and they are illustrated with an exhibition of views and objects manufactured in the country under study, and of everything else that may contribute to impart more or less complete information regarding the place supposed to be visited.

During the winter of 1887–88 Mexico was chosen as the country under study by the club, and for that reason I received at the beginning of the year 1888 an invitation to attend some of its sessions, and to say something about the Republic.   I accepted the invitation to attend some session, but stated to the invitation committee that, not having time to prepare a paper, I would only give some general notions on

---

[1] This article was published in the *Bulletin of the American Geographical Society of New York* of March 31, 1894, and it is inserted here without any changes.   Although the data contained in this article was published in the years 1887 and 1893, as it refers to the area which has not changed, I have not thought it necessary to revise the same.   So far as the Mexican States are concerned, I have later and more accurate data ; but the differences are insignificant, and it is not worth while to notice them.   As regards the population, the increase has been proportionate ; in respect to all the countries mentioned in this article there is no marked change in the general proportions.

Mexico, in a conversational form, and would be glad to answer any question that might be put to me by those attending the meeting who felt the desire to have further information and more details.

Accordingly, the evening of the 16th of January, 1888, I attended the meeting of the club and spoke for about an hour on the geographical position of Mexico, its physical conditions, its natural resources, and other matters connected with the situation of the country, but carefully avoiding to touch any political question, especially of an international character.

With a view to leave a record of what I intended to say, I had with me a stenographer to take down what I would say, and although his notes were not complete, by using them, and those taken by reporters, some extracts of my conversation were prepared and published the next morning.

Speaking of the geographical position of Mexico, I naturally stated, what is a fact, although not generally realized, that while the main portion of the territory of Mexico is located in North America it occupies a considerable portion of Central America, although politically it is considered as wholly situated in North America. On this subject I made the following remarks, taken from the newspapers, but which were correct:

"The isthmus of Panama divides the New World into two continents, one situated on the northern and the other on the southern hemisphere, but as the position of that isthmus does not correspond with the line of the equator, and lies considerably north of that line, a large portion of South America proper lies in the boreal hemisphere. North America proper is divided by the isthmus of Tehauntepec in two subdivisions—Central America from Panama to Tehauntepec, and North America from Tehauntepec to the North Pole.

"Central America in its present political organization includes the following States: Guatemala, Salvador, Honduras, Nicaragua, and Costa Rica, but from a geographical standpoint it has a much larger area, since it begins at the isthmus of Panama and ends at the isthmus of Tehuantepec. Taking this view, Mexico exercises sovereignty over a large portion of Central America, larger still than any single State of the five which are generally considered as the only components of the same, and representing a third of the total territorial area of Central America.

"The Mexican State of Chiapas and a part of Oaxaca, on the Pacific; of Yucatan, Campeche, and Tabasco, and a portion of the State of Vera Cruz on the Gulf of Mexico, are situated in geographical Central America.

"The following *résumé* of the territorial area and population of the several sections of Central America, taken from the *Statesman's Year Book*, London, 1887, shows that Mexico is a Central American as well as a North American power:

FIVE STATES OF CENTRAL AMERICA.

	Area in sq. miles.	Population.
Guatemala	46,800	1,224,602
Salvador	7,225	634,120
Honduras	46,400	458,000
Nicaragua	49,500	275,815
Costa Rica	23,200	213,785
Total	173,125	2,806,322

MEXICO.

State.	Area in sq. miles.	Population.
Chiapas..............................	16,048	242,029
Oaxaca (one-fifth).....................	6,718	152,255
Yucatan...............................	29,567	302,319
Campeche.............................	25,832	90,413
Tabasco..............................	11,815	140,747
Vera Cruz (one-fourth)..............	6,558	145,610
Total...........................	96,538	1,073,373

This shows that 36 per cent. of the total area of Central America belongs to Mexico.

In the foregoing list I omitted to take into account that, besides the States referred to, there are in Central America proper the British Colony of Belize or British Honduras, and that part of the State of Panama, in Colombia, which lies north of the isthmus of Panama.

Taking the area and population of those places from the statistical and geographical data published by the *Almanach de Gotha* for 1893, and from some official information in possession of Señor Doctor Don Manuel M. de Peralta, Costa Rican Minister to Washington, a gentleman very well versed in Central American affairs, the following results are obtained :

	Area in square miles.	Area in square kilometers.	Population.
Chiapas	16,048	41,565	270,000
Oaxaca (one-fifth)	6,718	17,400	158,800
Yucatan	29,567	76,579	330,000
Campeche	25,832	66,905	94,000
Tabasco	11,815	30,600	140,747
Veracruz (one-fourth) ...	6,558	16,986	181,000
	96,538	250,035	1,174,547
Guatemala............	48,300	125,100	1,520,000
Honduras............	46,262	119,820	400,000
Salvador..............	8,135	21,070	800,000
Nicaragua............	47,857	123,950	320,000
Costa Rica............	24,000	62,000	270,000
Panama (two-thirds).....	19,278	50,000	200,000
British Honduras.......	8,300	21,475	31,500
	202,132	523,415	3,541,500

GEOGRAPHICAL EXTENSION OF CENTRAL AMERICA.

	Square miles.	Square kilometers.
Mexican Central America.............	96,538	250,035
Five Republics of Central America.....	174,554	451,940
British Honduras....................	8,300	21,475
Panama (two-thirds)	19,278	50,000
	298,670	773,450

The foregoing table shows that a little more than 32 per cent. of the whole of Central America, geographically speaking, belongs to Mexico.

When those statements were translated into Spanish and published by *Las Novedades*, of New York, in its issue of the 18th of January, 1888, they were read by Señor Don Manuel Montufar, Secretary of the Guatemalan Legation in Washington, who, in the absence of the Minister, Señor Don Francisco Lainfiesta, was acting as Chargé d'Affaires, and he considered my statements in this connection as a geographical heresy, and as an evidence of the design of Mexico against the several States of Central America. His alarm was so great that he called the attention of the other representatives of the Central American States in Washington to this incident, in order to point out to them the serious dangers which he foresaw for their respective countries on account of my views, which he considered as more than extraordinary.

Fortunately, one of them, the representative of Costa Rica, Señor Doctor Don Manuel M. de Peralta, had attended the meeting of the Travellers' Club at which I spoke, and, I think, Doctor Don Horacio Guzman, the Nicaraguan Minister, was also present, although I am not sure of this, and both failed to see anything in what I stated in this connection that was not a geographical fact, and that, consequently, it could not be disputed; and therefore this incident, that threatened to assume certain proportions, died in its very cradle.

Señor Montufar showed himself over-sensitive at my remarks when there was not the slightest ground for such feeling. If I had made a geographical mistake in averring that a portion of the territory of Mexico was in Central America, geographically speaking, I would be the only sufferer by my mistake, because I would have been the laughing-stock of everybody, including the school-boy studying geography; and, on the contrary, if I had stated a fact, nobody had reason to complain, and much less to be alarmed.

My object in now mentioning this incident is to show the extreme sensitiveness of some Guatemalan gentlemen in regard to Mexico, which goes so far that they cannot listen sometimes to indisputable facts without umbrage, and without ascribing it to purposes and designs against their country. Fortunately this incident happened when the long-pending boundary dispute between Mexico and Guatemala had already been settled for several years, as, had it taken place before, when that question was opened, the situation would have been still more embarrassing and unpleasant.

M. Romero.

Washington, *December 29, 1893.*

In the chapter on Orography of this paper (page 31) I stated that I would give some profiles of the Mexican surface, which would show in an exact manner the different altitudes from the sea-level to the high plateaus of the country. I have selected for that purpose the principal measurements by railroads built in Mexico, as they naturally followed the easiest ascent and descent, both from the coast to the interior and back to the coast. I will also supplement those measurements with others made for wagon roads to and from important places.

FROM VERACRUZ TO MEXICO BY ORIZABA, BY THE MEXICAN RAILWAY.

STATIONS.	Distance between each station.		Distances.		Altitudes.	
	Kilom's.	Miles.	Kilom's.	Miles.	Metres.	Feet.
Veracruz.................	15.500	9.63	0.000	0.00	1.89	6.20
Tejeria.................	15.250	9.48	15.500	9.63	32.34	106.10
Purga..................	11.250	6.99	30.750	19.11	44.77	146.89
Soledad.................	21.250	13.21	42.000	26.10	93.08	305.39
Camaron.................	12.750	7.92	63.250	39.31	340.76	1116.47
Paso del Macho...........	10.000	6.22	76.000	47.23	475.55	1560.25
Atoyac	19.750	12.27	86.000	53.45	400.77	1314.91
Cordova	26.250	16.52	105.750	65.72	827.88	2713.61
Orizaba.................	20.250	12.58	132.000	82.04	1227.63	4027.80
Maltrata................	20.250	12.59	152.250	94.62	1601.79	5255.40
Boca del Monte..........	6.500	4.04	172.500	107.21	2415.36	7924.66
Esperanza	24.250	15.07	179.000	111.25	2451.79	8044.20
San Andres	20.500	12.74	203.250	126.32	2430.42	7974.08
Rinconada	18.000	11.19	223.750	139.06	2357.32	7734.24
San Marcos.............	17.250	10.72	241.750	150.25	2373.21	7786.37
Huamantla..............	25.500	15.84	259.000	160.97	2488.06	8164.97
Apizaco.................	27.000	16.79	284.500	176.81	2411.51	7912.03
Soltepec	19.500	12.12	311.500	193.60	2507.62	8227.37
Apam	15.500	9.63	331.000	205.72	2486.92	8159.45
Irolo	22.000	13.67	346.500	215.35	2452.58	8046.78
Otumba.................	11.500	7.15	368.500	229.02	2349.41	7708.28
Teotihuacan.............	11.250	6.99	380.000	236.17	2281.57	7485.71
Tepexpam	32.500	20.20	380.000	236.17	2244.99	7365.69
Mexico.................			423.750	263.36	2239.83	7348.76

FROM APIZACO TO PUEBLA, A BRANCH OF THE SAME ROAD.

Mexico..................	139.250	86.54	0.000	0.00	2239.83	7348.76
Apizaco.................	16.750	10.41	139.250	86.54	2411.51	7912.03
Santa Ana...............	18.250	11.29	156.000	96.95	2288.31	7507.82
Panzacola...............	12.000	7.52	174.250	108.24	2192.01	7191.86
Puebla			186.250	115.76	2154.63	7069.22

FROM VERACRUZ TO MEXICO BY JALAPA, BY THE INTEROCEANIC RAILWAY.

STATIONS.	Distance between each station.		Distances.		Altitudes.	
	Kilom's.	Miles.	Kilom's.	Miles.	Metres.	Feet.
Veracruz..................	20.234	12.58	0.000	0.00	2.00	6.56
Santa Fé.................	15.200	9.46	20.234	12.58	28.60	93.84
La Antigua..............	9.820	6.09	35.434	22.04	5.50	18.04
San Francisco...........	21.644	13.45	45.254	28.13	24.44	80.18
Rinconada...............	16.312	10.14	66.898	41.58	254.00	833.36
Colorado................	9.781	6.07	83.210	51.72	520.70	1708.39
El Palmar...............	15.603	9.70	92.991	57.79	690.08	2264.12
Chavarrillo..............	14.675	9.12	108.594	67.49	941.24	3088.16
Pacho...................	8.558	5.32	123.269	76.61	1170.44	3840.15
Jalapa..................	10.510	6.53	131.827	81.93	1336.18	4383.94
Banderilla..............	14.227	8.84	142.337	88.46	1490.00	4888.62
San Miguel.............	14.870	9.25	156.564	97.30	1780.22	5840.82
Cruz Verde.............	16.569	10.29	171.434	106.55	2073 09	6801.70
Las Vigas...............	20.827	12.95	188.003	116.84	2421.10	7943.50
Perote..................	29.476	18.31	208.830	129.79	2390.30	7842.44
Tepeyahualco...........	17.041	10.59	238.297	148.10	2321.50	7615.23
Virreyes................	17.064	10.61	255.338	158.69	2346.40	7698.41
Ojo de Agua............	11.303	7.02	272.402	169.30	2348.33	7704.74
San Marcos.............	14.014	8.71	283.705	176.32	2412.60	7915.61
La Venta...............	10.357	6.44	297.719	185.03	2559.05	8396.10
Acajete.................	11.344	7.05	308.076	191.47	2469.25	8101.48
Amozoc.................	19.391	12.05	319.420	198.52	2312.04	7585.67
Puebla.................	7.919	4.92	338.811	210.57	2155.60	7072.39
Los Arcos..............	15.586	9.69	346.730	215.49	2130.96	6991.56
Analco.................	15.231	9.47	362.316	225.18	2197.50	7209.88
San Martin Texmelucan...	12.721	7.91	377.547	234.65	2258.61	7410.38
Atotonilco.............	24.259	15.05	390.268	242.56	2472.10	8110.83
Nanacamilpa............	23.275	14.49	414.527	257.61	2740.16	8990.31
Calpulalpam............	9.302	5.78	437.802	272.10	2576.10	8990.31
San Lorenzo............	9.648	5.99	447.104	277.88	2484.22	8150.60
Irolo..................	15.617	9.71	456.752	283.87	2447.25	8029.30
Soapayuca..............	4.724	2.94	472.369	293.58	2409.05	7903.96
Otumba.................	31.209	19.39	477.093	296.52	2361.30	7747.29
Texcoco................	11.452	7.92	508.302	315.91	2249.10	7379.13
San Vicente............	9.353	5.19	519.754	323.03	2235.20	7333.52
Los Reyes..............	17.495	11.50	529.107	328.22	2240.10	7349.60
Mexico.................	....	....	546.602	339.72	2240.00	7349.27

FROM THE CITY OF MEXICO TO MORELOS, A BRANCH OF THE SAME ROAD.

Mexico.................	17.495	11.50	0.000	0.00	2240.00	7349.27
Los Reyes..............	7.005	3.73	17.495	11.50	2240.10	7349.60
Ayotla.................	9.300	5.77	24.500	15.23	2243.30	7360.09
La Compañia...........	12.900	8.02	33.800	21.00	2244.50	7364.03
Tenango...............	10.800	6.71	46.700	29.02	2324.20	7625.53
Amecameca............	12.200	7.59	57.500	35.73	2466.50	8092.42
Otumba................	22.900	14.23	69.700	43.32	2324.45	7626.33
Nepantla...............	26.800	16.66	92.600	57.55	1968.65	6459.04
Yecapixtla.............	16.500	10.25	119.400	74.21	1570.20	5151.75
Cuautla de Morelos.......	8.200	5.10	135.900	84.46	1216.48	3991.20
Calderon...............	14.000	8.70	144.100	89.56	1258.15	4127.92
Yautepec...............	18.000	11.19	158.100	98.26	1154.72	3788.59
Ticuman................	8.200	5.09	176.100	109.45	968.22	3176.69
Tlaltizapan............	8.700	5.41	184.300	114.54	934.10	3064.73
Tlalquitenango..........	2.300	1.43	193.000	119.95	900.20	2953.51
Jojutla................	12.100	7.52	195.300	121.38	890.64	2922.15
San Jose...............	7.600	4.73	207.400	128.90	992.35	3255.84
Puente de Ixtla.........	....	....	215.000	133.63	896.99	2942.99

FROM PUEBLA TO IZÚCAR DE MATAMOROS, A BRANCH OF THE SAME ROAD.

STATIONS.	Distance between each station.		Distances.		Altitudes.	
	Kilom's.	Miles.	Kilom's.	Miles.	Metres.	Feet.
Puebla..................	7.919	4.92	0.000	0.00	2155.60	7072.36
Los Arcos...............	5.000	3.11	7.919	4.92	2130.96	6991.52
Cholula.................	8.900	5.53	12.919	8.03	2145.00	7037.58
Santa María.............	18.100	11.25	21.819	13.56	2120.10	6955.89
San Augustin...........	5.850	3.64	39.919	24.81	2030.20	6660.94
Atlixco.................	19.150	11.90	45.769	28.45	1196.60	3925.99
San José Teruel.........	8.850	5.49	64.919	40.35	1685.18	5528.99
Tatetla.................	10.543	6.56	73.769	45.84	1584.94	5200.10
Matamoros..............	....	....	84.412	52.40	1443.80	4737.03

FROM MEXICO TO EL PASO DEL NORTE OR CIUDAD JUAREZ, BY THE CENTRAL MEXICAN RAILROAD.

STATIONS.	Kilom's.	Miles.	Kilom's.	Miles.	Metres.	Feet.
Mexico..................	11.700	7.27	0.000	0.00	2240.00	7349.32
Tlalnepantla............	5.900	3.67	11.700	7.27	2250.10	7392.46
Barrientos	3.300	2.05	17.600	10.94	2298.50	7541.26
Lechería................	6.800	4.23	20.900	12.99	2253.20	7392.63
Cuautitlan..............	8.300	5.15	27.700	17.22	2252.50	7390.33
Teoloyucan	10.500	6.52	36.000	22.37	2253.20	7392.63
Huehuetoca.............	6.000	3.74	46.500	28.89	2258.80	7411.00
Nochistongo.............	9.900	6.15	52.500	32.63	2248.00	7375.57
El Salto	17.600	10.96	62.400	38.78	2162.60	7095.37
Tula	13.500	8.39	80.000	49.72	2030.00	6660.32
San Antonio.............	24.300	15.10	93.500	58.11	2187.00	7175.43
Leña...................	3.800	2.37	117.800	73.21	2471.80	8109.84
Marquez................	8.300	5.15	121.600	75.58	2426.50	7961.22
Nopala.................	8.000	5.04	129.900	80.73	2341.40	7682.00
Dañú...................	14.000	8.63	137.900	85.77	2387.70	7833.92
Polotitlan..............	9.200	5.72	151.900	94.40	2292.30	7520.91
Cazadero...............	10.900	6.77	161.100	100.12	2249.50	7380.49
Palmillas...............	18.600	11.57	172.000	106.89	2162.00	7093.40
San Juan del Rio........	13.300	8.26	190.600	118.46	1905.50	6251.84
Chintepec	12.200	7.59	203.900	126.72	1894.90	6217.07
Ahorcado...............	24.400	15.16	216.100	134.31	1907.70	6259.07
Hércules................	5.000	3.11	240.500	149.47	1843.90	6049.74
Querétaro	18.500	11.50	245.500	152.58	1813.20	5949.02
Mariscala...............	14.500	9.01	264.000	164.08	1788.20	5867.00
Apaseo.................	13.000	8.08	278.500	173.09	1767.40	5798.75
Celaya.................	18.200	11.31	291.500	181.17	1757.40	5765.94
Guaje..................	22.800	14.17	309.700	192.48	1740.00	5708.85
Salamanca	11.100	6.90	332.500	206.65	1721.50	5648.15
Chico..................	9.200	5.72	343.600	213.55	1720.80	5645.85
Irapuato...............	16.600	10.31	352.800	219.27	1723.70	5655.37
Villalobos..............	13.200	8.20	369.400	229.58	1746.10	5728.87
Silao..................	19.000	11.82	382.600	237.78	1776.50	5828.61
Trinidad................	14.200	8.82	401.600	249.60	1818.00	5964.77
Leon...................	16.400	10.19	415.800	258.42	1785.80	5859.12
Francisco......	15.400	9.58	432.200	286.61	1765.00	5790.88
Pedrito............. ...	13.700	8.51	447.600	278.19	1795.00	5889.30
Loma..................	13.600	8.55	461.300	286.70	1890.40	6202.31
Lagos..................	10.600	6.59	474.900	295.15	1871.00	6138.66

FROM MEXICO TO EL PASO DEL NORTE OR CUIDAD JUAREZ, BY THE
CENTRAL MEXICAN RAILROAD.—*Continued.*

STATIONS.	Distance between each station.		Distances.		Altitudes.	
	Kilom's.	Miles.	Kilom's.	Miles.	Metres.	Feet.
Serrano (Altamira)	10.300	6.77	485.500	301.74	2015.80	6613.68
Los Salas	24.700	15.35	495.800	308.14	2035.00	6676.68
Santa María	16 700	10.38	520.500	323.49	1844.50	6051.71
Encarnacion	26.400	16.41	537.200	333.87	1851.00	6073.04
Peñuelas	21.500	13.36	563.600	350.28	1878.60	6163.60
Aguascalientes	30.100	18.71	585.100	363.64	1884.00	6181.31
Pabellon	8.500	5.28	615.200	382.35	1908.50	6261.69
Rincon de Romos	20.500	12.74	623.700	387.63	1296.60	6321.08
Soledad	5.800	32.20	644.200	400.37	1979.00	6493.00
Guadalupe	9.900	6.15	696.000	432.57	2330.20	7645.22
Zacatecas	13.500	8.39	705.900	438.72	2442.00	8012.03
Pimienta	16.100	10.00	719.400	447.11	2306.50	7567.46
Calera	28.000	17.41	735.500	457.11	2152.60	7062.52
Fresnillo	15.500	9.63	763.500	474.52	2091.50	6862.06
Mendoza	15.000	9.32	779.000	484.15	2103.20	6900.44
Gutierrez	22.100	13.74	794.000	493.47	2087.10	6847.63
Cañitas	13.500	8.39	816.100	507.21	2006.60	6583.51
Cedro	20.700	12.86	829.600	515.60	1962.40	6438.53
La Colorada	25.800	16.04	850.300	528.46	1957.20	6421.48
Pacheco	19.000	11.81	876.100	544.50	1889.00	6197.72
Guzman	19.700	12.24	895.100	556.31	1810.60	5940.49
Gonzalez	21.400	13.30	914.800	568.55	1757.30	5765.60
Camacho	21.900	13.61	936.200	581.85	1664.60	5461.47
San Isidro	23.200	14.42	958.100	595.46	1582.30	5191.44
Symon	24.000	14.92	981.300	609.88	1568.90	5147.48
La Mancha	21.000	13.05	1005.300	624.80	1557.60	5110.41
Calvo	23.900	14.85	1026.300	637.85	1525.00	5003.44
Peralta	15.500	9.64	1050.200	652.70	1353.10	4439.45
Jimulco	14.400	8.95	1065.700	662.34	1267.20	4157.63
Jalisco	14.300	8.88	1080.100	671.29	1232.10	4042.46
Picardias	25.200	15.67	1094.400	680.17	1205.10	3953.87
Matamoros	16.400	10.01	1119.600	695.84	1145.30	3757.66
Torreon	5.200	3.16	1136.000	705.85	1140.30	3741.13
Lerdo	17.700	11.25	1141.200	709.01	1135.50	3725.51
Noé	20.000	12.43	1158.900	720.26	1116.90	3664.49
Mapimí	24.000	14.92	1178.900	732.69	1125.70	3693.36
Peronal	22.200	13.79	1202.900	747.61	1114.20	3657.63
Conejos	22.700	14.11	1225.100	761.40	1146.50	3761.61
Yermo	18.900	11.75	1247.800	775.51	1158.70	3801.64
Cevallos	18.500	11.55	1266.700	787.26	1188.50	3899.41
Zavalza	14.600	9.07	1285.200	798.76	1201.60	3942.39
Escalon	18.000	10.57	1299.800	805.83	1263.20	4144.50
Rellano	21.400	13.30	1317.800	819.02	1330.00	4363.66
Corralitos	19.400	12.06	1339.200	832.32	1442.70	4733.43
Dolores	14.700	9.13	1358.600	844.38	1379.90	4527.38
Jimenez	19.100	11.87	1373.300	853.51	1381.20	4531.65
La Reforma	18.800	11.69	1392.400	865.38	1347.60	4421.41
Diaz	19.200	11.93	1411.200	877.07	1298.90	4261.63
Bustamante	15.700	9.76	1430.400	889.00	1257.70	4126.46
Santa Rosalia	16.000	9.94	1446.100	898.76	1226.00	4022.45
La Cruz	20.400	12.68	1462.100	908.70	1216.60	3991.61
Concho	15.600	9.70	1482.500	921.38	1219.90	4002.43
Saucillo	16.100	10.00	1498.100	931.08	1210.20	3970.61
Las Delicias	7.300	4.54	1514.200	941.08	1170.30	3839.69
Ortiz	24.300	15.08	1521.500	945.62	1157.10	3796.39

FROM MEXICO TO EL PASO DEL NORTE OR CIUDAD JUAREZ, BY THE CENTRAL MEXICAN RAILROAD.—*Continued.*

STATIONS.	Distance between each station.		Distances.		Altitudes.	
	Kilom's.	Miles.	Kilom's.	Miles.	Metres.	Feet.
Bachimba	17.400	10.76	1545.800	960.70	1264.10	4147.45
Horcasitas	22.400	13.91	1563.200	971.54	1366.50	4483.42
Mápula.................	22.900	14.24	1585.600	985.45	1514.40	4968.66
Chihuahua..............	23.100	14.36	1608.500	999.69	1412.30	4633.68
Sacramento	15.100	9.38	1631.600	1014.05	1519.90	4986.71
Ferragas................	11.600	7.21	1646.700	1023.43	1591.50	5221.63
Sauz...................	19.900	12.37	1658.300	1030.64	1564.40	5132.71
Encinillas	13.900	8.64	1678.200	1043.01	1533.60	5031.66
Agua Nueva.............	13.400	8.33	1692.100	1051.65	1527.50	5011.65
Laguna.................	20.400	12.67	1705.500	1059.98	1535.70	5038.55
Puerto.................	20.200	12.56	1725.900	1072.65	1618.90	5311.53
Gallego.................	29.000	18.02	1746.100	1085.21	1622.00	5321.71
Chivatito	15.400	9.57	1775.100	1103.23	1480.50	4857.45
Moctezuma.............	13.100	8.14	1790.500	1112.80	1382.80	4536.89
Las Minas	13.500	8.33	1803.600	1120.94	1318.10	4324.62
Ojo Caliente...........	11.300	7.09	1817.100	1129.27	1233.30	4046.39
Cármen................	22.800	14.17	1828.400	1136.36	1216.00	3989.64
San José...............	24.100	14.97	1851.200	1150.53	1194.60	3919.42
Ranchería..............	28.700	17.84	1875.300	1165.50	1281.80	4205.52
Los Médanos...........	18.200	11.32	1904.000	1183.34	1298.30	4259.66
Samalayuca	16.100	10.00	1922.200	1194.66	1274.50	4181.57
Tierra Blanca	14.400	8.95	1938.300	1204.66	1263.50	4145.48
Mesa..................	17.600	10.94	1952.700	1213.61	1207.10	3960.40
Ciudad Juarez..........			1970.300	1224.55	1133.10	3717.64

FROM AGUASCALIENTES TO TAMPICO, A BRANCH OF THE SAME ROAD.

Aguascalientes...........	14.300	8.90	0.000	0.00	1884.00	6181.31
Chicalote	6.200	3.84	14.300	8.90	1891.00	6204.28
Cañada.................	10.500	6.52	20.500	12.74	1921.50	6304.34
Gallardo................	4.600	2.86	31.000	19.26	1955.75	6416.71
El Tule.................	15.200	9.45	35.600	22.12	1962.75	6439.68
San Gil................	8.200	5.10	50.800	31.57	2011.50	6599.62
San Marcos.............	11.000	6.84	59.000	36.67	2031.25	6664.42
Garcia	12.800	7.95	70.000	43.71	2117.40	6947.07
La Honda..............	11.000	6.84	82.800	51.46	2138.50	7016.30
Peñon Blanco...........	16.200	10.07	93.800	58.30	2100.75	6892.44
Salinas	13.600	8.44	110.000	68.37	2075.63	6810.91
Zotol..................	13.500	8.39	123.600	76.81	2120.50	6957.24
Espíritu Santo..........	25.400	15.79	137.100	85.20	2038.25	6687.39
Solana	62.200	38.65	162.500	100.99	2234.80	7332.25
San Louis Potosi.........	17.300	10.96	224.700	139.64	1877.00	6158.35
Laguna Seca............	27.100	16.84	242.000	150.40	1827.00	5994.30
Corcovada	15.100	9.37	269.100	167.24	1700.00	5577.62
Peotillos	7.500	4.69	284.200	176.61	1740.00	5708.86
Silos	6.450	4.00	291.700	181.30	1509.00	4950.95
Puerto de San Jose.......	15.650	9.72	298.150	185.30	1566.00	5137.97
San Isidro..............	13.400	8.33	313.800	195.02	1257.00	4124.16
Cerritos................	11.200	6.97	327.200	203.35	1136.00	3727.16
Santa Toribia (El Gato)....	17.300	10.76	338.400	210.32	1100.00	3609.04
San Bartolo	43.300	26.90	355.700	221.08	1030.00	3379.38
Tanque de la Tinajilla.....	14.200	8.82	399.000	247.98	1190.00	3904.33
Cárdenas...............	14.700	9.14	413.200	256.80	1200.00	3937.14
La Labor...............	8.200	5.10	427.900	265.94	1200.00	3937.14

FROM AGUASCALIENTES TO TAMPICO, A BRANCH OF THE SAME ROAD.—
Continued.

STATIONS.	Distance between each station.		Distances.		Altitudes.	
	Kilom's.	Miles.	Kilom's.	Miles.	Metres.	Feet.
Las Canoas	7.900	4.91	436.100	271.04	990.00	3248.14
Los Llanos (Zacate).......	18.800	11.68	444.000	275.95	825.00	2706.78
Tamazopo (La Garita)......	16.800	10.44	462.800	287.63	350.00	1148.33
Rascon..................	15.100	9.38	479.600	298.07	295.00	967.88
Las Crucitas.............	9,500	5.91	494.700	307.45	275.00	902.26
El Salto (Micos)..........	10.700	6.65	504.200	313.36	218.00	715.25
San Mateo..............	13.800	8.58	514.900	320.01	175.00	574.16
Valles..................	11.900	7.39	528.700	328.59	75.00	246.07
San Felipe..............	2.300	1.43	540.600	335.98	160.00	524.95
El Abra.................	4.000	2.49	542.900	337.41	165.00	541.35
Taninul.................	8.000	4.98	546.900	339.90	125.00	410.11
Las Palmas..............	68,700	42.68	554.900	344.88	50.00	164.05
Chijol..................	13.700	8.52	623.600	387.56	65.00	213.25
Salinas (Chila)...........	17.900	11.13	637.300	396.08	5.00	16.40
Tamos..................	13.100	8.14	655.200	407.21	20.00	6.56
Tampico................	....	....	668.300	415.35	0.00	0.00

FROM IRAPUATO TO GUADALAJARA, A BRANCH OF THE SAME ROAD.

	Kilom's.	Miles.	Kilom's.	Miles.	Metres.	Feet.
Irapuato................	5.100	3.17	0.000	0.00	1724.00	5656.36
San Miguel..............	11.300	7.02	5.100	3.17	1721.00	5646.52
Rivera.................	7.600	4.73	16.400	10.19	1712.00	5616.99
Cuitzeo	8.000	4.96	24.000	14.92	1700.00	5577.62
Abasolo (Rio Turbio)......	6.200	3.85	32.000	19.88	1695.00	5561.21
San Rafael..............	11.600	7.22	38.200	23.73	1690.00	5544.81
Pénjamo................	14.300	8.89	49.800	30.95	1700.00	5577.62
Villaseñor..............	7.100	4.41	64.100	39.84	1690.00	5544.81
Palo Verde..............	13.500	8.40	71.200	44.25	1685.00	5528.40
Cortez.................	6.600	4.10	84.700	52.65	1675.00	5495.59
La Piedad..............	20.100	12.49	91.300	56.75	1675.00	5495.59
Patti..................	14.300	8.89	111.400	69.24	1665.00	5472.78
Yurecuaro..............	21.000	13.05	125.700	78.13	1540.00	5052.56
Negrete................	6.400	3.97	146.700	91.18	1531.00	5023.13
La Barca...............	4.700	2.93	153.100	95.15	1537.00	5042.82
Feliciano.	8.300	5.15	157.800	98.08	1540.00	5052.66
Limon..................	13.200	8.21	166.100	103.23	1543.00	5062.50
Ocotlan	17.500	10.88	179.300	111.44	1525.00	5003.44
Poncitlan	21.600	13.41	196.800	122.32	1522.00	4993.60
Atequiza	8.300	5.17	218.400	135.73	1512.00	4960.79
La Capilla..............	7.600	4.73	226.700	140.90	1515.00	4970.63
El Castillo..............	24.800	15.40	234.300	145.63	1525.00	5003.44
Guadalajara.............	....	....	259.100	161.03	1543.00	5062.50

FROM MEXICO TO LAREDO TAMAULIPAS, BY THE MEXICAN NATIONAL RAILWAY.

	Kilom's.	Miles.	Kilom's.	Miles.	Metres.	Feet.
Mexico..................	4.600	2.86	0.000	0.00	2240.00	7349.32
Tacuba.................	4.800	2.98	4.600	2.86	2250.00	7382.13
Naucalpan..............	3.900	2.42	9.400	5.84	2280.00	7480.56
Rio Hondo..............	8.700	5.41	13.300	8.26	2300.00	7546.17
San Bartolito............	5.500	3.42	22.000	13.67	2460.00	8071.13
Dos Rios...............	5.500	3.41	27.500	17.09	2680.00	8792.94
Laurel.................	5.900	3.68	33.000	20.50	2820.00	9252.27
Cumbre................	2.500	1.55	38.900	24.18	3050.00	10006.89

FROM MEXICO TO LAREDO TAMAULIPAS.—*Continued.*

STATIONS.	Distance between each station.		Distances.		Altitudes.	
	Kilom's.	Miles.	Kilom's.	Miles.	Metres.	Feet.
Salazar................	3.200	1.99	41.400	25.73	3000.00	9842.84
Carretera de Toluca.......	3.400	2.11	44.600	27.72	2900.00	9514.74
Fresno.................	2.500	1.56	48.000	29.83	2800.00	9186.75
Jajalpa................	5.600	3.48	50.500	31.39	2720.00	8924.18
Ocoyoacac.............	3.000	1.86	56.100	34.87	2600.00	8530.46
Lerma.................	13.900	8.64	59.100	36.73	2540.00	8333.60
Toluca................	7.400	4.60	73.000	45.37	2640.00	8661.70
Palmillas..............	16.700	10.38	80.400	49.97	2630.00	8628.89
Del Rio...............	14.700	9.14	97.100	60.35	2580.00	8464.84
Ixtlahuaca.............	12.300	7.64	111.800	69.49	2540.00	8333.60
Tepetitlan.............	9.800	6.09	124.100	77.13	2520.00	8267.98
Flor de María..........	20.200	12.56	133.900	83.22	2520.00	8267.98
Basoco................	4.000	2.48	154.100	95.78	2580.00	8464.84
Venta del Aire..........	5.800	3.60	158.100	98.26	2560.00	8399.22
Tultenango............	11.200	6.97	163.900	101.86	2540.00	8333.60
Solis.................	10.900	6.77	175.100	108.83	2430.00	7972.70
Tepetongo.............	7.100	4.41	186.000	115.60	2320.00	7611.79
Agua Buena (Buena Vista).	7.800	4.85	193.100	120.01	2240.00	7349.32
Mayor................	4.800	2.99	200.900	124.86	2160.00	7086.84
Pateo	3.400	2.10	225.700	127.85	2100.00	6889.98
Pomoca	14.100	8.76	209.100	129.95	2040.00	6693.13
Maravatío.............	12.000	7.47	223.200	138.71	2010.00	6594.70
San Antonio............	8.700	5.40	235.200	146.18	2080.00	6824.37
Zirizícuaro............	12.000	7.47	243.900	151.58	2010.00	6594.70
Tarandacuao...........	8.400	5.22	255.900	159.05	1920.00	6299.42
San José..............	8.500	5.28	264.300	164.27	1860.00	6102.57
Providencia............	12.900	8.02	272.800	169.55	1880.00	6168.19
Acámbaro.............	12.500	7.76	285.700	177.57	1860.00	6102.57
San Cristobal..........	17.500	10.88	298.200	185.33	1840.00	6036.95
Salvatierra............	15.500	9.63	315.700	196.21	1760.00	5774.48
Cascalote	8.900	5.53	331.200	205.84	1760.00	5774.48
Ojo Seno.............	14.200	8.84	340.100	211.37	1770.00	5807.29
Celaya...............	5.200	3.22	354.300	220.21	1740.00	5708.86
Santa Rita............	7.400	4.60	359.500	223.43	1760.00	5774.48
San Juan..............	3.800	2.37	366.900	228.03	1780.00	5840.10
Soria.................	7.200	4.47	370.700	230.40	1785.00	5856.50
Chamacuero	8.900	5.57	377.900	234.87	1790.00	5872.91
Rinconcillo............	13.000	8.08	386.800	240.40	1810.00	5938.52
Begoña...............	9.100	5.65	399.800	248.48	1825.00	5987.73
San Miguel de Allende.....	11.600	7.21	408.900	254.13	1870.00	6135.38
Atotonilco.............	11.300	7.03	420.500	261.34	1860.00	6102.57
Tequizquiapan	12.800	7.95	431.800	268.37	1870.00	6135.38
Dolores Hidalgo..........	7.200	4.48	444.600	276.32	1890.00	6201.00
Rincon	11.300	7.02	451.800	280.80	1900.00	6233.88
Peña Prieta	9.100	5.65	463.100	287.82	1930.00	6332.23
Trancas	9.000	5.59	472.200	293.47	1950.00	6397.85
Obregon..............	18.700	11.63	481.200	299.06	1990.00	6529.09
Ciudad Gonzalez (San Felipe)	14.400	8.95	499.900	310.69	2050.00	6725.94
Chirimoya.............	13.200	8.20	514.300	319.64	1860.00	6102.57
Jaral.................	16.700	10.38	527.500	327.84	1840.00	6036.95
Villa de Reyes...........	10.000	6.22	544.200	338.22	1830.00	6004.14
Jesus María............	14.800	9.19	554.200	344.44	1810.00	5938.52
La Pila...............	15.000	9.33	569.000	353.63	1900.00	6233.88
San Luis Potosí..........	13.400	8.33	584.000	362.96	1860.00	6102.57
Peñasco...............	15.100	9.37	597.400	371.29	1840.00	6036.95
Pinto.................	12.500	7.78	612.500	380.66	1820.00	5971.33
Bocas................	13.600	8.45	625.000	388.44	1700.00	5577.62
Enramada.............	15.200	9.45	638.600	396.89	1680.00	5512.00
Moctezuma............ ...	18.900	11.75	653.800	406.34	1660.00	5446.38

FROM MEXICO TO LAREDO TAMAULIPAS.—*Continuea.*

STATIONS.	Distance between each station.		Distances.		Altitudes.	
	Kilom's.	Miles.	Kilom's.	Miles.	Metres.	Feet.
El Venado	17.000	10.56	672.600	418.09	1740.00	5708.86
Los Charcos	16.300	10.13	689.700	428.65	1880.00	6168.19
Laguna Seca	11.600	7.20	706.000	438.78	2020.00	6627.51
Berrendo	15.400	9.58	717.600	445.98	1990.00	6529.09
La Maroma	16.000	9.94	733.000	455.56	1880.00	6168.19
Wadley	8.600	5.35	749.000	465.50	1840.00	6036.95
Catorce	6.800	4.23	757.600	470.85	1820.00	5971.33
Poblazon	15.200	9.44	764.400	475.08	1780.00	5840.10
Vanegas	16.400	10.20	779.600	484.52	1720.00	5643.24
La Trueba (La Parida)	15.800	9.81	796.000	494.72	1720.00	5643.24
San Vicente	15.700	9.76	811.800	504.53	1700.00	5577.62
El Salado	15.700	9.75	827.500	514.29	1720.00	5643.24
Lulu	20.200	12.56	843.200	524.04	1720.00	5643.24
La Ventura	20.000	12.43	863.400	536.60	1720.00	5643.24
Santa Elena	20.900	13.00	883.400	549.03	1760.00	5774.48
Gomes Farías	13.200	8.20	904.300	562.03	1940.00	6365.04
El Oro	17.300	10.77	917.500	570.23	1980.00	6496.28
Carneros	9.600	5.94	934.800	580.99	2080.00	6824.37
Agua Nueva	13.300	8.21	944.400	586.93	1920.00	6299.42
Encantada	6.300	3.92	957.600	595.14	1840.00	6036.95
Buena Vista	9.700	6.03	963.900	599.06	1750.00	5741.67
Saltillo	1.500	7.15	973.600	605.09	1600.00	5249.52
Los Bosques	3.500	2.17	985.100	612.24	1430.00	4691.76
Ramos Arizpe	7.300	4.55	988.600	614.41	1400.00	4593.33
Santa Maria	9.700	6.02	995.900	618.96	1320.00	4330.85
Ojo Caliente	7.000	4.35	1005.600	624.98	1220.00	4002.76
Los Muertos	2.300	1.40	1012.600	629.33	1160.00	3805.90
La Mariposa	10.400	6.46	1014.900	630.77	1120.00	3674.66
Rinconada	7.700	4.78	1025.300	637.23	1000.00	3280.95
Los Fierros	5.500	3.42	1033.000	642.01	930.00	3051.28
Soledad	10.200	6.34	1038.500	645.43	820.00	2693.38
Garcia	21.100	13.11	1048.700	651.77	740.00	2427.91
Santa Catarina	2.800	1.74	1069.800	664.88	640.00	2099.81
Leona	4.700	2.87	1072.600	666.62	600.00	1968.57
San Gerónimo	2.900	1.79	1077.300	669.55	590.00	1935.76
Gonzalitos	2.500	1.56	1080.200	671.34	580.00	1902.95
Monterey	7.600	4.73	1082.700	672.90	560.00	1837.33
Ramon Treviño	6.100	3.79	1090.300	677.63	510.00	1673.28
Topo	20.900	12.99	1096.400	681.42	480.00	1574.86
Salinas	8.100	5.03	1117.300	694.41	430.00	1410.81
Morales	16.300	10.13	1125.400	699.44	460.00	1509.24
Stevenson (Palmito)	8.700	5.40	1141.700	709.57	580.00	1902.95
Palo Blanco	13.300	8.20	1150.400	714.97	560.00	1837.33
Álamo	12.600	7.84	1163.600	723.17	490.00	1607.67
Villa Aldama	2.100	1.31	1176.200	731.01	420.00	1378.00
Guadalupe	3.400	2.11	1178.300	732.32	420.00	1378.00
Bustamante	9.800	6.09	1181.700	734.43	440.00	1443.62
Huizache	1.400	7.08	1191.500	740.52	470.00	1542.05
Golondrinas	12.000	7.46	1202.900	747.60	410.00	1345.19
Salome, Botello	12.100	7.52	1214.900	755.06	380.00	1246.76
Brasil	8.900	5.53	1227.000	762.58	340.00	1115.52
Lampazos	23.300	14.48	1235.900	768.11	300.09	984.28
Mojina	21.200	13.18	1259.200	782.59	240.00	787.43
Rodriguez	12.400	7.71	1280.400	795.77	200.00	656.19
Camaron	11.500	7.15	1292.800	803.48	200.00	656.19
Huizachito	16.500	10.25	1304.300	810.63	210.00	689.00
Jarita	13.100	8.14	1320.800	820.88	200.00	656.19
Sanchez	16.100	10.01	1333.900	829.02	160.00	524.95
Laredo de Tamaulipas			1350.000	839.03	130.00	426.52

FROM ACÁMBARO TO PÁTZCUARO, A BRANCH OF THE SAME ROAD.

STATIONS.	Distance between each station.		Distances.		Altitudes.	
	Kilom's.	Miles.	Kilom's.	Miles.	Metres.	Feet.
Acámbaro...............	13.250	8.23	0.000	0.00	1840.00	6036.95
La Cumbre..............	17.610	10.96	13.250	8.23	1960.00	6430.66
Andocutin...............	6.170	3.83	30.860	19.19	1840.00	6036.95
Huingo.................	12.360	7.68	37.030	23.02	1840.00	6036.95
Queréndaro.............	4.000	2.49	49.390	30.70	1840.00	6036.95
Zinzimeo...............	10.000	6.22	53.390	33.19	1840.00	6036.95
Quirio.................	7.610	4.73	63.390	39.41	1860.00	6102.57
Charo.................	5.920	3.67	71.000	44.14	1870.00	6135.38
La Goleta..............	3.150	1.95	76.920	47.81	1870.00	6135.38
Atapaneo...............	11.200	6.96	80.070	49.76	1880.00	6168.19
Morelia...............	19.900	12.37	91.270	56.72	1890.00	6201.00
Jacuaro...............	9.610	5.98	111.170	69.09	2000.00	6561.89
Coapa.................	6.800	4.22	120.780	75.07	2060.00	6758.75
Lagunillas	10.380	6.46	127.580	79.29	2100.00	6889.98
Ponce.................	2.910	1.80	137.960	85.75	2120.00	6955.60
Chapultepec............	12.530	7.79	140.870	87.55	2100.00	6889.98
Pátzcuaro..............	....	....	153.400	95.34	2040.00	6693.13

FROM PIEDRAS NEGRAS OR CIUDAD PORFIRIO DIAZ TO DURANGO, BY THE MEXICAN INTERNATIONAL RAILWAY.

STATIONS.	Kilom's.	Miles.	Kilom's.	Miles.	Metres.	Feet.
Ciudad Porfirio Diaz.......	6.540	4.06	0.000	0.00	220.00	721.81
Fuente.................	7.060	4.39	6.540	4.06	232.00	761.17
Rosa..................	26.200	16.29	13.600	8.45	278.00	912.11
Nava..................	11.960	7.44	39.800	24.74	324.00	1063.02
Allende...............	14.940	9.28	51.760	32.18	375.00	1230.35
Leona.................	15.640	9.71	66.700	41.46	455.00	1492.83
Peyotes...............	21.430	13.32	82.340	51.17	486.00	1594.55
Blanco................	12.850	7.99	103.770	64.49	387.00	1269.73
Sabinas...............	15.850	9.85	116.620	72.48	340.00	1115.52
Soledad...............	10.650	6.61	132.470	82.33	371.00	1217.23
Baroterán..............	14.120	8.78	143.120	88.94	425.00	1394.40
Aura..................	15.090	9.39	157.240	97.72	453.00	1486.27
Obayos................	15.330	9.52	172.330	107.11	396.00	1299.26
Baluarte...............	10.690	6.65	187.660	116.63	373.00	1223.79
Hermanas..............	21.230	13.18	198.350	123.28	396.00	1299.26
Adjuntas..............	13.570	8.44	219.580	136.46	465.00	1525.64
Estancia	4.770	2.97	233.150	144.90	547.00	1794.68
Monclova.............	18.560	11.54	237.920	147.87	587.00	1925.92
Castaño...............	14.920	9.29	256.480	159.41	748.00	2454.16
Gloria	19.590	12.16	271.400	168.70	823.00	2700.22
Bajan..	12.420	7.71	290.990	180.86	843.00	2765.84
Joya	20.410	12.68	303.410	188.57	829.00	2719.91
Espinazo..............	12.080	7.52	323.820	201.25	817.00	2680.54
Reata	22.860	14.21	335.900	208.77	900.00	2952.85
Treviño (Venadito)........	26.040	16.16	358.760	222.98	890.00	2920.05
Sauceda...............	24.760	15.40	384.800	239.14	997.00	3271.11
Jaral	23.020	14.31	409.560	254.54	1144.00	3753.40
Pastora	21.610	13.44	432.580	268.85	1157.00	3796.06
Cármen	23.970	14.89	454.190	282.29	1182.00	3878.08
Paila	19.670	12.23	478.160	297.18	1188.00	3897.77
Mimbre...............	16.540	10.28	497.830	309.41	1132.00	3714.03
Rafael	12.970	8.05	514.370	319.69	1102.00	3615.60
Pozo	11.290	7.02	527.340	327.74	1105.00	3625.44

FROM PIEDRAS NEGRAS OR CIUDAD PORFIRIO DIAZ TO DURANGO, BY THE MEXICAN INTERNATIONAL RAILWAY.—*Continued.*

STATIONS.	Distance between each station.		Distances.		Altitudes.	
	Kilom's.	Miles.	Kilom's.	Miles.	Metres.	Feet.
Bola....................	13.480	8.38	538.630	334.76	1089.00	3572.96
Mayran................	10.870	6.75	552.110	343.14	1094.00	3589.36
Hornos................	13.410	8.35	562.980	349.89	1096.00	3595.93
Colonia................	17.620	10.95	576.390	358.24	1105.00	3625.44
Matamoros.............	22.540	14.00	594.010	369.19	1112.00	3648.41
Torreon...............	8.050	5.00	616.550	383.19	1134.00	3720.59
San Carlos............	15.740	9.18	624.600	388.19	1137.71	3732.77
Loma	19.280	11.98	640.340	397.97	1181.52	3876.51
Chocolate.............	20.870	12.98	659.620	409.95	1377.25	4518.69
Huarichic.............	15.200	9.45	680.490	422.93	1325.37	4348.45
Pedriceña.............	25.640	15.93	695.690	432.38	1318.85	4327.07
Pasaje................	24.540	15.25	721.330	448.31	1605.28	5266.84
Yerbanís.............	21.580	13.41	745.870	463,56	1908.73	6262.53
Noria	12.760	7.93	767.450	476.97	1895.00	6217.40
Catalina..............	12.150	7.56	780.210	484.90	1969.47	6461.73
Tapona................	22.040	13.70	792.360	492.46	1982.72	6505.21
Gabriel	16.930	10.52	814.400	506.16	1955.20	9414.91
Chorro................	26.420	16.42	831.330	516.68	1868.10	6129.15
Labor.................	11.760	7.30	857.750	533.10	1864.38	6116.93
Durango...............	....	....	869.510	540.40	1880.13	6168.62

FROM SABINAS TO HONDO, A BRANCH OF THE SAME ROAD.

STATIONS.	Kilom's.	Miles.	Kilom's.	Miles.	Metres.	Feet.
Sabinas................	17.530	10.83	0.000	0.00	340.00	1115.52
San Felipe.............	2.380	1.48	17.430	10.83	313.00	1026.93
Hondo.................	....	....	19.810	12.31	319.00	1046.62

FROM THE CITY OF MEXICO TO CUERNAVACA AND ACAPULCO.
LINE FINISHED.

STATIONS.	Kilom's.	Miles.	Kilom's.	Miles.	Metres.	Feet.
Mexico................	28.060	17.44	0.000	0.00	2240.00	7349.27
Contreras..............	17.883	11.11	28.060	17.44	2480.00	8091.75
Ajusco................	15.191	9.44	45.943	28.55	2840.00	9272.89
La Cima...............	12.966	8 07	61.134	37.99	3040.00	9974.08
Xacapexco (Tres Marías)...	18.400	11.43	74.100	46.06	2800.00	9186.75

LINE IN CONSTRUCTION.

STATIONS.	Kilom's.	Miles.	Kilom's.	Miles.	Metres.	Feet.
San Juanico............	31.250	19.42	92.500	57.49	2290.00	7513.37
Cuernavaca.............	7.250	4.51	123.750	76.91	1520.00	4987.04
Jiutepec...............	6.750	4.20	131.000	82.42	1300.00	4265.23
San Vicente............	21.000	13.05	137.750	85.62	1260.00	4134.00
Xoxocotla.............	14.050	8.73	158.750	98.67	1030.00	3379.38
Puente de Ixtla..........	8.950	5.56	172.800	107.40	900.00	2952.85
Rio Amacusac..........	23.250	14.45	181.750	112.96	890.00	2920.05
Buena Vista............	21.000	13.05	205.000	127.41	1200.00	3937.14
Iguala................	11.000	6.84	226.000	140.46	720.00	2362.29
Tepecoacuilco...........	34.750	21.13	237.000	147.30	800.00	2624.76
Xalitla................	12.050	7.91	271.750	168.47	620.00	2034.19
Mexcala	28.700	17.84	283.800	176.38	480.00	1574.86
Venta del Zopilote........	11.500	7.15	312.500	194.22	760.00	2493.53
Zumpango	13.000	8.08	324.000	201.37	1000.00	3280.95

FROM THE CITY OF MEXICO TO CUERNAVACA AND ACAPULCO.
LINE IN CONSTRUCTION. (*Continued.*)

STATIONS.	Distance between each station.		Distances.		Altitudes.	
	Kilom's.	Miles.	Kilom's.	Miles.	Metre	Feet.
Tierras Prietas............	4.800	2.98	337.000	209.45	1320.00	4330.85
Chilpancingo.............	15.200	9.45	341.800	212.43	1200.00	3937.14
Cima de Valadez.........	8.250	5.12	357.000	221.88	1300.00	4265.23
La Imagen...............	11.750	7.31	365.250	227.00	1060.00	3477.81
Los Cajones.............	6.000	3.72	377.000	234.31	1000.00	3280.95
El Rincon...............	12.000	7.46	383.000	238.03	670.00	2198.24
Dos Caminos............	12.000	7.46	395.000	245.49	600.00	1968.57
Tierra Colorada..........	9.000	5.60	407.000	252.95	300.00	984.28
Rio Omitlan.............	4.000	2.48	416.000	258.55	180.00	590.57
Peregrino...............	32.000	19.89	420.000	261.03	140.00	459.33
Cacahuatepec............	24.500	15.23	452.000	280.92	60.00	196.86
Marquez................	16.500	10.25	476.500	296.15	20.00	65.62
Acapulco................			493.000	306.40	0.00	0.00

FROM PUEBLA TO OAXACA, BY THE MEXICAN SOUTHERN RAILWAY.

Puebla..................	18.400	11.43	0.000	0.00	2157.00	7077.00
Amozoc.................	7.600	4.73	18.400	11.43	2312.00	7585.54
Santa Rosa..............	11.200	6.95	26.000	16.16	2295.00	7529.77
Tepeaca	17.400	10.82	37.200	23.11	2244.60	7364.41
Rosendo Márquez........	10.500	6.53	54.600	33.93	2055.00	6742.34
Tecamachalco	12.600	7.83	65.100	40.46	2014.10	6608.15
Las Animas.............	9.400	5.84	77.700	48.29	2000.00	6561.89
Tlacotepec..............	31.300	19.46	87.100	54.13	1988.25	6523.35
Carnero................	8.900	5.53	118.400	73.59	1752.37	5749.43
Tehuacan...............	14.700	9.13	127.300	79.12	1662.57	5454.81
La Huerta..............	6.300	3.92	142.000	88.25	1453.29	4768.18
Santa Cruz.............	10.900	6.76	148.300	92.17	1370.31	4495.91
Pantzingo..............	14.600	9.09	159.200	98.93	1246.00	4088.07
Nopala.................	6.400	3.97	173.800	108.02	1060.56	3479.65
Venta Salada...........	15.200	9.46	180.200	111.99	972.07	3189.31
San Antonio............	8.700	5.40	195.400	121.45	787.92	2585.13
Mexía	20.300	12.62	204.100	126.85	695.00	2280.26
Tecomavaca.............	10.900	6.78	224.400	139.47	559.71	1836.38
Quiotepec..............	17.000	10.56	235.300	146.25	540.00	1771.71
Cuicatlan..............	4.800	2.98	252.300	156.81	592.00	1942.32
Tomellin...............	19.200	11.93	257.100	159.79	672.00	2204.80
Almoloyas..............	16.500	10.26	276.300	171.72	1055.00	3461.40
Santa Catarina..........	16.200	10.06	292.800	181.98	1332.00	4370.22
El Parian	13.700	8.52	309.000	192.04	1495.00	4905.02
Las Sedas..............	12.800	7.96	322.700	200.56	1927.00	6322.39
San Pablo Huitzo........	13.100	8.13	335.500	208.52	1695.00	5561.21
Villa de Etla	18.000	11.19	348.600	216.65	1642.00	5387.32
Oaxaca			366.600	227.84	1545.00	5069.06

FROM COATZACOALCOS TO SALINA CRUZ, BY THE NATIONAL
TEHUANTEPEC RAILWAY.

Coatzacoalcos	21.749	13.51	0.000	0.00	2.00	6.56
Los Llmones............	15.140	9.42	21.749	13.51	16.00	52.50
Chinameca..............	5.407	3.35	36.889	22.93	6.00	19.69
Jaltipan	20.547	12.77	42.296	26.28	40.00	131.24
Ojapa..................	12.568	7.83	62.843	39.05	32.00	104.99
Almagres....	11.589	7.19	75.411	46.88	48.00	157.49

STATIONS.	Distance between each station.		Distances.		Altitudes.	
	Kilom's.	Miles.	Kilom's.	Miles.	Metres.	Feet.
Juile.....................	9.284	5.77	87.000	54.07	40.00	131.24
Medias Aguas...........	9.672	6.01	96.284	59.84	32.00	104.99
Tortugas.................	21.044	13.08	105.956	65.85	44.00	144.36
Santa Lucrecia...........	7.000	4.36	127.000	78.93	30.00	98.43
Los Muertos.............	10.000	6.21	134.000	83.29	35.00	114.83
Ubero....................	14.801	9.20	144.000	89.50	25.00	82.02
Tolosa...................	7.199	4.47	158.801	98.70	52.00	170.61
Palomares................	20.570	12.78	166.000	103.17	88.00	288.73
Mogoñé..................	15.176	9.43	186.570	115.95	92.00	301.85
Rincon Antonio..........	13.254	8.25	201.746	125.38	176.00	577.45
Lagunas.................	17.764	11.04	215.000	133.63	260.00	853.05
Chivela.................	10.236	6.35	232.764	144.67	244.00	800.55
Rio Verde...............	17.186	10.68	243.000	151.02	115.00	377.30
San Gerónimo............	28.218	17.54	260.186	161.70	56.00	183.74
Tehuantepec.............	3.596	2.24	288.404	179.24	36.00	108.12
Santa Cruz..............	17.617	10.94	292.000	181.48	36.00	108.12
Salina Cruz.............	....	....	309.617	192.42	2.00	6.56

FROM THE CITY OF MEXICO TO PACHUCA, BY THE HIDALGO AND NORTHEASTERN MEXICAN RAILWAY.

LINE FINISHED.

NORTHEASTERN RAILWAY FROM MEXICO TO TIZAYUCA.

Station	Kilom's.	Miles	Kilom's.	Miles	Metres	Feet
Mexico..................	19.000	11.80	0.000	0.00	2264.76	7430.56
Canal...................	11.400	7.10	19.000	11.80	2266.01	7434.66
Ojo de Agua.............	5.200	3.23	30.400	18.90	2272.96	7457.46
Santa Ana...............	14.800	9.20	35.600	22.13	2271.36	7452.21
Tizayuca................	....	....	50.400	31.33	2294.65	7528.62

HIDALGO RAILWAY TO TUXPAN.

Station	Kilom's.	Miles	Kilom's.	Miles	Metres	Feet
Tizayuca................	16.100	10.00	....	....	....	....
Tezontepec..............	10.800	6.52	66.500	41.33	2344.87	7693.38
San Augustin............	6.000	3.92	77.300	47.85	2390.00	7841.46
Tepa...................	8.400	5.23	83.300	51.77	2438.08	7999.21
Tecajete................	11.900	7.38	91.700	57.00	2538.00	8327.04
Somo Riel...............	10.600	6.60	103.600	64.38	2638.50	8656.78
Las Lajas...............	7.000	4.34	114.200	70.98	2504.80	8218.10
Los Romeros.............	11.700	7.28	121.200	75.32	2392.80	7850.64
Santiago................	5.700	3.54	132.900	82.60	2221.72	7289.33
Tulancingo..............	7.200	4.48	138.600	86.14	2187.29	7176.39
Sototlan................	....	....	145.800	90.62	2171.46	7124.44

FROM TEPA TO PACHUCA, A BRANCH OF THE HIDALGO RAILROAD.

Station	Kilom's.	Miles	Kilom's.	Miles	Metres	Feet
Tepa....................	8.700	5.41	0.000	0.00	2438.08	7999.21
Xochihuacan.............	17.300	10.75	8.700	5.41	2380.06	7808.85
Pachuca.................	....	....	26.000	16.16	2420.99	7493.15

FROM SAN AUGUSTIN TO IROLO, A BRANCH OF THE HIDALGO RAILWAY.

Station	Kilom's.	Miles	Kilom's.	Miles	Metres	Feet
San Agustin.............	14.600	9.08	0.000	0.00	2390.00	7841.46
Tlanalapa...............	13.700	8.51	14.600	9.08	2437.39	7996.95
Irolo...................	....	....	28.300	17.59	2452.58	8046.78

FROM DURANGO TO MAZATLAN BY BRIDLE-PATH.

PLACES.	Altitudes.		PLACES.	Altitudes.	
	Metres.	Feet.		Metres.	Feet.
Durango............	1880.13	6168.62	La Ramona.........	1220.00	4002.76
Salitre	1925.00	6315.82	El Chapote.........	950.00	3116.90
El Salto	1900.00	6233.80	Rio del Baluarte......	630.00	2067.00
Arroyo Seco	1890.00	6201.00	La Ventanita.........	770.00	2526.34
Camino del Jaral.....	1890.00	6201.00	Sotolito..............	1550.00	5085.47
El Escalon...........	1980.00	6496.28	El Carrizo de Adentro.	1825.00	5987.73
Las Indias...........	2120.00	6955.60	El Carrizo de Afuera..	1860.00	6102.57
Calzon Roto	2180.00	7152.46	Las Loberas	1970.00	6463.47
El Pino	2260.00	7414.94	El Venteadero........	1930.00	6332.23
Rio Chico...........	2020.00	6627.51	Puerta de los Pilares..	1250.00	4101.19
La Palmita..........	2220.00	7283.70	Arroyo del Leon......	1120.00	3674.66
Los Cerritos	2260.00	7414.94	Palotillo.............	1010.00	3313.76
Los Mimbres........	2180.00	7152.46	Platanito	940.00	3084.09
Buena Vista.	2330.00	7644.60	Santa Catarina.......	210.00	689.00
Los Charcos.........	2340.00	7674.41	El Limon............	130.00	426.52
Los Navíos	2350.00	7710.22	El Tecomate.........	110.00	360.90
Navajas	2260.00	7414.94	Tagarete	85.00	278.88
Llano Grande........	2160.00	7086.84	Rio del Presidio......	55.00	180.45
Cruz de Piedra.......	2230.00	7316.51	Porras..............	65.00	213.26
Coyotes	2270.00	7447.75	Sigueros.............	50.00	164.05
El Salto.............	2280.00	7480.56	La Cofradia..........	45.00	147.64
Piloncillos..........	2390.00	7841.46	Confite..............	62.00	203.42
La Florida...........	2440.00	8005.51	La Escondida........	68.00	223.11
Junta de los Caminos..	2390.00	7841.46	Las Higueras.........	30.00	98.43
El Tecomate........	2100.00	6889.98	Las Conchas.........	22.30	73.16
Chavarria...........	1710.00	5610.43	Carboneras	15.50	50.85
La Cienega..........	2160.00	7086.84	Palos Prietos.........	1.54	5.05
Las Botijas	2050.00	6725.94	Mazatlan	0.00	0.00
La Escondida.......	2035.00	6676.72			

FROM MANZANILLO TO GUADALAJARA BY WAGON ROAD.

Manzanillo...........	0.00	0.00	Ciudad Guzman (Zapot-		
Cerro del Vigia.......	125.00	410.11	lan)................	1412.00	4632.70
Cola de Iguana.......	50.00	164.05	Santa Catarina.......	1412.00	4632.70
El Ciruelo...........	75.00	246.07	La Cuesta	1450.00	4767.38
Canoa Verde........	75.00	346.07	San Nicolás..........	1300.00	4265.23
Las Trojes...........	100.00	328.09	Amatitlan	1325.00	4347.25
Valenzuela...........	125.00	410.11	Sayula..............	1350.00	4429.28
Tecolapa............	175.00	574.16	Ojo de Agua.........	1360.00	4462.09
La Noria............	312.00	1023.65	Cofradia.............	1375.00	4511.30
La Presa	362.00	1187.70	Techolula	1375.00	4511.30
Colima.............	560.00	1837.33	Cuevitas.............	1360.00	4462.09
La Puerta	650.00	2132.62	El Cuemasate.......	1325.00	4347.25
San Joaquin	650.00	2132.62	El Crucero..........	1325.00	4347.25
Los Limones.........	850.00	2788.81	Cebollas.............	1350.00	4429.28
San Gerónimo...	900.00	2952.85	Los Pozos	1325.00	4347.25
Los Alcaracos........	1100.00	3609.04	Chimaltitan..........	1325.00	4347.25
La Quesería.........	1162.00	3812.46	Ocotan..............	1330.00	4363.66
Tonila	1175.00	3854.61	Santa Ana Acatlan....	1350.00	4429.28
Barranca Cachepehuate	975.00	3198.92	Puerta	1500.00	4921.42
San Márcos..........	985.00	3231.73	Cofradia.............	1512.00	4960.79
Barranca de Beltran...	850.00	2788.81	Santa Cruz..........	1475.00	4987.05
Playa	1025.00	3362.97	Arenal	1600.00	5429.52
Barranca Platanar....	950.00	3116.90	San Agustin.........	1575.00	5167.49
Loma...	1225.00	4019.16	La Calera...........	1575.00	5167.49
Barranca de Atenquique	1025.00	3362.97	Puente de Santa María.	1550.00	5085.47
Ocote Gacho........	1250.00	4101.19	Guadalajara.........	1500.00	4921.42
Pedregal............	1375.00	4511.30			

FROM TEHUACAN TO OAXACA AND PUERTO ANGEL BY WAGON ROAD.

PLACES.	Altitudes.		PLACES.	Altitudes.	
	Metres.	Feet.		Metres.	Feet.
Tehuacan............	1660.00	5446.38	Tierra Blanca........	2000.00	6561.89
La Huerta...........	1480.00	4855.81	Rio Atoyac..........	1660.00	5446.38
Arroyo de Buena Vista.	1320.00	4330.85	San Pablo Huitzo.....	1700.00	5577.62
San Sebastian........	1120.00	3674.66	Santiago Huitzo......	1680.00	5512.00
Camino de Calipán....	1060.00	3477.81	Villa de Etla.........	1660.00	5446.38
Calaveras...........	960.00	3149.71	Dolores	1640.00	5380.76
San Antonio...	900.00	2952.85	Panzacola	1540.00	5052.66
Hacienda de Ayotla...	860.00	2821.62	Oaxaca..............	1540.00	5052.66
Rio de Reyes	900.00	2952.85	San Agustin Juntas...	1530.00	5019.85
Tecomavaca	620.00	2034.19	Coyotepec...........	1600.00	5249.52
Rio Salado..........	600.00	1968.57	Cúspide	1900.00	6233.70
Campanario.........	730.00	2395.10	Santo Tomás Jaliera..	1830.00	6004.14
Organo.............	700.00	2296.67	Ocotlan	1720.00	5643.24
Pajarito............	680.00	2231.05	Magdalena...........	1700.00	5577.62
Gavilan	600.00	1968.57	San Martin..........	1700.00	5577.62
Paraje Blanco.......	580.00	1902.95	Rio Coapa...........	1590.00	5216.71
Rio Seco	560.00	1837.33	Ejutla..............	1540.00	5052.66
Chonoslar...........	700.00	2296.67	Arrogante	1600.00	5249.52
Rancho de Urrutia....	620.00	2034.19	Chichovo............	1840.00	6036.95
Rancho de Cuagulotal.	620.00	2034.19	Zopilote.............	1810.00	5938.52
Rancho de los Obos...	620.00	2034.19	Cúspide	1930.00	6332.23
Hacienda de Güendulain...............	620.00	2034.19	Tlacuache	1840.00	6036.95
Rio Apoala..........	540.00	1771.71	Tepehuaje...........	1780.00	5840.33
Rio Tomellin	540.00	1771.71	Miahuatlan..........	1800.00	5905.71
Balconcillo..........	680.00	2231.05	Chapaneco...........	2230.00	7316.51
Rancho del Chilar....	660.00	2165.43	Agua del Sol........	2400.00	7874.27
Infiernillo	660.00	2165.43	San José del Pacifico..	2600.00	8530.46
Don Dominguillo.....	750.00	2460.72	Garganta del Encino..	2800.00	9186.65
Arroyo Dominguillo ..	720.00	2362.29	Tres Cruces..........	3160.00	10367.79
Arroyo de Nopala....	710.00	2329.48	Rancho de Canoas ...	3000.00	9842.84
El Pochote	1240.00	4068.38	San Miguel Xuchistepec	2780.00	9121.04
Canton de Buena Vista.	1360.00	4462.09	Rio de San José......	2340.00	7677.41
Cúspide	1500.00	4921.42	Cerro de Santa Ana...	2720.00	8858.56
Puente de la Joya.....	1400.00	3412.19	Cerro de San Pedro...	2500.00	8202.36
Venta Vieja..........	1600.00	5249.52	El Porvenir..........	800.00	2624.76
Paredones	1840.00	6036.95	Garganta del Cerro de la Pluma..........	900.00	2952.85
Llano del Timbre....	1900.00	6233.70	La Providencia.......	830.00	2723.19
Cieneguilla	2020.00	6627.51	La Soledad	750.00	2460.72
Portezuelo..........	2220.00	7283.70	San José Totoltepec...	530.00	1738.90
Las Trancas.........	2080.00	6824.37	Rio Chacalapa	340.00	1115.52
Carbonera..........	2160.00	7086.84	Pochutla	160.00	524.95
Ojo de Agua........	2100.00	6889.98	Puerto Angel........	0.00	0.00

THE VALLEY OF MEXICO'S DRAINAGE.[1]

Mexico is finishing a great work, the drainage of the valley where the capital city is located, which has required for its completion nearly three hundred years and many millions of dollars, and has cost the lives of hundreds of thousands of men. The necessity, importance,

[1] This article was published in the *Engineering Magazine* of New York for January, 1895 (vol. viii., No 4), but has since been revised and considerably enlarged.

and magnitude of this work, which will be classed among the grandest achievements of men, and the nearness of its completion, induce me to write this paper, which I hope will give some idea of its scope and purpose.   I do not pretend to originality, as my work to some extent has been one of compilation from different monographs, which have appeared from time to time, and from some official publications of the Mexican Government.

Topographical Conditions of the Valley of Mexico.—The Valley of Mexico is an immense basin, of approximately circular shape with one extreme diameter of about sixty miles, completely bounded by high mountains, and having only two or three quite high passes out of it. No water drains out of the basin.   The surface of this valley has a mean altitude above the sea of 7413 feet and an area of about 2220 square miles.

Mountain ranges rise on every side, making a great corral of rock containing dozens of villages and hamlets, with the ancient capital in the centre.   In times past the fires of volcanoes licked up the earth, and such fires still live in the mammoth Popocatapetl, from whose great crater sulphur fumes and smoke with jets of flame have poured through the centuries.

The valley thus hemmed in with solid walls of rock had been an inland sea for many cycles, and during the early existence of man here the salt waters spread over a large extent of the depression.   The waters have been gradually lessening by seepage and evaporation, and the Aztec pilgrims coming from the north in the fourteenth century, having received a sign that they were to build their queen-of-the-world city on a small island of the sea, set about building dikes and combating the overflow of the waters.

Evaporation is so excessive at certain periods of the year that malaria, consequent on drought, was far more dreaded by the inhabitants than the periodical floods, and thousands perished annually, so that proper drainage was an absolute necessity for the preservation of health.

Work done by the Indians.—Nearly fifty years before the discovery of America, which took place in 1492, Netzahualcoyotl, saw the necessity for a drainage canal, and commenced the work in 1450. He constructed an immense dike to divide the fresh from the salt-water lakes of the valley.   The City of Mexico was at this time the centre of the Aztec nation, and was built on floating structures, like rafts, on the water in the numerous islets on the margins of the lakes, so that in the event of the water rising or the city being subjected to a state of siege, the whole city would float.   Mexico City now occupies the site of the old Aztec capital.

The waters of these lakes were liable to disturbances of all kinds;

thus it is recorded by Prescott in his *History of the Conquest of Mexico :* "In 1510 the great lake of Texcoco, without the occurrence of a tempest or earthquake, or any other visible cause, became violently agitated, overflowed its banks, and, pouring into the streets of Mexico, swept off many of the buildings by the fury of its water."

When Cortez arrived in Mexico from Spain in 1519 to take possession of the country in the name of the King of Spain, he found, to his great surprise, the defense of the city admirably arranged, and an almost enchanting view of flowering islets forming the floating capital. Little towns and villages lay half-concealed by the foliage, and from the distance these looked like companies of wild swans riding quietly on the waves.

A scene so new and wonderful filled the rude heart of the Spaniard with amazement. So astonished was he at the extent of the water of Lake Texcoco that he describes it as " a sea that embraces the whole valley," but upon hearing that it was a lake, with a mean depth of a few yards, he gave orders to cut a way through the dike and destroy the aqueduct of Chapultepec. The central dike dividing the fresh from the salt water lake was of such dimensions as to serve Cortez as a roadway for his army.

Prescott, in the work before alluded to, page 297, says: " Leaving the mainland, the Spaniards came on the great dike or causeway, which stretches some four or five miles in length, and divides Lake Chalco from Xochimilco on the west. It was a lance in breadth in the narrowest part, and in some places wide enough for eight horses to ride abreast. It was a solid structure of stone and lime, running directly through the lake, and struck the Spaniards as one of the most remarkable works they had seen in the country."

Having cut the dikes and drained the lake, the " floating city " was at once besieged, and where originally stood the great temple of the Aztecs a Christian temple was afterward raised. The Spaniards, finding themselves in complete possession, proceeded to erect the new City of Mexico, and building on the plan adopted by them at home, they cut down the points of the floating islands and by gradual extension soon placed the town below the mean average level of the lake. Hence arose the great difficulties of the drainage of the Valley of Mexico.

One of the immense dikes built by King Netzahualcoyotl was ten miles long. It divided Lake Texcoco into two parts. Of the two lakes thus formed one was allowed to remain salt, but the other was freshened by letting only fresh water enter by the streams flowing in, the water for the use of the city being taken from this latter. Little by little the waters have subsided since that period, and have been fought back, until now they are confined to six great lakes—Chalco, Xochimilco, Texcoco, Xaltocan, San Cristobal, and Zumpango. Each of these lakes is fed by streams which have little volume during the dry season, but which in the rainy season swell to considerable size, and at times overflow the valleys. The lake of Zumpango was the most dangerous of these, for it received the waters of the Cuautitlan River, —a river draining a large area of country, and having during the rainy season a great volume of water. This river has been turned into the cut of Nochistongo, and has ceased to threaten Mexico and its environs with its overflow.

From these topographical conditions frequent floodings of the old Aztec city and of the Spanish capital, situated almost at the lowest point of the valley, were sure to come in times of unusually heavy rains. In early days, when the Aztecs lived in the middle of Lake Mexico, when their temples and wigwams were built on piles and the streets were often only canals, the periodical overflows from the upper lakes were a matter of small concern, though even then the Nahua engineers were called upon to protect the city by dikes. But when by evaporation, by filling in at the site of the city, by lessened waters, due to the fissures caused by earthquakes, Lake Mexico had disappeared, and the city had come to be built on the spongy soil, above all, when the short-sighted choice of Cortez had been confirmed and the capital of New Spain had come to stand on the ruins of the Aztec town, increasing rapidly in population and wealth,—it became a serious matter that on an average of once in twenty-five years the streets should be from two to six feet under water for an indefinite time.

Work done by the Spaniards.—From 1519 to 1553 the Spaniards were busily engaged in building Mexico, and another grand dike, similar to that built by Netzahualcoyotl in 1450, was formed around the city; this protection proved insufficient, for in 1580 another inundation took place. The Viceroy of the day, Señor Don Martin Enriquez de Almanza, assisted by engineers, engaged to find an outlet for the waters north of the valley. During the time they were thus engaged, important facts were gleaned respecting the River Cuautitlan, and its curious behavior at the foot of Nochistongo, whence it doubled its course at a certain altitude and ran toward Lake Texcoco, instead of into its own lake of Xaltocan. The scheme formed by Enriquez de Almanza to remedy this evil was kept in abeyance, as his services were required in Peru.

In the year 1604 a serious inundation attacked Mexico City. The Marquis de Montes Claros did all in his power to carry out the plan of Señor Don Martin Enriquez to relieve the rivers of the north and of the valley of the excess of water from the central and south lakes, which are of higher altitudes. The *pros* and *cons* of this plan were beset with many great difficulties, and respecting one of the methods tried, mention must be made of a dike of great strength, constructed to prevent any excess or overflow of water from destroying the town of Zumpango and washing away its crops. This dike, which was to check the strong current of the river Pachuca, would also direct the river Cuautitlan to Mexico, direct the rivers north into Zumpango, and would inundate that verdant district, and probably submerge the town; whereas, to divert them into Lake Texcoco would submerge Mexico. To prevent this evil it was decided to make a tunnel; but here, as in all countries and in all ages, engineers, when engaged in any work of magnitude, and of a different character from that commonly known, always find theorists to offer objections, and thus stop the way to actual progress.   This was the case in Mexico City.

In 1607 another inundation, spreading over the whole valley, occurred, and, as all the dikes and other defences were swept away, caused a panic of terror among the inhabitants. The Marquis de Salinas was then Viceroy at Mexico City, and determined to carry out the plan of Señor Don Martin Enriquez, being assisted by an engineer of great repute named Enrico Martinez, and also solicited and obtained the co-operation of Father Sanchez, of the Society of Jesus. These three men, after many consultations, formulated the plan of embracing the whole of the lakes of the plain into one main channel of detention, and an outlet as required to keep the same under such control as to have at all times an abundance of water for use. The plan, broadly speaking, was to draw off the water from the south lakes which are at higher levels to those of the north, and to make them serve, by the scour the velocity of the water would cause, to deepen the passage for their exit, and, at the same time, assist the making of the grand canal.

Great opposition to this plan was offered on the score of economy, and many insisted that the inundations were solely due to the waters of Cuautitlan and the freshets of Pachuca, and if these were directed north no more was needed, while the people of Zumpango tried to show that no more was needed to inundate their town and submerge the district. The Viceroy then requested Enrico Martinez to induce Father Sanchez to submit some modifications of his former scheme.

The plan was modified, and on November 28, 1607, Enrico Martinez started operations on the modified plan, and in about eleven months 6600 metres ($4\frac{1}{10}$ miles) of tunnel, with a transverse section of 3.50 metres ($11\frac{1}{2}$ feet) wide, and a depth of 4.20 metres ($13\frac{3}{4}$ feet), was completed. At the same time other important drainage works were being made; the passage was opened from Boca de San Gregorio to Salto de Tula; this was 8600 metres ($5\frac{1}{3}$ miles) long, as well as two canals as aqueducts $6\frac{1}{2}$ miles long, one for Lake Zumpango and the other for the river Cuautitlan from Teoloyucan to Huehuetoca.

In December, 1608, in the presence of the Viceroy Don Luis de Velasco and the Archbishop of Mexico, Enrico Martinez inaugurated the outlet of the waters, the whole of the work just described being executed in one year.   Humboldt tells us that fifteen thousand native Indians were employed on these works.

In spite of the great good these works brought to the people, there was an outcry for economy, but it is certain that other motives prompted the disturbance and the attempt to harass and hamper the Viceroy.   The object was to prevent a grant of money from being made to pay for the lining of the tunnel with brick.   This was found to be necessary, as the greater part of the work was excavated in marl, and the liberated waters ran with such velocity that the symmetry of the tunnel was soon destroyed, and its passage and usefulness lessened by the *debris* that obstructed the fairway.   This state of things was brought so forcibly home to the objectors that a small sum of money was reluctantly granted, sufficient to patch up the tunnel in places where the rush of waters had made the most havoc, hydraulic cement or mortar being used, but the sum granted proved to be totally inadequate, and for want of more money the tunnel was rendered perfectly useless by falling obstructions.   This occurred in the year 1609. Gossips and theorists then united to run down the scheme, although it was conceded that the work had averted a terrible inundation or submergence of Mexico City.

A few years elapsed before the question of continuing the works for the tunnel again caused excitement; but a general feeling grew up that the work of the tunnel should be continued.   The opposition was strong enough to obtain the hearing of an appeal in Madrid, with the result that the Spanish Government in 1614 procured the services of a Dutch engineer, named Adrian van Boot, to proceed to Mexico City to examine and report on the canal works, and to submit a plan to remedy the evils.   As the result of his labors he condemned the plan of Father Sanchez, and recommended that the old means of defence used by the Indians should again be adopted, and that dams and dikes should be thrown up at once.   This report had the effect of annoying almost everybody, and was the means of much fruitless discussion.   In this dilemma the Spanish Government, when appealed to, confessed they were unable to advise the Viceroy of Mexico what to do, but sent the Marquis of Gelves to Mexico to see into matters, and he, having unbounded faith in the ability of the Dutch engineer, Adrian van Boot, and hoping to keep money in the treasury, ordered Enrico Martinez to close up the tunnel completely, and to return the rivers to their natural courses; but before these orders were half executed the enormous rush of waters grew so alarming that he had to accept again Enrico Martinez's plan over that of Adrian van Boot.   The

Marquis was soon after deposed, his place being taken by the Marquis de Cerralvo, whose first act was to set Martinez free at the request of the city council who provided him with means of continuing his work on the canal and tunnel. The Viceroy revoked his predecessor's order and issued another to open up the tunnel, and that with all speed, on his personal responsibility. Although Cerralvo gave these orders, he forgot to give Martinez the money to carry them out, and, as a consequence, the works remained in a deplorable condition.

The tunnel was blocked up by this cause, and Martinez was cruelly scored for not having done his work aright by the very ones who had refused to give him the necessary material for it. He bravely essayed to repair the damage, but the water-soaked condition of the ground gave no resistance for the building of the needed walls, while death mowed down the enslaved workers. They were crushed to death by the frequent cavings in of the loose soil, or were sent to the grave by the deadly damps. Finally, the charge being made that the builder was blocking up the tunnel in revenge, he was thrown into prison, where he languished for many months. As there was no one else available who could carry on the great work, he was afterwards released and again put in charge. It was then decided that, the tunnel being completely useless, the next thing to be done would be to make a great cut down to the tunnel and thus open it out. This entailed the making of an excavation fourteen miles in length with an average depth of one hundred and eighty feet and width of four hundred feet.

On June 20, 1629, the ever troublesome river Cuautitlan over flowed and inundated the north of the plain, and swept with it other streams into Lake Texcoco. In the September following the increase of the water was greater than ever had been known. The city was so suddenly and completely submerged that thirty thousand persons perished, the bodies floating about the streets for some time after. The destruction of property and life, consequent on the inundation, was so great generally, and affected the tunnel to such an extent, that during a period of five years there was scarcely any reduction in the height of the water, and the water in the city remained during all this time as high as the second story of the houses; the slight difference in the heighth of the water being caused by evaporation.

The Spanish Government at Madrid gave orders to change the capital to a better and more secure site. To this suggestion the citizens demurred, saying, in effect, that to insure complete security an outlay of only $3,000,000 was necessary, this being the estimated cost of completing the tunnel, whereas to build a new city would involve an outlay of $50,000,000, with a loss of another $50,000,000 in leaving the old one.

Several plans were now submitted in opposition to that of Enrico

Martinez, and one by Simon Mendez was accepted, his plan being to direct all the waters of the valley by one canal into the neck of the Tula, the spot selected by Martinez for his outlet.   It was soon discovered that the plan of Simon Mendez was far too costly, and as the money that could be spared was practically melting away without perceptible progress being made, Enrico Martinez was again requested to carry out the work as arranged with Father Sanchez.

The next Viceroy, the Marquis of Cadereita, was most desirous to see the work of the tunnel pushed on; but however enthusiastic he may have been, lack of funds prevented him from giving effect to his desires.   The work continued very slowly, Martinez being unable to do any work at the tunnel, and he contented himself with improving the canal by lining it in bad places with cement.   Martinez struggled on for thirty-seven years with this work, and died unnoticed and uncared for.   All trace of his place of final rest was lost.

In 1637 an earthquake made sad havoc with the tunnel works, and for lack of funds no repairs could take place; but when funds were obtainable workmen could not be procured, the earthquakes and inundations having carried off many thousands of these poor fellows.   The survivors lacked heart to return to such an unfortunate and, as they thought, accursed work.

In the year 1640 the work was being pressed on by men from the prisons, under the direction of the Franciscan monks, and carried on, with varying results, in this way for thirty-five years, until Señor Don Martin Solis was made head of the municipal council.   He being an avowed enemy to the Franciscans, sent them away, and undertook the superintendence of the work himself; but his method of treating the prisoners was so harsh and cruel that they broke out into open revolt, and the works were threatened.   Therefore, to save the works and his own life, he consented to the return of the Franciscans.   It is estimated that up to this time some two hundred thousand men lost their lives on this work.   The Franciscans steadily, but slowly, worked on, always with a very limited exchequer, until 1767, when there remained some 1935 metres (1¼ miles) still to be completed.   A contract was entered into to finish this work in five years for $800,000; but instead of five years it took twenty-two years, and, instead of 8 metres (25 feet wide), as contracted for, it was only 3 metres (9 feet 10 inches) wide.

The Spaniards continued the work in other hands for one hundred and fifty years before the task of opening the cut was completed. Spasmodic work for a century and a half led at last to the accomplishment of this project in 1789.   The old tunnel of Martinez is now a gigantic trench from 30 to 160 feet in depth and some 300 feet broad in some places, and is known as the Tajo de Nochistongo.   The immediate vicinity of the workings was depopulated of its native inhabitants by the insatiable demands of the killing labor, and recruits were then drawn from Puebla and other thickly populated Indian centres. Great prison barracks were built on the bare hills, and here all the criminals were sent to enter the work. The ones in charge were indifferent with regard to the lives entrusted to their care, and the slaughter, of which scant record remains in the parish burial books, and which resulted from a combination of defects in appliances for both the safety and the comfort of the workmen, was terrific. As the burial trenches were filled with new dead, the depths of the cut were tenanted by new laborers.

The victims of three years of bondage numbered fully two hundred thousand ere the work was done. Yet the results were but slight, only the excess of water from the highest lakes and streams being carried off. However, the danger from inundations of the city has been very materially decreased by the Nochistongo opening, and no more deluges have occurred since its completion.

Still the fact that the bottom of the cut was thirty feet higher than the surface of Texcoco, the lowest lying of the lakes, left the city in danger of inundation, as Lake Texcoco is constantly filling up at the rate of one and one-half inches a year and is now but a few feet below the level of the main plaza of the city.

The drainage works had long been a heavy burden upon the Mexican treasury. Up to 1637 Bancroft estimates that $3,000,000 had been expended. Up to the year 1800 the outlay had reached $6,247,670. Up to 1830 the total expenditure was $8,000,000.

Work done by the Mexican Government.—The problem which the Mexican Government had to face was very different from that which confronted Martinez in 1607. The question of preventing submergence is practically solved. The work of Martinez, unsatisfactory as it was, did a great deal to solve it. Since his day the area of the lakes has been gradually diminishing. The rapid evaporation in the rarefied air and under the direct sun of the valley partly accounts for this. Twice the water in Lake Texcoco has almost entirely disappeared, leaving only a sea of mud and a small pool. The great problem which the Mexican Government has now solved is not how to prevent an inflow of water, but how to provide an outlet for sewage. The danger to be averted was not that of drowning, but that of dying from the plague.

Lake Texcoco more than any other now menaces the security of the capital. The unwise cutting down of forests since the Spanish conquest permits the waters pouring down into the valley to bring with them annually great quantities of alluvial matter, which have so much raised the lake bottom and the water level that inundations have been of frequent occurrence. The general level of the City of Mexico is only 6.56 feet above the surface of the lake. The rainy season lasts

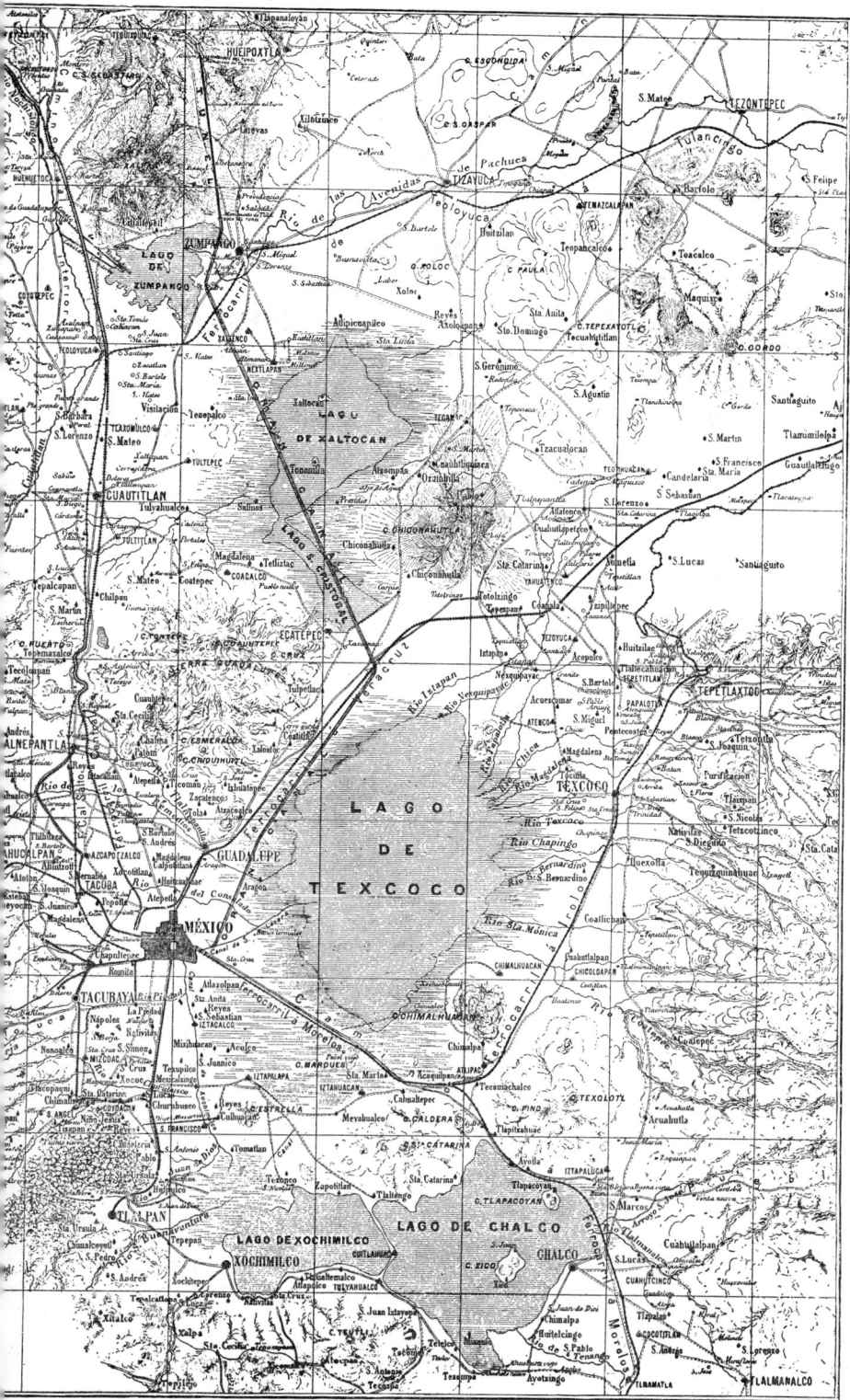

MAP OF THE VALLEY OF MEXICO, SHOWING THE CANAL AND TUNNEL.

from June to October inclusive. During this season five times as much water falls as during the rest of the year, evaporation can no longer compensate for rainfall, and the valley is more or less flooded.

Originally built in the midst of a lake, the city has been left on dry ground by the receding waters. Lakes Chalco and Xochimilco have altitudes nearly four feet greater than the pavement of the capital. Still more imperiously do the lakes to the north dominate the city. San Cristobal and Xaltocan are about five feet, while Zumpango is over thirteen feet, above it.

The project now almost completed is a modification of the scheme projected by Simon Mendez in the time of the Spanish Government, and which in 1849 was adopted by Captain Smith of the corps of American engineers which accompanied General Scott's army. The tunnel was ultimately located under the saddle and through the ravine of Acatlan, its mouth being in the Tequixquiac, near the village of that name. The works have been begun several times, and then suspended without effecting anything of importance. In 1866 the works now nearing completion were commenced. A project proposed by Señor Don Francisco de Garay, a well-known engineer of the City of Mexico, was pronounced the most feasible. But the revolutionary struggle succeeded, and for many years the work was relegated to the background.

In 1879 engineer Don Luis Espinosa, the present director of the works, took charge of the undertaking. In the first period mentioned the cutting of Tequixquiac was excavated, and the greater part of the shafts were begun; but at that point the work was stopped by political agitations.

The present gigantic work cannot have been considered to have been seriously undertaken, with a view of completion at any cost, until the year 1885, when the City Council of Mexico submitted a project to the Government to which they offered to contribute largely in the event of its being adopted.

A special commission, with ample authority to deal with the funds set aside for the work, was appointed by President Porfirio Diaz. The City Council set aside the sum of $400,000 per annum for the canal works, which sum was materially increased by the Federal Government.

In 1887 the City Council raised a loan in London of £2,400,000 to meet the cost of the work and guarantee its successful termination. The entire responsibility of the work was now assumed by the City Council, and the Government gave authority for the Council to make and collect new taxes. Still, there was not sufficient money forthcoming, so another loan was raised in London for £3,000,000, a portion of which was held for the work.

The drainage works, when carried out, will receive the surplus waters and sewage of the City of Mexico and carry them outside of the valley, and will also control the entire waters of the valley, affording an outlet, whenever found necessary, to those which might otherwise overflow fields and towns, rendering the soil stagnant and marshy. The work consists of three parts—1st, the tunnel; 2d, a canal starting from the gates of San Lázaro, and having a length of 47½ kilometres, or 43 miles, its line following on the eastern side of the Guadalupe range of hills and between that range and Lake Texcoco, changing its direction after arriving at the 20th kilometre to a northeasterly one, so as to diagonally cross Lake San Cristobal, a part of Lake Xaltocan, and a part of Lake Zumpango, and arriving finally at the mouth of the tunnel near the town of Zumpango; and 3d, the sewage of the City of Mexico.

The tunnel.—The contract for completing the tunnel was let to Messrs. Read & Campbell, of Mexico, but for some reason they were unable to finish the work. It was therefore continued and satisfactorily completed by the Drainage Board for a sum considerably less than the price contracted with Messrs. Read & Campbell under their superintendence as hereafter stated.

The tunnel has a length of 10,021.79 metres, or 32,869 feet (6⅛ miles), with a curved section formed by four curves respectively of the following dimensions: The upper part has a span of 4.185 metres, or 13 feet 9 inches, and a rise of 1.570 metres, or 5 feet 1½ inches; the two lateral arches have a chord each of 2.36 metres, or 7 feet 9 inches, a radius with a chord of 2.429 metres, or 8 feet, and a rise of 0.521 metre, or 1 foot 8½ inches; the elevation is 4.286 metres, or 14 feet, and the greatest width is the span of the upper arch. The accompanying drawings show this section. The tunnel is lined with brick, having a thickness in the upper part of 0.45 metre, or 1 foot 6 inches, and in the lower part over which the water runs, of 0.40 metre, or 1 foot 4 inches in the side arches, and of 0.30 metre, or 1 foot in the radius, this latter lining being of artificial stone made of sand and Portland cement. The elevation of the invert at the beginning of the tunnel is 9.20 metres, or 30 feet 1½ inches below datum; at the end of the tunnel, 17.53 metres, or 57 feet 6 inches below datum. The gradient is 0.00069 for the first 2170.74 metres, or 1 in 1500 for 7120 feet; 0.00072 for the following 5831 metres, or 1 in 1389 for 19,125 feet 6 inches; 0.001 for 4921.50 metres, or 1 in 1389 for 16,147 feet; and 0.00135, 1 in 520, for 1706 feet; these changes being in accordance with changes of details made from those of the original project, in some cases modifying the dimensions of the section. Twenty-five shafts, each 2 by 3 metres, or 16 feet 6¾ inches by 9 feet 10 inches, were opened at a distance of 400 metres, or 1312

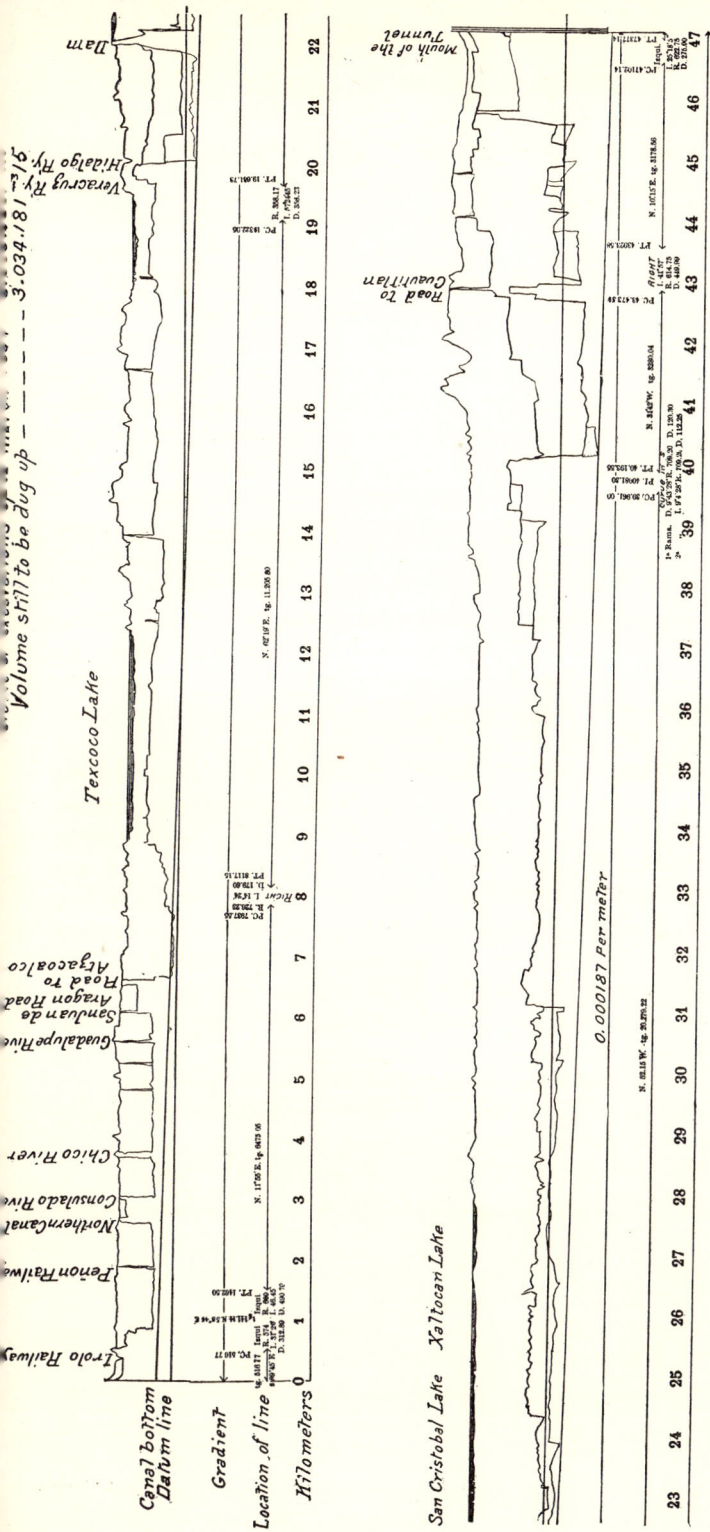

DRAINAGE OF THE VALLEY OF MEXICO
LONGITUDINAL SECTION OF THE MAIN CANAL

(This Cut was made in March, 1894, before the Canal was finished.)

feet from each other. These served to ventilate the tunnel and to facilitate the work. The deepest of these shafts, situated on the saddle of Acatlan, has a depth of 92 metres, or 301 feet 9 inches; the shallowest is 21 metres, or 68 feet 10 inches.

To give an idea of the labor involved beyond the mere tunneling, it is as well to mention that the quantity of materials required per lineal yard of tunnel was 1800 bricks, 94 cement blocks, 3 cubic yards of mortar, and 70 cubic feet of volcanic stone.

Maximum discharge through the tunnel = 18 cubic metres, $635\frac{2}{3}$ cubic feet per second.

When the drainage board took charge of the work, it was executed by day labor both in the canal and in the tunnel, the latter having the larger amounts expended on it. But, shortly afterwards, the contract for the tunnel was let to Messrs. Read & Campbell, of London, who, after having invested a considerable sum in the work, found themselves under the necessity of cancelling their contract at the beginning of the year 1892. The Drainage Board contracted in 1887 with the Bucyrus Co. for the excavation of 1,000,000 cubic metres from kilometre 22 of the canal, and continued to handle the work, as managers, on the remaining portion of the canal.

The Canal.—In 1887, the Drainage Board contracted with the Bucyrus Company, of the United States, of which Colonel Harris was the president, for the construction of the canal.

This company started with two spoon dredgers capable of raising a maximum of 1000 cubic metres, 1308 cubic yards, a day. They commenced operations at the twenty-second kilometre. In the opinion of the board of commissioners, the Bucyrus Company was not proceeding with the work at a suitable rate of speed, for at 1000 cubic metres, 1308 cubic yards, per day, the work of dredging alone, as there were some 12,000,000 of cubic metres, 15,696 cubic yards, of excavation to do, would take about forty-three years ; their contract was therefore cancelled.

In May, 1894, the Department of Public Works of Mexico contracted with Messrs. S. Pearson & Son, of London, for the completion of the canal, modifying their former contracts of December 25, 1889, March 30, 1891, and April 18, 1893, under the following bases: the unfinished excavation in the first nine kilometres, and that between kilometre 47 and the entrance of the tunnel of Tequixquiac, are to be continued by the Board of Drainage Directors, who must have the latter portion completed to 10 metres below the surface of the soil by December 31, 1894, and to the required depth of the canal by May 31, 1895, in order that the water in the canal may settle to that level and permit the contractors to slope the walls as required by the contract. The contractors are to complete the canal between kilometres 9 and 47 for the sum of $3,506,000. For making the monthly estimates of the canal will be divided into two sections—kilometres 9 to 22 and kilometres 22 to 47. In the first section the provisional estimate will be 40 cents per cubic metre; in the second a sum equal to the quotient obtained by dividing the remainder of the money by the number of cubic metres to be removed. The contractors may suspend the work of the dredgers when they fall below 40 cubic metres per hour, and can proceed with the excavation in any way they wish. The excavation had to be completed by May 1, 1896, except in the parts where the dredgers cannot work. Then for each day's delay the contractors must pay $500 fine, and after five months the contract will be rescinded.

These contractors carried out the work of the canal in two different ways—by hand work with centrifugal pumps to draw off the water which filtered into the work, and by means of enormously powerful Couloir dredgers which have a capacity for 3000 cubic metres of excavation per day, and which throw the excavated earth to a distance of more than 200 metres from the centre of the canal. They had five of these dredgers at work, and by means of them excavated to a depth of 20 metres or 65 feet, raising the earth to an elevation of more than 16 metres, 52½ feet, so as to empty it into the shoots, along which it was carried by a stream of water that delivered it at a considerable distance from the dredger. The dredgers have now done their work, and they have been taken to pieces and most of them sold as old iron, and some of their engines packed and transferred to the harbor works at Veracruz. The portion of the canal contracted for was completed to the satisfaction of all concerned in eight years.

The level of the bottom of the canal above the datum line adopted is 2.25 metres, or 7 feet 4 inches, and the mouth of the tunnel is 9.20 metres, or 30 feet ½ inch below the same datum, supposed to pass 10 metres, or 33.80 feet below the bottom of the Aztec calendar stone, since transferred to the National Museum, but marked on the wall of the Cathedral. The level of the ground at the beginning of the canal is 7.60 metres, or 24 feet 8 inches, and at the end 15.86 metres, or 52 feet above datum. The uniform slope of the canal is at the rate of 0.187 per kilometre.

The canal has a depth, at its commencement, of 5.50 metres, or 18 feet, which in the last few kilometres is increased to 20.50 metres, or 67 feet 3 inches. The side slopes were projected with a batter of 45 degrees, and the width of the bottom is 5. metres, or 18 feet for the first 20 kilometres, or 12½ miles, and 6.50 metres or 21 feet 2 inches in the rest of the canal. The first 20 kilometres, or 12½ miles, may be considered as a prolongation of the net of sewers in the city, and will receive only the water that passes through them. The flow is calculated for an average of 5 cubic metres, or 176½ cubic feet, although, when heavy

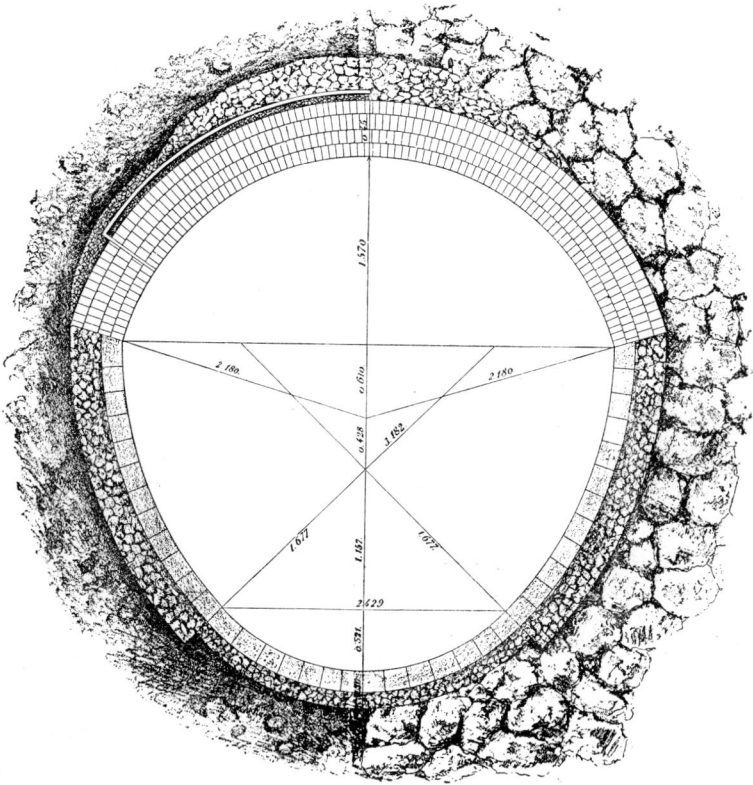

(Drainage of the Valley of Mexico.)

VERTICAL SECTION OF THE TUNNEL.

rains require it, they can receive a greater volume; the rest of the canal communicates with Lake Texcoco, and will be utilized in controlling its waters,—the lowest in the valley,—which can be made to flow into the canal from all parts. Hence the canal has been built to carry the largest flow that can pass through the tunnel, or 17.5 cubic metres, 618⅔cubic feet, per second. The cutting is through a strictly clay formation, comprising occasional thin strata of sand and sandstone.

For accommodation of railroads, wagon roads, and water-courses, it was necessary to construct five aqueducts of iron to carry rivers, four iron bridges for the passage of railroads, and seven bridges for vehicular traffic.

The sewage.—The sewers of the City of Mexico form a network of covered channels, located sometimes in the middle and sometimes on the sides of the streets, these being almost always gorges, communicating with a system of secondary sewers that empty into a collecting sewer discharging into the canal of San Lázaro, which transports the sewage to Lake Texcoco. If the water is high in the lake, water backs up into the sewers and saturates the soil under the houses and streets. As this has been the condition for several centuries, the state of the subsoil under the city can be better imagined than described. The death-rate touches 40 per 1000—the highest in the civilized world. Mexico's elevation of over 7000 feet is all that saves it from a pestilence. Malarial and gastric fevers are almost continually epidemic.

For a century the problem has been settling into one of pure sanitation. The plans which the Government has been working since about 1883, though called plans for draining the valley, really seek to get a fall sufficient to dispose of the sewage. In fact, in the original plan, from considerations of economy, care was to be taken to keep out of the projected canal all water both from the surface of the valley and from the rivers. The Consulado and the Guadalupe rivers were to be carried over the new canal in iron aqueducts. The drainage system was thus to be simply a part of the sewage system of the city.

The excavated materials have been tipped on each side of the canal at their natural slopes, and a towpath near the canal level provided. Sluice gates will direct the city drainage either to the canal or to Lake Texcoco. A sluice gate at the junction of the smaller with the larger part of the canal will control the flow of Lake Texcoco, and another sluice gate will be placed at the entrance of the tunnel.

Completion of the work.—As this paper goes to press, the drainage works of the Valley of Mexico are practically finished, as the waters of the valley have been for several years passing through the canal and the tunnel to their outlet in the river which takes them to the Gulf of Mexico, and the company with whom the canal was contracted is now giving the finishing touches to the sides and bottom of the canal and will deliver it to the Government Board of the Drainage Directors in January, 1898. It was agreed with the contractors that the portion of the canal between the City of Mexico and the 20th kilometre, which is comparatively difficult, because the ground is very loose, and the excavations to be made yet do not exceed 200,000 cubic metres, will be made directly by the Board as soon as the other portion of the canal has been finished ; this last section of the work is expected to be finished in June, 1898, when the waters of the City of Mexico will leave the valley by the drainage works here mentioned.

The canal and six-mile tunnel through the mountain range have a total length approaching thirty-seven miles. The present works will take rank with the great achievements of modern times, just as the immense " cut " of Nochistongo, their unsuccessful predecessor, was the leader among ancient earthworks in all the world. The completed system will have cost $20,000,000.

I have dwelt on these works at some length, because their importance to the City of Mexico can hardly be overestimated. Instead of being one of the healthiest cities in the world, as it should be with its magnificent climate and situation, Mexico, unfortunately, has a terribly heavy death-rate, due principally to want of drainage and generally bad sanitary condition. When the existing danger of floods is removed, and the sanitary evils are remedied by a proper system of drainage, the increased security that will be enjoyed by life and property will certainly have its effect on the prosperity of the city. Property will rise in value, the population will grow with rapidity, not to mention the tide of tourists that will set in from the United States, and this will mean larger revenues for the municipality.

I could not well finish this paper without paying General Diaz, President of Mexico, a just tribute for the great interest he has taken in having this gigantic work brought to a close during his administration. To his exertions in this regard, and to his commanding position in Mexico, more than to anything else, this happy result, now in sight, is due. So after a weary search of centuries for relief, the beautiful Valley of Mexico will gain its deliverance not only from the engulfing floods, but from the sanitary evils which have long resulted from defective drainage.

Contract for the Sewage System of the City of Mexico.—The complement of the drainage works is the construction of a proper sewage system in the City of Mexico, which will carry all its refuse out of the Valley of Mexico, and on June 8, 1898, a contract was signed at the City of Mexico by the Drainage Board with Messrs. Vezin & Co., of Paris, to do such work.

HISTORICAL NOTES ON MEXICO.

Mr. Walter S. Logan, a prominent lawyer of New York, with business interests in Mexico, chiefly in the State of Sonora, and a personal friend of mine, read a paper entitled "A Mexican Lawsuit" before the Law Department of the American Social Science Association, at their annual meeting at Saratoga, on the 5th of September, 1895, and requested me to be present at the same. I received at the same time an invitation to attend that meeting, which I suppose I owed to Mr. Logan, from Professor Francis Wayland, President of the Law Department of that Association. Wishing to oblige Mr. Logan, and at the same time to hear his paper read, for I had no doubt that it would do justice to Mexico, as Mr. Logan is friendly to that country, I determined to attend the meeting, and I reached Saratoga late on the afternoon of the day on which it was to be held. I found at the hotel at which Mr. Logan and most of the other gentlemen of the Association were stopping, and where I myself lodged, a printed notice that Mr. Logan would read his paper that evening, and that I would make some remarks afterwards. I was considerably disturbed by this, as it is always difficult for a diplomatic representative of a foreign country to speak in public, and I was not prepared to speak before so enlightened an audience.

At the appointed time we went to the meeting, and Mr. Logan read his paper. While he was reading it I noted certain incorrect statements made, in good faith, no doubt, by Mr. Logan, but which presented Mexico in a rather unfavorable light. I found myself in a very difficult position, because, considering myself as Mr. Logan's guest, I did not think it would be proper for me to criticise his paper; but, at the same time, being the official representative of Mexico, I could hardly permit his mistakes to pass unnoticed. I was placed in the same position as the guest who, while present at a dinner to which he had been invited, should hear his host make incorrect and even uncomplimentary remarks about his house or his family, although made unintentionally. No matter how bad taste such conduct showed if made intentionally, it would be still worse taste for the guest to notice such remarks. After some consideration, however, I concluded to avail myself of the opportunity which was given me to speak after Mr. Logan's paper was read, for the purpose of correcting some of the principal mistakes which he had made. When my turn came I embraced the opportunity to correct, in as careful, considerate, and polite a manner towards Mr. Logan, as was possible for me to do, what I considered were his chief mistakes.

At Mr. Logan's request, made to me just before he read his paper, I made some general remarks about the philosophy of the revolutions in Mexico, for the purpose of showing that the Mexican people were not actually inclined to revolt, that there had been ample cause for revolutions in the past; but that such causes had now disappeared, and it was not likely that any more disturbances would take place.

On all suitable opportunities which have been presented to me during my official residence in this country, I have tried to impress the same views in as concise and clear a manner as it was possible for me to do. On several occasions, and in different addresses delivered before distinguished audiences at public banquets and other places, I have presented these same views in the shape that it was possible to do in ten or fifteen minutes' time. I append to this paper a few of the addresses I have made with that purpose, beginning with one delivered in New York in 1864, and ending with another delivered in 1892 in the same city.

Some time after the Saratoga meeting had taken place I received from the American Social Science Association the stenographic notes of my remarks, accompanied by the request—made also by Mr. Logan, who published his remarks and mine in a special pamphlet—that I should correct mine for publication. With some reluctance I consented to revise them, but after they were published I saw that I had not done justice to the two subjects on which I had spoken, and that it would be expedient to revise my remarks and amplify them, so as to make two separate papers, one on the "Philosophy of the Mexican Revolutions," and the other on the "Criminal Jurisprudence of Mexico." I therefore prepared two articles, and they were published, the former in the January, and the latter in the July, 1895, number of the *North American Review*. Even after the publication in that Review I thought it advisable to further amplify and revise both articles, finally assuming the form in which they now appear.

In the meanwhile, Dr. Ricardo Becerra, a very distinguished man of letters from Colombia, South America, who for several years represented his country at Washington, and who is now living at Caracas, Venezuela, wrote recently a biography of General Don Francisco de Miranda, the principal promoter of the independence of the Spanish colonies of South America. I found in Dr. Becerra's book valuable information, that had not come to my knowledge before, about the work done in Europe in the latter part of the eighteenth century by native Americans and Spanish Jesuits, whom the father of the then reigning King of Spain had expelled from his dominions in America, to establish the independence of the Spanish colonies on this continent. I found that the promoters of that cause claimed to act in behalf of all the Spanish colonies of America, including Mexico, and as I was sure that Mexico had not been represented at the meetings which were held in Europe in the last quarter of the eighteenth century, I determined to rectify that statement, and with that purpose in view I wrote an article to vindicate the historical truth in regard to that important event in Spanish-American history.

When I began to write my paper I found that the course which the United States pursued towards the revolted colonies of Spain during their struggle for independence had a close connection with my subject, and about the same time, on January 11, 1897, Senator Hale, of Maine, presented to the Senate a paper entitled " Power to Recognize the Independence of a New State," which was published by order of the Senate, as Senate Document No. 56, Fifty-fourth Congress, Second Session. That paper, which I understood had been prepared at the State Department, contained a concise statement of the policy of the United States Government towards the Spanish-American republics, written especially with a view to support the contention that such recognition is an executive prerogative, and does not rest with Congress, and showing at the same time that the United States has always acted with deliberation in the recognition of belligerent rights or independence of a new foreign State, and tried to comply faithfully with her international obligations, a fact which shows that the policy of the present and last administrations regarding the disturbances in Cuba is in accordance with the precedents established by the fathers of the country at the beginning of the century. I found a great deal of valuable information collected in that paper, which I include in my article.

Reviewing the subject, I also found that the United States had prevented Mexico and Colombia from carrying to Cuba in 1825 the war against Spain, which in all probability might have resulted in the independence of that island, and thinking that that was a pertinent subject, I also embraced it in my paper.

I entitled my paper " The Origin of Mexican Independence," which I considered an appropriate title, but when I sent it to the editor of the *North American Review* for publication, he suggested a more pretentious one, namely, " The United States and the Liberation of the Spanish-American Colonies," and out of deference to his greater knowledge and experience I consented to make the change. This pretentious title caused wider circulation of some of the passages of the article than would otherwise have been the case, as it was telegraphed all over the country that I had written a paper censuring the United States for not having assisted the Spanish colonies in their war for independence, and for not having permitted Mexico and Colombia to make Cuba independent, when my article did not contain a word of censure against the United States Government, and was only a brief statement of historical facts with quotations from high American authorities.   I thought that the reason for this misunderstanding was the fact that my paper had not been read in its entirety by those who telegraph to us press extracts from the same, but only such extracts from it as were thought to be of importance, and thus its object was misapprehended.   I was under the impression that anybody who read carefully the whole text could find nothing incorrect or improper in it, much less disrespectful, either to the United States or to the Spanish Government.

I was therefore somewhat surprised when I saw that a man of Senator Money's great abilities shared such views, which he expressed in an answer to my article published in the *North American Review*, for September, 1897, under the title of "The United States and the Spanish-American Colonies.   A Reply."   In that paper Senator Money stated that my assertions were incorrect, and that the United States had materially and morally assisted in the liberation of the Spanish-American Republics.   It afforded me great pleasure to have the opportunity of making clear that my statements were correct, and that my article did not contain a word of censure against the Government of the United States, and with that purpose in view I published in the November number of the *North American Review* a rejoinder to Senator Money's article, amplifying what I had said in my first article, and showing, in my opinion in a very clear and conclusive manner, the correctness of my former statements.

I would much prefer to insert in this volume Senator Money's answer as well as my rejoinder, but as that would take a great deal of space and the question is not of such momentous importance as to warrant it, I have added to my first article such portions contained in the second as I think would make it more complete and clear, and consider in a few foot-notes some of Senator Money's principal objections.

As the paper relating to the origin of Mexican independence, which I have now entitled "Genesis of Mexican Independence," refers to a period which precedes our revolutions, I will insert it first, and it will be followed by the other entitled "Philosophy of the Mexican Revolutions."

PART I.

GENESIS OF MEXICAN INDEPENDENCE.

I. GENESIS OF MEXICAN INDEPENDENCE.[1]

The independence of the United States, proclaimed in 1776, and recognized by England in the treaty signed at Paris on September 3, 1783, based really on economic reasons, and, still more, the recognition of that independence by Spain, principally on account of her hostility to England and at the suggestion of her ally, France, at that time waging war upon England, could not fail to produce a profound impression in the Spanish colonies of America. These events showed the native Americans[2] that the European colonies of this continent had the right, recognized by Spain, to sever their connection with the mother-country, not only for political but for economic reasons. It was this consideration that caused Count de Aranda, a very able statesman, to advise Charles III., immediately upon the recognition of the United States by Spain, in a treaty signed at Paris in 1783, to establish among the Spanish colonies in America three great empires—one in Mexico, another in Peru, and a third on the Spanish Main, which should embrace New Granada, Venezuela, etc., each to be ruled by a member of the Spanish royal family. He proposed that the King should assume the title of Emperor, that the new sovereigns should intermarry into the Spanish royal family, and that each of them should pay an annual tribute into the Spanish treasury. Although this scheme might have proved difficult of realization, and might in the process of its execution have had to undergo radical changes, the final result would have certainly been less disastrous to Spain than the complete emancipation of her American colonies.

[1] This paper has been made up of the two articles published under the title of " The United States and the Liberation of the Spanish-American Colonies " in the *North American Review* of New York, for July and November, 1897, with several additions and revisions.

[2] It was my purpose to speak only about the origin of Mexican independence, but in preparing my paper I found that my subject was so closely related to the revolutionary movement in the other American Republics, that it would have been hardly possible for me to do full justice to it, without giving some account of the manner in which independence originated and was accomplished in the South American colonies. To do this has necessarily extended this paper beyond its intended limits, but I have endeavored to make my references to the wars of independence of the South American colonies as brief as possible.

The French Revolution, which to a certain extent was the result of the American independence,[1] must have exercised a great influence also on the minds of the native Spanish Americans, since it was a very serious blow to the theory of divine right by which it was then supposed in the Western World that nations were governed, as well as a recognition of the natural rights of the people; and this notwithstanding that the discreditable and sanguinary deeds of that revolution, and especially its acts of hostility to the Catholic religion, were represented by the Spanish authorities to the American colonists as being the acts of frenzied men, inspired by the worst passions, as well as illustrating the excesses to which the people were liable when unrestrained by their legitimate rulers. The fact that the Bourbons were not restored to power, but that the French Revolution took a conservative turn and was finally succeeded by the Empire of the First Napoleon, who ruled, not by divine right, but as the choice of the people for the benefit of the people, was the final blow to the principles on which the rule of the Spanish monarchy in America was based.

Spain did not hold her American colonies as forming a part with her of one common country, but as the fiefs or the personal property of the monarch, not so much by reason of her discovery and possession of them, as by reason of the Bull of Pope Alexander VI., which divided the ownership of the American continent between the Kings of Spain and Portugal, "in virtue of the jurisdiction which the Pope had over the world as the head of mankind," as expressed by the most learned commentator of the Spanish laws for the Indies (Solorzano, in his *Politica Indiana*, lib. i., cap. x. and xi., n. 8).

The American vassals of the King of Spain had no political rights of any kind, and no personal rights that the King could not ignore or

[1] The correctness of this assertion has been sometimes doubted, and although I think that its exactness has been proved, I will mention in support of it Mr. Henry Thomas Buckle's opinion, who, in speaking of the immediate cause of the French Revolution, says in his *History of Civilization in England*, vol. iii., pp. 291–293, edition of F. A. Brockhaus, Leipsic, 1865 :

"While all these things were conspiring to overthrow the old institutions, an event suddenly occurred which produced the most remarkable effects in France."

The event to which he refers is the American Revolution and the Declaration of Independence of the United States. He then adds :

"Indeed there is reason to believe that the final blow the French Government received was actually dealt by the hand of an American, for it is said that it was in consequence of the advice of Jefferson, that the popular part of the legislative body proclaimed itself the National Assembly, and thus set the crown at open defiance."

This assertion is supported by a letter which the Duke of Dorset, British Ambassador at Paris, addressed to Pitt on July 9, 1789, in which he says :

"Mr. Jefferson, the American Minister at this Court, has been a great deal consulted by the principal leaders of the *Tiers état;* and I have great reason to think that it was owing to his advice that order called itself ' L'Assemblée Nationale.' "

trample upon; they were, in fact, serfs; yet, by an inconsistency hardly to be accounted for, the Spanish Government established in its colonies municipal government; in this way laying unintentionally the foundation of the democratic institutions which were finally to prevail.

There was an unwritten colonial law, designed, no doubt, for the maintenance of the colonial system, but which was destined finally to put an end to it, in regard to which the Spaniards differed from the other European countries having colonies in America. This law concerned the status of the children of Spaniards born in America. The mere fact that they were born on this continent made them of an inferior caste, debarred from the enjoyment of any of the political or social rights of those born in Spain.

The Spaniards born in Spain formed a privileged class, and their children born in America were considered of an inferior race, born to oppression, who could not regard their parents as fathers, but as masters and oppressors.

The colonial economic system was also of so restrictive a nature as to make it impossible that it should permanently exist; and, more than any other grievance, it served to enlist in favor of the colonies the sympathy of the commercial nations of Europe, as it also affected their own interests. The commercial policy of the European nations with regard to their American colonies was essentially one of monopoly and protection, but the policy of Spain exceeded in point of fact all reasonable bounds, as it prohibited the colonies from raising or manufacturing any article produced or manufactured in the metropolis. To establish a complete monopoly, Spain undertook to provide her colonies with such goods as they needed, and to receive in return their natural products and specie. To carry out this policy, it was settled that only the port of Seville should be the one from which merchant vessels could be sent to the colonies; all commercial intercourse between the colonies was forbidden ; the natural products of the American colonies could be shipped only at certain ports, as Veracruz, on the Atlantic, and Acapulco, on the Pacific, for Mexico, and Panama and Portobelo for South America; and the merchant vessels could sail only once or twice a year in custody and escorted by war vessels, and the articles had to be transported overland to some remote place, as the City of Mexico in Mexico, and Potosi in South America, in the centre of the continent, from whence they were distributed to the several colonies where they were needed, sometimes at a cost of 500 or 600 per cent. above their original price. After a century of this policy, the merchant marine of Spain had disappeared, its capital and manufactures had considerably diminished, its commerce was conducted by foreigners by smuggling, and the gold and silver of the New World went everywhere except to Spain.

European Conspiracy to Accomplish Independence.—I have no information that would lead me to believe that the Mexicans who favored the independence of their country had organized, for the promotion of their cause, any secret society or political revolutionary centre, either in Mexico or in Europe, at the end of the eighteenth century. From a revolutionary manifesto [1] signed in Paris, on the 22d of December, 1797, by Don José del Poso y Sucre, Don Manuel José de Salas, and Don Francisco de Miranda, who called themselves " delegates from the Junta of Deputies from the Provinces and the people of South America, which convened at Madrid, Spain, on October 8, 1797, to settle upon the best means of effecting the independence of the American colonies of Spain," it appears that prominent men from South America had been endeavoring since 1782 to establish independence. To aid in attaining that object, the alliance of England, at that time at war with France, was recommended. They entered into several negotiations with England to that end, especially one initiated in London in 1790, with the British Premier, as a consequence of the conference held at Holliwood, which, it was stated, had been approved by the South American provinces, for the purpose of obtaining from Great Britain a naval force not exceeding 20 warships, 8000 infantry, and 2000 cavalry, the provinces promising to pay to England a pecuniary indemnity which the *Edinburgh Review* stated was to be 30,000,-000 pounds sterling, after their independence was accomplished, and to grant her besides certain commercial advantages.

In that manifesto it was suggested that the United States of America should be invited to make a treaty of friendship and alliance with South America, " on the basis that the possession of the two Floridas and of Louisiana should be guaranteed to the United States, so as to make the Mississippi the boundary between the two great nations, and that to the United States and Great Britain should be given all the islands of the American Archipelago, except Cuba, the key of the Gulf of Mexico." In return for these advantages it was proposed that the United States should furnish to South America an army of 5000 infantry and 2000 cavalry.

That document entrusted the leadership of the scheme, and the military operations necessary to carry it out, as well as the negotiations with England and the United States, to General Don Francisco de Miranda, born in 1750, in Caracas, the capital of Venezuela. Miranda entered the Spanish army, and served in the United States in the revo-

---

[1] This paper was published in 1815 by ex-President John Adams in the *Boston Advertiser*, with a letter addressed to the editor, Mr. Lloyd, in defence of his course in that incident, and reproduced in Spanish by Señor Don Ricardo Becerra, in the first volume of his book, *Vida de Don Francisco de Miranda*, published in Caracas, Venezuela, in 1896.

lutionary war against Great Britain. When the war was ended he was sent to Cuba, and while there he was accused of conspiring to deliver the island of Cuba to the British Government, and he was consequently court-martialled. Miranda then fled to Europe. He travelled in England, Germany, and Turkey, and finally visited Russia under the reign of Empress Catherine.

Miranda then went to France and enlisted in the revolutionary army. Serving under General Dumouriez, he was soon promoted to Brigadier-General, having achieved distinction in the Belgian campaign. The failure of the siege of Maelstrich which he conducted, the defeat of Nerwinden, in which battle he commanded the left wing, and the fall of the Girondists in Paris, caused Miranda's downfall, and he was arrested and court-martialled. But the reaction which followed the 9th Termidor gave him his liberty, and he went to London to renew his negotiations with Pitt to obtain England's assistance in the independence of the American colonies of Spain. He was the real head and centre of the conspiracy prepared in Europe to emancipate the American colonies of Spain. General Miranda believed that he had secured the assistance of the British Government, and it appears that he had some promises of assistance from Pitt, then the British Premier, which, however, were never carried out.

It seemed natural to suppose that, while Great Britain was waging war against Spain in 1798, the British Government would have been not only willing, but even anxious, to divert her attention by assisting the insurrection of her colonies. That was not exactly the case, however, because England expected that Spain would sever her alliance with France, and so aid England in her war against the French revolutionary government. With that object, England sent an agent to Madrid to give assurances to the Spanish Government that she would not assist in the colonial insurrection, if Spain gave up her alliance with France. At the same time instructions were sent to the English authorities in the island of Trinidad to assist in the South American insurrection and to prepare an expedition for that purpose, as Mr. Rufus King, the United States Minister in London, communicated to Mr. Pickering, the Secretary of State, in a despatch dated on February 26, 1798. Had England assisted directly in securing the independence of the Spanish colonies, that would have defeated her purpose of obtaining the support of Spain in her war against the French Government. This was especially the case after Napoleon obtained the ascendancy in France, and more so after the events of 1808, culminating in the treaty of Bayonne. When the Spanish nation rose against the French troops which occupied its territory, England naturally was not disposed to embarrass Spain, whom she considered and at length found to be a very valuable ally against Napoleon, and therefore all the efforts of Miranda and of the leaders of the insurrection in South America to obtain material assistance from England were unavailing.

Although the document above referred to seems to be restricted to South America, Central America is also mentioned in connection with a promise " to open to trade the isthmuses of Nicaragua and Panama "; and incidentally Mexico is also mentioned in a statement that " the deputies of the vice royalties of Mexico, Santa Fé, Lima, and Rio de la Plata, and of the Provinces of Caracas, Quito, Chile, etc., assembled in a legislative body, should decide definitively about the commercial advantages to be granted to England and the allies of South America." It is probable, however, that this reference to Mexico was made on the supposition that Mexico, by reason of similarity of race, language, and institutions, would follow the lead of South America. I have no knowledge of any Mexican having taken part in the conference.

It was further stated in that document that " Don José del Poso y Sucre and Don Manuel José de Salas should set out at once for Madrid to report to the Junta the result of their mission to Paris, carrying with them a copy of the same, and that as soon as this was done the Junta should adjourn and its members should go immediately to the American continent to promote simultaneously insurrections in all the towns of South America, to take place as soon as the assistance furnished by the allies should appear." A copy of that paper was given to General Miranda, as his credentials, to represent the Junta before the British and American Governments.

Mr. King, in his despatch to Mr. Pickering already referred to, reported that he had met in London several Jesuits of South America, from whom he learned that they were working for the emancipation of the Spanish colonies in America. They had lived for many years in London in the service and under the pay of the British Government, and they had shown Mr. King the papers that they had prepared for presentation to the British Government. From a letter addressed by ex-President Adams, on March 6, 1815, to Mr. Lloyd, editor of the *Morning Advertiser*, of Boston, explaining his conduct while President of the United States, in connection with the efforts of Miranda to obtain the assistance of the United States to emancipate the American colonies of Spain, it appears that Don José del Poso y Sucre and Don Manuel José de Salas, who signed the document in conjunction with General Miranda, were Jesuits, probably of the number mentioned by Mr. King; and to the fact, Mr. Adams intimated, that the immediate predecessor of Charles IV., who was at the time (1798) King of Spain, had expelled the Jesuits from his American dominions, was due their action in the matter, they being influenced by a desire to take revenge on the Spanish monarch. There is no doubt that Pitt had detained in London some Spanish Jesuits who took a very active part in the conspiracy to promote the insurrection, and who wrote several manifestoes and inflammatory documents which were to be distributed in the American colonies.

Expedition of General Miranda to Venezuela in 1806.—General Miranda sent to the United States in November, 1789, his friend and co-worker, Señor Caro, for the purpose of obtaining the assistance of this Government. It appears that the scheme had the good-will of Alexander Hamilton, who was at the time organizing a military force to be used in case of war with France, and that it also had the sympathy of Aaron Burr. President Adams, however, following a conservative policy, and having due regard for the neutrality laws, did not embark in the adventure, and did not receive Señor Caro. In November, 1805, General Miranda came to the United States, and was received both by President Jefferson and by Mr. Madison, the Secretary of State. He organized in New York an expedition of about two hundred men, which left that port on February 3, 1806, on the ship *Leander*, for Jaquemel in the island of Hayti, where he was joined by two transports, the *Bacchus* and the *Abeja*. Mr. William S. Smith, Jr., a grandson of ex-President John Adams, and a son of Colonel William S. Smith, Surveyor of the Port of New York, went in that expedition as aid to General Miranda. In consequence of that, Colonel Smith had to resign and he was indicted, and a noisy trial followed in which he was acquitted.

Miranda reached the coast of Venezuela, at Ocumare, but there he lost his two transports, which were captured by the Spaniards together with sixty-seven men, ten of whom were hanged at Puerto Cabello, the remaining fifty-seven being sent to the military prison of San Felipe el Real, in Cartagena.

Miranda met in the island of Barbadoes Sir Alexander Cochran, Admiral of the British Navy, who addressed him a letter dated June 6, 1806, on board his flagship, the *Northumberland*, in which he stated that Miranda's plan to achieve the independence of South America was advantageous to British interests, and agreed to assist in landing Miranda's forces on the coast of Venezuela, and to provide him with three small vessels and probably one frigate, and to defend Miranda's ships against any attacks from the Spanish naval forces. In exchange for his assistance he demanded certain commercial advantages to be granted when independence should be achieved. Miranda left Granada escorted by the English man-of-war *Lily*, the brig *Empress*, and the merchant schooner *Trimmer*. In Trinidad he had been reinforced, his army consisting of about four hundred men, and he landed at Coro. But nobody joined him, all the natives having fled to the interior on his arrival, and he was forced to leave the mainland and to return to the Antilles. This result showed the futility of the scheme to promote independence relying only or mainly on foreign aid. Independence did not make any headway until it relied only upon the support of the natives, and with them alone it was achieved.

In 1811, Miranda went again to Venezuela, and succeeded in organizing a force with which he began the war, but he was obliged to surrender, and was sent to a Spanish prison in Cadiz, where he died in 1816, without seeing his country's independence accomplished. But he had been the forerunner of Bolivar.

Origin of Mexican Independence.—What, in my opinion, contributed more than anything else to precipitate the independence of the American colonies were the disgraceful dissensions of the Spanish royal family in 1808 at Aranjuez and their subservience to Napoleon, which culminated in their abdication in favor of the Emperor. This was accomplished by the Treaty of Bayonne, which transferred to the French Emperor all the rights and titles of Charles IV. to the throne of Spain and the Indies, including the American colonies. The Spanish people strenuously resisted the French invasion and established Juntas in Spain and the colonies to rule the country in the name of Ferdinand VII., the heir of the King, whom Bonaparte had compelled to abdicate, the principal Junta acting as a regency.

The Spanish monarch was the head and centre of the government, and when he disappeared the people of Spain considered that the sovereignty had reverted to them, at least during the captivity of the King, and this view determined the organization of the several Juntas established in Spain, to which I have just referred. As a result of this doctrine, the Spanish subjects in America considered themselves entitled to organize Juntas for their own protection and to deny obedience to the Juntas, which without their representation and using the same right as they were now using, had been organized in Spain during the French invasion. In a communication which the City Council of Mexico addressed to the Viceroy on August 5, 1809, it was stated that [1] "under the present circumstances, the monarch being prevented from exercising the government, the sovereignty is represented by the nation, to accomplish in his name what may be most convenient."

It was in this manner that the native Americans acquired for the first time some control over their own affairs and began to realize that they could take care of themselves. Although the principal Spanish Junta, which met at Cadiz, called representatives to the Cortes from the Spanish colonies, the representation allowed to the latter was very meagre, and that step, instead of satisfying the colonists, only demonstrated to them that the Spaniards were determined not to allow them self-government. Thus the idea of independence gradually gained ground all over the American continent.

[1] *History of the Revolution of New Spain*, by José Guerra, vol. i., p. 41.

That such was the case is shown by the remarkable coincidence that the insurrections in all the American colonies of Spain took place within the same year and almost simultaneously, and, I think, without any previous concert among them.   The distances were so great and the means of communication so scanty, slow, and difficult, that news of an outbreak in one colony could not have been received in the others for several months, and, in some cases, for nearly a year after it had occurred.

This fact shows, in my opinion, that the colonies were ripe for independence, and that a condition of things had been reached which made independence a necessity that could not be suppressed, postponed, or evaded.   Although there had been several attempts at independence in the American colonies of Spain before the year 1810, more particularly the attempt at Chuquisaca, now Sucre, in Bolivia, on May 25, 1809, and some revolutionary movements which broke out in Quito and were easily subdued, independence was not proclaimed until the following year, 1810; on April 19th in Caracas, May 25th in Buenos Ayres, July 20th in Bogotá, on September 16th in Mexico, September 18th in Santiago, Chili, and in the same month of September in most of the other colonies.

It has been said by a distinguished South American historian [1] that ideas do not come without a cause; that they are the natural result of certain conditions, and that just as a plant which appears in an uncultivated soil is the manifestation of a combination of physical, chemical, climatological, and organic causes, so a new idea is a manifestation of a combination of intellectual forces, and appears at the same time in various individuals.   In support of this theory he adduces the saying of Emerson that there is a secret door by which ideas of reform enter the hearts of legislators and of the people, and thus the appearance of a new idea is a new hope which indicates that a new light has been kindled in the hearts of millions of persons.   This is proven by the fact that an idea will occur simultaneously to several persons living in different localities, and without any previous concert among them.

Without contesting the soundness of this view, what, in my opinion, produced the idea of independence in the American colonies was the common sense and natural reason of the inhabitants of the colonies, who had some education and whose minds were somewhat developed. They could not fail to perceive the injustice of being held in servitude by a comparatively small nation, and this view was strengthened by the example set by the United States when they proclaimed and achieved their independence.

In most of the Spanish colonies the independent movement began in the shape of a popular meeting, presided over by the leading persons

---

[1] General Bartolomé Mitre, *Historia de San Martin y de la Emancipacion Sud-Americana*, vol. i., chap. i., paragraph ix., p. 81, Buenos Ayres edition of 1887.

of the capital of the colony, for the purpose of opposing the French invasion of Spain, and supporting the rights of the Spanish royal family. It was thought necessary that the colonies should be armed and prepared, not only to repel the invasion of France, but also to assist the mother-country in her efforts to resist the Napoleonic aggression. In Mexico, however, this was not the case. The Viceroy, Iturrigaray, intended, no doubt in good faith, to arm the country for that purpose, but the jealousy of the " Audiencia " [1] and the native Spaniards inspired them with the suspicion that he intended to call a Popular Assembly, with the ultimate object of proclaiming the independence of Mexico; the ground for this supposition being that the Viceroy had refused to recognize the Junta established in Cadiz, Spain, and they accordingly deposed him, and sent him back to Spain, and appointed his successor. This, naturally, destroyed the respect which the Mexican people had for the representative of the Spanish King, and showed them that force, when successful, was justifiable, and could accomplish greater things. The way was thus paved for a series of military revolutions which continued to break out for about sixty years. The popular movement in all the other colonies drifted finally into a proclamation of independence, while in Mexico independence was proclaimed outright and without any semblance of submission to the Spanish Crown; the cry of Hidalgo, the originator of Mexican independence, being " Long live independence ! Down with the Spaniards! "

The War of Independence in South America.—It will be opportune and interesting to mention briefly when and how the Spanish colonies accomplished their independence.

The independence of South America proper, that is, from the Isthmus of Panama to Cape Horn, was accomplished mainly by two great military geniuses, as great as any the world has ever seen, assisted, of course, by several very able and distinguished lieutenants, among whom occupied the most conspicuous place as a star of the first magnitude General José Antonio Sucre, of Colombia, who achieved some of the most brilliant victories in the war, and who is considered by many as a soldier superior to Bolivar himself. [2] The two great generals were

[1] The Spanish colonies in America were governed by an executive officer, representative of the King, who was called Viceroy, Captain-General, President, etc., according to the importance of the colony, and an Audiencia, of from three to five members, which was a judicial court, acting at the same time as an advisory council to the Executive and intended in fact as a rival body to keep in check the Viceroy, often deposing him.

[2] One of Bolivar's most remarkable lieutenants was General José Antonio Paez, of Venezuela, whose prowess during the war of independence led to his being called the Venezuelan Achilles ; but he remained in Venezuela, while Bolivar went to Colombia, Ecuador, and Peru.

José de San Martin, born on February 25, 1778, in Yapeyú, a small town in the Argentine Republic, on the borders of Paraguay, who operated in the southern part of South America; and Simon Bolivar, born in Caracas, the capital of Venezuela, on July 25, 1783, whose field of operations covered the northern part of that continent, both finally meeting in Guayaquil. Both belonged to distinguished families of Spanish descent, both had received a military education in Spain and had served with distinction in the Spanish army, and both flew to their country's assistance when they heard that independence had been proclaimed. Bolivar was of an impulsive and reckless disposition, and suffered in consequence many serious defeats, while San Martin, being a much more cautious man, was only once defeated, at Cancharayada, Chili, on March 19, 1818, in a night sally made by the enemy, while he was changing the position that his army had occupied during the afternoon.

The La Plata Provinces, or the Argentine Republic, as it is now called, had not only practically established its independence in 1813, after the decisive victories of Tucuman, fought on September 24, 1812, and Salta, fought on February 20, 1813, although its independence was not formally declared until July 9, 1816, by a National Congress which met at Tucuman; but had also driven the Spaniards from Uruguay and Paraguay, and had assisted the adjoining provinces of Upper Peru, which had also rebelled against Spain, and before had shown great patriotism and determination in repulsing twice, in 1806 and 1808, the attacks of the English, then at war with Spain, for the purpose of capturing Buenos Ayres. The Argentine Republic was, therefore, the base of operations against the Spanish Government in the southern portion of South America, and her capital, Buenos Ayres, was the only capital on the continent which, once occupied by the patriots, since May 25, 1810, was never recaptured by the Spaniards.

Peru was at the time, after Mexico, the main seat of Spanish power in America. Lima, its capital, was called, for its enervating conditions and dissipations, the Capua [1] of South America. The Viceroy of Peru

[1] Lima is situated in a pleasant valley where rain never falls ; scarcely ever, about once in a hundred years, are there any thunder-storms, and the air is never impregnated with electricity. Generally, but more especially so in summer, the clouds temper the rays of the sun, while the soft and damp breezes from the south enervate its inhabitants and render active work irksome.

Unanue, in his *Observations on the Climate of Lima and its Influences*, second edition, p. 83, says: " Owing to the influence of the causes before stated (enervating conditions) the men necessarily lack manly traits of character. On the other hand, the same causes tend to the perfection of women ; their features are delicate, their expression soft, their eyes black, with large pupils full of fire and sensibility—the leading traits of a weak but nervous body."

It is a fact already noticed by Humboldt, that a moist, temperate climate prevail-

sent several expeditions, not only to subdue the insurgents of Upper Peru, which was a comparatively easy task, but also against those of Buenos Ayres, who suffered serious defeats in Vilcapujio, on October 1, 1813, and in Ayouma on November 14th of the same year. San Martin was for some months commander of the Argentine army in Upper Peru during 1814, after having obtained an important victory at San Lorenzo on February 3, 1813, and he soon became satisfied that the war could not end until a mortal blow was given to the Spanish power in Peru, and he realized that the only effectual way to accomplish that end was to march from Chili to Peru by the Pacific. He was therefore transferred, at his own request, to the Province of Cuyo, at whose capital, Mendoza, which commanded the main pass of the high cordillera dividing Argentina from Chili, he organized and disciplined his army, which he called the army of the Andes, availing himself of the assistance of the Chilian patriots who flocked to his banner, among whom was O'Higgins, who took such a leading part in the subsequent public events in Chili.

On January 17, 1817, San Martin's army left Mendoza and crossed the high cordillera by the Uspallata Pass, an undertaking accomplished in the face of the enemy, and which may well be compared with the crossing of the Alps by Hannibal, centuries before, when he invaded Italy. While in Chili, San Martin defeated the Spanish army at Chacabuco, on February 12, 1817, which permitted him to occupy Santiago, the capital of that country. The Viceroy sent from Lima another army of Spanish veterans, which joined the defeated Spaniards in Talcahuano, a strongly fortified place, and obtained at Cancharayada a victory on March 19, 1818. When both armies had arrived at the battle-field on the afternoon of that day, and while San Martin was changing during the night the position of his army, it was suddenly attacked by the enemy, dispersing a large portion of the same. San Martin had consequently to withdraw to Santiago, where he was followed by the Spanish general, and sixteen days later, on April 5, 1818, he fought and defeated the Spaniards at Maipo, near the City of Santiago, thus achieving the independence of Chili, and putting the Spanish Viceroy at Lima on the defensive.

The Governments of the La Plata Provinces and of Chili had agreed by a treaty signed at Buenos Ayres, on February 5, 1819, to send a joint expedition to liberate Peru; but before the expedition started a revolution broke out in the Argentine Provinces, requiring the presence of the Argentine army in Chili, and instructions were

ing in a country during the whole year, while very pleasant, does not have the invigorating properties of climates which have extremes of hot and cold weather, which act as a tonic and exercise a very healthy influence upon the body, making men stronger physically and more energetic and inclined to work.

sent to San Martin to return at once. San Martin, realizing that if he went back to Buenos Ayres his army would be demoralized and the cause of independence seriously jeopardized, resolved to disobey his instructions, and he resigned his command, but was recognized as general-in-chief by his army at Rancagua, in Chili, on April 2, 1820, and finally appointed general-in-chief of the joint Chilian-Argentine expeditionary army by the Chilian Government, who assumed the payment of the same. Before San Martin left Chili for Peru, the Argentine Government had been overthrown, and anarchy prevailed there. He found himself, therefore, without a government or nation to back his force, but acted as general-in-chief of the combined army by virtue of appointment of the Chilian Government and by the act of Rancagua, and under such circumstances only his personal worth and influence over the army, with Chili's assistance, could hold it together. San Martin knew that he could not march to Peru overland, and he therefore concentrated all his efforts on the task of providing Chili with a navy which would clear the Spanish Armada from the Pacific.

The geographical position of Chili, which is a long and narrow strip of land bounded by the Cordilleras on the east and bordering on the Pacific Ocean, made it indispensable for her to have a navy, and it is extraordinary how, being the poorest and the last of the Spanish-American Crown colonies, she could, under the able leadership of O'Higgins, a Chilian patriot of Irish descent, and while she was carrying on her war of independence against Spain, improvise a navy, a task in which the Chilian leader was very substantially assisted by San Martin and the Buenos Ayres Government with the man-of-war *Intrepido*, subsequently lost at the capture of Valdivia, by Lord Cochrane, on February 3, 1820. In September, 1818, O'Higgins had procured five men-of-war, manned by raw recruits with little or no naval discipline, and a few English and Americans who could not speak Spanish, which he put under the command of Colonel Manuel Blanco Encalada, born in Buenos Ayres, who had previously served in the Spanish navy, and who became afterwards Vice-President of Chili. Blanco Encalada attacked the frigate *Maria Isabel*, on October 28, 1818, while she was under the protection of the forts at the port of Talcahuano, and captured that vessel, as well as five Spanish transports, with seven hundred Spanish soldiers. The enlarged Chilian navy was placed under the command of the gallant Lord Cochrane, a very distinguished admiral of the British Royal Navy, then under a cloud at home, who took service under the Chilian flag, attacked and defeated the Spanish navy at the port of Callao, capturing the flagship *Esmeralda*, on November 5, 1820, and so established Chilian naval supremacy in the Southern Pacific among the American Republics.

During the year 1814, and before Chili had begun to organize her navy, the Argentine Independent Government had organized one which, under Admiral Brown, a gallant officer of Irish descent, defeated the Spanish navy at Montevideo, and established on the La Plata River the supremacy of the Argentine navy.

With the Chilian navy, consisting of nine men-of-war and sixteen transports, San Martin left Valparaiso for the Peruvian coast on August 20, 1820,[1] with an army of 4118 soldiers, of which 2313 were Argentines and 1805 Chilians. According to Miller, in his *Memoirs*, vol. i., page 243, one third of the Argentine division was composed of Chilians who had replaced the Argentine soldiers killed or disabled during the war, although all the officers were Argentines, and many of the Chilian contingent had the same nationality.

Eighteen days later San Martin landed in Peru, near the city of Pisco, to the south of Lima. The Viceroy had over 23,000 men under his command which he could concentrate against San Martin,

[1] It may be interesting to give a list of the ships which constituted the first Chilian navy, when the squadron left Valparaiso for Peru on August 20, 1820, under Lord Cochrane, and the way in which they were obtained.

Ship of the line *San Martin*, 1300 tons, of 64 guns, previously called *Cumberland*, which belonging to the English East India Company, was bought for $200,000 at Valparaiso by the Chilian government in 1818. Frigate *O'Higgins*, 1220 tons, 44 guns, formerly called *Maria Isabel*, captured at Talcahuano, October 28, 1818. Frigate *Lautaro*, 850 tons, 50 guns, previously called *Windham*, belonging to English and American merchants of Valparaiso, sold to the Chilian government for $180,000, June, 1818. Frigate *Independencia*, 580 tons, 28 guns, formerly called *Curacio*, bought in the United States for $150,000, June, 1819. Brig *Galvarino*, 398 tons, 18 guns, formerly called *Lucia*, bought by the Chilian government in 1818 for $70,000. Brig *Araucano*, 270 tons, 16 guns, called before *Columbus*, bought in the United States for $33,000. Brig *Pueyrredon*, 220 tons, 18 guns, called before *Aguila*, belonged to the Spanish navy and entered Valparaiso in February, 1817, without knowing that the port was in the possession of the patriots. Schooner *Montezuma*, 200 tons, 7 guns, captured at Callao in 1819. Sloop *Chacabuco*, 20 guns, called before *Coquimbo*, bought in Valparaiso in 1818. This ship remained to guard the Chilian coast.

The transports captured by the Chilian navy were the *Magdalena*, *Dolores*, *Carlota*, *Rosalia*, and *Helena*, formerly belonging to the Spanish government and captured by Admiral Blanco Encalada, and the merchant ships *Regina*, *Aguila*, *Victoria*, and *Jeresana*, captured by Lord Cochrane. Frigate *Thomas* was captured at Talcahuano, June 8, 1818. Brig *San Miguel* was captured by the *Lautaro* in 1817. *Perla* and *Potrillo* were Chilian vessels which had been captured by the Spanish and recaptured by Lord Cochrane.

Of these transports the *Dolores*, *Perla*, *Aguila*, *Jeresana*, and *Potrillo* accompanied the united expedition to Peru, and the Chilian government obtained in different ways the other transports which served for the same purpose, namely: *Gaditana*, *Consecuencia*, *Emprendedora*, *Santa Rosa*, *Mackenna*, *Peruana*, *Minerva*, *Golondrina*, *Libertad*, *Hercules*, and *Argentina*. The total tonnage of these transports was 7178 tons.

This expedition was manned by 1600 sailors and marines, of whom about 600 were foreigners, the greater portion of them being English and the balance Chilians.

and it required great generalship and fine manœuvring to baffle the Spanish army. After remaining a month and a half at Pisco, and sending a portion of his army, under General Las Heras, to the interior to raise the people in favor of independence, San Martin sailed with the remainder of his force, on October 29, 1820, to Ancon, a port twenty miles north of Lima, and when the Spanish army was being concentrated against him there he moved again, on November 8th, having possession of the sea, to Huacho, about seventy miles north of Lima, thus severing the communication of the Viceroy with his northern provinces. In the meantime the principal towns of Peru began to join the independent cause, and even a portion of the native army of the Viceroy joined San Martin. All this, together with the very able generalship of that great commander, forced the Viceroy to evacuate Lima on July 6, 1821, which was occupied by San Martin on the 10th of the same month. The port of Callao, the strongest fortified Spanish fort on the Pacific, remained in possession of the enemy up to September 21, 1821, when it surrendered to San Martin.

When San Martin arrived at the northern Peruvian coast, Guayaquil, a very important military and naval position on the Pacific, proclaimed its independence, considerably weakening the Spanish cause.

San Martin had several parleys with the Spanish officers and made different armistices with them. No agreement was reached at a conference held at Torre Blanca hacienda in Retes between San Martin's and La Serna's representatives, on February 23, 1821; but an armistice was signed at Punchauca on May 23, 1821, General San Martin having finally an interview with Viceroy La Serna on June 2, 1821, for the purpose that I will mention further on. Their representatives had met before at Miraflores.

The best proof that could be adduced of San Martin's generalship was his occupation of Peru. He arrived there with comparatively a handful of men, when the country was in full possession of the Spaniards, outnumbering him five to one, and without fighting a single battle he caused the enemy to evacuate its capital, Lima; he obtained the retreat of the army, under General Canterac, which the Viceroy had sent to relieve Callao, and the consequent surrender of this port, and he proceeded to proclaim the independence of Peru, on July 15, 1821. And, considering it indispensable for the success of the cause that he should be at the head of the Government, he proclaimed himself Protector, a title which had not been used since Cromwell, with military and civil control over the country, a position which he assumed on August 3, 1821, and which he kept to January, 1822, when he surrendered the authority to Torre Tagle, whom he had appointed before as Governor of Lima, and who remained in such capacity until San Martin's return to Chili in September of the same year.

On September 21, 1821, the strongly fortified port of Callao surrendered, after Admiral Cochrane had captured from inside the harbor, and from under the protection of the Spanish forts, on July 24, 1821, the Spanish war-ship *Resolucion*, of thirty-four guns, and the *San Fernando* and *Milagro*, both merchant vessels armed for war.

Although Cochrane and San Martin were collaborators in the same work, there was some jealousy between them, and they quarrelled at last, although the apparent immediate cause was that the navy had not been punctually paid by San Martin, and Cochrane, as Admiral of the Chilian navy, seized some money that San Martin had placed on board a ship for safe keeping, and distributed it among his men, finally abandoning the coast of Peru. Lord Cochrane blamed San Martin for assuming the government of Peru. He thought San Martin had betrayed the trust of the Chilian Government, under whose orders he was acting, although San Martin's course was fully approved by O'Higgins. He was also blamed for having abandoned Peru when the enemy was still strong, considering that step as equivalent to flight, and in his passion he even accused San Martin of cowardice and dishonesty, while in such matters he was above reproach.

San Martin was in favor of a monarchical form of government as the best way to insure the independence and prosperity of the new nations, while Bolivar was in favor of a republican form of government. Yet when the Civil War distracted Colombia, Bolivar himself was inclined to accept a monarchical government as an effectual way of putting an end to anarchy. Bolivar was the originator of the scheme that all the American Republics should act in concert for their common defence and in other matters affecting their welfare, and this was his object in proposing, in 1826, the meeting of an American Congress at Panama.

San Martin was not destined to complete the work he had undertaken, as that task was reserved for Bolivar. In 1822 San Martin's situation in Peru had become difficult, as his army had been considerably reduced by hard service and sickness, he having only 8500 men, many of them raw recruits, while the Viceroy had in Upper Peru about 19,000 men, which could be easily concentrated in a comparatively short time. That task was made still more difficult by the defeat of a detachment of San Martin's troops under General Tristan, at Ica, by General Canterac, on April 6, 1822, this being the only reverse that his troops suffered, and that when not commanded by himself in person. San Martin thought it necessary, therefore, to have the assistance of Bolivar to give the finishing blow to Spanish dominion in Peru, as otherwise he was afraid the war would be protracted for several years, and he proposed to meet Bolivar in Ecuador. They met in Guayaquil, on July 26 and 27, 1822.

No authentic report of that interview has ever been published, and this has given rise to many surmises about its objects and results. From the events which preceded and followed it, and from a letter written, soon after it took place, by San Martin to Bolivar, on August 29, 1822, and from conversations of the former with friends, there is room to form an idea of what took place in it. San Martin offered Bolivar to serve under his orders, if he would go with his victorious armies to Peru; but his proposal was not accepted, Bolivar saying that he could not leave Colombia without permission from the Colombian Congress, and agreeing only to send 1500 men of his army to aid San Martin. It is well known that San Martin and Bolivar differed greatly in their views on many subjects relating to the work that they had both undertaken. The difference of opinion between the two regarding the government of the new States was another factor which contributed to prevent their acting in accord. One cause of disagreement between them was the question of the port of Guayaquil, which San Martin thought ought either to belong to Peru, or that the question of its possession should have been settled by negotiation between the Colombian and Peruvian Governments, while Bolivar had already annexed it to Colombia. San Martin, believing that he was in Bolivar's way, and sincerely desiring the success of the cause of independence, proved himself a true patriot and a great man, and preferring to sacrifice his future, decided to withdraw from his field of operations, leaving his competitor alone and rendering him entirely responsible for the course of future events.

San Martin consequently returned to Lima, where he had previously, on December 17, 1821, convoked a National Congress to organize the State, and on the very day on which Congress met, September 20, 1822, he resigned his command in Peru, and sailed for Chili.

Bolivar's career was still more eventful. He fought the Spanish both in Venezuela and New Granada with very varying success from 1810 to 1817, being sometimes victorious and sometimes crushed and defeated, and being twice obliged to fly from the country and take refuge in foreign lands, until finally he asserted his supremacy, and at the battle of Boyacá, fought on August 7, 1819, in which he achieved the independence of New Granada and captured Bogotá, its capital, and at that of Carabobo, the Waterloo of the Spaniards in Colombia, which was fought on June 24, 1821, he achieved the independence of his native land, Venezuela, having previously occupied its capital, Caracas.

The most remarkable trait in Bolivar's character was his indomitable will, his unfaltering faith in his destiny, and in the final success of his cause, which, under the most adverse circumstances and after the worst defeats, when any one else would have despaired, sustained his hope and animated him to continue his efforts; his faith, in almost every instance, being justified soon afterwards by a great victory.[1]

Bolivar, like San Martin, realized that his success could not be permanent as long as the Spaniards were in possession of the neighboring countries, and more especially of Peru, the principal Spanish stronghold in South America, which they used as a base from which to assail the new nationalities, and he therefore decided to attack them first in Ecuador and afterwards in Peru. Both armies, each from opposite ends of South America, converged towards Peru with the same object in view, that of putting an end to the Spanish domination. He consequently marched his army to Ecuador, where he met and defeated the enemy in the battle of Bomboná, on April 7, 1822.

The victory of Bomboná was a very costly one to the patriots, on account of the severe losses they sustained, as out of their force of 2000 men they lost over 600, or about 30 per cent., while the Spaniards, having nearly the same number of troops, only lost about 250, or $12\frac{1}{2}$ per cent. The battle was of comparatively little result to the patriots, as immediately after it was gained Bolivar had to withdraw to his base of operations in Southern Colombia, where he remained until the 9th of June, 1822, when he succeeded in obtaining the surrender of the Province of Pasto, which, on account of its topography and the devotion of its inhabitants to the King of Spain, has been compared to La Vendeé during the French Revolution.

On May 13, 1821, General Sucre had asked the co-operation of San Martin to march against Quito, and in January, 1822, an agreement was made by which San Martin promised to assist Sucre with 1500 men to be paid by the Colombian Government, which troops he sent under the command of Colonel Lavalle, and so both armies, San Martin's and Bolivar's, met at the Equator on their march from opposite ends of South America.

General Sucre, with his own forces, left Guayaquil, marched against Quito, and after his junction with the Argentine contingent, he achieved, at Pichincha, in sight of Quito, on May 24, 1822, a complete victory over the royalists, which accomplished the independence of Ecuador.

As San Martin had predicted, the patriot army in Peru was defeated after he left the country, both at Torata and Moquegua, on January 20

---

[1] In General Mitre's opinion, as expressed in his *History of San Martin*, vol. iii., chap. i., p. 761, Buenos Ayres edition of 1887, Bolivar's tactics, if they can be so called, were the result of native warlike instinct, combined with European discipline. He used, indeed, but little tactics and less strategy ; his natural military instinct and genius for war prompted his movements, and he gained his victories chiefly by the audacity of his conceptions, the boldness and recklessness of his attacks, and his unflinching persistence after defeat. His military methods resembled in their reckless daring the tactics of Charles XII.

and 21, 1823. During the night of February 4, 1824, the Argentine garrison of the stronghold of Callao rebelled against the Government because they had not been paid, and finally delivered the place to the Spaniards, which was a very great blow to the cause of independence. Callao, like Veracruz, remained in possession of the Spaniards for some time after the independence of Mexico and Peru had been achieved.

After the defeats of Torata and Moquegua and the destruction of the army organized by Peru, under General Santa Cruz, the Peruvian Government made a treaty with Colombia, on April 12, 1823, by which it obtained the aid of 6000 troops; and, finally, after the country had fallen into anarchy, Bolivar made his appearance in Lima, where he was hailed as the liberator of the country, the Peruvian Congress appointing him, by a decree dated at Lima on August 10, 1823, Dictator and Liberator of Peru, thus giving him entire civil and military control over the country, so realizing San Martin's prediction.

General Abascal, Viceroy of Peru, had succeeded in organizing a native Peruvian army to oppose the independent cause, and among the officers who distinguished themselves in that army was General Valdez, who for his bravery and chivalry was called the Peruvian Bayard. The Spaniards had, besides, distinguished generals like General Canterac, famous for his talent to organize cavalry corps, and General La Serna, who became afterwards Viceroy. Generals Canterac and Valdez deprived Viceroy Pezuela of his military command, on January 29, 1821, at Asnapuquio, and appointed General La Serna in his place.

New dissensions broke out among the royalist troops, as most of them favored the Spanish Constitution of 1812, while General Valdez, with 5000 men, was in favor of an absolute monarchy, and hostilities broke out among the royalist troops, which caused them great loss, and assisted materially the patriots. By a strange phenomenon the Spanish officers belonged decidedly to the Liberal party, while the native Peruvian officers were enlisted on the side of the Absolutist party, this difference of opinion producing a rivalry in the army which affected seriously their *morale* and final success.

Bolivar, in full charge of the combined Peruvian, Chilian, and Argentine armies, as well as the whole of the Colombian army, marched against the Spaniards in Upper Peru. At Junin both armies met unexpectedly, on August 6, 1824, and only the cavalry took part in the engagement, the Spaniards having 1300 and the patriots 900 men, the Spanish cavalry being the flower of the Spanish army in Peru, and considered by the Spaniards invincible. The engagement lasted but three quarters of an hour,—no guns but only side arms were used,—but it was a bloody one, the Spaniards losing 250 men and the patriots 150 in killed and wounded. This defeat of the Spanish cavalry demoralized their army.

20

After Junin followed the battle of Ayacucho, fought on December 9, 1824, at which Bolivar was not present, although he had really directed its operations, having given his instructions to General Sucre, the commander of the patriot army. The Viceroy, La Serna, had collected the whole Spanish army, which was 10,000 men strong, while Sucre's army consisted only of 4500 Colombians, 1200 Peruvians, and 80 Argentines, the remnant of San Martin's army. Both armies had been for two weeks before the battle within sight of each other, manœuvring on a broken and difficult ground for the purpose of selecting their positions, and both fought with great bravery at Ayacucho, losing about twenty-five per cent. of their respective forces. The loss of the Spaniards was 2000 killed and wounded, and 3000 prisoners; the remainder of the army surrendered to Sucre, who sent them back home at Peru's expense. The result was a complete success for the patriots, who in that battle finally destroyed Spanish power in South America.

San Martin never had any political ambition and never administered the affairs of the government in the countries that he liberated, excepting the time when he exercised the government in Peru as protector. He respected the different nations which he found in America, that is, the political divisions established by the Spaniards during the colonial domination based on similarity of races and on natural geographical barriers, and did not attempt to annex Peru or any portion of it to his country or to Chili; while Bolivar had great political ambition, always assuming the reins of government in every country which he liberated, being at the same time Liberator and Dictator, and annexing some of them to Colombia.

Both San Martin and Bolivar died poor, the former having spent during the war a large fortune which he had inherited. San Martin ended his life in Europe in 1850 as a voluntary exile, while Bolivar died in Santa Marta in 1830, at the age of forty-seven, broken-hearted at the disruption of the Republic of Colombia, which he had founded, by the breaking out of civil war in that country, and at the ingratitude of many whom he had befriended.

Had they lived before Plutarch's time the lives of these two men were worthy of appearing in his *Parallel Lives of Celebrated Greeks and Romans*, and they would indeed have excelled in lustre many of those commemorated in his book.

When the enormous difficulties are considered that the liberating armies had to contend with, traversing immense distances in a very difficult and broken country without railways or even wagon-roads, having often to transport their artillery on mule-back, without any commissariat or money to pay the army, and often even without arms or ammunition, without any Government to lend its aid, as was the case with San Martin, and with constant changes of government, and even anarchy in some cases, what those men accomplished may be regarded as truly wonderful, and their march will bear favorable comparison with Alexander's invasion of Persia, with the difference in Alexander's favor that he went into a rich country, and had at his disposal the spoils of the Persian royal family, one of the richest at that time, while these men went into a poor and unsettled country, terribly ravaged by a destructive war.

In Mexico, as in all the other Spanish colonies, the war of independence had begun in 1810, and we consider that it ended on September 27, 1821, when Iturbide entered the City of Mexico with his victorious army, although the war had been practically ended when the Spanish Viceroy, O'Donoju, signed with Iturbide, at the city of Cordova, on August 24, 1821, a treaty in which he recognized on behalf of the Spanish Government the independence of Mexico. In a paper entitled " The Philosophy of the Mexican Revolutions " I have given more details about the war of independence in Mexico, which I think unnecessary to repeat here.

In what is now called Central America the people remained under the Spanish Government without any attempt to proclaim independence, very likely because they thought they could not cope with the power of the Spanish Viceroy in Mexico, until they heard of Iturbide's success, after which they proclaimed their independence and annexation to Mexico on September 15, 1821, seceding from Mexico in 1823, and establishing then the Central American Confederation, under the name of the United Provinces of Central America, a confederation which lasted until 1839, when each of the five States became an independent nation. In a paper entitled " Boundary Question between Mexico and Guatemala," I have spoken more at length about the independence of Guatemala.

It is a remarkable fact that almost all the leaders of the Spanish-American independence were shot either by the Spaniards, or by their own people on account of internal dissensions. Hidalgo, Morelos, and Iturbide in Mexico, and a long list of others in South America, suffered that fate. The Spaniards considered the insurgents as rebels and traitors, and gave them no quarter; they believed that by pursuing a sanguinary policy they would awe the masses and prevent them from taking part in the insurrection.

Many others met a violent death after independence had been achieved, like Iturbide and Guerrero in Mexico, Sucre and Cordoba in Colombia, and Bermudez in Venezuela. Many escaped death on the scaffold by ostracizing themselves, like O'Higgins in Chili, San Martin in Argentina, and even Bolivar was overtaken by death at the port of Santa Marta, on the eve of sailing for Europe.

While Spain was waging a war of independence against France, and the Spanish King was held in captivity by Napoleon, that is, from 1808 to 1814, she could with difficulty defend her American colonies, and only occasionally did she send reinforcements to the royalists maintaining their authority there; but when, with the assistance of England, the French were driven from Spain, after Napoleon's downfall in 1814, and Ferdinand VII. was restored to the throne, the Spanish monarch took active measures to subdue his American dominions and sent out large expeditions, the principal one, under General Morillo and consisting of 10,000 veterans, being intended for the La Plata Provinces, but finally landing in Venezuela; and with this expedition and others Spanish rule in America was almost restored.

In 1819 Ferdinand, assisted by the French, and as it appears by Russia also, straining every nerve, had collected at Cadiz a very large expedition, consisting of about 20,000 men, for the purpose of putting an end, as he anticipated, to the American insurrections; but the military chiefs of the expedition rebelled against the despotic government of the King, and proclaimed the restoration of the Liberal Constitution decreed by the Cortes in 1812, which constitution the King was obliged to accept, at least for the time being; and thus was frustrated Ferdinand's last serious attempt to subdue his rebellious subjects. During the insurrection the Spanish Government had sent out eighteen expeditions, consisting of about 45,000 men, at a cost of about $75,-000,000, which was then a very large force and a very large amount of money.

Spanish Overtures for Compromise.—The Liberal Cabinet, established after the restoration of the Constitution of 1820, believed that they could restore the Spanish power in America by compromising with the revolted colonies and granting them a degree of autonomy, or possibly by carrying out the plan proposed by Count Aranda, and, acting under authority granted to the King by the Cortes in two resolutions approved in 1820 and 1821, to enter into negotiations with the governments established in the American colonies, sent special commissioners to some of the colonies to offer them autonomy on condition that they should take the oath of allegiance to the King.

Ferdinand VII., then King of Spain, at the urgent solicitation of the Liberal leaders, or rather compelled by them, issued a proclamation in April, 1820, of which the following is an extract: "A sad experience of six years, and the excitement brought about by its energetic manifestations, had convinced everybody that the policy unwisely restored in 1814 had brought about greater evils, and had been a drawback to the advancement made until then." The King furthermore said that "the Spanish Americans, drawn aside from the pathway of rectitude, had succeeded in obtaining what they sought through war,—that is, tears and disaster." Wherefore he invited them to enter into peace negotiations with their metropolitan brethren on an equal footing. But, in order to attain this end, he offered them the rights they had under the Constitution of 1812, which they had rejected when they declared their independence. Finally, Ferdinand VII. said in this proclamation that he made his offer so "that there should be a renewal of the friendly relations existing during the past three centuries, and in conformity with the enlightenment of the age," and threatened that force should be employed if his paternal advice for harmony and union was not accepted.

The Spanish Cortes issued in 1820 a decree extending amnesty to all those who had taken part in the insurrection of the American colonies against Spain, and soon afterwards a second one, by which they authorized the sending of commissioners to the insurgent colonies for the purpose of ending the war by peaceful means.

Commissioners were sent to Bolivar in Colombia and San Martin in Peru. Bolivar accepted the invitation of the Spanish commissioners, and sent his own commissioners to Spain, but with instructions to treat under the basis of the recognition of the independence of Colombia, and he did so more to gain time than with any idea of coming to a satisfactory agreement.

The change of policy brought about in Spain by the success of the Liberals and the decision of the Cortes just referred to, explains why the Spanish representatives, both in Mexico and Peru, accepted the independence of those countries on condition of establishing there monarchies under a Spanish prince. But these agreements were finally rejected by the King of Spain, who, as a true Bourbon, would not hear of any suggestion tending to the independence of the colonies, but who, on the contrary, as long as he lived, was continually making efforts to fit out expeditions against them ; and in 1829 he sent a large one from Havana, under General Barradas, against Mexico, which landed at Tampico, but was defeated and obliged to return to that port. Ferdinand VII. was consistent in not recognizing the independence of the colonies, even after it had been for many years an accomplished fact, and recognition by Spain did not take place until 1836, after his death.

American Monarchical Views.—The Republican seed had been sown in America by the Pilgrims in New England, the Quakers in Pennsylvania, the cavaliers in Virginia; and when the United States established their independence under a republican form of government, it was almost impossible for the other new countries to adopt institutions of a less liberal character.

If Charles III. had accepted Count de Aranda's advice to establish three empires in America, all the turmoil and loss of life which were necessary to accomplish independence, and which followed the same, would have been avoided, and free institutions and a republican form of government would have finally been established peacefully and by evolution.

Several attempts were made to establish a monarchical form of government among the new nations of America. Godoy, the Prime Minister and guiding spirit of Charles IV., of Spain, advised his sovereign, after he had been dethroned by the Emperor Napoleon in 1808, to go to America and establish his empire there. Had Charles IV. followed that advice, the example of Brazil would have been repeated in the Spanish colonies, and this would have allowed them to pass from a despotic to a republican form of government without the serious disturbances, the turmoils, and the bloodshed which followed their independence, and liberal institutions would have finally prevailed, as was the case with Brazil. John VI. of Portugal, who did what was suggested to Charles IV. of Spain, that is, established his empire in Brazil, when he was driven from his country, was unable to found an absolute monarchy in America, and he returned to Portugal only to establish there a constitutional monarchy; and the Brazilian empire which succeeded him was really a Democratic government with a remarkably good man as a figure-head on the throne.

San Martin and the principal leaders of the Argentine revolution, forseeing the unrest and political disturbance which the adoption of republican institutions would necessarily entail on the new nations, they not being prepared for that form of government, which is adapted only for an enlightened people, capable of self-government, favored the establishment of a constitutional monarchy as affording the best guarantee of the life and stability of the new nations, and in those views they had the support of the Chilian Government under O'Higgins and of the Lautaro Lodge, a political secret society established in Buenos Ayres for the purpose of securing independence, which was afterwards extended by San Martin to Chili and Peru. In this they were largely influenced by Montesquieu, who, by his praises of the English Constitution, had inculcated in the French and Spanish speaking people of the world the opinion that it was a perfect form of government.

In 1814, at the suggestion of England, it was proposed by the Argentine Government that a Spanish infante, or son of the King of Spain, should be sent as king to the La Plata Provinces, a proposition which was not accepted by the Spanish King. The Argentine Congress, which declared the independence of their country in 1816, accepted secretly the monarchical form of government, and the Argentine representatives in Europe were authorized to enter into negotiations with the European powers for the purpose of establishing in the Argentine Provinces that form of government, the prevailing idea being to establish a monarchy with a native prince, a descendant of the old

Incas of Peru, on the throne, fixing the capital at the city of Cuzco. Between 1816 and 1819 the monarchical plan was again agitated. France was very anxious that a monarchical government should be established in Argentine, and the Argentine statesmen, believing that if they accepted that form of government, the European powers would support the independence of their country, favored it, and authorized their representatives in France and England to accept as king the French candidate, the Prince of Luca, a member of the Bourbon family and a nephew of the King of Spain.

While San Martin was Protector of Peru he sent to Europe, in December, 1821, Señor Don Juan Garcia del Rio to negotiate an alliance with Great Britain for the purpose of accepting a prince of the English royal family to be Emperor of Peru, on condition that he accepted the constitution which the nation's representatives should approve; and if the English Government was not disposed to accept this scheme, the same proposition was to be made to the Emperor of Russia, accepting a prince of his dynasty or any candidate whom he should propose, or finally any prince from the reigning houses of France and Portugal would be accepted, even the Prince of Luca.

But when in 1823 Mr. Canning stated to the French Government that England did not require the establishment of a monarchy as a condition of recognizing the independence of a new nation, the idea was given up. The appointment of a native as monarch, as in the case of Iturbide in Mexico, proved the futility of the idea of making any of the revolutionary leaders king or emperor.

Anarchy made such headway in Colombia that Bolivar in his message to the Colombian Congress, of January 20, 1830, said " I blush to say it, but independence is the only blessing we have obtained, and that at the cost of everything else," and it is believed that he became then a convert to the idea of a constitutional monarchy.

Many persons continued to be of the opinion that the best way to end anarchy was to establish a monarchy under European auspices. The futility of this theory has been since demonstrated by the tragic failure of Maximilian's experiment in Mexico. This experiment was undertaken under the best auspices. The Emperor Napoleon supported it with all the power of France, aided by that of Austria and Belgium, who contributed with armed contingencies to its establishment, and the so-called emperor was taken from the oldest and one of the noblest reigning families of Europe, the House of Hapsburg; its complete failure, therefore, proves conclusively the folly it would be to think of the establishment of a monarchy in America.

A distinguished Spanish-American historian [1] says that the United

[1] General Bartolome Mitre, *Historia de San Martin y de la Emancipacion Sud-Americana*, vol. i., chap. i., paragraph xv., p. 107, Buenos Ayres edition of 1887.

States in the first decade of the nineteenth century was a sun without planets, which shed light only upon its own sphere and that the appearance of a group of new nations which came out of the nebulous colonies of the South, formed for the first time in the history of the world a planetary system in the political order with natural laws, universal attractions, and democratic harmony, raising the United States to the rank of a first-class nation.

The simultaneous establishment of ten republics in the American continent just at the time when a very strong reaction was taking place in Europe in favor of absolute monarchical government, was indeed one of the most remarkable phenomena of the present century, and justified Mr. Canning in saying that the republics of the new world would restore the equilibrium of the old.

The psychological phenomena which marked the transplanting of the European races, Spanish and Anglo-Saxon, to the American continent, is very interesting, as most of the encumbrances, abuses, and wrongs prevailing in Europe as the result of the feudal system and of many centuries of hard struggles and oppression, were wiped out by their establishment in a new field with different environment. Class privilege, hereditary rank, the autocratic ideas, the complete disregard of the rights of the people which had become in Europe deeply-rooted institutions, were blotted out in the New World. Just as water that after many years of stagnation in a lake becomes polluted, by transferring it to another place loses through evaporation all its impurities and is restored to its pristine purity, so it happened with the transplanting of European races to the New World.

Differences between the Independence in Mexico and South America.— I think it worth while to notice some of the most striking differences which I find in the war of independence in Mexico and in South America. In the chapter, " Beginning of Mexican Independence," I have already stated the striking difference between the bold way in which independence was at once proclaimed in Mexico and the indirect manner in which it was done in almost every other country in South America, and here I will point out some of the most notable differences.

In South America the movement of independence began with the educated classes which were the higher classes, that is, the men of Spanish descent born in America, who had had the opportunity of acquiring some education by reading books forbidden by the Inquisition, but which in some way had found their way into their hands. They became impressed with the cause of independence, and finally were the leaders of that cause, while the lower classes by ignorance and prejudice generally favored the existing condition of things, and in the beginning opposed independence. But in Mexico the higher classes, either because they were more ignorant than in the South American colonies, or because the advantages they derived from the Spanish rule were greater, on the whole sided with the King, and offered the most decided opposition to the cause of independence. The leaders of this cause were the poor priests, who, of course had some education, and were great patriots, and they were assisted by the masses, including the Indians.

The movement for independence, which in the other Spanish colonies originated with the higher classes, in Mexico sprang originally from the lower classes, the higher classes always opposing it. Miranda, Bolivar, Mosquera, and Bermudez in Venezuela; Alvear, Belgrano, Pueyrredon, and Rivadavia in Buenos Ayres; Nariño, Caldas, Zea, Torres, and Gomez in Colombia; O'Higgins, Rozas, and the Carrera brothers in Chili; Riva Aguero, and Unanue in Peru; Montufar and Rocafuerte in Quito; Caro in Cuba, all belonged to the higher classes of those countries, while Hidalgo and Morelos were only humble Mexican priests.

A point in which the case of Mexico differs from the other Spanish colonies is in regard to the Indians. Several Indian insurrections took place in South America during the seventeenth and eighteenth centuries, which sometimes assumed a very serious character, but which were finally suppressed by the Spanish authorities. In all these cases the Indians intended to revert to their old form of government, that is, the one that they had before the conquest, thus really inaugurating a war of races, which deprived them of the assistance of the creoles, but in the war of independence in South America the Indians remained passive, and the movement was headed and carried out almost exclusively by the creoles. The gaucho of Argentina, the llanero of Venezuela, the roto of Chili, the cholo of Upper Peru were all creoles, while in Mexico we never had any Indian insurrection for the purpose of reverting to the Montezuma empire, and our Indians assisted manfully and bravely in our war of independence against Spain, being really our main reliance.

The principal difference between the war of independence as carried on in Mexico and in South America, was the attitude of the Catholic clergy. In Mexico the clergy was the mainstay of the Spanish Government, while in the South American colonies the clergy either remained passive or indifferent to the struggle, or sided with the patriots.

When one of the Mexican priests who sided with the independence, and especially if they were leaders like Hidalgo, Morelos, Matamoros, etc., fell into the hands of the Spaniards, they were at once placed at the disposal of the clergy, and tried by the Inquisition as transgressors of divine law and as heretics, and finally degraded in a very pompous public ceremony, before they were given up to the military authorities who tried them for the purpose of obtaining information about their plans and followers, and shot them without mercy. I am not aware that the process of degradation took place in the other Spanish-American colonies. The higher dignitaries of the Catholic clergy in Mexico attempted to make the common people believe that all patriots were heretics and devils, and that the object of the revolution was to destroy the Catholic religion, with the purpose of giving to the war of independence the character of a religious war.

The Spanish colony in South America which most resembled Mexico in this regard was Peru, where the higher clergy lived in opulence and were decidedly attached to the King, while the lower clergy were in favor of independence, and the participation of the clergy in Peru was of little consequence as compared with what took place in Mexico. The Peruvian clergy in general, and especially the parish priests, were decidedly in favor of independence. Not so, however, the higher dignitaries. During the uprising of Pumacahua, a leader in Upper Peru, which began at Cuzco, on August 3, 1814, the municipality and the ecclesiastical council elected a Junta to head the revolution, and the curates and monks preached rebellion in the adjoining provinces. The curate of the Sanctuary of Cuzco, Ildefonso Muñecas, having distinguished himself for his ardor, had been one of the principal promoters of the revolution, and took afterwards a leading part in the same. San Martin having due respect for his gray hairs did not repress him in any manner. The Archbishop of Charcas, the Bishops of Cuzco, Maynas, Huamango, and secretly the Bishop of Arequipa, had constituted themselves promoters of the movement against independence and ardent orators of the royalist cause. Lord Cochrane, in his *Memoirs*, of which I have seen a translation into Spanish, published in Lima in 1863, states that two monks incited the garrison of Chiloe and ran over the walls with a crucifix in one hand and a lance in the other to oppose the patriots. The Archbishop of Lima could not withdraw from the influence which surrounded and attracted him.

Archbishop Las Heras, although submitting to the inevitable, obeyed the impulse of his conscience and the commands of the Pope when " he recommended fidelity to the Spanish monarch and the uprooting and complete destruction of the seeds of disturbance and sedition that the enemy had sown in America, inspiring his flock with a just and stable hate, leaving no stone unturned," [1] for which he was exiled by San Martin. But even in Peru, the Archbishop himself, who was a native-born Spaniard, did not refrain from allowing a Te Deum to be sung in the Cathedral of Lima when independence was pro-

[1] *Encyclic of Pope Pius VII.,* of January 30, 1816. Later Pope Leo XII. issued in 1824, another encyclic against South American independence.

claimed, and he attended himself that Te Deum, something which no Mexican bishop would have consented to do.

The South American leaders, if we are to judge by the opinions expressed in the document above referred to, and more especially General Miranda, who had undoubted military talent, and was a distinguished soldier and an enthusiast in the cause of independence, believed that independence could not be achieved with native resources only, but that it required as an indispensable element of success the armed assistance of foreign nations, although they never succeeded in obtaining any. The views of the Mexican leaders were altogether different. They never dreamed of seeking any foreign assistance, but relied entirely upon the strength and resources of their own country. It is true that Hidalgo, soon after he proclaimed independence, and while he was retreating toward the north, sent a representative to the United States, but I believe that he had no intention of asking for material assistance, and desired only to obtain the good-will of a neighboring country in the contingency that, in the course of his military operations, he should reach its frontiers.

One of the differences between the struggle for independence in Mexico and that in South America, is that in the latter case the Argentine Provinces, Chili, and Colombia had diplomatic agents in Europe who worked steadily for the cause, and kept the leaders of the revolution well informed of the movements in Spain and in Europe against them, and even took part in the conspiracies in Spain for the purpose of preventing the sending of reinforcements to America, spending much money for that purpose, while Mexico was entirely isolated, had no representatives of any kind in Europe or the United States, and she depended entirely on her own resources, without even dreaming of foreign assistance of any kind. In the lists of official and unofficial agents sent by the colonies to the United States there does not appear any coming from Mexico, nor does it appear that the United States sent any commissioner or agent to Mexico, to inquire into the condition of the country.

As a consequence of the more intimate contact between the leaders of the independent movement in South America and Europe and of Mexico's isolation, the former had the active support, not only of foreign officers of high rank and even of private soldiers in the army as well as in the navy, but of whole regiments, like the Britannic Legion of Bolivar. The South American patriots had in their ranks some of the most distinguished European officers, among others Lord Cochrane in Chili, and Marshall Brayer, who had fought with Napoleon, and was with San Martin in Peru, while in Mexico, with the exception of Mina and his fellow-followers, who were not foreigners but Spaniards, I do not know of any foreigner who took part in our war of independence.

Another difference between the Mexican and South American wars of independence is that while some of the South American nations like Peru, Argentina, Chili, and others were able to organize navies, the Mexican patriots never were in possession of the coast, and therefore could never even think of having a navy before independence was actually accomplished.

Another matter in which I find a marked difference between the war of independence in South America and that in Mexico, is that in the former, although in the beginning the Spaniards gave no quarter to the patriots, yet they agreed early in the struggle to carry on a regular war, that is, not to shoot their prisoners, to make exchanges of such as they captured, and in general to allow their opponents the rights of belligerents, going so far as to receive commissioners from the leaders of the revolution and to grant armistice, and make formal treaties with them as the agreement signed between Bolivar and General Morillo at Santa Anna on November 27, 1820, for a truce of six months and to make thereafter a regular civilized war, while in Mexico they never waged a civilized war, and, with very few exceptions, shot every leader whom they captured and made no armistice or agreement of any kind with the chieftains of the revolution, considering them as traitors and outlaws, until the conclusion of the treaty between Iturbide and O'Donoju, signed at Cordova in 1821, which does not alter the case in any way, as it was signed after the patriots were in possession of the whole country.

Another material difference between the war of independence in Mexico and her South American sisters, was that the location of the Spanish colonies in South America being contiguous to each other, permitted them to be of mutual assistance in their struggle for independence, a fact which constituted a very great advantage; while Mexico, being entirely isolated, had to fight her own battles single-handed.

A last point of difference between the war of independence in Mexico and South America, is that we never had in Mexico any Lodge or any other political organization to aid the revolution, while the Lautaro Lodge in South America played a very important part in the war of independence on that continent.

Recognition of Independence by the United States.—The United States Government did not render any material or moral assistance to the cause of independence of the Spanish-American colonies,[1] excepting

---

[1] Senator Money considers in his article published in the *North American Review*, for September, 1897, that this assertion was not correct, and mentions the fact that several missions were sent by the United States Government to the struggling colonies to ascertain the true condition of things and act accordingly, as an act of moral support to the independent cause ; but this cannot be considered as an act of moral support,

the moral influence consequent to the recognition made by the United States Government of belligerency of the struggling colonies, and the moral assistance growing out of the fact that the United States having proclaimed and achieved their independence only a little over a quarter of a century before, could not help but sympathize with the cause of the Spanish American colonies, and that every American heart beat with real sympathy for that cause. The United States Government followed a strictly neutral policy, because being at peace with Spain, it considered that it would be a breach of neutrality to aid the movement to establish independence in her colonies.

Many of the leaders of the cause of independence in the Spanish-American colonies of America desired and expected assistance from

because if an agent or a commission is sent to inquire whether independence has been accomplished and no action is taken by the government after sending such agent or commission, the necessary inference is that the struggle was not in a condition to be recognized, and therefore the result of such measure had necessarily to be, although not intentionally so, against the struggling patriots and in favor of their enemy.

Senator Money, in support of his views that my assertion is incorrect, states that " as far as the law of nations would permit, we (the United States) certainly gave material support to the cause of freedom in South America," and also mentions " the curious spectacle afforded of two ships exactly alike, built at the same time, in the same American shipyard, one for the Spanish King, and one for his insurgent subjects." If the laws of this country allowed such a proceeding, it was not an act in support of the revolted Spanish colonies, and neither was it an act in support of the King of Spain. Anything that is done for both contending parties cannot be said to be in favor of either of them, or be looked upon as an act of great material or moral support.

The facts mentioned by Senator Money of the " tardiness and difficulties of communication at that time, the dissentions among the insurgents, the efforts of Peru, Chili, and La Plata to organize New Granada and Venezuela into a confederate republic, and those of the Central American states, in the same direction ; the continued talk of alliances, offensive and defensive ; the fear that early recognition of belligerency might prevent the negotiation or ratification of the treaty of 1819 ceding Florida to the United States ; the swarms of privateers who on the South Atlantic and on the Spanish Main flew the insurgent flags and committed the most atrocious acts of piracy," might have been sufficient to justify the United States in delaying recognition, if a complaint had been made on that point ; but the question is not whether the action of the United States is or is not justifiable, but whether the government of the United States rendered any assistance to the insurgents before independence was accomplished. The United States followed, in my opinion, a proper course under the circumstances.

Senator Money mentions the fact that several resolutions were introduced in the House of Representatives expressing sympathy with the insurrection in the Spanish-American colonies, but a resolution introduced in the House of Representatives, especially if it is voted down, as were most of Mr. Clay's resolutions, cannot, I think, be considered an act of moral support to the governments of the revolted colonies. To be sure Mr. Clay's resolution of May 10, 1820, and February 9 and 10, 1821, were carried by very small majorities in the House, but they did not pass the Senate, and they were approved by the House after independence had been an accomplished fact in most of the colonies.

the Government of the United States, as their cause was the same as that which this country had defended over thirty years before, and also for other obvious reasons. The United States Government was very careful to comply with its obligations, and not to give any well-grounded cause of complaint to the Spanish Government. The people of the United States and many prominent members of Congress heartily sympathized with the movement for independence in the Spanish-American colonies, and resolutions were introduced in the House of Representatives of the United States Congress asking their recognition, which were either not acted upon or voted down, as I will presently briefly state. The United States Government sent agents and commissioners to the revolted colonies to examine and report upon their situation; and the governments established in the new nations also sent commissioners to the United States for the purpose of asking recognition.

The facts which I have already presented show that on March 8, 1822, when Mr. Monroe asked Congress to recognize the independence of the Spanish colonies in America, Mexico, the Central American States, New Granada, Venezuela, Buenos Ayres, Paraguay, Uruguay, and Chili had fully accomplished their independence, and in Ecuador and Peru independence was practically accomplished, as Bolivar's army was then fighting under General Sucre in Ecuador, and the Spanish Viceroy had evacuated Lima, on July 6, 1821, as a result of San Martin's manœuvres.

I do not blame the United States for not having made that recognition, because the recognition of independence is the acknowledgment of a fact which cannot be recognized before it has actually occurred. Any other conduct would have implied an alliance between the revolted colonies and the United States, and it would have been unreasonable for the colonies to expect this country to enter into any such alliance with them.

It would take a great deal more space than it is proper for me to occupy, were I to quote the many declarations of American statesmen expressing the attitude of the United States Government in this case and the reasons for the same, and I will, therefore, only quote one of Mr. John Quincy Adams, from a report which he made as Secretary of State to President Monroe, dated August 24, 1816, published in *Wharton's International Law Digest*, paragraph 70, Chapter III., page 521, Volume I., second edition:

" There is a stage in such revolutionary contests when the party struggling for independence has, as I conceive, a right to demand its acknowledgment by neutral parties, and when the acknowledgment may be granted without departure from the obligations of neutrality. It is the stage when the independence is established as matter of fact, so as to leave the chances of the opposite party to recover their dominion utterly desperate. The neutral nation must, of course, judge for itself when this period has arrived; and as the belligerent nation has the same right to judge for itself, it is very likely to judge differently from the neutral, and to make it a cause of pretext for war, as Great Britain did expressly against France in our Revolution, and substantially against Holland. If war thus results, in point of fact, from the measure of recognizing the contested independence, the moral right or wrong of the war depends upon the justice and sincerity and prudence with which the recognizing nation took the step. I am satisfied that the cause of the South Americans, so far as it consists in the assertion of independence against Spain, is just. But the justice of a cause, however it may enlist individual feelings in its favor, is not sufficient to justify third parties in siding with it. The fact and the right combined can alone authorize a neutral to acknowledge a new and disputed sovereignty."

The cause of independence awoke in the people of the United States a very deep sympathy, which was felt in the House of Representatives of the United States Congress, as I will soon state.

The correctness of this statement appears very clearly from the following extract from a letter addressed by Mr. Gallatin, United States Minister at Paris, to Mr. John Quincy Adams, Secretary of State, on November 5, 1818, and published in *Wharton's International Law Digest*, paragraph 70, Chapter III., page 522, Volume I., second edition:

" I had upon every occasion stated that the general opinion of the United States must irresistibly lead to such a recognition; that it is a question, not of interest, but of feeling, and that this arose much less from the wish of seeing new republics established, than that of the emancipation of Spanish-America from Europe. . . . We have not, either directly or indirectly, excited the insurrection. It had been the spontaneous act of the inhabitants, and the natural effect of causes, which neither the United States nor Europe could have controlled. We had lent no assistance to either party; we had preserved a strict neutrality. But no European government could be surprised or displeased that in such a cause our wishes should be in favor of the success of the colonies, or that we should treat as independent powers those amongst them which had in fact established their independence."

On January 2, 1819, President Monroe's Cabinet considered the question of the recognition of Buenos Ayres. The Cabinet was divided on the question, Mr. Calhoun being of opinion that this country should act in concurrence with Great Britain, Mr. Crawford that it should send a minister to Buenos Ayres, and Mr. Adams thinking that the Minister should come from Buenos Ayres seeking recognition.

In 1822, when independence had been achieved in Mexico, Central America, and almost in all the South American colonies, President Monroe decided that it was time for the United States to recognize that fact, and in a very able message, which he sent to Congress on March 8th, of that year, he recommended that such recognition be made, supporting his recommendation with reasons as solid as they were unanswerable. The Committee on Foreign Affairs of the House of

20

Representatives acted at once on that recommendation, and, on the 19th of the same month, Mr. Russell, of Massachusetts, on behalf of that committee, presented to the House a very able report, recommending that the House of Representatives concur in the opinion expressed by the President in the above-mentioned message, that "the late American provinces of Spain that have declared their independence and are in the enjoyment of it, ought to be recognized by the United States as independent nations," and that "the Committee on Ways and Means be instructed to report a bill appropriating a sum not exceeding one hundred thousand dollars, to enable the President to give due effect to such provision." The House approved these resolutions, and, the appropriation having passed Congress, the independence of the American nations was thus recognized by the United States.

After this statement of facts, it is not strange that Mr. Lyman in his book, *Diplomacy of the United States*, should have said: "These revolutionary struggles did not awaken any great interest in our citizens." "Our Government," he adds, "was left free and unembarrassed to pursue its steady course of good faith and exact neutrality toward Spain, and of justice and policy towards the colonies." He further says: "Neither the vicinity of some portions of their respective territories, nor the circumstance of being members of the same continent, nor the benefit to be derived from commercial relations, nor the similarity of their struggles for independence, appears in the least to have influenced the definite arrangements of this Government. On the contrary, the business was conducted with the utmost caution and circumspection, and nothing was done to give offence to Spain, or awaken in other nations the slightest suspicion of the loyalty with which this country was determined to adhere to its system of neutrality."

Mr. Lyman concludes by saying that the United States was the first country to recognize the independence of the Spanish-American colonies, but that the recognition was delayed until not a shadow of hope for the restoration of Spanish dominion remained.

Recognition of Belligerency by the United States.—Long before the United States Government recognized the independence of the revolted colonies, it had recognized their belligerency.[1]

[1] Although Senator Money does not refer particularly to the recognition of belligerency of the revolted Spanish colonies in America by the United States, he presents the results of the same as proving the material assistance of the United States Government to the colonies. Far from tending to lessen the importance of the recognition of belligerency I, on the contrary, recognize it, not only as an act of justice, but also as a favor. Although, generally speaking, the granting of what one considers to be a right, is not regarded as a favor, nevertheless it is one, when the third party can, in the exercise of its sovereignty, ignore the right, as it can do, when it is the only judge of its obligations and when there is no way to compel its recognition except by force, which was in this case, of course, altogether out of the question.

I have not been able to find the date of any declaration, if any was formally made, by which the United States recognized the belligerency of the revolted Spanish colonies. In Mr. Monroe's message of March 8, 1822, he said that they had enjoyed belligerent rights. He made the same statement in his annual messages of December 2, 1817, and December 7, 1819, as in the former he said "that the United States has maintained impartial neutrality between Spain and its provinces, our ports have been open to both, etc.," a statement which he corroborates in the latter in the following words: "An impartial neutrality has been followed in the civil war between Spain and the Spanish Provinces in America, . . . and our ports have continued to be equally open to both parties, etc."

I must here observe that several of the revolted Spanish colonies had from the beginning of the struggle armies which could compete with and which often defeated the best troops of the Spanish army that had fought in the Peninsula against Napoleon ; had issued constitutions and organized regular governments, had in some cases improvised a navy which defeated the Spanish naval forces, and had captured and held their respective capitals, and that they were really engaged in making a lawful war of independence against the mother-country.

But that recognition did not, of course, prevent the United States Government from enforcing its neutrality laws, as appears from a list, transmitted by the Secretary of State on January 10, 1817, of the individuals and vessels prosecuted during 1815 for violating the neutrality of the United States in the United Provinces of New Granada and the United Provinces of Mexico.

The United States Congress on Recognition.—As early as December 10, 1811, a resolution was reported by a committee of the House of Representatives of the United States Congress, on the recognition of the independence of the South American Provinces, which was not acted upon. Several others were afterwards introduced in the House of Representatives expressing sympathy with the insurrection of the American colonies.

On March 24, 1818, Henry Clay, who felt great sympathy for the struggling Spanish colonies, and sought to obtain their recognition through legislative action, proposed an appropriation of $18,000 for the outfit and one year's salary of a minister to be deputed from the United States to the independent provinces of the River Plata in South America. This motion led to a discussion as to whether the power of recognizing foreign governments resided in the Executive or in Congress. The majority of the House seemed to be in favor of the Executive, and the motion was defeated on May 28th, by a vote of 115 to 45.

Mr. Clay renewed his resolution, which was discussed by the House on May 10, 1820, asserting " that it was expedient to provide by law a suitable outfit for such minister or ministers as the President, by and with the advice and consent of the Senate, may send to any of the governments of South America which have established and are maintaining their independence of Spain," and this resolution was carried by a vote of 80 to 75. On February 9, 1821, Mr. Clay again moved his \$10,000 appropriation bill for a minister to any South American government "which has established and is maintaining its independence of Spain." This was lost by a vote of 86 to 79. On the following day he introduced a resolution expressing " the interest of the people of the United States, which was shared by the House of Representatives, in the success of the Spanish provinces of South America struggling to establish their liberty and independence, and offering its constitutional support to the President of the United States, whenever he may deem it expedient to recognize the sovereignty and independence of any of said provinces." The first clause of this resolution was carried by a vote of 134 to 12 and the second by a vote of 87 to 68. A committee of two members was appointed to lay these resolutions before the President, and Mr. Clay, one of those members, in his report of February 19th, said " that the President assured the committee that he felt a great interest in the success of the provinces of South America and that he would take the resolution into deliberate consideration with the most perfect respect for the distinguished body from which it had emanated."

On January 31, 1822, Mr. Trimble of Kentucky introduced a joint resolution stating that the " President was authorized and requested to acknowledge the independence of the Republics of Colombia, and that the Spanish provinces of South America that had established and were maintaining their independence of Spain ought to be acknowledged." Before this resolution was acted upon, Mr. Nelson of Virginia introduced another resolution asking the President to lay before the House the documents relating to the South American question, and in response to this resolution President Monroe sent to the House his message of March 8, 1822, already referred to, in which he stated that, in his opinion, the time had come to recognize the South American provinces as independent countries. Thereupon Mr. Russell, of Massachusetts, in behalf of the Committee on Foreign Affairs, introduced two resolutions, also just referred to, which were approved by the House, and thus constituted the recognition by the United States Government of the independent nations of America.

Commissioners Sent by the Revolted Colonies to the United States.—The leaders of the independent cause in Spanish-America sent Commissioners to the United States for the purpose of obtaining the recognition by this Government of their independence, and, if possible, material assistance.

While Hidalgo, the promoter of Mexican independence, was in Guadalajara, in December, 1810, he appointed as his official representative in this country Señor Don Pascasio Ortiz de Letona, who was captured on his way, and committed suicide to escape death on the scaffold.

Don Juan Vicente Bolivar and Don Telésforo Orca were furnished with credentials dated at Caracas April 25, 1810, and full powers to transact business. A copy of the Declaration of Independence of the Province of Venezuela, made by the Congress composed of deputies assembled in Caracas, was communicated by them to the United States Government, and transmitted to Congress on December 9, 1811. These agents were not allowed to have any official intercourse with the United States Government.

On December 11, 1818, Señor Don Lino Clemente informed the Secretary of State that he had been appointed Venezuela's representative "near the United States," and requested an interview; but he was informed that no conference could be held with him and no communication received from him by this Government. His letters were submitted to the House of Representatives with the President's message of January 29, 1819, accompanied by a report from Mr. John Quincy Adams, Secretary of State, giving the reasons in full for delaying recognition at that time.

Don Manuel H. de Aguirre came to this country in 1817 as a public agent from La Plata and a private one from Chili, and addressed several letters to the Secretary of State, in 1817 and 1818, soliciting the acknowledgment of the Province of Buenos Ayres, which were transmitted to the House of Representatives, March 25, 1818, with a report from Secretary Adams, of that date. No answers were given to his letters, although conferences were held with him, and the President declined to enter into any negotiations with Señor Aguirre, because the latter did not appear furnished with powers to negotiate, and because he thought that the independence of the provinces had not yet been established.

A short time after the declination of Aguirre's application, in May, 1818, David C. de Forrest renewed the consideration of the same claim, by soliciting this Government to admit him as a consul general. The President did not grant the permission, because he thought it was not clear that the provinces even claimed entire independence, Buenos Ayres having the intention at that time to offer special commercial favors to Spain as a consideration for the relinquishment of her claims to sovereignty.

But neither the commissioners sent by the United States to the American colonies of Spain, nor those sent by those colonies to the United States, influenced in any way the attitude of strict neutrality observed by the United States Government in the war for independence of the Spanish colonies in America.

Commissioners Sent by the United States to the Revolted Colonies.—Between 1810 and 1820 the President of the United States sent commissioners on three different occasions to South America, in order to obtain reliable and exact information regarding the real situation of affairs there.   The first mission was entrusted by Mr. Monroe, as Secretary of State, to Mr. Joel R. Poinsett, as agent to Buenos Ayres, and was dated June 26, 1810.   Mr. Alexander Scott was sent as agent to Venezuela, on May 12, 1812.   Mr. Poinsett's report on the condition of South America was dated November 4, 1818.

The second commission was sent by the President in 1817, and consisted of Mr. Theodoric Bland, Mr. Cæsar A. Rodney, and Mr. John Graham, who were instructed to examine into the conditions of Buenos Ayres and Chili.   The reports of Mr. Rodney and Mr. Graham, dated November 5, 1818, and Mr. Bland's report, dated November 2, 1818, were transmitted to Congress on November 17th of the same year.   Appended to the first two reports is a " Historical Sketch of the Revolution of the United Provinces of South America, from the 25th of May, 1810, until the opening of the National Congress on the 25th of March, 1816, written by Doctor Gregorio Funes, and appended to his History of Buenos Ayres, Paraguay, and Tucuman."

The third commission was entrusted to Mr. T. B Prevost and Mr. John M. Forbes, sent in 1820 as commercial agents to Chili and Buenos Ayres.   Their reports were transmitted to Congress, the one on March 8th, and the other on April 26, 1822.   It is remarkable that no commission was sent to Mexico.

The Spanish-American Republics and Cuba.—The example of the Spanish colonies in America which had revolted against the mother-country and accomplished their independence, could not but influence the Cubans in attempting to attain the same object.   Mr. Ballou, of Massachusetts, who in 1854 visited the island of Cuba, and who remained there for a long time, wrote a book on that subject, in which he says:

" When the Cubans saw that their brothers in the Spanish-American colonies had revolted against the mother-country, and that most of them had secured their independence, they thought of following in their footsteps, and in 1823 the disaffected party conspired against Spain, relying on the promise of Simon Bolivar of throwing an invading force into the island.   The conspiracy was discovered and suppressed prematurely.   In 1826 some Cuban agitators residing in Caracas attempted a new expedition, which failed, and caused the execution of Don Francisco de Puero y Velazco and Don Bernabé Sanchez."

As I have before stated, both San Martin and Bolivar were of opinion, after they had accomplished the independence of their respective countries, Argentine and Colombia, that their task was not yet ended, and that their republics were not safe as long as the enemy was in possession of the adjoining country, and they both took their armies to Peru, the last stronghold of the Spaniards in America. Iturbide followed the same course in Mexico towards the neighboring countries. On the 27th of September, 1821, he entered victoriously the City of Mexico, after having achieved his country's independence from Spain, and in December following he sent an army to Guatemala, the country adjoining Mexico on the southeast, to secure her independence. Guatemala, which, as I have stated, had been quiet under the Spanish rule during the eleven years the war of independence in Mexico lasted, on the 15th of September, 1821, when Iturbide's success was a foregone conclusion, proclaimed her independence from Spain, which she achieved without any struggle, as there was only a small Spanish force in the country. Iturbide, however, wishing to assure the independence of Guatemala, which had already proclaimed her annexation to Mexico, sent there his army, under Colonel Filisola.

How well grounded were the fears of San Martin, Bolivar, and Iturbide is shown by the fact that in 1829 the Spanish Government sent to Mexico an armed expedition from Havana, under General Barradas, which landed at the port of Tampico, for the purpose of again subduing the colony of New Spain, as Mexico was formerly called. But the cause of independence had gained such a foothold that it was easy for us to defeat that expedition.

After Bolivar had accomplished in 1824 the independence of the northern half of South America, he still thought that his task was not ended until the Spanish were driven from Cuba and Porto Rico, as the possession by them of those controlling islands—especially the former —would give Spain an important foothold on this continent, from which she could at any time attack her revolted colonies. This danger was of more serious import to Mexico, on account of the proximity of Cuba to that country, and the Governments of both Mexico and Colombia contemplated a plan of military operations for the purpose of accomplishing the independence of the island of Cuba assisting the natives who desired independence. This step was in accordance with the course followed by Argentina, Colombia, and Mexico previous to the accomplishment of their independence.[1]

[1] Senator Money states that " there is no evidence that the inhabitants of Cuba had invited the invasion of Colombia and Mexico, nor that they desired to throw off the Spanish yoke ; that there was no outbreak there contemporaneous with the uprising in the other colonies in the hour of Spain's calamity and confusion at home, and that, in fact, the Spanish crown, in grateful acknowledgment of the loyalty of the Cubans in these years of general rebellion, designated her " The Ever Faithful Isle." It is an historical fact that the leaders of the independent movement in Cuba applied both to Bolivar and to Mexico for assistance to accomplish their independence, and it is an historical fact also that they conspired to declare their independence, but that their

It would be idle to speculate about the probable result of a combined Mexican-Colombian expedition against Cuba. Although Spain had then been conquered on land, she was, of course, stronger on sea than were some of her former colonies, as some of them had not a regular navy, and this would have been a great advantage to her if a naval war had been contemplated by Mexico and Colombia; but such was not the case. It was intended to collect a large land force, send it from a convenient point on the mainland to Cuba, and land it there, the assistance of the natives being, of course, counted upon in the fight for independence. The landing of such a force would probably have been an easy task.[1]

When the Government of the United States learned of the proposed plan of the Mexican and Colombian Governments for the liberation of Cuba, Mr. Clay, Secretary of State of the United States, wrote to the Mexican and Colombian Ministers at Washington, on December 20, 1825, requesting that their respective Governments should suspend any expedition that they might be preparing against the islands of Cuba and Porto Rico, on the ground that the United States could under no circumstances permit them to fall under the sovereignty of England, that they could not be indifferent to the islands passing into the possession of France, and that, therefore, the only solution of the question was to leave the islands in possession of Spain.[2]

work was discovered and their leaders shot, as stated by Mr. Ballou in the passage that I have just quoted.

[1] Senator Money says, regarding the naval forces of Mexico and Colombia, " It was not believed that Colombia or Mexico, separately or jointly, without navies and without resources, would be able to hold the island against the adverse contention of either France or Great Britain." To be sure the navies of Mexico and Colombia could not compete, either separately or jointly, against that of England or of France, but neither Mexico nor Colombia contemplated being drawn into a maritime war with those countries about Cuba. Had they been notified by England or France that such would be the result, they would have given up that expedition, as they did on the notification of the United States. Mexico and Colombia thought that they had the necessary navy and army armaments to invade Cuba and hold it, and the navy necessary to carry their troops.

[2] Senator Money expressed the opinion that the interposition of the United States in the case of Cuba was " really of the most vital service to Mexico and the other Republics, as it made Spain feel the necessity of terminating the war with the colonies already gone from her, in order to secure Cuba and Porto Rico that remained to her." As a matter of fact, Spain, far from changing her attitude of hostility towards Mexico after Mexico had, in 1826, given up her expedition to Cuba, sent in 1829 an armed expedition against Mexico, under General Barradas for the purpose of reconquering that country, which landed at Tampico as I have already stated.

Senator Money understood that in my remarks I considered Mr. Clay's action in this case unfriendly towards Mexico. He certainly misunderstood me, as far from expressing that opinion, on the contrary, I sincerely believe that Mr. Clay was a great friend of the Spanish-American Republics. The object of my paper was to mention a fact, without commenting on it in any manner whatsoever.

A copy of this communication was sent by Mr. Clay to Mr. Everett, United States Minister at Madrid, with a despatch dated at Washington, April 3, 1826, from which I have taken this information. In that despatch Mr. Clay stated that the United States Government thought that England was at the bottom of the scheme to liberate Cuba, and that, if Cuba were once independent from Spain, she would finally become an English colony or a State under French protection.[1]

I have not read the letter addressed by Mr. Clay to the Mexican Minister at Washington, nor could I, if it were in my possession, make use of it in this paper, without the consent of the Mexican Government. But although the only official document I have seen is Mr. Clay's letter to Mr. Everett, I have no doubt that Mr. Clay had other reasons besides those stated in that letter for the request made by him to the Mexican and Colombian Governments, but what those reasons were must remain a matter of surmise. In my opinion, one of them was that the United States Government believed that if Cuba were once independent, or were annexed to Mexico or Colombia, slavery would be abolished in that island, a step which would have been in conflict with the policy of the United States, then governed by the slave power, and which, therefore, naturally supported slavery. The question of slavery was then at the bottom of every important move in the United States, foreign and domestic, and it colored or discolored all her important transactions.[2] Perhaps the idea of acquiring, at some future time, the island of Cuba was another reason which dictated Mr. Clay's action.

[1] The following is a translation into English of the Spanish translation of Mr. Clay's letter to Mr. Everett, published in March, 1897, by *El Monitor*, of the City of Mexico. It being a re-translation, of course it cannot have the identical wording of the original :

" WASHINGTON, April 13, 1826.

" I addressed on the 20th of December last a note to the Ministers of Colombia and Mexico, copy whereof I enclose, for the purpose of inducing their respective governments to suspend any expedition which they might be preparing either individually or collectively against the Islands of Cuba and Porto Rico.

" Great Britain is firmly convinced that the United States will never consent that those islands should belong to England, no matter what might be the consequences of such policy. France is also aware that we would not be indifferent to her obtaining the possession of said islands.

" This situation of the great maritime powers (the United States, Great Britain, and France), is nearly equivalent to an absolute guarantee of the possession of those islands in favor of Spain, but it is impossible to enter into any agreement by treaty, guaranteeing such possession, and the President wishes you should let the Spanish government know that we cannot bind ourselves to any obligation whatever, looking to such guarantee. You must continue to decline any such proposition for that purpose, if any such is presented."

[2] Senator Money understood my remarks about Mr. Clay's reasons to recommend the governments of Mexico and Colombia not to carry out their intended expedition to liberate Cuba, as impeaching President John Quincy Adams and Mr. Clay of insincerity, which idea did not at all enter my mind. Both President John Quincy Adams and Mr.

In fact, the United States Government could not have acted in any other manner than it did in this case, for the simple reason that it had committed itself to follow that course. This fact appears very clearly in the following extract from a note by Mr. Richard Henry Dana, to paragraph 68, page 106, Chapter II. of Part II., of *Wheaton's Elements of International Law*, Boston edition of 1866, which shows at the same time that the people of Cuba, far from being entirely satisfied with the Spanish rule, desired their emancipation from the mother-country, at the time when the other American colonies of Spain had either already accomplished their independence or were fighting for it:

" The people of Cuba, already divided between the parties of the King and the Cortes, and terrified by symptoms of slave insurrections, had among them large numbers who, dissatisfied with Spanish rule, looked to other powers for protection—some to Great Britain, but far the larger part to the United States. About September, 1822, the latter party sent a secret agent to confer with President Monroe. They declared that if the United States Government would promise them protection, and ultimate admission into the Union, a revolution would be made to throw off the Spanish authority, of the success of which they had no doubt. While this proposition was before Mr. Monroe's Cabinet, he received an unofficial and circuitous communication from the French Minister, asserting that his Government had positive information of the design of Great Britain to take possession of Cuba. The American Government replied to the Cuban deputation that the friendly relations of the United States with Spain did not permit us to promise countenance or protection to insurrectional movements, and advised the people of Cuba to adhere to their Spanish allegiance; at the same time informing them that an attempt upon Cuba by either Great Britain or France would place the relations of Cuba with the United States in a very different position. Mr. Rush was instructed to inform Mr. Canning that the United States could not see with indifference the possession of Cuba by any European power other than Spain, and to inform him of the rumors that had reached the Cabinet. Mr. Canning disavowed emphatically all intention on the part of Great Britain to take possession of Cuba, but avowed her determination not to see with indifference its occupation by either France or the United States, and proposed an understanding between the British, French, and American Governments, without any formal convention, that Cuba should be left in the quiet possession of Spain. This was assented to by Mr. Monroe; but he had no communication with France on the subject, leaving that to the management of Great Britain."

Clay may have had many other reasons to take that course, but the only ones expressed in an official communication are those that I mentioned, and I ventured to add others which I thought might have been in their minds, although I only presented them as a surmise on my part, without vouching for their correctness. Senator Money mentions in support of his assertion that slavery had no connection with this case, and the fact that President John Quincy Adams was an anti-slavery man, which is quite correct ; but Mr. Clay was a Southern man, and President Adams's administration was the result of a compromise which precluded his supporting a policy affecting so directly the slavery question in the United States, then the leading one in this country. Senator Money asserts that Mr. Clay avowed other reasons besides those stated in his letter to Mr. Everett, but I have been unable to find any statement of such reasons in an official document.

The fact that the slavery question had some influence in this case, notwithstanding that President John Quincy Adams was an anti-slavery man, appears also stated in the following extract from a note of Mr. Dana's on the Monroe Doctrine appended to *Wheaton's Elements of International Law*, above quoted, paragraph 68, page 111, Chapter II., Part II.:

> "The slave-holding interest was clearly looking to Cuba, not only as an addition to its political power in the Union, but to prevent abolition of slavery there by some other power; and it is known that Mr. Adams had a noticeable leaning in favor of its importance to us in a military and commercial view."

The question of the independence of Cuba was considered in the American Congress which met at Panama in 1826, and the idea of sending an armed expedition to liberate that island was abandoned on account of the opposition of the Government of the United States, as appeared from a communication from Mr. Poinsett, United States Minister to Mexico, to Mr. Clay, Secretary of State, dated September 23, 1826,[1] the United States Government recognized that the request made to the Mexican and Colombian Governments resulted in the abandonment of the expedition, will be seen from the following extracts from a communication addressed by Mr. Clay to Baron de Maltitz, Russian *Chargé d'Affaires* in Washington, on December 23, 1826, which shows also that up to that date the United States Government discountenanced any attempt to wrest from Spain the islands of Cuba and Porto Rico:

> "The wishes of the United States in regard to Cuba and Porto Rico remain unchanged. They desire no disturbance of the possessions of Spain, believing it most compatible with the interests and harmony of all the great powers. They would see any such disturbance, at the instance and by the arms of any power, with great regret. The new States have hitherto forborne, and that principally in deference to the declared desire of the United States and Russia, to attack those islands. Whilst, on the other hand, Spain, instead of listening to the counsels of peace and moderation which the hopelessness of the war alone ought to have inspired, has sent forth from the port of Havana a formidable fleet for the manifest purpose of invasion, or other hostile operations, against the territories of some of the new States. It was dispersed and disabled in a storm; but neither the frowns of Providence, the distractions at home, nor the disasters which await her in a further prosecution of the war, appear yet to have awakened that unfortunate monarchy to a sense of the absolute necessity of terminating the existing hostilities.
> "Although the Government of the United States is extremely unwilling to see any attempt made, from any quarter, to wrest from Spain the possession of those islands, and may yet continue their exertions to prevent it, the undersigned is constrained in frankness to repeat what has already been communicated to the Government of Russia, that if Spain shall still unnecessarily prolong the war and drive the new States to the necessity of conquering peace in Cuba and Porto Rico, the Government

---

[1] *American State Papers*, Series of Foreign Relations, vol. vi., p. 361.

of the United States could not justly interpose unless a character should be given to the war of the invasion, which would render it, in reference to their own duties and interests improper that they should remain neutral spectators."

The Monroe Doctrine.[1]—President Monroe's famous message of December 2, 1823, in which he announced the American continental policy bearing his name, was, of course, issued almost two years after he had recognized, in his message of March 8, 1822, the independence of the American colonies of Spain. But that recognition was then only theoretical, as the United States neither sent to nor received from those countries any representative until some years later.

In that year, 1823, two specific dangers threatened the Western

[1] I cannot be expected in this paper more than merely to mention the Monroe Doctrine, its scope and objects, and the way in which it originated. There is perhaps no other American question upon which there has been so wide a difference of opinion as the interpretation of the Monroe Doctrine. Some American statesmen have restricted it very materially, while others have given to it a very large extent. But the fact remains that Congress has not sanctioned it by any legislative act, unless such a character be given to the act passed on December 21, 1895, making an appropriation for a commission to examine and report on the boundary between Venezuela and British Guiana. The policy of the different administrations has also varied very materially, in so far as the application of that doctrine is concerned. In the case of the seizure of Corinto, by British men-of-war, in March, 1895, as a preliminary step to coerce Nicaragua to pay an indemnity of $75,000 to Mr. Hatch, British Consular agent at Bluefields, for his imprisonment, the Monroe Doctrine was interpreted in a restricted way. while in the case of the boundary dispute between England, on behalf of British Guiana and Venezuela, the application given to it by President Cleveland was very wide. If later I shall have the time and opportunity to do so, I may undertake to make a review of the Monroe Doctrine and its applications, for the benefit of the Spanish-American readers, who are not entirely familiar with the same and somewhat bewildered at the widely different views prevailing here on that subject.

Senator Money misunderstood my remarks about the Monroe doctrine, as he thought that I said that it was of no material advantage to the new Republics, and did not give them any moral support. My remarks about the Monroe doctrine were only elementary, and were intended specially to make plain to the American Republics, its meaning and scope where in some cases it is misunderstood, being construed into a policy which has for its object the final absorption by the United States of all the American Republics. If the paragraph of my paper referring to this point is carefully read, it will be seen that my assertion to the effect that the recognition by the United States of the independence of the Spanish colonies in America was only theoretical, because it was not followed immediately by the appointment of official representatives from the United States to the new nations, referred to Mr. Monroe's message of March 8, 1822, in which he announced such recognition, and not to his message of December 2, 1823. All his remarks which bear on the subject of the Monroe doctrine are, therefore, irrelevant. I am perfectly aware of the importance and transcendency that the policy enunciated by President Monroe in his last-named Message, generally called the Monroe Doctrine, had on the fate of the American nations, and I certainly do not try to belittle or depreciate it in any manner whatever.

Hemisphere.   The northwest boundary between the Uinted States and Canada had not then been determined, and the territory in dispute had not been occupied or even fully explored.   Russia, by formal proclamation in 1821, had set up a claim to territory along the Pacific coast as far south as the fifty-first parallel, and had given unmistakable signs of her intention to plant a Russian colony within the disputed territory.   The movement was alarming to Great Britain as well as to the United States.

The other cause of alarm was that the Metternich-Bourbon reaction had set in, and there was good reason to fear that an attempt was about to be made to resubjugate the Spanish-American colonies.   This fear found ample justification in the attitude of the "holy alliance," formed immediately after the downfall of Napoleon, by Russia, Austria, Prussia, and France, for the avowed object of protecting the Catholic religion and the Divine Right of Kings.   This Alliance was offered for signature to all the monarchs of Europe except the Pope and the Sultan.   Of all the powers, Great Britain alone declined to join in the Alliance, but under the leadership of Metternich this combination proceeded with its reactionary work.[1]   In 1821 it sent an Austrian army into Italy to prevent the adoption of a constitution at Naples, and two years later it threw a French army into Spain to suppress a popular movement in behalf of the free constitution of 1812 and to reinstate the Bourbon dynasty.   Having thus put under its heel all opposition in Europe, the Alliance proposed a congress to consider the subjugation of the revolted Spanish colonies in America, and the re-establishment of Spanish authority in the Western Hemisphere.   Before matters were far advanced, the design became known to Great Britain, and word concerning it was at once sent by the British Minister to the Government of the United States.   President Monroe immediately consulted Jefferson and Madison, as well as his Cabinet, of whom John Quincy Adams and Calhoun were the most prominent members.   All agreed that the matter was of such momentous interest as to justify a

[1] I think it is an historical fact that Mr. George Canning, the Prime Minister of England in 1823, suggested to the United States a policy which culminated in the Monroe Doctrine, in the shape of an understanding between Great Britain and the United States to prevent the interference of the holy alliance on the part of the Spanish colonies of America.   It may be interesting, therefore, to know what Mr. Canning said in a letter which the papers assure has just come to light, and which is as follows :

"The great danger of the time—a danger which the policy of the European system would have fostered—was a division of the world into European and American, republican and monarchial : a league of worn out governments on the one hand and youthful and stirring nations, with the United States at their head, on the other.   We slip in between and plant ourselves in Mexico.   The United States have gotten the start of us in vain, and we link once more America to Europe.   Six months more and the mischief would have been done."

formal remonstrance. John Quincy Adams, the Secretary of State, wrote a declaration of policy relating to colonization, and Jefferson a similar declaration in regard to interference. These two were tacked together by President Monroe and embodied in his Message, which can be summarized in the following four propositions:

1. That the United States would not tolerate further colonization in the American continent by European powers.

2. That they would not permit the subjugation or subversion of any American Government by the Governments of Europe.

3. That they would not allow the extension to America of the monarchial system of the " holy alliance."

4. That the United States had not interfered and would not interfere with any of the existing colonies or dependencies of any European power on this continent.

I take from the note of Mr. Richard Henry Dana on the Monroe Doctrine, contained in the eighth edition, Boston, 1866, of *Elements of International Law*, by Henry Wheaton, paragraph 67, Part II., Chapter I., page 97, the following passages, which explain the object and scope of the Monroe Doctrine, supported by the ample authority further stated in detail in that note.

As a summary of this subject it would seem that the following positions may be safely taken :

" I. The declarations upon which Mr. Monroe consulted Mr. Jefferson and his own Cabinet related to the interposition of European powers in the affairs of American States.

" II. The kind of interposition declared against was that which may be made for the purpose of controlling their political affairs, or of extending to this hemisphere the system in operation upon the continent of Europe, by which the great powers exercise a control over the affairs of other European States.

" III. The declarations do not intimate any course of conduct to be pursued in case of such interpositions, but merely say that they would be ' considered as dangerous to our peace and safety,' and as ' the manifestation of an unfriendly disposition toward the United States,' which it would be impossible for us to ' behold with indifference ' ; thus leaving the nation to act at all times as its opinion of its policy or duty might require.

" IV. The declarations are only the opinion of the administration of 1823, and have acquired no legal force or sanction.

" V. The United States has never made any alliance with or pledge to any other American State on the subject covered by the declarations.

" VI. The declaration respecting non-colonization was on a subject distinct from European intervention with American States, and related to the acquisition of sovereign title by any European power, by new and original occupation or colonization thereafter. Whatever were the political motives for resisting such colonization, the principle of public law upon which it was placed was, that the continent must be considered as already within the occupation and jurisdiction of independent civilized nations."

Daniel Webster had still a more narrow view of the object and scope of the Monroe Doctrine, as appears from the following extract from a speech he delivered in the House of Representatives, on March 27, 1826:

" The amount of it (Mr. Monroe's declaration) was that this Government could not look with indifference on any combination to assist Spain in her war against the South American States; that we could not but consider any such combination as dangerous or unfriendly to us; and that if it should be formed it would be for the competent authorities of this Government to decide, when the case arose, what course our duty and our interest should require us to pursue."

The Panama Congress.—When Simon Bolivar proposed the assembling at Panama of a congress of the American nations to agree upon some continental policy, President John Quincy Adams laid before Congress, in his annual message of 1826, the question of the representation of the United States at that Congress. The coalition against the Adams Administration, which ultimately became the Jacksonian party, made its first great fight on this measure. It called forth long debates and aroused great excitement in the House of Representatives, because it was not an ordinary mission, and seemed to have far greater importance than any question of foreign relations that had previously come under discussion. It was believed to be an attempt to make a confederation or league of all the American countries, and thus to a certain extent to extinguish the individuality of the United States.

This discussion lasted from February 3 to April 21, 1826, when the Committee on Foreign Affairs reported a resolution declaring that it was expedient to appropriate the necessary funds to send representatives to the Panama Congress. This resolution was approved by a vote of 143 to 54, and passed the Senate by a vote of 24 to 19.

The United States delegates to the Panama Congress were instructed to attend the Congress merely in a diplomatic character, without discussing or accepting any proposition of alliance binding the United States. These restrictions had been embodied in an amendment presented both in the House and Senate, which had passed the House, but was finally rejected, because it was considered an infringement upon the prerogatives of the Executive. As it expressed the views of Congress, however, its provisions were embodied in the instructions to the Commissioners.

I understand that one of the objects of that Congress was to accomplish the independence of the island of Cuba, but the idea did not meet with the approval of the United States, and that fact prevented the Panama Congress from arriving at any practical result.

Mr. Buchanan, a Member of Congress from Pennsylvania, and afterwards President of the United States, introduced in 1826 a resolution which passed the House of Representatives by a vote of 99 to 95, and which reads as follows (see Wharton, *International Law Digest*, Volume I., Chapter III., paragraph 57, page 282):

"It is, therefore, the opinion of this House that the Government of the United States ought not to be represented at the Congress of Panama, except in a diplomatic character; nor ought they to form any alliance, offensive or defensive, or negotiate respecting such alliance, with all or any of the South American Republics; nor ought they to become parties with them, or either of them, to any joint declaration for the purpose of preventing the interference of any of the European powers with their independence or form of government, or to any compact for the purpose of preventing colonization upon the continents of America; but that the people of the United States should be left free to act, in any crisis, in such manner as their feelings of friendship towards these Republics, and as their own honor and policy, may at the time dictate."

It is interesting to quote here what Mr. J. C. B. Davis says in his *Notes on Treaties of the United States*, in regard to the Panama Congress, and which appears in Wharton's *International Law Digest*, Vol. I., Chapter II., paragraph 57, page 279.

"The Congress of Panama in 1826 was planned by Bolivar to secure the union of Spanish America against Spain. It had originally military as well as political purposes. In the military objects the United States could take no part; and indeed the necessity for such objects ceased when the full effects of Mr. Monroe's declarations were felt. But the specific objects of the Congress, the establishment of close and cordial relations of amity, the creation of commercial intercourse, of interchange of political thought and of habits of good understanding between the new republics and the United States and their respective citizens, might perhaps have been attained had the Administration of that day received the united support of the country. Unhappily they were lost; the new States were removed from the sympathetic and protecting influence of our example, and their commerce, which we might then have secured, passed into other hands unfriendly to the United States.

"In looking back upon the Panama Congress from this length of time it is easy to understand why the earnest and patriotic men who endeavored to crystallize an American system for this continent failed. . . . One of the questions proposed for discussion in the conference was ' The consideration of the means to be adopted for the entire abolition of the African slave trade,' to which proposition the Committee of the United States Senate of that day replied : ' The United States have not certainly the right, and ought never to feel the inclination, to dictate to others who may differ from them upon this subject ; nor do the Committee see the expediency of insulting other States with whom we are maintaining relations of perfect amity, by ascending the moral chair, and proclaiming from thence mere abstract principles, of the rectitude of which each nation enjoys the perfect right of deciding for itself.' The same Committee also alluded to the possibility that the conditions of the islands of Cuba and Porto Rico, still the possessions of Spain, and still slave-holding, might be made the subject of discussion and of contemplated action by the Panama Congress. ' If ever the United States' (they said) ' permit themselves to be associated with these nations in any general congress assembled for the discussion of common plans in any way affecting European interests, they will, by such act, not only deprive themselves of the ability they now possess of rendering useful assistance to the other American States, but also produce other effects prejudicial to their interests.'

"The printed correspondence respecting this mission will be found in the fifth volume of the *Foreign Relations*, folio edition, pages 834–905. It was the subject of animated discussion in Congress, which will be found in the second part of the second volume of the *Register of Congressional Debates for the Year 1826*."

Conclusion.—Circumstances have made this paper much longer than I expected, but it was necessary to speak of several subjects, all of which were closely connected with the independence of Mexico and the other Spanish colonies in America.

I hope that this statement of facts will serve to show that the Spanish colonies in America achieved their independence by their own efforts and without the aid of any foreign nation, and that if some of them expected such aid from England they never got it, and they had to rely upon the native element. I trust, also, that it will dispel some errors prevailing on that subject.

The Government of the United States maintained during the War of Independence a strict neutrality, although the recognition of belligerency of the revolted colonies was a decided advantage to them. But the people of the United States heartily sympathized with them, and in some cases personally assisted the cause of independence.

PART II.

PHILOSOPHY OF THE MEXICAN REVOLUTIONS.

II. PHILOSOPHY OF THE MEXICAN REVOLUTIONS.

It is always difficult for the outside world to understand fully, and to form a correct opinion in regard to the real condition of things existing in a country, especially so when that country is in an abnormal state, that is, when it is passing through a period of serious disturbances. This is particularly difficult in the case of Mexico, whose peculiar conditions make it so different from all other countries, that even educated Mexicans cannot always clearly understand the real situation of affairs in their country, unless they have made a special study of such matters. In this way I account for the general impression prevailing in the outside world that because Mexico has been disturbed by a long series of civil wars, which lasted for over half a century, we were constitutionally disposed to fight, and did so without any plausible cause or reason; but such a view is a very mistaken one, and the following remarks will, I hope, explain the philosophy of our civil wars.

In the first edition of this paper I passed very briefly on the war of independence in Mexico, because I intended to write an article as short as possible without sacrificing the end in view ; but, having been obliged to enter into some details of the war of independence of the South American Republics, I thought I could not afford to say less about the same war in Mexico. In the paper entitled "Genesis of Mexican Independence" I dealt at length on the war of independence in Mexico, and to avoid repetitions I will omit here the incidents and views there expressed.

To treat this subject methodically, I will divide this paper into three parts: the first embracing the war of independence, from 1810 to 1821, the second the revolutionary period from 1821 to 1855, and the third the war of reform and French intervention from 1856 to the present time.

WAR OF INDEPENDENCE.

During the Spanish rule in Mexico, which lasted exactly three centuries, from 1521 to 1821, there were three controlling privileged classes, the people counting for absolutely nothing. The first was the clergy, who, by obtaining bequests from persons who were about to die, and in various other ways had accumulated very large fortunes, owning directly or through mortgages over two thirds of the whole real estate of the country, and so absorbed the principal financial business. Their power was based not only upon their immense wealth, but also upon the religious influence which they exercised, and on the fact of their being the only educated class, for although they knew but little, they knew a great deal more than the other classes did, who were kept in ignorance. Their thorough discipline assisted the clergy very materially in wielding great influence. They were so powerful during the Spanish rule that a Viceroy once attempted to enforce his authority over a recalcitrant archbishop of the City of Mexico by arresting him and sending him to Spain. The Viceroy succeeded in making the arrest, but when it became known that the archbishop was on his way to Veracruz, so violent was the excitement of the people that he was speedily brought back to the City of Mexico, and the Viceroy was obliged to leave the country.

The Spanish Colonial Government of Mexico was an autotheocratic one, the civil and ecclesiastical administrations being as closely united as it was possible for them to be. Among the long list of Spanish Viceroys who ruled Mexico during the three hundred years of the colonial period, ten out of sixty-two, or over seventeen per cent.,[1] were archbishops of Mexico, the highest ecclesiastical dignitaries in the colony; and the archbishop was, in fact, the ex-officio Viceroy, as whenever a Viceroy died, or was removed and left the country before his successor arrived, generally the archbishop took his place.

The second privileged class were the Spaniards by birth, who formed a kind of aristocracy, a few of them having titles; and being the only one holding offices of trust, responsibility, or emolument in the country, and monopolizing the principal commercial business, they were also a wealthy class. They were so jealous of the native Mexicans that even the children of Spaniards born in Mexico of a Mexican mother were not considered on the same footing as the Spaniards; they were called creoles, had no rights whatever, and could not fill any public office or hold any position of importance. But few Spanish women ever went to Mexico. The men generally went there while very young, grew up in the country, and married Mexican women, occasionally pure-blooded Indians, but generally the daughters of Spaniards by Mexican mothers born in Mexico. From these unions came the creoles.

The third class was the army, which was comparatively small, but

[1] A nominal list of Viceroys in Mexico during the colonial period, stating the time that they remained in office, will be found at the end of this paper.

was a very important element in the country. Native Mexicans usually held very subordinate positions, only in a few cases being admitted among the commissioned officers.

These three classes were, of course, devotedly attached to the Spanish rule, because under it they prospered and had all the wealth and power they could possibly desire, while any change would only endanger their position and welfare. The higher clergy were, of course, heartily loyal to Spain, while a few members of the lower clergy, Mexicans by birth—the Church being almost the only career open to the natives—having on the other hand some patriotic feeling, were the only ones who could appreciate the condition of things, and longed for a change.

However much may be said against the Spanish colonial rule in Mexico, it must be borne in mind that it was only a necessary consequence of the ideas and conditions of things prevailing at that time, and although it was selfish and greedy, the Spaniards did nothing more than it was thought proper at the time to do; and it cannot be denied that the Madrid Government had a kindly feeling towards the natives, which was, however, not always shared by the authorities, and that, notwithstanding all the sufferings and degradation to which they were subjected they were not exterminated, as was the unhappy fate of those living in the northern part of the New World, settled by the Anglo-Saxon race.

Spain gave Mexico all she had—her religion, her language, her laws, her civilization, her genius; and not for the exclusive benefit of her subjects of Spanish descent; the conquered race also shared these advantages, and produced many men of note as lawyers, priests, mathematicians, astronomers, literary men and artists. The centralization of power and the common language began the work of assimilation, which although far from being wholly accomplished, yet had its beginning during the time of the Spanish conquest.

Opposition of Privileged Classes to Independence.—The opposition of the clergy to independence from Spain, and the alarm with which they viewed the movement in that direction were so great that its leaders were excommunicated by all the bishops of the country the moment the insurrection broke out. The Inquisition commenced proceedings against them, and several members of the higher clergy took up arms against the cause of independence. The Bishop of Oaxaca, forgetting the teachings of the founder of his religion, organized his clergy into a regiment to fight against the insurgents; but the martial prelate had no occasion to come into conflict with them, for he fled from the city, when Morelos approached it in 1812.

Something similar happened in Colombia, where the Bishop of Popayan, Jimenez de Padilla, incited the natives in favor of the

Spaniards by his preaching and fought the patriots with his sword, until the royalists capitulated to Bolivar, on June 8, 1822, after eleven years of hard fighting, for which it has been called the Colombian Vendée, comparing it with the resistance that the French Revolutionists met in that province.

The higher Catholic clergy in Peru took the same attitude. In Argentina a capitulation was signed, on February 20, 1813, by General Belgrano, commanding the Argentine troops, with General Tristan, commander of the Spanish army, by which the latter bound himself under oath not to take up arms during the war against the Argentine Government within the limits of the Viceroyalty of La Plata, and the Archbishop of Charcas in Argentina, and the Bishop of La Paz in Upper Peru, released the Spanish officer from his oath, under the plea that God did not consider binding treaties made with insurgents.

The example of the United States, and even that of Spain—where the people rebelled against the Government established by Napoleon in 1808, under his brother, Joseph Bonaparte, notwithstanding that it had the sanction of King Ferdinand VII., who had abdicated in favor of the French Emperor—could not but affect the Spanish colonies in America, and most of them proclaimed their independence in 1810.

In the preceding paper on " The Genesis of Mexican Independence," I dwelt upon the causes of the same, and upon the remarkable coincidence that it was proclaimed almost simultaneously in all the American colonies of Spain, and I therefore do not say here any more upon the subject.

Proclamation of Independence.—Independence was proclaimed in Mexico on September 16, 1810, in Dolores, an Indian village in the State of Guanajuato, by Miguel Hidalgo y Costilla, the aged curate of the town, with the co-operation of Allende, Aldama, and Abasolo, three inferior officers of the Mexican militia, born in Mexico. His undertaking had from the beginning all the leading classes of Mexico arrayed against it. He collected a very large number of Indians and peasants, and two or three regiments of the militia followed his lead. To enlist public sympathy on his side, he had put his cause under the protection of the Virgin of Guadalupe, who was supposed to have miraculously appeared two hundred years before to an humble Indian, as the patroness of his race, near the City of Mexico, and who was greatly reverenced throughout the country. His men were disorganized, without arms or ammunition, and undisciplined, and although he captured the important towns of Celaya, Guanajuato, Valladolid, and Toluca, and under good military leadership might have accomplished a great deal more, availing himself of the popular enthusiasm for independence and of the surprise and discomfiture of the Spaniards, he did not know how to make use of those advantages.

While Hidalgo was a great enthusiast, he had no military talents and no disciplined army. His assistants, Allende, Aldama, and Abasolo, who were only captains in the Spanish militia, proposed to him a plan of operations, which, if adopted, might have been successful, but he refused to accept it, and followed his own ideas which culminated in his complete defeat.

He marched against the City of Mexico, and fought a battle on October 30, 1810, at Monte de las Cruces, within sight of the capital, and, although he was successful, he did not enter the city, but remained inactive for some days, thus giving the Viceroy time to concentrate his troops, and when those coming from San Luis Potosi were approaching under General Calleja, Hidalgo retreated to Queretaro, having been attacked and defeated at Aculco on November 7th. Hidalgo retreated to Valladolid, and from there to Guadalajara, where he arrived on November 26th, and established there a regular government. Calleja followed him, and Hidalgo came out to fight Calleja and met him at Puente de Calderon, and on January 17, 1811, a battle took place in which Hidalgo was completely defeated. His military lieutenant advised Hidalgo not to offer a pitched battle to the enemy, as his forces could not compete with the Spanish veterans, but he did not follow that advice and this was the cause of his defeat, as the organization and discipline of the Spanish army at last prevailed against his large but disorganized masses. Hidalgo finally was captured in Acatita de Bajan, on May 21, 1811, and after having been degraded by the Inquisition and the higher clergy, he was shot at the City of Chihuahua on the 31st of the following July.

While Hidalgo was in Guadalajara, in December, 1810, he sent to the United States as his official representative Señor Don Pascasio Ortiz de Latona, as stated in the paper entitled "Genesis of Mexican Independence."

Morelos's Leadership.—Hidalgo was succeeded by another priest, a full-blooded Indian, José Maria Morelos, who had in him the elements of a great warrior.

Morelos, like Hidalgo, was a parish priest in the State of Michoacan, whose capital, Valladolid, is now called Morelia in his honor. He received his commission from Hidalgo when he passed through that State, and Morelos marched with a few men to capture the port of Acapulco, failing in that attempt, because that port was well fortified, but he attacked and defeated the Spanish in several encounters, capturing the towns of Chilpancingo, Tixtla, Chilapa, in the present State of Guerrero, Chiautla and Izucar in the State of Puebla, and Taxco in the State of Mexico. In the City of Cuautla, in the present State of Morelos, he resisted with 3000 men the 12,000 that the Viceroy had sent against him, from February 19th to May 2, 1812, fighting almost every day, and making that siege one of the most famous in the history of Mexico. He finally broke the lines of the enemy, and retreated with the remainder of his army.[1]

Morelos captured the city of Orizaba on October 26, 1812, and defeated the Spanish army which was besieging the town of Huajuapan in the State of Oaxaca, and also the city of Tehuacan in the State of Puebla, and from there he marched against the city of Oaxaca, which he captured on November 25, 1812. From Oaxaca he marched to Acapulco, which city he captured on April 12, 1813, after which he laid siege to the strong castle of San Diego, capturing it on August 20th of the same year.

Morelos organized a regular government, and convened a Congress, which met at Chilpancingo, on September 14, 1812, the first Congress we ever had, which declared independence on the 6th of November following. The Congress had to change the place of its meetings according to the fortunes of war, and on October 22, 1814, they issued a provisional constitution and established an executive government of three members, electing for that purpose Morelos, Liceaga, and Cos.

Morelos's fortunes began to wane at the end of 1813. On December 24th of that year he attacked the city of Valladolid and was repulsed with very heavy losses; in the following year his lieutenants suffered several defeats, Matamoros was defeated and captured at Puruaran, on February 3, 1814, and Galeana was defeated and killed at Coyuca on May 1st of the same year, and Don Miguel Bravo was also captured and shot at Puebla. Congress decided to continue its sessions at Tehuacan, and Morelos marched to that place escorting its members, but was overtaken by the Spanish troops, and to save the *personnel* of Congress he offered battle under disadvantageous circumstances at Texmalaca, on November 5, 1815, where he was defeated, captured, and taken to the City of Mexico, and, after being degraded by the Inquisition and higher clergy, he was shot at the Indian town of Ecatepec, near the City of Mexico, on December 22d of that year.

Slavery in Mexico.—The views about slavery of the Mexican revolution and its leaders will be shown by stating that Hidalgo issued, on December 6, 1810, not three months after he had proclaimed independence from Spain, a decree abolishing slavery in Mexico, and that our first Congress, which met in Chilpancingo in 1813, adopted at Apatzingan, on October 22, 1814, a constitution and promulgated a decree abolishing slavery. That decree, of course, could only be enforced in the few places which were occupied by the insurgents; but when inde-

[1] Mr. Walter S. Logan spoke on the subject in an address before the *New York Historical Society*, delivered April 4, 1893, entitled " *Cuautla*," which I consider well worth reading.

pendence was achieved, one of the first acts of the first Mexican Congress, convened at the City of Mexico to adopt a Constitution, was to issue a decree, on July 13, 1824, which abolished slavery, and it was then actually abolished in the whole country. The fact that our present Constitution of 1857 repeats the prohibition of holding slaves in Mexico, a prohibition which has appeared in all of our Constitutions, has caused the common opinion prevailing in this country, that we only abolished slavery in 1857, a mistake which I have often had occasion to to rectify.[1] In fact, every Mexican is born a strong anti-slavery man, so much so that we could not understand why the United States should have accepted slavery, and should have tried to sustain and extend it even at the cost of a tremendous civil war which imperilled the very existence of this country, and the great influence that it has to exercise upon the destinies of mankind, more especially when the very Declaration of American Independence proclaims the principle that all men are born free and equal, and when slavery is a contradiction of that great principle. But, fortunately, slavery has been abolished here, as it was in Mexico over seventy years ago, and the stain, which for a time tarnished the fair name of this country, has thus been completely effaced.

Bravo's Magnanimity.—In speaking of General Bravo, it will not be amiss to mention an incident which shows the magnanimity of the Mexican character and the temper of the men who were engaged in our war of independence. General Bravo had been detached by Morelos to the Province of Veracruz, and he attacked at San Agustin del Palmar, in December, 1812, a regiment of Spanish soldiers which had just landed from Spain and was escorting a military train to the City of Mexico, and defeated them, capturing three hundred men. Under the rules of war prevailing there at the time, all prisoners of war were shot without any mercy or discrimination. The Spaniards began that barbarous system, and the Mexicans thought they ought to retaliate. Bravo did not shoot these men at once, and on the evening of the day on which he captured them, he received the information from Morelos that his father, who had taken a prominent part in the war of independence, had been captured by the Spaniards and shot at the city of Mexico, accompanied by positive orders from Morelos to shoot all his Spanish prisoners. Bravo was a generous man, and while feeling deeply the blow he had received in his father's death, he yet hesitated as to

---

[1] Senator Money, misunderstood the position of Mexico on the slavery question when he said in his article : "Great Britain, lashed by the eloquence of Wilberforce, paid for and manumitted her slaves in 1838. France followed a slow second in 1848, and Mexico did not emancipate her own, of which she had very few, until several years after the events here considered." As appears from this paper, slavery was abolished in Mexico since 1810, and its abolition was carried into effect in 1824.

what he should do, and, after a sleepless night, he decided not only to pardon his prisoners, but to set them at liberty unconditionally. Such an act of generosity can only be fully appreciated when we consider the temper of the times, and the excitement under which both parties labored during that terrible struggle. It may be added that most of the prisoners, deeply touched by this act of magnanimity, joined Bravo's forces.

Mina's Expedition.—On April 15, 1817, General Francisco Xavier Mina, a Spanish soldier who had fought gallantly in Spain against the French, of broad-minded and liberal views, and a lover of liberty, went to Mexico to fight for her independence, as Lafayette had done several years before in the United States, landing in Soto de la Marina with five hundred men, and leaving a small detachment to guard the place, marched to the interior, defeating the Spanish army that opposed him. The Viceroy had to organize a large army under General Liñan to fight Mina, who advanced as far into the interior as the city of Leon, and, after several encounters in which he showed great military talent, he was defeated and made a prisoner at Venadito on October 27, 1817, and shot on the 11th of November of the same year.

After the capture of General Mina the revolutionary war in Mexico was almost ended, and in 1818 only small bands of disorganized men remained in the field, Vicente Guerrero in the south, and Guadalupe Victoria in the east, being almost the only leaders who had a regular force under their command. Guerrero was a muleteer, who joined the cause of independence from the beginning, fought under Morelos, and finally established his base of operations in the southern part of Mexico, which, favored by topographical conditions and climate, being very mountainous and in some places unhealthy, did not allow the Spanish regular troops to make much headway. He held his own until 1821 when the cause of independence finally succeeded.

Independence Achieved.—Such was the condition of things when, in 1820, the Spaniards at Madrid restored the Liberal Constitution adopted by the Cortes in 1812, when King Ferdinand VII. had fled from Spain and the country was in possession of the French, and that fact greatly alarmed the conservative Spanish element in Mexico, who, fearing that liberal principles might find a foothold in the mother-country and extend thence to Mexico, thought the best course they could pursue would be to proclaim independence from Spain, and establish a Catholic monarchy under a Spanish king, so that they would not be subject to the obnoxious changes which liberal ideas, that had begun to permeate Spain, might bring about. They addressed themselves, therefore, to Iturbide, who, although a native Mexican, had been one of the most successful leaders of the Spanish army against the insurrection, was a good soldier and an ambitious man. Iturbide fell in with their views, and, when appointed by the Viceroy to command the army sent to subdue the southern revolutionary leaders, he took all the available forces and money which the Viceroy could spare and joined Guerrero and the other revolutionary leaders, proclaiming on February 24, 1821, a political platform called "Plan de Iguala," which was a compromise between the revolution and its opponents, as it accomplished independence, but under a thoroughly Catholic monarchy, with a Spanish prince on the throne, and forbidding the exercise of any other religion. All the other commanding officers of the Spanish army in other sections of the country soon accepted this platform, and, as a consequence, independence was accomplished almost without a blow.

An incoming Viceroy, Don Juan O'Donojú, accepted the Plan of Iguala, and signed at Cordova, on August 24th of the same year, a treaty with Iturbide by which he recognized in behalf of the Spanish Government the independence of Mexico on condition that an empire be established in Mexico, calling to the throne a member of the Spanish family in compliance with the Plan of Iguala.[1]

It is a remarkable coincidence that only a little over three months before the treaty of Cordova, General San Martin agreed with the Spanish Viceroy, La Serna, on some terms of settlement, almost identical to the basis of that treaty. The Liberal Cabinet, organized in Spain in 1820 after the restoration of the Constitution of 1812, had sent special Commissioners to the revolted colonies to offer them autonomy, on condition that they take the oath of allegiance to the King. Don Manuel Abreu was the Spanish Commissioner sent to Peru, and under his authority the Spanish Viceroy, La Serna, met General San Martin at Punchauca, north of Lima, on May 3, 1821. San Martin offered to accept peace under the following conditions: 1. Spain to recognize the independence of Peru; 2. to appoint a regency of three members, one by San Martin, another by the Spanish Viceroy, La Serna, and the third elected by the people; and, 3. to send to Madrid two commissioners to ask the Spanish royal family to send one of its members as King of Peru. These conditions were approved by General La Serna, subject to the approval of the civil councils of Peru, but his army having disapproved of them, they were not carried out.

[1] It was reported that King Ferdinand VII. had written a confidential letter in 1820 to Viceroy Apodaca, the ruler of Mexico at that time, informing him that he considered himself held in captivity by the Spanish Liberals, and that fearing to share the fate of Louis XVI. of France, he had decided to go to Mexico to use there freely his royal authority, and therefore requested him to keep New Spain free from the constitutional movement, so that he could go there as absolute King. Although some have considered this letter as apocryphal, Alaman published the text of it in his *History of Mexico*, Volume V., pages 61, 62, and perhaps this explains why, in the Plan of Iguala and the treaty of Cordova, Ferdinand VII. was offered the throne of Mexico.

This short statement of facts shows that the first movement for independence, notwithstanding its popularity, was an apparent failure, because it had not the support of the higher classes; but as soon as it became for the interest of the higher classes themselves that Mexico should be independent of the Spanish rule, their influence turned the scale, and independence was at once achieved.

The ease with which the Spanish Government was overthrown in Mexico by the defections of the Spanish army tended greatly to the subversion of military discipline, which was instrumental in subsequent military mutinies against the constituted authorities. One of the worst effects of a successful rebellion is that it sanctions the principle that brute force shall rule, and awakens the personal ambition of unscrupulous and successful soldiers. All that was necessary to overthrow a government was to induce the general-in-chief of the government forces to join the rebels, and this offered so tempting a bait for promotion and power that few could resist it. It brought about the complete demoralization of the old Mexican army, as will presently be seen, and the overthrow of the several regular constituted governments, to the very great detriment of the country.

REVOLUTIONARY PERIOD.

Iturbide's Ephemeral Empire.—Iturbide entered victorious the City of Mexico on September 27, 1821. A regency of three members was established, of which he was elected President. He convoked a National Congress on February 24, 1822, and the Spanish Cortes having declared, on February 13th of the same year, null and void the treaty of Cordova, Congress, under some military pressure, declared Iturbide Emperor by 67 votes against 15, on May 19, 1822, and on July 21st he was formally crowned at the Cathedral. But the Mexican patriots, who had been fighting for ten years in favor of independence, material progress, and liberal principles, could not be satisfied with the success of their former enemies and the establishment of an empire. They thought that this was depriving the country and themselves of the fruits of their victory, and so they combined against Iturbide, and having a majority in Congress, he had it dissolved. In their efforts to overthrow the empire, the liberals were joined, strange to say, by the ultraconservatives, who were either jealous, or disagreed with Iturbide because he did not go as far as they intended, and they joined in the conspiracy against him, and thus his overthrow was made easy.

On December 6, 1822, Don Antonio Lopez de Santa Ana, of whom I shall presently have occasion to speak more at length, headed a rebellion in Veracruz against Iturbide, proclaiming a republican form of government. Iturbide sent an army under General Echavarri, but this General joined Santa Ana on February 1, 1823, in a platform (which we call plan) against Iturbide, called the "Plan of Casa Mata," which was adopted in many other sections of the country. Iturbide then restored the Congress that he had dissolved, and sent his resignation as Emperor. On April 7th, Congress decreed that Iturbide had not been regularly declared Emperor, that his resignation could not therefore be accepted, and he was ordered out of the country and sailed for Leghorn, Italy, on May 11, 1823, on the English brig *Rawlins*.

Iturbide was later induced by his friends to return to Mexico in the supposition that he would find the people in his favor. He landed at Soto de la Marina on the 14th of July, 1824, and the Legislature of the State of Tamaulipas sentenced him to death, as he had previously been declared an outlaw by an act of Congress, and he was shot at Padilla on the 19th of the same month.

Establishment of a Republic.—After Iturbide's downfall a republican form of government was unavoidable. Congress appointed an Executive Power of three members, electing for that position Generals Victoria, Bravo, and Negrete.

About this time Masonic lodges were established in Mexico, the first being of the Scottish Rite, which was joined by most of the conservative element of the country, but, unfortunately, that lodge was turned into a political organization, and played a very prominent part in the public disturbances of that period. The Liberal party was divided into two wings: the extreme Liberals, or Federalists, who were in favor of a government fashioned on the model of that of the United States, the powers of the Federal Government being limited; and the moderate Liberals, or Centralists, who favored a centralized republic, with a stronger government. This wing of the Liberal party united itself with the Monarchists and the friends of the Bourbons, and they all joined the lodge of the Scottish Rite, and were called "Escoceses" in Spanish. The Liberals were the old patriots who had fought for independence from the beginning and they were assisted by Iturbide's friends who out of hostility to the existing government had joined them, in their turn, and to meet their opponents with similar weapons, organized a lodge of the York Rite, whose members were called "Yorkinos." For some years the names by which the political parties were known in Mexico were "Escoceses" and "Yorkinos," equivalent to Conservatives and Liberals. Mr. Poinsett, the first United States Minister sent to Mexico, was at the time accused of being the instigator of the establishment of the lodges; but it seems that while he desired the success of the Yorkinos, he was not the founder of that Lodge.

Federal Constitution of 1824.—A National Congress to organize the country was convoked and met on November 7, 1823, and it issued on

January 21, 1824, the primary bases of a Federal Constitution, and on October 4th of the same year the final Constitution was adopted and promulgated. It was modelled on the Constitution of the United States, and was almost a copy of it, and I do not know whether, in imitating so closely the Constitution of this country we did not make a mistake. (The Constitution of a nation should be adapted to the conditions of that country. Here in the northern section of the continent, there were at the end of the last century thirteen colonies independent of each other, which made war against England, achieved their independence, and then found themselves little more than a confederacy of infantile nations, with all the weaknesses which have ever attended a simple confederation. They therefore decided to consolidate themselves into a single nation, under the name of " The United States of America." The Federal system of government was the only solution of the problems which then confronted the people of this country. It was the natural and inevitable outgrowth of the condition of things existing before the adoption of the Constitution. In Mexico there was a united country, subject to the same authorities and laws, and with only one head. In adopting a republican federal system there, the nation had to be artificially divided up into separate sections, to be called States, which had no separate existence before, and no individual history or experience in self-government. It is not to be wondered at, therefore, that when this Constitution went into operation it caused great disturbance. It is easy to find in this fact one of the causes of our prolonged civil wars. We were not alone in suffering such misfortunes, for almost every other nation on this continent, following in our footsteps, tried to adapt the republican federal system to a condition of things to which it was not suited. Brazil alone escaped this period of turmoil and experiment by establishing an empire, with a scion of the reigning house of Portugal on the throne, and by not adopting a federal republican form of government until nearly a century later, after the people had acquired some ideas of self-government and some capacity for carrying it out; and it is probably for these reasons that she has suffered less by civil commotion than any other country of similar origin in this hemisphere.

Unfortunately, very little regard was paid to the provisions of the Constitution of 1824 immediately after its promulgation, as the men then in power did not hesitate to infringe upon them, especially for the purpose of placing their own candidates in the high positions, thus setting a very bad example, which contributed greatly to the subsequent demoralization of the Mexican political parties, as will presently be seen.

Our Constitution of 1824 was a decided victory for the Liberal party, but very far from being a final one. The Church party, though

then defeated, was really the stronger of the two during the early years
of independent Mexico. The power of the Liberals was of short
duration ; the Conservative Church party prevailed upon some of
Mexico's numerous military leaders to rebel against the Government
and inaugurate a series of revolutions, which ended in 1835 in the overthrow of the Constitution of 1824, thus giving a pretext to the Texas
settlers to rebel against Mexico. Santa Ana and the Conservative
leaders held that a federal form of government was not that which was
best adapted to the country, and that a strong centralized government
was needed.

It would be too long and rather uninteresting to mention all the
military mutinies, or pronunciamientos as we called them, during the
revolutionary period from 1822 to 1855, as it would be a rather dry
and long list of names and dates almost unintelligible to any one not
very familiar with the history of Mexico. I will pass therefore over this
dark period, mentioning only the leading and most conspicuous of
them.

In a recent article published about Mexico by Justice Walter Clark,
of the Supreme Court of North Carolina,[1] it is stated that between 1821
and 1868 the form of the Mexican government was changed ten times;
that over fifty persons succeeded one another as presidents, dictators,
or emperors, and that more than three hundred successful or abortive
revolutions were recorded. I append to this paper a list of all the
rulers that Mexico has had before, during, and after the conquest by
the Spaniards, and that list contains the exact number of persons who
exercised the government in this country during the revolutionary
period, but even supposing that Justice Clark's figures be exact, they
will only show the correctness of the views just expressed on this subject—that the demoralized condition of the army made it easy to start
revolutions, that they occurred very frequently, and that the army had
naturally a great deal to do with them; but it is also plain that there
was often, if not always, some political motive or principle involved in
such revolutions, and although a great many were military mutinies,
others were popular uprisings, often under cover of military pronunciamientos.

All the military leaders during the whole period of our revolutions
pretended in their pronunciamientos that they only desired to carry
out the will of the people as interpreted by themselves, and that their
only object was to overthrow the existing government, which they considered either illegal or one which had abused its authority, claiming
always to act on behalf of the people and for their welfare, recognizing
in that way that the people are the source of all power.

[1] *Arena*, for February, 1896.—" The Land of the Noonday Sun. Mexico in
Midwinter."

22

After the adoption of the Federal Constitution hostilities between the two parties were renewed, the Liberal party, which had been the promoter of independence and which desired progress, and the Conservative or Church party, which aimed to maintain the status quo, and which was strongly averse to any change. It is not strange that the conflict between these two parties, representing ideas so antagonistic, should have lasted so long.

An election took place in September, 1824, and General Victoria was elected President, assuming that office on October 10, 1824, General Bravo being elected Vice-President. On January 1, 1825, the first Constitutional Congress opened its sessions, and on November 18, 1825, the fortress of Ulua, opposite Veracruz, surrendered to the Mexican Government. General Victoria finished his term of office in comparative peace, although some military pronunciamientos had taken place which he was able to subdue, among others one headed by General Bravo, the Vice-President, and another by General Santa Ana.

When the following presidential election took place, on September 1, 1828, General Guerrero was the candidate of the Federalist, or Yorkino party, and General Gomez Pedraza, Secretary of War in the Victoria administration, of the Scottish, or Centralist party, the former having had 9 and the latter 11 votes of the Legislatures of the States. The Yorkino party was not satisfied with the result of the election, and General Santa Ana placed himself at the head of a rebellion to nullify the election and make Guerrero president. Another pronunciamiento took place with the same object in view, in the City of Mexico, which was finally successful, and Congress, acting under such pressure, declared on January 12, 1829, Guerrero elected President, and General Bustamante, Vice-President. General Guerrero was inaugurated as President on April 1, 1829.

During Guerrero's presidency, the Captain-General of Havana sent an armed expedition with about 4000 selected Spanish troops under General Barradas, to reconquer Mexico, which landed near Tampico in July, 1829, and on the 4th of the following August captured that port. General Teran was sent by the Mexican Government against Barradas, and Santa Ana went from Veracruz of his own accord and without orders. Both attacked Barradas, who capitulated on September 11, 1829. Spain finally recognized the independence of Mexico after the death of Ferdinand VII., by a treaty signed at Madrid on December 28, 1836.

General Bustamante, the Vice-President, who was then in command of an army in Jalapa, rebelled against Guerrero, on December 4, 1829, proclaiming the restoration of the Constitution. Guerrero himself took the field against Bustamante, but as he left the City of Mexico, the garrison of the capital there rebelled against his authority, and his army having been disbanded, he abandoned the Government. Bustamante filled part of Guerrero's term. Guerrero rebelled in the South against Bustamante, but he was enticed to go on board an Italian vessel, whose master delivered him to Bustamante's agents, and he was shot on February 14, 1831. Several other uprisings took place against the Bustamante government, Santa Ana coming again at the head of them, and he defeated Bustamante's forces at Puebla in December, 1832, whereupon Bustamante signed an agreement with Santa Ana, called the "Zabaleta" agreement, by which it was stipulated that Gomez Pedraza, having been elected President, should be installed as such, and he therefore remained in power until the end of that term, on April 1, 1833.

Santa Ana's Leadership.—In the following election Santa Ana was elected President, and Valentin Gomez Farias, Vice-President, the new Government being inaugurated on April 1, 1833.

The military leaders continued to play a very important part in public affairs. The most remarkable instance was that of General Santa Anna. He was active, cunning, courageous, plausible, and even magnetic; but he was at the same time an ambitious, unprincipled, and selfish man, who sided with all parties and betrayed them all. He was a successful military leader in an irregular guerrilla warfare; but he had no ability as a soldier. He fought with the Spanish army against the independent cause up to 1821, and he went over to Iturbide, when the latter joined the independent leaders; in 1822 he rebelled against Iturbide, and proclaimed a federal republic, and in 1834 he abolished the Federal Constitution of 1824 and established a military dictatorship, which he reassumed at three different periods. From 1822 to 1855 he really had the fate of Mexico in his hands, having been President five different times, but he never served the country in any way except in his readiness to take part in our foreign wars, although his participation in them was often disastrous to Mexico. He began his political career as a Radical Liberal, and ended it as an ultra-reactionary leader of the Church party. In his campaigns against the Texans he allowed himself to be surprised at San Jacinto by a handful of men, when he had superior numbers; and he being then the President of Mexico committed the baseness of offering the recognition of Texan independence as the price of his personal liberation by the enemy, although secretly resolving not to carry out the agreement. His military incompetence was apparent in his campaigns against the armies of the United States under General Taylor at Angostura, and under General Scott at Cerro Gordo and the Valley of Mexico, where under better generalship we might have been victorious, having superior numbers. Although the final result of that war, under the then existing conditions, was of necessity against us, we certainly could have made a much better stand, had we had an abler man at the head of our armies. Santa Ana was often very easily discouraged, and more than once fled from the country, forsaking a power which he might have wielded longer, thus showing that he lacked tenacity of purpose. But this does not show, as a superficial observer might be disposed to believe, that the struggle was the result only of the personal ambition of unscrupulous military leaders, as what really happened was that the political parties used these leaders for their convenience, and had, of course, to share the power with them and to submit to some of their whims.

During Santa Ana's administration, military insurrections continued, but he was able to overpower them. Gomez Farias was an enlightened man of decidedly liberal tendencies, and, having a majority in Congress, he succeeded in passing several liberal measures, especially some destined to diminish the political influence of the clergy, like the repeal of the law making obligatory the payment of tithes. The Conservative party worked upon Santa Ana's susceptibilities to place him in antagonism to Gomez Farias. He therefore favored a revolution which broke out in Cuernavaca in 1834, proclaiming him as Dictator, and in April of that year he assumed the functions of such, dissolved Congress, repealed all the liberal laws which had just been issued, exiled from the country Gomez Farias, and convoked a new Congress, which met January 4, 1835, and which approved all that Santa Ana had done and declared him Dictator. Francisco Garcia, Governor of Zacatecas, rebelled against Santa Ana, but was defeated, and after his victory in Zacatecas he went to Texas. That Congress declared itself with authority to make a new Constitution.

Federal Constitution of 1835.—When the Church party had the ascendency under Santa Ana's first presidency, they repealed the Federal Constitution of 1824, and on October 23, 1835, they issued some bases for a new Constitution, which was finally proclaimed on December 29, 1836, under the title of " Constitutional Laws," and which abolished the Federal system of government, and several of the liberal features of the Federal Constitution of 1824. The " Constitutional Laws " of 1836 were, apparently, not conservative enough for the Church party, and they issued, on June 13, 1843, also under another one of Santa Ana's administrations, what was called the " Organic Bases," a still more conservative Constitution, as I will presently state.

The Church party being so wealthy and powerful, and having so much influence in the country, could very easily have brought about a civil war of so serious a character as would have made it difficult for the Liberal side to defeat them; but, as time elapsed, the Liberal party, which really represented the patriotic element of the country, grew stronger through education and contact with foreign nations, and was materially assisted in its task by the demoralization of the clergy and their unpatriotic conduct during our foreign wars—as, besides our civil wars, we had, in 1829, a war with Spain, already mentioned, which sent an expedition to reconquer Mexico; in 1838, a war with France; in 1846 and 1847, a war with the United States, and from 1862 to 1867, the war of the French Intervention.   It was not difficult, therefore, for the Liberal party to inaugurate in its turn a counter-revolution, which in the course of time was successful, and which finally restored it to power.   It was in this way that the period of our civil wars lasted so long, and that we came to have so many different Constitutions.

The Congress of 1836, finally convoked the people to elect a President and a new Congress.   In this election General Bustamante was elected President, and took his office on April 29, 1837.   Several insurrections broke out against centralism and the Bustamante administration, but they were easily subdued.   Bustamante himself marched with his army against General Urrea, who had pronounced in Tampico, and during his absence from the capital Santa Ana was appointed President *ad interim*.   Santa Ana himself marched against Generals Urrea and Mejia, and defeated them at Acajete, near the City of Mexico, capturing and shooting Mejia.   General Urrea pronounced again at the City of Mexico, on July 15, 1840, but he was finally defeated.   A final pronunciamiento against Bustamante took place in Guadalajara, on August 8, 1841, under General Paredes.   General Valencia soon afterwards revolted at the City of Mexico, and finally Santa Ana on the 9th of the following September pronounced himself at Perote, Veracruz.   Bustamante went to fight the rebels, but his troops abandoned him, and this gave success to the revolution.

Santa Ana's Third Presidency.—Santa Ana entered victorious the City of Mexico, and called a meeting of all the military leaders of the forces which had rebelled against Bustamante, which resulted in the agreement signed at Tacubaya on September 28, 1841, called the *Bases of Tacubaya,* by which it was provided that he should appoint a Junta to represent the several states, and that such Junta was to elect a President, who should have dictatorial powers until a national Congress should meet.   It is needless to say that Santa Ana was appointed Provisional President under that agreement, and such was the source of the dictatorial power he exercised for nearly three years, having taken the office on October 10, 1841, remaining in power with interruptions until June, 1844.   During his absence from the City of Mexico, Generals Bravo and Canalizo exercised the government.

Conservative Constitution of June 12, 1843.—Santa Ana's administration during that period was a military dictatorship under the plan proclaimed at Tacubaya on September 28, 1841, which gave him full legislative powers. A Congress was elected under this *régime*, which formulated a Constitution with some liberal tendencies, and for this reason it was not approved by the Administration, and Congress was dismissed in December, 1842. A Junta of notables was appointed by the Administration, and it issued a Constitution on June 12, 1843, establishing a strong centralized government, that Constitution being known by the name of "Organic Bases."

Under this Constitution a Congress was elected, and met on January 1, 1844, and Santa Ana was elected Constitutional President. The sixth of the Tacubaya Bases required the President to account to Congress for what he had done as Provisional President; and as Santa Ana did not comply with that duty, General Paredes rebelled against him, in Guadalajara, and Santa Ana went to subdue him, leaving as President *ad interim* General Canalizo. Canalizo dissolved Congress on November 29, 1844, and that caused a popular uprising in the City of Mexico on December 6th of the same year, the insurrectionists capturing Canalizo and his cabinet. Santa Ana returned from Guadalajara to attack the City of Mexico, but, finding it well fortified, went to Puebla, which had also rebelled against him, and finally left the country, being arrested at Jico, on his way to Veracruz. He was tried, but before his trial was over, a general amnesty was declared by Congress, in consequence of which he left the country.

General Herrera then assumed the government from December 6, 1844, until January 2, 1846. General Paredes, who had been given the command of a division sent to oppose the United States army which had invaded Mexico under General Taylor, rebelled against the Government on his way to the frontier at San Luis Potosi, on December 14, 1845, and marched against the City of Mexico, where he arrived on January 2, 1846, and the garrison of the city having joined him, General Herrera was deposed as President. A Junta of notables was convened by Paredes, and by them he was elected President, assuming that office on January 4, 1846. General Paredes thought of establishing a monarchical form of government; but on May 20, 1846, General Yañez rebelled at Guadalajara against him, taking the field. Paredes left the capital on July 29th. On August 4th, General Salas pronounced against Paredes at the citadel of Mexico, joined the rebels of Guadalajara, and asked the restoration of a Federal Republic. Paredes returned to the City of Mexico, but his troops abandoned him, and he had to fly for his safety.

Restoration of the Federal Constitution of 1824.—General Salas exercised the government from August 5 to December 24, 1846. By a decree of August 22d, he restored the Federal Constitution of October 4, 1824, and he convoked a National Congress, which met on December 6th, and elected President General Santa Ana, and Vice-President, Don Valentin Gomez Farias.

A Congress was elected for the purpose of issuing a Constitution, and on May 21, 1847, they restored the Constitution of October 4, 1824, with some amendments embraced in a statute called " Acta de Reformas " (act of amendments).

Santa Ana marched with his army towards the North to oppose General Taylor, and Gomez Farias exercised the government from December 24, 1846, to March 27, 1847. Under this Administration Congress, who had a liberal majority, decreed by an act of January 11, 1847, that ecclesiastical property should be nationalized for the purpose of using its proceeds in the defence of the integrity of the country in the war with the United States. But the clergy brought about a rebellion, headed by Generals Salas and Peña, and they succeeded in bribing some regular troops and most of the national guard, called "polkos," which Gomez Farias had organized, and which were ready to march to Veracruz to oppose General Scott, who had just landed there. From February 25 to March 21, 1847, the capital was the scene of daily battles, just at the moment when foreign troops were coming from the North, and when the squadron of the United States was bombarding Veracruz. After the battle of Buena Vista, Santa Ana returned from the North and assumed the government on March 21, 1847, and that put an end to the disturbances. But he sided with the clergy, because when he left again the capital on April 2d to meet General Scott he left General Anaya as President *ad interim,* instead of leaving Gomez Farias, who was the Vice-President.

War with the United States of 1846 and 1847.—The events of the war with the United States of 1846 and 1847 are well known in this country, and are not pertinent to my purpose in writing this paper, and I will therefore not attempt to relate them, and will only say that the incidents connected with the same afford the best proofs that could be adduced of the want of patriotism of the Mexican clergy, since, for the purpose of avoiding the execution of a law which affected their pecuniary interests, they did not hesitate to cause a revolution, when the country was invaded by a foreign nation, and to use for that rebellion the troops which were intended for the defence of the honor and integrity of the country.

It has been stated by prominent persons, among others Mr. Benton, that President Polk entered into a secret agreement with General Santa Ana, to the effect that the struggle would be confined to a few skirmishes to be followed by a treaty of peace, recognizing the Rio Grande as the western boundary of Texas, and that under this agreement President Polk forced Congress to declare war against Mexico. Mr. Benton is also authority for saying that the price offered to Santa Ana was two millions of dollars, and it is a fact that precisely that sum was appropriated by Congress to be used by the President at his discretion, in opening a way for peace negotiations, and that the declaration of war by the United States was immediately followed by orders to the Gulf Squadron blockading the Mexican coast to place no obstacle in the way of Santa Ana's return to Mexico, and he did return, landing at Veracruz after the war had been waged for some time. But whatever engagements Santa Ana might have entered into with the United States, it seems to me clear that he had not the intention of complying with them, and only entered into them for the sake of securing his safe return to Mexico.[1]

When the army of the United States occupied the City of Mexico, on September 14, 1847, General Santa Ana fled from the country, as he had done before, and Don Manuel de la Peña y Peña, a civilian President of the Supreme Court, and, under the Constitution of 1847, ex-officio Vice-President, assumed the government and established the capital at Queretaro, and under his administration peace was made with the United States by the treaty of Guadalupe Hidalgo, of February 2, 1848.

Anaya's, Peña y Peña's, Herrera's, and Arista's Administrations. — The Mexican Congress met at Queretaro on November 12, 1847, and appointed President *ad interim* General Anaya, who remained in office until January 18, 1848, when Peña y Peña was called again to fill that office.

---

[1] The *Midland Monthly* of Desmoines and Chicago, for May, 1897, published an article on General Grant's life by Mr. John W. Emerson, in which it was stated that overtures were made to General Scott to induce him to remain in Mexico, of which the following is an extract:

"It may surprise many readers to learn that overtures were made to General Scott by many Mexicans of position and by many American officers to permanently occupy Mexico and organize a new government. The scheme proposed to General Scott was in substance this : It was supposed that upon the conclusion of a treaty of peace at least three-fourths of the American army would be discharged, and that a large portion of the officers would resign, and with many of the men would enter the new army of Mexico, and enough others could be recruited in the United States to make the American contingent 15,000 strong, and to this might be added a like number of Mexican soldiers. With such an army it was suggested that Mexico could be held and governed in an orderly way and prosperity might be assured. The plan contemplated a *pronunciamiento*, in which General Scott should declare himself Dictator of the Republic for a term of five years or more, to give time for agitators to acquire pacific habits and to learn to govern themselves and to respect an orderly government, where the rights of property were not only respected, but fully protected. Already in possession of the forts, arsenals, foundries, cities, mines, and ports of entry, with nearly all the arms, it was not doubted that a general acquiesence would follow."

I have heard that the higher clergy in Mexico made some overtures of that kind to General Scott with the expectation of establishing under their control a firm government, but I am sure that that idea was not a popular one in Mexico.

An election was held under the existing Constitution, and General Herrera was elected President, and assumed that office on June 3, 1848, returning to the City of Mexico when it was evacuated by the troops of the United States. General Herrera finished his term of office, being the only such case after Victoria's administration, but several military uprisings occurred during his administration. General Paredes rebelled against Herrera, but was defeated, and Herrera's administration was noted for its simplicity and morality.

When General Herrera's term was over, General Arista, Herrera's Secretary of War, was elected President, assuming the government on January 15, 1851.   General Arista followed the traditions of his predecessor; but, his government being a remarkably good one with tendencies to a liberal policy, it had the opposition of the Church party, which organized several uprisings against him. Colonel Blancarte rebelled in Guadalajara on July 27, 1852, first against the Governor of the State of Jalisco, and finally proclaimed the return of Santa Ana as President. General Arista sent General Uraga against Blancarte; but, instead of attacking the rebels, Uraga joined them with the army that the President had entrusted to him. Several other uprisings occurred in different sections of the country, and, the rebels having a majority in Congress, General Arista's only alternative was either to dissolve Congress or resign, and, like a man of principle, he followed the second extreme, and on the 5th of January, 1853, he sent in his resignation, and left the City of Mexico.

Ceballos, the President of the Supreme Court, was called to assume the government ; but he dissolved Congress. Congress appointed Don Juan Mujica y Osorio, President, *ad interim*, and Ceballos sent against him an army under General Robles Pezuela, who joined the insurgents, and this finally ended in the recall of Santa Ana as Dictator, and with full powers.

Santa Ana's Last Administration.—Santa Ana landed at Veracruz on April 1, 1853, and sided entirely with the Church party, establishing a kind of empire, giving himself the title of Serene Highness. To procure himself means to remain in power he sold to the United States a portion of territory called the Messilla Valley, and ruled the country with an iron hand. The Liberal party could not stand such government, and the leaders of the South, under General Alvarez, proclaimed, on March 1, 1854, the Plan of Ayutla, which proposed the restoration of a Constitutional Government. Santa Ana took the field in person against the insurgents, and went as far as Acapulco, without being able to capture that city, and after several efforts on his part to subdue the insurrection, which had spread all over the country, abandoned the Government, and on the 9th of August, 1855, left the City of Mexico for Veracruz, where he sailed for his estate in Turbaco, New Granada.

WAR OF REFORM AND FRENCH INTERVENTION.

The Ayutla revolution finally succeeded, and General Alvarez was appointed President, assuming that office on October 4, 1855, when he organized a Liberal cabinet, of which Benito Juarez was Secretary of Justice, occupying soon afterwards the City of Mexico. Before an election could be held, General Alvarez appointed his successor as President *ad interim*, General Comonfort, one of the supporters of the Plan of Ayutla, and who belonged to the moderate wing of the Liberal party, and who assumed that office on December 12, 1855.

Federal Constitution of 1857.—Several military insurrections, promoted by the Church, took place against Comonfort in 1858, the city of Puebla having been twice the headquarters of the rebels ; but General Comonfort finally succeeded in subduing them. Under the Plan of Ayutla, a Constitutional Congress was convened on February 18, 1856, which issued the present Constitution of February 5, 1857. An election was held, and Comonfort was elected Constitutional President for four years, his inauguration taking place on December 1, 1857. He appointed Juarez his Secretary of the Interior during his new administration. Unfortunately, Comonfort wavered in his political views, and he was persuaded by the Church party to annul the Constitution, under the plea that it was impracticable, and that it would keep up political agitation, and on December 11, 1857, he dissolved the Constitutional Congress which had just convened, and on the 17th of the same month he abolished the Federal Constitution which he had sworn to support on the first of the month, and to which he owed his position, and declared himself Dictator. The Liberal party could not, of course, stand such conduct, and they raised as a man against Comonfort's usurpation. Soon afterwards he saw that he had been betrayed by the Church party, as they proclaimed President, General Zuluaga, one of Comonfort's most devout friends, and Comonfort left the country.

Juarez's Leadership.—Juarez was a most remarkable man. He was a full-blooded Indian, born in a small town, Guelatao, inhabited only by Indians, and where there was but one man—the parish priest—who spoke Spanish and could read and write. Juarez was so anxious to learn Spanish and to acquire an education that he offered his services as a domestic to the priest on condition that he should be taught. The priest found him so intelligent that he sent him to the adjoining City of Oaxaca to be educated. From such humble beginnings he rose to be a prominent lawyer and a distinguished statesman. He was, at different times, Secretary of State of his own state, member of the State Legislature, State Senator, Governor of his state for several terms, Representative to the Federal Congress, Secretary of Justice and of the Interior, Chief-Justice, Vice-President, and finally President of the Republic. His principal characteristics were his profound attachment to liberal principles, his clearness of intellect, his remarkably good common sense, his great moral courage, his unimpeachable integrity and honesty, his ardent patriotism, his tenacity of purpose, and his devotion to civil government. In time of war, when the destinies of the country often depended on the result of a battle, and when many others in his place would have led an army, he purposely abstained from exercising any military duties. These he left entirely to those of his associates who had shown talent for war, and he himself gave the example of a purely civil government. He had as much personal courage as any man in the world. I saw him more than once facing as near certain death as any man ever faced with perfect calmness and almost indifference, but without bravado. I am sure that he felt that it is best for a patriot to die in the service of his country, because in that case he wins for himself immortality, and on this theory I account for the fact that he was never afraid of death if it should come to him, while in the performance of a patriotic duty.[1]

[1] Mr. Seward's estimate of the character of Juarez shows how the Anglo-Saxon was impressed by the little Indian. When Mr. Seward visited Mexico on his trip around the world, he was heartily welcomed by my country, and in a remarkable speech that he made at the city of Puebla he said that Juarez was the greatest man that he had ever met in his life. His speech was taken down in shorthand, and Mr. Thomas H. Nelson of Terre Haute, Ind., then United States Minister to Mexico, noticing this phrase and thinking that in the excitement of the moment Mr. Seward had gone further than he intended, and further than he would like to have repeated on sober second thought, took it to Mr. Seward and said to him : " Governor, will you be willing to stand by what you said in your speech about Juarez being the greatest man you ever knew ? Remember that you have been the peer and contemporary of Webster, Clay, Calhoun, and many other distinguished men of our country, and that you place Juarez above them all." Mr. Seward answered : " What I said about Juarez was after mature consideration, and I am willing to stand by my opinion." This statement has been submitted to General Nelson and his reply, which I insert below, shows that he found it correct.

TERRE HAUTE, INDIANA, September 30, 1895.

His Excellency Matias Romero, etc., Washington, D. C.:
MY DEAR MR. ROMERO :
The receipt of your kind note would have been acknowledged sooner but for my absence from home.
During Mr. Seward's visit to Mexico he often spoke of President Juarez in terms of enthusiastic praise, in private conversation and in public speeches. In his speech at the banquet in Puebla especially he paid a lofty and eloquent tribute to the ability, statesmanship, and patriotism of the President, ranking him among the most illustrious names of the century. If I can find a copy it will afford me pleasure to send it to you; also some allusions of mine in public addresses to Mr. Seward's estimate of the exalted character and public services of that truly great man.
With kind regards, I remain, *como siempre,*
Very truly yours,   THOMAS H. NELSON.

As already stated, Benito Juarez was appointed Secretary of Justice by President Alvarez, and on November 23, 1855, he issued the first law against the clergy, which deprived them of the civil privileges they were enjoying in the exercise of their religious functions. Under the Spanish rule, and also after the independence of Mexico up to that date, the clergy had special courts made up of clergymen to try them for any offence that they might commit. This was a privilege which insured them almost perfect immunity, and exempted them from the control of the civil laws of the country. The Liberals thought that this was an outrage, but they could not change the condition of things until the Juarez law of 1855, although they had attempted it in 1833. The army enjoyed similar privileges, of which the Juarez law also deprived them, by restricting the jurisdiction of military courts to military offences.

The Juarez law was succeeded by the Lerdo law of June 25, 1856, which provided that no corporation — meaning the clergy, as the Church was the only corporation existing in Mexico—could hold real estate, and that such as was held then by any corporation should be sold to the actual tenants at a price which was to be arrived at by capitalizing the rent on a basis of six per cent. per annum rate of interest. Thereafter the tenant was to be the owner of the property, the corporation retaining a mortgage equal to the price fixed in this way. These two laws were the cause of the two insurrections already referred to, promoted by the Church and subdued by President Comonfort.

Juarez, after the enactment of the law which bore his name, had for a time been Governor of the State of Oaxaca, and while holding that office he had been elected Chief-Justice of the Republic and ex-officio Vice-President, and was at the time of the Comonfort rebellion acting as Secretary of the Interior. He became Comonfort's successor, and undertook to stem the tide of rebellion and reaction. In the City of Mexico most of the old regular army of the country were in favor of the Conservative or Church party, and the city, therefore, fell into the hands of Juarez' enemies, and he had to fly from it. He went to the interior, where he established his government, first at Queretaro and afterwards at Guanajuato and Guadalajara. Finally he sailed from Manzanillo, a Mexican port on the Pacific, to Panama, thence to New Orleans, and then back to Veracruz, on the Gulf of Mexico, where he remained for about two years. Veracruz was the stronghold of the Liberal party, as it was naturally a strong place and was well fortified. It was protected also by its bad climate and prevalence of yellow fever, and was the best place that Juarez could have selected to establish his government, and, being more in contact with foreigners, its inhabitants were Liberals. He remained at Veracruz from March, 1858, to January, 1861, the principal cities of the country being during that time in the hands of the Church party. The Liberal armies, though often defeated, were never destroyed, for the people were with them, and recruits came in abundance. After a defeat, the Liberal leaders reorganized their armies and were soon ready to meet the enemy again. Their courage and persistence were finally rewarded, and they were victorious in the decisive battle of Calpulalpan, on December 19, 1860.

Our old regular army, with very few exceptions, sided with the Church party, and that prolonged considerably the struggle, because the Liberals could only oppose disorganized and undisciplined masses to the regular troops of the Church party ; but after some time they succeeded in organizing armies as well disciplined as those of our enemies, and in that way the war was brought to a close in December, 1860.

Laws of Reform.—During the terrible struggle which we call the war of reform, Juarez issued, from Veracruz, on July 12 and 23, 1859, our reform laws, which had for their object to destroy the political power that the clergy had exercised before. The church property was declared National property, and was sold by the Government to the occupants of it at a nominal price, payable partially in National bonds, then selling at a very low price, about five per cent. of their face value. To prevent that in the future the Church should accumulate the real estate taken from her, she was disqualified to own real estate. The clergy were then deprived of all political rights—that is, they were disqualified to be elected for any office. Their convents, both of 'monks and nuns, were suppressed. The number of churches existing in the country was considerably reduced. Complete separation between Church and State was proclaimed. A civil registry of births, marriages, and deaths was established, taking from the clergy all interference with such subjects; which had been up to that time under their sole supervision. Processions and all other religious demonstrations outside of the church, as well as the ringing of bells, were prohibited. The number of feast days, which then amounted to nearly one fourth of all the days of the year, and tended to keep the people in idleness, were reduced to not more than two or three for the whole year. The wearing outside of the church of the priest's peculiar habit was prohibited, and many other stringent measures against the clergy were adopted, with a view to destroy their political power and to deprive them of the means to bring about another insurrection against the Government.

It is a remarkable fact that most of the Liberal leaders were lawyers, who, influenced by patriotism and a desire for the success of the Liberal cause, and without any military education, had to lead our armies during the long civil wars. Some of them became very distinguished soldiers in our war, as happened here in the United States.

So it can truly be said that the final success of the Liberal cause in Mexico was due in a great measure to the jurists of the nation; so much so, indeed, that they incurred the special hatred of the Church party, by whom the name of " lawyer " was wont to be used as a contemptuous designation for the Liberal leaders.

After the battle of Calpulalpan, fought on December 19, 1860, where General Miramon, the last Church party President, was defeated, Juarez left Veracruz and established his government at the City of Mexico. He then convened Congress, ordered an election, and in 1861 he was elected President for the first Constitutional term. The reform laws became operative when Juarez occupied the City of Mexico, and his rule was extended over the country.

The Church party did not give up the struggle, but began again with renewed vigor to start a new insurrection in 1861, directed especially against the execution of the reform laws. Although this insurrection was not of a serious character, and the insurgents could not capture any important places or defeat the Government troops, they did succeed in keeping up an unsettled condition of things throughout the whole country, involving great insecurity to life and property.

French Intervention in Mexico and Maximilian's Rule.—When the Church party became satisfied that the Liberal party had grown so much that they had not strength enough at home to overcome it, they went to Europe and continued their intrigues with European courts to secure foreign intervention in Mexico. Unfortunately, about that time the civil war broke out in the United States and insured the success of the Mexican Church leaders in obtaining European intervention, as the French Emperor was apparently quite certain of the success of the Confederacy, and was very well disposed to avail himself of the opportunity offered by the Mexican Church party of gaining a foothold in Mexico and effectually aiding in the permanent division of the United States. He had, besides, a dream of establishing a French empire in America, bordering on the Pacific. Under his influence an alliance was made between France, England, and Spain, by a treaty signed at London on October 1, 1861, and Maximilian was persuaded to come to Mexico. England and Spain withdrew before the war actually began, and Napoleon's first army, under General Lorencez, was defeated at Puebla on May 5, 1862; but, after being considerably reinforced, the French army, under Marshal Forey, succeeded in occupying both Puebla and the City of Mexico in 1863, and so began the French intervention. The details of that intervention are quite familiar in this country, and therefore it is not necessary to say anything more about it here.

When peace was restored in the United States after the collapse of the Confederacy, Louis Napoleon of course understood that he could not continue for an indefinite period his occupation of Mexico, and that he had to give up his Mexican plans and withdraw his army from the country. We could by our own efforts and without any foreign aid have finally driven the French from our country, but it would have taken us some time longer, as Napoleon could have kept his army in Mexico for one or perhaps two years longer; through the assistance of the United States it was withdrawn that much sooner, which was a great service to Mexico.[1] Maximilian well knew, also, that he could not remain in Mexico after the withdrawal of the French, and he decided to leave the country as soon as he heard that the French army was to be withdrawn, and was satisfied that his wife's mission to Europe (where she was overtaken by a dreadful calamity) to obtain a revocation of the order of withdrawal was fruitless; but, unfortunately, he was a dreamer, without force of character, and he was not a man equal to the occasion. He was not steady in his resolutions, and he was easily persuaded by the leaders of the Church party to return to the City of Mexico after he had already started on his homeward journey, and had gone in October, 1866, as far as Orizaba, two thirds of the way between the City of Mexico and Veracruz, where the *Novara*, the same Austrian man-of-war which had brought him to Mexico in 1864, lay ready to take him back to his native country, having been sent over at his request by the Emperor of Austria, and after he knew of the failure of his wife's mission to Europe to induce Napoleon III. to keep his army in Mexico. Early in February, 1867, Maximilian left the City of Mexico and went to Queretaro, where he was finally captured, tried, and shot on the 19th of the following June.

The fate of Maximilian was indeed a very sad one, but when it is considered that on October 2, 1866, a few months only before his execution, he had issued a decree ordering all Mexicans fighting for the independence of their country to be shot without any trial or other formality, and that had he lived he would have been a permanent centre of conspiracies of the monarchical party to overthrow the Republic in Mexico and restore the empire, it will be seen that his death might be considered as a political necessity. Besides, Maximilian's pardon would not have been considered in Europe as an act of generosity on the part of Mexico, but as a proof of weakness, and thus it might have encouraged the repetition of the experiment which ended his life, and it was thought necessary to give a lesson which would serve the purpose of discouraging, and thus preventing all such experiments in the future. The sadness of the tragedy was considerably increased by

[1] In the *Century Illustrated Monthly Magazine* for May, 1897, I published an article entitled, " The Fall of the Second Empire, as related to French Intervention in Mexico," which, in my opinion, shows that the French intervention was the primary cause of Napoleon's downfall.

the unhappy fate of his wife.[1]   It has been intimated sometimes that I had an important share in Maximilian's execution, but I had nothing whatever to do with it.

Restoration of the Republic.—In July 1867, the Juarez Government was again established at the City of Mexico, and another popular election took place, in which Juarez was almost unanimously elected by the people for another term, from 1867 to 1871.

The patriotism and firmness of Juarez were remarkable.   There was a time during the French intervention in which many seemed to despair of the fate of Mexico, and that feeling was not entirely unreasonable,

[1] Mme. Del Barrio, who was with Archduchess Carlotta in Mexico, and who journeyed with her to France, when she went to solicit the aid of Napoleon III., in the hope that the French emperor would assist Maximilian in the great task of crushing the Mexican patriots, gave in a letter the following details of the calamity which overtook her young friend: " Her majesty was in a state of great nervous excitement bordering on insanity even before we neared the coast of France in that unhappy summer of 1866.   It is generally assumed that her mental malady first asserted itself during her interview with the Pope, October 4th of that year.   The fact is that her majesty became a raving maniac in the castle of St. Cloud.

" These are the circumstances : When our steamer landed at Brest there was nobody to offer a royal welcome, or any kind of welcome.   Neither the French government nor the Belgian embassy was represented.   The same happened upon our arrival in Paris.   The empress trembled from head to foot as she stepped into the hired coach that brought us to our hotel.

" The day passed without a word from Emperor Napoleon,   On the second day the Empress Eugenie's chamberlain came to invite her majesty to breakfast at St. Cloud.   She refused the invitation, but said she would come to St. Cloud the following afternoon.   At the castle my mistress and their majesties of France were closeted for an hour longer, I remaining in the anteroom.

" Suddenly I heard the Empress Carlotta cry out in agonized tones, which were full of contempt at the same time, ' Indeed I should have known who you are and who I am.   I should not have dishonored the blood of the Bourbons in my veins by humbling myself before a Bonaparte, who is nothing but an adventurer.'

" A second later I heard a sound as if a heavy body had struck the floor.   I ran to the door, which was locked, but after a little while the Emperor Napoleon came out with a troubled face.   On entering, I found my mistress on a lounge, and kneeling by her side the Empress Eugenie, who was rubbing her hands and feet.   She had opened her corsets, had pulled off her stockings, and, in short, done everything to arouse her from the fainting spell.

" The emperor's statement that he could do nothing for his majesty of Mexico had brought on this trouble, said Eugenie.   Then she got up to get a glass of water, but, as she held it to my mistress' lips, the Empress Carlotta awoke and threw the water over her friend's dress, crying: ' Away, cursed murderer ; away with your poison ! ' and then, falling on my neck, she added : ' You are witness to this plot.   They want to poison me.   For God's sake do not leave me ! ' "

After that she had lucid intervals for some time, but she collapsed again during the historic interview with Pope Pius IX. and it was this scene at the Vatican which first attracted the attention of Europe to the mental irresponsibility of the unfortunate Carlotta.

considering that the country was invaded by a very large French army —some 60,000 or 80,000 men, I think. Besides, Napoleon and Maximilian had contrived to obtain an Austrian auxiliary corps, a corps from Hungary, and another from Belgium—Princess Carlotta, Maximilian's wife, was a daughter of the former King of Belgium and a sister of the present King—and Maximilian had also a contingent from the French colony of Algiers, and the command of the troops of the Church party, which were on his side, and which embraced most of our old regular army, and, finally, he had all the aristocratic element of Mexico in his favor. Altogether the array was so great that it was no wonder that many of our public men had at times little hope of success. But Juarez never despaired for a moment. He was perfectly certain of final success, and was ready to sacrifice his life for his country's cause.

Diaz's Leadership.—General Diaz was born in the city of Oaxaca, on September 15, 1830, of an humble but good family, having a small portion of Mixteco-Indian blood in his veins, of which he is very proud. He followed a literary career, and was near being graduated as a lawyer when he joined, in 1854, the Ayutla Revolution against Santa Ana, having followed since then a military career, for which he was especially fitted, and in which he soon achieved great distinction. From 1857 to 1860 he fought in the Tehuantepec District, under the most difficult and perilous circumstances, and holding his own in a very creditable campaign.

General Diaz began to take a very prominent part in the military affairs of Mexico during the war of reform and the war against the French intervention, having had an important command at the battle of May 5, 1862, and at the siege of Puebla in April and May, 1863.

During the war of intervention, the Mexican government divided the country into four military Departments, the eastern, western, northern, and southern, and General Diaz was given the command of the eastern Department, embracing the States of Oaxaca, Veracruz, Puebla, and others. In 1865 he defended the City of Oaxaca against the French, and General Bazaine had to take the field in person with a very large French force before he could capture that city. General Diaz was made prisoner and brought to Puebla, from where he escaped and went south, where he organized a new army with which he began operations against the French intervention. He defeated the Imperialists, who had been joined by a portion of the Austrian military contingent, at Carbonera on October 18, 1866, having previously obtained a great victory at Miahuatlan on the 3d of the same month, and afterwards captured successively the cities of Oaxaca, Puebla, and Mexico. After the restoration of the Republic he began to take a very prominent part in public affairs, and since 1877 his leadership has been undisputed.

Civil Wars from 1868 to 1875.—In a country where civil war and the disturbances consequent to it had lasted for so long a time it was natural that everything should be demoralized, and thus even after our complete success against the French intervention and the so-called Empire of Maximilian, some uprisings took place, which were headed by dissatisfied Liberal leaders; and although they were not of a serious nature, and were easily subdued by President Juarez, they kept the country in an unsettled condition, and contributed to support the opinion that we were unable to maintain peace.

The principal of these insurrections, that of La Noria, was headed by General Porfirio Diaz and other prominent members of the Liberal party, who were not satisfied with the policy of President Juarez, and who opposed his re-election in 1871, and proclaimed the principles of no re-election and a free ballot. His death on July 18, 1872, put an end to that insurrection, and the leaders submitted to the provisional government of Señor Don Sebastian Lerdo de Tejada, who, as Chief Justice of the Supreme Court, was the ex-officio President. A popular election took place in 1872, and Señor Lerdo de Tejada was elected Constitutional President. In the year 1876 he was a candidate for re-election, and that brought about the revolution of Tuxtepec, promoted by prominent leaders of the Liberal party, who again proclaimed the anti-election and free ballot principles, under the leadership of General Diaz, who placed himself at the head of that revolution. The battle of Tecoac, fought on November 16, 1876, decided the success of the Tuxtepec revolution, and General Diaz was installed as Chief Executive with full legislative powers. In April, 1877, he was elected Constitutional President, and since then he has been at the head of the Executive Department, excepting a four-years term, from 1880 to 1884, when General Don Manuel Gonzalez occupied the Executive office. The great progress which has taken place in Mexico in recent years is mainly due to the wise policy and earnest efforts of General Diaz. Among the many distinguished services that General Diaz has rendered to Mexico, perhaps the principal one is to have restored complete peace to the country. During the several terms in which he has filled the executive office he has earnestly encouraged the material development of the country, and firmly established peace and order. Material development always furnishes the best security that public peace will be maintained. It would be impossible, in the limited space at my command, to attempt, even, to give a superficial idea of the great services that General Diaz has rendered to Mexico, but as they are of recent date they are well known by all cotemporaries taking any interest in Mexican affairs.

It has sometimes been stated that Mexico is ruled by an oligarchy, and if by this it is meant that the nation is divided into classes, and that one of these classes is the ruling power, then the statement may be taken as correct, as Mexico is ruled by her educated class; but if by it it is meant that a few families have the ruling power by inheritance and do not allow others to share it, then it is altogether incorrect, as the humblest citizen in Mexico, belonging to any race whatsoever, even the pure Indian, can hold the highest position in the land, if his talents, his services, and his character entitle him to it. A case in point is that of Juarez, who was by birth an humble Indian, and, after being educated, became the foremost man in the country.

Disappearance of the Causes of Civil War.—It will be readily seen from this brief synopsis that the causes which brought about the civil wars in Mexico no longer exist. Ours was a contest for supremacy between the vital forces of the nation, between the old and the new ideas, which in other countries it has taken many years, and even centuries, to settle; but now our political problem is solved, the Church party is completely broken up as a political organization, and cannot cause again any serious disturbance, and the elements of civil war are now lacking.

The conditions in Mexico during the Spanish rule and even after the independence, and more or less up to the issue of our reform laws in 1859, were very similar to those existing in European countries during the feudal system. The clergy and their agents and followers were, in fact, the Mexican feudal barons, and their power and influence in the country were as great as those of the European barons, as they not only monopolized the wealth and education of the country, but also exercised great spiritual or religious influence upon the minds of the people. The position of the Mexican barons was perhaps even stronger, because, instead of being at cross purposes with the king or ruling power, as the European barons often were, they had a kind of alliance with the temporal power, by which each agreed to support and protect the other. When it is considered how long it took the kings of Europe to subdue the barons, how many efforts the people had to make to accomplish that end, and what protracted and bloody wars had to be fought before it was accomplished, which was not wholly until the French Revolution, it is rather a matter of surprise that Mexico and the other Spanish American countries similarly situated should have destroyed their feudalism in comparatively so short a time.

Mexico for nearly twenty years has been free from political disturbances and enjoying all the advantages of a permanent peace. Those who took part in former revolutions have either died off, disappeared, or are now interested in the maintenance of peace, because they are thriving in consequence of the development of the country. Even in case President Diaz's guidance should fail Mexico, I am sure peace would still be preserved, because there are very strong reasons in its

24

favor. Railways and telegraphs are great preservers of peace. In case of an insurrection it was not long ago that it took months before the Government could reach the insurgents, and in the meantime they could organize and fortify themselves and make considerable headway before they were confronted by an enemy. Now the Government can send troops at once to quell an insurrection.

Peace in Mexico is as assured as it is in any other country, and life and property are as safe there as anywhere else. Public opinion seems to share this view, and capital, especially foreign capital, which is so conservative and timid, is now being freely invested in Mexican enterprises.

Conclusion.—I intend to show that the Mexican revolutions have not been, as many have believed, the result of the turbulent character of the Mexican people and of their incapacity for self-government, but the necessary consequence of sociological laws, which, operating in a community with opposing interests and tendencies, produced in Mexico —as they have produced in almost every country under similar circumstances—serious crises which have been the necessary conditions and the preliminary steps toward the final political organization of the country. In fact, to judge Mexico, which is a young country, by the standard of older ones, like the English nation, for instance, which several centuries ago passed through similar crises, would not be reasonable. Several centuries passed before the Magna Charta could become operative in England. During her reign, Parliament yielded the most abject submission to the arrogant despotism of Queen Elizabeth, and later to the strong will of Cromwell; and Protestant intolerance there showed itself no less fierce than Catholic intolerance did in Spain under Philip II., and yet England has passed through crises similar to those of Mexico, until finally she has reached a normal condition of things, and is now perhaps the country where more real freedom is enjoyed, and where life and property are best protected in the world. To judge Mexico, which has been struggling to attain that condition after many years of war and disturbances, by the standard of England in her present condition, or of any other equally old country, would be unphilosophical and unjust.

RULERS OF MEXICO FROM THE MOST REMOTE PERIOD UP TO THE
PRESENT TIME.

First Period.

Before the Conquest ; Kingdom of Tula (Tollan).

The Toltecs were 117 years making their journey from Huehuetlapallan to Tollan.

The Toltec monarchy lasted 449 years—from 667 A.D. to 1116 A.D., and the successive sovereigns who reigned during that period were: Chalchinhtlatonac, founder of the dynasty; Izacatecatl, Huetzin, Totepeuh, Nacaxoc, Mitl, Queen Xiuhtlaltzin, Tecpancaltzin, and Topiltzin.

During the reign of the last king the destruction of the kingdom took place (1116), and the Toltecs were no longer a nation.

Kingdom of the Chichimecans (afterwards of Acolhuacan).

The Chichimecans made their appearance in the plateau of Anahuac in the year 1117 A.D.   Their capital was at first Tenayuca, then it was Texcoco.

Their kings reigned as follows:

		Year.
1.	Xolotl, the Great	1120
2.	Nopaltzin	1232
3.	Tlotzin—Pochotl	1263
4.	Quinantzin	1298
5.	Techotlata	1357
6.	Ixthlxochitl	1409
7.	Tezozomoc (usurper)	1418
8.	Maxtlaton (usurper)	1427
9.	Nezahuealcoyotl (legal ruler)	1431
10.	Nezahualpilli	1472
11.	Cacamatzin	1516
12.	Cuicuitzcatzin	1520
13.	Coanacotzin	1521
14.	Ixthlxochitl	1521

The kingdom of Texcoco, or Acolhuacan, ended with this sovereign, who was the most faithful ally of Cortez.

Aztec Kingdom.

The Aztecs settled in Anahuac in 1243 A.D., and after many years of servitude succeeded in establishing the City of Tenochtitlan in 1325. Before they established this city their leaders had been Huitzilihuitl and Xiuhtemoc.

Then their kings succeeded each other as follows:

		Year.
1.	Acamapichtly ascended the throne in	1376
2.	Huitzilihuitl	1396
3.	Chimalpopoca	1417
4.	Itzcoatl	1425

Year.

5. Motecutzoma I. (Ilhuicanina)......................... 1440
6. Axayacatl.. 1469
7. Tizoc... 1481
8. Ahuitzotl.. 1486
9. Motecutzoma II. (Xocoyotzin)......................... 1502
10. Cuitlahuatl... 1520
11. Cuauhtemoc... 1520

By the taking of the capital by the Spaniards in 1521 and the execution of Cuauhtemoc in 1525, the kingdom of the Aztecs or Mexicans
terminated.

Second Perioa.

From the Conquest until the End of the War of Independence.

1. Hernando Cortez, Governor and Captain-General......... 1521
2. Luis Ponce, Governor................................. 1526
3. Marcos de Aguilar, Governor.......................... 1526
4. Alonso de Estrada and Gonzalo de Sandoval, Governors.... 1527
5. Alonso de Estrada, Governor.......................... 1527
6. { Nuño de Guzman, Juan Ortiz Matienzo, Diego Delgadillo, } First Council................. 1528
7. { Sebastian Ramirez de Fuenleal, Vasco de Quiroga, Alonso Maldonado, Francisco Ceinos, Juan de Salmeron, } Second Council....... 1531

VICEROYS

During the Reign of Charles V.

1. Antonio de Mendoza.................................. 1535
2. Luis de Velasco...................................... 1550

During the Reign of Philip II.

3. Gaston de Peralta, Marquis of Falces.................. 1566
4. Martin Enriquez de Almanza.......................... 1568
5. Lorenzo de Mendoza, Count of Coruña................. 1580
6. Pedro Moya de Contreras, Archbishop of Mexico......... 1584
7. Alonso Manrique de Zuñiga, Marquis of Villa Manrique ... 1585
8. Luis de Velasco, the second.......................... 1590
9. Gaspar de Zuñiga y Acevedo, Count of Monterrey......... 1595

During the Reign of Philip III.

Year.
10. Juan de Mendoza y Luna, Marquis of Montes Claros....... 1603
11. Luis de Velasco, the second, for the second time.......... 1607
12. Francisco Garcia Guerra, Archbishop of Mexico........... 1611
13. Diego Fernandez de Cordoba, Marquis of Guadalcazar..... 1612

During the Reign of Philip IV.

14. Diego Carrillo Mendoza, Marquis of Gelves............. 1621
15. Rodrigo Pacheco Osorio, Marquis of Cerralvo........... 1624
16. Lope Diaz de Armendariz, Marquis of Cadereita.......... 1635
17. Diego Lopez Pacheco, Duke of Escalona................. 1640
18. Juan de Palafox y Mendoza, Archbishop of Mexico........ 1642
19. Garcia Sarmiento de Sotomayor, Count of Salvatierra...... 1642
20. Marcos Torres y Rueda, Bishop of Yucatan.............. 1648
21. Luis Enriquez de Guzman, Count of Alba de Liste........ 1650
22. Francisco Fernandez de la Cueva, Duke of Alburquerque... 1653
23. Juan de Leiva y de la Cerda, Marquis of Leiva........... 1660
24. Diego Osorio de Escobar, Bishop of Puebla.............. 1664
25. Antonio Sebastian de Toledo, Marquis of Mancera........ 1664

During the Reign of Charles II.

26. Pedro Nuño de Colon, Duke of Veragua................. 1673
27. Francisco Payo de Rivera Enriquez, Archbishop of Mexico. 1673
28. Tomas Antonio de la Cerda, Marquis of Laguna.......... 1680
29. Melchor Portocarrero, Count of Monclova............... 1686
30. Gaspar de la Cerda Sandoval, Count of Galvez........... 1688
31. Juan de Ortega Montañez, Bishop of Michoacan.......... 1696
32. José Sarmiento Valladares, Count of Montezuma......... 1696

During the Reign of Philip V.

33. Juan de Ortega Montañez, the second time 1701
34. Francisco Fernandez de la Cueva, Duke of Albuquerque.... 1702
35. Fernando de Alencastre, Duke of Linares................ 1711
36. Baltazar de Zuñiga, Marquis of Valero.................. 1716
37. Juan de Acuña, Marquis of Casafuerte 1722
38. Juan Antonio Vizarron, Archbishop of Mexico............ 1734
39. Pedro de Castro y Figueroa, Duke of Conquista 1740
40. Pedro Cebrian y Agustin, Count of Fuenclara............ 1742

During the Reign of Ferdinand VI.

41. Juan F. de Güemes y Horcasitas, Count of Revillagigedo... 1746
42. Agustin Ahumada y Villalon, Marquis of Amarillas........ 1755

During the Reign of Charles III.

Year.

43. Francisco Cajigal de la Vega............................ 1760
44. Joaquin de Monserrat, Marquis of Cruillas............... 1760
45. Carlos Francisco de Croix, Marquis of Croix............. 1766
46. Antonio Maria de Bucareli............................... 1771
47. Martin de Mayorga...................................... 1779
48. Matias de Galvez, Lieutenant-General................... 1783
49. Bernardo de Galvez, Count of Galvez.................... 1785
50. Alonso Nuñez de Haro, Archbishop of Mexico............. 1787
51. Manuel Antonio Flores.................................. 1787

During the Reign of Charles IV.

52. Juan Vicente Güemes Pacheco, Count of Revillagigedo..... 1789
53. Miguel de la Grua Salamanca, Marquis of Branceforte..... 1794
54. Miguel José de Azanza.................................. 1798
55. Felix Berenguer de Marquina........................... 1800
56. José de Iturrigaray................................... 1803
57. Pedro Garibay, Field-Marshal.......................... 1808

During the Reign of Ferdinand VII.

58. Francisco Javier de Lizana, Archbishop of Mexico........ 1809
59. Francisco Javier Venegas, Lieutenant-General........... 1810
60. Felix Calleja del Rey, Lieutenant-General.............. 1813
61. Juan Ruiz de Apodaca, Lieutenant-General.............. 1816
62. Juan O'Donojú 1821

Third Period.

After the Independence—The Regency.

1. { Agustin de Iturbide, President, Juan O'Donojú, Manuel de la Bárcena, José Isidro Yañez, Manuel Velazquez de Leon, } 1821

2. { Agustin de Iturbide, President, Count of Casa de Heras, General Nicolas Bravo, José Isidro Yañez, Doctor Valentin, } 1822

Empire.

3. Agustin I. (Iturbide), from May 19, 1822, to end of March.. 1823

Provisional Government.—Executive Power.

Year.

4. ⎰ General Nicolas Bravo,
General Guadalupe Victoria,
General Pedro C. Negrete,
General Vicente Guerrero (alternate),
General Mariano Michelena (alternate),
Miguel Dominguez (alternate), ⎱ 1823

Federal Republic—Presidents.

5. General Guadalupe Victoria..... 1824
6. General Vicente Guerrero............................. 1829
7. José Maria Bocanegra................................. 1829
8. ⎰ Pedro Velez,
General Luis Quintanar, ⎱ Triumvirate 1829
Lucas Alamán,
9. General Anastasio Bustamante......................... 1830
10. General Melchor Muzquiz, *ad interim*................ 1832
11. General Manuel Gomez Pedraza........................ 1832
12. Valentin Gomez Farias, Vice-President................ 1833
13. General Antonio Lopez de Santa Ana.................. 1833

Central Republic.

14. General Antonio Lopez de Santa Ana.................. 1835
15. General Miguel Barragan, *ad interim*............... 1835
16. José Justo Corro, *ad interim*...................... 1835
17. General Anastasio Bustamante........................ 1837
18. General Antonio Lopez de Santa Ana, *ad interim*.... 1839
19. Javier Echevarria, *ad interim*..................... 1841
20. General Antonio Lopez de Santa Ana, as Provisional
President.. 1841
21. General Nicolas Bravo and General Valentin Canalizo, as acting Presidents in place of Santa Ana from 1841 to..... 1843

Federal Republic.

22. General José Joaquin Herrera........................ 1844

Central Republic.

23. General Mariano Paredes y Arrillaga................. 1846
24. General Nicolas Bravo, *ad interim*................. 1846

Federal Republic.

Year.

25. General José Mariano Salas, as Provisional President....... 1846
26. General Antonio Lopez de Santa Ana.................... 1846
27. Valentin Gomez Farias, Vice-President. 1846
28. General Antonio Lopez de Santa-Anna................ 1847
29. General Pedro Maria Anaya, as substitute 1847
30. General Antonio Lopez de Santa Ana.................... 1847
31. Manuel de la Peña y Peña, as substitute................. 1847
32. General Pedro Maria Anaya, second time as substitute 1847
33. Manuel de la Peña y Peña, second time as substitute....... 1848
34. General José Joaquin de Herrera....................... 1848
35. General Mariano Arista 1851
36. Juan Bautista Ceballos, *ad interim* 1853

Central Republic.—Dictatorship.

37. General Manuel Maria Lombardini, President *ad interim*.... 1853
38. General Antonio Lopez Santa Ana, dictator, from April 1,
    1853, till August 9................................. 1855

Federal Republic.

39. General Martin Carrera as President *ad interim*........... 1855
40. General Juan Alvarez, *ad interim* 1855
41. General Ignacio Comonfort, as substitute at first and then as
    Constitutional President........................... 1855
42. Benito Juarez, *ad interim* at first..................... 1857
    The same as Constitutional President.................. 1861
    The same as Constitutional President.................. 1867
    The same as Constitutional President in.............. 1871
    and up to the time of his death, July 18, 1872.
43. Sebastian Lerdo de Tejada, as President *ad interim* at first
    and then as Constitutional President 1872
44. General Juan N. Mendez, in charge of the Executive Power
    (November) 1876
45. General Porfirio Diaz 1877
46. General Manuel Gonzalez.............................. 1880
47. General Porfirio Diaz (re-elected four times).............. 1884

Revolutionary leaders who, without legal title, held possession of the City of Mexico during the War of Reform.

1. Felix Zuloaga, from the 23d of January till the end of
   December.. 1858

Year.

2. Manuel Robles Pezuela, towards the end of 1858 and the
   beginning of 1859
3. Counsellor José Ignacio Pavon, a few days in 1859
4. Miguel Miramon, from March, 1859, till the 24th of December. 1859

*Administrations upheld by the French invaders, and who governed in the
places that were in the hands of the foreign army.—Regency.*

Pelagio de Labastida y Davalos, Archbishop of Mexico ; Juan
   N. Almonte ; Juan B. de Ormachea, Bishop of Tulancingo ; Mariano Salas ; and José Ignacio Pavon......... 1863
Archduke of Austria, Maximilian Ferdinand, from June, 1864,
   until May, 1867.

MEXICAN INTERVENTION AND NAPOLEON'S DOWNFALL.[1]

I have always thought that the downfall of the Napoleonic dynasty at
Sedan in 1870 was due to Louis Napoleon's intervention in Mexico.
But further to confirm this opinion I laid my views on the subject
before competent persons who knew a great deal more about the events
causing the crushing defeat of 1870 than myself.   One of these was
Señor Don Luis Maneyro, a Mexican gentleman who lived for many
years in France ; who resided there during the inception, progress, and
termination of the intervention, acting both before and after the intervention as Mexican consul at Bordeaux ; and who kept himself very well
posted about the political affairs of that country.   Another gentleman
whose opinion I regarded as carrying great weight was Mr. John Bigelow, United States Minister to France during the same period.   I
received answers from both gentlemen, which I do not feel at liberty to
publish, altogether confirming my views.   I append here a copy of the
memorandum which I submitted to both gentlemen for their criticism.

   Memorandum.—The defeat of the French army under General
Lorencez at Puebla, on May 5, 1862, and more particularly the complete failure of the French intervention in Mexico, ending with the
withdrawal of the French army, and the fall and execution of Maximilian in 1867, were in my opinion, the origin and the principal cause
of the humiliation of France in 1870, and the consequent downfall of
Louis Napoleon.   It seems to me that the French emperor, artfully
using the controlling power of France to further his own ends, was
always eager and ready to take part in the international troubles

---

[1] This article was published by the *Century Illustrated Monthly Magazine* of New
York, in vol. liv., No. 1, of May, 1897, under the title of " The Fall of the Second
Empire as Related to French Intervention in Mexico," and it is reproduced here with-
out any change.

arising in Europe, and very naturally the side to which he allied himself was in every instance the victorious one. Napoleon always made the best use of his victories, which gave him great prestige, thereby increasing proportionately his moral influence. He was considered by Europe as a great political genius who was leading France in the pathway of greatness and prosperity, and who could make no mistakes; and he became in fact the arbiter of the destinies of that continent. His military defeat in Mexico in 1862, the first one he had suffered, and which showed that he did not possess the foresight with which he was credited, and his moral and political defeat in 1867, caused by the fall and execution of Maximilian, showed the thinking men of the world that he also could fall into errors of judgment, and that he was not by any means the great man he had been supposed to be, causing him at once to descend from the high pedestal upon which his former success had placed him.

Men like Prince Bismarck saw that his reputation was usurped, and that he was not greatly above the average mortal, and prepared to strike the decisive blow which was dealt to him by Prussia in 1870. To deal this blow, Prince Bismarck took advantage of the complicated situation which Napoleon had created for himself in Mexico by declaring in 1866 the war against Austria which ended with the battle of Sadowa, thus strengthening Prussia, and putting her at the head of the North German Confederation at a time when Napoleon, engaged in Mexico, and in imminent danger of becoming involved in difficulties with the United States, could not well take part in that contest without running serious risks. The talent of Prince Bismarck consisted in taking advantage of the right moment. If Napoleon had not been engaged with the Mexican intervention, he undoubtedly would have taken the side either of Austria or of Prussia, and the war would have terminated in favor of the power backed by France, with territorial advantages for the latter; and thus he would have increased his reputation as a sagacious statesman. But had Napoleon supported either power, the probabilities are that the matter would have been settled without any war, or, if a war had broken out, it would have ended in favor of the allies of France. All this was swept away by the terrible collapse of 1867, which brought about his humiliation at Sedan and the fall of the. empire.

It is true that before declaring war on Austria, Bismarck obtained assurances from Napoleon that he would remain neutral; but the difficulties in which the French emperor had involved himself by his Mexican venture decided his course in this case, and Prince Bismarck knew very well that while the Mexican scheme was pending the Emperor of the French could not well afford to take part in any other undertaking of a serious character.

I believe that future historians, looking at these events without passion or prejudice, and inspired by a desire to present facts as they really are, can reason only in this way.   Mexico will have, as a reparation for the injustice done her by the French intervention, the sad satisfaction of having been the prime factor in the emancipation of Europe from the Napoleonic rule.   MATIAS ROMERO.

The foregoing paper caused Señor Don Luis Maneyro, Mexican Consul at Bordeaux, to write a memorandum confirming the assertions contained in the same, and considering the circumstances that Señor Maneyro has lived in France since his infancy, and that his father and himself had been prominently connected with public affairs, the former being a witness of the events connected with the French intervention in Mexico, and has had exceptional opportunities to know what took place there, his opinion has a great deal of weight.   I submitted to President Diaz this memorandum with the request that he should examine it and advise me whether it was correct in so far as the reported transactions between himself and Marshal Bazaine, commander of the French army, were concerned, and General Diaz in a letter, dated at the City of Mexico, June 5, 1897, answered me that before leaving the country, Marshal Bazaine offered to sell him, not his transportation material, but his powder, arms, and army clothing that he had in excess, and did not have the means of carrying with him.   I give below Señor Maneyro's memorandum.

MEMORANDUM BY SEÑOR DON LUIS MANEYRO, MEXICAN CONSUL AT BORDEAUX.

In 1866 France was not bound by any treaty or agreement that could have prevented her from taking part in the German struggle for supremacy.   She could have made the balance lean on the side she would have preferred, be it in favor of Prussia, be it in favor of the independent States of the German Confederation.

The consequences of such an intervention in the war of 1866, it is plainly to be seen, would have been most important for France and the empire; in fact it is impossible to exaggerate how far the result of events and the condition of affairs would have changed.

Perhaps merely the moral weight of French intervention on one side or the other would have given the final victory to her allies, perhaps Sadowa would not have taken place.   All these conjectures are allowable, and the preponderance of France would then have been undeniable.

At that time the French army enjoyed in Europe a well earned reputation, owing to its repeated triumphs after the fall of Napoleon I.

The restoration of Louis Philippe's Government and the Second Empire had been most successful in all their undertakings.

Everybody believed in the perfect organization and the easy mobilization of that most fortunate army, and although the system of Marshal Neil, who created the " Garde mobile " in imitation of the " landwehr," was not yet in existence, public confidence in the success of the French flag was thoroughly established.

The Luxembourg question presented a most plausible pretext for the intervention of France in the conflict. A very powerful party was inducing the Emperor to declare war, and the cabals nearest the two sovereigns at the Palace—those who influenced the Empress unfortunately comprised in their midst some Mexicans whose names are known to all, much to their disadvantage—were pushing them to form an alliance with Austria, Bavaria, Hanover, and against Prussia, then increasing in influence and power.

These courtiers who had had such disastrous influence during the period of hesitancy regarding the war of Mexico were then repaid for their former mistake.

Fate decreed that their unwholesome influence in 1862 should prevent the putting into practise their happy thought in 1866. That was really another of the evil consequences of the war of Mexico on unhappy France, and as determining the fall of the empire.

The following data which have been carefully examined were collected by a Mexican who is well acquainted with Paris, and mingled with the actors and spectators of those dramas of 1862–66 and 1870.

In May, 1866, the war party was very much in the majority at the Tuileries. Every day it was expected that the Luxembourg would be invaded by French troops, or at least that a declaration of war would be issued or some step taken which would admit of no backing out.

The reports of the French military attachés residing in various countries encouraged the hopes of success, and it was not to be supposed that Austria would be utterly defeated, on account of the number of her allies, but rather it could be well imagined that Prussia was about to be annihilated.

France had it in her power to give the victory to either side. The Emperor was determined, and the chiefs of his army corps who were consulted said that all reliance could be placed on their troops.

It was then that the grain of sand was visible, that grain of sand sent by God, as Bossuet terms it, which brings about the downfall of empires when they are most occupied with their glory and their pride.

That grain of sand became the retribution that Fate reserved for the unjust aggression against Mexico, it was the betrayal of the Commissary Department which made it impossible for France to undertake an European war.

When the Commissary Department was consulted, the scaffolding broke down, carrying with it all the combinations then made, and compelling France to remain passive, to paralyze her efforts, to reduce her to a mere spectator of a movement which changed the situation of Europe, built the powerful German nation threatening France at her very doors.   Germany was already hostile to France, was cognizant of her superiority, and wished to restore the old frontiers existing before the Palatinate War.

France had 50,000 men in Mexico.   Outside of Algiers, she still had 160,000 men distributed in four large military divisions.   If half of these troops would cross the Rhine, they might decide the princes who were hesitating to ally themselves to France, since, until the first victories of the Prussians took place and until the affair of Langensalz, many petty sovereigns and principalities were sorely troubled and did not know with what party they should side.

The answer given by the Commissary Department when consulted was as follows :

" It is impossible to undertake a campaign under existing conditions of things.   All the train material that could be used is in Mexico. We could not collect nor keep in store the necessary provisions, supplies, rations, ammunition, etc., for an army corps of six thousand men."

And yet the Commissaires Wolf and Friant kept up their urgent demand from Mexico for more train and artillery material!

The army corps of 50,000 men had required and absorbed war material sufficient for an army of 200,000 men in active campaign in Europe.

Everything had been taken away from the various warehouses, everything was in Mexico.   The lack of railways, the bad condition of the roads, the immense extent of land that the army had to cross, the army which was greatly subdivided and whose sections were at enormous distances from each other—the difficulty of providing the means of subsistence in a hostile country, where the places actually occupied were under the dominion of the invader, the necessities of an European army, which was not accustomed to the frugality and sobriety of the Mexican soldiers, all the above rendered necessary four times the amount of war material required in European countries.

The condition of the roads and the difficulties encountered in the moving of army trains had at times even brought about the destruction of war material which could not be carried away or had to remain buried in the mud.   The large pieces for siege artillery, which had been brought for the investment of Oaxaca, had to be carried on men's shoulders; and portions of them had to be left dismounted and scattered on the trunks of trees.   All the military trains were in Mexico, and still they were not sufficient to perform the work assigned to them.

The transport ships which carried that material would arrive one after the other, and immediately had to return to France to look for some more freight of a like nature, which could not be obtained.

The stormy passage of some of those vessels had resulted in the throwing overboard of a portion of their cargoes.

The transportation of the wounded, of provisions, and of ammunition was made under contract with the mule drivers of the country. No wagons or carts remained in France.

Upon the eve of abandoning Maximilian, Marshal Bazaine, when he knew that General Porfirio Diaz refused to buy his powder and the mules for his trains, had to drown the latter and burn the former. The French army was compelled to return to France, owing principally to the active influence brought to bear on Mr. Seward by Mr. Romero, Mexican Minister at Washington, which gave rise to the demand made by the United States on France to abandon Mexican territory gradually and at stated periods.

But that army returned to France without any war material and found none awaiting it in its native country.

The war against Germany was impossible, as was well understood by those who knew what an important part the Commissary Department plays in any war.

The Emperor and those who foresaw coming events, much against their will, had to abandon the opportunity that presented itself in the spring of 1866, and which was the only one which could possibly occur. The results of such a step we all know well enough; they were the disasters and fall of the empire, the humiliation of France, and the loss of a portion of her territory.

Mexico had obtained her full revenge.

ADDRESSES ON THE CAUSES OF THE MEXICAN REVOLUTIONS.

I have tried to make it clear in the minds of the people of the United States, availing myself of all the opportunities which have been presented to me, that there were sufficient causes for the revolutions that we had in Mexico, and that such causes having come to an end, there was no danger of any new outbreaks. It would be very long to insert here all the addresses that I have made with that object in view, in the many years of my official residence in this country, and I will therefore only mention such as, considering the occasion on which they were delivered, and the standing and character of the gentlemen participating in the same, I regard of more importance.

Banquet in New York City on March 29, 1864.—On March 29, 1864, after my return from Mexico as Envoy Extraordinary and Minister

Plenipotentiary, a banquet was given to me in the city of New York by prominent citizens, for the purpose of expressing their sympathy for the cause of Mexican independence and liberty.

The proceedings of this banquet were communicated by President Lincoln to the Senate of the United States with his Message of June 16, 1864, concerning Mexican affairs.

The citizens who tendered me that banquet were the following:

WILLIAM C. BRYANT.	FREDERICK DE PEYSTER.	C. A. BRISTED.
WILLIAM H. ASPINWALL.	W. BUTLER DUNCAN.	ALEXANDER VAN RENSSELAER.
HAMILTON FISH.	WILLIAM CURTIS NOYES.	GEORGE FOLSOM.
JOHN W. HAMERSLEY.	HENRY CLEWS.	WASHINGTON HUNT.
JONATHAN STURGES.	FREDERICK C. GEBHARD.	CHARLES KING.
JAMES W. BEEKMAN.	GEORGE T. STRONG.	WILLARD PARKER.
J. J. ASTOR, JR.	HENRY DELAFIELD.	ADRIAN ISELIN.
SMITH CLIFT.	HENRY E. PIERREPONT.	ROBERT J. LIVINGSTON.
W. E. DODGE, JR.	GEORGE OPDYKE.	SAMUEL B. RUGGLES.
DAVID HOADLEY.	DAVID DUDLEY FIELD.	JAMES T. BRADY.
	GEORGE BANCROFT.	

On that occasion I delivered the following address:

MR. CHAIRMAN—GENTLEMEN:—I feel entirely unable to express to you in a sufficient manner my sincere thanks for the great honor you have bestowed upon me and my country in this refined and splendid demonstration of your sympathy for struggling Mexico. It is, indeed, particularly gratifying to me that this significant demonstration is made by so many of the most distinguished and most eminent citizens, who are an ornament to this great metropolis, and whose virtues, learning, and enterprise have contributed so much to make your city in so brief a period the first, not only of the broad United States, but of the whole American continent, as well as to make your country one of the most powerful, wealthy, and civilized on the globe.

It is, indeed, another motive which greatly adds to my gratification, and for which, in the name of my country, I beg to express to you my gratitude for the kind words with which our distinguished friend has proposed the health of Benito Juarez, the Constitutional President of the Republic of Mexico, and for the prompt heartiness and cordiality with which that toast has been received. I perceive, with joy and gratitude, gentlemen, that you appreciate the high qualities of that statesman and patriot, and hold a strong and pure sympathy for the noble cause of which he is the leader.

I am rejoiced that I have the opportunity to see with my own eyes the proof that the eminent French statesman, M. Thiers, was somewhat mistaken when, in a speech he recently delivered before the *Corps Législatif*, of Paris, against the policy pursued by the Emperor Napoleon in Mexican affairs, he stated that the United States would not, under present circumstances, object in any way to that policy; and that, should the Archduke Maximilian come to this city *en route* to Mexico, he would meet with a cordial reception at your hands. It could scarcely be possible to have a more distinguished, complete, and genuine representation of the patriotism, intelligence, and wealth of the great city of New York—the leading city of the Union—than that I see assembled here this evening; yet, if I can trust my senses, gentlemen, I venture to assert that the sympathies of your great city run in a direction very different from that imagined by M. Thiers.

I am very happy to say that the kind of feeling you express for Mexico is fully reciprocated. In Mexico there are now but the sentiments of regard and admiration for the United States, and the desire to pursue such a course as will draw more closely all those powerful ties by which both nations should be united.

It has sometimes appeared to me, that the gentlemen who controlled the Government of the United States for thirty-five years previous to 1861, cared for nothing so much as for the acquisition of territory. Those gentlemen thus caused their country to appear in the character of a very covetous man, who, without knowing the boundaries of his own estate, or endeavoring to improve it, constantly exerts himself to enlarge its limits, without being very scrupulous as to the means of its accomplishment.

Just before the war with Mexico commenced, the United States had a boundary question with England, which threatened a rupture between the two countries, and I have been informed that the same documents which were prepared as a declaration of war against Great Britain were used when war was finally declared against Mexico. Thus, while the idea of acquiring domain from Great Britain by a dubious title, to say the least, was relinquished, the same scheme was carried out against Mexico, not only without any plausible reason, but, I must say, in violation of all principles of justice.

I beg of you, gentlemen, to excuse me if I have referred to an unpleasant point in the history of late events. But I wish to forcibly present to your minds the idea that the unfair policy I have alluded to led, in a great measure, to the troubles and complications in which you are now involved, and one of the consequences of which is French intervention in Mexico, as that intervention would never have been but for the civil war in the United States.

Those who have pursued this policy appear to have been, in the main, under the influence of the slave power, and to have had in view their own political influence and personal aggrandizement, rather than the great interests of their country. They very properly thought that, by extending the area of slavery, they would extend in proportion their influence and strength. For that reason they did not insist on increasing the territory of the United States in the far Northwest, where their *peculiar institution* could not be acclimated, but rather set their eyes toward the sunny regions of Mexico. By that means the institution of human slavery had so large an increase, that a short time afterward it was strong enough to commence a gigantic war against the Government of the United States. In my opinion, the leaders of the slavery party always had in view the separation of their own States from the free States of the North, and to replace the loss of Northern aimed at the acquisition of Southern territory.

I will not conceal from you, gentlemen, the fact that we have looked with deep apprehension upon such an aggressive policy, which threatened to deprive us of our independence and nationality—the highest and most precious rights that man can enjoy on earth. We were, of course, fully determined not to give up this precious inheritance, and we had resolved to fight to the last. In our present war with France, we are giving a proof of our determination. It may appear foolish and unavailing for Mexico, that has been so often exhausted in her struggles to obtain true liberty during the last forty years, to accept war with the greatest military power in Europe ; but there are circumstances in the life of nations which cause them to overlook all secondary considerations, and determine to exert themselves to overcome all difficulties. Besides, our situation is not so bad as many think.

Fortunately, the change of policy toward Mexico operated in the United States brought up a consequent change in the feelings of my country in regard to yours. We do not wish now to have any interest antagonistical to yours, because we mean to keep peace with you, and that object could scarcely be accomplished if our respective interests were in opposition. For that reason, among other very material ones that we had, we established a republican form of government and democratic institutions, modeled on the same basis as yours.

The Emperor of the French pretends that the object of his interference in Mexican affairs is to prevent the annexation of Mexico to the United States ; and yet that very result would, most likely, be ultimately accomplished if a monarchy were established in Mexico. Fortunately for us, that scheme is by no means a feasible one.

Mexico is most bountifully blessed by nature. She can produce of the best quality and in large quantities all of the principal agricultural staples of the world— cotton, coffee, sugar, tobacco, vanilla, wheat, and corn. Her mines have yielded the largest portion of all the silver which now circulates throughout the world, and there still remain to her mountains of that precious metal, as well as of gold, which only require labor, skill, and capital to make them available and valuable. The wealth of California is nothing when compared with what still remains in Mexico.

My country, therefore, opens a most desirable field for the enterprise of a commercial nation. Far-sighted England discovered this many years ago, and by establishing a line of mail steamers from Southampton to Veracruz and Tampico, and negotiating advantageous treaties of commerce, has, beyond all other nations, enjoyed the best of the Mexican trade. France, seeing this, and wishing to vie with England, has undertaken an enterprise which, besides being ruinous to her, will not produce the desired end, as the means adopted must surely cause the opposite result. The United States are the best situated to avail themselves of the immense wealth of Mexico. Being a neighbor nation, they have more advantages than any other for the frontier and coasting trade ; and, furthermore, being a nation second to none in wealth, activity, skill, and enterprise, they are called by nature to speculate in and enjoy the resources of Mexico.

We are willing to grant to the United States every commercial facility that will not be derogatory to our independence and sovereignty. This will give to the United States all possible advantages that could be derived from annexation, without any of its inconveniences. That once done, our common interests, political as well as commercial, will give us a common American continental policy which no European nation would dare disregard.

The bright future which I plainly see for both nations had made me forget for a moment the present troubles in which they are now involved. I consider these troubles of so transitory a nature as not to interfere materially with the common destiny I have foreshadowed ; but, as they have the interest of actuality, I beg to be allowed to make a few remarks in regard to them.

Every careful observer of events could not help noticing, when the expedition against Mexico was organized in Europe, that it would, sooner or later, draw the United States into the most serious complications, and involve them in the difficulty. The object of that expedition being no less than a direct and armed interference in the political affairs of an American nation, with a view to overthrow its republican institutions and establish on their ruins a monarchy, with a European prince on the throne,—the only question to be determined by the United States and the other nations concerned, was as to the time when they would be willing or ready to meet the issue thus boldly and openly held out by the antagonistic nations of Europe.

The United States could not be indifferent to this question ; just as a man who sees his neighbor's house set on fire by an incendiary, could not remain an unconcerned spectator, while his own house contains his family and all his fortune, and combustible matter lies in the basement. The only alternative left to him should be, whether it would be more convenient to his interests to help his neighbor in putting out the fire from the beginning, and with the same earnestness as if his own house were already caught by that destructive element, or to await inactive until the incendiary has succeeded in making a perfect blaze of his neighbor's property, by which all will inevitably be involved in one common ruin.

This, in my opinion, is the situation in which the United States is placed with

25

regard to Mexico. Taking into consideration the well-known sagacity of American statesmen, the often-proved devotion of the American people to republican institutions, and the patriotism and zeal of the Administration that presides over the destinies of the country, I cannot entertain the slightest doubt that the United States will act in this emergency as will conduce to the best interests they and mankind at large have at stake in the Mexican question.

In the meantime, however, I consider it of the highest importance that the delusion prevailing throughout Europe that the United States do not oppose, and rather favor, the establishment of a monarchy in Mexico by French bayonets, should be dispelled. The French government has been working steadily in causing that delusion to prevail on the other side of the water, and, so far, has succeeded more than could be expected, considering the absurdity of such an idea. The war against Mexico would be ten times more unpopular in France than it is now—in fact, it could not be maintained any longer—if the French people were made to understand that the people of the United States will never tolerate, much less favor or encourage, the establishment, by force of arms, of a European monarchy upon the ruins of a sister neighboring republic. The French people are friendly to the United States; old traditions, the common love of liberty, and the absence of opposing interests, make them friendly. They would, therefore, be wholly opposed to anything that, without bringing them any real benefit, might, sooner or later, lead to a war with this country. They very well know that such a war could not but be disastrous to France, since France would have everything to lose and nothing to gain by such a war, whatever may be her influence and power in the European continental politics.

The United States may find that they are brought squarely to the issue on the Mexican question sooner than they expected, should the report, lately reached here, of any understanding between Maximilian, as so-called Emperor of Mexico, and the insurgents in this country, prove correct. The archduke, it is stated, will inaugurate his administration by acknowledging the independence of the South, and, perhaps, he will go further; and this, of course, by the advice, consent, and support of the French Government, whose satellite, and nothing else, will the archduke be in Mexico.

The French official and semi-official papers assure us that Maximilian will soon depart for Mexico. All present appearances indicate that he is willing to change his high position in Europe for a hazardous one in Mexico. He cannot stay there unless supported by a French army, and he will not, therefore, be anything more than the shadow of the French emperor. Should he ever have a different view or desire from the French government, or even the French general-in-chief, he will be obliged to submit to the humiliating condition of forbearing to do that which he thinks best in a country where he will call himself emperor. As far as the personality of the Austrian duke is concerned, he is nothing. If he goes to Mexico to meddle in our affairs, we shall consider him as our enemy, and deal with him accordingly. We hold that in the political question which is being agitated in Mexico the person of the Austrian duke is not of much account; and whether he does or does not go there, that question can ultimately have only one possible solution—namely, the triumph and maintenance of republican institutions.

As far as I am concerned, I prefer that Maximilian should go to Mexico, so as to give the European dreamers on monarchies a fair chance to realize their dreams of America. As for Mexico, I can say that nothing that has transpired in my country should surprise any one who is familiar with our affairs. It is true that we have been unfortunate during the past year; we have lost nearly all the battles we have fought with the French; they have occupied some of our principal cities; they have blockaded our ports; but all these gains on the part of the French are nothing when compared with the elements of opposition and endurance which remains with the National

Government of Mexico, ruling a people numbering eight millions, determinedly opposed to intervention, ready to fight, and fighting already for their independence ; a country that will require half a million soldiers to subdue and possess ; naturally strong in defences, possessing inaccessible mountains, impracticable roads, where the patriots will be able to make a perpetual warfare upon the invader, until he is persuaded of the impossibility of accomplishing the conquest, or be compelled to leave for other causes. Such is the prospect before us, and that in case we could do nothing more than make a passive resistance. But we can do better than this.

Among the many events calculated to terminate immediately French intervention in Mexico, the European complications which threaten to cause a general war on that continent should be particularly mentioned. It is certainly wonderful that while Europe is in so insecure and agitated a condition, menaced by revolutions everywhere, and wrestling to recover its own existence and independence, the French emperor should be thinking about arranging other people's affairs, as if his own did not require his immediate and most particular attention.

The only serious support the French intervention had among the Mexicans was that afforded by the Church party, which was, in fact, the promoter and supporter of the intervention. The generals of the Church party have, with the aid of the French army, been conscripting Mexican citizens to make them fight with the foreign invader against their brothers and the independence of their country. The Church party expected, of course, as a small compensation for the services rendered to the intervention, that as soon as the French should take the City of Mexico they would restore the Church property confiscated by the National Government, and the *fueros* of the clergy, of which they had been deprived. But the French have thus far failed to do this. They discovered that the Church party was the weakest, and that with that party they had no chance of subduing the country. The French now wish to conciliate the Liberal party by sustaining and enforcing all the important measures and laws decreed by the National Government. But the Liberals of Mexico are true patriots, not partisans, and will not be conciliated, so long as the foot of the invader is on Mexican soil. The policy of the French so incensed the Church party that they broke altogether with the French. The Archbishop of Mexico, who was a member of the so-called regency, withdrew at once, and was afterward dismissed by General Bazaine. The so-called supreme tribunal protested against those measures, and shared the fate of the archbishop. All the archbishops and bishops in the republic then joined in signing a protest, in which they declared the condition of the Church to be far worse than it ever was under the rule of the Liberal Government ; that now they are not allowed even to issue their pastorals, a right never denied to them while the Liberals were in power in the City of Mexico. The protest concluded by excommunicating the French Government, the French army in Mexico, all Mexicans who take sides with the French, and everybody who supports the French cause in any way. These proceedings have left the French without the support of the only part of the native population they ever had in their favor, and have combined against them all the elements of the country.

I fear that I have already imposed too much upon your kindness, and, in concluding my remarks, I beg to express my earnest and sincere desire that this demonstration may be the beginning of a new era of perpetual peace and cordiality in the relations between the United States and Mexico. (Prolonged cheers.)

Banquet at New York City on October 2, 1867.—When the War of Intervention was over in Mexico, prominent citizens of New York City, desirous of testifying in some public manner their interest in the welfare of that country, and their esteem for my adhering to its cause amid the greatest discouragements, tendered me a banquet which took place at the city of New York on October 2, 1867, previous to my return home. The gentlemen who made the invitation and participated at the banquet were the following :

PETER COOPER,	WM. H. ASPINWALL,	PAUL SPOFFORD,
M. H. GRINNELL,	H. H. VAN DYCK,	HENRY CLEWS,
SAM'L G. COURTNEY,	JAMES ROBB,	CHAS. W. SANDFORD,
FRANCIS SKIDDY,	SHEPARD GANDY,	PARKE GODWIN
WM. R. GARRISON,	BENJ. HOLLIDAY,	ELLICOTT C. COWDIN,
WM. C. BRYANT,	JAMES W. BEEKMAN	HIRAM BARNEY,
WM. E. DODGE, Jr.,	JOHN JAY,	HENRY WARD BEECHER,
DAN'L BUTTERFIELD,	THEODORE ROOSEVELT	JOHN A. STEWART,
HENRY A. SMYTHE,	DAVID HOADLEY,	RUFUS INGALLS,
JAS. R. WHITING,	J. GRANT WILSON,	WM. G. FARGO.

On that occasion I made the following address :

Mr. CHAIRMAN—GENTLEMEN :—It is nearly eight years since I landed in an official capacity on this hospitable shore. Soon afterward, I became the representative of my country, or at least of such a portion of it, as believing that they had in the United States a great example to imitate, were eager to give Mexico the same advantages that this country enjoyed, by following the same line of policy.

About that very time, the elements of a gigantic political struggle were maturing, which produced soon afterward the great Civil War of the United States. This terrible shock was felt at once in Mexico, in the shape of an European intervention avowedly for the purpose of overthrowing the Republican institutions existing there. All of you, gentlemen, are quite familiar with what followed here as well as there. It pleased Heaven to crown with success the noble efforts of the patriots and philanthropists who, while defending in both countries the independence and integrity of their homes and the institutions of their choice, were also struggling for the advancement of humanity, and the amelioration of the social condition of the masses throughout the world.

I call your attention to this difficult crisis, only to express on this solemn occasion, before this distinguished assembly of representative men, my testimony of the high-toned, enlightened, and disinterested sympathy which the cause of Mexico awakened in the hearts of the people of the United States ; a sympathy which, while encouraging the Mexican people in the defense of their outraged rights, made European encroachments more guarded, and thus contributed in a great measure to the final success at which we now all rejoice.

In closing, or at least suspending, temporarily, my official duties at Washington, it behooves me to say that I carry home a very lively and most pleasant recollection of my long sojourn among you ; that I take also with me the lasting experience of eight years of political agitation, in which very momentous events have taken place; that, faithful to the political creed of the Liberal national party of Mexico, I will do all I can to contribute in establishing there the same political principles I have been taught to admire and appreciate here, and which, in my opinion, are indispensable to the welfare of Mexico ; and it will be my pride as well as my pleasure to be the friend of the United States so long as they entertain no hostile or unfriendly designs against my own country.

On a former occasion, and in this very place, I availed myself of the opportunity to express what I consider to be a philosophical view, based on facts, of the causes and objects of the civil wars in Mexico since the Declaration of its Independence. I do not believe that Nature has made different sets of rules for each people, or for each family of peoples, called races. It is, in my opinion, wiser to suppose that Providence controls mankind by the same code of rules, which are equally applicable to the Anglo-Saxon as to the Latin races—to the Indians as to the Africans.

In these modern times, political revolutions seem to have for their object the amelioration of the condition of the masses, by breaking or attempting to break down the old system of the organization of society when this becomes oppressive. Following this theory, it appears to me that in all modern revolutions there have been two sides : the aristocratic side, or the side of the few, who have in the course of time, accumulated wealth, power, and influence, often exercised to the disadvantage of the people ; and the popular side, or the side of the many, who lose those advantages in proportion as they are monopolized by their opponents. A point is reached where the exactions of the few become intolerable, and then comes a popular uprising ; or either the aristocratic element, foreseeing that this result is to happen, precipitates it by taking the initiative with a view to forcing the contest, before their enemies are fully organized and prepared. This was, in my opinion, the cause of the English revolution of the 17th century, which culminated in the establishment of the Commonwealth ; of the French revolution of the 18th century, which ended in a similar manner ; of the last civil war in the United States, and of the civil wars in Mexico and other Spanish-American Republics.

Our aristocracy in Mexico has been an ambitious and unscrupulous priesthood, who had wielded for centuries political power, and would rather see their country subjugated by a foreign despot than under the control of their political opponents who desire, in good faith, its advancement and prosperity, and its emancipation from religious intolerance, and from opposition to popular and free education. Fortunately for us, the question at home has been of a mere political character, notwithstanding the efforts of the clergy to make it also a religious one.

Our success against the French once achieved, I have very strong and well-grounded reasons to expect that we shall have peace and tranquillity, and that our country will be developed and enjoy fully their attending blessings.

Within a brief period we shall hold our election for the functionaries to be chosen by the people, and we shall then enter again into our constitutional existence, somewhat interrupted by the French intervention. Our policy will then be to enforce our laws which allow the free exercise of all religions, and give no preference to any ; which provide a perfect separation between Church and State ; to establish a system of free schools, which will educate the masses of our people, and make them productive and happy ; to encourage the immigration of peaceable and laboring citizens of the United States, which will assist us in developing our resources ; to invite the investment of the surplus capital of the United States in Mexican enterprises, and to look up to this privileged country as our eldest sister, affording us an example worthy of imitation. When these objects are attained, when both countries stand in the relation of friendly powers, with a common object and a common destiny, realizing the responsibility they have before the world as the guardians of republican institutions, my life-long ambition and my fondest wishes will have been realized.

The condition of the Mexican people is not fully understood outside of Mexico, and causes very many to distrust their capacity for self-government. It is certainly not so far advanced in civilization as the people of the United States. Education is not so much extended there as here ; there is little homogeneousness in the elements of which it is composed ; yet they are a peaceful, laborious people, well-meaning and docile, and they only need the establishment of free schools and the consolidation of peace, to become one of the best regulated people upon earth. The greater portion of our population has been purposely kept in the most complete ignorance by the

Spaniards and the Church party, with a view of controlling them more easily, and when we shall have educated them we shall double or treble the working energies of the country.

The conduct of the Mexican people during our late war with France shows, in my opinion, beyond all doubt, that they possess very many of the virtues which constitute a free people; their perseverance under the greatest discouragement, their courage and determination to fight constantly against an enemy vastly superior in resources, their moderation in the hour of success, their well-known endurance, are all facts which speak very clearly in their behalf. I have full confidence in them, and earnestly believe that, if they are not as advanced as it is desirable they should be they are capable and desirous of improvement.

As to their ability for self-government, I will only say that either republican institutions are adaptable to mankind, and calculated to promote their welfare and happiness, or they are not. If they are, I see no reason why the Mexican people should be considered unfit for them. If they are not, I could not explain their development in this country.

I think it is a mistaken view of the case to say that because we have had a civil war in Mexico, or rather a social war, which has lasted for many years, it should be concluded that we are incapable of self-government. None can suppose that we have been fighting all that time merely for the pleasure of it. We have had, to be sure, unscrupulous and designing men, who have ostensibly appeared as fighting to gratify their own ambition and self-aggrandizement; but, in fact, they have only been used by one or the other of the contending political parties; and principles have been involved at the bottom of our troubles.

As for the motives which prompted the late Maximilian to go to Mexico—much as I regret to speak of them, since he is now shielded by the sacred asylum of his grave—I, nevertheless, cannot help saying in defence of my own country, that whatever good intentions he may have entertained towards Mexico, if any, they have little to do with the question of his intervention there.

When he was asked to go to Mexico, it is charitable to suppose that he did not understand the true condition of the country so far removed from his own. But the mere fact that he was asked to go by a foreign state, at war with Mexico, and by a few Mexicans who were accomplices in the crime of overthrowing the institutions of their country by means of a foreign army, it seems to me, ought to have been sufficient to make him very careful before deciding to take part in and increase the political difficulties of Mexico. The inducements held out to him by the French emperor prevailed at last, and he determined to go under French protection and French auspices, notwithstanding that he never received a single vote from any place in Mexico not in possession of the French army of occupation.

The simple case was clearly before him. He may have supposed that if he succeeded in forcing the rule over the Mexican people, he would be the founder of a great European empire in the New World; if he failed, he would return to Europe with the prestige of having attempted to establish one, with the title of Emperor, with a higher position than he had ever had before, and a greater probability to succeed his brother as the ruler of the Austrian Empire, or to be the occupant of any vacant throne in that continent.

On leaving Miramar, and before arriving in Mexico, he went to Rome, to secure, as he said, the benediction of the Pope, and what we cannot understand in America, to consult with the Holy See about the temporal government of an American republic. The result was, that notwithstanding that consultation, he not only failed in establishing his rule in Mexico, but that soon after he arrived there he had almost an open rupture with the Pope and the Mexican clergy.

On arriving in Mexico he began to see that his task was more difficult than he had imagined. In the beginning, however, it was but light, as the French government had taken care to provide him with funds even before he left Europe, making so of this, another inducement for him to go. When these were exhausted, and the French emperor,—satisfied of the impracticability of his task,—made up his mind to withdraw his troops from Mexico, Maximilian thought of returning to Europe as the only alternative left him. I pass over, without comment, the unhappy though not unimportant rôle of the partner of his life. The result of this last and vain effort is well known to all.

Maximilian then determined to carry out his plan of leaving Mexico, and sailing from Veracruz, where an Austrian war vessel had been in readiness, awaiting to convey him to his home. He came almost by stealth from the City of Mexico to Orizaba, having previously shipped all his baggage and effects, which he took from the country.

On arriving at this latter place, he was overtaken by some of his supporters, who came to persuade him to remain, and who, as they were committed to the empire, saw in him at least one guarantee of foreign support. They represented to him, as they had done a few years before to the French emperor, and other European governments, that they controlled the Mexican people; that they could give him the men and money necessary to consolidate his rule in Mexico. They enlarged upon the glory he would achieve by accomplishing this result without the aid of the French, and availing themselves of the difficulties which had arisen between him and his supporters, they urged him, by exciting his wounded pride, to make at least another effort to remain ; in this instance they succeeded as well as in the former. Their efforts, however, would not have had this result, in my opinion, had they not been supported by the advice of one of Maximilian's most trusted counsellors—a Belgian—who accompanied him to Mexico, and who, on writing him a letter from Brussels, on the 17th of September, 1866, (the original of which has been in my hands), told him that he ought under no circumstances then to leave Mexico; that the French desired him to do so, to heap upon him the responsibility of their failure, and that he ought not to gratify them, but, by remaining, place this responsibility where it properly belonged. He advised his master furthermore, to call, after the withdrawal of the French, for a popular election to decide whether the Mexican people desired him or not, as the best means of leaving, without dishonor, a difficult position, and to return to Europe without prestige.

Maximilian's subsequent action showed that he undertook to carry out to the very letter this advice, given by a man entirely ignorant of the condition of Mexico. He returned to the City of Mexico, after having promised to call for a National Congress to decide whether the people desired the Republic or the Empire under him.

On arriving there he found that the National troops were closing their lines and carrying everything before them, and, supposing that he could arrest these advances by taking to the interior all the available forces accumulated in the City of Mexico, he marched to Queretaro. It would be unnecessary to say what happened there. Through the want of military ability he allowed our troops to concentrate upon and beseige Queretaro, until he was finally overcome. From the tenor of his communications while he was surrounded at Queretaro, it appears very clearly that he never realized the difficulties of his position, and much less the disastrous end of the campaign ; and his letters to President Juarez after he was captured, showed not less plainly that, until then, he had never dreamed of the sad fate which, by invading a harmless and innocent people in their American mountain homes, he had provoked and deserved.

But Maximilian, although a grand duke and heir of empire in Austria, was nothing of a Cæsar, and only a French automaton in the revolutionary drama of my country. Let this unhappy fate be accepted in extenuation of his crime, in consenting to be the automaton of the ambition of the French Cæsar in the revolution of Mexico.

Mexico can hereafter have no fears; for her safety against foreign invasion is secured; no revenges will follow the revolution which her enemies inaugurated, and
which has resulted in their own overthrow and ruin.

In concluding these remarks, I fear I have already intruded too long upon your
patience [cries of " No, no "], I must say that I believe the Mexican Government is
preparing several documents to be given to the world, in which its position and the
relations of Maximilian towards Mexico will be fully explained. I am certain when
these documents see the light, that all who doubted the correctness and propriety of
the policy adopted by the Mexican Government, will be inclined to change their minds.
I cannot resume my seat without again thanking the gentlemen present this evening
for their kindness and courtesy in tendering to me this demonstration. I shall always
remember it as one of the most pleasant evenings, and one of the most pleasing events
that has taken place in my life.

Banquet at New York City on December 16, 1891.—Mr. Walter S.
Logan, a prominent lawyer of New York, of whom I have before
spoken, was also kind enough to tender me a banquet in the Democratic Club of the City of New York, which took place on December
16, 1891, with the attendance of the following gentlemen :

Dr. Lyman Abbott,
Mr.Charles Frederick Adams,
Mr. Lawrence D. Alexander,
Mr. E. Ellery Anderson,
Hon. John H. V. Arnold,
Hon. William H. Arnoux,
Mr. Edward G. Bailey,
Mr. Peter T. Barlow,
Hon. Hiram Barney,
Mr. Henry W. Bean,
Hon. Henry R. Beekman,
Hon. James D. Bell,
Mr. William L. Bennett,
Señor Don Nicanor Bolet-
    Peraza,
Capt. E. C. Bowen,
Mr. Cephas Brainerd,
Mr. George W. Bramwell,
Mr. Eugene V. Brewster,
Mr. H. L. Bridgman,
Mr. Isaac H. Bromley,
Hon. William L. Brown,
Mr. Charles H. Brush,
Dr. Joseph D. Bryant,
Mr. Walter C. Cady,
Mr. John C. Calhoun,
Señor Don Joaquin Bernado
    Calvo,
Hon. Charles J. Canda,
Hon. Alfred C. Chapin,
Hon. Norton P. Chase,
Hon. L. E. Chittenden,
Mr. Gardner K. Clark, Jr.,
Mr. Salter S. Clark,
Mr. Charles W. Coleman,
Hon. Alfred R. Conkling,
Mr. Charles A. Coombs,
Mr. Magrane Coxe,
Hon. J. Sergeant Cram,

Mr. Thomas D. Crimmins,
Hon. William E. Curtis,
Hon. Noah Davis,
Mr. Charles W. Dayton,
Mr. Lewis L. Delafield,
Mr. Clarence Deming,
Mr. Charles M. Demond,
Mr. Rhinelander Dillon,
Mr. Augustus T. Docharty,
Hon. Daniel Dougherty,
Hon. C. T. Driscoll,
Mr. Frank J. Dupignac,
Hon. Dorman B. Eaton,
Col. M. V. B. Edgerly,
Mr. Walter Edwards,
Mr. George Cary Eggleston,
Mr. Rudolph Eickemeyer,
Hon. Smith Ely,
Mr. William T. Emmett,
Mr. J. Rockwell Fay,
Mr. Charles S. Findlay,
Prof. John Fiske,
Dr. Austin Flint,
Mr. Roger Foster,
Mr. A. B. de Frece,
Señor Don Jose G. Garcia,
Capt. Hugh R. Garden,
Mr. William J. Gardner,
Mr. James C. Goddard,
Rev. John C. Goddard,
Mr. Walter L. Goddard,
Hon. E. L. Godkin,
Mr. Antonio C. Gonzalez,
Mr. Frank C. Hatch,
Mr. Frederick H. Hatch,
Mr. John R. Hatch,
Mr. Marx E. Harby,
Hon. William F. Harrity,
Mr. Burton N. Harrison,

Hon. Michal D. Harter,
Mr. Henry W. Hayden,
Hon. Joseph C. Hendrix,
Hon. Abram S. Hewitt,
Mr. Thomas B. Hewitt,
Mr. Stephen R. Hewlett,
Mr. John R. Howard,
Mr. Edward C. Hurlbert,
Mr. Collis P. Huntington,
Hon. Thomas L. James,
Mr. George W. Kenyon,
Mr. John D. Kernan,
Hon. John Jay Knox,
Mr. Gilbert D. Lamb,
Col. Daniel S. Lamont,
Hon. Jefferson M. Levy,
Mr. Herbert H. Logan,
Mr. Grosvenor P. Lowrey,
Mr. Hart Lyman,
Hon. W. Gordon McCabe,
Mr. Walter L. McCorkle,
Mr. St. Clair McKelway,
Gen. James McLeer,
Mr. James F. Merriam,
Prof. John B. Moore,
Mr. Rollin M. Morgan,
Hon. Samuel D. Morris,
Hon. Theodore W. Myers,
Hon. Juan Navarro,
Hon. Henry L. Nelson,
Mr. Emmet B. Olcott,
Mr. A. C. Palmer,
Mr. George F. Parker,
Mr. Wheeler H. Peckham,
Hon. James J. Phelan,
Mr. Charles E. Phelps,
Hon. Orlando B. Potter,
Mr. Louis Prang,
Hon. Roger A. Pryor,

Mr. George Haven Putnam,
Mr. John E. Risley,
Mr. Oliver H. K. Risley,
Hon. Ellis H. Roberts,
Señor Don Matias Romero,
Hon. Horace Russell,
Mr. Louis H. Scott,
Mr. George H. Sexton,
Mr. John C. Sheehan,
Hon. Nelson Smith,
Mr. Santiago Smithers,
Mr. Henry B. Stapler,

Mr. Lucius P. Starr,
Mr. Simon Sterne,
Dr. George T. Stevens,
Mr. John Stewart,
Mr. Albert Stickney,
Hon. W. E. D. Stokes,
Mr. Isidor Straus,
Hon. Oscar S. Straus,
Hon. John A. Taylor,
Mr. Henry T. Thomas,
Mr. Daniel G. Thompson,
Mr. Hamilton B. Tompkins,
Prof. George A. Treadwell,

Hon. W. L. Trenholm,
Hon. John R. Voorhis,
Mr. Arthur E. Walradt,
Mr. J. Langdon Ward,
Hon. John DeWitt Warner,
Hon. Bartow S. Weeks,
Prof. Arthur M. Wheeler,
Hon. Everett P. Wheeler,
Hon. Andrew D. White,
Hon. Horace White,
Mr. T. C. Woodward,
Mr. Willis H. Young.

A great many speeches, and some of them of very great interest, were delivered on that occasion, and I am sorry that I do not have the space to insert here some of them, but I must confine myself to my address, which, although the humbler of the speeches then made, is relevant for the purpose that I now have in view. Fortunately they were all published in a very neat pamphlet which Mr. Logan gave to light under the title of *A Mexican Night.* My address in answer to a toast, " The Future of Mexico and its Relations with the United States," was the following :

Mr. Logan—Gentlemen :—I thank you very sincerely for this handsome and significant demonstration, in which the friends of Mexico have been so kindly treated. It has been the aim of my life to establish and cement the most cordial and friendly relations between the two great republics of the Western Hemisphere, and any demonstration like the present, calculated to produce such desirable results, is always very pleasing to me. In this case, specially, I feel particularly complimented, because I have been allowed the opportunity to meet so many of the most distinguished citizens of this city, the metropolis of the greatest republic of the world, which is destined to have a controlling influence in the welfare of mankind. (Applause.)

Although my participation in this banquet, as one of the friends of Mexico, is not a personal compliment to me, but due to the official position I now hold, as the diplomatic representative of my country near the government of the United States, I nevertheless keenly feel the whole kind meaning of this feast, and extend my heartfelt thanks to its originator, our amiable host, and to all the gentlemen who have honored us with their presence.

I hope I will be allowed, at a Mexican feast, to say a few words concerning the future of my country, in connection with the United States. You all know, gentlemen, that the wealth of Mexico is really astonishing. She has all the climates of the earth, from the frozen regions of the pole, in her snow-clad mountains, to the equatorial heat of her *tierras calientes*, and can produce, therefore, all the fruits which grow out of the earth ; and she alone can supply all the coffee, sugar, vanilla, india-rubber and other tropical products needed to provide the large market of the United States. Her mineral wealth is equally unbounded. Mexico has already yielded about two thirds of the whole silver which forms the stock of the white metal in the world, and her mines are, so far, merely scratched. Her mountains contain not only silver, but gold, iron, copper, lead, tin, cinnabar, and every other kind of metal. We have also large veins of coal, which are now being discovered, and only one has commenced to be developed. The configuration of the country, traversed by rugged and steep sierras, which come almost to the sea, while it prevents us from having large navigable streams of any length, furnishes thousands of torrents, which, in their precipitous course from the mountains to the sea, afford the largest amount of water-power I can conceive of, and will make of Mexico, in the course of time, one of the leading manufacturing countries of the world. We are bountifully blessed by Providence, as far as natural wealth is concerned, and we have all the elements to make us a self-supporting nation. All we need is peace and a just and patriotic government, willing to facilitate the development of the country ; and I think we have established the former permanently, and enjoy the latter fully. (Applause.)

Nature has made us neighbors, placing our respective countries in contiguity one to the other, for a distance of nearly two thousand miles. Our roads intermingle and make of both practically a single country for travelling and commercial purposes. We have no natural barriers to trade, all those existing being entirely artificial. Although the possibilities of Mexico are immense, we are not yet a manufacturing country, in the whole extent of this word, because our resources are still undeveloped.

We produce tropical fruits, specially raw materials, which you require as food for your large manufacturing interests, and we need a great many of the articles that you manufacture in this country. There is no reason, therefore, why we should not trade largely and to our mutual advantage. So far, and notwithstanding the artificial barriers existing on the frontier, over eighty per cent. of our exports come to the United States, and we take from this country nearly sixty per cent. of our imports ; and I have no doubt that with proper stimulus, and with a partial severance of the present barriers, traffic will double or treble before the lapse of many years. The development of trade will bring about not only the increase of business, but also of social relations between our respective countries. The capital, energy, and sagacity of the business men of this country will find a very large and profitable virgin field in Mexican enterprises.

Great doubts have been entertained about the stability of the government in Mexico, on account of our former political troubles. But it is quite plain, in my judgment, that as there was a reason for such troubles, and that said reason having now disappeared, there is no longer any danger that they will spring again. Mexico, while a colony of Spain three hundred years, was ruled by the Church then allied to the throne, which had a paramount influence, both moral and material. When Mexican independence was proclaimed in 1810, the leader being a member of the low clergy, Hidalgo, it was opposed by the Church, the aristocracy, and the Spaniards, and against such odds it could not make any headway. When in 1821 the Spanish Cortes adopted some liberal measures, which alarmed the conservative elements in Mexico, the Church thought that its interests would be better protected, having a home government that it could control, rather than one depending from the Court of Madrid, and its ruling spirits, joined the few scattered patriots which remained in the country, and independence was thus achieved, without bloodshed : this fact showing conclusively how great was the power of the Church in Mexico. As success was due to the adhesion of the Church party to the cause of independence, it was natural that they should form the new government, and the transitory Empire of Iturbide, their leader, was the outcome of their success. But the struggle then began between the liberal and progressive elements on one side, and the conservative party on the other, which culminated with the French intervention, supported by the Church party, and coinciding with the Civil War in the United States. The defeat of the intervention put an end to the armed struggle of the Church for political supremacy in Mexico. It is no wonder that such a struggle should last nearly fifty years, when it is taken into consideration that Mexico passed during that period through complete social and political evolution, while, in the old countries of Europe, similar changes have required the lapse of centuries and the shedding of torrents of human blood. The United

States, though a model country, as they began their national life under the best auspices, and have continued it with wonderful success, had the seeds of future trouble in slavery, and notwithstanding that slavery affected only the material interests of its supporters, they could not settle that difficulty but by the bloodiest civil war that the world ever beheld, and which lasted several years.

But, as the power of the Church has been completely broken down, thus bringing about the successful evolution of liberal and progressive ideas, there is no longer any danger of further political troubles, any more than there is in this country, or in any of the older nations of Europe, where stability is reasonably considered as an accomplished fact. Besides, the rapid means of communication afforded by telegraphic lines and railways, and the established credit of the country afford the Government effective means to promptly crush any outbreak, of which it was deprived before.

The business men of the older European nations seem to have taken this view of the situation, as they have invested largely in Mexican enterprises for the last fifteen years, and so far with benefit to themselves and profit to my country, which needs capital for the development of her immense sources of wealth. Citizens from this country have also invested largely, as it is attested by the three trunk railways now in operation in Mexico, connecting the country with the large railroad systems of the United States, and making them practically extensions of the same, and a large number of mining companies which have recently sprung up, taking hold principally of the old abandoned mines. Sometimes it has seemed to me that the European investors prefer to have their Mexican ventures in the name of citizens of this country, perhaps because they believe that their interests are better secured in that way. Every investor of any nationality is, in my opinion, perfectly guaranteed in Mexico. The lines already mentioned, and various others which are either finished or in process of construction, have relied on foreign capital, and specially on English money. Capital being so abundant in England, it is easier to find it there than anywhere else, for any enterprise requiring a large outlay, and even some of the railways in this country have been constructed with English capital.

When the settlement of the last territory of the United States shall make it difficult to find a new field for profitable enterprise, and before long it will be as difficult to find it here as it is now in Europe, the capital which this country is now so rapidly accumulating, and its enterprising activity, will have to look for new ventures. It will be an act of foresight to enter at once into the large and rich field offered by Mexico, at the very doors of the United States. I sincerely hope that you will avail yourselves of this bountiful opportunity, and that the result of our common efforts will be equally advantageous to both countries, as no one-sided bargain can ever be, in my opinion, satisfactory or lasting, and that the ultimate result of our combined efforts will be to create new bonds of cordiality, good will, and mutual profit between the citizens of these two great republics, making them lasting and true friends, and strengthening thus their respective positions among the family of nations, each preserving, of course, its own nationality. The height of my ambition would be satisfied if I could be allowed to see such a consummation. (Prolonged applause.)

Banquet at Boston on January 7, 1892.—On January 7, 1892, a banquet was given at the Hotel Vendome, in Boston, by the Merchants' Association of that city, to celebrate the eleventh anniversary of their organization, to which several of the diplomatic representatives of the Latin-American nations in Washington were invited.

The following is a list of the members of that association and the guests who attended the said banquet :

Beverly K. Moore,
H. G. Parker,
Weston Lewis,
H. Staples Potter,
John J. Henry,
Geo. O. Carpenter,
S. C. Lawrence,
J. H. Benton, Jr.,
John C. Paige,
Charles W. Parker,
Jas. L. Weson,
Cyrus A. Page,
John C. Lane,
Gardner W. Bullard,
Geo. W. Morse,
M. W. Richardson,
Geo. S. Burton,
Alfred Pierce,
A. L. Joslin,
W. W. Sias,
Joseph H. Wiley,
Frank L. Gross,
D. L. Bowers,
Ed. B. Wilson,
L. G. Burnham,
Stephen B. Simons,
Frank Jones,
S. N. D. North,
Dwight Prouty,
Henry C. Jackson,
John W. Chatham,
O. H. Alford,
C. H. Bacon,
M. Larrabee,
Jacob P. Bates,
Henry D. Yerxa,
J. Nelson Parker,
F. L. Walker,
W. E. Worcester,
Ed. P. Wilbur,
John Moir,
Caleb Chase,
Charles D. Sias,
Thomas Cunningham,
Col. Charles Weil,
Jacob Dreyfus,
C. A. Coffin,
Thomas P. Beal,
Wallace L. Pierce,
W. E. Simmons,
S. E. Shuman,
E. A. Shuman,
Thomas Doliber,
Charles S. Kelley,
W. H. Doliber,
C. A. Gilchrist,
Thomas Long,
Norman H. Spencer,
S. J. Kendall,
G. M. Preston,
G. K. Stratton,
Rufus F. Greeley,
J. E. Whitman,
Albert C. Manson,

B. W. Currier,
Geo. B. Carr,
Geo. McNeer,
W. M. Bunting,
F. A. Webster,
Edward E. Cole,
C. D. B. Fisk,
A. L. Richardson,
Dexter H. Follett,
Asa H. Caton,
L. A. Dodge,
C. A. Browning,
Wm. H. Lord,
W. Howard,
Wm. Lewis,
H. Whittington,
William B. Rice,
E. W. Anthony,
Geo. N. Talbot,
Joseph W. Hall,
H. L. Rice,
B. T. Thayer,
Hon. A. E. Pillsbury,
O. H. Sampson,
A. W. Finlayson,
Samuel Little,
Arthur W. Tufts,
S. W. Reynolds,
Hon. Alden Speare,
William H. Horton,
J. V. Spalding,
Jonathan Bigelow,
John Hopewell, Jr.,
O. F. Kendall,
Samuel P. Mandell,
Rodney P. Woodman,
William B. Lawrence,
D. W. Lawrence,
G. A. Leonard,
James Delano.
Theodore P. Spitz,
Ed. Bicknell,
J. Brodie,
F. R. Spalding,
Henry A. Pevear,
Eugene Griffin,
William E. Briant,
Parker B. Field,
H. W. Patterson,
M. N. Smith,
C. L. Watson,
H. A. Pemberton,
A. Shuman,
J. H. White,
Gen. J. P. Martin,
N. W. Rice,
C. S. Roberts,
J. H. Holmes,
Alexander Steinert,
James B. Forsyth,
E. C. Wheeler,
E. F. Dunham,
Col. Albert H. Pope,
John L. Whiting,

Hon. John Simkins,
Charles O. Dyer,
Jerome Jones,
R. H. Gardiner,
Hon. Albert Clarke,
Herbert Underwood,
Edwin S. Barret,
John Wales,
Geo. R. Wales,
John C. Wright,
A. O. Davidson,
James Phillips, Jr.,
John Bremer,
M. P. Clough,
John S. Bartlett,
E. L. Sanborn,
C. W. Whitten,
Henry S. Pratt,
F. Seavey,
Geo. A. Brigham,
Henry S. Howe,
W. H. Chipman,
W. A. Paine,
J. B. Leamy,
J. G. Ramsdell,
Frank W. Daniels,
W. B. Saul,
J. Alba Davis,
Rev. M. J. Savage,
N. B. Goodnow,
Cornelius P. Hatch,
John Sheppard, Jr.,
Frank M. Ames,
Frank F. Hodges,
G. H. B. Winship,
Senas Seares,
Charles S. Bartlett,
Alexis Torrey, L. G. B.,
J. C. Hollins,
Sol. P. Stratton,
Geo. S. Spaulding,
Geo. L. Sevens,
Byron S. Card,
Albert Irvings Croll,
Alfred M. Goodale,
C. P. F. Kellog,
W. A. Copeland,
E. T. Wendall,
Jas. M. Childs,
Lawrence C. Fenno,
C. W. Leonard,
J. S. Holden,
H. R. Turner,
Charles E. Adams,
Arthur W. Pope,
Joseph Lincoln,
Frederick H. Viaux,
Charles H. Clark,
F. W. Cheney,
F. H. Odiorne,
B. F. Larrabee,
C. Granville Way,
John F. Albree, Jr.,
W. H. Atwater,

HARRISON E. WOODWARD,
REV. J. H. WHITMORE,
A. E. WINSHIP,
W. L. TERHUNE,
GOV. H. A. TUTTLE,
JOHN SHEPARD,
OAKES A. AMES,
WILLIAM E. CURTIS,
M. HEWITT,

JOHN M. GRAHAM,
JOHN J. EATON,
FREDERICK ESTABROOK,
JOEL GOLDTHWAIT,
T. W. DELAND,
HON. J. C. BENNETT,
EDWIN W. INGALLS,
NICANOR BOLET PERAZA,
HENRY D. HYDE,

C. D. SMITH,
GUS ATWATER,
W. W. WAUGH,
R. J. MCCARTNEY,
E. A. BURNHAM,
JAMES F. MULLEN,
MATIAS ROMERO,
THEODORE NIKERSON,
LEWIS R. SPEARE.

At that banquet I delivered the following address in answer to the toast assigned to me :

MR. CHAIRMAN—GENTLEMEN :—I feel quite diffident in speaking before such a select audience, in this enlightened city, the Athens of America ; but I could not refrain from answering the sentiment which has been assigned to me, touching a subject in which I feel a most lively interest, and with which I consider myself fully identified.

Over one hundred years ago, after this continent had remained for nearly three centuries a dependency of the Western nations of Europe, the thirteen English colonies of North America, having arrived at their maturity, proclaimed and established their independence from the mother country. The Latin, or remaining portion of the continent, followed your example about thirty years later, a comparatively short period, taking into consideration the difficulties of communication at the time, and the momentous character of the undertaking, and from 1810 to 1824 we, too, proclaimed and established our independence. You realized in this privileged land the dream of the lovers of humanity in organizing a republican form of government, managed by the people, and intended for the good of the people, following the principles, and in many cases improving them materially, of the English unwritten constitution, which has assured them the best governments in the world. We also followed in this case your example and adopted a republican form of government, based substantially on the Constitution of the United States of America. It is true that Mexico had an ephemeral empire, which lasted not quite two years, and that Brazil had, until recently, a peaceful and progressive one ; but Mexico adopted, since 1823, a republican federal constitution, modelled on yours, and Brazil has just done the same, without the shedding of blood, and in fact without any opposition. If it is a source of great satisfaction to you that the eighteen nations into which this continent is divided, not including the United States, have followed your footsteps, not only in accomplishing independence, but also in adopting a republican government, there is imposed upon you, at the same time, the grave responsibility of setting a good example, which will contribute to the consolidation of popular government on this hemisphere.

We are following, besides, other equally meritorious examples which you have set for us. I speak of your love for peace and your untiring energy in developing your country, by which you have succeeded in making it one of the richest in the world. Your railroads, which surpass in extent those of Europe, notwithstanding that continent has three times your population, have been, in my opinion, the main element of your progress. The Latin portion of this continent has also been making strenuous efforts to build railroads. We have in Mexico one of the largest systems of the Latin-American countries, and it gives me pleasure to acknowledge on this occasion that in building it we have been greatly assisted by Boston capital, Boston enterprise, and Boston energy.

The first, and for several years the only railroad built in Mexico, from Veracruz to the City of Mexico, with a small branch to Puebla, was made wholly by English capital. It took the company over sixteen years to build 292 miles. That line did

not prove of special advantage to the country, mainly because the company would
make no branches to connect commercial centres, and because its tariffs were exceedingly high, the average of the import freights being twenty-two cents per mile per ton.
For the same reasons the road was not, in the beginning, a financial success, and its
stock was sold in London, in 1879, at six pounds sterling per share of one hundred
pounds ; but in 1883, when the line transported a great deal of railroad material for
the roads then under construction, which caused a dividend of 7 per cent. to be paid
on the stock, its price went up to 150, and this fact illustrates the possibilities of
Mexican roads.

In the face of such discouraging facts and prospects, Boston pluck undertook to
build a system of railways in Mexico, which then seemed a gigantic undertaking, but
Boston proved equal to the task. The enterprising men of Boston who built the
Santa Fe system were the pioneers of the Mexican railways. They built from May 1,
1880, to October 1, 1882, the 262 miles of the Sonora road, from Guaymas to Nogales,
where there is a branch to Benson, Arizona, connecting it with their main system.
Although, for reasons unknown to me, that road has not been a financial success, I
feel sure it will be, before long, a very valuable property.

About the same time several men of the Santa Fe system, and many other business men of Boston, organized in 1880 the Mexican Central Railway Company, and
after obtaining a liberal grant from the Mexican Government, built in less than four
years, from the 15th of September, 1880, to the 8th of March, 1884, a road from El
Paso del Norte to the City of Mexico, 1224 miles—a task which seemed then as ven-
turesome as the building of the Pacific road in this country during the Civil War—
to which new lines—they can hardly be called branches—have since been added, connecting their system with the Gulf of Mexico at Tampico, which, on account of the
deep water improvements now being carried out, will be one of the principal ports of
Mexico on the gulf, allowing the largest steamers to come into a bar which, before
the work commenced, only drew eight feet of water, and they have under construction
their line to the Pacific, as well as other important branches, which, when finished,
will make a completed system of 2100 miles.

One little incident will show the difficulties these pushing men had to contend
with. The late Samuel J. Tilden of New York was invited by his friends to invest in
this road. Not knowing much of Mexico, he decided, as a prudent man, before
making the investment to post himself about the condition of the country, and as he
could not go himself to Mexico, he requested his personal friend, the Hon. John
Bigelow, a most competent and worthy man, to take that trip and convey to him his
impressions. Unfortunately, Mr. Bigelow, notwithstanding his very high abilities
and qualifications, was unfavorably impressed with the country, either because he did
not remain there long enough, or because it is, in any case, very difficult for a
foreigner to understand a country with which he is not familiar ; and his report was
adverse to the investment. Mr. Bigelow published in *Harper's Magazine*, of New
York, for October, 1882, the result of his investigations, and thinking that he had misunderstood my country, and that his conclusions might be prejudicial to its development if I allowed it to go unchallenged, I answered his article. He then very
properly said, and I of course acquiesced in it, that between two conflicting opinions
about a future fact, whether investments in Mexican railroads would or would not be
profitable, time alone had to decide. I venture to say that sufficient time has now
elapsed to settle that question, and that although the Mexican Central Railway
securities have had, like those of any other large enterprise, their ups and downs, I
think their holders have every reason to be satisfied with their investment. I sincerely
think they own a very valuable property, whose price would be enhanced with the
lapse of time, and keep pace with the prosperity of Mexico.

The National Railway, another system almost as large as the Central, has also finished its main line, is already connected with the Gulf of Mexico at Tampico, and is building a branch to the Pacific, and I consider this line also as a very valuable one. The originator of the Southern Pacific Railway system has also built, and without subsidy, a trunk line to Mexico, the International, which is now being extended towards the Pacific, and which will also prove, I have no doubt, a very valuable property.

These four roads are really extensions into Mexico, and therefore Mexican feeders, of your large railway system, and they actually make of our two countries, for commercial purposes, a single territory. But owing to existing barriers to trade, the international traffic of the Mexican roads has only been about 20 per cent. of their total business.

Mexico subsidized for sometime her railways, and it was thought at first that the subsidies would be merely nominal, as the condition of her finances was such that few imagined that their payment could be effected. But the resources of the country are so great, that the subsidy was not only paid in yearly instalments as agreed upon, but last year the whole of it was advanced in cash to all roads willing to receive it in that way.

Let us see now how the building of roads has affected the prosperity of Mexico. The imports for the fiscal year ending the 30th of June, 1873, were $20,166,012 ; the exports for the same year, $31,594,005, most of them precious metals ; and the federal revenue was only $15,739,239. In about fifteen years, of which only six embrace the railroad era, the foreign trade and revenue of Mexico have increased over one hundred per centum, as the imports of the fiscal year ending on the 30th of June, 1889, the last one of which official statistics have been published in Mexico, amounted to $40,624,-894, the exports for the same year, two thirds being precious metals, to $60,158,423, and the federal revenue amounted to $32,745,981. The trade of Mexico with the United States has increased in still larger proportions. In the year ending June 30, 1873, we imported from the United States $5,231,254, and exported to this country $11,367,859, principally precious metals ; while in the last fiscal year of which the Mexican government has published statistics, our imports from this country amounted to $22,669,420, and we exported to the United States $43,022,440. We now buy from you nearly sixty per cent. of our imports, and we sell you over eighty per cent. of our exports, and this is merely the beginning of a large development of trade between the two countries, which will assume proportions that can hardly be anticipated.

But the building of roads in a country is only the beginning of its development. Mexico has entered into that path, and its results are already perceptible. Fortunately we have passed, I hope forever, the turbulent period of our revolutions. The causes which brought them about, namely, the influence of the Church in the destinies of the country, always exercised against its progress, having now disappeared, their effect will not be felt any longer, and with the assurance of peace and protection to life and property, there can be no doubt that large money investments will be made in Mexico. Since capital from this country, and especially from Boston, has assisted her in building her roads, it is to be hoped that such assistance will not stop there, but continue its wholesome work and build manufactories, operate mines, and take up many other new enterprises mutually profitable. The means of communication already being established, I hope that commercial development will follow. Two neighboring republics occupying the main portion, if not the whole, of the North American continent, which are contiguous for nearly two thousand miles, divided only by an imaginary line, producing each what the other needs, and connected by several systems of railways, must before long agree to lessen the present barriers to traffic, and when that is done the trade between the two will surprise the world. It is my wish that such a consummation shall not be delayed much longer.

THE ANGLO-SAXON AND ROMAN SYSTEMS OF CRIMINAL JURISPRUDENCE.

THE ANGLO-SAXON AND ROMAN SYSTEMS OF CRIMINAL JURISPRUDENCE.

The statements which preface the preceding chapter, under the head of "Historical Notes on Mexico," are also applicable to the present paper, as it is the second of the articles based on my remarks delivered at Saratoga on the 5th of September, 1895.

The subject to which this paper refers I consider of special importance, because my experience has shown me that a want of knowledge of the criminal jurisprudence of Mexico has often been the cause of irritation and misunderstanding in this country, as American citizens, when arrested in Mexico for any crime committed there, have frequently complained bitterly of Mexican criminal legislation, considering it unfair, unjust, and even inquisitorial, and alleging that the rights granted the accused by all civilized countries were denied them in Mexico. I believed it would further a good understanding between the United States and its Southern neighbors to show how mistaken these conclusions were, and I have no doubt that a clear statement of the case would prevent in the future the misunderstandings and dangers arising from such mistakes. This result will also affect most of the Latin-American States, as they all have similar criminal jurisprudence, derived from the Roman law. I, therefore, revised my remarks on the subject and put them in the shape of an article, which was published in the *North American Review*, for July, 1896, and later on in the *Green Bag*, of Boston, for October of the same year.

Before publishing this article I submitted it to various distinguished lawyers of this country, some of whom had occupied high official positions, because I feared that I might have fallen into some error in treating of a subject with which I was not entirely familiar, and I was, of course, very anxious to avoid any inaccuracy. I received different opinions—most of them highly favorable to the jury system; but the one that differs most from mine and contains the strongest reasons against my views, as expressed in my paper, comes from a very able gentleman from New York, the editor of one of the leading newspapers of that city, and as my purpose is to present both sides of the question, I have concluded to insert that letter, for whose publication I have been authorized by the author.

THE ANGLO-SAXON AND ROMAN SYSTEMS OF CRIMINAL JURISPRUDENCE.[1]

I have often heard, during my official residence in Washington, comparisons made between the Anglo-Saxon and Roman systems of criminal jurisprudence, generally very disparaging to the latter system, and this leads me to believe that our own, which is based on the Roman, is not quite well understood in this country. This, and not a desire to indulge in odious comparisons between the two systems, is my apology for writing a brief paper intended to show that our system is not so defective as some believe. I think that in doing this I render a service to the good understanding between the United States and its Southern neighbors.

This subject has always had a great interest for me. Having been educated at home as a lawyer, I have desired to study and practically to compare the various systems of jurisprudence of different countries, as one of the best ways to understand the philosophy of that science. I regret, however, that the public duties which have devolved upon me during my whole life, and my long absence from home, depriving me of the opportunity of practicing law in Mexico, have prevented my becoming better acquainted with all its provisions and my making a specialty of the study of jurisprudence. The same cause has prevented my studying fully the practical workings of the Anglo-Saxon system of jurisprudence, as existing in the United States. It is therefore with great reluctance that I approach such a difficult subject, believing, as I do, that I am not fully competent to treat it as thoroughly as I should like.

While I would not attempt to depreciate the Anglo-Saxon system of jurisprudence, I think the Roman system is also entitled to some regard. The most remarkable of the Roman institutions, and the one which we might say survived the downfall of the Roman Empire, and the incursions of the barbarians with their feudal system, was the civil

[1] This article was originally published by the *North American Review* of New York City for July, 1896, and with some additions in the *Green Bag*, of Boston, for October of the same year. The present edition has been revised and somewhat enlarged.

law; it contains all that was best of former ages and peoples. The advancement of old Etruria, the wisdom of Solon and Lycurgus, the principles of the legislation of Minos, and all that was of permanent value to Egypt, Phœnicia, Chaldea, and the foremost nations of the ancient times, were incorporated into the laws of the ten tables, which were engraved four hundred and fifty years before Christ; and therefrom was developed the wonderful legal system which culminated in the Institutes of Justinian in the year 534 of our era, a system which did more than anything else to assimilate to the Roman Republic the many dissimilar nations which became its provinces, and which were held together by the wonderful Roman civil law. The Roman law was really the result of freedom and free intellectual development, carried on during several centuries under the benign influence of republican institutions. On the other hand, the common law was the natural result of the feudal or military system of the Northern barbarians. The foundation, therefore, of the one is justice; the basis of the other is force.

The Jury System.—It is generally considered that the corner-stone of the Anglo-Saxon criminal jurisprudence is the system of trial by jury; and yet it appears from recent researches that the jury system was not indigenous to the common law of England, but was borrowed from the Franks.[1] In fact, the original idea of the jury system appears to have been borrowed from the Roman law.

The advantages of this system have been much enlarged upon by various writers, both in England and America, as well as upon the continent of Europe. I do not care to criticise it, even though it seems to me, at least under existing conditions, to be open to grave objections. I will only remark that when, eight hundred years ago, England was oppressed by a tyrannical king, the successful efforts of the English barons to wrest from him the Magna Charta, which gave to England no more than was already the common right of all the other nations of Central and Western Europe, were commendable, yet the concession was such that it was justly regarded as a most important step in securing human liberty. Even so, we know that the charter then granted was repeatedly violated by each and all the subsequent kings of England down to the accession of the Stuarts. The Magna Charta was procured from King John by the barons mainly for themselves, but it inured to the benefit of the Commons, since it secured to them the right to be tried by their peers. Now, however, that the power of the Commons has so greatly overshadowed that of the barons that the two classes are rapidly merging into one, the changed conditions do not warrant any undue laudation of the Great Charter. Cer-

---

[1] *History of English Law before the Time of Edward I.*, by Sir Frederick Pollock and Frederick William Maitland, Cambridge, 1895, vol. i., p. 117.

tainly, in the United States, where all differences of class have disappeared since slavery was abolished, there is no reason to fear oppression of the people by those in authority, since the people themselves by their representatives are in power; as a consequence, trial by jury of one's peers has no longer the significance which it might have had under Magna Charta. The arbitrary power of arrest and detention residing in the sovereign, and against which it was the purpose of Magna Charta to guard, has never existed in the United States, where the power of the President to order the arrest of a civilian exists only when the writ of *habeas corpus* is suspended in cases of rebellion, invasion, and other great public danger, and in extradition cases, as provided in the respective treaties.

While I should not like to express any decided convictions on this subject, I may safely say that the conditions under which the jury system was established or adopted, do not prevail at the present time, even in the country of its supposed origin; it cannot, therefore, have the importance it once had.

The jury system, as applied to criminal cases, is undoubtedly more favorable to the accused than to society.[1]

Up to this century the English people may be said to have regarded those of its members who were criminally prosecuted as in danger of becoming the victims of despotic power. It is proper to consider whether the changed relations of the people to the government have been accompanied with proper modifications of the common-law procedure. The criminal law of England is not less severe than that of the United States, but capital crimes and executions are far less frequent there than here. Yet in England there have been hardly any criminal appeals. Conviction before the trial court has been final, while in the United States there are appeals upon appeals, with a final resort to a writ of *habeas corpus* to the Supreme Court of the United States. In the State of New Jersey the Court of Errors and Appeals may be compelled to examine all the proceedings in a capital case, including the evidence, even if no exception has been taken, and although it does not have the prisoner before it or hear the witnesses or hear them testify, it must try the case to discover manifest errors like a court of equity balancing affidavits.

[1] From data contained in a report from the Committee on the Judiciary of the House of Representatives (No. 108, 54th Congress, 1st Session), presented by Mr. Thomas Updegraff of Iowa, on January 22, 1896, which contains several tables, compiled by the Department of Justice, of homicides perpetrated in the United States of which cognizance was taken by the Federal judicial authorities, stating the number of indictments, convictions, and acquittals, appears (Table No. 2) that in the year 1892, from twenty-nine judicial Federal districts, the Federal judicial authorities took cognizance of 112 homicides, of which 96 were indicted, 24 of the accused being convicted, 37 acquitted, and only one execution having taken place.

On psychological grounds it is well established that punishment, to be efficacious as a deterrent, must be prompt.[1] Some legislatures of the United States have gone so far as to provide that no one shall be hanged for a year after his conviction. In almost all of them a murderer may be sure of a year, perhaps several years, of life, after his arrest. He knows, the friends and family of the victim know, the

[1] Since this paper was written, the New York *Journal* of November 28, 1897, published the opinion of the Hon. Frederick R. Coudert, one of the most eminent lawyers of the city of New York, giving his views on the imperfections of criminal trials in the United States and England under the common-law system, as compared with the system prevailing in Continental Europe under the Roman system, from which I insert the following extract:

" I regard the present methods of our criminal law about as Jerry Bentham, the eminent English jurist, regarded the English criminal law, which, by the way, is much like the criminal law of this country. Bentham said: 'The English law of evidence is admirably adapted to the exclusion of truth.'

" There is no doubt to my mind that the methods used by criminal justices in getting jurors is deficient in many respects. One of the greatest deficiencies is that it excludes men from juries who read newspapers and have any knowledge of the case. Then, under the present system lawyers are allowed to wrangle and bring out all sorts of unimportant evidence. This only causes delays, and these delays are unfair to the person on trial, often keeping an innocent man in prison for months, and even years, before he gets a fair trial. In foreign countries, with the exception of England, the court will not listen to any evidence not important to the case. Lawyers are made to question the person on trial not hurriedly, but sufficiently fast to keep the case from dragging. If any question comes up which causes a wrangle, the justice before whom the case is being tried takes the witness in hand and questions him impartially, and to the point. By this practice the Continental methods reach rapid results, the guilty are punished more quickly, and the innocent do not suffer as they do under the system in vogue in America and England. When trials are delayed for months, and even years, it is a very costly thing to the State. Whenever there is a great criminal trial it takes weeks to get the jurors, and even after the jury box is filled the trial drags on, while lawyers are allowed to fight between themselves.

"One of the greatest hindrances to rapid trials in criminal cases is the *habeas corpus* proceedings, which are allowed in the majority of instances. The *habeas corpus* was the outgrowth of the clash between the classes in England, and was intended to protect the persons not high in favor with the crown. In those days the crown practically owned every judge and jurist, and a person who had caused offence to the king could be imprisoned and held as long as he lived, without any recourse. Crowns do not own judges and jurists in these civilized days, and every man can feel certain that he will get a fair and impartial trial as soon as he is arrested. Under the present system every judge in the State can be gone to for *habeas corpus* proceedings, and when they are granted they only serve to delay trial and hasty conviction or acquittal. *Habeas corpus* proceedings give an impetus to crime, and should be done away with. The Supreme Court, in its last three or four decisions regarding *habeas corpus* proceedings, has decided that the writs were not an appeal from the judge's decision, and were only to be allowed in rare cases.

" Do away with *habeas corpus* writs entirely and criminals will be brought much more quickly to trial."

people at large know, that before that time has passed many chances of escape may present themselves. The prisoner may break jail. Material witnesses may die or disappear. Resentment may be softened by the lapse of time; sympathy for the victim who has passed out of this world gives place to sympathy for the prisoner who is struggling to save his life. The longer punishment can be postponed, the greater the possibility that it may be evaded altogether; the greater the certainty, we may say, that it will be mitigated and eventually remitted. Such delays are dangerous, for in cases of atrocious crimes, particularly when violence is done to women, popular passions are always difficult to restrain, and if the penalty provided by law is uncertain or insufficient, the conservative element in the community finds itself deprived of its best argument for letting the law take its course.

That the jury system, as applied to criminal cases, has faults is evident from the fact that some of the States of this Union, like Maryland, for instance, have enacted statutes allowing the accused to select whether he shall be tried by jury or by a judge, and this notwithstanding the constitutional provision on the subject. I regard the Maryland statute as the first step to undermine the jury system.[1]

[1] The Bar Association of Texas held an annual convention at Galveston in 1896, and both the speeches delivered and the resolutions adopted show very clearly the inefficiency of the criminal system of jurisprudence in that State ; and the remarks then made apply also to the criminal jurisprudence under the common law.

Mr. F. W. Ball of Fort Worth read a paper before the association which was most emphatic in its arraignment of the existing system. "What can I say," he asked, "when I speak of our criminal law and procedure ? Can I do aught but voice the general sentiment of the people, and say that it is a stench in the nostrils of every honest and law-abiding man in Texas ? " He complained that " the solicitude of the courts for the Constitution and the bill of rights is such that they adjudge them to be invaded every time a red-handed murderer or a highway robber is convicted without observing all the formalities and niceties requisite under our beautifully complicated system of criminal procedure " ; and he declared that the decisions of the criminal appellate tribunal in hundreds of cases, by which known and notoriously guilty persons have escaped punishment, " fully and completely demonstrate one or the other of these two propositions, namely, that our criminal law is entirely insufficient for the purpose of preventing and punishing crime, or that the courts who have delivered the opinions in these cases are utterly imbecile and ignorant."

In speaking of practice and procedure in civil cases Mr. Ball declared that proper words of denunciation failed him, for the reason that " every kind of proceeding that is obsolete, every kind of method that is expensive, every kind of device that is dilatory or open to trickery, every kind of pleading and writ that is confusing and incomprehensible, is here foregathered for the benefit of the shyster lawyer, the greedy official, and the dilatory judge, and to the complete destruction of the miserable litigant." Judge Simpkins showed that a large proportion of these evils would have been avoided, if the Legislature had done its duty when the present appellate system was established by that body.

A striking address was delivered by Judge E. J. Simpkins of Corsicana. He enunciated the central truth, so often overlooked, that " the great aim of all judicial

I was told by a very prominent United States judge, that one of the leading advantages of the jury system is of an educational character, as in small towns, where people have few opportunities for education, the fact that ignorant men are impanelled in a jury, allows them the opportunity of hearing able arguments of the counsel, and considering difficult questions of law and fact, thus diffusing learning and education. While I agree in so far as that advantageous result of the jury system is concerned, I do not see that its educational advantages should be enough, by themselves, to establish or maintain that system.

Lynch Law.—The insufficiency of the common-law system of criminal jurisprudence to punish criminals is made evident, I think, by its practical results, which have, unfortunately, brought about what is commonly called lynch law, and by the fact that these in their turn have given rise to a practice which is based upon a defect in the existing law, and which, therefore, comes to be, in fact, the complement of criminal proceedings under the Anglo-Saxon system. It is hardly necessary to add that lynch law is highly demoralizing, that it is open to great abuses, and that, when the victim is an innocent person, it amounts to a grave crime.

When a community is satisfied that a crime has been committed, that a particular person is the author of that crime, and that he cannot be punished under the regular proceedings of a common-law trial, they often take the law into their own hands, and they administer swift justice in a manner that is often barbarous, but is the only way available. Where, as it sometimes happens, the victim is not the real perpetrator of the crime, the practice is indeed atrocious.[1] In any

procedure is to administer substantial justice," and he declared that, "when this result is accomplished, though errors are committed not injuriously affecting the real merits of the cause, the judgment ought to be affirmed."

Judge Simpkins held that it is of still greater importance in criminal than in civil cases that the controlling question should be the guilt or innocence of the defendant of the charge preferred, since criminal judgments more immediately affect the people, and therefore excite more comment than civil, and consequently whatever reasons exist for sustaining judgments in civil cases apply with tenfold force in criminal cases.

[1] As an instance of this, I will mention the case of Luis Moreno, who served in the Mexican army, was honorably discharged and came to California, where he worked in the Coggins Mill, near Sisson. On the night of the 5th of August, 1895, George Sears, the owner of a saloon at Bailley Hill, was mortally wounded in an affray, and Gaspar Mierhaus, a miner who was in the adjoining room to the saloon, came out to help Sears, there being no witness to that incident. Moreno and Stemler were suspected of having committed the crime and were consequently arrested. Mierhaus died of his wounds some days afterwards, and there was contradictory information as to whether he identified Moreno or not, as some said that he had, and others that he had said the assassin had a beard, Moreno having none. Before the preliminary examination took place, which had been fixed for the 26th of August, a mob attacked the jail, took out four prisoners, including Moreno, and lynched them all. When this lynch-

case the demoralizing effects of lynch law are so great, and I might say so shocking, that any system which seems to make such a law necessary as a consequence of its own defects ought to be revised, so as to put an end to that terrible practice.[1] Perhaps lynching is not only due to the imperfections of the jury system, but also to the imperfect system of procedure, that causes delays in bringing about a trial, and often to the chicane and deficient preparation of the prosecuting officer.

Up to recent date lynching in this country was only practised in the Southern States, and almost invariably on negroes guilty of the revolting crime of using violence against white women, but some have occurred recently in Central States, like Ohio and Maryland, and even in Connecticut, one of the New England States, which shows that the practice, far from being checked, is on the increase.[2]

ing was reported in the papers, a man who would not give his name for fear of being prosecuted, addressed a letter to the *San Francisco Examiner*, signing it John Doe, published by that paper in its issue of November 29, 1895, in which he confessed that he was the only author of the deed, and that he had killed Sears in self-defence, Moreno being thus exonerated from all participation in the crime.

[1] The extent lynching has reached in the United States is truly appalling. The report above quoted of the Committee of the Judiciary of the House of Representatives, containing several tables compiled by the Department of Justice of homicides perpetrated in the United States, shows (Table No. 3) that during 1895 there were 132 legal executions and 171 lynchings out of 10,500 homicides.

I find in a newspaper the following statistics about the number of judicial hangings and lynchings in the United States during five years. I am sorry that the years are not stated nor the source from which said statistics were taken, so as to verify them ; but I quote them on the supposition that they are correct :

"According to statistics, which are probably reliable, there have been only 723 judicial hangings in that country in five years, and 1118 lynchings in the same period. During this same five years there were 43,902 homicides. The number of illegal executions are not hard to account for. When there are but 723 executions by law out of nearly 44,000 murders, it cannot be wondered that the people should so frequently take matters in their own hands. The reason for this phenomenal miscarriage of justice will be imputed by some to the extraordinary smartness of the lawyers, and by others to the morbid sentimentality which exists towards murderers and cut-throats of the worst class."

[2] In support of these views, I quote the following extracts from an editorial from the *Washington Post*, one of the leading papers of this capital, on the recent Urbana, Ohio, lynching, which took place late in June, 1897 :

" . . . And when that crime is committed in localities where the law does not provide what public opinion regards as adequate punishment, or where the people have learned by experience that the machinery of justice is sluggish and uncertain, human nature asserts itself as certainly and as terribly as it did Friday in Ohio. . . .

" Preach of this thing of lynching as we may, the custom will survive all denunciation under existing circumstances. Until legislatures provide penalties which public opinion accepts as adequate, and until the courts convince the people that they can be relied upon to dispense speedy and unerring justice, communities will continue to protect themselves by punishing, with their own hands, the one crime which is unspeakable and unendurable.

It is very remarkable that the jury system has not produced in England the same results as in the United States in so far as lynching is concerned. Perhaps that is due to the fact that trials take a shorter time in England than they do here, and that the punishment follows the crime without much delay.

The Mexican Jury System.—The force of example and the great credit which Anglo-Saxon institutions have attained in the world, on account of their regard for individual rights, have induced some of the American nations of Latin origin to adopt the jury system, and we have done so in Mexico. Señor Mariscal, our present Secretary of State, who lived in the United States from 1863 to 1877, as Secretary of the Legation up to 1867, and afterwards as Minister from Mexico at Washington—and who is an eminent jurist, a thorough student, and a careful observer—made a special study of the jury system in the United States, and when he went home and became Secretary of Justice under President Juarez's administration, he established, in 1869, a jury system in the Federal District of Mexico for criminal cases, changing it somewhat, so as to adapt it to the peculiar conditions of the Mexican character. He provided, for instance, that a majority of the eleven jurors composing our jury should render a verdict, while under the Anglo-Saxon system the unanimous vote of the twelve jurors is required. It was provided, besides, by the Code of Criminal Procedure for the Federal District and Territories issued in 1880, with a view to prevent the failure of justice, that, if, in the opinion of the presiding judge, the verdict were clearly against the evidence, he should so report to the higher court, with a motion to set that verdict aside, and if the higher court should sustain his opinion, a new trial should be granted, unless eight jurors had concurred in the verdict, in which case it should be final and could not be set aside. These provisions were somewhat changed by the Act of June 24, 1891, which was incorporated in the new code of criminal procedure of July 6, 1891, which requires that the jury shall be composed of nine jurors, that a majority of them shall render a verdict, and that the decision of the jury shall be final if given by seven votes. Even with all these modifications in the system, I have seen cases in Mexico where criminals have gone unpunished, because, through the eloquence of their attorneys, the jury has been influenced in their favor.

Under the system of jurisprudence prevailing in the Federal District of Mexico all the preliminary proceedings in a criminal trial, such as the examination of the accused, the taking of testimony, etc., takes place before the judge who presides over such proceedings without a jury; when this has been completed and the case is ready to be submitted, the jury is empanelled and the evidence is read to it, as set forth in the record already formed; the prosecuting attorney then presents the charges, the defense is heard, and the witnesses of both parties are examined and cross-examined; thereupon the jury renders its verdict adjudging the accused either innocent or guilty, following substantially the practice under the common law of England and of the United States. In most of the Mexican States the old Spanish system of criminal jurisprudence yet prevails.

There are in Mexico some signs of reaction in regard to the jury system. Article VII. of our Constitution provided that all offences committed through the press should be tried by a jury which should decide as to the facts, and if the accused were convicted, another jury should apply the law and fix the penalty. But as the practical result of this system was that no offence of that kind could ever be punished, because the jury always acquitted the accused, our Constitution was amended on May 15, 1883, abrogating the jury system in these cases and submitting the offenders to the common courts, so that now offences committed through the press are tried and punished like crimes of any other character.

The Old Spanish System of Criminal Jurisprudence.—I often hear it asserted in this country that the proceedings under the Roman law are secret, and that the accused does not know what the witnesses have testified against him. This assertion is entirely incorrect, and often leads to very serious misunderstandings. One of the difficulties that the Spanish-American Republics have to contend with in this country, in cases where citizens of the United States are tried by the local judges in any of those Republics, is the great difference between their criminal legislation and procedure and the system prevailing in this country.

According to the Roman system, every criminal trial is divided into two stages; during the summary (*sumario*), which is the first, and the purpose of which is to ascertain the facts connected with the case, the testimony of the accused is taken down, sometimes without his knowing who may be the witnesses testifying against him, or even the crime with which he is charged. During this stage the accused is kept in solitary confinement, and not allowed to place himself in communication with others so that he cannot connive any scheme which might defeat the ends of justice, and while in such confinement we call him in Spanish "Incomunicado." During the plenary (*plenario*), or second stage, all the proceedings of the summary are made public; and thereafter all the proceedings are public, the accused enjoying the same rights which are guaranteed to him by the common law. To this latter statement there may be some slight exceptions, as, for instance, the fact that bail is allowed in only a few specified cases, determined by law, and never when the accused may, upon conviction, be liable to bodily punishment. It would take more space than is allowed in a paper of this character, to state the respective advantages of the two systems, and I shall, therefore, confine myself to briefly mentioning the principal differences between them.

The secret proceedings of the *sumario* are much criticised in the United States, it being forgotten that the English common law likewise provides a secret proceeding very similar to the *sumario*. Before any one is indicted in this country, the case is heard secretly by a grand jury, a body composed of persons who, in some cases at least, are secretly designated. The grand jury listens to such testimony as is offered, or as it may deem sufficient, without permitting the accused to be present or to know what transpires; and if, in their judgment, there is sufficient ground, an indictment is found; and thereafter the public trial begins before the court. It is very difficult, of course, to make any general statement which will be accurately true with respect to all of the forty-five commonwealths which compose this Union, since, as is well known, each of them has its own legislation. In some States, as in New York, a preliminary hearing may take place before a police magistrate, who has in some petty cases power to inflict punishment, release the accused, or hold him for action of the grand jury. Sometimes, however, no arrest is made until an indictment has been found by the grand jury, or in cases of misdemeanor, for trial by a court of judges if the defendant waives a jury.

So far, therefore, as a proceeding under one system may be said to correspond to a proceeding under the other, it may be said that the *sumario*, in countries where the Roman law prevails, corresponds practically to a grand jury indictment in Anglo-Saxon nations.

In the Latin countries testimony is taken down in writing, and, after being read to the witness, is signed by him and by the judge, in proof of the fact that his statements have been correctly recorded. That gives a degree of certainty to the correctness of the testimony which cannot be obtained by a stenographic report; and it renders it impossible for the judge or opposing counsel to put into the mouth of a witness language different from that which he has actually used. When the summary is ended, all the testimony is presented to the accused for his examination; and the right is then given him to cross-examine the witnesses who have appeared against him. The cross-examination is an old Spanish proceeding which we call " careo," and which in Spanish means that the accused is personally confronted with the witnesses in presence of the judge, for the purpose of cross-examining them. It is therefore quite incorrect to assert that, because the *sumario*, or first stage of the trial under the Latin system, is kept secret, therefore the accused does not know anything regarding the evidence against him; the fact being that during the second or plenary stage of the proceeding he is fully informed of all that has been done, and is given ample opportunity to refute it, either by presenting his own witnesses or by cross-examining such as have been presented by the other side, or called by the judge.

It should not be difficult to see which system of criminal jurisprudence is, on the whole, best calculated to do justice by ascertaining the real facts of the case, whether by a judge of long experience and proficiency in his profession, with no personal interest in the cases tried before him, or by a jury composed of men who have no experience in criminal jurisprudence. If the judge may sometimes be derelict in his duties, so also may the jury occasionally be controlled by their emotions. If the judge fails to do his duty, his failure will be corrected by an appellate court, as all cases must be reviewed upon appeal. For the improper verdict of a jury there is seldom any adequate remedy.

The Anglo-Saxon criminal jurisprudence is founded upon the principle that it is better to let one hundred criminals go unpunished than to inflict punishment upon a single innocent person. While the Latin system accepts that humanitarian principle, it is nevertheless better calculated to prevent the escape of a criminal unpunished.

Some American citizens who are tried in Spanish-American countries expect that the proceedings there will be conducted in accordance with the legislation of their own country, and, when they find it otherwise, they complain bitterly, considering the Latin proceedings as inquisitorial, outrageous, and even barbarous; and complaining that they are not tried under the laws in force in this country, as if the legislation of the United States should extend to foreign countries. My experience has shown me that this is sometimes the cause of serious difficulties and misunderstandings between the United States and some of the Spanish-American republics.[1]

Right of Appeal.—Another right guaranteed to the accused under the Mexican law, and which in its broadest sense is unknown to the common law as such, is the right of appeal; that is to say, the right in every case to have both the law and the facts reviewed by a higher

---

[1] As an instance of the kind of charges made against Mexico through the press by irresponsible parties, I will mention a case which recently occurred. A telegram dated at Omaha, Neb., on November 23, 1895, and published broadcast by the papers of this country, stated that Colonel W. A. Paxton, of that city, had received a letter from MacStewart, an old employee of his, who was under sentence of death at Parral, Chihuahua, Mexico, for shooting a policeman who was trying to kill him for a trivial offence, and stated that MacStewart desired to be placed in a court where he would be allowed to plead self-defence, which he pretended was not permitted under the Mexican law. What has already been said about the Mexican criminal jurisprudence is enough to show how entirely unfounded such a statement was.

Whenever I notice in the newspapers any complaint of this character, it is my custom to communicate the same to the Mexican Government and to request an official investigation of the case, so that I may rectify the statement if it should prove to be incorrect, or remedy the wrong before it assumes a serious aspect, if in fact there

court. Under the Mexican laws this right is very broad. Our laws provide that no decision made by judge or jury condemning the accused can be executed until after it has been affirmed by a higher court. Not only is the accused given the right to appeal once, and sometimes twice, from any decision against him, but it is also made the duty of the lower court to send the case with the record for review to the higher court in cases where the convicted person does not appeal. Such is the practice under the Roman and Spanish law; but in the Federal District of Mexico, where the jury system has been adopted, the case goes to the higher court only on appeal of the aggrieved party, and said appeal only affects questions of law, and not the facts as stated by the jury, which cannot be controverted.

It is true that under the common-law system of criminal jurisprudence the accused or his lawyer can take exceptions to points decided by the judge during the trial, and that these exceptions may be reviewed by a higher court, but this can hardly be said to be an appeal, in the sense contemplated by the Mexican law, because the decision of the appellate court is only limited to those points which may be covered by the exceptions taken at the trial. It is true that in some States, as, for instance, New York, an appeal can now be taken which will bring before the court for review, questions of fact as well as questions of law; but in so far as this procedure has been adopted, it is a departure from the strict rules of the common law and an adoption of the principles of the Roman law, since, according to the theory of the common law, a jury can make no mistake, and its findings are therefore final.

Writ of Habeas Corpus and Amparo.—We have copied in our Constitution from the Anglo-Saxon system of jurisprudence the writ of *habeas corpus*, the great conquest of the Anglo-Saxons, which guarantees life and liberty to man, and which places under the control of the judiciary the otherwise arbitrary orders of those in authority; but we have gone considerably farther in this direction, and under the

---

should be any real cause for complaint. In due course I generally receive an official statement which is almost always at great variance with the complaint. In this particular case, the facts turned out to be that MacStewart abused a policeman who was unarmed, and following him to the post-office at Parral, fired upon him without the slightest cause, killing him instantly ; that, not satisfied with this, he killed the policeman's horse, and then fired upon the chief of police who arrested him. It further appeared that this was his second offence of this character, as he had killed before, in Mexico, a United States citizen named Rogers. In the case of Rogers, MacStewart was acquitted, and upon the trial for the murder of the policeman he was allowed to plead self-defence, but failed utterly to establish it, as all the witnesses examined, including an American citizen by the name of Davis, a friend of MacStewart's, testified that there had been no provocation on the part of the policeman, and that the accused had committed a wilful and wanton murder.

name of *amparo* have extended this guarantee so that it is not limited to the protection of personal life and liberty, but embraces all rights under the Constitution—including the right of personal property, even when such rights have been defined by judicial decisions.   If, for instance, a man finds that his property, or any other of his Constitutional rights, are interfered with, either by civil or military authority, or even by a judicial sentence of a Federal or State court, he may apply to the respective Federal district court having jurisdiction thereof, asking it for an injunction to suspend the act complained of, and finally to decide the case, either in his favor or against him, the decision always going for revision to our Supreme Court.

Rights Guaranteed by the Mexican Constitution.—Our Constitution of 1857 is so careful not to allow anybody to be kept in prison for any extraordinary length of time, that Article XIX. specially provides that when a man is arrested the judge shall hold a preliminary examination, and shall within three days from the time of his arrest decide whether there is cause to try him, or whether he shall be set at liberty.   If the judge shall find that there is sufficient ground for continuing the investigation, the prisoner shall be remanded; otherwise he shall be set at liberty.   In the first instance the judge has to sign what is called in Spanish *auto de prision formal*, meaning an order of formal commitment.   In the second place the prisoner is set at liberty.   This proceeding corresponds in a measure to the grand jury investigation under the common law.   As I have already stated, in some States, like New York, a committing magistrate is authorized to examine the case as a preliminary step to the investigation of the grand jury. Where such a practice prevails, two examinations take place before the criminal charge upon which the accused is to be finally tried is definitely formulated, while under our system only one investigation is made, and even that must be completed within three days of the arrest.

The assertion, often heard, that American citizens tried in Mexico are not notified of the cause of their arrest; that they are not confronted with their accusers; and that they are not allowed to appear in self-defence, is in open contradiction to the express provisions of our statutes.   As a matter of fact, Article XX. of our Constitution of 1857 grants the following guarantees to the accused, in criminal cases:

1.   That the cause of the proceeding and the name of the accuser be made known to the accused.

2.   That the preliminary examination of the accused must be held within forty-eight hours from the time he is placed at the disposal of the judge.

3.   That he may cross-examine the witnesses who testify against him.

4.   That such information as the accused may need for the purpose of answering the indictment must be given him, if it be in the record.

5. That he must be heard in his own defence, either in person or by some attorney of his own selection, or by both, as he may choose; and if he should have nobody to appear for him, he will be furnished with a list of lawyers appointed for such cases and given the right to select as his attorney any one whom he may prefer.

Length of Trials under both Systems.—I often hear the complaint, too, that under the Roman system the trial proceeds very slowly, and it is asserted that criminal trials in the United States terminate more speedily. I am not prepared to say under which of the two systems of criminal procedure the trial is sooner brought to an end. When the trial actually begins, it may take a shorter time in the United States, because once begun, it cannot be interrupted. It often happens, however, that a long time elapses before a case is brought to trial; and this time is longer when a new trial is granted. It should be borne in mind that most of the courts in this country hold sessions but for a few weeks or months at a time, and that only during these sessions do they hear cases. In Latin-American countries, on the other hand, the courts are open and working all the year round. Moreover, under the common-law system, the whole of the trial takes place before the jury, so that the exclusive attention of the court is necessarily devoted to that case. Only one case, therefore, can be tried at a time. In Latin-American countries a judge may try several cases concurrently, because, even where the jury system has been adopted, as it has in Mexico, a great portion of the proceedings takes place before the judge without the jury. As a consequence of this, trials in this country, by reason of the crowded condition of the dockets, are often delayed for months at a time, while in the Latin countries trials begin as soon as the prisoners are arrested.

Summary Proceedings under the Mexican Constitution.—There is a provision in our Constitution which is often misunderstood, and which has given rise to the idea that we sometimes administer justice in too speedy a manner and with a complete disregard of the forms of law established for the protection of human life. Our Constitution commences with a declaration of the rights of man, taken in a great measure from the declaration of the French National Assembly during the Revolution, which in its turn was in a great measure taken from the Declaration of Independence of the United States. These rights secure the most ample liberty and immunity both to the person and property of the inhabitants of the country.

While our Constitution was being framed, however, it was contended that, on extraordinary occasions, as in case of war or other serious danger to society, the rights guaranteed by the Constitution might stand very much in the way of inflicting needed and speedy punishment. To obviate this, the Constitution provides, in Article XXIX., that the rights of man, as guaranteed by that instrument, excepting such as secure his life, may be suspended for a short time in certain emergencies, provided that suspension be upon the President's initiative, and with the consent of Congress; and provided, further, that the suspension shall be applicable to a class; that it shall not apply to an individual; and that it shall last for a brief period. If it should be found, for instance, that the crime of derailing railway cars, either for the purpose of robbing them or for any other unlawful end, should become frequent, and if it should be found that the emergency called for extraordinary measures, the President would ask Congress for the suspension of the personal guarantees of this class of criminals for a limited period, say six months; and if Congress should sanction this suspension, a summary criminal proceeding would be established, for the purpose of inflicting punishment without delay, thereby deterring others who might be disposed to commit the same crime. At the end of the period fixed public confidence would have been restored, and there being no further need for the unusual measures adopted, the suspension of Constitutional guarantees would come to an end. It will be seen that our Constitution provides a speedy way of punishing criminals in extraordinary cases, without the unfortunate need which the condition of things has sometimes made necessary in this country —as in California in former years—of establishing a committee of public safety to preserve order, a proceeding which meant that the people took the law into their own hands, acting without regard to the usual legal forms, and oftentimes in a manner closely resembling lynch law.

Mexican Prisons.—Great complaints are often made in this country against the Mexican prisons, which are said to be uncomfortable, and sometimes considered filthy. It is a fact that some prisons in Mexico are in a very poor condition; but that is due to the limited resources of the country. A poor country cannot afford to build magnificent prisons; yet notwithstanding that we have to contend with small means, the States of Jalisco and Puebla have built spacious and comfortable penitentiaries at Guadalajara and Puebla, their respective capitals, and the State of Guanajuato at the City of Salamanca. Other States, as San Luis Potosi, and Nuevo Leon [1] are constructing new

[1] Mr. E. G. Coffin, Warden of the Columbus, Ohio, Penitentiary, who recently visited Mexico with the members of the Prison Congress which met at Austin, Texas, wrote a pamphlet entitled, "The Prison Congress, and our Trip Through Mexico and Texas," in which he says of the penitentiary in the State of Nuevo Leon, established in the City of Monterey, as follows:

"At the Monterey Prison we were shown unusual courtesies by the governor and Mayor Jules Randle. There are 400 inmates. We found the prison scrupulously clean, the food pure, what there was of it, but no work for the inmates except trinket and lace making, in a desultory kind of a way. The prison seems to be conducted on a system of a continuous school, and the plan of confinement is a solitary one."

penitentiaries, and the Federal Government is concluding the erection of one at the City of Mexico which will compare favorably with any in this country.

Prisons cannot be as comfortable as palaces or hotels, and even in this country, with all its wealth, advancement, and prosperity, prisons are sometimes very objectionable.[1] If we had two sets of prisons in Mexico, one for Mexican citizens and the other for foreigners, and if the former were more comfortable than the latter, the citizens of this country would have reason to complain; but if we treat them on an equal footing with our own citizens, and if we give the best we can,—that is, if we keep them in the same building, provide the same food, and extend to them the same conditions that we do our own citizens, I fail to see how there can be any reasonable ground for complaint.

The Common Law and Roman Civil Jurisprudence.—When we pass from criminal to civil jurisprudence, the superiority of the Roman law is incontrovertible, and a few remarks on that subject will be pertinent in this case.[2]

---

[1] The *New York Herald* of the 29th of October, 1895, published the following statement, made to the Board of Estimate by Miss Rosa Butler of the State Charities Waif Association, about the deplorable condition of Blackwell's Island Almshouse :

"Among these evils are the terrible overcrowding at the almshouse, where, even during the past summer, more than three hundred persons slept on beds made on the floor ; unsuitability of the almshouse building, 1500 occupying buildings which have neither hot nor cold water, no bath-rooms, no lavatories ; the wretchedly inadequate nursing at the almshouse hospitals, there being but one untrained and incompetent nurse for every forty patients ; the unskilled and inadequate nursing on Randall's Island, where of 160 foundlings cared for in 1894, 119 died, and of 384 other infants— not foundlings—cared for without their mothers, 296 died ; the dilapidated condition of the City Hospital, to which no repairs have been made for several years ; the employment of workhouse prisoners in hospital kitchens ; placing the erysipelas wards in the dock house, which is old, noisy, and infested with vermin ; the lack of proper facilities of dealing with casual lodgers, and so forth."

If prisons that are in the heart of the city of New York, the largest and wealthiest of this country, and under its immediate supervision, are in that state, the bad condition of some of the Mexican prisons is certainly nothing extraordinary.

[2] In an admirable address that Judge Martin F. Morris, Associate Justice of the Court of Appeals of the District of Columbia and Professor of Constitutional and International Law, Admiralty, and Comparative Jurisprudence, in the Law School of Georgetown University, District of Columbia, delivered before the graduating class in 1891, he said, referring to the subject of the common law and the Roman law (pp. 30 and 31), the following :

"But, however it be in criminal cases, I have no hesitation whatever, after a long experience of it, to assert that, as a mode of determination of civil causes and private controversies, the genius of man has never yet devised anything more absurd than the organized ignorance and besotted prejudices of twelve men in a jury box. The man who has a good case is always desirous to have it taken away from the determination of a jury, and to submit it to the arbitrament of a court alone—to the arbitrament, in fact, of any one other than the twelve men in a jury box ; while the dishonest litigant,

The English common law is simply the law of usage and custom. Whatever is sanctioned by general usage becomes common law. Hence it is that in suits at common law the rights of parties are often determined by proof of custom. Upon this theory is based the idea of what is called a common-law marriage, which prevails in New York, and perhaps some other States of the Union, that cohabitation as husband and wife and public reputation as such, are sufficient *prima facie* proof of marriage. While this system has the great advantage that its provisions are in accordance with the tendencies and habits of the people, it also has the disadvantage that its provisions are uncertain, as habits may change on one side, and on the other they may not be so settled as to have the sanction of a rule under the common law. Under the civil law the good result of the common law is practically the same, but under a more systematic method, that is, the rules established by habit and justice combined, are collected into a Code of Laws, after they have been established by long years of practice, and have the advantage of being more precise on one side and more just on the other.

One of the most conclusive proofs that the Roman civil law is not inferior to the English common law is that England, the very country where it had its birth, was obliged to establish two systems of civil jurisprudence, one the common law proper, which was administered through the older and ordinary courts, and the other the Roman law, administered through the chancery or equity courts. Law is supposed to be the perfection of justice and the best expression of human reason; it should, then, embrace not only equity, but the very essence of justice itself. If, therefore, a particular law or system of laws fails to include equity, that law or system cannot be perfection. The very idea that equity can be a thing outside and different from law seems contradictory and absurd.

Although the chancery or equity courts were in the beginning estab-

the unprincipled lawyer, and the speculating knave, are ever loud in their demands for trial by jury ; for only upon the prejudices, the passions, the ignorance, or the corruption of juries can they base their hopes of success. This is the experience of every man who has had to do with courts of law, and it speaks volumes to the discredit of the system. Then the divided responsibility of court and jury, the necessity of immediate decision by the former of questions of law upon which appellate tribunals often deliberate for weeks and months without coming to a satisfactory conclusion, the consequent necessity of repeated trials before a final decision is reached—all contribute to render the system exceedingly unsatisfactory in its methods, no less than its results.

" We think we are fully justified in the assertion that there is no one feature of our jurisprudence that tends more in practice to a denial of justice than the system of trial by jury. It may, perhaps, have done well enough in a barbarous age, when judges may not have been more intelligent than juries, and may have been, in fact, the tools and minions of despotic power ; but in this age and country it is nothing more than a relic of feudal barbarism."

lished in England for the purpose of trying such cases as could not be reached by the common law, or in which the processes of the common-law courts afforded no adequate remedy, the Roman law came finally to be in reality the law which was intended to fill the gaps and remedy the defects of the common law. The common-law courts were always very jealous of the equity courts; but after the decision of King James I., in the controversy between Sir Edward Coke, on the one side, representing the common-law courts, and Lord Ellesmere, the Lord Chancellor, and Lord Bacon, on the other, representing the equity, or Roman-law courts, it was established that a man might have recourse to a court of equity in many cases after his rights had been adjudicated at the common-law courts. The establishment of this principle was equivalent in fact, though not in form, to giving an appeal from the courts of common law to the courts of equity, thus recognizing the superiority of the Roman over the common-law system. It is true that the equity courts could not reverse the decision of the common-law courts, but if, in the trial of the same case an equity court reached an opposite or different conclusion, the judgment of the common-law court could not be executed, and became therefore, in fact, nullified.

I am well aware that a common-law lawyer will not admit that the equity courts can reverse the judgment of the common-law courts, because legally and technically that cannot be done; but, as a matter of fact, such is the practical consequence of the system as it now exists. If a common-law court, for instance, decides a case against the defendant, and if after that decision the defendant finds proofs to establish his contentions, he may still go to the equity court, present his proofs, and ask that the plaintiff be enjoined from executing the judgment against him; and in such cases the equity court has jurisidiction to grant such an application. In a case like the one cited the equity court does not pretend technically to revise or reverse the judgment of the common-law court; but by granting the injunction against its execution it practically effects its reversal; and such a system therefore actually produces the same result as though the equity court were a court of appeals.[1]

[1] The following letters explain themselves and make this subject more clear:

"CHICAGO, July 17, 1896.

"SEÑOR DON MATIAS ROMERO,

"*Minister of the Republic of Mexico, Washington, D. C.*

"DEAR SIR,—I have read with deep interest your valuable article in the current number of the *North American Review*, contrasting the systems of criminal jurisprudence in force in your own country and in this, and am happy to say that I have gained from it much information which I had not before possessed, and of which very, very few of our American lawyers, and publicists even, have any adequate knowledge, and I desire, therefore, to sincerely thank you.

"May I, however, take the liberty of correcting a misstatement contained in the

The American people, with their practical common sense, have remedied a great many of the defects of the common-law practice in civil cases, changing it gradually to such an extent that now it can hardly be said that the English common-law system, as expounded by Blackstone, is in force in the United States. It is still called the common law, but for all practical purposes it is almost superseded by the Roman law.

Even as regards the jury system, and notwithstanding the fact that this has been considered the corner-stone of common-law criminal jurisprudence, some States of this country have, as I understand,

paragraph commencing at the bottom of page 88 ? It would seem that you regard the power of a court of equity to restrain the enforcement of a common-law judgment as equivalent to the power of a court of appeal. As a matter of fact, it is not so. A court of equity has no power whatever, under our system of jurisprudence, to interfere where an appeal would be the proper remedy. But where there has been fraud, or where it appears that judgment has been entered, when, in fact, no summons has been served on defendant, although the record recites that summons has been served, a court of equity may act, provided the question could not have been raised in the common law-suit, by reason of want of knowledge on the part of the defendant, until after the expiration of the term of court, or some similar reason. In addition, the defendant who seeks the aid of a court of equity in such case must show that the plaintiff had no cause of action ; but, if an appeal can be taken, an appeal must be taken, or defendant cannot complain.

" The error into which you have inadvertently fallen is, perhaps, a natural one, and does not detract in the least from the value of your article, for which I again express my appreciation.

" I trust you will not consider my remarks as impertinent, even though your attention has already been called to your error.

" I am, respectfully, your obedient servant,

" EDWIN I. FELSENTHAL, *Attorney-at-Law.*"

" WASHINGTON, Aug. 7, 1896.

" MR. EDWIN I. FELSENTHAL, *Attorney-at-Law, Chicago, Ill.*

" DEAR SIR,—In answer to your kind and appreciative note concerning my article in the *North American Review*, contrasting the criminal systems of the Roman and the English law, I have to say that I am entirely aware that, under the English or Anglo-American system of jurisprudence, there is technically no appeal from the courts of common law to the courts of equity, but that the concurrent jurisdiction of courts of common law and equity, and the power of courts of equity in many cases to annul or restrain the judgments of courts of law, had the practical effect of an appeal from the latter to the former. Probably I did not use the term appeal in the strict technical sense which it has in your jurisprudence, but rather in the common sense. However, your great commentator, Sir Edward Coke, in his famous controversy with Lord Bacon, concerning the jurisdiction of equity would seem to have regarded the exercise of the jurisdiction assumed by equity as an attempt to give an appeal to the courts of chancery from the courts of common law.

" Thanking you for the kind expressions concerning my article contained in your letter, I am very truly yours,

" M. ROMERO."

changed the foundation of that system by not requiring a unanimous verdict for the conviction of the accused.

The very country which established and for years maintained the common law has practically superseded it by the Roman jurisprudence. In one of the acts of the British Parliament passed in the years of 1873, 1874, and 1875 the whole system of English Courts of Justice was remodelled after the systems prevailing in countries which had adopted the Roman law, and it was provided that when the rules of common law and those of equity come into conflict, the latter shall prevail. Such a provision is almost equivalent to repealing the common law itself.

Literal Application of the Law.—The literal application of the common law is, I think, another of its disadvantages. A common-law judge is bound to apply the law in its literal meaning, even in cases when doing so may involve a denial of justice, while a Roman-law judge applies the letter of the law to the case where it fits exactly, and has some discretion to be guided by the meaning and object of its statute, rather than by its literal words, when its words conflict with justice or equity.

A result of the literal application of the statute, and of the strict observance of the formalities established by the statute, is the reversal of judgments upon the ground of purely technical errors, which in some States, like Texas, is carried to an excess, very difficult to understand by a Roman-law lawyer.[1]

Precedents and the Common Law.—American lawyers in arguing cases, and judges in deciding them according to the practice under the common-law system, are controlled almost entirely by precedents, and while considerations of justice and equity are sometimes indulged in, they have legally but little weight. Such a system is very unsatis-

---

[1] During the last meeting of the Bar Association of Texas, from which I have already quoted, it was mentioned that a robbery was committed in Groveton, the only town of that name in the State of Texas, and the county seat of Trinity County in said State. The robber was detected, tried, and convicted. There was no question either as to his guilt or as to the fairness of the proceedings against him in the court where he was arraigned. The case was carried up on exceptions to the Court of Appeals, and that tribunal set aside the verdict on the ground that the indictment only specified the crime as having been committed in the town of Groveton, State of Texas, instead of the town of Groveton, County of Trinity, State of Texas. It seems that the Court of Appeals is required by the Statutes to rule in that way. When the present appellate system was established by the Legislature of Texas, as originally submitted, the measure contained an article providing that, "if the court of civil appeals shall be of the opinion, in considering all the facts of a case, that the trial court failed to do substantial justice, it shall reverse the judgment, but it shall affirm the case if substantial justice has been done, though there be errors committed not affecting the merit of the case." This article provoked more debate in the Senate than any other in the bill, and it was passed by a large majority, but in the House it was stricken out without debate, and apparently without any apprehension of its importance.

factory, because each case being different from the other, the decisions in the one cannot be made to exactly fit the other. Moreover, it entails a herculean task upon the lawyers and judges, making it obligatory for them to search for precedents not only in the courts of their own country, but even in those of England. With the justices of the Supreme Court of the United States, this work is still more arduous, since they must examine and be familiar not only with all cases decided by the various Federal courts, but by all the courts of the forty-five different commonwealths which form this Union, each with its own distinct legislation, and with the Roman law also, adopted by the State of Louisiana; entailing besides the need of keeping a very large library. Doubtless, no public functionaries under the Federal Government have more arduous work imposed upon them. The day is not long enough to permit its completion, and I have personally known more than one who has broken down under that tremendous strain.

This condition of things shows that the common law is still in its rude and primary state, viz. : setting precedents. After sufficient precedents have been collected to form a code, they should be codified, if the United States shall not previously have accepted in its entirety the Roman law. The Roman law had to pass through these different stages, and it had passed them all, when it assumed the shape in which it is at present. It has been fully digested, and its principles formulated into simple rules, while the common law is yet in process of development, still passing through the primary stages.

Conclusion.—I hope that these few remarks, which have been written without preparation, will assist in dispelling the misapprehension which exists in this country regarding the criminal jurisprudence of Spanish-American nations, and in that way contribute to the better understanding between the United States and her sister Republics. A careful study of the Roman system of jurisprudence by Anglo-Saxon judges, lawyers, and statesmen has resulted in the adoption of many features of the Roman law, and a careful and comparative study of both systems would very likely lead to a conclusion in favor of an eclectic one which would combine the best features of each.

Mr. Godkin's opinions on the Jury System.—My desire to state facts correctly in this article, and hear opinions from different sources on the subject treated in the same, made me submit my paper to prominent gentlemen of this country in different stations, and hear their views and their criticisms. One of them, Mr. E. L. Godkin, a very able gentleman, a very forcible writer, and the editor of one of the leading New York papers, expressed views which entirely differed from mine, and as my object is to present the question in an impartial way, so that it can be well understood and considered on its merits, I take pleasure in inserting his letter on the subject:

" DEAR SEÑOR ROMERO:

" Although I read your article on the Roman and Anglo-Saxon Systems of Criminal Jurisprudence several days ago, I have retained it until I could find time to say a word or two about it.

" I think it will be useful in dissipating some popular prejudices here about your system which were painfully prevalent and influential at the time of our last dispute with Chili *apropos* of the attack on the American sailors in the streets of Valparaiso. I think your account of the real differences between the two systems will be most enlightening for the American public. But if I might venture to criticise, I should say that you do not do full justice to our jury system, and for these reasons: It was adopted in England as a protection against judges controlled or influenced by the Crown. It is used here for a similar reason. Judges who tried criminals in serious cases would have to be of a far higher character if their decisions were to command public confidence, than those which are given us by the elective system. If, for instance, I were tried in this city for criminal libel, before a Tammany judge without a jury I would stand no chance. It is almost of as much importance that the judgments of a court should command public confidence, as that they should be fair. People in this country would hardly ever acquiesce fully in the verdict of a single man. He would shrink from giving it on every side that seemed unpopular or seemed likely to affect his re-election. This democracy, which we have to take as we find it. Yours with all their faults have not this fault in so great a degree at least.

" In the next place, I should take exception to your ascribing lynch law to the imperfections of the jury system. I do not think lynching is due nearly as often to the faults of juries or to the faults of our system of procedure, than are the delays in the trial, or the failure of justice, caused by the chicane, corruption, and purposely defective preparation of the prosecuting officer. These would be just as great if not greater under the Roman system than ours. The efficient pursuit of crime depends far more on the vigilance, tenacity, and honesty of the District Attorney than in the way in which the criminal is tried.

" I should question, too, whether your account of the distinction between common law and equity either in this country or in England was correct. In this country certainly the two systems have long been merged, and I should doubt whether it was possible, in this State at least,[1] in either to arrest the execution of a common-law judgment by

[1] The code of procedure of the State of New York made a complete fusion between the two systems of common law and equity, and codes of other States have been modelled upon that basis ; but in the courts of the United States the two systems are separately administered on separate dockets and on distinct lines of procedure ; while in some of the States separate courts of chancery (equity) are still kept up.

an equity injunction, for the reason that the plaintiff in submitting his suit must always then select his remedy and ask for it. He must say, for instance, whether he seeks damages or equitable relief; whether the suit is one in equity or in common law is determined by the form of the complaint. Certainly this is the practice in this State, and unless you have done so already, I would suggest further inquiry among professional men on this point.

" What you say about the disadvantages of the precedent system as a body of law will be approved, I think, by most lawyers, but you will find much difference of opinion as to the value as well as possibility of a code. But on this point I think you would find much to interest you in one or two pamphlets written by Mr. James C. Carter, the leader of our bar here. His address is 271 or 277 Lexington Avenue, New York.

" With these small criticisms, I return you the article with many thanks for having given me the opportunity to read it, and with entire confidence in its usefulness.

" Yours very sincerely,
" Edwin L. Godkin."

MISTAKES OF MR. P. M. SMITH ABOUT JUDICIAL PROCEEDINGS IN MEXICO.[1]

The following article by the Hon. Matias Romero, Minister from Mexico at Washington appeared some years back in the *North American Review:*

It is truly lamentable to see the mistakes often made by able men of this country visiting Mexico regarding our institutions. I recently noticed a serious one about our judicial system, which appeared in the Lisbon, Ohio, *Leader*, of February 18, 1897, in a speech delivered by the Hon. P. M. Smith, in answer to a toast, " The Lawyer in Mexico," at a banquet of the Lisbon Bar and county officials, which took place in that city on Wednesday, February 2, 1897. It seems that Mr. Smith had visited Mexico, and seen the holding of a court, very likely in a very small Indian town, where the court " met in an adobe structure, containing a table, three chairs for the judge and lawyers, and a mud bench along the wall covered with cement, without books or file cases." He noticed that no oaths were administered to the witnesses, and without understanding the reason of this omission, he allowed his imagination and humor to get the better of his judgment, and offered the following explanation, showing not only his ignorance of the matter,

---

[1] This paper was published in the May, 1867, number of the *North American Review* of New York, in the " Notes and Comments," section.

but his undaunted courage in attempting to explain the meaning of something which he did not understand:

" Oaths were not administered on the theory, I assume, that an oath would add nothing to the natural truthfulness of the Mexican, and, if you are liable to be defeated by false testimony of two witnesses, for a small consideration you can secure three to contradict the two, and thus possibly win your case, and aid in securing justice to a worthy litigant."

If Mr. Smith had been better acquainted with the judicial system of Mexico he would have found that prior to 1873 we did administer oaths, as is now done in this country, in all judicial proceedings, and to all public officials on being qualified for their respective offices, and that in that year the oath was replaced by a formal promise to tell the truth. What we called our Laws of Reform, which had been enacted from 1855 to 1859, and which established full liberty of conscience and free exercise of any religious belief, and a complete separation between Church and State, were incorporated in our Constitution in 1873 as an amendment to the same, which made it necessary to suppress the oath, as the oath is a religious act, in which God and the Holy Scriptures are invoked in witness of the truth of a statement made, and it ought not to be required in judicial and other official matters, when some men might consider themselves forbidden by their creed to take an oath, and others look upon it as meaningless. When the oath was replaced by a formal promise to tell the truth, the law provided that said promise should have the same effect as the oath, its breach being punishable as a perjury. That promise is not only required in judicial proceedings, but in every case in which the oath was before administered, that is, in the qualification for public offices, and so forth. Had Mr. Smith taken the pains to understand the subject, he would have avoided the gross mistake alluded to.

Mr. Smith is also mistaken when he asserts " that whenever the authorities in Mexico want to get rid of a person who is obnoxious but does not violate any law that justifies his extermination, he is sentenced to the penitentiary for some criminal act, and while on his way to the prison he is advised by his guards to escape, and that when he attempts to do so, he is shot and reported lost on the road." In disturbed and lawless times, assassinations might have taken place in that manner, as they often do in other countries, because, unfortunately, men invested with authority, are sometimes apt to abuse it; but Mr. Smith may be sure that one or two cases that may have occurred in peaceful times could not justify his assertion, and that any person violating the laws in Mexico is always liable to trial and to suffer the proper punishment for his offence.

Another of Mr. Smith's errors, although one of less consequence, is his assertion that there is a Constitutional provision in Mexico guaranteeing a jury in criminal trials, but that in practice it is unknown. Our Constitution has no such provision, and it is only in the Federal District, by an Act of Congress, that we have established the jury system, which is now in force, notwithstanding Mr. Smith's statements. It is a fact that Article VII. of our Constitution provided that all offences committed through the press should be tried by a jury, who should decide as to the facts, and, if the accused was convicted, another jury should apply the law and fix the penalty; but the practical result of this system was that no offence of that kind could ever be punished, because the jury always acquitted the accused, and our Constitution was amended on May 15, 1883, abrogating the jury system and submitting the offenders to the common courts, so that now offences committed through the press are tried and punished like crimes of any other character. It is not likely that Mr. Smith could have referred to this occurrence, but even in case he had, his information was incorrect.

THE MEXICAN FREE ZONE.

THE MEXICAN FREE ZONE.

There is in the northern part of Mexico, along its border line with the United States, a belt of territory exempted from certain duties, and which is called " The Free Zone."

Mexico is a country of high import duties, which, added to the protection by her money having depreciated over fifty per cent., surrounds her people with an almost impassable tariff wall. Against this background the operations of the Free Zone are thrown into strong relief, and as the people of the United States are more concerned with this border commerce than any other people dealing with Mexico, the history of the Zone, its influence upon trade, and the question of its permanency become here questions of interest.

Unfortunately, the idea has prevailed in the United States that the Mexican Free Zone was established with a hostile spirit towards the United States, and for the main purpose of favoring smuggling against the interests of the Treasury and the bona fide merchants of this country.

As I was perfectly sure that such views were unsound and were based on grave misapprehensions, I thought it would be well—with a view to prevent misunderstandings, which are in the way of closer friendly and commercial relations between the two countries—to give a brief outline of the establishment of the Mexican Free Zone, and its practical results, and with that purpose I wrote an official letter to the Secretary of State of the United States, on February 10, 1888, supplementing it by another on the 14th of the same month, both of which were published with the President's Message of March 16, 1888, in answer to a resolution of the Senate of February 16th of the same year, asking for information on that subject. I insert at the end of this paper the President's Message and both of my letters. In writing the letters referred to I was prompted by a desire to promote a good understanding and harmonious relations between the two countries, and I believed that it would not be presumptuous on my part to offer some important statements on that subject. When, some time afterward, some public men, among others Mr. Crain, a Member of Congress from

431

Texas, asked me for some information about the Free Zone, I referred him to my official letters to the State Department, published by the Senate; and my statements seemed to him so satisfactory that when he spoke in the House on February 27, 1895, against the Cockrell resolution, on the subject of the Free Zone, most of his arguments were taken from my statements made to the State Department.

As public documents do not always attain a wide circulation among the people of this country, and as I desired that my statements in regard to the Free Zone should have in the United States as wide a circulation as possible, I thought it would be expedient to embody the views contained in my two official letters to the State Department, in an article for one of the leading magazines of this country, and I therefore prepared a paper, which was published in the *North American Review*, of April ,1892.

I give below that paper, which has been carefully revised and considerably enlarged, with a view to embrace a complete statement of this question and its bearings both towards Mexico and to the United States.

My opinions about the Free Zone are at least impartial, as the official records of Mexico show that far from being a friend of that institution, I have ever been its most earnest opponent, having been the leader of the opposition to the same both in the Mexican Congress and in the Mexican Cabinet, as I was the only Secretary of the Treasury who had so far officially advised its abolishment. I will not, therefore, belittle its advantages nor understate its disadvantages as I understand them, my object being to make a full and candid statement of the question in all its bearings for the aforesaid purpose.

The following is the revised paper referred to:

THE MEXICAN FREE ZONE.

Mexico has had for some years on its frontier with the United States what has been known as the " *Zona Libre*," or Free Zone. It is a strip of territory along the northern boundary of the republic, twenty kilometres, or about twelve and a half miles in width, and extending from the Gulf of Mexico to the Pacific coast, a distance of 1833 miles. Foreign goods entered for consumption within this Zone pay now only 18½ per cent. of the regular schedule of Mexican import duties. So, Mexico maintains along her northern boundary two custom lines. Goods passing the first line are assessed 18½ per cent. of the import duties, and when they pass the second, twenty kilometres to the south, they pay the remaining 81½ per cent. This applies only to goods entered for consumption within the Zone, for the full tariff is collected at the first line on all goods intended originally for shipment into the interior, thus necessitating only one collection. The Zone is therefore of small account to the Mexican Government as a revenue producer, but has been a constant source of trouble, inasmuch as it presents opportunities for smuggling, and it has been greatly misunderstood here.

It is a misnomer to call such institution a Free Zone, because foreign goods imported into it have never since its establishment been entirely free of duties. When the Free Zone was originally established and for some time later, foreign goods paid a duty of 2½ per cent. upon the import duties, destined to the respective municipalities, and since 1885 they have paid a portion of the import duties, which was in the beginning 10 per cent., and is now as high as 18½ per cent. The proper name for it might be, therefore, a zone with discriminating or reduced duties, and not a free zone. This exemption has been greatly misunderstood in this country, where the impression has prevailed that it was established by Mexico as an act of antagonism, if not of unfriendliness, towards the United States, and that its main, if not its sole purpose, was to encourage smuggling, to the prejudice of the merchants and the fiscal interests of this country.

To consider this matter impartially and fairly, it is proper first to state how the Free Zone originated in Mexico, what vicissitudes it has suffered, what action the United States Government has taken in the premises, and finally how it affects the interests of both countries.

Establishment of the Free Zone.—When in pursuance of the treaty of February 2, 1848, the Rio Grande from El Paso del Norte to the point where it flows into the Gulf of Mexico was accepted as the boundary line between Mexico and the United States, new settlements sprang up on the northern bank of the river, and things began to arrange themselves to the new conditions. The two nations, which so far had been separated by territory, very sparsely populated, were at once brought into close contact with each other, and it was found that the economical and commercial conditions on the north and south banks of the Rio Grande were in striking contrast to each other. In the towns of the United States along the north bank no taxes were levied and no restrictions of any kind were imposed upon internal trade. The import duties on foreign goods brought into the United States were at that time comparatively low, and this country was then attaining the full development of its unexampled career of material progress and prosperity. On the opposite bank, in Mexico, the towns were burdened by the oppressive system of taxation which had come down to us from the Spaniards. The heavy taxes which were levied on internal trade under the name of alcabalas largely increased the cost of foreign and domestic goods, and the collection of these taxes made a system of interior custom-houses, with all their attendant evils, a necessary institution. There were many and very onerous restrictions both upon foreign and domestic trade, and the import duties on foreign goods were so high as to be, in many cases, practically prohibitory. Many commodities were actually excluded from the country under the plea of protection to our national industries, and among these were articles of prime necessity, such as grain and provisions. The result of this condition of things was that radically different prices prevailed in the towns on the two sides of the river. At Brownsville, Texas, for instance, on the north bank of the Rio Grande, commodities and the necessaries of life, such as provisions and clothing, were bought at a low price, while in Matamoros and other Mexican towns, on the south bank, the same articles of domestic production, and often of an inferior quality, cost twice and even four times as much as at the stores just across the river. A still greater disproportion existed in the prices of foreign goods on the two sides of the river, and the cheapest commodities were always sold on the left bank of the Rio Grande.

The difference in taxation, and consequently in prices on the frontier, necessarily brought about one of two results. It either caused the inhabitants of the Mexican towns to emigrate to the settlements on the other side of the river, in order to enjoy the advantages which were to

be had in this country, or it induced them to purchase in the United
States the goods which they needed, and to smuggle them across the
Rio Grande to their homes in Mexico.

Besides, the physical characteristics of Mexico are such that a large
portion of the population of its Northern States contained in the Valley
of the Rio Grande depended for their supplies on the American side of
the river, notwithstanding the high tariff of the Mexican Government.

In 1849, the year following the adoption of the new boundary line
by the two countries, the situation on the Mexican frontier became so
intolerable and disquieting that our Federal Congress was obliged to
pass, on April 4th of that year, a law authorizing for three years the
importation, with reduced duties, through the frontier custom-houses of
the State of Tamaulipas—the only one, excepting Chihuahua, which
then had towns on the border—of such provisions as were needed for the
use of the people of the frontier.   Such goods had up to that time either
been prohibited by the existing tariff, or had been subject to almost prohibitory duties.   This law did not meet the exigencies of the situation,
because it was restricted to provisions, and these are not the only things
that men require for life and comfort.

On August 30, 1852, the United States Congress passed an act by
which the contrast between the conditions of the two sides of the Rio
Grande was made still greater, and the condition of things on the
Mexican side became worse than ever.   By that act foreign goods
could be sent in bond to Mexico over certain routes specified in the
act and others to be authorized by the Secretary of the Treasury.
These goods could be held on the frontier in the United States until a
favorable opportunity should present itself for their exportation into
Mexico, and they were exempted from all duties to the United States
when exported from them.   There was no similar privilege within the
territory of Mexico, as all foreign goods, of whatever kind they might
be, were there subject to the payment of duty upon their importation.

The result was that the inhabitants of the Mexican side of the river
were placed under such disadvantages that the public men of Tamaulipas, the State which at that time had towns on the border facing the
border villages of Texas, came to the belief that they could not live
there unless they had privileges similar to those existing in the United
States.   It was this belief that originated the Free Zone, and, in the
unsettled condition of Mexico, it did not take long for such men to find
an opportunity to bring about what they desired.

This statement of facts shows that the Free Zone was not really an
invention of the Mexican authorities of the State of Tamaulipas, but an
imitation, on a larger scale, of a similar measure enacted more than
five years previously by the United States Government for the benefit
of that portion of its territory bordering on Mexico.

28

On February 5, 1857, we adopted our present Constitution, which went into operation on the 16th of the following September. On the 1st of December of that year, General Ignacio Comonfort, who had just been elected President under the new Constitution, was inaugurated. Two weeks later he unfortunately issued a pronunciamiento against the very Constitution to which he owed his election, thus undermining the source of his authority, and he thereupon dissolved the Federal Congress then in session. Almost all of the Mexican States refused to consent to so daring a violation of the Constitution, and many of them, especially those far distant from the capital, reassumed their sovereignty, and their legislatures granted extraordinary powers to the governors, in order to enable them to defend their institutions against those who had betrayed their trust by trying to overthrow the Constitution, acting in this very much as some of the Brazilian States recently did when the President of that Republic, Marshal Diodoro Da Fonseca, attempted to assume the Dictatorship, and these States exercised, consequently, all the powers belonging to an independent state, as they were actually beyond the reach of the Federal Government.

By virtue of such powers, the Governor of the State of Tamaulipas issued, on March 17, 1858, a decree designed to afford a remedy for the hardships from which the frontier population of that State were then suffering. This decree established what has since that time been known in Mexico as the Free Zone. It exempted all foreign goods intended for the use of the frontier towns of that State or the ranches in their jurisdiction, or for trade between those towns, from all Federal duties, but not from municipal or State taxes. Such goods could remain in bond in the same towns, either at the house of the importer or at the public warehouse. The Federal Government not then having warehouses on the frontier, all packages had to go, of course, to the house of the importer. Thus, goods imported into the frontier towns could remain stored indefinitely without paying any storage or other charges to the Federal Treasury, and they only paid import duties when they were taken from the frontier towns to the interior of Mexico.

Nothing could give a better idea of the real object of the ordinance issued by the Governor of Tamaulipas, if there were any doubt about it, than the grounds on which he based his action, which he stated in the preamble of his decree in the following words:

" The citizen Ramon Guerra, Governor *ad interim* of the State of Tamaulipas ; Whereas, our towns on the northern frontier are in a state of actual decadence for the lack of laws to protect their commerce ; and, whereas, being situated in close proximity to a commercial nation which enjoys free trade, they need equal advantages in order not to lose their population, which is constantly emigrating to the neighboring country ; now, therefore, desiring to put an end to so serious an evil by means of franchises which have so long been demanded by the frontier trade ; favorably considering the petition of the inhabitants of Matamoros, and using the extraordinary faculties with which I am invested by the decree of December 28th, of the Honorable Legislature of the State, with the advice and consent of the council, I have seen fit to decree as follows," etc.

The following articles of the decree contain the main provisions in regard to the Free Zone, and show exactly how far it was intended to go :

"ARTICLE I.—Foreign goods designed for the consumption of the city of Matamoros and of the other towns on the bank of the Rio Bravo, Reynosa, Camargo, Mier, Guerrero, and Monterey Laredo, and for the trade which these towns carry on among themselves, shall be free from all duties, with the exception of municipal duties and such taxes as may be imposed, to the end that the burdens of the State may be borne. In like manner, goods deposited in government warehouses, or in warehouses belonging to private individuals, in the said towns, shall be free of duties so long as they are not conveyed inland to other towns of the State or of the Republic. The terms on which this trade is to be conducted are laid down in the following articles :

.   .   .   .

" ARTICLE 7.—Foreign goods leaving the privileged towns to be conveyed into the interior of the Republic shall, at the time of so doing, become subject to the duties laid upon them by the tariff, and they shall never be conveyed into the interior without having paid, at the custom-house of their place of departure, all duties which are required to be paid in the port, and without the observance of all the requirements and provisions of the laws in force, in order that they may not be molested or detained on their way."

The Governor of Tamaulipas foresaw that his decree would naturally facilitate smuggling, to the loss of the Federal Treasury of Mexico; but I am sure he little imagined that the Treasury of the United States would suffer in consequence thereof, and he earnestly recommended the citizens of the State to try to prevent such a result by all the means in their power, as appears from the following article of his decree:

"ARTICLE 8.—As the privilege granted by this decree ought not to cause any detriment to the national revenue, it is the duty of the inhabitants of the frontier to prevent, by all the means in their power, this privilege from being converted into a shameful smuggling traffic ; it is, therefore, the duty of every inhabitant of the frontier voluntarily to become a sentinel, constantly on the watch to prevent smuggling ; otherwise, the government will be under the painful necessity of withdrawing this privilege, by revoking the present decree."

The Governor's decree ended with the following article:

" ARTICLE 9.—This decree shall be subject to the revision and approval of the legislature of the State at its next meeting in ordinary session and to that of the Federal Congress when constitutional order shall be restored, although it shall go into force as soon as published in the privileged towns.

" Therefore, I order it to be printed, published, circulated, and duly enforced.

" Done at Ciudad Victoria, March 17, 1858.

" RAMON GUERRA.

" JOSE MARIA OLVERA, Chief Official."

The foregoing decree was confirmed and amplified on the plea of establishing regulations for its execution by another decree of the Governor of Tamaulipas, bearing date of October 29, 1860. The former decree was submitted, in compliance with the provisions of its last article, to the legislature of the State, and also to the Federal Congress for their approval, and was sanctioned by the latter body July 30, 1861.

New conditions are reducing very materially the scope and workings of the Free Zone. In former years, when the Free Zone duties were only $2\frac{1}{2}$ per cent. and the people were allowed to manufacture, the Free Zone was a benefit, and a very large number of articles of foreign manufacture were cheaper in the Free Zone than the same articles of domestic manufacture; but since the duties have been raised to $18\frac{1}{2}$ per cent., and exchange increased to 212, very few foreign articles can be consumed in the Free Zone in competition with Mexican domestic goods. Therefore, the rate of duties of $18\frac{1}{2}$ per cent., the decline in silver, and the progress of Mexico in manufacturing have practically nullified all advantages. Such articles as coffee, sugar, straw hats, shoes, vegetables, flour, beans, milk, fruits, meat, common clothing, blankets, etc., used and consumed by the poorer class of people are, if Mexican products or manufactures, cheaper than if imported from the United States; and as for the other articles which are generally consumed by the wealthier classes, the latter have the means to buy such articles and pay full duties.

The Mexican frontier labors under great disadvantages as compared with its neighbor, and a great drawback on that frontier is that the merchants have to pay on their invoices the State taxes on sales. Therefore, nearly all houses of consequence have an office on the United States side, in order to avoid paying this tax, which is, in some instances, out of proportion. This could be easily changed by allowing to the municipalities or States, instead of $1\frac{1}{2}$ per cent. which the present law provides, the additional 2 per cent. known as port duties, of which the frontier towns get no benefit. With this assistance of $3\frac{1}{2}$ per cent. to the municipalities or States, by the Federal Government, this tax on sales could be avoided, and the condition of things on the frontier would be considerably improved.

This brief statement will, I think, be sufficient to show that the establishment of the Free Zone was a step taken in what was then thought to be the duty of self-preservation, so to speak, and imitating similar measures adopted by the Congress of the United States, and that it was by no means a measure approved in a spirit of unfriendliness, much less of hostility, towards the United States, as has been generally believed in this country.

For more detailed information on this subject, and especially for the English translation of some of the official documents bearing on the same, I refer the reader to a Message which the President of the United States sent to the Senate on March 16, 1888 (*Senate Exec. Doc.*, No. 130, Fiftieth Congress, 1st Session), and to the report and accompanying documents of the Committee on Foreign Affairs of the House of Representatives, on the relations of the United States with Mexico, presented by Mr. Schleicher on the 25th of April, 1878 (*House Report*, No. 701, House of Representatives, Forty-fifth Congress, 2d Session).

Discussion of the Free Zone in the Mexican Congress.—I think it will not be amiss to say a few words about the different phases through which the Free Zone has passed in Mexico, since the restoration of the Republic in 1867. The Committee on Ways and Means of the Fifth Mexican Congress reported, in its session of 1870, a tariff bill which sanctioned the Free Zone, and this matter was fully discussed during the latter part of October and the beginning of November of that year. Members of the Cabinet have in Mexico not only the privilege of the floor in both Houses, as in the United States, but the right to participate in the debates and to express the views of the Executive. As Secretary of the Treasury of Mexico, I made a thorough study of this important and complicated subject, and I took part in the debate in question in the sessions of the House of the 28th and 29th of October, and the 4th and 5th of November, 1870, making lengthy remarks against the Free Zone, which were published in English in Mr. Schleicher's report. I at that time recommended its abolition to Congress, on behalf of the Executive. The reasons that led me to this conclusion were mainly of a constitutional nature, namely, that the Free Zone constituted a privilege in favor of a State, which is prohibited by our Constitution; and that although I was aware that the situation of the frontier towns of Mexico required the adoption of suitable remedies, I thought that one could be found of such a nature as would embrace the whole country, and be divested of the odious character of a privilege. My efforts were in vain; Congress voted in favor of the maintenance of the Free Zone and its extension to answer any objections of its unconstitutionality; and although the tariff then under discussion never became a law,[1] nevertheless the vote of Congress in favor of the Free Zone exercised great influence upon the existing and succeeding administrations, as it showed what was the opinion of the representatives of the people on that question.

[1] In the papers relating to Foreign Relations of the United States accompanying the President's Message to Congress of December 4, 1871 (pages 608–609), there is a letter from Mr. Thomas H. Nelson, United States Minister to Mexico, dated December 22, 1870, addressed to Mr. Fish, and annexed one addressed to me of December 21, 1870, and my answer of the same date, which states exactly the condition of things so far as the Free Zone was concerned after the Mexican Congress had voted in favor of the extension of the same.

The abolition of the Free Zone was agitated in Mexico after I left the Treasury Department in November, 1872. When, four years later, in 1878, I was again at the head of that department, and saw that it was not possible then to abolish the Free Zone, because the frontier influences were stronger than ever, I thought that we ought at least to make proper regulations to prevent, as far as was possible, any abuses of its franchises, and the regulations of June 17, 1878, were then issued with that object in view.

Extension of the Free Zone.—In the meanwhile there had been a strong reaction in favor of the Free Zone, as the State of Tamaulipas had taken a leading part in support of the revolution of Tuxtepec, which succeeded in 1876, and brought about the Administration then in power, and this was especially so during the Presidency of General Gonzalez, a citizen of that State, from 1880 to 1884.

General Diaz succeeded General Gonzalez on December 1, 1884, and in a new tariff act issued by him, January 24, 1885, the Free Zone, which had been up to that time restricted to the State of Tamaulipas, was extended to the whole frontier, namely, to the States of Coahuila, Chihuahua, and Sonora, and to the Territory of Lower California, for a distance of twenty kilometers from the boundary line, thereby placing it on a better footing than it had been before, when it appeared as a privilege confined to a single State and denied to others which were in exactly the same condition, an objection which I was the first to advance against the Free Zone. But the same tariff act, which so extended the Free Zone, limited considerably its franchises by the regulations contained in its Chapter XII.

The frontier towns and their representatives in Congress, however, exerted such pressure in the Federal Congress that by an act dated June 19, 1885, the limitations established in that tariff were suspended, and very liberal regulations were again adopted in the succeeding tariff of March 1, 1887, which remained in force until the present one of June 12, 1891, was issued. This act marked a new era, in so far as the Free Zone is concerned, as article 696 of the same subjects all foreign goods coming to the Free Zone, which had been previously free of all import duties, to a duty of ten per cent. of the import duties levied by the same tariff, excepting cattle of all kinds, which had to pay full duties. That rate has since been raised to 18½ per cent. of the import duties by a decree promulgated by the Treasury Department of Mexico, on May 12, 1896, which established a duty on foreign merchandise arriving in the country after the 1st of July of the same year, of seven per cent. upon import duties, to be paid in internal revenue stamps in substitution of the duties collected by the interior customhouses, which were abolished from that date. Another decree of the same department, dated June 4, 1896, established a municipal duty of

1½ per cent. upon import duties. I consider this provision as the beginning of a new system which will finally result in doing away with the institution.

The worst blow given by the Mexican Government to the Free Zone was the clause of Article 696 of our tariff act of June 12, 1891, to the effect that commodities manufactured in the Zone, whether of foreign or domestic raw materials should pay import duties coming into Mexico, outside of the Free Zone. This provision proved so detrimental to the interests of the people living in the Free Zone that after a time they would have to give up their privileges for the sake of enjoying the same rights as other Mexican citizens, so far as their products and manufactures were concerned. But recently, on October 31, 1896, regulations were established by the Mexican Treasury which allowed, with many restrictions, the introduction into Mexico free from import duties, of commodities manufactured in the Free Zone, and, although this is a marked advantage to the inhabitants of that zone, the conditions required for the free importation of their manufactures are very burdensome, and they are by no means put on the same footing as those manufactured by the other inhabitants of the country.

Public Opinion in Mexico about the Free Zone.—As I have already observed, the opinion of Mexican statesmen on the Free-Zone question has been divided, some entertaining the belief that it should be abolished because it grants to one section of the country privileges which are not authorized by the Constitution; and others, and by far the larger number, holding that, under the circumstances, its establishment was an imperative necessity, as its abolition would be equivalent to the destruction of the frontier. The friends of the Free Zone represented that the frontier towns of Mexico owed their existence to that institution, and that they could not exist without it. Through a concurrence of events, to which I shall refer later, many Mexicans were led to attribute to the Free Zone more beneficial results than it has really produced, and this has also had a decided influence in its maintenance and extension.

The situation of the Mexican frontier up to the beginning of the Civil War of the United States was, as I have already observed, one of poverty and even of misery, and formed a striking contrast to that existing on the other side of the Rio Grande. The war broke out almost simultaneously with the establishment of the Free Zone, and the situation of the Mexican frontier changed very materially as a consequence of the war, during its continuance, and for some time after its conclusion, prosperity deserted the left for the right bank of the Rio Grande, on account of the general prostration then prevailing in the South, while the Mexican border towns, and specially Matamoros, had something like a boom.[1] Superficial observers attributed that prosperity not to its true cause, which, in my opinion, was the war, but to the Free Zone; and feeling convinced that it had been productive of extraordinarily favorable results, they naturally considered it as a panacea for every ill, and its extension an imperative necessity for the frontier. The latter opinion finally prevailed in the councils of the Mexican Government, which debated the question from 1877 to 1885, with the result, already stated, of the extension of the Free Zone to all the boundary States.

The opinion of Mexican merchants to the south, at Saltillo, Monterrey, and other places, is decidedly opposed to the Free Zone, and they protested vigorously against the gross discrimination against their interests, for, as they contended, they cannot compete with the Zone merchants in selling goods to purchasers living within one hundred miles of the Zone, owing to the facility with which such goods can be bought therein, and carried out by the purchasers, or bought from the smugglers who make a business of furnishing the interior trade with contraband goods.

The merchants and the newspapers in the interior have always contended that the existence of the Free Zone on the frontier was contrary to the interests of the nation; even the people on the frontier, the property owners, and practically all persons having the welfare of the country at heart and who have given the subject some thought, share this opinion.

Right of Mexico to Establish the Free Zone.—There can be no doubt as to the right of the Government of Mexico to exempt from duties or levy them on the foreign trade of the country, even though they should injure the mercantile interests of other nations, and I therefore think it unnecessary to argue the right of Mexico to adopt and main-

[1] The following is the testimony of a spectator of the scenes in the Free Zone during the war :

"The law had but little effect upon our commerce until the opening of the civil war. With the Southern States in revolt, a free and neutral port on the border became at once of vast importance. Contrabands of war and supplies of all kinds could be bought in New York or Europe and sent to Matamoros, a neutral port. From a mere village Matamoros grew within three years to the third port of the world, with eighty vessels at a time anchored off the dangerous roads at the mouth of the Rio Grande. Bagdad, at the mouth, grew from nothing to 12,000 inhabitants, while Matamoros had 40,000, including representatives from every commercial nation in the world. The wickedness of the towns of Scripture fade away before that of these two during the years from 1861 to 1865. Men made or lost a fortune before breakfast buying or selling supplies or cotton. The smallest change for a gentleman was a $5 gold piece ; for a laborer a Mexican dollar. Cotton was wagoned from east of the Mississippi across the plains of Texas to seek a neutral port for export. When the Southern Confederacy collapsed, the *Zona Libre* lost all national importance and steadily declined in value. Matamoros still has the *Zona Libre*, but her commerce has become insignificant and her present population does not exceed 6,000."

tain the Free Zone, especially as regards the United States, which, in its tariff laws, does not have much consideration for the interests of the commerce of foreign nations, and only has in view the requirements of its own citizens, no matter how prejudicial they may be to foreign merchants, manufacturers, or producers; but I will only mention some reasons which seem to me rather plain.

The rates of duties established by the tariff laws of the United States have always been lower than those of Mexico. In a pamphlet, published at El Paso, Texas, in 1895, by Mr. C. R. Morehead, President of the State National Bank of El Paso, who is one of the most determined opponents of the Free Zone, entitled *The Free Zone of Mexico, Its Baneful Effects on the Commercial Interests of that Republic and those of the United States*, the author states as follows:

" In the year 1858 the United States of America only levied for the expenses of the Government an average import duty of 15 per cent. on all imported articles, while the import duties of Mexico were from 20 to 25 per cent., thus giving the American border an advantage over their Mexican neighbors of 5 to 10 per cent. in their commercial relations. Again, the Mexican border could only be reached by traversing a mountainous country for long distances, and the mode of transportation being the most primitive (burro trains), their goods could only be transported at great expense, as no such conveniences as a railroad existed in the Republic at that time. This apparent difference in the duties imposed upon the two banks of the river, and the resulting superiority of the one bank over the other in commercial intercourse, was the cause of the establishment of the Free Zone by the Government of Mexico."

This disproportion in the tariffs of the two countries, as Mr. Morehead acknowledged, made the commercial condition of the United States towns on the Mexican border a great deal more favorable than the condition of the Mexican towns. How would the Government of the United States have acted if Mexico had based on these great differences a remonstrance against the tariff in force in this country, and required that it should abolish it and establish one with the same or higher rates of duty than the Mexican tariff? And how would it have felt if remonstrances had been made against the building of railroads in this country, tapping the frontier, because thereby the condition of the inhabitants of the northern border of the Rio Grande would be bettered? What would the people of this country think if we should ask them to repeal the Act of August 20, 1852, because it encouraged smuggling in Mexico? The Mexican people feel exactly as the people of the United States would feel, if the circumstances were reversed.

It would be absurd to consider as an act hostile to this country the establishment by Mexico of absolute free trade, that is, the abolition of its custom-houses and import duties; in other words, the extension of the Free Zone throughout the whole country, because the United States, as a neighboring nation, would be the nation likely to profit most by such freedom of trade; and if such extension could not be justly a motive of complaint, how can it be so when the free trade is reduced to a very limited zone ?

How Far the Free Zone Favors Smuggling into the United States.— Having explained in what manner the Free Zone was established and what were its real purpose and scope, and before I consider the action of the United States Government on that subject, it will be proper to examine the main objections against it.

The second impression prevailing in the United States about the Free Zone, namely, that it was established to injure the United States, and that it causes a very large smuggling of foreign goods into this country is equally incorrect, as I will try to show.

It does not seem to me reasonable to suppose that the Free Zone was established for the purpose of encouraging smuggling, to the detriment of the United States Treasury, when in fact it harms Mexico to a much greater extent than it does this country, as, in order to injure the United States, Mexico would hardly be willing to injure itself ten times as much; and if the contraband trade carried on under the shadow of the Free Zone was a sufficient reason for its suppression, the interest of Mexico in this matter would long since have settled the question.

Any human institution can be abused by men. The goods stored in the frontier towns of the United States, in accordance with the Act of August 30, 1882, were easily smuggled into Mexico; and yet when the United States Congress passed that law, it did not intend, assuredly, to encourage smuggling to the detriment of Mexico, although such was practically its result. In the same manner the Governor of Tamaulipas at first, and the Mexican Congress afterwards, did not intend in establishing the Free Zone to encourage smuggling to the detriment of the United States.

Unfortunately, the mistaken impression that the Free Zone injures the United States has made a great headway among some of the American statesmen, no doubt because they have not carefully studied this subject. The annual loss caused to the United States Treasury, by the Free Zone, has been estimated to be as high as $6,000,000, as will presently appear. Secretary Fairchild, in a report to the Senate, to which I shall presently refer, expressed that opinion which was then the general impression of several other officials of the Treasury Department, and even of Committees in both Houses of Congress.

The only way to estimate the loss to the United States Treasury by smuggling through the Mexican frontier would be to examine what has been the amount of the importations of foreign goods from the United States into the Mexican Free Zone. But the United States custom-houses do not keep an account of foreign goods exported for consumption in the same, and as most of them go in transit to the interior, the amount of such goods as appears in the reports of the Bureau of Statistics of the United States Treasury Department only represents a small portion of the goods exported to the zone which might be smuggled back into the United States. With a view to ascertain the exact amount of such trade, Senator Morgan, who has always taken great interest in everything relating to Mexico, thought it proper to inquire how much that contraband trade amounted to, and on February 16, 1888, he introduced in the Senate [1] a resolution asking of the Treasury Department whether the Mexican Free Zone encouraged smuggling across that border into either country, and for the estimated loss to the United States; and in answer to that resolution the Secretary of the Treasury transmitted on the first of the following March a statement [2] from which it appears that the total value of the foreign mer-

[1] *Congressional Record,* vol. xix., part II., p. 1720. In the Senate of the United States, February 16, 1888.

THE MEXICAN FREE ZONE.

Mr. Morgan submitted the following resolution:

"*Resolved,* That the Secretary of the Treasury is directed to inform the Senate whether and to what extent the customs laws and regulations of Mexico, in the belt of country known as the Free Zone of Mexico, extending along our border, have encouraged smuggling across that border into either country; the estimated loss of revenue to the United States from that cause; the means employed, or that are necessary to prevent such smuggling; and the additional cost to the United States of the necessary agencies to prevent the violation of its laws in consequence of the existence of that Free Zone."

The resolution was considered by unanimous consent, and agreed to.

[2] Fiftieth Congress, 1st Session (Senate Executive Document No. 108), letter from the Secretary of the Treasury in response to Senate resolution of February 16, 1888, relative to smuggling in the Free Zone of Mexico. March 5, 1888, ordered to be printed and referred to the Committee on Foreign Relations:

"TREASURY DEPARTMENT, OFFICE OF THE SECRETARY,
"WASHINGTON, D. C., *March 1, 1888.*

"SIR,—I have the honor to acknowledge the receipt of Senate resolution, dated the 16th ultimo, directing me—

"'To inform the Senate whether and to what extent the customs laws and regulations of Mexico, in the belt of country known as the Free Zone of Mexico, extending along our border, have encouraged smuggling across that border into either country; the estimated loss of revenue to the United States from that cause; the means employed, or that were necessary, to prevent such smuggling; and the additional cost to the United States of the necessary agencies to prevent the violation of its laws in consequence of the existence of that Free Zone.'

"In reply I have to state that the only information in possession of this Department relative to the subject-matter of the resolution is of a general character. There is no doubt that the existence of the Free Zone of Mexico furnishes an opportunity for smuggling into the United States.

"Under the provisions of Section 3005, Revised Statutes, merchandise arriving in the United States and destined for places in the Republic of Mexico in transit may

chandise which had passed through the United States into Mexico during the fiscal year ending June 30, 1887, was $497,654; and adding to that amount merchandise to the value of $194,774, which was withdrawn from warehouse and exported to Mexico, making a total of $692,428, of which only $211,589 was dutiable, the balance of $480,839 was free under the tariff act of March 3d, 1883, then in force. So that, supposing that the whole of that amount had been smuggled back into Mexico, which could not possibly be the case, because some of those goods were needed in the Free Zone and near-by in Mexico, others legally imported and others smuggled into Mexico, the loss suffered by the Treasury of the United States would have been in reality insignificant.

The average amount of duties under the tariff act of March 3d, 1883, on the whole of the dutiable articles was 47.10 per cent., and the actual loss of revenue to the United States, supposing that all foreign goods imported into Mexico by the Free Zone should have been smuggled back into the United States, would only amount to $99,658, which is by no means as large as the amount estimated by the opponents of the Free Zone and not so much considering the facilities for smuggling which the frontier affords.

Secretary Fairchild in his answer expressed the views prevailing among the Treasury officials that there was no doubt that the existence of the Free Zone in Mexico furnished opportunities for smuggling into the United States; but the figures he gave showed that if any smuggling had been carried on, its amount was really insignificant.

From an official statement, published by the Bureau of Statistics of the United States Treasury Department, of imports and exports of merchandise from the United States during the year ending June 30,

be conveyed through the territory of the United States without payment of duties, under such regulations as the Secretary of the Treasury may prescribe. The total value of foreign merchandise which thus passed through the United States to Mexico during the last fiscal year was $497,654. In addition to that amount, merchandise of the value of $194,774 was withdrawn from warehouse and exported to Mexico, making a total of $692,428, of which $211,589 was dutiable and $480,839 free under our tariff.

" It has been alleged that a large proportion of the dutiable merchandise thus sent into Mexico is smuggled back into the United States. This Department has no means of ascertaining to what extent this is true.

" The principal articles, products of Mexico, which have been subjects of seizure by the customs officers on the Mexican border, are horses and cattle. So long as our present tariff on imports is continued, customs officers will be needed to collect duties and prevent smuggling, and I am not advised that the number and cost of such officials could be diminished if the Free Zone of Mexico were abolished.

" Respectfully yours,

" C. S. FAIRCHILD, *Secretary*

' Hon. JOHN J. INGALLS

" President *pro tempore* United States Senate.

1895, the first year after the Act of August 28, 1894, went into effect, it appears that the value of the foreign merchandise which passed by the frontier into Mexico was as follows: Through Brazos de Santiago $36,510; Corpus Christi, $26,738; Paso del Norte, $35,810; and Saluria, $32,868, making a total of $131,926. So that the total amount of foreign merchandise imported into the Free Zone from the United States in the first year after the Act of August 28, 1894, went into effect was $131,926, and supposing that the whole of it should have been smuggled back into the United States, the import duties on the same, at the rate of 41.75 per cent. under the tariff then in force, would amount to $55,080, which is a mere trifle, considering the conditions of the frontier.

For more details showing how insignificant is the smuggling from the Mexican Free Zone into the United States, and how great the advantages that this country derives from the Free Zone, I refer the reader to a letter that Mr. Frank B. Earnest, Collector of Customs at Laredo, Texas, addressed on February 23, 1895, to the Hon. W. H. Crain, Member of Congress from Texas, to an editorial from the *Lower Rio Grande*, a paper published in Brownsville, Texas, and to a letter from prominent citizens of Brownsville addressed also to Mr. Crain, all of which were read by him in the House of Representatives on February 27, 1895.

Even Mr. John W. Foster, who was, when United States Minister to Mexico, one of the most decided opponents to the Free Zone, and expressed in the different official communications addressed to the Department of State the opinion that the Free Zone was a great detriment to the United States, and had been established for the purpose of encouraging smuggling, changed his views when he went himself to the frontier for the purpose of making a personal examination of the subject, and in an official communication (No. 1077), addressed to Mr. Evarts, Secretary of State of the United States, dated City of Mexico, December 26, 1879, said as follows :

"In the past two or three years the situation has materially changed. The decline in price of manufactured goods in the United States, and our increased spirit of commercial enterprise, enables the American merchants on the Texas side of the river to compete successfully in many classes of goods with the merchants in Mexico, who import from Europe. The practical result is that, in cotton fabrics and many other articles, the Mexican frontier is supplied almost entirely from the United States, and the inducements for smuggling into Texas have greatly diminished. Our customs authorities along the Rio Grande, as well as the citizens in general, informed me on my recent visit to that region that the smuggling of foreign merchandise from the Mexican Free Zone had almost entirely ceased. On the other hand, my observation led me to the conclusion that this Zone was made the base of operations for quite an extensive system of smuggling of American (as well as European) goods into the interior of Mexico. It is the practice of the Mexicans to cross the river to the American towns and purchase our cotton and other goods, and introduce them without hindrance into the *Zona Libre*, whence they are clandestinely taken into the adjoining States of this Republic ; so that the measure which was originally intended to be a protection to Mexican interests and an obstruction to American commerce in its practical workings is just now proving to be the contrary. While I cannot regard the continuance of the *Zona Libre* as a friendly act toward the United States, my recent visit satisfied me that it was a much greater evil to Mexico than to our country. The existence of such a discriminating territory must always be a source of annoyance, and ought to be abolished if we are ever to have a legitimate and cordial commercial intercourse between the two countries, but at present it is the occasion of greater damage to the government and people who created it than to its neighbors."

Considering the matter from a disinterested point of view, it would certainly appear that, barring a possible increase in the temptation and opportunity to land and smuggle foreign goods into the United States, the Mexican Free Zone has been, and still continues to be, a benefit to American trade, and that any attempt to commit the United States Government to a hostile attitude toward that institution is only instigated by local interests.

Smuggling on the frontier will never be prevented, as it has recently happened that people were caught smuggling several sacks of potatoes, which pay practically no duties. Even sewing-machines and plows, which pay almost no duty at all, are smuggled. Perhaps this is due, in a great measure, to the conflicting and vexatious documentary requirements for the importation of small articles at the frontier. If the Government would allow bringing into Mexico small articles up to the value of, say, twenty dollars, without requiring any papers, then smuggling might be considerably reduced, and everybody would have the opportunity of accompanying the goods to the custom-house and paying the duties there, as is done on this side, and a great inducement to smuggling into Mexico would disappear.

Advantages of the Free Zone to the United States.—There is one aspect of this question which, as I believe, has so far passed entirely unnoticed. The Free Zone is really an advantage to the United States, since, as I have already stated, the Mexican system of legislation in the matter of customs and excise duties has generally been restrictive and even prohibitory, both by reason of the high import duties levied on foreign goods and of the existence of interior custom-houses, which prevailed up to the 30th of June, 1896, and also of State and municipal taxes, requiring vigilance and restrictions that must necessarily hamper business transactions. Any relaxation of such a system of restriction could not but be favorable to foreign nations trading with Mexico, and especially to a neighboring country like the United States, whose agricultural products and manufactures are mainly, if not exclusively, consumed on the Mexican frontier.

Under the Tariff Act, of October 1, 1890, and July 24, 1897, the Government of the United States has been trying very earnestly to obtain from foreign countries, and especially from the Spanish-American Republics, the free entry, or the admission at a reduced rate of duties, of some of its products and manufactures, and they naturally feel pleased when a new agreement is made. And yet the liberal terms provided by Mexico in favor of the free admission of all the products and manufactures of this country into our Free Zone has been taken here as an unfriendly act on our part towards this country.

It is a fact, which has already been commented upon by officials of the United States Government,[1] that the merchants on the north side of the Rio Grande River who clamored most loudly against the Free Zone were the European merchants, and the reason is very plain. The United States has, on account of its contiguity of territory, lines of railways, etc., almost the monopoly of the goods consumed in the Free Zone, while the European countries cannot send their goods there unless by long ocean routes and paying expensive railway freight, which add considerably to their cost and make their prices quite high. The advantages accruing from a free market are therefore almost exclusively enjoyed by merchants and citizens of the United States, and it would seem incredible that they should have often been so loud in their denunciations of that institution, which has really been a boon for many of them.

If the Free Zone has inconveniences for this country, although much less serious ones than those which it has for Mexico, it possesses, in my judgment, a decided advantage which has remained hitherto unnoticed. It practically makes a portion of Mexico a free market for all the products and manufactures of the United States, since merchandise of all kinds from this country may be imported into and consumed in Mexican territory almost duty free, and be warehoused in the region of the Zone for an unlimited time. No greater privilege can be asked for the commerce of a nation, and the only drawback in this respect that I can see to the Free Zone, in so far as the United States is concerned, is that it does not embrace the whole of Mexico. Supposing its privileges were extended to the whole of Mexico, would the United States consider the free admission of their products into that country as prejudicial to their interests? How strange, under this view of the question, does the idea prevailing here appear, that the Free Zone brings only injury to the United States and has been established to the advantage of European goods only, when ninety-five per cent. of the goods imported there under its franchises are from the United States.

Estimates of the present population of the Zone range from 60,000 to 80,000 souls. Allowing that 70,000 people find lodgment therein, it

[1] Mr. Warner P. Sutton, United States Consul General to New Laredo, in an official despatch dated April 25, 1890, addressed to the Secretary of State.

is evident the question is of importance both to Mexico and to the United States, on account of the peculiar trade conditions produced by this almost free-trade belt separating two high-tariff countries.

During the fiscal year ending on June 30, 1894, the United States exported to Mexico $12,441,805 in domestic manufactured goods and breadstuffs; of these exports, $6,715,688 went through the five customs districts on the northern border, Brazos de Santiago, Corpus Christi (Laredo), Saluria (Eagle Pass), El Paso del Norte, and Nogales, Arizona. Of the imports into the United States from Mexico, $8,228,892 came through these same ports. It is impossible to arrive at any exact figures as to the amount consumed by the inhabitants of the Zone, but it is estimated by the customs officers at the five points named that about twelve per cent., or about $813,890, is shipped into the Zone, and that only about three per cent. of this amount is re-entered for import to Mexico on the other side and pays the other eighty-two and a half per cent. of the Mexican tariffs. This would give as a result that about $800,000 in American goods were consumed by the residents of the Zone. These figures are comparatively valueless in arriving at any idea of the purchasing power of the Zone in the line of American products, for the reason that this $800,000 constitutes but an item of the real consumption. It is a well-known fact that the residents of the Zone buy most of the goods they consume of a staple character from the American merchants on the north side of the river. Allowing 70,000 people as the population of the Zone, it would be a conservative estimate to place the yearly trade at least as high as $3,200,000 in gold, for the Free Zone resident is very much dependent upon the American merchants. Based upon these estimates, the purchasing value of the Zone to the American trade is at least $4,000,000 each year, and by many who are in a position to be well informed in the premises, it is placed at a much higher figure.

Disadvantages of the Free Zone to Mexico.—The events connected with the foreign intervention in Mexico did not permit the natural effects of the Free Zone to be felt in the country until the Republic returned to its normal condition, that is, until after the termination of the French intervention and the downfall of the so-called Empire of Maximilian, events which took place during the year 1867. In January of 1868, I was called to the Treasury Department by President Juarez, and in my annual report to Congress, on September 16th of that year, I stated that one of the causes of the then depleted condition of the Mexican Treasury was the large contraband trade that was carried on through the Free Zone and enjoyed by the frontier towns of Tamaulipas; further remarking that the custom-houses of those towns were hardly able to meet their clerical and office expenses, and that this fact showed that the establishment of the Free Zone had not made that region prosper; and that, in my opinion, that institution was not the proper remedy for the evil which it was intended to cure.

It is true that the privilege of the Free Zone granted to the inhabitants of the northern portion of Tamaulipas to import and consume foreign goods without paying Federal duties, to store them in their own houses, and to keep them in bond for an unlimited time, was a powerful incentive to smuggling from the Free Zone either to Mexico or the United States; and that Mexico, which has suffered greatly from that result, has been obliged, with a view to the repression of smuggling, to establish a costly, oppressive, and complicated system of inspection; but protection to smuggling was not the object of the creators of the Free Zone, nor is it possible that smuggling should have been carried on to the prejudice of the United States, to the same extent to which it has been done to the disadvantage of Mexico.

As the duties levied by the Mexican tariff are much higher than those imposed in the United States, it is evident that the most lucrative contraband trade, and the easiest one to conduct, is that which is carried on to the detriment of the Mexican Treasury. Smuggling is more easily carried on in Mexico, because the Mexican frontier is very sparsely populated, and therefore the difficulty of guarding it is greatly increased, while the frontier of the United States is more thickly settled and thus better protected against illicit traffic.

To prevent smuggling from the Free Zone as far as this was possible, the Mexican Government has been obliged to double its frontier custom-houses of inspection of goods imported from the United States at great expense and considerable inconvenience to bona-fide merchants, as it has, in addition to the custom-houses directly on the boundary line, with proper inspection between each of them, another system of custom-houses and inspection some distance farther south, under the name of fiscal police, to prevent smuggling between the Free Zone and the rest of the country.

The Free Zone law has worked such a hardship on the property owners and manufacturers on the Mexican side that the losses they have sustained amount up into the millions, while the Republic has lost many thousands of inhabitants, as all the frontier towns have greatly decreased in population on account of its being impossible for them to provide work for the laboring classes. Matamoros, once a flourishing town of about 40,000 inhabitants, has decreased to about 4000 inhabitants; Nuevo Laredo and Piedras Negras have about held their own, on account of the railroads, but Laredo and Eagle Pass, Texas, have increased much more in proportion. This same comparison may be made between Nogales, Mexico, and Nogales, Arizona Territory. However, the greatest anomaly exists in El Paso del Norte. Before the Free Zone law went into effect, El Paso del Norte had a population of 15,000 people, and to-day the census shows only 8000.   In 1881, El Paso, Texas, was a village of 500 people; to-day it has a population of over 15,000 souls.

The existence of the Free Zone with its prohibitory laws as to manufactured articles has prevented the establishment of factories; without that law it is certain that ere this there would have been established along the frontier smelters, soap factories, glass factories, packing-houses, machine-shops, cracker factories, candle factories, brick factories, furniture factories, whiskey distilleries, etc.

In questions of this character there are, of course, a good many conflicting interests; but the main question is which interest the Government should really protect and which interest should be subordinate to others.   The people who have been fiercely contending for the continuation of the Free Zone and bringing about the old rate of two and a half per cent. duties, are principally owners of retail stores who import foreign goods, especially European and Asiatic goods, into the Free Zone and pretend to sell them to both United States and Mexican people.   It is well known that retail stores never employ any great number of clerks, whereas a factory of any kind would give employment to a large number of operatives and hands, and thus be of much more benefit to the people and to the city in general than a retail store employing only a few persons.

Action of the United States Government Adverse to the Free Zone.— It was for some time a matter of wonder to me that public opinion in this country could have been so grossly misled on the subject of the Free Zone; and that a measure which allowed a free market for all kinds of products and manufactures of this country into a large section of Mexican territory could be misunderstood to the extent of considering it as an offence to the United States.   I can imagine, however, how it was that public opinion came to be so grossly misled on this subject. The Southern States of the United States, and especially those close to the southeastern border of Mexico, enjoyed great prosperity before the War of the Rebellion.   All foreign merchandise was allowed to go free of duties to the border, and was smuggled into Mexico, and such transactions naturally established there a very large and prosperous commercial business.   The ravages of the war destroyed the wealth and commercial prosperity of the South, and when the war was over, towns which had been before rich and flourishing were prostrated and poor.   The Free Zone, which had then begun to be in operation, allowed the Mexican towns on the other side of the Rio Grande to have some commercial activity, especially with the importation of domestic commodities of the United States, and that naturally hurt the interests of some of the merchants established on the American side, especially those of European origin or connections.   It is not strange, therefore, that they should attribute entirely to the existence of the Free Zone in Mexico what was really the consequence of the civil war in the United States, and of the new condition of things brought about by the restoration of peace, and that they should account for their depressed condition by the existence of the Free Zone, although in that opinion they were utterly mistaken, and perhaps some others were guided by a feeling of jealousy or envy for the passing prosperity that the Mexican side of the line enjoyed during that war. Their complaints and murmurs naturally spread to the Members of Congress from the respective districts, and finally reached the highest officials of the United States Government. As Mexican affairs had been then so little understood in the United States, and this question had not been presented in its true light, the impression finally prevailed that the establishment of the Free Zone was an act of hostility on the part of Mexico towards the United States, intended to destroy its commerce and to favor smuggling into this country to the prejudice of its Treasury and bona-fide merchants. Of course the existence of this impression afforded a good opportunity to anybody who desired to attack or abuse Mexico to do so, as was the case with Mr. Schleicher, a Representative from Texas, of whom I shall presently speak.

It was in this way that almost all the representatives of the United States in Mexico since the restoration of the Republic in 1867, beginning with Mr. Edward Lee Plumb, General Rosecrans, Mr. Thomas H. Nelson, and especially Mr. John W. Foster, and some of their successors, seemed to labor under the impression—judging from the correspondence which they sent to the State Department on the subject, published afterwards by Congress—that the Mexican Free Zone was a very great injury to the United States; and several secretaries of state, including such distinguished men as Mr. Hamilton Fish, Mr. William M. Evarts, and others, seem—very likely for want of sufficient information—to have given the Free Zone more importance than it really deserved.

This impression extended even to President Grant who, in three of his annual messages to Congress, spoke of the Mexican Free Zone, expressing the mistaken opinion about that institution which prevailed for so long.[1]

[1] Extract from the annual message of President Grant, December 5, 1870:

"It is to be regretted that our representations in regard to the injurious effects, especially upon the revenue of the United States, of the policy of the Mexican Government, in exempting from impost duties a large tract of its territory on our borders, have not only been fruitless, but that it is even proposed in that country to extend the limits within which the privilege adverted to has hitherto been enjoyed.

"The expediency of taking into your serious consideration proper measures for countervailing the policy referred to will, it is presumed, engage your earnest attention."

Extract from the annual message of President Grant, December 4, 1871:

"The republic of Mexico has not yet repealed the very objectionable laws estab-

Mr. Samuel A. Belden, a citizen of the United States, residing at Brownsville, Texas, wrote a letter to the Secretary of the Treasury, dated in Washington on September 21, 1868,[1] in which he said that the effect of the Free Zone had been most disastrous to the commerce of lishing what is known as the 'Free Zone' on the frontier of the United States. It is hoped that this may yet be done, and also that more stringent measures may be taken by that republic for restraining lawless persons on its frontiers. I hope that Mexico, by its own action, will soon relieve this government of the difficulties experienced from these causes."

Extract from the annual message of President Grant, December 7, 1875:

" The Free Zone, so called, several years since established by the Mexican Government in several of the states of that republic adjacent to our frontier, remains in full operation. It has always been materially injurious to honest traffic, for it operates as an incentive to traders in Mexico to supply without customs-charges the wants of the inhabitants on this side the line, and prevents the same wants from being supplied by merchants of the United States, thereby, to a considerable extent, defrauding our revenue and checking honest commercial enterprise."

---

[1] "WASHINGTON, D. C., September 21, 1868.

" Some time in the year 1857 or '58 the governor of the State of Tamaulipas, Mexico, issued a decree authorizing the merchants and citizens inhabiting the strips of territory embraced in the portion of the State extending from the mouth of the Rio Grande to its farthest boundary, and from the river inland for two leagues, to introduce free of duty, merchandise of all classes.

" This is known as the *Zona Libre* (free belt), and the decree of the governor was in operation for three years before it was ratified by the general government, and is in full force at this time, notwithstanding the protest of the cities of Tampico and Veracruz against it as partial and unjust. The government was not in a condition to refuse any demand on the frontier, because of the heroic defenses which the inhabitants had made against Carvajal and other raiders. The merchandise introduced under this decree is required to pay duties only when exported from the *Zona Libre* to the interior of Mexico, or to the United States side of the Rio Grande, and its effect has been most disastrous to the commerce of the city of Brownsville, and other towns on our side of the Rio Grande, as well as to the revenue of the United States. No argument is required to prove this, nor can there be any doubt that it is the cause of the immense amount of contraband trade upon the frontier, the inducements to which are irresistible to such as are willing to engage in it, particularly in liquors and foreign merchandise, which can be purchased at Matamoros at a very small advance over the foreign cost, and their introduction into the United States at some point in an extended frontier of upwards of nine hundred miles, cannot be prevented.

" Prior to the existence of this decree the amount of merchandise in the United States bonded warehouses at Brazos de Santiago and Brownsville ranged from one to three millions of dollars, but since that period the trade has dwindled to such a point the custom-house there, instead of being a means of revenue, is an expense to the United States.

" For the removal of this incubus upon the trade of the citizens of our frontier they are without power, but think that the relations which have existed between the governments of Mexico and the United States, since the passage of the decree, will justify prompt action on the part of the United States to terminate so flagrant an injustice.   " Very respectfully,

" SAM. A. BELDEN, Brownville, Tex."

the city of Brownsville and other towns on the American side of the
Rio Grande, as well as to the revenue of the United States, and that
prior to the existence of the Free Zone the amount of merchandise in
the United States bonded warehouses at Brazos de Santiago and
Brownsville ranged from one to three millions of dollars, and that
since that period the trade has dwindled to such a point that the custom-house there, instead of being a means of revenue, was an expense
to the United States; calling the Free Zone a flagrant injustice, and
concluded by asking the prompt action on the part of the United
States to terminate the Free Zone.   Mr. Belden's personal interests
might have been adversely affected by the Free Zone, or he might have
shared in good faith the prejudices of his neighbors, due to the want of
a proper understanding of the case; he also forgot the changed condition of things in the South caused by the then recent civil war, but
be this as it will, such slender grounds as those stated in his letter were
made the subject of a communication addressed by the Secretary of
the Treasury, Mr. Hugh McCulloch, to the Department of State, on
September 26, 1868,[1] endorsing Mr. Belden's views, and asserting
that the Free Zone seriously affected the growth and prosperity of that
portion of the United States which borders on the Rio Grande.

This statement of facts shows how easy it is to mislead public
opinion, not only in complex, but even in simple questions, and how
difficult it is, when an error is allowed to spread and to prevail un-

[1] MR. MCCULLOCH TO MR. SEWARD.

"TREASURY DEPARTMENT, September 26, 1868.

"SIR:—I have the honor to transmit herewith a copy of a communication, dated
the 21st instant, from Mr. Samuel A. Belden, of Brownsville, Tex., in reference to the
existence on the Mexican side of the Rio Grande of a belt of country which is free to
commerce.

"It is alleged by Mr. Belden, and it has also been represented to the department
through other sources, that by reason of the existence of such free belt of country, the
loss to the revenue by means of smuggling is immense and continually increasing, and
that it seriously affects the growth and prosperity of that portion of the United States
which borders on the Rio Grande.

"In view of these representations, it is respectfully suggested whether it would
not be advisable to bring to the notice of the Mexican authorities the exemption of
that section of the country lying in immediate proximity to the United States, from
customs duties, and exactions which, so far as I am advised, are enforced throughout
the residue of the republic, thus inviting importation of merchandise with a view to its
introduction into the United States without the payment of duty, and imposing a heavy
expense on the United States Government for the protection of the revenue on that
frontier, without any corresponding benefit to Mexico, that I can perceive, which would
justify a measure so injurious to a neighboring and friendly power.

"I am, very respectfully,
"H. McCULLOCH, Secretary of the Treasury.

"Hon. WILLIAM H. SEWARD,
"Secretary of State."

challenged, to bring things back to their true condition, the result often being not only unpleasant, but highly dangerous.

Adverse Action of the United States Congress on the Free Zone.—The mistaken opinion that prevailed regarding the Free Zone was naturally reflected in Congress. As early as June 9, 1868, Mr. Blaine introduced in the House of Representatives a resolution,[1] which passed by unanimous consent, instructing the Committee on Foreign Affairs to inquire whether the action of the Mexican Government in establishing the free ports at Matamoros and other points on the Rio Grande was not in violation of treaty stipulations and unfriendly to the commercial rights of this country.

The Committee on Foreign Affairs called on the State Department for a copy of the papers relating to the subject of Mr. Blaine's resolution, and Mr. Seward sent to General Banks, chairman of that committee, such letters from Mr. Plumb and other diplomatic representatives of the United States in the City of Mexico, as were in possession of the State Department, with his letters of December 17, 1868, and January 2, 1869. With his clear mind, Mr. Seward understood at once, even with the meagre information then at hand, that Mexico had violated no right of the United States in establishing the Free Zone, and in his letter accompanying the correspondence in answer to the queries of the resolution he said : " I am under the impression that the establishment of the Free Zone, so-called, is not at variance with any existing treaty stipulation between the United States and the Mexican Republic."

After receiving the preceding letter the committee failed to make any report on Mr. Blaine's resolution.

On December 6, 1869, a meeting was held in the city of Brownsville, Texas, largely attended by citizens of that city and the adjoining country, and the meeting appointed Edward Downey, Mayor of Brownsville, a delegate to come to Washington to ask Congress that measures be taken to procure from the Mexican Government the abolition of the Free Zone, with a view to prevent smuggling into the United States, and for the protection of American interests on the frontier.

Mr. Downey, therefore, came to Washington and addressed a long memorial to Congress dated January 10, 1870,[2] in which he repeated the assertions of Mr. Belden, that the Free Zone had been established

---

[1] House of Representatives Journal, 2d Session, Fortieth Congress, p. 827.

"*Resolved*, That the Committee on Foreign Affairs be instructed to inquire whether the action of the Mexican Government in establishing free ports at Matamoros and other points on the Rio Grande is not in violation of treaty stipulations and unfriendly to the commercial rights of this country."

[2] Mr. Downey's memorial is published as Senate Miscellaneous Document No. 19, Forty-first Congress, 2d Session, and being a lengthy paper and full of errors and misrepresentations, I will not insert it here.

by the Mexican Government as an act of hostility to the United States, and for the main purpose of encouraging the smuggling of foreign goods into this country, adding that the Free Zone was the outcome of the efforts of European merchants on the Mexican side of the frontier ; that during the War of Rebellion the Mexican Government sympathized with the Southern Confederacy, and to assist it Mexico had reduced to one fourth the duties on munitions of war for the benefit of the Confederates, an assertion entirely at variance with the facts. He stated that the loss suffered by the United States Treasury in consequence of the smuggling carried on by the Free Zone, was estimated from one to six millions of dollars a year, and asserted that the Free Zone had been extended through the whole Mexican frontier with the United States, when that extension did not take place until 1885. How far was correct the assertion regarding the supposed sympathy of the Mexican Government with the Confederates will appear from what I have already stated, and from the facts that I will mention in considering Senator Patterson's report, which accepted the same assertion. This memorial was referred to the joint Select Committee on Retrenchment, which did not take any action on the same. Fortunately a remarkable change of feeling has taken place in Brownsville in so far as the Free Zone is concerned, as will be seen farther on.

Public men in the United States, or at least some of them, had been for some time under the impression that the way to abolish the Free Zone was to repeal the acts which allowed foreign merchandise to go in bond to frontier custom-houses, as if Mexico was very anxious, which was by no means the case, that the border towns of the United States should enjoy that privilege, and this accounts for the efforts made to repeal such acts, which were always unsuccessful until Mr. Cockrell passed his bill, to which I will presently refer.

In accordance with this view, Senator Patterson, of New Hampshire, introduced on April 9, 1870, in the second session of the Forty-first Congress, a bill [1] to repeal all existing laws authorizing the

---

[1] Forty-first Congress, 2d Session (Senate, 783). In the Senate of the United States, April 9, 1870, Mr. Patterson asked, and by unanimous consent obtained, leave to bring in the following bill, which was read twice, referred to the joint Select Committee on Retrenchment, and ordered to be printed :

" A Bill to repeal all existing laws authorizing the transportation and exportation of goods, wares, and merchandise in bond to Mexico, overland or by inland waters, and for other purposes.

" Be it enacted by the Senate and House of Representatives of the United States of America in Congress assembled, Sec. 1. That all existing laws authorizing the transportation and exportation of goods, wares, and merchandise in bond to Mexico, overland or by inland waters, be and the same are hereby repealed.

" Sec. 2. And be it further enacted, That all existing provisions of law authorizing the payment of drawback upon goods, wares, and merchandise exported from the

transportation and exportation of goods, wares, and merchandise in bond to Mexico overland, or by inland waters, and for other purposes, which was referred to the joint Select Committee on Retrenchment.

That committee reported favorably to the Senate Mr. Patterson's bill on May 16, 1870. The report was presented by Mr. Patterson himself, and shows a complete misunderstanding of the case. It repeats the charges made by Mr. Belden, Mr. Downey and others, giving them, on account of Mr. Patterson's position, a great deal more importance than they had before. It assumes that the establishment of the Free Zone in Mexico was a hostile act against the United States, decreed for the purpose of defrauding her revenues, that the Mexican Government had sympathized with the rebellion, and had, for the purpose of assisting it, altered her revenue laws, with a view to allowing contraband trade through Mexican territory; both statements being entirely incorrect.

The idea that the Mexican Government sympathized with the so-called Southern Confederacy and assisted it materially is simply preposterous, as everybody knows that Louis Napoleon, availing himself of the civil war in the United States, tried to establish an European empire in Mexico, with the ultimate purpose of acquiring a foothold in that country, and the Mexican people and the Mexican Government were therefore as anxious as the most patriotic of the Union men in this country to have the Union restored, if for no other reason than to obtain the restoration of the republic in Mexico, and the soundness of these views was fully confirmed by the subsequent facts.

I have reviewed carefully all the laws and regulations issued by the Federal Government of Mexico from 1861 to 1865, while the civil war lasted in the United States, and the only act that I find concerning either cotton or commerce with the Southern States, is one issued by President Juarez, under extraordinary powers at San Luis Potosi, on July 28, 1863, for the purpose of establishing an additional duty of one cent per pound on national, and two cents per pound on foreign raw cotton, to be paid at the place of consumption; and that duty, far from being a discrimination in favor of the Confederates, was, in the nature of things, a heavy tax on their principal product.

Under the regulations of the Free Zone, all goods that came to the

United States to ports or places in Mexico north of parallel twenty-three degrees thirty minutes north latitude, or the cancellation of bonds given for the exportation and landing of goods, wares, and merchandise at such ports and places be, and the same are hereby repealed ; and all authority to issue certificates in respect to the landing and delivery of goods, wares, and merchandise, conferred by law upon merchants and consuls of the United States resident at places in Mexico north of said parallel, is hereby revoked."

Passed the Senate without amendment, June 9, 1870, but failed in the House of Representatives.

same were free of import duties, and only paid them when they were taken outside of the Free Zone to be imported into Mexico. Any cotton imported into Mexico from the United States or from any other country, therefore, which did not go outside of the limits of the Free Zone, was not liable to the payment of duties, and could be freely exported. General Vidaurri, who in 1861 was the Governor and Military Commandant of the State of Nuevo Leon, with authority over Coahuila and Tamaulipas, issued an order, on April 5, 1862, levying transit duties of one cent per pound upon all cotton which had come free of duty to the Free Zone and was re-exported from the same.[1] The only object of General Vidaurri was, of course, to obtain revenue for his state government, and not to assist in the exportation of cotton through the Mexican frontier. If anybody had any right to complain of that duty it was the officials and the people of the so-called Confederate States, as the duty was a charge upon their main product, which at the time had a very high price, and was almost their only export abroad. I understand that even that duty was later increased to $1\frac{1}{2}$ cents per pound, but I have not been able to find the act establishing that increase.

Senator Patterson could not have understood fully the nature of the Free Zone and the conditions of the case, as otherwise I do not think he would have found fault with the Mexican officials for not forbidding the export of foreign cotton through Mexican ports. As no international law or act of comity could prevent the transit of such merchandise through Mexico, for the sole reason that the Southern States of this country had rebelled against the Federal Government, the Government of Mexico could not close its ports to the exportation of goods from the Southern States; and to do so, would have been equivalent to an alliance with the United States against the Southern States, and although the Federal Government of Mexico desired at heart the success of the Union, especially for the reason that its success

---

[1] I give below the order of General Vidaurri which created a tax on foreign cotton exported from Matamoros :

"MILITARY DEPARTMENT OF TAMAULIPAS.

"Taking into consideration the increased expenses that have to be incurred by merchants dealing in cotton who bring this article in order to re-export it, and it being desirable to increase, if possible, the arrival at this port of merchant vessels, I have deemed it proper to grant, in view of the petition presented for such purpose by the American citizen, J. A. Quintero, that hereafter all cotton imported to be re-exported shall pay as the only and entire duty the sum of one dollar per quintal or hundredweight. I communicate the same to you so that it may be duly complied with, and I renew you the assurances of my esteem.

"God and Liberty. MONTEREY, *April 5, 1862.*

"(Signed) SANTIAGO VIDAURRI.

"To the Citizen Collector of the Maritime and
Frontier Custom-House of Matamoros."

insured the prompt end of the French intervention in Mexico, it would not have been justified in taking that step.

Senator Patterson's Bill, reported favorably and without amendment by the Joint Committee on Retrenchment, on May 16, 1870,[1] passed the Senate without amendment, on June 9, 1870. In the House of

[1] Forty-first Congress, 2d Session. Senate *Report No. 166.* In the Senate of the United States, May 16, 1870. Ordered to be printed. Mr. Patterson made the following report. (To accompany Bill S. No. 783.)

" The Joint Select Committee on Retrenchment, to whom was referred Senate bill No. 783, 'to repeal all existing laws authorizing the transportation and exportation of goods, wares, and merchandise in bond to Mexico overland, or by inland waters, and for other purposes,' having considered the same, respectfully submit the following report :

" The object of the bill is to protect, so far as it can be done by legislation on our part, the revenue of the United States and the interests of our frontier bordering on the Rio Grande from the losses and injuries resulting from the facilities for smuggling afforded by the laws which it is proposed to repeal, and by the existence of the *Zona Libre*, or Free Belt, on the Mexican side of the Rio Grande.

" Prior to 1858 the American towns enjoyed greater commercial advantages and were much more thrifty and populous than their Mexican neighbors on the opposite side of the river.

" By the act of August 30, 1852, the transportation to Mexico of goods in bond was permitted by certain routes specified in the act, and by such others as the Secretary of the Treasury might prescribe. This enabled American merchants to store larger quantities of goods in our bonded warehouses, until a favorable opportunity arrived to withdraw them for consumption or for exportation in bond to Mexico.

" It is simply an impossibility to prevent smuggling on such a line as that formed by the Rio Grande, so long as a sufficient inducement to smuggle exists, and doubtless, at that time, there was considerable smuggling from the American side of the river, to the detriment of the revenue of Mexico and the legitimate commerce of her merchants, who were unable to compete successfully with those whose goods had paid only the lower rate of duty then required at the American ports, or having been exported from the United States in bond and smuggled into Mexico, had escaped payment of duties to either nation.

" On the 28th day of December, 1857, the legislature of the State of Tamaulipas passed an act creating the *Zona Libre*, which was promulgated March 17, 1858, by decree of Ramon Guerra, then provisional governor of Tamaulipas. The immense amount of smuggling on the Rio Grande, and the necessity for the repeal of our laws authorizing the exportation of goods in bond to Mexico, are mainly in consequence of that act.

" As the *Zona Libre* promises to be a matter of considerable interest to the country, we give the decree, establishing it in full in the appendix to this report ; also the testimony of competent witnesses showing its effects on our revenue and the prosperity of the frontier.

" The object of the act is clearly shown in the preamble, where it is recited ' that the villages on the northern frontier are found in a really ruinous state,' and that the decree is issued ' that they may not be entirely depopulated by emigration to the neighboring country.'

" By the first article of the decree foreign goods are admitted to Matamoros and other towns in the State of Tamaulipas on the Rio Grande, free of duty, except such

Representatives it was referred to the Committee on Commerce, but it was not reported by that Committee, and consequently failed.

Senator Reagan, from Texas, following in the footsteps of Senator as might be imposed for local purposes, which were mainly municipal and trifling in amount.

" Article second invites merchants established on the American bank of the river to transfer their business and effects to the other side, and grants special facilities and privileges for doing so. The other articles are mainly occupied with the regulations for the transfer of merchandise from the *Zona Libre* to the interior of Mexico.

" That the result of this decree was not unanticipated by its authors is clearly shown in Article eighth, in which the inhabitants are invoked ' to impede, by every means in their power, the conversion of this benefit granted to them into a shameless contraband traffic.'

" The purpose of the act was evidently to build up the Mexican towns at the expense of their American neighbors, which was to be accomplished by furnishing to smugglers, for hundreds of miles along a frontier that it is impossible to guard, a safe and convenient place of deposit for goods which they received free of duty, until a convenient opportunity should occur to smuggle them into the United States. The inevitable result was the destruction of the commerce and prosperity of the American towns, and great frauds, estimated at from $2,000,000 to $6,000,000 per annum, on the revenue of the United States.

" The general government of Mexico hesitated to approve an act so hostile to the interests of a friendly nation ; and it was not until July 30, 1861, when Texas was in the possession of the so-called Confederate States, to whom the *Zona Libre* would be of great advantage, that it received the sanction of President Juarez.

" During the war the towns of the *Zona Libre* furnished free ports of entry for the Confederates, through which they exported their cotton, and received in return large supplies of arms and other munitions of war. The Mexican Government, while professing friendship for the United States, sympathized with the rebels, and aided them by every means in its power. It modified its customs regulations so as to facilitate the exportation of cotton and the return of war material ; and while the Confederate ports were blockaded by our cruisers, permitted merchandise and munitions of war, imported into the *Zona Libre*, to be transferred to the Confederacy at one-fourth the rate of duty required on the same articles when shipped to other countries, or even taken to other places in Mexico. Under the guise of friendship and neutrality the Mexican Government did us more harm during the late war than it could have done if openly hostile ; for in that case we could have easily blockaded the mouth of the Rio Grande, and have completely cut off that great source of Confederate supplies.

" Since the close of the war the *Zona Libre* has served as a base from which smuggling into the United States can be safely carried on. The American towns have decayed, and the Mexican towns have flourished in proportion, so that instead of being in a ' really ruinous state,' and liable to be ' entirely depopulated by emigration to the neighboring country,' as they were in 1858, they contained in 1868 a population more than three times as large as that of their American neighbors, that ten years before were threatening to absorb them. Honest merchants, unable to compete with the smugglers, have been compelled to abandon the country or to engage in illicit trade themselves, and the whole community on both sides of the river has become so thoroughly demoralized that smuggling is generally considered a legitimate and honorable business. The desperate characters whom this condition of things has attracted or created, plunder private citizens as well as defraud the government, and frequently make raids into Texas and drive large herds of cattle across the river into Mexico. It

Patterson, introduced in the Senate of the United States, on January 6, 1890, a Bill to prevent the transportation of merchandise in bond

is estimated by well-informed men that the loss by these raids is sometimes as high as two hundred thousand head a year.

"The prosperity of the whole frontier is paralyzed by the existence of the *Zona Libre.* The revenue of Mexico suffers as well as our own. By the decree of Ramon Guerra, only goods consumed in the *Zona Libre* were exempted from duty ; but, although the importations exceed many times the amount that can be consumed by the population of that territory, the custom-houses collect barely enough to pay their own expenses.

"The Secretary of the Treasury of Mexico, in his Report, published in the fall of 1869, says :

"'Another of the causes which have contributed most powerfully to diminish the product of the public rents, and especially that of importation duties, has been the institution of the Free Zone, enjoyed by the frontier of Tamaulipas. The establishment of this institution, owing in the beginning to the desire of favoring the frontier population of Tamaulipas, constitutes an exception which can with difficulty be sustained according to good economical principles, and which has given and will still give margin for abuses and frauds of importance by which suffer greatly the commerce of good faith and the Federal exchequer.'

"Soon after the restoration of order, the attention of the Mexican Government was called to the injuries resulting to both countries from the existence of the *Zona Libre,* and to the unfriendly spirit shown by enacting for the territory bordering on our frontier different customs regulations from those which existed in other parts of the country, by which the enforcement of our laws and the prevention of frauds on our revenue were made impossible. The President and heads of the executive departments admitted the justice of our complaints, and gave reason to hope that the decree establishing the *Zona Libre* would be abrogated at the next session of Congress. No action was taken by the Mexican Congress until December last, when, instead of abrogating the decree, they extended it so as to include the States of Nuevo Leon and Coahuila.

"The following extract from an article which appeared in *La Cronica,* March 18, 1870, and which it is understood was written by a distinguished member of the Mexican Congress, will show the spirit in which this extension was made and the manner in which the *Zona Libre* is regarded by the enlightened statesmen of Mexico :

"'The newspapers of the United States are full of complaints against the institution of the Free Zone on our northern frontier. The evils resulting therefrom to the treasury and the commerce of their country are serious, and they denounce the measure as contrary to the reciprocity which should exist between the two countries. For ourselves, from the time the establishment of the Free Zone was discussed in Congress, it never seemed to us a measure favorable to the interests of Mexico, and we believed further that it would tend to destroy the relations of friendship existing between the two nations.

"'We remember that Congress was deluded by the assurance that the institution of the Free Zone injured the commerce of the United States, and for this reason favored the interests of Mexico. We admit the former proposition, but are far from expecting that the latter will prove true. We do believe, after having studied the question, that the Free Zone injures both nations ; the United States, because all that frontier being a free port, the merchants of the American side will come to our territory to store their goods, and watch for an opportunity to introduce them in a clandestine manner into Texas. Thus Mexico will be in the position of a person who injures himself and at the same time injures his neighbor.

through the ports and territory of the United States into the Republic of Mexico, and to restore that privilege whenever the *Zona Libre* along the boundary line between the two countries shall be

" 'It was said in Congress that Mexico was free to dictate her own laws. Nobody can doubt that she has this right, but neither can we disregard the obligations imposed upon nations by natural law not to make themselves bad neighbors, one to the other.'

"With a knowledge of the course pursued by Mexico during the war and of the feeling toward the United States which now animates the majority of her Congress, it is useless to expect anything from her friendship or her justice.

" We must depend wholly on ourselves and must protect our revenue by the best means in our power. This can be partially effected by the passage of the proposed Bill. Large quantities of merchandise are transported in bond from other parts of the United States, mainly from Indianola, Galveston, and Corpus Christi, to the bank of the Rio Grande, and ostensibly crossed over into Mexico. Of this the certificate of an American consul, or, where there is no consul, that of two merchants, is considered sufficient evidence, and on the return of such a certificate the bond is cancelled. Where nearly all the inhabitants are engaged in smuggling, such certificates are not difficult to obtain. No inconsiderable portion of those goods ever cross the river, but after proceeding for a few miles in the direction of the place to which they are professedly destined, they are carried into the *chaparral*, taken from the original packages, and thereafter transported with perfect impunity into the interior. After the requisite time the certificate that they have been landed in Mexico is returned, signed, as required, by two merchants, and the bond is cancelled. Sometimes the goods are actually carried across the river, but the greater portion soon find their way back into the United States without the payment of duties.

" The Northern States of Mexico are mainly dependent for their supplies on goods transported in bond across a portion of our territory.

" The Secretary of the Treasury has lately issued orders discontinuing routes designated by the Treasury Department pursuant to the provisions of the Act of August 30, 1852. By the passage of the proposed bill the other routes authorized by that act will be closed, and the transit trade in bond, with all the smuggling resulting therefrom, entirely stopped.

" The cost of supplies for the Northern States of Mexico will be increased by the expense of transportation over long, difficult, and unsafe routes, or, if received by the same routes as at present, by the addition of the United States duty, which must then be paid, so that it will be for the interest of the people of those States to join with the party already opposed to the *Zona Libre* in demanding its abolishment.

" The passage of the proposed bill will prevent smuggling, so far as it is perpetrated under cover of our laws authorizing the exportation of goods in bond, but it will not prevent the smuggling into the United States of goods originally imported into Mexico, and will therefore prove only a partial remedy. No effectual prevention of smuggling across the Rio Grande can be devised, except such as will require the concurrent action of Mexico.

" The State Department has been in correspondence with the Mexican Government for two years past in relation to the *Zona Libre*, and, although the President and executive officers of that Government have expressed their sense of its injurious effects on both countries, and their desire for its abolishment, the only practical result has been, as was before stated, its extension by Congress over two more States.

" The hope of successful negotiations seems to have been exhausted. In viola-

abolished,[1] which was referred to the Committee on Commerce, and reported adversely on June 25, 1890, by Mr. Cullom of that Committee, and after being debated was recommitted on July 1, 1890. Senator Reagan was not satisfied with that decision, and on the same day, July 1, 1890, he presented substantially the same Bill with only a few verbal alterations, as an amendment to Senate Bill 1642,[2] which was referred

tion of her own Constitution, which prohibits the enactment of revenue laws unequal in their effect, Mexico still persists in maintaining along our frontier a belt of territory to which goods are admitted free, while imports to all other portions of the country are required to pay a heavy duty. Unfriendly is the mildest term by which such conduct can be characterized. A due consideration for the protection of our own interests may render other measures requisite to induce Mexico to regard the comity of nations, and observe toward us such a course of conduct as is essential to the maintenance of friendly relations between neighboring countries. In so delicate and important a matter, the Committee offer no suggestions, but simply report the facts connected with the existence of the *Zona Libre* for the consideration of Congress, and recommend the passage of the proposed Bill without amendment."

[1] Fifty-first Congress, 1st Session (S. 1642). In the Senate of the United States, January 6, 1890. Mr. Reagan introduced the following Bill, which was read twice and referred to the Committee on Commerce, June 25, 1890. Reported by Mr. Cullom adversely.

"A Bill to prevent the transportation of merchandise in bond through the ports and territory of the United States into the Republic of Mexico, and to restore that privilege whenever the *Zona Libre* along the boundary between the two countries shall be abolished.

"Be it enacted by the Senate and House of Representatives of the United States of America in Congress assembled, That after thirty days from the passage of this act it shall be unlawful for any person, firm, or corporation to transport any merchandise in bond through the ports or territory of the United States into the territory of the Republic of Mexico ; and any person, firm, or corporation violating the provisions of this section shall be liable to a fine of not less than one thousand dollars, and to imprisonment for a term not exceeding one year.

"Sec. 2. That if the Republic of Mexico shall at any time abolish said *Zona Libre*, and shall give notice of that fact to the President of the United States, he shall, upon the receipt of such notice, by proclamation restore the right to transport merchandise through the ports and territory of the United States in bond into the territory of the Republic of Mexico as now permitted by law."

[2] Fifty-first Congress, 1st Session. (S. 1642.) In the Senate of the United States, July 1, 1890. Referred to the Committee on Commerce and ordered to be printed.

AMENDMENT

Intended to be proposed by Mr. Reagan to the Bill (S. 1642) to prevent the transportation of merchandise in bond through the ports and territory of the United States into the Republic of Mexico, and to restore that privilege whenever the *Zona Libre* along the boundary between the two countries shall be abolished, viz., strike out all after the enacting clause and insert the following :

"That after thirty days from the passage of this act it shall be unlawful for any person, firm, or corporation to transport any merchandise in bond through the ports or territory of the United States into the *Zona Libre* or Free Zone of the Republic of Mexico ; and any person, firm, or corporation violating the provisions of this section

to the Committee on Commerce, but that Committee did not take any further action on the subject, and the matter rested there.

A similar measure finally passed Congress on February 27, 1895, and became the joint resolution signed by the President March 1, 1895, and of which I will presently speak.

Marauding on the Frontier.—The close connection that marauding on the frontier had with the Free-Zone question from 1872 to 1879, makes it necessary to say a few words about this incident.

The unsettled condition of the frontier at the time caused marauders to prey upon both sides of the border, Texas often being the victim; and for this the Mexican Government was not responsible, but on the contrary exerted itself as far as it could to prevent and punish such offenders. There were at the time also Indian raids, made especially by the Indians living in the United States, which at times were given permission to leave their reservations and hunt in Mexico, where they committed terrible crimes, from which sometimes the Texas settlements suffered, and all this contributed to establish a condition of unrest on the frontier. Members of Congress from Texas thought very likely the Mexican Government was somewhat responsible for such occurrences, and they exerted themselves to place the responsibility upon Mexico.

Mr. John Hancock, a Member of Congress from Texas, succeeded in having a joint [1] resolution passed by Congress, which was approved

shall be liable to a fine of not less than one thousand dollars and to imprisonment to a term not exceeding one year. But this act shall not be construed to prohibit the transportation of such merchandise into any part of the territory of Mexico where duties on imports are required to be paid by that country; and the Secretary of the Treasury shall make such rules and regulations as may be necessary to carry into effect the provisions of this act.

"Sec. 2. That if the Republic of Mexico shall at any time abolish said *Zona Libre*, and shall give notice of that fact to the President of the United States, he shall, upon the receipt of said notice, by proclamation, restore the right to transport merchandise through the ports and territory of the United States in bond into any port of the territory of the Republic of Mexico as now permitted by law."

[1] [RESOLUTION NOT OF GENERAL NATURE—No. 4.]

JOINT RESOLUTION appointing commissioners to inquire into depredations on the frontiers of the State of Texas.

Whereas there are complaints of many depredations having been committed for several years past upon the frontiers of the State of Texas, by bands of Indians and Mexicans who crossed the Rio Grande River into the State of Texas, murdering the inhabitants or carrying them into captivity, and destroying or carrying away the property of the citizens of said State; as also that bands of Indians have committed and continue to commit like depredations on the property, lives, and liberty of the citizens along the northern and northwestern frontiers of said State: Therefore,

Resolved by the Senate and House of Representatives of the United States of America in Congress assembled, That the President of the United States be, and he is

on May 7, 1872, to appoint a Special Commission of three persons to inquire into depredations by bands of Indians and Mexicans who crossed the Rio Grande into the State of Texas, and in pursuance of that resolution President Grant appointed Messrs. Thomas P. Robb, Richard H. Savage, and Thomas O. Osborn as commissioners to investigate such depredations. Mexico, on her part, appointed a similar commission for the purpose of ascertaining the marauding which had taken place in her territory.

The United States Commission presented in 1872 a preliminary report, which was submitted to Congress by President Grant with his Message of December 16, 1872. In that report the Commissioners said, referring to the Free Zone, as follows :

" The harassing question of the *Zona Libre*, it does not fall within the province of the Commissioners to examine, but they feel called to notice the extension of this Zone in opposition to the most friendly remonstrances of the United States, as another evidence of the spirit which has characterized the policy of the Mexican Government in its dealings with the United States for a series of years."

What has already been said about the extension of the Free Zone, shows how greatly misinformed were the United States Commissioners on the subject.

The final report of the Commission made on June 30, 1873, to the Secretary of State containing no proposal on the Free Zone, was communicated by President Grant to Congress with his Message of May 26, 1874.

President Grant, in his Annual Message of December 7, 1874, said in reference to the marauding on the frontier :

" . . . Marauding on the frontier, between Mexico and Texas, still frequently takes place despite the vigilance of the civil and military authorities in that quarter.

hereby, authorized and empowered to appoint three persons to act as commissioners to inquire into the extent and character of said depredations, by whom committed, their residence, or country inhabited by them, the persons murdered or carried into captivity, the character and value or the property destroyed or carried away, from what portions of said State, and to whom the same belonged.

Sec. 2. That it shall be the duty of said commissioners, or a majority of them, as soon as practicable, to proceed to the frontiers of said State and take the testimony, under oath, of such witnesses as may appear before them, after having given notice for ten days previous, by publication in the nearest newspaper, of the time and place of their meeting, of all such depredations, when, where, by, and upon whom committed, and shall make up and transmit to the President full reports of their said investigations.

Sec. 3. That said commissioners shall be entitled to and receive as compensation for their services, the sum of ten dollars per day each, and their travelling expenses to each, for and during the time they shall be engaged in said service ; and the sum of six thousand dollars, or so much thereof as may be necessary, be, and the same is hereby appropriated, to pay the expenses of said investigation and said commissioners.

Approved, May 7, 1872.

. . . . It is hoped that the efforts of this Government will be seconded by those of Mexico to the effectual suppression of these acts of wrong.

Which shows that in President Grant's opinion the Mexican frontier had also suffered by the marauding.

From 1876 to 1878 the relations between Mexico and the United States were in a critical condition, owing especially to the efforts of Mr. Gustav Schleicher, a Member of Congress from the Sixth District of Texas, born in Darmstadt, Germany, and who had served in the House of Representatives and Senate of the Texas Legislature, having been elected to the Forty-fourth Congress and re-elected to the Forty-fifth and Forty-sixth Congresses of the United States, although he died before the beginning of his last term. Guided either by a great zeal to serve the interests of his State, or because he desired to precipitate some trouble with Mexico, he exerted himself in an extraordinary manner to make it appear that Mexico was giving great cause of offense to the United States, and that this country had to take the necessary means, even at the cost of war, to stop such imaginary aggressions.

On January 6, 1876, the House of Representatives passed a resolution introduced by Mr. Schleicher, to the effect :

" That the portion of the President's Message which refers to the inroads, robberies, and murders along the Mexican border in Texas be referred to a Special Committee of five members, with instructions to inquire into the causes and the nature and extent of these depredations, and the measures that might prevent their continuance, with power to send for persons and papers, and to report at as early a date as possible."

As is usual in such cases, Mr. Schleicher was appointed Chairman of that Special Committee, which gave him, of course, a commanding position in the same.

On February 9, 1876, the Special Committee appointed in conformity with the resolution approved by the House on January 6th submitted its report,[1] which concerned especially the raids on the frontier.

On the 1st of November, 1877, the House of Representatives passed a resolution introduced by Mr. Schleicher, asking the President to communicate to the House any information in his possession relative to the Mexican border in Texas, and any recent violations of the territory of the United States by incursions by Mexicans, and in answer to that resolution President Hayes sent to the House, with his message of November 12, 1877, reports of the Secretaries of State and of War, of the same date, with their accompanying papers. This Message was referred by the House to the Committee of Foreign Affairs, and on December 10th of the same year a resolution presented by Mr. Schleicher was adopted by the House of Representatives, referring to

[1] Forty-third Congress, 1st Session. House of Representatives Ex. Doc. No. 257.

the same Committee so much of the Annual Message of the President of the United States to the two Houses of Congress at that session, together with the accompanying documents, as related to the difficulties on the Rio Grande border.

The report of the Committee on Foreign Affairs of the House of Representatives of the Forty-fifth Congress, 2d Session, presented on April 25, 1878, by Mr. Schleicher, accompanying a resolution [1] which was equivalent to a declaration of war against Mexico, was based, among other imaginary insults, on the supposition that the Free Zone in Mexico was very injurious to the United States, and its establishment almost an act of hostility on the part of Mexico.

Mr. Schleicher died at Washington on January 10, 1879, and this incident ended with him, his death having coincided with the consolidation of peace in Mexico.

Joint Resolution of March 1, 1895.—When some of the most prominent men of the United States misunderstood the scope and purpose of the Free Zone, it is not strange that some of the inhabitants of the Texas border should have done so also, and should, for that reason, have shown a strong dislike and opposition to it. Some citizens of Texas, living on the frontier, and prejudiced against the Free Zone, presented a petition, on January 24, 1895, to the Texas Legislature, which was afterwards approved by that body, in the shape of a resolution calling upon

[1] Forty-ninth Congress, 1st Session, House of Representatives. (Report No. 2615.)

JOINT RESOLUTION.

Be it resolved by the Senate and House of Representatives of the United States of America in Congress assembled :

1.	That experience has fully demonstrated the necessity, under existing conditions, for the presence of an adequate military force on the Mexican border in Texas, as the only guarantee of the lives and property of our citizens against the cattle-thieves, robbers, and murderers who cross from the Mexican side of the Rio Grande ; and that the President is therefore requested to keep on that border, from the mouth of the Rio Grande to El Paso, a military force of not less than five thousand men, of which at least three thousand shall be cavalry.

2.	That the orders of the President, issued by the Secretary of War June 1, 1877, authorizing the crossing of the border by our troops in certain cases, are necessary for an efficient defense of the lives and property of our citizens, and should not be withdrawn or modified until treaty stipulations shall have been agreed to by Mexico that will secure an equally efficient protection.

3.	That the following should be secured by treaty stipulations :

First.	Indemnity for injuries to the persons and losses to the property of citizens of the United States for which the Government of Mexico shall be found liable.

Second.	The abolition of the Free Zone.

Third.	Such provisions as will hereafter secure on the border the speedy trial and punishment of criminals, residents, or citizens of Mexico, as well as others, in the courts within whose jurisdiction the crimes have been committed.

Fourth.	The exemption of American citizens residing in Mexico from forced loans and all other illegal exactions.

the Members of Congress from that State to urge upon Mexico to abolish the Free Zone, and, in case of a refusal, then for the United States to close its bonded warehouse against all goods entering Mexico through any of our ports. Mr. Jeremiah V. Cockrell, a member of Congress from the 13th District of Texas, undertook with more zeal than discretion to carry out the wishes of the Texas Legislature, and on January 17, 1895, he introduced a joint resolution [1] with a long preamble, asserting that the Free Zone was detrimental to the interests of American merchants doing business near the said Zone, by reason of their inability to compete with the untaxed importations of foreign countries; that it was depriving this Government of much revenue by reason of the increasing evil of smuggling on the frontier of the Rio Grande, where an increased force of customs inspectors adequate to prevent this contraband trade would entail an enormous expense, and that all the free importations landed on the Free Zone caused loss of revenue to this Government.

[1] Fifty-third Congress, 3d Session (House of Representatives, 260). In the House of Representatives, January 17, 1895. Referred to the Committee on Ways and Means and ordered to be printed. Mr. Cockrell introduced the following joint resolution :

" Joint resolution in reference to the Free Zone along the northern frontier of Mexico and adjacent to the United States.

" *Whereas*, the so-called ' Free Zone' along the northern frontier of Mexico and adjacent to the United States, in which all foreign goods are admitted free of duty by the Mexican Government, has had for years past a detrimental effect on the interests of American merchants doing business near the said Zone, by reason of their inability to compete with the untaxed importations from China, Japan, France, Italy, Germany, England, and all Europe ; and

" *Whereas*, The said Free Zone has for years and is daily depriving the Government of much revenue by reason of the increased and growing evil of smuggling on that frontier of the Rio Grande where an increased force of customs inspectors adequate to prevent this contraband trade would entail an enormous expense not commensurate with the revenues there collected ; and

" *Whereas*, All the free importations that are landed on that Zone, which cause the loss of revenue to this Government and the humiliation of daily violations of its customs laws, which it is impossible to correct, are carried in bond through this country and delivered in said Zone. Therefore, be it

" *Resolved*, by the Senate and House of Representatives of the United States of America in Congress assembled, That the Secretary of the Treasury be, and is hereby, directed to suspend, so long as the Mexican Free-Zone law exists, obedience to the laws that permit merchandise in bond to be landed thereon, as the only means this Government has to prevent loss of revenue and to protect the honest importers of the United States from the unjust discrimination which the Free Zone of Mexico occasions against them, without, however, impairing, hindering, or impeding the *bona fide* importations into the interior of Mexico beyond the Free-Zone frontier, or in any manner disturbing the commercial relations of the two countries, excepting so far as the Free Zone of Mexico is concerned, which has proven to be inimical to the interests of the United States, and after long toleration has justified this course.

From what I have already stated from official information obtained from the Secretary of the Treasury, and from the testimonials of gentlemen from Texas, holding high official positions, who know all about the Free Zone, Mr. Cockrell's assertions will be seen to be destitute of foundation.

Both the preamble and enacting clause were so objectionable to the Committee of Ways and Means that, when they reported this resolution [1] to the House on February 18, 1895, they had to omit the former and leave of the latter only the provision that the Secretary of the Treasury "should suspend the operation of Section 3005 of the Revised Statutes, in so far as the same permits foreign goods, wares, and merchandise to be transported in bond through the United States into the Free Zone of Mexico, so long as the Mexican Free-Zone law exists." [2]

[1] Fifty-third Congress, 3d Session, House of Representatives. *Report No. 1850.* Mexican Free Zone. February 18, 1895. Committed to the Committee of the Whole House on the State of the Union, and ordered to be printed. Mr. Bynum, from the Committee on Ways and Means, submitted the following Report. (To accompany H. Res. 277):

"The Committee on Ways and Means, to whom was referred the House Resolution (H. Res. 260) entitled, 'A joint resolution in reference to the Free Zone along the northern frontier of Mexico and adjacent to the United States,' having had the same under consideration, respectfully report the same back with the recommendation that the accompanying substitute be adopted in its stead.

"The design of the resolution was to prevent the transportation of merchandise in bond through the United States into the Free Zone of Mexico. The Free Zone of Mexico is a narrow strip extending along the northern boundary of Mexico from the Gulf of Mexico to the Pacific Ocean. The Government of Mexico does not allow shipments in bond through its territory into the Free Zone, hence all shipments into this territory are made through the United States. The sparsely-settled country along the line between the United States and Mexico makes smuggling easy, and the officers of the Government have found it impossible to prevent the same. The exemption of that portion of *Zona Libre*, between the Gulf of Mexico and Laredo, is deemed advisable by reason of the navigability of the river between those points. There is no objection upon the part of the Mexican Government to the passage of this resolution and the action proposed to be taken by this Government."

[2] Fifty-third Congress, 3d Session (H. Res. 277). In the Senate of the United States, February 20, 1895. Read twice and referred to the Committee on Finance, February 21, 1895. *Resolved*, That this joint resolution pass (February 25, 1895). Vote on third reading, and passage reconsidered and referred to the Committee on Finance.

"Joint resolution in reference to the Free Zone along the northern frontier of Mexico and adjacent to the United States:

"*Resolved*, by the Senate and House of Representatives of the United States of America in Congress assembled, That the Secretary of the Treasury be, and is hereby, authorized and directed to suspend the operation of Section 3005 of the Revised Statutes, in so far as the same permits goods, wares, and merchandise to be transported in bond through the United States into the Free Zone of Mexico, so long as the Mexican Free-Zone law exists, at any point between the western boundary of the city of Laredo, in the State of Texas, and the Pacific Ocean · Provided that

In justice to other Members from Texas, I must say that some of them objected to Mr. Cockrell's resolution, and Mr. William H. Crain, a young and very promising Member from that State, representing the 11th District, who, unfortunately, has since died, spoke in favor of the Free Zone, showing that it was not prejudicial to the United States, and he qualified Mr. Cockrell's resolution as an attempt to coerce Mexico into the abolition of the Free Zone. Finally, when he found that he could not stem the current, he amended the resolution to the effect that it should not embrace his Congressional district, extending from Laredo, Texas, to the Gulf of Mexico; and the resolution so amended was approved by the House of Representatives, reported favorably by the Committee on Finance of the Senate on February 20th, and approved by the Senate on February 25th; but when the directors of the railways running to the excluded district learned of this discrimination, they naturally objected to it, on the ground that it discriminated against them, and this objection was so strong that the resolution had to be reconsidered by the Senate, and amended to make the prohibition general, and in this form it was finally approved by both Houses of Congress and by the President on March 1, 1895.[1]

Commissioner Lyman, of the United States Civil Service Commission, made a trip to the frontier, and hearing only parties inimical to the Free Zone, and giving full credence to their statements, made a report to the Commission on his return to Washington in February, 1895, in which he repeated the assertions that the Free Zone was prejudicial to the interests of the United States, that it encouraged smuggling, and suggested that for the purpose of stopping it, the bonded privilege for foreign merchandise sent to the frontier should be withdrawn. How ungrounded these views were, will appear by reading the opinion of the Collector of Customs at Laredo, of citizens of El Paso and other prominent parties on the frontier better informed than Mr. Lyman of

nothing herein contained shall be construed so as to prevent the transportation of merchandise in bond to be delivered at points in the territory of Mexico beyond the limits of said Free Zone."

Passed the House of Representatives, February 19, 1895.

(Attest)   JAMES KERR, Clerk.

[1] Public Resolution, No. 23. Joint resolution in reference to the Free Zone along the northern frontier of Mexico and adjacent to the United States:

" Resolved, by the Senate and the House of Representatives of the United States of America in Congress assembled, That the Secretary of the Treasury be, and is hereby, authorized and directed to suspend the operation of Section 3005 of the Revised Statutes, in so far as the same permits goods, wares, and merchandise to be transported in bond through the United States into the Free Zone of Mexico, so long as the Mexican Free-Zone law exists ; Provided, That nothing herein contained shall be construed so as to prevent the transportation of merchandise in bond to be delivered at points in the territory of Mexico beyond the limits of said **Free Zone.**"

Approved, March 1, 1895.

the condition of things there. His opinion, however, could not fail to assist the friends of the measure proposed in the House by Mr. Cockrell.

Mr. Cockrell's resolution, after all his exertions, was inoperative because of its imperfect wording, to the effect " that the Secretary of the Treasury should suspend Section 3005 of the Revised Statutes in so far as the same permitted goods, wares, and merchandise to be transported through the United States into the Free Zone of Mexico so long as the Free-Zone law exists."

When this resolution went to the Treasury Department, it was found that Section 3005 of the United States Revised Statutes, which was the only one repealed by the same, was insufficient to accomplish the purpose intended by its originators, as it ought to have repealed, also, Sections 3002, 3003, and 3004. Section 3005 allowed foreign goods to enter in transit in bond directly to the place of destination without examination; while the others allowed the same goods to enter for warehouse and transportation with examination at the port of arrival. As the other three sections had been left in force, the only result accomplished by the Act was that goods sent to the frontier, intended for the Mexican Free Zone would now be required to be examined, when before they could be passed without examination. Therefore, the efforts of Mr. Cockrell were entirely ineffective; but even if they had been successful, their practical result would have been that European goods intended for the Free Zone, which formerly came through the United States, paying freight to the American railways, would be imported through Mexican ports, and from there transported to the Free Zone, to the advantage of the Mexican railways and Mexican merchants, and that the American merchants on the frontier who formerly handled such goods and gained the commission on the same, would be deprived of that business which would be transferred to the Mexican merchants and the right bank of the Rio Grande.

Prior to the attempt of the United States to put an end to the bonding privilege allowing the shipping of goods through the United States, Mexico extended no bonded privilege from her ports of entry. This forced all shipments from foreign countries to American ports and over American railroads. The Mexican entry ports of Tampico, Veracruz, and Guaymas did not recognize the Zone, and full duties were required on all goods entered regardless of their ultimate destination. The people of the United States, therefore, had up to April 1st, 1895, an absolute monopoly of the carrying trade of the Zone and a monopoly of the selling trade of that territory in nearly every line of goods. Such is the result of ill-advised legislation.

The danger that foreign goods transported in bond from or to the frontier and passed into Mexico should be smuggled back into the

United States could not be remedied by that Act, because the same danger exists in regard to the same goods, once in the Free Zone, whether they come through the United States or through Mexican territory, and therefore the measure enacted was entirely inadequate to accomplish the object intended.

These reasons were so plain that on December 18, 1896, Mr. Seth W. Cobb, a member of Congress from Missouri, introduced by request in the House of Representatives a joint resolution for the repeal of the Act of March 1, 1895, which was referred to the Committee on Ways and Means of the House.[1]

If the purpose of that Act was to obtain from Mexico a repeal of the Free Zone, as might be inferred from its wording, and especially in the form in which it was originally submitted, that purpose entirely failed, and I can affirm that this and similar measures will be new and serious obstacles for the abolition of the Free Zone.

An incident happened in this connection which I think worth mentioning. In the report of the Committee on Ways and Means, submitted to the House of Representatives on February 18th, 1895, Mr. Bynum, who had this matter in charge, stated that there was no objection on the part of the Mexican Government to the passage of that resolution and to the action proposed to be taken by the Government of the United States. While this matter was pending in Congress, I purposely refrained from speaking to any member on the subject, or taking any action in regard to it, notwithstanding that I was sure that Mr. Bynum was misinformed, lest my interference might be considered as an attempt to influence legislation, and because, as we have objected to the United States Government interfering in our legislation on the Free Zone, to be consistent, I thought we ought not to interfere when the United States attempted to legislate on the same subject. But, after the joint resolution had been approved by the President and it was placed in the statutes of this country, I thought I would make this matter clear, and I wrote to Mr. Bynum the following letter:

" WASHINGTON, *March 6, 1895.*

" *Hon. William D. Bynum, Indianapolis, Indiana :*

" MY DEAR SIR,—I noticed that you stated, both in the report submitted by yourself on the 18th of February ultimo in behalf of the Committee of Ways and Means

---

[1] Fifty-fourth Congress, 2d Session (H. Res. 222). In the House of Representatives, December 18, 1896. Mr. Cobb (by request) introduced the following joint resolution, which was referred to the Committee on Ways and Means and ordered to be printed :

" Joint resolution to repeal the joint resolution in reference to the Free Zone :

" *Resolved*, by the Senate and House of Representatives of the United States of America in Congress assembled, That the joint resolution entitled, ' Joint resolution in reference to the Free Zone along the northern frontier of Mexico and adjacent to the United States,' approved March 1, 1895, be, and the same is, hereby repealed.

of the House of Representatives, and during the discussion on the subject in the House, that there was no objection on the part of the Mexican Government to the passage of the resolution to suspend the transportation of our merchandise in bond, through the United States, destined to the Free Zone in Mexico. As I am not aware that my Government has made any declaration concerning this matter, you will confer a favor on me if you will kindly inform me what was your foundation for this statement.

"Apologizing for the trouble I am giving you, I remain,

"Very faithfully yours,　　　M. ROMERO."

In due time I received from Mr. Bynum the following answer:

"COMMITTEE OF WAYS AND MEANS,
"HOUSE OF REPRESENTATIVES,
"WASHINGTON, D. C., *March 27, 1895.*

"*Mr. M. Romero, Washington, D. C.:*

"MY DEAR SIR,—Yours of the 6th instant addressed to me at Indianapolis was returned—hence the delay in answering. The report upon the bill for abolition of the shipment of goods in bond through the United States into the Free Zone of Mexico was written very hastily in the closing hours of the session. The statement therein that the Government of Mexico had no objections to the measure, was based upon representations made to the Committee by parties who appeared before it in advocacy of the passage. It was not based upon anything purporting to come from any official or representative of the Mexican Government.

"Very respectfully,　　　W. D. BYNUM."

Reaction in Favor of the Free Zone.—There are some symptoms of reaction against the hostility of the Free Zone developed in the United States, and I will mention here briefly in what they consist. I have already referred to the resolution introduced by Senator Morgan in the Senate of the United States, asking the Secretary of the Treasury for information as to whether and to what extent the Free Zone in Mexico encouraged smuggling into this country, and to Secretary Fairchild's answer which showed how insignificant was the foreign trade through the Free Zone. At the same time, on February 16, 1888, Senator Morgan introduced another resolution calling "on the Secretary of State for all correspondence with the Government of Mexico or its diplomatic representatives, respecting the laws and regulations of that Republic relating to customs duties and their collection in the belt of border country extending along the frontier of the United States from the mouth of the Rio Grande to the Pacific Ocean, known as the Free Zone of Mexico." This last resolution was intended to bring out my two official communications to the Secretary of State, of February 10th and 14th, 1888, respectively, which were sent to the Senate with the President's Message of March 16, 1888,[1] and which I append to this paper.

---

[1] In the Senate of the United States, February 16, 1888. *Congressional Record,* vol. xix., part ii., p. 1261.

THE MEXICAN FREE ZONE.

" *Mr. Morgan.*—I submit the following resolution :

"'*Resolved,* That the Secretary of State is directed to send to the Senate copies of all correspondence with the Government of Mexico, or its diplomatic representatives,

There are also signs of a reaction in Congress on this subject, as is shown by the fact already stated that Mr. Seth Cobb introduced a resolution to repeal the joint resolution of March 1, 1895; which shows that members of Congress are becoming satisfied of the injurious results to the interests of their own country brought about by said joint resolution.

Notwithstanding the preponderance of opinion against the Free Zone, to which I have just alluded, the facts in the case are so plain that it will hardly be possible to misrepresent and agitate it much longer. When some of the public men of this country took the pains to study the scope and purpose of the Free Zone they at first expressed opinions in regard to that institution which were greatly at variance with those I have quoted, but after the question had been discussed it is pleasant to find that the false impression that prevailed in the United States regarding the Free Zone is being materially changed.

not heretofore published, respecting the laws and regulations of that Republic relating to customs duties and their collection in the belt of border country extending with our frontier from the mouth of the Rio Grande to the Pacific Ocean, known as the Free Zone of Mexico.'

"*Mr. Edmunds.*—I suggest to the Senator from Alabama that the ordinary course has been, and I think it ought to be, in calling for diplomatic correspondence, that the request should be addressed to the President with the usual clause, 'If not in his opinion incompatible with the public interest.'

"*Mr. Morgan.*—I had been informed that the Minister from Mexico had made a voluntary communication to the Secretary of State setting forth what the laws and regulations were.

"*Mr. Edmunds.*—I dare say that may be true as a matter of fact, but, officially, we do not know it. I think we had better preserve the usual form.

"*Mr. Morgan.*—That was the reason why I put the resolution in the form I did, knowing that there was no secret about the matter. I am quite willing to change it so as to direct the resolution to the President, 'if not incompatible with the public interest.'

"*The President pro tempore.*—The modification of the resolution will be read.

" The Chief Clerk read as follows :

"'*Resolved*, That the President, if not incompatible with the public interest, is requested to send to the Senate copies of all correspondence with the Government of Mexico, etc.'

"*Mr. Edmunds.*—It should be, 'if in his opinion not incompatible with the public interest.'

"*The President pro tempore.*—The resolution as proposed to be modified will be read.

" The Chief Clerk read as follows :

"'*Resolved*, That the President, if in his opinion not incompatible with the public interest, is requested to send to the Senate copies of all correspondence with the Government of Mexico, etc.'

" The resolution, as modified, was agreed to.

" The replies to these resolutions are printed respectively as Senate Executive Documents Nos. 109 and 130, 1st Session, Fiftieth Congress."

Mr. Warner P. Sutton, an able Consular officer of the United States, who represented his country for fifteen years as Consul on the frontier, serving for five years as Consul and ten years as Consul-General in Mexico—the first eleven at Matamoros and the remainder of the time at New Laredo—holds that the Free Zone in Mexico is advantageous, rather than in any way detrimental to the commercial and revenue interests of the United States, and he expressed those views in an interview, which was published by the New York *Evening Post*, of May 19, 1894. I attach so much importance to Mr. Sutton's views that I append his interview to this paper.

As I have already stated, Mr. Crain, a Member of Congress from Texas, delivered a speech in the House of Representatives on February 27, 1895, in which he plainly demonstrated that the Free Zone in Mexico is in no way prejudicial to the interests of the United States; and to the letters addressed to him on February 25, 1895, by the Collector of Customs at Laredo, which express exactly the same views, and on January 27, 1895, by the leading citizens of Brownsville, Texas, including the Mayor and other public men—a city which had been the hot-bed of the opposition to the Free Zone—asserting that the Free Zone was advantageous to the commercial interests of the United States.

The feeling on the frontier of the United States in so far as the Free Zone is concerned is at present quite different from what it was thirty years ago. Brownsville, Rio Grande City, and Nogales have no railroad outlet to the north, and in these places few opponents of the Zone as an institution can now be found. The American opposition to the Zone is to be found in the cities of Laredo, Eagle Pass, and El Paso, as it is claimed there that the trade of the American merchants in European goods, such as silks and other luxuries, is ruined by the proximity of the Free Zone and the towns across the river. Nuevo Laredo, opposite Laredo; Piedras Negras, opposite Eagle Pass; and El Paso del Norte, opposite El Paso, Texas, are built up at the expense of those on the American side. Another class which has opposed the Free Zone is a limited number of real estate owners in the border towns of the United States, who imagine that if they could ruin their rivals on the other side of the river they would enjoy a perpetual boom of prosperity.

United States Opposition to the Free Zone has been in the Way of its Abolition.—I think it is proper on this occasion to state that the misunderstanding which has prevailed here with regard to the object and tendencies of the Free Zone and the manner in which that misunderstanding has been expressed by Federal and State officials, has really served as a powerful argument to the Mexican defenders of the Free Zone, to keep up that institution, as they accuse their opponents of subserviency to this country, attributing to them a design to sacrifice the interests of Mexico to the demands of the United States. It may not be out of place for me to quote here certain views regarding this aspect of the question which I expressed as Secretary of the Treasury of Mexico, in my annual report submitted to the Federal Congress, under date of September 16, 1870, and which are the following:

" The friendly representations made by the United States Government to that of the Republic in relation to the injury accruing to the United States from the Free Zone are also worthy of being taken into consideration by Congress, not that it may seek to please the neighboring nation in a spirit of servility, at the expense of the rights and interests of the Republic, which it is under obligations to care for and uphold above everything else (which spirit would be unworthy of our national representatives); but as a neighborly act, and in order to have a right to be heard and treated with consideration in case that in the process of time some difficulty may arise on our northern frontier of such a nature as to possess, regarding Mexico, the character which the Free Zone possesses, as regards our neighboring nation ; in order, moreover, that Mexico may acquire a new title to be heard and considered in a cordial and friendly, as well as just and equitable, manner when she may have occasion to offer remonstrances with a view to the protection of her interests. A nation's dignity is not so well upheld by refusing to consider the moderate and amicable remonstrances of a neighboring nation, as it is by hearing and considering such remonstrances and then acting according to the requirements of justice."

The Free Zone and the Hanseatic Cities.—The Free-Zone question had a precedent in the Hanseatic cities of Germany, which it is proper to consider, as showing that the Free Zone was not a Mexican invention and what may be its probable outcome. The Hanseatic cities, especially Hamburg and Bremen, had practically the same thing as the Free Zone, and it is perhaps well to compare the situation which existed in these Hanseatic cities of Germany with that of the Free Zone in Mexico. The Hanseatic cities were, from a customs and financial point of view, treated as a foreign country; and all goods, whether of foreign or of domestic manufacture, had to pay full duties upon entering Prussia.

After the war between France and Germany, Prince Bismarck considered it necessary that the rich populations of Hamburg and Bremen, consisting of over half a million of people, should contribute to the national expenses in revenue, and was persistent in that the mentioned cities should abandon their privileges. The Hanseatic cities did not take the initiative step for a customs union with the remaining part of Germany, and the people at large were opposed to any change; but the manufacturers of Hamburg, who could not ship goods into the remaining part of Germany, without paying duties, had for several years been advocating such a union with the other part of the empire. Prince Bismarck contended that the privileges enjoyed by the Hanseatic cities, from a national and financial point of view, were a drawback to the interests at large of Germany, as it was very difficult to prevent smuggling from the free territory into the territory paying duties, and thus the Imperial Government was deprived of a good deal of revenue.

Finally Prince Bismarck's views prevailed, the desired change was accomplished : but when the Hanseatic cities were brought into the customs union, there existed very little sympathy for the new state of affairs. However, time has shown that the people are now fully satisfied with the existing conditions; and if to-day a movement should be inaugurated to go back to the old system, it is extremely doubtful if a majority could be found in favor of the old conditions.

Since the formation of this customs union with Prussia, manufacturing, both for export and domestic consumption, has increased enormously in the Hanseatic cities, a good deal of the manufacturing being done in the bonded warehouse or free district, where everything enters free and there is no interference by the Government.

The prices of some articles in the Hanseatic cities, of course, increased when they had to pay duties, but the increased manufacturing created a demand for labor and consequent increase of wages, so that the people were thus fully compensated for the increase in the prices of some articles on account of their having to pay duties.

In the German cities of this union there are certain districts containing from three to twelve square kilometres, where foreign goods are stored or deposited without any customs requirements excepting for statistical purposes.[1]   In Hamburg this free district or territory contains

[1] Messrs. Ketlesen & Degetau, of El Paso del Norte, Mexico, having asked, on February 24, 1897, Messrs. Oetling Gebruder, of Hamburg, several questions about the free city of Hamburg, they received the following answer, which shows how the Free Zone could be adjusted in Mexico :

1.   The free territory of the city of Hamburg, before it became included in the Custom-House Union with Prussia, comprised an area of 413.71 square kilometres.

2.   When leaving the free territory, all merchandise, including agricultural products, had to pay import duties in conformity with the Prussian tariff.

3.   From the time that Hamburg formed part of the Custom-House Union with Prussia, there was a great improvement noticeable in the State of Hamburg, and all its industries greatly increased.

4.   The prices of the necessaries of life did not increase, as a general rule, as they were controlled by the prices ruling in the principal markets of Europe.

5.   The area of the present jurisdiction granted to bonded warehouses, where articles may be kept without paying duties, is 10.44 square kilometres.

6.   A portion of these warehouses belongs to the Government, and a portion to private individuals.

7.   The Government does not interfere in any way with any merchandise entered at the free warehouse.

8.   Duties in conformity with the tariff have to be paid on all articles taken from the bonded warehouse for home consumption in Germany.   No duties have to be paid on any articles taken out to be exported.

OETLING GEBRUDER.

HAMBURG, March 20, 1897.

twelve square kilometres, and, while Hamburg, before entering the customs union with Germany, was the fifth most important port of the world, it has since then become one among the first in importance.

This may be the way to solve the problem in Mexico, that is, the Government might designate a certain territory, say, two or three square kilometres, for instance, in Matamoros, Laredo, Piedras Negras, El Paso del Norte, and Nogales, where merchants would be allowed to store their goods without duties and then, upon their withdrawing the same for home consumption, pay full duties; and if they should be exported, to be free of any expense for duties. This would give the frontier towns an opportunity to develop a large trade in commerce, and even sell to parties in the United States.

Conclusion.—I sincerely hope that the foregoing remarks will in some measure contribute to dispel the false impressions prevailing in the United States in regard to the Mexican Free Zone, and that in consequence when the agitation on the subject shall have completely disappeared, it will be easier to adjust this matter in such a manner as will be honorable and satisfactory to all concerned.

APPENDIX TO THE MEXICAN FREE ZONE.

PRESIDENT'S MESSAGE OF MARCH 16, 1888, ON THE FREE ZONE.

Senate, 50th Congress, 1st Session, Ex. Doc. No. 130.

Message from the President of the United States, transmitting a letter of the Secretary of State, in response to Senate resolution of February 16, 1888, relative to the Mexican *Zona Libre*.

March 19, 1888.—Read and referred to the Committee on Printing. March 27, 1888.—Ordered to be printed.

To the Senate of the United States :

I herewith transmit, in compliance with the resolution of the Senate of the 16th ultimo, a report from the Secretary of State, accompanied by certain correspondence in regard to the Mexican *Zona Libre*.

GROVER CLEVELAND.

EXECUTIVE MANSION, WASHINGTON,
March 16, 1888.

To the President :

The undersigned, Secretary of State, to whom was referred a resolution adopted by the Senate of the United States on the 16th ultimo, requesting the President, "if in his opinion not incompatible with the public interest, to send to the Senate copies of all correspondence with the Government of Mexico, or its diplomatic representatives, not heretofore published, respecting the laws and regulations of that Republic in its belt of border country extending with our frontier from the mouth of the Rio Grande to the Pacific Ocean, known as the Free Zone of Mexico," has the honor to submit to the President, with a view to its communication to the Senate in response to that resolution, copies of certain unpublished correspondence on file in the Department of State which cover the inquiry of that body.

A copy of the important tariff laws and customs regulations of Mexico, which went into effect July 1, 1887, and which include many special provisions relative to importation, bonding, consumption, and travel in the *Zona Libre*, is also transmitted, as essential to a knowledge of its workings.

Two of the inclosures,* with the note of the Mexican minister at this capital, dated February 10, 1888, on the subject of the *Zona Libre* from a historical view, are unavoidably communicated in the original Spanish.

Respectfully submitted,

T. F. BAYARD.

DEPARTMENT OF STATE, WASHINGTON,
March 16, 1888.

* While this document was passing through the press an opportunity was found to translate these inclosures, and they therefore appear translated into the English language.

480

No. 7. MR. ROMERO TO MR. BAYARD.

[*Translation.*]

LEGATION OF MEXICO, WASHINGTON,
February 10, 1888.

MR. SECRETARY :—I have observed both in the correspondence of the representatives of the United States in Mexico, which has been published by their Government, and in statements made by prominent persons in this country, expressions and opinions respecting the Free Zone which exists in the portion of Mexico bordering on the United States, which I consider wholly unfounded ; it has consequently seemed proper to me, from a due regard to the good understanding and harmony between our two countries, to offer some explanations whereby I trust that the erroneous impressions that now prevail on this subject will be rectified.

I think I do not hazard much in saying that both in official circles in the United States and outside of those circles it is believed that the Free Zone was established in Mexico as an act of antagonism, if not of hostility, to the United States and mainly, if not solely, for the purpose of encouraging smuggling, to the prejudice of the fiscal interest of this country.   It will not be difficult to show how unfounded these opinions are.

When in pursuance of the treaty of February 2, 1848, the Rio Grande from El Paso del Norte to the point where it flows into the sea was accepted as the boundary line between Mexico and the United States, and when American settlements began to be made on the left bank of that river, two peoples were brought into contact with each other whose economical and commercial conditions offered a striking contrast. In the United States no taxes were levied upon internal trade, and it was not otherwise restricted ; the import duties on foreign goods were at that time relatively low, and the country was just entering upon an unexampled career of progress, while in Mexico, which had inherited the Spanish system of taxation, taxes were levied which largely increased the cost of domestic goods ; the collection of these taxes rendered internal custom-houses necessary, and the restrictions placed upon trade were numberless ; import duties on foreign goods were so high as to be prohibitory ; in addition to this, the importation of various kinds of goods was prohibited, among them some of prime necessity, such as provisions.

The result of this state of things was that while in Brownsville, and other towns on the left bank of the Rio Grande, domestic articles of daily use, such as provisions, clothing, etc., were sold at a comparatively low price, in the Mexican towns on the right bank they cost twice and even four times as much, and that foreign goods also were much cheaper on the one than on the other side of the river.

This difference of circumstances necessarily brought about one of these two results: It either caused the inhabitants of the Mexican towns to emigrate to those of the United States in order to enjoy the advantages which were to be had in that country, or it induced them to purchase the goods which they needed in the United States and then to smuggle them over to the Mexican side.

In 1849, that is to say, in the year following that in which the new boundary line was adopted, the situation on the Mexican frontier became so disquieting that the Federal Congress was obliged to pass a law, on the 14th of April, which may be considered as the first step toward the establishment of the Free Zone. This law authorized, for a term of three years, the importation through the frontier custom-houses of the State of Tamaulipas of such provisions as were for the use of the people of the frontier, which goods, up to that time, had been prohibited by the existing tariff or had been subject to very heavy duties.

This law did not meet the exigencies of the situation; and in 1858 the Free Zone was established by the governor of Tamaulipas as an absolute necessity of the State.

On the 5th of February, 1857, the constitution was adopted which is now in force in Mexico, and which went into operation on the 16th of September following. On the first of September, Don Ignacio Comonfort, the constitutional President, was inaugurated, and, unfortunately, a pronunciamiento was issued by him on the 17th of the same month against the Constitution; he also dissolved the Federal Congress which was then in session. For this reason several Mexican States, especially such as were at a distance from the centre, reassumed their sovereignty, and their legislatures granted extraordinary powers to the governors, in order to enable those officers to protect their institutions.

In virtue of these powers the governor of the State of Tamaulipas issued, on the 17th of March, 1858, a decree which was designed to afford a remedy for the hardships that were then suffered by the frontier population of that State. This decree established what has since that time been known as the "Free Zone," in which foreign goods intended for the use of the frontier towns of the State, and of the ranches in their jurisdiction, or for trade between those towns, were to be exempt from all Federal duties, but not from municipal or State taxes, an unlimited right of bonding being, moreover, granted to those towns. Thus it was that foreign goods imported there could remain stored indefinitely without paying any duties to the Federal treasury. The said goods paid no import duties, except when they were removed from those towns to be shipped to the interior of Mexico.

Nothing could furnish a better explanation of the true object of the decree issued by the governor of Tamaulipas, if there were room for any well-founded doubt with regard to it, than the grounds on which he based his action, which were as follows:

"Whereas the towns on our northern frontier are in a state of actual decadence owing to the want of laws to protect their trade; and whereas, being situated in close proximity to a commercial nation which enjoys free trade, they need similar advantages in order to avoid losing their population, which is constantly emigrating to the neighboring country; now, therefore, desiring to arrest this serious evil by means of franchises which have so long been demanded by the frontier trade."

The decree of the Governor of Tamaulipas of March 17, 1858, was submitted to the legislature of the State and also to the Federal Congress for their approval, and it was approved by the latter body July 30, 1861.

This brief statement will, I think, be sufficient to show that the establishment of the Free Zone was a step taken in fulfilment of the duty of self-preservation, so to speak, and that it was by no means a measure adopted in a spirit of unfriendliness, much less of hostility toward the United States, as has been believed in this country.

The second impression which prevails here with regard to the Free Zone is equally unfounded.

The events connected with the foreign intervention did not permit the effects of the Free Zone to be felt in Mexico until the republic returned to its normal condition, as it did when peace was restored.

In the report made by the Secretary of the Treasury to the Congress of the United States, September 16, 1869, that officer stated that one of the causes of the then depleted condition of the Mexican treasury was the large contraband trade that was carried on through the Free Zone enjoyed by the frontier towns of Tamaulipas. The Secretary remarked at the same time that the custom-houses of those towns were scarcely able to meet their expenses, which showed that that region had not prospered, notwithstanding the franchises granted to it by the Free Zone, and that the said Zone was not the proper remedy for the evil which it was intended to cure.

It is true that the privilege granted by the Free Zone to the inhabitants of the northern portion of Tamaulipas to import foreign goods without paying import duties, to store them in their own houses, and to keep them in bond for an unlimited time was, and has been, a powerful incentive to smuggling, with a view to repressing which recourse has been had in Mexico to a costly and complicated system of inspection. Protection to smuggling was not, however, the object had in view by the creators of the Free Zone, nor has it been possible for smuggling to be carried on to the prejudice of the United States to the same extent to which this has been done to the prejudice of Mexico.

Inasmuch as the duties levied by the Mexican tariff are much higher than those of the United States, it is evident that the most lucrative contraband trade is that which is carried on to the detriment of the Mexican treasury. That trade is, at the same time, carried on with less difficulty, because the Mexican frontier is very sparsely populated, in consequence of which the difficulty of guarding it is greatly increased, while the frontier of the United States is more thickly settled and better defended against smuggling.

It does not seem to me conceivable that, in order to encourage smuggling, to the detriment of the United States Treasury, which might be counted as one, smuggling could be encouraged to the detriment of the Mexican Treasury, which might be counted as ten [i.e., in order to injure the United States the Mexicans would not be willing to injure themselves ten times as much] ; and if the smuggling which is carried on through the Free Zone were a sufficient reason for the abolition of the latter, the interest of Mexico in this matter would long since have settled this question.

There is another consideration to which I think proper to call your attention before concluding this note, and which, in my judgment, may be regarded as an advantage to the United States accruing from the Free Zone. As I have already stated, the Mexican system of legislation concerning customs and excise duties has generally been restrictive and even prohibitory, both by reason of the high import duties established in my country and of the existence of interior custom-houses ; also on account of State and municipal taxes, which necessitate vigilance and restrictions that cannot do otherwise than hamper business transactions. I have frequently seen complaints on this account in official documents of this Government, and I confess that some of them have appeared to me to be not without foundation, although we are the party that suffers most from those restrictions. If the Free Zone in Mexico has inconveniences for this country much less serious than those which it has for Mexico, it has, in my judgment, one advantage which has hitherto remained unnoticed. That advantage is that goods from the United States may be impoited into Mexican territory duty free, and be warehoused in the region of the Zone for an unlimited time. No greater privileges to the commerce of a nation can be asked for. If these privileges, which are confined to a limited zone, were extended to the whole country, I do not think that the United States would consider the free admission of their productions into Mexico as being prejudicial to their interests.

As I have already remarked, the opinion of Mexican statesmen with regard to the Free Zone has been divided, some having thought that it should be abolished, because it grants to one section of the country privileges which are not authorized by the Constitution, and others having maintained that, under the circumstances, it was an imperative necessity, and that its abolition would be equivalent to the destruction of the frontier. The latter opinion finally prevailed in the councils of the Mexican Government, and, in accordance therewith the Free Zone was extended to the States of Coahuila, Chihuahua, Sonora, and the territory of Lower California, for a distance of 20 kilometres from the boundary-line; and thus, so far from any encouragement being afforded to those who favored the abolition of the Free Zone, the opposite system triumphed completely.

The Free Zone was subjected to regulations, or rather it was confirmed and amplified, by another decree of the Governor of Tamaulipas, bearing date of October 29, 1860, and the Federal Government did not subject it to regulations until June 17, 1878. Chapter XII. of the tariff of January 24, 1885, subjected the Free Zone to regulations in a restrictive way. Such, however, was the pressure exerted by the frontier towns and by their representatives in the Congress of the Union that, by a decree dated June 19, 1885, the limitations established in that chapter were suspended and more liberal regulations were again adopted in the tariff of March 1, 1887, which is still in force.

I think it proper for me to state in this connection that when I was obliged to study this question thoroughly, owing to the fact of my filling the office of the Secretary of the Treasury of the United States of Mexico, I formed an opinion which was decidedly adverse to the Free Zone, which opinion I expressed in official documents, and recommended its abolition to Congress ; so that instead of having been an advocate of the Zone I have probably been its most earnest opponent. The reasons which led me to this conclusion were of a constitutional character, and although I was aware that the situation of the frontier towns of Mexico required the adoption of suitable remedies, I always exerted myself to have measures adopted of such a nature that they could be extended to the whole country, they thereby being divested of their odiousness as privileges.

There can be no doubt as to the right of the Government of Mexico to establish rules relative to domestic and foreign trade in the country and the misunderstanding which has prevailed here with regard to the object and tendencies of the Free Zone, and the manner in which that misunderstanding has been expressed by certain Federal and State officers, has really served as an argument to the advocates of the Free Zone, who attribute to their opponents a design in advocating its abolition to sacrifice the interests of Mexico to satisfy the demands of the United States.

It may not be out of place for me to quote here certain views that were expressed by the Secretary of the Treasury of Mexico in the report submitted by him to the Congress of the Union under date of September 16, 1870. They are as follows :

3679. The friendly representations made by the United States Government to that of the Republic in relation to the injury accruing to the United States from the Free

Zone are also worthy of being taken into consideration by the Congress, not that it may seek to please the neighboring nation in a spirit of servility at the expense of the rights and interests of the Republic, which it is under obligations to care for and uphold above everything else (which spirit would be unworthy of our national representatives), but as a neighborly act, and in order to have a right to be heard and treated with consideration in case that in process of time some difficulty arise on our northern frontier of such a nature as to possess, as regards Mexico, the character which the Free Zone possesses as regards our neighboring nation ; in order, moreover, that Mexico may acquire a new title to be heard and considered in a cordial and friendly as well as just and equitable manner when she may have occasion to offer remonstrances with a view to the protection of her interests.

" A nation's dignity is not so well upheld by refusing to consider the moderate and amicable remonstrances of a neighboring nation as it is by hearing and considering such remonstrances and then acting according to the requirements of justice."

As a supplement to this note I have the honor to enclose a pamphlet containing the following documents :

(1) Text of the decree of the Governor of Tamaulipas, dated March 17, 1858, establishing the Free Zone.

(2) A law passed by the Federal Congress of Mexico, dated July 30, 1861, confirming the above decree.

(3) Regulations concerning the Free Zone, promulgated by the Governor of Tamaulipas, October 29, 1860.

(4) The first regulations concerning the aforesaid Zone, promulgated by the Federal Government June 17, 1878.

Fuller details on this subject will be found in the speeches delivered by the Secretary of the Treasury in the Mexican Congress on the 28th and 29th of October, and on the 4th and 5th of November, 1870, which are contained in the " verbal reports of the Secretary of the Treasury to the Congress of the Union during the first period of the second year of its sessions," printed in the City of Mexico in 1870, a copy of which I sent to you as an enclosure to my note of January 4, 1886.

Be pleased to accept, Mr. Secretary, the assurances of my most distinguished consideration.

M. ROMERO.

Hon. THOMAS F. BAYARD.

NO. 8.   MR. ROMERO TO MR. BAYARD.

LEGATION OF MEXICO, WASHINGTON,
February 14, 1888.

Mr. SECRETARY :—In the note which I addressed to you on the 10th instant relative to the Free Zone established in Mexico, I omitted to state two facts, which I think proper to mention here with a view to throwing additional light upon this matter and to dispelling certain prejudices which prevail in this country with regard to it, and which might affect the friendly relations between Mexico and the United States.

The first of these facts is that the Free Zone was not really an invention of the Mexican authorities of the State of Tamaulipas, but an imitation on a larger scale of similar measures which had been adopted more than five years previously by the United States Government for the benefit of that portion of its territory which bordered on Mexico.

The law of the United States Congress, of August 30, 1852, authorized the transportation to Mexico of goods sent in bond by certain routes specified in that law, and by all such others as the Secretary of the Treasury might see fit to authorize. This rendered it possible to send large quantities of goods to the frontier towns of the

United States without paying duties, and to keep them there in bond until a favorable opportunity offered for their exportation to Mexico.

As everything may be abused, the goods that were stored in the frontier towns of the United States were smuggled into Mexico. The United States Congress, when it passed that law, of course did not intend to encourage smuggling to the detriment of Mexico, although such was, practically, its result ; just as the Governor of Tamaulipas at first, and the Mexican Congress afterwards, did not intend, in establishing the Free Zone, to facilitate smuggling to the detriment of the United States.

There was no such privilege within the territory of Mexico. All foreign goods, of whatever kind they might be, were subjected to the payment of duty when they were imported.

This difference of circumstances led the public men of Tamaulipas to believe that in order to place both sides of the frontier on the same footing in respect to commercial privileges, they needed to establish privileges similar to those which existed in the United States, although those which they did establish by the decree of March 17, 1858, were much more extensive than those which existed on the left bank of the Rio Grande.

The second fact which I desire to mention is a coincidence which is one of the causes that have induced the inhabitants of the Mexican frontier to attribute to the Free Zone more beneficial results than it has really produced, which circumstance has, perhaps, led to its maintenance and extension.

The situation of the Mexican frontier, up to the beginning of the Civil War in the United States, was, as I have already remarked, one of poverty and even of misery, and formed a striking contrast to the other side of the Rio Grande. That war broke out almost simultaneously with the establishment of the Free Zone. The situation of the Mexican frontier thereupon changed very much, and welfare and prosperity crossed from the left to the right bank of the Rio Grande during that war, and for some time afterwards, owing to the general prostration which prevailed in the South. Superficial observers attributed that prosperity not to its true cause, which, in my opinion, was the aforesaid war, but to the Free Zone, and feeling convinced that it has been pro-ductive of extraordinary results, they naturally considered it as a panacea for all evils, and its extension as an imperative necessity for the country.

I hope that these brief explanations will serve to rectify some of the errors and prejudices which prevail in this country in reference to this matter.

Be pleased to accept, etc.,

M. ROMERO.

S. Ex. 130—11.

MR. CRAIN'S SPEECH IN THE HOUSE OF REPRESENTATIVES.

Congressional Record, vol. xxvii., No. 65, Fifty-third Congress, 3d Session, Washington, Wednesday, February 27, 1895.

House of Representatives, Wednesday, February 27, 1895. The House met at 11 o'clock A.M. Prayer by the Chaplain, Rev. E. B. Bagby. The Journal of the proceedings of yesterday was read and approved.

MEXICAN FREE ZONE.

THE SPEAKER also laid before the House the amendments of the Senate to the joint resolution (H. Res. 277) in reference to the Free Zone along the northern frontier of Mexico and adjacent to the United States.

MR. COCKRELL.—I move to concur in the Senate amendment.

MR. CRAIN.—Would it be in order to move to refer this matter to a committee ?

THE SPEAKER.—It would.

MR. CRAIN.—I move its reference to the Committee on Ways and Means.

THE SPEAKER.—The amendment of the Senate will be read.

The Clerk read as follows :

" Strike out, after the word ' exists,' in line 8, the following words : ' At any point between the western boundary of the city of Laredo, in the State of Texas, and the Pacific Ocean.' "

THE SPEAKER.—The motion to refer will first be submitted to the House.

The question was taken ; and on a division (demanded by Mr. Crain) there were —ayes 7, noes 43.

MR. CRAIN.—No quorum.

THE SPEAKER.—The point of order being made that no quorum has voted, the Chair will appoint tellers.

Mr. Crain and Mr. Cockrell were appointed tellers.

Before the announcement of the result of the division

MR. CRAIN said : Mr. Speaker, I withdraw the point of no quorum, with the understanding that I am to have time to explain my position in reference to this matter.

THE SPEAKER.—The point of no quorum is withdrawn. The noes have it and the motion to refer is lost.

The question now recurs on the motion to concur in the Senate amendment.

MR. CABANISS.—I would ask that this amendment be again reported.

The amendment was again read.

MR. CRAIN.—Mr. Speaker—

THE SPEAKER.—The Chair recognizes the gentleman from Texas [Mr. Cockrell] in charge of the resolution.

MR. COCKRELL.—I yield to my colleague thirty minutes.

MR. CRAIN.—Mr. Speaker, the history of this resolution is a very peculiar one. Originally, without the amendment proposed by the Senate, it was an agreed settlement of all of the differences between my colleague from Texas and myself upon the subject of the disestablishment of the Free Zone by the coercion of a neighboring Government on the part of the Congress of the United States. The amended resolution of the House was agreed to by my colleague [Mr. Cockrell], my colleague [Mr. Paschal], and myself, and was adopted unanimously, I believe, by the Committee on Ways and Means of the House. The House passed it by unanimous consent, and it was passed in the Senate without objection, and was signed by the Speaker of the House and by the President of the Senate, and would doubtless to-day be the law of the land but for the fact that Washington's birthday intervened, and the resolution, as thus signed, failed to reach the hands of the President.

The resolution as amended was recalled by the Senate without objection, and an amendment inserted by that body providing that the coercive measure suggested in the resolution should apply to the entire boundary between the Republic of Mexico and the Republic of the United States. I have no objection to the gentlemen who represent other portions of the Rio Grande having their wishes carried out in that regard, but I do protest in the name of the constituency I have the honor to represent against the imposition of a coercive measure like this upon their neighbors on the other side of the Rio Grande.

I cannot understand, Mr. Speaker, how Democrats who are theoretically and who are assumed to be practically free traders can favor a measure which has for its ultimate effect, as stated in the body of it, the coercion of a sister Republic into the disestablishment of free trade and the establishment in lieu thereof of a protective tariff system. I can readily understand how logically and consistently our Republican brethren can support such a proposition, but I fail to understand how gentlemen claiming to be Democrats and who are willing to put wool upon the free list and sugar upon the free list and iron upon the free list, and other raw materials upon the free list, can support a measure which declares to the Mexican Government that it must discontinue free trade along our frontier and substitute in place of it a protective tariff system.

The Mexican Free Zone includes a strip of territory varying in width from three to twelve or thirteen miles. In that territory all goods coming from any country in the world, whether from Japan, China, or the United States, are entered by the payment of one-tenth of the regular Mexican tariff rate. After those goods leave that Zone they are compelled by each municipality, by each State, and by the Federal Government through whose territory they pass to pay the regular tariff rate imposed.

Now, Mexican wool comes into Texas free. Why? Because we have established a *Zona Libre*, not three miles in extent, but coextensive with the limits of the United States, because we have made wool free. I say to this House, Mr. Speaker, that by the adoption of this resolution we affect not the people of Mexico alone, not those who are charged with being smugglers, but foreign governments, whose importers have the advantage of the bonded system and also every mode of transportation of foreign goods in bond across the territory of the United States intended for consumption in the Republic of Mexico.

The opposition to the proposition as agreed upon and unanimously passed by this House, which opposition was raised in the Senate, was not based upon any political or economical ground, but upon the pretext that the carrying trade of all these goods in bond would enter Mexico by one railroad, the Mexican National, or by the International and Great Northern, and would be taken away from the Southern Pacific, the Texas Pacific, and other roads running into and through the territory represented by my colleagues who favor this resolution.

It is an injustice to foreign Governments. Why? Because the subjects of these Governments who are manufacturers, who are producers, are prohibited from carrying their goods in bond across the territory of the United States into the Republic of Mexico. Gentlemen in the other Chamber of this legislative body have said, " We are Americans ; we do not intend to be compelled by Germany or by France to remove the differential tax on sugar, when they seek to compel us to do it by retaliation by refusing importations of American breadstuffs, American beef, or American meat products of any kind, character, or description." And yet we propose by this resolution to say to Mexico, " Until you abolish the Free Zone you shall not have the privilege of the bonded system across our country." Will any gentleman rise now—and I pause for a reply—and give any sound, truthful reason for this proposition? Nobody suggests a reason.

It is said that the Mexican Government wants this Free Zone disestablished. It is within their own province. It is within their own territorial jurisdiction, and if they desire to have it abolished, why does not the Mexican Congress, acting with the Mexican President, abolish it? Is it possible that in order to accomplish this result they appeal to the American Congress? We might as well say that until Great Britain does away with comparative free trade we will keep up our high protective-tariff system. We repel the idea of coercion on the part of European Governments, and yet we attempt to establish a similar policy by our legislative enactment.

Only twelve per cent. of the entire importations into Mexico remain in the Free Zone. It has been said that it is a hiding place, a nesting place for smugglers. Mr. Speaker, I have in my possession a letter from the collector of customs at Laredo which is an answer to this base, calumniatory charge against my constituents. I do not stand here to speak for others. If colleagues of mine say that their constituents are smugglers, I do not attempt to dispute the suggestion, for I have no knowledge on the subject; but as to my own constituents I do repel the insinuation, or the charge, in whatever form made or whencesoever it comes, with all the power of language I can command.

I ask, Mr. Speaker, that the Clerk of the House read this communication.

THE SPEAKER.—The Clerk will read.

The Clerk read as follows:

"CUSTOM HOUSE, COLLECTOR'S OFFICE,
"LAREDO, TEX., *February 23, 1895.*

"MY DEAR SIR,—I am just in receipt of the marked copy of the *Washington Post* of the 12th instant, sent me by you, containing an extract from the report of Civil Service Commissioner Lyman on his recent tour of inspection along the Mexican frontier. With the greater part of the conclusions reached by Commissioner Lyman I very heartily agree, but I am unable to see what benefit will accrue to the United States from the abolition of the Free Zone. It is true that petty smuggling is constantly carried on between the towns in the Free Zone just across the river and those on this bank. This petty smuggling is annoying and it is almost impossible to prevent it. The purchases of foreign goods in Nuevo Laredo, for instance, made by persons from this side are usually small in quantity and value. I think that in most cases the petty smuggling of this character is done by ladies who conceal about their persons a few pairs of silk hose, of kid gloves, small quantities of lace, and in some instances silk dress patterns. As the majority of the people here, however, do not indulge in silk goods of any character these purchases are not extensive. On the other hand the people who live across the river buy very largely on this side, their purchases consisting of groceries, prints, hardware, and articles of like character.

"One gentleman who lives in Nuevo Laredo told me yesterday that his monthly bills on this side of the river amounted to $60. Numbers of families living in Nuevo Laredo buy practically all of their groceries from merchants on this side of the river. The commission merchants here tell me that they have in the Free Zone one of their best markets. Flour, bacon, and many other American products are sold in Nuevo Laredo and the territory above and below that point. In fact, the balance of trade is very largely in our favor. I can not assent to the proposition that the existence of the Free Zone has inured very largely to the benefit of the Mexican border towns, and that business is 'dead and unprofitable' in the American towns opposite them. This is not true of Laredo. This place has been steadily growing in importance as a business point for the past several years. Our merchants have been doing a large and profitable business, and all of them are prosperous.

"During the long period of depression that has prevailed everywhere we have not had a single failure among our business men. There is not a single storehouse on this side of the river that is unoccupied. There are numbers of vacant houses in Nuevo Laredo, across the river, and they have only two general dealers whose business is of any importance. On the Mexican side of the river the towns of Guerrero, Mier, Camargo, and Matamoras, all in the Free Zone, are dead towns. Guerrero was formerly a fine little city of about 6000 population and with a thriving trade. I visited it some two months ago, and found it a 'deserted village' of about 800 people. Its storehouses are closed and its trade is dead. I learn that this is true in a large measure of the other towns named.

"If the proposition now before Congress to withdraw from the Mexican merchants the privilege of transporting goods in bond across our territory become a law, it will divert from our American railroads a large part of the freight traffic now enjoyed by them and will send it permanently to the Mexican ports of Tampico and Veracruz. Should it be enacted and the result be the abolition of the Free Zone, what benefit will the United States derive? I can think of none. Those of our people who understand this matter are obliged to you for your amendment excepting our territory from the operation of this law. I inclose a note from Special Inspector Izard on this subject and a letter recently published by Mr. Shafter, of Eagle Pass.

"Yours very truly,   FRANK B. EARNEST.

"Hon. W. H. CRAIN, Washington, D. C."

MR. CRAIN.—Now, Mr. Speaker, I should like to have an editorial read from the *Lower Rio Grande*, a paper which is published at Brownsville, Texas.

The Clerk read as follows:

"THE *ZONA LIBRE*."

"On the 24th instant we published a resolution to be presented to the Texas legislature, which has since passed that body, and which calls upon our members of Congress to urge upon Mexico to abolish the Mexican *Zona Libre*, or Free Zone, and in case of a refusal, then for the United States to close its bonded warehouses against all goods entering Mexico through any of our ports.

"We have been at a loss to understand how or why such a ruinous measure could ever be proposed and why or how it could pass the Texas legislature, and, astonishing to relate, we are told that it was not opposed by our immediate representatives even, and such a mass of absolute misstatements is permitted to be sent as a basis for future Congressional legislation.

"*Apropos* of this resolution we have been shown a pamphlet written by Mr. C. R. Morehead, President State National Bank, El Paso, Tex., which is possibly the basis of the resolution passed by the Texas legislature, which is a statement against the Free Zone, urging its abolishment. Were Mr. Morehead a citizen of the interior of Mexico, or a European manufacturer, there might be some reason to justify his statements, but as an American a more suicidal effort was never made. The opening of his pamphlet is as follows: .

"'Along the Rio Grande River, the divide between the territory of the United States and that of Mexico, are many causes which result in an ill-feeling between the border inhabitants which is daily growing in intensity and magnitude. These causes and the consequent estrangement are the growth of many years and have a tendency to result in a complete alienation.

"'This immediate section, having once formed a portion of the dominion of Mexico, and having gained its independence by the sword, is naturally antagonized by that Government, and to such an extent that forbearance almost ceases to be a virtue.

"'The conditions which cause the intensity of feeling are mainly the result of long years of Mexican legislation which has operated against the commercial interests of the entire border. This legislation was first conceived on March 17, 1858, when the Governor of the State of Tamaulipas, Mexico, issued a decree establishing what is known as the *Zona Libre*, or Free Zone along the northern boundary of his States.'

"Here is a broad statement which is not justified by a single condition of existing affairs. Never in the history of this frontier was there less cause for 'ill-feeling' than there is to-day, and there is no more ill-feeling commercially and socially than there is between New York and Brooklyn, hence the 'consequent estrangement' is no more or less than genuine fol-de-rol. No more amicable condition is possible to exist than is existing to-day. The above statement, though, is the groundwork for a bombastic appeal for the abolition of the *Zona Libre*.

"The statements of Mr. Morehead are too many to have their absurdities exposed in a newspaper article, but as his basis is all wrong the superstructure must necessarily be false and visionary, as a few statements of facts will show.

"The *Zona Libre* is a belt of land along the Mexican side of the Rio Grande, thirteen miles wide, and not some forty-three miles wide, as stated by Mr. Morehead, into which foreign goods can be imported almost free of duty. Under the operation of actual conditions that belt is the great mart in all Mexico for goods of American manufacture, and when such goods are taken into Mexico the sending of them into the interior of Mexico has to take place under the immediate care of officers of the revenue service of Mexico. In this Free Zone American manufactures have successfully competed for the trade to the exclusion of foreign goods. To close the *Zona Libre*, or Free Zone, is simply to kill off this large trade in American fabrics. Why? Because the Mexican tariff would exclude American fabrics, and nothing but the lower priced foreign goods could enter and pay duties in competition with the fabrics of Mexico. American goods would be upon the American border to be smuggled into Mexico, but while the *Zona Libre* lasts Mexico is in no danger of such frauds being perpetrated upon her revenues, as was the actual condition before the *Zona* was established.

"To close the bonded system of the United States against Mexico would be to force all of the commerce that now travels over American railroads and American ships to enter Mexico in foreign bottoms at the port of Tampico and at the mouth of the Rio Grande by rail, to be carried to the very same places where it is now taken over American lines. The feeling, therefore, which would deprive Mexico of the bonded accommodation is one of hatred to Mexico and one of destruction to American industries and trade.

"Mexico is to-day in no wise dependent upon facilities in the United States to carry on her trade and commerce with foreign countries, as she formerly was, and this changed condition many seem not to understand. The resolution passed by the Texas legislature and the Morehead pamphlet, if carried into effect, would positively kill every American interest along the Rio Grande and destroy the great and growing trade now existing between the two countries. More hatred, malice, and folly, from an American standpoint, could not be imagined than those two dangerous papers contain."

MR. CRAIN.—Mr. Speaker, I further ask leave to read from a communication sent to me from some leading citizens of Brownsville in reference to this subject :

"BROWNSVILLE, TEX., *January 27, 1895.*

"The arguments favoring the abolition of the *Zona Libre* do not apply here. The importations into the *Zona Libre* from Brownsville, Rio Grande City, and Roma are chiefly breadstuffs, agricultural implements, and other goods of American production ; hence there is no smuggling back from Mexico to the United States of foreign goods. This is abundantly shown by the character of the seizures made by our customs officers, which seldom embrace anything but articles of Mexican origin, and this no change or modification in the *Zona Libre* would affect. But our whole transportation system depends on our continuing to supply Matamoras and the adjacent territory with the class of goods they now purchase from us. If the inhabitants of that section are compelled to pay Mexican import duties on their flour, lard, soap, sugar, beans, cotton goods, clothing, plows, harness, hardware, agricultural implements, and machinery, all of which American manufactures they now buy from us, they will use similar articles of Mexican origin and production, although of inferior quality and higher first cost, because they can get those native articles without the payment of import duties. The result is, we lose our market for a large and constantly increasing quantity of our own products, and in losing this market we so decrease the volume of our trade that we would cease to have direct communication by steamer and otherwise with the great centres of American production, our own local wants not being sufficient to justify the continuance of the steamer line to supply them alone.

"You will thus see the matter is of vital importance to us. We therefore ask you to exert all your influence, official, legislative, and personal, to aid us.

"There is another phase of the question. The threat to suspend the operation of our bonded system on the northern frontier of Mexico unless that country shall abolish the *Zona Libre* is a very serious one. Suppose (and the supposition is fully warranted) Mexico declines to be coerced; then the American railroads running to the Mexican frontier lose the carrying of the best-paying and most valuable portion of their traffic, as the transportation of all goods of European origin would be forced into vessels direct to Mexican ports, and not only our railroads but our coastwise carrying companies would suffer severely, and in order to fully load those vessels for Mexican ports direct, the Mexican merchant would be compelled to purchase in Europe many goods he now procures from the United States. In point of fact, the suspension of our bonded system to the northern frontier of Mexico would benefit only European producers, merchants, and carriers, and would work a corresponding injury to those interests of our own country.

"We are, very respectfully,

"Thomas Carson,
"James B. Wells,
"John I. Kleiber,
"Wm. J. Russell,
"G. M. Raphael,
"William Kelly."

The Speaker.—The time of the gentleman has expired.

Mr. Crain.—Inasmuch as five minutes of my time has been interrupted by the receiving of a message from the Senate, I will ask an extension of five minutes.

The Speaker.—The Chair hears no objection.

Mr. Crain.—Mr. Speaker, I just wanted five minutes to explain the proposition submitted by the gentleman from Indiana [Mr. Bynum]. He has stated to the House that this will not affect the importation in the Free Zone of American goods. If gentlemen will examine the resolution, they will find that it is distinctly stated that until the Free Zone is abolished the bonded system of the United States shall be suspended as to Mexico. Now, if the Free Zone is abolished, then American goods going into Mexico have to pay the full rate of duty. That is all I have to say, Mr. Speaker.

The previous question was then ordered, and under the operation thereof the Senate amendment was concurred in.

On motion of Mr. Cockrell, a motion to reconsider the vote by which the Senate amendment was concurred in was laid on the table.

MR. SUTTON'S OPINION ON THE FREE ZONE.

The *New York Evening Post*, May 19, 1894. The Free Zone. Agitation of Texas Citizens for its abolition. What the Zone is; advantages which Mexicans have under existing conditions.

"Washington, *May 19, 1894.*

"The agitation by citizens of Texas in favor of abolishing the Free Zone between this country and Mexico has got as far as a resolution of inquiry brought into the House by Representative Crain, calling for the correspondence between our Government and that of Mexico on the subject of the Zone. Warner P. Sutton, who for many years was a Consul-General of the United States in Mexico, was asked by the *Evening Post* correspondent to-day for some account of the Free Zone.

" ' It is a narrow strip of territory,' he answered, 'nowhere more than twelve and one half miles wide, along the northern border of Mexico. Into the ports of this Zone goods may be imported on payment of only 10 per cent. of the regular duty. The people on the Mexican side of the border can thus get French wines, liquors, silks, and laces and similar goods from other foreign countries, cheaper than those on the American side. The merchants on the Mexican side have to pay only one tenth of the Mexican duty on these goods, while those on our side pay the whole of our duty. As a consequence, there is a strong temptation for residents on the American side to buy these things on the Mexican side and run them over without paying duties. A substantial advantage is reaped in this way by the Mexican merchants.

" ' This advantage, however, is largely offset by the high taxes levied on the Mexican side. They have a stamp tax there which would make the internal-revenue provisions of the Wilson-Voorhees bill green with envy ; and every time a dollar shows itself it is loaded with a new tax. If one or two houses go out of business, their tax is usually added on to the quota of those remaining, so that the *Zona Libre* benefits are largely eaten up by higher taxes.

" ' Aside from the class of European goods I have mentioned, we supply this frontier market with nearly everything sold there. Take it all around, we probably outsell the rest of the world three to one, all along this border line of Mexico from the Pacific Ocean to the Gulf. As our goods are free on our side and pay 10 per cent. of the high Mexican duty on the Mexican side, our merchants can and do compete with the Europeans in everything we produce. We almost hold our own against many European goods.'

" ' These conditions must reflect themselves in the prosperity of the towns on the two sides of the border ? '

" ' They do. Matamoras, which was formerly the gate to Mexico, has now very little business; Brownsville, on our side of the river, has it all. Nuevo Laredo, Mexico, has less business every year, while Laredo, Texas, gains steadily. Most of the chief buyers of Nuevo Laredo come over and buy groceries, dry goods, furniture, etc., on the American side, and get them across on verbal permits or on the regular invoices of importers. The largest stocks are carried on the American side. There are two or three large stores on the Mexican side ; but even with the *Zona* privilege the advantages, except on a few lines of European goods, are with our people. At Piedras Negras and Eagle Pass business is about equally divided ; but this is because the railway shops are located on the Mexican side. At El Paso, Texas, and Juarez, Mexico, the American side has three times the trade of the Mexican side.'

" ' In all these cases the Rio Grande is the boundary, is it not ? '

" ' Yes; but at Nogales, Arizona, and Sonora, Mexico, the boundary is an imaginary line, and you have to get your bearings by the hills and other landmarks from time to time to tell whether you are in Mexico or the United States. This gives rise to many oddities. One dramseller has the line running through his bar-room. As the license laws are easier in Mexico, he has his drinking bar on that side, and his customers cross the room into the United States to wipe off their perspiration.'

" ' The idea of abolishing the *Zona Libre* is not new ? '

" ' By no means. It has been discussed for thirty-five years at least. During our Civil War the free belt made Matamoras the third port in the world. As we have increased our production of goods which Mexico needs, the benefits of the Zone have diminished, until now it serves only to keep alive the towns on the Mexican side. The Mexicans, except along the border, think no more of it than we do. They would be very glad of some convenient way to get rid of it. But they know that if it were abolished summarily it would utterly kill out what little mercantile life now remains on their side. What ought to be done is to negotiate a treaty by which the products of each country, at least in small amounts, could cross the border without payment of duties on either side. If that were done Mexico could afford to wipe out the Free Zone and dispense with European goods."

" ' How would the summary abolition of the Zone affect us ? '

" ' It would not do for us to urge its abolition without this local free interchange of products, because the Zone is now a large consumer of many of our goods. Wheat, flour, corn, bacon, lard, etc., are supplied by us exclusively, as well as many other necessaries. So long as the inhabitants of the Zone can import these at 10 per cent. of the regular duties, they can eat them ; but if the full duties were exacted, they would be too expensive. For instance, some five million pounds of our flour are imported every year at Matamoras, Nuevo Laredo, Piedras Negras, Juarez, and Nogales, exclusively for consumption in the Zone, for scarcely a barrel goes into the interior. The full duty is more than two cents a pound on wheat and four cents on wheat flour. Those who live in the Zone can pay 10 per cent. of this duty and eat our flour ; those farther back have to buy Mexican flour or eat corn-meal.'

" ' How would you advise going about the improvement of present conditions ? '

" ' What we have long needed in our relations with Mexico is to put political questions in the background and study and treat with Mexico on a friendly commercial basis. Do you know that we have absolutely no treaties of any sort in force with Mexico to-day except an extradition treaty—an extremely faulty one—dated away back in 1861 ? It is high time to negotiate at least a commercial treaty. Mexico needs our products and has always been disposed to meet us half way. Too much protection buncombe by one party and too much free-trade theorizing by the other have prevented our doing five or ten million dollars' worth of commerce with Mexico every year, to the great benefit of both countries.

" ' We had the Grant-Romero treaty in 1883. I worked on that with General Grant, and hoped that even so small a step in the right direction would be followed by others. The House proceeded to pitch the treaty out of court, while some individuals added insult to injury by saying mean things about Mexico. We ought now to pass a general resolution reciting what should be done, intrust the plan to a non-partisan commission to work out, and, when they have made a report, enact the necessary legislation promptly, with such conditions that it will stay in force not less than ten years.'

" ' Why not have complete free trade with Mexico, as our next neighbor ? '

" ' It would be idle to talk about that for the present. Mexico is too poor even to consider such a suggestion. She could afford, however, and I believe would be willing, to try a system of limited reciprocity, with such local border interchange of national products as would enable her to abolish the *Zona Libre.* Both countries would reap the advantage of a cessation of smuggling, and Mexico would be enabled to do away with most of her interior customs guards, and save a half-million dollars or more in salaries every year. Along with such a system some articles could be made free in each country, and a few others given lower duties. The subject is of great importance, and one to which I have given much study for fifteen years. I earnestly hope a change in present conditions will be inaugurated soon.' "

Supplement to the Free Zone.—At the end of this book I will append a Supplement to the Free Zone paper, containing recent official information received from the Mexican Government since this paper went to press, on the extent of the foreign trade in the Free Zone, and a brief review of the action taken on the same subject by the Fifty-fifth Congress of the United States, resulting in the repeal by the House of Representatives of the Joint Resolution of March 1, 1895, and causing the production of important official documents.

LABOR AND WAGES IN MEXICO.

LABOR AND WAGES IN MEXICO.

I have often heard it stated, in this country, as the chief reason for advocating restrictions on its trade with Mexico, that we pay low wages to our laborers, who are sometimes called paupers and peons, and that the maintenance of the high wages prevailing here requires that the free entrance of Mexican products similar to those of the United States be prohibited by the imposition of high duties.

As long as I did not hear these ideas expressed by Federal functionaries, I did not think that I was called upon to rectify them, but when Mr. Thomas H. Carter, formerly a Member of Congress, and now a Senator from Montana, in a speech delivered in the House of Representatives, on May 15, 1890, in support of the provisions of the tariff bill which became the Act of October 1, 1890, levying a duty upon lead in ores, based his arguments on the fact that we had in Mexico peon or slave labor, and that the United States had to protect her own citizens against the pauper labor of Mexico, I believed it was my duty to explain what we meant in Spanish by peon, and what was the condition of the Mexican laborers, thus rectifying the mistaken opinions in that regard prevailing in this country. I considered myself specially called upon to do so, as the same objection is repeated whenever it is proposed to adopt liberal measures for the promotion of trade between the two neighboring Republics. It seemed to me that I might contribute to the better understanding of each other and to a reciprocally advantageous increase of their trade relations, if I should give some idea of the condition of the Mexican laborer ; of the wages which are paid in Mexico ; of the causes which control their amount ; of the manner in which these causes affect the cost and therefore the price of the commodities we produce; and of the price of Mexican articles obtained with low wages, as compared with the price of the same commodities produced here with high wages, and finally of the cost of living in Mexico.

Before writing on the subject, I waited until some time had elapsed after the tariff bill, approved October 1, 1890, had become a law, to avoid incurring the imputation of desiring to interfere in the internal legislation of this country; and even then I was careful not to allude to Mr. Carter's remarks as having in any way influenced me in writing the article, which appeared in the *North American Review* for January, 1892.

The campaign for the Presidential election held in November, 1895, began over three years after my article was published by the *North American Review*, and the cardinal point in that campaign was the standard of money in this country, that is, whether the United States should adhere to the gold standard, or return to the free coinage of silver, and possibly come finally to the single silver standard. As Mexico is a silver country and adjoins the United States, it afforded an example to judge of the results of the silver standard, *pro* and *con*, according to the views entertained by the respective parties. Several committees and numerous newspaper correspondents were sent to Mexico to study this question, with a view to use the information gathered in the electoral campaign. Some of them had made up their minds before they left this country, either in favor of the gold or silver standard, and none of them remained in Mexico long enough to understand it thoroughly. Their reports, therefore, while most of them were undoubtedly written in good faith, contained but little information of real value, with many errors that led to serious mistakes and misunderstandings. They sometimes presented the cheap products of Mexico as a proof of her poverty and a reason operating against her prosperity; and at the same time when in some cases her products were high, that fact was mentioned as a reason for the same result. The silver standard was made responsible for many results in which it had nothing to do.

My desire to rectify the main errors published, induced me to revise my article, availing myself of the data which came to light since it was first published, especially from official sources like the reports of the Minister and of the Consul-General of the United States at the City of Mexico, and of the arguments presented during the last canvass on both sides of the question, so far as they involve serious mistakes in matters of fact affecting Mexico.

My main and only object in writing this paper was to show that poorly paid Mexican labor cannot compete with well-paid American labor ; but as this subject is so closely connected with the rate of import duties, I had to allude to this incidentally. I understand very well that in my position it would be an intrusion on my part to discuss this question, which is one pertaining to the internal affairs of the United States, and I will only refer to it in so far as it affects the rate of wages. In this connection I consider it proper to state here that, while my personal views lead me rather to lean on duties for revenue, I was not able in either of the three different times in which I served as Secretary of the Treasury of Mexico, to make any material reductions on our very heavy import duties, much higher than those prevailing in this country, that notwithstanding that sometimes I had legislative authority to do so, and that therefore I could not consistently find fault with, and much less criticise, the prevailing high tariff views of the public men in the United States, who think them indispensable for the prosperity and welfare of their country, and that my whole and only object was to show that the low Mexican labor ought not to alarm the United States with any fear of competition.

I should be very glad if with this contribution I could in some way dispel some of the mistaken ideas prevailing in this country in regard to labor and wages in Mexico, which so far have stood in the way of measures tending to increase our mutual trade.

Since my article was published I have paid more attention to this subject, and have read all I could obtain on the same, as *Wages*, by Francis Walker; *Wages and Capital*, by F. W. Taussig; *The Labor Movement in America*, by Richard T. Ely; *A History of Money and Prices, The Industrial Situation*, and *The Economy of High Wages*, by J. Schoenhof ; *Who Pays your Taxes ?* by Bolton Hall; *Wages vs. 16 to 1*, by John de Witt Warner ; *Relation of Tariff to Wages*, by David A. Wells; *The Bargain Theory of Wages*, by John Davidson ; *Production and Distribution*, by M. Cannan ; *The Law of Wages, the Rate and Amount*, by Mr. John Richards of San Francisco ; Mr. Henry George's books relating to the labor question: *A Perplexed Philosopher, Progress and Poverty, Social Problems, Protection or Free Trade, Property in Land, The Condition of Labor, The Land Question*, and his posthumous book just published, *The Science of Political Economy ;* the several chapters on labor of Mr. Edward Atkinson's *Industrial Progress of the Nation*, and several other pamphlets, including the valuable statistics on labor published by the United States Labor Department, and the statistics on Farm Labor in the United States, issued by the Department of Agriculture.

The revised article is the following.

LABOR AND WAGES IN MEXICO.

To do justice to this complex matter, I will have to speak separately of the different subjects affecting the wage question in Mexico, but I will try to be as concise as possible regarding each of them, as I do not intend to write a long treatise.

Different Theories on Wages.—There are several theories about wages, their sociological character, and their relation to production and wealth. It would be foreign to my purpose to dwell upon the different theories of wages, and I will therefore only state here that the oldest one, called "The Subsistence Theory," inaugurated by Ricardo, consists in fixing wages to an amount sufficient to provide for a man's subsistence, and this theory is considered as a remnant of the servitude in which the wage-earner was held up to the beginning of the present century. "The Productivity-of-Labor Theory," which is a forward step in the evolution of wages, intended to emancipate the wage-earner from his employer, consists in making wages depend on the value of the commodities they produce. "The Bargain Theory of Wages," as stated by Mr. Davidson in his book entitled *The Bargain Theory of Wages*, considers wages as any other commodity which is bought and sold, and whose price is determined both by the seller and buyer with equal voice in the bargain. "The Wages-Fund Theory" considers labor as regulated by the supply and the demand, and has as its complement the theory of "The Mobility of Labor," namely, to transport labor from where it is cheap to places where it is better paid.

I do not think that the last word on this subject has yet been spoken. I imagine that each theory on wages has some sound principle which really and actually affects wages, and I think that an eclectic system combining all theories will be a sound one.

A Main Factor Regulating Wages.—Without attempting to support any special theory, I think that there is a factor which invariably affects labor. I will enunciate this factor, which consists in a very simple principle that my experience shows me to be perfectly correct, and which I think I fully demonstrate in this paper, namely, that wages are regulated by the amount of work that they produce, and, conse-

501

quently, that low wages bring about high cost, and high wages low cost in the product of labor.

As the fear of competition by the cheap Mexican labor, or peon labor, as it is often called in this country, has played such an important part in adjusting duties on Mexican products imported into the United States, I consider it my duty to dwell somewhat on this point.

For a long period of time there was great fear of competition in manufactures from England. The advocates of high duties never wearied of describing the " pauper " labor of England, and the necessity of high duties here to prevent labor in the United States from falling to the same level of wages—to them one of indescribable misery and extreme poverty. Even within a few years an account of the hand nail-makers in the iron districts was circulated, which was regarded as the best evidence of what " free trade " in England had done for the workingmen. The question of labor cost is now discussed from a more scientific standpoint, and the fallacy of basing conclusions upon money wages has been demonstrated. Experience has shown that high wages in the United States mean high productive ability, and when American manufactures meet similar foreign products in neutral markets, and control those markets, the old theory cannot stand.

As the exporter of manufactures, England was looked upon as the country most to be feared. When Continental nations began to manufacture on so large a scale as to provide a surplus for export, the " pauper labor of Europe " was a new reason for fear, and the wages of the Continent, much lower in money than the wages of England, were quoted by the friends of high wages in the United States. For some years the sums of money received weekly by the glass-makers of Belgium, the ribbon-makers of France, and the textile-workers of Germany did yeoman service in supporting the demands of manufacturers in this country, that duties should be maintained because of " high-priced and dear labor " prevailing here. It was useless to repeat that money wages did not express labor cost, or that England would long since have been driven from the field by this " pauper " labor of Europe if such arguments were true. A table was prepared, showing a remarkable difference in money wages, and this table was looked upon as unanswerable proof of that theory.

Signs of another change of base are now visible. Continental Europe may still serve to frighten a few who may not have been enlightened, and even English wages are quoted occasionally as a memorial of the old days, when such an argument was accepted without question. But neither of these excites the same horror that it once did, and the pauper labor of Asia and Mexico is now the main reason advanced. Manufacturers urged duties that would protect them and the labor they employed from the products of China, Japan, and of British India, the East Indies, and Mexico. The harrowing condition of labor in those countries has been dwelt upon as an apparently strong argument, and any wages—a few cents a day—were named as representing the earnings of these peoples. Textile fibres grown by " pauper labor or labor paid in the most niggardly manner "; chemicals made, or to be made in China, with labor at starvation wages ; machinery and machine products, the outcome of Japanese ingenuity in applying their ridiculously cheap labor to copying American inventions and trade-marks, the influx of Eastern copies of Western manufactures, were presented as the reason for a nearly prohibitive legislation enacted to protect the infant industries of the United States.

The fear over the possible competition in the East has grown in recent years, but a study of the commerce between the United States and Asia fails to disclose any evidence of this competition, as the official returns of the Bureau of Statistics of the United States Treasury Department shows that during the last five years the trade with China and Japan has increased slowly in so far as the imports from those countries are concerned, while the increase of the exports from the United States to them has been very material,[1] and the trade with British India and the British East Indies has decreased.

The tariff of March 3, 1883, was determined by a fear of European competition. An average duty of forty-five per cent. was regarded as good protection against the Continent of Europe as well as England; against the machine products of Great Britain, France, and Germany, as well as against the home industries of Russia and Austria. If that rate was required against Europe, what rate will be demanded against Asia and Mexico ?

It is very strange that while many in the United States thought it necessary to protect their manufactures from foreign competition by high duties, Count Goluchowski, Premier of Austria, should be so much afraid about the competition of American manufactories in European markets, and should call on Europe to unite in a commercial league

---

[1] In the last five years imports from China have gained $1,600,000 ; but this increase is almost entirely to be found in the single item of raw silk. In the same period the imports from British India and the British East Indies decreased $4,400,000, and not a single item of manufactures shows a larger import in the year 1896 than in that of 1892. With Japan, the country most to be feared in manufactures, United States imports have gained $1,800,000 in five years, and in manufactures of silk, flax, and hemp, there has been a small increase : yet it is an increase too small to weigh in the supply of such a market as the United States. United States exports to Japan have gained $4,300,000 in five years, to China $1,300,000, and to British India have lost $400,000. On the face of the returns these countries are better customers for American products than the United States is for theirs. The gains with Mexico are still larger.

against the United States and Japan, in a speech delivered in Vienna in November, 1897.

Agricultural products of this country, like wheat, cotton, and others, notwithstanding the high wages paid here to field laborers, successfully sustain in the English and other neutral foreign markets, a sharp competition with similar foreign products obtained with low wages, in some cases even lower than those in Mexico, as in the case of China and the East Indies, as is shown by the very large increase of the exports of this country. The exports of the year 1897 exceeded those of 1896, which were abnormally large, by $93,292,278, or 9 per cent. There need, therefore, be no fear of competition from Mexico.

I believe that the people of the United States have the necessary enterprise and capacity to compete with any other people in the world in the production of manufactured articles. It is true that the high wages paid here, the import duties upon raw materials, and the high price of coal as compared with its price in some other countries, increase the cost of the production of certain commodities as compared with similar ones manufactured in England, France, Germany, and Belgium; but it must at the same time be remembered that the application of machinery, which is used here on a much larger scale than in any other country, cheapens production so greatly that it enables this country to manufacture many articles at a less cost than any other. An instance of this is the manufacture of steel rails in the Edgar Thompson Factory at Pittsburg, Penn., where, the entire production being mechanical, few hands are employed, and where natural gas is used as fuel.

High import duties are not enough, by themselves, to keep up high wages. If that were so, the wages in Mexico should be higher than in the United States, because our tariff is still more protective than the tariff of this country. It is true that our products did not use to compete with foreign manufactures in our home markets, and that may account in some way for that fact. But we are beginning now to manufacture largely a coarser kind of goods, like textiles, iron, and others which compete with similar foreign manufactures, and are driving them from our markets, and if that principle were true, our wages paid for such manufactures ought to be higher than in the United States because our tariff is higher.

High import duties collected in Mexico, amounting in some cases to over three hundred per cent. ad valorem, have neither increased nor cheapened our productions, nor raised our wages. Our imports in the fiscal year ending on the 30th of June, 1889, amounted to $40,024,-894.32; if we deduct from this the free articles, valued at $13,506,230.23, we shall have, as the dutiable merchandise, $26,518,664.09, yielding a revenue of $32,477,962.95, or an average of 122 per cent. upon dutiable and 81.14 per cent. upon the total imports, which is larger in proportion than that of any other American nation, and almost double that of the United States, where the average was 44.41 per cent. for the fiscal year ending on the 30th of June, 1890, the last fiscal year before the tariff, approved on October 1, 1890, was in operation; the value of the dutiable articles amounting to $507,511,764, and the import duties to $226,540,-037. This contrast appears still greater in the case of the foreign trade in the fiscal year ended June 30, 1896, of both countries. According to the information conveyed in the President's Message of December 6, 1896, the proportion on dutiable goods imported in the fiscal year ending June 30, 1896—during which the Wilson Bill was in operation—was 39.94 per cent.; and on all articles, dutiable and free together, it was 20.55 per cent.; while in Mexico the imports of the same fiscal year amounted to $42,253,938, out of which $37,249,405 were dutiable, the proportion being 57.6 per cent. upon dutiable goods and 50.8 upon the total imports. Notwithstanding all this, and although our wages are lower than those in this country, our production, as compared with similar articles produced in this country, is considerably dearer.

At the end of 1897 over 50,000 workmen employed in the cotton mills in Fall River and other places of Massachusetts had their wages reduced ten per cent., and a similar reduction was made in other mills in New Hampshire and Rhode Island, as well as in Lewiston, Auburn, and Biddeford, Maine, a reduction having also taken place in the wages of a great shoe factory in New Bedford, Massachusetts.

It would be unreasonable and unfair to make the present tariff accountable for that reduction, with which it has nothing to do, and the most satisfactory explanation given of it is, in my opinion, the one advanced by a committee of New England manufacturers sent South to investigate the subject, who have reported that the New England mills, in their effort to secure cheaper labor, have substituted French-Canadian and other foreign for American hands, presumably at lower rates, but not necessarily at lower cost of production, and that the Southern mills with which they compete employ American workmen and are getting excellent work.

In an Appendix to this paper I will present the views of distinguished American statesmen on this subject, which seem to support the views here contained, to the effect that the main factor of wages is the amount of commodities they produce, and that wages are higher in the United States than anywhere else because labor here is more efficient than in other countries.

The Mexican Laborer.—In Mexico we call a laborer any kind of wage-earner, and peon, a farm wage-earner, although the word peon is going into disuse, because it does not mean now what it did under the Spanish rule. I will speak in another portion of this paper of the peonage system, and here I will only make general considerations regarding the wage-earners of Mexico and their present condition.

It is impossible to institute a comparison between a laborer of the United States and one of Mexico. Any such attempt would be futile; they are wholly different in habits of thought and in mode of life. Their ambitions are diverse, and their education and tendencies are dissimilar. There is no common plane of comparison. Mexico must be measured by Mexican standards. Erroneous conclusions would be reached were we to apply the English, French, German, or American systems to the Mexican laborer.

No one will dispute that the average American workingman is better off in many ways than his counterpart in Mexico. The public school educates the American workingman, and he has many wants to satisfy, and we are glad for it. Otherwise he would not be what he is, the most intelligent, on the average, of all the world's toilers. He is a great consumer of tropical products, and this fact makes him tributary to Mexico. The better his wages the more he will consume, and the better it would be for our hot-country planters.

The social and physical status of most of the Mexican toilers is very unsatisfactory, and is attributable to various causes. In the first place, they are the descendants of practically enslaved sons of the soil, conquered by the early Spaniards; in the second place, they have been practically and until recently living under conditions similar to feudalism; and, in the third place, education has not yet penetrated among the adult laborers. But public schools are multiplying all over Mexico, and in many regions the minds of the little children of the laborer are being trained and disciplined as well as informed. Railways, by making it easy for the laborer to go from one part of the country to another, are destroying the centuries-old state of serfdom among the laborers. Slowly, very slowly, but none the less surely, is the educational policy of the Mexican Government raising the level of the toilers of Mexico.

The laborer in Mexico is passing from peonage under the Spaniards, which was a very mild and tolerable form of feudal servitude, to absolute freedom of action, with a horizon that is continually expanding. He was contented in his former sphere, for the Spaniards, especially those engaged in agriculture, were generally good to their hands. They did not educate them nor attempt to elevate them, neither did they try to elevate themselves. The whole of Mexico was plunged into apathy, but it was the apathy of supreme indifference, not of despair. Now they can go where they like, serve whom they like, and return to their village when they like. And they use their liberty to the point of abuse. Yet still the horizon keeps enlarging. The rate of wages keeps moving upwards, and there is no sign that it has reached its limit. The number of Mexicans whose fathers were either virtual or actual peons, and who are now receiving a dollar a day, is constantly increasing. It is easy to picture the satisfaction felt by a man whose boyhood was nurtured on the simple food of corn-cakes and beans, and who now receives a Mexican dollar, day in and day out, except upon Sunday, and then as well if he is willing to work on that day.

While the Mexican laborers are deprived of most of the comforts enjoyed by their brethren in the United States, it is the opinion of some thoughtful Americans who have visited Mexico that they are happier, because their needs are fewer, the necessaries of life for them are cheaper, and their employment is constant—conditions which sometimes do not exist in this country.

Mexican Peonage.—Peon in Spanish means a laborer who performs rough work that does not require either art nor any special fitness, and it does not give at all the idea of servitude, but under the Spanish rule the conquerors were given the ownership of a certain territory, where they exercised quasi-feudal rights upon the natives living there, and as they required their services to till the land, a very mild form of servitude was established, consisting in the landlord's providing for the needs of his laborers ; that is, furnishing them money, in the shape of an advance for future services, whenever they had any special need in the families, such as marriage, birth, sickness, death, etc., they, of course, being obliged to repay their indebtedness to their employer. In some cases this obligation passed to the descendant of the laborer, who had to work to discharge his parent's debt. Since Mexico achieved her independence this condition of things has changed very materially. I never knew or heard of any case in which the descendant of a man had to discharge with his labor the debts of his parents, and the Mexican laws from the beginning have been directed to destroy that system, as I will presently state. I can therefore say with perfect truth, that peonage, in the meaning in which it is understood in this country—that is, a kind of slavery—never existed in Mexico, and that even the Spanish peonage system is not now in existence, although there are some districts which still have slight remnants of peonage, as will be seen farther on, but the laborers suffer there no more than they do in some other countries, as up to the end of the last century laborers were everywhere, as a general rule, held in a kind of slavery or peonage.

The early history of the United States shows that even white men were held in bondage in all the States to work out debts, and to expiate offences, and it is only a generation back that slavery on a great scale was abolished. There are, to-day, the "convict-camp" abuses in the Southern States of the American Union, against which influential journals in that section are strongly protesting. In Pennsylvania, one reads of the poverty-stricken condition of the imported foreign miners, who try to maintain families on fifty and sixty cents a day.

In all countries there are plenty of abuses; children are over-worked, and women forced into coarse pursuits. Mexico is able to show as good a record as any country in these matters, and a strong public opinion is growing there against all forms of oppression of human beings.

All over the civilized world men are becoming humaner in senti-ment, the fundamental rights of men are more regarded, and the struggle against selfish greed on the part of the minority of employers is making good progress.

Peonage never meant a low system of wages, as is understood in the United States. The prevailing impression in this country regarding the Mexican peon is an erroneous one. It is supposed here that peon-age is, as a matter of fact, sheer slavery, and that it extends throughout the whole country. I have shown that it is not slavery, and now I will say that it exists principally in a comparatively reduced area where laborers are very scarce, and this fact shows that, while the system is liable to abuse, it has some advantages for the laborer.

Meantime our peons are not starving, and are, for the most part, a quiet and philosophic people, enjoying their frequent respites from toil, and complaining very little, while a patriotic Government has their interests at heart and is planning for their welfare, and especially for that of their children.

What follows will show how much the evils of the peonage system in Mexico have been exaggerated, and how they all are being now radi-cally corrected ; but before proceeding any farther, I will state what is the condition of the Mexican farm laborer, or peon, in the different localities of Mexico.

The largest portion of the Mexican population is located on the mountains, central table-lands, and other high regions, which enjoy a cold and healthful climate on account of their elevation above the sea. Only the products of the cold zone can grow there, and these were formerly cultivated on a limited scale, solely for local con-sumption, as the high cost of transportation prevented their being carried to any distance. In this region labor is abundant, and until recent years it exceeded the demand; consequently, wages were low, and the peonage system only existed to a small extent; because of the number of working hands being greater than the demand, the laborers were exposed to disadvantages that fortunately are now beginning to disappear, as prosperity of the country increases the demand for labor.

The temperate region embraces the land situated at from three to five thousand feet above the level of the sea, and it is sparsely popu-lated; but it yields valuable products, such as coffee, sugar, and other tropical fruits. It is very difficult to find in this region the necessary hands to till the land on a large scale.   For these reasons, and, above all, because of the high cost of transportation, tropical products could not be grown before the railways were built, except in a few places favorably located, and then in a limited quantity.   This explains why some of these products commanded a higher price in some localities of the country where they are produced than in foreign markets, to which they are transported from great distances.   Sugar, for instance, which is retailed in New York at 4½ cents a pound, costs in the City of Mexico from 12 to 18 cents, and it is not so well refined as the article sold here, although it probably has for that reason a greater amount of saccharine matter.

The hot region, which embraces the coast on both oceans and the low valleys situated in the interior of the country, is very sparsely inhabited; labor is therefore very scarce, and wages are higher here than in any other region.   While in the high and cold regions wages were often 12½ cents a day and rations, on the coast they are sometimes $1 a day.   The inhabitants of the cold and temperate regions do not like to descend to the warm zone, because they are exposed to maladies prevailing there, such as yellow fever and intermittent and remittent fevers, and because they are terribly annoyed by mosquitoes, and they can hardly endure the heat.   If at any time they do go down there, it is only to remain a few days.   It has been thought that as the lowlands are the most fertile and rich, and are almost uninhabited, they could be cultivated only by means of negro or Asiatic labor; and this idea has induced some Mexican planters to try Chinese immigration, as Article II. of our Constitution grants to all men the right freely to enter and leave Mexico.

The laborers living in the warm lands have, on account of the smallness of their number, advantages which are not shared by their fellow-laborers inhabiting the higher regions.   The first of these advantages is, as I have already stated, larger wages; the second is that they can obtain advances, in reasonable amounts, for any needs they may have, as marriages, births, sickness, or death in their families, since the small amount of their wages does not allow them to economize for such emergencies, and these advances are willingly made by their employers and set to the account of future services, without interest or security.

Unfortunately, the very advantages which the laborers living in the hot lands of Mexico enjoy, and the smallness of their numbers, which I have just mentioned, are sometimes the causes of great abuses on the part of some employers, of which the laborer is the victim on account of his ignorance and complete destitution, on the one hand, and the influence and wealth of his employer on the other.

I speak of this subject from personal experience, because, having spent several years as a planter in the District of Soconusco, State of Chiapas, where these conditions prevail, I saw the practical workings of the peonage system. It was not possible to obtain there a laborer, either as a domestic or a field hand, without first paying the debt of from one to five hundred dollars that he had contracted with his former employer; so that it is easy to understand what an expenditure of money was required before a large number of hands could be obtained. Lapse of time increases the debt instead of diminishing it, since the laborer asks each week, as a rule, for more than the amount of his wages. Whenever the hands are displeased with their work—either because they quarrel among themselves, because their employer does not treat them well, because they do not get all the money advances they ask, or for any other reason—they have entire freedom to offer their services to anybody else, who willingly pays their debt, as everybody is always in need of help; but often, and especially when the employer does not live permanently in the country, as was my case when I was in Soconusco, laborers whose debts reach a considerable sum conceal themselves, fly to another district where they are not known, or in some other manner evade the payment of their indebtedness; with the result that it is a total loss to their employer. The same is the case when the indebted laborer dies or becomes disabled for work.

These are the practical results of the peonage system, so far as my experience goes, although I do not deny that it is liable to great abuse on the part of the employers, who are favored in a few cases by the tolerance of the local authorities and by the ignorance and poverty of the laborers.

There are some places—especially in the States of Tabasco and Campeche, where mahogany, cedar, ebony and dyewoods are cut in uninhabited spots, which change as the wood is exhausted—where the employer assumes, in the absence of any magistrate or other authority, and generally through an overseer, for he himself seldom remains at such places, all the powers of government. Of course, opportunities for doing injustice are very much increased, in view of the fact that there an employer is hardly ever called to account for abuse of authority. In most of these cases the employer is obliged to set up, for the convenience of his laborers—as I have heard, though I have no personal knowledge in the matter—a store where they can provide themselves, there being no other near by, with provisions, groceries, and such dry-goods as they may need in the ordinary course of life, paying for them with the scrip issued to them by the employer over his signature in settlement of their wages. It is easy to see how greatly this system is liable to abuse, since the laborer has to purchase at the store of his employer everything he wants, and at such prices as the owner may think fit to charge, thus losing all the benefits of competition.[1]

But the peonage system has no legal existence in Mexico, because Article V. of our Constitution of 1857, enacted for the purpose of abolishing it, provides that "nobody should be obliged to render personal service without proper compensation and his full consent," and forbids the issuance of any law to authorize any contract which might have for its object the "loss or irreparable sacrifice of the freedom of man through work, education, or religious vows." This article was amended on the 25th of September, 1873, chiefly with a view of prohibiting the taking of religious vows in Mexico, and also of making it more explicit, and it reads now, so far as work is concerned, as follows: "The state cannot allow the fulfilment of any agreement, contract, or covenant which may, in any manner, impair, destroy, or irrevocably sacrifice man's liberty, either through work, education, or religious vows."

Whatever abuses might have been committed under the peonage system in Mexico in former years when laborers were abundant and occupation scarce, and the laborers were ignorant and destitute, they have either disappeared altogether or been very materially reduced with the changing conditions of the country, as labor is now in great demand, so much so that in very many places the demand exceeds the supply. The laborers began to be educated with the restoration of peace. The local authorities vie with each other to enforce the laws which guarantee the personal rights of every inhabitant of the country.

Rate of Agricultural Mexican Wages.—The broken surface of Mexico gives us all the climates of the world, frequently at very short distances from each other, and enables us to produce the fruits of all the zones, while placing at our disposal, at the same time, an immense hy-

---

[1] It seems that something similar to this is done in the United States, as is shown by the following extract from Gen. Rush C. Hawkins's article, entitled "Brutality and Avarice Triumphant," published in the June, 1896, number of the *North American Review*, page 660:

"One of the most facile means in the hands of avarice for cheating the poor and helpless is the 'corporation and contractor's' store. It is usually owned by corporations whose employees are the only patrons, and the rule is to sell the poorest possible quality of supplies at the highest price obtainable. In many instances employees are given to understand that they are expected to trade at the company and contract stores, or, failing to do so, will be discharged. This oppressive method of cheating is not confined to any particular part of the country, but prevails, with varying degrees of malignancy, wherever under one management, either corporate, partnership, or individual, any considerable number of employees are assembled together. Since the close of the Civil War many thousands of ignorant blacks have been made the victims of this common and heartless swindle, which has absorbed their scant earnings. At the end of each month, year in and year out, it has proved to their untrained minds an astonishing fact that the longer and the harder they worked the more they got in debt to their employers."

draulic power, of which for the present we hardly avail ourselves. But, on the other hand, this condition of things made transportation very expensive, and rendered the interchange of products exceedingly difficult. The obstacles to communication between the various sections of the country, and the diversity of conditions existing in each, cause a great difference in the wages paid in different localities.

The Department of Public Works of the Mexican Government has been for some time past collecting data regarding the wages paid to field laborers, and during one of my visits in 1891, to the City of Mexico, I obtained a summary of such data. It is very difficult to present it in a complete and correct form, because there are several systems of wages. In some places a fixed amount is paid for one day's work; in others, again, besides the wages, rations are given,[1] consisting of a certain quantity of grain, sufficient for the subsistence of the laborer and his family; the quality and quantity of these rations vary, as well as their value, for grain has different prices in the various localities; and all these causes render it very difficult to make an entirely accurate *résumé* of the official data.

The most complete that I was able to prepare, during my visit to Mexico in 1891, is the following, which embraces the maximum and minimum field wages paid in the different States of the Mexican Confederation, in cents and per day:

[1] This assertion is confirmed by the following statement from Mr. Ransom's (U. S. Minister to Mexico) report on Prices and Labor in Mexico, of September 26, 1896, published in vol. xiii., part 1, page 117, of *Special Consular Reports*, on Money and Prices of Foreign Countries :

" A large portion of the farming in Mexico is carried on under the ' share system.' The Government reports show that, in many instances, rations of corn are furnished to the hired laborer ; in some cases we find that he is allowed a small amount per day for his board in addition to wages ; again, he is furnished by the landlord with a small piece of land to cultivate for his own benefit."

These views are confirmed by a report on the condition of Mexico, dated at its capital city, on September 4, 1896, from Governor Thomas T. Crittenden, then Consul-General of the United States in the City of Mexico, and published by the *Journal* of New York, in its issue of September 17, 1896:

" The wages paid laborers and artisans are largely improved. Formerly workmen, particularly agricultural laborers, were paid in ' kind ' ; now they are paid in money. In the case of farm laborers, it is the custom of the country for the employer, in addition to the regular wages, to allow the laborer the use of a certain acreage to raise his own food. In many of the agricultural districts, instead of employing labor directly, the owners of haciendas follow what is known in the United States as the share system of cultivating their land. Those who were formerly practically serfs now receive half the crop they raise. Corn is the great staple of the country.

" In considering the labor and wage question it should be borne in mind that the American skilled workman possesses on the average a much higher degree of skill in his trade than the Mexican employed in a similar vocation. The American skilled workman also performs much more work in a day than the workman in this country."

DAILY WAGES PAID TO FIELD HANDS IN MEXICO IN 1891.

STATES.	Minimum. Cts.	Maximum. Cts.	Average.[1] Cts.
Aguascalientes	$0.18¾	$0.18¾	$0.18¾
Lower California (T)	.50	.50	.50
Chiapas	.25	.75	.50
Chihuahua	.18¾	.25	.21⅞
Coahuila	.31¼	.75	.53⅛
Colima	.25	.37½	.31¼
Durango	.25	.75	.50
Federal District	.31¼	.37½	.34⅜
Guanajuato	.18¾	.31¼	.25
Guerrero	.18¾	.50	.24⅜
Hidalgo	.12½	.37½	.25
Jalisco	.18¾	.50	.34⅜
Mexico	.12½	.37½	.25
Michoacan	.15½	.75	.45¼
Morelos	.25	.75	.50
Nuevo Leon	.18¾	.18¾	.18¾
Oaxaca	.18¾	.50	.34⅜
Puebla	.18¾	.50	.34⅜
Queretaro	.18¾	.37½	.28⅛
San Luis Potosi	.18¾	.25	.22¼
Sonora	.30	1.00	.65
Tabasco	.37½	.50	.43¾
Tamaulipas	.25	.50	.37½
Tepic (T)	.25	.50	.37½
Tlaxcala	.25	.50	.37½
Veracruz	.25	.62½	.43¾
Yucatan	.25	.37½	.31¼
Zacatecas	.18¾	.50	.34⅜
Average in the whole country	.23⅓	.50	.36

Before giving an account of the causes of the diversity of wages paid in Mexico for field work, and showing why these wages are so low, it is opportune to say that it is not in Mexico only that such diversity of wages exists, for something similar is the case in this country. According to information published by the Wisconsin Labor Bureau, in 1891, a common laborer in Atlanta earns 7½ cents per hour, while the same laborer in Galveston, also a Southern city, earns 25 cents per hour, or three times as much.

The Division of Statistics of the Department of Agriculture of the United States issued, in 1892, a report (Miscellaneous Series, Report No. 4) on the "Wages of Farm Labor in the United States. Re-

[1] The averages in this table are not properly made, because they are obtained by adding the minimum and maximum wages and dividing the result by two, and that does not give the true average. To secure an average rate, each rate should be multiplied by the number of persons receiving it, then the total number receiving all rates should be divided into the aggregate amount, as shown by the multiplication. The total average in the preceding table was obtained by adding all rates in each column and dividing by the number of rates, which gives only an arithmetical mean and not an average, but not having the data necessary to make a true average, I only did what I could.

sult of nine statistical investigations, from 1866 to 1892, with extensive inquiries concerning wages from 1840 to 1865," which contains (page 16) a tabular statement showing that in 1892 the average wages for farm labor, without board, was $12.50 per month in South Carolina, $13.30 in North Carolina, $13.50 in Georgia, and $13.75 in Alabama, while in California the wages paid were $36.50 and in the State of Washington $37.50, the average for all the States for that year being $18.60. For farm labor, with board, the wages varied from $8.40 to $25, and averaged $12.54.

Mr. Ransom's and Mr. Crittenden's Reports on Wages.—On September 26, 1896, Mr. Matthew M. Ransom, United States Minister at the City of Mexico, sent to the State Department a report on the currency, prices, and condition of labor in that country, which was published in the *Special Consular Report* (vol. xiii., part 1) on Money and Prices in Foreign Countries, and to which he appended a statement of wages paid to men for agricultural labor in 1893, stating that the rates were taken from the Government statistics for that year, and that they were expressed in Mexican currency. As that statement is a little more comprehensive than mine and somewhat later, and although it is not complete and cannot, I think, be taken as entirely correct, because it would be exceedingly difficult to make an altogether reliable statement, I consider it a fair one and insert it here:

WAGES PER DAY OF AGRICULTURAL LABOR IN 1893—MEN.[1]

STATE.	Major-domos.	Overseers.	Herders.	Shepherds.	Pulque Hands.	Peons.
Aguascalientes...	$0.25 to $0.37	$0.25 to $0.37	$0.13 to $0.20	....	....	$0.13 to $0.25
Campeche.......	.50 to 1.50	.25 to .31	.25 to .75	$0.25	....	.25 to .50
Mexico..........	.37 to 1.00	.25 to .50	.18 to .50	$0.18 to .25	$0.28 to $0.37	.18 to .50
Guerrero........	.75 to 1.00	.... .50	.37 to .50	....	....	.12 to .31
Hidalgo.........	.37 to 1.00	.18 to .50	.18 to .50	.18 to .31	.37	.18 to .50
Jalisco..........	.37 to 1.00	.25 to .50	.25 to .50	.25 to .50	.37	.25 to .50
Michoacan.......	.50 to 2.00	.25 to .50	.25 to .50	.18 to .37	.18 to .50	.18 to .75
Sonora..........	.62 to 1.00	.50 to 1.75	.37 to 1.00	.37 to 1.00	....	.37 to 1.00
Tabasco	.75 to 1.00	.50 to .75	.25 to .50	.25 to .50	....	.37 to 1.00
Coahuila	.50 to .75	.37 to .50	.37 to .50	.25	.37	.25 to .37
Colima.........	1.00	....	....	.25 to .37	....	.37 to .75
Tamaulipas	.50	.18 to .25	.18 to .25	....	....	.18 to .25
Chihuahua......	....	.50 to .75	.50 to .75	....	....	.37 to .62
Durango........	.50 to 1.00	.31 to .62	.31 to .50	.25 to .37	....	.25 to .37
Guanajuato	.37 to 1.00	.37 to .62	.37	.18 to .25	.18 to .25	.18 to .25
Nuevo Leon.....	.75 to 1.00	.25 to 1.00	.25 to .75	.18 to .50	.37 to .50	.18 to .50
Oaxaca.........	.50 to 1.00	.37 to .50	.... .50	....	....	.25 to .50
Puebla	.50 to 1.00	.37 to .50	.25 to .60	.18 to .31	.25 to .66	.18 to .50
Veracruz........	.50 to 1.00	.37 to 1.00	.37 to 1.00	.37 to 1.00	....	.18 to .37
Yucatan........	1.00 to 1.25	....	.50 to .75	.25 to .50	....	.25 to .75
Zacatecas	.37 to .75	.25 to 1.00	.25 to .75	.37 to .50	.18 to .50	.18 to .50
Federal District.	1.00 to 1.50	.... .50	.... .50	.37 to .50	.37 to .50	.37 to .40
San Luis Potosi..	.50 to .83	.... .40	.... .20	.18 to .20	.18 to .25	.18 to .25
Morelos.........	1.00 to 2.00	.... .50	.... .50	....	....	.37 to 1.00

[1] These rates are taken from the Government statistics for the year 1893. They are expressed in Mexican currency; in United States currency they are about one-half.

In some of the States rations of corn and bacon are furnished; very seldom any meat.

Besides Mr. Ransom's report, another with the same purpose, made by Mr. Thomas T. Crittenden, United States Consul-General at the City of Mexico, dated September 1, 1896, containing important data, was published in the same number of the *Special Consular Reports* of the United States. Both reports embrace data about wages in the factories, mines, and railroads that, while I believe they are correct as far as they go, are not comprehensive enough, as they relate only to certain factories and mining districts. So far as the railroads are concerned, they are entirely reliable, because the railway companies are but few, and most of them furnished directly to Mr. Ransom a correct schedule of their wages. As they serve to show the rate of Mexican wages, I append to this article such tabular statements sent by Mr. Ransom as I think of interest.

Mr. Crittenden's report contains the following table of wages and salaries paid in and about the City of Mexico on September 1, 1896:

MEXICAN WAGES.

EMPLOYMENT.	MEXICAN CURRENCY.	UNITED STATES CURRENCY.
Agents, railway................per month..	$75.00 –$150.00	$39.00 – $78.00
Boiler makers....................per day..	4.00 – 8.00	2.08 – 4.16
Brakemen....................per month..	35.00 – 75.00	18.20 – 39.00
Bricklayers (native)...............per day..	1.00 – 1.50	.52 – .78
Clerks (office).................per month..	40.00 – 200.00	20.00 – 104.00
Cooks, women [1]....................do....	6.00 – 12.00	3.12 – 6.24
Cooks, men........................do....	25.00 – 75.00	13.00 – 39.00
Carpenters ....per day..	1.50 – 4.75	.78 – 2.37
Conductors, passenger...........per month..	100.00 – 160.00	52.00 – 83.20
Conductors, freight.................do....	100.00 – 200.00	52.00 – 104.00
Conductors, street-car...........per day..	.50 – 1.00	.26 – .52
Coachmen, private (native).......per month..	15.00 – 30.00	7.80 – 15.60
Coachmen, public (native)...........do....	[2]15.00	7.80
Division (railway) superintendents......do....	250.00 – 350.00	130.00 – 192.00
Drivers, street-car.................per day..	.50 – 1.00	.26 – .52
Engineers :		
Locomotive.................per month..	150.00 – 250.00	78.00 – 130.00
Stationary, with board [3].........per day..	2.50 – 3.35	1.30 – 1.82
Stationary, without board [3] ....do....	3.50 – 5.00	1.82 – 2.60
Engravers ....do....	5.00 – 10.00	2.60 – 5.20
Firemen, locomotive.............per month..	75.00 – 100.00	39.44 – 52.00
Firemen, ordinary...................do....	20.00 – 50.00	10.44 – 26.00
Furnace men......................per day..	1.00 – 1.50	.52 – .78
Harness makers, etc.................do....	.50 – 2.00	.26 – 1.04
Iron workers.......................do....	2.00 – 2.50	1.04 – 1.30
Jewellers ....do....	2.00 – 5.00	1.04 – 2.60
Laborers, in large cities............do....	.37½– .67½	.19½– .353
Laborers, in the country [4]............do....	.10 – .15	.052– .078

[1] And 9 cents (4.68 cents, United States) per day for rations.

[2] Maximum ; these depend largely on tips.

[3] In mines and on large plantations.

[4] Laborers (day) in the country, from 19 to 50 cents per day. In some instances meals are furnished, or an allowance of from 10 to 15 cents a day to cover the cost of the meals. The average laborer will live well and in good strength on from 10 to 15 cents per day, and will support his family

MEXICAN WAGES—*Continued.*

EMPLOYMENT.	MEXICAN CURRENCY.		UNITED STATES CURRENCY.	
Laborers in factories (10 to 11 hours).per day..	$0.50 –	$1.00	$0.26 –	$0.52
Laborers, skilled (10 to 11 hours).......do....	1.50 –	2.00	.78 –	1.04
Mechanics............................do....	3.50 –	5.00	1.82 –	2.60
Machinists (shop)....................do....	3.50 –	5.00	1.82 –	2.60
Miners, skilled......................do....	1.00 –	1.50	.52 –	.78
Miners, ordinary.....................do....	.50 –	.80	.26 –	.416
Maids, house....................per month..	4.00 –	7.00	2.08 –	3.64
Operators, telegraph.................do....	50.00 –	150.00	26.00 –	78.00
Plumbers:				
Native......................per day..	2.00 –	2.50	1.04 –	1.30
American.....................do....	6.00 –	8.00	3.12 –	4.16
Printers:				
Native ....per week..	7.00 –	8.00	3.64 –	4.16
Pressmen.......................do....	8.00 –	11.00	4.16 –	5.72
Compositors ....do....	10.00 –	12.00	5.20 –	6.24
Policemen....................per month..	30.00 –	50.00	13.60 –	26.00
Switchmen ....per day..		1.50		.78
Blacksmiths..........................do....	3.50 –	4.00	1.82 –	2.34
Gold- and silver-smiths..............do....	2.25 –	3.50	1.17 –	1.82
Stone masons .... do....	1.00 –	1.50	.52 –	.78
Seamstresses.......................do....	.37 –	.50	.29 –	.26
Train masters.................per month..	150.00 –	175.00	73.00 –	91.00
Tailors:				
Repairers ....per day..	1.00 –	1.25	.52 –	.65
Coat makers ....per coat..	5.00 –	12.00	2.60 –	6.24
Vest makers.................per vest..	1.35 –	1.50	.71 –	.78
Pantaloonists.................per pair..	1.75 –	2.50		.91

Low Wages in Mexico.—A great deal has been written about the low scale of wages prevailing in Mexico. The laborer in that country has been held up to his brethren in the United States as an object of great pity and commiseration, and his condition has been depicted in most realistic colors. He has been compared with the well-fed, well-clothed, and well-housed workmen of this Republic, and the comparison was not made to appear greatly to his advantage. Wages in Mexico are certainly very low, although, fortunately, they are rising; but biased persons from this country who visit Mexico and remain there only a few days, unacquainted with the language, the people, and the conditions of the country, completely misunderstand the case, and are apt to come to general conclusions from some special instance that may come to their notice, and return to the United States supposing that

on from 10 to 20 cents per day. Of course he will have his little patch of corn, beans, and chiles planted near his hut, which is the largest part of his "bill of fare" three times a day, and for three hundred and sixty-five days in the year. Five to ten dollars per year will clothe him, except, perhaps, his hat, and for that, he will, if he can get the money, pay from $5 to $20. As to wages paid for farm labor, it is well to add that a large part of the farming in this country is done on shares; almost the entire corn crop of Mexico—and it is one of the largest and most important—is raised by the "peons" on shares. The landowner furnishes everything, including a house to live in, and for this receives one-half of the crop. Others of the poorer class who are employed directly by the owner receive, besides their daily wages, a small plot of ground and a certain number of hours each week to cultivate it.

they know all about the subject, and make incorrect and ungrounded statements about the laboring classes in Mexico.[1]

Farther on I will show the difference in the cost of life between Mexico and the United States, and, as a consequence of the same, how much more can be obtained in Mexico by a smaller amount of wages than in the United States. Those who work in Mexico live fairly well according to the value of their services and the necessaries of life. Those who are out of employment find existence much more tolerable in tropical Mexico than in this country, where fires and warm clothing are for the greater part of the year indispensable. Both in Mexico and the United States the very poor are wretched. But, from a hygienic point of view, the Mexican laborer's adobe hut is no more squalid and unwholesome than the swarming tenements and sweat-shops of New York City.

When one speaks of wages in the United States he always refers to wages in the Northern and Western States, which are the highest paid in this country and in the world, but not to the largest section of this country where wages are comparatively small, especially those paid to the negroes in the South. It is true that the latter enjoy advantages that the Northern laborers do not: a more benign climate and the privilege of cultivating a small plot of ground where they can obtain vegetables, fruits, corn, etc., and raise some domestic animals, and find easy and cheap shelter, which contributes, of course, to reduce the expense of the necessaries of life; but the Mexican laborers are very much in the same condition with a great many decided advantages over the Southern negroes, in so far as the climate is concerned, and if the wages and the

---

[1] One instance of this is the case of Mr. Theodore Knauff, who is a student of sociology and recently visited Mexico, and in December, 1896, delivered a lecture at the Franklin Institute of Philadelphia, under the joint auspices of that Institute and the Young Men's Christian Association of that city, upon the conditions of Mexico as he thought he found them, in which, at the outset, he declares "that of the 12,500,000 people composing the population of Mexico, at least 8,000,000 have never slept in a bed or worn stockings. They are forced to live at a less expense per diem than it takes to keep the meanest American farm-horse. Millions of Mexicans have never worn anything but a single garment, called a 'sarappe,' which is roughly described as a sack with a hole in the top, through which the wearer protrudes his head. This garment," continues Mr. Knauff, "forms at the same time the Mexican's coat, hat, and even his bed. The feet are usually bare or clothed in domestic sandals. The women wear a kind of cotton shawl over their heads and shoulders, called a 'rebozo.' The Mexican farm laborers' conditions are inferior to those of the late slaves of our Southern States. Their huts have but one opening, no windows, and dirt floors. When wishing to go to bed, they simply unroll their mats, and, without removing their clothing, lie down and go to sleep. The laborer has a certain wage and is given time and place to build himself a house. If he does not build it he has nothing with which to cover his head. The houses are built by the people who live in them. Some of the houses are mud-roofed and others roofed by palms or banana leaves."

Anybody familiar with Mexico knows that this statement has as many mistakes as lines.

condition of living and happiness between the two classes are compared, I do not think that any material advantage to the latter would be
found.   Their social condition is, of course, infinitely better in Mexico
because there they can rise to the highest position in the country. The
condition of some of the working classes in this country is not as satisfactory as it might be.   The recent clothing strike in New York City has
shown beyond all denial that the pay of certain classes of workmen
engaged in the making of clothing has been as follows: Tailors, from
$3 to $5 a week; children's jacket-makers, about $3 a week; knee-
pants makers, $5 a week; vest-makers, $4 a week.   In other words,
these people have been receiving from thirty-three to eighty-three
cents per day.

Recently, there has been a tendency to reduce the compensation
of working girls in the great shops of the big towns.   I understand that
in New York the wages of $3 a week is now considered quite enough,
and a working girl could hardly afford to live there on $3 a week.

The Mexican laborer is receiving wages quite equal in amount to
those received by his poorly paid unfortunate brethren in this country,
but his wages are far more powerful than theirs in the purchasing of those
necessaries which go to make up his life.   With his 37½ cents per day,
he can live, according to his notions, in comparative comfort; with
their 37½ cents per day, it is not possible to live with comfort in this
country.   His climate is also mild and delightful; he needs not the fuel
and the clothing which are necessary to the New York workmen.

It is not possible in every country to pay high wages to the laborers.
Even in this great country, where laborers are better paid than anywhere else, and where they have sometimes been called princes—and
they deserve that name, if compared with others—wages are sometimes
quite low.

To ensure for the workingman of Mexico higher wages many things
have to be accomplished.   He has first to be technically trained, to be
made more intelligent by education, to unlearn his habits of dawdling
and procrastination, in a word, to put more conscience into his work.
There are mechanics there who are getting good pay because they have
learned the lesson of the times; they are diligent and efficient.   Foreign
mechanics are well paid in Mexico when they are engaged by responsible concerns.   In some lines of endeavor, wages are very good there
as compared with the cost of subsistence.

Mexico is a southern land with a benign climate, a winterless land,
a land of easy habits, and its masses are not yet inclined to put forth
the exertion necessary to gain high wages.

High Wages to Skilled Laborers.—Everybody admits, even those
who most harshly disparage Mexico because of her silver standard,
that railway engineers, conductors, and in fact all skilled laborers, re-

ceive in Mexico higher wages than such laborers receive in the United States under a gold basis, that is, that the wages of such men in silver are more than its equivalent in gold at the corresponding price of silver; while the native unskilled labor is paid a very low price, a price considerably lower than similar labor is paid in this country. This fact proves very conclusively, in my opinion, that labor, independently of the demand, which is one of the principal factors to regulate its value, has a fixed price; that is, that the more it can produce the higher is the price it can obtain. A company, for instance, finds that it is very profitable to establish in Mexico cotton or woollen mills, smelters, or any other similar plant, and as there are not experts in Mexico to establish the plant and work it, it has to send for them either to the United States or to Europe; and the expert, of course, would not go to Mexico unless he expected to receive something more than he can get at home, and, naturally, in money having the same value. If the expert gets $4 a day in gold in the United States or England, he would certainly not go to Mexico to receive $4 in silver, which would be equivalent, at the present price of silver, to less than $2 in gold, so losing more than fifty per cent. of his present wages; but he would demand at least from $8 to $10 in silver, which is more than he receives at home, and the company starting the plant has necessarily to pay those wages or it would be unable to carry on its business. This explains why experts and skilled laborers get higher wages in Mexico than in the United States, while the unskilled laborers, for reasons already stated, get a great deal less.

Skilled labor in Mexico commands, of course, the same or higher price as in the old countries, and it is paid in its equivalent in silver, and it is paid much better than in Italy, Spain, and Turkey, and about as well as in England, all of which are old countries. Of course, no workingman in Mexico can get, or can expect, such wages as are paid in Homestead, Bethlehem, and Pittsburg ; namely, $10, $15, and $25 per diem, for the simple reason that in Mexico no such establishments exist as the Carnegie Works, and, therefore, no opening for the specialties referred to.

Why Mexican Labor is Cheap.—The question of wages is undoubtedly settled by fixed laws, but these laws are so complex and affected by so many factors that there is a very wide difference of opinion about their true nature. Undoubtedly the amount and quality of the work produced by the wage-earner in a given time is one of the principal factors regulating wages ; but when a country is isolated by the condition of its civilization, by tariff barriers, by very high cost of transportation, or by other causes, preventing it from receiving the manufactures of the commercial nations which compete in the world's markets, wages may be affected by different principles, like the cost

of living and others.   The isolation of Mexico during several centuries, and the want of cheap and easy means of communication,
prevented the development of agriculture, trade, and industries and
made many communities self-supporting; that is, they had to raise
the necessary articles of food for their own maintenance, and sometimes to weave the cotton and woollen goods required for clothing.
This isolation, of course, prevented the development of the natural resources of the country and kept wages necessarily very low; because
the demand for its products being very limited—just enough to supply
the needs of a small community—and the supply very great, the price
of labor had necessarily to be very low.   The question of wages is settled by natural laws, and there is a natural level for them.   In isolated
districts, not subject to the general law governing wages, as most of
Mexico was before the railway era, the rule is that in a cheap country,
where the necessaries of life are but little, wages are comparatively
low, while in a dear country wages have to be proportionately high, because in any case a man has to earn enough to sustain life.   When a
laborer can satisfy his needs by working little he has no inducement to
go beyond that; but when to support himself and his family, he needs to
exert himself as much as he can then he has to produce a comparatively
large amount of commodities to earn higher wages.   The laborer's wants
not only depend, in such isolated districts, upon the natural conditions
of the country, but also on the degree of civilization which the people
have reached.   Of course, competition in manufactures which go to
international markets controls wages in commercial and manufacturing
countries.   These considerations explain why wages in Mexico are so
low, as compared with wages in the United States, and it suffices to
say that, now that our railways are built and the country has entered
on the path of prosperity, as the old conditions are changing, wages are
increasing and tend to increase considerably.

It must be borne in mind that the climatic influences in both
countries are so different that their respective inhabitants, and especially the wage-earning classes, cannot be judged by the same standard.
The mild climate of Mexico, for instance, does not require all the provisions for winter and the corresponding increased expense for that
season that are needed in this latitude.   Almost all over that country,
excepting in the most northern States, the difference in the seasons is
so slight that we do not need to change our style of clothing from
winter to summer.   We do not need to heat our houses, not even in
the City of Mexico, which is nearly 8000 feet above the level of the sea
and located in what we call the cold region; and, therefore, we do not
have the expenses unavoidable in a northern climate where houses
have to be heated during the winter.   The benignity of the Mexican
climate renders unnecessary expensive houses for the poor people, that

is, houses which can be hermetically closed in winter to keep them warm; on the contrary, in the temperate and hot climates, what is desirable is to keep the houses cool.   Building materials, namely, adobe, which is unburnt brick of very large size, is very cheap, and all this contributes to make living in Mexico much cheaper than in the United States.   In a great many localities in Mexico even shoes are not indispensable, and may be considered as an article of convenience or luxury, not a necessity.   So far as food is concerned, nature has provided, too, an abundant supply of fruits, a fertile soil, which in some localities yields as many as four crops a year; and the maintenance of a family is, as compared with the same needs in the United States, exceedingly cheap.   Therefore, what would be considered as starvation wages in this country would supply a working family in Mexico with all the necessaries and even with some of the luxuries of life; and these natural conditions cannot be altered or changed by legislation, or by any artificial means.

I consider the assumption that the tendency of wages in Mexico is to become lower as a very mistaken one.   The contrary assumption is the correct one.   Wages in Mexico could not be any lower than they are, and in every kind of work there is a marked tendency to increase, and I know by personal experience that an increase, and a very decided one, has taken place during the past fifteen years.

Difference in Amount of Work Accomplished by Mexican and American Workmen.—It is a fact that wages in Mexico are far lower in many instances than those paid for the same industries in the United States, although sometimes, that is, in the case of skilled laborers, they are as high or higher; but this ought not to appear strange when it is considered that this country pays probably the highest wages in the world; not even the foremost manufacturing nations of Europe, as England, France, Germany, and Belgium, being equal in this regard.   Yet while it is true that labor in European countries is not so well remunerated as in the United States, it must be taken into account that the same amount of labor produces there less than here.   I am assured by competent persons that a bank-bill printer, for instance, does not print in England more than 1000 sheets per week, while the average work done by the American workman is 6000 sheets per week; and it is stated in the *Journal des Economistes* that a French weaver can take care of only four looms, a Belgian of five, an English weaver of six, and one from this country of eight, while a Mexican weaver cannot attend to more than two looms.   But the actual production during a given working time is in Mexico far less than in the United States, or even in Europe.

The day's work of a Mexican laborer, very likely, represents in many cases only one-fourth of what is accomplished during the same time by a laborer in the United States.   A Mexican laborer working from ten to eleven hours a day, for instance, accomplishes less work, or produces less, than a European or an American laborer in seven or nine hours, and in some instances the disproportion is as great as one to five.   I have been assured that a Mexican bricklayer in eleven hours' work does not lay more than 500 bricks, while a bricklayer in the United States lays 2500 in nine hours.   Mr. Enrique Creel, of Chihuahua, a prominent Mexican gentleman, of American parentage, stated in an interview published by the Denver, Colorado, *News*, of October 25, 1896, that a St. Louis contractor, who was executing a large contract for the Mexican Government, told him that a Mexican bricklayer could lay, on an average, 500 bricks daily, while an American bricklayer is able to lay 5000 daily.   Under such conditions the high wages of $3 a day paid in the United States are no higher than the wages of 50 cents paid in Mexico, so far as the product of labor is concerned.

The principal causes for this difference in working capacity are, in my opinion, the following: (1) the Mexican laborer is not so well fed as his fellow-laborer in this country; (2) he generally works until he is exhausted, and his work is not, therefore, so productive; (3) he is not, on the whole, so well educated as the average laborer in the United States; (4) he has fewer wants to satisfy, and therefore less inducement to work.   Perhaps there is, in addition to these causes, at least in some localities, another, a climatic influence, the enervating character of the tropical climate and the high altitude above the level of the sea, and the consequent lower atmospheric pressure at which a large portion of the population of Mexico is located.   I am inclined to believe that this is a factor in the case, as a similar difference is noticed among animals.   A plough drawn by one horse in this country would, in Mexico, require two or three horses to accomplish the same work in similar soil; and this shows that the difference in working strength may be due, at least in part and in some places, to natural causes or climatic influences.

Low Wages Mean High Cost of Production.—It is now time to show that the low wages paid in Mexico do not always produce cheap commodities, and could not therefore, by competition, lower the compensation of labor, or the cost of similar articles manufactured in the United States.

We pay in Mexico, in some cases, wages amounting to about a sixth of what is paid here for similar work, and yet production in Mexico, with such low wages, is a great deal more costly than the production of similar articles in the United States, with probably the highest wages in the world.

It is true that wages are one of the principal factors in the cost of production of all kinds of merchandise, but they are not the only, and, in many cases, not even the principal one.   The question of wages is very complex, and it seems that, in comparing the wages of this country with those paid in Mexico, two important factors are generally over-looked: first, the amount of commodities produced in each country by the same unit of work, either because of the greater capacity or the greater physical strength of the laborer, or through the use of machinery, which increases the amount of production and cheapens it enormous-ly; and, second, the cost of living in each country, and, as a conse-quence of the same, the purchasing power of the currency in each. When these two factors are taken into account it will be found that the high wages paid here are often no higher for the work performed, perhaps in some cases even lower, than those paid in Mexico and in other countries; and only in that way can we explain how this country, with its high wages, can produce many articles—as, for instance, watches and clocks—which compete successfully with those made in Switzerland, where wages are comparatively low.

The cost of production, too, depends on other circumstances, vary-ing in different countries, all of which must be considered in order to arrive at a proper understanding of the subject. I should need more space than I can reasonably use in this article to mention all the causes which affect wages, and to show how far they influence the cost of production; and I shall only present some practical and suggestive examples taken from the tables of the cost of living which I will pres-ently insert, to show that some commodities produced in this country, with high wages, cost less, and therefore are sold at a lower price, than similar articles produced in Mexico with low wages.

One of the best illustrations of the correctness of this statement is afforded by the working of the mines in both countries. Although the wages of miners in Mexico are probably one-third or one-fourth of those paid in the United States, the production of silver costs much less here than there. Mr. Thomas H. Carter, a very competent judge, stated, during the first session of the Fifty-first Congress, that miners' wages here were $3 a day, while he fixes at 50 cents per day the wages of the Mexican miners. I do not think his statement correct so far as Mexican mining wages are concerned, as miners there can earn larger wages than field hands. That our production of silver is more costly than it is here is shown by the fact that mines similar to those which we abandon because it does not pay for us to work them, either on ac-count of the low grade of silver which they yield, or for other reasons, are operated in the United States with profit. This is in a great measure because in the United States machinery is largely used in mines, which diminishes the cost of production and increases its amount; but this very fact shows that wages are not the only factor affecting the cost of production, and also that with high wages it is possible, and even easy, to produce at a less cost than with low wages.

Cotton culture is another example. I am aware that the cotton-growers of the United States hold that what they call their cotton belt has peculiar conditions for the production of their staple, which in their opinion do not exist in any other portion of the world, and they believe, therefore, that nobody can compete with them in this regard. Without any intention on my part to depreciate the advantages of the cotton belt of this country, I am yet of the opinion that there are in Mexico lands as well adapted to the production of cotton as the best in this country, and in some other regions perhaps even better; yet, notwithstanding these advantages and although our wages are low, cotton is produced at less cost in this country, and is sold with profit by the planters for one-half the price that it commands in Mexico. So great is the difference in the price of this staple in the two countries that notwithstanding an import duty on cotton of seven cents per kilogram, gross weight, or nearly four cents per pound, which is equivalent to fifty per cent. ad valorem, we import from this country almost one-half of the cotton used in our home manufactures. I do not overlook the fact that cotton is raised here by negro labor, which is considerably cheaper than white labor; but, even assuming that wages in this case be the same in both countries, the difference in cost is so great that labor is not the only factor in the expense of production.

Something similar happens with sugar. Here it is produced with high wages, and—although the culture of the sugar-cane in Louisiana is an artificial one, since frosts prevail there, since the cane has to be planted every year or two, and the ground tilled at considerable expense several times a year, so that such culture is an artificial one—yet the Louisiana planters sell their sugar in New York with profit at from six to seven cents per pound, while in the City of Mexico and other places in my country it commands twice and even three times that price.

The same is the case with tobacco. Although the climate and soil are very likely better fitted for its culture in Mexico than in this country, tobacco costs there, on an average, $24\frac{1}{2}$ cents per pound, while it is sold here at $8\frac{1}{2}$ cents per pound.

I shall not speak of the products of the cold climate, such as wheat, barley, oats, etc., because the climate and soil of this country are naturally adapted for such culture, while for tropical products the conditions are decidedly in favor of Mexico; but despite the fact that we also have cold regions in Mexico, and notwithstanding the difference in wages, wheat is worth there twice as much as here, and there is about the same difference in the price of corn.

It is much the same with manufactured articles, like common printing-paper, which in the United States is worth about three cents a pound and in Mexico fifteen cents, although we have abundant raw material and water-power for its manufacture. To encourage the making of paper, we established an import duty on foreign unsized and half-sized paper of ten cents per kilogram, or over five cents per pound, equivalent to almost one hundred per cent. ad valorem, which was reduced by our present tariff to five cents per kilogram for the unsized, keeping the duty of ten cents on the half-sized paper; and notwithstanding this, we import printing-paper from this country, where the wages are so high compared with ours.   Something similar happens with cotton and cotton prints, the former being worth five cents per yard in this country and from ten to fifteen cents per *vara* of thirty-three English inches in Mexico, and the latter, which are sold here at eight cents per yard, being worth in Mexico about twenty cents per yard.

The same exactly happens with almost everything else produced in Mexico as compared with this country.   I have built houses in both countries, and by personal experience I can assure that substantially the same house will cost in the United States about one-third of what it costs in Mexico, notwithstanding that the wages of bricklayers, carpenters, and other mechanics employed in building a house are very much lower there than they are here.[1]

It is a well-known principle that the fewer the hands employed in the manufacturing of a commodity, the less will be the cost of such commodity.   If in manufacturing a commodity a skilled man can do in a factory the work requiring five men in another, the former factory will need a much smaller building to accommodate its operatives than the latter, and that implies a large saving of expense, not only in constructing its buildings, in heating, lighting, cleaning, and repairing them, but also in insurance, taxes, etc., the difference being so great that the smaller building can afford to produce the same commodity at a much lower rate than the larger building, independently of the amount paid in wages.

[1] These facts, in my opinion, support Mr. John Richards's theory on wages, as laid down in his book, *The Law of Wages, the Rate and Amount*, in which he asserts that wages are controlled by certain principles uniform all over the world, and that wages could not be high or low from any other cause than the efficiency of workmen, the implements they employ, and what they produce.   He naturally makes a distinction between the amount of wages and the rate of wages, showing that the amount does not depend upon the rate.   By amount of wages he designates that part of the cost of commodities which is paid for labor.   By rate of wages he designates the rate per day, week, or month, paid to workmen for their services.   He appears to prove that a high tariff and dear material do not produce high wages, as is the general belief, and that the labor cost of products is less in this than in any other country.   He sets forth the following principles :

First.—All manufactured articles of every kind are made up of three elements or components, namely : material, wages, and expenses.

Second.—All staple articles of manufacture, such as enter into the world's trade, must have a nearly uniform value or international value.

Third.—The amount of wages entering into the cost of manufactured commodities is also nearly uniform, irrespective of the rate of wages paid for their production.

I believe that the preceding facts show beyond all doubt that unless there is a material change in the present conditions of Mexico, there need be no fear of competition in the United States from Mexican manufactures or agricultural or mining products obtained by us with cheap labor.

One reason why Mexican products were so high was that before they reached the markets they had to pay the local duty called alcabala, levied in coming into the cities. Unfortunately, the internal commerce of Mexico was not free, as in the United States, where such freedom has contributed very much, in my opinion, to the marvellous prosperity of the people. Our Constitution of 1857 prescribed the abolition, from the first of July, 1858, of the interior duties and custom-houses throughout the country, but it was not until recently that this measure could be carried out. Since the first of July, 1895, commerce in Mexico is as free as in the United States, the interior duties and custom-houses having been abolished.

Use of Modern Implements and Machinery by Mexicans.—I have often heard the remark made by public men of the United States, also contained in Mr. Foster's report of October 9, 1878, to Mr. Carlisle Mason, President of the Manufacturers' Association of Chicago, that the Mexicans were generally opposed to the use of agricultural implements, and I considered this an error arising from want of sufficient knowledge of the Mexican laborer.[1] As the Mexican people have not

Fourth.—The rate of wages depends mainly upon what workmen produce, varying with efficiency of labor and cost of material and expense.

Mr. Richards asserts that prices are subject to general principles which tend to make them uniform, and that it would not be possible to have high wages in a country while others paid low ones, because labor from the latter countries would flow to the former and establish the proper level, and he further states that if the rate of wages is lower in some countries, it is because workmen produce there less than in others.

Long before I read Mr. Richards's book, I had come to adopt views similar to his, although they did not occur to me exactly in the same manner in which he presents them in his book.

[1] Mr. Foster's report was communicated to Mr. Evarts, Secretary of State of the United States, on October 9, 1878, and published among "Papers relating to Foreign Relations of the United States, Transmitted to Congress with the Annual Message of the President of December 2, 1878," pp. 636–654. This report, which in my opinion contains several serious mistakes concerning Mexico, compelled me to write, as Secretary of the Treasury of that country, an official and full answer to the same, dated January 15, 1879, addressed to our Department of State, for the purpose of rectifying Mr. Foster's mistakes, and explaining points which were not made sufficiently clear in his report. My answer, entitled "Report of the Secretary of Finance of the United States of Mexico of the 15th of January, 1879, on the Actual Condition of Mexico, and the Increase of Commerce with the United States, Rectifying the Report of the Hon. John W. Foster, Envoy Extraordinary and Minister Plenipotentiary of the United States in Mexico, the 9th of October, 1878, to Mr. Carlisle Mason, President of the Manufacturers' Association of the City of Chicago, in the State of Illinois, of the United States of America," was published in English in New York in 1890, in a book in quarto of 325 pages, and was freely circulated in this country.

used machinery or implements for hundreds of years, not only because most of them have been invented or applied only recently, but because the cheapness of labor there made them unnecessary in many cases, it is natural that they should not have shown a preference for their use. Some have, besides, the fear, natural in ignorant men, that the use of machinery might diminish the number of hands employed on the farms or in industries, and that therefore a great many of them might be left without employment. But this is a natural feeling, prevailing not only in Mexico, but in every other country. Whenever the Mexican people have seen, however, that the use of machinery or implements diminishes their labor, not only without destroying, but, on the contrary, rather increasing their wages, they have shown themselves as willing to use them as any people in the world, and so far as their ability to handle them is concerned, they are second to none. A proof of this is the fact that we have now in Mexico quite a large number of cotton and woollen mills and other manufacturing plants using improved machinery and worked entirely by Mexican hands. A Mexican laborer may not be so expert as one from this country in attending to several looms at the same time, but he is quite competent to attend to a few, and in the course of time his ability will be developed, and he will be able to do whatever anyone else can do.

One of the reasons why agricultural machinery has not been more used in Mexico is a very simple one, which I know by personal experience, as I myself was engaged in agricultural pursuits for some years. I believe it is a fact well known to farmers and also to manufacturers in this country that agricultural machines and implements have to vary according to the conditions of the soil, that is, not only in accordance with the heaviness or lightness of the soil, but with the topographical position of the ground. It must be considered whether it is level, undulating, or hilly; whether stumps remain in the ground or whether it has been cultivated for some time, and so is entirely free from them; whether stones are or are not mixed with the vegetable earth; and implements which work well in soil possessing certain conditions, may be utterly useless in other ground having different conditions, requiring perhaps only some slight changes to adapt them to a different soil. When an order is sent to the United States for agricultural implements or machinery, sufficient care is not taken to explain the conditions of the ground, and the manufacturer may send—and does so frequently—articles which are utterly useless when they arrive at their destination. I myself found that my invoices of machinery and agricultural implements were often entirely useless, doubtless because they were not adapted to the condition of the soil to which they were applied.

Another objection to the extensive use of agricultural machinery and implements in Mexico—which is also serious, but easily overcome —is that not everywhere are there shops to repair them or replace broken pieces; therefore, when a spring, a screw, or any other part of a machine, no matter how insignificant it may be, is broken or out of order, the whole machine is thrown away because it is no longer of any use, so causing the loss of a large amount of money; and when these reasons are taken into consideration, and especially when the lack of acquaintance of the Mexican laborers with such machines and implements and the lowness of their wages are considered, it will not appear surprising that they are not much used in that country. But the field there is a very large one, and one whose importance increases every day, and I have no doubt that the time will come, especially if due care is taken by manufacturers in this country to understand the special needs of each locality in supplying them with machines and implements manufactured in this country, when that trade will be very valuable, and it is already becoming so.

It will be seen that these difficulties could not be appreciated by a tourist who only spends a few days or weeks in Mexico, and comes back saying that the Mexicans are utterly incompetent and unwilling to handle agricultural machinery and implements, or implements of any kind; or by United States representatives living in cities where they have no opportunity to come into close contact with the farming element, and only report what they may hear and occasionally see in their excursions from those cities.

Mexican Wages and Silver.—The impression generally prevails in this country that Mexican wages are reduced to one-half of their old amount in consequence of the depreciation of silver, reasoning that if wages were twenty-five cents a day, for instance, when silver was on a par with gold at the ratio of 16 to 1, now that it has declined about one hundred per cent., wages of twenty-five cents in silver are equivalent to about twelve and a half cents in gold, and that wages not having increased in the same proportion that silver has depreciated, the result must be that they have been reduced to one-half. This is a mistaken conclusion.[1] In an article which I published in the *North*

---

[1] This assertion is confirmed by the following statement in Mr. Crittenden's report on the currency, prices and condition of labor in Mexico, dated September 1st, 1896, and sent to the State Department and published in the *Special Consular Report*, vol. xiii., Part I, already referred to :

"Wages of unskilled labor has been almost unaffected by the premium on gold. The great stimulation of all enterprises, the building of thousands of miles of railroads, the establishment of numerous factories, and the bringing under cultivation of thousands of acres of land, has given employment to a vast number of men. This, of course, has had its effect in raising wages and bettering the condition of the laboring classes, at the same time reducing the revolutionary spirit that heretofore had great sway in this country. It has been a most difficult matter to make this roving class of

American Review, of June, 1895, I explained the results of the silver standard in Mexico, and showed that the purchasing power of the silver dollar remains there the same as it was when silver was on a par with gold, in so far as Mexican commodities and services are concerned, and that prices have only increased somewhat for imported articles, or for such Mexican products as have their prices regulated in foreign markets. I refer, therefore, the reader to that article, which will be found in this volume, and here I will only say that within the boundaries of Mexico there has been no such thing as a depreciation in silver, as silver has maintained its old level with regard to commodities. It purchases as much now as it did before its decline in value relative to gold began. It pays for as much labor as before, and in the hands of the laborer it purchases as much of the necessaries of life. It is only in connection with imports that the premium on gold or the decline in silver has caused an advance in price.[1] But the laboring population purchase little that is imported, and so whether imported goods cost more or not is of little or no consequence to persons of that class. In many cases even the price of imported articles has not enhanced, notwithstanding the depreciation of silver.[2]

people, by whom this country is largely populated, think and believe that prosperity and plenty only come with peace; now that they understand, with but few exceptions they are thoroughly contented."

[1] Mr. Crittenden says on the subject in the report just quoted as follows:

"Their value has in no way been affected by the rise and fall of silver. As to imported luxuries and fineries, they are, when the difference in the price of silver is taken into consideration, more expensive now than in 1873. The increased railroad facilities and cheapness of transportation have been more than offset by increased duties, stamp tax, rent, and clerk hire. However, the consumption and use of imported articles is limited almost entirely to the rich and travelled natives and foreigners. Finally, it can be generally proven that the cost of living and wearing apparel of the native was as low, and in many cases lower, in 1873 than at the present time."

[2] This assertion appears fully corroborated by the following interview of ex-Consul Crittenden, published by the *Star*, Kansas City, Mo., May 2, 1895:

"People who go from Kansas City to Old Mexico almost invariably buy supplies of clothing there and come back to tell how much cheaper goods can be bought in the City of Mexico than in any American city. This has occurred so often that Consul-General Crittenden, who is at home on a brief leave of absence, was asked yesterday for an explanation:

"'Such a condition exists,' he said, 'but the explanation is yet to be found. The Mexican dollar is worth about fifty-two cents in American money, but I can buy just as good gloves for $1.50, Mexican money, in Old Mexico, as I can buy anywhere in America for $1.50, American money. On one of my trips here I wore a very good suit of clothes, made to order in a very satisfactory manner, which cost me just $12 in the Mexican capital. You can get an elegant suit of clothes made to order there, in the best style, for $35, Mexican money. Shoes that cost $5 a pair here, bring $3 a pair there, no matter whether they were made in Paris or in Mexico. A very

Very many believe that the low rate of wages in Mexico is due to the depreciation of silver, and those professing this opinion are very much mistaken, because when, thirty years ago, silver was at a par and even at a premium with gold at the ratio of 16 to 1, the wages in Mexico were lower than they are now, and the Mexican laborer was not so well off as he is to-day.

To make a proper investigation about the condition of the Mexican laborers in connection with the money standard, it would be necessary to extend that investigation to gold countries such as Spain, Italy, Germany, Turkey, etc., etc., so as to see to what extent the money standard affects the prosperity of the working classes. I think that the standard of money has very little to do with the condition of labor. The silver standard has nothing to do with their reward; they would earn no more, in proportion, were the country on a gold basis. In fact, tens of thousands of them would be out of employment by reason of the impossibility of competing with the workers of gold-standard countries.

Under the operation of the gold standard farm labor received three times as much in one part of the Union as it did in another part, as is shown by the above-quoted publication of the Agricultural Department, entitled, " Wages of Farm Labor of the United States." The

large proportion of the shoes sold in that country come from France. They seem to be as good as ours, although I do not like the fit quite so well, and I usually buy my shoes here. What seems remarkable to me is that goods of American manufacture sell for less in Mexico than in the United States. My wife does most of the buying, and from her I learn that she can buy the finest silk underwear—she bought some for me recently—for 25 per cent. less in Mexico than in this country. I understand, too, that the Jaeger underwear is much cheaper there than in American cities. I don't pretend to account for it. The goods are made in New York and they pay a high duty, certainly not less than 25 per cent. ad valorem, in the Mexican ports of entry.

" ' My wife gets the very finest Irish linen for fifty cents a yard in Old Mexico. In fact, we buy everything in the clothing line, except shoes, in Mexico, in preference to buying here, as goods are so much cheaper there.

" ' The Mexicans are very fond of jewelry, and get it very much cheaper than we do. There are jewelry stores in the City of Mexico finer than any that I ever saw in an American city. Last winter one of the Lucases of St. Louis—James Lucas, I believe—made a trip around the world, and finally reached the City of Mexico. His daughter was with him. While in Paris the young woman saw a very fine gold watch, which she wanted. The price there was $225 in American money, and her father decided not to buy it. When they reached Mexico she saw an exact duplicate of the watch she had seen in Paris, and again asked her father to buy it. They inquired the price and found that it was $225 in Mexican money, or just half the price asked by the Paris jeweler. Mr. Lucas offered his check for it and referred the jeweler to me. Now, why such a piece of jewelry should be sold in Mexico for half the price asked in Paris I don't know, nor can I explain why American-made goods should sell for less there than in St. Louis or Kansas City, but it is a fact. The Mexicans are shrewd buyers, for one thing, and our jobbers and merchants desire big profits. That is the only explanation of the matter that I know.' "

fact that wages paid in each State were ascertained by averages, shows that the difference between the best-paid labor and the poorest-paid labor is still greater.   That report also shows that in the United States Caucasian farm labor receives more than three times as much as the same labor receives in Germany, although both countries have a gold standard and a protective tariff.   Between 1816 and 1834 England had a gold standard and the United States had a double standard, with silver as the money in common use, and laboring men were better off here than in England.   Turkey is one of the gold-standard nations, and Japan, until recently, coined silver at a ratio almost identical to that of the United States, and yet the progress of Japan was really remarkable. All this shows that silver is not the cause of the low wages of Mexico.

Transportation in Mexico.—In the paper entitled " Geographical and Statistical Notes on Mexico " (pages 9, 53, and 154), I have dwelt upon the impediments to commerce and the consequent reduction in proportion caused by the high cost of transportation in Mexico, be-fore railroads were built, in consequence of the broken surface of that country, and upon the results of such conditions which prevented any article from being profitably exported, unless raised near the coast or unless it had a very high price and small bulk, like precious metals, these facts reducing the exports of Mexico practically to the precious metals, indigo, cochineal, and similar articles of high price and small bulk.   The final consequence of such a condition of things was, there-fore, to reduce the production to the amount necessary for local con-sumption, and as a consequence of this to establish different prices for the same article, varying according to the distances it had to be trans-ported, establishing in this manner a monopoly to the local production for local consumption.

Merchandise could not be transported from one place to another at any distance in Mexico without increasing the cost very largely. Sugar, for instance, which in some localities was produced at the cost of one cent a pound, was sold in others at twenty-five cents a pound. Such a condition of things reduced the consumption and consequently the production within very narrow limits, and very often a year's abundant crops was a calamity to the farmers, as the abundance of products without an increase of consumption caused a great fall in prices.   Under such circumstances the wages paid to the field laborers had necessarily to be low; and although they now begin to improve with the greater demand for labor brought about by the construction of railroads, and the consequent development of the country's natural resources, they are yet far from being what is to be desired, and what I am sure they will be before long.

Even now, when Mexico had, on October 31, 1897, in operation 6,731.30 miles of railways, and when the depreciation in the value of silver has established a bounty of over one hundred per cent. on the exportation of commodities, the proportion during the fiscal year ended June 30, 1896, was $64,838,596 of precious metals, and $40,178,306 of commodities, the precious metals amounting to sixty-one per cent. of the total exports, and the total amount exported from Mexico during the last fiscal year ended June 30, 1897, was $111,346,494.

Cost of Living in Mexico.—It is time now to speak of the prices of Mexican commodities and to compare them with such as are produced here. Our Department of Public Works has been for some time collecting data concerning the prices of agricultural products in Mexico, and during the visit I made to the capital of the Republic, in 1891, I obtained a *résumé* of such data, which I give below, reducing the weights and measures used in Mexico to the same standard as those used in this country, and stating the price of each article in each country.

It has been very difficult to make this table, for the complete accuracy of which I cannot vouch, notwithstanding that I have used much care and availed myself of all the means within my reach to make it as complete as possible; but the difficulty of obtaining the average price of certain articles in both countries is very great, and also the reduction to a common standard of the weights and measures used in each. So far as commodities in the United States are concerned, I have taken as the basis for fixing their price the data contained in No. 12 of the Statistical Abstract of the United States for the year 1889, prepared by the Bureau of Statistics, under the direction of the Secretary of the Treasury, and sent by him to the House of Representatives on the 4th of December of the same year. In regard to such commodities as were not embraced in that document, I have used the data contained in the thirty-second annual report of the Chamber of Commerce of the City of New York for the fiscal year 1889–90, and in the report of the Produce Exchange of New York for the same period, and such other data as I have been able to obtain from reliable sources.

PRICES OF WEARING APPAREL IN 1896.

ARTICLES.	MEXICAN CURRENCY.	UNITED STATES CURRENCY.
Flannel (54 inches wide) ....per vara [1]..	$1.00	$0.51
Gingham (26 inches wide). ....do.....	$0.20 to .25	$0.10 to .13
Ordinary cassimere (52 inches wide)........do.....	1.75	.90
Prints and calicoes (33 inches wide)........do.....	.18¾	.10
Complete suit of woollen clothes, the cheapest........	10.00	5.10
Bleaching blouses.............................	1.50	.77
Pantaloons, cheap.............................	1.50	.77
Woollen hats.................................	1.50 to 25.00	.77 to 12.75
Straw hats...................................	.50	.26

[1] Vara equals 33 inches.

AVERAGE PRICES OF COMMODITIES IN MEXICO AND THE UNITED STATES IN 1891.

ARTICLES.	PRICES IN MEXICO.	PRICES IN THE UNITED STATES.
Bacon	50c. per lb.	20c. per lb.
Beeves	8c. per lb. gross weight.	4½ per lb. gross weight.
Coal	$16 per ton.	$3.18 per ton.
Coffee	22c. per lb.	19c. per lb.
Corn	2c. per lb.	⅘c. per lb., or 43c. per bushel of 56 lbs.
Cotton prints	10½c. per yard.	3⅘c. per yard.
Cottons	19c. per lb.	10c. per lb.
Flour	5c. per lb.	1½c. per lb., or $2.75 per bbl. of 196 lbs.
Ham	50c. per lb.	18c. per lb.
Hogs (alive)	9c. per lb. gross weight.	3¾c. per lb. gross weight.
Iron, pig	$32 per ton.	$19 per ton.
Lard	18c. per lb.	8⅓c. per lb.
Meats:		
Beef	12c. per lb.	7c. per lb.
Mutton	14c. per lb.	8¼c. per lb.
Pork	11c. per lb.	5¾c. per lb.
Paper, printing	15c. per lb.	5c. per lb.
Prints	8½c. per yard.	6¼c. per yard.
Rice	7c. per lb.	5c. per lb.
Salt	7c. per lb.	4c. per lb.
Sheep	9c. per lb. gross weight.	5c. per lb. gross weight.
Sugar	21c. per lb.	5c. per lb.
Tallow	15c. per lb.	4⅗c. per lb.
Tobacco	24c. per lb.	6¼c. per lb.
Wheat	3c. per lb.	1⅖c. per lb., or 83c. per bushel of 60 lbs.
Whiskey	$16 a cask of 20.0787 galls., or 80c. per gall.; 36c. per gall. in bond.	

RETAIL PRICES OF FOOD PRODUCTS IN THE CITY OF MEXICO.

ARTICLES.		MEXICAN CURRENCY.	UNITED STATES CURRENCY.
Jerked beef	per pound	$0.65	$0 33
Salt fish	do.	.45	.23
Salt pork	do.	$0.32 to .40	$0.16½ to .21
Hams, native	do.	.33	.17½
Hams, imported	do.	.55	.28
Eggs	per dozen	.25	.13¾
Flour, native	per pound	.07	.03
Flour, American	do.	.15	.08
Wheat	per bushel	1.50 to 1.80	.76 to .91
Corn	do.	1.00 to 1.40	.51 to .71
Corn meal, American	per pound	.15	.08
Beans, American	do.	.09	.04½
Beans, Mexican	do.	.07	.03¾
Butter, native	do.	.35 to .50	.18 to .26
Butter, American	do.	.60 to .75	.31 to .37½
Sugar, native (uncut)	do.	.08 to .10	.04¼ to .05

RETAIL PRICES OF FOOD PRODUCTS IN THE CITY OF MEXICO.—*Continued.*

ARTICLES.	MEXICAN CURRENCY.	UNITED STATES CURRENCY.
Sugar, native (cut)....................per pound..	$0.14	$0.07⅛
Sugar, American (refined)................do......	.25	.13
Molasses, native........................per gallon..	1.00	.51
Maple sirup..............................do......	4.00	2.04
Dripped sirup, imported..................do......	8.00	4.08
Salt (table)..........................per pound..	.08	.04½
Coarse salt...............................do......	.03	.01½
Pepper (black)...........................do......	$0.70 to 2.50	$0.35½ to .40¾
Tea, choice...............................do......	1.25 to .80	1.27 to 1.28
Coffee, raw..............................do......	.68	.21
Coffee, roasted and ground...............do......	.60	.31
Kerosene oil, good...................per gallon..	.40	.34⅛

Mr. Ransom's report on money and prices in Mexico, to which I have already alluded, contains a statement of prices in Mexico, and, although I cannot vouch for their correctness, I think it proper to give them here. Mr. Ransom's statements are the following:

RETAIL PRICES OF FOOD PRODUCTS CONSUMED IN MEXICO AND EXPORTED IN 1896.

ARTICLES.	MEXICAN CURRENCY.	UNITED STATES CURRENCY.
Jerked beef..........................per pound..	$0.12 to $0.20	$0.07 to $0.12
Fresh beef (cities)......................do......	.12 to .25	.07 to .13
Fresh beef (ranch).......................do......	.06	.03¼
Fresh pork...............................do......	.15 to .25	.08 to .13
Salt pork................................do......	.25 to .45	.13 to .23
Native hams..............................do......	.40 to .55	.20 to .28
Flour....................................do......	.06 to .10	.03¼ to .04½
Corn:		
Usually..................................do......	.01½	.00¾
Now......................................do......	.04	.02⅕
Native beans.............................do......	.07 to .14	.03½ to .08
Native butter............................do......	.50	.26
Native cheese............................do......	.25 to .55	.13 to .28
Native soap (laundry)....................do......	.08 to .15	.05 to .08
Native sugar (white).....................do......	.08 to .15	.04½ to .08
Native sugar (brown).....................do......	.04 to .08	.02¼ to .04
Coffee (raw).............................do......	.35 to .45	.18 to .23
Irish potatoes...........................do......	.03 to .07	.01¾ to .03¼
Rice.....................................do......	.08 to .10	.04¼ to .05
Lard.....................................do......	.20 to .26	.11 to .13
Kerosene oil........................per gallon..	.60 to .75	.31 to .38
Tea (common)........................per pound..	.50	.26
Tea (good and choice)....................do......	1.50 to 2.00	.76 to 1.02
Molasses (ordinary).................per gallon..	1.00	.57
Wheat:		
Per bushel....................................	1.50	.76
Generally.....................................	1.80	.91

Mr. Crittenden's statement is the following:

PRICES.
WHOLESALE AND RETAIL PRICES OF ARTICLES.
[Where wholesale price is not given, the retail prices can be reckoned on from 15 to 40 per cent. higher.]

ARTICLES.	MEXICAN CURRENCY.	UNITED STATES CURRENCY.
Corned beef..............................	Not used.	
Jerked beef...........................per pound..	$0.65	$0.34
Salted fish................................do......	.45	.235
Salted pork.............................do......	$0.32– .40	$0.166– .208
Ham :		
American..........................do......	.55	.286
American, wholesale..................do......	.42	.218
Mexican...........................do......	.35	.192
Mexican, wholesale..................do......	.27	.14
Eggs...............................per dozen..	.25	.13
Flour :		
American..........................per pound..	.15	.078
Mexican...........................do......	.07	.036
Wheat.............................per bushel..	1.50– 1.80	.78 – .936
Corn (high on account of short crop)........do......	1.50– 1.80	.78 – .936
Corn meal, American.................per pound..	.15	.078
Beans :		
American..........................per pound..	.09	.047
Mexican (frijoles).....................do......	.07	.036
Butter :		
American creamery...................do......	.50– .75	.26 – .39
Mexican, unsalted...................do......	.35– .50	.192– .26
Sugar :		
Foreign .. ..do......	.25	.13
Mexican, uncut.......................do......	.08– .10	.042– .051
Mexican, cut...........................do......	.14	.073
Molasses, ordinary...................per gallon..	1.00	.52
Sirup, maple.............................do......	4.00	2.08
Sirup, imported ....do......	8.00	4.16
Salt :		
Table.............................per pound..	.10	.052
Coarse..............................do......	.03	.016
Pepper..............................do......	.70– .80	.364– .418
Tea................................do......	1.25– 2.50	.65 – 1.306
Coffee, green, retail..................do......	.40	.20
Coffee, ground, retail.................do......	.50	.26
Coffee, wholesale.....................do......	.19– .31	.099– .161
Kerosene .. ..per gallon..	.56– .66	.291– .343
Gasoline...............................do......	.37	.192

PRICES OF MEXICAN MANUFACTURES.

ARTICLES.	WHOLESALE.		RETAIL.	
	Mexican Currency.	United States Currency.	Mexican Currency.	United States Currency.
Flannel, 54 inches wide........per vara[1]..	$0.75	$0.39	$1.00	$0.52
Ginghams, 25 inches wide........do......	$0.18– .20	$0.09 – .104	$0.20– .25	$0.104– .13
Cassimeres, 52 inches wide......do......	1.25– 1.50	.65 – .78	1.75	.91
Prints, 33 inches wide.............do......	.15– .16	.078– .483	.19	.094
Prints, 27 inches wide............do......	.11– .11¾	.057– .058	.13	.067
Sheetings, 66 inches wide.......do......	.28– .30	.145– .156	.32	.166
Shirting, 26 inches wide.........do......	.07– .11	.036– .057	.08– .13	.042– .067

[1] The vara is 33 inches.

WHOLESALE PRICES, CITY OF MEXICO, 1886 AND 1896, MEXICAN
CURRENCY.[1]

ARTICLES.	QUANTITY.	1886.	1896.
	Pounds.		
Olive oil.................................	25	$5.00 to $5.50	$6.00
Beneseed oil...........................	25	3.25	3.50
Linseed oil.............................	25	2.75	5.00
Cotton..................................	1	.18 to .19	.18
Rice.....................................	100	6.50 to 7.00	$8.00 to 10.00
Sugar (uncut)...........................	25	2.17 to 2.25	1.68 to 1.81
Coffee..................................	100	11.00	29.00
Barley..................................	300	3.50	4.50
Beans...................................	300	13.00	14.00 to 15.00
Peas	300	14.00 to 15.00	11.00 to 17.00
Flour....................................	25	1.31	1.00 to 1.09
Ham	25	5.00 to 5.50	5.00 to 6.00
Corn	300	5.50	7.50
Piloncillo	300	7.50 to 8.00	8.25 to 8.50
Cheese..................................	25	5.25	6.00 to 6.50
Salt	25	.62 to .66	.56 to .88
Tallow..................................	25	4.25	3.50
Tobacco	25	3.50 to 4.25	6.50 to 7.50
Wheat...................................	300	11.25 to 11.50	11.00 to 12.50

On account of its natural conditions, the cost of living in Mexico
is considerably cheaper than in the United States[2]; and, taking into
consideration that the Mexican dollar has not lost any of its purchasing

[1] Expressed in United States currency will be about one-half in 1896, but in 1886
the Mexican dollar was valued by the United States Mint at 81.7 cents.

[2] In the report that Mr. Thomas T. Crittenden, while he was U. S. Consul-General to the City of Mexico, sent to the New York *Journal*, dated at the City of Mexico,
on September 4, 1896, he stated on this subject the following, published by that paper
in its issue of September 17, 1896 :

" *Cost of Living in Mexico.*—As to the cost of living in Mexico, I find it in many
respects much cheaper than in the United States. The manner of life made possible,
and even necessary, by the climatic conditions simplifies the problem. Fuel, for instance, so considerable an item of expense in the North, is an unimportant feature
here. I doubt if many families expend so much as $15 per year each for their char-
coal. The average expense for fuel for the better classes is about $1.25 per week.
The use of fires for heating alone is almost unknown. Meats and fatty foods of whatever kind, heavy woollen clothing and other items, absolutely indispensable to life and
comfort in Northern climates, are not needed here ; on the contrary, they are even
detrimental to health. In general, I find living in the City of Mexico about as reasonable as at my home in Kansas City. There are many articles that enter into home
consumption that are much higher, especially those not grown or produced in Mexico,
but when those are considered the costs average quite well. Servants are much
cheaper, and when good ones are obtained they are as serviceable and more contented,
seldom leaving the premises and never complaining of the work. Hotel and board-
ing-house rates are about the same in Mexican money as they are in the United States
in American coin. I have heard tourists say they could get meals here as good and
cheaper than in cities in the United States."

power for domestic commodities, Mexican wages go considerably farther than the same amount would go in the United States.

The cost of living, that is, of food, clothing, house-rent, and everything else that enters into the daily life of a workingman, differs so greatly in the two countries that the only comparison possible to make intelligently is one between the present conditions in Mexico and those existing ten or fifteen years ago, in the matter of the income and the expenses representing the cost of living, and the opportunity of earning such living. The cost of livelihood in Mexico for the working classes has not materially increased during that time, while the wages have increased considerably.

During the discussion which preceded the last Presidential election Mexico was on the tapis, and the opinions expressed on the subject of prices of commodities were of a very contradictory nature. Sometimes the price of Mexican commodities was represented as exceedingly high, and therefore beyond the reach of the poorer classes, and when compared with similar commodities in the United States it showed the great advantage that this country had in producing cheaply the necessaries of life. That reason was alleged when it was intended to show that the silver standard in Mexico raised the price of commodities and made the country wretchedly poor. At the same time, when commodities were cheaper in Mexico than in the United States, that fact was presented to show that labor was very badly remunerated in that country, a result which was also attributed to the silver standard prevailing there.

Therefore, whatever might be the result of a comparison of prices between the two countries, it always was unfavorable to Mexico. If commodities were cheaper there than in the United States it showed that labor was very badly remunerated, and it was presented as the cause of the so-called pauper or peon labor prevailing there. If, on the contrary, commodities were there higher than in the United States, that was supposed to be the result of the silver standard, which made everything higher and reduced considerably the purchasing power of the low wages of Mexican laborers. This very fact shows the fallacy of such doctrines. Such comparisons are not fair, because some commodities which are comparatively cheap here and could not be easily obtained in Mexico had to be imported from the United States, paying for them in gold, besides heavy import duties, and that made them, of course, exceedingly high there; while other commodities which were easily raised in Mexico were considerably lower than they could be obtained in this country, and that reasoning did not prove, therefore, what it was intended to show.

Several comparisons have been recently made in this regard between Mexico and the United States that are very disparaging to the former, but, as I have just stated, domestic commodities in Mexico have not increased in price since the depreciation of silver, excepting those that, like coffee, have their price regulated in foreign markets, but which are not very much used by the poorer classes. So far as foreign commodities are concerned, of course they have almost duplicated their value, because they have to be paid in gold.

Report of Labor Assembly.—The labor question in Mexico was so earnestly agitated during the last Presidential election in the United States that the Chicago Trade and Labor Assembly, desiring reliable information on the subject, sent to Mexico a special committee of two, Mr. Paul J. Maas, who organized the American Confederation of Labor, and Mr. Patrick Enright, of the Executive Board of the Moulders' Union, for the purpose of examining the question on the spot, and that committee presented a report on October 10, 1896,[1] which was widely circulated in this country, and taken as a conclusive proof of the bad results of the silver standard in Mexico, so far as the laboring classes were concerned. That report, however, failed to present the question in a proper light, for the reason that the gentlemen who made it did not know enough of Mexico to fully comprehend what they saw, and they did not remain long enough there for that purpose.

The report of these gentlemen shows their good faith and their

---

[1] I quote the following extract from that report, which shows how much the gentlemen who made it misunderstood Mexico:

" Wages in Mexico, except to skilled and steady mechanics—always foreigners—are very low. On railroads engineers (Americans) on passenger trains receive $210 per month, while the firemen (Mexicans) receive $1.85 per day ; freight engineers (Americans), $250 per month ; firemen (Mexicans), $1.50 to $1.75 per day ; passenger conductors (Americans), $160 per month ; brakemen (Mexicans), $1.50 per day ; freight conductors (Americans), $200 per month ; brakemen (Mexicans), $57 to $63 per month ; Pullman conductors, $80 per month (American money), and the porters, $38 per month (American money), with $5 per month extra for being able to talk Spanish. The national soldiers (or regular army) of Mexico, called rurales, and who are all ex-bandits, receive $1 per day. In a broom factory near the depot at Jimenez the men are paid 50 cents, and women and children 25 to 37½ cents per day. In the cotton mills, cotton-seed oil mills, and soap factory at Torreon men are paid 37½ to 50 cents, and women and children 25 cents per day. A cargador (public carrier) has a rate of 12½ cents per hour, but you can hire him for from 25 to 37½ cents per day.

" At Leon, where nearly all the leather goods in Mexico are manufactured, the peon gets his leather cut for shoes, harness, or other goods to be made by him, and takes the material to his hut, where the whole family assists him, the same as in the sweatshops of Chicago. For making shoes he receives $1 and upward per dozen pairs ; on the other leather goods he receives 37½ to 50 cents per day for his labors, working as long as daylight lasts, averaging twelve to fourteen hours per day. Common laborers can be hired for 18 to 50 cents per day. House servants, male or female, receive $3 to $5 per month and board themselves. In or near cities peons live in adobe houses and pay a rental of $3 a year for the ground that the house stands on. When leaving this for another location all ' improvements ' the peon has made go to the landlord, or owner of the land, who pays no taxes whatever on the land."

earnest purpose to present fairly the condition of the Mexican work-men, but they seem to have gone to Mexico with a very exalted idea of the condition of the Mexican wage-earner, imagining that it might rival the situation of his fellow-workman in the United States. This was a complete delusion, as there cannot be any comparison between the two; and when they found the true condition of the Mexican workman, they concluded that the American workingman was a prince in comparison with his Mexican brother—a conclusion which I do not consider very far wrong. Their principal mistake, however, was to attribute to the silver standard in Mexico the poor condition of the Mexican workman. If they had been in Mexico when silver was on a par with gold, at the ratio of 16 to 1, that is, when the Mexican dollar had one hundred cents of gold value in silver bullion, they would have found that the Mexican workman was then a great deal worse than he is now, when the Mexican dollar has less than fifty cents of the gold value of silver in it, and they would have come to more just conculsions.

While they understood some matters in Mexico tolerably well, as when they said, for instance, that there was greater security to life and property in that country than in the City of Chicago, they made serious mistakes in others, as when they stated that all transactions were made in cash, when, as a matter of fact, all mercantile operations of any consequence are made on credit; and long credit, too, as credit is the basis of both the foreign and internal trade in Mexico; and as when they said that it is but five years since a law was passed in the City of Mexico compelling men to wear trousers; with many other almost laughable mistakes to point out, which would take too long and would divert me from my principal object in this paper.

I will consider in the two following chapters of this paper, two of the main objections that the committee made to the Mexican laborer.

Mexican Labor is not Organized.—It has been observed that Mexican labor is not organized, and this assertion is entirely correct. I have no doubt that in the course of time Mexican labor will be properly organized, and that then it will enjoy all the benefits of organization; and while I recognize that organization is a very great advantage to the laboring man as long as he does not become the instrument of unscrupulous persons who occasionally are at the head of such organizations, they so far have met with serious objections in this country, and it is yet the problem how this matter will turn out, there being great probability that the present conditions of labor and capital may suffer material changes.[1]

It is hardly possible for the present that organized labor will be

[1] The danger that the working people will take active steps to change the present conditions of labor appears very plain from the following extract from one of Mr. Henry George's books, a man remarkable for his rare character of simplicity and devotion to duty :

able to dominate the industrial situation to enforce its demands against associated capital which has the entire industrial plant under its control. Socialists believe that the large monopolies which have grown up in the last few years are but the pioneers of their system of a better economical organization of industries, whereby products will be cheapened, enabling everyone to live in comfort. The trusts say they do away with waste and with reckless competition, and the socialists are with them in this. But those who are watching the great social and political movement in the United States cannot venture to predict how huge labor unions and the industrial monopolies are going to find common ground to stand on. It is hardly possible that they can work out a scheme to operate in harmony.

Very many prominent men in this country believe that a great change in social conditions is coming, that labor will have to be given a larger share in the profits of organized industry as the only means of preventing an upheaval of society by the accumulating forces of discontent. Some wealthy men seem to be looking forward to some inevitable readjustment of conditions and are striving to enlist the thinking workingmen with them in the development of a plan for the betterment of the condition of the masses of the people.[1]

" Near the window by which I write a great bull is tethered by a ring in his nose. Grazing, round and round, he has wound his rope about the stake until now he stands a close prisoner, tantalized by rich grass he cannot reach, unable even to toss his head to rid himself of the flies that cluster on his shoulders. Now and again he struggles vainly, and then, after pitiful bellowings, relapses into silent misery. This bull, a very type of massive strength, who, because he has not wit enough to see how he might be free, suffers want in sight of plenty, and is helplessly preyed upon by weaker creatures, seems to me no unfit emblem of the working masses. In all lands men whose toil creates abounding wealth are pinched with poverty, and, while advancing civilization opens wider vistas and awakens new desires, are held down to brutish levels by animal needs. Bitterly conscious of injustice, feeling in their inmost souls that they were made for more than so narrow a life, they, too, spasmodically struggle and cry out. But until they trace effect to cause, until they see how they are fettered and may be freed, their struggles and outcries are as vain as those of the bull. Nay, they are vainer. I shall go out and drive the bull in the way that will untwist his rope. But who shall drive men into freedom? Till they use the reason with which they have been gifted nothing can avail. For them there is no special providence. Under all forms of government the ultimate power lies with the masses. It is not kings nor aristocracies nor landowners nor capitalists that anywhere really enslave the people. It is their own ignorance."

[1] An article in *Gunton's Magazine* for October, 1897, on what workingmen really need, significant as coming from a periodical generally supposed to receive its financial support from some of the millionaires and trust magnates who are seeking to guide the opinion of the laboring men of the country, and to keep them from drifting into the ranks of the Socialists, or enlisting under the single-tax banner of Henry George, is an argument for the raising of the condition of the workingmen by means

I am sure that any ground gained or any change obtained by the laboring classes of the United States will react in Mexico, and that the Mexican laborer will finally share in more or less degree the same advantages gained here.

Trade unionism has been carried to lengths in England never known in any other country in modern times, and employers assert that the evils promoted by it have now become intolerable, and that further submission to its exactions means the destruction of the manufacturing interests and of the immense foreign trade of the country.

The savings-banks were established with the idea of assisting working people and encouraging them to save as much money as they could, giving them the opportunity to invest it profitably.

The evil that underlies the present savings-banks everywhere is that the money of the depositors is not employed lucratively. Everywhere is a glut of deposits in the other banks, and they have invaded the domain which once belonged exclusively to the savings-banks. In Mexico City the three principal banks have on deposit more than one hundred million dollars, the owners of which wanted to lend upon first mortgage to any amount at seven per cent. The National Bank alone has from ten to twelve millions in specie of its own for which it can find no use, and naturally cannot assist its depositors in their search

of the organization of labor in trades unions, the only form of " trust " possible for those who have merely their skill and labor to sell for wages :

" The writer says : ' The great fact about the whole matter is that the material progress of labor can be achieved only as wages rise, and prices, through the use of improved methods of production, decline. Nothing can be of real service to labor which does not promote one or the other of these movements. The single tax will not do it. Socialism will not do it. Whatever will create among laborers new desires, habits, and tastes, new demands for comforts and refinements, new ambitions for higher individual and social life, strong enough to make them organize to enforce these demands, will do it. Starting from this basis, we find a wide range of benificent influences which can be utilized to our end. Clean and well-lighted streets, public parks and baths, model tenements and good sanitation will promote discontent with vile conditions of home life. Free museums, libraries, and art galleries will instill a higher range of tastes and wants. Kindergartens and ample school facilities will do the same. A shorter working day will give the rest and leisure necessary for an adequate home and social life."

Continuing, Mr. Gunton remarks : " Public policies which encourage the increase of manufacturing industries will thereby promote the growth of towns and cities, and thus give the environment so necessary to the operation of high-wage forces. Trades unions offer the medium through which these forces can be centralized and brought to bear upon the industrial situation with a power and effectiveness which cannot be resisted." . . .

Still another distinctively Socialistic device is adopted by Mr. Gunton, who remarks that " labor insurance will remove the necessity of rigid self-denial and parsimony through all the years when men should be enjoying the full benefit of their earnings, and taking advantage of those opportunities which disappear as age comes on."

for a form of investment that is exceedingly limited. Of course these banks offered the Monte de Piedad [1] all the money it could use at three per cent., and the depositors in its own savings-banks suffered accordingly. If the saving habit had been developed in the Mexican working man this would have been a terrible blow, but, unfortunately, he has not yet arrived at that point. He is still wasting his daily dollar, confident that he will earn another to-morrow, but forgetting that he will not always be young and strong, agile, clear-sighted, and of steady nerve.

We must create the saving habit by tempting the well-paid Mexican workingman to save. This can easily be done by inverting the action of the Monte de Piedad, which created a savings-bank to furnish it with cheap capital for its business. What is wanted is a universal system of savings-banks throughout the Republic of Mexico, whose deposits will be used for lending upon pledges at the French and Belgian rates for the profit of the depositors. This is a new departure, but it is the old wholesome law of mutuality which has proved so successful. This system is known in Europe as the Scotch bank, where all the profits of banking above expenses and working capital go to the depositors.

Feast Days in Mexico.—The Catholic clergy of Mexico encouraged the custom of having a great many feast days, which were, besides, very profitable to the church. Over one-third of the year, not counting the Sabbath, was given up to religious festivals, during which all work was stopped. So objectionable were the results of this system that, when, in 1858, the laws of reform were enacted separating the church from the state, the feast days were reduced by law to a very limited number —about six only in the year; but, as happens with all legislation in conflict with the actual habits of the people, the law has not been faithfully complied with, more especially because it does not provide any punishment for the offenders. This fact makes foreigners in Mexico consider native labor unreliable.

Immigration from the United States into Mexico.—It has been also stated that the condition of things in Mexico would not warrant the emigration to it of citizens of this country. To be sure, I would not advise anybody without capital or who is not an expert workman to go there, because he certainly could not compete with native labor; but to those having small fortunes and willing to put up with the inconveniences and discomforts of a new and foreign country, Mexico offers a field for profitable labor and investment hardly to be equalled anywhere else.

If the laborer in the United States goes to Mexico and drawing the same pay in silver as he did in gold, goes down to live in the same style and on the same food as the native laborer, occupying the same class of

[1] A national establishment to loan money to the poor, at low rate of interest.

position or work, he will find it cheaper than in the United States, but to go to Mexico to eat the same food, to wear similar clothes, and have the same comforts as in the States, he will require two silver dollars for every one dollar received in the United States, and then be worse off in that he has no society and no pleasures.

Not to repeat what I have stated on this subject, I refer the reader who would like to know more fully my views about emigrating to Mexico to the chapter on " Immigration from the United States," in the paper entitled " Geographical and Statistical Notes on Mexico," pages 125 to 129.

Conclusion.—I should be very glad if the explanations made in this article result in dispelling some of the errors prevailing in this country in regard to the conditions of labor in Mexico; and I hope that, in case restrictions against Mexican trade are discussed, they will not be urged on the ground that our articles are produced with peon labor. I sincerely hope that both countries, instead of acting in a manner contrary to the ends of nature, which has placed the one beside the other, and has given them different climates, productions, and possibilities, will co-operate with the purpose of nature, and not interpose other obstacles to reciprocal trade than those that are absolutely necessary for their mutual well-being and progress.

APPENDIX No. 1.

The following tables of wages paid in Mexico are taken from Mr. Ransom's report on *Money and Prices in Mexico*, dated at the City of Mexico on September 26, 1896:

WAGES PAID IN THE CITY OF MEXICO IN 1896.

[Per day, except when otherwise stated.]

	MEXICAN CURRENCY.			UNITED STATES CURRENCY.		
Day laborers [1].....................	$0.25, $0.37 to	$0.67		$0.08, $0.12½ to $0.34		
Blacksmiths [1]......................	.75, 1.25 to	1.50		.63	to	.76
Carpenters (ordinary)...............	1.25 to	1.50		.62	to	.76
Carpenters (foremen)...............	2.50 to	5.00		1.27	to	2.25
Printers :						
Pressmen.....................		1.50		.76		
Job printers..................		1.25		.62		
Compositors..................		1.43		.72		
Engravers.........................	5.00 to	10.00		2.25	to	5.50
Masons...........................	.75, 1.00 to	1.50		.57	to	.76
Bricklayers.......................	1.00 to	1.50		.51	to	.76
Iron workers......................	2.00 to	2.50		1.02	to	1.28
Private coachmen........per month..	15.00 to	25.00		7.65	to 12.25	
Public coachmen.............do....		10.00		5.50		
Policemen...................do....	30.00 to	50.00		15.30	to 25.50	
Wagon drivers....................		1.25		.62		
Butchers..........................		1.50		.76		
Shoemakers.......................	1.00 to	1.25		.62		
Laborers in factories..............	.40, .63 to	1.00		.31	to	.51
Skilled mechanics.................		5.00		2.25		
Plumbers.........................	2.00 to	2.50		1.02	to	1.27
Miners...........................	.40, .60 to	1.00		.31	to	.56
Skilled miners....................	1.00 to	1.50		.51	to	.71
Furnace men, smelters............	1.00 to	1.50		.51	to	.76
Section men on railroads........	.50 to	.62		.26	to	.31
Section foremen..................	1.00 to	1.50		.51	to	.76
Train masters..........per month..	150.00 to 175.00			....		
Tailors :						
Repairers.....................	1.00 to	1.25		.51	to	.63
Coat makers..........per coat..	5.00 to	12.00		2.55	to	6.10
Vest makers..........per vest..	1.35 to	1.60		.65	to	.82
Pants makers.........per pair..	1.75 to	2.50		.90	to	1.28
Harness and saddle makers..........	.50 to	2.00		.26	to	1.02

[1] Wages of laborers range from 25 to 67 cents per day ; wages of blacksmiths range from 75 cents to $1.50 per day.

WAGES PER DAY PAID IN THE REPUBLIC OF MEXICO IN 1896.

	MEXICAN CURRENCY.	UNITED STATES CURRENCY.
Carpenters......................	$0.75 to $1.25	$0.38 to $0.63
Carpenters, foremen...............	1.75 to 3.00	.89 to 1.53
Masons.........................	.75 to 1.25	.38 to .63
Masons, foremen..................	1.25 to 3.00	.89 to 1.53
Painters	.75 to 1.00	.38 to .51
Painters, foremen.................	1.00 to 2.00	.51 to 1.02
Miners :		
Ordinary.....................	.62 to 1.50	.31 to .76
Skilled	1.25 to 1.80	.89 to .91
Hatters........................	.75 to 1.00	.38 to .51
Hatters, skilled..................	1.50 to 2.50	.76 to 1.27
Shoemakers.....................	1.25 to 2.50	.89 to 1.27
Shoemakers, ordinary..............	.75 to 1.25	.38 to .89
Blacksmiths (mines)..............	1.50 to 3.00	.76 to 1.53
Carpenters (mines)...............	1.50 to 3.00	.76 to 1.53
Machinists......................	3.00 to 4.00	1.53 to 2.04
Head miners	2.00 to 2.50	1.02 to 1.27
Watchmen......................	.75 to 1.00	.38 to .51
Factories :		
Girls and boys.................	$0.18, .25 to .37	$0.09, .13 to .18½
Men	.40 to 1.00	.20½ to .51
Women.......................	.18 to .50	.09 to .25¼

WAGES PER DAY PAID IN TEN MEXICAN COTTON FACTORIES—ORDINARY
FACTORY HANDS—IN 1896, MEXICAN CURRENCY.[1]

NAME OF FACTORY.	TOTAL OPERA- TIVES.	MEN.	WOMEN.	CHILDREN.
Rio Blanco..............	1,220	$0.45	$0.45	$0.20
Hercules................				
La Priussima............	1,880	$0.50 to .75	$0.37 to .50	$0.12½ to .25
San Antonio............				
Baron y La Colimena.....	500	.37	.37	.25
San Ildefonso...........	451	.37 to 1.00	.37 to .50	.18 to .25
La Reforma.............	500	.65	.50	.25
La Estrella.............	600	.50 to .60	.25 to .50	.20 to .25
Bella Vista.............	600	.50 to .60	.25 to .50	.20 to .25
San Fernando...........	500	.65	.50	.25
La Amistad.............	150	.50 to 2.50	.50 to .75	.25
Industric Nacional.......	....	.37 to 1.50	.37 to .50	.20 to .25

Lowest paid men, 25 cents ; highest paid men, $2.50 ; lowest paid women, 12½ cents ; highest paid women, 75 cents ; lowest paid children, 12½ cents ; highest paid children, 37 cents.

[1] These rates expressed in United States currency will be about one-half. (The Mexican dollar equals 51 cents in United States currency.)

WAGES PER DAY PAID TO MEXICAN COTTON FACTORY OPERATIVES
ACCORDING TO THEIR RESPECTIVE OCCUPATIONS, IN
1896, IN MEXICAN CURRENCY.[1]

STATE.	FOREMEN.	SPINNERS.	CARDERS.	WASHERS.
Aguascalientes...............	....	$0.50	$0.50	$0.50
Mexico......................	$1.50	$0.50 to .75	$0.37 to .50	$0.37 to .50
Oaxaca.....................	$1.00 to 5.00	.50 to 2.00	.50 to 1.00	.50 to .75
Puebla.....................	1.00 to 3.00	.50 to 1.12	.50 to 1.12	.50 to 1.12
San Luis Potosi.............	....	.25	.25	.25
Sinaloa....................	2.00 to 3.00	.62 to 1.50	.62 to 1.00	.62
Nuevo Leon................	1.00	.75	.37 to 1.00	.37 to .75
Coahuila...................	1.00 to 2.00	.50 to 1.00	.50 to 1.00	.75
Chihuahua.................	1.00	.50 to .75	.50 to .75	.50 to .75
Durango...................	1.00 to 3.00	.37 to 1.00	.37 to 1.00	.37 to 1.00
Guanajuato................	.62 to 3.00	.37 to 1.00	.37 to 1.00	.37 to .75
Guerrero..................	1.00	.75	.50	.75
Hidalgo...................	1.12	.18 to .75	.18 to .75	.18 to .75
Jalisco....................	1.00	.31 to 1.00	.25 to .75	.37 to .50
Michoacan.................	1.00	.50	.50	.37
Federal district............	2.00 to 3.00	.50 to 1.00	.50 to 1.00	.50 to 1.00

STATE.	WEAVERS.	DYERS.	MACHINISTS.	FIREMEN.	HANDS.
Aguascalientes ..	$.50	$0.50	....	....	....
Mexico.........	$0.37 to .50	$0.50 to .75	$1.00	$0.50	$0.25 to $0.37
Oaxaca.........	.50 to .75	1.00 to 2.00	....	....	.50 to .75
Puebla.........	.37 to 1.00	.37 to 1.00	....	....	.50
San Luis Potosi..	.25	....	....	....	.25
Sinaloa.........	.62 to 1.00	1.00 to 2.00	$2.00 to 3.00	$0.75 to 1.00	.62
Nuevo Leon....	....	....	....	....	.37 to .50
Coahuila	.50 to 1.00	.50 to 2.00	1.50	.50	.37 to .50
Chihuahua......	.50 to .75	.50 to .75	....	.50 to .75	.37 to .50
Durango........	.37 to 1.00	.37 to 1.00	....	....	.37 to .75
Guanajuato.....	....	.37 to 2.00	....	.37	.37
Guerrero........	.75	.75	....	....	.50 to .75
Hidalgo.	.18 to .50	.50 to .75	....	....	.18 to .50
Jalisco.........	.37 to 1.00	....	....	....	.25 to .31
Michoacan......	.50	.75	....	.50	.25
Federal district..	.50 to 1.00	1.00 to 1.50	2.00 to 3.00	.75 to 1.00	.50 to .75

[1] At present rate of exchange these rates, expressed in American currency, are about one-half (51 cents to the dollar).

WAGES OF RAILWAY EMPLOYEES IN 1896.
MEXICAN INTERNATIONAL RAILWAY.

	MEXICAN CURRENCY.	UNITED STATES CURRENCY.
Passenger conductors [1]..........per month..	$165.00	$83.00
Passenger brakemen [1]...............do......	60.00	31.00
Freight conductors [2].................do......	$185.00 to 220.00	$94.00 to 113.00
Freight brakemen [2]..................do......	60.00 to 120.00	31.00 to 62.00
All engineers [2].....................do......	190.00 to 210.00	96.00 to 108.00
All firemen [2] ....do......	120.00 to 160.00	31.00 to 81.00
Telegraphers.....................do......	60.00 to 125.00	31.00 to 65.00
Section men.....................per day..	.50 to .62½	.26 to .31¼

[1] Three thousand miles is a month's run.   [2] Mileage.

WAGES OF RAILWAY EMPLOYEES IN 1896.
MEXICAN CENTRAL.

	MEXICAN CURRENCY.	UNITED STATES CURRENCY.
Passenger conductors...........per month..	$225.00	$114.00
Passenger engineers................do......	225.00	114.00
Freight conductors................do......	150.00	76.00
Freight engineers.................do......	150.00	76.00
Brakemen ....do......	60.00	31.00
Firemen.......................do......	90.00	45.00
Bill clerks ....do......	75.00	37.00
Clerks ....do......	50.00	26.00
Telegraphers:		
American......................do......	100.00	51.00
Mexican......................do......	$60.00 to 75.00	$31.00 to 37.00
Railroad laborers................. per day..	.62 to 1.00	.31 to .51

MEXICAN NATIONAL.

Passenger conductors...........per month..	$150.00	$76.00
Freight conductors................do......	$140.00 to 180.00	$71.00 to 91.00
Engineers, full time................do......	240.00	142.00
Section foremen..................do......	90.00	45.00
Firemen..........................do......	75.00 to 100.00	37.00 to 57.00
Telegraph operators:		
On line of road........ ....do......	60.00	31.00
Main offices....................do......	90.00 to 150.00	45.00 to 76.00
Bridge carpenters:		
Native........................per day..	1.00 to 1.50	.51 to .76
American.......................do....	2.75 to 4.15	1.38 to 2.08
Section men......................do....	.50 to .75	.26 to .38
Laborers..........................do....	.62½	.31

WAGES PER DAY PAID TO MINERS IN THE DIFFERENT STATES.[1]

[In Mexican currency, equal in United States currency to about one-half.]

STATE.	ORE BREAKER.	TIMBER MAN.	WATCHMAN.	PEON.
Coahuila	$0.75	$0.75	$0.75 to $1.00	$0.50 to $0.75
Chihuahua..........	1.50	$1.00 to 1.50	1.00 to 1.50	1.00 to 1.50
Durango............	$0.50 to 1.50	.40 to 1.00	.37 to 1.00	.37 to 1.00
Guanajuato.........	.18 to .50	.50	....	.18 to .37
Guerrero	.37	.37	.37 to .50	.37
Hidalgo............	.31 to .75	.31 to .75	.50 to 1.00	.25 to .50
Michoacan	.50 to 1.00	.37 to .75	.25 to .75	.37 to .75
Mexico	.50 to .75	.50	.50	.25 to .50
Nuevo Leon	.50 to 1.00	.75 to 1.00	.75 to 1.00	.50 to .75
Oaxaca.............	.25 to .75	.25 to .50	.25 to .31	.25 to .50
Queretaro..........	.50	....	....	.25 to .37
San Luis Potosi	.25 to .66	....	.66	.25 to .50
Sonora.............	1.00 to 2.00	1.20	1.00 to 2.00	.45 to 2.00
Zacatecas	.50 to 1.75	.50 to 1.75	.37 to .72	.37 to .50

[1] From Government reports.

WAGES PER DAY PAID TO MINERS IN THE DIFFERENT STATES.

STATE.	QUICKSILVER MIXERS.	DRILLERS AND PICKMEN.	FURNACEMEN (HORNERO).	TROWEL WORKERS (PLANILLERS).
Coahuila..............	....	$0.75 to $1.00	$0.75	$0.75 to $1.00
Chihuahua..........	$2.00 to $3.00	.51 to 2.50	1.50	1.50 to 2.00
Durango............	1.00 to 2.00	.40 to 1.50	$0.75 to 1.00	1.00 to 2.50
Guanajuato.........	....	.50	....	.50
Guerrero	....	.50 to .75	.37	.50
Hidalgo.............	....	.31 to 1.00	....	.31 to 1.00
Michoacan..........	.50 to 1.00	.50 to 1.00	.37 to 1.00	.50 to 1.18
Mexico.............	2.00 to 3.00	.50 to .75	1.00	1.00
Nuevo Leon........	1.00 to 2.00	.66 to 1.00	.75 to 1.00	.75 to 1.00
Oaxaca.............	1.75	.25 to 1.00	.50	.75 to 1.00
Queretaro	....	.50 to 1.00	....	.50
San Luis Potosi	....	1.00 to 1.60	.50	1.00
Sonora.............	1.00 to 3.00	.45 to 1.00	1.00 to 2.00	.75 to 2.00
Zacatecas..........	1.00 to 3.00	.70 to 1.00	.70 to 1.50	.66 to 1.20

DAILY WAGES OF STREET-CAR EMPLOYEES IN THE CITY OF MEXICO IN 1896.[1]

[Obtained from the Compañia de Ferrocarriles del Distrito Federal de Mexico, S. A.]

CHARACTER OF EMPLOYEE.	MEXICAN CURRENCY.		AVERAGE HOURS OF WORK.
Conductors of trains..............................		$1.50	13
Ticket sellers....................................		1.00	13
Ticket collectors on urban lines.....................	$1.25 to	1.75	13
Drivers		.75	13
Foremen at stations..............................	1.00 to	1.75	....
Stablemen.......................................		.63	....
Foremen of repair gangs	1.00 to	1.50	9
Peons...		.44	9
Pavers..		.69	9
Switchmen, guards, watchmen, etc..................	.50 to	.94	12
Carpenters......................................	.75 to	2.00	10
Blacksmiths	.75 to	2.25	10
Mechanics	.75 to	1.75	10
Painters..	.75 to	2.25	10
Harness makers..................................	.83 to	2.00	10
Engine drivers [1]................................	100.00 to	150.00	13
Firemen		1.25	13
Brakemen.......................................		1.00	13

[1] Per month.

[1] All these are paid by the day, except engine drivers. Wages are paid in Mexican silver, without rations. At present rate of exchange, these wages in American money amount to one-half.

II. COST OF LIVING.

The following statement of prices and cost of living in Mexico is also taken from Mr. Ransom's report, above quoted, on *Money and Prices in Mexico :*

PRICES OF AGRICULTURAL AND PASTORAL PRODUCTS EXPORTED IN 1896.

ARTICLES.	MEXICAN CURRENCY.	UNITED STATES CURRENCY.
Indigo..................per pound..	75 cents to $1.25.....	38 to 62 cents.
Sugar, fine.................do....	10 to 14 cents........	5 to 8 cents.
Sugar, brown...............do....	7 cents..............	3½ cents.
Cocoa.......................do....	40 cents.............	21 cents.
Tobacco.....................do....	12, 20, 24, to 28 cents	6, 11, 13, to 14½ cents.
Coffee......................do....	25 to 35 cents........	13 to 18 cents.
Flour.......................do....	4 to 6 cents..........	2 to 3 cents.
Beans.......................do....	5 cents..............	2¾ cents.
Wax.............every 25 pounds..	16 to 20 cents a pound	8 to 13 cents.
Honey..........every 100 pounds..	20 cents a pound.....	10½ cents.
Hennequen. ....per ton..	$80, gold...........	....
Fiber and cordage.......per pound..	6 cents.............	3¼ cents.
Oil................for 25 pounds..	$3..................	$1.53.
Rubber...............per pound..	25 cents............	13 cents.
Dyewoods..........................	$35 a ton, gold.......	....
Ixtle.............per 100 pounds..	$5..................	$2.55.
Vanilla......................do....	$12 to $16...........	$6.10 to $8.16.
Lemons..................per 100..	20 cents............	11 cents.
Oranges.....................do....	$1 to $1.50..........	51 to 77 cents.
Bananas.....................do....	60 cents............	31 cents.

PRICES OF PRODUCTS CONSUMED IN THE COUNTRY (MEXICO).

PRODUCTS.	MEXICAN CURRENCY.	UNITED STATES CURRENCY.
Wheat...........................per pound..	$0.02 to $0.04	$0.01 to $0.02⅕
Cotton..............................do....	.13 to .18	.06½ to .09
Wool (choice)........................do....	.60	.31
Butter:		
Ordinary..........................do....	.50	.26
Choice............................do....	.75	.38
Beans...............................do....	.06	.03
Eggs............................per dozen..	.25	.13
Lard............................per pound..	.16 to .24	.08 to .12
Rice................................do....	.06 to .08	.03 to .04
Cheese..............................do....	.50	.26
Chick pease.........................do....	.03	.01½
Soap, common........................do....	.08	.04¼
Barley..............................do....	.01½	. ¾
Pepper..............................do....	.16	.08¼
Sulphur.............................do....	.07 to .10	.03½ to .03½
Grapes..............................do....	.10 to .15	.05 to .08
Beef:		
On ranch..........................do....	.06	.03
Good, in cities...................do....	.12	.06
Best, in cities...................do....	.25	.13
In City of Mexico, good...........do....	.16	.08

COMPARATIVE TABLE SETTING FORTH THE CURRENT PRICES OF MANU-
FACTURES AND MERCHANDISE FOR THE YEARS ENUMERATED, AS
PUBLISHED BY THE BOARD OF COMMISSION AGENTS (MEXICAN
CURRENCY).

ARTICLES.	MILLS.	DESCRIPTION.	QUANTITY.	PRICE MAY 20, 1886.	PRICE JUNE 28, 1895.
Carpet.........	San Ildefonso..	....	Per vara [1]..	$1.12	$0.88
Flannel.........	......do.......	Cash price.........	.....do.....	$0.94 to 1.00	1.00
Do	Aguila.........	......do.......	.....do....	.94 to 1.00	1.00
Socks...........		Mexican..........	Per dozen..	1.00 to 1.25	$1.00 to 1.25
Drawers....		Knitted Mexican..	.....do....	9.00	7.00
Undershirts.....		Knitted, various classes..........	.....do.....	4.50 to 10.00	4.00 to 10.00

[1] Vara equals 33 inches.

PRICES OF GOODS MANUFACTURED IN MEXICO, WHOLESALE, MEXICAN
CURRENCY.

Carpeting ....per 33 inches..		$0.88
Flannel.................................do......		1.00
Socks.............................per dozen..	$1.00 to	1.25
Drawers...............................do......		7.00
Undershirts, woven (cotton)..............do......	4.00 to	10.00
Cassimere.....................per garment..		2.00
White blankets (cotton)....................each..		2.50
Bedspreads.........................per dozen..	26.00 to	45.00
Prints, 33 inches wide ....per vara [1]..	.15 to	.16
Blankets............................per dozen..		16.00
Colored wool yarn thread............per pound..		1.00
Cotton thread.........................do......	0.34 to	.50
Colored prints, 33 inches wide..........per vara..	.15 to	.18
Mexican stockings ....per dozen..		1.37
Gray and blue cloth (wool) ....per vara..	1.75 to	2.25
Plaids of Tulancingo.....................do....	.15 to	.18
Ginghams, 26 inches wide.. ....do....	.18 to	.20

[1] Vara equals 33 inches.

WHOLESALE PRICES PER POUND IN MEXICO (FOURTEEN STATES).[1]

STATES.	White sugar.	Brown sugar.	Coffee.	Beans.	Flour.	Butter.	Corn.	Irish pota- toes.	Wheat.	Rice.
	Cents.	Cents.	Cents.	Cents.	Cents.	Cents.	Cents.	Cents.	Cents.	Cents.
Michoacan............	8	7	25	8	4	22	2¼	4	2¹¹⁄₁₀	......
Zacatecas.............	9	8	....	7	....	21	4		2¼	9¼
Mexico	.....	.....	....	4	....	20	1⅜	4	....	....
Jalisco.....	7	6½	28	2¼	4½	13	1	3	....	3¼
Chihuahua............	14	12	40	3	4½	24	2½	2	2½	12
Oaxaca...........	11	10	24	4	9	45	2	8	....	8
Guerrero	12	9	50	12	10	15	4½		....	....
Hidalgo..............	12	10	....	5	7	28	2⅓	4	4⅜	6
Coahuila.............	10	9	36	3⅓	4½	......	2		....	8
Aguascalientes.......	11	10	....	5	5⅜	20	3½		3⅜	7
Durango.............	11	10	38	4	4½	20	2⅜		2⅜	....
Puebla..............	8	7	28	5	6	23	3		3½	....
Colima..............	8	6	24	2½	5	......	2	3	....	3½
Veracruz.............	10	7	30	6	7	22	3¼		3⅜	10

[1] Taken from Government Report, May and September, 1896, and expressed in
Mexican currency ; $1 equals 51 cents United States currency.

TABLE OF PRICES OF COMMODITIES IN CERTAIN CITIES.

ARTICLES.	VERACRUZ.		TAMPICO.		DURANGO.		CHIHUAHUA.	
	Mexican currency.	United States currency.	Mexican currency.	United States currency.	Mexican currency.	United States currency.	Mexican currency.	United States currency.
Jerked beef....per pound..	$0.25	$0.13	$0.12	$0.06	....	....	$0.12	$0.06
Salt fish..........do......	.30	.16	.30	.16	$0.40	$0.21	[1].25	.13
Salt pork..........do......	.25	.13	....	....	.25	.13	....	......
Hams..............do......	.50	.26	.50	.26	.45	.23	.25	.13
Eggs...........per dozen..	.35	.18	.48	.25	$0.18 to .60	$0.10 to .31	.25	.13
Flour..........per pound..	.10	.05½	.08	.04	.05	.02½	.03	.01½
Corn ....do......	.04	.02	.02¾	.01¾	.02½	.01¾	.01½	.00¾
Beans..............do......	.06	.03¼	.06	.03¼	.04	.02	.03	.01¾
Butter ....do......	.55	.28	.75	.38	[1]	[1]	.40	.21
Sugar..............do......	.10	.05½	.10	.05½	.10	.05½	.10	.05
Salt...............do......	.05	....	.05	....	.02½	.01¾	.01	.00½
Tea:								
Ordinary........do......	.30	.16	.50	.26	1.00	.51	.25	.13
Choice..........do......	2.50	1.28	2.00	1.02	2.50	1.27	1.20	.61
Coffee.............do......	.35	.18	.37	.18½	.38 to .45	.19 to .23	.38	.19
Wood............per cord..	7.50	3.83	4.00	2.04	5.50	2.52	[2].25	[2].13
Kerosene oil......per gall..	.60	.31	.60	.31	.80	.40	.80	.40
Soap, common..per pound..	.10	.05¼	....	....	.12½	.07	....	....
Lard ....do......	....	....	.25	.13	.22	.12	....	....
Fresh beef........do......	....	....	.10	.05½	.15 to .25	.08 to .13	....	....
Irish potatoes.....do......	....	......	.10	.05½	....	....	....	....
Candles...........do......	....	....	....	....	.25	.12	....	....
Cheese............do......	....	....	....	....	.31	.16	....	....

[1] Imported. [2] Hundredweight.

III. PRICES AND WAGES.

The following statement of prices and wages in several cities of Mexico appears in Appendix G to Mr. Ransom's report on *Money and Prices in Mexico*:

PRICES AND WAGES AT VARIOUS POINTS IN MEXICO (IN MEXICAN CURRENCY).

[Summary of reports from United States consuls to the legation in Mexico.]

DURANGO.

PRICES.	PRICES.	WAGES PER DAY.
Fresh beef, 15 to 25c. per lb. Salt fish (imported), 40c. per lb. Fresh fish, 12½c. per lb. Salt pork, 25c. per lb. Ham, 40 to 50c. per lb. Eggs, 1¼ to 4c. each. Flour, 5 to 6c. per lb. Corn, 1¾ to 2¾c. per lb. Wheat, 4 to 6c. per lb. Beans, 3 to 4c. per lb. American cheese, 50 to 55c. per lb. Domestic cheese, 25 to 75c. per lb. White sugar, 10c. per lb.	Brown sugar, 7c. per lb. Salt (table), 2 to 3c. per lb. Tea, $1 to $2.50 per lb. Coffee, 38 to 45c. per lb. Lard, 20 to 25c. per lb. Olive oil, 30 to 40c. per pint. Soap (laundry), 10 to 15c. per lb. Candles, 25 to 30c. per lb. WAGES PER DAY. Carpenters, $1 to $1.50. Masons, $1.25 to $2.	Painters, 75c. to $1. Miscellaneous laborers, 50c. Miners, 75c. to $1. Mine blacksmiths, $1 to $1.50. Hoisters, $1.25 to $2. Pumpers, $1.25 to $2. Engineers, 75c. to $1. Firemen, 75c. to $1. Dynamo tenders, $1 to $1.50. American machinists, $5 to $10. Mexican machinists, $1 to $3. Molders, 75c. to $2.50.

MATAMOROS.

PRICES.	PRICES.	WAGES.
Corn, $1 per bushel.	Mutton, 12c. per lb.	Engineers, $80 per month.
Coffee, 30 to 40c. per lb.	Molasses, $2 per gallon.	Carpenters, 75c. per day.
Beans, $2.18 per bushel.	Rice, 7c. per lb.	Bricklayers, 75c. per day.
Sugar, 10 to 15c. per lb.	Salt, 2½c. per lb.	Painters, $1 per day.
Beef, 8 to 12c. per lb.	All these products are Ameri-	Saddlers, $1 to $1.50 per day.
Lard, 14c. per lb.	can except coffee, beans,	Blacksmiths, 75c. per day.
Flour, 4 to 7c. per lb.	beef, corn, eggs, and chick-	Farm hands, 37c. per day.
Potatoes, 4 to 7c. per lb.	ens ; sugar is from Germany.	Cooks, $5 to $7 per month.
Bacon, 25c. per lb.		Bakers, 75c. to $1 per day.
Candles, 24c. per lb.		Waiters, $5 to $7 per month.
Cheese, 35c. per lb.		Common labor, 50c. per day.
Eggs, 30 to 36c. per dozen.		Wharf hands, $1 per day.
Chickens, 25c. per lb.		Car drivers, 50c. per day.

PIEDRAS NEGRAS.

PRICES.	PRICES.	PRICES.
Lard, 15c. per lb.	Pork (salt), 25c. per lb.	Beans, 5c. per lb.
Corn, 2c. per lb.	Ham, 30c. per lb.	Butter, 60c. per lb.
Coffee, 35 to 40c. per lb.	Eggs, 36c. per dozen.	Sugar, 15c. per lb.
Rice, 8c. per lb.	Flour, 4 to 6c. per lb.	Salt, 2c. per lb.
Potatoes, 5c. per lb.	Meal, 3½ to 4c. per lb.	

PIEDRAS NEGRAS (FREE ZONE).

PRICES.	PRICES.	PRICES.
Lard, 15c. per lb.	Beans, 5c. per lb.	Underwear (imported), $3.50 per suit.
Corn, 2c. per lb.	Butter, 60c. per lb.	Underwear, woollen (imported), $5.50 per suit.
Coffee, 35 to 40c. per lb.	Sugar, 15c. per lb.	American overshirts, $1.50 to $3.50 each.
Rice, 8c. per lb.	Salt, 2c. per lb.	Overshoes, $1.75 per pair.
Potatoes, 5c. per lb.	Tea, $1 per lb.	American hats, $2 to $10 each.
Salt pork, 25c. per lb.	Douglas shoes, $4.50 to $11.25 per pair.	Handkerchiefs, $1 to $9 per doz.
Ham, 38c. per lb.	Ready-made clothing, $10.50 to $30 per suit.	Half hose, $2.50 to $10 per doz.
Eggs, 3c. each.		
Flour, 4 to 6c. per lb.		
Meal, 3½ to 4c. per lb.		

ZACATECAS.

PRICES.	PRICES.	WAGES PER DAY.
Corn, $1.25 per bushel.	Common wool pants, $4 to $8 per pair.	Firemen :
Wheat, $4 per 100 lbs.	Blouses, common cotton, $1 to $1.50 each.	Skilled, $1.50 to $2.
Oats, 90c. per bushel.	Coats, common cotton, $3 to $4 each.	Unskilled, $1 to $1.25.
Beans, $1.66 to $2 per bushel.		Blacksmiths :
Potatoes (Irish), 3 to 4c. per lb.		Skilled, $1.50 to $2.
Chilis, 90c. per bushel.	**WAGES PER DAY.**	Unskilled, 75c.
Pork, 10c. per lb.		Carpenters :
Beef, 12c. per lb.	Peons, 37½ to 50c.	Skilled, $1.25 to $1.50.
Mutton, 10c. per lb.	Skilled :	Unskilled, 75c.
Flour :	Miners, 75c.	Tinsmiths :
First-class, 6c. per lb.	Head miners, $2 to $2.50.	Skilled, $1 to $1.25.
Second-class, 4c. per lb.	Carpenters, under ground, $2 to $2.50.	Unskilled, 75c. to $1.
Hats, straw (common), $1 to $3 per dozen.	Carpenters, above ground, $1.25 to $1.50.	Shoemakers :
Hats, felt (Mexican), $12 to $18 per dozen.	Blacksmiths, $1.25 to $1.50.	Skilled, $1.50 to $2.
Hats, felt (imported), $48 to $60 per dozen.	Machinists, $3 to $4.	Unskilled, 75c. to $1.
Shoes (women's common), $6 to $12 per dozen.	Firemen, $1 to $1.50.	Hatters :
Shoes (women's medium), $18 to $24 per dozen.	Ore sorters, 75c.	Skilled, $2 to $2.50.
Shoes (women's fine), $30 to $36 per dozen.	Overseers, $1.50 to $1.75.	Unskilled, 75c. to $1.
Sandals (men's), $2 to $3 per doz.	Unskilled :	Bakers :
Common shoes (men's), $24 to $30 per dozen.	Carpenters, above ground, 75c.	Skilled, $1.25 to $1.50.
Fine shoes (men's), $36 per dozen.	Blacksmiths, 75c.	Unskilled, 75c.
Common cotton pants, 50c. to $1.50 per pair.	Watchmen, 75c.	Masons :
	Labor on haciendas :	Skilled, $1.50 to $2.
	Machinists :	Unskilled, 75c.
	Skilled, $3 to $5.	House painters :
		Skilled, $1.50 to $2.
		Unskilled, 75c.

SAN LUIS POTOSI.

PRICES.	WAGES.	WAGES.
Corn, 2½c. per lb.	Farm hands, table-lands (no board), 18 to 25c. per day.	Foremen painters, $1 to $1.50 per day.
Beans, 15c. per lb.	Farm hands, low-lands (no board, 37 to 50c. per day.	Ordinary painters, 37 to 75c. per day.
Beef, 12c. per lb.	Foremen carpenters, $1.50 to $2 per day.	Coachmen, $10 to $15 per month.
Pork, 14c. per lb.	Ordinary carpenters, 75c. to $1 per day.	Clerks in dry-goods stores, $20 to $50 per month.
Lard, 26c. per lb.	Foremen masons, $1.50 to $2 per day.	Clerks in groceries, $15 to $50 per month.
Coffee, 37½ to 40c. per lb.	Ordinary masons, 75c. to $1 per day.	Miners, 50 to 75c. per day.
White sugar, 9 to 10c. per lb.	Foremen blacksmiths, $1.50 to $2.50 per day.	Railroad laborers, 37 to 75c. per day.
Brown sugar, 3 to 8c. per lb.	Ordinary blacksmiths, 50c. to $1.50 per day.	
Shoes for laborers, $1 per pair.		
American shoes (good), $5 per pair.		
Native shoes (good), $2.50 per pair.		
Unbleached domestic, 6 to 12c. per 33 inches.		
Native cassimeres, $1.75 to $2.25 per 33 inches.		

MONTEREY.

PRICES.	PRICES.	WAGES.
Men's shoes, 75c. to $6 per pair.	Men's half hose, 25c. to $1 pair.	Laborers, 63c. per day.
Hats, 50c. to $10 each.	Ladies' stockings, 50c. to $1.50 per pair.	Skilled carpenters, $5 per day.
Men's suits, $10 to $50 each.	Flannels, 75c. to $1.25 per yard.	Unskilled carpenters, $1 to $2 per day.
Domestic, 24 inches, 12 to 18c. per yard.		Skilled masons, $6 per day.
Calicoes, 22 inches, 12 to 18c. per yard.	**WAGES.**	Unskilled masons, $1 to $3 per day.
Ginghams, 12 to 15c. per yard.	Machinists, $6 per day.	Painters, skilled, $3.50 per day.
Shirtings, 22 to 24 inches, 10 to 15c. per yard.	Superintendent mines, $150 per month.	Painters, unskilled, 50c. to $2 per day.
Blankets, $2 to $8 per pair.	Civil engineers, $150 per month.	Farm hands, $12 per month.

TAMPICO.

PRICES.	WAGES.	WAGES.
Sun-dried beef, 12c per lb.	Railroads:	Farm labor:[1]
Ham (imported), 50c. per lb.	Conductors, $135 per month.	Laborers, 50c. per day.
Bacon, 45c. per lb.	Engineers, $165 per month.	Laborers (skilled), 75c. per day.
Lard, 25c. per lb.	Firemen, $45 per month.	Foremen, $1 per day.
Eggs, two-thirds of a cent each; now 4c. each.	Brakemen, $55 per month.	Farm hands (no rations), 18 to 25c. per day.
Flour (domestic), 6¼c. per lb.	Foremen section, $35 per month.	Carpenters, masons, etc., 38c. per day.
Corn, 2⅜c. per lb.	Hands, 63c. per day.	Foremen, 50c. per day.
Beans, 6c. per lb.	Mechanics:	Field hands in suburbs, 21c. per day.
Butter, 75c. per lb.	Machinists, $2.75 per day.	
Sugar, 8½ to 10c. per lb.	Metal workers, $1.37 per day.	
Coffee, 37c. per lb.	Carpenters, $1.50 per day.	
Irish potatoes, 10c. per lb.	Masons, $1.88 per day.	
Onions, 7c. per lb.	Painters, $1.37 per day.	
Rice, 8c. per lb.	Stevedores, $1.13 per day.	
Beef (wholesale), 10c per lb.	Farm hands, 37 to 50c. per day.	
Mutton, 15c. per lb.		
Pork, 20c. per lb.		

[1] In the coffee districts hands will take 7 pounds of corn for a day's labor.

PASO DEL NORTE (IN THE FREE ZONE).

PRICES.	PRICES.	PRICES.
Flour, $3.75 per 100 lbs.	Men's calf shoes, $3.50 to $4.50 per pair.	Straw hats, 40c. to $3 each.
Sugar, 10c. per lb.	Men's boots, $3 to $5 per pair.	Wool hats, $1 to $5.
Coffee, 40c. per lb.	Men's overalls, $1.20 to $2.25 per pair.	Wool blankets, 3 lb. weight, 50 by 82 inches, $3.75 each.
Rice, 12½c. per lb.	Jean coats, $2.25 to $3.50 each.	Unbleached muslin, 33 inches wide, 13½c. per 33 inches.
Butter, 60c. per lb.	Cassimere pants, $3.50 to $5 per pair.	Calico, 28 inches wide, 15c. per 33 inches.
Eggs, 37½c. per dozen.	Cassimere suits, $10.50 to $16 each.	Flannel, 48 inches, common, $1.10 per 33 inches.
Meal, 2½c. per lb.	Cassimere suits, fine, $21 to $35 each.	Flannel, 54 inches, fine, $2 per 33 inches.
Beans, 4c. per lb.		
Slippers, $1 to $3 per pair.		
Heavy brogans, $1.50 to $2 per pair.		

CHIHUAHUA.

Prices.

WHOLESALE.	RETAIL.	WHOLESALE.	RETAIL.
Jerked beef, 8c. per lb.............	12c. per lb.	Corn, 55c. per bushel.............	60c. per bu.
Salt fish, 20c. per lb................	25c. per lb.	Beans, 2c. per lb.................	3c. per lb.
Ham (imported), 35c. per lb........	40c. per lb.	Butter, 35c. per lb................	40c. per lb.
Ham (domestic), 18c. per lb.......	25c. per lb.	Salt, 75c. per cwt................	$1 per cwt.
Eggs, 18c. per dozen..............	25c. per doz.	Tea (domestic), 18c. per lb........	25c. per lb.
Flour, $5 per barrel...............	$6 per barrel.	Tea (imported), $1.10 per lb........	$1.20 per lb.
Wheat, $1 per bushel.............	$1.15 per bu.	Coffee, 30c. per lb................	38c. per lb.

Sheeting, unbleached, 33 inches wide, 12½c. per 33 inches.
Sheeting, bleached, 26 inches wide, 12½c. per 33 inches.
Gingham, 28 inches wide, 15c. per 33 inches.
Cassimere, 55 inches wide, $1.27 per 33 inches.
Calicoes, 24 inches wide, 12½c. per 33 inches.

CHIHUAHUA (*Continued*).

Wages (City).

CLASS.	AMERICAN.	MEXICAN.
Heater in rolling mills...............................	$5 per day.	$3 per day.
Rollers in rolling mills..............................	$20 per day.	
Nail makers	$15 per day.	
Blacksmiths...	$6 per day.	$3 per day.
Molders..	$5 per day.	$3 per day.
Pattern makers		$4 per day.
Carpenters..		$2.50 to $3 per day.
Masons		$2 to $2.50 per day.
Painters		$2 to $2.50 per day.
Railroad laborers....................................		$1 to $1.50 per day.
Factory employees (boys and girls)...................		25 to 50 cents per day.
House servants (with food)...........................		$8 to $10 per month.
Miners...		$1.50 to $2 per day.

APPENDIX NO. 2.

I now append the views of American statesmen on the subject of the rate of wages that I referred to in this paper (page 505), namely, that the main factor of the rate of wages is the amount of commodities they produce, and not the rate of import duties on foreign merchandise.

I could cite the views of many other public men of the United States bearing on the same subject, but as that would take a great deal more space than I have at my command, I will only append two which I consider fully sustain my views.

The Hon. John G. Carlisle expressed the views just referred to with his usual lucidity in the following extract from his Annual Report, as Secretary of the Treasury, of December 15, 1896, to the House of Representatives, on the state of the finances in the fiscal year ended June 30, 1896 :

" The danger of a large foreign competition in our home market, and the alleged injurious effects of such competition upon the interests of domestic labor, have not only been greatly exaggerated in the past, but are less now than at any time heretofore, and must continue to grow less hereafter.

" In 1886, three statisticians and economists of high standing, at the request of one of my predecessors, Mr. Secretary Manning, made and submitted to him a careful estimate of the number of persons engaged in gainful occupations in the United States, who could be subjected to foreign competition, and, although they worked by different methods and conducted their investigations independently of one another, their several estimates agreed within a fraction of 1 per cent. In their opinions, about 5 per cent. of our population so engaged were subject to competition from other countries, and one of the gentlemen said : ' The general conclusion that if trade were entirely free, the fraction of our present industrial population injuriously subject to foreign competition would not exceed 6 or 7 per cent., seems to me unquestionable.' Those estimates were based upon the census of 1880 and the trade of 1886. Since that time, great changes have taken place in our international trade and in the cost of production and subsistence in this country, and it cannot be doubted that the principal industries in the United States are relatively and actually stronger now than they were then, and, therefore, better able now than they were then to compete with foreign products, not only in the home market, but in the markets abroad, where no special privileges or advantages are conferred upon their rivals by treaties or differential tariffs.

" The number of our people engaged in gainful occupations increased from 17,-392,099 in 1880 to 22,735,661 in 1890, a gain of 5,343,562 ; and, while the increase in all such occupations during the ten years was 30.72 per cent., the increase in manufacturing and mechanical industries, which are supposed to be most subject to foreign competition, was 49.13 per cent. A further and most gratifying evidence of our growing industrial power is to be found in the greatly increased exports of the products of domestic manufacture, which now constitute, for the first time in our history, more than one fourth the total value of all our sales in foreign markets. If these products were not, at least, equal in quality to similar products of other parts of the world, and if the prices at which they are sold were not as low as the prices demanded by our foreign competitors, they could not find a market outside the limits of our own country. The exportation of manufactured products would not go on continuously year after year at an increasing rate, unless there was a profit for our people in the operation, nor unless the markets in which they are sold are in some manner benefited by giving a preference to the American article over like articles produced elsewhere. The annual increases since 1892 in the quantities and values of exported manufactures, notwithstanding the extremely low prices which have prevailed in all the markets of the world, are without a parallel in our commercial history, and furnish such conclusive evidence of industrial power and a capacity to compete successfully with the outside world in production and trade as ought to convince our people that protective duties on imported goods cannot be hereafter justified or excused upon the plea that they are necessary for the encouragement of capital or the security of labor in this country. With a healthy internal growth and a constantly increasing export trade, the influence of foreign competition in our home market must continue to diminish, and there is no reason to fear that our domestic industries could be seriously interfered with, even under schedules of duties much lower than we now have.

"But an examination of the various gainful pursuits in which the people of the United States were engaged in 1890, which is the date of the latest official returns upon the subject, will show that, even if we are not more independent of foreign competition now than we were then, the number of those who can be adversely affected by the importation of products from abroad is so small, in comparison with our total population, that it would be both impolitic and unjust to persist in a system of taxation designed for the special protection of their interests at the expense of all others. Of the five great classes or groups into which the total population engaged in gainful occupations (22,735,661) is divided, three—professionals, 944,328, domestic and personal servants, 4,360,506, and persons engaged in trade and transportation, 3,325,962— may be excluded at the outset as exempt from foreign competition. No tariff duties can affect these classes, except by increasing the cost of many of the commodities which they are compelled to buy and use.

"Of the agricultural, mining, and fishing group, numbering 9,013,669, only a very small percentage can be subjected to direct competition with the foreigner, and this part is located on or near the seacoast or other borders of our country. In some parts of New England, in Northern New York, and in a few other localities on the border, Canadian competition in agricultural products must sometimes be met to a certain extent, but the people in all these places are able to export other kinds of products, similar to those of their Canadian neighbors, and sell them at a profit in the Dominion and in other parts of the world, in competition with all others. In fact, the traffic in agricultural products across the Canadian line includes large sales by our citizens to the people of the Dominion, as well as purchases from them, and the official statistics of our whole trade with that country in this character of products show that we annually export more than three times as much as we import, our exports last year being $17,400,000, and our imports only $5,500,000. It is safe to say that not more than 500,000 persons, or about five and a half per cent. of those engaged in agriculture, mining, and fishing in this country, can be in any degree adversely affected by competition from abroad, and all these are wholly or partially compensated for foreign interference in their home market by the increased sales which international trade secures for their own products in foreign markets.

" In considering the manufacturing and mechanical industries, for the purpose of ascertaining to what extent they can be subject to foreign competition, the following general propositions may, I think, be accepted as the basis for just conclusions :

" (1) A large and continuous export of a particular class of articles proves an ability to manufacture as cheaply as any foreign competing nation.

" (2) Natural advantages, such as the proximity or cheapness of raw materials, inventiveness, special aptitudes, and facilities secured by an extensive use of superior machinery, are sufficient in most cases to exclude foreign competition.

" (3) Many occupations, such as those of bakers, blacksmiths, carpenters, masons, and others, are necessarily local ; the work must be done at a particular place, and, consequently, foreign competition is impossible.

" (4) The expenses of importation—the cost of transportation, insurance, loss of interest, etc.—prevent competition from abroad in many kinds of manufacturing and mechanical products.

" Applying these propositions in the investigation of the industries known as ' manufacturing and mechanical,' the result may be most briefly and conveniently stated in the form of a table, in which the interests subject to more or less foreign competition are classified as nearly as possible according to the tariff schedules and in accordance with an extremely liberal view of the question.

INDUSTRIES.	NUMBER OF EMPLOYEES.	WAGES.
Clay and pottery, etc...........................	71,619	$35,786,320
Textiles.........	589,048	201,350,485
Paints, etc.....................................	11,511	7,840,510
Chemicals......................................	19,474	11,019,322
Paper, etc......................................	16,745	10,395,436
Metals...	160,555	88,662,796
Food..	38,920	12,087,501
Miscellaneous.., ...	79,707	36,396,382
Total...............................	987,573	$403,538,752

" These constitute about 21 per cent. of the 4,712,622 persons engaged in all our manufacturing and mechanical industries, and, adding to them the 500,000 employed in agriculture, mining, and fishing, a total of 1,487,573 is obtained, which is about 6½ per cent. of the total population engaged in all gainful occupations, according to the returns of 1890. A more thorough investigation would doubtless show that considerable deductions ought to be made from this total. Geographical position, proximity to materials or markets, or the existence of cheap and efficient transportation facilities, operate as a strong natural protection against foreign as well as domestic competition. There is a constant internal movement of our industries, seeking more favorable situations, in order to reduce the cost of production and secure better access to the markets, and every such change, when judiciously made, strengthens our industrial system and reduces the danger of possible interference by the introduction of foreign products. If the full effect of these movements could be ascertained, it would be found that they have during the last few years contributed largely to the independence and prosperity of our manufacturing industries, and that on this account great numbers of our people who were formerly subjected to more or less foreign competition are now entirely exempt from it. The failures of many of our industries in the past have been attributed to insufficient protection against competition from abroad, when the real causes were unfavorable locations and lack of skill and experience on the part of their managers, or oversupply of products by domestic establishments.

" In view of the comparatively small and constantly decreasing part of our laboring population that could be affected even by a repeal of all duties, a movement for the imposition of higher duties upon imported goods cannot be regarded as justifiable upon any of the grounds usually urged in support of such measures by the advocates of the protective theory.

" The cost of production in all the great manufacturing nations has been so nearly equalized by modern inventions and economies, that movements of their several products from one to another cannot take place upon a large scale, or for any considerable length of time, if these products are burdened in the markets to which they are sent with charges to which they are not subjected in the countries of their origin ; and this tendency toward equalization of cost is still going on and must continue. A very small tax or charge will now entirely prevent the importation of many articles which a few years ago constituted a large proportion of our total dutiable merchandise and contributed very materially to our public revenues.

" Of all the great manufacturing nations, ours is the only one which annually produces a surplus of food and raw materials, and, unless we fail to utilize our resources, we must become the great exporting country of the world. No very considerable part of our natural material can be much longer profitably carried to other countries and returned to us in the form of manufactures, but it will be converted into the finished product by our people in their own shops and factories, and, after supplying the home demand, the surplus will go abroad, to compete successfully with like products of other peoples not so favorably situated. This is the result toward which we have been rapidly advancing since 1892, and, unless our progress is seriously checked by unusual adverse influences, the time can not be very far distant when the importation of manufactured products as one of the sources of revenue must be substantially excluded from our estimates."

The Minority Report of the Committee on Ways and Means of the House of Representatives on March 27, 1897, expressed the same views in a very clear and concise manner in the following extract :

" The labor argument of the protectionist can be reduced to an absurdity which makes it amazing that it should ever have been seriously advanced. To say in one breath that the welfare of labor depends upon its wages and that its wages in turn depends upon its skill and intelligence, and in the next breath to say that the very intelligent and highly skilled laborers of this country cannot successfully compete with the ignorant and unskilled laborers of the Old World, is equivalent to saying that skill and intelligence are not of great advantage to the laborers who possess them. To our minds, it involves a contradiction in history, as well as in economic theory, to hold that the factory labor of a civilized country needs protection against the factory labor of an uncivilized country. The fact that the unskilled laborers of a half-civilized country live more cheaply than the skilled laborers of a highly civilized country is more than counterbalanced by the greater productiveness of the skilled and intelligent laborer. If this view of the question needed further support than the mere statement of it, it can be found in those excellent works which assert that the skill and intelligence of the American laborer are such that he is able to produce seven times as much as the less skilful and less intelligent laborer of Continental Europe and fifteen times as much as the ignorant and unskilled laborers of Asia. Surely it will be admitted that a productive capacity seven times as great as the one and fifteen times as great as the other should be all that the American laborer needs to protect himself against the competition of European drudges and Asiatic serfs."

THE SILVER STANDARD IN MEXICO.

THE SILVER STANDARD IN MEXICO.

INTRODUCTION.

I published in the *North American Review* for June, 1895, a paper entitled " The Silver Standard in Mexico," which I now insert here.

In the preceding papers I have followed the system of revising them carefully and adding to them all the incidents on the same subject which had taken place after each was written, answering such objec- tions as have since come to my knowledge and were not consid- ered in the original article. I have embodied all these additions in the revised paper and preceded it by a short introduction, stating only how it originated and what were the reasons which induced me to write it. In the case of the "Silver Standard," however, I have thought it more prudent not to alter what I originally wrote and published in the *North American Review*, because that paper had the sanction of the then Secretary of State of the United States. I furthermore de- termined to embrace in the form of an introduction, such incidents connected with the silver standard in Mexico as have occurred since the paper was originally printed, as well as my answers to such objec- tions or misstatements as have since come to my knowledge. The foregoing explains why this introduction is more lengthy than those preceding the other papers, having the anomaly of being longer than the paper itself, and also why I had in a few cases to speak more fully of incidents which had already been discussed in the original paper, making unavoidable repetitions, as in the cases of the reasons why we have adopted the silver standard, of our difficulties in the way of changing it for the gold standard, and of one or two other subjects.

I will now state the manner in which my article on this subject originated.

Senator Morgan's Request for Information.—On March 22, 1895, Senator John T. Morgan of Alabama, wrote me the following letter:

" UNITED STATES SENATE, *March 22, 1895.*
" *His Excellency, Matias Romero, Washington, D. C.*
" MY DEAR MR. ROMERO :—So much has been said recently about the growth of Mexico, in prosperity, as it concerns the industries of your people and their freedom

from embarrassment of domestic indebtedness, that I wish to ask whether this matter is real, or whether it is overstated. I know that your agriculture, manufacture, and mining must be your chief reliance for prosperity, since you have not the advantages of a great commerce or the profits of an economic carrying-trade ; so I conclude that if your people are prosperous and free from the burdens of a heavy domestic indebtedness it must be the result of your domestic policy, relating to finance, taxation, or the economy of public administration. Yet I see that the rate of exchange between Mexico and the United States and the European countries is very heavy, to the apparent disadvantage of Mexico. I am also aware that you must use a heavy percentage of manufactures, consumed in Mexico, from other countries.

"I suppose it is true, also, that very large sums of gold coin are sent abroad annually to pay the interest of your national debt and your railroad securities and other bonded indebtedness, guaranteed or otherwise.

"The like demands upon our resources produce depression and stagnation of business in the United States, and the question I would present to your attention is whether the same causes, operating in Mexico, produce the same results. And, if they do not disturb or destroy the prosperity of your people, what is the cause of the difference in these results? I will very highly appreciate the answers you may be able to give to these suggestions, knowing that that they will be sincere, and that they will come from an able and enlightened source.

"With high regard, truly yours,
"JOHN T. MORGAN."

It has been my habit during my official residence in this country to refrain from writing, or even saying, anything that might be construed as the expression of an opinion on any political question being agitated in this country, and more especially on issues which assume great importance in the heated canvass that precedes Presidential elections. For this reason, when Senator Morgan, an earnest friend of silver, addressed to me the letter just inserted, I hesitated very much about answering it, because I knew that he intended to use my answer in his campaign in Alabama in favor of the free coinage of silver, and although he only asked for facts—and nobody could possibly object to my giving facts regarding the actual condition of things in Mexico, as the result of our silver standard—I was afraid that my answer might be construed as an attempt on my part to interfere in the political questions of this country, and I desire to be entirely free from such imputations. But, at the same time, as Senator Morgan was a prominent member of the Senate, and was at the time the Chairman of the Committee on Foreign Affairs in that branch of the legislative power, and, besides, was and has been for many years a warm personal friend of mine and a sincere friend to Mexico, and has obliged me in different ways, I was very reluctant to leave his letter unanswered, or even to give him verbally the information that he desired. To satisfy my mind, however, I decided to consult Judge Gresham, then the Secretary of State of the United States, as to whether it would be proper for me to answer in writing Senator Morgan's letter, and whether my answer stating such facts as I understood to be the results produced by the silver standard in Mexico, would be liable to misconstruction.

Secretary Gresham read carefully Senator Morgan's letter, and told me that he saw no objection to my replying to it, as it referred to a matter of general interest which had no connection with diplomatic affairs. I therefore prepared an answer, which I read to Mr. Gresham before sending it to Senator Morgan. Secretary Gresham found it adequate, impartial, and safe, and consequently I sent it to Senator Morgan, who forwarded copies of his letter and my answer to the *Daily State*, a newspaper of Birmingham, Alabama, in which they were published on April 7, 1895.

Paper for the North American Review.—General Lloyd Bryce, then editor of the *North American Review*, had requested me, several months before I wrote my letter to Senator Morgan, to prepare an article for publication in his paper on the Silver Standard in Mexico. Notwithstanding my desire to oblige General Bryce, as I was under obligations to him for his kindness and promptness in publishing my articles in his paper, I thought that the matter was a very delicate one, and that it was better for me not to discuss it. But when I had already written a letter on that subject which had been published, although by a local paper of Alabama, I thought that it was becoming for me to put my letter in the shape of an article for the *North American Review*, to comply with General Bryce's request, and I consequently did so. Besides, as my letter to Senator Morgan contained information which I thought was of interest to all citizens of this country, I thought there could be no impropriety in putting into the shape of an article the information contained in my letter. My article was published in the issue of the *North American Review* of June, 1895, and it drew many comments from the public press of this country, a part of which accused me of interfering in a question of internal policy of the United States, notwithstanding that I had been very careful to anticipate such a charge. Both in my letter to Senator Morgan and in my article in the *North American Review*, I had stated that the conditions of the two countries were so different that what was good for Mexico might not be so for the United States, and I had concluded by saying that the restoration of silver to its old price or ratio with gold was desirable for Mexico, showing in this way that I did not favor a depreciated currency.

President Cleveland had long before taken a decided attitude on the silver question, and I have since heard that some of his friends complained that my article had been written in the interests of silver. Mr. Gresham's unfortunate demise, which took place only two or three days before my article appeared in the *North American Review*, deprived me of my chief defence before the Government of the United

States, had I been charged with having taken any part in this controversy, and this fact confirmed me in my belief that it is dangerous for a diplomat to write about any topic which is a matter of political discussion in the country to which he is accredited.

In preparing my article for the *North American Review* I prefaced it by a paragraph stating that I had not written it voluntarily, but under the compulsion of having to answer a letter of Senator Morgan's, but the editor of that periodical, desiring it to appear as an original contribution, omitted this paragraph, and, for want of space, other portions of my article, especially the foot-notes I had appended to it. These will all be included in the present edition.

Senator Allen's Request for Information.—On March 11, 1896, Senator William V. Allen, from Nebraska, asked me for data relative to the development of Mexican industries within the last few years to enable him to demonstrate that Mexico had realized great prosperity in her material development within a comparatively short time, especially in the increase of railroads, factories, and other industries. I was somewhat embarrassed by the receipt of this letter, because, after my experience in answering Senator Morgan's letter, even with the advice and approval of the Administration, I was not willing to furnish the information desired, especially when it was asked for the purpose of using it in debate in the Senate; but, at the same time, I did not like to be discourteous to the Senator, and I thought, besides, that the mere fact of furnishing information published by the Mexican Government, which is within the reach of everybody, could in no way be taken as a breach of courtesy on my part. I therefore, after consulting with Secretary of State Olney, answered Senator Allen's letter, referring him to the paper on "The Silver Standard in Mexico," published in the *North American Review* for June, 1895.[1]

How the Paper was Quoted.—I was particularly careful to state in my paper all the advantages and disavantages of the silver standard

---

[1] The following is the text of Senator Allen's letter to me and of my reply :

"COMMITTEE ON FOREST RESERVATIONS AND THE PROTECTION OF GAME,
"UNITED STATES SENATE,
"WASHINGTON, D. C., March 11, 1896.

" *Señor Don Matias Romero,*
" *Envoy Extraordinary and Minister Plenipotentiary,*
" *1413 I Street, N. W., Washington, D. C.*

" SIR :—I have the honor to direct your attention to an editorial appearing in the Washington *Post*, March 7th current, entitled " The Silver Dollar in Mexico," and also a paper in the current March number of the *Arena*, published at Boston, Massachusetts, by Mr. Justice Walter Clark, of the Supreme Bench of North Carolina.

" I write for the purpose of obtaining from you such data and information along the lines indicated in this editorial and paper as you may feel disposed to furnish me. I am desirous of taking up and considering thoroughly and exhaustively in the United

in Mexico, as I had practically studied them during the year 1892, when I was in the City of Mexico at the head of the Treasury department. I had then the best opportunities to see practically the workings

States Senate at an early day, the silver question in Mexico, and I should be pleased to be placed in possession of such views as you may possess on the subject.

"You no doubt understand fully the argument made by gold monometallists in this country and illustrated by what they are pleased to state as the condition in Mexico resulting from silver monometallism.

"I should be pleased to be furnished with such data, in as compact form as possible, as may be in your possession, relative to the development of Mexican industries within the last few years, to enable me to demonstrate that Mexico has realized great prosperity in her material development within a comparatively short time. The increase of railroads, factories, and other industries would be important.

"I have the honor to be, Very truly yours,

"W. V. ALLEN, U. S. S."

"WASHINGTON, March 12, 1896.

"*Hon. William V. Allen, United States Senator, Washington, D. C.*

"SIR,—I have received your letter of yesterday, in which you direct my attention to an editorial which appeared in the Washington *Post* of the 7th instant, entitled "The Silver Dollar in Mexico," and also to a paper in the current number of the *Arena* published at Boston, Mass., by Mr. Justice Walter Clark of the Supreme Bench of North Carolina, and ask me for such information as I may have on the lines of those articles, as you wish to take up in the Senate, at an early date, the silver question in Mexico.

"I do not think it would be proper for me to furnish information to be used in the discussion before the United States Senate, of a question pending in this country and which divides its political parties and is therefore in the nature of a domestic concern, as there is danger that any information furnished by me for such purpose might be taken as a desire of intruding into the domestic affairs of the United States. As the representative of a foreign country, and especially of one which is a friend of the United States, it would not become me to appear meddling in the domestic affairs of this country.

"But, at the same time, as what you desire are facts, and as the facts relating to this subject have already been stated in a way which I think would not be liable to misconstruction, I beg leave to refer you to an article which I published in the *North American Review* for June, 1895, which states in a conscientious and concise manner, the advantages and disadvantages of the silver standard in Mexico.

"I have read with interest Justice Clark's article mentioned by you, and it is very interesting for me to see how the same facts strike so differently different public men of the United States, according to their preconceived ideas on the money question. The friend of silver, like Justice Clark, finds in Mexico an example of the remarkably favorable results of the silver standard, while on the contrary, the friends of the gold standard, like Mr. W. H. Scott, editor of the *Oregonian* of Portland, Oregon, who published in his paper on the 28th ultimo a letter dated at the City of Mexico on the 20th of the same month, relating his experiences and impressions of Mexico during his visit to that country, find in Mexico an example of the bad results and terrible consequences produced by the silver standard.

"It will afford me great pleasure to know that the facts, as presented in the *North American Review*, will fulfill your desire for information contained in your letter that I have the pleasure to answer. "I am, very truly yours,

"M. ROMERO."

of the silver standard, and, if anything, I was over conservative in my estimate of its advantages.   It would have been foolish in me to have attempted to exaggerate these advantages, because it could very easily be shown that my statements were incorrect, and this would have placed me in a very disagreeable position, independently of my desire to be always honest about everything.

As my paper presented in a very just and impartial manner both the advantages and disadvantages of the silver standard in Mexico, in the United States the friends as well as the opponents of the free coinage of silver found in the article many reasons to defend their views, by exaggerating the advantages and underrating the disadvantages of the policy that they preferred.

My article was often quoted by several newspapers and public men in this country, and even in the legislative halls of the Republic, although mainly by the advocates of the free coinage of silver.   In the session of the Senate of the United States of the 10th of January, 1896, Senator Jones, of Arkansas, read several extracts from the same, and I have received frequent requests for copies of it from distinguished quarters.

President Diaz's Views on Silver.—Since that time General Diaz, President of the Mexican Republic, in an interview published in the New York *Journal,* of September 11, 1896, expressed exactly the same views as those put forth by me in my paper.[1]

[1] The following is a letter from Mr. W. E. Lewis, the *Journal* special correspondent in Mexico, dated at the City of Mexico on September 9, 1896, and addressed to Mr. W. R. Hearst, editor of the New York *Journal,* and enclosing the so-called interview with President Diaz.

" CITY OF MEXICO, *September 9.*

" What President Diaz sends herewith on the effect of free silver coinage in Mexico is given double importance by the facts that Mexico is one of the most prosperous of the silver-using nations, and that its prosperity has been attained under the statesman-like administration of the veteran Executive who now sends this personal message to the *Journal.*   Shallow observers who have been shaken by the sight of Mexican dollars selling in the United States for 53 cents, while ignoring the fact that in Mexico they buy as much, and only as much, wheat now as in 1860, will learn from the President of the Mexican Republic how stimulating upon productive industry is a dollar which it does not pay to hoard, but to spend ; which keeps ever its normal value, and so doing keeps always stable the prices of commodities for which it is exchanged.

" W. E. LEWIS,
" *The ' Journal's ' Special Commissioner to Mexico."*

" FROM PORFIRIO DIAZ.
" CITY OF MEXICO, *September 9, 1896.*
" *To W. R. Hearst, New York 'Journal' :*
" I do not care to discuss the effect of the silver coinage on the material interests of Mexico with a view to influencing the result of the coming national election in the United States.   Such course on my part would be wholly improper, considering the friendly and peaceful relations existing between the United States and Mexico.   The

When I called President Diaz's attention to his message published by the New York *Journal*, he informed me in a letter dated at the City of Mexico on the 6th of October, 1896, that the San Francisco present political issue in the former country is the question of the money standard, and I do not wish to be regarded as in any wise attempting to affect the outcome.

"I can give the facts relative to existing industries and the establishment of new ones in Mexico under our financial system, and each may draw his own conclusions as to the causes which have produced such awakening in commercial and industrial affairs. Ocular demonstrations of the vast development may be found by visiting the cotton and woollen mills in our various cities. Some are old, others recently opened. Our paper mills and their output also furnish evidence of our material prosperity. Until a comparatively recent period all the pulp used in the manufacture of paper in this country was imported, and the paper only was made in Mexico ; now the pulp and everything that enters into the composition of the paper is made here. The departments of the government will furnish the exact data and statistics showing the growth of domestic manufactures and commerce.

"*Growth of Mexico's Commercial Interests.*—While our material interests have increased steadily and healthfully for the last twenty years, since the close of the Indian mints and the repeal of the Sherman law, so called, in the United States, the growth of Mexico's commercial and industrial interests has been particularly marked. The consequent appreciation in the price of gold and the increase in exchange between Mexico and the gold standard countries at once operated to reduce importations and stimulate home manufactures.

"The added price of exchange was in effect an addition to the tariff. The importer added to the original cost the duty and cost of exchange. Our cotton and woollen mills already in operation were obliged to enlarge their capacity and new ones were established. The number of operatives necessarily had to be greatly increased.

"To show the falling off in the consumption of foreign merchandise, it may be said that the year prior to the increase of foreign exchange on silver our customs collections at the ports of entry amounted to $22,000,000. The next year they were $14,000,000. In the fiscal year ending in 1890 our importations exceeded $52,000,000. In the fiscal year ending in 1895 they were slightly in excess of $34,000,000. On the other hand, our exportations increased. In 1890-91 they amounted to $63,000,000, and in 1894-95 to $90,000,000. There was nothing in the nature of a commercial panic consequent upon the sharp advance in silver exchange.

"*Bank and Business Failures Rare in Mexico.*—Our merchants are conservative and careful, and bank and business failures are happily rare in Mexico under any circumstances. As to wages and the condition of laboring men, considering the nature of work and classes of industry, they compare favorably with those in other countries.

"The demand for skilled labor has grown with the great increase in the number of mills and manufactories. This demand in all branches of labor is strong. The added exchange has not impaired the value of our dollar as applied to the purchase of articles of home manufacture. Its buying power is unchanged in this respect, and prices for domestic merchandise and produce vary only according to the supply and the demand.

"Heavy investments of foreign capital in Mexican enterprises have been made since the appreciation of gold elsewhere.

"There is another point of view. The foreign debt of the country is payable in gold. The duties on imported merchandise are collected in silver, or on that basis. The high rates of exchange, together with the decrease in our customs collections before alluded to, have caused a considerable shrinkage in this source of revenue."

Examiner had asked, by cable, his views on the silver question in Mexico, and that he had sent by mail in answer some tables and other data bearing on that subject. When, some time later, Mr. Lewis made a similar request, the President answered him that, these questions being agitated in the political canvas in the United States, in which he thought it would not be proper for him to take a part, he declined giving his views. This was the extent of his communication with the *Journal*, but from such data the telegram was made up, which I suppose was substantially correct.

When it was stated by the public press, in the middle of 1897, that Mexico was going to adopt the gold standard, I asked President Diaz, at the request of prominent men of this country, whether this was the case, and in a letter from him dated at the City of Mexico on August 11, 1897, he answered me that for the time being he did not intend to recommend that measure, as Mexico was waiting for the result of the adoption of the gold standard in other countries before deciding whether or not to make that move.

The Silver Question Became the Leading Political Question in the United States.—Soon after the publication of my article in the *North American Review*, the silver question became the leading question in the United States, on account of the National Democratic Convention, which met at Chicago on the 7th of July, 1896, having accepted a plank in its platform in favor of the free and unlimited coinage of silver at the ratio of 16 to 1; while the National Republican Convention, which had met at St. Louis a few days before declared in favor of the gold standard.

The silver question became, therefore, the leading question of both parties in the presidential election of 1896, and in their canvass the spokesmen of both mentioned Mexico as an instance supporting their respective views; some of the Democratic orators tried to show that the prosperity of Mexico was due solely to the silver standard, and some of the Republicans to demonstrate that the many disadvantages under which we labor in Mexico, as compared with the United States, were due to the same standard.

Newspaper Agents Sent to Mexico to Study the Silver Question.— Some of the leading newspapers of this country sent special representatives to Mexico for the purpose of studying on the spot the effect of the silver standard in that country, and although these were men of unquestionable general ability, they were at a disadvantage amidst strange conditions, and among a people with whose language, history, and genius they were unfamiliar; notwithstanding which they expected in two or three weeks' stay in the country to arrive at sound or useful conclusions on the social and economical questions in all their aspects which they had been sent to study. Many went there, besides, already prejudiced in favor of some particular view, and none remained there long enough to form just opinions on those complex questions. The result, as was natural to expect, was that each side made a great many mistakes and that the good name of Mexico suffered a great deal for that reason.

The unsatisfactory result of the missions referred to was increased by the fact that such agents, in some cases, were sent to Mexico to seek for facts in support of conclusions which were irrevocably formed, so that their minds were open to only one set of facts and observations, and in the published accounts of some of these investigations one is not impressed by their sense of relevancy to the facts observed or to the questions under discussion.

The same thing happened in their case as in that of my paper, that Mexico was presented by both sides as supporting their respective theories, that is, the silver men exaggerated the advantages of the silver standard, as they are developed in Mexico, and considered that standard as the sole cause of the prosperity of that country; while the gold men exaggerated the disadvantages of the silver standard and pointed out the many lines in which Mexico is far behind the United States, attributing these drawbacks to the silver standard.

It was stated in this country, and with great effect, that anybody going to Mexico could buy with an American silver dollar one dollar's worth of goods, or pay for a dinner of that price, and have besides one Mexican dollar returned in exchange.   While this statement may be in some respects substantially correct, as a matter of fact it was not so. It may have happened only once or twice, and for a very few days each time, since the depreciation of silver began, that the Mexican dollar has been worth exactly 50 cents in gold, when exchanged for gold or sold for the silver bullion contained in the same.   The price until recently, and not considering the last great fall of that metal, was generally from 53 to 58 cents and sometimes higher, and therefore it would not be possible to pay with an American dollar, worth from $1.85 to $1.90 in Mexican money, for the value of one Mexican dollar and have another Mexican dollar returned in exchange, although that operation might have been made on two or three days during all that time when the price of the silver bullion in the Mexican dollar was exactly 50 cents.   The keepers of restaurants, shops, etc., are not informed about the price of silver in London, which varies almost every day, and they would not attempt to exchange a foreign coin for the exact market price of the bullion contained in the same, running the risk of losing by the operation.   If anybody should offer in Mexico a United States silver dollar in payment of one dollar's worth of goods, the shopkeeper very likely would not receive the coin, because he would not be aware of its value; or, if he received it, knowing that it was worth more than a Mexican dollar, he would not give in exchange the full value of the gold dollar at the price of silver bullion on that day for fear of losing money. But, of course, any one having a United States silver dollar could go to an exchange office, have it exchanged for, say 190 cents, pay for his breakfast or his goods the value of 100 Mexican cents, and have 90 cents in change left; and so far the statement may be substantially correct. In the paper published by the *North American Review*, and which follows this introduction, I explained why this happens, namely, that the United States silver dollar is the representative of a gold dollar, while the Mexican dollar is not redeemed in gold.

Comments on the Silver Standard in Mexico.—It would be unfair to consider the silver standard of Mexico as the only factor in the progress of that country. Its present prosperity is due principally to the building of a system of railways which makes transportation easy and comparatively cheap, to the complete peace that has prevailed there for twenty years, to the investment of foreign capital, and more especially to the unlimited natural resources of the country. The silver standard has been, too, a factor in the prosperity of Mexico, because without sufficient circulation we could not have developed our resources to the extent that we have done, as is shown by the advantages which have accrued to Mexico on account of that standard as stated in the accompanying paper; but that progress is not due solely to the silver standard, as was alleged by some of the orators and newspaper writers favoring the free coinage of silver.[1] The other side made a similar mistake in attributing to the silver standard all the disadvantages

---

[1] The following extract from a book published in 1897 by the Mexican Central Railway Company Bureau of Information, under Mr. A. V. Temple, entitled *Facts and Figures About Mexico*, fully confirms these views, as well as those expressed in other portions of this paper :

"*Causes of Prosperity.*—While Mexico's prosperity is unquestionably due to a large number of causes, prominent among which are the suppression of disorder, the extension of railroads, and the liberal policy of the government towards foreign capitalists and emigrants, it is very evident that her industrial growth has been powerfully stimulated by the existing monetary standard.

When silver and gold, as valued in the world's commodities, parted company, and Mexican dollars (which were being exported to Europe) were sold for a less price as measured in the currency of the gold standard countries, a rise in the price of all imported articles began in Mexico. From this time dates the development of Mexico's cotton and woollen industries, as well as the increase in the exportation of articles other than precious metals. The demand and the margin of profit for home-made goods increased as Mexican dollars depreciated. The native manufacturer enlarged his operations, introduced improved machinery, and began to compete successfully with many grades of imported goods.

The consumer now purchases from the Mexican manufacturer at the same price in silver as when silver was at par with gold, instead of being exported to Europe, as

under which we labor in Mexico.   It is true, that we have not yet attained the same degree of civilization, wealth, and industrial and mercantile prosperity that this country has, but that is because we have difficult problems to solve which are well known here.   We have been without means of communication for centuries; we have a heterogeneous population, most of which is, so far, entirely uneducated; and above all, we have been contending with long and disastrous civil

formerly.   Many millions of dollars have thus been kept at home and added to the capital of the country.

Cotton mills have been constructed in all parts of the republic.   The acreage of cotton is constantly increasing, but the native crop is not yet sufficient to supply the demand, and large quantities of cotton are imported from the United States.

The history of the woollen trade has been almost identical with that of cotton.

The Mexican manufacturer of woollens produces now a very good article, although he cannot yet compete with the finer fabrics of France and England.   In former years there was a considerable exportation of wool to the United States ; now there is a considerable importation of it from the United States into Mexico.

While it is true that the Mexican dollar, as measured in francs, marks, or pounds sterling, has decreased in value nearly 50 per cent., it is also true that prices of almost every class of foreign goods have also decreased 50 per cent.   A suit of clothes made from the finest quality of imported goods costs only the same number of Mexican silver dollars to-day that it cost twenty-five years ago.

Note also the effect on real estate.   Coffee plantations have risen in value from $75 or $80 an acre, the price when gold was at par with silver, to from $200 to $800 an acre.   The annual profits of these plantations have risen from $10 or $15 an acre to from $50 to $150 an acre.   Similar advances are true also in sugar and tobacco haciendas.

The premium on gold has been the cause of immense internal improvements throughout the country.   The capital kept at home has been invested in irrigation schemes, in improving large tracts of fallow land, and in other enterprises of a like character.   The premium has also brought much foreign capital here, which has been invested in various branches of industry, particularly in the production of articles for exportation.

The foreign investor doubles his capital when he brings it to Mexico.   He gets the advantage of cheap and docile labor for silver, and sells his exported product for gold.

This great stimulation to all industrial enterprises, the building of railroads, the establishment of factories, and the cultivation of thousands of acres of land—all these have had a notable effect upon the people.   The great demand for labor has benefited them immensely, and has promoted peace and prosperity throughout the country.

The resources and opportunities of Mexico have only been recently revealed to her own people, as well as to foreigners.   It is much easier now than it ever was before to get capital here at a relatively low rate of interest for any legitimate enterprise, because, first, there is more money in the country than when we were importing so largely ; and because, second, the business man is willing, under present conditions, to take risks which would be considered too great in an era of low prices and a contracted currency.

The native producer has prospered under silver at the expense of the foreign merchant and of the importer.   Silver in Mexico has stimulated exports and contracted imports."

wars, from which this country has been almost altogether free—and these factors are the real causes of our present economic conditions.

The low Mexican wages were also attributed to our silver standard. To be sure the wages that we pay our laborers are not quite as high as those paid to similar laborers in this country, but that is not due to the silver standard, as has already been stated, since wages were no higher when silver and gold were at par at the ratio of 16 to 1, but, on the contrary, have since increased, and I have no doubt they will continue to increase in the future. In a paper entitled "Labor and Wages in Mexico," which appears in this book (pages 495–543), I have dealt fully with this subject and I have also tried to explain the condition of our wage-earning classes (pages 528–531).

Pessimists who have visited Mexico or studied its present conditions predict that our prosperity is not of a permanent character, as they think that it will be followed by a tremendous crash, similar to that which took place not long ago in Australia and later in the Argentine Republic, because they think that investments in Mexico have been overdone, and that when the time comes to liquidate our indebtedness and we have to pay them in gold, we will not be able to do so, and then we shall be in the same condition as those countries after the crash. I do not entertain any such view of the situation. I think investments in Mexico so far have been prudently made, and they are sure to bring a reasonable interest, even if paid in gold. Of course it would have been better if we could have accomplished the development of our country with our own means and without using any foreign money ; but there was not capital enough in Mexico to do so, and besides, the Mexicans had no experience and therefore no confidence in large collective enterprises, and would not invest their money in them. The problem for us was therefore to decide whether we would continue in the unsettled conditions of stagnation, poverty, and danger in which we had been for many years, and not owe anything abroad, or whether we should build railways, enlarge our mining interests, build our manufactories, and extend our agricultural productions with the aid of foreign capital. The United States afforded a very encouraging example to us, for this country has really been developed by European capital, and yet nobody doubts the wisdom of that policy. Besides, the Mexican people are getting richer by the development of their country with the assistance of foreign capital, and in the course of time they will be able to buy their own securities now in foreign markets, and in that way save the interest or tribute which now they pay to Europe and to the United States, just as this country has done under similar circumstances.

I hope that if in the future the example of Mexico is again brought into the internal politics of this country, the information embraced in this paper, and in some of the others contained in this volume, which is entirely reliable and impartial, will contribute to dispel the many mistakes that prevailed in the presidential canvass of 1896.

Mr. Kennedy's Misstatement.—To show my impartiality in this matter I will state that when my attention was called, during the last political canvass, to an affidavit signed by J. H. Kennedy,[1] who called himself a resident of the town of Sinaloa, Mexico, to the effect that the United States silver dollar could not be exchanged for two Mexican dollars in Mexico; that the national debt of Mexico was not paid in gold, and that Mexico could redeem her debt at once without any difficulty, I had no hesitation in correcting those misstatements, as appears from the following letter that I addressed on September 27, 1896, to Mr. Arthur E. Fletcher, of Milwaukee, in answer to an inquiry from him on the subject. My letter was

[1] Mr. Kennedy's affidavit is the following, taken from the *Times* of Minneapolis, Minn., of October 12, 1896 :

" *Silver Dollars in Mexico.*—J. H. Kennedy, a former resident of Iowa, has attacked the statement so generally made regarding Mexico and silver by making the following affidavit before E. H. English, a notary public at Valley Junction :

" I, James H. Kennedy, now a resident of the town of Sinaloa, Mexico, do solemnly swear that I am an American by birth ; that I served three years in the Seventh Iowa during the late Civil War ; that I have always been a republican ; that I have resided in Mexico for twenty-five years ; that I speak the Spanish language as well or better than I now do the English. I have travelled through twenty-four of the twenty-seven states in Mexico in an official capacity and as an interpreter for numerous syndicates. I have had access to almost all the archives of that country. I am better acquainted with the customs and usages of that country than I am of my mother country. I left Mexico on the 2d day of March, 1896, coming to this country to visit my friends, relatives, and old comrades. During the last month in Iowa I have heard more absurd and utterly false statements made in regard to Mexico than I ever thought could be conjured up by mortal man, all to deceive the voter.

" One most heard is that you can take one American silver dollar into Mexico and get two Mexican silver dollars for it, or that you can get a 50-cent meal and throw down an American dollar and they will give you back in change a Mexican dollar. I brand this as utterly false in every respect, a lie manufactured out of whole cloth. I assert that a Mexican will not accept an American dollar, either gold, silver, or paper, for any amount, but will refer you to a broker, where you can sell your silver dollars as bullion for Mexican money ; then they will trade with you. The largest hotel in the City of Mexico will not accept American money under any circumstances, but will invariably refer you to a broker.

" By paying the mintage any one can take silver bullion to either of the mints in Mexico and get Mexican silver dollars for it, and for two hundred and fifty years silver bullion has never fluctuated to exceed two cents.

" I hear it asserted that the national debt is payable in gold. I brand this as utterly false. Every dollar of the debt, $46,000,000, is, and always has been, payable in the lawful money of that country, and we are now paying our debt in Mexican silver dollars, the money of the contract.

" I assert that Mexico in the present decade is making strides in advancement

published by the Milwaukee *Sentinel* on the 4th of the following October, adding to my name the prefix of "Minister of the Mexican
Republic" in Washington, an official designation which I never use
and which is not correct, because the official name of Mexico is the
"United States of Mexico," not "Mexican Republic."

The following is a copy of my answer to Mr. Fletcher:

"WASHINGTON, D. C., *September 27, 1896.*
"*Mr. Arthur E. Fletcher, Plankington Bank, Milwaukee, Wis.:*

"DEAR SIR :—I am in receipt of your letter of the 25th instant and in answer
have to inform you that the President's Message, read to the Mexican Congress on the
16th inst., explains fully the case you mention. Our gold debt, or foreign debt, as
we call it, because all of it is held in Europe, amounts to more than $100,000,000, and
is payable in gold, both interest and principal, and our silver debt, a large portion of
which is held in Europe and some of it in Mexico, is payable in silver, both interest
and principal.

"I doubt very much whether Mexico could pay her whole debt even in silver,
because that would require about $200,000,000, and our revenue is only about $50,-
000,000 and the expenses reach about the same amount, but it might be redeemed by
issuing new bonds with less interest, and that is very likely what will be done by
Mexico at the proper time.   I am, very truly yours,   M. ROMERO."

Official Declarations of Mexico on the Monetary Question.—One of
the objects for which the International American Conference that
assembled in Washington in 1889 and 1890 was convened, under
Act of Congress of May 24, 1888, was (Section 6th) "the adoption of
a common silver coin to be issued by the different Governments, the
same to be legal tender in all commercial transactions between the citizens of all the American States." A committee was therefore appointed to consider the subject of a Monetary Union, and not being
able to agree upon any project with such purpose in view, because the
United States delegates did not favor any, the committee decided to
recommend the convening of a Special Commission of the American
nations for the purpose, a recommendation which was finally adopted,
because the other American nations considered that the United States
being the largest of the American countries, ought to take the lead,
and the others ought not to act in opposition to its wishes and policy.

greater than any other nation on earth. Twenty-five years ago we had eighty miles
of railroad, now we have near eight thousand miles of railroad. We are building
factories on every hand. Twenty-eight years ago, when the French army was driven
out, the Mexican government was left penniless—not a dollar in the treasury. We
can now pay our entire national debt any day a demand would be made for it.

"I am now on my way to Mexico to spend the rest of my life. Any one can find
me by addressing a letter to James H. Kennedy, Sinaloa, Mexico.

"In conclusion, I invite an honest and thorough investigation into the facts of
my statement, and I defy successful contradiction. I am not the owner of mining
stocks and no personal interest has caused me to make this statement, but have given
it by request of an old comrade.   JAMES H. KENNEDY."

During the discussion of that report I suggested the adoption of a common coin by all the American nations, to be legal tender in payment of all debts, and the coining of a certain amount of silver dollars of the same weight and fineness, to be issued in proportion to their population—for instance, $1 for each inhabitant that each country had,—such dollars to be legal tender for the payment of all debts of all the American nations, redeemable on presentation in gold by the respective countries and stated the inconveniences that would accrue to Mexico by the adoption of a common silver coin. [1]

When the Special Commission of the Monetary Union assembled in Washington from January 7 to April 4, 1891, it appeared that the

[1] I expressed on that occasion the willingness of Mexico to agree to a common silver coin of the same fineness and weight, to be legal tender in all American nations, if they all should accept that agreement, notwithstanding the great drawbacks that Mexico would suffer in that case.   In the remarks that I made before the Conference in the meeting of March 27, 1890, when the Monetary Union recommendation was discussed, I said on the subject what follows :

" It would be difficult for the American nations to agree that the international silver dollar should have the same fineness and weight as the Mexican dollar, because in that case they would create a coin of more value than their own.   And this would necessarily have to be depreciated if they should accept the same fineness and weight as that of the dollar of the United States of America, which is substantially the same as that of several other of the American States.   Then we should have in Mexico two silver coins ; the international one, with the weight and fineness which should be agreed upon, and the Mexican one with higher weight and fineness.   This difference in weight and fineness in two coins of the same nominal value, coined in the same country, could not but cause serious embarrassments.   Notwithstanding all this, Mexico, wishing to contribute as far as it is in her power, and even at the expense of any reasonable effort, to the unifications of institutions and interests with all the other American Republics, has been disposed to accept the coinage of an international silver coin, without undervaluing the fact that any step towards increasing the value of silver will finally be advantageous to us.   .   .   ."

My opinion on the rehabilitation of silver by the United States was expressed in the following words :

" This gentleman fears that if an international silver dollar should be coined by all the American nations, that coin would come to the United States to be exchanged for gold, and that in that way all the gold now in the Treasury should be lost and the United States be obliged to give up their gold standard and become monometallist. In my opinion this fear is ungrounded, because the United States buy from the American nations to the amount of several millions of dollars in raw materials, and the difference between the amount bought and the American goods exported to those countries, which is paid by them in cash, could be paid in international silver coin which they might receive.   Besides, we could agree, as the Latin Monetary Union did, that each American nation should be bound to redeem in gold the international silver dollar that each might coin.   If the basis for coinage should be as the minimum one dollar per each inhabitant in each country, there should be a demand at once for 120,000,000 ounces of silver, which would necessarily increase the value of this metal and have a very great moral influence in the solution of this problem by the other commercial nations of the world."

American delegates would not be in favor of any Monetary Union among the American nations, and that the only way to overcome the difficulties of the case was to recommend the meeting of a Monetary Conference, where all the nations of the world should be represented, which motion was adopted, and led to the meeting of the Monetary Conference which assembled at Brussels from November 22d to December 17th, 1892.

At the fifth meeting of the American International Monetary Commission, which took place on March 30, 1891, I delivered an address in which I again stated the position of Mexico so far as monetary matters were concerned, and foreshadowed the same views expressed in my answer to Senator Morgan, and in my paper published in the *North American Review* for June, 1895. That answer will be found in an appendix to the present paper.

The American countries have different kinds of coin. Venezuela for instance, has as a monetary unit, the *Bolivar*, equal to a franc, and other countries have two kinds of dollars, *peso duro*, and one of less value called *peso feble*, and in each country the dollar has different names. In Ecuador it is called *Sucre*, in Peru, *Sol*, in Bolivia, *Boliviano*, and in Brazil, *Milreis*. The weight and fineness of the silver dollar varies in almost every one of them : some have 9/10 of silver and 1/10 of alloy ; others have less, and others, like Mexico, more than that proportion, and it would be of great advantage if the coins of all American nations, by having the same fineness and weight, should be of the same denomination and value.

Mexican Opinion Favorable to the Silver Standard.—Everybody in Mexico, that is, from the educated to the ignorant, from the rich to the poor, from the natives to the foreigners, and even the bankers [1] who in other countries are decidedly favorable to the gold standard,

---

[1] This assertion is confirmed by the following extracts from an editorial of the *Mexican Herald*, a newspaper published in English in the City of Mexico by very able American editors, in its issue of November 4, 1897.

" *Mexican Bankers and Silver.*—Why are our great bankers so loyal to the cause of silver? Why are they not gold monometalists as are the bankers of England, the United States, and the continent of Europe? It is because they are not merely bankers ; they are heavy investors and directors in new manufacturing industries dependent for their prosperity on the continued use of silver as money in this country. They take a broader view of the currency situation than do bankers abroad, because they are factors in a great manufacturing movement, which has for its ultimate purpose the achieving of Mexico's industrial independence.

" Being something more than lenders of money, they are liberal in their ideas and are not blinded by prejudice. They can see all sides of the currency question. There are many able and sagacious men among the bankers of Mexico and they are, with hardly an exception, bimetallists. They are not trying to make money dear, they are not wrecking properties, but rather are creating industries. . . ."

are all in favor of silver.   The Government holds the same opinion. As Mexico is now prosperous a large portion of the people attribute its prosperity to the silver standard and are therefore decidedly favorable to the continuance of that standard.

It is not strange that Mexicans think so when prominent and able foreigners living there hold the same opinion.

Mr. Lionel E. G. Carden, the very able British Consul at the City of Mexico, who has been in Mexico for nearly eighteen years and understands the country well, has expressed official views on this subject which go much further than my own.   He holds that, while the first effects of the depreciation of silver on the Mexican Government and on the Mexican railroads were unfavorable, the ultimate result will be beneficial and will tend to increase the country's agricultural resources and consequently the republic's export trade, provided that a price shall be arrived at not subject to fluctuations; and that the greatest disadvantages that the Mexican Government and the railways suffer from the depreciation are therefore the constant fluctuations in the market price of silver.   Mr. Carden's views appear in a report on the effect of the depreciation of silver in Mexico, addressed to Lord Rosebery on August 4, 1893.[1]

[1] It would occupy too much space to give here the chief portions of Mr. Carden's report, and I will only insert, therefore some of its main points :

" A low price of silver," Mr. Carden says, " if permanent, would not only not be prejudicial to Mexico as a whole, but would conduce to its ultimate benefit by the stimulus it would afford to the development of its immense agricultural resources." His conclusions are that " the losses which would be sustained by the government and the railway companies are essentially limited in their amount, the benefits which would accrue to certain of the productive industries are susceptible of indefinite extension," and that such extension would " at once make itself felt in an increase in the revenues of the government as well as of the railways."

The reasoning by which these interesting conclusions are supported is somewhat too extensive for full quotation here.   Mr. Carden's report is supplemented by exhaustive tabulations of the statistics on which he formed his views.   He points out that the fall in the exchange value of the Mexican silver dollar from 37d. (its average for some years) to about 33d. (the present level), involved an additional loss to the government of about $2,000,000 in meeting the gold payment on its external debt, while to make good the effect of the silver depreciation on the indebtedness of the railroads on which gold must be paid, the lines would have to increase their earnings by over 23 per cent.   At the same time it is figured out that an increase in the premium on gold from 30 per cent. to 50 per cent. produces, all other things being equal, a loss of 10 per cent. in customs duties to the Government.

Coming to the other and more favorable side of this question, Mr. Carden contends that the fall in silver would be accompanied by an increase in the purchasing power of the country.   The amount of foreign goods imported depends chiefly, he argues, on the number of dollars available for the purchase of such goods, which, in its turn, depends upon the general prosperity of the country.   As the present year, 1893, promises well for the agricultural interests, there are good grounds for expecting that the consequent increased movement of trade will to some extent compensate the

Mr. Carden in a later report to the Foreign Office on the trade of Mexico in 1895 attributes to the depreciation of silver the expansion of that trade and of the general prosperity of the country, as follows:

" This favorable condition of things must be attributed in great measure to the stimulus afforded to the development of the agricultural resources of the country by the depreciation of silver, which, far from being prejudicial, has proved to be of the greatest benefit to Mexico, as I predicted it would in my report on that subject of August, 1893."

I will give now some of the reasons that Mexico has to be so far favorable to the silver standard and not to lose all hope that silver may yet be reinstated as a money metal by the great commercial nations of the world.

The Natural Ratio and the World's Production of Precious Metals. —We have not yet lost all hope of the rehabilitation of silver as one of the money metals of the world, because, although modern machinery and improved methods have cheapened the production of silver, the same causes, and especially the discovery of new and rich gold fields, like South Africa and the Klondike, have increased very largely the proportions of the production of gold.

I will enter into some details on this subject to show that the position of Mexico is not entirely destitute of foundation and sound reason.

loss arising from the fall in value of the silver dollar.   Supposing this fall should continue—as is most likely to be the case when the Sherman act is repealed—the development of agricultural enterprise and the increased movement of trade will have to be considerable to offset the loss in revenue of the government.   Mr. Carden thinks that in four years that movement may increase to the extent of from 10 per cent. to 15 per cent.   Then there has been a notable increase in the exports, not only in amount, but also in the silver value of these articles, the selling price of which, being in gold, is improved by a rise in exchange.   Calculated at 60 per cent. premium as regards the gold values (*i.e.*, taking the silver dollar at 30*d*.), the exports in 1891–92 would show an increase of $21,897,522 over those of 1889–90.   This calculation shows that what would be gained by the increased gold value of the exports more than covers what would be lost in connection with the greater silver cost of the imports ; that is to say, the increased purchasing power of $16,599,800, which a gold premium of 60 per cent. would require, would be met by an increase of $21,897,522 in the value of the exports.   As stocks of merchandise on hand were then considerably reduced, Mr. Carden thought the commercial classes would not suffer much actual loss by a further fall of silver, provided it were fixed and permanent, and that prices would soon adapt themselves to the altered condition of exchange.   The railways, he thought, would find compensation in the ordinary development of their traffic and by the opening up of new traffic for export, while, as for the silver mining enterprise, which is an important factor in Mexico, the profits are not affected by a reduction in the gold value of silver, while the increase in the cost of supplies imported from abroad is offset by the very general existence of a small proportion of gold in the silver ores.   On the other hand, a depreciation of silver would greatly stimulate the mining of gold, copper, and the base metals.

Among the advocates of gold monometallism, and I am not speaking of the intelligent advocates of a single standard, it is commonly said that the reason why most of the nations of civilization have demonetized silver is its excessive production of late years as compared with gold. They always declared that silver is mined so abundantly and so cheaply by modern processes that it has become useless except as token money. But the facts regarding production do not bear out this assertion. Silver, as I will show by unimpeachable statistical authority, is *not* produced in excess at the present time.

It used to be affirmed that, to preserve the parity of exchange between gold and silver, the production of the latter should be as sixteen ounces to one of the former. But since the discovery, in the middle of our century, of the Australian and Californian gold-fields, the output of the yellow metal has been excessive, and that of silver, as Mulhall, the statistician, points out, relatively short. If, he urges, the *production* of the two metals determined their value, silver should be worth at present *33 per cent. more than in 1850*, for from 1850 to the close of 1894 the production of silver, in weight, has been, approximately, but twelve times that of gold—93,714 tons of silver to 8108 of gold.

But the depreciation of silver has been more than 50 per cent., for it sold in London in 1850 at $60\frac{1}{8}$ pence an ounce, and to-day it ranges below 28 pence!

The silver production of the world from 1850 to the beginning of 1895 was as follows:

	SILVER. Tons.	VALUE. Millions of £.
United States...............	30,350	226
Mexico......................	29,910	217
South America..............	13,410	103
Other Countries............	20,044	156
Total	93,714	702

The annual average output of silver at the present time is 5,000 tons, and it is interesting to bear in mind that, in twenty years, from 1850 down to 1870, the average production was only 1050 tons yearly. Taking this fact in connection with its demonetization and the decline of silver in value is explained. There are some curious facts regarding the precious metals, and the following table shows that the world's stock of silver, as compared with gold, was in 1848 as 32 to 1, whereas at present it is less than 20 to 1. The world has taken advantage of the increasing supply of gold to employ it more extensively in money.

THE WORLD'S STOCK OF THE MONEY METALS.

| YEAR. | GOLD. TONS. | | |
	Coined.	Uncoined.	Total.
1800	908	1,822	2,730
1848	1,125	2,450	3,575
1894	5,840	3,460	9,300

| YEAR. | SILVER. TONS. | | |
	Coined.	Uncoined.	Total.
1800	42,000	46,000	88,000
1848	45,200	67,800	113,000
1894	92,000	89,000	181,000

These figures show how, relatively, gold has outdistanced silver ; how slight, in comparison, has been the increase in the world's stock of silver to that of its stock of gold.

And while gold is being mined in a ratio to silver far beyond the averages of former years, the arts are taking up a large proportion of the product. In 1894, the gold mined was 273 tons, and Soetbeer estimates, on a carefully ascertained mass of data, that 100 tons are yearly absorbed in the arts. Silver is being mined at the rate of 5000 tons a year, and 500 tons are consumed in the arts. And, although as silver declines in price the manufacturing use of it increases, it remains a fact that a vastly greater proportion than of gold is available for monetary use.

Mr. Francis B. Forbes, of Boston, a careful student of the currency question, has taken the trouble to compile a series of tables of great value, and, incidentally, he confirms Mulhall's statistics, which I have just given, demonstrating indubitably that silver is not being produced in excess of a just ratio to gold.

TABLE A.—WORLD'S PRODUCTION OF GOLD AND SILVER, 1493–1896.

| | GOLD. | SILVER. | WEIGHT |
	Kilograms.	Kilograms.	Ratio of Silver.
Total production, 50 years, 1801–1850...	118,487	3,272,345	27.6
Total production, 25 years, 1851–1875...	4,775,625	31,003,825	6.5
Total production, 21 years, 1876-1896...	3,991,614	70,841,365	17.7
Total production, 96 years, 1801–1896...	8,885,726	105,117,535	11.8
Add total production from discovery of America by Columbus to beginning of this century, according to best estimates, 308 years, 1493–1800.....	4,633,583	146,554,405	31.6
Aggregate production, 404 years, 1493–1896..........................	13,519,309	251,671,940	18.6

TABLE B.—WORLD'S ANNUAL PRODUCTION OF GOLD AND SILVER
FOR THE ELEVEN YEARS, 1886–1896.

YEARS.	GOLD. Product. Kilograms.	SILVER. Product. Kilograms.	WEIGHT. Ratio of Silver.
1886............................	159,735	2,901,826	18.2
1887............................	159,150	2,989,732	18.8
1888............................	165,803	3,384,865	20.4
1889............................	185,803	3,739,004	20.1
1890............................	178,821	3,921,935	21.9
1891............................	196,577	4,226,427	21.5
1892............................	220,899	4,763,479	21.6
1893............................	236,662	5,165,961	21.8
1894............................	271,768	5,217,608	19.2
1895............................	301,544	5,235,096	17.3
1896............................	316,158	5,008,874	15.8
Total production, 11 years, 1886–1896,	2,392,920	46,554,807	19.5

The remarkable increase in gold extraction in recent years has not been met by a corresponding increase of the silver output. The ratio of silver to gold mined last year is better than the 16 to 1 proportion over which the recent presidential campaign in the United States was fought.

From the beginning of this century down to 1850 the total product of silver weighed 27.6 times as much as the gold output; then came the great gold discoveries in California and Australia, and the next twenty-five years saw the relative weight of the world's production of silver to gold reduced to 6.5, when in Europe a movement began, headed by Michel Chevalier in France, to demonetize gold. Luckily this was not done, and the great flood of the money metal enriched the world and marvellously stimulated commerce, manufacturing, and colonization. In the next period, 1876–96, silver again began to be mined in a normal ratio to the gold output, but the hue and cry against it grew louder and deeper, resulting in the general demonetization of silver in Europe. The fact of greatest significance is that during the ninety-six years of our century ended December, 1896, the ratio of silver to gold was only 11.8.

Mulhall puts it concisely, saying, " If the production of the two metals determined their value, silver ought to be now worth thirty-three per cent. more than in 1850!" And another fact bearing on the great controversy: " The stock of silver as compared to gold in 1848 was as 31 to 1, whereas at present it is less than 20 to 1, and yet silver has fallen fifty per cent. in price."

Why, then, has silver been so discredited, and why is its commercial value so low at present ? There is one obvious answer; it has been legally shorn, that is, artificially, of its value, just as gold, if demonetized, would be accorded a lower price as an article of commerce.

Two facts have been made clear by statistics, one that silver is not extracted, the world over, out of proportion to gold, and, second, the world's stock of silver is, proportionally to gold, less than it was forty-nine years ago.

The old-school political economists maintained stoutly that a monetary standard, to be satisfactory, must have a stable and permanent value. The theory is a very dazzling one for the man who makes up a text-book of political economy and an outline of monetary systems in the quiet of his study, aided by any sound author on logic; but when coming to real life it does not look well. They have assumed that gold is permanent in value and therefore the only reliable monetary yardstick. Practical and accurate observers find fault with the theory that gold is the best possible standard of value because "it does not fluctuate."

It has been shown by laborious students of prices, like Mr. Sauerbeck, that, during the past quarter of a century, gold has risen in value sixty to seventy per cent. as compared with commodities in general, while silver has fallen in relation to staple articles twenty-five to thirty per cent. Gold has been even more unsteady than silver. One great cause of the rise in value of gold is the demonetization of silver, throwing more of the world's monetary work on the yellow metal, while, for exactly the same cause, silver has been discredited. I find the editor of the *Statist*, of London, a trustworthy authority and an advocate of gold, admitting that "*Neither gold nor silver has a stable value independent of its monetary use*, and neither, therefore, satisfies the condition laid down by the older economists." But, as might be expected, the editor of the *Statist* adds: "This is only another illustration of the numberless blunders into which the older economists were led by the deductive method to which they adhered."

Gold makes a very good currency basis for old and wealthy nations, where the banking system is highly developed and credit is perfected, but for young and poor nations, busily engaged in developing their resources, it remains to be seen if it will serve their purpose. The gold and silver question is not one to be studied in a partisan spirit. Perhaps, some day, people will admit that both metals are useful money bases, and the *Statist* itself, a few years ago, wanted to divide the nations into gold-using and silver-using. It was not a bad idea, could it have been arranged by international agreement.

England and Silver.—Another reason why Mexico has not yet given up all hope that silver may be reinstated as a money metal, is the belief that the manufacturing interests of Great Britain would suffer so much by the bounty to manufacturing produced by the depreciation of silver in silver countries that she would have to co-operate with the United States, France, and other nations favoring the restoration of silver. I do not myself share such belief; but in justice to Mexico I think I ought to mention this fact.

There can be no doubt that the manufacturing interests of England are suffering very seriously by the depreciation of silver. In the opinion of competent observers in England the dulness in the cotton textile industry is due largely to the depreciation of silver which has stimulated the manufacture of cotton goods in various other parts of the world. Lancashire, the seat of Britain's cotton manufacturing industry, had, up to July, 1867, 1700 firms engaged in the business, the total spindles being 62,000,000, and the total number of looms 641,547. In this great centre of industry there has been witnessed the extraordinary spectacle of " every department of the cotton trade being under a cloud. The balance sheet of the firms are bound to show serious losses save in a few exceptional cases.'' The cotton exportation to India has fallen off heavily, owing to the famine, the plague, and the diminished purchasing power of silver, and, meantime, most of the machine shops of the North of England have been busy in turning out looms and spindles, " but the bulk of it goes abroad to swell the volume of production, and to furnish grave problems for the textile districts of the North to solve in the future." This is said by the *London Daily Chronicle*, which remarks that there is a general opinion that wages must come down quite ten per cent.

Another English paper that speaks with authority on this subject is the *Cotton Factory Times*, which says:

" So far as Continental markets are concerned, we may practically give them up, except in such classes of yarn and cloth as they cannot conveniently produce themselves. But in Asia and in the South American Republics—which are also mill-building—there is yet room for good business were our currency put on a right footing. Here we have all the Lancashire authorities wringing their hands at what they almost term a deadlock, and yet it is only now and again that they whisper to themselves the true cause."

And then the same journal utters the following sentiment:

" With the purchasing power of the money of our leading customers reduced by nearly one-half, as compared with little over twenty years ago, is it any wonder that they cannot keep increasing their purchases of our goods, and run after producers whose goods are produced under the same currency conditions as their own ? Twenty odd years ago the Asiatic rupee was worth two shillings, and ten of them were worth a pound. Now ten of them are worth, in England, little more than half a sovereign, and as the Hindoo has no more rupees to spend than before, he wants the same quantity of stuff or thereabouts for his rupee, or he won't buy. We do not assert that had silver not been demonetized in 1873 we could have gone on increasing our trade at the rate we had previously done, but there can be no doubt we should have done, and could now, were things altered, be doing a steady trade."

Mexico [1] offers a clear demonstration of the truth of what the *Cotton Factory Times* said, as new cotton mills are built equipped with English machinery, the inevitable result being the supplying to a still greater extent by domestic mills the demand for cotton goods. England is furnishing the weapons wherewith her own great trade is to be reduced in volume.

It would seem to be for the interest of England to do something for silver, in conjunction with the United States, France, and Germany. Possibly, as Dr. Karl Peters, the distinguished German historian, says, in a remarkable article published in 1897 in the *Zukunft*, of Berlin, England need not foster her manufactures as sedulously as formerly, for with the demonetization of silver she gains in the volume of imports needed to pay the interest due her on capital placed abroad, and so is becoming an enormously wealthy banker-nation which can live on her world-wide investments regardless of losses to her manufacturers and merchants.

Dr. Peters is so strong a believer in the eventual preponderance on this planet of the Anglo-Saxon race that he has been criticised sharply for his anglomania by contemporary German writers.

Dr. Peters sees nothing for England to fear in becoming less powerful in manufacturing; she is, in his opinion, destined to change into a purely capitalist country. He adds:

"The time is approaching when Glasgow and Manchester will be unable to compete with foreign rivals, but the capital heaped together in the city of London will control all foreign industry, monopolizing all private property. Already India, America, Australia, and South Africa are forced to send their produce at cheap rates to England, in part payment of dividends and interest. British imperialism is not founded on cannons ; it rests upon money alone, and ancient Rome never exploited her provinces in a more relentless manner than Great Britain her possessions or any country subject to the influence of her capital."

The German historian reckons up the " tribute money " yearly paid in London. India contributes $100,000,000; Australia and South Africa at present $75,000,000, and the United States, at the least calculation, $250,000,000, although French statisticians estimate the " Yankee tribute " at $400,000,000 annually!

[1] Mr. Carden, however, expresses the opinion, in a very able report to the London Foreign Office on *Cotton Manufacturing Industry in Mexico*, dated at the City of Mexico on March 10, 1898 (*British Diplomatic and Consular Reports*, No. 453, *Miscellaneous Series*), that the abundance of money in Mexico seeking investment, and not the depreciation of silver, is the cause of the great increase of the cotton industry in that country, although in another portion of his report he says that the Mexican cotton industry, favored as it is by the very heavy premium on gold, has practically nothing to fear from foreign competition. It seems obvious that the abundance of money seeking investment in Mexico might be due to our silver standard, which has increased so much our exports of commodities, leaving our coin at home.

It seems to me beyond all doubt that for the reason assigned by Dr. Peters, or for other considerations, England will not consent, under the present condition of things, to the rehabilitation of silver.

The United States and Silver from a Mexican Standpoint.—I will not finish this introduction without stating that the opinion prevailing in the United States that Mexico desires this country to adopt the silver standard for the purpose of being helped in the way of less fluctuations and a material increase in the price of silver, is a very mistaken one.   A great many think that should the United States adopt the silver standard, the large profits now derived by selling here in gold the articles produced by us under a silver basis will cease, to the great detriment of Mexico, and they are therefore averse to seeing the United States under the silver basis.

I am sure that nobody in Mexico would like to see the United States debase its currency for the sake of their keeping company with silver standard nations.   We are sure that the great importance of the United States as a commercial and industrial nation will always make its money, whether gold or silver, as good as any other in the world, and while if they favor silver they might contribute to increase the price of that metal, or at least to avoid the present fluctuations, such policy will hardly bring about the debasement of the United States' currency.

The Mexican government and the Mexican people at large would be glad of course if the United States Government, with its commanding position among the great commercial nations of the world, would assist in the restoration of the price of silver, or at least in preventing its falling any lower; but many would rather see the United States adhere to the gold standard, as it means for Mexico exemption from competition, and also a gold premium bounty ' on tropical products.

[1] A great many in Mexico consider as an advantage the permanent depreciation of silver, and this statement is borne out by the following remarks of Mr. William J. Bryan in a letter, on his recent visit to Mexico, that was published in the New York *World* of January 23, 1898, in which he says :

" I found quite a number of Mexicans who went so far as to express the hope that the United States would continue the gold standard because of the advantage which Mexican manufacturers find in a high rate of exchange, but the majority of the people with whom I talked desire the restoration of bimetalism in the United States in order that stability in exchange may be added to stability in prices "

My statement is also confirmed by the following extract from an interview which Captain W. G. Raóul, President of the Mexican National R. R. Co., had with a New Orleans *Times-Democrat* correspondent published in the issue of that paper of September 4, 1896 :

" Mexican merchants do not want to see the United States go on a silver basis. Mexico has a good thing as matters are now, and she don't want to share the silver pudding with the people on the north of her.   Free silver is a blessing to any community or country . . ."

Mexico and the Gold Standard.—I have been often asked why Mexico does not adopt the gold standard and place herself abreast with the great commercial nations of the world. On this account I think it proper to present some views on the subject.

It would be a great deal more difficult for Mexico to accept the gold standard than for the United States to adopt the silver standard, because, the silver standard having been in operation in Mexico for four hundred years, to abandon it and come to the gold standard, a higher standard of value, would entail untold losses, a great disturbance of business, many failures, and almost universal ruin; while the adoption of the silver standard in the United States, although undoubtedly it would be accompanied by very serious disturbances in business and by heavy losses, might ultimately result, considering the great importance of this country as a commercial and manufacturing nation, in the restoration of silver as a money metal by the other commercial nations of the world, although without a reasonable certainty that such should be the result, a certainty not easy to obtain, it would not be prudent to make hastily such a change.

Although we have suffered so far all the drawbacks of the silver standard that I will presently mention, we are satisfied with it, because it has not been an unmitigated evil, as it has brought us decided advantages. We are willing, therefore, to wait and see what is the final outcome of this question, and watch the result of several experiments in adopting the gold standard which are now being made by some of the recent silver standard nations, like Japan, Chili, and especially India.[1] It is my personal opinion that the commercial nations of the world will finally reinstate silver as a money metal, going

[1] I think it would be interesting to state what has been, so far, the result of the adoption of the gold standard by Chili and Japan, and of the closing of the Indian mints to the free coinage of silver. Perhaps the data that I have on that subject is not entirely impartial, as in every country where the silver standard prevails public opinion is divided on that question, a strong party advocating the adoption of the gold standard and the other the permanence of the silver or paper money currency, and perhaps the friends of the old system exaggerate the inconveniences of the change.

The adoption of the gold standard may necessarily bring about, at least for some time, serious disturbances consequent to such an important change in the monetary system of the country, and perhaps, notwithstanding the disadvantages stated in the information that I have received, such changes would in the end be beneficial to the nations which have adopted it, but that would only appear with the lapse of a reasonable time. In the case of Chili, that country, like Argentina and Brazil, was really under a paper money basis, which, as compared with gold, was worth a great deal less than silver, and therefore the change that Chili has made may ultimately be beneficial to her, because it is an advantage to change from a paper money to a coin money.

Japan has adopted the gold standard in so far as to redeem in gold her silver coins at the ratio of 1 to 32, and Chili has done the same at the ratio of 1 to 42. Both in-back to the bimetallic standard which long prevailed for so long, but if that should not be so, and all the nations of the world would accept the gold standard, and if silver should command as low a price as any of the base metals, like lead or copper, we of course would accept the gold standard, especially if by that time we can produce, as I have

tended to equal the legal with the commercial ratio of silver, but as the market price of silver changes so often, their object so far has been frustrated.

In the case of India, undoubtedly the Colonial Government has saved, by closing the mints to the free coinage of silver, large amounts of money in buying exchange on London ; but whether the closing of the mints is beneficial to the country at large, I think cannot yet be ascertained, and is a matter subject to further developments.

The following is the information referred to :

Japan.—Some newspapers of the Mikado's Empire are lamenting that the gold standard was ever thought of. In recent reviews of the year 1897 appearing in the native papers, there is a general condemnation of the gold standard. It is admitted that the financial situation in Japan is worse than it was in 1896. Public securities have fallen, railway and industrial shares are very low, and many new undertakings have stopped for lack of funds. And worse than all, the exportation of cotton yarns to silver-using China has come to a standstill. The Japanese papers ascribe this to the gold standard.

The *Tiji Shimpo*, an important paper, says :

" The adoption of the gold standard is the worst mistake ever committed by the government in the long history of the thirty years that have passed since the present Meiji era began. The Matsukata ministry, however, must bear the full responsibility for it. The prospect which the country had of still further developing her industries owing to the depreciation of silver compared with gold has now been ruthlessly thrown away. Our trade with silver-using countries has already been greatly injured. In China, Corea, and the Strait settlements, where at one time Japanese products found a good market and were rapidly expelling foreign goods, Japan is now losing ground and is likely soon to have little footing left. Many of the factories in the western part of Japan are closing or only running on half time."

And *Greater Japan* remarks in the same tone :

" We can speak only in gloomy terms of the year just past. Commercial affairs and political affairs reached their lowest depths of depression and mismanagement. The introduction of the gold standard proved a complete failure. It was to have opened the door to an inflow of foreign capital, thus succoring the distress of the industrial classes and producing an appreciation in the price of public securities. But foreign capital has not come in, neither have public securities appreciated. On the contrary, we have seen an ever-increasing preponderance on the side of imports, a corresponding outflow of specie, and a steady fall in the price of bonds. Nor is this all. The effect of the demonetization of silver has been fatal to the most promising of all Japan's industrial enterprises—cotton spinning. Its chief market has been closed against it, and the prosperity that distinguished it at the close of 1896 was replaced by adversity at the end of 1897."

The gold standard is not probably the sole cause of the bad times in Japan, for the people there have become imbued with a speculative spirit and the rage for easily made fortunes is to be noted there as in Europe and the United States.

Chili.—According to a well-informed financial paper of Chili, *La Tribuna de Valparaiso*, the adoption of the gold standard in that country, some two years ago, has not given satisfactory results. In point of fact, it is asserted that since the former

no doubt we will, a large amount of gold, namely, from $20,000,000 to $25,000,000 a year, which will be the basis of our gold currency.

Another reason which makes it difficult for Mexico to adopt the gold standard, is that we are very large producers of silver, the United States only being ahead of us; therefore it would be injurious to our interests to depreciate that metal in our own market, such being the

financial policy was discarded and gold has become the only circulating medium, poverty and a paralyzation of business seems to have fallen to the lot of many districts that heretofore were very flourishing. There is a noticeable scarcity of circulating medium all over the country, public and private securities have depreciated, and the rate of interest which some years ago was 7 or 8 per cent. is now as high as 12 per cent. Furthermore, since the gold standard was introduced, five banks, with an aggregated capital of $3,300,000, have failed, and three, with capital amounting to $12,300,000 have gone into liquidation. Thus it is said that 25 per cent. of the money invested in banking in that country has been lost, and a similar result has obtained with regard to many mining and industrial enterprises which heretofore had been in a most flourishing condition.

India.—The opinion of many intelligent bankers and merchants of India seems to be favorable to silver. The *Indian Spectator*, reflecting accurately this opinion, said recently : '' The attitude of the government of India is indeed too plainly one of a pronouncedly uncompromising character. They have pinned their faith on the great experiment of 1893, believing too optimistically that the day is come when it will succeed, and we shall have gold brought to our mints at 1*s.* 4*d.* a rupee, and are delighted at the prospect of having the Indian currency assimilated with the English, which indeed it would do if we had gold sovereigns in India in quantity large enough to make the rupee in reality a mere token coin. We are not at all confident that such a consummation is very near to us now. Nor can we pay exclusive attention to our trade with England alone, and be blind to the fact that the present currency arrangements have told very injuriously upon our growing trade with the silver-using East.''

And confirming the views of Chairman Yule of the Bank of Calcutta, one of the ablest advocates of silver-coinage resumption in all India, the *Indian Spectator* goes on to say : '' The unrestricted inflow of silver bullion and the tightness of the money market are other effects of the currency legislation of 1893 which we cannot view with equanimity. We cannot, therefore, approve of the attitude taken by our government or their determination, expressed in their dispatch in so many words, to persist in their policy of introducing a gold standard in the country and not to go back and be a party to any problematic scheme of bi-metallism. Nor can we believe that we would be worse off if, with our mints open, we could by any means raise silver up and be content with a purely silver currency.''

The following is an abstract of the opinion of the Anglo-Indian press on the present financial conditions in the second week of February, 1898, published by the London *Times :*

'' Since the closure of the Indian mints the rupee has had an artificial value on an intermediate level between gold and silver. It has been a scarcity rupee, not representing the market value of silver, but the lack of an adequate supply of currency. The Indian government, having large gold payments to make in England every year, has profited by an artificial scarcity of money. If the rupee had been on a par with silver in its downward course the remittances would have been heavily increased. The Indian government, since the closing of the mints to silver, has produced a money

necessary consequence of our accepting the gold standard. Now, it has not been depreciated at home, for it has the same purchasing power that it had when silver was at a par with gold, at a ratio of 16 to 1 ; silver has only depreciated in foreign markets, but should we accept a gold standard we necessarily would depreciate it in our own country, which is our largest and most important market.

famine for the sake of obtaining more favorable rates of exchange in its own transactions with London."

The results of this policy as explained by financial writers in India have been disastrous to all classes. The average rate of interest has risen from $4\frac{1}{2}$ in 1895 and $5\frac{3}{4}$ in 1896 to $7\frac{11}{12}$ in 1897. How high it will go in 1898 no expert ventures to forecast. In Calcutta loans have been negotiated as high as 14 per cent., while in Bombay, according to *The Times*, of India, even " 24 per cent. would not bring out an advance upon the most solid of all securities, namely gold bars." With a bank rate of 10 per cent. merchants have been embarrassed in selling their bills, and commercial enterprise has been paralyzed. This continuous money stringency, while fatal to economic progress, has also affected the capacity of the masses for purchasing food in famine times. Mr. B. M. Malabari, in his pamphlet on *India in 1897*, discusses the vital question whether the famine results from the absence of foodstuffs or from the want of means of buying food. The London *Times* makes this weighty summary of financial opinion in India :

" If the conviction once possesses the Indian mind that the artificial enhancement of the rupee is a contributory cause of famine, it will furnish a common rallying cry for all classes—peasant and townsman, rich and poor—such as has never before been raised. Put in economic terms, the contention is that the government, in order more easily to discharge its own gold obligations, has subjected India to an artificial currency that bears down the producing industries on which the present and the future of the people depend. Thus stated, the question is open to fair argument. But if it passes from the Anglo-Indian to the vernacular press, it will cease to be stated in economic terms, and become a popular cry of the spoliation of the peasant,—that cry for which it has hitherto been our endeavor to avoid giving any just cause."

Financial writers in Calcutta and Bombay do not hesitate to say that there is imminent danger lest the idea that the famine in food as connected with the famine in money may take hold of the Indian mind.

From some statements made by Lord George Hamilton, Secretary of State for India, in a debate on the Indian currency, which took place in the House of Commons of the British Parliament on March 29, 1898, it appears that in the opinion of the Indian Office it would be impossible to reopen the Indian mints without some international arrangement, which at present is considered out of the question, and that the British Government was so perfectly satisfied with the closing of the Indian mints that the attempt to reopen them was qualified as an act of lunacy. The Liberal element in the House of Commons seemed to be entirely satisfied with Lord George Hamilton's views, as Sir William Vernon Harcourt, Liberal leader in the House, congratulated Lord George Hamilton upon his speech in which he expressed the views just quoted, and the House then adopted Lord George Hamilton's motion, appointing a committee which will have practically all the powers of a royal commission to inquire into the practicability of the Indian Government's proposals for a gold standard. At the same time, during the discussion of the budget debate in the Indian Legislative Council, Sir James Westland, the financial member of the Council, announced that he could declare that a silver standard or the reopening of the Indian mints was now impossible.

It would seem easy for Mexico to overcome all the drawbacks of the silver standard by decreeing the payment in gold of the whole or of a portion of its import duties; but such a scheme would establish two different kinds of currency in Mexico, and, gold being the more valuable, would tend to depreciate within the limits of Mexico our silver currency, with disadvantages to all the interests in the country. There is another serious objection to that plan: our import duties are already so high that they do not admit of any further increase. If we collected them in gold, we should have to reduce them to about fifty per cent. of the present rates, now payable in silver, and then we should have gained nothing, but increased the disadvantage of the fluctuations in the price of silver bullion; while if we should leave the import duties at or about their present rates, and make them payable in gold, we should practically double them, and they would become so burdensome as to afford great encouragement to smuggling, and so reduce very considerably their proceeds, especially considering the high increase in the value of foreign commodities caused by the depreciation of silver.[1]

[1] In this regard, I think it interesting to insert here a letter from Señor Don Jose Yvés Limantour, the Secretary of the Treasury of Mexico, addressed on August 18, 1897, to Mr. Ottoman Haupt, a well known French currency authority and gold monometallist, who has advocated the adoption of the gold standard in Mexico, and even suggested a practical way to do it, in which letter the policy of the Mexican Government on the subject is clearly outlined, and the difficulties of adopting the gold standard ably presented.

" *Mexico City, August* 18, 1897.

" *D. Ottoman Haupt, Esq., Paris :*

" MY DEAR SIR :—Your esteemed letter of July 21st last came duly to hand, and I answer the same with pleasure, anxious to meet the laudable intentions that have no doubt prompted you to communicate to me your opinions in regard to the monetary question in Mexico.

" Let me begin by assuring you that you made no mistake when you thought that your special studies upon the subject were known to me. In fact, your principal works have a prominent place in my library, and I always read the same with interest and frequently consult them.

" You are furthermore right when you assure me that it is not at present an academical discussion upon the convenience of a single unit or a double unit, but of an essentially practical problem whose solution is every day more urgently needed. Some time has already elapsed since this study was taken up by the Secretaryship under my charge, and, as you can readily understand, the Government follows closely the general phases under which the monetary question presents itself, as well as it tries to follow under its various hues the consequences that are likely to follow.

" There is no doubt that on account of this subject a panic reigns the world over, under which influence many nations, with or without cause, be it for lucrative purposes or on account of an immitative mania, have changed their monetary system and have put silver in the shade.

" It is also true that other nations such as India and China, which were enormous consumers of the white metal, have diminished or stopped buying it, and the fact is

Mexico and the Ratio.—I think it is beyond all question that the main, if not the only, cause of the depreciation of silver is the fact of its having been demonetized, and there can be no doubt that should the mints of the world be again open to the free coinage of silver, as they were before 1872, at the ratio then existing, the market price of that metal would be again as it was then as compared with gold, in the proportion of sixteen to one.

I am sure the Mexican Government would accept any ratio that the commercial nations of the world should be willing to agree upon, even in case it differs from the old one. So far as my personal views are concerned I would rather stand by this ratio, because it is the natural ratio, and because it stood for four hundred years with almost no break or difficulty, but serving a good purpose. Should any other ratio, whether eighteen, twenty, or more, to one, be adopted, it would be an artificial one, having to stand upon only the statute books of the commercial nations of the world opening their mints to the free coinage of silver at such ratio.

Important Papers on Silver Printed by the United States Senate.— The Senate of the United States has ordered, on motion of several of its members holding opposite views, the printing of many very inter-

also true, beyond any doubt, that its production has constantly increased and in a progression most rapid. All of these circumstances combined have tended to, or at least hastened, the depreciation of silver.

" Is this question, however, settled fatally and definitely, or does it not admit of any remedy or relief? You seem to think so, but I, for my part, am not yet convinced of it, and independently of any opinion that may be had on this important subject, many powerful reasons exist why Mexico should not change its silver monetary unit, at least whilst some of its economic peculiarities remain.

" In my answer to Mr. Jacoby, which you read, I brought forward and tried to give in detail the two sorts of difficulties that would beset us in order to exchange the silver for the gold unit. The first of these difficulties involves the means to procure the necessary gold for our circulation, and the second (and evidently the most serious) almost borders on the impossible, for it means no less than the necessity for keeping the gold in the country and suppressing its exportation.

" Mexico's commercial balance is very unfavorable, its exportations far exceeding its importations, and besides the value of these latter it has to pay in gold the service of its foreign debt, the interest on its bonds, its railroad dividends, and those of many other industrial and mining enterprises, which have been established or are worked with foreign capital. In favorable years this unequilibrium is partially neutralized with the new European capital coming to seek investment in the country, but this compensating factor disappears completely in feverish times, and, moreover, when silver is suffering continual depreciations.

" Well, taking altogether the exportations necessary to pay up these various sums : silver represents from 55 to 60 per cent., and the remaining 45 or 40 per cent. other products ; in other words, 65,000,000 of silver against 45,000,000 or 50,000,000 of all other export articles put together.

" Under these conditions, what expedient must we resort to in order to retain the necessary gold bought, and not to suffer the deception, which other nations have had

esting papers bearing on bimetallism and specially on the silver question and on the effects of the depreciation of silver in the Eastern nations, which form now a very instructive collection, containing a great deal of very useful information on that subject. On motion of Senator Chandler, presented on June 6, 1898, a list of such papers has just been published (55th Congress, 2d Session. Senate. Doc. No. 286), and for the benefit of the readers who desire a source of information, I append that list to this paper. Special mention is due to two of these papers, namely : A summary of the results of the injuries which the world has suffered by the depreciation of silver, presented in a very concise manner by Baron de Courcel, French Ambassador at London, at a meeting held at the Foreign Office on July 15, 1897, where the three American commissioners sent to Europe to negotiate an international bimetallic agreement were present, besides Ambassador Hay, Lord Salisbury, and several other members of the British Cabinet, which appears in the Minutes of that meeting, published among the papers presented to Parliament in October, 1897, and which the Senate of the United States ordered to be printed on January 17, 1898, on motion of Senator Chandler (55th Congress, 2d Session. Senate. Doc. No. 69) ; and an extract from the speech of Monsieur Méline, President of the Council and Minister of Agriculture, delivered in the French Chamber of Deputies on the 20th of November, 1897, which shows very clearly the evils resulting to the world at large from the depreciation of silver, and that such depreciation is not due to the increased production of that metal (55th Congress, 2d Session. Senate. Doc. No. 26).

The Paper as Published in the North American Review.—After having made the foregoing statements and explanations in this rather lengthy introduction, it is time to insert the paper as it appeared in the *North American Review* for June, 1895.

that have adopted the gold unit, of seeing, powerless to avoid it, the exodus of their gold to foreign nations?

"Truly, I have been unable to satisfactorily answer to myself this question. As long as silver remains in circulation, it is well known by Gresham's law that gold is invariably exported, and to limit the circulation of silver is not to be thought of in a country that produces it, perhaps, in more abundance than any other in the world.

"To issue gold certificates to keep the metal on hand is not in my opinion practical, because if such certificates are not redeemable at the will of the bearer it entails a very delicate question of credit, and would expose us to unfavorable unforseen disasters and contingencies, and if it were otherwise the certificates would at once be converted into gold and immediately exported.

"I finish this letter assuring you that it will always be a pleasure to me to hear your opinion upon subjects that to you are so familiar and that you cultivate and elucidate with such a recognized ability.

"Believe me, yours sincerely.

J. Y. LIMANTOUR."

THE SILVER STANDARD IN MEXICO.

The editor of the *North American Review* asked me some time ago for an article about the industrial, agricultural, and commercial conditions of Mexico, as compared with the same conditions in the United States, in connection with the monetary systems existing in both countries. I was very reluctant to write on that subject, fearing that my remarks might be construed as showing a desire on my part to meddle in the important currency questions then pending in this country, or as an attempt to institute a comparison between Mexico and the United States, in which Mexico should appear in an advantageous position,[1] nothing being further from my mind than either of these purposes. Senator Morgan from Alabama subsequently made some inquiries of me on the same subject, and I could not refuse to give him the information he desired; after which I saw no objection to furnishing it to the *North American Review*, and I used in the preparation of this article everything that I said to Senator Morgan in answer to his inquiry:

No Possible Comparison Between Mexico and the United States.—I must begin, however, by saying that it would be neither desirable nor proper for me to enter into a comparison between Mexico and the United States. This country is so far in advance of Mexico in material progress, commerce, manufactures, improved methods of agriculture, high wages, public education, accumulation of wealth, banking and banking facilities, and so many other things, that such a comparison would be unfair, although in some respects Mexico has suffered less than this country during the present financial crisis. I shall, therefore, confine myself to stating the advantages and disadvantages produced in Mexico by the silver standard prevailing there, without drawing any conclusions from the facts presented, so that every reader can draw his own.

[1] This article was written and published at the time when the financial crisis of 1893 was producing its direst effects in the United States, that is, when prices had come down, factories were closed, operatives dismissed, wages reduced, strikes occurring everywhere, business depressed, many men were without employment, and in consequence of all that a very unsatisfactory condition of things prevailed all over the country. It is to that condition of things that the article refers in stating that Mexico had not suffered so much as the United States during that period.

But in doing so, I must disclaim all purpose of commenting in any manner, even by implication, on the monetary question in the United States. My position here, both as an alien and more especially as the official representative of a friendly foreign country, precludes me from meddling in any way in a public question pending in the United States. Besides the conditions of the two countries are so widely different, that they can hardly be compared with each other, and what is advantageous to one might be inconvenient, or even hurtful, to the other. My statements have therefore reference to Mexico alone and in no way to the United States.

Reasons why Mexico has the Silver Standard.—Mexico is legally a bimetallic country, because we have free coinage of both gold and silver at the ratio of 16 to 1 ; but practically we are a silver monometallic country, because under the operation of the Gresham Law all the gold bullion and the gold coin existing in Mexico is exported as merchandise, having a much greater market value than its legal value in Mexico, and silver is therefore the only metallic money used there in payment of debts or for any other purpose. The silver standard prevailing in Mexico was not adopted from choice. Mexico being the largest silver-producing country, over two thirds of the whole silver stock of the world having come out of its mines, silver has been our only currency for nearly four hundred years. We have kept so far our monetary standard, because, as will be seen farther on, it has not been an unmitigated evil for Mexico, because we have hoped that the commercial nations of the world would find it to their interest to rehabilitate silver in some way, and also because we have been anxious to avoid the derangements and disadvantages consequent to a change of monetary standard which would be also felt, although not in such a degree, by the United States, should they attempt to change their present gold standard for a silver one. A change from the silver to the gold standard would cause in Mexico general ruin, as we do not yet produce gold enough to base our currency on that metal, and as our exports of commodities are not yet sufficiently large to allow us to buy all the gold we need for that purpose. The high price of gold is a great incentive to gold-mining, and if gold continues at the present high price for some time, I am sure Mexico will before long be a large producer of that metal.

We never had any paper currency, either national, state, or issued by banks. Two or three banks, indeed, have now issued notes, but they are not legal tender. They are convertible into silver coin at the holder's pleasure, and while they circulate freely in the large cities and for convenience' sake are preferred to the hard dollar, they are almost unknown in the small towns and in the country. The bank issues special notes for each place, which are redeemable only in that place, thus keeping up in effect the old system of charging a high premium for the exchange of money from one place to another, the item of profit to the banks corresponding with what used to be the charge for transporting silver money.

Advantages of the Silver Standard to Mexico.—The advantages to Mexico of the silver basis are the following, most of which could not be applicable to the United States on account of the different conditions prevailing in each country : [1]

[1] The effects of the silver standard for all countries, and without taking into consideration the peculiar conditions of any one, are very clearly stated in the Report of the Committee appointed by the Japanese Government to study the question of standard, previous to their adoption of the gold standard, which was printed by order of the Senate of July 7, 1897, as Senate Document No. 176, 55th Congress, 1st Session. I take from that report the following heads on the subject of such advantages, without giving in detail the explanations and reasons of the report to sustain its views.

The effects of the silver standard are :

1. Increase of exports.
2. Rise in prices of commodities.
3. Light burden of debtors and taxpayers.
4. Good condition of agriculture.
5. Development of commerce and industry.
6. Increase in revenue from taxes and other sources.
7. Increase in demand for labor.
8. Increase of national expenditure.
9. Distress of those who receive fixed wages.
10. Disadvantages to creditors.
11. Growth of speculative enterprise.
12. Rise in prices of commodities imported from gold countries and decrease in imports.

The effects of the gold standard as enumerated in that report are the following :

1. Profits to creditors.
2. Fall in prices of commodities imported from silver countries.
3. Decrease of national expenditure.
4. Depreciation of prices of commodities.
5. Loss to debtors and taxpayers.
6. Depression of commerce and industry.
7. Decline of rate of interest.
8. Distress of farmers.
9. Decrease in revenue.
10. Distress of employers.
11. Decrease in demand of labor.
12. Increase of imports from silver countries.

The report concludes by enumerating the effects in Japan of the recent change of ratio between gold and silver.

1. Radical change in the relative prices of gold and silver.
2. Gold appreciated more than silver depreciated.
3. The chief cause of change in the ratio of gold and silver is the increased demand for gold in several countries.
4. The change in the ratio of gold and silver gives advantages to the silver countries and disadvantages to the gold countries.

1st. The silver standard encourages very materially, so long as other leading commercial nations have the single gold standard, the increase of exports of domestic products, because the expenses of producing them, land, wages, rent, taxes, etc., are paid in silver, and therefore their cost, as compared with their market value, is considerably less than that of similar articles produced or raised in single gold standard countries. When sold in gold markets, therefore, they bring very profitable prices, as they are converted into silver, at a high rate of exchange. These conditions have caused a great development in the exportation of some of our agricultural products, because they yield very large profits; coffee, for instance, which costs on an average about ten cents a pound to produce it, all expenses included, has been sold at about twenty cents in gold in foreign markets. The export of other agricultural products which did not pay when gold and silver were at par, that is, at the ratio of one to sixteen, is now remunerative, because there is returned to us in exchange more than we lose in the gold price of the article.

The same is the result of some agricultural products that we could not export before because their price in foreign markets was not remunerative. Such is the case, for instance, with beans, which at eight cents would not pay when silver and gold were at par, but now that eight cents in gold make about sixteen cents in silver, it is a profitable price. Our exports for several years preceding 1869 were about, a year $20,000,000 00

1872–73	31,594,005 14
1888–89	60,158,423 02
1891–92	75,467,714 95
1892–93	87,509,207 00 [1]

The Statistical Bureau of the Mexican Government quotes the price of our exports in silver, and therefore to find them in gold they have to be reduced to the market price of silver, but, even reduced to one-half, the increase is very remarkable.

Formerly we used to export only silver and gold ; because of their

5. Japan has made great economic progress.
6. Increase of national expenditures.
7. Distress of those who receive fixed wages.
8. Loss of creditors.
9. Prevalence of speculative enterprise.
10. Rise in prices of goods imported from gold countries.
11. Tendency to luxury.
12. The opening of the mint invites the import of silver.
13. Stagnation in commercial dealings with Japan and gold countries.
14. Decrease of capital investments from gold countries.

[1] For the last two fiscal years our exports were : 1895–96, $105,016,902.00 ; 1896–97, $111,346,494.00.

small weight and bulk relatively to their value, they were the only articles that paid for transportation. But the proportion of other commodities has been increased recently to fifteen, twenty, thirty, and forty per cent. of the export of our precious metals, and during the fiscal year ending June 30, 1896, the proportion was sixty-one per cent., as the exports of precious metals amounted to $64,838,596, and the exports of commodities to $40,178,306.

2d. The silver standard is a great stimulus to the development of home manufactures, because foreign commodities have to be paid for in gold, and, owing to the high rate of exchange, their prices are so high that it pays well to manufacture some of them at home, our low wages also contributing to this result.[1]

For these reasons we are increasing considerably our manufacturing plants, especially our cotton mills, smelters, etc., and we begin now to manufacture several articles that formerly we used to buy from foreign countries, and all this, notwithstanding that the mountainous character of our country, the want of interior navigable watercourses, and the scarcity of fuel, make manufacturing very expensive in Mexico. But we are finding abundant coal deposits, and, when our railroads tap our coal-fields, that objection will be considerably diminished. One of our railroads, the International, built by Mr. C. P. Huntington and his associates, has already reached a very large coal-field at Salinas, near Piedras Negras, which is now supplying with coal a part of the country, and even some sections of the Southern Pacific system of this country, but of course it cannot supply the whole of Mexico. When that need is satisfied, we shall have to contend only with the increased expenses of transporting the raw material to the factories and the

[1] Mr. Ransom, United States Minister in the City of Mexico, confirms this statement in the following paragraph from his report on the Currency, Prices, and Condition of Labor in Mexico, dated at the City of Mexico, September 26, 1896, and published in Vol. XIII., Part I., of the *Special Consular Reports :*

" Manufacturing in Mexico has been developed to a considerable extent, especially in the manufacture of the coarser grades of cotton and woollen goods, ordinary bleachings, goods for shawls, prints, and calicoes, woollen cloth ; also in the manufacture of the products of sugar-cane, alcohol, paper, cigars, and cigarettes. Many well-informed persons believe that the depreciation of the price of silver has been the main cause of the development of these industries. To some extent this is doubtless true ; the large discount on silver has had its influence in depressing foreign importation and stimulating domestic production. But other powerful causes have had their effect in this direction—an able, wise, and just administration of the government during the presidency of General Diaz, the confidence of the Mexican people and foreigners in the stability of the government, the building of railroads (all but the one from Veracruz to the City of Mexico having been completed since 1883), the improvement of coast harbors, the enlargement of commerce, the liberal action of the government toward new industries ; in fact, the general influences of law, liberty, peace, and commerce, have all contributed to this result."

manufactured goods to the place of consumption over a mountainous country with high grades and many sharp curves, unless some new means of transportation may be hereafter devised which shall overcome those obstacles. Eventually Mexico will utilize for manufacturing the many streams, almost torrents, which come down the steep mountains, and which constitute a very large water-power.

One of the leading directors of the Mexican Central Railroad, has informed me that about ten years ago the supplies imported to operate that road amounted to sixty per cent. of all the material used, and that to save the loss on exchange, the company has been following the system of manufacturing in Mexico all that they possibly can, and that the proportion of foreign supplies imported during the last year has been reduced now to twenty per cent., and that they have decided to use Mexican rails, as soon as they can be manufactued in Mexico, which will still further considerably reduce that percentage.

As it is now, some manufacturing plants of the United States are being taken to Mexico, as appears in the following extract from the annual report of Mr. W. G. Raoul, President of the Mexican National Railroad Company, for the year 1894 [1]:

"The most extensive and best equipped shops owned by the company are on the north side of the Rio Grande, in the United States, but the greater expense of operating them has caused the withdrawal of much of the work from them to the shops of Mexico. Our shops in Mexico are not adequate for the entire work of the road, and the removal of the Texas plant into Mexico becomes an economic necessity, if the peculiar trade and the industrial conditions now existing respectively in the two countries are to continue."

A like result has been obtained in other countries which are or were on a silver basis, such as Japan, China, and India, the depreciation of silver, or the high rates of exchange having forced those countries to manufacture staple goods for home consumption and in some cases even for export, and this fact begins to be sorely felt in England and other old manufacturing countries.[2]

The development of manufactures in Mexico has also brought about an increase in the production of raw materials consumed in our

---

[1] In 1896 the Mexican National Railroad had continued the same policy, as is shown by the following extract from an interview which Mr. Raoul had with a New Orleans *Times-Democrat* correspondent, and which appears in the issue of that paper of September 4, 1896:

"We find it to the interest of our company to do all our repairing and building of cars in Mexico. Our shops are located at Laredo, Texas, but they are practically closed, and we do nearly everything at the City of Mexico and other points. In this way free silver benefits a community, gives its citizens plenty of work, draws it away from gold-standard countries, and thus furnishes a continual stream of prosperity."

[2] The following remarks contained in a paper read at a recent session (1897) of the Royal Colonial Institute in London, by the Hon. T. H. Whitehead, of Hong Kong, China, which deals with the effects of the depreciation in the value of silver, on the trade of Great Britain with the Orient, confirms my statement about the great stimulus that the

manufactories, and which before we used to buy from foreign countries, as is the case with cotton. The price of such articles in gold makes them so high that it is cheaper to raise them at home.

low price of silver is to manufacturing in silver countries, and he presents the case with such clearness that I think it worth while to insert his remarks here.

"In Oriental countries we are witnessing remarkable industrial progress, and unequalled prosperity among their people, when simultaneously serious losses are attending similar industries in England ; while under the present system it is highly probable that there will be a further fall in the present very low level of gold prices, which will still more prejudice the position of the British manufactures. What is also of unquestionable great concern in the Empire, is that it may lead to the transference of a large part of our principal industries to silver-using countries. So long as the gold value of silver continues to be as it is now, liable to violent fluctuations, the more perilous must become the conditions of the principal British industries, and the more possible must it be to prevent disaster from overtaking them. British labor and gold capital can no longer compete on equal terms with Asiatic labor and silver capital, and the position of British industries is growing more critical every day.

"Turning to the jute manufacture, we find that about thirty years ago nearly the whole of it centered in Dundee, whereas now about one third is conducted on the banks of the Hoogly, near Calcutta. The removal of this trade from our shores has been most detrimental to British interests. Its transfer is unquestionably due in very great measure to the fall in the gold price of silver, and to the subtle advantages arising therefrom in favor of the manufacturer in silver countries. On a falling exchange, *i. e.*, when the gold price of silver is declining, and it has been doing so for upwards of twenty years, the Dundee manufacturer is placed at a relative disadvantage compared with the Calcutta manufacturer. To clearly explain how this arises is not very easy. However, take one example, and let it be supposed that both manufacturers buy the raw jute at the same slver price, and that the cost of manufacturing it in both countries is similar. The cost includes (1) jute ; (2) wages ; and (3) locally produced stores for the mills, and taxes, etc. If each manufacturer realizes the same gold price for his product, the Dundee manufacturer closes the transaction at once. Before the Dundee product arrives in Australia or New York, and before payment can be made therefor in those countries, the gold value of silver falls, and the Calcutta manufacturer consequently thereby receives more silver for the gold price of his product. To that extent does he derive an advantage for, though he received a large number of rupees, he pays away no more for wages, locally produced stores, and taxes. For instance, say a ton of manufactures produced in Calcutta is sold for 50£, and that exchange on the day of sale is 1s. 4d. per rupee ; the equivalent would be Rs. 750, of which Rs. 500 would be required to defray the cost of manufacturing, including profit, and that Rs. 250 would represent wages, mill stores and taxes, all payable in rupees ; but before the Calcutta manufacturer is paid in New York or Australia, and before he is able to convert the gold price, 50£, he obtained for his goods, exchange, or the gold price of silver, falls, say to 1s. 2d. per rupee. This would give him for his 50£, Rs. 857.14, instead of Rs. 750 ; the surplus of Rs., 107.14, equal to 6£, 5s., would be a further profit and additional to what the Dundee manufacturer would receive. To that extent, viz., 12 per cent., does the silver-using country derive an unequal advantage. The more the gold price of silver falls after the sale of the product is effected in sterling, and previous to converting gold into silver, the greater will be his advantage over the British manufacturer, and there are other and more subtle benefits favorable to the Oriental and detrimental to the home industries, of sufficient importance to explain the transfer of so much of the trade from Dundee to Calcutta."

3d. While the fall of silver and free coinage in Mexico have not given to the Mexican silver coins, when converted into foreign exchange or sold for gold, any value other than that of the silver bullion contained in the same, nevertheless the purchasing power of the silver dollar is now, on the whole, as great as it ever was in Mexico, and it has only been reduced in the case of foreign articles, so that one can buy now almost the same amount of home commodities for the same number of dollars that they cost when gold and silver were at par,[1] that is, at

[1] The paper already mentioned, " Labor and Wages in Mexico" (pages 536 to 538), contains sufficient evidence to show the correctness of my statement, namely, that the silver dollar has not any less purchasing power in Mexico than it had when silver and gold were at par, at the ratio of 16 to 1, and that only foreign commodities have increased in price, although in many cases they are sold at a much lower price than they had in 1872, before the demonetization of silver took place, because by the use of machinery and owing to other causes said commodities are manufactured now much cheaper that they were twenty-five years ago, and here I will only add the following article taken from *The Trader* of Mexico vol. vii., No. 4, of April, 1898, which confirms fully my assertion to the effect that the Mexican silver dollar has not lost any of its purchasing power notwithstanding the depreciation of silver.

" *Labor and Products.*—In reply to the statements that are frequently put forth by the American Press—and particularly that portion of it which represents the commercial interests—that the food products and manufactured articles generally consumed by the common people in this country have risen in price in the same proportion as the exchange has risen, we give the following table, representing the prices for the first quarter of 1893 as compared with those of the first quarter of 1898. These figures are taken from *The Trader* for the periods mentioned, and correspond with the official returns for the articles quoted. Prior to 1893 *The Trader* published no market reports, and as there are no other reliable sources at hand from which to quote we are necessarily compelled to confine ourselves to the dates above mentioned :

Articles.	First quarter of 1893.	1898.	Percentages.
Corn, 300 lbs......	$7.00	$4.75	31
Beans, " "	17.00	9.00	47
Wheat, " "	10.25	10.25	..
Rice, 100 lbs.....................	7.50	7.50	..
Coffee, " "	30.50	17.00	44
Lard, 25 lbs.....................	6.12	4.00	34
Tallow, " "	4.00	2.37	40
Sugar, " "	2.25	2.00	10
Cotton Cloth, per piece.............	3.50	2.08	20
Prints, " "	2.31	2.75	14
Woollens, per metre................	2.25	2.00	11

Average decrease over 20 per cent.

It will be observed that in the eleven articles quoted, only one—prints—has increased in price, while in the ten remaining articles the average decrease was over 20 per cent. The absolute necessities, therefore, regardless of the fluctuations in exchange, have varied but little in price in the past five years. While the price of gold has more than doubled in the same length of time, the Mexican dollar has not decreased in value when measured by the amount of home products it will exchange for, and which are the staple articles of 10,000,000 of the 13,000,000 population of Mexico."

the ratio of 1 to 16, excepting such Mexican commodities as have their price fixed in foreign gold markets.[1]

It is not a little puzzling to some travellers who go from this country to Mexico to see a United States silver dollar containing less silver bullion than a Mexican silver dollar, exchanged there for two Mexican silver dollars when silver is at about fifty-six cents an ounce; but they do not bear in mind that in making such an exchange, the Mexican silver dollar is sold for the market price of the silver bullion it contains, just as if it was not coined, while the United States silver dollar is the representative of a gold dollar, received as such in this country, and is therefore an article of merchandise bought to pay debts in the United States or Europe; but notwithstanding that fact, the Mexican silver dollar has not lost any of its purchasing power in Mexico.

4th. The fact that foreign commodities have to be paid for in gold makes them so high that this operates as a protective duty against them, equal to the price of exchange, or the difference between the market value of the gold and silver bullion. Protectionists would count this as a very important advantage, although I myself do not

[1] The following statement of remarks of Mr. Maitland, delivered on March last before a meeting of the China Mutual Steamship Co., confirms fully what I have stated here:

"Mr. Maitland remarked that the working expenses of the China Mutual Steamship Co. had been considerably reduced, almost entirely by the great fall in the gold price of silver, which, however, was not altogether an unmixed good, as the very same causes had brought about an enormous falling off in the British export trade to the far East. For the repairs of their steamers very large amounts of money were annually needed, and they had already commenced to make the repairs in Singapore, China, and Japan. With the dollar at 2s., the skilled Asiatic will work for a month for less than a skilled British subject will work for a week. The labor leaders in this country are rapidly becoming aware of the danger to labor caused by a currency system which is driving work from this country to the extent of millions of pounds sterling per annum, which must seriously reduce wages and increase the already large numbers of unemployed persons, and they are beginning to favor a policy of monetary reform.

"Let me explain that silver will still employ the same quantity of Oriental labor as it did twenty or thirty years ago. The inadequacy of our monetary standard, therefore, allows the Eastern countries to now employ 100 per cent. more labor for a given amount of gold than they could do twenty-five years ago. To make this important statement quite clear allow me to give the following example: In 1870 ten rupees were the equivalent of one sovereign under the joint standard of gold and silver, and employed twenty men for one day. To-day twenty rupees are about the equivalent of one sovereign; so that for twenty rupees forty men can be engaged for one day, instead of twenty men as in 1870. Against such a disability, British labor cannot possibly compete. On the other hand, the effect of this disability is that gold prices of commodities have fallen to nearly one-half of their former level, while in Oriental countries silver prices are still practically in most cases on their old level. Therefore, the more gold appreciates, the greater will be the tendency to still further lower gold prices.

"In connection with the decline in the value of China's foreign import trade, it

attach much importance to it in that sense, as I believe in low duties, unless in certain cases and for certain reasons, high duties are rendered necessary.

5th. Our silver standard encourages the investment in Mexico of capital from rich countries having the gold standard, since every gold dollar when sent to Mexico is converted into two silver dollars, at the present rate of exchange, and, when invested in lands, wages, and other expenses for the raising of agricultural products which are sold for gold in foreign markets, like coffee, the proceeds are so large that they constitute a very great inducement for the investment of capital. Besides, if at any time in the future silver should be reinstated as a money metal by the leading commercial nations of the world, and rise in price, the capital invested in a silver country would be actually duplicated in gold.

6th. The development of the country has increased considerably the local traffic of our railroads, and that increase is very encouraging, and goes far to compensate the companies owning them for the losses which the depreciation of silver entailed on them in the payment of interest on their bonded debts.[1]

may not be out of place to remark that, to the observer in the East, it seems inexplicable that the gold-currency countries, while striving to extend their trade, should resolutely ignore the fact, so clearly demonstrated by the decline in the demand for piece goods, that to the millions in China the tael, or ounce of silver, is still a tael of undiminished purchasing power, whether the sterling value be 6s. or 3s. ; and that so soon as the discredited tael fails to buy the same quantity of foreign goods as heretofore, the consumer ceases to be a customer, and will supply his own wants by manufacturing textiles from home-grown materials. Indications are not wanting that the erection of cotton mills at ports extending from the Gulf of Tonking to Chungking (some 900 miles up the Yangtse) is contemplated, and there is abundant evidence of great local activity in that direction. A nation whose inexhaustible supply of laborers excites such alarm among Western people and governments, is not likely to prove less formidable when it brings similar forces of cheap, silver-paid skilled operatives into competition with the textile industries of the gold wage-earning classes of Europe and America, and the effect will be felt more acutely and cause greater consternation than the presence of Chinese labor abroad whenever it comes into rivalry with the handicrafts of Occidental races. The condition of Indian finance is known to be precarious, owing chiefly to the increasing cost in silver of India's gold obligations, together with the perilous growth of Indian State expenditure. On the latter subject, Sir David Barbour spoke at the Mansion House last May in very positive terms, while another ex-finance member of the Viceroy's Council in India (Sir Auchland Colcin) wrote to the same effect in the *Nineteenth Century* of October last. The masses of the population are poor, and they have been impoverished by additional taxation to provide for the increasing burdens caused by the falling exchange. Further new taxes may lead to serious discontent among the people, for it is generally believed that the extreme limit of taxation has been reached."

[1] In the chapter on the railways in Mexico, pages 193–220 of the first paper of this volume, entitled " Geographical and Statistical Notes on Mexico," I give the full details of the increased earnings of the Mexican railroads. In foot notes to the Silver

7th. There is another very great advantage that Mexico has derived from the silver standard, although this may be peculiar to us. Before our railroads were built the only articles which we could export were silver and gold dollars—coinage being then made compulsory by law—because no other product could pay the very high expense of transportation. The result was that to pay for our imports we had to export almost all of our annual output of silver, so that very little was left for our home circulation. Thus we were almost constantly suffering from a contraction of currency; money became very dear, while the price of labor was very low. But now the conditions are reversed· The low price of silver abroad makes it unprofitable to export it, and its value at home makes it useful in all industries, and we send out our agricultural products to pay for our imports and for our gold obligations, keeping at home our silver and thus increasing our circulation,

Standard paper which I prepared for the *North American Review,* I inserted a statement of the earnings of the Mexican International and Mexican Northern Railways for the year 1892, which the editor of the *North American Review* did not publish, and which will be found in the present edition of the paper.

I now give a statement of the earnings in 1897 of the Mexican Central, National and International Railroads, taken from the respective reports and not embraced in the data above mentioned.

Mexican Central Railroad.—The following table, taken from the report of the company for 1897, shows the gross earnings for each of the last thirteen years, both with and without the amount derived from the carriage of construction material, and also states the average mileage operated each year on which the earnings were based, and the earnings per mile.

YEAR.	AVERAGE MILEAGE.	GROSS EARNINGS.	LESS CONSTRUCTION MATERIAL.	GROSS COMMERCIAL.	EARNINGS PER MILE.
1885	1235.90	$3,559,560	$26,741	$3,532,819	$2,858
1886	1235.90	3,857,705	none	3,857,705	3,121
1887	1235.90	4,886,578	301,317	4,585,261	3,710
1888	1316.40	5,774,331	471,831	5,302,500	4,028
1889	1461.85	6,337,225	475,451	5,861,774	4,009
1890	1527.20	6,425,694	303,020	6,122,674	4,009
1891	1665.11	7,374,538	431,798	6,942,740	4,169
1892	1824.83	7,963,253	397,376	7,565,877	4,146
1893	1846.64	7,981,768	none	7,981,768	4,322
1894	1859.83	8,426,025	none	8,426,025	4,530
1895	1859.83	9,495,865	68,256	9,427,609	5,069
1896	1869.60	10,208,020	200,442	10,007,578	5,352
1897	1955.66	12,845,819	31,198	12,814,621	6,552

It will be observed that over the gains in all the previous years there was in 1897 a further increase in amount of over $2,807,043, or about 28 per cent. The gross earnings per mile rose from $5352 in 1896 to $6552 in 1897, the addition in this case being nearly 22½ per cent., which is the most striking evidence of the growth that has been going on and is still in progress. The report well says the showing is a most reso that we now have an ample supply of money in our banks. That fact, of course, stimulates industry, keeps up prices, and increases the demand for labor.

8th. Most of our millionaires, and many rich Mexicans having large fixed incomes, preferred formerly to live in Europe, and used to spend their money there, but the higher rate of exchange has reduced their incomes so materially that a great many of them are returning home, and now spend their incomes in Mexico.

Disadvantages of the Silver Standard to Mexico.—The disadvantages brought to Mexico by the silver standard are the following:

1st. Importations are considerably reduced, because foreign commodities almost double their price when sold for silver, and they are therefore beyond the reach of the middle classes with limited means, while the poorer classes have never used them.

While the amount of import duties in Mexico has not decreased, it has not increased in the same proportion as the other taxes, especially the internal revenue. They formerly amounted to from seventy-five to eighty per cent. of the Federal revenue of Mexico and are now reduced to about forty per cent., the internal revenue having increased greatly. The through freight going to Mexico from the United States markable one, indicating great industrial activity and development in Mexico. The report also states that all classes of commercial traffic, and traffic in both directions on all parts of the system, record substantial and gratifying increases.

Mexican National Railway.—The following table shows the earnings, gross and net, year by year, since 1889.

	GROSS EARNINGS.	NET EARNINGS.
1889	$3,660,124.24	$666,692.70
1890	3,754,966.36	827,004.47
1891	4,206,422.74	1,159,021.18
1892	4,756,029.94	1,700,613.39
1893	4,224,804.11	1,638,437.66
1894	4,329,078.65	1,891,962.24
1895	4,513,205.91	2,071,408.50
1896	5,299,025.77	2,525,957.71
1897	6,080,663.28	2,986,237.92

It will be observed that there was a further increase in the gross earnings in the year 1897 of $781,638 (nearly 15 per cent.) and a further increase of $460,280 (over 18 per cent.) in the net. Since 1889 the gross earnings have risen from $3,660,124 to $6,080,663 and the net earnings from $666,693 to $2,986,238. In this last instance the total for 1897 is about four and a half times what it was in 1889. While the receipts have increased, there has been also economy and efficiency in the operation of the road. In 1889 the ratio of expenses to earnings was 81.78 per cent. ; in 1897 it was only 50.89 per cent. In other words, while in 1889 it took over eighty-one cents to earn a dollar, in 1897 the expenditure of money to earn a dollar was but little in excess of fifty cents. It actually cost only $101,000 more money to earn 6 million dollars in 1897 than it

is decreasing on all the roads, while the local traffic is increasing considerably, the difference being such as to result in increased yearly earnings of all the Mexican roads.

2d. The constant fluctuations in the market price of silver is another drawback of the silver standard, greater than the depreciation of that metal, and it has contributed still more than the low price of that metal to reduce the importations of foreign commodities in Mexico during recent years, because there has been no safe basis for any calculation.[1]

A Mexican merchant, for instance, buys foreign goods, at six months' credit, when silver is at thirty pence per ounce, and sells did to earn 3⅝ million dollars in 1889. In exact figures, with gross of $3,660,124 in 1889, expenses were $2,993,432, and with gross earnings of $6,080,663 in 1897, expenses were $3,094,425.

Mexican International Railway.—This road shows also a large increase in its earnings during 1897. This fact, as well as the steady rising year by year of the gross and net earnings of the road, appears from the following table :

YEAR.	AVERAGE KILOMETERS OPERATED.	GROSS EARNINGS.	AVERAGE EARNINGS PER KILOMETER.	AVERAGE EARNINGS PER MILE.
1884.................	245.20	$103,307 98	$421 49	$612 37
1885.................	273.58	153,916 18	562 59	905 39
1886.................	273.58	185,150 25	676 76	1,098 11
1887.................	273.58	237,394 13	867 73	1,396 43
1888.................	573.97	656,781 41	1,144 28	1,841 47
1889.................	636.34	911,698 51	1,432 73	2,305 64
1890.................	637.38	1,126,366 41	1,745 64	2,839 77
1891.................	658.30	1,197,856 55	1,819 69	2,924 02
1892.................	746.37	2,095,726 14	2,107 89	4,518 67
1893.................	922.19	2,050,934 01	2,226 15	3,579 04
1894.................	922.19	2,169,121 47	2,352 14	3,785 29
1895.................	947.23	2,664,126 08	2,812 54	4,526 28
1896.................	1,011.02	2,900,925 33	2,869 30	4,617 69
1897.................	1,060.60	3,034,126 04	2,860 76	4,603 88

It will be seen that there has been but one year when the upward movement was interrupted. The further increase in the last year, though small, is certainly worthy of note.

From the report of this road in 1897, for the year ending December 31, 1897, it appears that the aggregate freight tonnage in 1897 was 561,636 tons, and it is interesting to note that 71 per cent. of this total was composed of products of mines, the two largest items being 258,428 tons coal and coke, and 122,084 tons silver ore. Some of the items of the agricultural tonnage are also showing expansion, though the agricultural tonnage as a whole fell off in 1897, owing to the diminished importations of corn into Mexico. The cotton tonnage furnishes an illustration. Across the United States frontier there were shipped to the interior of Mexico 5197 bales, against 1573 bales the year before ; while from the Laguna region the shipments were 24,133 bales, against 21,209 bales.

The following table shows how great were these fluctuations during a recent period. From the end of December, 1896, to the end of March, 1898, the prices and

them, charging duties, freight, insurance, etc., at a certain price, which includes his profit; but when the time comes to pay his debt silver has fallen to twenty-seven pence, say, and he finds that instead of having made any profit he has sustained a heavy loss. For this reason, and to prevent any serious loss, importing merchants have to charge very high prices to cover all contingencies, keeping always a very reduced stock of goods, and this is another serious obstacle to the development of foreign trade.[1]

index numbers of silver were as follows (60.84d. per ounce being the parity of 1 gold to 15½ silver = 100).

		AVERAGE.
End December, 1896	29 13–16d.,	equal to 49.0
" August, 1897	23 7– 8d.,	" " 39.2
" December, 1897	26 5– 8d.,	" " 43.8
" January, 1898	26 3–16d.,	" " 43.0
" March, 1898	25 11–16d.,	" " 42.2

[1] Mr. Maitland's remarks on this subject, already quoted, confirm the correctness of my statement, although they are meant to show the drawbacks suffered by gold countries through the great and constant fluctuations in the market price of silver.

These views are also confirmed and other drawbacks resulting from the contraction in the price of silver are made apparent by the remarks of Mr. Jamieson, British Consul at Shanghai, China, at a meeting of the British Bimetallic League held in London in 1897, where, discussing the growth of cotton manufacturing in China and Japan, he points out that when one observes the amount of cotton spinning and weaving machinery that is now being exported to silver-using countries, a conviction forces itself on the mind that a change is going on which will in the end have grave consequences. This class of machinery exportation from Great Britain has risen, since 1893, some 86 per cent. By the end of this year (1897) there will be running in China and Japan close on to 2,000,000 cotton spindles. This activity in cotton manufacturing in these countries, Mr. Jamieson says, would never have come, if it had not been for the fall in silver. Great Britain is exporting cotton machinery, but at the ultimate cost of her own export trade.

Mr. Jamieson also says that in the Chinese ports the middlemen, the old-fashioned merchants, bear the brunt of the petty and incessant fluctuations of silver. They have been forced into the position of mere commission agents, and he adds :

"Much of the business now is done in that way, viz., by selling to China and buying in Manchester simultaneously, and at the same time settling exchange forward through one of the banks. In this way the merchant runs no risk at all ; but, per contra, he gets little profit. As it requires little or no capital to do that sort of business, a crowd of small men have come forward who have cut down commissions almost to the vanishing point. Now, some of you manufacturers may say that is all the better for us—the cheaper they do business out there the more will they want to buy. But there is another side to the question. The extension of your business into new fields depends solely on those whom I may term your agents, the merchants out in foreign parts. The manufacturer sits at his door till somebody comes to buy. The middleman goes out into the world seeking new outlets for British products. They are the people who conquer the world for you, whose energy and push have made British trade what it is. But they won't do that for nothing. If you starve them they wont work. Now, that is largely the position that the destruction of the par of exchange has

3d. The reduction of imports referred to diminishes proportionately the import duties, which, until very recently, were in Mexico the chief source of the federal revenue.

4th. The national expenses are considerably increased by the payment in gold of the interest of the national debt held abroad, and other expenses of minor account, such as salaries of diplomatic and consular officials. As we have to buy exchange to pay that interest it is, at the present rate of exchange, actually increased from six to twelve per cent. when paid in gold. But we can now purchase exchange from our own people, drawn against their own agricultural exports, and they make some of the profit.[1]

5th. To meet the reduction in the import duties and the increased expenses of the gold obligations, it is indispensable to increase the burden of direct taxation to make up for both losses.

6th. Our railroads are similarly affected. They collect their freights in silver, but pay in gold the interest on their securities, and for the foreign articles needed for their roads.

7th. The transportation of foreign commodities by railroads is much reduced, but the local traffic has increased in such a way as not only to make up for that loss, but to leave a large surplus.

8th. While the prices of the necessaries of life for the poorer classes

brought our merchants to. The uncertainty of the trade has chilled their energies. They work on the lines to make bread and butter, hardly venturing to initiate any new. They hesitate to invest their money in new enterprises, not knowing how it will come back to them. This, though it may seem a small matter and rather savoring of personality, is, in my opinion, one of great importance. It is essential to the development of British trade that your merchants, the great distributors, should be men of wealth and intelligence and energy, and this you can only secure by making it worth their while—in other words, when there is money to be made in it."

Mr. Jamieson's remarks are applicable to Mexican conditions. The lack of stability in exchange has transformed our trade there ; the telegraph and the railways have made the new way of doing business possible ; competition has been vastly increased and the strong mercantile houses of the old-fashioned sort are not multiplying in Mexico, and, in so far as those existing fail to adopt the new methods, they lose trade.

[1] The burden of this charge to the Mexican Treasury appears quite clearly from the following figures taken from the report that President Diaz addressed to his fellow-citizens on November 30, 1896, giving an account of his administration in Mexico during the last twelve years.

The Treasury Department estimated the expenses of exchange to pay the interest of the gold bonds in London during the fiscal year 1888–1889 to be $729,178.14. These expenses amounted in the following years as follows :

1890–91	$2,314,477 77
1891–92	3,225,246 77
1892–93	5,101,223 57

Similar losses are suffered by the railroads, that have to pay in gold the interest on their bonds and the supplies they buy abroad. I take from the report of the Mexican Central Railroad for 1897 the following table, which shows in a graphic way

who do not consume foreign commodities, have not increased, except
in the case of a small number of home products whose prices are fixed
by foreign gold markets, the living expenses of the middle and wealthy
classes who use foreign commodities have been increased.

There are many other disadvantages resulting to Mexico from our
having a silver standard; but I have mentioned the most noteworthy
and important ones, and most of the disadvantages omitted by me are
the results of those already pointed out.

Conditions Resulting in Mexico from the Silver Standard.—The disadvantages of the silver standard are considerably lessened in Mexico
because of the fact that we have used coined silver for over three hundred years as our currency, and therefore we have not had to suffer
the disturbances and drawbacks of changing the standard, but have
continued with the same currency, regardless of the market price of
silver bullion in foreign countries and this of course has prevented any
serious derangement in business and in prices.

In consequence of these causes, we have had fewer business failures
than other countries; our internal traffic has greatly increased, with much
benefit to our railroads, which, with only one exception, have not gone

how the growing premium on gold has added to the expenses of the company on
purchases made in the United States.

| YEARS. | COST IN UNITED STATES MONEY. | PREMIUM | | COST IN MEXICAN CURRENCY. |
		AVERAGE RATE.	AMOUNT.	
1891.....................	$1,549,998 60	128.83	$446,841 39	$1,996,839 99
1892.....................	1,386,065 68	143.16	598,277 01	1,984,342 69
1893.....................	1,213,270 38	160.04	728,475 62	1,941,746 00
1894.....................	1,089,472 37	192.69	1,009,829 98	2,099,302 35
1895.....................	929,677 49	188.94	826,880 83	1,756,558 32
1896.....	1,048,481 21	188.65	929,442 18	1,977,923 39
1897.....	1,447,530 13	209.39	1,583,446 21	3,030,976 34

The foregoing brings out the fact that in United States money—that is, in gold—
the purchases made in 1897 actually cost less than those made in 1891, the comparison
being $1,447,530 against $1,549,998.   But as the purchasing power of the silver
dollar has in the meantime so seriously declined, it took $3,030,976 of Mexican money
to pay for the purchases in 1897, against only $1,996,840 in 1891. The loss in the
comparison of these two years, it will be observed, is over a million dollars.

The International Railroad suffers in the same way from the steady depreciation
in the price of silver, which diminishes the gold value of the Mexican silver dollar.
The average price received for the dollar in 1897 was only 47.80 cents, against 51.31
cents in 1896. Working expenses increased $107,072 over the year preceding (on a gain
in gross earnings of $133,201), and the report notes that the fall in the price of silver
contributed in part to this increase by the arbitrary augmentation of cost thus forced
upon all imported supplies consumed during the year.

into the hands of receivers, notwithstanding that they have to pay in gold the interest of their bonds and the increased price of the foreign commodities which they need to operate the roads.[1]

We do not suffer in Mexico from one of the principal causes of the present (June, 1895) financial distress in other countries—the low prices of agricultural products. In fact, in some cases, the prices of domestic commodities have gone up considerably, when they are fixed by the value of the commodity in gold markets. This is the case with coffee, for instance. As the largest portion of our crop is exported and commands cash, its price is fixed by its value in gold markets, and in con-

[1] The conditions of our railroads appears very clearly from the following extract of Mr. Raoul's report, December 31, 1894, to which I have already alluded :

" It was observed in the last report that there had been no appreciable diminution in the purchasing power of the Mexican silver dollar, as applied to labor and materials of Mexican origin, and that this had stimulated the effort and had made it practicable to neutralize, in some degree, the bad effects of the fall in the bullion value of silver outside the country, by increasing the number of articles we can economically manufacture in our own shops, and the quantity and variety of native supplies and materials that can be advantageously purchased in the country, as against buying in a foreign country for gold. This condition remains practically unchanged, and to it is due, in large part, whatever success has attended the efforts of the managing officers in Mexico in maintaining economies already established and effecting others to the same purpose. . . .

"A comparison of the traffic with last year shows that, with the exception of passengers, a loss has been suffered only on those classes that are affected by the condition of the exchange market between Mexico and gold standard countries. The local traffic, which fairly is a register of the internal trade, has made satisfactory progress—sufficient to offset the losses on the external traffic, and yield the increase shown in the general result.

" The increase and decrease on the several classes of business have been as follows :

Revenue from imports has decreased . . . . .15.14 per cent.
Revenue from export of silver ores has decreased . . . . . . 49.18 per cent.
Revenue from other exports has increased . . . . 7.80 per cent.
Revenue from internal traffic has increased . . . . .13.23 per cent.
Revenue from express business has increased . . . . .14.12 per cent.
Revenue from passengers has decreased. . . . . 6.14 per cent."

" The Mexican Northern Railway, running from Escalon, a station on the Mexican Central Railway, to the mining region of Sierra Mojada, in the State of Coahuila, was organized in 1890 under the provisions of Chapter 468 of the Laws of 1881 of the State of New York, the articles of association being dated on the 24th of June of 1890, and the certificate of incorporation on June 26th, 1890. The following is taken from the last report of the Company :

" The whole line of the road is completed ; gauge, standard ; rails, steel, 56 and 60 lbs.; equipment, seven locomotives, two caboose cars, two combination passenger cars, five water cars.

" The capital stock is $3,000,000, the number of shares 30,000, par value $100.

" Bonded debt, $1,660,000, represented by 1,660 first mortgage twenty-year coupon bonds of the par value of $1,000 each.

' A portion of the line of the road was first opened for freight on December 15,

sequence of this its price in Mexico has been almost doubled, with great advantage to the producer.

We have greater stability of prices, wages, rents, etc. Although our wages are low, there has been in recent years a marked tendency to their increase. Our factories are not only in operation, but they

1890, and during the remaining period of construction until September 30, 1891, the road was operated by or for the account of the construction company.

" STATEMENT OF THE YEAR ENDING JUNE 30, 1893."

Gross earnings		$1,160,147 89
Operating expenses		604,595 88
		555,552 01
Miscellaneous receipts		2,133 87
Net earnings		557,685 88
Fixed charges :		
Payments to sinking fund	$58,007 39	
One year's interest on bonds	99,600 00	
Betterments :		
New construction and rolling stock	$73,572 50	
		231,179 89
Surplus earnings		$ 326,505 99

" From which our quarterly dividends of 1½ per cent. each and one extra dividend of 2 per cent., amounting altogether to $240,000, were paid."

The annual report of the Mexican International Railway Co., for the year ending December 31, 1894, made by its president, Mr. C. P. Huntington, and dated at New York City on March 6, 1895, is not less satisfactory. After stating that the total length of the road is 629.93 English miles, and speaking of the earnings of the road, Mr. Huntington says :

" The transportation earnings and expenses (in Mexican currency) for the year have been as follows :

" EARNINGS.

	1894.	1893.	Increase.	Decrease.
Passenger earnings ..	$ 208,551 86	$ 219,624 38		$11,072 52
Express " ..	20,073 78	20,598 10		524 31
Freight " ..	1,873,974 91	1,743,140 42	$130,834 49	
Car mileage " ..	25,273 86	19,896 99	5,376 87	
Locomotive mileage earnings	7,993 13	4,681 91	3,311 22	
Telegraph earnings ..	7,558 43	7,094 02	464 41	
Sundry " ..	6,200 35	16,391 84		10,191 49
Rental " ..	16,447 95	13,776 42	2,671 53	
International bridge earnings	3,047 20	5,729 93		2,682 73
Totals	$2,169,121 47	$2,050,934 01	$118,187 46	
Operating expenses..	1,281,815 83	1,301,394 33		$19,578 50

are being greatly extended, and new plants and industries are being established.   Instead of diminishing the demand for our laborers, we find occupation for them all, and we need to import them for the work to be done in some localities, and, as our laborers find occupation and increased wages, we have no strikes.   Our silver mines have not stopped work, and we find them still quite profitable.   We have more ready money with which to transact our increased business; we offer greater inducements to foreign investors than formerly; and the country is undoubtedly more prosperous than it has ever before been, although the silver standard is not the only cause of our prosperity. One of its principal causes is, undoubtedly the building of railroads, as already stated, but they could not have been as remunerative as they are without the production and coinage of silver.

CONCLUSION.—Summing up the effects produced in Mexico by the

Earnings over operating expenses. $887,305 64	$749,539 68	$137,765 96
Earnings over operating expenses as above.	887,305 64	
Exchange estimated at 200 per cent. on purchases in U. S. currency and charged to operating expenses at that rate.	209,838 66	1,097,144 30
Less stamp tax paid.		13,712 42
Leaving in Mexican currency		$1,083,431 88
which, converted into U. S. currency at the rate of 53.13 cents for the silver dollar, would be.		575,627 36
And balance for account of express contract.		52,000 00
Interest on deposits.		14,660 30
Miscellaneous receipts.		4,777 44
Total U. S. currency.		$647,065 10
Against this is chargeable in U. S. currency, viz. :		
One year's interest on bonded debt. .	$560,000 00	
General expenses.	10,112 85	570,112 85
Balance U. S. currency. . . .		$76,952 25 "

After explaining the manner in which Mexican silver is reduced to United States currency, Mr. Huntington says in his report :

" The net results from the year's operations show an increase in the gross earnings of $118,187.46 or 5.76 per cent., and a decrease in operating expenses of $19,578.50 or 1.50 per cent., making a total gain of $137,765.96 or 18.38 per cent. over 1893.   This is quite a gratifying showing, when it is considered that the general business depression in the United States, and the low price of silver, have not been without their unfavorable effect upon the year's business."

silver standard, I can say, with perfect truth, that while it is a drawback, a great inconvenience, and a serious loss to the government and to the railroads to have our currency depreciated when we have to use it abroad, either to pay for foreign merchandise or the interest on our gold obligations, and while that depreciation increases our burdens to some extent, because our gold obligations and the price of foreign commodities are nearly doubled by it, the advantages we derive from the use of silver money in all our transactions are so great as, in my opinion, to fully compensate, if they do not outweigh, its disadvantages.

Notwithstanding the views of those who desire that the present depreciation of the Mexican money should continue in Mexico, I, for one, and I think that I express the views of a majority of my fellow-citizens, would like to see our silver commanding the same price as it had before it was demonetized in 1873, and we believe that the world will have to come back sooner or later to bimetallism, as the only way to have a common and a more stable level of values and to avoid most of the financial troubles from which the commercial nations of the world are now so keenly suffering.

APPENDIX.

I will insert in this supplement the following papers: 1st, my remarks delivered on March 30, 1891, at the fifth meeting of the American International Monetary Commission on the position of Mexico on the monetary question; 2d, a list of papers bearing on the silver question, printed by order of the Senate, from 1893 to 1898, published by the Senate on June 6, 1898; and 3d, comments on the Mexican Central Railway earnings in silver and reduced to gold, and on the deficit of that road to pay the interest of its bonded indebtedness.

I.—M. ROMERO'S REMARKS ON THE POSITION OF MEXICO ON THE MONETARY QUESTION.

Remarks of M. Romero, delivered on March 30, 1891, at the fifth meeting of the American International Monetary Commission, on the position of Mexico on the monetary question :

GENTLEMEN : While I shall cast my vote in favor of the propositions of the Delegates of the United States to this Conference, because I think they are advisable, and because they come from the representatives of the inviting country, still I cannot refrain from expressing my regret that said propositions were not introduced after some attempt had been made for all the American nations represented at this Conference to come to an understanding on the subject of a common coin.

The American nations are all bimetallists, but they have adopted different ratios between gold and silver, and they have coins differing in weight and alloy, and, therefore, in my opinion, it would be desirable at least to arrive at some understanding which should secure the establishment of a common ratio between gold and silver, and a unit of coin of the same weight and fineness, even though the coin of each country should not be a legal tender outside of its own limits, in case it be found impossible to agree upon its being received as a legal tender in all the American countries.

I, for one, would have had no difficulty in accepting the ratio of 1 to 15½, which prevails in the other countries of America, and I venture to presume that the United States might accept this same ratio, since one of its most distinguished Senators, well versed in financial and monetary matters, recently introduced a bill for that purpose, to which I imagine the country is not averse. In that case we might secure the advantage of at least having a uniform ratio in America to be the same as that prevailing in Europe.

There is no doubt that an international agreement upon a common coin, to be a legal tender in all the contracting countries, would require the concurrence of the nations of the world to make it complete and work smoothly ; but for the present it seems unlikely and quite difficult to obtain this concurrence, so far as England and Germany, and especially England, are concerned. This matter has been discussed several times in conference wherein Great Britain was represented, and she has never given her assent, and I see no new reason why she would give it now.

I have been for some time of opinion that if all the American nations should reach an agreement which would secure to them a common coin, and especially if this were to be a legal tender in all of them, the effect of such agreement would be so marked in Europe, and especially in England, that it would be likely to induce that power to join in the agreement, as she could not afford to allow the United States to have commercial advantages in the American continent which she could not share.

I am afraid that the advances the United States are making every day in the world as a commercial nation are hardly realized in this country; and I think that for this reason they are slow in taking the lead in some important commercial matters. Besides, all indications seem to show that one of the first acts of the Fifty-second Congress of the United States, which meets on the first Monday in December next, will be to authorize the free coinage of silver, and, in case that is done, all the objections they now have against the legal-tender clause of a common American coin will disappear. Would it not be more prudent, under such circumstances, to adjourn this Conference until the first of January, 1892, when this subject will, in all probability, have been decided by the Government of the United States.

I beg to be allowed to grasp this opportunity to state the position of Mexico on this question, repeating, perhaps, what I previously stated on a similar occasion, as Delegate from Mexico to the International American Conference.

Mexico is legally a bimetallic country, because we have both gold and silver coins, both being legal tender ; but practically it is a silver nation, because all our business is carried on exclusively with silver, since, owing to the difference of the price in the markets of the world of both metals, all of our gold (and we do not yet produce much) is exported, while a considerable part of our silver remains in the country in the form of coin.

I will mention, briefly, the disadvantages the depreciation of silver in the markets of the world produces in Mexico, and at the same time (be not astonished) the advantages accruing therefrom.

The disadvantages are three :

(1)   An increase in the price in Mexico of foreign goods which has to be paid in gold.

(2)   A loss to the national treasury in the funds sent abroad to pay the interest on the Mexican bonds held in Europe, which loss is equivalent to an increase in the rate of that interest.

(3)   A loss to wealthy Mexicans living in Europe, when their capitals or revenues are sent to them, equivalent to the depreciation of silver, between twenty-five and thirty-three per cent.

The depreciation of silver has not affected in any perceptible way the working of our silver mines, but, on the contrary, our production of that metal has considerably increased since 1871, when the depreciation began, although this increase is due, of course, to the construction of railways, to the long peace the country has enjoyed, and to the restoration of our public credit. I do not know of any silver mine where work has been stopped owing to the depreciation of silver.

These disadvantages are, however, of but little account when compared to the benefits we have received from the depreciation of silver, and which are the following :

(1)   As the Mexican commodities we export, such as coffee, indigo, hennequen, etc., are sold in the foreign markets in gold, they command now a higher price at home, where they are bought for silver, which really amounts to a bounty, when exported, equal to the difference between the actual price of silver at home and their price in gold in the markets of the world, which has been between twenty-five and thirty-three per cent. This bounty has produced the effect of considerably increasing the production and exportation of commodities which could not be exported before.

(2)   And perhaps the most important advantage has been to keep in Mexico a very large amount of money which formerly used to go out of the country as soon as coined, it being the only article of export with which imported foreign goods were purchased,

thus leaving a very limited amount to transact the business of the country. The reason why this money does not go out now is because it has become more profitable to export commodities in the place of silver, which remains in the country in the form of coin, to the great benefit of business.

It is natural that when the Mexican dollar loses from one fourth to one third of its value in Mexico by sending it abroad, that it should be kept in the country, and that in its stead other articles should be exported, thus considerably increasing the circulating medium in Mexico, to the great benefit of all ; and the country, therefore, is perfectly satisfied with the present condition of things.

(3) A great many rich men in Mexico, both native and foreign, used to realize on what they had in the country and send the proceeds to Europe, where they found a safer, if not more a profitable field for investment. But they cannot afford to do so now, because their capital would be reduced one third or one fourth ; and as besides there is now perfect security to life and property in Mexico, and a large field for profitable investment has been opened by the building of railways and the consolidation of peace and order in the country, capital is entering instead of leaving Mexico.

When these facts are taken into consideration, it does not seem strange that we are in no great haste to seek any change in the present condition of things, because the depreciation of silver has actually produced very favorable results. Yet, when we consider that silver has been for nearly three hundred years almost our only article of export, and that it now represents two-thirds of our total exports, we cannot be indifferent to any measure adopted, either by treaty or legislation, which may produce the effect of enhancing the value of that metal ; and for this reason we might be willing to join in any agreement which may be likely to bring about that result, provided it would not materially affect our interests.

We are peculiarly situated as regards our silver coin, possessing advantages that are enjoyed by no other country. This fact becomes patent when we consider the great demand there is for our silver dollar in the world, owing to its having a larger amount of pure metal than any similar foreign coin, and therefore commanding a higher price than any other dollar. We have, besides, a special market for our silver dollar in the East, where it has been used for many years as the national coin, and where it is in great demand. This circumstance causes us to be very slow to accept any changes in our own coin which may deprive us of those markets and those advantages.

The preceding remarks will show the Conference that while Mexico is disposed to co-operate with her sisters, the American Republics, in any measures which would be beneficial to the interests of those concerned, she is not willing to accept anything which would not be clearly advantageous and useful to all, and she is in no particular hurry to change the actual condition of things.

2.—LIST OF PAPERS BEARING ON THE SILVER QUESTION.

Fifty-fifth Congress, 2d Session, Senate Document No. 286. June 6, 1898. Ordered to be printed. Mr. Chandler presented the following list of papers bearing on the silver question, printed by order of the Senate, 1893-1898. (Prepared in the Senate Library by Mr. Clifford Warden.)

This list of papers bearing upon the silver question embraces the principal papers printed by order of the Senate during the period since the beginning of the Fifty-third Congress, 1893. It includes several important papers which were printed by order of the Senate during the consideration, in 1893, of the bill to repeal the silver-purchasing portion of the Sherman law of 1890.

Subject.	Congress.	Session.	Document number (Senate).
* Give us free silver. An editorial printed in the New York *Recorder*, August 13, 1893.	53d.	1st.	Mis. 11.
Production of gold and silver in the world since the discovery of America. Presented by Mr. Vest.	53d.	1st.	Mis. 17.
Report of the commission appointed to inquire into the Indian currency, commonly known as the Herschell report on the coinage of silver in India, with the accompanying correspondence and testimony.	53d.	1st.	Mis. 23, 3 parts.
* Letter from F. C. Waite to Hon. Henry M. Teller, relative to cause of financial and industrial depression.	53d.	1st.	Mis. 25.
* Letter from Ernest Seyd to Hon. Samuel Hooper on the subject of coinage.	53d.	1st.	Mis. 29.
Letter from R. E. Preston, Acting Director of the Mint, transmitting statements of the production and coinages of the principal countries of the world, for the years 1873–1892. Presented by Mr. Cockrell.	53d.	1st.	Mis. 34.
Monetary systems and approximate stocks of money in the aggregate and per capita in the principal countries of the world. Presented by Mr. Cockrell.	53d.	1st.	Mis. 35.
Production of gold and silver in the world, 1792–1892. (Statement.) Presented by Mr. Cockrell.	53d.	1st.	Mis. 36.
No international bimetallism including Great Britain is possible. Memorial of A. Wolcott. Presented by Mr. Allen.	53d.	1st.	Mis. 47.
Official statement of production of gold and silver of Arizona, Colorado, California, Idaho, Montana, Nevada, Utah, and New Mexico, 1873–1892. Presented by Mr. Teller.	53d.	1st.	Mis. 52.
Memorial from the buisness men of Philadelphia in relation to tariff and financial legislation. Presented by Mr. Cameron.	53d.	1st.	Mis. 68.
* The currency problem, by J. Barr Robertson ; a paper quoted from the *Journal of the Society of Arts*. Presented by Mr. Teller.	53d.	1st.	Mis. 89.
Seigniorage arising from the coinage of silver purchased under the act of July 14, 1890 : Correspondence with the Secretary of the Treasury relative to.	53d.	1st.	Mis. 91.
* The future of silver, by Eduard Suess, professor of geology at the University of Vienna, member of the Austrian Parliament, etc. Published by permission of the author and by direction of the Committee on Finance.	53d.	1st.	Mis. 95.
* Memorial of the legislature of Utah in favor of silver coinage (at 16 to 1).	53d.	2d.	Mis. 80.
Census distribution of the gold and silver, by States. Article prepared by Frederick C. Waite. Presented by Mr. Kyle.	53d.	2d.	Mis. 210.
The evidence of a Crown colony on gold and silver prices—Bimetallism in relation to agricultural depression. Address delivered before the London Chamber of Commerce, July 24, 1894. Presented by Mr. Teller.	53d.	2d.	Mis. 262.

* Published also in Coinage Laws of the United States, 1792–1894 (Fifty-third Congress, 2d Session, Senate Report 235).

Subject.	Congress.	Session.	Document number (Senate).
Berlin Silver Commission, 1894. Report of the proceedings, to which is appended the report of the proceedings of the International Bimetallic Conference at London, May 2–3, 1894. Translated and prepared under direction of the Committee on Finance, by authority of Senate resolution of June 18, 1894.	53d.	2d.	Mis. 274.
Statement to accompany Senate bill 2439, "A bill to provide for the establishment and maintenance of a bimetallic monetary basis, and to secure the adjustment to business requirements of the volume and distribution of the national currency," etc. Presented by Mr. Manderson.	53d.	3d.	Mis. 31.
Resolutions adopted by the Farmers' National Congress of America at its annual meeting at Parkersburg, W. Va., Oct. 3–6, 1894. Presented by Mr. George.	53d.	3d.	Mis. 35.
Memorial of Anson Wolcott on the state of the national finances. Presented by Mr. Turpie.	53d.	3d.	Mis. 86.
The real causes of agricultural distress. Papers. Presented by Mr. Teller.	53d.	3d.	Mis. 94.
The fall of prices—the cause and the cure. Address by President E. Benjamin Andrews before the Manufacturers' Club of Philadelphia, Feb. 18, 1894. Presented by Mr. Cockrell.	53d.	3d.	Mis. 136.
Bill to provide in connection with other nations for the unlimited coinage of gold and silver at the ratio of 1 to 15½, and letter of Mr. Robert Stein in relation to the bill. Presented by Mr. Chandler, Dec. 12, 1895.	54th.	1st.	Doc. 24.
Papers on bimetallism, by George Jameison, and on the rise in the value of gold, by Thomas Holyoake Box; on the fall in silver and its effects on British trade, by David Octavius Croal, and comments by Sir Henry Meysey-Thompson. Presented by Mr. Stewart.	54th.	1st.	Doc. 30.
Gold monometallism; the upas tree of Great Britain; blighting effect on British industries; hypothetical example of the cost of monometallism. Presented by Mr. Teller.	54th.	1st.	Doc. 29.
Resolution of the Camden County, N. J., Farmer's Institute, favoring the free and unlimited coinage of silver. Presented by Mr. Teller.	54th.	1st.	Doc. 124.
Memorial of Anson Wolcott on the monetary laws and monetary conditions of the United States. Presented by Mr. Stewart.	54th.	1st.	Doc. 177.
Letter of the Secretary of the Treasury, Jan. 16, 1896, relative to the amount of silver bullion on hand, the cost of same, and coinage value if coined into dollars, and amount of seigniorage if so coined, etc. Presented by Mr. Cockrell.	54th.	1st.	Doc. 184.
Letters of Hon. Ben. Butterworth and Samuel J. Ritchie upon the silver question and upon the general financial policy of the Government, as of late pursued. Presented by Mr. Teller.	54th.	1st.	Doc. 235.
Speech of Hon. John G. Carlisle before the workingmen of Chicago, April 15, 1896.	54th.	1st.	Doc. 256.
Speech of John P. Altgeld, governor of Illinois, at the Auditorium, Chicago, May 16, 1896. Presented by Mr. Cockrell.	54th.	1st.	Doc. 284.

Subject.	Congress.	Session.	Document number (Senate).
Gold and the world's wheat farmers, by L. G. Powers. Presented by Mr. Lodge.	54th.	1st.	Doc. 306.
The Orientals as manufacturing competitors. "A silver menace." Letters of John P. Young, published in the San Francisco *Chronicle*. Presented by Mr. Teller.	54th.	1st.	Doc. 311.
Memorial of Henry Nelson Loud, containing an argument for a universal standard dollar. Presented by Mr. McMillan.	54th.	2d.	Doc. 99.
Arguments by eminent French, German, and English writers in favor of bimetallism, published by the *National Review*, February, 1897. Presented by Mr. Chandler.	54th.	2d.	Doc. 131.
Memorial of John M. Mott, praying that the mints of the United States be opened to the free coinage of silver. Presented by Mr. Turpie.	55th.	1st.	Doc. 20.
Memorial of clergymen of Philadelphia, petitioning for the removal of the inequalities of the present protective system. Presented by Mr. Cannon.	55th.	1st.	Doc. 60.
Reports of the metallists of the French and English Bimetallic League on international bimetallism. Presented by Mr. Chandler.	55th.	1st.	Doc. 156.
Papers relating to the adoption of the gold standard by Japan. Presented by Mr. Pettigrew.	55th.	1st.	Doc. 176.
Speech by Hon. Charles A. Towne, chairman of the National Committee, Silver Republican Party, April 24, 1897. Presented by Mr. Pettigrew.	55th.	1st.	Doc. 177.
Appointment of a monetary commission to investigate and report upon a revision of the financial system of the United States. Recommended in message from the President of the United States.	55th.	1st.	Doc. 190.
Extracts from a speech of Monsieur Meline, President of the French Cabinet, delivered in the Chamber of Deputies, November 20, 1897. Presented by Mr. Wolcott.	55th.	2d.	Doc. 26.
Correspondence submitted, July 27, 1897, by the British Government to the House of Commons on the currency proposals made by the United States special envoys. Presented by Mr. Chandler.	55th.	2d.	Doc. 69.
Statement by Prof. J. A. Collins relative to the distribution of wealth in the United States. Presented by Mr. Allen.	55th.	2d.	Doc. 75.
Silver and wheat, a paper published by Mr. R. Lacey Everett. Presented by Mr. Pettigrew.	55th.	2d.	Doc. 86.
Monetary changes in Japan, by Mr. Garrett Droppers, of Tokyo, Japan. Presented by Mr. Wolcott.	55th.	2d.	Doc. 126.
The crime of 1873—Why the silver dollar was omitted in the law of 1873—Frank G. Winn, of Claremont, N. H., reviews the coinage laws and shows why the silver dollar was omitted. Presented by Mr. Gallinger.	55th.	2d.	Doc. 147.
Amount, cost, etc., in standard silver dollars, of silver bullion purchased under act of July 14, 1890, etc. Letter from the Secretary of the Treasury in response to a Senate resolution.	55th.	2d.	Doc. 163.

Subject.	Congress.	Session.	Document number (Senate).
Monetary question in Russia, a paper published by *L'Economiste Europeen*, of Paris, May 7, 1897. Presented by Mr. Pettigrew.	55th.	2d.	Doc. 167.
The currency question. Communication from Mr. Charles A. Towne, published in the *Post-Intelligencer*, of Seattle, Wash. Presented by Mr. Pettigrew.	55th.	2d.	Doc. 227.
Coinage value of silver bullion in the Treasury, etc. Letter from the Secretary of the Treasury in response to a Senate resolution of May 4, 1898.			
Certain silver bullion in the United States Treasury. Letter from the Secretary of the Treasury in response to a Senate resolution of April 27, 1898.	55th.	2d.	Doc. 268.
The Indian Currency, an article by Sir Robert Giffen, published in the London *Times*, May 19, 1898. Presented by Mr. Chandler.	55th.	2d.	Doc. 279.

3. LOSS OF MEXICAN ROADS IN REDUCING THEIR EARNINGS TO GOLD.

After this paper had been printed I found in a newspaper of this country a comparison of the earnings of the Mexican Central Railway in silver with their equivalent in gold, from which it appears that the increase of earnings has not been constant when measured in gold, as the price of exchange has varied considerably, having had always an upward tendency. I also found a statement of the deficit of that road to pay all its gold obligations and the interest on its bonds during the last five years, which has been published to show how much the Mexican roads are suffering on account of our silver standard.

As I desire to be perfectly fair and impartial and to present both sides of the case, I give here the above-mentioned figures, as follows :

MEXICAN CENTRAL RAILWAY.

	EARNINGS PER MILE.	
	Mexican Currency.	Gold.
1891..............................	$4,169	$3,236
1892..............................	4,146	2,896
1893..............................	4,322	2,701
1894..............................	4,530	2,351
1895..............................	5,069	2,683
1896..............................	5,352	2,837
1897..............................	6,552	3,129

DEFICIT OF THE MEXICAN CENTRAL RAILWAY.

In 1893...	$546,401
" 1894...	814,185
" 1895...	265,252
" 1896...	483,011
" 1897...	538,947

I take the above figures to be correct, although I do not think they embrace such profits as the Mexican Central road made by carrying their own construction material, and I have to remark that I do not consider it fair to reduce to gold the earnings of the Mexican railways, because the largest portion of their expenses—namely, those paid in Mexico, including all operating expenses—are paid in silver, and it is only for rolling-stock and other foreign commodities that they have to pay in gold as well as the interest on their bonded indebtedness. The proper course in this case would be to deduct from the total earnings of the road the operating and other expenses incurred in silver, and to reduce to gold such amount as is left for the purpose of paying for foreign commodities and the interest on its debt. When that operation is done the above-quoted figures will appear in a very different aspect. That is just what the Mexican National Road does. That Company keeps its accounts in Mexican money, and in order to avoid having the cost of operation fluctuate back and forth with the fluctuations of silver, it adopted several years ago an arbitrary rate of exchange, which was 20 per cent. discount, then the actual rate of exchange. In this way the income account is debited with the actual cost of purchasing gold and the net shown is consequently the amount reducible to gold, so giving a clear idea of the gold earnings of the road. I think the other roads do something similar.

I would further remark that the Mexican Central Railway has a very large bonded indebtedness, and although it only pays 4 per cent. interest on most of it, that interest has to be paid in gold ; and on account of the depreciation of silver the road has not yet earned money enough to pay the whole of that interest, and every year it has a deficit, which has been paid with a large amount of subsidy granted by the Mexican Government to the Company, and which has been kept in trust for such emergencies as this.

Notwithstanding such deficit, the Mexican Central Railway Company must consider its property very valuable, since it is increasing considerably its mileage every year.

The Mexican National Railway Company has also a very large bonded indebtedness in proportion to its mileage, having four different kinds of bonds. The interest of the first series has been punctually paid. There are outstanding Series " A " Bonds, Second Mortgage, for $12,265,000, cumulative ; $12,265,00 Second Mortgage Series " B," purely income bonds, and $7,040,000 Third Mortgage Income Bonds. While the Second Mortgage Series " A " Bonds bear coupons and are cumulative, they are not, by the terms of the Trust, entitled to have the mortgage foreclosed for a certain period, or under certain conditions. During the last year the Company paid upon these bonds out of its earnings $3\frac{1}{2}$ per cent., which is the largest payment made on them since their issue. If silver had not been depreciated the Mexican National would have been able to pay in full the interest on their bonds. As it is now, the increase in the traffic has been remarkably uniform year by year, and has been sufficient to a little more than compensate for the depreciation of silver : that is to say, the net returns of the Company as measured by gold have been a little greater each year.

The Mexican International Railway Company, which has issued a reasonable amount of bonds in proportion to its mileage, earns enough to pay in gold the interest on its bonds, with its receipts in silver.

The following statement shows the bonded indebtedness of each of the three leading Mexican roads, their mileage, and the bonded indebtedness per mile :

	Bonded Indebtedness.	Mileage.	Bonded Indebtedness per mile.
Mexican Central Railway	$95,051,712.50	1,877.15	$50,636.18
Mexican National Railway	42,879,000.00	1,056.16	40,598.96
Mexican International Railway	14,984,000.00	658.28	22,762.34

THE PAN-AMERICAN CONFERENCE
OF 1889.

THE PAN-AMERICAN CONFERENCE
OF 1889.

INTRODUCTION.

The meeting in Washington in October, 1889, of a Congress in which all the American States were represented was an event of great moment and concern, not only to the United States, but to every one of the nations of this hemisphere. In that way the project originated by Bolivar, immediately after the independence of the Spanish colonies in America, of forming a confederation among all the American nations for their mutual advancement, was partially realized. It is therefore of great importance to record what took place in that Conference, as I am sure it will not be the last one, and a knowledge of the circumstances attending the same and of its main discussions and decisions will be of great use in future meetings. It is now nearly ten years since that meeting took place, and the idea has been suggested of calling a similar conference, as it is thought proper that the American nations should convene to consult among themselves on subjects affecting their common interests and welfare at least once in every ten years.

I thought that an impartial, conscientious, and concise analysis of what took place in that Conference presented by a Spanish-American delegate, especially from the point of view of the Latin-American nations, which is not quite fully understood in the United States, would be of great interest to all concerned, and especially so to this country, and with such object in view I wrote a paper which appeared in the September and October numbers of 1890 of the *North American Review*, of New York, under the heading of "The Pan-American Conference."

I now reprint this paper substantially as it was then published; but giving only a few more details about the way in which the Act of May 24, 1888, which convened the Conference, originated, and about other points of personal interest, and rectifying a statement regarding Mr. Henderson, Chairman of the United States delegation to the Conference, which

623

appeared in the original article, and which was not exactly fair to him. This edition of the paper gives me also the opportunity of mentioning what have been so far some of the permanent results of the Conference. I have thought it advisable also to append the principal documents which are referred to in the paper, as the Act convening the Conference, a full list of the delegates, a list of the committees, and the text of the project of arbitration, and another against conquest, reported by the Committee on General Welfare, which finally ended in a Treaty of Arbitration, signed by most of the delegates to the same on April 19, 1890, and several other important documents bearing on the results of the Conference.

I published this paper almost immediately after the Conference adjourned, and when Mr. Blaine and all the members of the Conference were not only living, but had fresh in their memory the events that happened in the same, and when Mr. Blaine was yet Secretary of State. With the exception of Mr. Henderson, to whom I have already alluded, neither Mr. Blaine nor any one of the delegates in any manner, directly or indirectly, intimated to me or to anybody else, to my knowledge, that there was any misstatement or misunderstanding on my part about the incidents which I had commented upon, and this shows very clearly to my mind that my statements were correct.

Complete information on this subject will be found in the following official publications of the proceedings of the Pan-American Conference : 1st, a volume of 906 pages, containing the Minutes, signed by the President and the two Secretaries, of the seventy meetings held by the Conference, under the title of *Minutes of the International American Conference in English and Spanish, 1890.* 2d, a publication in four volumes entitled *International American Conference*, printed by the United States Government under the direction of the Executive Committee and by order of the Conference, approved March 7, 1890. Volumes I. and II. of said publication contain the reports of the committees and discussions thereon ; Vol. III. contains the narrative of the tour of the delegates through the United States, descriptions of places visited, and reports of addresses delivered ; and Vol. IV. an historical appendix, beginning with the Congress of Panama of 1826, and subsequent movements toward a conference of American nations. And 3d, a volume containing the recommendations approved by the Pan-American Conference sent to Congress by President Harrison, each with a special Message, accompanied in every case by a report of Mr. Blaine as Secretary of State. In some cases, as in regard to reciprocity treaties, Mr. Blaine wrote a full report, going into details of the subject, and in others he merely prepared a letter of transmittal. The following is a complete list of the subjects recommended by the Pan-American Conference, as communicated by President Harrison to Congress, with the dates of his Messages in the chronological order in which they were sent, all of which are bound in one volume :

Inter-Continental Railway, President's Message to the Senate, May 19, 1890.

International American Bank, President's Message to the Senate, May 27, 1890. Senate Ex. Doc., No. 129, Fifty-first Congress, 1st Session.

Customs Regulations, President's Message to the Senate, June 2, 1890. Senate Ex. Doc., No. 135, Fifty-first Congress, 1st Session.

Reciprocity Treaties, President's Message to the Senate, June 19, 1890. Senate Ex. Doc., No. 158, Fifty-first Congress, 1st Session.

Colombian Exposition, President's Message to the Senate, July 2, 1890. Senate Ex. Doc., No. 173, Fifty-first Congress, 1st Session.

Postal and Cable Communications, President's Message to the Senate, July 2, 1890. Senate Ex. Doc., No. 174, Fifty-first Congress, 1st Session.

Sanitary and Quarantine Regulations, President's Message to the Senate, July 11, 1890. Senate Ex. Doc., No. 176, Fifty-first Congress, 1st Session.

Patents and Trade-Marks, President's Message to the Senate, July 11, 1890. Senate Ex. Doc., No. 177, Fifty-first Congress, 1st Session.

International Monetary Union, President's Message to the Senate, July 12, 1890. Senate Ex. Doc., No. 180, Fifty-first Congress, 1st Session.

Uniform System of Weights and Measures, President's Message to the Senate, July 12, 1890. Senate Ex. Doc., No. 181, Fifty-first Congress, 1st Session.

Uniform System of Port Dues, President's Message to the Senate, July 14, 1890. Senate Ex. Doc., No. 182, Fifty-first Congress, 1st Session.

Uniform Code of International Law, President's Message to the Senate, July 14, 1890. Senate Ex. Doc., No. 183, Fifty-first Congress, 1st Session.

Uniform Treaties for the Extradition of Criminals, President's Message to the Senate, July 15, 1890. Senate Ex. Doc., No. 187, Fifty-first Congress, 1st Session.

Erection of Memorial Tablet, President's Message to the Senate, July 15, 1890. Senate Ex. Doc., No. 188, Fifty-first Congress, 1st Session.

Plan of Arbitration, President's Message to the Senate, September 3, 1890. Senate Ex. Doc., No. 224, Fifty-first Congress, 1st Session.

THE PAN-AMERICAN CONFERENCE OF 1889.

Although the idea of assembling a congress in which all the American nations should be represented was not a new one—as it had originated in South America with its liberator, Bolivar, after the Spanish colonies had accomplished their independence, and was put into effect by his calling in 1826 a congress to meet at Panama, a project very heartily supported in this country by Henry Clay, then Secretary of State—Mr. James G. Blaine can be properly considered as the originator in the United States of the movement which resulted in convening the International American Conference which met in October, 1889. He proposed it in 1881, when he served as Secretary of State for the first time, under President Garfield's Administration, but reduced to narrow limits the object of such a conference: namely, to the negotiation of an agreement for the purpose of settling by arbitration all differences that might arise between the American nations.

The change of Administration which soon afterwards took place, in consequence of the assassination of President Garfield, caused this idea to be abandoned, as at that time it had not been well received. Chili was then engaged in a war with Peru and Bolivia, and some thought that the proposed conference was an attempt to interfere in that difficulty. Mexico also received it very coolly, for she had then a boundary question pending with Guatemala, and Mr. Blaine had proposed that the President of the United States should arbitrate thereon; but, unfortunately, in making that offer, he had expressed an opinion unfavorable to the rights of Mexico, which were based on undeniable historical facts; and for this and other reasons the proposal was not then accepted.

Act Convening the Conference.—The idea remained latent in this country, however, and it was revived by President Arthur, who, coming from the commercial metropolis, and being in close association with the mercantile community, thought of adding a commercial feature to the original proposition, and sent a Commission to the several other Republics to ascertain how another invitation would be received, and to ask suggestions as to the topics that might be considered at a conference of

American nations.   A draft of the law authorizing the President of the United States to call such an assembly was submitted to Congress with the report of that Commission, and full abstracts of interviews with the Presidents of ten of the American nations concerning the meeting and subjects to be discussed.   Nine endorsed the project with cordial approval.   Chili reserved its reply, being reluctant, while certain political complications were pending, to give a positive answer.   The report of the Commission and its recommendations reflected the policy of President Arthur, but were nevertheless transmitted to Congress by President Cleveland without endorsement.   The proposed law calling a conference was therefore brought forward under President Cleveland's first Administration, although without any intervention on Mr. Blaine's part.   It was introduced in the House of Representatives by Governor McCreary, a Democratic Representative from Kentucky, and in the Senate by Mr. W. P. Frye, a distinguished Republican Senator from Maine, both members of the Foreign Affairs Committee in their respective Houses.   These facts show that it was not introduced and approved as a political measure, since it was supported by the two parties struggling for ascendancy in this country.   President Cleveland's Administration did not second the proposal in an active manner, seeming to content itself with passive indifference.

The Act was finally approved by Congress on May 10, 1888, but President Cleveland withheld his approval of the same, and when the ten days fixed by the Constitution had elapsed without its having been approved by the President, it was announced on May 24th that the Bill had become a law without the sanction of the President.

It will be interesting to state that the arbitration clause of the Act of May 24, 1888, was introduced on January 4, 1888, in the House of Representatives of the 50th Congress, 1st Session, by Hon. William McKinley, then a Member of Congress from Ohio, and now President of the United States,[1] and this fact shows the trend of his views in

---

[1] Fiftieth Congress, 1st Session, H. R. 1715.   In the House of Representatives, January 4, 1888.   Read twice, referred to the Committee on Foreign Affairs, and ordered to be printed.   Mr. McKinley introduced the following bill : " A Bill to authorize the President of the United States to invite the autonomic governments of America to send delegates to an international congress to arrange the settlement of national differences by arbitration."

" *Be it enacted by the Senate and House of Representatives of the United States of America in Congress assembled,* That the President of the United States be, and he is hereby, authorized to invite the autonomic governments of America to send delegates to a congress to be held at Washington or New York, and at such time as he may designate, for the purpose of devising and formulating and recommending a definite and fixed plan of arbitration of all differences now existing or that may hereafter exist between them, with the understanding that the delegation from each government shall have but one vote in said convention ; and that the President is hereby authorized to

favor of arbitration, which he proclaimed and defended so vigorously as President of the United States when the arbitration treaty between the United States and Great Britain was pending in the Senate.

The personal views of the new promoters of the project were not limited to arbitration, but embraced every subject which might affect the relations of the United States with the other American Republics. To prevent opposition in Congress the promoters of the measure had to accept new suggestions which came up during the discussion of the bill, and which enlarged considerably the subjects upon which the Conference had to act. Finally, the Act of May 24, 1888, embraced eight different subjects which the Conference was called upon to consider, some of them covering as many as four subdivisions. On account of these amendments, provisions were incorporated into the Act which did not meet with the support of President Cleveland's Administration or that of his successor, President Harrison, under whose Administration the Conference was held; such, for instance, as the one referring to the adoption of a silver coin to be legal tender in all the American Republics.

From this statement of facts it appears that Mr. Blaine had nothing to do with the enactment of the law which convened the Conference, and therefore he is not, and cannot be, responsible for the form in which it was finally approved.

As this law was passed during a Democratic Administration, by a Congress having a Democratic majority in the House of Representatives, although the Republican party had control of the Senate, it was natural that it should embrace several of the principles contained in the platform of the dominant party, as, for instance, those referring to the development of foreign trade, which might directly or indirectly conflict with the political views and the ideas of political economy of their opponents, and to the coinage of a silver coin of uniform fineness and weight to be a legal tender in all the American nations. It was natural, too, that the delegates of the United States, appointed by a Republican Administration, should represent the protection principles of that party, and that, therefore, they would not be eager to accept the measures concerning the development of foreign trade, and would look with concern on the coining of silver into legal-tender money. This resulted from the diversity of political and economic views in the two parties which control this country, and which in turn attain ascendancy; as it happens some-

appoint delegates, who shall not exceed twelve in number, equally from the two leading political parties, six of them being learned in international law ; and that such delegates shall serve without compensation other than their expenses ; and that the President is hereby authorized to take such other action as may be necessary for the purposes of this act ; and the sum of thirty thousand dollars is hereby appropriated, out of any money in the Treasury not otherwise appropriated, to defray the expenses that may be incurred under this Act."

times that one House of Congress is controlled by one party and the other House by the other party. For these reasons, and from the frequent rotation of political parties in the government of the United States, it is very difficult to bring to a successful termination any transaction of a complex character which requires complete continuity of views and effort on the part of all the branches of the government for any length of time.

Fears of the Spanish-American Nations.—It may be assumed that, as a general rule, the Latin-American nations, except, perhaps, the Central American and two or three of the South American States, looked with distrust on the meeting in Washington of an International American Conference, fearing that its object might be to secure the political and commercial ascendancy of the United States on this continent, to the disadvantage of those nations; but this distrust did not go so far as to make them refuse the invitation. Fortunately, when they were invited, there was no serious question pending between the Latin-American States which could prevent their acceptance, as was the case when a conference was suggested in 1881. The invitation was therefore accepted by all the American nations, with the single exception of San Domingo. The answer of the Dominican Government was a very courteous one, as it stated that that Government had agreed, in a treaty recently signed with the United States, upon arbitration, extradition, reciprocity, and the other subjects mentioned in the law convening the Conference; that these subjects had therefore been considered and decided in said treaty under the Dominican point of view, embracing stipulations which were already decided by the Dominican Government and could not be modified by the Conference, as it was not proper to modify treaty stipulations in an indirect manner by recommendations of the Conference; and therefore, as long as the pending treaty would not be acted upon by the United States, the Dominican Government felt that it could not send delegates to the Conference. This letter was mistranslated, as the phrase *causaban estado*, which meant that as the Dominican Government was "committed to a definite policy on all the points of the program of the Conference, it was useless that it should attend that Conference," was translated "*caused a hitch* in the relations between the two countries." That naturally created some feeling on the part of the United States, because if the translation had been correct the Dominican answer would certainly have been discourteous; thus showing what are the consequences of a mistranslation. Chili accepted in so far as economic questions were concerned, but stated that she would take no part in political questions or in arbitration. An unofficial intimation that an invitation for the representation of Cuba and Porto Rico in the Conference might be accepted was overlooked for obvious reasons.

It was apprehended by some, as already intimated, that the object of the United States in convening the Conference was to obtain decided political and commercial advantages over the other nations of this continent, making them almost its dependencies; and this view caused decided opposition to the project.   There was nothing to show that this was the purpose of the United States, and it probably never entered the mind of either President Arthur or Secretary Frelinghuysen, who formulated the plan.   Their motives, as expressed to their confidential associates, were to promote the peace and the material development of the American countries, and divert their trade from Europe to the United States.   Mr. Blaine, whose boundless ambition grasped at all possibilities, may have desired a political alliance in which " The Great Republic " should figure as a protector of its smaller sisters, but he was violently opposed to the mixture of races, and never favored the annexation to the United States of any foreign territory, except Canada.   The delegates from the United States did not propose in the Conference anything seemingly designed to accomplish such an end.   Judging, therefore, by facts and results, these apprehensions were entirely groundless.   In speaking of arbitration and commercial union, this will appear more plainly.

My personal knowledge of what took place in the Conference leads me to think that there was not on the part of Mr. Blaine any preconceived plan about the subjects that were to be considered, except, perhaps, that of arbitration, and that he not only had no prearranged plan, but even refused to express an opinion on any subject, or even to give instructions to the United States delegates when called on for them.   Mr. Blaine's purpose, as it appears to me, was not to curtail in any manner whatever the full freedom of all the Latin-American nations represented in the Conference, but to allow equal freedom to the United States delegates, so that all might propose and agree on such points as they should think most advantageous to the interests of their respective countries, without any pressure and without even suggestions from the United States Government.

Even in regard to the question of arbitration, Mr. Blaine's wish was only that an agreement should be arrived at that all disputes arising among American nations should be ended by arbitration, with the very laudable and humane object of abolishing war; and he did not seem to have any special plan of his own.   When he had to act upon one, he tried to harmonize the discordant opinions of the delegates, without intending to press it upon any one.   His interference on this subject was only for the purpose of revising the plan which was accepted by a majority of the Conference; and to carry out this purpose he had to request one of the United States delegates to give up his opposition to the form in which the project was finally accepted.

It was understood and asserted at the time that even the general idea of arbitration was not unanimously supported by the representatives of the United States.

Personnel of the Conference.—Mexico, Guatemala, Nicaragua, Colombia, Venezuela, Peru, Chili, the Argentine Republic, and Brazil accredited as delegates to the Conference their diplomatic representatives residing at Washington; Colombia, Venezuela, the Argentine Republic, and Brazil each sent two more delegates, while Mexico and Chili each sent only one more; all the other Republics were represented by one delegate each. The delegates from Honduras, Ecuador, and Bolivia were, besides, accredited to the United States Government as Envoys Extraordinary, and those from Chili and Brazil had a similar character before the Conference. The representatives of Salvador, Costa Rica, Paraguay, and Uruguay came only as delegates, as did also the first representative from Hayti. The Uruguayan delegate was the only one who left before the close of the session. The first delegate from Hayti was obliged to return home on account of sickness, and his place was filled by the Haytian Minister Resident at Washington.

On the very day the Conference closed its session, that is, on April 19, 1890, there was received the acceptance by Hawaii of an invitation sent by Mr. Blaine, as Secretary of State of the United States, to send a representative to the Conference, and the announcement was made that Mr. Carter, then Hawaiian Minister in Washington, had been appointed a delegate. There was therefore no opportunity to pass upon Mr. Carter's credentials, thus avoiding the discussion of the question, regarding which the Argentine delegates were disposed to object, as they thought that Hawaii could not be represented in the Conference, because the Act of Congress authorizing the meeting of the Conference only referred to American nations, and the Hawaiian group is not in the American continents or their adjacent islands.

The delegates who were accredited as Ministers at Washington found very soon that their official relations to the United States Government considerably restricted their liberty of action as compared with that enjoyed by those of their colleagues who came on a transient mission.

Although President Cleveland issued the invitation for the Conference, he refrained, out of deference to his successor, from naming the United States delegates, and their appointment was made soon after President Harrison's inauguration. These appointments were severely censured in some quarters, because it was thought that some of the gentlemen named were not the best fitted for the mission, and some went so far as to think that their selection was an act of disrespect to the Latin-American nations. Whatever may have been the motive which governed the President of the United States in making the appointments, I am sure that he did not intend to choose as representatives of this country gentlemen of little worth, much less to show any disrespect to the nations which the Government of the United States had invited to send delegates to Washington. The appointments were made in the manner usual in connection with offices of the highest rank. They were all ratified by the Senate. The gentlemen appointed represented all political parties, all sections of the country, and all branches of its industries; and they were all honorable gentlemen. Among them were two ex-Senators, four manufacturers, and two merchants; from which it seems that the intention was to select business men rather than diplomats.

It is entirely unnecessary, so far as the Latin-American nations are concerned, to inquire whether this Government could have selected gentlemen better fitted for the work, because if those appointed had not the necessary qualifications, the United States would have been the principal sufferer from any embarrassment that might have resulted.

The habits and manners of the two races represented in the Conference were so widely different; the urbanity of the Latin race is so exquisite, and it attaches so much importance to forms of courtesy and personal attention, which, as a general rule, are somewhat disregarded by the Anglo-Saxon race, that when they came in contact the contrast was very apparent. It was natural that the Latin-Americans, who did not know the Anglo-Saxon Americans well, should wonder at the simplicity of their manners, which almost looked like discourtesy, and that they should have attributed to impoliteness what was only the result of different customs and ways of life. The daily intercourse of the delegates during several months dispelled this impression, which had disappeared almost completely when the Conference adjourned. There were, however, among the United States delegates several who distinguished themselves by their courtesy and conciliatory spirit, especially Mr. Carnegie, Mr. Bliss, and Mr. Flint, very likely because they were somewhat acquainted with the Latin race.

Difficulties Growing Out of the Use of Different Languages.—One of the principal difficulties which arose in the Conference, and which, although apparently insignificant, had an influence that can hardly be over-estimated, was caused by the different languages spoken by the delegates. Only one of the United States delegates, Mr. Flint, had a meagre knowledge of colloquial Spanish, gained in commercial intercourse; one, Mr. Trescot, could read it; but the other delegates of the United States knew nothing of it. Several of the Latin-American members, and among them the Argentine delegates, who took so important a part in the proceedings of the Conference, did not speak English, although one of them by the end of the session understood it tolerably well. It certainly would have been preferable if all the

United States delegates had spoken Spanish, and been conversant with diplomatic affairs in general, especially with those of the Latin-American nations. It would have been desirable, also, that all the Latin-American delegates had spoken English and been familiar with the United States; but the inconvenience which resulted from these drawbacks was not essential, and was remedied in some degree by means of interpreters. Besides, the advantage of knowing both languages was a secondary one compared with all the other qualifications of a delegate. These circumstances made the services of interpreters indispensable.

My personal experience has shown me how difficult it is to make a good translation. Besides a perfect knowledge of the original language and of that in which the translation is made, other conditions are required, which are not always found in any one person, as, for instance, perfect familiarity with the subject-matter to which the translation refers, and a good command of language. This explains why it is almost impossible to translate a masterpiece, like Shakespeare's works. The best proof that can be presented of this difficulty is shown by retranslating a translation into its original language: for instance, take any masterpiece, either of English or Spanish, translate it to the other language, and then retranslate it into its original language, and the imperfections of the first translation will be apparent.

The above - stated difficulties of making a good translation are greatly enhanced when applied to the oral language. It is hard to realize how difficult it is to translate fairly a good speech until one has undertaken to do it. So far as speeches worthy of that name are concerned, they are generally made by good orators, and to do justice to the speeches the translator ought himself to possess high oratorical qualifications, because it is plain that if a man has not perfect command of his own language, and is not able to speak it elegantly, he much less can do so when using a foreign language, and even if he translates into his own language, he cannot do justice to an eloquent speech made in the other when he has not equal qualification as a speaker with the orator himself.

Another great difficulty in translating a speech is the fact that it requires a wonderfully good memory. A speech generally embraces several subjects, and in order that none be omitted the memory must grasp and retain them all, even in case notes are taken to avoid any omission.

The difficulty of correct translations, which was felt more especially in the early sessions of the Conference, caused the delegates of quick temper, when they did not fully understand the ideas expressed in the other language, to misinterpret them, and sometimes to consider them offensive and to return sharp answers, which provoked sharp retorts, and not only disturbed the harmony among the delegates, but in some cases seemed even to threaten the success of the Conference.[1]

The interpreters were required by Article IX. of the rules of the Conference, to interpret the speeches made at the discussions of the meetings as soon as they were delivered, stating the substance of the remarks made by the respective delegates.

The preceding remarks are not intended to cast any reflections on the ability of the gentlemen who served as interpreters in the Pan-American Conference, who were both able and competent, and who made very creditable translations, as such remarks only express my own conclusions, based on my personal experience when I have had to make translations and act as an interpreter. The qualifications as a Spanish and English scholar of Doctor Don José Ignacio Rodriguez, who succeeded Señor Pierra as the Spanish Secretary of the Conference, are too well known to be questioned. Dr. Rodriguez was such an efficient interpreter that I remember I thought on one occasion that he had misunderstood in interpreting into Spanish the remarks made in English by one of the United States delegates, and the speaker being requested to repeat his remarks, I found that I was the one who had misunderstood him and that Dr. Rodriguez's version was the correct one.

Reported Agreement between the Latin-American Countries.—It has been stated that the Chilian Government laid its views before the Governments of the Argentine Republic and the Empire of Brazil, proposing that the three nations should act in concert in the Conference, and that it had answers which it understood to mean that those Governments shared its views in regard to arbitration, and that they all would stand together. Probably this was the reason why the Chilian delegates consented to take part in some of the discussions relating to arbitration, and did not refrain from voting on that subject, except in the last days of the Conference, when the question had assumed a definite shape, and it was plain that their views in this regard were not shared by any of the other South American nations. The Argentine delegates declared, however, that their Government had not committed itself to Chili on this question. If the Brazilian Government gave Chili such assurance, it instructed its delegates in Washington, after the Empire was overthrown in Brazil in November, 1889, and the

---

[1] In an answer I wrote in June, 1890, to severe strictures against the United States and Mexican delegates made by Señor Don Fidel G. Pierra, and published on May 4th of that year in *La Nacion*, a newspaper of Buenos Ayres, Argentina, and which will be found in the Appendix at the end of this paper, I dwelt especially on the inconveniences, serious troubles, and frequent misunderstandings caused in the early sessions of the Pan-American Conference by the use of different languages spoken by its members.

Republican Government established, to act in perfect accord with those of Argentina, as at that time the relations between the two countries had assumed a very cordial and intimate character. That, of course, increased very considerably the strength of the Argentine delegates, as the Brazilians were able men, and represented the largest country in South America, and up to that time it was understood that their instructions required them to act in concert with the Chilian delegates.

The delegates from Paraguay and Uruguay had been instructed by their respective Governments to act in accord with the Argentine delegates, and so they did; but the delegate from Uruguay found it difficult to act in that way, and rather than disobey the instructions of his Government, he soon decided to give up his position, and to return to London, where he was accredited as Uruguayan diplomatic representative.

Jealousy among the South American Nations.—There are in South America two nations which have acquired very great importance—one on account of its large territorial extent, its immense natural resources, favored by an excellent system of navigable rivers, and its extraordinary material progress; the other by its unrivalled position on the Pacific, by possessing as it does almost one half of the western coast of South America, by its habits of order and industry, and by its rapid acquisition of national and individual wealth. I refer to the Argentine Republic and to Chili. Although Brazil has a larger territory and population than these two nations together, the political transition which was in progress in that country prevented it, then, from being a centre of political combinations. The last war on the Pacific, the results of which were not yet an accomplished fact, naturally caused very great excitement. It is only natural that the nations which were conquered in that war should look upon the Argentine Republic as the centre of strength for the maintenance of the political equilibrium or *statu quo ;* and that, for the same reasons, they should look with distrust upon Chili, and apprehend a repetition of events similar to the war of 1879–1883. It was natural, too, that this political excitement, which is merely alluded to here, should be felt in the workings of the Conference, and it is absolutely necessary to take it into consideration to explain some of the incidents which took place in that assembly.

This conflict of political views and interests did not, however, prevent personal and official relations among the South American delegates from being so courteous and cordial that no one who was not aware of the feelings and tendencies of the various countries could perceive that any difference existed among them. On almost all questions presented in the Conference they acted in accord; even the Chilian and

Argentine delegates did so in the discussion of the rules, and, especially, the one concerning the minority report on customs union and reciprocity treaties.

Central America is too far from Chili and the Argentine Republic to take part in the political complications of South America, but she has a pending question of her own—the confederation of the five Central American States—which is a transcendent one, on which, it seems, all the States are not in complete accord, and this fact could not fail to influence the conduct of their representatives in the Conference. The projected Nicaragua Canal was also a source of difference between Nicaragua and Costa Rica.

I would not convey an exact idea of the tendencies and apprehensions which prevailed in the Conference, should I omit to say that Guatemala looked upon Mexico with distrust,[1] because she imagined that the Mexican Government cherished certain designs against her—a supposition by no means correct—and this notwithstanding that the long boundary dispute between Mexico and Guatemala had then been settled, first by the preliminary bases signed in New York, on August 12, 1882, between General J. Rufino Barrios, President of Guatemala, and myself, and by the final boundary treaty signed in the City of Mexico on the 27th of the following September. It was inevitable that this fear should also be felt in the Conference.

Mexico, if not the only one, was nevertheless one of the few Latin-American nations which could properly be considered as really impartial in regard to South American questions. On account of the immense distance which separates her from her southern sisters, and the lack of means of communication, which almost wholly prevents commercial relations with them, Mexico has no political interest in the subjects agitated in those countries. Hence she looks upon all the nations of the southern continent as friends and sisters, and has a most cordial and sincere wish for the prosperity and welfare of each of them. Although Mexico ardently desires that the principles of equity and justice should prevail among the American nations, and although she might disapprove of the conduct of any of them which, in her opinion, was subversive of those principles, and might even go so far as to express her disapproval, she is not called upon to take any active part in regard to questions which may arise in South America, and, therefore, she is not only neutral, but perfectly impartial.

---

[1] Fortunately the condition of things which existed in 1889 is rapidly disappearing. The last boundary question between Mexico and Guatemala, growing out of the interpretation of the treaty of September 27, 1882, was amicably settled by the convention of April 1, 1896, and the late enlightened ruler of Guatemala, General José Maria Reyna Barrios, inaugurated a change of policy which I consider very beneficial to that country.

Perhaps in the beginning a misunderstanding of this position caused the Mexican delegates to be looked upon with distrust by some of their colleagues, who feared that they might be disposed to interfere in the South American questions, or be too partial to the United States; but the impartial and friendly conduct of those delegates in regard to the sister-Republics of South America ought to have satisfied them that Mexico, far from having any feeling against, or design upon, any South American nation, or any wish to interfere in their policies, had, on the contrary, the most sincere wishes for the preservation of their peace and the promotion of their common welfare.

The Argentine delegates seemed to be under the impression that the Mexican delegates had formed a compact with their Chilian colleagues to act together in the Conference.   Such impression, if it ever existed, was entirely unfounded.   There was no compact, understanding, or agreement of any kind whatsoever, expressed or implied, between the Mexican and the Chilian delegates to act together, in all or in any question before the Conference, and much less in antagonism to any of the other States, and when their votes happened to be in accord, it was due only to similarity of views or instructions from their respective Governments, and never to any compact among them.

Preliminary Meeting of the Conference.—The President of the United States fixed the 2d of October, 1889, as the date for the meeting of the Conference.   Two days previous to this date, the delegates, excepting those of Ecuador, Paraguay, and Hayti, who had not arrived, assembled in Washington, and held a preliminary meeting to agree upon their organization.   The first question which was presented to them was the election of a president.

Election of Mr. Blaine as President.—It is an act of courtesy, sanctioned by the example of diplomatic congresses and conferences which have met hitherto, that a representative of the inviting Government, on whose territory the conference meets, shall be elected President; and therefore all the delegates agreed that the President should be a member of the United States delegation.   The Latin-American delegates were not in accord as to the gentleman whom they desired to elect President; some thought that Mr. Henderson, being the Chairman of the United States delegation, ought to be chosen; others were disposed to vote for Mr. Trescot, because he had had great experience in diplomatic affairs, and was supposed to be better fitted for the position. Mr. Blaine was suggested for President by Mr. Curtis because of the supposed antagonism between Mr. Henderson and Mr. Trescot.   This suggestion was originally made to Mr. Blaine, who was pleased with the prospect of participating in the Conference.   He sent Mr. Curtis to President Harrison to submit the proposition and the reasons.   President Harrison approved, and requested Mr. Bliss and Mr. Davis to express his wish to the United States delegates and to the Conference if necessary. A technical objection at once presented itself—whether a functionary of this Government who was not a member of the Conference, not being a delegate, could be made President; but this objection, which was only one of form, was happily solved, since the Secretary of State represented his country in a truer sense than the ten United States delegates together. Hence if the election was to be made with the purpose of fulfilling a duty of courtesy towards the inviting Government, that duty could be most satisfactorily performed by choosing the Secretary of State, even though he were not a delegate. On the other hand, the high position of this functionary made his election as President an act befitting the dignity of the Conference. Although several delegates objected at first to his election, all were satisfied with the foregoing explanation, excepting the Argentine representatives, who stated that they could not vote for him because he was not a member of the Conference. To avoid casting a negative vote, they decided not to be present at the first meeting of the Conference, when the President was elected ; but both of them attended the official banquet which Mr. Blaine gave on that day to the delegates. The judgment of the Argentine delegates was certainly entitled to great weight, but it is not likely that they alone were right in this matter; and if this incident involved a question of the dignity and independence of the delegates, it is not probable that only the delegates of one among the fourteen States represented in the Conference would have entertained such an opinion. If this objection had been a valid one, those presenting it would not have attended the subsequent meetings of the Conference, as they were presided over by a gentleman who, in their opinion, was not qualified to be its President.

I think that the Argentine delegates were misled by a memorandum prepared under Mr. Trescot's direction by Mr. Warner P. Sutton, who was at the time Chief Clerk of the Conference, mentioning all the precedents of the European diplomatic conferences which unanimously establish the practice to be that the Secretary of State of the inviting Government, being a member of the Conference, should be elected President.

This memorandum was intended for the exclusive use of Secretary Blaine and the American delegates, but by some means knowledge of its contents reached Señor Quintana, and as Mr. Blaine was not a member of the United States delegation, Señor Quintana naturally thought that Mr. Blaine was not eligible for President. Señor Quintana afterwards made a very handsome explanation and apology to Mr. Blaine, and the Sutton memorandum was frequently the subject of jest between them. There was another important memorandum to the effect that this Conference was the first one ever held in the United States, and ought to be held under such conditions as would justify the making of precedents, and not follow exactly those hitherto made in Europe.

Subsequent events, and especially those which occurred during the last meetings of the Conference, showed clearly how wise was the election of Mr. Blaine, because he was invested with full powers to negotiate with the Latin-American delegates—powers which were really broader than those of the United States delegation—and because, on the other hand, possessing exquisite tact and a strong desire to prevent the failure of a high purpose in an assembly of which he was the originator, he went farther in order to come to an agreement with the Latin-American delegates than in all probability the United States delegation would have deemed themselves authorized to go.

Question of Precedence.—The question of the precedence of the nations represented in the Conference was next brought up. Some thought that the alphabetical order should be adopted, and others that this matter should be decided by lot. The latter view prevailed, and in the third meeting of the Conference all the nations represented were placed in ballot, and thus the precedence given to their delegates was decided.

Formal Opening of the Conference.—After the preliminary meetings in which the Conference elected its President, it was formally organized on October 2, 1889. Mr. Blaine delivered on that occasion a very remarkable address which was one of his happiest compositions, and then he took the delegates to the White House to present them to President Harrison. In the evening he gave a banquet to the delegates which was attended by them all, and early the next morning the delegates left Washington for New York and West Point on their excursion through the principal cities of the United States.

The Excursion of the Delegates.—The Conference, immediately after its formal opening, adjourned to enter upon the railway excursion which lasted from October 3 to November 13, 1889. That excursion covered more than nine thousand miles of travel, and included visits to all of the large cities east of the Missouri and north of the Ohio River. It was suggested by Mr. William E. Curtis, whose connection with the Conference will presently appear, and heartily favored by President Harrison and Secretary Blaine, and it had several objects in view: First, to give the delegates an opportunity to become acquainted with each other, and to establish friendly personal relations among themselves before entering upon the serious business of the Conference; second, to impress them with the magnitude, the wealth, the prosperity, and the commercial advantages of the United States; third, to soften, and if possible to remove the prejudices and distrust that have been alluded to, by hospitality and social intercourse; and, finally, to awaken among the people of the United States an interest in the proceedings of the Conference and an appreciation of its importance.

However, after the excursion took place, I thought it did not produce the results expected, as many of the delegates knew this country well, and those who did not, could hardly form an adequate idea of it in such a rapid trip. Some of those who took an active part in the proceedings of the Conference, among them the Argentine delegates, did not join it, but about three-fourths of the delegates and almost all the attachés made the entire journey, it being the particular desire of Mr. Blaine that all the young men should go, because, as he said, they would learn more than the older men and would make better use of their information. The only delegate who did not accompany the excursion at all was Señor Saenz Peña, who excused himself because his wife and child were absolute strangers in Washington, unable to speak the language, and dissatisfied with hotel life, and he felt that he must remain and get them settled in a private dwelling as soon as possible. Señor Quintana accompanied the excursion only a few days; he joined the delegates at Chicago, but left the next day and was not present at the banquet given there to the delegates, and where he had been invited to speak; he excused his return by saying that he had been unexpectedly appointed a delegate, and felt that he should make use of the interval to prepare himself for his labors.

I only accompanied the excursion to West Point and then returned to Washington. When the delegates reached Chicago I went there, at the special request of Mr. Blaine, and accompanied the excursion to Council Bluffs and Omaha, returning from there to Washington. When the excursion reached Pittsburg, I, with most of the delegates who had not joined it, went to that place and we all came together to Philadelphia, Wilmington, and Baltimore.

If any favorable result grew out of the excursion, it was most likely among the inhabitants of the cities visited by the delegates, on account of the good impression which may have been produced by personal intercourse with them, although this was, of course, very slight. This, too, may have dispelled some wrong views that had been entertained. Those who most enjoyed the excursion were the young men, attachés of delegations and others who joined it.

On the return of the delegates after their excursion, just mentioned, the organization of the Conference was perfected by approving the rules of the same, electing Vice-Presidents, committees, etc., on which subjects I shall presently speak.

Election of Vice-Presidents.—If Mr. Blaine had been a man of fewer engagements than fall to the lot of a Secretary of State, and able to attend all the meetings of the Conference and remain as long as they lasted, his election would very likely have proved satisfactory during the remaining sessions of the Conference; but, this not being the case, it was soon found that the change of the presiding officer every day created many difficulties, because there was no uniformity in the decisions of the chair; and this caused delay and inconvenience in the workings of the Conference. For this reason, Señor Alfonso, a Chilian delegate, reported on behalf of the Committee of Rules on December 4, 1889, a resolution to the effect that two Vice-Presidents should be elected, who should be called to the chair by turns in the absence of the President, the chair to be filled in their absence by the other delegates in regular order adopted by the Conference. That resolution was approved on the following day.

The United States delegates, viewing the election of Mr. Blaine as an act of deference and courtesy to themselves, decided to reciprocate it by offering their support in carrying out any plan the Latin-American delegates might suggest for the appointment of one or more Vice-Presidents. With the best intention of pleasing their colleagues, and following the parliamentary practices which prevail in this country, the United States delegates made a suggestion, which did not find favor, to the effect that, there being three different sections of America represented in the Conference, a Vice-President should be elected for each of them—to wit, one from the delegates of Central America, two from the delegates of South America (one representing the eastern side, or the nations bordering on the Atlantic, and the other the western side, or the nations bordering on the Pacific), and a fourth to represent the Latin portion of North America.

Although I do not believe that any of the delegates desired to be elected Vice-President on personal grounds, the matter was regarded with a great deal of interest by all of them, on account of the political bearing which it might have on the relations between their respective countries. The above suggestion was not accepted, owing to the difficulty of coming to an agreement about the appointment of one or more Vice-Presidents; and it was first decided that none should be elected, but that in the absence of the President his place should be filled by each delegate in turn as designated by lot. Later, however, it was decided to elect two Vice-Presidents.

The jealousies prevailing in some of the South American Republics, to which I have already alluded, increased by the ill feeling caused by the war which had taken place a few years before between Chili on one side and Bolivia and Peru on the other, had created such a condition of things that it was very difficult for the South American delegates to agree upon a Vice-President of the Conference, and that threatened to be a bone of contention between them. Señor Lafayette Rodriguez Pereira, a Brazilian delegate and a man of very clear judgment and great experience, who out of regard for the personal feelings of the

Emperor vacated his office as soon as he heard that the Emperor had been dethroned, thought that one of the Mexican delegates was the only possible candidate which could have the support of the South American delegates, because, while Mexico is inhabited by the same race and having the same conditions as the South American Republics, she was by the great distance from her sisters and the scanty means of communication between them, entirely neutral to their differences and friendly to all; but the nucleus formed around the Argentine delegates would not be satisfied with a neutral Vice-President, and they desired one who was willing to act in accord with their views on the subject of arbitration and conquest. So when the time came to elect a Vice-President, the Argentine delegates, together with their friends, had as their candidate the Peruvian delegate, who was very well fitted for the position, as he had been partially educated in the United States, spoke English very well, had lived many years in this country, and was perfectly familiar with the same, besides being a man of great ability and remarkably good sense; while some of the other delegates, like the Chilian, Brazilian, and others, who opposed the preponderance of the Argentines, and could not see with indifference that they should have control of the Conference, tried to have a neutral delegate as Vice-President, and their choice was in favor of one of the Mexican representatives.

The election of the first Vice-President took place on December 6, 1889, and on the first ballot Señor Zegarra, the Peruvian representative, received six votes, a Mexican representative five, Señor Hurtado three votes, Señor Quintana and Señor Cruz one vote each, and nobody having obtained a majority, the question was presented whether some of the absent delegates had a right to vote, but finally it was decided to take another ballot the following day. At this ballot, which took place on December 7, 1889, Señor Zegarra and myself received eight votes each, and Señor Aragon, a delegate from Costa Rica, proposed that chance should decide which of the two should be first and second Vice-Presidents respectively.

A recess was taken and two ballots deposited in a box, one bearing the name of Señor Zegarra and the other mine. A ballot was drawn, bearing the name of Señor Zegarra, and he was thereupon declared first Vice-President.[1]

The Peruvian delegate, who knew well the programme of his friends, did not attend the Conference during the two days in which

[1] It may be interesting to know how the delegates voted on that occasion, and although the ballot was secret and I cannot be sure of the way in which each delegation voted, I think from what I knew and heard at the time that the most approximate version is the following: For Señor Zegarra, The Argentine Republic, Uruguay, Paraguay, Bolivia, Venezuela, Guatemala, Nicaragua, and Honduras; for myself, the United States, Brazil, Chili, Colombia, Ecuador, Costa Rica, Salvador, and Hayti.

the ballots were taken, but as I did not consider myself a candidate, I attended both meetings, but was not in the hall of the Conference when the ballot was taken on the second day.

As Mexico had two delegates, one of them intended to vote for his colleague, not as an honor to him personally, but to their country, which course would have been perfectly proper; but he was induced by me to give up his intention and the election was decided by lot. I had no desire to act as presiding officer of the Conference, because that would have curtailed considerably my freedom of action on the floor. Señor Zegarra made a model presiding officer.[1]

On that occasion an incident occurred, insignificant in itself, but which caused a misunderstanding that I do not think is yet fully dispelled. As the United States delegates were disposed to accept and support anything that their colleagues might determine upon in regard to the vice-presidency, as an act of courtesy towards them and in exchange for their having elected as President the Secretary of State, they thought that the Latin-American delegates would be more free to discuss and decide this point, which was a delicate one, being somewhat personal, if they consulted by themselves; and for this reason the United States delegates were not present in the room where their colleagues met. Their absence, however, was considered by some of the Latin-American delegates as an act of discourtesy, because they took as a want of consideration to them the fact of their not assembling in the same room with their colleagues, whereas the true reason was a desire to show consideration for their associates.

Right of Delegates to Express Personal Opinions.—Another incident which threatened to disturb the good understanding of the Conference was the view entertained by the Argentine delegation that the delegates should express only the official opinion of their Governments, and that personal views ought not to be taken into account, either in the Conference or in the committees. The law providing for the meeting of the Conference had authorized each nation to send as many delegates as it thought proper, but prescribed at the same time that each country should have only one vote; so that whatever might have been the opinions of the delegates from any State, in casting their vote only one opinion was expressed, which was the opinion of the majority, and therefore the official opinion of their Government.

It was natural to suppose and to expect that each delegate would express the opinion of his Government contained in his instructions when the case under consideration was embraced in such instructions, or an opinion as nearly as possible in accord with the wishes and interests

[1] In my answer to Señor Pierra, to which I have already alluded and which appears among the documents forming the Appendix to this paper, I give further details about the election of the Vice-Presidents.

of his country, as each one could form when he had not specific instructions on any particular question. In many cases the American Governments either did not give instructions to their delegates or gave them very broad ones, preferring that they should exercise their own personal judgment and discretion on such questions as might arise. To assert, therefore, that the delegates ought to express only the official opinion of their Governments was to interfere in a measure with the relations of the delegates with their respective Governments, and to limit their right to say what they thought proper. This opinion did not meet with favor in the Conference, since, while it arrived at no decision on this point, it never refused to hear any personal opinion, or contrary opinions from two or more members of the same delegation.

Appointment of Committees.—The appointment of the committees was a very important matter, since a great deal of the success of the Conference depended thereon, and, with a view to avoiding any unpleasantness among the delegates on this account, they agreed to request the President to appoint them. Mr. Blaine performed that duty without consulting any of the delegates, only exercising his own discretion on the subject. As I understand, Señor Quintana was the only man consulted as to his own wishes, believing that he would turn out to be a " punctilious gentleman," as Mr. Blaine expressed it. His preference was ascertained, and then he was placed on the Committee of General Welfare. I do not know that the appointment of the committees gave rise to any well-grounded complaint, or caused embarrassment in the transaction of the business which they had in charge. The only embarrassment I have heard of in the committees was caused by the discordant opinions of the delegates from one country who were members of the same committees, and by the fact that the United States delegates had no instructions from their Government, and could therefore express only their own personal views. In the Committee on Monetary Union there were two United States delegates who held opposite views in regard to the coining of silver, and this made it difficult for the other members of the committee to find out what was the view of the United States Government on this subject. I understand there was a similar difficulty, although in a less degree, in the Committee on Communications by Railways; but the most serious misunderstanding arose in the General Welfare Committee, which had the subject of arbitration in charge, because the United States member expressed personal views which were not shared by the other members of the committee.

Rules of the Conference.—The Conference, when organized, decided, very prudently, to frame a code of rules for its deliberations and decisions, and the committee appointed for that purpose took as a model the rules approved by the South American Congress that met at

Montevideo in 1888, which had the advantage of having been put in practice successfully at that congress. Señor Quintana, and a member of the Committee on Rules, who was also a member of that congress, was requested by the committee to prepare the rules and to support them in the discussion before the Conference.

The parliamentary practices of the Latin and the Anglo-Saxon nations being so widely different, the rules reported by the committee of seven, of whom six were Latin members and only one Anglo-Saxon member, met with great opposition on the part of the United States delegates. A long discussion of each article, which lasted for several weeks, ensued. This discussion, which was mainly sustained by the Argentine delegates, warmly supported by Señor Alfonso, the chairman of the committee, showed at once the firmness of character of both sets of delegates, and especially of the United States delegates, who were not quite disposed to accept the modifications suggested to them, even though these were not of much consequence. This was an indication of what was to happen later with more important subjects. The rules were finally approved substantially as they were presented by the committee.

Señor Quintana, conscious of his own merits, and influenced always by firm convictions, was never willing to yield even in such points as might be considered of a secondary nature, as in some cases it is quite desirable to do for the purpose of obtaining the cordial and spontaneous support of an assembly wherein, necessarily, different views exist. Tact, which in such a case consists in yielding on secondary points for the purpose of securing the principal ones,—although frequently there are differences of opinion as to which are the principal and which the secondary points,—possibly, after all, is a characteristic of weaker minds.

Mr. Henderson, the Chairman of the United States delegation, possessed somewhat similar strong convictions, and for this reason the discussions which had the liveliest character, and which sometimes went so far as to be personal, were those which took place between this gentleman and Señor Quintana. The Argentine delegates, inspired by the great progress of their country, and having no political relations and no business of any importance with the United States, showed an independence which in every case was very laudable, but they sometimes, perhaps on account of their personal characteristics, displayed an extraordinary and exquisite susceptibility. Whatever may have been disagreeable in the discussions of the Conference was disposed of, however, in a satisfactory manner by the following remark of Mr. Henderson in closing the session: " If in that freedom of speech a word of acrimony has been used, let us now consider it expunged from the record, and resolve to forget it forever.''

Soon after the Conference met, some newspapers in this country, prompted by jealous politicians at Buenos Ayres, began to attack the Argentine delegates with extraordinary and unjustifiable rudeness, even going so far as to say that they were paid agents of England acting with the purpose of preventing the success of the Conference. Such uncalled-for and ungrounded attacks caused, as was only natural, a strong reaction, by which the merits of those gentlemen were made plain and the reflections cast upon them were disposed of in so successful a manner that such insinuations were never again referred to. Any unpleasant feeling which these aspersions may have caused the Argentine delegates was certainly abundantly compensated for by the satisfaction they must have felt when they were so triumphantly and successfully vindicated.

The attitude of the Argentine delegates, who, during the discussions of the Conference, had frequent encounters with the United States delegates, especially with Mr. Henderson, and spoke of their country as being on a parallel with the United States, was of course a source of great satisfaction to many more patriotic than discreet Spanish-Americans, who did not realize the objects of the Conference and the best means to accomplish these objects to the advantage of the Latin-American nations. Not only the Argentine papers, but the papers of other Spanish-American countries, praised very highly the attitude of the Argentine delegates, and those who like myself had followed a different course were severely censured by Mexican papers, and I was criticised even by a distinguished Mexican writer. I had, therefore, to enter into a discussion with a prominent literary man of Mexico, who regretted that I did not assume the more than independent attitude of the Argentine delegates, and that discussion was ended by the Mexican Government stating that I had acted under their instructions and in a manner entirely satisfactory to them. I append extracts from a letter written by me at the time to my critic explaining my course.

Mr. William E. Curtis.—Although I realize how disagreeable it is to descend to personal matters, I think it indispensable, with a view to a better understanding of what happened in the Conference, to make some explanation of certain incidents of this nature. Mr. William E. Curtis, who had acted as Secretary and finally as a member of the South American Commission sent by President Arthur, in 1884, for the purpose of promoting trade with South America, was appointed by Mr. Blaine to take charge of the work preparatory to the meeting of the Conference, and more especially to supervise the excursion which the Government of the United States arranged in honor of the delegates.

According to the original plan of the Conference Mr. Curtis was to be Chief Secretary, or Executive Officer, with three Under-Secretaries

—Spanish, Portuguese, and English; but Mr. Curtis was not a *persona grata* to all the delegates, and the opposition to him was prompted by some Spanish-Americans in New York whom Mr. Curtis had offended: the Argentine delegates were much displeased with a magazine article Mr. Curtis had written concerning the financial credit of their country; the Colombians because of an article concerning the family relations of President Nuñez, and his concordat with the Pope; the delegates from Chili were offended because of his comments upon the then recent war with Peru; and Señor Caamaño, of Ecuador, disliked some humorous personal allusions in the *Capitals of South America*. The publication of this book was the principal cause of the opposition, as it contained allusions to other Spanish-American countries which had in some way offended their respective delegates, who thought he had committed many serious mistakes and made many uncomplimentary remarks in speaking of their capital cities. This would not seem strange, taking into consideration that the time Mr. Curtis spent in each city was very short, and remembering how difficult it is under such circumstances to know and understand a country, and, still more, to write about it without making mistakes, which are generally to the prejudice of the country treated of. All of the delegates at the close of the Convention were generous enough to write Mr. Curtis congratulatory letters upon his management, with assurances of their personal regard.

The Committee on Rules presented a resolution, which was approved by the Conference at its second meeting, to elect two Secretaries, one to take charge of the Spanish work and the other of the English, both to be conversant with each language, and both to be elected directly by the Conference. The Secretary of State accepted this resolution out of deference to the Conference, notwithstanding that the law which convened the assembly gave him the appointment of all its clerks; and his right to do this was still more clear because the salaries of the Secretaries were paid by the United States Government. As Mr. Curtis did not know Spanish, he was precluded from being a secretary; Mr. Blaine then appointed him Executive Officer of the Conference, and he acted until the end as chief of all the clerks. I must state here, in justice to Mr. Curtis, that during the time he served in this capacity he succeeded in dispelling many of the unfavorable views which existed regarding him.

Señor Don Fidel G. Pierra.—The notoriety acquired by the Spanish Secretary of the Conference makes it necessary to say a few words about him. Señor Don Fidel G. Pierra is a Cuban who lived many years in New York, where, I understand, he had some commercial business. He accompanied the Spanish-American delegates on the excursion which preceded the Conference, as representative of the

Spanish-American Commercial Union of New York, and secured their acquaintance and friendship by rendering them services as an interpreter and in other ways. The Conference elected him Spanish Secretary; but on account of his peculiar temperament and disposition he was not able to remain long in that place, although he had the good-will and support of the Latin-American delegates. He complained that he had not competent clerks to assist him, and he thought the Executive Clerk, Mr. Curtis, was unfriendly; he also alleged that the salary assigned to him by the Department of State was not sufficient compensation for his work, although it was higher than the salary assigned to the Assistant Secretaries of State, and as high as the highest paid to clerks of the Conference. Finally his resignation was accepted, and soon afterwards Señor Pierra addressed to *La Nacion*, of Buenos Ayres, Argentina, a letter dated at Washington, on March 10, 1890, in which he gave an account of the proceedings of the Conference, making many incorrect and some slanderous assertions in regard to incidents which occurred in the Conference, and more especially respecting some of the delegates of the United States and Mexico.[1] I thought it proper on my part to publish a correction of such misstatements, and I wrote a correct statement of such incidents, which was published by *Las Novedades*, a Spanish newspaper of the city of New York, in its issue of July 7, 1890. Señor Pierra's assertions were incidentally considered in the Senate of

---

[1] When Señor Pierra's letter to *La Nacion* of Buenos Ayres reached New York, a few extracts from the same were printed by the *New York Herald* of June 28, 1890, and in its issue of July 3, 1890, it published fuller extracts of such portions of the letter as contained abuse to the representatives of the United States, as well as to myself. As soon as I had the first intimation of that letter, by the first publication of the *New York Herald*, I obtained a copy of *La Nacion* of Buenos Ayres which had the letter in full, prepared at once an answer, which was intended to be read especially among the Spanish-American people, to dispel inaccuracies of Señor Pierra, and sent it to *Las Novedades* of New York, which published it in its issue of July 7, 1890.

In a discussion in the Senate of the United States, which took place on July 3, 1890, on a bill to subsidize a line of steamers from New York to Buenos Ayres, Senator Vest, under the misapprehension that Señor Pierra was the Secretary of a society in the city of Buenos Ayres and had accompanied to Washington the delegation from the Argentine Republic to the Pan-American Conference, and believing that Señor Pierra expressed the views of the Argentine delegates about their colleagues representing the United States, read some extracts from Señor Pierra's letter in which he abused the United States delegates. This abuse so excited Senator Hawley that he qualified the aspersions of Señor Pierra with most forcible and strong language, as appears on pages 7495, 7496, and 7497 of the *Congressional Record* for July 4, 1890; and finally Senator Frye, in the session of the Senate of the 14th of the same month, spoke on this subject for the purpose of dispelling Senator Vest's misapprehensions about the position of Señor Pierra in the Argentine Republic, using, like Senator Hawley, very strong language to characterize Señor Pierra's conduct, and then Senator Vest disclaimed all responsibility or endorsement of any of Señor Pierra's statements.

the United States on July 14, 1890, and qualified in the harshest possible manner, although fully deserved, considering the impropriety of his conduct. I append to this paper a copy of my communication to *Las Novedades* of New York.

Arbitration.—Arbitration is a very difficult and complicated subject. It cannot be denied that during the present century mankind has advanced very rapidly in civilization and moral sense, and it is to be hoped that, at no distant period, such advancement will make war impossible, for war has been thus far one of the greatest scourges which has afflicted the human race. But so long as the moral sense of highly advanced countries does not disapprove of war as an uncivilized way of adjusting differences among themselves, not much progress can be made by accepting arbitration in solemn treaties, especially if no method of coercion is agreed upon against such nations as may refuse to compromise their differences, and such a method cannot be established without attempts against the sovereignty and independence of the respective states.

It was thought by some Spanish Americans that the purpose of the United States was to establish a permanent court of arbitration at Washington, and this was looked upon as a way of giving the United States a decided preponderance in all questions affecting this continent. Although I understand that the United States delegate who was chairman of the Committee on General Welfare looked favorably upon the idea of having a permanent tribunal, and his views on this subject were shared by his Colombian colleague, the plan was not accepted by the other Latin-American delegates, nor by the Secretary of State of the United States, and had therefore to be abandoned.

Mr. Blaine wished arbitration without limitations which might nullify its principle. Chili did not favor arbitration, except in a very restricted manner. Mexico and the Argentine Republic desired reasonable limitations, while all the other States accepted the idea without any limitation. The Argentine and Brazilian delegates introduced, on January 15, 1890, an arbitration project which contained, besides, declarations and stipulations against conquest.

The Argentine delegates were the nucleus of the opposition to the acquisition of territory by conquest, and naturally were joined by the South American nations which had lost territory in the then recent war with Chili, namely, Peru and Bolivia. The object of the Argentine delegates was to have the Conference declare that territory could not in any case, past or future, be acquired as a consequence of war. Such declaration would interfere with the acquisition by Chili of territory belonging to Peru and Bolivia. The United States delegate in the committee thought it inexpedient that the Conference should join in any such declaration, among other reasons because that would be equivalent to condemning the acquisition of Mexican territory after the war of 1847 and 1848, and he could not therefore join the Argentines in accomplishing that object.

The text of the Argentine and Brazilian project appears in Mr. Henderson's letter of February 14, 1898, which will be found among the documents (No. 4) annexed to this paper, taken from the minutes of the meeting of the Conference held January 15, 1890. The Argentine-Brazilian project was referred, upon its presentation, to the Committee on General Welfare, and was not reported by that committee [1] until April 14th, near the close of the session of the Conference, which finished its work on the 18th and adjourned on the 19th of the same month.

While this project was in committee Mr. Blaine had two meetings with delegates at his residence; the first one with the representatives of Chili, the Argentine Republic, Brazil, and Mexico, whose views were supposed not to be in entire accord with Mr. Blaine's, although the Republican Government of Brazil had then authorized its delegates to accept the broadest possible plan of arbitration; and the second meeting with all the other delegates, who fully accepted the views of the Secretary of State.

The divergence of views between the United States and the Latin-American delegates about the details of the project was so great that Mr. Blaine had to take the matter into his own hands, and summoned all the members of the Committee on General Welfare to discuss the subject with him at his private residence, spending the greater part of two nights in that work. He suggested several changes to the Argentine-Brazilian project, which had been accepted by all the Latin-American members of the committee, and suggested further, as the only way in which matters could be adjusted, to divide the project into two parts, confining the first to a general arbitration, and the second to a declaration against conquest, which the Argentine delegates made a condition *sine qua non* to accept arbitration.

After the committee had accepted Mr. Blaine's suggestion they agreed upon a draft for the first project, which when completed was handed to Mr. Curtis with instructions to have a clean copy made of the same and submit it to Mr. Blaine for his information. Mr. Curtis did so and Mr. Blaine amended it considerably, and with such amendments, and others afterward made, it was reported by the committee. Mr. Curtis keeps in his office in this city (Washington) the original type-

---

[1] The verbal incorrections which are noticed in the Plan of Arbitration as reported by the committee, were due to the fact that Señor Cruz, the Guatemalean delegate to the Conference, and a member of the Committee of General Welfare, was entrusted to put into English the Spanish text of the project, who, although a good linguist and having a fair knowledge of the English language, was not then entirely proficient in the same.

written copy of the project as agreed upon by the committee, with the amendments made by Mr. Blaine in his own handwriting, and he has kindly allowed me to make a facsimile of the first page of that paper (Document No. 5 of the Appendix), which was the one most substantially amended, and from which it appears exactly how much and how materially the Argentine-Brazilian project was altered by Mr. Blaine, and shows at the same time the trend of his mind on the subject of arbitration and the interest he took in the same. At Mr. Blaine's request Mr. Henderson signed the report of the committee as modified and approved by Mr. Blaine.

On the 14th of April, 1890, the report of the committee, bearing date of the 9th, was presented to the Conference, and was first discussed and approved under the rule called in Spanish " *Discusion en lo general*," which in English might be " discussion on the whole," and by which the adoption of the general idea of a measure is first discussed, since, if that idea is not accepted, it is useless to enter into its details, and if the idea is accepted then the discussion and approval of the details of the measure are in order, under our parliamentary practice accepted by the rules of the Conference. The project reported by the committee was approved on the whole on the day of its presentation, as were also the first eleven articles, excepting the 2d and 4th, which were discussed and approved at the meeting of the Conference which took place on the 16th of April. The Preamble was considerably modified, and it was finally approved at the meeting of the 17th.

The Argentine delegates voted in favor of arbitration when the project was discussed on the whole ; but when the final vote on the specific project proposed by the committee was submitted to the Conference on April 18th, they abstained from voting.

The fact that Mr. Henderson did not sign the report on the right of conquest, that it had suffered substantial changes from the form in which it was presented by the Argentine delegates, and the fear that after the agreement was signed it might not be ratified by the contracting parties, were, in all probability, the causes why they did not vote for the arbitration plan nor sign the respective treaty. Mr. Henderson's refusal came near causing a failure of arbitration, and to avoid such failure Mr. Blaine had to accept the scheme against conquest.

Before the arbitration project was finally approved, important changes were made in the same, which appear in Document No. 8 of the Appendix to this paper, which is the text of the treaty signed in Washington April 28, 1890. This treaty as well as two other recommendations of the Conference were submitted to Congress by the President with his Message of September 3, 1890.

At the meeting of April 18th the Committee on General Welfare presented their project against conquest, the final text of that project being approved in very different shape from that in which it was reported by the committee. In the annexed document, No. 7, appears the text as reported by the committee, and in No. 8 the text of the project as approved by the Conference.

The Conference also approved a recommendation to the European nations to accept the principle of arbitration, which appears among the papers embraced in Document No. 8.

The report of the committee was presented to the Conference so late that it could only be taken up partially in three meetings, and there was not sufficient time to consider it carefully, or even to adopt verbal amendments which were necessary to make it more clear and precise. It can therefore be properly said that there was no discussion on the subject of arbitration, since the delegates could only give their views in the debate which followed for the purpose of explaining their votes and the position of their respective Governments.

From what I heard at the time especially from Señor Quintana, and judging from the natural disposition of Mr. Henderson to be deliberate and careful in anything he does, I thought, and expressed in rather harsh terms in the first edition of this paper, that he was responsible for the delay of the Committee of General Welfare in reporting to the Conference the arbitration project. When my article was published, Mr. Henderson told me that I had done him an injustice, and that he was in no way responsible for that delay. I assured him that I did not have any intention to be unfair to him or to anybody else connected with the Conference, and that if he would do me the favor of writing a memorandum of the case, I would publish it at once as a correction of my statement. He did not do so at the time, and when I was preparing the present edition of this paper, I begged of him again to make his statement of the case, and he kindly sent me a letter containing the history of his connection with the arbitration project presented by the committee of which he was chairman, with two enclosures, which in justice to Mr. Henderson I published in the *North American Review* for April, 1898, so that those who had read my article could read Mr. Henderson's explanation, and I now append to this paper what I published in that *Review*. (Document No. 4.)

Mr. Blaine desired that the delegates who had accepted the report of the committee should sign it in the shape of a treaty before the Conference closed its sessions. His grounds were that Article I. of the Act convening the Conference mentioned as its principal object the consideration and recommendation of a plan of arbitration. Several delegates, among them the Argentines, were of the opinion that this subject ought not to be disconnected from the others, and were willing to sign in the shape of a treaty the recommendation relative to arbitration, provided all the other recommendations adopted by the Conference were signed at the same time. As there was no time to engross all of them, the formality of signature was, on motion of a delegate from the United States, limited to that concerning arbitration, and this constituted another reason why the Argentine delegates would not sign it. Other delegates who would have signed the arbitration project in the shape of a recommendation did not consider themselves authorized to sign it in the shape of a treaty, and this explains why some of the delegates who voted for the agreement did not sign the treaty. On that occasion Mr. Blaine's earnestness carried him so far that he thought it necessary to come down from the chair and take the place of a delegate in supporting the motion, which was finally carried.[1]

After the Conference approved the arbitration project on the 18th of April, 1890, it was necessary to engross the same in the form of a treaty written in the four languages spoken by the American nations, namely, English, Spanish, Portuguese, and French ; and after the proper translations were made, a work done at the State Department, Mr. Blaine ordered twenty-five copies of the same printed at the Government Printing Office, on large paper, with four parallel columns, one of them for each of the respective languages, and when all this work was finished, the treaty was signed at the State Department on April 28, 1890, exactly in the shape in which it appears in Document No. 8 of the Appendix to this paper. The treaty was signed by the representatives of the Governments of Bolivia, Ecuador, Guatemala, Hayti, Honduras, Nicaragua, Salvador, the United States of America, the United States of Brazil, the United States of Venezuela, and Uruguay. The States that failed to sign the treaty were, therefore, Mexico, Costa Rica, Colombia, Peru, Chili, the Argentine Republic, and Paraguay. The Costa Rican delegate left Washington before the treaty was signed, and the Venezuelan delegates received instructions to sign the treaty after it had been executed by the other delegates.

As Article XIX. of the treaty provided that the ratifications of the same should be exchanged in Washington on or before the 1st day of May, 1891, and as that time expired before the treaty could be ratified by the respective nations, another convention extending the time for such a purpose was signed in Washington on October 22, 1891. The only Governments which signified to the United States Government

---

[1] In a paper which I published in the *Bulletin of the American Geographical Society*, of New York, for September 30, 1897, vol. xxix., No. 3, entitled, "*Mr. Blaine and the Boundary Question between Mexico and Guatemala*," I stated at length how earnest a friend of arbitration Mr. Blaine was, and how hard he worked to substitute arbitration for war in the settlement of international disputes, making this almost the object of his life, and how his devotion to arbitration shown on different occasions and under very different circumstances enlisted his sympathies in favor of Guatemala in our boundary question with that State.

their willingness to renew the treaty were Ecuador, Guatemala, Honduras, Venezuela, Nicaragua, Salvador, and Bolivia.

I understood the treaty had been submitted to the United States Senate for its ratification ; but after having made inquiries on the subject I found that it was never sent to the Senate. I cannot understand, knowing as I do how earnest a friend of arbitration, and how anxious to have it reduced to a tangible shape in the form of a treaty, Mr. Blaine was, that when the treaty was actually signed, at his earnest request and through his decided efforts, he should leave it in the files of the State Department, without sending it to the Senate as is always done with all treaties negotiated by representatives of the United States Government, unless disapproved by the President. When he had it in his power as Secretary of State to submit the same to the Senate, it is beyond my comprehension why he did not do so. Possibly President Harrison objected to the treaty, and that may be the explanation of his failure.

Although Mr. Blaine was the leading spirit of the arbitration project, he cannot be considered as the author of the form in which it was finally approved by the Conference, because he had to give up much for the purpose of securing the acceptance of the principle of arbitration; but the Preamble to that paper was due almost entirely to him.

The population, territorial extension, trade, wealth, and advanced civilization of the United States make them the greatest and most powerful nation on this continent, and on this account they had decided advantages over some of the smaller nations, which they could easily bring to bear in case of difficulties with them. The plan approved by the Conference deprived them of all these advantages, and placed them in the same position as the weakest American nation. It is true that this agreement, equitable as it is in all its bearings, as all the countries participate in it under the most absolute equality, might be used hereafter in establishing the preponderance of the United States; but should they have intended to undertake this, they would not have been willing to bind themselves by an agreement which they would have to break more or less openly before they could take other steps. This appeared so clear to my mind that when the agreement was made I expressed the opinion that it would not be ratified by the Senate of the United States.

I was sure that a treaty of arbitration which had been approved in such a hasty manner, and in my opinion without due deliberation and without fully considering the serious objections presented against it, would not be approved by the Senate of the United States, and I so expressed in the first edition of this paper published in October, 1890. My prediction could not be fully verified, because the treaty was not submitted to the Senate for ratification, and to my surprise not only the United States but other governments whose delegates signed the treaty did not ratify it, and so the treaty failed.

Since that time the arbitration views of the United States Government have received a great set-back in the rejection by the Senate of the United States on May 5, 1897, of the Treaty of Arbitration with Great Britain signed in Washington on January 11th of the same year. It seems to me that if the United States are not willing to enter into a general plan of arbitration with a nation at least as powerful as themselves it is not likely that they will do so with smaller and weaker nations. I am sure, however, that the arbitration idea will be developed, beginning in a limited way, until finally, possibly after some centuries, it may supersede war.

Mexico on the Treaty of General Arbitration.—The Mexican Government did not look with good-will, for obvious reasons, upon the idea of forced and unrestricted arbitration; and as Article XXI. of the treaty of February 2, 1848, between Mexico and the United States provided ample arbitration with this country, Mexico thought it prudent not to have it extended any further, and instructed its delegates accordingly. We did not intend, therefore, to take any part in the discussion on this subject, but only to cast our votes in accordance with our instructions when the question came up. But when the Mexican Government heard that several South American nations were disposed to go much farther than Mexico in the premises, not wishing to appear in disaccord with her sister Republics, it authorized its delegates to extend the scope of arbitration, but not to accept it without limitation.

I had, however, to give up the intention of taking a passive position on this question, because the Secretary of State requested me particularly to prepare a draft of arbitration, which, in my opinion, would be acceptable to the Mexican Government and the Latin-American States which were not disposed to accept arbitration without limitation. I stated to him, with all candor and sincerity, the obstacles which were in the way of my drafting a project which I was not sure would have the support even of my own Government; but, in order not to disregard his repeated requests, and because I thought that I might possibly draft something which would be acceptable to all, I consented to take up the matter and to speak on the subject with several of my colleagues. Soon afterwards, however, I found that the difficulties in the way of coming to a general agreement were insurmountable, and I wholly gave up the attempt. When the report of the committee was discussed in the Conference the Mexican delegates expressed only the opinion of their Government, and voted in accordance with their instructions, when they had specific instructions, or with what they understood to be the wishes of their Government on new points regarding which there had been no time to receive instructions.

There were besides some subjects connected with arbitration which were looked upon in a very different way by Mexico and the South American nations. I refer to boundary questions, and, in fact, to all territorial questions. In the immense territorial area, very thinly populated, of the South American nations, their people being of a homogeneous race and having the same religion, habits, and language, and those nations not having, as a general rule, clearly marked territorial limits, the boundary questions which have sprung up among them are relatively of little importance. A district of land practically uninhabited does not diminish in any perceptible manner the domain of the nation that may lose it, nor increase greatly the power of the nation which may acquire it, nor make any material change of language, habits, education, social condition, and political status of its inhabitants. This is not the case as between Mexico and the United States, because they are countries inhabited by different races, speaking different languages, having different customs, religions, and habits, and because the proportion of population, wealth, and material strength between them constitutes a very different condition of things. The boundary disputes in South America have generally been decided, and with a great deal of reason, by arbitration, and its statesmen hold the view that, if arbitration is good for anything, it is good to end such disputes. Perhaps it is the best way to solve them in any case ; but to make arbitration obligatory as to all questions, including boundary difficulties, which may arise between Mexico and the United States, would be equivalent to placing Mexico in an unfavorable position. Therefore so broad a stipulation, which is not only desirable, but even necessary, in South America, might well not be accepted by Mexico. This explains why Mexico did not follow her sister-Republics in the whole length to which they were willing to go on this subject.

Subsequent action by the United States on the subject justifies the position of Mexico in this case. The United States has had since the arbitration treaty was signed, serious questions threatening war, with various countries, as with Chili in 1891, growing out of the Valparaiso riot which resulted in the wounding of some sailors of the United States cruiser *Baltimore*. Chili proposed arbitration to settle that difficulty, and it was not accepted by President Harrison. In a later question which unfortunately could not be settled by peaceful means, arbitration was again proposed and refused by this government. The reason that questions affecting the honor of a country are not fit subjects for arbitration was not mentioned in either of those two cases, but I have no doubt that it was the controlling reason which decided the policy of this Government in both instances, and that was exactly the position assumed by Mexico on the subject in the Pan-American Conference when arbitration was discussed.

Reciprocity Treaties.—Reciprocity treaties have a great *rôle* to perform in the development of commercial relations between the Spanish-American nations and the United States, but, unfortunately, public opinion is not yet prepared in this country to accept them. The subject of reciprocity is far more complicated than it appears to be, since it has become connected with the protection and free-trade questions which are now so earnestly agitated in this country. The United States, as an eminently Anglo-Saxon nation, has always followed, although sometimes with slowness, the footsteps of the mother-country, in many cases even going beyond her; and, although thus far they do not seem disposed to accept free trade, which has done so much to secure the commercial preponderance of England, I have no doubt that before long they will not remain behind Great Britain in this regard; but as the ultra-protective policy prevails here at present, it is not possible to establish and maintain reciprocity successfully. The United States, from an agricultural country which it was a few years ago, has reached the condition of a manufacturing one, and in this stage is making very rapid strides. Now when the production of manufactured articles is exceeding the needs of the home market, the foundation of the protective system is receiving a great blow; production is now cheapened; new foreign markets are now sought for the surplus products; and when all this is attained, this country will be a great commercial nation. Reciprocity treaties will represent the transition between these two stages, and until the second is fully attained there will be many difficulties in the way.

The fate of the reciprocity treaty signed with Mexico in 1883 demonstrates the correctness of this view. That treaty, which was initiated by this Government, was made with a country contiguous to it for nearly two thousand miles, inhabited by twelve millions of people, who produce, in proportion to their population, very few manufactured articles, but who have all the elements of soil, climate, and labor necessary to produce the raw materials needed by the manufacturing industries of the United States. That nation, too, is connected with the United States by four trunk railways built by United States companies, which are really extensions and feeders of the trunk lines of this country. It is clear that, if reciprocity could not be established with Mexico, much less can it be adopted with the other American nations, which have not as favorable conditions, excepting perhaps Brazil, which has developed a very large trade with the United States. It has been found impossible to carry out the reciprocity treaty with Mexico, which was intended, by the exemption of duty on Mexican sugar, to open new sources of production and trade. Moreover, the tariff Act of October 1, 1890, intended to close this market to the chief article of Mexican export—silver in lead-ore,—an industry which was developed by the construction of railroads in Mexico, this ore being the principal article that they transport, and which was encouraged and increased by the capital and skill of this country.

The main reason why the reciprocity treaty with Mexico was not put in operation was the opposition to receiving, free of duty, Mexican sugar, notwithstanding the fact that, as compensation for such advantage, Mexico made valuable concessions to this country; and yet in the Tariff Bill enacted October 1, 1890, foreign sugar was exempted from all import duties, without any compensation or advantage in favor of the national production of other articles.

Reciprocity was, undoubtedly, the subject most fully considered in the Conference, and the one which commanded the most earnest attention. The committee agreed as to the difficulty of establishing a customs union, in the sense of a *Zollverein*, and as to the desirability of making reciprocity treaties to promote trade between the respective countries. On the latter point, however, the committee was divided, as the Brazilian, Colombian, Venezuelan, Nicaraguan, and Mexican members of it recommended the negotiation of such treaties, not upon a uniform basis, but in accordance with the circumstances and needs of each country, while the Argentine and Chilian delegates thought it officiousness on the part of the Conference to make any such recommendation. The Argentine Government had favored reciprocity treaties, as in 1875 it proposed to the United States the negotiation of one, and the same suggestion was renewed by the Argentine delegation to the chairman of the United States delegation in the Conference, as stated in the discussion by Señor Saenz Peña, an Argentine delegate who was a member of that committee, who also favored reciprocity personally, but he did not think that the Conference had authority, under the law convening it, to consider the subject of reciprocity, as it was not mentioned in the program of its labors. He therefore did not sign the report of the majority, and made with Señor Alfonso a minority report.

The essential difference between the views of the majority and the minority of the committee was that the majority thought that they ought not to discourage the negotiation of reciprocity treaties, even if this was only for the purpose of leaving on the United States the responsibility of their failure, while the minority preferred not to commit itself to any given policy, leaving the whole matter to the respective governments, although in reality they seemed convinced of the advantage of such treaties and wished to negotiate them.

The discussion on this subject in the Conference was carried on mainly between the delegates of the Argentine Republic and of the United States, who were members of the committee; but the economic policy of both countries rather than that of negotiating reciprocity treaties was the subject really discussed. The Conference finally approved the recommendation of the majority in favor of such treaties, and refused to give a vote against customs union, because they regarded this as a step which might be misunderstood, in the sense of acting against one of the objects of the law convening the Conference, and because the United States delegates were among the first to acknowledge the impracticability of such a union. The minority had to reconsider the abrupt manner in which they rejected the customs union.

Mr. Blaine attached a great deal of importance to this matter, and the deep interest he finally took in it was only revealed several months after the adjournment of the Conference. Conscious of the many advantages which would accrue to his country by the negotiation of such treaties, he did all that was in his power before the Committee on Ways and Means of the House of Representatives, which was at the time preparing the tariff bill approved by the President, October 1, 1890, to induce it to leave the duties on sugar as a good basis to negotiate such treaties. The official and private utterances of Mr. Blaine, which soon afterwards were made public, show very plainly the great importance he attached to the subject, and the interest he felt in it was so great that he even went so far as to antagonize his own political party. For the failure of reciprocity treaties he, therefore, cannot be responsible. The Argentine delegates, who were not aware of all his efforts, very likely thought that he was indifferent to this matter, but subsequent events have shown that this was not the case, although I understand that he did not favor free wool, which was what they desired.

Mr. Blaine's suggestions in favor of reciprocity made to the Committee on Ways and Means of the House of Representatives, with a view to favor reciprocity with the Latin-American countries, were not accepted, and instead of that, sugar, which was the principal inducement that the United States could offer to those nations, was placed in the free list.

Instead of the commercial reciprocity, as understood in the treaties with Canada, concluded June 5, 1854, with the Hawaiian Islands on January 30, 1875, and the unexecuted treaty with Mexico of January 20, 1883, namely, the admission into the United States free of duty of commodities produced in the Latin-American countries paying high duties under the tariff bill, and *vice versa*, which was equivalent to a partial free trade applicable only to a few commodities, and which was what Mr. Blaine recommended to the Committee on Ways and Means of the House of Representatives, Congress approved a measure which was really retaliation instead of reciprocity, namely, that whenever the President should be satisfied that the government of any country producing and exporting sugars, molasses, coffee, tea, and hides, raw and uncured, or any of such articles, imposed duties or other exactions upon the agricultural or other products of the United States, which in view of the introduction of such articles into the United States he might deem to be reciprocally unequal and unreasonable, he should have the power to suspend the free importation of such articles into the United States, for such time as he should deem just, and to levy a duty upon the same, which was specified in Section 3 of the Tariff Act of October 1, 1890.

I can say with perfect certainty that none of the Latin-American countries ever established import duties with a view to discriminate against the United States, and that if sometimes they levy high duties on commodities from this country, which are paid also by similar commodities from other countries, it is because they need such duties as revenue to defray their public expenses, and in no manner are they intended to discriminate against the United States or to act as an obstacle to the trade with this country.

The United States succeeded through their able diplomacy in making reciprocity agreements with Brazil on January 31, 1891, and Spain in behalf of Cuba and Porto Rico on June 16, 1891. As the largest portion of the sugar and coffee imported into the United States came respectively from Cuba and Brazil, the other American countries which exported those products had either to enter into similar reciprocity agreements or be subject to a differential duty, and many of them had to accept the very slight advantage offered by that tariff. The European nations which had colonies in America producing sugar and coffee had also, for the same reasons, to enter into similar arrangements.

Mexico, Colombia, Venezuela, the Argentine Republic, Hayti, and other nations did not enter into any diplomatic agreement,—some, like Mexico, because they thought there was not sufficient compensation in the reciprocity provisions of the tariff, and others, like Colombia and Venezuela, because they depended almost exclusively on their import duties and could not possibly reduce them. President Harrison issued a proclamation on the 15th of March, 1892, levying differential duties of three cents per pound on the coffee imported from Colombia, Venezuela, and Hayti.

I have reason to know that neither of the countries which entered into such agreements were at all satisfied with them, and in fact the Brazilian agreement was the source of great dissatisfaction to the people of that country and of severe censure to Señor Mendonça, the Brazilian Minister in Washington, who negotiated it. Señor Mendonça stated that Mr. Blaine had promised him that he would not make reciprocity agreements in so far as sugar was concerned with any other country, which would have given to Brazil the monopoly of the sugar trade with the United States, this being the principal inducement which the Brazilian Government had to accept the agreement; but when this fact was brought unofficially to the notice of Mr. Blaine, he denied having ever made any such promise.

President Cleveland was understood not to be in favor of the reciprocity agreement, but he could not take upon himself the responsibility of nullifying them by a mere executive act. This object was attained however, by the tariff bill of August 28, 1894, which terminated said agreements by ignoring them.

Sections 3d and 4th of the tariff Act approved on July 24, 1897, now in force, gives a larger scope for reciprocity agreements, but even that does not have enough inducement for the American countries to enter into such agreements, and I am not aware that so far any has been made.

There is an impression in this country that the Latin-American nations were very well satisfied with the reciprocity agreements and that they were very anxious to renew them, but I know that impression is ungrounded. Some of the American republics have the impression that through reciprocity they may obtain a very large reduction of duties, as compared with other nations, on the sugar imported to the United States, and that is the reason why some of them are favorably disposed to make such agreements.

The result proves very clearly how little the real condition of things was appreciated by some of the manufacturing nations of Europe, when they feared that the outcome of the Conference might be the negotiation by the United States of reciprocity treaties with American republics that might interfere with their own existing commercial relations.

Lasting Results of the Conference.—I consider as the lasting results of the Pan-American Conference; the railway project, out of which came a Railway Commission which has done very important work; the Monetary Commission, which led to the meeting of the Brussels Conference, although its result so far has been nugatory; and the organization of the Bureau of American Republics.

I will speak especially of each of these three subjects, and before ending this paper I will mention others which the Conference took up but which were not quite as important, namely, the Montevideo Treaties and Commercial Nomenclature.

Intercontinental Railway Project.—The Committee on this subject appointed by the International American Conference recommended that a special International American Commission of engineers should meet in Washington to ascertain the routes, determine their true length, estimate the cost of each, and compare their respective advantages for the purpose of deciding upon the construction of an international railway connecting all the nations. That recommendation, which was approved by the Conference on February 26, 1890, appears in Appendix No. 8 to this paper.   The Railway Commission met in Washington and had its first session at the Department of State on December 4, 1890.[1]

The Commission held eighteen other sessions between December 4, 1890, and the 22d of April, 1891, and eleven of the American nations were represented by delegates, who remained as the final representatives of their respective countries.[2]

The Commission, after organization and the appointment of the necessary committees, determined to send as many surveying parties into the field as the state of its funds would permit.

Before the Commission adjourned they left the work to be done in the hands of the Executive Committee, composed of five members, of which Mr. Cassatt was the chairman.   The business of the central

[1] The following commissioners were present at the first meeting of the Commission : Mr. A. J. Cassatt and Mr. Henry G. Davis, representing the United States ; Señor Don Leandro Fernández, representing Mexico ; Señor Don Clímaco Calderón, Señor Don Julio Rengifo, and Señor Don C. Frederico Párraga, representing Colombia ; Señor Don Matías Romero, representing Ecuador ; Mr. John Stewart, representing Paraguay ; and Señor Don Manuel Elguera, representing Peru.

As several of the representatives of the American Republics had not arrived at Washington when the Conference met, the Secretary of State authorized their diplomatic representatives to represent their respective countries, and in that capacity the following gentlemen were present at that meeting : Señor Don Jacobo Baiz, Consul General and Chargé d'Affaires of Guatemala ; Señor Don Nicanor Bolet Peraza, Envoy Extraordinary, etc., from Venezuela ; Dr. Don F. C. C. Zegarra, Envoy Extraordinary, etc., from Peru ; Señor Don J. G. do Amaral Valente, Envoy Extraordinary, etc., from Brazil ; and Señor Don Anselmo Volio, Chargé d'Affaires of Costa Rica, met at the invitation of the Secretary of State, to witness the proceedings, in the absence of the Commissioners from these countries.

The Mexican government sent to the Commission an engineer, but the Ecuatorian government did me the honor of appointing me their representative, notwithstanding I was not an engineer, until the special representative sent by that government reached Washington, so I was not present at all the meetings of the Conference.

[2] The following is a list of the permanent delegates to the railway convention : Argentina, by Señores Don Carlos Agote, Julio Krause, and Miguel Tedín ; Brazil, by Señores Don Pedro Betim Paes Leme, Francisco de Monlevade, and Francisco Leite Lobo Pereira ; Colombia, by Señores Don C. Frederico Párraga, Julio Rengifo, and Clímaco Calderón ; Ecuador and Peru, by Señor Don Leffert L. Buck ; Guatemala, by Señor Don Antonio Batres ; Mexico, by Señor Don Leandro Fernández ; Paraguay, by Mr. John Stewart ; Salvador, by Señor Don Benjamin Molina Guirola ; the United States, by Messrs. Alexander J. Cassatt, Henry G. Davis, and Richard C. Kerens ; Uruguay, by Señor Don Francisco A. Lanza, and Venezuela, by Señor Don Luis J. Blanco.   Señor Hector de Castro was appointed Secretary in January, 1891, but resigned to take effect June 30, 1892.   Lieut. R. M. G. Brown, U. S. Navy, was appointed Executive and Disbursing Officer, March 10, 1891, and on the 20th of December, 1892, the Executive Committee unanimously elected Capt. E. Z. Steever, U. S. Army, who had been serving in the office as engineer since April 1, 1891, Secretary of the Commission, the duties of said position to be performed in addition to his other duties.

office at Washington has been conducted by Messrs. A. J. Cassatt, President, R. M. G. Brown, Executive Officer, E. Z. Steever, Secretary. The amount of money on hand only warranted the despatch of three such parties, viz.:

Corps No. 1, composed almost entirely of officers of the U. S. Army, under the command of Capt. E. Z. Steever, U. S. Army, was to proceed to Central America and survey a line from the western boundary of Mexico through Guatemala, Salvador, Honduras, Nicaragua, and Costa Rica, then through the Isthmus of Panamá into Colombia until it should meet Corps No. 2, coming northward. Corps No. 2, under the direction of Mr. William F. Shank, was to proceed to Quito, Ecuador, and thence survey northward to Colombia and through that Republic and the Isthmus of Panamá until it should meet Corps No. 1 coming from the north. Corps No. 3, under Mr. J. Imbrie Miller, in conjunction with Corps No. 2, was likewise to proceed to Quito and thence survey southward through Ecuador and Perú to Lake Titicaca on the confines of Bolivia. As already stated, the above three parties were the only ones actually despatched to the field, but the scheme of the Committee on Surveys included three other parties which, if funds permitted, were to be sent out at a later date. Party No. 4 was to enter the field by way of the port of Antofagasta, Chile, and, proceeding northeasterly, was to begin its surveys near the city of Oruro, Bolivia, working towards La Paz, Bolivia, Puno and Cuzco, Perú, until it should meet Party No. 3 coming southward. Party No. 5 was expected to commence its surveys at Huanchaca, Bolivia, and work to the neighborhood of Potosí, crossing the river Pilcomayo, entering Brazil by way of Corumbá, and extending its surveys via Coxim until a connection should be made with the railroads having communication with the capital, Río de Janeiro. Party No. 6, commencing its work at Potosí, Bolivia, was to follow the course of the Pilcomayo River and proceed towards Asunción, Paraguay, thus making connection with the railroads of that Republic and of Uruguay.

The several parties sailed from the United States in the spring of 1891, and after remaining in the field from one and a half to two years, returned to Washington, and several years were then devoted to the preparation of the necessary maps, reduction of the data collected, and the preparation of the reports of the chief engineers. Each party reported the feasibility of constructing an intercontinental trunk-line, although the ease with which such a line could be constructed would, naturally, vary in different countries, according to the character of the region traversed and the obstacles to be encountered. In Central America the construction would be comparatively easy and at a moderate cost. This would be true to a greater or less extent through Colombia and into Ecuador, and through the latter Republic well into

Perú; but in the southern section of Perú, where but one route was surveyed, many difficulties were encountered, owing to the deep chasms formed by several rivers, the direction of which being nearly at right angles to the proposed road, maximum grades would be necessary. However, there are a number of alternative routes which present less difficulties, although requiring a longer development. In Central America, the line from Ayutla, on the Río Suchiate, to Río Savegre, in Costa Rica, would be in length about 890 miles, of which 187 are already built. A proposed location from the Río Savegre through the Isthmus of Panamá and Colombia to Quito, in Ecuador, would be 1663 miles. From Quito, through Ecuador and Perú, to Puno, on Lake Titicaca, the location proposed would be 2170 miles, of which 151 miles are already built.

The Commission has already published the *Minutes of the Commission* in both English and Spanish, a book of 132 pages with a map; *Preliminary Report of the Executive Committee*, in both English and Spanish, with five maps, dated January 31, 1893, and the *Report of the Committee on Trade and Resources*, in English, which documents have already been distributed ; in addition it has printed, in both English and Spanish, the report of Corps No. 3, and its accompanying portfolio of maps, the report of Corps No. 2 and a portfolio of maps accompanying the same, and has nearly finished the report of Corps No. 1 and its portfolio of maps. When all these reports are finished a condensed report of the Commission proper will be prepared, giving a summary of the work accomplished and results attained, part of which is now in the hands of the printer.

Monetary Union.—The action of the Conference on this important question was a step backward. The law of Congress which convened it submitted to the Conference the consideration of the advisability of " coining a silver coin of the same weight and fineness, which would be a legal tender in all the American nations." The Conference decided to recommend the convening in Washington of another special commission for the purpose of deciding about the coining of one or more coins, without stating the metal of which they should be coined, of the same weight and fineness, to be used in the nations represented in the Conference, without stating whether they should be a legal tender in all the countries. A majority, if not all, of the Latin-American nations preferred the basis laid down in the convening law, but they had to yield on this point so as to act in accordance with the United States, whose delegates, excepting one, Mr. Estee, were decidedly opposed to the coining of legal-tender silver money.

In accordance with the recommendation of the Pan-American Conference to the effect that an International American Commission should be especially convened for the purpose of considering the question of a monetary union among themselves, President Harrison sent invitations to the American Republics for such Commission. The Commission had eight meetings in Washington from January 7 to April 4, 1891, I representing Mexico, having been honored with the appointment of presiding officer of the Commission, notwithstanding that it is the universal rule that the president of an international conference should be a delegate of the inviting nation.[1] The Minutes of this Commission were published in English and Spanish in a book of 123 pages entitled *Minutes of the American International Monetary Commission of 1891.* It was of course impossible to come to any satisfactory conclusion in that Commission, as had been the case before in the Pan-American Conference, and the only way to overcome the difficulty was to agree upon a recommendation to the Government of the United States that it should propose to all nations of the world the meeting of an International Monetary Conference.[2] This recommendation led to the meeting of a monetary conference at Brussels from November 22 to December 17, 1892, which, as is well known, did not produce any satisfactory result, but rather was a setback to the idea of arriving at an

---

[1] The following is a list of the delegates to the American International Monetary Commission :

Argentine Republic, Señor Don Miguel Tedin ; Bolivia, Señor Don Melchor Obarrio ; Brazil, Señor Don Salvador de Mendonça ; Colombia, Señors Don Julio Rengifo and Don Clímaco Calderón ; Chile, Señor Don Prudencio Lazcano ; the United States, the Hon. N. P. Hill, the Hon. Lambert Tree, and the Hon. W. A. Russell ; Hawaii, the Hon. H. A. P. Carter ; Hayti, the Hon. Hannibal Price ; Honduras, the Hon. Rowan W. Stevens ; Mexico, Señor Don Matías Romero ; Nicaragua, Señor Don Horacio Guzmán ; Uruguay, Señor Don José Marti ; Peru, Señor Don Felix Cipriano C. Zegarra ; Costa Rica, Señor Don Joaquin B. Calvo ; Venezuela, Señor Don Estanislao Vetancourt Rendon.

[2] The following is a copy of a resolution introduced by Señor Mendonça, recommending the meeting of an International Monetary Commission, reported favorably by the committee to which it was referred, and approved by the Commission on April 3, 1891 :

WHEREAS, first, in the opinion of the Commission the establishment of a fixed ratio between gold and silver, the adoption of coins of both metals and of a common monetary unit would be of great benefit to the commerce of the world ;

Secondly, these ends could be accomplished by means of an international agreement entered into by all the commercial nations of the world ; and

Thirdly, in view of the efforts recently made in this behalf it does not appear probable that under present circumstances the desired ends can be obtained ; be it therefore

Resolved, That this Commission bring its sessions to a close, expressing the wish that before long another Commission may meet which shall reach an agreement that will secure the adoption of a uniform monetary system between the nations of America, advantageous to each and all.

M. ROMERO,	JULIO RENGIFO,
SALVADOR DE MENDONÇA,	JOSÉ MARTI,
MIGUEL TEDIN,	H. GUZMÁN.

WASHINGTON, D. C., *April 3, 1891.*

international agreement on some proposition intended to restore silver as a money metal by the commercial nations of the world.

The report of the Commissioners of the United States to the Brussels Conference, dated at Washington February 14, 1893, together with the Minutes of the ten meetings of the Conference, were printed, with the President's Message to Congress of February 21, 1893, in a volume of 384 pages.

Bureau of American Republics.—Another lasting result of the Pan-American Conference was the establishment in the city of Washington, supported by all the American countries, with a quota in proportion to their population, of an American Commercial Bureau for the purpose of disseminating commercial information among the American nations and so to increase their mercantile relations. Although that bureau has not done all that was expected of it, with the experience already gained it could be hereafter a very useful institution to promote trade between the American nations.

Mr. Curtis was at the head of the Bureau during President Harrison's administration. When Mr. Cleveland entered into his second term Mr. Clinton Furbish was appointed Director, and he remained as such all through that administration. On the inauguration of President McKinley, Mr. Joseph P. Smith was appointed Director, and he greatly exerted himself to fulfil the duties of his office and make his mark, but unfortunately he contracted a disease which, much to the regret of all, resulted in his premature death.

The recommendation approved by the Pan-American Conference in regard to the Bureau entrusted the direction of the same to the Secretary of State of the United States; but while Mr. Olney held that office he desired that the American republics should have more direct participation in the control of the Bureau, and he summoned a meeting of their representatives in Washington, who appointed a committee to propose some regulations with the view of establishing civil service for the Bureau, and so having more stability in its employees, avoiding the rotation of other offices in this country, the personnel of which changes almost with every new administration. On the 4th of June, 1896, new regulations were approved at a meeting of the American representatives in Washington, establishing an Executive Committee of four representatives, each of them to serve for four years in the alphabetical order of their country, under the presidency of the Secretary of State, to decide all matters pertaining to the Bureau, and providing that appointments of its employees should be made by the Secretary of State after examination by a Board of Examiners, composed of five members, three appointed by the Latin-American members of the Executive Committee and two by the Secretary of State.

The Bureau is supported by the contributions of all the American republics who accepted the agreement apportioned *pro rata* to their population, and with a view to diminish the respective quota the Director of the Bureau was authorized to publish advertisements in the *Monthly Bulletin*, a source which was expected would yield some revenue.

The Bureau of American Republics has made several publications, to some of which I have especially referred, and the others are the following : It edits a *Monthly Bulletin*, or magazine of 150 pages, containing current information of interest relating to the various countries represented by the Bureau, printed in the four languages spoken by the American nations, and besides it has published handbooks of all the American Republics, and also of Hawaii and Alaska; it has printed a Newspaper Directory of Latin-America, a Commercial Directory of most of the American Republics, and especially a general *Commercial Directory* in two large volumes, and the *Commercial Nomenclature* to which I shall presently allude. All the regular publications issued by the Bureau amount to ninety, up to March 1, 1898.

There has been from time to time in the Congress of the United States some opposition to the Bureau, but whenever the respective committees have investigated the subject, they have decided to support the Bureau, and there is no doubt that it will stand for the ten years agreed upon, and possibly that it will be extended for a similar period.

The Montevideo Treaties.—The part which the Montevidean treaties played in the Conference ought not to be omitted. It is known that the principal nations of South America met in congress in Montevideo in 1888, and recommended the conclusion of treaties on international civil law, international commercial law, international law of penal procedure, patents, trade-marks, copyright, extradition, etc., etc. The extended scope and details of the provisions therein contained have prevented some of the nations which attended that congress, and whose plenipotentiaries signed the treaties, from accepting them all. The Mexican Government, which, at the request of the Argentine Republic, had been studying those treaties for more than a year, had not then come to any conclusion about them. The rules accepted in those treaties are the same as those prevailing in the nations which follow the Roman law, and as the United States is governed generally by the common law of England, and subjects of municipal law in the several states do not fall under the federal jurisdiction, it is very difficult for this country to accept said treaties in all their details, since that would be equivalent to changing the basis of their legislation. This explains the opposition of the United States delegation to these treaties. Notwithstanding all this, three of them—those relating to copyrights, trade-marks, and patents—were accepted by the United States delegate who was a member of the committee, and, finally by the delegation when the matter was brought to a vote before the Conference.

The Conference also agreed to recommend the study by all the American nations of the Montevideo Treaties, with a view to their final adoption.

Commercial Nomenclature. — There is an incident which, although not of serious consequence, shows how easy it is to misunderstand the plainest enactment, even in case that all pains are taken to make its object perfectly clear.   I will briefly mention that incident before ending this paper.

I always thought it would be very advisable for the American nations to agree upon a common nomenclature in their tariff laws, each of them reserving, of course, the right to tax foreign goods according to their own views and convenience.   If this idea were carried out, a central bureau, located, for instance, in Washington, could publish from time to time the tariffs of all American countries, in a single book having several columns, one set apart for each country, showing the rate of duty that each levied upon a given commodity.   It would, of course, be very difficult to agree on a common nomenclature, and that ought to be the work of experts, one from each of the interested nations. This could be done, accepting, for instance, the United States tariff, or such other as might be advisable, as the basis of the work, and then adding to it such merchandise as is quoted in the tariffs of the other countries and not mentioned in the United States tariff.   In this case, such commodities, if not taxed in the United States, would be left blank in the column belonging to the United States, and also in the columns of the countries that did not levy any duty upon them.   While such tariff book containing all the data would be rather cumbersome, as it would have to be in the four languages spoken by the American nations, it would have the advantage of showing the exact amount of duties levied by each one, upon every specific imported commodity.

With this object in view I introduced in the Conference on January 2, 1890, the following resolution, which was referred to the Committee on Customs Regulations, of which I was a member:

" *Resolved*, That the proper committee of this Conference be requested to examine and report about the convenience and practicability of adopting a common schedule of foreign goods, to be used by the several nations represented in this Conference for the purpose of collecting import duties, making invoices, bills of lading, etc., each country having the exclusive right to fix the amount of duties to be levied on each article, but the schedule of the articles to be common to all.

" M. ROMERO,
" Delegate from Mexico.

" WASHINGTON, *January 2, 1890.*"

My resolution was carefully examined by the committee, and after I explained to them its object it was written over again, to make it man-

datory and plainer, in the following terms, in which it was reported
to the Conference, and agreed upon by the same on February 10, 1890.

" *Resolved*, That the International American Conference recommends to the Governments represented therein the adoption of a common nomenclature which shall
designate in alphabetical order in equivalent terms, in English, Spanish, Portuguese,
and French, the commodities on which import duties are levied, to be used respectively
by all the American nations for the purpose of levying customs imposts which are or may
hereafter be established, and also to be used in shipping manifests, consular invoices,
entries, clearance petitions, and other customs documents ; but not to effect in any
manner the right of each nation to levy the import duties now in force, or which may
hereafter be established.

" J. Alfonso. Charles R. Flint. M. Romero.
" H. G. Davis. Salvador de Mendonça. Clímaco Calderón."

When the time to carry this motion into effect arrived, the Bureau
of American Republics, misunderstanding completely its object,
printed, while Mr. Curtis was Director of the Bureau, a list of commercial terms in the four languages spoken by the American nations,
with a parallel blank column. This work was printed for the purpose
of submitting it to the respective governments for their remarks,
additions, and revisions, and when they all had been heard from, then
to give it to the public as an official work; but Mr. Curtis's successor
did not quite wait to hear such views, and the book was issued as it
finally came out, something like a vocabulary or dictionary of commercial terms used in the American countries, which was published in
three volumes under the name of *The Commercial Nomenclature of the
American Republics*, and which, while it is a very commendable work
and very useful in the mercantile intercourse between the American
countries, is by no means what my motion intended or what I had in
view.

Discussion of Other Subjects by the Conference.—The Conference
took up, besides, several other subjects which, although important in
themselves, appear in a secondary light when compared with those I
have mentioned. I refer to the recommendation favoring a uniform
system of weights and measures; and those to adopt uniform and
liberal rules for the valuation of merchandise at the custom-houses; to
simplify the import and consular dues; to adopt any of the South
American conventions for sanitary purposes; to establish railways and
lines of steamers among the several nations; to negotiate extradition
treaties ; to establish an American international bank for the purpose
of carrying on the exchanges then made through London. The recommendations of the Conference bearing on those subjects were inserted in the different publications of the Conference, and I therefore
deem it unnecessary to say anything more about them.

Final Results of the Conference.—The most important result of the
Conference—and I mention it in the first place because all the others

depended on the ratification of the respective agreements by the American governments, which generally was not given, while the one I refer to was and is an effective one and likely to exercise great influence for some time to come — was the mutual acquaintance through the representatives of the different nations, which, situated far apart and without easy and close communication among themselves, were almost unknown to each other. The constant intercourse of the delegates for nearly six months, and their daily discussion of important questions affecting the paramount interests of their respective countries, was to many of them quite a surprising revelation of the importance and progress, resources and education of the several states represented in the Conference. There is, therefore, no mistake in regarding as its first and best result the sentiment of mutual respect and consideration with which each delegate was inspired for his colleagues and for the nations represented by them; and so far as the United States is concerned, this result was accepted and acknowledged not only by its delegates, but also by its government and people who from day to day were informed of the doings of the Conference.

The second result in importance is the agreement on arbitration, which would have been, if ratified by the various nations, a measure of transcendent importance. This of itself would have been enough to make the Conference highly memorable and fruitful.

The other results of the Conference, although important in themselves, are not so far-reaching as those that I have already mentioned.

At first sight it might appear that the results of the Conference were disappointing; but I think it can be safely said that its success was greater than there was any reason to expect. Almost all of the Latin-American nations came to Washington with a fear that the United States intended to dictate to them by means of its great power and its material superiority, and they went back satisfied that, so far from this being the case, this country had only sentiments of respect and consideration for her sister-republics, and that its aim had simply been to accomplish what was of mutual advantage to all, she acting on the same footing as the smallest of the nations represented.

On the other hand, I believe that the Latin-American Republics have left on the Government and the people of the United States a more lasting and favorable impression than they had before been able to make. The occasion afforded an opportunity to the people of the United States to form a better idea of the civilization and the material progress of the Latin-American countries, and of the worth and patriotism of their sons; and soon afterwards it became an admitted fact that liberality of action, mutual regard, and a good understanding are almost a necessity among the American nations. Remembering that great results in behalf of mankind cannot be reached in a day, and much less when success depends on the action of several countries affected by different influences and conditions, I have no doubt that the meeting in Washington of an assembly of all the American nations was as greatly advantageous both to the Government and the people who promoted the meeting as to the Governments and countries who participated in the same more for its future than for its present results.

Conclusion.—I sincerely hope that the preceding paper will be taken as a proof of my interest in anything affecting closer social, political, and commercial relations between the United States and her sister American Republics, even in case that all the views which I have expressed and I hold in good faith are not accepted as sound or correct.

The documents which are included in the following Appendix, I consider as the complement of this paper.

APPENDIX.

I now append the most important of the several documents mentioned in the foregoing paper, which I consider useful to form a complete idea of what is stated in the same, namely : 1. Act of May 24, 1888, Convening the American International Conference ; 2. List of Delegates, Secretaries, and Attachés ; 3. List of Committees ; 4. Ex-Senator Henderson and the Arbitration Project ; 5. Facsimile Copy of the Amendments made by Mr. Blaine to the Argentine Plan of Arbitration ; 6. Arbitration Plan of the Pan-American Conference as reported by the Committee ; 7. Right of Conquest ; 8. Treaty of Arbitration signed by the Delegates to the Pan-American Conference, recommendation to European Powers to accept Arbitration, and recommendation on the right of conquest ; 9. Recommendation of Reciprocity Treaties ; 10. Recommendation on Railway Communication ; 11. Recommendation of the meeting of an American International Monetary Commission ; 12. Censure from Mexican Press and a Mexican Writer because a Mexican Delegate did not follow in the footsteps of the Argentines ; 13. My answer to Señor Pierra published in *Las Novedades*, of New York, of July 7, 1890.

1. ACT OF MAY 24, 1888, CONVENING THE AMERICAN INTERNATIONAL CONFERENCE.

An Act authorizing the President of the United States to arrange a Conference between the United States of America and the Republics of Mexico, Central and South America, Hayti, San Domingo, and the Empire of Brazil.

Be it enacted by the Senate and House of Representaves of the United States of America in Congress assembled, That the President of the United States be, and he is hereby, requested and authorized to invite the several Governments of the Republics of Mexico, Central and South America, Hayti, San Domingo, and the Empire of Brazil, to join the United States in a Conference to be held at Washington, in the United States, at such time as he may deem proper, in the year eighteen hundred and eighty-nine, for the purpose of discussing and recommending for adoption to their respective Governments some plan of arbitration for the settlement of disagreements and disputes that may hereafter arise between them, and for considering questions relating to the improvement of business intercourse and means of direct communication between said countries, and to encourage such reciprocal commercial relations as will be beneficial to all and secure more extensive markets for the products of each of said countries.

SEC. 2. That in forwarding the invitations to the said Governments the President of the United States shall set forth that the conference is called to consider :—

First.   Measures that shall tend to preserve the peace and promote the prosperity of the several American states.

Second.   Measures toward the formation of an American customs union, under which the trade of the American nations with each other shall, so far as possible and profitable, be promoted.

Third. The establishment of regular and frequent communication between the ports of the several American States and the ports of each other.

Fourth. The establishment of a uniform system of customs regulations in each of the independent American States to govern the mode of importation and exportation of merchandise and port dues and charges, a uniform method of determining the classification and valuation of such merchandise in the ports of each country, and a uniform system of invoices, and the subject of the sanitation of ships and quarantine.

Fifth. The adoption of a uniform system of weights and measures, and laws to protect the patent rights, copyrights, and trade-marks of citizens of either country in the other, and for the extradition of criminals.

Sixth. The adoption of a common silver coin, to be issued by each Government, the same to be legal tender in all commercial transactions between the citizens of all the American States.

Seventh. An agreement upon and recommendation for adoption to their respective Governments of a definite plan of arbitration of all questions, disputes, and differences that may now or hereafter exist between them, to the end that all difficulties and disputes between such Nations may be peacefully settled and wars prevented.

Eighth. And to consider such other subjects relating to the welfare of the several States represented as may be presented by any of said States which are hereby invited to participate in said Conference.

SEC. 3. That the sum of seventy-five thousand dollars, or so much thereof as may be necessary, is hereby appropriated, out of any money in the Treasury not otherwise appropriated, the same to be disbursed under the direction and in the discretion of the Secretary of State, for expenses incidental to the Conference.

SEC. 4. That the President of the United States shall appoint, by and with the advice and consent of the Senate, ten delegates to said Conference, who shall serve without compensation other than their actual necessary expenses, and the several other States participating in said Conference shall be represented by as many delegates as each may elect. Provided, however, That in the disposition of questions to come before said Conference no State shall be entitled to more than one vote.

SEC. 5. That the Secretary of State shall appoint such clerks and other assistants as shall be necessary, at a compensation to be determined by him, and provide for the daily publication by the Public Printer, in the English, Spanish, and Portuguese languages, of so much of the proceedings of the Conference as it shall determine, and upon the conclusion of said Conference shall transmit a report of the same to the Congress of the United States, together with a statement of the disbursements of the appropriation herein provided for.

Approved, May 24, 1888.

2. LIST OF DELEGATES, SECRETARIES, AND ATTACHÉS.

(Arranged in order of precedence, as determined by lot, November 20, 1889.)

President, JAMES G. BLAINE.

Secretaries: { H. Remsen Whitehouse, Fidel G. Pierra,[1] José Ignacio Rodriguez (succeeding Mr. Pierra).

HAYTI.	NICARAGUA.
Delegates :	*Delegate :*
Arthur Laforestrie,[2]	Horacio Guzmán.
Hannibal Price.[3]	*Secretary :*
Secretary :	R. Mayorga.
H. Aristide Preston.	

[1] Resigned February 14, 1890.   [2] To March 5, 1890.   [3] From April 1, 1890.

PERU.
Delegate :
Felix C. C. Zegarra.
Secretary :
Leopoldo Oyague y Soyer.
Attaché :
Manuel Elguera.

GUATEMALA.
Delegate :
Fernando Cruz.
Secretary :
Domingo Estrada.
Attaché :
Javier A. Arroyo.

URUGUAY.
Delegate :
Alberto Nin.
Secretaries :
Dionisio Ramos Montero,
Henry Dauber.

COLOMBIA.
Delegates :
José M. Hurtado,
Carlos Martinez Silva,
Clímaco Calderón.
Secretary :
Julio Rengifo.

ARGENTINE REPUBLIC.
Delegates :
Roque Saenz Peña,
Manuel Quintana.
Secretaries :
Federico Pinedo,
Ernesto Bosch.

COSTA RICA.
Delegate :
Manuel Aragón.
Secretary :
Joaquín Bernardo Calvo.

PARAGUAY.
Delegate :
José S. Decoud.

BRAZIL.
Delegates :
Lafayette Rodrigues Pereira, [1]
J. G. do Amaral Valente,
Salvador de Mendonça.

Secretaries :
José Augusto Ferreira de Costa,
Joaquim de Freitas Vasconcellos.
Attachés :
Alfredo de Moraes Gomes Ferreira,
Mario de Mendonça.

HONDURAS.
Delegate :
Jerónimo Zelaya.
Secretaries :
E. Constantino Fiallos,
Richard Villafranca.

MEXICO.
Delegates :
Matias Romero,
Enrique A. Mexia.
Secretary :
Enrique Santibañez.

BOLIVIA.
Delegate :
Juan F. Velarde.
Seeretary :
Melchor Obarrio.
Attachés :
Alcibiades Velarde,
Mariano Velarde.

UNITED STATES.
Delegates :
John B. Henderson,
Cornelius N. Bliss,
Clement Studebaker,
T. Jefferson Coolidge,
William Henry Trescot,
Andrew Carnegie,
Morris M. Estee,
John F. Hanson,
Henry G. Davis,
Charles R. Flint.
Secretaries :
Edmund W. P. Smith,
Edward A. Trescot.

VENEZUELA.
Delegates :
Nicanor Bolet Peraza,
José Andrade,
Francisco Antonio Silva.
Secretary :
Nicanor Bolet Monagas.

[1] Resigned November 27, 1889.

CHILI.
Delegates :
  Emilio C. Varas,
  José Alfonso.
Secretaries :
  Carlos Zañartu,
  Paulino Alfonso,
  Domingo Peña Toro.

SALVADOR.
Delegate :
  Jacinto Castellanos.

Secretary :
  Samuel Valdivieso.
Attaché :
  J. Arrieta Rossi.

ECUADOR.
Delegate :
  José María Plácido Caamaño.
Secretary :
  Antonio Echeverría.

Executive Officer :
  William Eleroy Curtis.
Disbursing Officer :
  Haughwout Howe.
Sergeants-at-Arms :
  John G. Bourke, Captain, U. S. Army,
  Henry R. Lemly, First Lieutenant
    U. S. Army.
Surgeon :
  H. C. Yarrow, Acting Assistant Surgeon, U. S. Army.
Consulting Engineer to the Committee on Railway Communication :
  George A. Zinn, First Lieutenant,
    Corps of Engineers.
Official Interpreters :
  José Ignacio Rodriguez,
  Arthur W. Fergusson.

Publication Clerk :
  Carlos Federico Adams-Michelena.
Translators :
  Mary F. Foster,
  Ambrosio J. Gonzalez,
  Marathon M. Ramsey,
  José R. Villalon,
  J. Vicente Serrano,
  Miss M. E. Torrence.
Official Stenographers :
  Hudson C. Tanner,
  Manuel Trillanes,
  Mauro Durán,
  Walter C. Bryne.
Stenographers :
  John T. Suter, Jr.
  Imogen A. Hanna.

---

3.   LIST OF COMMITTEES

(Appointed December 13, 1889.)

Executive Committee.

Mr. Zegarra, First Vice-President, of Peru.
Mr. Romero, Second Vice-President, of Mexico.
Mr. Bliss, of the United States.
Mr. Hurtado, of Colombia.
Mr. Mendonça, of Brazil.
The President of the Conference, ex-officio.

Secretary, William Eleroy Curtis.

Committee on Customs Union.

Mr. Valente, of Brazil.
Mr. Henderson, of the United States.
Mr. Saenz Peña, of the Argentine Republic.
Mr. Romero, of Mexico.
Mr. Martinez Silva, of Columbia.
Mr. Alfonso, of Chili.
Mr. Guzmán, of Nicaragua.
Mr. Bolet Peraza, of Venezuela.

Secretary, J. Vicente Serrano.

Committee on Communication on the Atlantic.

Mr. Saenz Peña, of the Argentine Republic.
Mr. Coolidge, of the United States.

Mr. Mendonça, of Brazil.
Mr. Decoud, of Paraguay.
Mr. Laforestrie, of Hayti.

Secretary, Arthur W. Fergusson.

Committee on Communication on the Pacific.

Mr. Caamaño, of Ecuador.
Mr. Varas, of Chili.
Mr. Estee, of the United States.

Mr. Castellanos, of Salvador.
Mr. Mexia, of Mexico.

Secretary, Arthur W. Fergusson.

Committee on Communication on the Gulf of Mexico and the Caribbean Sea.

Mr. Aragón, of Costa Rica.
Mr. Guzmán, of Nicaragua.
Mr. Calderón, of Colombia.

Mr. Hanson, of the United States.
Mr. Antonio Francisco Silva, of Venezuela.

Secretary, William Eleroy Curtis.

Committee on Railway Communications.

Mr. Velarde, of Bolivia.
Mr. Davis, of the United States.
Mr. Mexia, of Mexico.
Mr. Cruz, of Guatemala.
Mr. Zelaya, of Honduras.
Mr. Castellanos, of Salvador.
Mr. Carnegie, of the United States.
Mr. Aragón, of Costa Rica.
Mr. Martinez Silva, of Colombia.

Mr. Andrade, of Venezuela.
Mr. Caamaño, of Ecuador.
Mr. Zegarra, of Peru.
Mr. Varas, of Chili.
Mr. Quintana, of the Argentine Republic.
Mr. Nin, of Uruguay.
Mr. Valente, of Brazil.
Mr. Decoud, of Paraguay.
Mr. Guzmán, of Nicaragua.

Secretary, Arthur W. Fergusson.

Committee on Customs Regulations.

Mr. Nin, of Uruguay.
Mr. Alfonso, of Chili.
Mr. Romero, of Mexico.
Mr. Calderón, of Colombia.
Mr. Flint, of the United States.

Mr. Mendonça, of Brazil.
Mr. Davis, of the United States.
Mr. Aragón, of Costa Rica.
Mr. Bolet Peraza, of Venezuela.

Secretary, Edmund W. P. Smith.

Committee on Port Dues.

Mr. Bolet Peraza, of Venezuela.
Mr. Laforestrie, of Hayti.
Mr. Varas, of Chili.
Mr. Studebaker, of the United States.

Mr. Nin, of Uruguay.
Mr. Mendonça, of Brazil.
Mr. Quintana, of the Argentine Republic.
Mr. Guzmán, of Nicaragua.

Secretary, Edmund W. P. Smith.

Committee on Sanitary Regulations.

Mr. Guzmán, of Nicaragua.
Mr. Valente, of Brazil.
Mr. Zegarra, of Peru.
Mr. Hanson, of the United States.

Mr. Andrade, of Venezuela.
Mr. Laforestrie, of Hayti.
Mr. Nin, of Uruguay.

Secretary, Henry R. Lemly, U. S. A.

Committee on Patents and Trade-Marks.

Mr. Decoud, of Paraguay.
Mr. Carnegie, of the United States.

Mr. Calderón, of Colombia.

Secretary, Edmund W. P. Smith.

Committee on Weights and Measures.

Mr. Castellanos, of Salvador.
Mr. Antonio Francisco Silva, of Venezuela.

Mr. Studebaker, of the United States.

Secretary, Edmund W. P. Smith.

Committee on Extradition.

Mr. Zelaya, of Honduras.
Mr. Trescot, of the United States.

Mr. Saenz Peña, of the Argentine Republic.
Mr. Quintana, of the Argentine Republic.

Secretary, José Ignacio Rodriguez.

Committee on Monetary Convention.

Mr. Mexia, of Mexico.
Mr. Estee, of the United States.
Mr. Martinez Silva, of Colombia.
Mr. Alfonso, of Chili.

Mr. Coolidge, of the United States.
Mr. Velarde, of Bolivia.
Mr. Zelaya, of Honduras.

Secretary, J. Vicente Serrano.

Committee on Banking.

Mr. Hurtado, of Colombia.
Mr. Mendonça, of Brazil.
Mr. Varas, of Chili.

Mr. Flint, of the United States.
Mr. Aragón, of Costa Rica.

Secretary, Henry R. Lemly, U. S. A.

Committee on International Law.

Mr. Cruz, of Guatemala.
Mr. Quintana, of the Argentine Republic.
Mr. Trescot, of the United States.

Mr. Alfonso, of Chili.
Mr. Caamaño, of Ecuador.

Secretary, José Ignacio Rodriguez.

Committee on General Welfare.

Mr. Henderson, of the United States.

Dr. Quintana, of the Argentine Republic.

Mr. Velarde, of Bolivia.

Mr. Bolet Peraza, of Venezuela.

Mr. Hurtado, of Columbia.

Mr. Valente, of Brazil.

Mr. Cruz, of Guatemala.

Secretary, Edmund W. P. Smith.

Committee on Rules.

Mr. Alfonso, of Chili.

Mr. Quintana, of the Argentine Republic.

Mr. Trescot, of the United States.

Mr. Caamaño, of Ecuador.

Mr. Romero, of Mexico.

Mr. Castellanos, of Salvador.

Mr. Valente, of Brazil.

Committee on Credentials.

Mr. Romero, of Mexico.

Mr. Quintana, of the Argentine Republic.

Mr. Coolidge, of the United States.

---

4. EX-SENATOR HENDERSON AND THE ARBITRATION PROJECT OF THE PAN-AMERICAN CONFERENCE.

From the North American Review, April, 1898.

In *The North American Review* for September and October, 1890, I published a paper on the Pan-American Conference, which had then just met, and wherein I tried to give an idea of what took place in the same, from the point of view of one of the Latin-American delegates, which I thought would be of interest for the government and citizens of the United States, especially in case that at a future time a similar Conference should be convened. In the second part of that paper, speaking about the arbitration project reported by the Committee on General Welfare of that Conference, of which ex-Senator Henderson, the first of the United States delegates, was the Chairman, I mentioned the fact that said project was reported in the last session of the Conference, and therefore too late for a fair discussion, and judging from what I had heard at the time, especially from an Argentine delegate, member of the same Committee, and from the natural disposition of Mr. Henderson to be deliberate and careful in anything he does, I thought, and expressed it in rather harsh terms in the first edition of this paper, that he was responsible for the delay of the Committee on General Welfare in reporting to the Conference the arbitration project.

When my article was published, Mr. Henderson informed me that I had done him an injustice, and that he was in no way responsible for that delay. I assured him that I did not have any intention to be unfair with him or with anybody else connected with the Conference, and that if he would do me the favor of writing a memorandum of the case, I would publish it at once as a correction of my statement. He did not do so at the time, and when I prepared a second edition of this paper, I begged of him again to make his statement of the case, and he kindly sent me a letter dated on the 14th instant, containing the history of his connection with the arbitration project presented by the Committee of which he was chairman, with two annexes referred to by him, all of which I am glad in justice to Mr. Henderson to append to this paper.

M. ROMERO.

WASHINGTON, *February 24, 1898.*

WASHINGTON, D. C., *February 14, 1898.*

MY DEAR MR. ROMERO :

In compliance with my promise to that effect, I herewith forward you a brief explanation of the action of the Committee on General Welfare in the International Conference on the subject of arbitration.

In February, 1890, two plans for arbitrating controversies between the American Republics were pending, one known as the plan of the Argentine and Brazilian delegates, and the other as that of the United States.

The Argentine-Brazilian plan is enclosed, marked A. The plan offered by myself is enclosed and marked B.

At a meeting of the Committee, held on February 19, 1890, it was unanimously agreed that the general principle of arbitration for the settlement of disputes should be accepted.

Dr. Quintana, of the Argentine Republic, then propounded the following proposition to be voted on by the Committee, to wit : " Shall arbitration include all questions of controversy present and future ? "

The discussion which followed its introduction drew forth the admission of its friends that its adoption was intended to operate as an approval of the principles enunciated in the 5th, 6th, 7th, and 8th clauses of the Argentine-Brazilian scheme of arbitration.

A declaration of this character was, of course, offensive to the representatives from Chili ; and would necessarily make all the states, under any general plan of arbitration, parties to the controversy between Chili on the one side and Peru and Bolivia on the other. Its adoption, in my judgment, meant even more than this. It would suggest an invitation to wage wars by pledging to the aggressor total immunity against any possible loss of territory as the result of such wars.

My first object was to exclude the construction so palpably offensive to Chili. I therefore moved to amend the proposition as follows, to wit : " Shall arbitration include all *new* questions of dispute which may arise after these articles shall be accepted, whether growing out of disagreements, past or present?" The vote on this (my amendment) was as follows :

Ayes—Henderson.

Noes—Cruz, Velarde, Hurtado, Quintana, Valente, Bolet Peraza.

When the Committee reached the question of the formation of the tribunals of arbitration, I offered the plan embodied in the first four articles of the bill or ordinance presented by me and herein referred to as B.

Ayes—Henderson and Hurtado.

Noes—Cruz, Velarde, Valente, Quintana, and Bolet Peraza.

Dr. Quintana then proposed the third and fourth articles of the Argentine-Brazilian plan, and his proposition was adopted by the same vote as the one last recorded, the ayes and noes being of course reversed.

It will be seen that my views were entirely overruled, and that such was the understanding of the Committee ; and thereupon Mr. Velarde, of Bolivia, moved a special committee, consisting of Quintana, Hurtado, and Cruz, " to put into shape and form the articles voted upon." The Committee again met on February 27, 1890, to receive the report of the sub-committee. The secretary's report of the proceedings of the Committee on this occasion reads as follows : " Mr. Quintana, Chairman (of sub-committee), stated that, as it was understood that a plan would be presented by the Honorable, the Secretary of State, on arbitration, to the various members of the Committee on General Welfare, the sub-committee had deemed it advisable to defer its report until said plan had been duly considered ; but his committee (sub) would endeavor to present its report before Mr. Henderson's departure for the

West." Immediately after this announcement Mr. Valente again called up the Argentine-Brazilian plan, and moved that Articles 2, 6, 7, and 8 thereof be considered and adopted.

I at once moved to amend Article 6 by inserting between the words "convey" and "any" the words "to the offending nation." I also moved to amend Article 7 by striking out "the" between the words "to" and "hostilities" in the first line, and in the fourth line of Article 7 to insert between the words "territory" and "they" the words "to the offending nation." I also moved to amend the first line of Article 8 by striking out the word "whether" and inserting the word "when," and in the same line to strike out the words "or the consequence" and insert the words "and purpose." After long discussion the original resolutions, together with my amendments as aforesaid, were referred to the sub-committee to be considered and reported on as early as practicable.

If my motions had been adopted Section Six would have read as follows, to wit:

"Sixth. In cases of war a victory of arms shall not convey to the offending nation any rights to the territory of the conquered."

And Section Seven would have read as follows, to wit:

"Seventh. The treaties of peace which put an end to hostilities may fix the pecuniary indemnifications which the belligerents may owe to each other, but if they contain cessions or abandonment of territory to the offending nation, they will not be concluded," etc.

And Section Eight would have read as follows, to wit:

"Eight. Acts of Conquest, when the object and purpose of the war, shall be considered to be in violation of the public law of America."

I now declare to you that the great delay of my Committee on General Welfare to make report on the subject of arbitration was wholly and entirely caused by the failure of this sub-committee to formulate the plan or scheme of arbitration for the action of the Conference. Why this delay was adopted as the seeming policy of this sub-committee I have no reason to assign. It was appointed on February 19th, and did not report until April 9th. This neglect is not, in any sense, chargeable to me. I repeatedly called on Dr. Quintana and the other members of the Committee, both before going to St. Louis and after my return, and urged immediate action in order that ample time might be given to the Conference for consideration of so important a subject. My views had been overruled and the whole subject removed from my charge by the deliberate action of the Committee. Principles had been enunciated by the Committee as the basis of action by the sub-committee to which I could never give my assent. At my solicitation much of this objectionable matter was rejected and thrown out by Mr. Blaine as wholly impracticable and impossible of acceptance by the people of the United States. So far from Mr. Blaine's commanding or even requesting me or my colleagues to support the Argentine-Brazilian plan, he at all times considered it in its original form as wholly indefeasible, if not absurd.

Yours truly,

J. B. HENDERSON.

A.—PLAN OF ARBITRATION SUBMITTED BY THE MEMBERS FROM ARGENTINE AND BRAZIL.

Considering, That the international policy of the American Conference should be characterized by reciprocal principles and declarations of mutual security and respect among all the states of the continent;

That this feeling of security should be inspired from the very moment in which the representatives of the three Americas meet for the first time, so as to show that their acts and resolutions are in accordance with sentiments of mutual respect and cordiality ;

The Conference being also desirous of giving assent to the principles which, to the honor of the strong states, have been established by public law for the support of the weak, and which are confirmed by the ethics of nations and proclaimed by humanity, it is hereby declared :

First. That international arbitration is a principle of American public law, to which the nations in this Conference bind themselves, for decision, not only in their questions on territorial limits, but also in all those in which arbitration be compatible with sovereignty.

Second. The armed occupation of the disputed territory, without having first resorted to arbitration, shall be considered contrary to the present declarations and to the engagements entered into thereby, but resistance offered to such act of occupation shall not have the same character.

Third. The arbitration may take place in an unipersonal form whenever the states agree to the election of only one arbitrator ; but if it takes place in a collective form, there shall be appointed an equal number of judges by each party, with power to elect an umpire in case of disagreement ; said election to be made at the first meeting of the Tribunal.

Fourth. The election of arbitrators shall not be subject to any limitations or exclusions ; it may devolve either on the governments represented in this Conference, or on any other government deserving the confidence of the parties, and also on scientific corporations, or on high functionaries either of the interested states themselves or of other neutral states.

Fifth. The present declarations are applicable not only to differences which in the future may arise in the relations of the states, but also to those which, in a direct form, are now in actual discussion between the governments ; but the rules to be made shall have no bearing upon the arbitrations already constituted.

Sixth. In cases of war, a victory of arms shall not convey any rights to the territory of the conquered.

Seventh. The treaties of peace which put an end to the hostilities may fix the pecuniary indemnifications which the belligerents may owe to each other, but if they contain cessions or abandonment of territory they will not be concluded, as far as this particular point is concerned, without the previous evacuation of the territory of the conquered power by the troops of the other belligerent.

Eighth. Acts of conquest, whether the object or the consequence of the war, shall be considered to be in violation of the public law of America.

Washington, *January 15, 1890.*

B.—ARBITRATION PROJECT SUBMITTED BY MR. HENDERSON TO THE COMMITTEE OF GENERAL WELFARE OF THE INTERNATIONAL AMERICAN CONFERENCE ON FEBRUARY 19, 1890.

1. If any of the nations assenting to these articles shall have cause of complaint against another, it shall cause formal notice thereof to be given to the offending nation, specifying in detail the origin and character of such complaint and also the redress which it seeks.

2. The nation receiving notice of such complaint shall as soon as practicable, and within a period not exceeding three months thereafter, furnish a full and explicit answer to such complaint, and cause the same to be delivered to the State Department or other especially accredited agent of the complaining nation.

3. If within three months from the time of delivering such answer no agreement shall have been made for the final settlement of the questions in dispute, then each of said nations shall appoint five members of a Joint High Commission, who shall meet together as soon as possible after their appointment for the purpose of hearing and considering the questions of difference. They shall adopt for themselves rules of procedure and notify each nation thereof; and they shall hear and consider the case presented by each, and within six months from the time of their first meeting they shall report to the nations interested the result of their deliberations.

If, in determining any question coming before them, the members of the Joint High Commission fail to agree, they shall select an umpire who shall then and thereafter become a member of the Commission.

4. Whenever the Joint High Commission, appointed as hereinbefore provided, shall fail to agree, or where the nations appointing them shall fail to accept and abide by their decision, either or both of the contending nations may give notice of such failure to all the nations signing these articles and becoming parties thereto, and there shall then be formed a High Tribunal of Arbitration in manner following, to wit: Each nation receiving the said notice shall immediately transmit to the nations in controversy the names of four persons, to be selected by the Executive Department of the Government so selecting them, and from the list of such persons the nations in controversy, beginning with the complaining nation, shall alternately strike out one name until the number shall be reduced to nine, which nine persons shall constitute a Tribunal.

The Tribunal thus constituted shall, by writing signed by the members or by a majority of them, appoint a time and place of meeting and give notice thereof to the parties in controversy; and at such time and place, or at other times and places to which an adjournment may be had, it shall determine the rules of its proceedings and thereupon hear the parties and decide between them; and the decision when made or signed by the majority of the members thereof and delivered to the nations in controversy, shall be final and conclusive.

If any nation receiving the notice and request to appoint members of such Tribunal shall fail to transmit the names of the four persons as herein provided within two months after receipt of notice to do so, then the states in controversy shall each appoint two persons in their places, who shall be subject to ultimate rejection in the same manner as those appointed by the neutral states; and if either of the parties to the controversy shall fail to signify its rejection of a name from the list, as herein required, within one month after request from the other to do so, such other may reject for it. If any of the persons selected to constitute this Tribunal shall die, or for any cause fail to serve, the vacancy shall immediately be filled by the nation making the original appointment.

5. Each nation signing these articles as a party binds itself to unite in forming a Joint High Commission and a High Tribunal of Arbitration in all proper cases and to submit to the decisions thereof, when constituted and conducted as herein required.

6. If any of the said nations shall begin and prosecute war against another wrongfully and in disregard of the provisions hereby adopted for the preservation of peace, such nation shall have no right to insist on the performance of neutral duties by the governments of any of the other states; and in such a case the offending nation shall have no lawful right to take or hold property, real or personal, by way of conquest, from its adversary.

5. FACSIMILE COPY OF THE AMENDMENTS MADE BY MR. BLAINE
THE ARGENTINE PLAN OF ARBITRATION.

The delegates ~~of~~ *from* the Republics of North, South and Central America ~~and the Republic of Hayti,~~ assembled in the International American Conference --

Believing that war is the most costly, the most ~~unsatisfactory,~~ *dangerous* and *expedient* and the most ~~perilous experiment~~ for the ~~permanent~~ *cruel* settlement of international differences -

~~Recognizing~~ *Believing* that the growth of moral principle in the world has induced a public opinion that there are no questions of international interest which cannot be ~~promptly and~~ amicably ~~settled~~ *adjusted* by the intervention of impartial counsel -

~~Encouraged~~ *Believing* ~~by the great benefit to mankind which has thus far attended the establishment of Republican institutions, and confident (that the present condition of their respective countries - free from the conflicting political interests and entanglements which disturb other countries - is especially favorable to the substitution of Arbitration for war -~~ *Believing that the*

~~Convinced by their~~ friendly and cordial association in ~~the present Conference~~ that the American Republics, sharing alike the principles, the ~~????~~ obligations and responsibilities of popular constitutional government, and bound together by vast, ~~largely~~ increasing, ~~and ever concentrating~~ *so much to* common interests, may within their own circle, establish pea on earth and good will towards men -- *by the establishment of*

Do ~~hereby~~ ~~recommend~~ ~~to~~ ~~all~~ ~~the~~ ~~governments~~ ~~by~~ ~~which~~ ~~they~~
Have herself some agreed upon & concluded
~~are~~ ~~accredited~~ ~~to~~ ~~celebrate~~ a uniform treaty of Arbitration

in the articles following:

Do hereby recommend that a uniform Treaty of Arbitration in the articles following be celebrated and confirmed

---

6. PLAN OF ARBITRATION.

REPORT OF THE COMMITTEE ON GENERAL WELFARE, SUBMITTED TO THE CONFERENCE, APRIL 14, 1890.

The delegates from North, Central, and South America in Conference Assembled :

Believing that war is the most costly, the most cruel, the most fruitless, and the most dangerous expedient for the settlement of international differences ;

Believing that the growth of moral principle in the world has awakened a public opinion in favor of the amicable adjustment of all questions of international interest by the intervention of impartial counsel ;

Animated by a realization of the great moral and material benefits that peace offers to mankind, and that the existing conditions of the several nations is especially propitious for the adoption of arbitration as a substitute for armed struggles ;

Believing that the American Republics, sharing alike the principles, the obligations, and the responsibilities of popular constitutional government, and bound together by vast and increasing mutual interests, may, within their own circle, do much to establish peace on earth and good will to men ;

And considering it their duty to declare their assent to the high principles which tradition has authorized, public reason supports, and the whole of mankind proclaims, in protection of the weak states, in honor of the strong, and to the benefit of all ;

Do solemnly recommend all the Governments by which they are accredited to celebrate a uniform treaty of arbitration in the articles following, namely :

ARTICLE I.   The Republics of North, Central, and South America hereby adopt arbitration as a principle of American international law for the settlement of all differences, disputes, or controversies that may arise between them.

ARTICLE II.   Arbitration shall be obligatory in all controversies concerning diplomatic rights and privileges, boundaries, territories, indemnities, the right of navigation, and the validity, construction, and enforcement of treaties.

ARTICLE III.   Arbitration shall be equally obligatory in all cases, other than those mentioned in the foregoing article, whatever may be their origin, nature, or occasion, with the single exception mentioned in the next following article.

ARTICLE IV.   Such exception shall be when, in the judgment of any nation involved in the controversy, its independence might be endangered by the result of arbitration ; for such nation, arbitration shall be optional, but it shall be obligatory upon the adversary power.

ARTICLE V.   All controversies, or differences, with the exception stated in Article IV., whether pending or hereafter arising, shall be submitted to arbitration, even though they may have originated in occurrences antedating the present treaty.

Article VI. No question shall be revived by virtue of this treaty concerning which a definite agreement shall already have been reached. In such cases arbitration shall be resorted to only for the settlement of questions concerning the validity, interpretation, or enforcement of such agreement.

Article VII. Any government may serve in the capacity of arbitrator which maintains friendly relations with the nation opposed to the one selecting it. The office of arbitrator may also be entrusted to tribunals of justice, to scientific bodies, to public officials, or to private individuals, whether citizens or not of the states selecting them.

Article VIII. The court of arbitration may consist of one or more persons. If of one person, the arbitrator shall be selected jointly by the nations concerned. If of several persons, their selection may be jointly made by the nations concerned. Should no choice be made, each nation claiming a distinct interest in the question at issue shall have the right to appoint one arbitrator on its own behalf.

Article IX. Whenever the court shall consist of an even number of arbitrators, the nations concerned shall appoint an umpire, who shall decide all questions upon which the arbitrators may disagree. If the nations interested fail to agree in the selection of an umpire, such umpire shall be selected by the arbitrators already appointed.

Article X. The appointment of an umpire, and his acceptance, shall take place before the arbitrators enter upon the hearing of the questions in dispute.

Article XI. The umpire shall not act as a member of the court, but his duties and powers shall be limited to the decision of questions upon which the arbitrators shall be unable to agree.

Article XII. Should an arbitrator, or an umpire, be prevented from serving by reason of death, resignation, or other cause, such arbitrator or umpire shall be replaced by a substitute, to be selected in the same manner in which the original arbitrator or umpire shall have been chosen.

Article XIII. The court shall hold its sessions at such place as the parties in interest may agree upon, and in case of disagreement or failure to name a place the court itself may determine the location.

Article XIV. When the court shall consist of several arbitrators, a majority of the whole number may act, notwithstanding the absence or withdrawal of the minority. In such case the majority shall continue in the performance of their duties until they shall have reached a final determination of the questions submitted for their consideration.

Article XV. The decision of a majority of a whole number of arbitrators shall be final both on the main and incidental issues, unless in the agreement to arbitrate it shall have been expressly provided that unanimity is essential.

Article XVI. The general expenses of arbitration proceedings shall be paid in equal proportion by the governments that are parties thereto; but the expenses incurred by either party in the preparation and prosecution of its case shall be defrayed by it individually.

Article XVII. Whenever disputes arise the nations involved shall appoint courts of arbitration in accordance with the provisions of the preceding articles. Only by the mutual and free consent of all such nations may those provisions be disregarded, and courts of arbitration appointed under different arrangements.

Article XVIII. This treaty shall remain in force for twenty years from the date of the exchange of ratifications. After the expiration of that period it shall continue in operation until one of the contracting parties shall have notified all the others of its desire to terminate it. In the event of such notice the treaty shall continue obligatory upon the party giving it for at least one year thereafter, but the withdrawal of one or more nations shall not invalidate the treaty with respect to the other nations concerned.

ARTICLE XIX.   This treaty shall be ratified by all the nations approving it, according to their respective constitutional methods ; and the ratifications shall be exchanged in the city of Washington on or before the first day of May, A.D. 1891. Any other nation may accept this treaty and become a party thereto by signing a copy thereof and depositing the same with the Government of the United States : whereupon the said Government shall communicate this fact to the other contracting parties.

In testimony whereof the undersigned plenipotentiaries have hereunto affixed their signatures and seals.

Done in the city of Washington, in   copies in English, Spanish, and Portuguese, on this   day of the month of   , one thousand eight hundred and ninety.

JOHN B. HENDERSON,   MANUEL QUINTANA,
JUAN FRANCISCO VELARDE,   N. BOLET PERAZA,
J. M. HURTADO,   J. G. DO AMARAL VALENTE,
                   FERNANDO CRUZ.
WASHINGTON, *April 9, 1890.*

---

7.   THE RIGHT OF CONQUEST.

SUPPLEMENTARY REPORT OF THE COMMITTEE ON GENERAL WELFARE.

Whereas there is in America no territory which can be deemed *res nullius ;* and

Whereas, in view of this, a war of conquest of one American nation against another would constitute a clearly unjustifiable act of violence and spoliation ; and

Whereas, the possibilities of aggressions upon national territory would inevitably involve a recourse to the ruinous system of war armaments in time of peace ; and

Whereas, the Conference feels that it would fall short of the most exalted conception of its mission were it to abstain from embodying its pacific and fraternal sentiments in declarations tending to promote national stability, and guarantee just international relations among the nations of the continent :

BE IT THEREFORE RESOLVED BY THE INTERNATIONAL AMERICAN CONFERENCE, That it earnestly recommends to the Governments therein represented the adoption of the following declarations :

First.   That the principle of conquest shall never hereafter be recognized as admissible under American public law.

Second.   That all cessions of territory made subsequent to the present declaration shall be absolutely void if made under threats of war or the presence of an armed force.

Third.   Any nation from which such cessions shall have been exacted may demand that the question of the validity of the cessions so made shall be submitted to arbitration.

Fourth.   Any renunciation of the right to have recourse to arbitration shall be null and void whatever the time, circumstances, and conditions may be under which such renunciation shall have been effected.

MANUEL QUINTANA,
JUAN FRANCISCO VELARDE,
N. BOLET PERAZA,

The delegations from Colombia, Brazil, and Guatemala approve the preamble and the first article or declaration of the resolutions.

J. M. HURTADO,
J. G. DO AMARAL VALENTE,
FERNANDO CRUZ.

8. TREATY OF ARBITRATION SIGNED BY THE DELEGATES TO THE PAN-AMERICAN CONFERENCE.

I.—TREATY OF ARBITRATION.

The Delegates from North, Central, and South America in Conference assembled :

Believing that war is the most cruel, the most fruitless, and the most dangerous expedient for the settlement of international differences ;

Recognizing that the growth of the moral principles which govern political societies has created an earnest desire in favor of the amicable adjustment of such differences ;

Animated by the conviction of the great moral and material benefits that peace offers to mankind, and trusting that the existing conditions of the respective nations are especially propitious for the adoption of arbitration as a substitute for armed struggles ;

Convinced by reason of their friendly and cordial meeting in the present Conference, that the American Republics, controlled alike by the principles, duties, and responsibilities of popular Government, and bound together by vast and increasing mutual interests, can, within the sphere of their own action, maintain the peace of the continent, and the good-will of all its inhabitants ;

And considering it their duty to lend their assent to the lofty principles of peace which the most enlightened public sentiment of the world approves ;

Do solemnly recommend all the Governments by which they are accredited to conclude a uniform treaty of arbitration in the articles following :

ARTICLE I.—The Republics of North, Central, and South America hereby adopt arbitration as a principle of American international law for the settlement of the differences, disputes, or controversies that may arise between two or more of them.

ARTICLE II.—Arbitration shall be obligatory in all controversies concerning diplomatic and consular privileges, boundaries, territories, indemnities, the right of navigation, and the validity, construction, and enforcement of treaties.

ARTICLE III.—Arbitration shall be equally obligatory in all cases other than those mentioned in the foregoing article, whatever may be their origin, nature, or object, with the single exception mentioned in the next following article.

ARTICLE IV.—The sole questions excepted from the provisions of the preceding articles are those which, in the judgment of any one of the nations involved in the controversy, may imperil its independence. In which case, for such nation, arbitration shall be optional ; but it shall be obligatory upon the adversary power.

ARTICLE V.—All controversies or differences, whether pending or hereafter arising, shall be submitted to arbitration, even though they may have originated in occurrences antedating the present treaty.

ARTICLE VI.—No question shall be revived by virtue of this treaty concerning which a definite agreement shall already have been reached. In such cases arbitration shall be resorted to only for the settlement of questions concerning the validity, interpretation, or enforcement of such agreements.

ARTICLE VII.—The choice of arbitrators shall not be limited or confined to American States. Any government may serve in the capacity of arbitrator which maintains friendly relations with the nation opposed to the one selecting it. The office of arbitrator may also be intrusted to tribunals of justice, to scientific bodies, to public officials, or to private individuals, whether citizens or not of the States selecting them.

ARTICLE VIII.—The court of arbitration may consist of one or more persons.

If of one person, he shall be selected jointly by the nations concerned. If of several persons, their selection may be jointly made by the nations concerned. Should no choice be agreed upon, each nation showing a distinct interest in the question at issue shall have the right to appoint one arbitrator on its own behalf.

ARTICLE IX.—Whenever the court shall consist of an even number of arbitrators, the nations concerned shall appoint an umpire, who shall decide all questions upon which the arbitrators may disagree. If the nations interested fail to agree in the selection of an umpire, such umpire shall be selected by the arbitrators already appointed.

ARTICLE X.—The appointment of an umpire, and his acceptance, shall take place before the arbitrators enter upon the hearing of the questions in dispute.

ARTICLE XI.—The umpire shall not act as a member of the court, but his duties and powers shall be limited to the decision of questions, whether principal or incidental, upon which the arbitrators shall be unable to agree.

ARTICLE XII.—Should an arbitrator or an umpire be prevented from serving by reason of death, resignation, or other cause, such arbitrator or umpire shall be replaced by a substitute to be selected in the same manner in which the original arbitrator or umpire shall have been chosen.

ARTICLE XIII.—The court shall hold its sessions at such place as the parties in interest may agree upon, and in case of disagreement or failure to name a place the court itself may determine the location.

ARTICLE XIV.—When the court shall consist of several arbitrators, a majority of the whole number may act notwithstanding the absence or withdrawal of the minority. In such case the majority shall continue in the performance of their duties until they shall have reached a final determination of the questions submitted for their consideration.

ARTICLE XV.—The decision of a majority of the whole number of arbitrators shall be final both on the main and incidental issues, unless in the agreement to arbitrate it shall have been expressly provided that unanimity is essential.

ARTICLE XVI.—The general expenses of arbitration proceedings shall be paid in equal proportions by the governments that are parties thereto; but expenses incurred by either party in the preparation and prosecution of its case shall be defrayed by it individually.

ARTICLE XVII.—Whenever disputes arise the nations involved shall appoint courts of arbitration in accordance with the provisions of the preceding articles. Only by the mutual and free consent of all of such nations may those provisions be disregarded, and courts of arbitration appointed under different arrangements.

ARTICLE XVIII.—This treaty shall remain in force for twenty years from the date of the exchange of ratifications. After the expiration of that period, it shall continue in operation until one of the contracting parties shall have notified all the others of its desire to terminate it. In the event of such notice the treaty shall continue obligatory upon the party giving it for one year thereafter, but the withdrawal of one or more nations shall not invalidate the treaty with respect to the other nations concerned.

ARTICLE XIX.—This treaty shall be ratified by all the nations approving it, according to their respective constitutional methods; and the ratifications shall be exchanged in the city of Washington on or before the first day of May, A.D. 1891.

Any other nation may accept this treaty and become a party thereto, by signing a copy thereof and depositing the same with the Government of the United States; whereupon the said Government shall communicate this fact to the other contracting parties.

In testimony whereof the undersigned plenipotentiaries have hereunto affixed their signatures and seals.

Done in the city of Washington, in copies in English, Spanish, and Portuguese, on this 28th day of the month of April, one thousand eight hundred and ninety.

JUAN FRANCISCO VELARDE,
    For the Republic of Bolivia.

J. M. P. CAAMAÑO,
    For the Republic of Ecuador.

FERNANDO CRUZ,
    For the Republic of Guatemala.

HANNIBAL PRICE,
    For the Republic of Haiti.

JERONIMO ZELAYA,
    For Honduras.

H. GUZMÁN,
    For Nicaragua.

JACINTO CASTELLANOS,
    For Salvador.

JAMES G. BLAINE,
    For the United States of America.
    (Signed after April 28, 1890, on receipt of instructions.)

SALVADOR DE MENDONÇA,
    For the United States of Brazil.

N. BOLET PERAZA,
JOSÉ ANDRADE,
    For the United States of Venezuela.

ALBERTO NIN,
    For the Oriental Republic of Uruguay.

II.—RECOMMENDATION TO EUROPEAN POWERS TO ACCEPT ARBITRATION.

The International American Conference Resolves : That this Conference, having recommended arbitration for the settlement of disputes among the Republics of America, begs leave to express the wish that controversies between them and the nations of Europe may be settled in the same friendly manner.

It is further recommended that the government of each nation herein represented communicate this wish to all friendly powers.

III.—RECOMMENDATION OF THE CONFERENCE REGARDING THE RIGHT OF CONQUEST.

Whereas the International American Conference feels that it would fall short of the most exalted conception of its mission were it to abstain from embodying its pacific and fraternal sentiments in declarations tending to promote national stability and guarantee just international relations among the nations of the continent : Be it therefore

Resolved, That it earnestly recommends to the Governments therein represented the adoption of the following declarations :

First. That the principle of conquest shall not, during the continuance of the Treaty of Arbitration, be recognized as admissible under American public law.

Second. That all cessions of territory made during the continuance of the Treaty of Arbitration shall be void, if made under threats of war or the presence of an armed force.

Third. Any nation from which such cessions shall be exacted may demand that the validity of the cessions so made shall be submitted to arbitration.

Fourth. Any renunciation of the right to arbitration made under the conditions named in the second section shall be null and void.

---

9. RECOMMENDATION ADOPTED BY THE PAN-AMERICAN CONFERENCE ON APRIL 10, 1890, IN FAVOR OF RECIPROCITY TREATIES.

The Committee on Customs Union has made a careful study of the questions submitted to its consideration by the International American Conference, in reference to forming a customs union among the several nations of this continent.

It is generally understood by customs union the establishing among the several nations of a single customs territory, to wit, that the nations forming the union shall collect import duties on foreign goods, under substantially the same tariff laws; divide the proceeds thereof in a given proportion, and mutually receive, free of duty, their respective natural or manufactured products.

The acceptance of this plan would demand, as a previous requirement, a change in the fundamental laws of the countries accepting the union. Even after they were ready to make such changes, a great many other difficulties, almost insurmountable, would have to be overcome ; as, for instance, fixing the representation of each nation at the international assembly empowered to frame a common tariff and amend it in the future. The territorial extent, the populations, and the national wealth differ so much among the American Republics that if these conditions should be taken as the basis of representation at said assembly, the small States would not have sufficient protection for their interests ; and, if all the nations were admitted as sovereign on an equal footing, the large ones would be insufficiently protected. It might be necessary, to obviate this difficulty, to create two bodies, one representing the population and the other the States, in the manner in which a like problem was solved in the Constitution of the United States of America. But this step would, in the opinion of the committee, require a partial sacrifice of the national sovereignty of the American nations, and more radical changes in their respective constitutions than in its judgment they are willing to accept.

If by customs union is meant the free-trade between the American nations of all their natural or manufactured products, which is, properly speaking, unrestricted reciprocity, the committee believes it is in principle acceptable, because all measures looking to the freedom of commerce must necessarily increase the trade and the development of the material resources of the countries accepting that system, and it would in all probability bring about as favorable results as those obtained by free-trade among the different States of this Union.

But while the committee believes that such a union is at present impracticable as a continental system, among other reasons because the import duties levied on foreign trade constitute the main sources of revenue of all the American nations, and such of them as are not manufacturing countries would thus lose more or less of such revenue, on which they depend in a great measure to defray their national expenses ; while the manufacturing countries, such as the United States of America, would have to abandon, at least partially, the protective policy which they have adopted to more or less extent, and they do not seem yet prepared to change that system. Besides, a reciprocity treaty mutually advantageous between two contiguous countries might prove onerous if extended to all as a continental compact, especially as the products of many of the American Republics are similar. Therefore, while these obstacles are in the way, it seems premature to propose free-trade among the nations of this hemisphere.

But although it is not easy, in the opinion of the committee, to reach at once unrestricted reciprocity, that end might be obtained gradually and partially. The first and most efficient step in that direction is the negotiation of partial reciprocity treaties among the American nations, whereby each may agree to remove or diminish their respective import duties on some of the natural or manufactured products of one or more of the other nations in exchange for similar and equivalent advantages, as, if the mutual concessions were not equivalent, the treaties would soon become odious, and could not last but for a limited time, and would discredit the system. If after this has been tried for some reasonable time a good result should follow, as it is to be expected, the number of articles on the free list might be enlarged in each case, from time to time, until they attain, through the development of the natural elements of wealth, other sources of revenue or an increase of the existing ones, which would allow the contracting nations to reach unrestricted reciprocity or a free-trade among some or all the American nations.

RECOMMENDATION OF THE CONFERENCE.

Therefore the committee proposes :

To recommend to such of the Governments represented in the Conference as may be interested in the concluding of partial reciprocity commercial treaties, to negotiate such treaties with one or more of the American countries as it may be in their interest to make them, under such a basis as may be acceptable in each case, taking into consideration the special situation, conditions, and interests of each country, and with a view to promote their common welfare.

10. RECOMMENDATION OF THE PAN-AMERICAN CONFERENCE APPROVED ON FEBRUARY 26, 1898, ON RAILWAY COMMUNICATION.

REPORT OF THE COMMITTEE ON RAILWAY COMMUNICATION.

The International American Conference is of the opinion:

First. That a railroad connecting all or a majority of the nations represented in this Conference will contribute greatly to the development of cordial relations between said nations and the growth of their material interests.

Second. That the best method of facilitating its execution is the appointment of an international commission of engineers to ascertain the possible routes, to determine their true length, to estimate the cost of each, and to compare their respective advantages.

Third. That the said commission should consist of a body of engineers of whom each nation should appoint three, and which should have authority to divide into subcommissions and appoint as many other engineers and employees as may be considered necessary for the more rapid execution of the work.

Fourth. That each of the Governments accepting may appoint, at its own expense, commissioners or engineers to serve as auxiliaries to the sub-commissions charged with the sectional surveys of the line.

Fifth. That the railroad, in so far as the common interests will permit, should connect the principal cities lying in the vicinity of its route.

Sixth. That if the general direction of the line cannot be altered without great inconvenience, for the purpose mentioned in the preceding article, branch lines should be surveyed to connect those cities with the main line.

Seventh. That for the purpose of reducing the cost of the enterprise the existing railways should be utilized as far as is practicable and compatible with the route and conditions of the continental railroad.

Eighth. That in case the results of the survey demonstrate the practicability and advisability of the railroad, proposals for the construction either of the whole line or of sections thereof should be solicited.

Ninth. That the construction, management, and operation of the line should be at the expense of the concessionaires, or of the persons to whom they sublet the work or transfer their rights, with all due formalities, the consent of the respective Governments being first obtained.

Tenth. That all materials necessary for the construction and operation of the railroad should be exempt from import duties, subject to such regulations as may be necessary to prevent the abuse of this privilege.

Eleventh. That all personal and real property of the railroad employed in its construction and operation should be exempt from all taxation, either national, provincial (State), or municipal.

Twelfth. That the execution of a work of such magnitude deserves to be further encouraged by subsidies, grants of land, or guarantee of a minimum of interest.

Thirteenth. That the salaries of the commission, as well as the expense incident to the preliminary and final surveys, should be assumed by all the nations accepting, in proportion to population according to the latest official census, or, in the absence of a census, by agreement between their several Governments.

Fourteenth. That the railroad should be declared forever neutral for the purpose of securing freedom of traffic.

Fifteenth. That the approval of the surveys, the terms of the proposals, the protection of the concessionaires, the inspection of the work, the legislation affecting it, the neutrality of the road, and the free passage of merchandise in transit, should be (in the event contemplated by article eighth) the subject of special agreement between all the nations interested.

Sixteenth. That as soon as the Government of the United States shall receive notice of the acceptance of these recommendations by the other Governments, it shall invite them to appoint the commission of engineers referred to in the second article, in order that it may meet in the city of Washington, at the earliest possible date.

JUAN FRANCISCO VELARDE.	H. G. DAVIS.
E. A. MEXIA.	FERNANDO CRUZ.
JERÓNIMO ZELAYA.	JACINTO CASTELLANOS.
ANDREW CARNEGIE.	CARLOS MARTINEZ SILVA.
JOSÉ ANDRADE.	J. M. P. CAAMAÑO.
F. C. C. ZEGARRA.	E. C. VARAS.
MANUEL QUINTANA.	J. G. DO AMARAL VALENTE.
JOSÉ S. DECOUD.	H. GUZMÁN.

---

11. MR. BLAINE'S REPORT TO THE PRESIDENT, CONTAINING THE RECOMMENDATIONS OF THE INTERNATIONAL AMERICAN CONFERENCE OF APRIL 7, 1890, ON AN AMERICAN INTERNATIONAL MONETARY UNION.

DEPARTMENT OF STATE,
WASHINGTON, *July 10, 1890.*

THE PRESIDENT:

The International American Conference, recently in session at this capital, adopted the following report:

" The International American Conference is of opinion that great advantages would accrue to the commerce between the nations of this continent by the use of a coin or coins that would be current at the same value in all the countries represented in this Conference, and therefore recommends—

" (1) That an international American monetary union be established.

" (2) That as a basis for this union an international coin or coins be issued which shall be uniform in weight and fineness, and which may be used in all the countries represented in this Conference.

" (3) That to give full effect to this recommendation there shall meet in Washington a commission composed of one delegate or more from each nation represented in this Conference, which shall consider the quantity, the kind of currency, the uses it shall have, and the value and proportion of the international silver coin or coins, and their relations to gold.

" (4) That the Government of the United States shall invite the commission to meet in Washington within a year from the date of the adjournment of this Conference."

It was hoped and expected by the Conference that the recommendations would be transmitted to Congress with a recommendation that the several nations interested be invited to send delegates to a meeting of the international American monetary union at Washington on the first Wednesday of January next; that authority be granted for the appointment of three delegates on the part of the United States, and that an appropriation be made to meet the necessary expenses.

Respectfully submitted.

JAMES G. BLAINE.

---

12. CENSURE OF A MEXICAN DELEGATE BY THE MEXICAN PRESS AND A PROMINENT WRITER.

Señor Don Francisco Sosa, a prominent literary man of Mexico, published in the third volume of *La Revista Nacional de Ciencias y Letras* a biographical sketch of Señor Don Nicanor Bolet Peraza, a delegate from Venezuela, in which he censured him and myself for not having followed in the footsteps of the Argentine delegates in the discussion before the International American Conference. He said among other things the following:

As our countryman, Mr. Romero, has a great love for his native land, he vehemently desires to see her great and prosperous; but he has not been able to entirely shake off the influence that American habits have exerted on his mind. That is the reason why, during the Conference, neither Bolet Peraza nor Romero were among those who in round periods, with loud emphasis, and with the fire natural to the great orators of Spanish America, united their efforts with the Argentine Delegates, Quintana and Saenz Peña, zealous guardians of the autonomy, and legitimate and sacred rights of Latin America. To them, that is to say, to Bolet Peraza and Romero, the fraternal feelings of this great Republic are above suspicion, and no fear should be entertained, that, under the cloak of union, the stronger might dominate the weaker, and *quia dominat leo*, become the arbiter of their destinies, the judge of their controversies, in fine be their lord and master.

When Señor Sosa's paper came to my knowledge, I wrote to him, on June 10, 1890, a letter in which I explained my conduct in the Conference, and from which I insert the following extracts:

The opinions of the Latin-American Delegates were expressed in two different ways. The first was during the excursion, to which they had been invited by the Government of the United States, as its guests, and were received as such by all the cities of this country that they visited; and the second as representatives of their Governments, at the International American Conference. . . . .

In the first case, do you consider that it would have been proper and polite to make any comparison between what the Delegates were seeing here and what they left in their countries, even if what they left at home was superior to what they found here? The greater the advancement and progress of their respective countries, the more impropriety there would have been to make reference to them under such circumstances, as all comparisons are odious. The fact that we were Delegates did not deprive us of the attributes of gentlemen, and when a gentleman invites another to his house, and attends to him as his guest, it would be at least very poor taste on the part of the person invited to expatiate to his host on the superiority of his own household, and on the condition of his own business affairs as compared with what he finds where he is in the capacity of a guest. That is so very true, that the Argentine Delegate himself, who was situated in a more advantageous position than ourselves, as I will explain farther on, did not deem it proper to say a single word at several banquets and receptions at which he was present.

Notwithstanding this, as I desired to avail myself of some opportunity to make a few remarks before some one of the distinguished audiences of this country regarding the commercial relations between Mexico and the United States, I read at the banquet given by the "Spanish-American Commercial Union," of New York, on the 20th of December, 1889, in honor of the Delegates, an address, which I suppose you may have seen, as it was published in all the papers of that city, wherein, without offending any one, and with the utmost moderation, as is shown by the fact that instead of being censured it was well received by nearly all the newspapers of this country, I made some remarks which can favorably compare in frankness and vigor with the speeches delivered during the excursion and in the meetings of the Conference.

If we now turn our attention to what the Delegates said at the meetings of the Conference, it seems proper to state that there were two sets of Delegates : one comprising gentlemen who had no permanent position near this Government, but who merely came to this country to stay during the meetings of the Conference ; and the other comprising gentlemen who, besides being Delegates, were representatives permanently accredited, and who at the end of the sessions of the Conference would have to stay here and continue discussing official matters of importance with the Government of the United States, and whose duty it was to preserve cordial personal relations with the members of this Government, not to jeopardize the success of very important affairs of their respective countries. This second class of Delegates could still be subdivided into two classes, the first of which comprised those who represented countries that, owing to their being situated at the extreme southern portion of the American Continent, with scarcely any commercial, political, or social relations with the United States, and having no questions, affairs, or complications of any kind, enjoyed greater freedom to express their opinions without reservation or circumlocution, and who made free use of such freedom, in such a way that they pleased even the most exacting ; and the second class was composed of representatives of countries situated near the United States—and in one instance, of a country adjoining it throughout a large extent of territory, and connected by several trunk railway lines, as is the case with Mexico—with intimate relations of every kind, who had to look beyond the immediate results of the Conference, and who could not, through misplaced patriotism or improper egotism, compromise not only the affairs pending before the Conference but the more weighty ones that were daily being discussed between their respective countries and the United States. . . . .

A very well-known proverb says that "speech is silver but silence is gold," and if this is not always true, it is so when prudence succeeds in overcoming a desire to obtain a victory by words, merely, which is often only a temporary one. Be it as it may, I think that in diplomacy especially, men are judged by their deeds and not by their words.

You think that the long residence of Mr. Bolet Peraza and myself in this country renders us unable " to shake off entirely the influence exercised upon us by our long residence in this country," and you imagine that on that account we have not been "zealous defenders of the autonomy and sacred rights of Latin-America," and by interpreting our minds you attribute to us the opinion that we believe that " the fraternal feelings of this great Republic are above suspicion " and that "no fear should be entertained that under the cloak of union the stronger might dominate the weaker, and *quia dominor leo*, become the arbiter of their destinies, the judge of their controversies, in fine be their lord and master."

I am very sure that if you were better informed regarding what took place at the Conference, you would not have written those phrases, which are not only unjust, but that have no foundation to stand upon.

---

13. M. ROMERO'S ANSWER TO SEÑOR PIERRA'S ATTACKS.

(From *Las Novedades*, New York, July 7, 1890.)[1]

In a letter signed by Mr. Fidel G. Pierra, dated at Washington, on March 10, 1890, addressed to the editor of *La Nacion*, of Buenos Ayres, published on the 4th of May following, several assertions are made, some incorrect and some slanderous, regarding incidents which occurred in the International American Conference, and more especially respecting some of its Delegates. Had he referred to a matter of less importance, I would not condescend to notice the utterances of a man so blinded by his self-esteem that, not satisfied with the censure that he brought upon himself and with having placed some Delegates in an unpleasant position, now wishes to avenge his supposed grievances on others, although I am sure that his utterances cannot reach the gentlemen he attempts to offend ; but as this incident refers to serious and grave matters, in which the cordial relations and good understanding of all the American nations are involved, I think it advisable, as an eye-witness of the events connected with the Conference, to make some corrections of the letter already mentioned.

No wonder, then, that *La Nacion*, of Buenos Ayres, upon inserting that letter in its columns, "leaves the responsibility of the article to its author," and that it does not confine itself to this, but states that the time for fully judging the Conference is not yet at hand, since, even supposing that it had not attained any material results, a thing which cannot yet be known, it believes, and rightly, too, that the Conference must produce moral results which must be, perforce, favorable.

Señor Pierra's Personality.—I shall begin with the personality of Mr. Pierra. This gentleman, who, owing to the fact that he had a commission house in New York, and therefore something to lose, it would seem should act with some caution and circumspection, has descended to a level upon which probably no person having a mercantile or social position would like to place himself, for not only does he show that he is as little loyal to a government he has served and from whom he has received a salary, by revealing matters of which he probably had knowledge by virtue of his office, but he attacks, without reason, the very persons who appointed him to perform its duties.

[1] As Señor Pierra wrote and published his letter in Spanish, my answer to him was also written in Spanish, and the one inserted here is a translation from the original publication. My letter appeared in *Las Novedades* without any headings ; but as it is somewhat lengthy and embraces several subjects, I thought it better, for the convenience of the reader, to add to it some side headings. Extracts of my letter were published by several papers of the United States.

In the capacity of Secretary of the Spanish-American Union of New York, he accompanied the Delegates on the excursion to which the Government of the United States invited them, having received ample remuneration for this service.   During this excursion he was in touch with the greater number of the Delegates, and having the advantage of knowing this country and of speaking Spanish and English, he tried to render them services which would make them grateful to him, and which paved the way to his election as Secretary.

His Appointment as Spanish Secretary of the Conference.—The Conference resolved upon the appointment of two Secretaries, both versed in the English and Spanish languages, one to take charge of the Spanish, and the other of the English work.   By request of the Department of State I proposed for English Secretary, on the 25th of November last, Mr. Remsen Whitehouse, whose appointment was unanimously agreed to.   But before making this nomination, I took care to personally speak to all the Delegates, or at least to one member from each Delegation, explaining the motives which led me to suggest the nomination, and to know if a unanimous agreement could be reached thereon.   What, then, was my surprise, when, without extending to me the courtesy shown by me to my colleagues, immediately after the election of Mr. Whitehouse, one of the Spanish-American Delegates nominated Mr. Pierra for Spanish Secretary !   This circumstance, or rather the desire to show that I resented what I considered an uncalled-for slight on the part of a colleague, made me give my vote against the election of Mr. Pierra ; although, not to offend his susceptibility, I stated clearly that my vote did not imply any want of confidence in the ability or integrity of the candidate, and I explained the reasons that impelled me to vote as I did.   This vote, however, severely wounded the self-esteem of Mr. Pierra, who considered it as a mortal offence, and this is the only explanation I can find for his utterances regarding me.

It is true that Mr. Pierra was not appointed Secretary to the Conference by the Government of the United States, but by the vote of the Delegates ; but, besides having the vote of the Delegates from this country in his favor in the election, and that for this reason he should consider himself as much under obligations to them as to all the others who voted for him, there is the circumstance that Section V. of the law pursuant to which the Conference was called together, provided that the Secretary of State of the United States should designate the employees, and that Mr. Blaine, through deference to the Latin-American Delegates, consented that the appointment of Secretaries should be made by the Conference itself ; but these employees, being paid by the United States Government, contracted obligations regarding it, which, I think, have been completely ignored by Mr. Pierra.

Although aware of his abilities, it was natural that in a new, arduous, and complicated matter, he should at first make mistakes, although of little consequence, and for the purpose of showing him that I was not actuated by any personal feeling against him, I refrained on many occasions from criticising at the meetings of the Conference the inaccuracies or errors that I discovered in the minutes prepared by him, and in order to avoid wounding his sensitiveness, called his attention to them in a personal and private way.

Mr. Pierra's Resignations.—Mr. Pierra, who probably imagined that, because he had the position of Secretary to the Conference, he was entitled to the same privileges as the Delegates, commenced to experience some disappointments, as when he discovered that he could not consult directly with Mr. Blaine upon what he might have to propose regarding the business of the Secretary's office, but had to do it through the official whom the Secretary of State had appointed to serve as intermediary in matters of routine, that is, through Mr. William E. Curtis, and this circumstance wounded his pride to such an extent that he repeatedly, verbally as well as in writing, presented his resignation to the Executive Committee, of which, unfortunately, in so far as this incident is concerned, I was a member. He set forth the reasons he had for resigning, which were principally two : first, because he thought he was not treated with due consideration, but was rather annoyed, and that he was not provided with competent employees ; and second, because he believed he did not receive sufficient pecuniary remuneration.

As a member of the Executive Committee, I did all I could to induce Mr. Pierra not to insist in his resignation and to remove the difficulties which had prompted him to present it, excepting the one regarding the salary which had been assigned him by the Department of State,—of ten dollars a day, or three hundred a month,—because this was the highest salary paid any of the employees, (for salaries are as a rule low in this country, and that of three hundred dollars was equal to or greater than those paid to the second and third Assistant Secretaries of State), and above all because as the Latin-American nations did not pay the salaries it would have been improper for their representatives to ask for an increase of the same. On the 29th of January, 1890, Mr. Pierra was paid his salary up to the 31st of that month, and on the following day he returned the money, stating in writing that the Executive Committee knew the reasons for his non-acceptance of it. On the 14th of February he presented his formal resignation, and at the meeting held by the Executive Committee to consider it, I advised that it should not be accepted, and I even made up my mind to speak with the Secretary of State upon the subject, with the view of overcoming the reasons advanced by Mr. Pierra. I can state without divulging any secret or agreement, that I was the only member of the Executive Committee who did not favor the immediate acceptance of his resignation, as the only means to avoid the difficulties he had created for himself and for the Delegates who were his personal friends. Mr. Blaine expressed the desire that the resignation be not accepted, and offered to do all he could to retain Mr. Pierra as Secretary, although he suggested the impossibility of paying him a larger salary for the reasons already stated, and because he believed that a higher salary might cause serious inconveniences, as the auditing officers of the Treasury Department might find it too high, and thereby subject the Secretary of State to criticism and open censure.

It would take too long to relate all the other incidents which occurred in this connection, and I shall simply say that some of the Latin-American Delegates, believing that Mr. Pierra might be the victim of supposed intrigues on the part of Mr. Curtis, took up his defence with great earnestness in the matter of the resignation ; they addressed him a letter asking that he should not resign his position of Secretary and made other efforts to retain him in that office. Deceived by these manifestations of good will he thought, probably, that he could treat the United States Government, whose employee he was, with contempt, and he determined to withdraw his resignation, upon the condition that he be allowed to serve without pay. As this condition was incompatible with the dignity of the Conference, the Executive Committee decided that it could not be accepted, but without saying anything regarding the resignation proper, and upon being informed of the decision Mr. Pierra wrote another communication in which he withdrew the objectionable part of the preceding one, and thereupon received the salary which he had before declined.

At this stage of the incident the Executive Committee met again and directed me to draft a report containing a statement of what had taken place, and reporting in favor of accepting the resignation of Mr. Pierra. I wrote such report setting forth exactly what had transpired ; but instead of recommending the acceptance of his resignation, I recommended that it be not accepted. This part was changed by the majority of the Committee who thought it advisable, in view of the stage the subject had reached, not to make any recommendation as to the acceptance of the resignation, but rather to leave the whole matter to the decision of the Conference, and the committee made other amendments in the last paragraph of my draft of the report, which, carefully examined, are less favorable to Mr. Pierra than the phrases I had written.

The amendments introduced in my report appear in the original text of that document, and are well known to the other members of the Committee. For greater clearness I here insert both texts. Mine reads thus :

" But as *from letters which some Honorable Delegates* have addressed to this gentleman, *and from resolutions introduced* in the Conference, it appears that there are several Honorable Delegates who earnestly desire that Mr. Pierra return to perform the duties of Secretary, and who believe that, if returning, he will permanently remain, the Committee does not desire to oppose the wishes of these Honorable Delegates and consequently it proposes *that Mr. Pierra be allowed to withdraw his resignation and return, to perform the duties of Spanish-American Secretary of the Conference.*"

This was modified by the majority of the Committee, so as to read as follows :

" But it appears from *resolutions introduced* in this Conference, and *other documents,* that some of the Delegates earnestly desire, because they think the business of the Conference would be facilitated thereby, that Mr. Pierra should return to his duties as Secretary, believing, also, that his return would be permanent. The Committee, therefore, not wishing to oppose the desires of the said Delegates, *refers the matter to the decision of the Conference without recommendation.*"

The other statements in the report written by me were perfectly correct, for, had it been otherwise, the report would not have been signed by the other Spanish-American members of the Committee, who were earnest friends of Mr. Pierra, and one of whom had signed the letter to which I have alluded, in which he was requested that he should not leave his office as Secretary.

The Conference terminated this incident by authorizing the Executive Committee, upon motion of a Delegate from the United States, to decide what they might think best regarding Mr. Pierra's resignation. Such resignation was accepted by the Committee, without any action or interference whatever on my part, and thus Mr. Pierra ceased to be Secretary.

My efforts to retain Mr. Pierra as Secretary.—From his letter to *La Nacion,* of Buenos Ayres, I infer that he considers me as the instigator of his withdrawal, and that he qualifies my efforts to retain him as Secretary as refined intrigues ; whereas if I had any hand at all in his leaving the office, it was that of delaying it for some time, and to obtain that his withdrawal should take place in a less disagreeable way for him than it otherwise might have been. If his separation had been due to my intrigues, as he indicates, this would be a very serious charge against the intelligence, not only of all the members of the Conference, but more especially of the three Latin-Americans who were members of the Executive Committee, two at least of whom, as I have already stated, were personal friends of Mr. Pierra, who would have become the instruments of my supposed intrigues, or against their loyalty had they made themselves my accomplices. Besides the Delegates signing the report, Mr. Mendonça, a Delegate from Brazil, was a member of the Committee, whose signature does not appear on that document because he was not present at the meeting on that day ; but as is well known to the other members of the Committee, he expressed from the very first the most decided opinions in favor of the acceptance of the resignation.

Mr. Pierra's Imputations.—I shall say very little regarding the personal imputations which Mr. Pierra hurls against me. He attributes to me the desire to be elected President of the Conference, whereas, as he himself acknowledges, the President had to be a Delegate from the United States. And this could not have been otherwise without committing an act of serious discourtesy towards the inviting Government. Since I was not an United States Delegate, how could the idea of being elected President of the Congress ever have been entertained by me ? Had I entertained the desire to preside over the Conference, I could have attained it by failing to ask my colleague to refrain from voting for me in the election for Vice-President, which was a tie, and thus the vote of Mexico would have decided it in my favor.

Mr. Pierra asserts that for the purpose of obtaining that position I interpreted erroneously the remarks made by the United States Delegates. This assertion implies not only a slander on me, but an insult to all the other delegates who were present, whom it would be necessary to consider as childishly inexpert or ignorant, to have been the victims of such a gross deception. Many of the Latin-Americans spoke English better than I—for I am the first to recognize that I do not know it perfectly, as Mr. Pierra states, and I should add that I have never boasted of being a linguist, and, on the contrary, have always been aware that I do not possess the gift of eloquence nor that of languages—and all the other Delegates who did not speak English, spoke French. Among the American Delegates there was one, Mr. Flint, who spoke Spanish correctly, and at least one more, Mr. Trescot, who understood it sufficiently well, and two or three more, like Mr. Coolidge and Mr. Carnegie, who spoke French correctly. All the Delegates were in intimate and constant communication with each other, and under these circumstances it was not possible that what was said to me by the United States Delegates could be intentionally misinterpreted by me, for if I were capable of such an abuse, I would have been corrected and reproved on the spot.

My efforts to avoid misunderstandings among the Delegates.—The fact of my having resided in this country for a longer time than any other of the Latin-American Delegates, and of being personally acquainted with most of the United States Delegates long before the meeting of the Conference, and perhaps also because I was the member of the Latin-American Diplomatic Corps who had resided longest in Washington, they applied to me in the beginning of the session in order to make known their desires and wishes to the other Delegates. This state of things, which I by no means sought, and which I only considered as a service to the Latin-American Delegates who did not speak English, which I could not refuse, is the foundation for Mr. Pierra to assert that I made distorted interpretations and that I interfered in matters with which he thinks I had nothing to do.

The difficulty of understanding each other, owing to the lack of good interpreters, especially during the first sessions of the Conference, was the cause of misunderstandings, which might have even assumed a disagreeable character, among the Latin-American Delegates and their colleagues of the United States. As I could readily see the cause of such misunderstandings—owing to the limited knowledge I have of both languages, which, although imperfect, as averred by Mr. Pierra, enables me to understand sufficiently all that is said in English, and to make myself understood, although imperfectly, in that language—I essayed to prevent it, making the necessary explanations, sometimes to the United States Delegates when the misunderstandings were on their side, and sometimes to the Latin-Americans. I thought that I rendered in this way a service to my colleagues, assuming a task somewhat disagreeable, which I was really not called upon to perform, and which probably I should not have accepted had I been guided by selfish motives. These efforts on my part to prevent misunderstandings and to render services to some of my colleagues, which, had I been in their place, I would have greatly appreciated, serve also as a foundation for Mr. Pierra's imputation that I desired to become a righter of wrongs, redresser of injuries, etc., etc. When the Delegates knew and understood each other better, when the interpreters improved, and when I saw that there was no necessity for explanations nor interference on my part, I ceased completely to assume the task or render the services which I had undertaken at the beginning of the sessions of the Conference. I believe that all the Delegates can bear witness that, instead of trying to divide them, as Mr. Pierra asserts, my purpose was to unite them and prevent misunderstandings among them, which principally arose from the lack of knowledge of the respective languages and the customs of the countries represented.

Alleged subsidy of New York Papers.—Mr. Pierra asserts that I pay newspapers in New York to eulogize me. I will merely refute that other slander by saying that I never purchased a single eulogy nor have I ever paid a Spanish or Anglo-American paper issued at New York, or at any other place, a single cent beyond the subscription price when I was a subscriber.

I think the praise which Mr. Pierra extends to the Latin-American Delegates is well merited, and that even in some cases it falls short. But it seems strange that only two out of the twenty-three Latin-Americans who met in the Conference failed to deserve his praise, and that those two should be the only Delegates who denied him their votes for Secretary; respecting one of them, Mr. Mexia, my colleague, he does not see fit to say one word for or against, but regarding me, he unbosoms himself to his full satisfaction.

Mr. Sutton's Memorandum.[1]—I had no knowledge of the private instructions which Mr. Pierra asserts were addressed by the Department of State to the United States Delegates regarding the election of President. I had been assured by well-informed persons that the document, which Mr. Pierra obtained probably in his capacity as Secretary, and whose publication with the object he gives should be considered, at the very least, as an act of discourtesy, was not written in the Department of State, and much less bore the character of private instructions, but that it was prepared by an employee to whom the Secretary of State gave in charge the work preliminary to the meeting of the Conference. When carefully examined we find, on the other hand, that it contains nothing new, nothing irregular, nor anything which might be considered as offensive to the rights and interests of the Latin-American nations represented in the Conference, for the reason that it only states that the office of President of the Conference belonged, as an act of courtesy, usual among civilized nations, to a representative of the United States.

Conclusion.—I think it unnecessary to consider the other statements contained in Mr. Pierra's letter which do not refer to me personally, although I expect later to have the opportunity to make some explanations regarding the proceedings of the Conference, which will show, although indirectly, the biased and untenable character of Mr. Pierra's assertions.

[1] The document, to which Señor Pierra gave such great importance, was the Sutton Memorandum, to which I refer on page 639 of this book. I had not heard anything at all about that paper, until after Señor Pierra's letter reached Washington, and then on inquiry I found out what appears both in my answer to Señor Pierra, and in the preceding paper.

SUPPLEMENT TO THE FREE ZONE PAPER.

Since this paper went to press, the Congress of the United States has acted again on the Free Zone question, causing important congressional documents to come out, and the House of Representatives passed a Joint Resolution repealing the Joint Resolution of March 1st, 1898. I have also received valuable official information from the Mexican Government bearing on the amount of foreign merchandise, not from the United States, imported into the Free Zone, during the fiscal years 1895–96 and 1896–97. I have thought proper, therefore, to embrace that information, as well as the action of Congress and papers referred to, in the present supplement.

Foreign Commodities Imported into the Free Zone.—With a view of finding out the exact value of foreign merchandise, except the products and manufactures of the United States imported into the Mexican Free Zone, with the payment of eighteen and one half per cent. of the full import duties, and in that way show what is the exact amount of that trade, I requested the Mexican Government to prepare a statement of the extent of that trade from the official data furnished by the respective custom houses, which I received after my paper on the subject had been printed.

We have twelve custom houses on our frontier with the United States, between the mouth of the Rio Grande River and the Pacific Ocean. Seven of them, Mier, Guerrero, Camargo, Boquillas, La Morita, Tijuana and Sásabe imported during the two fiscal years 1895–96 and 1896–97 only foreign merchandise, the product and manufacture of the United States, and none from Europe or any other country. The importations from the other five custom houses were as follows:

CUSTOM HOUSES.	YEARS.	VALUE.	18½ PER CENT. OF DUTIES PAID.	TOTAL DUTIES.
Matamoros	1895–96	$49,124	$14,919.01	$80,643.33
"	1896–97			
Laredo de Tamaulipas.....	1895–96	210,862	48,530.31	262,326.00
" " "	1896–97			
Piedras Negras :				
(Ciudad Porfirio Diaz) ...	1895–96	21,660	14,969.65	2,813.43
" " " ...	1896–97	34,620		5,278.27
El Paso del Norte[1] :				
(Ciudad Juarez)	1895196	102,507	18,643.14	100,773.70
" "	1896–97			
Nogales..................	1895–96	41,460	15,388.57	75,164.26
"	1896–97	6,161		8,017.21
Total...............		$466,394	$112,450.68	$535,016.20

[1] In the figures of the El Paso del Norte custom house are embraced both the commodities imported from the United States and those arrived in transit from Veracruz, Tampico, and Guaymas.

I regret that the data sent by the Matamoros, Laredo, and El Paso del Norte custom houses do not state separately the importation of foreign merchandise not from the United States, during the fiscal years 1895–96 and 1896–97, but give the figures of both years together.   To avoid the delay necessary to have this data revised, I will take as the importation of each year, one half of the importation of the two years.   The total value of foreign merchandise, not produced or manufactured in the United States, imported into the Mexican Free Zone during the two years mentioned was $466,394, which would give an average for one year of $233,197.   A large portion of these commodities, fifty per cent. of them at least, goes to places in Mexico outside of the Free Zone limits in so far as those imported by the Laredo and El Paso del Norte custom houses are concerned, and about twenty-five per cent. of those imported by the Piedras Negras and Nogales custom houses, leaving in those districts about seventy-five per cent.; and supposing that all the merchandise imported by the Matamoros custom house is consumed in the Free Zone of that locality, the value of the merchandise left in the Free Zone would be $141,868. But out of this amount ought to be deducted such commodities as are consumed in the Free Zone, which would be at least fifty per cent., and that will leave $70,934, which might be smuggled into the adjoining countries, the largest portion of which will likely go into Mexico; but supposing that all should be smuggled into the United States, which I consider is not at all probable, the value of merchandise smuggled into this country would have been $70,934, which at the average rate of duty in the United States in the year ending June 30, 1896, was 39.95 per cent., and the average for the following year ending June 30, 1897, which was 42.17 per cent., making an average rate of 41.06 per cent. would amount $29,125.50 as the loss suffered by the United States Treasury on account of the Mexican Free Zone.

Even supposing that all the commodities imported into the Mexican Free Zone should be smuggled into the United States, which is certainly almost an impossibility, because some of them are consumed in the Free Zone, and the largest portion if smuggled at all is smuggled into Mexico, the value of merchandise smuggled into this country during each of the mentioned fiscal years would be $233,197, which at the average duty paid in this country during the said years of 41.06 per cent. would amount to $95,750.97.

This information, which is official and therefore correct, corroborates Secretary of the Treasury Fairchild's Report of March 1, 1888, and which I give in full in the foregoing paper, and sustains my contention of how much the smuggling which can be carried on from Mexico to the United States on account of the Free Zone has been exaggerated, even in case that every cent of European manufactures imported to the Free Zone was smuggled into this country.

Action of the Fifty-fifth Congress on the Free Zone.—The members of Congress from Texas renewed their efforts during the 1st Session of the Fifty-fifth Congress to repeal the Joint Resolution approved March 1, 1895, forbidding the transportation of goods in bond into the Free Zone of Mexico, and Mr. Samuel B. Cooper, representing the 2d District of Texas, introduced by request on March 20, 1897,[1] a Joint Resolution to that effect, which was referred to the Committee on Ways and Means and ordered to be printed. As the 1st Session of the Fifty-fifth Congress was specially devoted to the tariff, and for that reason the Speaker did not appoint any committees until the end of the session, excepting the one on Ways and Means, who had to report the tariff bill, this Committee did not take any action on Mr. Cooper's resolution until the 2d Session of the Fifty-fifth Congress, when, on March 11, 1898, it was favorably reported by the Committee, referred to the House Calendar and ordered to be printed. When the Committee had thus to take some action on the subject of the Free Zone, not being familiar with the bearings of that institution on the interests of the United States, they addressed, on January 21, 1898, a communication to the Secretary of the Treasury, asking his views on said resolution.

Secretary Gage sent to the Hon. Nelson Dingley, Chairman of the Ways and Means Committee of the House, on January 26, 1898,[2] his

---

[1] Fifty-fifth Congress, 2d Session, H. Res. 27. [Report No. 702.] In the House of Representatives, March 20, 1897, Mr. Cooper of Texas, (by request) introduced the following joint resolution ; which was referred to the Committee on Ways and Means and ordered to be printed. March 11, 1898, referred to the House Calendar and ordered to be printed.

"Joint resolution. To repeal the joint resolution in reference to the Free Zone :

"*Resolved by the Senate and House of Representatives of the United States of America in Congress assembled*, That the joint resolution entitled ' Joint resolution in reference to the Free Zone along the northern frontier of Mexico and adjacent to the United States,' approved March first, eighteen hundred and ninety-five, be, and the same is hereby, repealed, and the full operation of section three thousand and five of the Revised Statutes as existing prior to the adoption of such joint resolution is hereby revived."

[2] "TREASURY DEPARTMENT, OFFICE OF THE SECRETARY,
"WASHINGTON, D. C., *January 26, 1898.*

"SIR : I have the honor to acknowledge the receipt of a letter, dated the 21st instant, from the clerk of your committee, with which was transmitted, for an expression of my views thereon, House joint resolution 27, providing for the repeal of the joint resolution in reference to the Free Zone.

"On the 2d of February last, in reply to a letter from you, inclosing, for an expression of the views of this Department thereon, House joint resolution 222, which is substantially the same as that under consideration, you were advised that there is abundant opportunity for the perpetration of frauds on the revenue by reason of the Free Zone of Mexico, and until the privileges pertaining to said Zone are abolished

answer to the Committee's inquiries, stating that on the 2d of February, 1897, he had given the views of the Department on the Joint Resolution introduced for the same purpose by Mr. Cobb on December 18, 1896, and he repeated his opinion that the only practical result of the Act of March 1, 1895, "had been the loss of business to American railway companies by reason of the diversion of the traffic to points in the Free Zone, by way of Mexican seaports." He also reiterated such views as he had expressed before, to the effect that he saw no objection to the passage of Mr. Cooper's Joint Resolution. Secretary Gage's letter, expressing the views of the Treasury Department officials, further stated "that there is abundant opportunity for the perpetration of frauds on the revenue by reason of the Free Zone of Mexico, and that until the privileges pertaining to the said Zone are abolished by the Mexican Government, the danger to the revenue will continue to exist."

Mr. James L. Slayden, another member of Congress from Texas, representing the 12th Congressional District, embracing San Antonio, introduced in the House of Representatives, on January 31, 1898,[1] during its 2d Session, a Joint Resolution, having in view the same object as Mr. Cooper's, namely, to repeal the Joint Resolution approved March 1, 1895, forbidding the transportation of goods in bond to the Free Zone in Mexico, and his resolution was also referred to the Committee on Ways and Means.

General Grosvenor, a member of the Committee, to whom both resolutions were referred, introduced in the House on February 16,

---

by the Mexican Government the danger to the revenue will continue to exist. The opinion was also expressed that the only practical result of the legislation which it is intended to repeal has been loss of business to American railway companies by reason of the diversion of the traffic to points in the Free Zone by way of Mexican seaports. The views then expressed are reiterated, and I see no objection to the passage of House resolution No. 27.

" Respectfully yours,
" L. J. GAGE, Secretary."

" HON. NELSON DINGLEY,
　" Chairman Committee on Ways and Means, House of Representatives."

[1] Fifty-fifth Congress, 2d Session, H. Res. 139. In the House of Representatives, January 31, 1898, Mr. Slayden introduced the following joint resolution ; which was referred to the Committee on Ways and Means and ordered to be printed :

" Joint Resolution. To repeal joint resolution numbered twenty, approved March first, eighteen hundred and ninety-five, forbidding the transportation of goods in bond to the Free Zone in Mexico.

" *Resolved by the Senate and House of Representatives of the United States of America in Congress assembled*, That joint resolution numbered twenty, approved March first, eighteen hundred and ninety-five, which authorized and directed the Secretary of the Treasury to suspend the operation of section three thousand and five of the Revised Statutes, having reference to the transportation of goods, wares, and merchandise in bond to the Free Zone in Mexico be, and the same is hereby, repealed."

1898,[1] on behalf of that Committee, a Resolution asking " the Secretary of the Treasury to inform the House whether frauds upon the customs of the United States have been, and are being, committed through the Free Zone of Mexico by reason of the existence of the same and the existing laws and regulations, and if so, that said Secretary report what, if any, change in law or regulations is necessary to protect the revenues of the United States from such frauds."

General Grosvenor's Resolution having been approved by the House after some explanations made by him, the Secretary of the Treasury answered the same, in a communication addressed on March 11, 1898,[2]

[1] Fifty-fifth Congress, 2d Session, House of Representatives. Resolution No. 226. In the House of Representatives. February 16, 1898.—Ordered to be printed. Mr. Grosvenor submitted the following resolution :

" *Resolved by the House of Represent~tives*, That the Secretary of the Treasury be, and he is, requested to inform the House whether frauds upon the customs of the United States have been, and are being, committed through the Free Zone of Mexico, or by reason of the existence of the same and the existing laws and regulations, and if so, that said Secretary report what, if any, change in law or regulations is necessary to protect the revenues of the United States from such frauds."

[2] Fifty-fifth Congress, 2d Session, House of Representatives. Document No. 342. Mexico Free Zone. Letter from the Secretary of the Treasury, transmitting a reply to the House resolution of the 16th ultimo in regard to frauds upon the customs through the Free Zone of Mexico. March 14, 1898.—Referred to the Committee on Ways and Means and ordered to be printed.

" Treasury Department, Office of the Secretary,
" Washington, D. C., *March 11, 1898.*

" Sir : I have the honor to acknowledge the receipt of copy of a resolution, dated the 16th ultimo, of the House of Representatives, wherein I am directed to inform the House whether frauds upon the customs of the United States have been and are being committed through the free zone of Mexico or by reason of the existence of the same, and the existing laws and regulations ; and, if so, that I report what, if any, changes in law or regulations are necessary to protect the revenues of the United States from such frauds.

" In reply I have to state that no doubt there is opportunity for the perpetration of frauds upon the revenue by reason of the continuance of the free zone of Mexico, and until the privileges pertaining to said zone are abolished by the Mexican Government the danger to our revenue will continue to exist. On March 1, 1895, a joint resolution authorizing the Secretary of the Treasury to suspend the operation of section 3005, Revised Statutes, in so far as the same permits goods, wares, and merchandise to be transported in bond through the United States into the free zone of Mexico so long as said zone exists, was approved, but the only apparent result of such resolution has been loss of business to American railway companies, by reason of the diversion of the traffic to places in the free zone by way of Mexican seaports. In March, 1888, an investigation was made with the view to ascertaining the value of merchandise which passed through the United States to Mexico during the preceding year. As a result of the inquiries it was found that the total value of foreign merchandise passing in transit was $497,654, and in addition to that amount merchandise of the value of

to the Speaker of the House of Representatives, in which he reiterated his views " that there is opportunity for the perpetration of frauds on the revenue of the United States by reason of the continuance of the Free Zone of Mexico, and that until the privileges pertaining to the said Zone are abolished by the Mexican Government the danger to our revenue will continue to exist."   I have to remark that the Secretary of the Treasury only said that dangers existed for the perpetration of frauds, and he did not aver that frauds were actually perpetrated, as was the ground taken by his predecessors.   Secretary Gage also reiterated in that report the views expressed in his former letter of January 26, 1898, that " the adoption of the Resolution of March 1, 1895, has caused a loss of business to American railway companies by reason of the diversion of the traffic to points in the Free Zone by way of Mexican seaports."   Secretary Gage referred also to the Report of Secretary Fairchild of March 1, 1898, which I have given in full in the foregoing paper, and stated that " the official records of the frontier ports, while showing the quantity and value of goods exported to Mexico, do not indicate the proportionate quantity or value of the merchandise sent to the Free Zone of Mexico," and concluded by saying that he was not prepared to suggest any changes in the existing law regulations which may be necessary to protect the revenues of the United States from the perpetration of frauds with the existence of the Free Zone of Mexico.

$194,774 was withdrawn from warehouse and exported to Mexico, making a total of $692,428, of which $211,589 was dutiable.

" Since the passage of the joint resolution above referred to, no merchandise is forwarded through the United States to places in the free zone under the regulations which were made pursuant to the provisions of section 3005 of the Revised Statutes, but goods destined for Mexico arriving at the seaports are allowed to be forwarded to ports on the Southwestern frontier after appraisement and entry at the port of first arrival.   Entry of such merchandise for exportation to Mexico is made at the port of exit.   The official records of said ports, while showing the quantity and value of goods exported to Mexico, do not indicate the proportionate quantity or value of the merchandise sent to the free zone of that country.   This information, if desired, may be obtained by special inquiries at the several ports on the Southwestern border.

" In reply to the request for a report as to any changes in existing law or regulations which may be necessary to protect the revenues of the United States from the perpetration of frauds through the existence of the free zone of Mexico, I have to state that officers of this department stationed on the border have from time to time been instructed to be specially vigilant in protecting the revenue against the unlawful introduction of goods from places in the free zone, and I am unable to indicate any measure which would afford additional protection to the revenues of the United States against the smuggling of merchandise from the free zone.   I am, however, of opinion that the joint resolution approved March 1, 1895, should be repealed.

" Respectfully yours,

" L. J. GAGE, Secretary."

THE SPEAKER OF THE HOUSE OF REPRESENTATIVES."

When I saw in the *Congressional Record* of February 16, 1898, Mr. Grosvenor's Resolution, I thought it proper to submit both to Mr. Grosvenor himself, and to the Secretary of the Treasury, the press proofs of my paper on the Free Zone, as it contained full and impartial statements on the subject, and in doing so I informed both of them that I was well aware that I had no right to interfere in the internal legislation of this country, and that therefore I did not ask for nor suggest anything at all, my object being merely to allow them the opportunity of reading a complete, and, in my opinion, impartial statement of the Free Zone question, so that they could understandingly make up their minds on the subject and arrive at a fair and just conclusion.

My paper does not seem to have made much impression upon Secretary Gage, if he really had an opportunity of reading it carefully, as, after it had been in his possession several days, he reiterates in his Report of March 11, 1898, the same views that he and his predecessors had before expressed upon the opportunity of committing frauds upon the revenue of the United States as allowed by the Mexican Free Zone.

The Committee on Ways and Means of the House did me the honor to ask my consent to insert in their Report my paper on the Free Zone, and as my object in writing and publishing it was to dispel misapprehensions existing here on that subject, which were in the way of a better understanding between the two countries, I was very glad that my paper should be published in an official document, as in that way it could be within the reach of Senators, Members of Congress, and other high officials of this Government, for whose benefit it was specially written.

The Committee on Ways and Means presented on March 11, 1898,[1]

---

[1] Fifty-fifth Congress, 2d Session, House of Representatives. Report No. 702. Mexican Free Zone.   March 11, 1898, referred to the House Calendar and ordered to be printed.   Mr. Grosvenor, from the Committee on Ways and Means, submitted the following report. [To accompany H. Res. 27.]

" The Committees on Ways and Means, to whom was referred the joint resolution (H. Res. 27) ' to repeal the joint resolution in reference to the Free Zone,' having had the same under consideration, beg leave to report :

" By section 3005 of the Revised Statutes, the right of ' free ' transportation in bond is accorded to adjoining countries through the United States and upon its railroads and other transportation systems, under regulations made by the Secretary of the Treasury.   This right extended to the Republic of Mexico.   The Republic of Mexico, in the exercise of its sovereignty, created a district of territory along its entire frontier bordering on the United States, about 13 miles wide, in which territory goods and merchandise were and are admitted free of duty.   It is called and known as the ' Free Zone ' or ' Zona Libre.'   This right of shipment was enjoyed until March 1 1895, when a joint resolution was passed authorizing and directing the Secre-

their Report on Mr. Cooper's Resolution, and that Report was accompanied by the Secretary of the Treasury's letter of January 26, 1898, to which I have already referred, and by my paper on the Free Zone as it appears in this book.

The House of Representatives repeals the Joint Resolution of March 1st, 1895.—On May 4, 1898, Mr. Grosvenor on behalf of the Committee on Ways and Means of the House of Representatives moved to consider Mr. Cooper's resolution. Messrs. Grosvenor, Dingley, and Slayden sustained the privileged character of the resolution, while the motion was opposed by three representatives from Texas, Messrs. Lanham, Bailey, and Stephens, who contended that the resolution was not privileged; but the Speaker having decided in favor of the Committee's

tary of the Treasury to suspend this right so far as the Free Zone was concerned, and in pursuance thereof the Secretary did suspend said right.

" The reason for the passage of that joint resolution (vol. 28, United States Statutes at Large, page 973, No. 23) was to prevent what was represented as a large 'smuggling' trade back into the United States from the 'free' goods admitted into this zone. Earnest protest was at the time made against the passage of the resolution, and for the facts bearing upon the matter reference is here made to *Congressional Record*, volume 27, part 4, page 2850 et. seq., Fifty-third Congress, third session. Since that time three years have elapsed, and the purpose for which the resolution was passed shows that it has failed. Mexico has not repealed the 'Free Zone,' and the United States has not been better protected. On the contrary, the only effect of the resolution has been to drive from our own transportation lines a large traffic into European and foreign lines—a very large and profitable business—without any return whatever. The goods that should and would be shipped in bond over our lines into the territory of Mexico are now shipped by vessels to Vera Cruz and other Mexican ports, in foreign bottoms, and over the Mexican railroads into the Free Zone, thus depriving our railroads of their legitimate business. These facts have been submitted to the Secretary of the Treasury and his opinion taken upon the adoption of the resolution now before the committee, and he sees no objection to such action. His letter, dated January 26, 1898, addressed to Hon. Nelson Dingley, Chairman Committee on Ways and Means, is attached hereto and made a part hereof.

" We therefore recommend the adoption of the joint resolution (No. 27) now before the Committee, and report the same back to the House with a recommendation that it do pass.

" The subject of the Free Zone, with its history and the variety of historical data connected therewith, is a very interesting subject ; and inasmuch as it affects the relations between this Government and the Republic of Mexico, and inasmuch as the whole subject-matter is one of great interest, the committee have seen fit to embody in this report a very able and comprehensive paper prepared by Señor Don Matias Romero, the distinguished representative of the Republic of Mexico at this capital. That gentleman has had ample opportunity to know whereof he writes in this behalf, having been a member of the Mexican Government and intimate with everything connected with the subject. Your committee take pleasure, therefore, with the consent of that distinguished gentleman, in here presenting his paper as a part of this report. It is taken from the proofs of a series of papers bearing on the relations between Mexico and the United States that the Mexican minister is now about to publish in book form.

contention, the resolution was taken up and passed in Committee of the Whole.   During the short discussion which took place previous to the passage of the resolution, the members from Texas representing the districts adjoining the Mexican frontier were in favor of the same, excepting Mr. Stephens, who contended that Mr. Cooper favored it because it only benefitted the railroads to the prejudice of the merchants on the frontier.   Messrs. Slayden and Kleberg, the two representing the districts in Texas bordering on the Rio Grande, excepting El Paso represented by Mr. Stephens, contended that the Joint Resolution of March 1, 1895, had injured the interests not only of the United States railways but of the local merchants on the border, and that they all were anxious for the repeal of such Joint Resolution.

Mr. Slayden considered the Mexican Free Zone as a real advantage to the United States and expressed a desire that it should be extended to a larger area, so as to increase its benefits,[1] and that is the first time that I have heard an American statesman express an opinion on that subject which agrees entirely with mine.   Mr. Lanham objected to the consideration of the resolution, but did say that he was not opposed to it although he finally so voted, and the only one who spoke against it was Mr. Stephens, who contended that his constituents objected to the resolution.

Mr. Stephens's only argument worthy of such a name was that, under the present conditions, the United States merchants on the frontier had the advantage of low freight rates, because there are several competing lines to the respective border towns, while the merchants on the Mexican side of the frontier, having only one line to each town, pay high rates over the Mexican roads for want of competition, and that it was not wise to give the Mexican merchants the advantage of low freight rates obtained by the United States merchants resulting from the present law.   But supposing that it would be a sound principal to regulate railway freight rates by the nationality of the shippers, Mr. Stephens did not take into consideration the fact that the haul from Tampico to El Paso, Mexico, which is the furthest town on the frontier from the Atlantic seaboard, is about one third of the distance of the haul from New York to El Paso, Texas, and that the Mexican railroads are interested in establishing their freights in such a way

---

[1] The following is an extract from Mr. Slayden's speech relating to this subject :

" MR. SPEAKER : So far from desiring the abolition of the Free Zone, I would, if I could, exercise any influence whatever upon the Mexican Government, ask it to extend that zone three, four, or five hundred miles farther back.   This territory adjacent to us has a duty of only $17\frac{1}{2}$ per cent. of the normal Mexican duty ; and on the other side it backs up against a part of Mexico which has a tremendously high duty, so that the extension of this Free Zone would certainly be a benefit to the trade of this country.   Therefore, I say that so far from asking the abolition of the Free Zone, I would vastly prefer to have it extended farther back into the interior."

as to encourage instead of destroying their business, which would be the result if exorbitantly high rates were collected.

Mr. Stephens brought my paper on the Free Zone into the discussion, saying that I criticized General Grant and Mr. Blaine on account of their views on the Free Zone, while I only stated their action on the subject without commenting on it at all. Mr. Grosvenor closed the discussion, making a very clear, concise, and conclusive speech; the vote resulted in the approval of the resolution by forty-eight votes against four. Mr. Grosvenor mentioned the fact that two different Secretaries of the Treasury had expressed their opinion in favor of the repeal of the resolution of March 1, 1895. He also recognized the right of the Mexican Government to establish the Free Zone, saying: "It is a matter that the United States Government cannot control. It is the prerogative of the sovereignty of the Mexican Republic. . . . This is a matter for her. It is not our revenue. It does not in that way affect our revenue, theoretically, at least." Although Mr. Grosvenor stated that he was himself against the Free Zone.

Mr. Stephens seemed to be under the impression that the Committee on Ways and Means had asked my opinion on the subject, and that I had written an argument for their benefit, and under that supposition he complained that his side had not been heard. Mr. Grosvenor disposed conclusively of that contention, stating what appears from my paper, namely, that it was written and published long before the Committee on Ways and Means of the Fifty-fifth Congress took up that matter, and is only a review of the whole question, stating the contention on both sides, for the benefit of those who desire reliable information on the subject.

It is a fact which cannot be denied that the Joint Resolution of March 1, 1895, was passed with the object of inducing Mexico to abolish the Free Zone, and as such object has not been obtained it is beyond all question that the purpose of that legislation has entirely failed and brought about only injury to the railways and merchants of the United States, a point which Mr. Grosvenor made very clear in his remarks.

Far from having any interest in the repeal of the Joint Resolution of March 1, 1895, Mexico would rather let it remain in force, as it constitutes a real benefit to the Mexican railways. I personally was pleased to see the tenor and result of the discussion in the House, because it showed me that the question was treated more intelligently than ever before, and because it showed a more friendly sentiment toward Mexico than on former occasions. Mr. Slayden qualified in his speech the Joint Resolution of March 1, 1896, as a "deliberate affront by a petty annoyance to the Republic of Mexico, which lies on yonder side of the Rio Grande."

The Joint Resolution as approved by the House of Representatives passed to the Senate and was referred to the Committee on Finance, but as the Senate has had very important matters to consider during the present session, especially those affecting the war with Spain, the House Resolution has not been taken up in the Senate up to the time that this paper goes to press. I would like to give here the outcome of this incident, that is, the final action of Congress on the pending Joint Resolution; but I am afraid that under the present political conditions of this country no conclusion will be reached for some time, and it would not be reasonable to delay indefinitely the printing of this volume in expectation of such action.

As this paper goes to press the fifty-fifth Congress of the United States has closed its second Session without the Senate having taken any action on the Joint Resolution approved by the House of Representatives to repeal the Joint Resolution of April 1, 1896.

LIST OF PRESIDENT'S MESSAGES ON MEXICO SENT TO CONGRESS
DURING THE PERIOD OF THE FRENCH INTERVENTION, FROM
1861 TO 1867, PREPARED BY MR. CLIFFORD WARREN, ASSISTANT
LIBRARIAN OF THE UNITED STATES SENATE.

1861.

Official instructions from Secretary of State William H. Seward to Hon. Thomas Corwin,
the United States Minister to Mexico, dated April 6, 1861 :

.   .   .   .

" Taking into view the actual condition and circumstances of Mexico, as well
as those of the United States, the President is fully satisfied that the safety, welfare, and happiness of the latter would be more effectually promoted if the former
should retain its complete integrity and independence, than they could be by any
dismemberment of Mexico, with a transfer or diminution of its sovereignty, even
though thereby a portion or the whole of the country or its sovereignty should be
transferred to the United States themselves.   .   .   .   Mexico really has, or ought
to have, no enemies.   The world is deeply interested in the development of her
agricultural, and especially her mineral and commercial, resources, while it holds
in high respect the simple virtues and heroism of her people, and, above all, their
inextinguishable love of civil liberty.

" The President, therefore, will use all proper influence to favor the restoration
of order and authority in Mexico.   .   .   .   If, on the other hand, it shall appear
in the sequel that the Mexican people are only now resting a brief season to recover their wasted energies sufficiently to lacerate themselves with new domestic
conflicts, then it is to be feared that not only the Government of the United States
but many other governments will find it impossible to prevent a resort to that
magnificent country of a class of persons, unhappily too numerous everywhere,
who are accustomed to suppose that visionary schemes of public interest, aggrandizement, or reform will justify even lawless invasion and aggression.

" For a few years past, the condition of Mexico has been so unsettled as to
raise the question on both sides of the Atlantic whether the time has not come
when some foreign power ought, in the general interest of society, to intervene to
establish a protectorate or some other form of government in that country and
guaranty its continuance there.   Such schemes may even now be held under consideration by some European nations.   .   .   .   You will not fail to assure the
Government of Mexico that the President neither has, nor can ever have, any
sympathy with such designs, in whatever quarter they may arise or whatever
character they may take on."   (Foreign Relations, 1861, pages 65–70, Senate
Executive Document No. 1, 37th Congress, 2d Session.   6 pages.)

713

President's Message to the House of Representatives, December 9, 1861, transmitting "a report from the Secretary of State, in reply to the resolution of the House of the 4th instant, relative to the intervention of certain European powers in the affairs of Mexico," saying that "it would be inexpedient at this juncture to make public the papers referred to." (37th Congress, 2d Session, House Executive Document No. 4. 1 page.)

1862.

President's Message to the Senate, January 24, 1862, communicating "a dispatch which has just been received from Mr. Corwin, our Minister to Mexico. It communicates important information concerning the war which is waged against Mexico by the combined powers of Spain, France, and Great Britain." (Senate Executive Journal, Vol. 12, page 102.)

President's Message to the Senate, January 28, 1862, submitting for ratification a treaty of extradition with the Mexican Government ; also submitting a postal convention with Mexico, and correspondence in relation thereto. (Senate Executive Journal, Vol. 12, page 102.)

President's Message to the Senate, February 27, 1862, informing the Senate that Lieutenant-General Scott had advised the President that, "while he (Gen. Scott) would cheerfully accept a commission as additional Minister to Mexico, with a view to promote the interests of the United States and of peace, yet his infirmities are such that he could not be able to reach the capital of that country by any existing mode of travel, and he therefore deems it his duty to decline the important mission I had proposed for him," etc. (Senate Executive Journal, Vol. 12, page 136.)

President's Message to the House of Representatives, April 14, 1862, enclosing papers on the present condition of Mexico. (37th Congress, 2d Session, House Executive Document No. 100. 434 pages.)

President's Message to the Senate, April 15, 1862, relating to the delay attending the approval by the Senate of the extradition treaty and the postal convention with Mexico, and recommending the passage of a resolution extending the time specified for the exchange of ratifications for sixty days from and after the 11th of June proximo, the date of the expiration of the period named for that purpose in both instruments. (Senate Executive Journal, Vol. 12, pages 237, 238.)

President's Message to the House of Representatives, May 23, 1862, transmitting a report from the Secretary of State, in answer to the resolution of the House of the 22d instant, calling for " copies of such correspondence as may have been received by this Government since that accompanied by the Message of April 14, 1862, relating to the condition of affairs in Mexico, and the breaking up of the treaty with the latter by the allied powers,"—the Secretary of State reporting " that it is not deemed expedient to comply with the request at the present time." (37th Congress, 2d Session, House Executive Document No. 120, Vol. 9. 1 page.)

President's Message to the Senate, June 23, 1862, relative to a project of a treaty between the United States and Mexico, submitted to the Senate, Dec. 7, 1861, as to which the Senate, on February 25, 1862, adopted a resolution to the effect " that it is not advisable to negotiate a treaty that will require the United States to assume any portion of the principal or interest of the debt of Mexico, or that will require the concurrence of European powers." Before the facts relative to the action of the Senate reached the United States Minister in Mexico, that official proceeded to negotiate further with Mexico. The President stated in his Message to the Senate (above cited) that " In view of the very important events occurring there, he has thought that the interests of the United States would be promoted by the conclusion of two treaties, which should provide for a loan to that Republic. He has, therefore, signed such treaties, and they having been duly ratified by the Government of Mexico he has transmitted them to me for my consideration. The action of the Senate is of course conclusive against an acceptance of the treaties on my part. I have nevertheless thought it just to our excellent minister in Mexico, and respectful to the Government of that Republic, to lay the treaties before the Senate, together with the correspondence which has occurred in relation to them. In performing this duty I have only to add that the importance of the subject thus submitted to the Senate cannot be overestimated, and I shall cheerfully receive and consider with the highest respect any further advice the Senate may think proper to give upon the subject." (Senate Executive Journal, Vol. 12, page 370.)

President's Message to the House of Representatives, July 12, 1862, transmitting a report of the Secretary of State upon the subject of the House resolution of the 9th ultimo, requesting " whatever information he (the President) possesses concerning the relations existing between this country and foreign powers," the Secretary of State reporting that, although considerable progress had been made in preparing an answer to the resolution, the correspondence upon the subject was so voluminous, and the indispensable current of business of the Department of State was so pressing in proportion to its force, that it was impracticable to comply with the resolution at that session of Congress. (37th Congress, 2d Session, House Executive Document No. 148, Vol. 10. 1 page.)

President Lincoln, in his Annual Message to Congress, December 1, 1862, stated that there had " not only been no change of our previous relations with the independent states of our continent, but more friendly sentiments than have heretofore existed, are believed to be entertained by these neighbors, whose safety and progress are so intimately connected with our own. This statement especially applies to Mexico, Nicaragua, Costa Rica, Honduras, Peru, and Chili."

Near the opening of this Message, President Lincoln stated that " The correspondence touching foreign affairs which has taken place during the last year is herewith submitted, in virtual compliance with a request to that effect, made by the House of Representatives near the close of the last session of Congress."

The correspondence relating to the state of affairs in Mexico, the negotiations between Mexico and the allied powers, the prospects of the French in Mexico, the proposed treaties between Mexico and the United States for a loan to Mexico, etc., covers 45 pages (pages 729-774) in same volume with the President's Message. (37th Congress, 3d Session, House Executive Document No. 1, Vol. 1, Diplomatic Correspondence, 1862.)

1863.

President's Message to the House of Representatives of January 5, 1863, in relation to the alleged interference of the United States Minister to Mexico in favor of the French. (37th Congress, 3d Session, House Executive Document No. 23. 27 pages.)

President's Message to the Senate, January 20, 1863, enclosing correspondence between the United States Government and Mexican Minister in relation to the exportation of articles contraband of war for the use of the French army in Mexico. (37th Congress, 3d Session, Senate Executive Document No. 24. 17 pages.)

President's Message to the House of Representatives, February 4, 1863, enclosing report of Secretary of State and accompanying papers on present condition of Mexico. (37th Congress, 3d Session, House Executive Document No. 54. 802 pages.)

President's Message to the Senate, February 13, 1863, transmitting a report from the Secretary of State in answer to the resolution of the Senate of the 12th instant, requesting the President to communicate to that body "any information he may have relative to the use of negroes by the French army in Mexico." (37th Congress, 3d Session, Senate Executive Document No. 40. 3 pages.)

President's Annual Message, December 8, 1863, and accompanying documents, embracing the Diplomatic Correspondence for the years 1862–63, relating to Mexican affairs, French invasion of Mexico, battles, etc. (38th Congress, 1st Session, House Ex. Doc. No. 1, Vol. 2, pages 1229 to 1256. 27 pages.)

Mexico...........................Pages 1229 to 1256.
France.......................... " 707 to 838.
        " .... " 1320 to 1329.
Netherlands...................... " 877 to 903.
Spain........................... " 985.
Austria......................... " 997 to 1016.

1864.

President's Message, March 24, 1864, in reply to the resolution of the Senate of the 15th instant, in relation to the establishment of monarchical governments in Central and South America, and transmitting a report from the Secretary of State, to whom the subject was referred. (38th Congress, 1st Session, Senate Ex. Doc. No. 30. 1 page.)

President's Message, May 24, 1864, in answer to a resolution of the House of Representatives of the day preceding, on the subject of a joint resolution of the 4th of the previous month, relative to Mexico, transmitting a report from the Secretary of State, to whom the resolution was referred.

The resolution of the House of Representatives requested the President to communicate to that body, "if not inconsistent with the public interest, any explanations given by the Government of the United States to the Government of France respecting the sense and bearing of the joint resolution relating to Mexico, which passed the House of Representatives, unanimously, on the 4th of April, 1864." The Secretary of State laid before the President "a copy of all the correspondence on file, or on record in this Department, on the subject of the joint resolution referred to," which joint resolution declared the opposition of that body to a recognition of a monarchy in Mexico. (38th Congress, 1st Session, House Ex. Doc. No. 92. 4 pages.)

President's Special Message to the Senate, May 28, 1864, in reply to a Senate resolution of the 25th instant, relating to Mexican affairs, transmitting a partial report from the Secretary of State, with accompanying papers, in response to the request of the Senate for all correspondence between the Secretary of State and the Mexican Minister in relation to the course of trade between France and the United States while France and Mexico were at war with each other, in articles supposed to be in derogation of the rights of neutrals ; also, other information "relative to the present condition of affairs in the Republic of Mexico, and especially upon the attempt of any European powers to overthrow republican institutions on this continent with a view of establishing monarchical forms of government in their stead."

Also, copies of correspondence which had taken place with the Minister of Mexico, in relation to articles of trade, since that communicated to the Senate with the Message of the President of 20th January, 1863 (printed as Senate Ex. Doc. No. 24, 37th Congress, 3d Session).   (38th Congress, 1st Session, Senate Ex. Doc. No. 47.   6 pages.)

President's Message to the Senate, June 16, 1864, transmitting a further report from the Secretary of State, in answer to the resolution of the Senate of the 25th ultimo, relative to Mexican affairs, with the papers therein referred to.   (38th Congress, 1st Session, Senate Ex. Doc. No. 11.   496 pages.)

President Lincoln's fourth Annual Message, December 6, 1864, stated that "Mexico continues to be a theatre of civil war.   While our political relations with that country have undergone no change, we have at the same time strictly maintained neutrality between the belligerents." (Foreign Relations, 1864, page 1.   38th Congress, 2d Session, House Ex. Doc. No. 1, Vol. 1.)

      Vol. 1, see page 399 (1 to 399).
      Vol. 2, pages   1 to 253, France.
      Vol. 2,   "   304 to 331, Netherlands, see page 314.
      Vol. 4,   "   1 to 106, Spain.
      Vol. 4,   "   107 to 190, Austria.
      Vol. 4,   "   191 to 224, Prussia, see page 212.
      Vol. 4,   "   226 to 265, Belgium.
      Vol. 4,   "   267 to 324, Portugal, see page 273.
      Vol. 4,   "   338 to 345, Denmark, see page 344.
      Vol. 4,   "   346 to 363, Sweden and Norway.
      Vol. 4,   "   386 to 401, Switzerland.

1865.

President's Message, February 4, 1865, in compliance with the resolution of the Senate of the 13th ultimo, requesting information upon the present condition of Mexico and the case of the French war transport steamer Rhine, transmitting a report from the Secretary of State and the papers by which it was accompanied.   The French war transport steamer Rhine, it was alleged, "took articles contraband of war from San Francisco to the French forces at Acapulco, in the Mexican Republic." (38th Congress, 2d Session, Senate Ex. Doc. No. 33.   14 pages.)

President Johnson submitted to Congress, with his first Annual Message, December 4, 1865, the Diplomatic Correspondence of the past year, including that relating to Mexican affairs, namely :

    Mexico...................... Vol. 3, pages 356 to 849.
    Mexico...................... Vol. 4,   "   480 to 482.
    Great Britain............... Vol. 1,   "   1 to 670.
    Great Britain............... Vol. 2,   "   1 to 196.
    France...................... Vol. 2,   "   197 to 362.
    Austria..................... Vol. 3,   "   1 to 39.
    Belgium..................... Vol. 3,   "   70 to 89.
    Italy....................... Vol. 3,   "   139 to 149.
    Rome........................ Vol. 3,   "   150 to 164.
    Egypt....................... Vol. 3,   "   313 to 338.
    Sweden and Norway........... Vol. 3,   "   184 to 206.

(39th Congress, 1st Session, House Ex. Doc. No. 1, Vols. 1, 2, and 3.)
Appendix, Vol. 4 : "Expressions of condolence and sympathy inspired by

the assassination of Abraham Lincoln, late President of the United States of America, and the attempted assassination of William H. Seward, Secretary of State, and Frederick W. Seward, Assistant Secretary of State, on the evening of the 14th of April, 1865."

President's Message to the Senate, December 13, 1865, containing information of a decree of the so-called Emperor of Mexico. (39th Congress, 1st Session, Senate Ex. Doc. No. 5. 20 pages.)

President's Message to the House of Representatives, December 14, 1865, bearing on the so-called decree re-establishing slavery or peonage in Mexico. (39th Congress, 1st Session, House Ex. Doc. No. 13. 14 pages.)

President's Message to the Senate, December 21, 1865, containing information respecting the occupation by French troops of the Republic of Mexico, and the establishment of a monarchy there. (39th Congress, 1st Session, Senate Ex. Doc. No. 6. 100 pages.)

1866.

President's Message to the Senate, January 5, 1866, containing information of plans to induce the dissatisfied citizens of the United States to emigrate into Mexico. (39th Congress, 1st Session, Senate Ex. Doc. No. 8. 44 pages.)

President's Message to the House of Representatives, January 5, 1866, on the steps taken by the so-called Emperor of Mexico to obtain a recognition. (39th Congress, 1st Session, House Ex. Doc. No. 20. 12 pages.)

President's Message to the House of Representatives, January 10, 1866, on the alleged kidnapping in Mexico of the child (Iturbide) of an American lady. (39th Congress, 1st Session, House Ex. Doc. No. 21. 1 page.)

President's Message to the Senate, January 26, 1866, containing information regarding the present condition of affairs on the southwestern frontier of the United States, and any violation of neutrality on the part of the army on the right bank of the Rio Grande. (39th Congress, 1st Session, Senate Ex. Doc. No. 16. 1 page.)

President's Message to the Senate, January 26, 1866, enclosing the report of the Secretary of State regarding the transit of United States troops, in 1861, through Mexican territory. (39th Congress, 1st Session, Senate Ex. Doc. No. 17. 8 pages.)

President's Message to the House of Representatives, January 26, 1866, in regard to any demonstration in honor of President Juarez of Mexico. (39th Congress, 1st Session, House Ex. Doc. No. 31. 20 pages.)

President's Message to the House of Representatives, February 1, 1866, on the "Imperial Mexican Express Company." (39th Congress, 1st Session, House Ex. Doc. No. 38. 17 pages.)

President's Message to the House of Representatives, March 6, 1866, in regard to the term of office of President Juarez of Mexico. (39th Congress, 1st Session, House Ex. Doc. No. 64. 1 page.)

President's Message to the House of Representatives, March 20, 1866, enclosing information upon the present condition of affairs in Mexico. (39th Congress, 1st Session, House Ex. Doc. No. 73, in two volumes : Part 1, 706 pages ; Part 2, 613 pages.)

President's Message to the Senate, April 20, 1866, transmitting, in compliance with a Senate resolution of the 8th instant, a communication from the Secretary of War, of the 19th instant, covering copies of the correspondence respecting General Orders No. 17, issued by the commander of the Department of California, and, also, the Attorney-General's opinion "as to the question whether the order involves a breach of neutrality towards Mexico." General Orders No. 17 instructed commanders on the southern frontiers within the Department of California "to take the necessary measures to preserve the neutrality of the United States with respect to the parties engaged in the existing war in Mexico, and to suffer no armed parties to pass the frontier from the United States, nor suffer any arms or munitions of war to be sent over the frontier to either belligerent," etc. (39th Congress, 1st Session, Senate Ex. Doc. No. 40. 10 pages.)

President's Message to the House of Representatives, April 23, 1866, on the evacuation of Mexico by the French. (39th Congress, 1st Session, House Ex. Doc. No. 93. 47 pages.)

President's Message to the House of Representatives, May 10, 1866, on discriminations against American commerce by the so-called Maximilian Government. (39th Congress, 1st Session, House Ex. Doc. No. 110. 2 pages.)

President's Message to the Senate, June 15, 1866, regarding the departure of troops from Austria for Mexico. (39th Congress, 1st Session, Senate Ex. Doc. No. 54. 21 pages.)

President's Message to the House of Representatives, June 18, 1866, regarding the dispatch of military forces from Austria for service in Mexico. (39th Congress, 1st Session, House Ex. Doc. No. 130. 1 page.)

President's Message to Congress, June 22, 1866, regarding employment of European troops in Mexico. (39th Congress, 1st Session, House Ex. Doc. No. 137. 2 pages.)

President's Proclamation, August 17, 1866, reciting the existence of war in the Republic of Mexico, "aggravated by foreign military intervention"; that the United States, in accordance with their settled habits and policy, are a neutral power in regard to the war which thus afflicts the Republic of Mexico; that one of the belligerents in the said war, namely, the Prince Maximilian, who asserts himself to be Emperor in Mexico, has issued a decree in regard to the port of Matamoras and other ports which are in the occupation and possession of another of the said belligerents, namely, the United States of Mexico; that "the decree thus recited, by declaring a belligerent blockade unsupported by competent military or naval force, is in violation of the neutral rights of the United States as defined by the law of nations, as well as to the treaties existing between the United States of America and the aforesaid United States of Mexico." Therefore, the President of the United States proclaimed and declared "that the aforesaid decree is held and will be held by the United States to be absolutely null and void as against the Government and citizens of the United States, and that any attempt which shall be made to enforce the same against the Government or the citizens of the United States will be disallowed." ("Messages and Papers of the Presidents," Vol. vi., pages 433, 434.)

President's Executive Order, October 26, 1866, to Hon. Edwin M. Stanton, Secretary of War, saying: "Recent advices indicate an early evacuation of Mexico by the French expeditionary forces and that the time has arrived when our Minister to Mexico should place himself in communication with that Republic. In furtherance of the objects of his mission and as evidence of the earnest desire felt by the United States for the proper adjustment of the questions involved, I deem it of great importance that General Grant should by his presence and advice co-operate with our Minister.

"I have therefore to ask that you will request General Grant to proceed to some point on our Mexican frontier most suitable and convenient for communication with our Minister, or (if General Grant deems it best) to accompany him to his destination in Mexico, and to give him the aid of his advice in carrying out the instructions of the Secretary of State, a copy of which is herewith sent for the General's information. General Grant will make report to the Secretary of War of such matters as, in his discretion, ought to be communicated to the Department." (" Messages and Papers of the Presidents," Vol. vi., page 443.)

President's Executive Order, October 30, 1866, addressed to Hon. Edwin M. Stanton, Secretary of War, saying : "General Ulysses S. Grant having found it inconvenient to assume the duties specified in my letter to you of the 26th instant, you will please relieve him from the same and assign them in all respects to William T. Sherman, Lieutenant-General of the army of the United States. By way of guiding General Sherman in the performance of his duties, you will furnish him with a copy of your special orders to General Grant, made in compliance with my letter of the 26th instant, together with a copy of the instructions of the Secretary of State to Lewis D. Campbell, Esq., therein mentioned. The Lieutenant-General will proceed to the execution of his duties without delay." (" Messages and Papers of the Presidents," Vol. vi., pages 443, 444.)

President's Annual Message, December 3, 1866, informed Congress that—"In the month of April last, as Congress is aware, a friendly arrangement was made between the Emperor of France and the President of the United States for the withdrawal from Mexico of the French expeditionary military forces. This withdrawal was to be effected in three detachments, the first of which, it was understood, would leave Mexico in November, now past, the second in March next, and the third and last in November, 1867. Immediately upon the completion of the evacuation, the French Government was to assume the same attitude of non-intervention in regard to Mexico as is held by the Government of the United States. Repeated assurances have been given by the Emperor since that agreement that he would complete the promised evacuation within the period mentioned, or sooner.

"It was reasonably expected that the proceedings thus contemplated would produce a crisis of great political interest in the Republic of Mexico. The newly appointed Minister of the United States, Mr. Campbell, was therefore sent forward on the 9th day of November last, to assume his proper functions as Minister Plenipotentiary of the United States to that Republic. It was also thought expedient that he should be attended in the vicinity of Mexico by the Lieutenant-General of the Army of the United States, with the view of obtaining such information as might be important to determine the course to be pursued by the United States in re-establishing and maintaining necessary and proper intercourse with the Republic of Mexico. Deeply interested in the cause of liberty and humanity, it seemed an obvious duty on our part to exercise whatever influence we possessed for the restoration and permanent establishment in that country of a domestic and republican form of government.

"Such was the condition of our affairs in regard to Mexico when, on the 22d of November last, official information was received from Paris that the Emperor of France had some time before decided not to withdraw a detachment of his forces in the month of November past, according to engagement, but that his decision was made with the purpose of withdrawing the whole of those forces in the ensuing spring. Of this determination, however, the United States had not received any notice or intimation ; and, so soon as the information was received by the government, care was taken to make known its dissent to the Emperor of France.

"I cannot forego the hope that France will reconsider the subject, and adopt some resolution in regard to the evacuation of Mexico which will conform as nearly as practicable with the existing engagement, and thus meet the just expectations of the United States.

"The papers relating to the subject will be laid before you.

"It is believed that, with the evacuation of Mexico by the expeditionary forces, no subject for serious differences between France and the United States would remain. The expressions of the Emperor and people of France warrant a hope that the traditionary friendship between the two countries might in that case be renewed and permanently restored.

"A claim of a citizen of the United States for indemnity for spoliations committed on the high seas by the French authorities, in the exercise of a belligerent power against Mexico, has been met by the Government of France with a proposition to defer settlement until a mutual convention for the adjustment of all claims of citizens of both countries, arising out of the recent wars on this continent, shall be agreed upon by the two countries. The suggestion is not deemed unreasonable, but it belongs to Congress to direct the manner in which claims for indemnity by foreigners, as well as by citizens of the United States, arising out of the late civil war, shall be adjudicated and determined. I have no doubt that the subject of all such claims will engage your attention at a convenient and proper time." (39th Congress, 2d Session, House Executive Document No. 1, Part 1, pages 11, 12.)

(Diplomatic Correspondence relating to Mexican affairs, 1865–66, is contained in House Ex. Doc. No. 1, Parts 1, 2, and 3, 39th Congress, 2d Session.)

President's Special Message, December 8, 1866, in reply to resolution of the House of Representatives of the 5th instant, inquiring if any portion of Mexican territory had been occupied by United States troops, transmitting the accompanying report upon the subject from the Secretary of War. (39th Congress, 2d Session, House Executive Document No 8.   4 pages.)

President's Special Message, December 20, 1866, in reply to resolution of the House of Representatives of the 4th instant, supplying information "relating to the attempt of Santa Anna and Ortega to organize armed expeditions within the United States for the purpose of overthrowing the National Government of the Republic of Mexico." (39th Congress, 2d Session, House Executive Document No. 17. 179 pages.)

1867.

President's Special Message to the House of Representatives, January 14, 1867, in reply to House resolutions of the 19th ultimo, supplying information regarding the occupation of Mexican territory by the troops of the United States. (39th Congress, 2d Session, House Executive Document No. 37.   6 pages.)

President's Message to the House of Representatives, January 29th, 1867, transmitting, in compliance with House resolutions of 4th of December and 18th of December, 1866, information "upon the present condition of affairs in the Republic of Mexico," and "copies of all correspondence on the subject of the evacuation of Mexico by the French troops, not before officially published." (39th Congress, 2d Session, House Executive Document No. 76.   735 pages.)

President's Special Message to the Senate, February 11, 1867, in answer to Senate resolution of the 6th instant, requesting " copies of all correspondence not heretofore communicated on the subject of grants to American citizens for railroad and telegraph lines across the territory of the Republic of Mexico." (39th Congress, 2d Session, Senate Executive Document No. 25. 30 pages.)

President's Message to the House of Representatives, March 20, 1867, relative to the withdrawal of French troops from Mexico. (40th Congress, 1st Session, House Executive Document No. 11. 2 pages.)

President's Special Message to the Senate, April 12, 1867, in answer to Senate resolution of the 10th instant, calling for "information relative to prisoners of war taken by belligerents in the Republic of Mexico." (40th Congress, Special Session of Senate, Senate Executive Document No. 5. 4 pages.)

President's Special Message to the House of Representatives, July 10, 1867, "in compliance with so much of the resolution of the House of Representatives of the 8th instant as requests information in regard to certain agreements said to have been entered into between the United States, European, and West Virginia Land and Mining Company and certain reputed agents of the Republic of Mexico." (40th Congress, 1st Session, House Executive Document No. 23. 250 pages.)

President's Special Message, July 11, 1867, in reply to resolution of the House of Representatives of the 3d instant, requesting " all the official correspondence between the Department of State and the Hon. Lewis D. Campbell, late Minister to Mexico, and also with his successor," communicates a report from the Secretary of State and the papers accompanying it. (40th Congress, 1st Session, House Executive Document No. 30. 76 pages.)

President's Special Message, July 12, 1867, in compliance with resolution of the Senate of the 8th instant (to same effect and purpose as House resolution of the 3d instant). Informs the Senate that " the correspondence called for by the Senate has already been communicated to the House of Representatives." (40th Congress, 1st Session, Senate Executive Document No. 15. 1 page.)

President's Special Message, July 18, 1867, in compliance with Senate resolution of 8th instant requesting " copies of any correspondence on the files of the Department of State relating to any recent event in Mexico." (40th Congress, 1st Session, Senate Executive Document No. 20. 298 pages.)

(This document includes 12 pages " Index to papers relating to Mexican Affairs, in 1867,—Capture, trial, and execution of Maximilian.")

President's Message, July 18, 1867, in compliance with that part of House resolution of 8th instant which requested " any official correspondence or other information relating to the capture and execution of Maximilian and the arrest and reported execution of Santa Anna in Mexico," transmits a report from the Secretary of State, from which it appears that the correspondence called for by the House resolution had been already communicated to the Senate. (40th Congress, 1st Session, House Executive Document No. 31. 1 page.)

President's Annual Message, December 3, 1867, informed Congress that " The Republic of Mexico, having been relieved from foreign intervention, is earnestly engaged in efforts to re-establish her constitutional system of government." (40th Congress, 2d Session, House Executive Document No. 1, Part 1, page 19.)

(Diplomatic Correspondence, 1866–67, relating to affairs in Mexico, etc., in Vols. i. and ii., House Executive Document No. 1, 40th Congress, 2d Session. Mexico, Vol. ii., pages 334–685.)

President's Special Message, December 5, 1867, in compliance with House resolution of July 17th last, requesting " all information received at the several departments of the Government touching the organization within or near the territory of the United States of armed bodies of men for the purpose of avenging the death of Archduke Maximilian or of intervening in Mexican affairs, and what measures have been taken to prevent the organization or departure of such organized bodies for the purpose of carrying out such objects," transmits a report from the Secretary of State, and the papers accompanying it. (40th Congress, 2d Session, House Executive Document No. 25, 6 pages.)

1868.

President's Annual Message, December 9, 1868, informed Congress that "Our relations with Mexico during the year have been marked by an increasing growth of mutual confidence." (40th Congress, 3d Session, House Executive Document No. 1, Part 1, page 13.)

(Diplomatic Correspondence, 1867–68, relating to affairs in Mexico, Vol. ii., pages 378–640.)

INDEX TO GEOGRAPHICAL AND
STATISTICAL NOTES.

Index.

HISTORICAL NOTES ON MEXICO.

A

Abascal, General, Viceroy of Peru, 305
Abasolo, Captain, who joined Hidalgo, his plan of military operations to free Mexico, 343
Absolutist Party, Peruvian officers enlisted in, 305
Aculco, Hidalgo attacked and defeated at, by the Spanish army under Calleja, November 7, 1810, 343
Adams, John, Ex-President, published revolutionary manifesto signed in Paris on December 22, 1797, to explain his conduct, 290 ; letter referred to in which he explains his conduct toward Mexico, 292
Adams, John Quincy, Ex-President, Report of, as Secretary of State, on sympathy of United States for Mexico in movement for independence, 318 ; letter to, of November 5, 1818, from Mr. Gallatin, United States Minister at Paris, showing sympathy United States felt for Mexico in cause of independence, 319 ; report of, published in President's Message, showing why United States delayed recognition, wrong motives attributed to M. Romero in regard to remarks about, 327, 328 ; an anti-slavery man, 329 ; his views regarding the Panama Congress, 333
Aguirre, Manuel H. de, agent from La Plata and Chili to United States, asking recognition of Province of Buenos Ayres, 323
Aldama, Captain, who joined Hidalgo, 342 ; proposed plan of military operations to free Mexico, 343
Alexander, compared with San Martin, 306, 307
Allende, Captain, who joined Hidalgo, 342 ; proposed plan of military operations to free Mexico, 343
Alliance, Holy, its purposes regarding the American colonies of Spain, 331
Alvarez, Juan, leader of Liberal Party in Mexico, 359
American Social Science Association,

meeting of, at Saratoga in 1895, Mr. Walter S. Logan's remarks regarding Mexico at, 281 ; M. Romero's speech at meeting of, 281 ; article on Mexico enlarging speech at, 282
Anaya, Pedro Maria, President, *ad interim*, of Mexico, 357, 358
Aranda, Count de, his plan for the independence of the Spanish colonies in America, 287 ; Liberal Cabinet wanted to carry out plan of, 308 ; had Charles III. accepted plan of, Mexico would have accomplished independence sooner, 309
Arista, Mariano, President of Mexico in 1851, resigned 1853, 359
Army of the Andes, organized and disciplined by San Martin at Mendoza, 298.
Ayacucho, Upper Peru, battle of, fought on December 9, 1824, between General Sucre, commanding patriot army, and Viceroy La Serna, on the Spanish side and destroyed Spanish power in South America, 306

B

Banquet at New York, March 29, 1864, M. Romero's speech about the conditions in Mexico and the French Intervention, 383–387
Banquet at New York, October 2, 1867, M. Romero's speech at, on the success of Mexico over Maximilian and French Intervention, 387–392
Banquet at New York, December 16, 1891, tendered by Walter S. Logan to M. Romero, 392 ; M. Romero's speech on future of Mexico and United States, 393–395
Banquet at Boston, January 7, 1892, address of M. Romero on the prosperity of Mexico and the share that Boston has in the same, 397–399
Barradas, General, commander of Spanish expedition to Tampico, 309 ; sent from Havana to reconquer Mexico, 352

731

San Martin—*Continued.*
General-in-Chief of Chilian-Argentine army, helped to provide Chili with a navy, 299; invaded Peru, 308; conquered Lima 301; Protector of Peru, 325; armistice at Miraflores, 301; disagreement with Bolivar, 303; resigned and ostracised himself, 306; his generalship, 301; his relations with Lord Cochrane, favored a monarchial constitutional form of government, 302; compared with Alexander, 306, 307; death, 306

Santa Anna, Antonio Lopez de, disposition of, fought with Spain against independent cause to 1821, when he joined independent leaders, 323; headed rebellion against Iturbide, 348; headed several military rebellions, 352; President five times, military career, and competence, 353; easily discouraged, became antagonistic to Farias, favored revolution and abolished Federal Constitution and was proclaimed as Dictator in 1834, convoked new Congress on July 4, 1835, 354; appointed President on October 10, 1841, 355; elected Constitutional President in 1844, 356; appointed President in 1846, marched against General Taylor, returned to the City of Mexico and assumed government, marched against General Scott and fought the United States army in the Valley of Mexico, 357; fled from country in 1847, 358; President in 1853, sold Mesilla Valley to the United States, left Mexico in 1855, 359

Santa Cruz, General, head of Peruvian army, 305

Scott, Alexander, agent sent by the United States in 1812 to Venezuela, 324

Scott, Winfield, his battles at Cerro Gordo and Valley of Mexico, 353

Seward, William H., his estimate of Juarez's character, 361

Slavery, fear by the United States that it might be abolished in Cuba if independent, 329; Cuba in regard to, 327–329; abolished in Mexico, 344, 345

Smith, W. S., Jr., a grandson of Ex-President John Adams accompanied General Miranda in his expedition against Venezuela, his father tried and acquitted for violation of neutrality laws, 293

Solorzano, his *Politica Indiana*, 288

Spanish Cortes, issued Liberal Constitution of 1812, 308; re-issued decree of 1820, 309

Spanish rule, length in American colonies of, 339; good done in Mexico by, 341

Sucre, José Antonio, of Venezuela, a great soldier, 296; asked co-operation of San Martin to march against Quito, 304;

commanded at battle of Ayacucho, 306; death, 307

Sucre, José del Poso y, a Jesuit, 292; delegate to Junta of October 8, 1797, 290; commissioned to report to Junta the result of mission to Paris, 292

T

Taylor, Zachariah, fought battle at Angostura, 353

Teran, General Manuel de Mier y, sent by Mexican Government against Barradas, 352

Tilden, Samuel J., invited to invest in Mexico, sent Mr. John Bigelow to study the field, 398

Torres, of Colombia, leader in War of Independence, 313

Torre Tagle, Governor of Lima, 301

Treaties, of Paris, recognizing the independence of the United States, by England in 1783, 286; of Bayonne, 301; of Cordova, 347; of Madrid, recognizing the independence of Mexico, 352

Trimble, Representative, resolution introduced, 1822, recognizing the independence of the Spanish colonies in America, 322

Tristan, general in San Martin's army, defeated at Ica, in Peru, 302

Tucuman, battle at, contributed very materially to establish independence of Argentine Republic, 297

U

Unanue, of Peru, leader in War of Independence, 313; *Observations of the Climate of Lima and Its Influences* cited, 297

United Provinces of Central America, Mexico recognized its independence, 307

United States, attitude of, towards Mexico, 316–318; Senator Money on attitude of United States towards Mexico, 316, 317; sympathy towards Mexico of, 319, 320; recognized belligerency of revolted colonies, 320, 321; commissioners sent to by revolted colonies, 322, 323; neutrality observed by, 323, 324; commissioners sent by the, to the revolted Spanish colonies, 324; policy of, toward Cuba, 328; slavery in, 345

Uraga, General José Lopez, sent against Blancarte in Mexico, but joined insurgents, 359

Urrea, General, pronounced at Tampico against the Central Government of Mexico on July 15, 1840, 355

V

Valdez, General, Peruvian Bayard, favored absolute monarchy, 305

THE ANGLO-SAXON AND ROMAN SYSTEMS OF CRIMINAL JURISPRUDENCE.

A

Advantages of jury system, in small towns is of educational character, 409

Americans in Mexico, often expect to be tried by laws similar to those of the United States, 414

Amparo, writ of, an extension of the *habeas corpus* under the common law, 416

Anglo-Saxon and Roman Systems of Criminal Jurisprudence paper, why written, 403 ; submitted to various distinguished lawyers before publishing, editors in New York not in accord with M. Romero's views in regard to, first published in *North American Review* for July, 1896, and in *Green Bag* for October, same year, 403

Appeal, right of, definition of, 414, 415 ; provisions of under Mexican law, provisions in Federal District of Mexico, exceptions to in Common Law, 415

B

Bacon, Lord, represented the Roman law in equity controversy, 421 ; his controversy with Sir Edward Coke, 422

Ball, T. W., read paper before Bar Association of Galveston, Texas, 1896, against present criminal jurisprudence under common law, 408

Blackstone, cannot be said that English common-law system as expounded by, is used in United States, 422

Butler, Rosa, extract from statement of almshouses and hospitals in New York, 419

C

" Careo," corresponds to cross-examination under common law trials, 413

Carter, James C., written several pamphlets on precedence in law, 426

Coffin, E. G., his *The Prison Congress, and Our Trip Through Mexico and Texas*, 418

Coke, Sir Edward, represented common law in equity controversy, 421 ; great commentator, 422

Comparison between Anglo-Saxon and Roman Criminal Jurisprudence, cannot be compared, Roman entitled to regard, 404 ; which system is best calculated to do justice, principles of each, 405

Conclusion of Criminal Jurisprudence paper, 424

Constitution of Mexico, Article I. of, similar to Declaration of Independence of the United States, 417 ; Article XIX. of, provisions of, comparison between and law in New York, 416 ; Article XX. of, assertions that Americans tried in Mexico are not notified of cause of their arrest contradicted by, 416, provisions of, 416, 417 ; Article XXIX. of, what to obviate, 417, provisions of, 418

Coudert, Frederick R., extract from on imperfections of criminal trials under common-law system as compared with Roman system prevailing in Continental Europe, 407

Criminal law in England and United States, how English used to regard criminals, crimes less frequent now in England than in United States, appeals in England and United States, 406

D

Difference between law in this country and Roman law, *sumario* criticised, 413

Disadvantages of common law, literal application of, result of, instance to explain, 423

E

Ellesmere, Lord, represented the equity of Roman law in controversy between common law and equity, 421

English common law, law of usage and custom, marriage law prevailing in New York and advantages and disadvantages

740

THE MEXICAN FREE ZONE.

A

Abolition of Free Zone, agitated in 1872, but impossible on account of frontier influences, regulations issued, 440 ; asked for by citizens of Brownsville, Texas, 456; opposition from the United States made it difficult for Mexico to accomplish, 476, 477

Advantages to United States of Free Zone, relaxation of restrictions of custom and excise duties, 448 ; free market for products and manufactures of United States, 449 ; nearly all goods manufactured in United States purchased in Free Zone, 450

B

Bailey, Joseph W., Member of Congress from Texas, contended that Mr. Cooper's resolution on the Free Zone was not privileged, 709

Bayard, Thomas F., Secretary of State, letter from M. Romero to, of February 10, 1888, on Mexican Free Zone, 485, 486 ; his letter of March 16, 1888, to the President, transmitting all correspondence of State Department on Mexican Free Zone, 480, 481

Belden, Samuel A., extract of letter of, in which he states that Free Zone has been disastrous to Brownsville, Texas, and other American towns, and asks prompt action on part of United States to terminate Free Zone, 454 ; letter of, caused Secretary McCulloch to write letter to Secretary of State, saying Free Zone was established in hostility to United States, 456, 457

Bismarck, Prince, thought that the Hanseatic privileges of Hamburg and Bremen should be abolished, 477, 478

Blaine, James G., resolution of, inquiring on the Free Zone, 456 ; M. Romero improperly accused of criticising, on account of his Free Zone resolution, 711

Bonded privilege, prior to attempt of United States to put an end to Free Zone, Mexico had none, 472 ; danger ot, in smuggling, 472, 473

Bynum, Mr., Member of Congress, letter to, from M. Romero, on the Free Zone of Mexico, 473, 474 ; answer from, to M. Romero on Free Zone question, 474

C

Civil War of United States, effect on Mexican frontier, made towns flourish, 441 ; prosperity of towns attributed by many to Free Zone, and resulted in extension of Free Zone, views from a witness of scenes in the Free Zone during war, 442 ; made southern towns less prosperous after war, 452, 453

Cobb, Seth W., Member of Congress, introduced Joint Resolution in House of Representatives to repeal Free Zone law, 473, 475

Cockrell, Jeremiah V., Member of Congress, resolution against Free Zone, 432, 469–471 ; resolution inoperative on account of imperfect wording, 472

Commissioners on marauding on the frontier, extract of their report, first published in General Grant's Message of December 16, 1872, finally committed by President Grant to Congress with his Message of May 26, 1874, 465

Comonfort, General, Ignacio, inaugurated pronunciamiento against Constitution under which he had been elected, 436

Cooper, Samuel B., Member of Congress, resolution to repeal Joint Resolution of March 1, 1895, forbidding transportation of goods in bond into Free Zone of Mexico, resolution of, favorably reported, 704 ; report on resolution of, 709 ; resolution of, 709, 710

Cotton, regulations on the Free Zone, 458, 459

743

LABOR AND WAGES IN MEXICO.

Fear of United States of cheap labor, Mexico used for that purpose more so than now, England most to be feared, pauper labor of Europe feared, pauper labor of Mexico and Asia now feared, 502 ; study fails to discern any evidence of competition, gain of United States in exports and imports, 503

Feast days in Mexico, why objectionable, reduced, 542

Foster, John W., United States Minister to Mexico, report of, in which he asserted that Mexicans were generally opposed to use of agricultural implements, 526

G

George, Henry, extract from his book, *Progress and Poverty*, 539, 540

Goluchowski, Count, called on Europe to unite in commercial league against United States and Japan, 503, 504

Gunton, Mr., article on what workingmen really need, 540, 541

H

Hawkins, Rush C., *Brutality and Avarice Triumphant*, extract from, 511

High import duties cannot alone keep up high wages, and why, 504 ; in Mexico have neither increased nor cheapened wages, and figures showing, 504, 505

High wages, how can be obtained in Mexico, 518

I

Immigration from United States into Mexico, who advised to go, 542, 543

K

Knauft, Theodore, on the conditions of Mexican people, 517

L

Labor higher in United States because more efficient, 505

Laboring classes in United States, any change for the better will react in Mexico, 541

Low wages mean high cost of production, 522

Low wages of Mexico, do not compare favorably with high wages paid in the United States, 516 ; why misunderstood, 516, 517 ; cannot be any lower than now, and tendency is to become higher, 521

Lucas, Charles, incident showing cheapness of Mexican products, 530

M

Maas, Paul J., sent to Mexico by Labor Assembly to obtain information on Labor, report of, 538

Machinery in Mexico, use of, why not used heretofore, number of cotton and woolen mills run by machinery, not usually suited to soil of Mexico, 527 ; not everywhere shops to repair, difficulties of, cannot be appreciated by tourists or United States representatives living in cities, 528

Manning, Daniel, Secretary of the Treasury, estimate of number of persons engaged in gainful occupations in United States submitted to, 555

Manufacturers of the United States, argument urged by, for levying heavy import duties, 502, 505

Mason, Carlisle, President of Manufacturers' Association of Chicago, asked information about Mexico of Mr. Foster, and received a report from him, 526

Mexican labor, why cheap, wants few in isolated districts, 519, 520 ; climate, 520, 521 ; difference of transportation, 531

Mexican laborers, some think are happier than American, and why, 507 ; in somewhat similar condition as Southern negroes, 517, 518 ; can buy more with money than United States laborer, 518 ; descendants of slaves, until recently have been living under feudal conditions, not educated, are now free, 506 ; wages rising, 506, 507; work of, as compared with United States, 521, 522

Mexican peonage, what it is, M. Romero's experience of, 509, 510 ; when liable to abuse, 510, 511 ; why not legal, Article V. of Mexican Constitution and amendment, abuses are disappearing, 511 ; does not mean now what it did under Spanish rule, 505 ; meaning of, in Spanish labor consisted in, why no better in United States, 507 ; why abused, 508, 509

Mexican products, had to pay Alcabala tax, tax abolished in 1895, 526

Mexican wages go farther than in United States, 537

O

Organized Labor, Mexico has none, will in time probably have it, 539 ; in United States, 540

P

Paper on Labor and Wages, why it was written, 497, 498

THE SILVER STANDARD.

A

Adoption of common silver coin, one of the objects not obtained at the International American Conference of 1889, 574 ; extract from M. Romero's remarks in regard to, 575

Advantage of silver standard to Mexico, encourages exports, 596, 597 ; stimulates the development of home manufactures, 597, 598 ; purchasing power of the silver dollar has not decreased in Mexico, 600, 601 ; gold price of foreign commodities making them so high, equivalent to protection, 601 ; exchange in gold countries encourages investment in Mexico, 602 ; low price of silver makes it unprofitable to export it, 604

Agents sent to Mexico to study silver question, unfamiliar with the language, history, and conditions of the country, 568 ; many already prejudiced against Mexico, 569

Agricultural products, have not suffered in Mexico from fallen prices, 609

Allen, Senator William V., letter to M. Romero on March 11, 1896, asking for information on silver standard in Mexico, 564, 565 ; answer of M. Romero to letter of, 565

American International Monetary Commission, address delivered at, by M. Romero, 576, 613, 614 ; difficulties it had to contend with, 575, 576

B

Brussels Monetary Conference, why necessary, report of the United States Commissioners, 576

Bryan, William J., extract from letter of, to *New York World* of January 23, 1898, saying that some Mexicans desire that the United States do not go under the silver standard, but that on the whole they desire restoration of bimetalism in the United States, 585

Bryce, Lloyd, request for a paper on silver standard in Mexico for the *North*

American Review made of M. Romero and answer, 563

Business failures, few in Mexico, 608, 609

C

Carden, Lionel E. G., British Consul-General in Mexico, thinks silver will in the end be beneficial to Mexico, 577 ; his views from his report on silver in Mexico, 577, 578 ; extract from report of, on trade of Mexico in 1895, 578

Chevalier, Michel, headed movement in France to demonetize gold, 581

Clark, Justice Walter, article in *Arena*, of Boston, of March, 1896, presenting Mexico as an example of the favorable results of the silver standard, 564, 565

Cleveland, President, stand on silver question of, 563

Coal, scarce now in Mexico but large deposits being found, 597

Coins of different American countries, 576

Conditions in Mexico, satisfactory notwithstanding the silver standard, 610, 611

Cotton industry in Mexico, Lionel E. G. Carden's report on, 584

Courcel, Baron de, French Ambassador in London, on injuries world has suffered by depreciation of silver, 592

Currency of Mexico, free coinage of silver, why silver was adopted, why cannot be changed, no paper money used, 594 ; system used by banks 594, 595

D

Depreciation of silver, 579 ; its effect on England, 583, 584 ; extracts from *Cotton Factory Times* on, 583 ; Mexico satisfied with silver standard, 586

Diaz, President, his views on silver, 566 ; interview published in *New York Journal* on effect of silver coinage in Mexico, 566, 567 ; on growth of commercial interests in Mexico, wages, labor, 567 ; letter from, to M. Romero,

THE PAN-AMERICAN CONFERENCE.